Index of Notation

One can buy dozens of books on ray-tracing and physically based rendering, but when you actually sit down to write rendering code yourself, you may suddenly realize those books are only telling you half the story. At every turn you will face design and engineering decisions about everything from data structures to sampling patterns, any one of which can impact system performance drastically. Most people who have worked in the innards of rendering systems have learned this esoterica by hearsay and a lot of trial and error.

Matt Pharr and Greg Humphreys have decided to tell the rest of the story, by publishing and annotating the breadth and depth of a fully-functional physically based renderer, using the literate programming approach. Applying this approach—which interleaves source code and descriptive text—to the construction and documentation of even a simple computer program can be a daunting task, but its application here is Herculean and quite possibly historic.

In spite of their attention to engineering detail, the authors haven't skimped on their coverage of the theoretical underpinnings of physically based rendering. Their chapters on sampling theory and material models are among the best in print. However, the inclusion of a working artifact that implements the theory using corresponding notation and structure is an incomparable learning and teaching tool.

Dan Goldman
computer graphics supervisor for visual effects

We have been using early versions of this book and its accompanying source code in our graduate courses and in our research for the past two semesters, and we've been thrilled with them. The book has an excellent blend of the theoretical and practical information needed to build an efficient physically based renderer. Much of the information contained in the book is not available in any other reference book; an example is the description of practical methods for anisotropic filtering. The code that accompanies the book satisfies at least as great a need—it's well written, well commented, and strikes a good balance between performance and extensibility. As a result, we have already adopted the code as the software infrastructure for two different research projects within our group. I enthusiastically recommend that any researcher or practitioner who works on rendering systems buy a copy of this book.

Bill Mark
Assistant Professor
University of Texas at Austin

This book is the only place to my knowledge where the implementation details of several advanced global illumination algorithms are actually shown. Not only details, but code! That is a tremendous benefit to the community and a major strength of the book.

Timothy Purcell
Stanford University / NVIDIA

Designing and implementing a production-quality ray tracer that is based on the physical principles of light transport is difficult. Writing a book that clearly explains the underlying principles and algorithms, from radiative transfer theory to Loop subdivision and photon mapping, is hard. Combining these explanations with source code using Knuth's literate programming methodology to produce a beautifully-designed, full-featured, and wonderfully extensible rendering system might seem NP-hard, but this book proves that it can be done. Whether you are a computer science student or computer graphics researcher, there is simply no better book on the topic.

Ian Ashdown
President
byHeart Consultants Limited

A good textbook should inspire, and also inform the reader and allow him or her to go beyond the covers of the book. Matt and Greg have done a yeoman's job of creating a very comprehensive source of knowledge on the topics of global illumination and physically based rendering. The book certainly informs the reader. It does not simplify the material and that is a good thing. Rather, through careful exposition and very useful illustrations it provides several learning aids. There are several chapters on several fundamental topics replete with examples, figures and illustrations. Also, the treatment of various algorithms is simultaneously both comprehensive and in great depth. Most importantly, the book relies on a carefully developed programming environment that allows the reader to experiment. pbrt *is easy to use and yet allows for rendition of complex scenes. As a result one can learn the material in a pedagogically sound way and also venture beyond the confines of the text. It is easy to be inspired by the effort. I have used a version of the book and software as a text for an advanced course in computer graphics. Both my students and I found the text very useful.*

Raghu Machiraju
Associate Professor
Department of Computer Science and Engineering
The Ohio State University

This book is a great tool for anyone looking to get into advanced ray tracing techniques. It is the best guide to architecting a photorealistic renderer that I have seen.

Brian Budge
Ph.D. student
graphics and visualization research group
UC Davis

THE MORGAN KAUFMANN SERIES IN INTERACTIVE 3D TECHNOLOGY

SERIES EDITOR: DAVID H. EBERLY, MAGIC SOFTWARE, INC.

The game industry is a powerful and driving force in the evolution of computer technology. As the capabilities of personal computers, peripheral hardware, and game consoles have grown, so has the demand for quality information about the algorithms, tools, and descriptions needed to take advantage of this new technology. To satisfy this demand and establish a new level of professional reference for the game developer, we created the **Morgan Kaufmann Series in Interactive 3D Technology**. Books in the series are written for developers by leading industry professionals and academic researchers, and cover the state of the art in real-time 3D. The series emphasizes practical, working solutions and solid software-engineering principles. The goal is for the developer to be able to implement real systems from the fundamental ideas, whether it be for games or other applications.

Physically Based Rendering: From Theory to Implementation
Matt Pharr and Greg Humphreys

Essential Mathematics for Games and Interactive Applications: A Programmer's Guide
James M. Van Verth and Lars M. Bishop

Game Physics
David H. Eberly

Collision Detection in Interactive 3D Environments
Gino van den Bergen

3D Game Engine Design: A Practical Approach to Real-Time Computer Graphics
David H. Eberly

Forthcoming

Real-Time Collision Detection
Christer Ericson

3D Game Engine Architecture: Engineering Real-Time Applications with Wild Magic
David H. Eberly

Artificial Intelligence for Computer Games
Ian Millington

Physically Based Rendering

FROM THEORY TO IMPLEMENTATION

MATT PHARR
NVIDIA

GREG HUMPHREYS
Department of Computer Science
University of Virginia

AMSTERDAM · BOSTON · HEIDELBERG · LONDON
NEW YORK · OXFORD · PARIS · SAN DIEGO
SAN FRANCISCO · SINGAPORE · SYDNEY · TOKYO

ELSEVIER

Morgan Kaufmann is an imprint of Elsevier

MORGAN KAUFMANN PUBLISHERS

Senior Editor Tim Cox
Publishing Services Manager Simon Crump
Project Editor Kyle Sarofeen
Project Management Elisabeth Beller
Editorial Coordinator Rick Camp
Cover Design Chen Design Associates, San Francisco
Cover Image scene modeled by Oliver Deussen and Bernd Lintermann; rendered by pbrt
Text Design Chen Design
Composition Windfall Software, using ZzTeX
Technical Illustration Dartmouth Publishing
Copyeditor Ken DellaPenta
Proofreader Jennifer McClain
Indexer Steve Rath
Interior and Cover Printer Hing Yip (China) Printing & Binding Co. Ltd.

Morgan Kaufmann Publishers is an imprint of Elsevier.
500 Sansome Street, Suite 400, San Francisco, CA 94111

This book is printed on acid-free paper.

Library of Congress Cataloguing-in-Publication: applied for

ISBN: 0-12-553180-X

For information on all Morgan Kaufmann publications,
visit our Web site at www.mkp.com.

Printed in China
08 07 06 05 04   5 4 3 2 1

To **Deirdre**, who even let me bring the manuscript on our honeymoon.

M. P.

To **Jessica**, for her endless support, encouragement, and love, and for pointing out that "smaple" is not a word, no matter how many times I typed it.

G. H.

ABOUT THE AUTHORS

Matt Pharr is a member of the technical staff at NVIDIA, where he works on interactive graphics and programmable shading as part of the Software Architecture group. Previously, he was a cofounder of Exluna, where he developed offline rendering software and investigated applications of graphics hardware to high-quality rendering. He holds a B.S. degree from Yale University and is a Ph.D. candidate in the Stanford Graphics Laboratory under the supervision of Pat Hanrahan, where he has researched both theoretical and systems issues related to rendering and has written a series of SIGGRAPH papers on these topics.

Greg Humphreys is an assistant professor of computer science at the University of Virginia, where his research focuses on interactive visualization of very large datasets. Greg has a B.S. degree from Princeton University and a Ph.D. in computer science from Stanford University under the supervision of Pat Hanrahan. His doctoral dissertation, "A Stream Processing Approach to Interactive Graphics on Clusters of Workstations," showed that it was possible to build scalable interactive graphics systems using only commodity components. His cluster-rendering software called "Chromium" is in widespread use in research and industry labs around the world.

Contents

* An asterisk denotes a section with advanced content that can be skipped on a first reading.

CHAPTER 15. MONTE CARLO INTEGRATION II: IMPROVING EFFICIENCY — 663

APPENDIXES

Foreword

Over the last 10 years, I've had the pleasure of teaching a course in image synthesis at Princeton and Stanford. That course provides a broad overview of the theory and practice of rendering, concentrating on the algorithms and techniques needed to make realistic imagery. Typically, it is the second course in computer graphics (assuming as a prerequisite an introductory computer graphics course) and is taken by upper-level undergraduates and first-year graduate students.

Like my colleagues around the world, I initially had the students build a ray tracer from scratch, step by step, over the term. Writing a ray tracer is an excellent way to learn computer graphics since it includes modules for geometry, materials, lighting, imaging—all the basic concepts. In fact, the process of writing a ray tracer has become a rite of passage for computer graphics students.

Eventually, however, a few problems with this approach became clear. First, everyone spent way too much time building support libraries. This included code for reading geometric file formats and for writing images to files. The wise students also invested time building solid utility libraries, like foundation classes for matrices, points, and vectors. At the end of the term I would ask them whether they thought writing a ray tracer was worth all the time. They all agreed they learned a lot by writing all this infrastructural code. However, they also complained that they had very little time for the more interesting aspects of rendering—the actual topics of the course. The fun parts that I wanted them to work on—like lighting simulation, participating media, photon mapping, and so on—were left behind.

Another problem was that while I had many students who wrote beautiful code, some students produced "spaghetti code." Once they got going in the wrong direction, it was very hard for them to recover. They learned after each new assignment that the way the previous assignment had been implemented may not have been such a good idea after all, since it was difficult to extend. Unfortunately, there was not enough time to go back and rewrite the original libraries. It became apparent that it was important that students learn how to develop systems that are well-structured, robust, and extensible—skills that often aren't explicitly taught.

Gradually over the years, I provided better and more complete support libraries so that students had more time to concentrate on the subject material. Then Matt and Greg, both former teaching assistants, had the idea of building a ray tracer using literate programming. One day they said to me, "Suppose we wrote a literate ray tracer. Would you use it in the course?" I said, "That's a great idea—sign me up!" The book before you documents pbrt, the sixth version of the system. We have used it since 2000 at Stanford.

The idea of literate programming was invented by Donald Knuth. He believed that programs were works of literature in the eyes of the nerdy beholder and could be presented to the reader as a book. He invented the system web for writing literate programs. Using web, the programmer uses a language like TeX for formatting the text and a programming language like C++ for writing the program. The program is embedded in the text as a graph of interconnected parts, which Knuth called a "web," similar in spirit to the way that web pages are interconnected using links. To compile and run the program, the program is extracted automatically from the text. Donald Knuth has published several books documenting TeX and Metafont as literate programs. Another great example of a literate program is lcc, the subject of the book *A Retargetable C Compiler* written by Christopher Fraser and David Hanson. They document a complete ANSI C compiler in the literate style. The lcc book in many ways is the model for this book.

Writing a literate program is a *lot* more work than writing a normal program. After all, who ever documents their programs in the first place!? Moreover, who documents them in a pedagogical style that is easy to understand? And finally, who ever provides commentary on the theory and design issues behind the code as they write the documentation? All of that is here in the pages that follow.

The real value of pbrt is not just that it is a well-documented ray tracer. There are two other important reasons to read this book.

First, computer graphics, and rendering in particular, is full of beautiful theory. The theory covers physical concepts, such as light fields and the interaction of light with different materials, and mathematical concepts, such as integral equations and Monte Carlo integration. The great thing about computers is that they allow us to build rendering systems based on the best theory. pbrt in essence turns the theory of image-making into a practical method for creating images. Each physical process or mathematical abstraction is translated into a class, with methods that implement algorithms that model the corresponding concept. There is a direct correspondence between the architecture of the system and the theory. Good theory thus leads to good architectures. Seeing in detail how theory is transformed into practice is perhaps the strongest reason for reading this book.

Second, it is really, really hard to build a good rendering system. The best system designers pay attention to every detail. They are craftsmen who polish every pixel, prevent every crack between triangles, and stamp out every aliasing and quantization artifact. They also build robust systems that handle every case, not just the easy ones. Choosing algorithms that work is an art in itself. Finally, there are many subtle issues in handling large models (by conserving memory in the right places) and efficient execution (optimizing the right code) that only come from experience building and using real systems. There are not many opportunities to learn about these issues, and seeing how they have been solved by others is one of the best ways to do so.

Matt and Greg are skilled programmers. Matt worked with the RenderMan team at Pixar, is one of the cofounders of Exluna, and is a designer and implementor of their Entropy renderer. Greg has also developed many systems, including WireGL and Chromium, a large open-source project to support parallel rendering. Greg also wrote the tangling and untangling software used to produce this book. They are both master craftsmen who will convert you from a rendering journeyman to a rendering master.

Pat Hanrahan
Canon USA Professor
Stanford University

Preface

[Just as] other information should be available to those who want to learn and understand, program source code is the only means for programmers to learn the art from their predecessors. It would be unthinkable for playwrights not to allow other playwrights to read their plays [or to allow them] at theater performances where they would be barred even from taking notes. Likewise, any good author is well read, as every child who learns to write will read hundreds of times more than it writes. Programmers, however, are expected to invent the alphabet and learn to write long novels all on their own. Programming cannot grow and learn unless the next generation of programmers has access to the knowledge and information gathered by other programmers before them. —Erik Naggum

Rendering is a fundamental component of computer graphics. At the highest level of abstraction, rendering is the process of converting a description of a three-dimensional scene into an image. Algorithms for animation, geometric modeling, texturing, and other areas of computer graphics all must pass their results through some sort of rendering process so that they can be made visible in an image. Rendering has become ubiquitous; from movies to games and beyond, it has opened new frontiers for creative expression, entertainment, and visualization.

In the early years of the field, research in rendering focused on solving fundamental problems such as determining which objects are visible from a given viewpoint. As effective solutions to these problems have been found and as richer and more realistic scene descriptions have become available thanks to continued progress in other areas of graphics, modern rendering has grown to include ideas from a broad range of disciplines, including physics and astrophysics, astronomy, biology, psychology and the study of perception, and pure and applied mathematics. The interdisciplinary nature of rendering is one of the reasons that it is such a fascinating area of study.

This book presents a selection of modern rendering algorithms through the documented source code for a complete rendering system. All of the images in this book, including the one on the front and back covers, were rendered by this software. All of the algorithms that came together to generate these images are described in these pages. The system, pbrt, is written using a programming methodology called *literate programming* that mixes prose describing the system with the source code that implements it. We believe that the literate programming approach is a valuable way to introduce ideas in computer graphics and computer science in general. Often, some of the subtleties of an algorithm can be unclear or hidden until it is implemented, so seeing an actual implementation is a good way to acquire a solid understanding of that algorithm's details. Indeed, we believe that deep understanding of a small number of algorithms in this manner provides a stronger base for further study of computer graphics than does superficial understanding of many.

In addition to clarifying how an algorithm is implemented in practice, presenting these algorithms in the context of a complete and nontrivial software system also allows us to address issues in the design and implementation of medium-sized rendering systems. The design of a rendering system's basic abstractions and interfaces has substantial implications for both the elegance of the implementation and the ability to extend it later, yet the trade-offs in this design space are rarely discussed.

pbrt and the contents of this book focus exclusively on *photorealistic rendering*, which can be defined variously as the task of generating images that are indistinguishable from those that a camera would capture in a photograph, or as the task of generating images that evoke the same response from a human observer as looking at the actual scene. There are many reasons to focus on photorealism. Photorealistic images are crucial for the movie special-effects industry because computer-generated imagery must often be mixed seamlessly with footage of the real world. In entertainment applications where all of the imagery is synthetic, photorealism is an effective tool for making the observer forget that he or she is looking at an environment that does not actually exist. Finally, photorealism gives a reasonably well-defined metric for evaluating the quality of the rendering system's output.

A consequence of our approach is that this book and the system it describes do not exhaustively cover the state of the art in rendering; many interesting topics in photorealistic rendering will not be introduced either because they don't fit well with the architecture of the software system (e.g., finite-element radiosity algorithms) or because we believed that the pedagogical value of explaining the algorithm was outweighed by the complexity of its implementation (e.g., Metropolis light transport). We will note these decisions as they come up and provide pointers to further resources so that the reader can follow up on topics of interest. Many other areas of rendering, including interactive rendering, visualization, and illustrative forms of rendering such as pen-and-ink styles, aren't covered in this book at all. Nevertheless, many of the algorithms and ideas in this system (e.g., algorithms for texture map anti-aliasing) are applicable to a wider set of rendering styles.

AUDIENCE

Our primary intended audience for this book is students in graduate or upper-level undergraduate computer graphics classes. This book assumes existing knowledge of computer graphics at the level of an introductory college-level course, although certain key concepts such as basic vector geometry and transformations will be reviewed here. For students who do not have experience with programs that have tens of thousands of lines of source code, the literate programming style gives a gentle introduction to this complexity. We pay special attention to explaining the reasoning behind some of the key interfaces and abstractions in the system in order to give these readers a sense of why the system is structured in the way that it is.

Our secondary, but equally important, audiences are advanced graduate students and researchers, software developers in industry, and individuals interested in the fun of writing their own rendering systems. Although many of the ideas in this book will likely be familiar to these readers, seeing explanations of the algorithms presented in the literate style may provide new perspectives. pbrt includes implementations of a number of newer and/or difficult-to-implement algorithms and techniques, such as subdivision surfaces, Monte Carlo light transport, and volumetric scattering models; these should be of particular interest to experienced practitioners in rendering. We hope that delving into one particular organization of a complete and nontrivial rendering system will also be thought provoking to this audience.

OVERVIEW AND GOALS

pbrt is based on the *ray-tracing* algorithm. Ray tracing is an elegant technique that has its origins in lens making; Carl Freidrich Gauss traced rays through lenses by hand in the 19th century. Ray-tracing algorithms on computers follow the path of infinitesimal rays of light through the scene until they intersect a surface. This approach gives a simple method for finding the first visible object as seen from any particular position and direction, and is the basis for many rendering algorithms.

pbrt was designed and implemented with three main goals in mind: it should be *complete*, it should be *illustrative*, and it should be *physically based*.

Completeness implies that the system should not lack key features found in high-quality commercial rendering systems. In particular, it means that important practical issues, such as antialiasing, robustness, and the ability to efficiently render complex scenes, should all be addressed thoroughly. It is important to consider these issues from the start of the system's design, since these features can have subtle implications for all components of the system and can be quite difficult to retrofit into the system at a later stage of implementation.

Our second goal means that we tried to choose algorithms, data structures, and rendering techniques with care and with an eye toward readability and clarity. Since their implementations will be examined by more readers than is the case for many other rendering systems, we tried to select the most elegant algorithms that we were aware of and implement them as well as possible. This goal also required that the system be small enough for a single person to understand completely. We have implemented pbrt using a plug-in architecture, with only a small core of basic glue, and as much of the functionality as possible in external modules. The result is that one doesn't need to understand all of the various plug-ins in order to understand the basic structure of the system. This makes it easier to delve deeply into parts of interest and skip others, without losing sight of how the overall system fits together.

There is a tension between the two goals of being complete and being illustrative. Implementing and describing every possible useful technique would not only make this book extremely long, but also would make the system prohibitively complex for most readers. In cases where pbrt lacks a particularly useful feature, we have attempted to design the architecture so that the feature could be added without altering the overall system design.

The basic foundations for physically based rendering are the laws of physics and their mathematical expression. pbrt was designed to use the correct physical units and concepts for the quantities it computes and the algorithms it implements. When configured to do so, pbrt can compute images that are *physically correct;* they accurately reflect the lighting as it would be in a real-world version of the scene. One advantage of the decision to use a physical basis is that it gives a concrete standard of program correctness: for simple scenes, where the expected result can be computed in closed form, if pbrt doesn't compute the same result, we know there must be a bug in the implementation. Similarly, if different physically based lighting algorithms in pbrt give different results for the same scene, or if pbrt doesn't give the same results as another physically based renderer, there is certainly an error in one of them. Finally, we believe that this physically based approach to rendering is valuable because it is rigorous. When it is not clear how a particular computation should be performed, physics gives an answer that guarantees a consistent result.

Efficiency was given lower priority than these three goals. Since rendering systems often run for many minutes or hours in the course of generating an image, efficiency is clearly important. However, we have mostly confined ourselves to *algorithmic* efficiency rather than low-level code optimization. In some cases, obvious micro-optimizations take a backseat to clear, well-organized code, although we did make some effort to optimize the parts of the system where most of the computation occurs. For this reason, as well as to ensure portability, pbrt is not presented as a parallel or multithreaded application, although parallelizing pbrt would not be very difficult.

In the course of presenting pbrt and discussing its implementation, we hope to convey some hard-learned lessons from years of rendering research and development. There is more to writing a good renderer than stringing together a set of fast algorithms; making the system both flexible and robust is a difficult task. The system's performance must degrade gracefully as more geometry or light sources are added to it, or as any other axis of complexity is pushed. Numeric stability must be handled carefully, and algorithms that don't waste floating-point precision are critical.

The rewards for developing a system that addresses all these issues are enormous–it is a great pleasure to write a new renderer or add a new feature to an existing renderer and use it to create an image that couldn't be generated before. Our most fundamental goal in writing this book was to bring this opportunity to a wider audience. Readers are encouraged to use the system to render the example scenes on the companion CD as they progress through the book. Exercises at the end of each chapter suggest modifications to the system that will help clarify its inner workings, and more complex projects to extend the system by adding new features.

The Web site for this book is located at *www.pbrt.org*. There we will post errata and bug fixes, updates to pbrt's source code, additional scenes to render, supplemental utilities, and new plug-in modules. Any bugs in pbrt or errors in this text that are not listed at the Web site can be reported to the email address *bugs@pbrt.org*. We greatly value your feedback!

ACKNOWLEDGMENTS

Pat Hanrahan has contributed to this book in more ways than we could hope to acknowledge; we owe a profound debt to him. He tirelessly argued for clean interfaces and finding the right abstractions to use throughout the system, and his understanding of and approach to rendering deeply influenced its design. His willingness to use pbrt and this manuscript in his rendering course at Stanford was enormously helpful, particularly in the early years of its life when it was still in very rough form; his feedback throughout this process has been crucial for bringing the text to its current state. Finally, the group of people that Pat helped assemble at the Stanford Graphics Lab, and the open environment that he fostered, made for an exciting, stimulating, and fertile environment. We feel extremely privileged to have been there.

Marc Levoy, Leonidas Guibas, and Ron Fedkiw were similarly instrumental in making Stanford such an extraordinary place to study. We thank them for everything they have done to create this truly unique place.

We owe a debt of gratitude to the many students who used early drafts of this book in courses at Stanford and the University of Virginia between 1999 and 2004. These students provided an enormous amount of feedback about the book and pbrt. The teaching assistants for these courses deserve special mention: Tim Purcell, Mike Cammarano, Ian Buck, and Ren Ng at Stanford, and Nolan Goodnight at Virginia. A number of students in those classes gave particularly valuable feedback and sent bug reports and bug fixes; we would especially like to thank Evan Parker and Phil Beatty. A draft of the manuscript of this book was used in classes taught by Bill Mark and Don Fussell at the University of Texas, Austin, and Raghu Machiraju at Ohio State University; their feedback was invaluable, and we are grateful for their adventurousness in incorporating this system into their courses, even while it was still being edited and revised.

Matt Pharr would like to specifically acknowledge colleagues and coworkers in rendering-related endeavors who have been a great source of education and who have substantially influenced his approach to writing renderers and his understanding of the field: notably, Tony Apodaca, Tom Duff, Doug Epps, Reid Gershbein, Larry Gritz, Craig Kolb, Tom Lokovic, Mark VandeWettering, and Eric Veach. Particular thanks go to Craig Kolb, who provided a cornerstone of Matt's early computer graphics education through the freely available source code to the rayshade ray-tracing system and who has been a great colleague to have the opportunity to work with through a series of rendering research projects and commercial adventures. Eric Veach has also been generous with his time and expertise; his insistence on the importance of continuing to work on problems and software designs until robust, clean, and correct solutions have been found has been an influential lesson. Thanks also to Doug Shult and Stan Eisenstat for formative lessons in mathematics and computer science during high school and college, respectively, and most importantly to Matt's parents, for the education they've provided and continued encouragement along the way. Finally, thanks also to Nick Triantos, Jayant Kolhe, and NVIDIA for their understanding and support through the final stages of this project.

Greg Humphreys is very grateful to all the professors and TAs who tolerated him when he was an undergraduate at Princeton. Many people encouraged his interest in graphics, specifically Michael Cohen, David Dobkin, Adam Finkelstein, Michael Cox, Gordon Stoll, Patrick Min, and Dan Wallach. Doug Clark, Steve Lyon, and Andy Wolfe also supervised various independent research boondoggles without even laughing once. Once, in a group meeting about a year-long robotics project, Steve Lyon became exasperated and yelled, "Stop telling me why it can't be done, and figure out how to do it!"—an impromptu lesson that will never be forgotten. Eric Ristad fired Greg as a summer research assistant after his freshman year (before the summer even began), pawning him off on an unsuspecting Pat Hanrahan and beginning an advising relationship that would span 10 years and both coasts. Finally, Dave Hanson taught Greg that literate programming was a great way to work, and that computer programming can be a beautiful and subtle art form.

We would also like to thank the many friends and colleagues who made the Stanford Graphics Lab such a rich environment to work in and such a fun place to be: Maneesh Agrawala, Ian Buck, Milton Chen, Brian Curless, James Davis, Matthew Eldridge, Brian Freyburger, Chase Garfinkle, Reid Gershbein, John Gerth, François Guimbretière, Olaf Hall-Holt, Chris Holt, Mike Houston, Homan Igehy, Henrik Wann Jensen, Brad Johanson, Craig Kolb, Venkat Krishnamurthy, Phil Lacroute, Tolis Lerios, Bill Lorensen, Bill Mark, Steve Marschner, Tamara Munzner, Ren Ng, John Owens, Hans Pedersen, Kekoa Proudfoot, Tim Purcell, Jonathan Ragan-Kelley, Ravi Ramamoorthi, Szymon Rusinkiewicz, Philipp Slusallek, Jeff Solomon, Gordon Stoll, Maureen Stone, Diane Tang, and Li-Yi Wei.

We are also grateful to Don Mitchell, for his help with understanding some of the details of sampling and reconstruction; Thomas Kollig and Alexander Keller, for explaining the finer points of low-discrepancy sampling; and Dave Eberly, "Just d'FAQs," Hans-Bernhard Broeker, Steve Westin, and Gernot Hoffmann, for many interesting threads on *comp.graphics.algorithms*. Christer Ericson had a number of suggestions for improving our kd-tree implementation and generously made available a chapter from his upcoming book on collision detection that pointed us to a number of techniques that helped improve our implementation.

Many people and organizations have generously in supplyied us with scenes and models for use in this book and the accompanying CD. Their generosity has been invaluable in helping us create interesting example images throughout the text. The bunny, Buddha, and dragon models are courtesy of the Stanford Computer Graphics Laboratory's scanning repository at *graphics.stanford.edu/data/3Dscanrep/*. The ecosystem scene was created by Oliver Deussen and Bernd Lintermann for a paper by them and collaborators (Deussen, Hanrahan, Lintermann, Mech, Pharr, and Prusinkiewicz 1998). The "killeroo" model is included with permission of Phil Dench and Martin Rezard (3D scan and digital representations by headus, design and clay sculpt by Rezard). The physically accurate smoke data sets were created by Duc Nguyen and Ron Fedkiw. Nolan Goodnight created environment maps with a realistic skylight model. Finally, the Cornell Program of Computer Graphics Light Measurement Laboratory allowed us to include measured BRDF data.

We would especially like to thank Marko Dabrovic and Mihovil Odak at RNA Studios, *www.rna.hr*, who supplied us with a bounty of excellent models and scenes, including the Sponza atrium, the Sibenik cathedral, the Audi TT car model, and others that we were unable to incorporate into the book by the publication deadline.

We would also like to thank the book's reviewers, all of whom had insightful and constructive feedback about the manuscript at various stages of its progress: Ian Ashdown, Per Christensen, Doug Epps, Dan Goldman, Eric Haines, Erik Reinhard, Pete Shirley, Peter-Pike Sloan, Greg Ward, and a host of anonymous reviewers.

Finally, we would also like to thank Tim Cox (senior editor), for his willingness to take on this slightly unorthodox project and for both his direction and patience throughout the process. We are very grateful to Elisabeth Beller (project manager), who has gone well beyond the call of duty for this book; her ability to keep this complex project in control and on schedule has been remarkable, and we particularly thank her for the measurable impact she has had on the quality of the final result. Thanks also to Rick Camp (editorial assistant) for his many contributions along the way. Paul Anagnostopoulos and Jacqui Scarlott at Windfall Software did the book's composition; their ability to take the authors' homebrew literate programming file format and turn it into high-quality final output while also juggling the multiple unusual types of indexing we asked for is greatly appreciated. Thanks also to Ken DellaPenta (copyeditor) and Jennifer McClain (proofreader) as well as to Max Spector at Chen Design (text and cover designer), and Steve Rath (indexer).

ADDITIONAL READING

Donald Knuth's article *Literate Programming* (Knuth 1984) describes the main ideas behind literate programming as well as his web programming environment. The seminal TEX typesetting system was written with web and has been published as a series of books (Knuth 1986, Knuth 1993a). More recently, Knuth has published a collection of graph algorithms in literate format in *The Stanford GraphBase* (Knuth 1993b). These programs are enjoyable to read and are excellent presentations of their respective algorithms. The Web site *www.literateprogramming.com* has pointers to many articles about literate programming, literate programs to download, and a variety of literate programming systems; many refinements have been made since Knuth's original development of the idea.

The only other literate program we know of that has been published as a book is the implementation of the lcc compiler, which was written by Christopher Fraser and David Hanson and published as *A Retargetable C Compiler: Design and Implementation* (Fraser and Hanson 1995).

Physically Based Rendering

FROM THEORY TO IMPLEMENTATION

CHAPTER ONE

01 INTRODUCTION

Rendering is the process of producing a 2D image from a description of a 3D scene. Obviously, this is a very broad task, and there are many ways to approach it. *Physically based* techniques attempt to simulate reality; that is, they use principles of physics to model the interaction of light and matter. In physically based rendering, realism is usually the primary goal. This approach is in contrast to *interactive* rendering, which sacrifices realism for high performance and low latency, or *nonphotorealistic* rendering, which strives for artistic freedom and expressiveness.

This book describes pbrt, a physically based rendering system based on the ray-tracing algorithm. Most computer graphics books present algorithms and theory, sometimes combined with snippets of code. In contrast, this book couples the theory with a complete implementation of a fully functional rendering system.

1.1 LITERATE PROGRAMMING

While writing the TEX typesetting system, Donald Knuth developed a new programming methodology based on the simple but revolutionary idea that *programs should be written more for people's consumption than for computers' consumption*. He named this methodology *literate programming*. This book (including the chapter you're reading now) is a long literate program. This means that in the course of reading this book, you will read the *full* implementation of the pbrt rendering system, not just a high-level description of it.

1

Literate programs are written in a metalanguage that mixes a document formatting language (e.g., TEX or HTML) and a programming language (e.g., C++). Two separate systems process the program: a "weaver" that transforms the literate program into a document suitable for typesetting, and a "tangler" that produces source code suitable for compilation. Our literate programming system is homegrown, but it was heavily influenced by Norman Ramsey's noweb system.

The literate programming metalanguage provides two important features. The first is the ability to mix prose with source code. This feature makes the description of the program just as important as its actual source code, encouraging careful design and documentation. Second, the language provides mechanisms for presenting the program code to the reader in an entirely different order than it is supplied to the compiler. Thus, the program can be described in a logical manner. Each named block of code is called a *fragment*, and each fragment can refer to other fragments by name.

As a simple example, consider a function InitGlobals() that is responsible for initializing all of a program's global variables:[1]

```
void InitGlobals(void) {
    num_marbles = 25.7;
    shoe_size = 13;
    dielectric = true;
    my_senator = REPUBLICAN;
}
```

Despite its brevity, this function is hard to understand without any context. Why, for example, can the variable num_marbles take on floating-point values? Just looking at the code, one would need to search through the entire program to see where each variable is declared and how it is used in order to understand its purpose and the meanings of its legal values. Although this structuring of the system is fine for a compiler, a human reader would much rather see the initialization code for each variable presented separately, near the code that actually declares and uses the variable.

In a literate program, one can instead write InitGlobals() like this:

⟨*Function Definitions*⟩ ≡
```
    void InitGlobals() {
        ⟨Initialize Global Variables  3⟩
    }
```

This defines a fragment, called ⟨*Function Definitions*⟩, that contains the definition of the InitGlobals() function. The InitGlobals() function itself refers to another fragment, ⟨*Initialize Global Variables*⟩. Because the initialization fragment has not yet been defined,

---

1   The example code in this section is merely illustrative and is not part of pbrt itself.

we don't know anything about this function except that it will contain assignments to global variables. This is just the right level of abstraction for now, since no variables have been declared yet. When we introduce the global variable shoe_size somewhere later in the program, we can then write

⟨*Initialize Global Variables*⟩ ≡   2
```
shoe_size = 13;
```

Here we have started to define the contents of ⟨*Initialize Global Variables*⟩. When the literate program is tangled into source code for compilation, the literate programming system will substitute the code shoe_size = 13; inside the definition of the InitGlobals() function. Later in the text, we may define another global variable, dielectric, and we can append its initialization to the fragment:

⟨*Initialize Global Variables*⟩+≡   2
```
dielectric = true;
```

The +≡ symbol after the fragment name shows that we have added to a previously defined fragment. When tangled, the result of these three fragments is the code

```
void InitGlobals() {
    shoe_size = 13;
    dielectric = true;
}
```

In this way, we can decompose complex functions into logically distinct parts, making them much easier to understand. For example, we can write a complicated function as a series of fragments:

⟨*Function Definitions*⟩+≡
```
void complex_func(int x, int y, double *data) {
    ⟨Check validity of arguments⟩
    if (x < y) {
        ⟨Swap parameter values⟩
    }
    ⟨Do precomputation before loop⟩
    ⟨Loop through and update data array⟩
}
```

Again, the contents of each fragment are expanded inline in complex_func() for compilation. In the document, we can introduce each fragment and its implementation in turn. This decomposition lets us present code a few lines at a time, making it easier to understand. Another advantage of this style of programming is that by separating the function into logical fragments, each with a single and well-delineated purpose, each one can then be written and verified independently. In general, we will try to make each fragment less than 10 lines long.

In some sense, the literate programming system is just an enhanced macro substitution package tuned to the task of rearranging program source code. This may seem like a trivial change, but in fact literate programming is quite different from other ways of structuring software systems.

1.1.1 INDEXING AND CROSS-REFERENCING

The following features are designed to make the text easier to navigate. Indices in the page margins give page numbers where the functions, variables, and methods used on that page are defined. Indices at the end of the book collect all of these identifiers so that it's possible to find definitions by name. Appendix D, "Index of Fragments," lists the pages where each fragment is defined and the pages where it is used. Within the text, a defined fragment name is followed by a list of page numbers on which that fragment is used. For example, a fragment definition such as

⟨*A fascinating fragment*⟩ ≡   184, 690
```
    num_marbles += .001;
```

indicates that this fragment is used on pages 184 and 690. If the fragments that use this fragment are not included in the book text, no page numbers will be listed. When a fragment is used inside another fragment, the page number on which it is first defined appears after the fragment name. For example,

⟨*Do something interesting*⟩+≡   500
```
    InitializeSomethingInteresting();
```
    ⟨*Do something else interesting* 486⟩
```
    CleanUp();
```

indicates that the ⟨*Do something else interesting*⟩ fragment is defined on page 486. If the definition of the fragment is not included in the book, no page number will be listed. When a fragment is adding code to a previously defined fragment, +≡ appears to the right of the fragment name. This is illustrated in the preceding example.

1.2 PHOTOREALISTIC RENDERING AND THE RAY-TRACING ALGORITHM

The goal of photorealistic rendering is to create an image of a 3D scene that is indistinguishable from a photograph of the same scene. Before we describe the rendering process, it is important to understand that in this context the word "indistinguishable" is imprecise because it involves a human observer, and different observers may perceive the same image differently. Although we will cover a few perceptual issues in this book, accounting for the precise characteristics of a given observer is a very difficult and largely unsolved problem. For the most part, we will be satisfied with an accurate simulation of the physics of light and its interaction with matter, relying on our understanding of display technology to present a "good" image to the viewer.

Most photorealistic rendering systems are based on the ray-tracing algorithm. Ray tracing is actually a very simple algorithm; it is based on following the path of a ray of light through a scene as it interacts with and bounces off objects in an environment. Although there are many ways to write a ray tracer, all such systems simulate at least the following objects and phenomena:

- *Cameras:* How and from where is the scene being viewed? Cameras generate rays from the viewing point into the scene.
- *Ray-object intersections*: We must be able to tell precisely where a given ray pierces a geometric object. In addition, we need to determine certain properties of the object at the intersection point, such as a surface normal. Most ray tracers also have some facility for finding the intersection of a ray with multiple objects, typically returning the closest intersection along the ray.
- *Light distribution:* Without lighting, there would be little point in rendering a scene. A ray tracer must model the distribution of light throughout the scene, including not only the locations of the lights themselves, but also the way in which they distribute their energy throughout space.
- *Visibility:* In order to know whether a given light deposits energy at a point on a surface, we must know whether there is an uninterrupted path from the point to the light source. Fortunately, this question is easy to answer in a ray tracer, since we can just construct the ray from the surface to the light, find the closest ray-object intersection, and compare the intersection distance to the light distance.
- *Surface scattering:* Each object must provide a description of its appearance, including information about how light interacts with the object's surface, as well as the nature of the reradiated (or *scattered*) light. We are usually interested in the properties of the light that is scattered directly toward the camera. Models for surface scattering are typically parameterized so that they can simulate a variety of appearances.
- *Recursive ray tracing:* Because light can arrive at a surface after bouncing off several other surfaces, it is usually necessary to trace additional rays originating at the surface to fully capture this effect. This is particularly important for shiny surfaces like metal or glass.
- *Ray propagation:* We need to know what happens to the light traveling along a ray as it passes through space. If we are rendering a scene in a vacuum, light energy remains constant along a ray. Although most human observers have never been in a vacuum, this is the typical assumption made by most ray tracers. More sophisticated models are available for tracing rays through fog, smoke, the Earth's atmosphere, and so on.

We will briefly discuss each of these simulation tasks in this section. In the next section, we will show pbrt's high-level interface to the underlying simulation components and follow the progress of a single ray through the main rendering loop. We will also show one specific surface scattering model based on Turner Whitted's original ray-tracing algorithm.

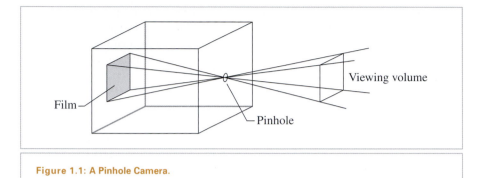

Figure 1.1: A Pinhole Camera.

1.2.1 CAMERAS

Nearly everyone has used a camera and is familiar with its basic functionality: you indicate your desire to record an image of the world (usually by pressing a button), and the image is recorded onto a piece of film. One of the simplest devices for taking photographs in the real world is called the *pinhole camera*. Pinhole cameras consist of a light-tight box with a tiny hole at one end (Figure 1.1). When the hole is uncovered, light enters this hole and falls on a piece of photographic paper that is affixed to the other end of the box. Despite its simplicity, this kind of camera is still used today, frequently for artistic reasons. Very long exposure times are necessary to get enough light on the film to form an image.

Although most cameras are substantially more complex than the pinhole camera, it is a convenient starting point for simulation. The most important function of the camera is to define the portion of the scene that will be recorded onto the film. In Figure 1.1, it is easy to see that connecting the pinhole to the edges of the film creates a double pyramid that extends into the scene. Objects that are not inside this pyramid cannot be imaged onto the film. Because modern cameras image a more complex shape than a pyramid, we will refer to the region of space that can potentially be imaged onto the film as the *viewing volume*.

Another way to think about the pinhole camera is to place the film plane in front of the pinhole, at the same distance (Figure 1.2). Note that connecting the hole to the film defines exactly the same viewing volume as before. Of course, this is not a practical way to build a real camera, but for simulation purposes it is a convenient abstraction. When the film (or image) plane is in front of the pinhole, the pinhole is frequently referred to as the *eye*.

Now we come to the crucial issue in rendering: at each point in the image, what color value do we display? If we recall the original pinhole camera, it is clear that light rays that do not travel along the vector between the pinhole and a point on the film cannot contribute to that film location. In our simulated camera with the film plane in front of

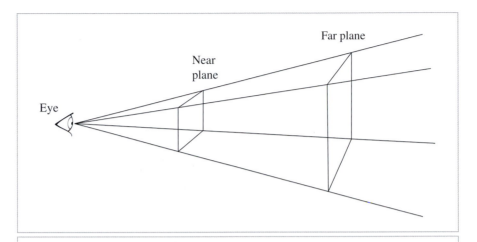

Figure 1.2: When we simulate a pinhole camera, we place the film in front of the hole at the near plane, and the hole is renamed the "eye."

the eye, we are interested in the amount of light traveling from the image point to the eye.

Therefore, the task of the camera simulator is to take a point on the image and generate *rays* along which light is known to contribute to that image location. Because a ray consists of an origin point and a direction vector, this is particularly simple for the pinhole camera model of Figure 1.2: it simply uses the near plane for the origin, and the vector from the eye to the near plane as the ray's direction. For more complex camera models involving multiple lenses, this calculation can be more involved. However, if the process of converting image locations to rays is completely encapsulated in the camera module, the rest of the rendering system can focus on evaluating the lighting along those rays, and a variety of camera models can be supported. pbrt's camera abstraction is described in detail in Chapter 6.

1.2.2 RAY-OBJECT INTERSECTIONS

Each time the camera generates a ray, the first task of the renderer is to determine which object, if any, that ray intersects first, and where the intersection occurs. This intersection point is the visible point along the ray, and we will want to simulate the interaction of light with the object at this point. To find the intersection, we must test the ray for intersection against all objects in the scene and select the one that the ray intersects first. Given a ray r, we first start by writing it in *parametric form:*

$$r(t) = o + t\mathbf{d},$$

where o is the ray's origin, **d** is its direction vector, and t is a parameter whose legal range is $[0, \infty)$. We can obtain a point along the ray by specifying its parametric t value and evaluating the above equation.

It is often easy to find the intersection between the ray r and a surface defined by an implicit function $F(x, y, z) = 0$. We first substitute the ray equation into the implicit equation, producing a new function whose only parameter is t. We then solve this function for t and substitute the smallest positive root into the ray equation to find the desired point. For example, the implicit equation of a sphere centered at the origin with radius r is

$$x^2 + y^2 + z^2 - r^2 = 0,$$

so substituting the ray equation, we have

$$\left(o + t\mathbf{d}\right)_x^2 + \left(o + t\mathbf{d}\right)_y^2 + \left(o + t\mathbf{d}\right)_z^2 - r^2 = 0.$$

This is just a quadratic equation in t, so we can easily solve it. If there are no real roots, the ray must miss the sphere. If there are roots, we simply select the smaller positive one.

The intersection point is not enough information for the rest of the ray tracer; it needs to know certain properties of the surface at the point. First, the appearance model needs to be extracted and passed along to later stages of the ray-tracing algorithm, and additional geometric information about the intersection point will also be required in order to shade the point. For example, the surface normal **n** is always required. Although many ray tracers operate with only **n**, more sophisticated rendering systems like pbrt require even more information, such as various partial derivatives with respect to the local parameterization of the surface.

Of course, most scenes are made up of multiple objects. The brute-force intersection approach would be to test the ray against each object in turn, choosing the minimum t value of the intersections found. This approach, while correct, is very slow, even for scenes of modest complexity. A solution is to incorporate an *acceleration structure* that quickly rejects whole groups of objects during the ray intersection process. This ability to quickly cull irrelevant geometry means that ray tracing frequently runs in $O(I \log N)$ time, where I is the number of pixels in the image and N is the number of objects in the scene.[2] (Building the acceleration structure is necessarily at least $O(N)$ time.)

The geometric interface supported by pbrt is described in Chapter 3, and the acceleration interface is shown in Chapter 4.

---

2   Although ray tracing's logarithmic complexity is often heralded as one of its key strengths, this is typically only true on average. The computational geometry literature has shown ray-tracing algorithms that have worst-case logarithmic running time, but these algorithms only work for certain types of scenes and have very expensive preprocessing and storage requirements. Szirmay-Kalos and Márton provide pointers to the relevant literature (Szirmay-Kalos and Márton 1998). In practice, the ray-tracing algorithms presented in this book are sublinear, but without expensive preprocessing and huge memory usage, it is always possible to construct worst-case scenes where ray tracing runs in $O(IN)$ time.

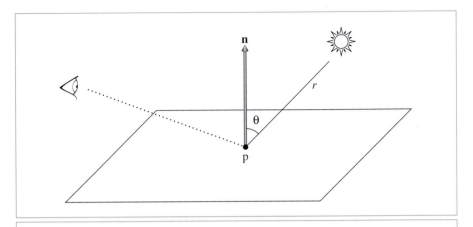

Figure 1.3: Geometric construction for evaluating the light energy at a point due to a point light source. The distance from the point to the light source is denoted by r.

1.2.3 LIGHT DISTRIBUTION

The ray-object intersection stage gives us a point to be shaded and some information about the geometry at that point. Recall that our eventual goal is to find the amount of light leaving this point in the direction of the eye. In order to do this, we need to know how much light is *arriving* at this point. This involves both the *geometric* and *radiometric* distribution of light in the scene. For very simple light sources (e.g., point lights), the geometric distribution of lighting is a simple matter of knowing the position of the lights. However, point lights do not exist in the real world, and so physically based lighting is often based on *area* light sources. This means that the light source is associated with a geometric object that emits illumination from its surface. However, we will use point lights in this section to illustrate the components of light distribution; rigorous discussion of light measurement and distribution is the topic of Chapters 5 and 13.

We would like to know the amount of light energy being deposited on the differential area surrounding the intersection point (Figure 1.3). We will assume that the light source has some power Φ associated with it, and that it radiates light equally in all directions. This means that the total amount of energy on a sphere surrounding the light is $\Phi/(4\pi)$. (All of these measurements will be explained and formalized in Chapter 13.) But if we consider two such spheres (Figure 1.4), it is clear that the energy at a point on the larger sphere must be less than the energy at a point on the smaller sphere because the same total energy is distributed over a larger area. Specifically, the amount of energy at a point on a sphere of radius r is proportional to $1/r^2$. Furthermore, it can be shown that if the tiny surface patch dA is tilted by an angle θ away from the vector from the surface point to the light, the amount of energy deposited on dA is proportional to $\cos\theta$.

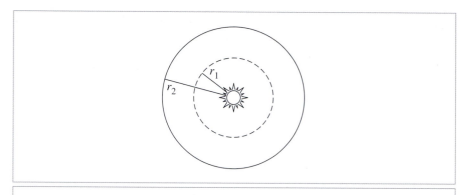

Figure 1.4: Since the point light radiates light equally in all directions, the same total energy is deposited on all spheres centered at the light.

Putting this all together, the total light energy dE (the *differential irradiance*) deposited on dA is

$$dE = \frac{\Phi \cos \theta}{4\pi r^2}.$$

Readers already familiar with basic lighting in computer graphics will notice two familiar laws encoded in this equation: the cosine falloff of light for tilted surfaces mentioned above, and the one-over-r-squared falloff of light with distance.

Scenes with multiple lights are easily handled because illumination is *linear*: the contribution of each light can be computed separately and summed to obtain the overall contribution.

1.2.4 VISIBILITY

The lighting distribution described in the previous section ignores one very important component: *shadows*. Each light contributes illumination to the point being shaded only if the path from the point to the light's position is unobstructed (Figure 1.5).

Fortunately, in a ray tracer it is trivial to determine if the light is visible from the point being shaded. We simply construct a new ray whose origin is at the surface point and whose direction points toward the light. These special rays are called *shadow rays*. If we trace this ray through the environment, we can use the parametric t value found by the intersection routines to determine the distance to the shadow ray's intersection point. If this distance is greater than the distance to the light or if no intersection is found, there is no blocking object between the light and the surface, and the light's contribution is included.

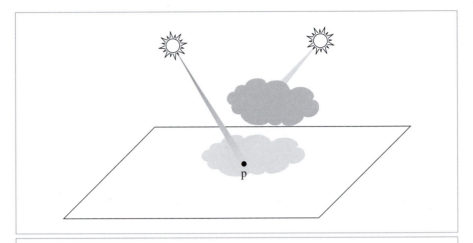

Figure 1.5: A light source only deposits energy on surfaces if the source is not obscured. The light source on the left illuminates the point p, but the light source on the right does not.

1.2.5 SURFACE SCATTERING

We now have the two pieces of information that are vital for proper shading of a point: its location and the incident lighting.[3] Now we need to determine how the incident lighting is *scattered* at the surface. Specifically, we are interested in the amount of light energy scattered back along the ray that we originally traced to find the intersection point, since that ray leads to the eye (Figure 1.6).

Each object in the scene provides a *material*, which is a description of its appearance properties at each point on the surface. This description is given by the *Bidirectional Reflectance Distribution Function* (BRDF). This function tells us how much energy is reflected from a given incoming direction ω_i to a given outgoing direction ω_o. We will write the BRDF at p as $f_r(p, \omega_o, \omega_i)$. Now, computing the amount of light L scattered back toward the eye is straightforward:

```
for each light:
    if light is not blocked:
        incident_light = light.L( point )
        amount_reflected =
            surface.BRDF( hit_point, light_vector, eye_vector )
        L += amount_reflected * incident_light
```

---

3   Readers already familiar with rendering might object that the discussion in this section considers only direct lighting. Rest assured that pbrt does support global illumination.

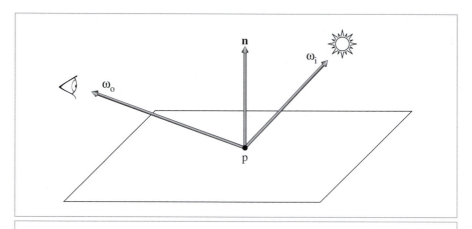

Figure 1.6: The Geometry of Surface Scattering. Incident light arriving along direction ω_i interacts with the surface at point p and is scattered back toward the eye along direction ω_o. The amount of light scattered toward the eye is given by the product of the incident light energy and the BRDF.

Here we are using L to represent the light; this represents a slightly different unit for measuring light than dE, which was used before.

It is easy to generalize the notion of a BRDF to transmitted light (obtaining a BTDF) or to general scattering of light arriving from either side of the surface. A function that describes general scattering is called a *Bidirectional Scattering Distribution Function*, (BSDF). pbrt supports a variety of both physically and phenomenologically based BSDF models; they are described in Chapter 9.

1.2.6 RECURSIVE RAY TRACING

Turner Whitted's original paper on ray tracing emphasized its *recursive* nature. For example, if a ray from the eye hits a shiny object like a mirror, we can *reflect* the ray about the surface normal at the intersection point and recursively call the ray-tracing routine to find the light arriving at the point on the mirror, adding its contribution to the original camera ray. This same technique can be used to trace transmitted rays that intersect transparent objects. For a long time, most early ray-tracing examples showcased mirrors and glass balls (Figure 1.7) because these types of effects are difficult to capture with other rendering techniques.

In general, the amount of light that reaches the eye from a point on an object is given by the sum of emitted light and reflected light. This idea is formalized by the *light transport equation* (also often known as the *rendering equation*), which says that the outgoing radiance $L_o(p, \omega_o)$ from a point p in direction ω_o is the emitted radiance at that point in that direction, $L_e(p, \omega_o)$, plus the incident radiance from all directions on the sphere $\mathbb{S}^2$ around p scaled by the BSDF $f(p, \omega_o, \omega_i)$ and a cosine term:

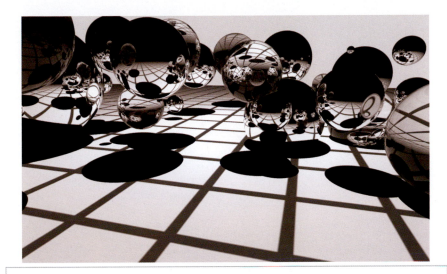

Figure 1.7: A Prototypical Example of Early Ray Tracing. Note the use of mirrored and glass objects, which emphasize the algorithm's ability to handle these kinds of surfaces.

$$L_o(p, \omega_o) = L_e(p, \omega_o) + \int_{\mathbb{S}^2} f(p, \omega_o, \omega_i)\, L_i(p, \omega_i)|\cos\theta_i|\mathrm{d}\omega_i. \tag{1.1}$$

We will show a more complete derivation of this equation later, in Sections 5.4 and 16.2. Solving this integral analytically is not possible except for the simplest of scenes, so we must either make simplifying assumptions or use numerical integration techniques.

Whitted's algorithm approximates this integral by ignoring incoming light from most directions and only evaluating $L_i(p, \omega_i)$ for directions to light sources and for the directions of perfect reflection and refraction. In other words, it turns the integral into a sum over a small number of directions.

Whitted's method can be extended to capture more effects than just perfect mirrors and glass. For example, by tracing many recursive rays near the mirror-reflection direction and averaging their contributions, we obtain an approximation of glossy reflection. In fact, we can *always* recursively trace a ray whenever we hit an object. For example, we can randomly choose a reflection direction ω_i and weight the contribution of this newly spawned ray by evaluating the BRDF $f_r(p, \omega_o, \omega_i)$. This simple but powerful idea can lead to very realistic images because it captures all of the interreflection of light between objects. Of course, we need to know when to terminate the recursion, and choosing directions completely at random may make the rendering algorithm slow to converge to a reasonable result. These problems can be addressed, however; these issues are the topic of Chapters 14–16.

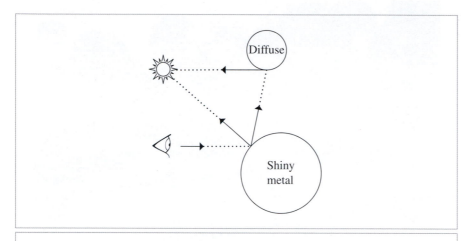

Figure 1.8: Recursive ray tracing associates an entire tree of rays with each image location.

When we trace rays recursively in this manner, we are really associating a *tree* of rays with each image location (Figure 1.8). The ray from the eye always appears at the root of this tree. Note that each ray in this tree can have a *weight* associated with it; this allows us to model, for example, shiny surfaces that do not reflect 100% of the incoming light.

1.2.7 RAY PROPAGATION

The prior discussion has assumed that rays are traveling through a vacuum. For example, when describing the distribution of light from a point source, we assumed that the energy was distributed equally on the surface of a sphere centered at the light without decreasing along the way. The presence of *participating media* such as smoke, fog, or dust can invalidate this assumption. Many ray tracers ignore these phenomena, though doing so is quite limiting. Even if we are not making a rendering of a smoke-filled room, almost all outdoor scenes are affected substantially by participating media. For example, the Earth's atmosphere causes objects that are farther away to appear less saturated (Figure 1.9).

There are two ways in which a participating medium can affect the light propagating along a ray. First, the medium can *extinguish* (or *attenuate*) light, either by absorbing it or by scattering it in a different direction. We can capture this effect by computing the *transmittance T* between the ray origin and the intersection point. The transmittance tells us how much of the light scattered at the intersection point makes it back to the ray origin.

A participating medium can also add to the light along a ray. This can happen either if the medium emits light (as with a flame), or if the medium scatters light from other directions back along the ray (Figure 1.10). We can find this quantity by numerically

Figure 1.9: The Earth's Atmosphere Decreases Saturation with Distance. The scene on the top is rendered without simulating this phenomenon, while the scene on the bottom includes an atmospheric model. This sort of atmospheric attenuation is an important depth cue when viewing real scenes and adds a sense of scale to the rendering on the bottom.

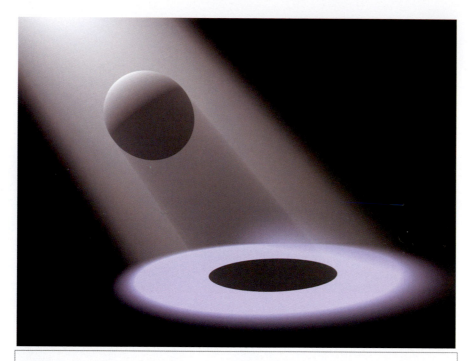

Figure 1.10: A Spotlight Shining on a Sphere through Fog. Notice that the shape of the spotlight's lighting distribution and the sphere's shadow are clearly visible due to the additional scattering in the participating medium.

evaluating the *volume light transport equation*, in the same way we evaluated the light transport equation to find the amount of light reflected from a surface. We will leave the description of participating media and volume rendering until Chapters 12 and 17. For now, it will suffice to say that we can compute the effect of participating media and add it to the ray's contribution.

1.3 pbrt: SYSTEM OVERVIEW

pbrt is written using a plug-in architecture. The pbrt executable consists of the core code that drives the system's main flow of control, but contains no code related to specific elements like spheres or spotlights. The core renderer is written in terms of the abstract base classes that define the interfaces to the plug-in types. At run time, modules are loaded to provide the child classes needed for the particular scene being rendered. This method of organization makes it easy to extend the system; substantial new functionality can be added by just writing a new plug-in. Of course, it is impossible to foresee all of

> **Table 1.1: Plug-ins.** pbrt supports 13 types of plug-in objects that can be loaded at run time based on the contents of the scene description file. The system can be extended with new plug-ins without needing to be recompiled itself.

Base class	Directory 💿	Section
Shape	shapes/	3.1
Primitive	accelerators/	4.1
Camera	cameras/	6.1
Sampler	samplers/	7.2
Filter	filters/	7.6
Film	film/	8.1
ToneMap	tonemaps/	8.4
Material	materials/	10.2
Texture	textures/	11.3
VolumeRegion	volumes/	12.3
Light	lights/	13.1
SurfaceIntegrator	integrators/	Ch. 16 intro
VolumeIntegrator	integrators/	17.2

the ways that a developer might want to extend the system, so more far-reaching projects may require modifications to the core renderer.

The source code to pbrt is distributed across a small directory hierarchy that can be found on the accompanying CD. All of the code for the pbrt core is in the core/💿 directory, and the main() function is contained in the short file renderer/pbrt.cpp.💿 pbrt supports 13 different types of plug-ins, summarized in Table 1.1. Low-level details of the routines that load these modules are discussed in Section B.4 in Appendix B. Section B.4.1 describes the process for adding new plug-ins to the system.

Throughout this section are a number of images rendered with pbrt. Of them, Figures 1.11 through 1.14 are notable: not only are they visually impressive, but each of them was created by a student in a rendering course where the final class project was to extend pbrt with new functionality in order to render an interesting image. These images are among the best from those courses.

1.3.1 PHASES OF EXECUTION

pbrt can be conceptually divided into three phases of execution. First, it parses the scene description file provided by the user. This is a text file that specifies the geometric shapes that make up the scene, their material properties, the lights that illuminate them, where the virtual camera is positioned in the scene, and parameters to all of the individual algorithms used throughout the system. Each statement in the input file has a direct

Figure 1.11: Guillaume Poncin and Pramod Sharma extended `pbrt` in numerous ways, implementing a number of complex rendering algorithms, to make this prize-winning image for Stanford's cs348b rendering competition. The trees are modeled procedurally with L-systems, a glow image processing filter increases the apparent realism of the lights on the tree, snow was modeled procedurally with metaballs, and a subsurface scattering algorithm gave the snow its realistic appearance by accounting for the effect of light that travels beneath the snow for some distance before leaving it.

mapping to one of the routines in Appendix B; these routines comprise the procedural interface for describing a scene to `pbrt`. A number of example scenes are provided in the `examples/` directory in the `pbrt` distribution; Appendix C describes the scene file format. The end result of the parsing phase is an instance of the Scene class.

Once the scene has been specified, the main rendering loop begins. This phase is where `pbrt` usually spends the majority of its running time, and most of this book describes code that executes during this phase. The rendering loop is implemented in the `Scene::Render()` method, which is be the focus of Section 1.3.3. This method determines the light arriving at a virtual film plane for a large number of rays in order to model the process of image formation.

Finally, once the contributions of all of these film samples have been computed, the third phase of execution performs postprocessing of the image before it is written to disk. Statistics about the various rendering algorithms used are printed, and the scene

Scene 23

Scene::Render() 24

Figure 1.12: Rui Wang won the rendering competition in UVA's advanced rendering course by extending pbrt with an implementation of a subsurface scattering algorithm, which efficiently models the effect of light that enters a surface at one point and exits elsewhere (Jensen, Marschner, Levoy, and Hanrahan 2001). This effect leads to a very convincing rendering of jade with a complex geometric model.

description data in memory is deallocated. The renderer then resumes processing statements from the scene description file until no more remain, allowing the user to specify another scene to be rendered, if desired.

1.3.2 SCENE REPRESENTATION

pbrt's main() function can be found in the file renderer/pbrt.cpp. This function is quite simple; after calling pbrtInit(), which does systemwide initialization, it parses the given scene description(s), leading to the creation of a Scene object that represents all of the elements (shapes, lights, etc.) that make up the scene. Because the input can specify multiple scenes to be rendered, rendering actually begins as soon as the appropriate input directive is parsed. After all rendering is done, pbrtCleanup() does final cleanup before the system exits.

The pbrtInit() and pbrtCleanup() functions appear in a *mini-index* in the page margin, along with the number of the page where they are actually defined. The mini-indices have

(a)

(b)

(c)

Figure 1.13: This image was created by Eric Lee, who extended `pbrt` in order to be able to render these two cars using image-based lighting algorithms and composite them onto a photograph of the Stanford Quad (a) using techniques first proposed by Paul Debevec (1998). First, he created a high-dynamic range light map by photographing a mirrored ball in the original environment at various exposures and assembling the images together (b). This light map was then used to synthetically light the 3D models during rendering (c). Finally, the rendered objects were composited onto the original photograph of the background using differential rendering (note the shadows that the cars cast on the ground). *Car models are copyright Fabrice Heillouis dmi.chez.tiscali.fr, and used with permission. Images are copyright Eric Lee homepage.mac.com/eric.lee.*

Figure 1.14: Jared Jacobs and Michael Turitzin added an implementation of Kajiya and Kay's texel-based fur rendering algorithm (Kajiya and Kay 1989) to pbrt and rendered this image, where both the fur on the dog and the shag carpet are rendered with the texel fur algorithm.

pointers to the definitions of almost all of the functions, classes, methods, and member variables used or referred to on each page.

⟨*main program*⟩ ≡
```
int main(int argc, char *argv[]) {
    pbrtInit();
    ⟨Process scene description 22⟩
    pbrtCleanup();
    return 0;
}
```

pbrtCleanup() 883

pbrtInit() 883

If pbrt is run with no command line arguments, then the scene description is read from standard input. Otherwise it loops through the command line arguments, processing each input filename in turn. No command line arguments other than filenames are supported.

⟨*Process scene description*⟩ ≡   21
```
    if (argc == 1) {
        ⟨Parse scene from standard input  22⟩
    } else {
        ⟨Parse scene from input files  22⟩
    }
```

The ParseFile() function parses a scene description file, either from standard input or from a file on disk; it returns false if it was unable to open the file. The mechanics of parsing scene description files will not be described in this book; the parser implementation can be found in the lex and yacc files core/pbrtlex.l🔴 and core/pbrtparse.y,🔴 respectively. Readers who want to understand the parsing subsystem but are not familiar with these tools may wish to consult Levine, Mason, and Brown (1992). We use the common UNIX idiom that a file named "-" represents standard input:

⟨*Parse scene from standard input*⟩ ≡   22
```
    ParseFile("-");
```

If a particular input file can't be opened, the Error() routine reports this information to the user. Error() uses the same format string semantics as printf().

⟨*Parse scene from input files*⟩ ≡   22
```
    for (int i = 1; i < argc; i++)
        if (!ParseFile(argv[i]))
            Error("Couldn't open scene file \"%s\"\n", argv[i]);
```

As the scene file is parsed, objects are created that represent the camera, lights, and geometric primitives in the scene. Along with other objects that manage the rendering process itself, these are all grouped together in the Scene object, which is allocated by the RenderOptions::MakeScene() method in Section B.3.7 in Appendix B. The Scene class is declared in core/scene.h🔴 and defined in core/scene.cpp. 🔴 Notice the COREDLL macro in its class declaration; this explicitly identifies this class as one that we would like to export from the core rendering library, and is necessary on the Windows platform. More information about dynamic libraries can be found in Section B.4.

We will not include the implementation of the Scene constructor here; it just stores copies of its arguments in the various member variables inside the class.

⟨*Scene Declarations*⟩ ≡
```
class COREDLL Scene {
public:
    ⟨Scene Public Methods 29⟩
    ⟨Scene Data 23⟩
};
```

Each geometric object in the scene is represented by a `Primitive`, which combines two objects: a `Shape` that specifies its geometry, and a `Material` that describes its appearance (e.g., the object's color, whether it has a dull or glossy finish, etc.). All of these geometric primitives are collected into a single `Primitive` called `Scene::aggregate`. This is represented by a special kind of primitive that itself holds references to many other primitives. To the rest of the system, however, it appears no different than a regular primitive. The specific class used to implement `Scene::aggregate` stores all the scene's primitives in an acceleration data structure that reduces unnecessary ray intersection tests.

⟨*Scene Data*⟩ ≡   **23**
```
Primitive *aggregate;
```

Each light source in the scene is represented by a `Light` object, which specifies the shape of a light and the distribution of energy that it emits. The `Scene` stores all of the lights in a `vector` class from the C++ standard library. While some renderers support separate light lists per geometric object, allowing a light to illuminate only some of the objects in the scene, this idea does not map well to the physically based rendering approach taken in pbrt, so we use only this per-scene list.

⟨*Scene Data*⟩+≡   **23**
```
vector<Light *> lights;
```

The `Camera` object controls the viewing and lens parameters such as position, orientation, focus, and field of view. A `Film` member variable inside the `Camera` class handles image storage. The `Camera` classes are described in Chapter 6, and `Film` is described in Chapter 8. After the image has been computed, the `Film` is responsible for writing the image to disk.

⟨*Scene Data*⟩+≡   **23**
```
Camera *camera;
```

In addition to geometric primitives, pbrt also supports participating media, or *volumetric* primitives. These types of primitives are supported through the `VolumeRegion` interface. The system's support for participating media is described in Chapter 12. Like `Primitives`, multiple `VolumeRegions` are all stored together in a single aggregate region `Scene::volumeRegion`.

⟨*Scene Data*⟩+≡   **23**
```
VolumeRegion *volumeRegion;
```

Integrators handle the task of simulating the propagation of light in the scene in order to compute how much light arrives at image sample positions on the film plane. They are so named because they numerically evaluate the integrals in the surface and volume light transport equations that describe the distribution of light in the environment. SurfaceIntegrators compute reflected light from geometric surfaces, while VolumeIntegrators handle the scattering from volumetric primitives. Integrators are described in Chapters 16 and 17.

⟨*Scene Data*⟩+≡   23
```
SurfaceIntegrator *surfaceIntegrator;
VolumeIntegrator *volumeIntegrator;
```

Finally, each Scene contains a class called Sampler. The role of this class is subtle, but its implementation can substantially affect the quality of the images that the system generates. First, the sampler is responsible for choosing the points on the image plane from which rays are traced. Second, it is responsible for supplying the sample positions used by the integrators in their light transport computations; for example, some integrators need to choose random points on light sources to compute illumination from area lights. Generating a good distribution of samples is an important part of the rendering process and is discussed in Chapter 7.

⟨*Scene Data*⟩+≡   23
```
Sampler *sampler;
```

1.3.3 MAIN RENDERING LOOP

After the Scene has been allocated and initialized, the Scene::Render() method is invoked, starting the second phase of pbrt's execution: the main rendering loop. For each of a series of positions on the image plane, this method uses the Camera and the Sampler to generate a ray into the scene, and then uses the SurfaceIntegrator and VolumeIntegrator to determine the amount of light arriving at the image plane along that ray. This value is passed to the Film, which records the light's contribution. Figure 1.15 summarizes the main classes used in this method and the flow of data among them.

⟨*Scene Methods*⟩≡
```
void Scene::Render() {
    ⟨Allocate and initialize sample 25⟩
    ⟨Allow integrators to do pre-processing for the scene 25⟩
    ⟨Trace rays: The main loop 26⟩
    ⟨Clean up after rendering and store final image 28⟩
}
```

Before rendering starts, the Render() method constructs a Sample object, into which the Sampler will store the samples it generates during the main loop. Because the number and types of samples that need to be generated are partially dependent on the integrators, the Sample constructor takes pointers to the integrators so they can be queried for their

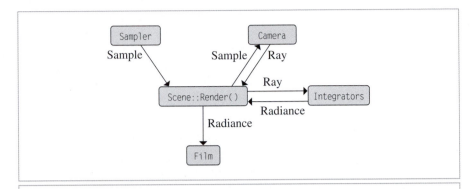

Figure 1.15: Class Relationships for the Main Rendering Loop in the `Scene::Render()` Method in `core/scene.cpp`. The `Sampler` provides a sequence of sample values, one for each image sample to be taken. The `Camera` turns a sample into a corresponding ray from the film plane, and the `Integrators` compute the radiance along that ray arriving at the film. The sample and its radiance are given to the `Film`, which stores their contribution in an image. This process repeats until the `Sampler` has provided as many samples as are necessary to generate the final image.

requirements. See Section 7.2.1 for more information about how integrators request particular sets of samples.

⟨*Allocate and initialize* `sample`⟩ ≡   24
```
    Sample *sample = new Sample(surfaceIntegrator,
                                volumeIntegrator,
                                this);
```

The only other task to complete before rendering can begin is to call the `Preprocess()` methods of the integrators. Because information like the specific light sources and geometry of the scene aren't known when the integrators are first created, the `Preprocess()` method gives them an opportunity to do the necessary scene-dependent initialization. For example, the `PhotonIntegrator` in Section 16.5 uses this opportunity to create data structures that hold a representation of the distribution of illumination in the scene.

⟨*Allow integrators to do pre-processing for the scene*⟩ ≡   24
```
    surfaceIntegrator->Preprocess(this);
    volumeIntegrator->Preprocess(this);
```

Ray tracing can be a slow algorithm, particularly for complex scenes with complex lighting. The `ProgressReporter` object gives the user visual feedback regarding *pbrt's* progress; this can make waiting for a long rendering job much less frustrating. The `ProgressReporter` constructor takes the total number of "work steps" as a parameter, so that it knows the total amount of work to be done.

Finally, the main rendering loop begins. Each time through the loop, `Sampler::GetNextSample()` is called to initialize `sample` with the next image sample value; it returns `false` when there are no more samples. The fragments in the loop body find the corresponding camera ray and pass it to the integrators to compute the radiance along the ray arriving at the film plane. Finally, they add the result to the image, deallocate some memory allocated along the way, and update the `ProgressReporter`.

⟨*Trace rays: The main loop*⟩ ≡   24
```
    ProgressReporter progress(sampler->TotalSamples(), "Rendering");
    while (sampler->GetNextSample(sample)) {
        ⟨Find camera ray for sample 26⟩
        ⟨Evaluate radiance along camera ray  27⟩
        ⟨Add sample contribution to image  28⟩
        ⟨Free BSDF memory from computing image sample value  28⟩
        ⟨Report rendering progress  28⟩
    }
```

The only method in the `Camera` interface is `Camera::GenerateRay()`, which returns the ray to trace for a given image sample position. This method is passed a sample and a pointer to a ray; it initializes all of the fields of the ray based on the contents of the sample. The direction vector of the generated ray must be of unit length; most of the integrators depend on this property.

The camera also returns a floating-point weight associated with the ray. For simple camera models, each ray is weighted equally, but more complex `Cameras` may generate some rays that contribute more than others. For example, in a real camera, less light arrives at the edges of the film plane than at the center, an effect called *vignetting*. The returned weight is used to scale the ray's contribution to the image.

Notice that the class we use to represent the camera ray is called `RayDifferential`; this is a subclass of the parent `Ray` class and will be explained shortly.

⟨*Find camera ray for* `sample`⟩ ≡   26
```
    RayDifferential ray;
    float rayWeight = camera->GenerateRay(*sample, &ray);
    ⟨Generate ray differentials for camera ray  27⟩
```

In order to get better results from some of the texture functions defined in Chapter 11, it is useful to have the rays that the `Camera` would generate for samples that are one pixel away on the image plane in both the *x* and *y* directions. The additional rays will allow us to compute how quickly a texture varies with respect to the pixel spacing, a key component of texture antialiasing. While the `Ray` class just holds the origin and direction of a single ray, `RayDifferential` inherits from `Ray` so that it has not only those member variables, but also two additional `Rays`, rx and ry, to hold these neighbors.

⟨*Generate ray differentials for camera ray*⟩ ≡   26
```
++(sample->imageX);
camera->GenerateRay(*sample, &ray.rx);
--(sample->imageX);
++(sample->imageY);
camera->GenerateRay(*sample, &ray.ry);
ray.hasDifferentials = true;
--(sample->imageY);
```

Now that we have a ray, the next task is to determine the amount of light arriving at the image plane along that ray. The unit that describes the strength of this light is called *radiance*. The symbol for radiance arriving along a ray is L_i, so the method to compute radiance is Scene::Li(). The implementation of this method is shown in the next section. Radiance values are represented by the Spectrum class, which is pbrt's abstraction for energy distributions that vary over wavelength—in other words, *color*.

In addition to returning radiance, Scene::Li() sets the alpha variable to the *alpha value* for this ray. Alpha encodes the cumulative *opacity* along the ray. If the ray hits an opaque object, alpha is 1, indicating that nothing behind the intersection point is visible. If the ray passed through something partially transparent, like fog, but never hit an opaque object, alpha is between 0 and 1. If the ray didn't hit anything, alpha is 0. Storing an alpha value with each pixel can be useful for a variety of postprocessing effects. For example, alpha makes it possible to composite a rendered object on top of a photograph, using each pixel's alpha value to interpolate between the rendering and the photograph.

⟨*Evaluate radiance along camera ray*⟩ ≡   26
```
float alpha;
Spectrum Ls = 0.f;
if (rayWeight > 0.f)
    Ls = rayWeight * Li(ray, sample, &alpha);
```
⟨*Issue warning if unexpected radiance value returned*⟩

A common side effect of bugs in the rendering process is that impossible radiance values are computed. For example, division by zero often results in radiance values equal to the IEEE floating-point "not a number" value. The renderer looks for this possibility, as well as spectra with infinite or negative contributions, and prints an error message when it encounters them. Here we won't include the fragment that does this, ⟨*Issue warning if unexpected radiance value returned*⟩, since it is straightforward and not very interesting. See the implementation in core/scene.cpp if you're interested in its details.

After the ray's contribution is known, the image can be updated. The Film::AddSample() method updates the pixels in the image given the results from this sample. The details of this process are explained in Sections 7.6, 8.1, and 8.2.

⟨*Add sample contribution to image*⟩ ≡   26
```
    camera->film->AddSample(*sample, ray, Ls, alpha);
```

pbrt uses the BSDF class to describe the material properties of a point on a surface; they will be described in more detail later in this chapter and also in Chapter 9. During rendering, it is necessary to dynamically allocate memory to store the BSDFs used to compute the contribution of each sample. In order to avoid calling the system's memory allocation routines many times to do this, the system uses the MemoryArena class to manage pools of memory for BSDFs. Section 10.1.1 describes this process in more detail. Once the contribution for a sample has been computed, the rendering loop here can inform the BSDF class that all of the memory allocated for the sample is no longer needed.

⟨*Free BSDF memory from computing image sample value*⟩ ≡   26
```
    BSDF::FreeAll();
```

In order to simplify the task of gathering statistics that are meaningful or interesting to the user, a few statistics-tracking classes are defined in Section A.1.3 in Appendix A. StatsCounter overloads the ++ operator to increment the counter. Finally, a call to ProgressReporter::Update() lets the ProgressReporter know that one step of the task that it is tracking has been completed. Except in this introduction, code to gather statistics will be omitted from this book.

⟨*Report rendering progress*⟩ ≡   26
```
    static StatsCounter cameraRaysTraced("Camera", "Camera Rays Traced");
    ++cameraRaysTraced;
    progress.Update();
```

At the end of the main loop, Scene::Render() frees the sample memory, lets the progress reporter know that the task has completed, and begins the third phase of pbrt's execution with a call to Film::WriteImage(), where the imaging pipeline prepares the final image for storage.

⟨*Clean up after rendering and store final image*⟩ ≡   24
```
    delete sample;
    progress.Done();
    camera->film->WriteImage();
```

1.3.4 SCENE METHODS

The Scene class has only a handful of additional methods besides Render(); its main purpose is to hold variables that represent the scene. The methods it does have just forward requests to methods of the Scene's member variables.

The Scene::Intersect() method traces the given ray into the scene and returns a boolean value indicating whether the ray intersected any of the primitives. If so, it fills in the provided Intersection structure with information about the closest intersection point along the ray. The Intersection structure is defined in Section 4.1.

⟨*Scene Public Methods*⟩ ≡   23
```
bool Intersect(const Ray &ray, Intersection *isect) const {
    return aggregate->Intersect(ray, isect);
}
```

A closely related method is Scene::IntersectP(), which checks for the existence of intersections along the ray, but does not return any information about those intersections. Because this routine doesn't need to search for the closest intersection or compute any additional information about the intersections, it is more efficient than Scene::Intersect() when this additional information isn't needed. This routine is used for shadow rays.

⟨*Scene Public Methods*⟩ + ≡   23
```
bool IntersectP(const Ray &ray) const {
    return aggregate->IntersectP(ray);
}
```

Scene::WorldBound() returns a 3D box that bounds all of the geometry in the scene, which is simply the bounding box of Scene::aggregate. The Scene class caches this bound to avoid having to repeatedly compute it.

⟨*Scene Data*⟩ + ≡   23
```
BBox bound;
```

⟨*Scene Constructor Implementation*⟩ ≡
```
bound = aggregate->WorldBound();
```

⟨*Scene Methods*⟩ + ≡
```
const BBox &Scene::WorldBound() const {
    return bound;
}
```

The Scene::Li() method computes the radiance along the given ray. This method first calls SurfaceIntegrator::Li() to compute the outgoing radiance L_o from the first surface that the ray intersects and then stores the result in Lo. It then invokes VolumeIntegrator::Transmittance() to compute the fraction of light T that is extinguished between the surface and the camera due to participating media. Finally, VolumeIntegrator::Li() determines the radiance L_v added along the ray due to interactions with participating media. The net effect of these interactions is $T L_o + L_v$; this calculation is explained further in Sections 17.1 and 17.2.

⟨*Scene Methods*⟩+≡
```
Spectrum Scene::Li(const RayDifferential &ray,
                   const Sample *sample, float *alpha) const {
    Spectrum Lo = surfaceIntegrator->Li(this, ray, sample, alpha);
    Spectrum T = volumeIntegrator->Transmittance(this, ray, sample, alpha);
    Spectrum Lv = volumeIntegrator->Li(this, ray, sample, alpha);
    return T * Lo + Lv;
}
```

It is also useful to isolate the computation of attenuation along a ray due to participating media; the `Scene::Transmittance()` method returns this quantity by forwarding the request to the `VolumeIntegrator::Transmittance()` method.

⟨*Scene Methods*⟩+≡
```
Spectrum Scene::Transmittance(const Ray &ray) const {
    return volumeIntegrator->Transmittance(this, ray, NULL, NULL);
}
```

1.3.5 AN INTEGRATOR FOR WHITTED-STYLE RAY TRACING

Chapters 16 and 17 include the implementations of many different surface and volume integrators, based on a variety of algorithms with differing levels of accuracy. Here we will present a surface integrator based on Whitted's ray-tracing algorithm. This integrator accurately computes reflected and transmitted light from specular surfaces like glass, mirrors, and water, although it doesn't account for other types of indirect lighting effects like light bouncing off a wall and illuminating a room. The more complex integrators later in the book build on the ideas in this integrator to implement more sophisticated light transport algorithms. The `WhittedIntegrator` class can be found in the `integrators/whitted.cpp`⊙ file in the pbrt distribution.

⟨*WhittedIntegrator Declarations*⟩≡
```
class WhittedIntegrator : public SurfaceIntegrator {
public:
    ⟨WhittedIntegrator Public Methods⟩
private:
    ⟨WhittedIntegrator Private Data  32⟩
};
```

The key method that all integrators must provide is `Integrator::Li()`, which returns the radiance along a ray. Figure 1.16 summarizes the data flow among the main classes used during integration at surfaces.

⟨*WhittedIntegrator Method Definitions*⟩ ≡
```
Spectrum WhittedIntegrator::Li(const Scene *scene,
        const RayDifferential &ray, const Sample *sample,
        float *alpha) const {
    Intersection isect;
    Spectrum L(0.);
    bool hitSomething;
    ⟨Search for ray-primitive intersection 31⟩
    if (!hitSomething) {
        ⟨Handle ray with no intersection 31⟩
    }
    else {
        ⟨Initialize alpha for ray hit 32⟩
        ⟨Compute emitted and reflected light at ray intersection point 33⟩
    }
    return L;
}
```

The integrator first needs to determine what primitive was hit by the ray, so it calls
`Scene::Intersect()`:

⟨*Search for ray-primitive intersection*⟩ ≡   31
```
hitSomething = scene->Intersect(ray, &isect);
```

Handling rays that don't hit any geometry is quite simple. We initially set their alpha value
to be fully transparent. However, certain types of light sources may not be associated
with any geometry but can still contribute radiance to rays that do not hit anything. For
example, the Earth's sky illuminates points on the Earth's surface with blue light, even
though there isn't geometry associated with the sky per se. Therefore, for rays that do
not hit anything, each light's `Light::Le()` method is called so that these particular lights
can contribute to the ray's radiance. Most light sources will not contribute in this way,
but in certain cases this is very useful. See Section 13.5 for an example of a light that can
illuminate the film plane directly. If any light has fallen on the film plane, the alpha value
is set to be one (fully opaque).

⟨*Handle ray with no intersection*⟩ ≡   31
```
if (alpha) *alpha = 0.;
for (u_int i = 0; i < scene->lights.size(); ++i)
    L += scene->lights[i]->Le(ray);
if (alpha && !L.Black()) *alpha = 1.;
return L;
```

The Whitted integrator works by recursively evaluating radiance along reflected and refracted ray directions. It keeps track of the depth of recursion in the variable
`WhittedIntegrator::rayDepth` and stops the recursion at a predetermined maximum

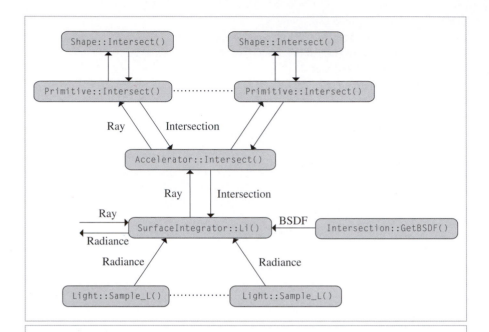

Figure 1.16: Class Relationships for Surface Integration. The main rendering loop passes a camera ray to the `SurfaceIntegrator`, which returns the radiance along that ray arriving at the film plane. The integrator uses the `Scene::Intersect()` method to find the first surface that the ray intersects; this method in turn passes the request on to an accelerator `Primitive`. The accelerator performs ray-primitive intersection tests with the geometric `Primitives` that the ray potentially intersects, using each shape's `Shape::Intersect()` routine. Once the `Intersection` is returned to the integrator, it gets the material properties at the intersection point in the form of a `BSDF` and uses the `Lights` in the `Scene` to determine the illumination there. This gives the information needed to compute the radiance reflected back along the ray at the intersection point.

depth, `WhittedIntegrator::maxDepth`. By default, the maximum recursion depth is five. Without this termination criterion, the recursion might never terminate (imagine a hall-of-mirrors scene). These two member variables are initialized in the `WhittedIntegrator` constructor, which we will not show here.

⟨*WhittedIntegrator Private Data*⟩ ≡   30
```
int maxDepth;
mutable int rayDepth;
```

If an intersection is found, the first task is to initialize the output variable `alpha`. Remember that `alpha` records the opacity of the hit point. Here it is initialized to one:

⟨*Initialize* alpha *for ray hit*⟩ ≡   31
```
if (alpha) *alpha = 1.;
```

Now we reach the heart of the Whitted integrator, which sums the contribution of each light source and models perfect reflection and refraction:

⟨*Compute emitted and reflected light at ray intersection point*⟩ ≡   31
    ⟨*Evaluate BSDF at hit point* **33**⟩
    ⟨*Initialize common variables for Whitted integrator* **33**⟩
    ⟨*Compute emitted light if ray hit an area light source* **34**⟩
    ⟨*Add contribution of each light source* **35**⟩
    if (rayDepth++ < maxDepth) {
        ⟨*Trace rays for specular reflection and refraction* **36**⟩
    }
    --rayDepth;

Bidirectional Scattering Distribution Functions are represented in pbrt by the BSDF class. pbrt provides BSDF implementations for several standard scattering functions used in computer graphics, such as Lambertian reflection and the Torrance-Sparrow microfacet model. These and other reflection models are described in Chapter 9.

The BSDF interface makes it possible to shade a particular surface point, but BSDFs may vary across a surface. Surfaces with complex material properties, such as wood or marble, have a different BSDF at each point. Even if wood is modeled as perfectly diffuse, the color at each point will depend on the wood's grain. These spatial variations of shading parameters are described with Textures, which in turn may be described procedurally or stored in image maps (Chapter 11).

To obtain the BSDF at the hit point, the integrator calls the Intersection::GetBSDF() method:

⟨*Evaluate BSDF at hit point*⟩ ≡   **33, 750**
    BSDF *bsdf = isect.GetBSDF(ray);

Figure 1.17 shows a few quantities that will be used frequently in the fragments to come; p represents the position of the ray-primitive intersection, and n is the surface normal at the intersection point. The normalized direction from the hit point back to the ray origin is stored in wo; because Cameras are responsible for normalizing the direction component of generated rays, there's no need to renormalize it here. Normalized directions are denoted by the ω symbol in this book, and in pbrt's code we will use the shorthand wo for ω_o, the outgoing direction of scattered light.

⟨*Initialize common variables for Whitted integrator*⟩ ≡   **33**
    const Point &p = bsdf->dgShading.p;
    const Normal &n = bsdf->dgShading.nn;
    Vector wo = -ray.d;

In case the ray happened to hit geometry that is emissive (such as an area light source), the integrator computes the emitted radiance by calling the Intersection::Le() method.

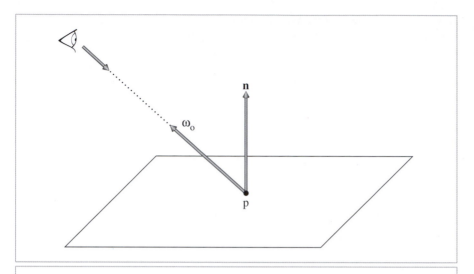

Figure 1.17: Geometric Setting for the Whitted Integrator. p is the ray intersection point and **n** is the surface normal there. The direction in which we'd like to compute reflected radiance is ω_o; it is the vector pointing in the opposite direction of the incident ray.

This gives us the first term of the light transport equation, Equation (1.1) on page 13. If the object is not emissive, this method returns a black spectrum.

⟨*Compute emitted light if ray hit an area light source*⟩ ≡   33
```
L += isect.Le(wo);
```

For each light, the integrator calls the `Light::Sample_L()` method to compute the radiance from that light falling on the surface at the point being shaded. This method also returns the direction vector from the point being shaded to the light source, which is stored in the variable `wi`. This method does not account for the possibility that some other shape may block light from the light and prevent it from reaching the point being shaded. Instead, it returns a `VisibilityTester` object that can be used to determine if any primitives block the surface point from the light source. This test is done by tracing a shadow ray between the point being shaded and the light to verify that the path is clear.

Intersection::Le() 620

Light::Sample_L() 695

VisibilityTester 600

pbrt's code is organized in this way in order to be able to avoid having to trace the shadow ray unless necessary. Specifically, it can first make sure that the light falling on the surface *would* be scattered in the direction ω_o if the light isn't blocked. For example, if the surface is not transmissive, then light arriving at the back side of the surface doesn't contribute to reflection.

If the arriving radiance is nonzero and the BSDF indicates a nonzero contribution for the pair of directions (ω_o, ω_i), the integrator multiplies the radiance value L_i by the value of the BSDF, a cosine term, as well as the transmittance between the intersection point and the light. This product represents the light's contribution to the light transport equation integral, and it is added to the total reflected radiance L_o. After all lights have been considered, the integrator has computed the total contribution of *direct lighting*— light that arrives at the surface directly from emissive objects (as opposed to light that has reflected off other objects in the scene before arriving at the point).

⟨*Add contribution of each light source*⟩ ≡   33

```
Vector wi;
for (u_int i = 0; i < scene->lights.size(); ++i) {
    VisibilityTester visibility;
    Spectrum Li = scene->lights[i]->Sample_L(p, &wi, &visibility);
    if (Li.Black()) continue;
    Spectrum f = bsdf->f(wo, wi);
    if (!f.Black() && visibility.Unoccluded(scene))
        L += f * Li * AbsDot(wi, n) *
        visibility.Transmittance(scene);
}
```

This integrator also handles light scattered by perfectly specular surfaces like mirrors or glass. It is fairly simple to use properties of mirrors to find the reflected directions (Figure 1.18), and Snell's law to find the transmitted directions. The integrator can then recursively follow the appropriate ray in the new direction and add its contribution to the reflected radiance at the point originally seen from the camera.

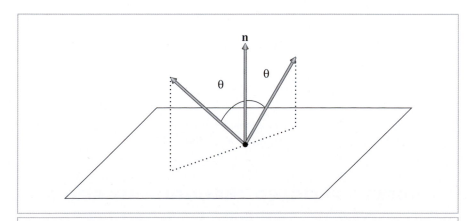

Figure 1.18: Reflected rays due to perfect specular reflection make the same angle with the surface normal as the incident ray.

The `BSDF::Sample_f()` method returns an incident ray direction for a given outgoing direction and a given mode of light scattering. It is one of the foundations of the Monte Carlo light transport algorithms that will be the subject of the last few chapters of this book. Here, we will use it to find only outgoing directions corresponding to perfect specular reflection or refraction, using flags to indicate to `BSDF::Sample_f()` that other types of reflection should be ignored. Although `BSDF::Sample_f()` can sample random directions leaving the surface for probabilistic integration algorithms, the randomness is constrained to be consistent with the BSDF's scattering properties. In the case of perfect specular reflection or refraction, only one direction is possible, so there is no randomness at all.

The two calls to `BSDF::Sample_f()` in the following fragment initialize wi with the chosen direction and return the BSDF's value for the directions (ω_o, ω_i). If the value of the BSDF is nonzero, the integrator uses the `Scene::Li()` method to get the incoming radiance along ω_i, which will eventually cause the `WhittedIntegrator::Li()` method to be called again. To compute the cosine term of the reflection integral, the integrator calls the `AbsDot()` function, which returns the absolute value of the dot product between two vectors. If the vectors are normalized, as both wi and n are here, this is equal to the cosine of the angle between them.

In order to use ray differentials to antialias textures that are seen in reflections or refractions, it is necessary to know how reflection and transmission affect the screen-space footprint of rays. The fragments that compute the ray differentials for these rays are defined in Section 11.1.3.

⟨*Trace rays for specular reflection and refraction*⟩ ≡   **33, 760**
```
    Spectrum f = bsdf->Sample_f(wo, &wi,
        BxDFType(BSDF_REFLECTION | BSDF_SPECULAR));
    if (!f.Black()) {
        ⟨Compute ray differential rd for specular reflection  496⟩
        L += f * scene->Li(rd, sample) * AbsDot(wi, n);
    }
    f = bsdf->Sample_f(wo, &wi,
        BxDFType(BSDF_TRANSMISSION | BSDF_SPECULAR));
    if (!f.Black()) {
        ⟨Compute ray differential rd for specular transmission⟩
        L += f * scene->Li(rd, sample) * AbsDot(wi, n);
    }
```

AbsDot() 52
BSDF 462
BSDF::Sample_f() 691
BSDF_REFLECTION 415
BSDF_SPECULAR 415
BSDF_TRANSMISSION 415
BxDFType 415
Scene::Li() 30
Spectrum 230
WhittedIntegrator::Li() 31

1.4 HOW TO PROCEED THROUGH THIS BOOK

We have written this book assuming it will be read in roughly front-to-back order. We have tried to minimize the number of forward references to ideas and interfaces that haven't yet been introduced, but do assume that the reader is acquainted with the previous content at any particular point in the text. However, some sections go into depth about advanced topics that some readers may wish to skip over (particularly on first reading); each advanced section is identified by an asterisk in its title.

Because of the modular nature of the system, the main requirement is that the reader be familiar with the low-level classes like `Point`, `Ray`, and `Spectrum`; the interfaces defined by the abstract base classes listed in Table 1.1; and the main rendering loop in `Scene::Render()`. Given that knowledge, for example, the reader who doesn't care about precisely how a camera model based on a perspective projection matrix maps samples to rays can skip over the implementation of that camera and can just remember that the `Camera::GenerateRay()` method somehow turns a `Sample` into a `Ray`.

The rest of this book is divided into four main parts of a few chapters each. First, Chapters 2 through 4 define the main geometric functionality in the system. Chapter 2 has the low-level classes like `Point`, `Ray`, and `BBox`. Chapter 3 defines the `Shape` interface, gives implementations of a number of shapes, and shows how to perform ray-shape intersection tests. Chapter 4 has the implementations of the acceleration structures for speeding up ray tracing by avoiding tests with primitives that a ray can be shown to definitely not intersect.

The second part covers the image formation process. First, Chapter 5 introduces the physical units used to measure light, and the `Spectrum` class that represents wavelength-varying distributions (i.e., color). Chapter 6 defines the `Camera` interface and has a few different camera implementations. The `Sampler` classes that place samples on the image plane are the topic of Chapter 7, and the overall process of turning radiance values on the film into images suitable for display is explained in Chapter 8.

The third part of the book is about light and how it scatters from surfaces and participating media. Chapter 9 includes a set of building-block classes that define a variety of types of reflection from surfaces. Materials, described in Chapter 10, use these reflection functions to implement a number of different surface materials, such as plastic, glass, and metal. Chapter 11 introduces texture, which describes variation in material properties (color, roughness, etc.) over surfaces, and Chapter 12 has the abstractions that describe how light is scattered and absorbed in participating media. Finally, Chapter 13 has the interface for light sources and light source implementations.

The last part brings all of the ideas from the rest of the book together to implement a number of integrators. Chapters 14 and 15 introduce the theory of Monte Carlo integration, a statistical technique for estimating the value of complex integrals, and have low-level routines for applying Monte Carlo to illumination and light scattering. The surface and volume integrators in Chapters 16 and 17 use Monte Carlo integration to compute more accurate approximations of the light transport equation than the `WhittedIntegrator`, using techniques like path tracing, irradiance caching, and photon mapping. The final chapter of the book has a brief retrospective and discussion of system

BBox 60
Camera 256
Camera::GenerateRay() 256
Point 54
Ray 59
Sample 299
Sampler 296
Scene::Render() 24
Shape 90
Spectrum 230
WhittedIntegrator 30

design decisions along with a number of suggestions for more far-reaching projects than those in the exercises.

1.4.1 THE EXERCISES

At the end of each chapter you will find exercises related to the material covered in that chapter. Each exercise is marked as one of three levels of difficulty:

- ❶ an exercise that should take only an hour or two
- ❷ a reading and/or implementation task that would be suitable for a course assignment and should take between 10 and 20 hours of work
- ❸ a suggested final project for a course that will likely take 40 hours or more to complete

1.5 USING AND UNDERSTANDING THE CODE

We have written pbrt in C++. However, we have used only a subset of the language, both to make the code easy to understand, as well as to maximize the system's portability. In particular, we have avoided multiple inheritance and run time exception handling, and have used only a small subset of C++'s extensive standard library.

We will occasionally omit short sections of pbrt's source code from this document. For example, when there are a number of cases to be handled, all with nearly identical code, we will present one case and note that the code for the remaining cases has been omitted from the text. Of course, all the omitted code can be found on the companion CD.

1.5.1 POINTER OR REFERENCE?

C++ provides two different mechanisms for passing the address of a data structure to a function: pointers and references. If a function argument is not intended as an output variable, either can be used to save the expense of passing the entire structure on the stack. By convention, pbrt uses pointers when the function argument will be modified in some way, and const references when it won't. One important exception to this rule is that we will always use a pointer when we want to be able to pass NULL to indicate that a parameter is not available or should not be used.

1.5.2 CODE OPTIMIZATION

We have tried to make pbrt efficient through the use of well-chosen algorithms rather than through local micro-optimizations. However, we have applied some local optimizations to the parts of pbrt that account for the most execution time, as long as doing so didn't make the code confusing. There are two main local optimization principles used throughout the code:

- • On current CPU architectures, the slowest mathematical operations are divides, square roots, and trigonometric functions. Addition, subtraction, and multiplication are generally 10–50 times faster than those operations. Reducing the number of slow mathematical operations can help performance substantially; for example, instead of repeatedly dividing by some value v, we will tend to precompute the reciprocal $1/v$ and multiply by that instead.

- The speed of CPUs continues to grow more quickly than the speed at which data can be loaded from main memory into the CPU. This means that waiting for values to be fetched from memory can be a major performance limitation. Organizing algorithms and data structures in ways that give good performance from memory caches can speed up program execution much more than reducing the total number of instructions executed. Section A.2 in Appendix A discusses general principles for memory-efficient programming; these ideas are mostly applied in the ray intersection acceleration structures of Chapter 4 and the image map representation in Section 11.4.2, although they influence many of the design decisions throughout the system.

1.5.3 THE BOOK WEB SITE

We have created a companion Web site for this book, located at *www.pbrt.org*. The Web site includes supplementary material such as updates to the source code, additional modules, example scenes, and errata. We will also host contributed pbrt modules from readers.

All readers are encouraged to visit the Web site and follow the instructions to subscribe to the *pbrt-announce@pbrt.org* mailing list. We will occasionally send announcements of software updates to this list, so readers can always have the latest version of pbrt and all the latest modules. We will also host other mailing lists relating to pbrt, as well as an online discussion forum and a bug-tracking system.

1.5.4 BUGS

Although we have made every effort to make pbrt as correct as possible through extensive testing, it is inevitable that some bugs are still present. If you believe you have found a bug, please do the following:

1. Make sure you test with an unmodified copy of the latest version of pbrt. We will not debug modified versions of pbrt, even if you believe that the error is unrelated to your changes.
2. Check the online discussion forum and the bug-tracking system at *www.pbrt.org*. Your issue may be a known bug, or it may be a commonly misunderstood feature.
3. Remove as much as you can from the input file that demonstrates the bug. Many bugs can be demonstrated by input files that are just a few lines long.
4. Submit a detailed bug report using our online bug-tracking system. Make sure that you include the short input file that demonstrates the bug and a detailed description of why you think pbrt is not behaving correctly on your input.

FURTHER READING

In a seminal early paper, Arthur Appel (1968) first described the basic idea of ray tracing to solve the hidden surface problem and to compute shadows in polygonal scenes. Goldstein and Nagel (1971) later showed how ray tracing could be used to render scenes with quadric surfaces. Kay and Greenberg (1979) described a ray-tracing approach to rendering transparency, and Whitted's seminal *CACM* article described the general recursive ray-tracing algorithm we have outlined in this chapter, accurately simulating reflection and refraction from specular surfaces and shadows from point light sources (Whitted 1980). Heckbert (1987) was the first to explore realistic rendering of dessert.

Notable books on physically based rendering and image synthesis include Cohen and Wallace's *Radiosity and Realistic Image Synthesis* (Cohen and Wallace 1993), Sillion and Puech's *Radiosity and Global Illumination* (Sillion and Puech 1994), and Ashdown's *Radiosity: A Programmer's Perspective* (Ashdown 1994), all of which primarily describe the finite-element radiosity method. Glassner's *Principles of Digital Image Synthesis* (Glassner 1995) is an encyclopedic two-volume summary of theoretical foundations for realistic rendering. Hall's *Illumination and Color in Computer Generated Imagery* (Hall 1989) is one of the first books to present rendering in a physically based framework. Dutré et al.'s *Advanced Global Illumination* has extensive and up-to-date coverage of these topics (Dutré, Bekaert, and Bala 2003).

Greenberg et al. (1997) make a strong argument for a physically accurate rendering based on measurements of the material properties of real-world objects and on deep understanding of the human visual system. These ideas have served as a basis for much of the rendering research done at Cornell over the past two decades.

In a paper on ray-tracing system design, Kirk and Arvo (1988) suggested many principles that have now become classic in renderer design. Their renderer was implemented as a core kernel that encapsulated the basic rendering algorithms and interacted with primitives and shading routines via a carefully constructed object-oriented interface. This approach made it easy to extend the system with new primitives and acceleration methods. pbrt's plug-in design is based on these ideas.

Another good reference on ray tracer design is *Introduction to Ray Tracing* (Glassner 1989a), which describes the state of the art in ray tracing at that time and has a chapter by Heckbert that sketches the design of a basic ray tracer. Also, Shirley and Morley's *Realistic Ray Tracing* gives an easy-to-understand introduction to ray tracing and includes the complete source code to a basic ray tracer (Shirley and Morley 2003).

Researchers at Cornell University have developed a rendering testbed over many years; its design and overall structure is described by Trumbore, Lytle, and Greenberg (1993). Its predecessor was described by Hall and Greenberg (1983). This system is a loosely coupled set of modules and libraries, each designed to handle a single task (ray-object intersection acceleration, image storage, etc.) and written in a way that makes it easy to combine appropriate modules to investigate and develop new rendering algorithms. This testbed has been quite successful, serving as the foundation for much of the rendering research done at Cornell.

Many papers have been written that describe the design and implementation of other rendering systems, including renderers for entertainment and artistic applications. The REYES architecture, which forms the basis for Pixar's RenderMan renderer, was first described by Cook, Carpenter, and Catmull (1987), and a number of improvements to the original algorithm are summarized by Apodaca and Gritz (2000). Gritz and Hahn (1996) describe the BMRT ray tracer. The renderer in the Maya modeling and animation system is described by Sung et al. (1998), and some of the internal structure of the *mental ray* renderer is described in Driemeyer and Herken's book on its API (Driemeyer and Herken 2002).

Another category of renderer focuses on physically based rendering, like pbrt. One of the first renderers based fundamentally on physical quantities is called *Radiance*, and it has been used widely in lighting simulation applications. Ward describes its design and history in a paper and a book (Ward 1994b; Larson and Shakespeare 1998). Radiance is designed in the UNIX style, as a set of interacting programs, each handling a different part of the rendering process. This general type of rendering architecture was first described by Duff (1985).

Glassner's *Spectrum* rendering architecture also focuses on physically based rendering (Glassner 1993), approached through a signal-processing-based formulation of the problem. It is an extensible system built with a plug-in architecture; pbrt's approach of using parameter/value lists for initializing plug-in objects is similar to *Spectrum*'s. One notable feature of *Spectrum* is that all parameters that describe the scene can be functions of time.

Slusallek and Seidel describe the architecture of the *Vision* rendering system, which is also physically based and designed to support a wide variety of light transport algorithms (Slusallek and Seidel 1995, 1996; Slusallek 1996). In particular, it has the ambitious goal of supporting both Monte Carlo and finite-element-based light transport algorithms. The *RenderPark* rendering system also supports a variety of physically based rendering algorithms, including both Monte Carlo and finite-element approaches. It was developed by Bekaert, Suykens, Peers, and Masselus and is available from *www.cs.kuleuven.ac.be/cwis/research/graphics/RENDERPARK*.

The source code to a number of other ray tracers and renderers is available on the Web. Notable ones include Mark VandeWettering's *MTV*, which was the first freely available ray tracer to be widely distributed; it was posted to the *comp.sources.unix* newsgroup in 1988. Craig Kolb's *rayshade* had a number of releases during the 1990s; its current homepage is *graphics.stanford.edu/~cek/rayshade/rayshade.html*. The *Radiance* system is available from *radsite.lbl.gov/radiance/HOME.html*. POV-Ray is used by a large number of individuals and is available from *www.povray.org*.

A good introduction to the C++ programming language and C++ standard library is the third edition of Stroustrup's *The C++ Programming Language* (Stroustrup 1997).

EXERCISE

● **1.1**   A good way to gain understanding of pbrt is to follow the process of computing the radiance value for a single ray in a debugger. Build a version of pbrt with debugging symbols and set up your debugger to run pbrt with the killeroo-simple.pbrt scene from the examples/⊙ directory. Set a breakpoint in the Scene::Render() method and trace through the process of how a ray is generated, how its radiance value is computed, and how its contribution is added to the image.

As you gain more understanding about the details of the system later in the book, repeat this process and trace through particular parts of the system more carefully.

Scene::Render() 24

CHAPTER TWO

02 GEOMETRY AND TRANSFORMATIONS

Almost all nontrivial graphics programs are built on a foundation of geometric classes. These classes represent mathematical constructs like points, vectors, and rays. Because these classes are ubiquitous throughout the system, good abstractions and efficient implementations are critical. This chapter presents the interface to and implementation of pbrt's geometric foundation. Note that these are not the classes that represent the actual scene geometry (triangles, spheres, etc.); those classes are the topic of Chapter 3.

The geometric classes in this chapter are defined in the files `core/geometry.h` and `core/geometry.cpp`, and transformation matrices (Section 2.7) can be found in the files `core/transform.h` and `core/transform.cpp`.

2.1 COORDINATE SYSTEMS

As is typical in computer graphics, pbrt represents three-dimensional points, vectors, and normal vectors with three floating-point coordinate values: x, y, and z. Of course, these values are meaningless without a *coordinate system* that defines the origin of the space and gives three nonparallel vectors that define the x, y, and z axes of the space. Together, the origin and three vectors are called the *frame* that defines the coordinate system. Given an arbitrary point or direction in 3D, its (x, y, z) coordinate values depend

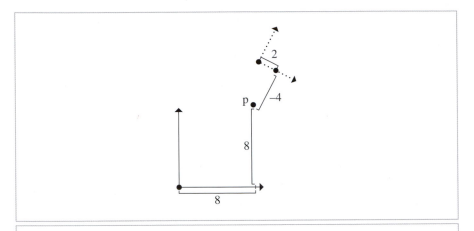

Figure 2.1: In 2D, the (x, y) coordinates of a point p are defined by the relationship of the point to a particular 2D coordinate system. Here, two coordinate systems are shown; the point might have coordinates (8, 8) with respect to the coordinate system with its coordinate axes drawn in solid lines, but have coordinates (2, −4) with respect to the coordinate system with dashed axes. In either case, the 2D point p is at the same absolute position in space.

on its relationship to the frame. Figure 2.1 shows an example that illustrates this idea in 2D.

In the general n-dimensional case, a frame's origin p_o and its n linearly independent basis vectors define an n-dimensional *affine space*. All vectors **v** in the space can be expressed as a linear combination of the basis vectors. Given a vector **v** and the basis vectors v_i, there is a unique set of scalar values s_i such that

$$\mathbf{v} = s_1\mathbf{v}_1 + \cdots + s_n\mathbf{v}_n.$$

The scalars s_i are the *representation* of **v** with respect to the basis $\{\mathbf{v}_1, \mathbf{v}_2, \ldots, \mathbf{v}_n\}$ and are the coordinate values that we store with the vector. Similarly, for all points p, there are unique scalars s_i such that the point can be expressed in terms of the origin p_o and the basis vectors

$$\mathbf{p} = p_o + s_1\mathbf{v}_1 + \cdots + s_n\mathbf{v}_n.$$

Thus, although points and vectors are both represented by x, y, and z coordinates in 3D, they are distinct mathematical entities and are not freely interchangeable.

This definition of points and vectors in terms of coordinate systems reveals a paradox: to define a frame we need a point and a set of vectors. But we can only meaningfully talk about points and vectors with respect to a particular frame. Therefore, we need a *standard frame* with origin (0, 0, 0) and basis vectors (1, 0, 0), (0, 1, 0), and (0, 0, 1). All

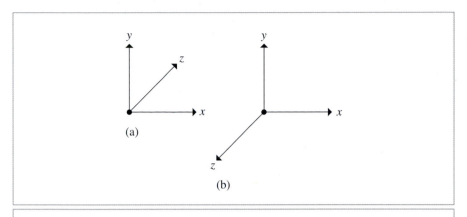

Figure 2.2: (a) In a left-handed coordinate system, the z axis points into the page when the x and y axes are oriented with x pointing to the right and y pointing up. (b) In a right-handed system, the z axis points out of the page.

other frames will be defined with respect to this canonical coordinate system. We will call this coordinate system *world space*.

2.1.1 COORDINATE SYSTEM HANDEDNESS

There are two different ways that the three coordinate axes can be arranged, as shown in Figure 2.2. Given perpendicular x and y coordinate axes, the z axis can point in one of two directions. These two choices are called *left-handed* and *right-handed*. The choice between the two is arbitrary, but has a number of implications for how some of the geometric operations throughout the chapter are defined. pbrt uses a left-handed coordinate system.

2.2 VECTORS

⟨*Geometry Declarations*⟩ ≡
```
    class COREDLL Vector {
    public:
        ⟨Vector Public Methods  48⟩
        ⟨Vector Public Data  48⟩
    };
```

COREDLL 904

Vector 47

A Vector in pbrt represents a direction in 3D space. As described earlier, vectors are represented with a three-tuple of components that give its representation in terms of the x, y, and z axes of the space it is defined in. The individual components of a vector $\mathbf{v}$ will be written $\mathbf{v}_x$, $\mathbf{v}_y$, and $\mathbf{v}_z$.

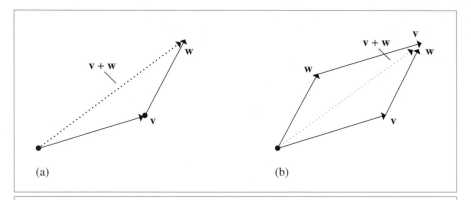

Figure 2.3: (a) Vector addition: $\mathbf{v} + \mathbf{w}$. (b) Notice that the sum $\mathbf{v} + \mathbf{w}$ forms the diagonal of the parallelogram formed by $\mathbf{v}$ and $\mathbf{w}$, which shows the commutativity of vector addition: $\mathbf{v} + \mathbf{w} = \mathbf{w} + \mathbf{v}$.

⟨*Vector Public Data*⟩ ≡   **47**
```
float x, y, z;
```

Readers who are experienced in object-oriented design might object to our decision to make the Vector data publicly accessible. Typically, data members are only accessible inside the class, and external code that wishes to access or modify the contents of a class must do so through a well-defined API of selector and mutator functions. Although we generally agree with this design principle, it is not appropriate here. The purpose of selector and mutator functions is to hide the class's internal implementation details. In the case of Vectors, hiding this basic part of their design gains nothing and adds bulk to the class usage.

By default, the (x, y, z) values are set to zero, although the user of the class can optionally supply values for each of the components:

⟨*Vector Public Methods*⟩ ≡   **47**
```
Vector(float _x=0, float _y=0, float _z=0)
   : x(_x), y(_y), z(_z) {
}
```

2.2.1 ARITHMETIC

Vector 47

Addition and subtraction of vectors is done component-wise. The usual geometric interpretation of vector addition and subtraction is shown in Figures 2.3 and 2.4.

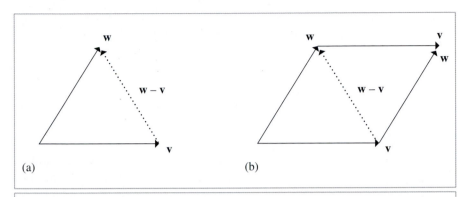

Figure 2.4: (a) Vector subtraction. (b) The difference $-\mathbf{v} - \mathbf{w}$ is the other diagonal of the parallelogram formed by $\mathbf{v}$ and $\mathbf{w}$.

⟨*Vector Public Methods*⟩+≡   **47**
```
Vector operator+(const Vector &v) const {
    return Vector(x + v.x, y + v.y, z + v.z);
}

Vector& operator+=(const Vector &v) {
    x += v.x; y += v.y; z += v.z;
    return *this;
}
```

The code for subtracting two vectors is similar, and therefore not shown here.

2.2.2 SCALING

A vector can be multiplied component-wise by a scalar, thereby changing its length. Three functions are needed in order to cover all of the different ways that this operation may be written in source code (i.e., v*s, s*v, and v *= s):

⟨*Vector Public Methods*⟩+≡   **47**
```
Vector operator*(float f) const {
    return Vector(f*x, f*y, f*z);
}

Vector &operator*=(float f) {
    x *= f; y *= f; z *= f;
    return *this;
}
```

Vector 47

⟨*Geometry Inline Functions*⟩ ≡
```
inline Vector operator*(float f, const Vector &v) {
    return v*f;
}
```

Similarly, a vector can be divided component-wise by a scalar. The code for scalar division is similar to scalar multiplication, although division of a scalar by a vector is not well defined, and so is not permitted.

In the implementation of these methods, we use a single division to compute the scalar's reciprocal, then perform three component-wise multiplications. This is a useful trick for avoiding division operations, which are generally much slower than multiplies on modern CPUs.[1]

We use the Assert() macro to make sure that the given scale is not zero; this should never happen and would indicate a bug elsewhere in the system. When compiled in optimized mode, this macro will not perform the check, saving the expense of verifying this case. Assert() is defined in Section A.1.1 in Appendix A.

⟨*Vector Public Methods*⟩+≡   47
```
Vector operator/(float f) const {
    Assert(f!=0);
    float inv = 1.f / f;
    return Vector(x * inv, y * inv, z * inv);
}

Vector &operator/=(float f) {
    Assert(f!=0);
    float inv = 1.f / f;
    x *= inv; y *= inv; z *= inv;
    return *this;
}
```

The Vector class also provides a unary negation operator that returns a new vector pointing in the opposite direction of the original one:

---

1   It is a common misconception that these sorts of optimizations are unnecessary because the compiler will perform the necessary analysis. Compilers are frequently unable to perform optimizations that require symbolic manipulation of expressions. For example, given two floating-point numbers, the quantities a+b and b+a are not candidates for common subexpression elimination because the IEEE floating-point standard (which is standard on modern architectures) does not guarantee that the two sums will be identical. In fact, compilers are limited in their ability to legally make these substitutions because expressions may have been carefully ordered in order to minimize round-off error.

⟨*Vector Public Methods*⟩+≡   47
```
Vector operator-() const {
    return Vector(-x, -y, -z);
}
```

Some routines will find it useful to be able to easily loop over the components of a Vector; the Vector class also provides a C++ operator so that given a vector v, then v[0] == v.x and so forth.

⟨*Vector Public Methods*⟩+≡   47
```
float operator[](int i) const {
    Assert(i >= 0 && i <= 2);
    return (&x)[i];
}


float &operator[](int i) {
    Assert(i >= 0 && i <= 2);
    return (&x)[i];
}
```

2.2.3 DOT AND CROSS PRODUCT

Two useful operations on vectors are the dot product (also known as the scalar or inner product) and the cross product. For two vectors **v** and **w**, their *dot product* (**v** · **w**) is defined as

$$\mathbf{v}_x\mathbf{w}_x + \mathbf{v}_y\mathbf{w}_y + \mathbf{v}_z\mathbf{w}_z.$$

⟨*Geometry Inline Functions*⟩+≡
```
inline float Dot(const Vector &v1, const Vector &v2) {
    return v1.x * v2.x + v1.y * v2.y + v1.z * v2.z;
}
```

The dot product has a simple relationship to the angle between the two vectors:

$$(\mathbf{v} \cdot \mathbf{w}) = \|\mathbf{v}\|\|\mathbf{w}\|\cos\theta, \tag{2.1}$$

where θ is the angle between **v** and **w**, and $\|\mathbf{v}\|$ denotes the length of the vector **v**. It follows from this that (**v** · **w**) is zero if and only if **v** and **w** are perpendicular, provided that neither **v** nor **w** is *degenerate*—equal to $(0, 0, 0)$. A set of two or more mutually perpendicular vectors is said to be *orthogonal*. An orthogonal set of unit vectors is called *orthonormal*.

Assert() 835

Vector 47

It immediately follows from Equation (2.1) that if **v** and **w** are unit vectors, their dot product is exactly the cosine of the angle between them. As the cosine of the angle between two vectors often needs to be computed in computer graphics, we will frequently make use of this property.

A few basic properties directly follow from the definition. For example, if $\mathbf{u}$, $\mathbf{v}$, and $\mathbf{w}$ are vectors and s is a scalar value, then

$$(\mathbf{u} \cdot \mathbf{v}) = (\mathbf{v} \cdot \mathbf{u})$$
$$(s\mathbf{u} \cdot \mathbf{v}) = s(\mathbf{v} \cdot \mathbf{u})$$
$$(\mathbf{u} \cdot (\mathbf{v} + \mathbf{w})) = (\mathbf{u} \cdot \mathbf{v}) + (\mathbf{u} \cdot \mathbf{w}).$$

We will frequently need to compute the absolute value of the dot product as well. The `AbsDot()` function does this for us so that we don't need a separate call to `fabsf()`:

⟨*Geometry Inline Functions*⟩+≡
```
inline float AbsDot(const Vector &v1, const Vector &v2) {
    return fabsf(Dot(v1, v2));
}
```

The *cross product* is another useful vector operation. Given two vectors in 3D, the cross product $\mathbf{v} \times \mathbf{w}$ is a vector that is perpendicular to both of them. Note that this new vector can point in one of two directions; the coordinate system's handedness determines which is appropriate. Given orthogonal vectors $\mathbf{v}$ and $\mathbf{w}$, then $\mathbf{v} \times \mathbf{w}$ is defined to be a vector such that $(\mathbf{v}, \mathbf{w}, \mathbf{v} \times \mathbf{w})$ form a coordinate system of the appropriate handedness.

In a left-handed coordinate system, the cross product is defined as

$$(\mathbf{v} \times \mathbf{w})_x = \mathbf{v}_y \mathbf{w}_z - \mathbf{v}_z \mathbf{w}_y$$
$$(\mathbf{v} \times \mathbf{w})_y = \mathbf{v}_z \mathbf{w}_x - \mathbf{v}_x \mathbf{w}_z$$
$$(\mathbf{v} \times \mathbf{w})_z = \mathbf{v}_x \mathbf{w}_y - \mathbf{v}_y \mathbf{w}_x.$$

An easy way to remember this is to compute the determinant of the matrix

$$\mathbf{v} \times \mathbf{w} = \begin{vmatrix} i & j & k \\ \mathbf{v}_x & \mathbf{v}_y & \mathbf{v}_z \\ \mathbf{w}_x & \mathbf{w}_y & \mathbf{w}_z \end{vmatrix},$$

where i, j, and k represent the axes $(1, 0, 0)$, $(0, 1, 0)$, and $(0, 0, 1)$, respectively. Note that this equation is merely a memory aid and not a rigorous mathematical construction, since the matrix entries are a mix of scalars and vectors.

⟨*Geometry Inline Functions*⟩+≡
```
inline Vector Cross(const Vector &v1, const Vector &v2) {
    return Vector((v1.y * v2.z) - (v1.z * v2.y),
                  (v1.z * v2.x) - (v1.x * v2.z),
                  (v1.x * v2.y) - (v1.y * v2.x));
}
```

From the definition of the cross product, we can derive

$$\|\mathbf{v} \times \mathbf{w}\| = \|\mathbf{v}\| \|\mathbf{w}\| \sin\theta, \qquad\qquad [2.2]$$

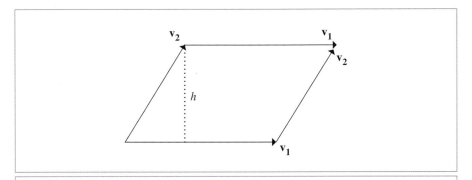

Figure 2.5: The area of a parallelogram with edges given by vectors v_1 and v_2 is equal to $v_1 h$. The cross product can easily compute this value as $\|v_1 \times v_2\|$.

where θ is the angle between **v** and **w**. An important implication of this is that the cross product of two perpendicular unit vectors is itself a unit vector. Note also that the result of the cross product is a degenerate vector if **v** and **w** are parallel.

This definition also shows a convenient way to compute the area of a parallelogram (Figure 2.5). If the two edges of the parallelogram are given by vectors v_2 and v_1, and it has height h, the area is given by $\|v_2\| h$. Since $h = \sin \theta \|v_1\|$, we can use Equation (2.2) to see that the area is $\|v_1 \times v_2\|$.

2.2.4 NORMALIZATION

It is often necessary to *normalize* a vector—that is, to compute a new vector pointing in the same direction but with unit length. A normalized vector is often called a *unit vector*. The function to do this is called `Normalize()`. The notation used in this book for normalized vectors is that $\hat{v}$ is the normalized version of **v**. `Vector::Normalize()` divides each component by the length of the vector, denoted in text by $\|v\|$.

⟨*Vector Public Methods*⟩+≡   47
```
    float LengthSquared() const { return x*x + y*y + z*z; }
    float Length() const { return sqrtf(LengthSquared()); }
```

`Vector::Normalize()` returns a new vector; it does *not* normalize the vector in place:

⟨*Geometry Inline Functions*⟩+≡
```
    inline Vector Normalize(const Vector &v) {
        return v / v.Length();
    }
```

2.2.5 COORDINATE SYSTEM FROM A VECTOR

We will frequently want to construct a local coordinate system given only a single vector. Because the cross product of two vectors is orthogonal to both, we can apply the cross product two times to get a set of three orthogonal vectors for the coordinate system. Note that the two vectors generated by this technique are unique only up to a rotation about the given vector.

The implementation of this function assumes that the vector passed in, v1, has already been normalized. It first constructs a perpendicular vector by zeroing one of the two components of the original vector and swapping the remaining two. Inspection of the two cases should make clear that v2 will be normalized and that the dot product $(\mathbf{v}_1 \cdot \mathbf{v}_2)$ is equal to zero. Given these two perpendicular vectors, a single cross product gives the third, which by definition will be perpendicular to the first two.

⟨*Geometry Inline Functions*⟩+≡
```
inline void CoordinateSystem(const Vector &v1, Vector *v2, Vector *v3) {
    if (fabsf(v1.x) > fabsf(v1.y)) {
        float invLen = 1.f / sqrtf(v1.x*v1.x + v1.z*v1.z);
        *v2 = Vector(-v1.z * invLen, 0.f, v1.x * invLen);
    }
    else {
        float invLen = 1.f / sqrtf(v1.y*v1.y + v1.z*v1.z);
        *v2 = Vector(0.f, v1.z * invLen, -v1.y * invLen);
    }
    *v3 = Cross(v1, *v2);
}
```

2.3 POINTS

⟨*Geometry Declarations*⟩+≡
```
class COREDLL Point {
public:
    ⟨Point Methods  55⟩
    ⟨Point Public Data  55⟩
};
```

A point is a zero-dimensional location in 3D space. The Point class in pbrt represents points in the obvious way: using *x*, *y*, and *z* coordinates with respect to their coordinate system. Although the same (x, y, z) representation is used for vectors, the fact that a point represents a position, whereas a vector represents a direction, leads to a number of important differences in how they are treated. Points are denoted in text by p.

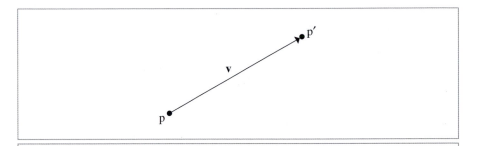

Figure 2.6: Obtaining the Vector between Two Points. The vector p′ − p is the component-wise subtraction of the points p′ and p.

⟨*Point Public Data*⟩ ≡   54
```
float x,y,z;
```

Like the Vector constructor, the Point constructor takes optional parameters to set the x, y, and z coordinate values.

⟨*Point Methods*⟩ ≡   54
```
Point(float _x=0, float _y=0, float _z=0)
    : x(_x), y(_y), z(_z) {
}
```

There are certain Point methods that either return or take a Vector. For instance, one can add a vector to a point, offsetting it in the given direction and obtaining a new point. Alternately, one can subtract one point from another, obtaining the vector between them, as shown in Figure 2.6.

⟨*Point Methods*⟩+≡   54
```
Point operator+(const Vector &v) const {
    return Point(x + v.x, y + v.y, z + v.z);
}

Point &operator+=(const Vector &v) {
    x += v.x; y += v.y; z += v.z;
    return *this;
}
```

Point 54
Vector 47

⟨*Point Methods*⟩+≡   **54**

```
Vector operator-(const Point &p) const {
    return Vector(x - p.x, y - p.y, z - p.z);
}

Point operator-(const Vector &v) const {
    return Point(x - v.x, y - v.y, z - v.z);
}

Point &operator-=(const Vector &v) {
    x -= v.x; y -= v.y; z -= v.z;
    return *this;
}
```

The distance between two points is easily computed by subtracting them to compute the vector between them and then finding the length of that vector:

⟨*Geometry Inline Functions*⟩+≡

```
inline float Distance(const Point &p1, const Point &p2) {
    return (p1 - p2).Length();
}
inline float DistanceSquared(const Point &p1, const Point &p2) {
    return (p1 - p2).LengthSquared();
}
```

Although in general it doesn't make sense mathematically to weight points by a scalar or add two points together, the Point class still allows these operations in order to be able to compute weighted sums of points, which is mathematically meaningful as long as the weights used all sum to one. The code for scalar multiplication and addition with Points is identical to Vectors, so it is not shown here.

2.4 NORMALS

⟨*Geometry Declarations*⟩+≡

```
class COREDLL Normal {
public:
    ⟨Normal Methods 57⟩
    ⟨Normal Public Data⟩
};
```

COREDLL 904
Point 54
Vector 47

A *surface normal* (or just *normal*) is a vector that is perpendicular to a surface at a particular position. It can be defined as the cross product of any two nonparallel vectors that are tangent to the surface at a point. Although normals are superficially similar to vectors, it is important to distinguish between the two of them: because normals are defined in terms of their relationship to a particular surface, they behave differently than vectors in some situations, particularly when applying transformations. This difference is discussed in Section 2.8.

The implementations of Normals and Vectors are very similar: like vectors, normals are represented by three floats x, y, and z; they can be added and subtracted to compute new normals; and they can be scaled and normalized. However, a normal cannot be added to a point, and one cannot take the cross product of two normals. Note that, in an unfortunate turn of terminology, normals are *not* necessarily normalized.

The Normal provides an extra constructor that initializes a Normal from a Vector. Because Normals and Vectors are different in subtle ways, we want to make sure that this conversion doesn't happen when we don't intend it to, but we'd like it to be possible where it is appropriate. Fortunately, the C++ explicit keyword ensures that conversion between two compatible types only happens when the programmer explicitly requests such a conversion. Vector also provides a constructor that converts the other way.

⟨*Normal Methods*⟩ ≡   56
```
explicit Normal(const Vector &v)
  : x(v.x), y(v.y), z(v.z) {}
```

⟨*Vector Public Methods*⟩+≡   47
```
explicit Vector(const Normal &n);
```

⟨*Geometry Inline Functions*⟩+≡
```
inline Vector::Vector(const Normal &n)
  : x(n.x), y(n.y), z(n.z) { }
```

Thus, given the declarations Vector v; Normal n;, the assignment n = v is illegal, so it is necessary to explicitly convert the vector, as in n = Normal(v).

The Dot() and AbsDot() functions are also overloaded to compute dot products between the various possible combinations of normals and vectors. This code won't be included in the text here. We also won't include implementations of all of the various other Normal methods here, since they are similar to those for vectors.

2.5 RAYS

⟨*Geometry Declarations*⟩+≡
```
class COREDLL Ray {
public:
    ⟨Ray Public Methods 59⟩
    ⟨Ray Public Data 58⟩
};
```

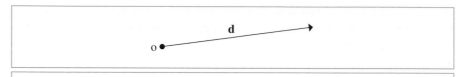

A *ray* is a semi-infinite line specified by its origin and direction. pbrt represents a Ray with a Point for the origin and a Vector for the direction. A ray is denoted by r; it has origin o and direction **d**, as shown in Figure 2.7. Because we will be referring to these variables often throughout the code, the origin and direction members of a Ray are named o and d. Note that we again choose to make the data publicly available for convenience.

⟨*Ray Public Data*⟩ ≡   57
```
    Point o;
    Vector d;
```

The *parametric form* of a ray expresses it as a function of a scalar value t, giving the set of points that the ray passes through:

$$r(t) = o + t\mathbf{d} \qquad 0 \le t \le \infty. \qquad [2.3]$$

The Ray also includes fields to limit the ray to a particular segment along its infinite extent. These fields, called mint and maxt, allow us to restrict the ray to a segment of points [r(mint), r(maxt)]. Notice that these fields are declared as mutable, meaning that they can be changed even if the Ray structure that contains them is const.

Thus, when a ray is passed to a method that takes a const Ray &, that method is not allowed to modify its origin or direction, but can modify its parametric range. This convention fits one of the most common uses of rays in the system, as parameters to ray-object intersection testing routines, which will record the offsets to the closest intersection in maxt.

⟨*Ray Public Data*⟩+≡   57
```
    mutable float mint, maxt;
```

For simulating motion blur, each ray may have a time value associated with it, so a data member to store time is available as well. The rest of the renderer is responsible for constructing a representation of the scene at the appropriate time for each ray.

⟨*Ray Public Data*⟩+≡   57
```
    float time;
```

Point 54
Ray 59
Vector 47

Constructing Rays is straightforward. The default constructor relies on the Point and Vector constructors to set the origin and direction to (0, 0, 0). Alternately, a particular point and direction can be provided. Also note that mint is initialized to a small constant rather than 0. The reason for this is discussed in Section 3.1.4—it is a classic ray-tracing hack to avoid false self-intersections due to floating-point precision limitations.

⟨*Ray Public Methods*⟩ ≡   57
```
Ray() : mint(RAY_EPSILON), maxt(INFINITY), time(0.f) { }
Ray(const Point &origin, const Vector &direction,
    float start = RAY_EPSILON, float end = INFINITY, float t = 0.f)
    : o(origin), d(direction), mint(start), maxt(end), time(t) { }
```

⟨*Global Constants*⟩ ≡
```
#define RAY_EPSILON 1e-3f
```

Because a ray can be thought of as a function of a single parameter t, the Ray class overloads the function application operator for rays. This way, when we need to find the point at a particular position along a ray, we can write code like

```
Ray r(Point(0,0,0), Vector(1,2,3));
Point p = r(1.7);
```

⟨*Ray Public Methods*⟩+≡   57
```
Point operator()(float t) const { return o + d * t; }
```

2.5.1 RAY DIFFERENTIALS

In order to be able to perform better antialiasing with the texture functions defined in Chapter 11, pbrt keeps track of some additional information with each ray that is traced. In Section 11.1, this information will be used to compute information so that the Texture class can estimate the projected area on the image plane of a small part of the scene. From this, the Texture can compute the texture's average value over that area, leading to a better final image.

RayDifferential is a subclass of Ray that contains additional information about two auxiliary rays. These extra rays represent camera rays offset one pixel in the x and y direction from the main ray. By determining the area that these three rays project to on an object being shaded, the Texture can estimate an area to average over for proper antialiasing.

Because the RayDifferential class inherits from Ray, geometric interfaces in the system are written to take const Ray & parameters, so that either a Ray or RayDifferential can be passed to them. Only the routines related to antialiasing and texturing require RayDifferential parameters.

⟨*Geometry Declarations*⟩+≡
```
class COREDLL RayDifferential : public Ray {
public:
    ⟨RayDifferential Methods 60⟩
    ⟨RayDifferential Public Data 60⟩
};
```

⟨*RayDifferential Methods*⟩≡   60
```
RayDifferential() { hasDifferentials = false; }
RayDifferential(const Point &org, const Vector &dir)
        : Ray(org, dir) {
    hasDifferentials = false;
}
```

Note that we again use the `explicit` keyword to prevent Rays from accidentally being converted to RayDifferentials. The constructor sets `hasDifferentials` to false initially because the neighboring rays are not yet known. These fields are initialized by the renderer's main loop, in the code fragment ⟨*Generate ray differentials for camera ray*⟩ defined on page 27.

⟨*RayDifferential Methods*⟩+≡   60
```
explicit RayDifferential(const Ray &ray) : Ray(ray) {
    hasDifferentials = false;
}
```

⟨*RayDifferential Public Data*⟩≡   60
```
bool hasDifferentials;
Ray rx, ry;
```

2.6 THREE-DIMENSIONAL BOUNDING BOXES

⟨*Geometry Declarations*⟩+≡
```
class COREDLL BBox {
public:
    ⟨BBox Public Methods 61⟩
    ⟨BBox Public Data 61⟩
};
```

COREDLL 904
Point 54
Ray 59
RayDifferential 60
Vector 47

The scenes that pbrt will render will often contain objects that are computationally expensive to process. For many operations, it is often useful to have a three-dimensional *bounding volume* that encloses an object. For example, if a ray does not pass through a particular bounding volume, pbrt can avoid processing all of the objects inside of it for that ray.

The measurable benefit of this technique is related to two factors: the expense of processing the bounding volume compared to the expense of processing the objects inside of it,

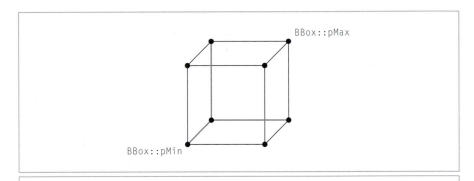

Figure 2.8: An Example Axis-Aligned Bounding Box. The BBox class stores only the coordinates of the minimum and maximum points of the box. All other box corners are implicit in this representation.

and the tightness of the fit of the bounding box. If we have a very loose bound around an object, we will often incorrectly determine that its contents need to be examined further. However, in order to make the bounding volume a closer fit, it may be necessary to make the volume a complex object itself, thus increasing the expense of processing it.

There are many choices for bounding volumes; pbrt uses *axis-aligned bounding boxes* (AABBs). Other popular choices are spheres and *oriented bounding boxes* (OBBs). An AABB can be described by one of its vertices and three lengths, each representing the distance spanned along the x, y, and z coordinate axes. Alternatively, two opposite vertices of the box describe it. We chose the two-point representation for pbrt's BBox class; it stores the positions of the vertex with minimum x, y, and z values and of the one with maximum x, y, and z. A 2D illustration of a bounding box and its representation is shown in Figure 2.8.

The default BBox constructor sets the extent to be degenerate; by violating the invariant that pMin.x <= pMax.x, and so on, this convention ensures that any operations done with this box will have the correct result for a completely empty box.

⟨*BBox Public Methods*⟩ ≡   60
```
BBox() {
    pMin = Point( INFINITY,  INFINITY,  INFINITY);
    pMax = Point(-INFINITY, -INFINITY, -INFINITY);
}
```

⟨*BBox Public Data*⟩ ≡   60
```
Point pMin, pMax;
```

It is also useful to be able to initialize a BBox to enclose a single point:

⟨*BBox Public Methods*⟩+≡   60
```
BBox(const Point &p) : pMin(p), pMax(p) { }
```

If the caller passes two corner points (p1 and p2) to define the box, since p1 and p2 are not necessarily chosen so that p1.x <= p2.x, and so on, the constructor needs to find their component-wise minimum and maximum values:

⟨*BBox Public Methods*⟩+≡   60

```
BBox(const Point &p1, const Point &p2) {
    pMin = Point(min(p1.x, p2.x),
                 min(p1.y, p2.y),
                 min(p1.z, p2.z));
    pMax = Point(max(p1.x, p2.x),
                 max(p1.y, p2.y),
                 max(p1.z, p2.z));
}
```

Given a bounding box and a point, the BBox::Union() function computes and returns a new bounding box that encompasses that point as well as the space that the original box encompassed:

⟨*BBox Method Definitions*⟩≡

```
COREDLL BBox Union(const BBox &b, const Point &p) {
    BBox ret = b;
    ret.pMin.x = min(b.pMin.x, p.x);
    ret.pMin.y = min(b.pMin.y, p.y);
    ret.pMin.z = min(b.pMin.z, p.z);
    ret.pMax.x = max(b.pMax.x, p.x);
    ret.pMax.y = max(b.pMax.y, p.y);
    ret.pMax.z = max(b.pMax.z, p.z);
    return ret;
}
```

It is similarly possible to construct a new box that bounds the space encompassed by two other bounding boxes. The definition of this function is similar to the earlier Union() method that takes a Point; the difference is that the pMin and pMax of the second box are used for the min() and max() tests, respectively.

⟨*BBox Public Methods*⟩+≡   60

```
friend COREDLL BBox Union(const BBox &b, const BBox &b2);
```

It is easy to determine if two BBoxes overlap by seeing if their extents overlap in all of x, y, and z:

⟨*BBox Public Methods*⟩+≡   60

```
bool Overlaps(const BBox &b) const {
    bool x = (pMax.x >= b.pMin.x) && (pMin.x <= b.pMax.x);
    bool y = (pMax.y >= b.pMin.y) && (pMin.y <= b.pMax.y);
    bool z = (pMax.z >= b.pMin.z) && (pMin.z <= b.pMax.z);
    return (x && y && z);
}
```

Three simple 1D containment tests determine if a given point is inside the bounding box:

⟨*BBox Public Methods*⟩+≡   60

```
bool Inside(const Point &pt) const {
    return (pt.x >= pMin.x && pt.x <= pMax.x &&
            pt.y >= pMin.y && pt.y <= pMax.y &&
            pt.z >= pMin.z && pt.z <= pMax.z);
}
```

The `BBox::Expand()` method pads the bounding box by a constant factor, and `BBox::Volume()` returns the volume of the space inside the box:

⟨*BBox Public Methods*⟩+≡   60

```
void Expand(float delta) {
    pMin -= Vector(delta, delta, delta);
    pMax += Vector(delta, delta, delta);
}
```

⟨*BBox Public Methods*⟩+≡   60

```
float Volume() const {
    Vector d = pMax - pMin;
    return d.x * d.y * d.z;
}
```

The `BBox::MaximumExtent()` method tells the caller which of the three axes is longest. This is useful, for example, when deciding along which axis to subdivide when building a kd-tree (see Section A.5, for example).

⟨*BBox Public Methods*⟩+≡   60

```
int MaximumExtent() const {
    Vector diag = pMax - pMin;
    if (diag.x > diag.y && diag.x > diag.z)
        return 0;
    else if (diag.y > diag.z)
        return 1;
    else
        return 2;
}
```

Finally, the BBox provides a method that returns the center and radius of a sphere that bounds the bounding box. In general, this may give a far looser fit than a sphere that bounded the original contents of the BBox directly, although it is a useful method to have available. For example, in Chapter 15, we use this method to get a sphere that completely bounds the scene in order to generate a random ray that is likely to intersect the scene geometry.

⟨*BBox Method Definitions*⟩+≡
```
void BBox::BoundingSphere(Point *c, float *rad) const {
    *c = .5f * pMin + .5f * pMax;
    *rad = Distance(*c, pMax);
}
```

2.7 TRANSFORMATIONS

In general, a *transformation* **T** is a mapping from points to points and from vectors to vectors:

$$p' = T(p) \qquad v' = T(v).$$

The transformation **T** may be an arbitrary procedure. However, we will consider a subset of all possible transformations in this chapter. In particular, they will be

- *Linear:* If **T** is an arbitrary linear transformation and s is an arbitrary scalar, then $T(sv) = sT(v)$ and $T(v_1 + v_2) = T(v_1) + T(v_2)$. These two properties can greatly simplify reasoning about transformations.
- *Continuous:* Roughly speaking, **T** maps the neighborhoods around p and **v** to ones around p′ and **v**′.
- *One-to-one and invertible:* For each p, **T** maps p to a single unique p′. Furthermore, there exists an inverse transform T^{-1} that maps p′ back to p.

We will often want to take a point, vector, or normal defined with respect to one coordinate frame and find its coordinate values with respect to another frame. Using basic properties of linear algebra, a 4×4 matrix can be shown to express the linear transformation of a point or vector from one frame to another. Furthermore, such a 4×4 matrix suffices to express all linear transformations of points and vectors within a fixed frame, such as translation in space or rotation around a point. Therefore, there are different (and incompatible!) ways that a matrix can be interpreted:

- *Transformation of the frame:* Given a point, the matrix could express how to compute a *new* point in the same frame that represents the transformation of the original point (e.g., by translating it in some direction).
- *Transformation from one frame to another:* A matrix can express the coordinates of a point or vector in a new frame in terms of the coordinates in the original frame.

In general, transformations make it possible to work in the most convenient coordinate space. For example, we can write routines that define a virtual camera assuming that the camera is located at the origin, looks down the z axis, and has the y axis pointing up and the x axis pointing right. These assumptions greatly simplify the camera implementation. Then to place the camera at any point in the scene looking in any direction, we just construct a transformation that maps points in the scene's coordinate system to the camera's coordinate system.

2.7.1 HOMOGENEOUS COORDINATES

Given a frame defined by $(p, \mathbf{v}_1, \mathbf{v}_2, \mathbf{v}_3)$, there is ambiguity between the representation of a point (p_x, p_y, p_z) and a vector (v_x, v_y, v_z) with the same (x, y, z) coordinates. Using the representations of points and vectors introduced at the start of the chapter, we can write the point as the inner product $[s_1 \ s_2 \ s_3 \ 1][\mathbf{v}_1 \ \mathbf{v}_2 \ \mathbf{v}_3 \ p_o]^T$ and the vector as the inner product $[s_1' \ s_2' \ s_3' \ 0][\mathbf{v}_1 \ \mathbf{v}_2 \ \mathbf{v}_3 \ p_o]^T$. These four vectors of three s_i values and a zero or one are called the *homogeneous* representations of the point and the vector. The fourth coordinate of the homogeneous representation is sometimes called the *weight*. For a point, its value can be any scalar other than zero: the homogeneous points $[1, 3, -2, 1]$ and $[-2, -6, 4, -2]$ describe the same Cartesian point $(1, 3, -2)$. In general, homogeneous points obey the identity

$$(x, y, z, w) = \left(\frac{x}{w}, \frac{y}{w}, \frac{z}{w} \right).$$

We will use these facts to see how a transformation matrix can describe how points and vectors in one frame can be mapped to another frame. Consider a matrix $\mathbf{M}$ that describes the transformation from one coordinate system to another:

$$\mathbf{M} = \begin{pmatrix} m_{00} & m_{01} & m_{02} & m_{03} \\ m_{10} & m_{11} & m_{12} & m_{13} \\ m_{20} & m_{21} & m_{22} & m_{23} \\ m_{30} & m_{31} & m_{32} & m_{33} \end{pmatrix}.$$

Then if the transformation represented by $\mathbf{M}$ is applied to the x axis vector $(1, 0, 0)$, we have

$$\mathbf{M}[1\,0\,0\,0]^T = [m_{00} \ m_{10} \ m_{20} \ m_{30}]^T.$$

Thus, directly reading the columns of the matrix shows how the basis vectors and the origin of the current coordinate system are transformed by the matrix:

$$\mathbf{x} = [1\,0\,0\,0]^T$$
$$\mathbf{y} = [0\,1\,0\,0]^T$$
$$\mathbf{z} = [0\,0\,1\,0]^T$$
$$\mathbf{p} = [0\,0\,0\,1]^T.$$

In general, by characterizing how the basis is transformed, we know how any point or vector specified in terms of that basis is transformed. Because points and vectors in the current coordinate system are expressed in terms of the current coordinate system's frame, applying the transformation to them directly is equivalent to applying the transformation to the current coordinate system's basis and finding their coordinates in terms of the transformed basis.

We will not use homogeneous coordinates explicitly in our code; there is no Homogeneous class. However, the various transformation routines in the next section will implicitly convert points, vectors, and normals to homogeneous form, transform the homogeneous points, and then convert them back before returning the result. This isolates the details of homogeneous coordinates in one place (namely, the implementation of transformations).

⟨*Transform Declarations*⟩ ≡
```
class COREDLL Transform {
public:
    ⟨Transform Public Methods 67⟩
private:
    ⟨Transform Private Data 67⟩
};
```

A transformation is represented by the elements of the matrix m[4][4], a Reference to a Matrix4x4 object. The low-level Matrix4x4 class is defined in Section A.3.2. m is stored in *row-major* form, so element m[i][j] corresponds to $m_{i,j}$, where i is the row number and j is the column number. For convenience, the Transform also stores the inverse of the matrix m in the Transform::mInv member; it is better to have the inverse easily available than to repeatedly compute it as needed.

The reference-counting template class Reference is described in Section A.2.2. It tracks how many objects hold a reference to the reference-counted object and automatically frees its memory when no more references are held.

The Transform class stores references to matrices rather than storing them directly so that multiple Transforms can point to the same matrix. This means that any instance of the Transform class takes up very little memory on its own. If a huge number of shapes in the scene have the same object-to-world transformation, then they can all have their own Transform objects but share the same Matrix4x4s. Since the Transform only stores pointers to the matrices, a second transform that can reuse an existing matrix saves 72 bytes of storage over an implementation where each shape has its own Matrix4x4 (assuming floats are 4 bytes). This savings can be substantial in large scenes.

However, a certain amount of flexibility is lost by allowing matrices to be shared between transformations. Specifically, the elements of a Matrix4x4 cannot be modified after it is created. This isn't a problem in practice, since the transformations in a scene are typically created when pbrt parses the scene description file and don't need to change later at rendering time. This design decision leads to a programming style where whenever the matrices in a Transform need to be updated, a new Matrix4x4 is dynamically allocated for the new value. Thanks to the automatic memory management from reference counting, this process isn't too unwieldy.

⟨*Transform Private Data*⟩ ≡   66
```
Reference<Matrix4x4> m, mInv;
```

2.7.2 BASIC OPERATIONS

When a new Transform is created, it defaults to the *identity transformation*—the transformation that maps each point and each vector to itself. This transformation is represented by the *identity matrix:*

$$
\mathbf{I} = \begin{pmatrix} 1 & 0 & 0 & 0 \\ 0 & 1 & 0 & 0 \\ 0 & 0 & 1 & 0 \\ 0 & 0 & 0 & 1 \end{pmatrix}.
$$

The implementation here relies on the default Matrix4x4 constructor to fill in the identity matrix. Because of the convention that Matrix4x4s cannot be modified by Transforms after creation, it's safe for m and mInv to reference the same matrix in this case.

⟨*Transform Public Methods*⟩ ≡   66
```
Transform() {
    m = mInv = new Matrix4x4;
}
```

A Transform can also be created from a given matrix. In this case, the given matrix must be explicitly inverted.

⟨*Transform Public Methods*⟩+≡   66
```
Transform(float mat[4][4]) {
    m = new Matrix4x4(mat[0][0], mat[0][1], mat[0][2], mat[0][3],
                      mat[1][0], mat[1][1], mat[1][2], mat[1][3],
                      mat[2][0], mat[2][1], mat[2][2], mat[2][3],
                      mat[3][0], mat[3][1], mat[3][2], mat[3][3]);
    mInv = m->Inverse();
}
```

⟨*Transform Public Methods*⟩+≡   66
```
Transform(const Reference<Matrix4x4> &mat) {
    m = mat;
    mInv = m->Inverse();
}
```

Finally, the most commonly used constructor takes a reference to the transformation matrix along with an explicitly provided inverse. This is a superior approach to computing the inverse in the constructor because many geometric transformations have very simple inverses and we can avoid the expense of computing a general 4×4 matrix inverse. Of course, this places the burden on the caller to make sure that the supplied inverse is correct.

⟨*Transform Public Methods*⟩+≡   66
```
Transform(const Reference<Matrix4x4> &mat,
          const Reference<Matrix4x4> &minv) {
    m = mat;
    mInv = minv;
}
```

⟨*Transform Public Methods*⟩+≡   66
```
Transform GetInverse() const {
    return Transform(mInv, m);
}
```

2.7.3 TRANSLATIONS

One of the simplest transformations is the *translation transformation* $\mathbf{T}(\Delta x, \Delta y, \Delta z)$. When applied to a point p, it translates p's coordinates by Δx, Δy, and Δz, as shown in Figure 2.9. As an example, $\mathbf{T}(2, 2, 1)(x, y, z) = (x + 2, y + 2, z + 1)$.

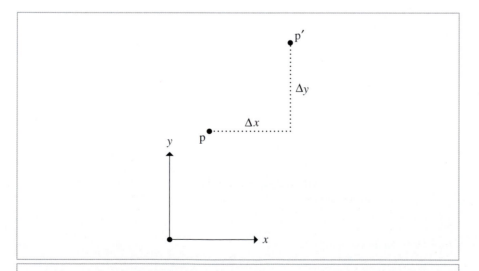

Matrix4x4 852
Reference 839
Transform 66

Figure 2.9: Translation in 2D. Adding offsets Δx and Δy to a point's coordinates correspondingly changes its position in space.

Translation has some simple properties:

$$\mathbf{T}(0, 0, 0) = \mathbf{I}$$
$$\mathbf{T}(x_1, y_1, z_1)\mathbf{T}(x_2, y_2, z_2) = \mathbf{T}(x_1 + x_2, y_1 + y_2, z_1 + z_2)$$
$$\mathbf{T}(x_1, y_1, z_1)\mathbf{T}(x_2, y_2, z_2) = \mathbf{T}(x_2, y_2, z_2)\mathbf{T}(x_1, y_1, z_1)$$
$$\mathbf{T}^{-1}(x, y, z) = \mathbf{T}(-x, -y, -z).$$

Translation only affects points, leaving vectors unchanged. In matrix form, the translation transformation is

$$\mathbf{T}(\Delta x, \Delta y, \Delta z) = \begin{pmatrix} 1 & 0 & 0 & \Delta x \\ 0 & 1 & 0 & \Delta y \\ 0 & 0 & 1 & \Delta z \\ 0 & 0 & 0 & 1 \end{pmatrix}.$$

When we consider the operation of a translation matrix on a point, we see the value of homogeneous coordinates. Consider the product of the matrix for $\mathbf{T}(\Delta x, \Delta y, \Delta z)$ with a point p in homogeneous coordinates $[x \ y \ z \ 1]$:

$$\begin{pmatrix} 1 & 0 & 0 & \Delta x \\ 0 & 1 & 0 & \Delta y \\ 0 & 0 & 1 & \Delta z \\ 0 & 0 & 0 & 1 \end{pmatrix} \begin{pmatrix} x \\ y \\ z \\ 1 \end{pmatrix} = \begin{pmatrix} x + \Delta x \\ y + \Delta y \\ z + \Delta z \\ 1 \end{pmatrix}.$$

As expected, we have computed a new point with its coordinates offset by $(\Delta x, \Delta y, \Delta z)$. However, if we apply $\mathbf{T}$ to a vector $\mathbf{v}$, we have

$$\begin{pmatrix} 1 & 0 & 0 & \Delta x \\ 0 & 1 & 0 & \Delta y \\ 0 & 0 & 1 & \Delta z \\ 0 & 0 & 0 & 1 \end{pmatrix} \begin{pmatrix} x \\ y \\ z \\ 0 \end{pmatrix} = \begin{pmatrix} x \\ y \\ z \\ 0 \end{pmatrix}.$$

The result is the same vector $\mathbf{v}$. This makes sense because vectors represent directions, so translation leaves them unchanged.

Transform 66

We will define a routine that creates a new Transform matrix to represent a given translation—it is a straightforward application of the translation matrix equation. These routines fully initialize the Transform that is returned, also initializing the matrix that represents the inverse of the translation.

⟨*Transform Method Definitions*⟩ ≡
```
COREDLL Transform Translate(const Vector &delta) {
    Matrix4x4 *m, *minv;
    m = new Matrix4x4(1, 0, 0, delta.x,
                      0, 1, 0, delta.y,
                      0, 0, 1, delta.z,
                      0, 0, 0,       1);
    minv = new Matrix4x4(1, 0, 0, -delta.x,
                         0, 1, 0, -delta.y,
                         0, 0, 1, -delta.z,
                         0, 0, 0,        1);
    return Transform(m, minv);
}
```

2.7.4 SCALING

Another basic transformation is the *scale transformation*, $S(s_x, s_y, s_z)$. It has the effect of taking a point or vector and multiplying its components by scale factors in x, y, and z: $S(2, 2, 1)(x, y, z) = (2x, 2y, z)$. It has the following basic properties:

$$S(1, 1, 1) = I$$
$$S(x_1, y_1, z_1)S(x_2, y_2, z_2) = S(x_1x_2, y_1y_2, z_1z_2)$$
$$S^{-1}(x, y, z) = S\left(\frac{1}{x}, \frac{1}{y}, \frac{1}{z}\right).$$

We can differentiate between *uniform scaling*, where all three scale factors have the same value, and *nonuniform scaling*, where they may have different values. The general scale matrix is

$$S(x, y, z) = \begin{pmatrix} x & 0 & 0 & 0 \\ 0 & y & 0 & 0 \\ 0 & 0 & z & 0 \\ 0 & 0 & 0 & 1 \end{pmatrix}.$$

⟨*Transform Method Definitions*⟩+≡
```
COREDLL Transform Scale(float x, float y, float z) {
    Matrix4x4 *m, *minv;
    m = new Matrix4x4(x, 0, 0, 0,
                      0, y, 0, 0,
                      0, 0, z, 0,
                      0, 0, 0, 1);
```

COREDLL 904
Matrix4x4 852
Transform 66
Vector 47

```
minv = new Matrix4x4(1.f/x,      0,      0, 0,
                         0, 1.f/y,      0, 0,
                         0,      0, 1.f/z, 0,
                         0,      0,      0, 1);
    return Transform(m, minv);
}
```

2.7.5 x, y, AND z AXIS ROTATIONS

Another useful type of transformation is the *rotation transformation* R. In general, we can define an arbitrary axis from the origin in any direction and then rotate around that axis by a given angle. The most common rotations of this type are around the x, y, and z coordinate axes. We will write these rotations as $\mathbf{R}_x(\theta)$, $\mathbf{R}_y(\theta)$, and so on. The rotation around an arbitrary axis (x, y, z) is denoted by $\mathbf{R}_{(x,y,z)}(\theta)$.

Rotations also have some basic properties:

$$\mathbf{R}_a(0) = \mathbf{I}$$
$$\mathbf{R}_a(\theta_1)\mathbf{R}_a(\theta_2) = \mathbf{R}_a(\theta_1 + \theta_2)$$
$$\mathbf{R}_a(\theta_1)\mathbf{R}_a(\theta_2) = \mathbf{R}_a(\theta_2)\mathbf{R}_a(\theta_1)$$
$$\mathbf{R}_a^{-1}(\theta) = \mathbf{R}_a(-\theta) = \mathbf{R}_a^T(\theta),$$

where $\mathbf{R}^T$ is the matrix transpose of $\mathbf{R}$. This last property, that the inverse of $\mathbf{R}$ is equal to its transpose, stems from the fact that $\mathbf{R}$ is an *orthogonal matrix*; its upper 3×3 components are all orthogonal to each other. Fortunately, the transpose is much easier to compute than a full matrix inverse.

For a left-handed coordinate system, the matrix for rotation around the x axis is

$$\mathbf{R}_x(\theta) = \begin{pmatrix} 1 & 0 & 0 & 0 \\ 0 & \cos\theta & -\sin\theta & 0 \\ 0 & \sin\theta & \cos\theta & 0 \\ 0 & 0 & 0 & 1 \end{pmatrix}.$$

Figure 2.10 gives an intuition for how this matrix works. It's easy to see that it leaves the x axis unchanged:

$$\mathbf{R}_x(\theta)[1\,0\,0\,0]^T = [1\,0\,0\,0].$$

It maps the y axis $(0, 1, 0)$ to $(0, \cos\theta, \sin\theta)$ and the z axis to $(0, -\sin\theta, \cos\theta)$. The y and z axes remain in the same plane, perpendicular to the x axis, but are rotated by the given angle. An arbitrary point in space is similarly rotated about the x axis by this transformation while staying in the same yz plane as it was originally.

RotateX() 72

The implementation of the RotateX() function is straightforward.

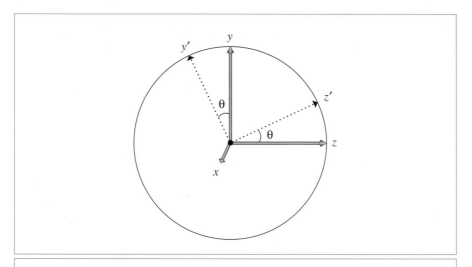

Figure 2.10: Rotation by an angle θ about the x axis leaves the x coordinate unchanged. The y and z axes are mapped to the vectors given by the dashed lines; y and z coordinates move accordingly.

⟨*Transform Method Definitions*⟩+≡

```
Transform RotateX(float angle) {
    float sin_t = sinf(Radians(angle));
    float cos_t = cosf(Radians(angle));
    Matrix4x4 *m = new Matrix4x4(1,     0,      0, 0,
                                 0, cos_t, -sin_t, 0,
                                 0, sin_t,  cos_t, 0,
                                 0,     0,      0, 1);
    return Transform(m, m->Transpose());
}
```

Similarly, for rotation around y and z, we have

$$
\mathbf{R}_y(\theta) = \begin{pmatrix} \cos\theta & 0 & \sin\theta & 0 \\ 0 & 1 & 0 & 0 \\ -\sin\theta & 0 & \cos\theta & 0 \\ 0 & 0 & 0 & 1 \end{pmatrix} \qquad \mathbf{R}_z(\theta) = \begin{pmatrix} \cos\theta & -\sin\theta & 0 & 0 \\ \sin\theta & \cos\theta & 0 & 0 \\ 0 & 0 & 1 & 0 \\ 0 & 0 & 0 & 1 \end{pmatrix}.
$$

The implementations of RotateY() and RotateZ() follow directly and are not included here.

Matrix4x4 852

Transform 66

2.7.6 ROTATION AROUND AN ARBITRARY AXIS

We also provide a routine to compute the transformation that represents rotation around an arbitrary axis. The usual derivation of this matrix is based on computing rotations

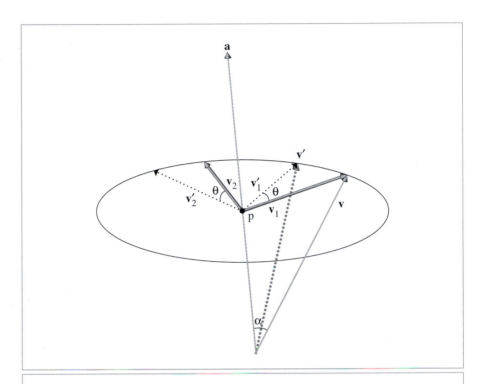

Figure 2.11: A vector **v** can be rotated around an arbitrary axis **a** by constructing a coordinate system (p, $\mathbf{v}_1$, $\mathbf{v}_2$) in the plane perpendicular to the axis that passes through **v**'s end point and rotating the vectors $\mathbf{v}_1$ and $\mathbf{v}_2$ about p. Applying this rotation to the axes of the coordinate system $(1, 0, 0)$, $(0, 1, 0)$, and $(0, 0, 1)$ gives the general rotation matrix for this rotation.

that map the given axis to a fixed axis (e.g., z), performing the rotation there, and then rotating the fixed axis back to the original axis. A more elegant derivation can be constructed with vector algebra.

Consider a normalized direction vector **a** that gives the axis to rotate around by angle θ, and a vector **v** to be rotated (Figure 2.11). First, we can compute the point p along the axis **a** that is in the plane through the end point of **v** and is perpendicular to **a**. Assuming **v** and **a** form an angle α, we have

$$p = \mathbf{a} \cos \alpha = \mathbf{a}(\mathbf{v} \cdot \mathbf{a}).$$

We now compute a pair of basis vectors $\mathbf{v}_1$ and $\mathbf{v}_2$ in this plane. Trivially, one of them is

$$\mathbf{v}_1 = \mathbf{v} - \mathbf{p},$$

and the other can be computed with a cross product

$$\mathbf{v}_2 = (\mathbf{v}_1 \times \mathbf{a}).$$

Because **a** is normalized, $\mathbf{v}_1$ and $\mathbf{v}_2$ have the same length, equal to the distance from **v** to p. To now compute the rotation by an angle θ about the point p in the plane of rotation, the rotation formulas earlier give us

$$\mathbf{v}' = \mathbf{p} + \mathbf{v}_1 \cos\theta + \mathbf{v}_2 \sin\theta.$$

To convert this to a rotation matrix, we apply this formula to the basis vectors $\mathbf{v}_1 = (1, 0, 0)$, $\mathbf{v}_2 = (0, 1, 0)$, and $\mathbf{v}_3 = (0, 0, 1)$ to get the values of the rows of the matrix. The result of all this is encapsulated in the following function. As with the other rotation matrices, the inverse is equal to the transpose.

⟨Transform Method Definitions⟩+≡
```
    Transform Rotate(float angle, const Vector &axis) {
        Vector a = Normalize(axis);
        float s = sinf(Radians(angle));
        float c = cosf(Radians(angle));
        float m[4][4];

        m[0][0] = a.x * a.x + (1.f - a.x * a.x) * c;
        m[0][1] = a.x * a.y * (1.f - c) - a.z * s;
        m[0][2] = a.x * a.z * (1.f - c) + a.y * s;
        m[0][3] = 0;

        m[1][0] = a.x * a.y * (1.f - c) + a.z * s;
        m[1][1] = a.y * a.y + (1.f - a.y * a.y) * c;
        m[1][2] = a.y * a.z * (1.f - c) - a.x * s;
        m[1][3] = 0;

        m[2][0] = a.x * a.z * (1.f - c) - a.y * s;
        m[2][1] = a.y * a.z * (1.f - c) + a.x * s;
        m[2][2] = a.z * a.z + (1.f - a.z * a.z) * c;
        m[2][3] = 0;

        m[3][0] = 0;
        m[3][1] = 0;
        m[3][2] = 0;
        m[3][3] = 1;

        Matrix4x4 *mat = new Matrix4x4(m);
        return Transform(mat, mat->Transpose());
    }
```

Matrix4x4 852
Transform 66
Vector 47
Vector::Normalize() 53

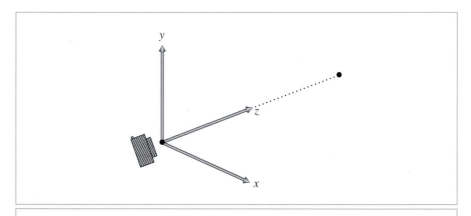

Figure 2.12: Given a camera position, the position being looked at from the camera, and an "up" direction, the look-at transformation describes a transformation from a viewing coordinate system where the camera is at the origin looking down the $+z$ axis and the $+y$ axis is along the up direction.

2.7.7 THE LOOK-AT TRANSFORMATION

The *look-at transformation* is particularly useful for placing a camera in the scene. The caller specifies the desired position of the camera, a point the camera is looking at, and an "up" vector that orients the camera along the viewing direction implied by the first two parameters. All of these values are given in world space coordinates. The look-at construction then gives a transformation between camera space and world space (Figure 2.12).

In order to find the entries of the look-at transformation matrix, we use principles described earlier in this section: the columns of a transformation matrix give the effect of the transformation on the basis of a coordinate system.

⟨*Transform Method Definitions*⟩+≡
```
Transform LookAt(const Point &pos, const Point &look, const Vector &up) {
    float m[4][4];
    ⟨Initialize fourth column of viewing matrix 76⟩
    ⟨Initialize first three columns of viewing matrix 76⟩
    Matrix4x4 *camToWorld = new Matrix4x4(m);
    return Transform(camToWorld->Inverse(), camToWorld);
}
```

Matrix4x4 852
Matrix4x4::Inverse() 853
Point 54
Transform 66
Vector 47

The easiest column is the fourth one, which gives the point that the camera space origin, $[0\ 0\ 0\ 1]^T$, maps to in world space. This is clearly just the camera position, supplied by the user.

⟨*Initialize fourth column of viewing matrix*⟩ ≡   **75**

```
m[0][3] = pos.x;
m[1][3] = pos.y;
m[2][3] = pos.z;
m[3][3] = 1;
```

The other three columns aren't much more difficult. First, LookAt() computes the normalized direction vector from the camera location to the look-at point; this gives the vector coordinates that the *z* axis should map to and, thus, the third column of the matrix. (Camera space is defined with the viewing direction down the +*z* axis.) The first column, giving the world space direction that the +*x* axis in camera space maps to, is found by taking the cross product of the user-supplied "up" vector with the recently computed viewing direction vector. Finally, the "up" vector is recomputed by taking the cross product of the viewing direction vector with the transformed *x* axis vector, thus ensuring that the *y* and *z* axes are perpendicular and we have an orthonormal viewing coordinate system.

⟨*Initialize first three columns of viewing matrix*⟩ ≡   **75**

```
Vector dir = Normalize(look - pos);
Vector right = Cross(dir, Normalize(up));
Vector newUp = Cross(right, dir);
m[0][0] = right.x;
m[1][0] = right.y;
m[2][0] = right.z;
m[3][0] = 0.;
m[0][1] = newUp.x;
m[1][1] = newUp.y;
m[2][1] = newUp.z;
m[3][1] = 0.;
m[0][2] = dir.x;
m[1][2] = dir.y;
m[2][2] = dir.z;
m[3][2] = 0.;
```

2.8 APPLYING TRANSFORMATIONS

We can now define routines that perform the appropriate matrix multiplications to transform points and vectors. We will overload the function application operator to describe these transformations; this lets us write code like

```
Point P = ...;
Transform T = ...;
Point new_P = T(P);
```

2.8.1 POINTS

The point transformation routine takes a point (x, y, z) and implicitly represents it as the homogeneous column vector $[x\ y\ z\ 1]^T$. It then transforms the point by premultiplying this vector with the transformation matrix. Finally, it divides by w to convert back to a nonhomogeneous point representation. For efficiency, this method skips the divide by the homogeneous weight w when $w = 1$, which is common for most of the transformations that will be used in pbrt—only the projective transformations defined in Chapter 6 will require this divide.

⟨*Transform Inline Functions*⟩ ≡
```
inline Point Transform::operator()(const Point &pt) const {
    float x = pt.x, y = pt.y, z = pt.z;
    float xp = m->m[0][0]*x + m->m[0][1]*y + m->m[0][2]*z + m->m[0][3];
    float yp = m->m[1][0]*x + m->m[1][1]*y + m->m[1][2]*z + m->m[1][3];
    float zp = m->m[2][0]*x + m->m[2][1]*y + m->m[2][2]*z + m->m[2][3];
    float wp = m->m[3][0]*x + m->m[3][1]*y + m->m[3][2]*z + m->m[3][3];

    Assert(wp != 0);
    if (wp == 1.) return Point(xp, yp, zp);
    else          return Point(xp, yp, zp)/wp;
}
```

We also provide transformation methods that let the caller pass a pointer to an object for the result. This saves the expense of returning structures by value on the stack. Note that we copy the original (x, y, z) coordinates to local variables in case the result pointer points to the same location as pt. This way, these routines can be used even if a point is being transformed in place.

⟨*Transform Inline Functions*⟩+≡
```
inline void Transform::operator()(const Point &pt,
                                  Point *ptrans) const {
    float x = pt.x, y = pt.y, z = pt.z;
    ptrans->x = m->m[0][0]*x + m->m[0][1]*y + m->m[0][2]*z + m->m[0][3];
    ptrans->y = m->m[1][0]*x + m->m[1][1]*y + m->m[1][2]*z + m->m[1][3];
    ptrans->z = m->m[2][0]*x + m->m[2][1]*y + m->m[2][2]*z + m->m[2][3];
    float w   = m->m[3][0]*x + m->m[3][1]*y + m->m[3][2]*z + m->m[3][3];
    if (w != 1.) *ptrans /= w;
}
```

Point 54
Transform 66

2.8.2 VECTORS

The transformations of vectors can be computed in a similar fashion. However, the multiplication of the matrix and the row vector is simplified since the implicit homogeneous w coordinate is zero.

⟨*Transform Inline Functions*⟩+≡
```
inline Vector Transform::operator()(const Vector &v) const {
    float x = v.x, y = v.y, z = v.z;
    return Vector(m->m[0][0]*x + m->m[0][1]*y + m->m[0][2]*z,
                  m->m[1][0]*x + m->m[1][1]*y + m->m[1][2]*z,
                  m->m[2][0]*x + m->m[2][1]*y + m->m[2][2]*z);
}
```

There is also a method allowing the caller to pass a pointer to the result object. The code to do this has a similar design to the `Point` transformation code and is not shown here. This code will also be omitted for subsequent transformation methods.

2.8.3 NORMALS

Normals do not transform in the same way that vectors do, as shown in Figure 2.13. Although tangent vectors transform in the straightforward way, normals require special treatment. Because the normal vector **n** and any tangent vector **t** on the surface are orthogonal by construction, we know that

$$\mathbf{n} \cdot \mathbf{t} = \mathbf{n}^T \mathbf{t} = 0.$$

When we transform a point on the surface by some matrix **M**, the new tangent vector **t**′ at the transformed point is **Mt**. The transformed normal **n**′ should be equal to **Sn** for some 4×4 matrix **S**. To maintain the orthogonality requirement, we must have

$$0 = (\mathbf{n}')^T \mathbf{t}'$$
$$= (\mathbf{Sn})^T \mathbf{Mt}$$
$$= (\mathbf{n})^T \mathbf{S}^T \mathbf{Mt}.$$

This condition holds if $\mathbf{S}^T \mathbf{M} = \mathbf{I}$, the identity matrix. Therefore, $\mathbf{S}^T = \mathbf{M}^{-1}$, and so $\mathbf{S} = \mathbf{M}^{-1^T}$, and we see that normals must be transformed by the inverse transpose of the transformation matrix. This detail is one of the main reasons why `Transform`s maintain their inverses.

Note that this method does not explicitly compute the transpose of the inverse when transforming normals. It just indexes into the inverse matrix in a different order (compare to the code for transforming `Vector`s).

⟨*Transform Inline Functions*⟩+≡
```
inline Normal Transform::operator()(const Normal &n) const {
    float x = n.x, y = n.y, z = n.z;
    return Normal(mInv->m[0][0]*x + mInv->m[1][0]*y + mInv->m[2][0]*z,
                  mInv->m[0][1]*x + mInv->m[1][1]*y + mInv->m[2][1]*z,
                  mInv->m[0][2]*x + mInv->m[1][2]*y + mInv->m[2][2]*z);
}
```

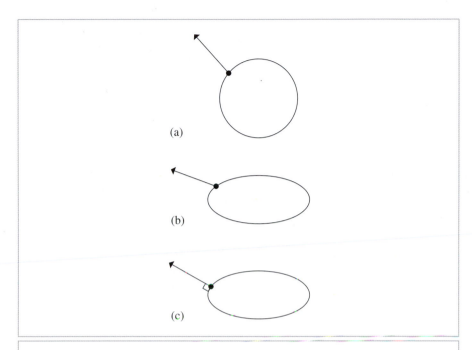

Figure 2.13: Transforming Surface Normals. (a) Original circle. (b) When scaling the circle to be half as tall in the y direction, simply treating the normal as a direction and scaling it in the same manner will lead to incorrect results. (c) A properly transformed normal.

2.8.4 RAYS

Transforming rays is straightforward: the method to do this transforms the constituent origin and direction and copies the other data members.

⟨*Transform Inline Functions*⟩+≡
```
inline Ray Transform::operator()(const Ray &r) const {
    Ray ret;
    (*this)(r.o, &ret.o);
    (*this)(r.d, &ret.d);
    ret.mint = r.mint;
    ret.maxt = r.maxt;
    ret.time = r.time;
    return ret;
}
```

Ray 59
Transform 66

2.8.5 BOUNDING BOXES

The easiest way to transform an axis-aligned bounding box is to transform all eight of its corner vertices and then compute a new bounding box that encompasses those points. We will present code for this method below; one of the exercises for this chapter is to implement a technique to do this computation more efficiently.

⟨*Transform Method Definitions*⟩+≡
```
BBox Transform::operator()(const BBox &b) const {
    const Transform &M = *this;
    BBox ret(        M(Point(b.pMin.x, b.pMin.y, b.pMin.z)));
    ret = Union(ret, M(Point(b.pMax.x, b.pMin.y, b.pMin.z)));
    ret = Union(ret, M(Point(b.pMin.x, b.pMax.y, b.pMin.z)));
    ret = Union(ret, M(Point(b.pMin.x, b.pMin.y, b.pMax.z)));
    ret = Union(ret, M(Point(b.pMin.x, b.pMax.y, b.pMax.z)));
    ret = Union(ret, M(Point(b.pMax.x, b.pMax.y, b.pMin.z)));
    ret = Union(ret, M(Point(b.pMax.x, b.pMin.y, b.pMax.z)));
    ret = Union(ret, M(Point(b.pMax.x, b.pMax.y, b.pMax.z)));
    return ret;
}
```

2.8.6 COMPOSITION OF TRANSFORMATIONS

Having defined how the matrices representing individual types of transformations are constructed, we can now consider an aggregate transformation resulting from a series of individual transformations. Finally, we can see the real value of representing transformations with matrices.

Consider a series of transformations **ABC**. We'd like to compute a new transformation **T** such that applying **T** gives the same result as applying each of **A**, **B**, and **C** in reverse order; that is, $\mathbf{A}(\mathbf{B}(\mathbf{C}(p))) = \mathbf{T}(p)$. Such a transformation **T** can be computed by multiplying the matrices of the transformations **A**, **B**, and **C** together. In pbrt, we can write

```
Transform T = A * B * C;
```

Then we can apply T to Points p as usual, Point pp = T(p), instead of applying each transformation in turn: Point pp = A(B(C(p))).

We use the C++ * operator to compute the new transformation that results from post-multiplying a transformation with another transformation t2. In matrix multiplication, the (i, j)th element of the resulting matrix ret is the inner product of the ith row of the first matrix with the jth column of the second.

The inverse of the resulting transformation is equal to the product of t2.mInv * mInv. This is a result of the matrix identity

$$(\mathbf{AB})^{-1} = \mathbf{B}^{-1}\mathbf{A}^{-1}.$$

⟨*Transform Method Definitions*⟩+≡
```
Transform Transform::operator*(const Transform &t2) const {
    Reference<Matrix4x4> m1 = Matrix4x4::Mul(m, t2.m);
    Reference<Matrix4x4> m2 = Matrix4x4::Mul(t2.mInv, mInv);
    return Transform(m1, m2);
}
```

2.8.7 TRANSFORMATIONS AND COORDINATE SYSTEM HANDEDNESS

Certain types of transformations change a left-handed coordinate system into a right-handed one, or vice versa. Some routines will need to know if the handedness of the source coordinate system is different from that of the destination. In particular, routines that want to ensure that a surface normal always points "outside" of a surface might need to flip the normal's direction after transformation if the handedness changes.

Fortunately, it is easy to tell if handedness is changed by a transformation: it happens only when the determinant of the transformation's upper-left 3×3 submatrix is negative.

⟨*Transform Method Definitions*⟩+≡
```
bool Transform::SwapsHandedness() const {
    float det = ((m->m[0][0] *
                  (m->m[1][1] * m->m[2][2] -
                   m->m[1][2] * m->m[2][1])) -
                 (m->m[0][1] *
                  (m->m[1][0] * m->m[2][2] -
                   m->m[1][2] * m->m[2][0])) +
                 (m->m[0][2] *
                  (m->m[1][0] * m->m[2][1] -
                   m->m[1][1] * m->m[2][0])));
    return det < 0.f;
}
```

2.9 DIFFERENTIAL GEOMETRY

We will wrap up this chapter by developing a self-contained representation for the geometry of a particular point on a surface (typically the point of a ray intersection). This abstraction needs to hide the particular type of geometric shape the point lies on, supplying enough information about the surface point to allow the shading and geometric operations in the rest of pbrt to be implemented generically, without the need to distinguish between different shape types such as spheres and triangles. The DifferentialGeometry class implements just such an abstraction.

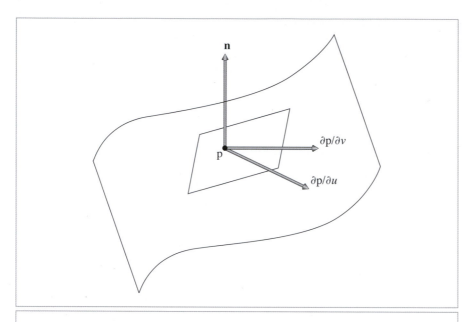

Figure 2.14: The Local Differential Geometry around a Point p. The parametric partial derivatives of the surface, $\partial p/\partial u$ and $\partial p/\partial v$, lie in the tangent plane but are not necessarily orthogonal. The surface normal **n** is given by the cross product of $\partial p/\partial u$ and $\partial p/\partial v$. The vectors $\partial n/\partial u$ and $\partial n/\partial v$ (not shown here) record the differential change in surface normal as we move u and v along the surface.

The information needed by the rest of the system includes

- the position of the 3D point p
- the surface normal **n** at the point
- (u, v) coordinates from the parameterization of the surface
- the parametric partial derivatives $\partial p/\partial u$ and $\partial p/\partial v$
- the partial derivatives of the change in surface normal $\partial n/\partial u$ and $\partial n/\partial v$
- a pointer to the Shape that the differential geometry lies on (the Shape class will be introduced in the next chapter)

See Figure 2.14 for a depiction of these values.

This representation assumes that shapes have a parametric description—that for some range of (u, v) values, points on the surface are given by some function f such that $p = f(u, v)$. Although this isn't true for all shapes, all of the shapes that pbrt supports do have at least a local parametric description, so we will stick with the parametric representation since this assumption is helpful elsewhere (e.g., for antialiasing of textures in Chapter 11).

Shape 90

⟨*DifferentialGeometry Declarations*⟩ ≡
```
struct COREDLL DifferentialGeometry {
    DifferentialGeometry() { u = v = 0.; shape = NULL; }
    ⟨DifferentialGeometry Public Methods⟩
    ⟨DifferentialGeometry Public Data 83⟩
};
```

The names of the member variables directly correspond to the quantities they represent. Here we have named the `Normal` member variable `nn` with a second "n" to reflect the fact that it is a normalized version of the surface normal.

⟨*DifferentialGeometry Public Data*⟩ ≡   83
```
Point p;
Normal nn;
float u, v;
const Shape *shape;
```

We also need to store the partial derivatives of the surface position and the surface normal:

⟨*DifferentialGeometry Public Data*⟩+≡   83
```
Vector dpdu, dpdv;
Vector dndu, dndv;
```

The `DifferentialGeometry` constructor only needs a few parameters—the point of interest, the partial derivatives of position and normal, and the (u, v) coordinates. It computes the normal as the cross product of the partial derivatives.

⟨*DifferentialGeometry Method Definitions*⟩ ≡
```
DifferentialGeometry::DifferentialGeometry(const Point &P,
        const Vector &DPDU, const Vector &DPDV,
        const Vector &DNDU, const Vector &DNDV,
        float uu, float vv, const Shape *sh)
    : p(P), dpdu(DPDU), dpdv(DPDV), dndu(DNDU), dndv(DNDV) {
    ⟨Initialize DifferentialGeometry from parameters 83⟩
    ⟨Adjust normal based on orientation and handedness 84⟩
}
```

⟨*Initialize* `DifferentialGeometry` *from parameters*⟩ ≡   83
```
nn = Normal(Normalize(Cross(dpdu, dpdv)));
u = uu;
v = vv;
shape = sh;
```

The surface normal has special meaning to pbrt, which assumes that for closed shapes, the normal is oriented such that it points to the "outside" of the shape. For example, this assumption will be used later when we need to decide if a ray is entering or leaving the volume enclosed by a shape. Furthermore, for geometry used as an area light source, light is emitted from only the side of the two-sided surface that the normal lies in; the other side is black.

Because normals have this special meaning, pbrt provides a mechansim for the user to reverse the orientation of the normal, flipping it to point in the opposite direction. The ReverseOrientation directive in pbrt's input file flips the normal to point in the opposite, nondefault direction. Therefore, it will be necessary to check if the given Shape has this flag set and, if so, switch the normal's direction.

However, one other factor plays into the orientation of the normal and must be accounted for here as well. If the Shape's transformation matrix has switched the handedness of the object coordinate system from pbrt's default left-handed coordinate system to a right-handed one, we need to switch the orientation of the normal as well. To see why this is so, consider a scale matrix $S(1, 1, -1)$. We would naturally expect this scale to switch the direction of the normal, although because we compute the normal by $\mathbf{n} = \partial p/\partial u \times \partial p/\partial v$, it can be shown that

$$S(1, 1, -1)\frac{\partial \mathrm{p}}{\partial u} \times S(1, 1, -1)\frac{\partial \mathrm{p}}{\partial v} = \frac{\partial \mathrm{p}}{\partial u} \times \frac{\partial \mathrm{p}}{\partial v} = \mathbf{n} \neq S(1, 1, -1)\mathbf{n}.$$

Therefore, it is also necessary to manually flip the normal's direction if the transformation switches the handedness of the coordinate system, since the flip won't be accounted for by the computation of the normal's direction using the cross product.

The normal's direction is swapped if one but not both of these two conditions is met; if both were met, their effect would cancel out. The exclusive-OR operation tests this condition.

⟨*Adjust normal based on orientation and handedness*⟩ ≡   83
```
    if (shape->reverseOrientation ^ shape->transformSwapsHandedness)
        nn *= -1.f;
```

FURTHER READING

DeRose, Goldman, and their collaborators have argued for an elegant "coordinate-free" approach to describing vector geometry for graphics, where the fact that positions and directions happen to be represented by (x, y, z) coordinates with respect to a particular coordinate system is deemphasized and where points and vectors themselves record which coordinate system they are expressed in terms of (Goldman 1985; DeRose 1989; Mann, Litke, and DeRose 1997). This makes it possible for a software layer to ensure that common errors like adding a vector in one coordinate system to a point in another coordinate system are transparently handled by transforming them to a common coordinate system first. We have not followed this approach in pbrt, although the principles behind

Shape::reverseOrientation 90

Shape::
    transformSwapsHandedness 90

this approach are well worth understanding and keeping in mind when working with coordinate systems in computer graphics.

Schneider and Eberly's *Geometric Tools for Computer Graphics* is influenced by the coordinate-free approach and covers the topics of this chapter in much greater depth (Schneider and Eberly 2003). It is also full of useful geometric algorithms for graphics. A classic and more traditional introduction to the topics of this chapter is *Mathematical Elements for Computer Graphics* by Rogers and Adams (1990). Note that their book uses a row-vector representation of points and vectors, however, which means that our matrices would be transposed when expressed in their framework, and that they multiply points and vectors by matrices to transform them, pM, rather than multiplying matrices by points as we do, Mp. Homogeneous coordinates were only briefly mentioned in this chapter, although they are the basis of projective geometry, where they are the foundation of many elegant algorithms. Stolfi's book is an excellent introduction to this topic (Stolfi 1991).

There are many good books on linear algebra and vector geometry. We have found Lang (1986) and Buck (1978) to be good references on these respective topics. See also Akenine-Möller and Haines (2002) for a solid graphics-based introduction to linear algebra.

The subtleties of how normal vectors are transformed were first widely understood in the graphics community after articles by Wallis (1990) and Turkowski (1990c).

EXERCISES

● 2.1   Find a more efficient way to transform axis-aligned bounding boxes by taking advantage of the symmetries of the problem: because the eight corner points are linear combinations of three axis-aligned basis vectors and a single corner point, their transformed bounding box can be found much more efficiently than by the method we presented (Arvo 1990).

❷ 2.2   Reimplement the core geometry classes using a vector instruction set such as Intel's SSE. Evaluate the performance implications on scenes with a variety of characteristics. What can you conclude about the effectiveness of this approach?

❷ 2.3   Instead of boxes, tighter bounds around objects could be computed by using the intersections of many nonorthogonal slabs. Extend the bounding box class in pbrt to allow the user to specify a bound comprised of arbitrary slabs.

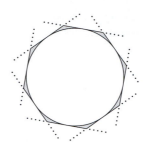

Axis-aligned   Non-axis-aligned   Arbitrary
bounding box   bounding box   bounding slabs

● 2.4   Change pbrt so that it transforms Normals just like Vectors and create a scene
          that gives a clearly incorrect image due to this bug. (Don't forget to eliminate
          this change from your copy of the source code when you're done!)

● 2.5   In practice, many elements of transformation matrices are zero or one, ren-
          dering many of the mathematical operations in the Point, Vector, Normal, and
          Ray transformation routines unnecessary. Modify pbrt to track this property
          of Transforms and write specialized transformation methods that use this in-
          formation to avoid unnecessary operations. (See Arvo (1991) for an elegant
          approach.) How do your changes affect performance for typical scenes? In
          what ways does this technique have the potential to reduce performance in-
          stead?

● 2.6   Research more robust ways to avoid the self-intersection problem in ray tracing.
          Implement such a technique in pbrt, and remove the initial assignment of
          RAY_EPSILON to Ray::mint. Construct a scene where your new approach gives
          a correct image but the current implementation does not.

CHAPTER THREE

03 SHAPES

In this chapter, we will present pbrt's abstraction for geometric primitives such as spheres and triangles. Careful abstraction of geometric shapes in a ray tracer is a key component of a clean system design, and shapes are the ideal candidate for an object-oriented approach. All geometric primitives implement a common interface, and the rest of the renderer can use this interface without needing any details about the underlying shape. This makes it possible to isolate the geometric and shading subsystems of pbrt. Without this isolation, adding new shapes to an existing renderer can be difficult and error prone.

pbrt hides details about its primitives behind a two-level abstraction. The Shape class provides access to the raw geometric properties of the primitive, such as its surface area and bounding box, and provides a ray intersection routine. The Primitive class provides additional nongeometric information about the primitive, such as its material properties. The rest of the renderer then deals only with the abstract Primitive interface. This chapter will focus on the geometry-only Shape class; the Primitive interface is the topic of Chapter 4.

The interface for Shapes is in the source file core/shape.h, and definitions of common Shape methods can be found in core/shape.cpp.

3.1 BASIC SHAPE INTERFACE

The Shape class in pbrt is *reference counted*—pbrt keeps track of the number of outstanding pointers to a particular shape and automatically deletes the shape when that reference count goes to zero. Although not completely foolproof, this is a form of *garbage collection* that eliminates the need to have to worry about freeing shape memory at the wrong time. The ReferenceCounted class handles all of the underlying mechanisms; its implementation is in Section A.2.2 in Appendix A.

⟨*Shape Declarations*⟩ ≡
```
    class COREDLL Shape : public ReferenceCounted {
    public:
        ⟨Shape Interface  91⟩
        ⟨Shape Public Data  90⟩
    };
```

All shapes are defined in object coordinate space; for example, all spheres are defined in a coordinate system where the center of the sphere is at the origin. In order to place a sphere at another position in the scene, a transformation that describes the mapping from object space to world space must be provided. The Shape class stores both this transformation and its inverse. Shapes also take a boolean parameter, reverseOrientation, that indicates whether their surface normal directions should be reversed from the default. This capability is useful because the orientation of the surface normal is used to determine which side of a shape is "outside." For example, shapes that emit illumination are emissive only on the side the surface normal lies on. The value of this parameter is set via the ReverseOrientation statement in pbrt input files.

Shapes also store the result of the Transform::SwapsHandedness() call for their object-to-world transformation. This value is needed by the DifferentialGeometry constructor that will be called each time a ray intersection is found, so the Shape constructor computes it once and stores it.

⟨*Shape Method Definitions*⟩ ≡
```
    Shape::Shape(const Transform &o2w, bool ro)
        : ObjectToWorld(o2w), WorldToObject(o2w.GetInverse()),
        reverseOrientation(ro),
        transformSwapsHandedness(o2w.SwapsHandedness()) {
    }
```

COREDLL 904
ReferenceCounted 839
Shape 90
Transform 66
Transform::GetInverse() 68
Transform::
  SwapsHandedness() 81

⟨*Shape Public Data*⟩ ≡   90
```
    const Transform ObjectToWorld, WorldToObject;
    const bool reverseOrientation, transformSwapsHandedness;
```

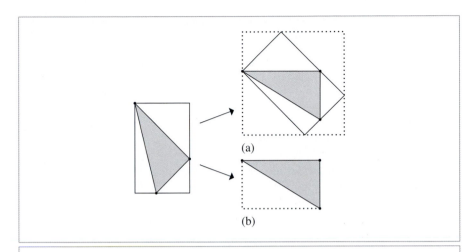

Figure 3.1: A world space bounding box of a triangle is computed by transforming its object space bounding box to world space and then finding the bounding box that encloses the resulting bounding box; a sloppy bound may result. (a) However, if the triangle's vertices are first transformed from object space to world space and then bounded (b), the fit of the bounding box can be much better.

3.1.1 BOUNDING

Each Shape subclass must be capable of bounding itself with a BBox. There are two different bounding methods. The first, ObjectBound(), returns a bounding box in the shape's object space, and the second, WorldBound(), returns a bounding box in world space. The implementation of the first method is left up to each individual shape, but there is a default implementation of the second method that transforms the object bound to world space. Shapes that can easily compute a tighter world space bound should override this method, however. An example of such a shape is a triangle (Figure 3.1).

⟨*Shape Interface*⟩ ≡   90
```
virtual BBox ObjectBound() const = 0;
```

⟨*Shape Interface*⟩+≡   90
```
virtual BBox WorldBound() const {
    return ObjectToWorld(ObjectBound());
}
```

3.1.2 REFINEMENT

Not every shape needs to be capable of determining whether a ray intersects it. For example, a complex surface might first be tessellated into triangles, which can then be intersected directly. Another possibility is a shape that is a placeholder for a large amount of geometry that is stored on disk. We could store just the filename of the geometry file and the bounding box of the geometry in memory, and read the geometry in from disk only if a ray pierces the bounding box.

The default implementation of the Shape::CanIntersect() function indicates that a shape *can* compute ray intersections, so only shapes that are nonintersectable need to override this method.

⟨*Shape Interface*⟩+≡   90
```
virtual bool CanIntersect() const { return true; }
```

If the shape cannot be intersected directly, it must provide a Shape::Refine() method that splits the shape into a group of new shapes, some of which may be intersectable and some of which may need further refinement. The default implementation of the Shape::Refine() method issues an error message; thus, shapes that are intersectable (which is the common case) do not have to provide an empty instance of this method. pbrt will never call Shape::Refine() if Shape::CanIntersect() returns true.

⟨*Shape Interface*⟩+≡   90
```
virtual void Refine(vector<Reference<Shape> > &refined) const {
    Severe("Unimplemented Shape::Refine() method called");
}
```

3.1.3 INTERSECTION

The Shape class provides two different intersection routines. The first, Shape::Intersect(), returns geometric information about a single ray-shape intersection corresponding to the first intersection, if any, in the [mint, maxt] parametric range along the ray. The other, Shape::IntersectP(), is a predicate function that determines whether or not an intersection occurs, without returning any details about the intersection itself. Some shape implementations provide a more efficient implementation for IntersectP() that can determine whether an intersection exists without computing all of its details.

There are a few important things to keep in mind when reading (and writing) intersection routines:

- The Ray structure contains Ray::mint and Ray::maxt variables that define a ray *segment*. Intersection routines must ignore any intersections that do not occur along this segment.
- If an intersection is found, its parametric distance along the ray should be stored in the pointer tHit that is passed into the intersection routine. If there are multiple intersections along the ray, the closest one should be reported.
- Information about an intersection is stored in the DifferentialGeometry structure, which completely captures the local geometric properties of a surface. This class is used heavily throughout pbrt, and it serves to cleanly isolate the geomet-

ric portion of the ray tracer from the shading and illumination portions. The DifferentialGeometry class was defined in Section 2.9.[1]

- The rays passed into intersection routines will be in world space, so shapes are responsible for transforming them to object space if needed for intersection tests. The differential geometry returned should be in world space.

Rather than making the intersection routines pure virtual functions, the Shape class provides default implementations of the intersect routines that print an error message if they are called. All Shapes that return true from Shape::CanIntersect() must provide implementations of these functions; those that return false can depend on pbrt not to call these routines on nonintersectable shapes. If these were pure virtual functions, then each nonintersectable shape would have to implement a similar default function.

⟨*Shape Interface*⟩+≡   90
```
virtual bool Intersect(const Ray &ray, float *tHit,
                       DifferentialGeometry *dg) const {
    Severe("Unimplemented Shape::Intersect() method called");
    return false;
}
```

⟨*Shape Interface*⟩+≡   90
```
virtual bool IntersectP(const Ray &ray) const {
    Severe("Unimplemented Shape::IntersectP() method called");
    return false;
}
```

3.1.4 AVOIDING INCORRECT SELF-INTERSECTIONS

A classic issue in ray tracing is the self-intersection problem, where floating-point errors can lead to incorrect self-intersections when rays are traced starting from a previously computed ray-surface intersection point (e.g., shadow rays, rays for specular reflection or refraction, etc.). Figure 3.2 illustrates the problem: Represented in finite-precision floating-point numbers, the computed intersection point may lie slightly below the actual surface. If new rays are traced with this point as their origin, it's possible that they may intersect the surface even though a ray actually starting from the surface would not.

DifferentialGeometry 83

Ray 59

Severe() 834

Shape 90

Shape::CanIntersect() 92

---

1   Almost all ray tracers use this general idiom for returning geometric information about intersections with shapes. As an optimization, many will only partially initialize the intersection information when an intersection is found, storing just enough information so that the rest of the values can be computed later if actually needed. This approach saves work in the case where a closer intersection is later found with another shape. In our experience, the extra work to compute all the information isn't substantial, and for renderers that have complex scene data management algorithms (e.g., discarding geometry from main memory when too much memory is being used and writing it to disk), the deferred approach may fail because the shape is no longer in memory.

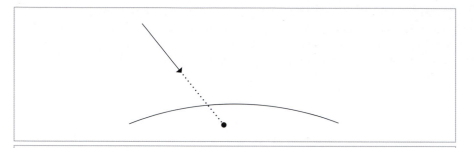

Figure 3.2: Due to finite floating-point precision and round-off error, when the intersection of a ray is found with a shape, the computed intersection point may lie slightly above or slightly below the true intersection point. This can lead to rendering errors when reflected and shadow rays are traced starting from the computed intersection point, as incorrect self-intersections with the surface may be detected.

pbrt addresses this issue with a hack, although one that generally works well in practice: the Ray::mint values of the reflected rays will be set to a small "epsilon" value, chosen to be large enough to eliminate this problem for many scenes in practice. The RAY_EPSILON value, defined in Section 2.5, is the compile time constant value used.

Unfortunately, no single constant can reliably solve the self-intersection problem. It needs to be small enough not to miss true intersections, but large enough to overcome most precision errors. For any given constant, it is easy to construct a scene for which it will not work. In particular, for scenes with very large scales or very tiny scales, this constant will be ineffective, since the error in the computed intersection point is related to each of the magnitudes of the components of the ray, the magnitudes of the numbers that describe the particular shape, and the particular computations done in computing the intersection point.

3.1.5 SHADING GEOMETRY

Some shapes (notably triangle meshes) support the idea of having two types of differential geometry at a point on the surface: the true geometry, which accurately reflects the local properties of the surface, and the *shading geometry*, which may have normals and tangents that are different than those in the true differential geometry. For triangle meshes, the user can provide normal vectors and primary tangents at the vertices of the mesh that are interpolated to give normals and tangents at points across the faces of triangles.

The Shape::GetShadingGeometry() method returns the shading geometry corresponding to the DifferentialGeometry returned by the Shape::Intersect() routine. By default, the shading geometry matches the true geometry, so the default implementation just copies the true geometry. One subtlety is that an object-to-world transformation is passed to this routine; if the routine needs to transform data from object space to world space to compute the shading geometry, it must use this transformation rather than the Shape::ObjectToWorld transformation. This allows object instancing to be implemented in pbrt (see Section 4.1.2).

⟨*Shape Interface*⟩+≡   90
```
    virtual void GetShadingGeometry(const Transform &obj2world,
            const DifferentialGeometry &dg,
            DifferentialGeometry *dgShading) const {
        *dgShading = dg;
    }
```

3.1.6 SURFACE AREA

In order to properly use Shapes as area lights, it is necessary to be able to compute the surface area of a shape in object space. As with the intersection methods, this method will only be called for intersectable shapes.

⟨*Shape Interface*⟩+≡   90
```
    virtual float Area() const {
        Severe("Unimplemented Shape::Area() method called");
        return 0.;
    }
```

3.1.7 SIDEDNESS

Many rendering systems, particularly those based on scan line or z-buffer algorithms, support the concept of shapes being "one-sided"—the shape is visible if seen from the front but disappears when viewed from behind. In particular, if a geometric object is closed and always viewed from the outside, then the back-facing parts of it can be discarded without changing the resulting image. This optimization can substantially improve the speed of these types of hidden surface removal algorithms. The potential for improved performance is reduced when using this technique with ray tracing, however, since it is often necessary to perform the ray-object intersection before determining the surface normal to do the back-facing test. Furthermore, this feature can lead to a physically inconsistent scene description if one-sided objects are not in fact closed. For example, a surface might block light when a shadow ray is traced from a light source to a point on another surface, but not if the shadow ray is traced in the other direction. For all of these reasons, pbrt doesn't support this feature.

DifferentialGeometry 83
Severe() 834
Shape::ObjectToWorld 90
Transform 66

3.2 SPHERES

⟨*Sphere Declarations*⟩ ≡
```
class Sphere : public Shape {
public:
    ⟨Sphere Public Methods 705⟩
private:
    ⟨Sphere Private Data 98⟩
};
```

Spheres are a special case of a general type of surface called *quadrics*—surfaces described by quadratic polynomials in x, y, and z. They are the simplest type of curved surface that is useful to a ray tracer and are a good starting point for general ray intersection routines. pbrt supports six types of quadrics: spheres, cones, disks (a special case of a cone), cylinders, hyperboloids, and paraboloids.

Many surfaces can be described in one of two main ways: in *implicit form* and in *parametric form*. An implicit function describes a 3D surface as

$$f(x, y, z) = 0.$$

The set of all points (x, y, z) that fulfill this condition define the surface. For a unit sphere at the origin, the familiar implicit equation is $x^2 + y^2 + z^2 - 1 = 0$. Only the set of points one unit from the origin satisfies this constraint, giving the unit sphere's surface.

Many surfaces can also be described parametrically using a function to map 2D points to 3D points on the surface. For example, a sphere of radius r can be described as a function of 2D spherical coordinates (θ, ϕ), where θ ranges from 0 to π and ϕ ranges from 0 to 2π (Figure 3.3):

$$x = r \, \sin \theta \, \cos \phi$$
$$y = r \, \sin \theta \, \sin \phi$$
$$z = r \, \cos \theta.$$

We can transform this function $f(\theta, \phi)$ into a function $f(u, v)$ over $[0, 1]^2$ with the substitution

$$\phi = u\phi_{max}$$
$$\theta = \theta_{min} + v(\theta_{max} - \theta_{min}).$$

This form is particularly useful for texture mapping, where it can be directly used to map a texture defined over $[0, 1]^2$ to the sphere. Figure 3.4 shows an image of two spheres; a grid image map has been used to show the (u, v) parameterization.

As we describe the implementation of the sphere shape, we will make use of both the implicit and parametric descriptions of the shape, depending on which is a more natural way to approach the particular problem we're facing.

Shape 90

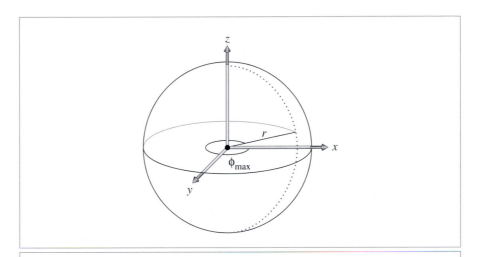

Figure 3.3: Basic Setting for the Sphere Shape. It has a radius of r and is centered at the object space origin. A partial sphere may be described by specifying a maximum ϕ value.

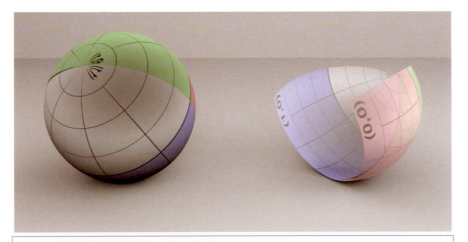

Figure 3.4: Two Spheres. On the left is a complete sphere, and on the right is a partial sphere (with $z_{max} < r$ and $\phi_{max} < 2\pi$). Note that the texture map used shows the (u, v) parameterization of the shape; the singularity at one of the poles is visible in the complete sphere.

3.2.1 CONSTRUCTION

The Sphere class specifies a shape that is centered at the origin in object space. To place it elsewhere in the scene, the user must apply an appropriate transformation when specifying the sphere in the input file.

The radius of the sphere can have an arbitrary positive value, and the sphere's extent can be truncated in two different ways. First, minimum and maximum z values may be set; the parts of the sphere below and above these, respectively, are cut off. Second, considering the parameterization of the sphere in spherical coordinates, a maximum ϕ value can be set. The sphere sweeps out ϕ values from 0 to the given ϕ_{max} such that the section of the sphere with spherical ϕ values above ϕ_{max} is also removed.

⟨*Sphere Method Definitions*⟩ ≡

```
Sphere::Sphere(const Transform &o2w, bool ro, float rad,
               float z0, float z1, float pm)
    : Shape(o2w, ro) {
    radius = rad;
    zmin = Clamp(min(z0, z1), -radius, radius);
    zmax = Clamp(max(z0, z1), -radius, radius);
    thetaMin = acosf(zmin/radius);
    thetaMax = acosf(zmax/radius);
    phiMax = Radians(Clamp(pm, 0.0f, 360.0f));
}
```

⟨*Sphere Private Data*⟩ ≡   96

```
float radius;
float phiMax;
float zmin, zmax;
float thetaMin, thetaMax;
```

3.2.2 BOUNDING

Computing a bounding box for a sphere is straightforward. The implementation here will use the values of z_{min} and z_{max} provided by the user to tighten up the bound when less than an entire sphere is being rendered. However, it won't do the extra work to look at θ_{max} and see if it can compute a tighter bounding box when θ_{max} is less than 2π. This improvement is left as an exercise.

⟨*Sphere Method Definitions*⟩ + ≡

```
BBox Sphere::ObjectBound() const {
    return BBox(Point(-radius, -radius, zmin),
                Point( radius,  radius, zmax));
}
```

3.2.3 INTERSECTION

The task of deriving an intersection test is simplified by the fact that the sphere is centered at the origin. However, if the sphere has been transformed to another position in world space, then it is necessary to transform rays to object space before intersecting them with the sphere, using the world-to-object transformation. Given a ray in object space, the intersection computation can be performed in object space instead.[2]

The following fragment shows the entire intersection method:

⟨*Sphere Method Definitions*⟩+≡
```
    bool Sphere::Intersect(const Ray &r, float *tHit,
                              DifferentialGeometry *dg) const {
        float phi;
        Point phit;
        ⟨Transform Ray to object space  99⟩
        ⟨Compute quadratic sphere coefficients  100⟩
        ⟨Solve quadratic equation for t values  100⟩
        ⟨Compute sphere hit position and φ  102⟩
        ⟨Test sphere intersection against clipping parameters  102⟩
        ⟨Find parametric representation of sphere hit  103⟩
        ⟨Initialize DifferentialGeometry from parametric information  106⟩
        ⟨Update tHit for quadric intersection  106⟩
        return true;
    }
```

First, the given world space ray is transformed to the sphere's object space. The remainder of the intersection test will take place in that coordinate system.

⟨*Transform* Ray *to object space*⟩≡   **99, 107, 111, 115**
```
    Ray ray;
    WorldToObject(r, &ray);
```

If a sphere is centered at the origin with radius r, its implicit representation is

$$x^2 + y^2 + z^2 - r^2 = 0.$$

By substituting the parametric representation of the ray, given in Equation (2.3), into the implicit sphere equation, we have

$$\left(o_x + t\mathbf{d}_x\right)^2 + \left(o_y + t\mathbf{d}_y\right)^2 + \left(o_z + t\mathbf{d}_z\right)^2 = r^2.$$

---

[2] This is something of a classic theme in computer graphics: by transforming the problem to a particular restricted case, it is possible to more easily and efficiently do an intersection test: that is, many terms of the equations cancel out since the sphere is always at $(0, 0, 0)$. No overall generality is lost, since an appropriate translation can be applied to the ray for spheres at other positions.

Note that all elements of this equation besides t are known values. The t values where the equation holds give the parametric positions along the ray where the implicit sphere equation holds and thus the points along the ray where it intersects the sphere. We can expand this equation and gather the coefficients for a general quadratic equation in t,

$$At^2 + Bt + C = 0,$$

where[3]

$$A = \mathbf{d}_x^2 + \mathbf{d}_y^2 + \mathbf{d}_z^2$$
$$B = 2(\mathbf{d}_x o_x + \mathbf{d}_y o_y + \mathbf{d}_z o_z)$$
$$C = o_x^2 + o_y^2 + o_z^2 - r^2.$$

This directly translates to this fragment of source code:

⟨*Compute quadratic sphere coefficients*⟩ ≡   99, 107
```
    float A = ray.d.x*ray.d.x + ray.d.y*ray.d.y + ray.d.z*ray.d.z;
    float B = 2 * (ray.d.x*ray.o.x + ray.d.y*ray.o.y + ray.d.z*ray.o.z);
    float C = ray.o.x*ray.o.x + ray.o.y*ray.o.y +
              ray.o.z*ray.o.z - radius*radius;
```

There are two possible solutions to this quadratic equation, giving zero, one, or two nonimaginary t values where the ray intersects the sphere:

$$t_0 = \frac{-B - \sqrt{B^2 - 4AC}}{2A}$$
$$t_1 = \frac{-B + \sqrt{B^2 - 4AC}}{2A}.$$

The `Quadratic()` utility function solves a quadratic equation, returning `false` if there are no real solutions and returning `true` and setting `t0` and `t1` appropriately if there are solutions:

⟨*Solve quadratic equation for* t *values*⟩ ≡   99, 107, 111
```
    float t0, t1;
    if (!Quadratic(A, B, C, &t0, &t1))
        return false;
```
    ⟨*Compute intersection distance along ray* 102⟩

Quadratic() 101

Sphere::radius 98

3   Some ray tracers require that the direction vector of a ray be normalized, meaning $A = 1$. This can lead to subtle errors, however, if the caller forgets to normalize the ray direction. Of course, these errors can be avoided by normalizing the direction in the ray constructor, but this wastes effort when the provided direction is *already* normalized. To avoid this needless complexity, pbrt never insists on vector normalization in intersection routines. This is particularly helpful since it reduces the amount of computation needed to transform rays to object space, since no normalization is necessary there.

⟨*Global Inline Functions*⟩ ≡
```
inline bool Quadratic(float A, float B, float C, float *t0, float *t1) {
    ⟨Find quadratic discriminant 101⟩
    ⟨Compute quadratic t values 101⟩
}
```

If the discriminant ($B^2 - 4AC$) is negative, then there are no real roots and the ray must miss the sphere:

⟨*Find quadratic discriminant*⟩ ≡   101
```
float discrim = B * B - 4.f * A * C;
if (discrim < 0.) return false;
float rootDiscrim = sqrtf(discrim);
```

The usual version of the quadratic equation can give poor numeric precision when $B \approx \pm\sqrt{B^2 - 4AC}$ due to cancellation error. It can be rewritten algebraically to a more stable form:

$$t_0 = \frac{q}{A}$$
$$t_1 = \frac{C}{q},$$

where

$$q = \begin{cases} -.5(B - \sqrt{B^2 - 4AC}) & : B < 0 \\ -.5(B + \sqrt{B^2 - 4AC}) & : \text{otherwise.} \end{cases}$$

⟨*Compute quadratic t values*⟩ ≡   101
```
float q;
if (B < 0) q = -.5f * (B - rootDiscrim);
else       q = -.5f * (B + rootDiscrim);
*t0 = q / A;
*t1 = C / q;
if (*t0 > *t1) swap(*t0, *t1);
return true;
```

Given the two intersection t values, the intersection method checks them against the ray segment from mint to maxt. Since t_0 is guaranteed to be less than t_1 (and mint less than maxt), if t_0 is greater than maxt or t_1 is less than mint, then it is certain that both hits are out of the range of interest. Otherwise, t_0 is the tentative hit distance. It may be less than mint, however, in which case we ignore it and try t_1. If that is also out of range, we have no valid intersection. If there is an intersection, thit holds the distance to the hit.

⟨*Compute intersection distance along ray*⟩ ≡   **100**
```
if (t0 > ray.maxt || t1 < ray.mint)
    return false;
float thit = t0;
if (t0 < ray.mint) {
    thit = t1;
    if (thit > ray.maxt) return false;
}
```

3.2.4 PARTIAL SPHERES

Given the parametric distance along the ray to the intersection with a full sphere, it is necessary to handle partial spheres with clipped z or ϕ ranges. Intersections that are in clipped areas need to be ignored. The implementation starts by computing the object space position of the intersection, `phit`, and the ϕ value for the hit point. Using the parametric representation of the sphere,

$$\frac{y}{x} = \frac{r \, \sin \theta \, \sin \phi}{r \sin \theta \cos \phi} = \tan \phi,$$

so $\phi = \arctan y/x$. It is necessary to remap the result of the C standard library's `atan2f` function to a value between 0 and 2π, to match the sphere's original definition.

⟨*Compute sphere hit position and* ϕ⟩ ≡   **99, 102, 107**
```
phit = ray(thit);
phi = atan2f(phit.y, phit.x);
if (phi < 0.) phi += 2.f*M_PI;
```

The hit point can now be tested against the specified minima and maxima for z and ϕ. If the t_0 intersection wasn't actually valid, the routine tries again with t_1.

⟨*Test sphere intersection against clipping parameters*⟩ ≡   **99, 107**
```
if (phit.z < zmin || phit.z > zmax || phi > phiMax) {
    if (thit == t1) return false;
    if (t1 > ray.maxt) return false;
    thit = t1;
    ⟨Compute sphere hit position and φ 102⟩
    if (phit.z < zmin || phit.z > zmax || phi > phiMax)
        return false;
}
```

At this point, it is certain that the ray hits the sphere, and the `DifferentialGeometry` structure can be initialized. The method computes u and v values by scaling the previously computed ϕ value for the hit to lie between 0 and 1 and by computing a θ value between 0 and 1 for the hit point, based on the range of θ values for the given sphere.

Then, it finds the parametric partial derivatives of position $\partial p/\partial u$ and $\partial p/\partial v$ and surface normal $\partial \mathbf{n}/\partial u$ and $\partial \mathbf{n}/\partial v$.

⟨*Find parametric representation of sphere hit*⟩ ≡   99
```
float u = phi / phiMax;
float theta = acosf(phit.z / radius);
float v = (theta - thetaMin) / (thetaMax - thetaMin);
```
⟨*Compute sphere $\partial p/\partial u$ and $\partial p/\partial v$* **104**⟩
⟨*Compute sphere $\partial \mathbf{n}/\partial u$ and $\partial \mathbf{n}/\partial v$* **105**⟩

Computing the partial derivatives of a point on the sphere is a short exercise in algebra. Here we will show how the x component of $\partial p/\partial u$, $\partial p_x/\partial u$, is calculated; the other components are found similarly. Using the parametric definition of the sphere, we have

$$x = r \sin \theta \cos \phi$$

$$\frac{\partial p_x}{\partial u} = \frac{\partial}{\partial u} (r \sin \theta \cos \phi)$$

$$= r \sin \theta \frac{\partial}{\partial u} (\cos \phi)$$

$$= r \sin \theta (-\phi_{max} \sin \phi).$$

Using a substitution based on the parametric definition of the sphere's y coordinate, this simplifies to

$$\frac{\partial p_x}{\partial u} = -\phi_{max} y.$$

Similarly

$$\frac{\partial p_y}{\partial u} = \phi_{max} x,$$

and

$$\frac{\partial p_z}{\partial u} = 0.$$

A similar process gives $\partial p/\partial v$. The complete result is

Sphere::phiMax 98
Sphere::radius 98
Sphere::thetaMax 98
Sphere::thetaMin 98

$$\frac{\partial p}{\partial u} = (-\phi_{max} y, \phi_{max} x, 0)$$

$$\frac{\partial p}{\partial v} = (\theta_{max} - \theta_{min})(z \cos \phi, z \sin \phi, -r \sin \theta).$$

⟨*Compute sphere ∂p/∂u and ∂p/∂v*⟩ ≡ **103**

```
float zradius = sqrtf(phit.x*phit.x + phit.y*phit.y);
float invzradius = 1.f / zradius;
float cosphi = phit.x * invzradius;
float sinphi = phit.y * invzradius;
Vector dpdu(-phiMax * phit.y, phiMax * phit.x, 0);
Vector dpdv = (thetaMax-thetaMin) *
    Vector(phit.z * cosphi, phit.z * sinphi,
           -radius * sinf(thetaMin + v*(thetaMax - thetaMin)));
```

⋆3.2.5 PARTIAL DERIVATIVES OF NORMAL VECTORS

It is also useful to determine how the normal changes as we move along the surface in the u and v directions. For example, the antialiasing techniques in Chapter 11 are dependent on this information to antialias textures on objects that are seen reflected in curved surfaces. The differential changes in normal $\partial\mathbf{n}/\partial u$ and $\partial\mathbf{n}/\partial v$ are given by the *Weingarten equations* from differential geometry:

$$\frac{\partial\mathbf{n}}{\partial u} = \frac{fF - eG}{EG - F^2}\frac{\partial\mathbf{p}}{\partial u} + \frac{eF - fE}{EG - F^2}\frac{\partial\mathbf{p}}{\partial v}$$

$$\frac{\partial\mathbf{n}}{\partial v} = \frac{gF - fG}{EG - F^2}\frac{\partial\mathbf{p}}{\partial u} + \frac{fF - gE}{EG - F^2}\frac{\partial\mathbf{p}}{\partial v},$$

where E, F, and G are coefficients of the *first fundamental form* and are given by

$$E = \left|\frac{\partial\mathbf{p}}{\partial u}\right|^2$$

$$F = \left(\frac{\partial\mathbf{p}}{\partial u} \cdot \frac{\partial\mathbf{p}}{\partial v}\right)$$

$$G = \left|\frac{\partial\mathbf{p}}{\partial v}\right|^2.$$

These are easily computed with the $\partial\mathbf{p}/\partial u$ and $\partial\mathbf{p}/\partial v$ values found earlier. The e, f, and g are coefficients of the *second fundamental form*,

---

⋆ This section covers advanced topics and may be skipped on a first reading.

$$e = \left(\mathbf{n} \cdot \frac{\partial^2 \mathbf{p}}{\partial u^2} \right)$$

$$f = \left(\mathbf{n} \cdot \frac{\partial^2 \mathbf{p}}{\partial u \partial v} \right)$$

$$g = \left(\mathbf{n} \cdot \frac{\partial^2 \mathbf{p}}{\partial v^2} \right).$$

The two fundamental forms have basic connections with the local curvature of a surface; see a differential geometry textbook such as Gray (1993) for details. To find e, f, and g, it is necessary to compute the second-order partial derivatives $\partial^2 \mathbf{p}/\partial u^2$ and so on.

For spheres, a little more algebra gives the required second derivatives:

$$\frac{\partial^2 \mathbf{p}}{\partial u^2} = -\phi_{\max}^2 (x, y, 0)$$

$$\frac{\partial^2 \mathbf{p}}{\partial u \partial v} = (\theta_{\max} - \theta_{\min}) z \phi_{\max} (-\sin \phi, \cos \phi, 0)$$

$$\frac{\partial^2 \mathbf{p}}{\partial v^2} = -(\theta_{\max} - \theta_{\min})^2 (x, y, z).$$

⟨*Compute sphere* $\partial \mathbf{n}/\partial u$ *and* $\partial \mathbf{n}/\partial v$⟩ ≡   103

```
Vector d2Pduu = -phiMax * phiMax * Vector(phit.x, phit.y, 0);
Vector d2Pduv = (thetaMax - thetaMin) * phit.z * phiMax *
                Vector(-sinphi, cosphi, 0.);
Vector d2Pdvv = -(thetaMax - thetaMin) * (thetaMax - thetaMin) *
                Vector(phit.x, phit.y, phit.z);
```
⟨*Compute coefficients for fundamental forms* **105**⟩
⟨*Compute* $\partial \mathbf{n}/\partial u$ *and* $\partial \mathbf{n}/\partial v$ *from fundamental form coefficients* **106**⟩

⟨*Compute coefficients for fundamental forms*⟩ ≡   **105, 113**

```
float E = Dot(dpdu, dpdu);
float F = Dot(dpdu, dpdv);
float G = Dot(dpdv, dpdv);
Vector N = Cross(dpdu, dpdv);
float e = Dot(N, d2Pduu);
float f = Dot(N, d2Pduv);
float g = Dot(N, d2Pdvv);
```

⟨*Compute* ∂**n**/∂*u and* ∂**n**/∂*v from fundamental form coefficients*⟩ ≡   **105, 113**

```
    float invEGF2 = 1.f / (E*G - F*F);
    Vector dndu = (f*F - e*G) * invEGF2 * dpdu +
                  (e*F - f*E) * invEGF2 * dpdv;
    Vector dndv = (g*F - f*G) * invEGF2 * dpdu +
                  (f*F - g*E) * invEGF2 * dpdv;
```

3.2.6 `DifferentialGeometry` INITIALIZATION

Having computed the surface parameterization and all the relevant partial derivatives, the `DifferentialGeometry` structure can be initialized with the geometric information for this intersection:

⟨*Initialize* `DifferentialGeometry` *from parametric information*⟩ ≡   **99, 111, 115**

```
    *dg = DifferentialGeometry(ObjectToWorld(phit),
                               ObjectToWorld(dpdu),
                               ObjectToWorld(dpdv),
                               ObjectToWorld(dndu),
                               ObjectToWorld(dndv),
                               u, v, this);
```

Since there is an intersection, the `tHit` parameter is updated with the parametric hit distance along the ray, which was stored in `thit`. This will allow subsequent intersection tests to terminate early if the potential hit would be farther away than the existing intersection.

A natural question to ask at this point is, "What effect does the world-to-object transformation have on the correct parametric distance to return?" Indeed, the intersection method has found a parametric distance to the intersection for the object space ray, which may have been translated, rotated, scaled, or worse when it was transformed from world space. However, it can be shown that the parametric distance to an intersection in object space is exactly the same as it would have been if the ray was left in world space and the intersection had been done there and, thus, `tHit` can be initialized directly. Note that if the object space ray's direction had been normalized after the transformation, then this would no longer be the case and a correction factor related to the unnormalized ray's length would be needed. This is another motivation for not normalizing the object space ray's direction after transformation.

⟨*Update* `tHit` *for quadric intersection*⟩ ≡   **99, 111, 115**

```
    *tHit = thit;
```

The `Sphere::IntersectP()` routine is almost identical to `Sphere::Intersect()`, but it does not fill in the `DifferentialGeometry` structure. Because `Intersect` and `IntersectP` are always so closely related, we will not show `IntersectP` for the remaining shapes.

⟨*Sphere Method Definitions*⟩+≡
```
bool Sphere::IntersectP(const Ray &r) const {
    float phi;
    Point phit;
```
⟨*Transform* Ray *to object space* **99**⟩
⟨*Compute quadratic sphere coefficients* **100**⟩
⟨*Solve quadratic equation for* t *values* **100**⟩
⟨*Compute sphere hit position and* φ **102**⟩
⟨*Test sphere intersection against clipping parameters* **102**⟩
```
    return true;
}
```

3.2.7 SURFACE AREA

To compute the surface area of quadrics, we use a standard formula from integral calculus. If a curve $y = f(x)$ from $y = a$ to $y = b$ is revolved around the x axis, the surface area of the resulting swept surface is

$$2\pi \int_a^b f(x)\sqrt{1 + \left(f'(x)\right)^2}\, dx,$$

where $f'(x)$ denotes the derivative df/dx.[4] Since most of our surfaces of revolution are only partially swept around the axis, we will instead use the formula

$$\phi_{max} \int_a^b f(x)\sqrt{1 + \left(f'(x)\right)^2}\, dx.$$

The sphere is a surface of revolution of a circular arc. The function that defines the profile curve of the sphere is

$$f(x) = \sqrt{r^2 - x^2},$$

and its derivative is

$$f'(x) = -\frac{x}{\sqrt{r^2 - x^2}}.$$

Recall that the sphere is clipped at z_{min} and z_{max}. The surface area is therefore

---

4 See Anton, Bivens, and Davis (2001) for a derivation.

$$A = \phi_{max} \int_{z_{min}}^{z_{max}} \sqrt{r^2 - x^2} \sqrt{1 + \frac{x^2}{r^2 - x^2}} \, dx$$

$$= \phi_{max} \int_{z_{min}}^{z_{max}} \sqrt{r^2 - x^2 + x^2} \, dx$$

$$= \phi_{max} \int_{z_{min}}^{z_{max}} r \, dx$$

$$= \phi_{max} r (z_{max} - z_{min}).$$

For the full sphere $\phi_{max} = 2\pi$, $z_{min} = -r$ and $z_{max} = r$, so we have the standard formula $A = 4\pi r^2$, confirming that the formula is correct.

⟨*Sphere Method Definitions*⟩+≡

```
float Sphere::Area() const {
    return phiMax * radius * (zmax-zmin);
}
```

3.3 CYLINDERS

⟨*Cylinder Declarations*⟩≡

```
class Cylinder : public Shape {
public:
    ⟨Cylinder Public Methods 705⟩
protected:
    ⟨Cylinder Private Data 110⟩
};
```

3.3.1 CONSTRUCTION

Another useful quadric is the cylinder; pbrt provides cylinder Shapes that are centered around the z axis. The implementation is in the file shapes/cylinder.cpp. 🔴 The user supplies a minimum and maximum z value for the cylinder, as well as a radius and maximum ϕ sweep value (Figure 3.5). In parametric form, a cylinder is described by the following equations:

$$\phi = u\phi_{max}$$
$$x = r\cos\phi$$
$$y = r\sin\phi$$
$$z = z_{min} + v(z_{max} - z_{min}).$$

Figure 3.6 shows a rendered image of two cylinders. Like the spheres image, the left cylinder is a complete cylinder, while the right one is a partial cylinder due to having a ϕ_{max} value less than 2π.

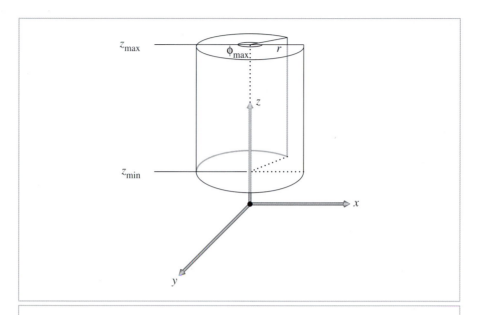

Figure 3.5: Basic Setting for the Cylinder Shape. It has a radius of r and covers a range along the z axis. A partial cylinder may be swept by specifying a maximum ϕ value.

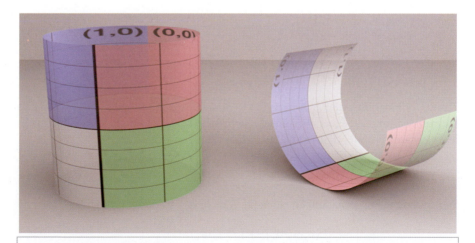

Figure 3.6: Two Cylinders. A complete cylinder is on the left, and a partial cylinder is on the right.

⟨*Cylinder Method Definitions*⟩ ≡
```
Cylinder::Cylinder(const Transform &o2w, bool ro, float rad,
                   float z0, float z1, float pm)
    : Shape(o2w, ro) {
    radius = rad;
    zmin = min(z0, z1);
    zmax = max(z0, z1);
    phiMax = Radians(Clamp(pm, 0.0f, 360.0f));
}
```

⟨*Cylinder Private Data*⟩ ≡   **108**
```
float radius;
float zmin, zmax;
float phiMax;
```

3.3.2 BOUNDING

As was done with the sphere, the bounding method computes a conservative bounding box for the cylinder using the z range but without taking into account the maximum ϕ.

⟨*Cylinder Method Definitions*⟩+≡
```
BBox Cylinder::ObjectBound() const {
    Point p1 = Point(-radius, -radius, zmin);
    Point p2 = Point( radius,  radius, zmax);
    return BBox(p1, p2);
}
```

3.3.3 INTERSECTION

The ray-cylinder intersection formula can be found by substituting the ray equation into the cylinder's implicit equation, similarly to the sphere case. The implicit equation for an infinitely long cylinder centered on the z axis with radius r is

$$x^2 + y^2 - r^2 = 0.$$

Substituting the ray equation, Equation (2.3), we have

$$\left(o_x + t\mathbf{d}_x\right)^2 + \left(o_y + t\mathbf{d}_y\right)^2 = r^2.$$

When we expand this and find the coefficients of the quadratic equation $At^2 + Bt + C$, we have

$$A = \mathbf{d}_x^2 + \mathbf{d}_y^2$$
$$B = 2(\mathbf{d}_x o_x + \mathbf{d}_y o_y)$$
$$C = o_x^2 + o_y^2 - r^2.$$

⟨*Compute quadratic cylinder coefficients*⟩ ≡   **111**

```
float A = ray.d.x*ray.d.x + ray.d.y*ray.d.y;
float B = 2 * (ray.d.x*ray.o.x + ray.d.y*ray.o.y);
float C = ray.o.x*ray.o.x + ray.o.y*ray.o.y - radius*radius;
```

The solution process for the quadratic equation is similar for all quadric shapes, so some fragments from the Sphere intersection method will be reused in the following.

⟨*Cylinder Method Definitions*⟩+≡

```
bool Cylinder::Intersect(const Ray &r, float *tHit,
                         DifferentialGeometry *dg) const {
    float phi;
    Point phit;
```
⟨*Transform* Ray *to object space* **99**⟩
⟨*Compute quadratic cylinder coefficients* **111**⟩
⟨*Solve quadratic equation for* t *values* **100**⟩
⟨*Compute cylinder hit point and* φ **111**⟩
⟨*Test cylinder intersection against clipping parameters* **112**⟩
⟨*Find parametric representation of cylinder hit* **112**⟩
⟨*Initialize* DifferentialGeometry *from parametric information* **106**⟩
⟨*Update* tHit *for quadric intersection* **106**⟩
```
    return true;
}
```

3.3.4 PARTIAL CYLINDERS

As with the sphere, we can invert the parametric description of the cylinder to compute a ϕ value by inverting the x and y parametric equations to solve for ϕ. In fact, the result is the same as for the sphere.

⟨*Compute cylinder hit point and* φ⟩ ≡   **111, 112**

```
phit = ray(thit);
phi = atan2f(phit.y, phit.x);
if (phi < 0.) phi += 2.f*M_PI;
```

The intersection routine now makes sure that the hit is in the specified z range, and that the angle is acceptable. If not, it rejects the hit and tries with t_1, if it hasn't already, just like the sphere.

⟨*Test cylinder intersection against clipping parameters*⟩ ≡   **111**

```
if (phit.z < zmin || phit.z > zmax || phi > phiMax) {
    if (thit == t1) return false;
    thit = t1;
    if (t1 > ray.maxt) return false;
    ⟨Compute cylinder hit point and φ 111⟩
    if (phit.z < zmin || phit.z > zmax || phi > phiMax)
        return false;
}
```

Again the u value is computed by scaling ϕ to lie between 0 and 1. Straightforward inversion of the parametric equation for the cylinder's z value gives the v parametric coordinate.

⟨*Find parametric representation of cylinder hit*⟩ ≡   **111**

```
float u = phi / phiMax;
float v = (phit.z - zmin) / (zmax - zmin);
⟨Compute cylinder ∂p/∂u and ∂p/∂v 112⟩
⟨Compute cylinder ∂n/∂u and ∂n/∂v 113⟩
```

The partial derivatives for a cylinder are quite easy to derive:

$$\frac{\partial \mathrm{p}}{\partial u} = (-\phi_{\max} y, \ \phi_{\max} x, \ 0)$$

$$\frac{\partial \mathrm{p}}{\partial v} = (0, \ 0, \ z_{\max} - z_{\min}).$$

⟨*Compute cylinder ∂p/∂u and ∂p/∂v*⟩ ≡   **112**

```
Vector dpdu(-phiMax * phit.y, phiMax * phit.x, 0);
Vector dpdv(0, 0, zmax - zmin);
```

We again use the Weingarten equations to compute the parametric change in the cylinder normal. The relevant partial derivatives are

$$\frac{\partial^2 \mathrm{p}}{\partial u^2} = -\phi_{\max}^2 (x, y, 0)$$

$$\frac{\partial^2 \mathrm{p}}{\partial u \partial v} = (0, 0, 0)$$

$$\frac{\partial^2 \mathrm{p}}{\partial v^2} = (0, 0, 0).$$

⟨*Compute cylinder* ∂**n**/∂*u* *and* ∂**n**/∂*v*⟩ ≡   **112**
```
    Vector d2Pduu = -phiMax * phiMax *
                       Vector(phit.x, phit.y, 0);
    Vector d2Pduv(0, 0, 0), d2Pdvv(0, 0, 0);
```
    ⟨*Compute coefficients for fundamental forms* **105**⟩
    ⟨*Compute* ∂**n**/∂*u* *and* ∂**n**/∂*v from fundamental form coefficients* **106**⟩

3.3.5 SURFACE AREA

A cylinder is just a rolled-up rectangle. If you unroll the rectangle, its height is $z_{max} - z_{min}$, and its width is $r\phi_{max}$:

⟨*Cylinder Method Definitions*⟩+≡
```
    float Cylinder::Area() const {
        return (zmax-zmin)*phiMax*radius;
    }
```

3.4 DISKS

⟨*Disk Declarations*⟩ ≡
```
    class Disk : public Shape {
    public:
        ⟨Disk Public Methods 704⟩
    private:
        ⟨Disk Private Data 115⟩
    };
```

The disk is an interesting quadric since it has a particularly straightforward intersection routine that avoids solving the quadratic equation. In pbrt, a Disk is a circular disk of radius *r* at height *h* along the *z* axis. It is implemented in the file shapes/disk.cpp.ⓒⓓ In order to make partial disks, the user may specify a maximum ϕ value beyond which the disk is cut off (Figure 3.7). The disk can also be generalized to an annulus by specifying an inner radius r_i. In parametric form, it is described by

$$\phi = u\,\phi_{max}$$
$$x = ((1-v)r_i + vr)\cos\phi$$
$$y = ((1-v)r_i + vr)\sin\phi$$
$$z = h.$$

Figure 3.8 is a rendered image of two disks.

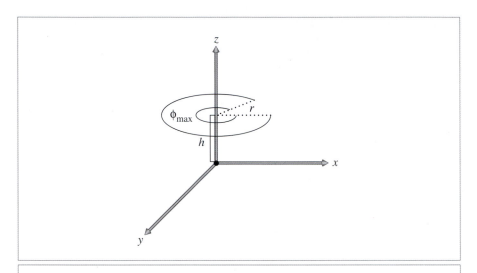

Figure 3.7: Basic Setting for the Disk Shape. The disk has radius r and is located at height h along the z axis. A partial disk may be swept by specifying a maximum ϕ value and an inner radius r_i.

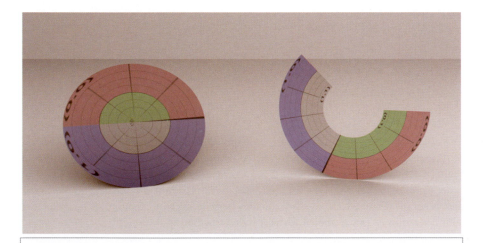

Figure 3.8: Two Disks. A complete disk is on the left, and a partial disk is on the right.

3.4.1 CONSTRUCTION

⟨*Disk Method Definitions*⟩ ≡

```
Disk::Disk(const Transform &o2w, bool ro, float ht,
           float r, float ri, float tmax)
    : Shape(o2w, ro) {
    height = ht;
    radius = r;
    innerRadius = ri;
    phiMax = Radians(Clamp(tmax, 0.0f, 360.0f));
}
```

⟨*Disk Private Data*⟩ ≡   **113**

```
float height, radius, innerRadius, phiMax;
```

3.4.2 BOUNDING

The bounding method is quite straightforward; it computes a bounding box centered at the height of the disk along *z*, with extent of radius in both the *x* and *y* directions.

⟨*Disk Method Definitions*⟩+≡

```
BBox Disk::ObjectBound() const {
    return BBox(Point(-radius, -radius, height),
                Point( radius,  radius, height));
}
```

3.4.3 INTERSECTION

Intersecting a ray with a disk is also quite easy. The intersection of the ray with the $z = h$ plane that the disk lies in is found and the intersection point is checked to see if it lies inside the disk.

⟨*Disk Method Definitions*⟩+≡

```
bool Disk::Intersect(const Ray &r, float *tHit,
                     DifferentialGeometry *dg) const {
    ⟨Transform Ray to object space  99⟩
    ⟨Compute plane intersection for disk  116⟩
    ⟨See if hit point is inside disk radii and φmax  116⟩
    ⟨Find parametric representation of disk hit  117⟩
    ⟨Initialize DifferentialGeometry from parametric information  106⟩
    ⟨Update tHit for quadric intersection  106⟩
    return true;
}
```

The first step is to compute the parametric *t* value where the ray intersects the plane that the disk lies in. Using the same approach as we did for intersecting rays with boxes, we want to find t such that the z component of the ray's position is equal to the height of the disk. Thus,

$$h = o_z + t\mathbf{d}_z$$

and

$$t = \frac{h - o_z}{\mathbf{d}_z}.$$

If the ray is parallel to the disk's plane (i.e., the z component of its direction is zero), there is no intersection. Otherwise the intersection method then checks if t is inside the legal range of values [mint, maxt]. If not, the routine can return false.

⟨*Compute plane intersection for disk*⟩ ≡   **115**
```
if (ray.d.z==0) return false;
float thit = (height - ray.o.z) / ray.d.z;
if (thit < ray.mint || thit > ray.maxt)
    return false;
```

Now the intersection method can compute the point phit where the ray intersects the plane. Once the plane intersection is known, false is returned if the distance from the hit to the center of the disk is more than Disk::radius or less than Disk::innerRadius. This process can be optimized by actually computing the squared distance to the center, taking advantage of the fact that the x and y coordinates of the center point (0, 0, height) are zero, and the z coordinate of phit is equal to height.

⟨*See if hit point is inside disk radii and* ϕ_{max}⟩ ≡   **115**
```
Point phit = ray(thit);
float dist2 = phit.x * phit.x + phit.y * phit.y;
if (dist2 > radius * radius || dist2 < innerRadius * innerRadius)
    return false;
```
⟨*Test disk ϕ value against* ϕ_{max} **116**⟩

If the distance check passes, a final test makes sure that the ϕ value of the hit point is between zero and ϕ_{max}, specified by the caller. Inverting the disk's parameterization gives the same expression for ϕ as the other quadric shapes.

⟨*Test disk ϕ value against* ϕ_{max}⟩ ≡   **116**
```
float phi = atan2f(phit.y, phit.x);
if (phi < 0) phi += 2. * M_PI;
if (phi > phiMax)
    return false;
```

If we've gotten this far, there is an intersection with the disk. The parameter u is scaled to reflect the partial disk specified by ϕ_{max}, and v is computed by inverting the parametric equation. The equations for the partial derivatives at the hit point can be derived with a similar process to that used for the previous quadrics. Because the normal of a disk is the same everywhere, the partial derivatives $\partial\mathbf{n}/\partial u$ and $\partial\mathbf{n}/\partial v$ are both trivially $(0, 0, 0)$.

⟨*Find parametric representation of disk hit*⟩ ≡   115

```
float u = phi / phiMax;
float v = 1.f - ((sqrtf(dist2)-innerRadius) /
                  (radius-innerRadius));
Vector dpdu(-phiMax * phit.y, phiMax * phit.x, 0.);
Vector dpdv(-phit.x / (1-v), -phit.y / (1-v), 0.);
Vector dndu(0,0,0), dndv(0,0,0);
```

3.4.4 SURFACE AREA

Disks have trivially computed surface area, since they're just portions of an annulus:

$$A = \frac{\phi_{\max}}{2}(r^2 - r_i^2).$$

⟨*Disk Method Definitions*⟩+≡

```
float Disk::Area() const {
    return phiMax * 0.5f *
        (radius * radius - innerRadius * innerRadius);
}
```

3.5 OTHER QUADRICS

pbrt supports three more quadrics: cones, paraboloids, and hyperboloids. They are implemented in the source files shapes/cone.cpp,⓪ shapes/paraboloid.cpp,⓪ and shapes/hyperboloid.cpp.⓪ We won't include their full implementations here, since the techniques used to derive their quadratic intersection coefficients, parametric coordinates, and partial derivatives should now be familiar. However, we will briefly summarize the implicit and parametric forms of these shapes. A rendered image of the three of them is in Figure 3.9.

3.5.1 CONES

The implicit equation of a cone centered on the z axis with radius r and height h is

$$\left(\frac{hx}{r}\right)^2 + \left(\frac{hy}{r}\right)^2 - (z - h)^2 = 0.$$

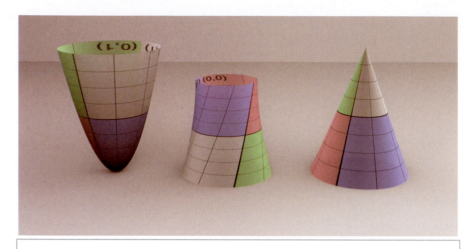

Figure 3.9: The Remaining Quadric Shapes. From left to right: the paraboloid, the hyperboloid, and the cone.

Cones are also described parametrically:

$$\phi = u\phi_{max}$$
$$x = r(1 - v)\cos\phi$$
$$y = r(1 - v)\sin\phi$$
$$z = vh.$$

The partial derivatives at a point on a cone are

$$\frac{\partial p}{\partial u} = (-\phi_{max}y, \phi_{max}x, 0)$$
$$\frac{\partial p}{\partial v} = \left(-\frac{x}{1 - v}, \frac{y}{1 - v}, h\right),$$

and the second partial derivatives are

$$\frac{\partial^2 p}{\partial u^2} = -\phi_{max}^2(x, y, 0)$$
$$\frac{\partial^2 p}{\partial u \partial v} = \frac{\phi_{max}}{1 - v}(y, -x, 0)$$
$$\frac{\partial^2 p}{\partial v^2} = (0, 0, 0).$$

3.5.2 PARABOLOIDS

The implicit equation of a paraboloid centered on the z axis with radius r and height h is

$$\frac{hx^2}{r^2} + \frac{hy^2}{r^2} - z = 0,$$

and its parametric form is

$$\phi = u\phi_{max}$$
$$z = v(z_{max} - z_{min})$$
$$r = r_{max}\sqrt{\frac{z}{z_{max}}}$$
$$x = r\cos\phi$$
$$y = r\sin\phi.$$

The partial derivatives are

$$\frac{\partial \mathbf{p}}{\partial u} = (-\phi_{max}y, \phi_{max}x, 0)$$
$$\frac{\partial \mathbf{p}}{\partial v} = (z_{max} - z_{min})\left(\frac{x}{2z}, \frac{y}{2z}, 1\right),$$

and

$$\frac{\partial^2 \mathbf{p}}{\partial u^2} = -\phi_{max}^2(x, y, 0)$$
$$\frac{\partial^2 \mathbf{p}}{\partial u \partial v} = \phi_{max}(z_{max} - z_{min})\left(-\frac{y}{2z}, \frac{x}{2z}, 0\right)$$
$$\frac{\partial^2 \mathbf{p}}{\partial v^2} = -(z_{max} - z_{min})^2\left(\frac{x}{4z^2}, \frac{y}{4z^2}, 0\right)$$

3.5.3 HYPERBOLOIDS

Finally, the implicit form of the hyperboloid is

$$x^2 + y^2 - z^2 = -1,$$

and the parametric form is

$$\phi = u\phi_{max}$$
$$x_r = (1 - v)x_1 + vx_2$$
$$y_r = (1 - v)y_1 + vy_2$$
$$x = x_r\cos\phi - y_r\sin\phi$$
$$y = x_r\sin\phi + y_r\cos\phi$$
$$z = (1 - v)z_1 + vz_2.$$

The partial derivatives are

$$\frac{\partial \mathbf{p}}{\partial u} = (-\phi_{max} y, \phi_{max} x, 0)$$

$$\frac{\partial \mathbf{p}}{\partial v} = ((x_2 - x_1) \cos \phi - (y_2 - y_1) \sin \phi, (x_2 - x_1) \sin \phi + (y_2 - y_1) \cos \phi, z_2 - z_1),$$

and

$$\frac{\partial^2 \mathbf{p}}{\partial u^2} = -\phi_{max}^2 (x, y, 0)$$

$$\frac{\partial^2 \mathbf{p}}{\partial u \partial v} = \phi_{max} \left(-\frac{\partial \mathbf{p}_y}{\partial v}, \frac{\partial \mathbf{p}_x}{\partial v} 0 \right)$$

$$\frac{\partial^2 \mathbf{p}}{\partial v^2} = (0, 0, 0).$$

3.6 TRIANGLES AND MESHES

⟨*TriangleMesh Declarations*⟩ ≡
```
class TriangleMesh : public Shape {
public:
    ⟨TriangleMesh Public Methods 123⟩
protected:
    ⟨TriangleMesh Data 122⟩
};
```

The triangle is one of the most commonly used shapes in computer graphics. pbrt supports *triangle meshes*, where a number of triangles are stored together so that their per-vertex data can be shared among multiple triangles. Single triangles are simply treated as degenerate meshes. Figure 3.10 shows an image of a complex triangle mesh of over one million triangles.

The arguments to the TriangleMesh constructor are as follows:

- nt: Number of triangles.
- nv: Number of vertices.
- vi: Pointer to an array of vertex indices. For the ith triangle, its three vertex positions are P[vi[3*i]], P[vi[3*i+1]], and P[vi[3*i+2]].
- P: Array of nv vertex positions.
- N: An optional array of normal vectors, one per vertex in the mesh. If present, these are interpolated across triangle faces to compute shading differential geometry.
- S: An optional array of tangent vectors, one per vertex in the mesh. These are also used to compute shading geometry.
- uv: An optional array of parametric (u, v) values, one for each vertex.

Figure 3.10: Happy Buddha Model. This triangle mesh contains over one million individual triangles. It was created from a real statue using a 3D laser scanner. *(Model courtesy Stanford Computer Graphics Laboratory Scanning Repository.)*

The constructor copies the relevant information and stores it in the `TriangleMesh` object. In particular, it must make its own copies of `vi`, `P`, `N`, and `S`, since the caller retains ownership of the data being passed in.

TriangleMesh 120

Triangles have a dual role among the primitives in `pbrt`: not only are they a user-supplied primitive, but other primitives often tessellate themselves into triangle meshes. For example, subdivision surfaces end up creating a mesh of triangles to approximate the smooth limit surface. Ray intersections are performed against these triangles, rather than directly against the subdivision surface.

Because of this second role, it's important that a routine that is creating a triangle mesh be able to specify the parameterization of the triangles. If a triangle was created by evaluating the position of a parametric surface at three particular (u, v) coordinate values, for example, those (u, v) values should be interpolated to compute the (u, v) value at ray intersection points inside the triangle; hence the uv parameter.

⟨*TriangleMesh Method Definitions*⟩ ≡
```
TriangleMesh::TriangleMesh(const Transform &o2w, bool ro,
        int nt, int nv, const int *vi, const Point *P,
        const Normal *N, const Vector *S, const float *uv)
    : Shape(o2w, ro) {
    ntris = nt;
    nverts = nv;
    vertexIndex = new int[3 * ntris];
    memcpy(vertexIndex, vi, 3 * ntris * sizeof(int));
    ⟨Copy uv, N, and S vertex data, if present⟩
    ⟨Transform mesh vertices to world space  123⟩
}
```

The ⟨*Copy* uv, N, *and* S *vertex data, if present*⟩ fragment just allocates the appropriate amount of space and copies the data, if it is present. Its implementation isn't included here.

⟨*TriangleMesh Data*⟩ ≡   **120**
```
int ntris, nverts;
int *vertexIndex;
Point *p;
Normal *n;
Vector *s;
float *uvs;
```

Unlike the other shapes that leave the primitive description in object space and then transform incoming rays from world space to object space, triangle meshes transform the shape into world space and save the work of transforming the incoming rays into the object space or the intersection's differential geometry out to world space. This is a good idea because this operation can be performed once at start-up, avoiding transforming rays many times during rendering. Doing this with quadrics is more complicated, although possible—see Exercise 3.1 at the end of the chapter for more information. Normal and tangent vectors for shading geometry are left in object space, since the `GetShadingGeometry()` method must transform them to world space with the transformation matrix supplied to that method, which may not necessarily be the one stored by the Shape.

⟨*Transform mesh vertices to world space*⟩ ≡   **122**
```
for (int i  = 0; i < nverts; ++i)
    p[i] = ObjectToWorld(P[i]);
```

The object space bound of a triangle mesh is easily found by computing a bounding box that encompasses all of the vertices of the mesh. Because the vertex positions p are transformed to world space in the constructor, the implementation here has to transform them back to object space before computing their bound. Note that these bounds are fairly expensive to compute. The implementation assumes that the caller will cache the results of these computations if they will be reused, which is the case elsewhere in pbrt where the bounding methods are called.

⟨*TriangleMesh Method Definitions*⟩+≡
```
BBox TriangleMesh::ObjectBound() const {
    BBox bobj;
    for (int i = 0; i < nverts; i++)
        bobj = Union(bobj, WorldToObject(p[i]));
    return bobj;
}
```

The TriangleMesh shape is one of the shapes that can compute a better world space bound than can be found by transforming its object space bounding box to world space. Its world space bound can be directly computed from the world space vertices.

⟨*TriangleMesh Method Definitions*⟩+≡
```
BBox TriangleMesh::WorldBound() const {
    BBox worldBounds;
    for (int i = 0; i < nverts; i++)
        worldBounds = Union(worldBounds, p[i]);
    return worldBounds;
}
```

The TriangleMesh shape does not directly compute intersections. Instead, it splits itself into many separate Triangles, each representing a single triangle. All of the individual triangles reference the shared set of vertices in p, avoiding per-triangle replication of the shared data. The TriangleMesh class therefore overrides the Shape::CanIntersect() method to indicate that TriangleMeshes cannot be intersected directly.

⟨*TriangleMesh Public Methods*⟩ ≡   **120**
```
bool CanIntersect() const { return false; }
```

When pbrt encounters a shape that cannot be intersected directly, it calls its Refine() method. Shape::Refine() is expected to produce a list of simpler shapes in the vector passed in, refined. The implementation here is simple; it creates a new Triangle for each of the triangles in the mesh.

⟨*TriangleMesh Method Definitions*⟩+≡
```
    void TriangleMesh::Refine(vector<Reference<Shape> > &refined) const {
        for (int i = 0; i < ntris; ++i)
            refined.push_back(new Triangle(ObjectToWorld, reverseOrientation,
                                           (TriangleMesh *)this, i));
    }
```

3.6.1 TRIANGLE

⟨*TriangleMesh Declarations*⟩+≡
```
    class Triangle : public Shape {
    public:
        ⟨Triangle Public Methods  124⟩
    private:
        ⟨Triangle Data  124⟩
    };
```

The `Triangle` doesn't store much data—just a pointer to the parent `TriangleMesh` that it came from and a pointer to its three vertex indices in the mesh:

⟨*Triangle Public Methods*⟩≡   **124**
```
    Triangle(const Transform &o2w, bool ro, TriangleMesh *m, int n)
        : Shape(o2w, ro) {
        mesh = m;
        v = &mesh->vertexIndex[3*n];
    }
```

Note that the implementation stores a pointer to the first vertex *index*, instead of storing three pointers to the vertices themselves. This reduces the amount of storage required for each `Triangle` at a cost of another level of indirection.

⟨*Triangle Data*⟩≡   **124**
```
    Reference<TriangleMesh> mesh;
    int *v;
```

As with `TriangleMesh`es, it is possible to compute better world space bounding boxes for individual triangles by bounding the world space vertices directly.

⟨*TriangleMesh Method Definitions*⟩+≡
```
    BBox Triangle::ObjectBound() const {
        ⟨Get triangle vertices in p1, p2, and p3  125⟩
        return Union(BBox(WorldToObject(p1), WorldToObject(p2)),
                     WorldToObject(p3));
    }
```

⟨*TriangleMesh Method Definitions*⟩+≡
```
BBox Triangle::WorldBound() const {
    ⟨Get triangle vertices in p1, p2, and p3 125⟩
    return Union(BBox(p1, p2), p3);
}
```

⟨*Get triangle vertices in* p1, p2, *and* p3⟩≡   124, 125, 127, 130, 705
```
const Point &p1 = mesh->p[v[0]];
const Point &p2 = mesh->p[v[1]];
const Point &p3 = mesh->p[v[2]];
```

3.6.2 TRIANGLE INTERSECTION

An efficient algorithm for ray-triangle intersection can be derived using *barycentric coordinates*. Barycentric coordinates provide a way to parameterize a triangle in terms of two variables, b_1 and b_2:

$$p(b_1, b_2) = (1 - b_1 - b_2)p_0 + b_1 p_1 + b_2 p_2.$$

The conditions on b_1 and b_2 are that $b_1 \geq 0$, $b_2 \geq 0$, and $b_1 + b_2 \leq 1$. The barycentric coordinates are also a natural way to interpolate across the surface of the triangle. Given values a_0, a_1, and a_2 defined at the vertices and given the barycentric coordinates for a point on the triangle, we can compute an interpolated value of a at that point as $(1 - b_1 - b_2)a_0 + b_1 a_1 + b_2 a_2$.

To derive an algorithm for intersecting a ray with a triangle, we insert the parametric ray equation into the triangle equation:

$$o + t\mathbf{d} = (1 - b_1 - b_2)p_0 + b_1 p_1 + b_2 p_2. \tag{3.1}$$

Following the technique described by Möller and Trumbore (1997), we use the shorthand notation $\mathbf{e}_1 = p_1 - p_0$, $\mathbf{e}_2 = p_2 - p_0$, and $\mathbf{s} = o - p_0$. We can now rearrange the terms of Equation (3.1) to obtain the matrix equation

$$\left(-\mathbf{d} \quad \mathbf{e}_1 \quad \mathbf{e}_2 \right) \begin{bmatrix} t \\ b_1 \\ b_2 \end{bmatrix} = \mathbf{s}. \tag{3.2}$$

Solving this linear system will give us both the barycentric coordinates of the intersection point as well as the parametric distance along the ray. Geometrically, we can interpret this system as a translation of the triangle to the origin, and a transformation of the triangle to a unit triangle in y and z.

We can easily solve Equation (3.2) using Cramer's rule. Note that we are introducing a bit of notation for brevity here; we write $|\, \mathbf{a} \quad \mathbf{b} \quad \mathbf{c} \,|$ to mean the determinant of the matrix having $\mathbf{a}$, $\mathbf{b}$, and $\mathbf{c}$ as its columns. Cramer's rule gives

BBox 60
Point 54
Triangle 124
TriangleMesh::p 122

$$\begin{bmatrix} t \\ b_1 \\ b_2 \end{bmatrix} = \frac{1}{|-d \quad e_1 \quad e_2|} \begin{bmatrix} |\quad s \quad e_1 \quad e_2| \\ |-d \quad s \quad e_2| \\ |-d \quad e_1 \quad s| \end{bmatrix}. \tag{3.3}$$

This can be rewritten using the identity $|a \quad b \quad c| = -(a \times c) \cdot b = -(c \times b) \cdot a$. We then obtain

$$\begin{bmatrix} t \\ b_1 \\ b_2 \end{bmatrix} = \frac{1}{(d \times e_2) \cdot e_1} \begin{bmatrix} (s \times e_1) \cdot e_2 \\ (d \times e_2) \cdot s \\ (s \times e_1) \cdot d \end{bmatrix}. \tag{3.4}$$

If we use the substitution $s_1 = d \times e_2$ and $s_2 = s \times e_1$, the common subexpressions are made more explicit:

$$\begin{bmatrix} t \\ b_1 \\ b_2 \end{bmatrix} = \frac{1}{s_1 \cdot e_1} \begin{bmatrix} s_2 \cdot e_2 \\ s_1 \cdot s \\ s_2 \cdot d \end{bmatrix}. \tag{3.5}$$

In order to compute e_1, e_2, and s we need 9 subtractions. To compute s_1 and s_2, we need 2 cross products, which is a total of 12 multiplications and 6 subtractions. Finally, to compute t, b_1, and b_2, we need 4 dot products (12 multiplications and 8 additions), 1 reciprocal, and 3 multiplications. Thus, the total cost of ray-triangle intersection is 1 divide, 27 multiplies, and 17 adds (counting adds and subtracts together). Note that some of these operations can be avoided if it is determined midcalculation that the ray does not intersect the triangle.

⟨*TriangleMesh Method Definitions*⟩+≡
```
    bool Triangle::Intersect(const Ray &ray, float *tHit,
                          DifferentialGeometry *dg) const {
        ⟨Compute s₁ 127⟩
        ⟨Compute first barycentric coordinate 127⟩
        ⟨Compute second barycentric coordinate 127⟩
        ⟨Compute t to intersection point 127⟩
        ⟨Fill in DifferentialGeometry from triangle hit 128⟩
        *tHit = t;
        return true;
    }
```

The implementation first computes the divisor from Equation (3.5). It finds the three mesh vertices that make up this particular Triangle, and then computes the edge vectors and divisor. Note that if the divisor is zero, this triangle is degenerate and therefore cannot intersect a ray.

⟨*Compute* s_1⟩ ≡   126
 ⟨*Get triangle vertices in* p1, p2, *and* p3 **125**⟩
 ```
Vector e1 = p2 - p1;
Vector e2 = p3 - p1;
Vector s1 = Cross(ray.d, e2);
float divisor = Dot(s1, e1);
if (divisor == 0.)
    return false;
float invDivisor = 1.f / divisor;
```

Now the routine can compute the barycentric coordinate b_1. Recall that barycentric coordinates that are less than zero or greater than one represent points outside the triangle, indicating no intersection.

⟨*Compute first barycentric coordinate*⟩ ≡   126
 ```
Vector d = ray.o - p1;
float b1 = Dot(d, s1) * invDivisor;
if (b1 < 0. || b1 > 1.)
    return false;
```

The second barycentric coordinate, b_2, is computed in a similar way:

⟨*Compute second barycentric coordinate*⟩ ≡   126
 ```
Vector s2 = Cross(d, e1);
float b2 = Dot(ray.d, s2) * invDivisor;
if (b2 < 0. || b1 + b2 > 1.)
    return false;
```

Now that we know the ray intersects the triangle, we compute the distance along the ray at which the intersection occurs. This gives a last opportunity to exit the procedure early, in the case where the t value falls outside the Ray::mint and Ray::maxt bounds.

⟨*Compute* t *to intersection point*⟩ ≡   126
 ```
float t = Dot(e2, s2) * invDivisor;
if (t < ray.mint || t > ray.maxt)
    return false;
```

We now have all the information we need to initialize the DifferentialGeometry structure for this intersection. In contrast to previous shapes, it's not necessary to transform the partial derivatives to world space, since the triangle's vertices were already transformed to world space. Like the disk, the partial derivatives of the triangle's normal are also both $(0, 0, 0)$, since it is flat.

Cross() 52
DifferentialGeometry 83
Dot() 51
Ray::maxt 58
Ray::mint 58
Ray::o 58
Vector 47

⟨*Fill in* DifferentialGeometry *from triangle hit*⟩ ≡   **126**
  ⟨*Compute triangle partial derivatives* **129**⟩
  ⟨*Interpolate* (*u*, *v*) *triangle parametric coordinates* **129**⟩
  *dg = DifferentialGeometry(ray(t), dpdu, dpdv,
                      Vector(0,0,0), Vector(0,0,0),
                      tu, tv, this);

In order to generate consistent tangent vectors over triangle meshes, it is necessary to compute the partial derivatives $\partial p/\partial u$ and $\partial p/\partial v$ using the parametric (u, v) values at the triangle vertices, if provided. Although the partial derivatives are the same at all points on the triangle, the implementation here recomputes them each time an intersection is found. Although this results in redundant computation, the storage savings for large triangle meshes can be substantial.

The triangle is the set of points

$$p_o + u \frac{\partial p}{\partial u} + v \frac{\partial p}{\partial v},$$

for some p_o, where u and v range over the parametric coordinates of the triangle. We also know the three vertex positions p_i, $i = 1, \ 2, \ 3$, and the texture coordinates (u_i, v_i) at each vertex. From this it follows that the partial derivatives of p must satisfy

$$p_i = p_o + u_i \frac{\partial p}{\partial u} + v_i \frac{\partial p}{\partial v}.$$

In other words, there is a unique affine mapping from the two-dimensional (u, v) space to points on the triangle (such a mapping exists even though the triangle is specified in 3D space because the triangle is planar). To compute expressions for $\partial p/\partial u$ and $\partial p/\partial v$, we start by computing the differences $p_1 - p_3$ and $p_2 - p_3$, giving the matrix equation

$$\begin{pmatrix} u_1 - u_3 & v_1 - v_3 \\ u_2 - u_3 & v_2 - v_3 \end{pmatrix} \begin{pmatrix} \partial p/\partial u \\ \partial p/\partial v \end{pmatrix} = \begin{pmatrix} p_1 - p_3 \\ p_2 - p_3 \end{pmatrix}.$$

Thus,

$$\begin{pmatrix} \partial p/\partial u \\ \partial p/\partial v \end{pmatrix} = \begin{pmatrix} u_1 - u_3 & v_1 - v_3 \\ u_2 - u_3 & v_2 - v_3 \end{pmatrix}^{-1} \begin{pmatrix} p_1 - p_3 \\ p_2 - p_3 \end{pmatrix}.$$

DifferentialGeometry 83

Vector 47

Inverting a 2×2 matrix is straightforward. The inverse of the (u, v) differences matrix is

$$\frac{1}{(u_1 - u_3)(v_2 - v_3) - (v_1 - v_3)(u_2 - u_3)} \begin{pmatrix} v_2 - v_3 & -(v_1 - v_3) \\ -(u_2 - u_3) & u_1 - u_3 \end{pmatrix}.$$

⟨*Compute triangle partial derivatives*⟩ ≡   128
```
Vector dpdu, dpdv;
float uvs[3][2];
GetUVs(uvs);
```
⟨*Compute deltas for triangle partial derivatives* 129⟩
```
float determinant = du1 * dv2 - dv1 * du2;
if (determinant == 0.f) {
```
    ⟨*Handle zero determinant for triangle partial derivative matrix* 129⟩
```
}
else {
    float invdet = 1.f / determinant;
    dpdu = ( dv2 * dp1 - dv1 * dp2) * invdet;
    dpdv = (-du2 * dp1 + du1 * dp2) * invdet;
}
```

⟨*Compute deltas for triangle partial derivatives*⟩ ≡   129
```
float du1 = uvs[0][0] - uvs[2][0];
float du2 = uvs[1][0] - uvs[2][0];
float dv1 = uvs[0][1] - uvs[2][1];
float dv2 = uvs[1][1] - uvs[2][1];
Vector dp1 = p1 - p3, dp2 = p2 - p3;
```

Finally, it is necessary to handle the case when the matrix is singular and therefore cannot be inverted. Note that this only happens when the user-supplied per-vertex parameterization values are degenerate. In this case, the Triangle just chooses an arbitrary coordinate system about the triangle's surface normal, making sure that it is orthonormal:

⟨*Handle zero determinant for triangle partial derivative matrix*⟩ ≡   129
```
CoordinateSystem(Normalize(Cross(e2, e1)), &dpdu, &dpdv);
```

To compute the (u, v) parametric coordinates at the hit point, the barycentric interpolation formula is applied to the (u, v) parametric coordinates at the vertices.

⟨*Interpolate (u, v) triangle parametric coordinates*⟩ ≡   128
```
float b0 = 1 - b1 - b2;
float tu = b0*uvs[0][0] + b1*uvs[1][0] + b2*uvs[2][0];
float tv = b0*uvs[0][1] + b1*uvs[1][1] + b2*uvs[2][1];
```

The utility routine GetUVs() returns the (u, v) coordinates for the three vertices of the triangle, either from the TriangleMesh, if it has them, or returning default values if none were specified with the mesh.

⟨*TriangleMesh Method Definitions*⟩+≡
```
void Triangle::GetUVs(float uv[3][2]) const {
    if (mesh->uvs) {
        uv[0][0] = mesh->uvs[2*v[0]];
        uv[0][1] = mesh->uvs[2*v[0]+1];
        uv[1][0] = mesh->uvs[2*v[1]];
        uv[1][1] = mesh->uvs[2*v[1]+1];
        uv[2][0] = mesh->uvs[2*v[2]];
        uv[2][1] = mesh->uvs[2*v[2]+1];
    }
    else {
        uv[0][0] = 0.; uv[0][1] = 0.;
        uv[1][0] = 1.; uv[1][1] = 0.;
        uv[2][0] = 1.; uv[2][1] = 1.;
    }
}
```

3.6.3 SURFACE AREA

Recall from Section 2.2 that the area of a parallelogram is given by the length of the cross product of the two vectors along its sides. From this, it's easy to see that given the vectors for two edges of a triangle, its area is half of the area of the parallelogram given by those two vectors (Figure 3.11).

⟨*TriangleMesh Method Definitions*⟩+≡
```
float Triangle::Area() const {
    ⟨Get triangle vertices in p1, p2, and p3 125⟩
    return 0.5f * Cross(p2-p1, p3-p1).Length();
}
```

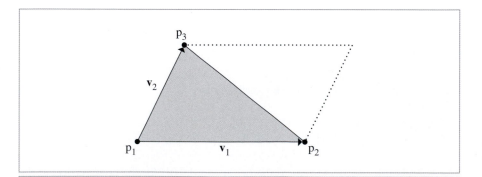

Triangle 124
TriangleMesh::uvs 122

Figure 3.11: The area of a triangle with two edges given by vectors v_1 and v_2 is one-half of the area of the parallelogram. The parallelogram area is given by the length of the cross product of $\mathbf{v}_1$ and $\mathbf{v}_2$.

3.6.4 SHADING GEOMETRY

If the `TriangleMesh` has per-vertex normals or tangent vectors, the `GetShadingGeometry()` method uses them to initialize the shading geometry appropriately:

⟨*Triangle Public Methods*⟩+≡   **124**
```
    virtual void GetShadingGeometry(const Transform &obj2world,
            const DifferentialGeometry &dg,
            DifferentialGeometry *dgShading) const {
        if (!mesh->n && !mesh->s) {
            *dgShading = dg;
            return;
        }
        ⟨Initialize Triangle shading geometry with n and s 131⟩
    }
```

Because the `DifferentialGeometry` from a ray-triangle intersection stores parametric (u, v) coordinates but doesn't have the barycentric coordinates of the intersection point, the first task is to determine what the barycentric coordinates are. These are then used to compute an interpolated normal vector and **s** vector, which are converted to two tangent vectors that give the same normal, since the `DifferentialGeometry` constructor takes two tangent vectors rather than the normal. Finally, the partial derivatives of the shading normal are found and the shading geometry structure can be initialized.

⟨*Initialize* `Triangle` *shading geometry with* n *and* s⟩ ≡   **131**
```
    ⟨Compute barycentric coordinates for point  132⟩
    ⟨Use n and s to compute shading tangents for triangle, ss and ts 133⟩
    Vector dndu, dndv;
    ⟨Compute ∂n/∂u and ∂n/∂v for triangle shading geometry⟩
    *dgShading = DifferentialGeometry(dg.p, ss, ts,
        dndu, dndv, dg.u, dg.v, dg.shape);
```

Recall that the (u, v) parametric coordinates in the `DifferentialGeometry` for a triangle are computed with barycentric interpolation of parametric coordinates at the triangle vertices:

$$u = b_0 u_0 + b_1 u_1 + b_2 u_2$$
$$v = b_0 v_0 + b_1 v_1 + b_2 v_2,$$

where $b_0 = 1 - b_1 - b_2$. Here, the values of u, v, u_i, and v_i are all known, u and v from the `DifferentialGeometry` and u_i and v_i from the `Triangle`. We can substitute for the b_0 term and rewrite the above equations, giving a linear system in two unknowns b_1 and b_2:

$$\begin{pmatrix} u_1 - u_0 & u_2 - u_1 \\ v_1 - v_0 & v_2 - v_1 \end{pmatrix} \begin{pmatrix} b_1 \\ b_2 \end{pmatrix} = \begin{pmatrix} u - u_0 \\ v - v_0 \end{pmatrix}.$$

This is a linear system of the basic form $\mathbf{AB} = \mathbf{C}$. We can solve for $\mathbf{B}$ by inverting $\mathbf{A}$, giving the two barycentric coordinates

$$\mathbf{B} = \mathbf{A}^{-1}\mathbf{C}.$$

The closed-form solution for linear systems of this form is implemented in the utility routine `SolveLinearSystem2x2()`.

⟨*Compute barycentric coordinates for point*⟩ ≡   131
```
float b[3];
⟨Initialize A and C matrices for barycentrics 132⟩
if (!SolveLinearSystem2x2(A, C, &b[1])) {
    ⟨Handle degenerate parametric mapping 132⟩
}
else
    b[0] = 1.f - b[1] - b[2];
```

⟨*Initialize* A *and* C *matrices for barycentrics*⟩ ≡   132
```
float uv[3][2];
GetUVs(uv);
float A[2][2] =
    { { uv[1][0] - uv[0][0], uv[2][0] - uv[0][0] },
      { uv[1][1] - uv[0][1], uv[2][1] - uv[0][1] } };
float C[2] = { dg.u - uv[0][0], dg.v - uv[0][1] };
```

If the determinant of $\mathbf{A}$ is zero, the solution is undefined and `SolveLinearSystem2x2()` returns `false`. This case happens if all three triangle vertices had the same texture coordinates, for example. In this case, the barycentric coordinates are all set arbitrarily to $\frac{1}{3}$:

⟨*Handle degenerate parametric mapping*⟩ ≡   132
```
b[0] = b[1] = b[2] = 1.f/3.f;
```

Given the barycentrics, it's straightforward to compute the shading normal and shading **s** tangent vector by interpolating among the appropriate vertex normals and tangents. First, the vector `ts` for the differential geometry constructor is found using the cross product of `ss` and `ns`, giving an orthogonal vector to the two of them. Next, `ss` is overwritten with the cross product of `ns` and `ts`; this ensures that the cross product of `ss` and `ts` gives `ns`.

Thus, if per-vertex **n** and **s** values are provided and if the interpolated **n** and **s** values aren't perfectly orthogonal, **n** will be preserved and **s** will be modified so that the coordinate system is orthogonal.

⟨*Use* n *and* s *to compute shading tangents for triangle,* ss *and* ts⟩ ≡   131

```
Normal ns;
Vector ss, ts;
if (mesh->n) ns = Normalize(b[0] * mesh->n[v[0]] +
                            b[1] * mesh->n[v[1]] +
                            b[2] * mesh->n[v[2]]);
else   ns = dg.nn;
if (mesh->s) ss = Normalize(b[0] * mesh->s[v[0]] +
                            b[1] * mesh->s[v[1]] +
                            b[2] * mesh->s[v[2]]);
else   ss = Normalize(dg.dpdu);
ts = Cross(ss, ns);
ss = Cross(ts, ns);
ts = Normalize(obj2world(ts));
ss = Normalize(obj2world(ss));
```

The code to compute the partial derivatives $\partial n/\partial u$ and $\partial n/\partial v$ is almost identical to the code to compute the partial derivatives $\partial p/\partial u$ and $\partial p/\partial v$ on a triangle. Therefore, it has been elided from the text here.

*3.7 SUBDIVISION SURFACES

We will wrap up this chapter by defining a Shape that implements *subdivision surfaces*, a representation that is particularly well-suited to describing complex smooth shapes. The subdivision surface for a particular mesh is defined by repeatedly subdividing the faces of the mesh into smaller faces and then finding the new vertex locations using weighted combinations of the old vertex positions.

For appropriately chosen subdivision rules, this process converges to give a smooth *limit surface* as the number of subdivision steps goes to infinity. In practice, just a few levels of subdivision typically suffice to give a good approximation of the limit surface. Figure 3.12 shows a simple example of a subdivision, where a tetrahedron has been subdivided zero, one, two, and six times. Figure 3.13 shows the effect of applying subdivision to the Killeroo model; on the top is the original control mesh, and below is the subdivision surface that the control mesh represents.

Although originally developed in the 1970s, subdivision surfaces have recently received a fair amount of attention in computer graphics thanks to some important advantages over polygonal and spline-based representations of surfaces. The advantages of subdivision include the following:

Cross() 52
Normal 56
Shape 90
Vector 47
Vector::Normalize() 53

Figure 3.12: Subdivision of a Tetrahedron. From left to right, zero, one, two, and six subdivision steps have been used. (At zero levels, the vertices are just moved to lie on the limit surface.) As more subdivision is done, the mesh approaches the limit surface, the smooth surface described by the original mesh. Notice how the specular highlights become progressively more accurate and the silhouette edges appear smoother as more levels of subdivision are performed.

- Subdivision surfaces are smooth, as opposed to polygon meshes, which appear faceted when viewed close up, regardless of how finely they are modeled.
- A lot of existing infrastructure in modeling systems can be retargeted to subdivision. The classic toolbox of techniques for modeling polygon meshes can be applied to modeling subdivision control meshes.
- Subdivision surfaces are well-suited to describing objects with complex topology, since they start with a control mesh of arbitrary (manifold) topology. Parametric surface models generally don't handle complex topology well.
- Subdivision methods are often generalizations of spline-based surface representations, so spline surfaces can often just be run through general subdivision surface renderers.
- It is easy to add detail to a localized region of a subdivision surface, simply by adding faces to appropriate parts of the control mesh. This is much harder with spline representations.

Here, we will describe an implementation of *Loop subdivision surfaces*.[5] The Loop subdivision rules are based on triangular faces in the control mesh; faces with more than three vertices are triangulated at the start. At each subdivision step, all faces split into four child faces (Figure 3.14). New vertices are added along all of the edges of the original mesh, with positions computed using weighted averages of nearby vertices. Furthermore, the position of each original vertex is updated with a weighted average of its position and its new neighbors' positions. The implementation here uses weights based on improvements to Loop's method developed by Hoppe et al. (1994). We will not include discussion here about how these weights are derived. They must be chosen carefully to ensure that the limit surface actually has particular desirable

---

5   Named after the inventor of the subdivision rules used, Charles Loop.

Figure 3.13: Subdivision Applied to the Killeroo Model. The control mesh (top) describes the subdivision surface shown below it. Subdivision is well-suited to modeling shapes like this one, since it's easy to add detail locally by refining the control mesh, and there are no limitations on the topology of the final surface. *Model courtesy headus/Rezard.*

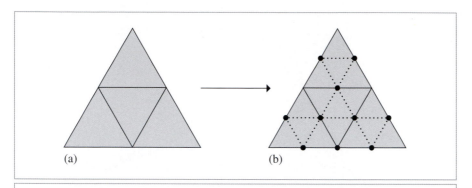

(a)   (b)

Figure 3.14: Basic Refinement Process for Loop Subdivision. (a) The control mesh before sub-division. (b) The new mesh after one subdivision step. Each triangular face of the mesh has been subdivided into four new faces by splitting each of the edges and connecting the new vertices with new edges.

smoothness properties, although subtle mathematics are necessary to prove that they indeed do this.

3.7.1 MESH REPRESENTATION

⟨*LoopSubdiv Declarations*⟩ ≡
```
    class LoopSubdiv : public Shape {
    public:
        ⟨LoopSubdiv Public Methods  146⟩
    private:
        ⟨LoopSubdiv Private Methods  150⟩
        ⟨LoopSubdiv Private Data  137⟩
    };
```

We will start by describing the data structures used to represent the subdivision mesh. These data structures need to be carefully designed in order to support all of the oper-ations necessary to cleanly implement the subdivision algorithm. The parameters to the LoopSubdiv constructor specify a triangle mesh in exactly the same format used in the TriangleMesh constructor (Section 3.6): each face is described by three integer vertex in-dices, giving offsets into the vertex array P for the face's three vertices. We will need to process this data to determine which faces are adjacent to each other, which faces are adjacent to which vertices, and so on.

⟨*LoopSubdiv Method Definitions*⟩ ≡
```
LoopSubdiv::LoopSubdiv(const Transform &o2w, bool ro,
                        int nfaces, int nvertices,
                        const int *vertexIndices,
                        const Point *P, int nl)
    : Shape(o2w, ro) {
    nLevels = nl;
    ⟨Allocate LoopSubdiv vertices and faces 137⟩
    ⟨Set face to vertex pointers 140⟩
    ⟨Set neighbor pointers in faces 142⟩
    ⟨Finish vertex initialization 143⟩
}
```

We will shortly define `SDVertex` and `SDFace` structures, which hold data for vertices and faces in the subdivision mesh. The constructor starts by allocating one instance of the `SDVertex` class for each vertex in the mesh and an `SDFace` for each face. For now, these are mostly uninitialized.

⟨*Allocate* LoopSubdiv *vertices and faces*⟩ ≡   137
```
int i;
SDVertex *verts = new SDVertex[nvertices];
for (i = 0; i < nvertices; ++i) {
    verts[i] = SDVertex(P[i]);
    vertices.push_back(&verts[i]);
}
SDFace *fs = new SDFace[nfaces];
for (i = 0; i < nfaces; ++i)
    faces.push_back(&fs[i]);
```

The `LoopSubdiv` destructor, which we won't include here, deletes all of the faces and vertices allocated above.

⟨*LoopSubdiv Private Data*⟩ ≡   136
```
int nLevels;
vector<SDVertex *> vertices;
vector<SDFace *> faces;
```

The Loop subdivision scheme, like most other subdivision schemes, assumes that the control mesh is *manifold*—no more than two faces share any given edge. Such a mesh may be closed or open: A *closed mesh* has no boundary, and all faces have adjacent faces across each of their edges. An *open mesh* has some faces that do not have all three neighbors. The `LoopSubdiv` implementation here supports both closed and open meshes.

In the interior of a triangle mesh, most vertices are adjacent to six faces and have six neighbor vertices directly connected to them with edges. On the boundaries of an open mesh, most vertices are adjacent to three faces and four vertices. The number of vertices directly adjacent to a vertex is called the vertex's *valence*. Interior vertices with valence other than six, or boundary vertices with valence other than four, are called *extraordinary vertices*; otherwise they are called *regular*.[6] Loop subdivision surfaces are smooth everywhere except at their extraordinary vertices.

Each SDVertex stores its position P, a boolean that indicates whether it is a regular or extraordinary vertex, and a boolean that records if it lies on the boundary of the mesh. It also holds a pointer to an arbitrary face adjacent to it; this pointer gives a starting point for finding all of the adjacent faces. Finally, there is a pointer to store the new SDVertex for the next level of subdivision, if any.

⟨*LoopSubdiv Local Structures*⟩ ≡
```
    struct SDVertex {
        ⟨SDVertex Constructor 138⟩
        ⟨SDVertex Methods⟩
        Point P;
        SDFace *startFace;
        SDVertex *child;
        bool regular, boundary;
    };
```

The constructor for SDVertex does the obvious initialization. Note that the value of SDVertex::startFace is initially set to NULL.

⟨*SDVertex Constructor*⟩ ≡   **138**
```
    SDVertex(Point pt = Point(0,0,0))
        : P(pt), startFace(NULL), child(NULL),
          regular(false), boundary(false) { }
```

The SDFace structure is where most of the topological information about the mesh is maintained. Because all faces are triangular, faces always store pointers to their three vertices and pointers to the adjacent faces across its three edges. The corresponding face neighbor pointers will be NULL if the face is on the boundary of an open mesh.

The face neighbor pointers are indexed such that if we label the edge from v[i] to v[(i+1)%3] as the *i*th edge, then the neighbor face across that edge is stored in f[i] (Figure 3.15). This labeling convention is important to keep in mind. Later when we are updating the topology of a newly subdivided mesh, we will make extensive use of it to navigate around the mesh. Similarly to the SDVertex class, the SDFace also stores pointers to child faces at the next level of subdivision.

---

6   These terms are commonly used in the modeling literature, although "irregular" versus "regular" or "extraordinary" versus "ordinary" might be more intuitive.

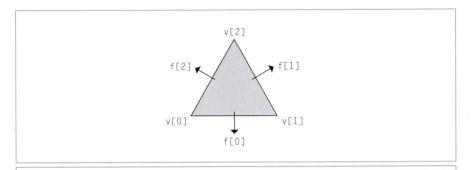

Figure 3.15: Each triangular face stores three pointers to SDVertex objects v[i] and three pointers to neighboring faces f[i]. Neighboring faces are indexed using the convention that the *i*th edge is the edge from v[i] to v[(i+1)%3], and the neighbor across the *i*th edge is in f[i].

⟨*LoopSubdiv Local Structures*⟩+≡
```
struct SDFace {
    ⟨SDFace Constructor⟩
    ⟨SDFace Methods  145⟩
    SDVertex *v[3];
    SDFace *f[3];
    SDFace *children[4];
};
```

The SDFace constructor is straightforward—it simply sets these various pointers to NULL—so it is not shown here.

In order to simplify navigation of the SDFace data structure, we'll provide macros that make it easy to determine the vertex and face indices before or after a particular index. These macros add appropriate offsets and compute the result modulus three to handle cycling around. To compute the previous index, they add 2 instead of subtracting 1, which avoids possibly taking the modulus of a negative number, the result of which is implementation dependent in C++.

⟨*LoopSubdiv Macros*⟩≡
```
#define NEXT(i) (((i)+1)%3)
#define PREV(i) (((i)+2)%3)
```

In addition to requiring a manifold mesh, the LoopSubdiv class expects that the control mesh specified by the user will be *consistently ordered*—each *directed edge* in the mesh can be present only once. An edge that is shared by two faces should be specified in a different direction by each face. Consider two vertices, v_0 and v_1, with an edge between them. We expect that one of the triangular faces that has this edge will specify its three vertices so that v_0 is before v_1, and that the other face will specify its vertices so that v_1 is before

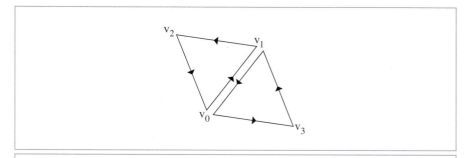

Figure 3.16: All of the faces in the input mesh must be specified so that each shared edge is given no more than once in each direction. Here, the edge from v_0 to v_1 is traversed from v_0 to v_1 by one face and from v_1 to v_0 by the other. Another way to think of this is in terms of face orientation: all faces' vertices should be given consistently in either clockwise or counterclockwise order, as seen from outside the mesh.

v_0 (Figure 3.16). A Möbius strip is one example of a surface that cannot be consistently ordered, but such surfaces come up rarely in rendering so in practice this restriction is not a problem. Poorly formed mesh data from other programs that don't create consistently ordered meshes can be troublesome, however.

Given this assumption about the input data, the constructor can now initialize this mesh's topological data structures. It first loops over all of the faces and sets their v pointers to point to their three vertices. It also sets each vertex's SDVertex::startFace pointer to point to one of the vertex's neighboring faces. It doesn't matter which of its adjacent faces is used, so the implementation just keeps resetting it each time it comes across another face that the vertex is incident to, thus ensuring that all vertices have some non-NULL face pointer by the time the loop is complete.

⟨*Set face to vertex pointers*⟩ ≡   137

```
const int *vp = vertexIndices;
for (i = 0; i < nfaces; ++i) {
    SDFace *f = faces[i];
    for (int j = 0; j < 3; ++j) {
        SDVertex *v = vertices[vp[j]];
        f->v[j] = v;
        v->startFace = f;
    }
    vp += 3;
}
```

SDFace 139
SDFace::v 139
SDVertex 138
SDVertex::startFace 138

Now it is necessary to set each face's f pointer to point to its neighboring faces. This is a bit trickier, since face adjacency information isn't directly specified by the user. The constructor loops over the faces and creates an SDEdge object for each of their three edges. When it comes to another face that shares the same edge, it can update both faces' neighbor pointers.

⟨*LoopSubdiv Local Structures*⟩+≡
```
struct SDEdge {
    ⟨SDEdge Constructor 141⟩
    ⟨SDEdge Comparison Function 141⟩
    SDVertex *v[2];
    SDFace *f[2];
    int f0edgeNum;
};
```

The SDEdge constructor takes pointers to the two vertices at each end of the edge. It orders them so that v[0] holds the one that is first in memory. This code may seem strange, but it is simply relying on the fact that pointers in C++ are effectively numbers that can be manipulated like integers,[7] and that the ordering of vertices on an edge is arbitrary. Sorting vertices on the address of the pointer guarantees that the edge (v_a, v_b) is correctly recognized as the same as the edge (v_b, v_a), regardless of what order the vertices are given in.

⟨*SDEdge Constructor*⟩≡   141
```
SDEdge(SDVertex *v0 = NULL, SDVertex *v1 = NULL) {
    v[0] = min(v0, v1);
    v[1] = max(v0, v1);
    f[0] = f[1] = NULL;
    f0edgeNum = -1;
}
```

The class also defines an ordering operation for SDEdge objects so that they can be stored in other data structures that rely on ordering being well-defined.

⟨*SDEdge Comparison Function*⟩≡   141
```
bool operator<(const SDEdge &e2) const {
    if (v[0] == e2.v[0]) return v[1] < e2.v[1];
    return v[0] < e2.v[0];
}
```

Now the constructor can get to work, looping over the edges in all of the faces and updating the neighbor pointers as it goes. It uses a set to store the edges that have only one adjacent face so far. The set makes it possible to search for a particular edge in $O(\log n)$ time.

---

7   Segmented architectures notwithstanding.

⟨*Set neighbor pointers in* faces⟩ ≡   **137**
```
    set<SDEdge> edges;
    for (i = 0; i < nfaces; ++i) {
        SDFace *f = faces[i];
        for (int edgeNum = 0; edgeNum < 3; ++edgeNum) {
            ⟨Update neighbor pointer for edgeNum 142⟩
        }
    }
```

For each edge in each face, the loop body creates an edge object and sees if the same edge has been seen previously. If so, it initializes both faces' neighbor pointers across the edge. If not, it adds the edge to the set of edges. The indices of the two vertices at the ends of the edge, v0 and v1, are equal to the edge index and the edge index plus one.

⟨*Update neighbor pointer for* edgeNum⟩ ≡   **142**
```
    int v0 = edgeNum, v1 = NEXT(edgeNum);
    SDEdge e(f->v[v0], f->v[v1]);
    if (edges.find(e) == edges.end()) {
        ⟨Handle new edge 142⟩
    }
    else {
        ⟨Handle previously seen edge 142⟩
    }
```

Given an edge that hasn't been encountered before, the current face's pointer is stored in the edge object's f[0] member. Because the input mesh is manifold, there can be at most one other face that shares this edge. When such a face is discovered, it can be used to initialize the neighboring face field. Storing the edge number of this edge in the current face allows the neighboring face to initialize its corresponding edge neighbor pointer.

⟨*Handle new edge*⟩ ≡   **142**
```
    e.f[0] = f;
    e.f0edgeNum = edgeNum;
    edges.insert(e);
```

When the second face on an edge is found, the neighbor pointers for each of the two faces are set. The edge is then removed from the edge set, since no edge can be shared by more than two faces.

⟨*Handle previously seen edge*⟩ ≡   **142**
```
    e = *edges.find(e);
    e.f[0]->f[e.f0edgeNum] = f;
    f->f[edgeNum] = e.f[0];
    edges.erase(e);
```

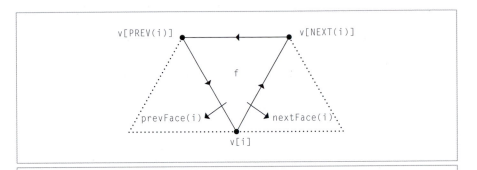

Figure 3.17: Given a vertex v[i] and a face that it is incident to, f, we define the *next face* as the face adjacent to f across the edge from v[i] to v[NEXT(i)]. The previous face is defined analogously.

Now that all faces have proper neighbor pointers, the boundary and regular flags in each of the vertices can be set. In order to determine if a vertex is a boundary vertex, we'll define an ordering of faces around a vertex (Figure 3.17). For a vertex v[i] on a face f, we define the vertex's *next face* as the face across the edge from v[i] to v[NEXT(i)] and the *previous face* as the face across the edge from v[PREV(i)] to v[i].

By successively going to the next face around v, we can iterate over the faces adjacent to it. If we eventually return to the face we started at, then we are at an interior vertex; if we come to an edge with a NULL neighbor pointer, then we're at a boundary vertex (Figure 3.18). Once the initialization routine has determined if this is a boundary vertex, it computes the valence of the vertex and sets the regular flag if the valence is 6 for an interior vertex or 4 for a boundary vertex; otherwise it is an extraordinary vertex.

⟨*Finish vertex initialization*⟩ ≡ 137

```
for (i = 0; i < nvertices; ++i) {
    SDVertex *v = vertices[i];
    SDFace *f = v->startFace;
    do {
        f = f->nextFace(v);
    } while (f && f != v->startFace);
    v->boundary = (f == NULL);
    if (!v->boundary && v->valence() == 6)
        v->regular = true;
    else if (v->boundary && v->valence() == 4)
        v->regular = true;
    else
        v->regular = false;
}
```

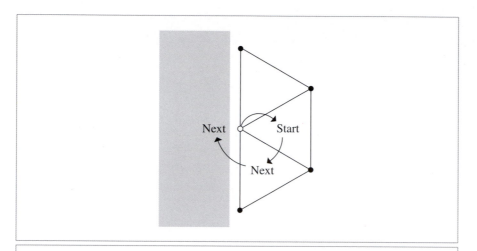

Figure 3.18: We can determine if a vertex is a boundary vertex by starting from the adjacent face `startFace` and following next face pointers around the vertex. If we come to a face that has no next neighbor face, then the vertex is on a boundary. If we return to `startFace`, it's an interior vertex.

Because the valence of a vertex is frequently needed, we will provide the method `SDVertex::valence()`.

⟨*LoopSubdiv Inline Functions*⟩ ≡
```
inline int SDVertex::valence() {
    SDFace *f = startFace;
    if (!boundary) {
        ⟨Compute valence of interior vertex 144⟩
    }
    else {
        ⟨Compute valence of boundary vertex 145⟩
    }
}
```

To compute the valence of a nonboundary vertex, this method counts the number of the adjacent faces starting by following each face's neighbor pointers around the vertex until it reaches the starting face. The valence is equal to the number of faces visited.

⟨*Compute valence of interior vertex*⟩ ≡   **144**
```
int nf = 1;
while ((f = f->nextFace(this)) != startFace)
    ++nf;
return nf;
```

For boundary vertices we can use the same approach, although in this case, the valence is one more than the number of adjacent faces. The loop over adjacent faces is slightly more complicated here: it follows pointers to the next face around the vertex until it reaches the boundary, counting the number of faces seen. It then starts again at startFace and follows previous face pointers until it encounters the boundary in the other direction.

⟨*Compute valence of boundary vertex*⟩ ≡   **144**
```
int nf = 1;
while ((f = f->nextFace(this)) != NULL)
    ++nf;
f = startFace;
while ((f = f->prevFace(this)) != NULL)
    ++nf;
return nf+1;
```

SDFace::vnum() is a utility function that finds the index of a given vertex pointer. It is a fatal error to pass a pointer to a vertex that isn't part of the current face—this case would represent a bug elsewhere in the subdivision code.

⟨*SDFace Methods*⟩ ≡   **139**
```
int vnum(SDVertex *vert) const {
    for (int i = 0; i < 3; ++i)
        if (v[i] == vert) return i;
    Severe("Basic logic error in SDFace::vnum()");
    return -1;
}
```

Since the next face for a vertex v[i] on a face f is over the ith edge (recall the mapping of edge neighbor pointers from Figure 3.15), we can find the appropriate face neighbor pointer easily given the index i for the vertex, which the vnum() utility function provides. The previous face is across the edge from PREV(i) to i, so the method returns f[PREV(i)] for the previous face.

⟨*SDFace Methods*⟩+≡   **139**
```
SDFace *nextFace(SDVertex *vert) {
    return f[vnum(vert)];
}
```

⟨*SDFace Methods*⟩+≡   **139**
```
SDFace *prevFace(SDVertex *vert) {
    return f[PREV(vnum(vert))];
}
```

It is also useful to be able to get the next and previous vertices around a face starting at any vertex. The SDFace::nextVert() and SDFace::prevVert() methods do just that (Figure 3.19).

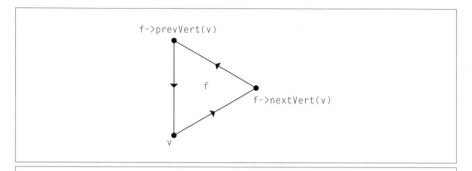

Figure 3.19: Given a vertex v on a face f, the method `f->prevVert(v)` returns the previous vertex around the face from v, and `f->nextVert(v)` returns the next vertex, where "next" and "previous" are defined by the original ordering of vertices when this face was defined.

⟨*SDFace Methods*⟩+≡   **139**
```
SDVertex *nextVert(SDVertex *vert) {
    return v[NEXT(vnum(vert))];
}
```

⟨*SDFace Methods*⟩+≡   **139**
```
SDVertex *prevVert(SDVertex *vert) {
    return v[PREV(vnum(vert))];
}
```

3.7.2 BOUNDS

Loop subdivision surfaces have the *convex hull property:* the limit surface is guaranteed to be inside the convex hull of the original control mesh. Thus, for the bounding methods, we can just bound the original control vertices. The bounding methods are essentially equivalent to those in `TriangleMesh`, so we won't include them here.

⟨*LoopSubdiv Public Methods*⟩≡   **136**
```
BBox ObjectBound() const;
BBox WorldBound() const;
```

3.7.3 SUBDIVISON

Now we can show how subdivision proceeds with the modified Loop rules. The `LoopSubdiv` shape doesn't support intersection directly, but applies subdivision a fixed number of times to generate a `TriangleMesh` for rendering. Exercise 3.10 at the end of the chapter discusses adaptive subdivision, where each original face is subdivided enough times so that the result looks smooth from a particular viewpoint rather than just using a fixed number of levels of subdivision, which can over-subdivide some areas while simultaneously under-subdividing others.

⟨*LoopSubdiv Method Definitions*⟩+≡
```
bool LoopSubdiv::CanIntersect() const {
    return false;
}
```

The Refine() method handles all of the subdivision. It repeatedly applies the subdivision rules to the mesh, each time generating a new mesh to be used as the input to the next step. After each subdivision step, the f and v arrays in the Refine() method are updated to point to the faces and vertices from the level of subdivision just computed. When the LoopSubdiv is done subdividing, it creates a TriangleMesh representation of the surface and returns to the caller. The ObjectArena class, defined in Section A.2.4 in Appendix A, provides a custom memory allocation method that quickly allocates objects of a particular type and automatically frees their memory when it goes out of scope.

⟨*LoopSubdiv Method Definitions*⟩+≡
```
void LoopSubdiv::Refine(vector<Reference<Shape> > &refined) const {
    vector<SDFace *> f = faces;
    vector<SDVertex *> v = vertices;
    ObjectArena<SDVertex> vertexArena;
    ObjectArena<SDFace> faceArena;
    for (int i = 0; i < nLevels; ++i) {
        ⟨Update f and v for next level of subdivision 147⟩
    }
    ⟨Push vertices to limit surface 158⟩
    ⟨Compute vertex tangents on limit surface 159⟩
    ⟨Create TriangleMesh from subdivision mesh⟩
}
```

The main loop of a subdivision step proceeds as follows: it creates vectors for all of the vertices and faces at the current level of subdivision and then proceeds to compute new vertex positions and update the topological representation for the refined mesh. Figure 3.20 shows the basic refinement rules for faces in the mesh. Each face is split into four child faces, such that the *i*th child face is next to the *i*th vertex of the input face and the final face is in the center. Three new vertices are then computed along the split edges of the original face.

⟨*Update f and v for next level of subdivision*⟩≡   147
```
vector<SDFace *> newFaces;
vector<SDVertex *> newVertices;
⟨Allocate next level of children in mesh tree 148⟩
⟨Update vertex positions and create new edge vertices 149⟩
⟨Update new mesh topology 156⟩
⟨Prepare for next level of subdivision 158⟩
```

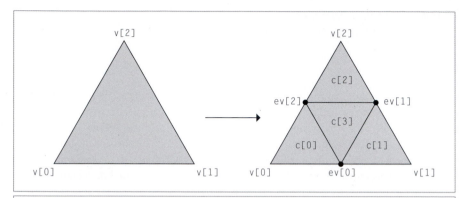

Figure 3.20: Basic Subdivision of a Single Triangular Face. Four child faces are created, ordered such that the *i*th child face is adjacent to the *i*th vertex of the original face and the fourth child face is in the center of the subdivided face. Three edge vertices need to be computed; they are numbered so that the *i*th edge vertex is along the *i*th edge of the original face.

First, storage is allocated for the updated values of the vertices already present in the input mesh. The method also allocates storage for the child faces. It doesn't yet do any initialization of the new vertices and faces other than setting the regular and boundary flags for the vertices since subdivision leaves boundary vertices on the boundary and interior vertices in the interior and it doesn't change the valence of vertices in the mesh.

⟨*Allocate next level of children in mesh tree*⟩ ≡   147
```
for (u_int j = 0; j < v.size(); ++j) {
    v[j]->child = new (vertexArena) SDVertex;
    v[j]->child->regular = v[j]->regular;
    v[j]->child->boundary = v[j]->boundary;
    newVertices.push_back(v[j]->child);
}
for (u_int j = 0; j < f.size(); ++j)
    for (int k = 0; k < 4; ++k) {
        f[j]->children[k] = new (faceArena) SDFace;
        newFaces.push_back(f[j]->children[k]);
    }
```

Computing New Vertex Positions

Before worrying about initializing the topology of the subdivided mesh, the refinement method computes positions for all of the vertices in the mesh. First, it considers the problem of computing updated positions for all of the vertices that were already present in the mesh; these vertices are called *even vertices*. It then computes the new vertices on the split edges. These are called *odd vertices*.

⟨*Update vertex positions and create new edge vertices*⟩ ≡   **147**
    ⟨*Update vertex positions for even vertices* **149**⟩
    ⟨*Compute new odd edge vertices* **153**⟩

Different techniques are used to compute the updated positions for each of the different types of even vertices—regular and extraordinary, boundary and interior. This gives four cases to handle.

⟨*Update vertex positions for even vertices*⟩ ≡   **149**

```
for (u_int j = 0; j < v.size(); ++j) {
    if (!v[j]->boundary) {
        ⟨Apply one-ring rule for even vertex  150⟩
    }
    else {
        ⟨Apply boundary rule for even vertex  152⟩
    }
}
```

For both types of interior vertices, we take the set of vertices adjacent to each vertex (called the *one-ring* around it, reflecting the fact that it's a ring of neighbors) and weight each of the neighbor vertices by a weight β (Figure 3.21). The vertex we are updating, in the center, is weighted by $1 - n\beta$, where n is the valence of the vertex. Thus, the new position v' for a vertex v is

$$v' = (1 - n\beta)v + \sum_{i=1}^{N} \beta v_i.$$

This formulation ensures that the sum of weights is one, which guarantees the convex hull property that was used earlier for bounding the surface. The position of the vertex being updated is only affected by vertices that are nearby; this is known as *local support*. Loop subdivision is particularly efficient because its subdivision rules all have this property.

The particular weight β used for this step is a key component of the subdivision method and must be chosen carefully in order to ensure smoothness of the limit surface among other desirable properties.[8] The LoopSubdiv::beta() method that follows computes a β value based on the vertex's valence that ensures smoothness. For regular interior vertices, LoopSubdiv::beta() returns $\frac{1}{16}$. Since this is a common case, the implementation uses $\frac{1}{16}$ directly instead of calling LoopSubdiv::beta() every time.

---

8   Again, see the papers cited at the start of this section and in the "Further Reading" section for information about how values like β are derived.

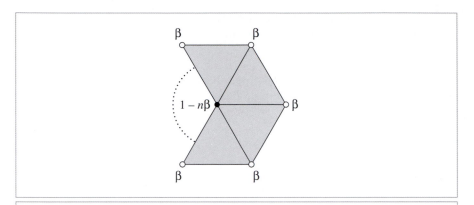

Figure 3.21: The new position v′ for a vertex v is computed by weighting the adjacent vertices v$_i$ by a weight β and weighting v by $(1 - n\beta)$, where n is the valence of v. The adjacent vertices v$_i$ are collectively referred to as the *one-ring* around v.

⟨*Apply one-ring rule for even vertex*⟩ ≡   **149**
```
if (v[j]->regular)
    v[j]->child->P = weightOneRing(v[j], 1.f/16.f);
else
    v[j]->child->P = weightOneRing(v[j], beta(v[j]->valence()));
```

⟨*LoopSubdiv Private Methods*⟩ ≡   **136**
```
static float beta(int valence) {
    if (valence == 3) return 3.f/16.f;
    else return 3.f / (8.f * valence);
}
```

The LoopSubdiv::weightOneRing() function loops over the one-ring of adjacent vertices and applies the given weight to compute a new vertex position. It uses the SDVertex::oneRing() function, defined in the following, which returns the positions of the vertices around the vertex vert.

⟨*LoopSubdiv Method Definitions*⟩+≡
```
Point LoopSubdiv::weightOneRing(SDVertex *vert, float beta) {
    ⟨Put vert one-ring in Pring 151⟩
    Point P = (1 - valence * beta) * vert->P;
    for (int i = 0; i < valence; ++i)
        P += beta * Pring[i];
    return P;
}
```

Because a variable number of vertices are in the one-rings, we use `alloca()` to quickly dynamically allocate space to store their positions.

⟨*Put* vert *one-ring in* Pring⟩ ≡   150, 153
```
int valence = vert->valence();
Point *Pring = (Point *)alloca(valence * sizeof(Point));
vert->oneRing(Pring);
```

The `oneRing()` method assumes that the pointer passed in points to an area of memory large enough to hold the one-ring around the vertex.

⟨*LoopSubdiv Method Definitions*⟩+≡
```
void SDVertex::oneRing(Point *P) {
    if (!boundary) {
        ⟨Get one-ring vertices for interior vertex  151⟩
    }
    else {
        ⟨Get one-ring vertices for boundary vertex  152⟩
    }
}
```

It's relatively easy to get the one-ring around an interior vertex by looping over the faces adjacent to the vertex, and for each face retaining the vertex after the center vertex. (Brief sketching with pencil and paper should convince you that this process returns all of the vertices in the one-ring.)

⟨*Get one-ring vertices for interior vertex*⟩ ≡   151
```
SDFace *face = startFace;
do {
    *P++ = face->nextVert(this)->P;
    face = face->nextFace(this);
} while (face != startFace);
```

The one-ring around a boundary vertex is a bit more tricky. The implementation here carefully stores the one-ring in the given `Point` array so that the first and last entries in the array are the two adjacent vertices along the boundary. This ordering is important because the adjacent boundary vertices will often be weighted differently than the adjacent vertices that are in the interior of the mesh. Doing so requires that we first loop around neighbor faces until we reach a face on the boundary and then loop around the other way, storing vertices one by one.

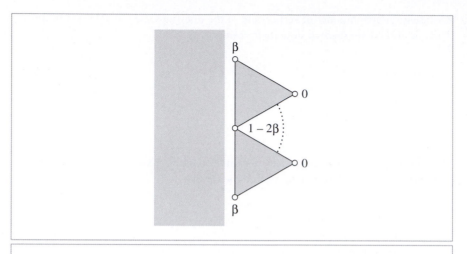

Figure 3.22: Subdivision on a Boundary Edge. The new position for the vertex in the center is computed by weighting it and its two neighbor vertices by the weights shown.

⟨*Get one-ring vertices for boundary vertex*⟩ ≡   151

```
SDFace *face = startFace, *f2;
while ((f2 = face->nextFace(this)) != NULL)
    face = f2;
*P++ = face->nextVert(this)->P;
do {
    *P++ = face->prevVert(this)->P;
    face = face->prevFace(this);
} while (face != NULL);
```

For vertices on the boundary, the new vertex's position is based only on the two neighboring boundary vertices (Figure 3.22). Not depending on interior vertices ensures that two abutting surfaces that share the same vertices on the boundary will have abutting limit surfaces. The weightBoundary() utility function applies the given weighting on the two neighbor vertices v_1 and v_2 to compute the new position v' as

$$v' = (1 - 2\beta)v + \beta v_1 + \beta v_2.$$

The same weight of $\frac{1}{8}$ is used for both regular and extraordinary vertices.

⟨*Apply boundary rule for even vertex*⟩ ≡   149

```
v[j]->child->P = weightBoundary(v[j], 1.f/8.f);
```

The weightBoundary() utility function applies the given weights at a boundary vertex. Because the SDVertex::oneRing() function orders the boundary vertex's one-ring such that the first and last entries are the boundary neighbors, the implementation here is particularly straightforward.

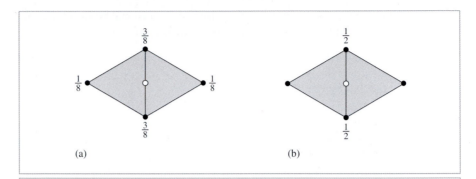

Figure 3.23: Subdivision Rule for Edge Split. The position of the new odd vertex, marked with an open circle, is found by weighting the two vertices at the ends of the edge and the two vertices opposite it on the adjacent triangles. (a) The weights for an interior vertex; (b) the weights for a boundary vertex.

⟨*LoopSubdiv Method Definitions*⟩+≡

```
Point LoopSubdiv::weightBoundary(SDVertex *vert, float beta) {
    ⟨Put vert one-ring in Pring 151⟩
    Point P = (1-2*beta) * vert->P;
    P += beta * Pring[0];
    P += beta * Pring[valence-1];
    return P;
}
```

Now the refinement method computes the positions of the odd vertices—the new vertices along the split edges of the mesh. It loops over each edge of each face in the mesh, computing the new vertex that splits the edge (Figure 3.23). For interior edges, the new vertex is found by weighting the two vertices at the ends of the edge and the two vertices across from the edge on the adjacent faces. It loops through all three edges of each face, and each time it comes to an edge that hasn't been seen before, it computes and stores the new odd vertex for the edge in the edgeVerts associative array.

⟨*Compute new odd edge vertices*⟩≡   **149**

```
map<SDEdge, SDVertex *> edgeVerts;
for (u_int j = 0; j < f.size(); ++j) {
    SDFace *face = f[j];
    for (int k = 0; k < 3; ++k) {
        ⟨Compute odd vertex on kth edge 154⟩
    }
}
```

As was done when setting the face neighbor pointers in the original mesh, an SDEdge object is created for the edge and checked to see if it is in the set of edges that have already been visited. If it isn't, the new vertex on this edge is computed and added to the map, which is an associative array structure that performs efficient lookups.

⟨*Compute odd vertex on kth edge*⟩ ≡   **153**
```
    SDEdge edge(face->v[k], face->v[NEXT(k)]);
    SDVertex *vert = edgeVerts[edge];
    if (!vert) {
        ⟨Create and initialize new odd vertex 154⟩
        ⟨Apply edge rules to compute new vertex position 154⟩
        edgeVerts[edge] = vert;
    }
```

In Loop subdivision, the new vertices added by subdivision are always regular. (This means that the proportion of extraordinary vertices with respect to regular vertices will decrease with each level of subdivision.) Therefore the `regular` member of the new vertex can immediately be set to `true`. The `boundary` member can also be easily initialized, by checking to see if there is a neighbor face across the edge that is being split. Finally, the new vertex's `startFace` pointer can also be set here. For all odd vertices on the edges of a face, the center child (child face number three) is guaranteed to be adjacent to the new vertex.

⟨*Create and initialize new odd vertex*⟩ ≡   **154**
```
    vert = new (vertexArena) SDVertex;
    newVertices.push_back(vert);
    vert->regular = true;
    vert->boundary = (face->f[k] == NULL);
    vert->startFace = face->children[3];
```

For odd boundary vertices, the new vertex is just the average of the two adjacent vertices. For odd interior vertices, the two vertices at the ends of the edge are given weight $\frac{3}{8}$, and the two vertices opposite the edge are given weight $\frac{1}{8}$ (Figure 3.23). These last two vertices can be found using the `SDFace::otherVert()` utility function, which returns the vertex opposite a given edge of a face.

⟨*Apply edge rules to compute new vertex position*⟩ ≡   **154**
```
    if (vert->boundary) {
        vert->P =  0.5f * edge.v[0]->P;
        vert->P += 0.5f * edge.v[1]->P;
    }
    else {
        vert->P =  3.f/8.f * edge.v[0]->P;
        vert->P += 3.f/8.f * edge.v[1]->P;
        vert->P += 1.f/8.f * face->otherVert(edge.v[0], edge.v[1])->P;
        vert->P += 1.f/8.f *
            face->f[k]->otherVert(edge.v[0], edge.v[1])->P;
    }
```

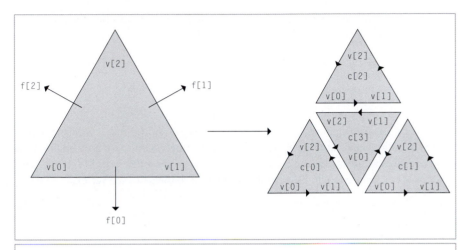

Figure 3.24: Each face is split into four child faces, such that the ith child is adjacent to the ith vertex of the original face, and such that the ith child face's ith vertex is the child of the ith vertex of the original face. The vertices of the center child are oriented such that the ith vertex is the odd vertex along the ith edge of the parent face.

The `SDFace::otherVert()` method is self-explanatory:

⟨*SDFace Methods*⟩+≡   139
```
SDVertex *otherVert(SDVertex *v0, SDVertex *v1) {
    for (int i = 0; i < 3; ++i)
        if (v[i] != v0 && v[i] != v1)
            return v[i];
    Severe("Basic logic error in SDVertex::otherVert()");
    return NULL;
}
```

Updating Mesh Topology

In order to keep the details of the topology update as straightforward as possible, the numbering scheme for the subdivided faces and their vertices has been chosen carefully (Figure 3.24). Review that figure carefully; the conventions shown there are key to the next few pages.

There are four main tasks required to update the topological pointers of the refined mesh:

1. The odd vertices' `SDVertex::startFace` pointers need to store a pointer to one of their adjacent faces.
2. Similarly, the even vertices' `SDVertex::startFace` pointers must be set.
3. The new faces' neighbor `f[i]` pointers need to be set to point to the neighboring faces.
4. The new faces' `v[i]` pointers need to point to the appropriate vertices.

The startFace pointers of the odd vertices were already initialized when they were first created. We'll handle the other three tasks in order here.

⟨*Update new mesh topology*⟩ ≡   **147**
    ⟨*Update even vertex face pointers* **156**⟩
    ⟨*Update face neighbor pointers* **156**⟩
    ⟨*Update face vertex pointers* **157**⟩

If a vertex is the *i*th vertex of its startFace, then it is guaranteed that it will be adjacent to the *i*th child face of startFace. Therefore it is just necessary to loop through all the parent vertices in the mesh, and for each one find its vertex index in its startFace. This index can then be used to find the child face adjacent to the new even vertex.

⟨*Update even vertex face pointers*⟩ ≡   **156**
```
for (u_int j = 0; j < v.size(); ++j) {
    SDVertex *vert = v[j];
    int vertNum = vert->startFace->vnum(vert);
    vert->child->startFace =
        vert->startFace->children[vertNum];
}
```

Next the face neighbor pointers for the newly created faces are updated. We break this into two steps: one to update neighbors among children of the same parent, and one to do neighbors across children of different parents. This involves some tricky pointer manipulation.

⟨*Update face neighbor pointers*⟩ ≡   **156**
```
for (u_int j = 0; j < f.size(); ++j) {
    SDFace *face = f[j];
    for (int k = 0; k < 3; ++k) {
        ⟨Update children f pointers for siblings  156⟩
        ⟨Update children f pointers for neighbor children  157⟩
    }
}
```

For the first step, recall that the interior child face is always stored in children[3]. Furthermore, the *k* + 1st child face (for *k* = 0, 1, 2) is across the *k*th edge of the interior face, and the interior face is across the *k* + 1st edge of the *k*th face.

⟨*Update children f pointers for siblings*⟩ ≡   **156**
```
face->children[3]->f[k] = face->children[NEXT(k)];
face->children[k]->f[NEXT(k)] = face->children[3];
```

We'll now update the children's face neighbor pointers that point to children of other parents. Only the first three children need to be addressed here; the interior child's neighbor pointers have already been fully initialized. Inspection of Figure 3.24 reveals that the *k*th and PREV(*k*)th edges of the *i*th child need to be set. To set the *k*th edge of the *k*th child, we first find the *k*th edge of the parent face, then the neighbor parent f2 across that edge. If f2 exists (meaning we aren't on a boundary), the neighbor parent index for the vertex v[k] is found. That index is equal to the index of the neighbor child we are searching for. This process is then repeated to find the child across the PREV(*k*)th edge.

⟨*Update children f pointers for neighbor children*⟩ ≡   156
```
    SDFace *f2 = face->f[k];
    face->children[k]->f[k] =
        f2 ? f2->children[f2->vnum(face->v[k])] : NULL;
    f2 = face->f[PREV(k)];
    face->children[k]->f[PREV(k)] =
        f2 ? f2->children[f2->vnum(face->v[k])] : NULL;
```

Finally, we handle the fourth step in the topological updates: setting the children faces' vertex pointers.

⟨*Update face vertex pointers*⟩ ≡   156
```
    for (u_int j = 0; j < f.size(); ++j) {
        SDFace *face = f[j];
        for (int k = 0; k < 3; ++k) {
            ⟨Update child vertex pointer to new even vertex 157⟩
            ⟨Update child vertex pointer to new odd vertex 157⟩
        }
    }
```

For the *k*th child face (for *k* = 0, 1, 2), the *k*th vertex corresponds to the even vertex that is adjacent to the child face. For the noninterior child faces, there is one even vertex and two odd vertices; for the interior child face, there are three odd vertices. This vertex can be found by following the child pointer of the parent vertex, available from the parent face.

⟨*Update child vertex pointer to new even vertex*⟩ ≡   157
```
    face->children[k]->v[k] = face->v[k]->child;
```

To update the rest of the vertex pointers, the edgeVerts associative array is reused to find the odd vertex for each split edge of the parent face. Three child faces have that vertex as an incident vertex. The vertex indices for the three faces are easily found, again based on the numbering scheme established in Figure 3.24.

⟨*Update child vertex pointer to new odd vertex*⟩ ≡   157
```
    SDVertex *vert = edgeVerts[SDEdge(face->v[k], face->v[NEXT(k)])];
    face->children[k]->v[NEXT(k)] = vert;
    face->children[NEXT(k)]->v[k] = vert;
    face->children[3]->v[k] = vert;
```

After the geometric and topological work has been done for a subdivision step, the newly created vertices and faces are moved into the v and f arrays:

⟨*Prepare for next level of subdivision*⟩ ≡   147
```
f = newFaces;
v = newVertices;
```

To the Limit Surface and Output

One of the remarkable properties of subdivision surfaces is that there are special subdivision rules that give the positions that the vertices of the mesh would have if we continued subdividing forever. We apply these rules here to initialize an array of limit surface positions, Plimit. Note that it's important to temporarily store the limit surface positions somewhere other than in the vertices while the computation is taking place. Because the limit surface position of each vertex depends on the original positions of its surrounding vertices, the original positions of all vertices must remain unchanged until the computation is complete.

The limit rule for a boundary vertex weights the two neighbor vertices by $\frac{1}{5}$ and the center vertex by $\frac{3}{5}$. The rule for interior vertices is based on a function gamma(), which computes appropriate vertex weights based on the valence of the vertex.

⟨*Push vertices to limit surface*⟩ ≡   147
```
Point *Plimit = new Point[v.size()];
for (u_int i = 0; i < v.size(); ++i) {
    if (v[i]->boundary)
        Plimit[i] =  weightBoundary(v[i], 1.f/5.f);
    else
        Plimit[i] =  weightOneRing(v[i], gamma(v[i]->valence()));
}
for (u_int i = 0; i < v.size(); ++i)
    v[i]->P = Plimit[i];
```

⟨*LoopSubdiv Private Methods*⟩ +≡   136
```
static float gamma(int valence) {
    return 1.f / (valence + 3.f / (8.f * beta(valence)));
}
```

In order to generate a smooth-looking triangle mesh with per-vertex surface normals, a pair of nonparallel tangent vectors to the limit surface are computed at each vertex. As with the limit rule for positions, this is an analytic computation that gives the precise tangents on the actual limit surface.

⟨*Compute vertex tangents on limit surface*⟩ ≡   **147**

```
vector<Normal> Ns;
Ns.reserve(v.size());
int ringSize = 16;
Point *Pring = new Point[ringSize];
for (u_int i = 0; i < v.size(); ++i) {
    SDVertex *vert = v[i];
    Vector S(0,0,0), T(0,0,0);
    int valence = vert->valence();
    if (valence > ringSize) {
        ringSize = valence;
        delete[] Pring;
        Pring = new Point[ringSize];
    }
    vert->oneRing(Pring);

    if (!vert->boundary) {
        ⟨Compute tangents of interior face 159⟩
    }
    else {
        ⟨Compute tangents of boundary face 161⟩
    }
    Ns.push_back(Normal(Cross(S, T)));
}
```

Figure 3.25 shows the setting for computing tangents in the mesh interior. The center vertex is given a weight of zero and the neighbors are given weights w_i. To compute the first tangent vector **s**, the weights are

$$w_i = \cos\left(\frac{2\pi i}{n}\right),$$

where n is the valence of the vertex. The second tangent **t** is computed with weights

$$w_i = \sin\left(\frac{2\pi i}{n}\right).$$

⟨*Compute tangents of interior face*⟩ ≡   **159**

```
for (int k = 0; k < valence; ++k) {
    S += cosf(2.f*M_PI*k/valence) * Vector(Pring[k]);
    T += sinf(2.f*M_PI*k/valence) * Vector(Pring[k]);
}
```

Tangents on boundary vertices are a bit trickier. Figure 3.26 shows the ordering of vertices in the one-ring expected in the following discussion.

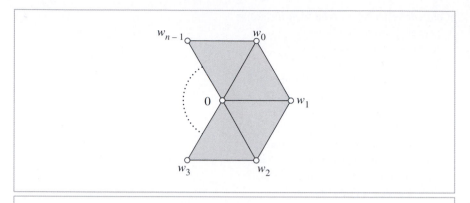

Figure 3.25: To compute tangents for interior vertices, the one-ring vertices are weighted with weights w_i. The center vertex, where the tangent is being computed, always has a weight of 0.

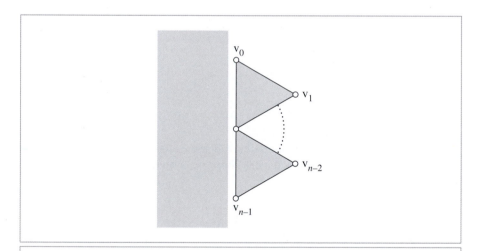

Figure 3.26: Tangents at boundary vertices are also computed as weighted averages of the adjacent vertices. However, some of the boundary tangent rules incorporate the value of the center vertex.

The first tangent, known as the *across tangent*, is given by the vector between the two neighboring boundary vertices:

$$\mathbf{s} = \mathbf{v}_{n-1} - \mathbf{v}_0.$$

The second tangent, known as the *transverse tangent,* is computed based on the vertex's valence. The center vertex is given a weight w_c and the one-ring vertices are given weights specified by a vector $(w_0, w_1, \ldots, w_{n-1})$. The transverse tangent rules we will use are

Valence	w_c	w_i
2	-2	$(1, 1)$
3	-1	$(0, 1, 0)$
4 (regular)	-2	$(-1, 2, 2, -1)$

For valences of 5 and higher, $w_c = 0$ and

$$w_0 = w_{n-1} = \sin \theta$$

$$w_i = (2 \cos \theta - 2) \, \sin(\theta i),$$

where

$$\theta = \frac{\pi}{n - 1}.$$

Although we will not prove it here, these weights sum to zero for all values of i. This guarantees that the weighted sum is in fact a tangent vector.

⟨*Compute tangents of boundary face*⟩ ≡   159
```
  S = Pring[valence-1] - Pring[0];
  if (valence == 2)
      T = Vector(Pring[0] + Pring[1] - 2 * vert->P);
  else if (valence == 3)
      T = Pring[1] - vert->P;
  else if (valence == 4) // regular
      T = Vector(-1*Pring[0] + 2*Pring[1] + 2*Pring[2] +
                  -1*Pring[3] + -2*vert->P);
  else {
      float theta = M_PI / float(valence-1);
      T = Vector(sinf(theta) * (Pring[0] + Pring[valence-1]));
      for (int k = 1; k < valence-1; ++k) {
          float wt = (2*cosf(theta) - 2) * sinf((k) * theta);
          T += Vector(wt * Pring[k]);
      }
      T = -T;
  }
```

Finally, the fragment ⟨*Create* `TriangleMesh` *from subdivision mesh*⟩ creates the triangle mesh object and adds it to the `refined` vector passed to the `LoopSubdiv::Refine()` method. We won't include it here, since it's just a straightforward transformation of the subdivided mesh into an indexed triangle mesh.

M_PI 855

Vector 47

FURTHER READING

An Introduction to Ray Tracing has an extensive survey of algorithms for ray-shape intersection (Glassner 1989a). Goldstein and Nagel (1971) discuss ray-quadric intersections, and Heckbert (1984) discusses the mathematics of quadrics for graphics applications in detail, with many citations to literature in mathematics and other fields. Hanrahan (1983) describes a system that automates the process of deriving a ray intersection routine for surfaces defined by implicit polynomials; his system emits C source code to perform the intersection test and normal computation for a surface described by a given equation. Mitchell (1990) showed that interval arithmetic could be applied to develop algorithms for robustly computing intersections with implicit surfaces that can not be described by polynomials and are thus more difficult to accurately compute intersections for. See Moore's book (1966) for an introduction to interval arithmetic.

Other notable early papers related to ray-shape intersection include Kajiya's work on computing intersections with surfaces of revolution and procedurally generated fractal terrains (Kajiya 1983) and his algorithm for computing intersections with parametric patches (Kajiya 1982). Recent work on more efficient techniques for direct ray intersection with patches includes papers by Stürzlinger (1998) and Martin et al. (2000). The ray-triangle intersection test in Section 3.6 was developed by Möller and Trumbore (1997). Fournier et al.'s paper on rendering procedural stochastic models (Fournier, Fussel, and Carpenter 1982) and Hart et al.'s paper on finding intersections with fractals (Hart, Sandin, and Kauffman 1989) illustrate the broad range of shape representations that can be used with ray-tracing algorithms.

Subdivision surfaces were invented by Doo and Sabin (1978) and Catmull and Clark (1978). The Loop subdivision method was originally developed by Charles Loop (1987), although the implementation in pbrt uses the improved rules for subdivision and tangents along boundary edges developed by Hoppe et al. (1994). There has been extensive work in subdivision surfaces recently. The SIGGRAPH course notes give a good summary of the state of the art and also have extensive references (Zorin et al. 2000). See also Warren's recent book on the topic (Warren 2002).

An exciting recent development in subdivision surfaces is the ability to evaluate them at arbitrary points on the surface (Stam 1998). Subdivision surface implementations like the one in this chapter are often relatively inefficient, spending as much time dereferencing pointers as they do applying subdivision rules. Stam's approach also reduces the impact of this problem. Bolz and Schröder (2002) suggest a much more efficient implementation approach that precomputes a number of quantities that make it possible to compute the final mesh much more efficiently.

Phong and Crow (1975) first introduced the idea of interpolating per-vertex shading normals to give the appearance of smooth surfaces from polygonal meshes.

The notion of shapes that repeatedly refine themselves into collections of other shapes until ready for rendering was first introduced in the REYES renderer (Cook, Carpenter, and Catmull 1987).

An excellent introduction to differential geometry is Gray (1993); Section 14.3 of that book presents the Weingarten equations. Turkowski (1990a) has expressions for first and second partial derivatives of a handful of parametric primitives.

EXERCISES

❷ 3.1 One nice property of mesh-based shapes like triangle meshes and subdivision surfaces is that the shape's vertices can be transformed into world space, so that it isn't necessary to transform rays into object space before performing ray intersection tests. Interestingly enough, it is possible to do the same thing for ray-quadric intersections.

The implicit forms of the quadrics in this chapter were all of the form

$$Ax^2 + Bxy + Cxz + Dy^2 + Eyz + Fz^2 + G = 0,$$

where some of the constants $A \ldots G$ were zero. More generally, we can define quadric surfaces by the equation

$$Ax^2 + By^2 + Cz^2 + 2Dxy + 2Eyz + 2Fxz + 2Gz + 2Hy + 2Iz + J = 0,$$

where most of the parameters $A \ldots J$ don't directly correspond to the earlier $A \ldots G$. In this form, the quadric can be represented by a 4×4 symmetric matrix $\mathbf{Q}$:

$$\begin{bmatrix} x & y & z & 1 \end{bmatrix} \begin{pmatrix} A & D & F & G \\ D & B & E & H \\ F & E & C & I \\ G & H & I & J \end{pmatrix} \begin{bmatrix} x \\ y \\ z \\ 1 \end{bmatrix} = \mathbf{p}^T \mathbf{Q} \mathbf{p} = 0.$$

Given this representation, first show that the matrix $\mathbf{Q}'$ representing a quadric transformed by the matrix $\mathbf{M}$ is

$$\mathbf{Q}' = (\mathbf{M}^T)^{-1} \mathbf{Q} \mathbf{M}^{-1}.$$

To do so, show that for any point p where $\mathbf{p}^T \mathbf{Q} \mathbf{p} = 0$, if we apply a transformation $\mathbf{M}$ to p and compute $\mathbf{p}' = \mathbf{M} \mathbf{p}$, we'd like to find $\mathbf{Q}'$ so that $(\mathbf{p}')^T \mathbf{Q}' \mathbf{p}' = 0$.

Next, substitute the ray equation into the earlier more general quadric equation to compute coefficients for the quadratic equation $at^2 + bt + c = 0$ in terms of entries of the matrix $\mathbf{Q}$ to pass to the Quadratic() function.

Now implement this approach in pbrt and use it instead of the original quadric intersection routines. Note that you will still need to transform the resulting world space hit points into object space to test against θ_{max}, if it is not 2π, and so on. How does performance compare to the original scheme?

Quadratic() 101

❶ 3.2 Improve the object space bounding box routines for the quadrics to properly account for $\phi_{max} < 2\pi$ and compute tighter bounding boxes when possible. How much does this improve performance when rendering scenes with partial quadric shapes?

● 3.3 There is room to optimize the implementations of the various quadric primitives in pbrt in a number of ways. For example, for complete spheres some of the tests in the intersection routine related to partial spheres are unnecessary. Furthermore, some of the quadrics have calls to trigonometric functions that could be turned into simpler expressions using insight about the geometry of the particular primitives. Investigate ways to speed up these methods. How much does doing so improve the overall run time of pbrt?

● 3.4 Currently pbrt recomputes the partial derivatives $\partial p/\partial u$ and $\partial p/\partial v$ for triangles every time they are needed, even though they are constant for each triangle. Precompute these vectors and analyze the speed/storage trade-off, especially for large triangle meshes. How does the depth complexity of the scene and the size of triangles in the image affect this trade-off?

● 3.5 Implement a general polygon primitive that supports an arbitrary number of vertices and convex or concave polygons as a new plug-in to pbrt. You can assume that a valid polygon has been provided and that all of the vertices of the polygon lie on the same plane, although you might want to issue a warning when this is not the case.

An efficient technique for computing ray-polygon intersections is to find the plane equation for the polygon from its normal and a point on the plane. Then compute the intersection of the ray with that plane and project the intersection point and the polygon vertices to 2D. Then apply a 2D point-in-polygon test to determine if the point is inside the polygon. An easy way to do this is to effectively do a 2D ray-tracing computation and intersect the ray with each of the edge segments and count how many it goes through. If it goes through an odd number of them, the point is inside the polygon and there is an intersection. See Figure 3.27 for an illustration of this idea.

You may find it helpful to read the article by Haines (1994) that surveys a number of approaches for efficient point-in-polygon tests. Some of the techniques described there may be helpful for optimizing this test. Furthermore, Section 13.3.3 of Schneider and Eberly (2003) discusses strategies for getting all the corner cases right, for example, when the 2D ray is aligned precisely with an edge or passes through a vertex of the polygon.

● 3.6 Constructive solid geometry (CSG) is a classic solid modeling technique, where complex shapes are built up by considering the union, intersection, and differences of more primitive shapes. For example, a sphere could be used to create pits in a cylinder if a shape was modeled as the difference of a cylinder and set of spheres that partially overlapped it. See Hoffmann (1989) for further information about CSG.

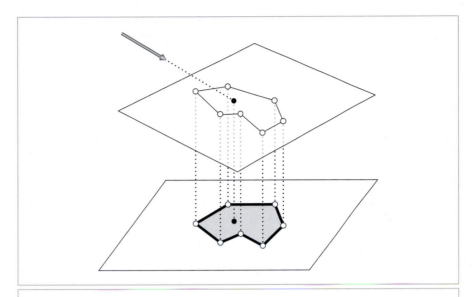

Figure 3.27: A ray-polygon intersection test can be performed by finding the point where the ray intersects the polygon's plane, projecting the hit point and polygon vertices onto an axis-aligned plane, and doing a 2D point-in-polygon test there.

Add support for CSG to pbrt and render images that demonstrate interesting shapes that can be rendered using CSG. You may want to read Roth (1982), which first described how ray tracing could be used to render models described by CSG, as well as Amanatides and Mitchell (1990), which discusses precision-related issues for CSG ray tracing.

❷ 3.7   Procedurally described parametric surfaces: Write a Shape that takes a general mathematical expression of the form $f(u, v) \rightarrow (x, y, z)$ that describes a parametric surface as a function of (u, v). Evaluate the given function at a grid of (u, v) positions and create a TriangleMesh that approximates the given surface when the Shape::Refine() method is called.

❸ 3.8   Almost all methods for subdivision surfaces are based on either refining a mesh of triangles or a mesh of quadrilaterals. If a rendering system only supports one type of mesh, meshes of the other type are typically tessellated to make faces of the expected type in a preprocessing step. However, doing this can introduce artifacts in the final subdivision surface. Read Stam and Loop's paper on a hybrid subdivision scheme that supports meshes with both quadrilateral and triangular faces (Stam and Loop 2003) and implement a Shape based on their method. Demonstrate cases where the subdivision surface that your implementation creates does not have artifacts that are present in the output from LoopSubdiv.

❷ 3.9 The smoothness of subdivision surfaces isn't always desirable. Sometimes it is useful to be able to flag some edges of a subdivision control mesh as "creases" and apply different subdivision rules there to preserve a sharp edge. Extend the LoopSubdiv implementation so that some edges can be denoted as creases, and use the boundary subdivision rules to compute the positions of vertices along those edges. Render images showing the difference this makes.

❸ 3.10 Implement adaptive subdivision for the LoopSubdiv Shape. A weakness of the basic implementation in Section 3.7 is that each face is always refined a fixed number of times: this may mean that some faces are underrefined, leading to visible faceting in the triangle mesh, and some faces are overrefined, leading to excessive memory use and rendering time. With adaptive subdivision, individual faces are no longer subdivided once a particular error threshold has been reached.

An easy error threshold to implement computes the face normals of each face and its directly adjacent faces. If they are sufficiently close to each other (e.g., as tested via dot products), then the limit surface for that face will be reasonably flat and further refinement will likely make little difference to the final surface. Alternatively, you might want to approximate the area that a subdivided face covers on the image plane and continue subdividing until this area becomes sufficiently small. This approximation could be done using ray differentials; see Section 11.1.1 for an explanation of how to relate the ray differential to the screen space footprint.

The trickiest part of this exercise is that some faces that don't need subdivision due to the flatness test will still need to be subdivided in order to provide vertices so that neighboring faces that do need to subdivide can get their vertex one-rings. In particular, adjacent faces can differ by no more than one level of subdivision.

❸ 3.11 Ray-tracing point-sampled geometry: Extending methods for rendering complex models represented as a collection of point samples (Levoy and Whitted 1985; Pfister et al. 2000; Rusinkiewicz and Levoy 2000), Schaufler and Jensen (2000) have described a method for intersecting rays with collections of oriented point samples in space. They probabilistically determine that an intersection has occurred when a ray approaches a sufficient local density of point samples and compute a surface normal with a weighted average of the nearby samples. Read their paper and extend pbrt to support a point-sampled geometry shape. Do any of pbrt's basic interfaces need to be extended or generalized to support a shape like this?

❸ **3.12** Ray-tracing ribbons: Hair is often modeled as a collection of *generalized cylinders*, which are defined as the shape that results from sweeping a disk along a given curve. Because there are often a large number of individual hairs, an efficient method for intersecting rays with generalized cylinders is needed for ray-tracing hair. A number of methods have been developed to compute ray intersections with generalized cylinders (Bronsvoort and Klok 1985; de Voogt, van der Helm, and Bronsvoort 2000); investigate these algorithms and extend pbrt to support a fast hair primitive with one of them. Alternatively, investigate the generalization of Schaufler and Jensen's approach for probabilistic point intersection (Schaufler and Jensen 2000) to probabilistic line intersection and apply this to fast ray tracing of hair.

❸ **3.13** Implicit functions: Just as implicit definitions of the quadric shapes are a useful starting point for deriving ray intersection algorithms, more complex implicit functions can also be used to define interesting shapes. In particular, difficult-to-model organic shapes, water drops, and so on, can be well-represented by implicit surfaces. Blinn (1982a) introduced the idea of directly rendering implicit surfaces, and Wyvill and Wyvill (1989) give a basis function for implicit surfaces with a number of advantages compared to Blinn's.

Implement a method for finding ray intersections with general implicit surfaces and add it to pbrt. You may wish to read papers by Kalra and Barr (1989) and Hart (1996) for methods for ray-tracing them. Mitchell's algorithm for robust ray intersections with implicit surfaces gives another effective method for finding these intersections (Mitchell 1990); his method may be easier to implement than the others. For his technique, you may find Moore's book on interval arithmetic a useful reference (Moore 1966).

❸ **3.14** L-systems: A very successful technique for procedurally modeling plants was introduced to graphics by Alvy Ray Smith (1984), who applied *Lindenmayer systems* (L-systems) to model branching plant structures. Prusinkiewicz and collaborators have generalized this approach to encompass a much wider variety of types of plants and effects that determine their appearance (Prusinkiewicz 1986; Prusinkiewicz, James, and Mech 1994; Deussen et al. 1998; Prusinkiewicz et al. 2001). L-systems describe the branching structure of these types of shapes via a grammar. The grammar can be evaluated to form expressions that describe a topological representation of a plant, which can then be translated into a geometric representation. Add an L-system primitive to pbrt that takes a grammar as input and evaluates it on demand at rendering time to create the plant described by it.

CHAPTER FOUR

04 PRIMITIVES AND INTERSECTION ACCELERATION

The classes described in the last chapter focus exclusively on representing geometric properties of 3D objects. Although the Shape class is a convenient abstraction for geometric operations such as intersection and bounding, it doesn't contain enough information to fully describe an object in a scene. For example, it is necessary to bind material properties to each shape in order to specify its appearance. To accomplish these goals, this chapter introduces the Primitive class and provides a number of implementations.

Shapes to be rendered directly are represented by the GeometricPrimitive class. This class combines a Shape with a description of its appearance properties. So that the geometric and shading portions of pbrt can be cleanly separated, these appearance properties are encapsulated in the Material class, which is described in Chapter 10.

Some scenes contain many instances of the same geometry at different locations. Direct support for instancing can greatly reduce the memory requirements for representing such scenes, since it is only necessary to store a pointer to the geometry and a unique transformation for each instance of the primitive. pbrt provides the InstancePrimitive class for this task. Each InstancePrimitive has a separate Transform to place it in the scene but can share geometry with other InstancePrimitives. This allows the system to efficiently render extremely complex scenes such as the one in Figure 4.1.

Figure 4.1: This ecosystem scene makes heavy use of instancing as a mechanism for compressing the scene's description. There are only 1.1 million unique triangles in the scene, although thanks to object reuse through instancing, the total geometric complexity is 19.5 million triangles.

This chapter also introduces the Aggregate base class, which represents a container that can hold many Primitives. pbrt uses this class to implement *acceleration structures*—data structures that help reduce the otherwise $O(n)$ complexity of testing a ray for intersection with all n objects in a scene. Most rays will intersect only a few primitives and miss the others by a large distance. If an intersection acceleration technique can reject whole groups of primitives at once, there will be a substantial performance improvement compared to simply testing each ray against each primitive in turn. One benefit from reusing the Primitive interface for these acceleration structures is that pbrt can support hybrid approaches where an accelerator of one type holds accelerators of other types.

This chapter describes the implementation of two accelerators, one (GridAccel) based on overlaying a uniform grid over the scene, and the other (KdTreeAccel) based on adaptive recursive spatial subdivision.

4.1 PRIMITIVE INTERFACE AND GEOMETRIC PRIMITIVES

The abstract `Primitive` base class is the bridge between the geometry processing and shading subsystems of pbrt. It inherits from the `ReferenceCounted` base class, which automatically tracks how many references there are to an object, freeing its storage when the last reference goes out of scope. Other classes that store `Primitives` shouldn't store pointers to them, but instead hold a `Reference<Primitive>`, which ensures that reference counts are computed correctly. The `Reference` class otherwise behaves as if it was a pointer to a `Primitive`.

⟨*Primitive Declarations*⟩ ≡
```
class COREDLL Primitive : public ReferenceCounted {
public:
    ⟨Primitive Interface 171⟩
};
```

Because the `Primitive` class connects geometry and shading, its interface contains methods related to both. There are five geometric routines, all of which are similar to a corresponding Shape method. The first, `Primitive::WorldBound()`, returns a box that encloses the primitive's geometry in world space. There are many uses for such a bound; one of the most important is to place the `Primitive` in the acceleration data structures.

⟨*Primitive Interface*⟩ ≡   171
```
virtual BBox WorldBound() const = 0;
```

Similarly to the Shape class, all primitives must be able to either determine if a given ray intersects their geometry or else refine themselves into one or more new primitives. Like the Shape interface, `Primitive` has a `Primitive::CanIntersect()` method so that pbrt can determine whether the underlying geometry is intersectable or not.

One difference from the Shape interface is that the `Primitive` intersection methods return `Intersection` structures rather than `DifferentialGeometry`. These `Intersection` structures hold more information about the intersection than just the local geometric information, such as information about the material properties at the hit point.

Another difference is that `Shape::Intersect()` returns the parametric distance along the ray to the intersection in a `float *` output variable, while `Primitive::Intersect()` is responsible for updating `Ray::maxt` with this value if an intersection is found. This way, the geometric routines from the last chapter do not need to know how the parametric distance will be used by the rest of the system.

⟨*Primitive Interface*⟩+≡   **171**
```
virtual bool CanIntersect() const;
virtual bool Intersect(const Ray &r, Intersection *in) const = 0;
virtual bool IntersectP(const Ray &r) const = 0;
virtual void Refine(vector<Reference<Primitive> > &refined) const;
```

The Intersection structure holds information about a ray-primitive intersection, including information about the differential geometry of the point on the surface, a pointer to the Primitive that the ray hit, and its world-to-object-space transformation.

⟨*Primitive Declarations*⟩+≡
```
struct COREDLL Intersection {
    ⟨Intersection Public Methods⟩
    DifferentialGeometry dg;
    const Primitive *primitive;
    Transform WorldToObject;
};
```

It may be necessary to repeatedly refine a primitive until all of the primitives it has returned are themselves intersectable. The Primitive::FullyRefine() utility method handles this task. Its implementation is straightforward. It maintains a queue of primitives to be refined (called todo in the following code) and invokes the Primitive::Refine() method repeatedly on entries in that queue. Intersectable Primitives returned by Primitive::Refine() are placed on the output queue, while nonintersectable ones are placed on the todo list by the Refine() routine.

⟨*Primitive Interface*⟩+≡   **171**
```
void FullyRefine(vector<Reference<Primitive> > &refined) const;
```

⟨*Primitive Method Definitions*⟩≡
```
void
Primitive::FullyRefine(vector<Reference<Primitive> > &refined) const {
    vector<Reference<Primitive> > todo;
    todo.push_back(const_cast<Primitive *>(this));
    while (todo.size()) {
        ⟨Refine last primitive in todo list 172⟩
    }
}
```

⟨*Refine last primitive in todo list*⟩≡   **172**
```
Reference<Primitive> prim = todo.back();
todo.pop_back();
if (prim->CanIntersect())
    refined.push_back(prim);
else
    prim->Refine(todo);
```

In addition to the geometric methods, a `Primitive` object has two methods related to its material properties. The first, `Primitive::GetAreaLight()`, returns a pointer to the `AreaLight` that describes the primitive's emission distribution, if the primitive is itself a light source. If the primitive is not emissive, this method returns `NULL`.

The second method, `Primitive::GetBSDF()`, returns a representation of the light-scattering properties of the material at the given point on the surface in a BSDF object (which is introduced in Section 10.1). In addition to the differential geometry at the hit point, it takes the world-to-object-space transformation as a parameter. This informa-tion will be required by the `InstancePrimitive` class, described later in this chapter.

⟨*Primitive Interface*⟩+≡   171
```
virtual const AreaLight *GetAreaLight() const = 0;
virtual BSDF *GetBSDF(const DifferentialGeometry &dg,
    const Transform &WorldToObject) const = 0;
```

4.1.1 GEOMETRIC PRIMITIVES

The `GeometricPrimitive` class represents a single shape (e.g., a sphere) in the scene. One `GeometricPrimitive` is allocated for each shape in the scene description provided by the user. It is implemented in the files core/primitive.h🔴 and core/primitive.cpp. 🔴

⟨*Primitive Declarations*⟩+≡
```
class GeometricPrimitive : public Primitive {
public:
    ⟨GeometricPrimitive Public Methods 173⟩
private:
    ⟨GeometricPrimitive Private Data 173⟩
};
```

Each `GeometricPrimitive` holds a reference to a `Shape` and its `Material`. In addition, because primitives in pbrt may be area light sources, it stores a pointer to an `AreaLight` object that describes its emission characteristics (this pointer is set to `NULL` if the primitive does not emit light).

⟨*GeometricPrimitive Private Data*⟩≡   173
```
Reference<Shape> shape;
Reference<Material> material;
AreaLight *areaLight;
```

The `GeometricPrimitive` constructor initializes these variables from the parameters passed to it. Its implementation is omitted.

⟨*GeometricPrimitive Public Methods*⟩≡   173
```
GeometricPrimitive(const Reference<Shape> &s,
                   const Reference<Material> &m,
                   AreaLight *a);
```

Most of the methods of the `Primitive` interface related to geometric processing are simply forwarded to the corresponding Shape method. For example, `GeometricPrimitive::Intersect()` calls the `Shape::Intersect()` method of its enclosed `Shape` to do the actual geometric intersection and initializes an `Intersection` object to describe the intersection, if any. It also uses the returned parametric hit distance to update the `Ray::maxt` member. The primary advantage of storing the distance to the closest hit in `Ray::maxt` is that it may be possible to stop performing intersection tests with any primitives that lie farther along the ray than any already found.

⟨*GeometricPrimitive Method Definitions*⟩ ≡

```
bool GeometricPrimitive::Intersect(const Ray &r,
                                   Intersection *isect) const {
    float thit;
    if (!shape->Intersect(r, &thit, &isect->dg))
        return false;
    isect->primitive = this;
    isect->WorldToObject = shape->WorldToObject;
    r.maxt = thit;
    return true;
}
```

We won't include the implementations of the `GeometricPrimitive`'s `WorldBound()`, `IntersectP()`, `CanIntersect()`, or `Refine()` methods here; they just forward these requests on to the `Shape` in a similar manner. Similarly, `GetAreaLight()` just returns the `GeometricPrimitive::areaLight` member.

Finally, the `GetBSDF()` method calls to its `Shape` to find the shading geometry at the point and forwards the request on to the `Material`.

⟨*GeometricPrimitive Method Definitions*⟩+≡

```
BSDF *GeometricPrimitive::GetBSDF(const DifferentialGeometry &dg,
                                 const Transform &WorldToObject) const {
    DifferentialGeometry dgs;
    shape->GetShadingGeometry(WorldToObject.GetInverse(), dg, &dgs);
    return material->GetBSDF(dg, dgs);
}
```

4.1.2 OBJECT INSTANCING

Object instancing is a classic technique in rendering that reuses transformed copies of a single collection of geometry at multiple positions in a scene. For example, in a model of a concert hall with thousands of identical seats, the scene description can be compressed substantially if all of the seats refer to a shared geometric representation of a single seat. The ecosystem scene in Figure 4.1 has over 4000 individual plants of various types, although only 61 unique plant models. Because each plant model is instanced multiple times, the complete scene has 19.5 million triangles total, although only 1.1 million triangles are stored in memory, thanks to primitive reuse through object instancing. pbrt uses approximately 300 MB of memory when rendering this scene.

Object instancing is handled by the InstancePrimitive class. It takes a reference to the shared Primitive that represents the instanced model, and the instance-to-world-space transformation that places it in the scene. If the geometry to be instanced is described by multiple Primitives, the calling code is responsible for placing them in an Aggregate class so that only a single Primitive needs to be stored here.

The InstancePrimitive similarly requires that the primitive be intersectable. It would be a waste of time and memory for all of the instances to individually refine the primitive. See the pbrtObjectInstance() function in Section B.3.6 of Appendix B for the code that creates instances based on the scene description file, refining and creating aggregates as described here.

⟨*Primitive Declarations*⟩ +≡
```
classInstancePrimitive : public Primitive {
public:
    ⟨InstancePrimitive Public Methods 175⟩
private:
    ⟨InstancePrimitive Private Data 175⟩
};
```

⟨*InstancePrimitive Public Methods*⟩ ≡   **175**
```
InstancePrimitive(Reference<Primitive> &i, const Transform &i2w) {
    instance = i;
    InstanceToWorld = i2w;
    WorldToInstance = i2w.GetInverse();
}
```

⟨*InstancePrimitive Private Data*⟩ ≡   **175**
```
Reference<Primitive> instance;
Transform InstanceToWorld, WorldToInstance;
```

The key task of the InstancePrimitive is to mediate between the Primitive interface that it implements and the Primitive that it holds a reference to, accounting for the effects of the additional transformation matrix that it holds. The InstancePrimitive's WorldToInstance transformation defines the transformation from world space to the coordinate system of this particular instance of the shared geometry. The shared geometry in instance has its own transformation that should be interpreted as the transformation from an InstancePrimitive's coordinate system to object space. The complete transformation to world space requires both of these transformations together.

Thus, the InstancePrimitive::Intersect() method transforms the given ray to the shared geometry's coordinate system and passes the transformed ray to the Intersect()

routine of the shared geometry. If a hit is found, the DifferentialGeometry at the intersection point needs to be transformed to world space. This task is handled by the straightforward ⟨*Transform instance's differential geometry to world space*⟩ fragment, not included here. This way, the instanced primitive is unaware that its concept of "world space" is actually not the real scene world space; the InstancePrimitive does the necessary work so that instances behave as expected.

⟨*InstancePrimitive Method Definitions*⟩ ≡
```
  bool InstancePrimitive::Intersect(const Ray &r,
                                    Intersection *isect) const {
    Ray ray = WorldToInstance(r);
    if (!instance->Intersect(ray, isect))
        return false;
    r.maxt = ray.maxt;
    isect->WorldToObject = isect->WorldToObject * WorldToInstance;
    ⟨Transform instance's differential geometry to world space⟩
    return true;
  }
```

The rest of the geometric Primitive methods are forwarded on to the shared instance, with the results similarly transformed as appropriate by the InstancePrimitive's transformation.

⟨*InstancePrimitive Public Methods*⟩+≡   **175**
```
  BBox WorldBound() const {
    return InstanceToWorld(instance->WorldBound());
  }
```

The InstancePrimitive::GetAreaLight() and InstancePrimitive::GetBSDF() methods should never be called. The corresponding methods in the primitive that the ray actually hit will be called instead. Calling the InstancePrimitve implementations (not shown here) results in a run time error.

4.2 AGGREGATES

Acceleration structures are one of the components at the heart of any ray tracer. Without algorithms to reduce the number of unnecessary ray intersection tests, tracing a single ray through a scene would take time linear in the number of primitives in the scene, since the ray would need to be tested against each primitive in turn to find the closest intersection. However, doing so is extremely wasteful in most scenes, since the ray passes nowhere near the vast majority of primitives. The goal of acceleration structures is to allow the quick, simultaneous rejection of *groups* of primitives and also to order the search process so that nearby intersections are likely to be found first and farther away ones can potentially be ignored.

Because ray-object intersections often account for the bulk of execution time in ray tracers, there has been a substantial amount of research into algorithms for ray intersection acceleration. We will not try to explore all of this work here, but refer the interested reader to references in the "Further Reading" section at the end of this chapter and in particular Arvo and Kirk's chapter in *An Introduction to Ray Tracing* (Glassner 1989a), which has a useful taxonomy for organizing different approaches to ray-tracing acceleration.

Broadly speaking, there are two main approaches to this problem: spatial subdivision and object subdivision. Spatial subdivision algorithms decompose 3D space into regions (e.g., by superimposing a grid of axis-aligned boxes on the scene) and record which `Primitives` overlap which regions. In some algorithms, the regions may also be adaptively subdivided based on the number of primitives that overlap them. When a ray intersection needs to be found, the sequence of these regions that the ray passes through is computed and only the primitives in the overlapping regions are tested for intersection.

In contrast, object subdivision is based on progressively breaking the objects in the scene down into smaller sets of constituent objects. For example, a model of a room might be broken down into four walls, a ceiling, and a chair. If a ray doesn't intersect the room's bounding volume, then all of its `Primitives` can be culled. Otherwise the ray is tested against each of them. If it hit the chair's bounding volume, for example, then it might be tested against each of its legs, the seat, and the back. Otherwise the chair is culled.

Both of these approaches have been quite successful at solving the general problem of ray intersection computational requirements; there's no fundamental reason to prefer one over the other. The `GridAccel` and `KdTreeAccel` in this chapter are both based on the spatial subdivision approach.

The `Aggregate` class provides an interface for grouping multiple `Primitive` objects together. Because `Aggregate`s themselves implement the `Primitive` interface, no special support is required elsewhere in pbrt for acceleration. `Integrator`s can be written as if there was just a single `Primitive` in the scene, checking for intersections without needing to be concerned about how they're actually found. Furthermore, by implementing acceleration in this way, it is easy to experiment with new acceleration techniques by simply adding a new `Aggregate` primitive to pbrt.

⟨*Primitive Declarations*⟩+≡
```
class COREDLL Aggregate : public Primitive {
public:
    ⟨Aggregate Public Methods⟩
};
```

Like `InstancePrimitive`s, the `Aggregate` intersection routines set the `Intersection::primitive` pointer to the primitive that the ray actually hit, not the aggregate that holds the primitive. Because pbrt uses this pointer to obtain information about the primitive being hit (its reflection and emission properties), the `Aggregate::GetAreaLight()` and

`Aggregate::GetBSDF()` methods should never be called, so the implementations of those methods (not shown here) will simply report a run time error.

4.2.1 RAY-BOX INTERSECTIONS

Both the `GridAccel` and the `KdTreeAccel` in the next two sections store a `BBox` that surrounds all of their primitives. This box can be used to quickly determine if a ray doesn't intersect any of the primitives; if the ray misses the box, it also must miss all of the primitives inside it. Furthermore, both of these accelerators use the point at which the ray enters the bounding box and the point at which it exits as part of the input to their traversal algorithms. Therefore, we will add a `BBox` method, `BBox::IntersectP()`, that checks for a ray-box intersection and returns the two parametric t values of the intersection, if any.

One way to think of bounding boxes is as the intersection of three slabs, where a slab is the region of space between two parallel planes. To intersect a ray against a box, we intersect the ray against each of the box's three slabs in turn. Because the slabs are aligned with the three coordinate axes, a number of optimizations can be made in the ray-slab tests.

The basic ray–bounding box intersection algorithm works as follows: We start with a parametric interval that covers that range of positions t along the ray where we're interested in finding intersections; typically, this is $[0, \infty)$. We will then successively compute the two parametric t positions where the ray intersects each axis-aligned slab. We compute the set intersection of the per-slab intersection interval with our `BBox` intersection interval, returning failure if we find that the resulting interval is degenerate. If, after checking all three slabs, the interval is nondegenerate, we have the parametric range of the ray that is inside the box. Figure 4.2 illustrates this process, and Figure 4.3 shows the basic geometry of a ray and a slab.

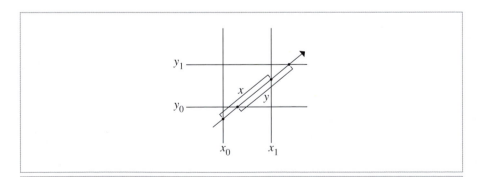

Figure 4.2: Intersecting a Ray with an Axis-Aligned Bounding Box. We compute intersection points with each slab in turn, progressively narrowing the parametric interval. Here in 2D, the intersection of the x and y extents along the ray gives the extent where the ray is inside the box.

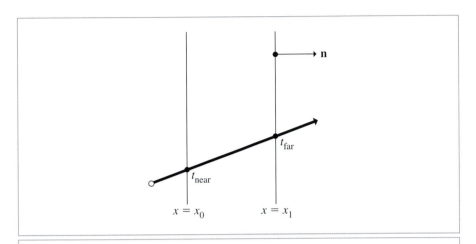

Figure 4.3: Intersecting a Ray with an Axis-Aligned Slab. The two planes shown here are described by $x = c$ for some constant value c. The normal of each plane is $(1, 0, 0)$. Unless the ray is parallel to the planes, it will intersect the slab twice, at parametric positions t_{near} and t_{far}.

If the `BBox::IntersectP()` method returns true, the intersection's parametric range is returned in the optional arguments `hitt0` and `hitt1`. Intersections outside of the `Ray::mint/Ray::maxt` range of the ray are ignored. If the ray's starting point, `ray(ray.mint)`, is inside the box, `ray.mint` is returned for `hitt0`.

⟨*BBox Method Definitions*⟩+≡
```
bool BBox::IntersectP(const Ray &ray, float *hitt0,
                      float *hitt1) const {
    float t0 = ray.mint, t1 = ray.maxt;
    for (int i = 0; i < 3; ++i) {
        ⟨Update interval for ith bounding box slab 180⟩
    }
    if (hitt0) *hitt0 = t0;
    if (hitt1) *hitt1 = t1;
    return true;
}
```

BBox 60
BBox::IntersectP() 179
Ray 59
Ray::maxt 58
Ray::mint 58

For each pair of planes, this routine needs to compute two ray-plane intersections, giving the parametric t values where the intersections occur. Consider the slab along the x axis: it can be described by the two planes through the points $(x_1, 0, 0)$ and $(x_2, 0, 0)$, each with normal $(1, 0, 0)$. Consider the first t value for a plane intersection, t_1. From the ray-plane intersection equation from Section 3.4.3, we have

$$t_1 = -\frac{((o - (x_1, 0, 0)) \cdot (1, 0, 0))}{(\mathbf{d} \cdot (1, 0, 0))}.$$

Because the y and z components of the normal are zero, we can use the definition of the dot product to simplify this substantially:

$$t_1 = -\frac{o_x - x_1}{d_x} = \frac{x_1 - o_x}{d_x}.$$

The code to compute these values starts by computing the reciprocal of the corresponding component of the ray direction so that it can multiply by this factor instead of performing multiple divisions. Note that although it divides by this component, it is not necessary to verify that it is nonzero. If it is zero, then invRayDir will hold an infinite value, either $-\infty$ or ∞, and the rest of the algorithm still works correctly.[1]

⟨*Update interval for* i*th bounding box slab*⟩ ≡   179
```
    float invRayDir = 1.f / ray.d[i];
    float tNear = (pMin[i] - ray.o[i]) * invRayDir;
    float tFar  = (pMax[i] - ray.o[i]) * invRayDir;
    ⟨Update parametric interval from slab intersection ts  180⟩
```

The two distances are reordered so that t_{near} holds the closer intersection and t_{far} the farther one. This gives a parametric range $[t_{near}, t_{far}]$, which is used to compute the set intersection with the current range $[t_0, t_1]$ to compute a new range. If this new range is empty (i.e., $t_0 > t_1$), then the code can immediately return failure. There is another floating-point related subtlety here: in the case where the ray origin is in the plane of one of the bounding box slabs and the ray lies in the plane of the slab, it is possible that tNear or tFar will be computed by an expression of the form 0/0, which results in an IEEE floating-point "not a number" (NaN) value. Like infinity values, NaNs have well-specified semantics: for example, any logical comparison involving a NaN always evaluates to false. Therefore, the code that updates the values of t0 and t1 is carefully written so that if tNear or tFar is NaN, then t0 or t1 won't ever take on a NaN value but will always remain unchanged.

⟨*Update parametric interval from slab intersection t s*⟩ ≡   180
```
    if (tNear > tFar) swap(tNear, tFar);
    t0 = tNear > t0 ? tNear : t0;
    t1 = tFar  < t1 ? tFar  : t1;
    if (t0 > t1) return false;
```

---

1   This assumes that the architecture being used supports IEEE floating-point arithmetic (Institute of Electrical and Electronic Engineers 1985), which is universal on modern systems. The relevant properties of IEEE floating-point arithmetic are that for all $v > 0$, $v/0 = \infty$ and for all $w < 0$, $w/0 = -\infty$, where ∞ is a special value such that any positive number multiplied by ∞ gives ∞, any negative number multiplied by ∞ gives $-\infty$, and so on.

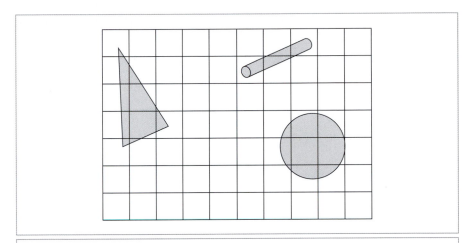

Figure 4.4: The regular grid accelerator divides space into regularly sized cells. Each one stores a reference to the `Primitives` that overlap it.

4.3 GRID ACCELERATOR

`GridAccel` is an accelerator that divides an axis-aligned region of space into equal-sized chunks (called *voxels*). Each voxel stores references to the primitives that overlap it (Figure 4.4). Given a ray, the grid steps through each of the voxels that the ray passes through in order, checking for intersections with only the primitives in each voxel. Useless ray intersection tests are reduced substantially because primitives far away from the ray aren't considered at all. Furthermore, because the voxels are considered from near to far along the ray, it is possible to stop performing intersection tests once an intersection has been found and it is certain that it is not possible for there to be any closer intersections.

The `GridAccel` structure can be initialized quickly, and a simple computation determines the sequence of voxels through which a given ray passes. However, this simplicity is a doubled-edged sword. `GridAccel` can suffer from poor performance when the primitives in the scene aren't distributed evenly throughout space. If there's a small region of space with a lot of geometry in it, all that geometry might fall in a single voxel, and performance will suffer when a ray passes through that voxel, as many intersection tests will be performed. This is sometimes referred to as the "teapot in a stadium" problem. The basic problem is that the data structure cannot adapt well to the distribution of the data that it is storing: if a very fine grid is used, too much time is spent stepping through empty space, and if the grid is too coarse, there is little benefit from the grid at all. The `KdTreeAccel` in the next section adapts to the distribution of geometry such that it doesn't suffer from this problem.

The implementation of pbrt's grid accelerator is defined in `accelerators/grid.cpp`. ⊕

⟨*GridAccel Declarations*⟩ ≡
```
    class  GridAccel : public Aggregate {
    public:
        ⟨GridAccel Public Methods  198⟩
    private:
        ⟨GridAccel Private Methods  187⟩
        ⟨GridAccel Private Data  183⟩
    };
```

4.3.1 CREATION

The `GridAccel` constructor takes a vector of `Primitives` to be stored in the grid. It automatically determines the number of voxels to store in the grid based on the number of primitives.

One factor that adds to the complexity of the grid's implementation is the fact that some of these primitives may not be directly intersectable (they may return `false` from `Primitive::CanIntersect()`) and need to refine themselves into subprimitives before intersection tests can be performed. This is a problem because when the grid is being built, we might have a scene with a single primitive in it and choose to build a coarse grid with few voxels. However, if the primitive is later refined for intersection tests, it might turn into millions of primitives, and the original grid resolution would be far too small to efficiently find intersections. pbrt addresses this problem in one of two ways:

- If the `refineImmediately` flag to the grid constructor is `true`, all of the `Primitives` are refined until they have turned into intersectable primitives. This may waste time and memory for scenes where some of the primitives wouldn't ever need to be refined since no rays approached them.
- Otherwise, primitives are refined only when a ray enters one of the voxels they are stored in. If they create multiple `Primitives` when refined, the new primitives are stored in a new instance of a `GridAccel` that replaces the original `Primitive` in the top-level grid. This allows the implementation to handle primitive refinement without needing to rebuild the entire grid each time another primitive is refined. A flag to the constructor indicates whether this grid was constructed explicitly by pbrt or implicitly by a `Refine()` method. This is worth tracking for subtle issues related to statistics collection.

⟨*GridAccel Method Definitions*⟩ ≡
```
    GridAccel::GridAccel(const vector<Reference<Primitive> > &p,
                         bool forRefined, bool refineImmediately)
        : gridForRefined(forRefined) {
```
⟨*Initialize* prims *with primitives for grid* **183**⟩
⟨*Initialize mailboxes for grid* **184**⟩
⟨*Compute bounds and choose grid resolution* **185**⟩
⟨*Compute voxel widths and allocate voxels* **186**⟩
⟨*Add primitives to grid voxels* **186**⟩
```
    }
```

⟨*GridAccel Private Data*⟩ ≡   **182**
```
    bool gridForRefined;
```

First, the constructor determines the final set of `Primitives` to store in the grid, either directly using the primitives passed in or refining all of them until they are intersectable.

⟨*Initialize* prims *with primitives for grid*⟩ ≡   **183**
```
    vector<Reference<Primitive> > prims;
    if (refineImmediately)
        for (u_int i = 0; i < p.size(); ++i)
            p[i]->FullyRefine(prims);
    else
        prims = p;
```

Because primitives may overlap multiple grid voxels, there is the possibility that a ray will be tested multiple times against the same primitive as it passes through those voxels (Figure 4.5). A technique called *mailboxing* makes it possible to quickly determine if a ray has already been tested for intersection with a particular primitive, so these extra tests can be avoided. In this technique, each ray is assigned a unique integer id. The id of the last ray that was tested against each primitive is stored along with the primitive itself. As the ray passes through voxels in the grid, the ray's id is compared with the primitives' ids; if they are different, the ray-primitive intersection test is performed and the primitive's id is updated to match the ray's. If the ray encounters the same primitive in later voxels, the ids will match and the test is trivially skipped.[2]

The `GridAccel` constructor creates a `MailboxPrim` structure for each primitive. Grid voxels store pointers to the `MailboxPrims` of the primitives that overlap them. The `MailboxPrim` stores both a reference to the primitive as well as the integer tag that identifies the last

2   This approach depends on the fact that the grid finds the intersection for a ray and returns before any other rays are passed to `GridAccel::Intersect()`; if this was not the case, the grid would still find the right ray-primitive intersections, although unnecessary tests might be performed as multiple rays overwrote the mailbox ids in primitives that they passed by. In particular, if pbrt was multithreaded, the mailboxing scheme would need to be revisited as rays from different threads would sometimes be passing through the grid simultaneously. In general, parallel ray tracing makes mailboxing much more complicated.

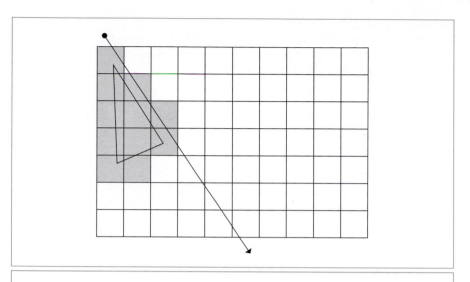

Figure 4.5: The triangle primitive overlaps multiple voxels in the grid, indicated here by shaded cells. Mailboxing eliminates the redundant intersection tests for rays like the one shown here that pass through multiple cells that the triangle overlaps as well.

ray that was tested against it. All of the mailboxes are allocated in a single contiguous cache-aligned block for improved memory performance.

⟨*Initialize mailboxes for grid*⟩ ≡   **183**
```
nMailboxes = prims.size();
mailboxes = (MailboxPrim *)AllocAligned(nMailboxes *
                                 sizeof(MailboxPrim));
for (u_int i = 0; i < nMailboxes; ++i)
    new (&mailboxes[i]) MailboxPrim(prims[i]);
```

⟨*MailboxPrim Declarations*⟩ ≡
```
struct MailboxPrim {
    MailboxPrim(const Reference<Primitive> &p) {
        primitive = p;
        lastMailboxId = -1;
    }
    Reference<Primitive> primitive;
    int lastMailboxId;
};
```

AllocAligned() 842
MailboxPrim 184
Primitive 171
Reference 839

⟨*GridAccel Private Data*⟩ + ≡   **182**
```
u_int nMailboxes;
MailboxPrim *mailboxes;
```

The constructor next computes the overall bounds of the primitives and determines how many voxels to create along each of the x, y, and z axes. The voxelsPerUnitDist variable is computed in a later fragment, giving the average number of voxels that should be created per unit distance in each of the three directions. Given that value, multiplication by the grid's extent in each direction gives the number of voxels to make. The number of voxels in any direction is capped at 64 to avoid creating enormous data structures for complex scenes.

⟨*Compute bounds and choose grid resolution*⟩ ≡   **183**
```
for (u_int i = 0; i < prims.size(); ++i)
    bounds = Union(bounds, prims[i]->WorldBound());
Vector delta = bounds.pMax - bounds.pMin;
```
⟨*Find* voxelsPerUnitDist *for grid* **186**⟩
```
for (int axis = 0; axis < 3; ++axis) {
    NVoxels[axis] = Round2Int(delta[axis] * voxelsPerUnitDist);
    NVoxels[axis] = Clamp(NVoxels[axis], 1, 64);
}
```

⟨*GridAccel Private Data*⟩+≡   **182**
```
int NVoxels[3];
BBox bounds;
```

As a first approximation to choosing a grid size, the total number of voxels should be roughly proportional to the total number of primitives. If the primitives were uniformly distributed, this would mean that a constant number of primitives were in each voxel. While increasing the number of voxels improves efficiency by reducing the average number of primitives per voxel (and thus reducing the number of ray-object intersection tests that need to be performed), doing so also increases memory use, hurts cache performance, and increases the time spent tracing the ray's path through the greater number of voxels it overlaps. On the other hand, too few voxels obviously leads to poor performance, due to an increased number of ray-primitive intersection tests to be performed.

Given the goal of having the number of voxels be proportional to the number of primitives, the cube root of the number of objects is an appropriate starting point for the grid resolution in each direction. In practice, this value is typically scaled by an empirically chosen factor; in pbrt we use a scale of three. Whichever of the x, y, or z dimensions has the largest extent will have exactly $3\sqrt[3]{N}$ voxels for a scene with N primitives. The number of voxels in the other two directions are set in an effort to create voxels that are as close to cubes as possible. The voxelsPerUnitDist variable is the foundation of these computations; it gives the number of voxels to create per unit distance. Its value is set such that cubeRoot voxels will be created along the axis with the largest extent.

⟨*Find* voxelsPerUnitDist *for grid*⟩ ≡   **185**

```
int maxAxis = bounds.MaximumExtent();
float invMaxWidth = 1.f / delta[maxAxis];
float cubeRoot = 3.f * powf(float(prims.size()), 1.f/3.f);
float voxelsPerUnitDist = cubeRoot * invMaxWidth;
```

Given the number of voxels in each dimension, the constructor sets GridAccel::Width, which holds the world space widths of the voxels in each direction. It also precomputes the GridAccel::InvWidth values, so that routines that would otherwise divide by the Width value can perform a multiplication rather than dividing. Finally, it allocates an array of pointers to Voxel structures for each of the voxels in the grid. These pointers are set to NULL initially and will only be allocated for any voxel with one or more overlapping primitives.[3]

⟨*Compute voxel widths and allocate voxels*⟩ ≡   **183**

```
for (int axis = 0; axis < 3; ++axis) {
    Width[axis] = delta[axis] / NVoxels[axis];
    InvWidth[axis] = (Width[axis] == 0.f) ? 0.f : 1.f / Width[axis];
}
int nVoxels = NVoxels[0] * NVoxels[1] * NVoxels[2];
voxels = (Voxel **)AllocAligned(nVoxels * sizeof(Voxel *));
memset(voxels, 0, nVoxels * sizeof(Voxel *));
```

⟨*GridAccel Private Data*⟩+≡   **182**

```
Vector Width, InvWidth;
Voxel **voxels;
```

Once the voxels themselves have been allocated, primitives can be added to the voxels that they overlap. The GridAccel constructor adds each primitive's corresponding MailboxPrim to the voxels that its bounding box overlaps.

⟨*Add primitives to grid voxels*⟩ ≡   **183**

```
for (u_int i = 0; i < prims.size(); ++i) {
    ⟨Find voxel extent of primitive 187⟩
    ⟨Add primitive to overlapping voxels 188⟩
}
```

First, the world space bounds of the primitive are converted to the integer voxel coordinates that contain its two opposite corners. This is done by the utility function

---

3   Some grid implementations try to save even more memory by using a hash table from (x, y, z) voxel number to voxel structures. This saves the memory for the voxels array, which may be substantial if the grid has very small voxels, and the vast majority of them are empty. However, this approach increases the computational expense of finding the Voxel structure for each voxel that a ray passes through.

GridAccel::PosToVoxel(), which turns a world space (x, y, z) position into the coordinates of the voxel that contains that point.

⟨*Find voxel extent of primitive*⟩ ≡   186
```
BBox pb = prims[i]->WorldBound();
int vmin[3], vmax[3];
for (int axis = 0; axis < 3; ++axis) {
    vmin[axis] = PosToVoxel(pb.pMin, axis);
    vmax[axis] = PosToVoxel(pb.pMax, axis);
}
```

⟨*GridAccel Private Methods*⟩ ≡   182
```
int PosToVoxel(const Point &P, int axis) const {
    int v = Float2Int((P[axis] - bounds.pMin[axis]) *
                          InvWidth[axis]);
    return Clamp(v, 0, NVoxels[axis]-1);
}
```

The GridAccel::VoxelToPos() method is the opposite of GridAccel::PosToVoxel(); it returns the position of a particular voxel's lower corner. For efficiency it has two forms—the first does this calculation for only a single axis, while the second does it for all three simultaneously.

⟨*GridAccel Private Methods*⟩+≡   182
```
float VoxelToPos(int p, int axis) const {
    return bounds.pMin[axis] + p * Width[axis];
}
```

⟨*GridAccel Private Methods*⟩+≡   182
```
Point VoxelToPos(int x, int y, int z) const {
    return bounds.pMin +
        Vector(x * Width[0], y * Width[1], z * Width[2]);
}
```

The primitive is now added to all of the voxels that its bounds overlap. Using its bounds for this test is a conservative test for voxel overlap—at worst it will overestimate the voxels that the primitive overlaps. Figure 4.6 shows an example of two cases where this method leads to primitives being stored in more voxels than necessary. Exercise 4.11 at the end of this chapter describes a more accurate method for associating primitives with voxels.

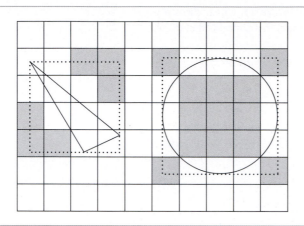

Figure 4.6: Two examples of cases where using the bounding box of a primitive to determine which grid voxels it should be stored in will cause it to be stored in a number of voxels unnecessarily: On the left, a long skinny triangle has a lot of empty space inside its axis-aligned bounding box, and it is unnecessarily added to the shaded voxels. On the right, the surface of the sphere doesn't intersect many of the voxels inside its bound, and they are also inaccurately included in the sphere's extent. While this error degrades performance, it doesn't lead to incorrect ray intersection results.

⟨*Add primitive to overlapping voxels*⟩ ≡   186
```
for (int z = vmin[2]; z <= vmax[2]; ++z)
    for (int y = vmin[1]; y <= vmax[1]; ++y)
        for (int x = vmin[0]; x <= vmax[0]; ++x) {
            int offset = Offset(x, y, z);
            if (!voxels[offset]) {
                ⟨Allocate new voxel and store primitive in it  189⟩
            }
            else {
                ⟨Add primitive to already-allocated voxel  189⟩
            }
        }
```

The `GridAccel::Offset()` utility functions give the offset into the `voxels` array for a particular (x, y, z) voxel. It is the standard indexing scheme in C++ for encoding a multidimensional array in a 1D array. We have localized this computation into a separate function, however, in order to make it easier to experiment with different array layouts, such as blocked schemes for improved cache performance.

⟨*GridAccel Private Methods*⟩+≡   182
```
inline int Offset(int x, int y, int z) const {
    return z*NVoxels[0]*NVoxels[1] + y*NVoxels[0] + x;
}
```

To further reduce memory used for dynamically allocated voxels and to improve their memory locality, the grid constructor uses an ObjectArena to hand out memory for voxels. The ObjectArena, implemented in Section A.2.4 in Appendix A, provides custom allocation routines based on allocating large blocks of memory and using them to service memory allocation requests. It doesn't support freeing memory from individual allocations; it will only free all of them at once. This improves allocation performance and practically eliminates memory overhead for bookkeeping, thus reducing the system's overall memory use as well.

⟨*Allocate new voxel and store primitive in it*⟩ ≡   **188**
```
voxels[offset] = new (voxelArena) Voxel(&mailboxes[i]);
```

⟨*GridAccel Private Data*⟩+≡   **182**
```
ObjectArena<Voxel> voxelArena;
```

If this isn't the first primitive to overlap this voxel, the Voxel has already been allocated and the primitive is handed off to the Voxel::AddPrimitive() method.

⟨*Add primitive to already-allocated voxel*⟩ ≡   **188**
```
voxels[offset]->AddPrimitive(&mailboxes[i]);
```

The Voxel structure records which primitives overlap its extent. Because many Voxels may be allocated for a grid, we use a few simple techniques to keep the size of a Voxel small: variables that record its basic properties are packed into a single 32-bit word, and we use a union to overlap two pointers only one of which will actually be used depending on the number of overlapping primitives. An added reward for reducing memory use in this manner is that the system's performance may improve due to better cache performance.

⟨*Voxel Declarations*⟩ ≡
```
struct Voxel {
    ⟨Voxel Public Methods 190⟩
    union {
        MailboxPrim *onePrimitive;
        MailboxPrim **primitives;
    };
    u_int allCanIntersect:1;
    u_int nPrimitives:31;
};
```

When a Voxel is first allocated, only a single primitive has been found that overlaps it, so Voxel::nPrimitives is one, and Voxel::onePrimitive is used to store a pointer to its MailboxPrim. As more primitives are found to overlap, Voxel::nPrimitives will be greater than one, and Voxel::primitives is set to point to a dynamically allocated array of pointers to MailboxPrim structures. Because these conditions are mutually exclusive, the pointer to the single primitive and pointer to the array of pointers to primitives can share the same memory by being stored in a union. Voxel::allCanIntersect is used to record if all of the primitives in the voxel are intersectable or if some need refinement. Initially, it is conservatively set to false.

⟨*Voxel Public Methods*⟩ ≡   **189**
```
    Voxel(MailboxPrim *op) {
        allCanIntersect = false;
        nPrimitives = 1;
        onePrimitive = op;
    }
```

When `Voxel::AddPrimitive()` is called, this must mean that two or more primitives overlap the voxel, so the primitives' `MailboxPrim` pointers will be stored in its `Voxel::primitives` array. Memory for this array must be allocated in two cases: if the voxel currently holds a single primitive and it is necessary to store a second, or if the allocated array is full. Rather than using more space in the voxel structure to store the current size of the array, the code here follows the convention that the array size will always be a power of two. Thus, whenever the `Voxel::nPrimitives` count is a power of two, the array has been filled and more memory is needed.

⟨*Voxel Public Methods*⟩+≡   **189**
```
    void AddPrimitive(MailboxPrim *prim) {
        if (nPrimitives == 1) {
            ⟨Allocate initial primitives array in voxel 190⟩
        }
        else if (IsPowerOf2(nPrimitives)) {
            ⟨Increase size of primitives array in voxel 191⟩
        }
        primitives[nPrimitives] = prim;
        ++nPrimitives;
    }
```

Recall that `Voxel::onePrimitive` and `Voxel::primitives` are stored in a union. Therefore, it is important to store the new memory for the array of pointers in a local variable on the stack and initialize its first entry from `Voxel::onePrimitive` before `Voxel::primitives` is initialized with the array pointer. Otherwise, the value of `Voxel::onePrimitive` would be clobbered before it was added to the new array, since `Voxel::onePrimitive` and `Voxel::primitives` share the same memory.

⟨*Allocate initial primitives array in voxel*⟩ ≡   **190**
```
    MailboxPrim **p = new MailboxPrim *[2];
    p[0] = onePrimitive;
    primitives = p;
```

Similarly, it's necessary to be careful when setting `Voxel::primitives` to the pointer to the expanded array of `MailboxPrim` pointers.

⟨*Increase size of* primitives *array in voxel*⟩ ≡   **190**
```
int nAlloc = 2 * nPrimitives;
MailboxPrim **p = new MailboxPrim *[nAlloc];
for (u_int i = 0; i < nPrimitives; ++i)
    p[i] = primitives[i];
delete[] primitives;
primitives = p;
```

We won't show the straightforward implementations of the `GridAccel::WorldBound()` or `GridAccel::CanIntersect()` methods or its destructor.

4.3.2 TRAVERSAL

The `GridAccel::Intersect()` method handles the task of determining which voxels a ray passes through and calling the appropriate ray-primitive intersection routines.

⟨*GridAccel Method Definitions*⟩ + ≡
```
bool GridAccel::Intersect(const Ray &ray,
                          Intersection *isect) const {
    ⟨Check ray against overall grid bounds 191⟩
    ⟨Get ray mailbox id 192⟩
    ⟨Set up 3D DDA for ray 193⟩
    ⟨Walk ray through voxel grid 194⟩
}
```

The first task is to determine where the ray enters the grid, which gives the starting point for traversal through the voxels. If the ray's origin is inside the grid's bounding box, then clearly it begins there. Otherwise the `GridAccel::Intersect()` method finds the intersection of the ray with the grid's bounding box. If it hits, the first intersection along the ray is the starting point. If the ray misses the grid's bounding box, there can be no intersection with any of the geometry in the grid so `GridAccel::Intersect()` returns immediately.

⟨*Check ray against overall grid bounds*⟩ ≡   **191**
```
float rayT;
if (bounds.Inside(ray(ray.mint)))
    rayT = ray.mint;
else if (!bounds.IntersectP(ray, &rayT))
    return false;
Point gridIntersect = ray(rayT);
```

Once we know that there is work to do, the next task is to find a unique ray identifier for mailboxing. The `GridAccel` uses a monotonic sequence of ray identifiers sorted in the `GridAccel::curMailboxId` member.

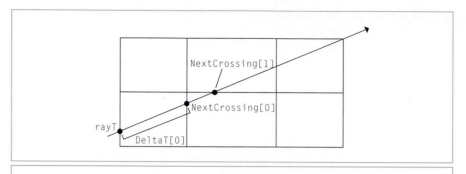

Figure 4.7: Stepping a Ray through a Voxel Grid. rayT is the parametric distance along the ray to the first intersection with the grid. The parametric distance along the ray to the point where it crosses into the next voxel in the x direction is stored in NextCrossing[0], and similarly for the y and z directions (not shown). When the ray crosses into the next x voxel, for example, it is immediately possible to update the value of NextCrossingT[0] by adding a fixed value, the voxel width in x divided by the ray's x direction, DeltaT[0].

⟨*Get ray mailbox id*⟩ ≡   **191**
```
int rayId = ++curMailboxId;
```

⟨*GridAccel Private Data*⟩+≡   **182**
```
static int curMailboxId;
```

The intersection method now computes the initial (x, y, z) integer voxel coordinates for this ray as well as a number of auxiliary values that will make it efficient to incrementally compute the set of voxels that the ray passes through. The ray-voxel traversal computation is similar in spirit to Bresenham's classic line drawing algorithm, where the series of pixels that a line passes through are found incrementally using just addition and comparisons to step from one pixel to the next. The main difference between the ray marching algorithm and Bresenham's are that we would like to find *all* of the voxels that the ray passes through, while Bresenham's algorithm typically only turns on one pixel per row or column that a line passes through. This type of algorithm is known as a *digital differential analyzer* (DDA)."

The values that the ray-voxel stepping algorithm needs to keep track of are the following:

1. The coordinates of the voxel currently being considered, Pos.
2. The parametric t position along the ray where it makes its next crossing into another voxel in each of the x, y, and z directions, NextCrossingT (Figure 4.7). For example, for a ray with a positive x direction component, the parametric value along the ray where it crosses into the next voxel in x, NextCrossingT[0] is the parametric starting point rayT plus the x distance to the next voxel divided

GridAccel::curMailboxId 192

by the ray's x direction component. (This is similar to the ray-plane intersection formula.)

3. The change in the current voxel coordinates after a step in each direction (1 or −1), stored in Step.
4. The distance along the ray between voxels in each direction, DeltaT. These values are found by dividing the width of a voxel in a particular direction by the ray's corresponding direction component, giving the parametric distance along the ray to travel to get from one side of a voxel to the other in the particular direction.
5. The coordinates of the voxel after the last one the ray passes through when it exits the grid, Out.

The first two items will be updated as we step through the grid, while the last three are constant for each ray.

⟨*Set up 3D DDA for ray*⟩ ≡   **191**
```
float NextCrossingT[3], DeltaT[3];
int Step[3], Out[3], Pos[3];
for (int axis = 0; axis < 3; ++axis) {
    ⟨Compute current voxel for axis 193⟩
    if (ray.d[axis] >= 0) {
        ⟨Handle ray with positive direction for voxel stepping 194⟩
    }
    else {
        ⟨Handle ray with negative direction for voxel stepping 194⟩
    }
}
```

Computing the voxel address that the ray starts out in is easy since this method has already determined the position where the ray enters the grid. Thus, it can simply use the utility routine GridAccel::PosToVoxel() defined earlier.

⟨*Compute current voxel for axis*⟩ ≡   **193**
```
Pos[axis] = PosToVoxel(gridIntersect, axis);
```

If the ray's direction component is zero for a particular axis, then the NextCrossingT value for that axis will be initialized to the IEEE floating-point ∞ value by the following computation. The voxel stepping logic later in this section will always decide to step in one of the other directions and will correctly never step in this direction. This is convenient because it can handle rays that are perpendicular to any axis without any special code to test for division by zero.

GridAccel::PosToVoxel() 187
Ray::d 58

⟨*Handle ray with positive direction for voxel stepping*⟩ ≡   **193**
```
NextCrossingT[axis] = rayT +
    (VoxelToPos(Pos[axis]+1, axis) - gridIntersect[axis]) / ray.d[axis];
DeltaT[axis] = Width[axis] / ray.d[axis];
Step[axis] = 1;
Out[axis] = NVoxels[axis];
```

Similar computations compute these values for rays with negative direction components:

⟨*Handle ray with negative direction for voxel stepping*⟩ ≡   **193**
```
NextCrossingT[axis] = rayT +
    (VoxelToPos(Pos[axis], axis) - gridIntersect[axis]) / ray.d[axis];
DeltaT[axis] = -Width[axis] / ray.d[axis];
Step[axis] = -1;
Out[axis] = -1;
```

Once all the preprocessing is done for the ray, stepping through the grid can start. Starting with the first voxel that the ray passes through, the intersection routine checks for intersections with the primitives inside that voxel. If it finds a hit, the boolean flag hitSomething is set to true. It is necessary to be careful, however, because the intersection point may be outside the current voxel since primitives may overlap multiple voxels. Therefore, the method doesn't immediately return when done processing a voxel where an intersection was found. Instead, it uses the fact that the primitive's intersection routine will update the Ray::maxt member variable. Therefore, when stepping through voxels, it will return only when it enters a voxel at a point that is beyond the closest found intersection.

⟨*Walk ray through voxel grid*⟩ ≡   **191**
```
bool hitSomething = false;
for (;;) {
    Voxel *voxel = voxels[Offset(Pos[0], Pos[1], Pos[2])];
    if (voxel != NULL)
        hitSomething |= voxel->Intersect(ray, isect, rayId);
    ⟨Advance to next voxel 197⟩
}
return hitSomething;
```

For each nonempty voxel, the grid traversal method calls the Voxel's Intersect() routine, which handles the details of mailboxing and calling the Primitive::Intersect() methods.

⟨*GridAccel Method Definitions*⟩+≡

```
bool Voxel::Intersect(const Ray &ray, Intersection *isect, int rayId) {
    ⟨Refine primitives in voxel if needed 195⟩
    ⟨Loop over primitives in voxel and find intersections 196⟩
}
```

The boolean `Voxel::allCanIntersect` member indicates whether all of the primitives in the voxel are known to be intersectable. If its value is `false`, the `Intersect()` routine must loop over all of the primitives, calling their refinement routines as needed until only intersectable geometry remains. The logic for finding the ith `MailboxPrim` in the loop over primitives is slightly complicated by a level of pointer indirection, since a single primitive and multiple primitives are stored differently in voxels. Handling this case in the way done in the following is worthwhile since it moves the test for whether the loop should be using the `Voxel::onePrimitive` item for a single primitive or the `Voxel::primitives` array for multiple primitives outside of the loop body.

⟨*Refine primitives in voxel if needed*⟩≡   195

```
if (!allCanIntersect) {
    MailboxPrim **mpp;
    if (nPrimitives == 1) mpp = &onePrimitive;
    else mpp = primitives;
    for (u_int i = 0; i < nPrimitives; ++i) {
        MailboxPrim *mp = mpp[i];
        ⟨Refine primitive in mp if it's not intersectable 196⟩
    }
    allCanIntersect = true;
}
```

Primitives that need refinement are refined until only intersectable primitives remain, and a new `GridAccel` is created to hold the returned primitives if more than one was returned. One reason to always make a `GridAccel` for multiple refined primitives is that doing so simplifies primitive refinement. A single `Primitive` always turns into a single object that represents all of the new `Primitives`, so it's never necessary to increase the number of primitives in the voxel. If this primitive overlaps multiple voxels, then because all of them hold a pointer to a single `MailboxPrim` for it, it suffices to just update the primitive reference in the shared `MailboxPrim` directly, and there's no need to loop over all of the voxels.[4]

---

4   The bounding box of the original unrefined primitive must encompass the refined geometry as well, so there's no danger that the refined geometry will overlap more voxels than before. On the other hand, it also may overlap many fewer voxels, which would lead to unnecessary intersection tests, since the grid implementation doesn't try to remove references to the primitive from voxels that it no longer overlaps.

⟨*Refine primitive in* mp *if it's not intersectable*⟩ ≡ 195

```
if (!mp->primitive->CanIntersect()) {
    vector<Reference<Primitive> > p;
    mp->primitive->FullyRefine(p);
    if (p.size() == 1)
        mp->primitive = p[0];
    else
        mp->primitive = new GridAccel(p, true, false);
}
```

Once it is certain that there are only intersectable primitives in the voxel, the loop over MailboxPrims for performing intersection tests again has to deal with the difference between voxels with one primitive and voxels with multiple primitives in the same manner that the primitive refinement code did.

⟨*Loop over primitives in voxel and find intersections*⟩ ≡ 195

```
bool hitSomething = false;
MailboxPrim **mpp;
if (nPrimitives == 1) mpp = &onePrimitive;
else mpp = primitives;
for (u_int i = 0; i < nPrimitives; ++i) {
    MailboxPrim *mp = mpp[i];
    ⟨Do mailbox check between ray and primitive 196⟩
    ⟨Check for ray-primitive intersection⟩
}
return hitSomething;
```

Here now is the mailbox check. If this ray was previously tested against this primitive in another voxel, the redundant intersection test can be trivially skipped.

⟨*Do mailbox check between ray and primitive*⟩ ≡ 196

```
if (mp->lastMailboxId == rayId)
    continue;
```

Finally, if a ray-primitive intersection test is necessary, the primitive's mailbox needs to be updated.

⟨*Check for ray–primitive intersection*⟩ ≡

```
mp->lastMailboxId = rayId;
if (mp->primitive->Intersect(ray, isect)) {
    hitSomething = true;
}
```

After doing the intersection tests for the primitives in the current voxel, it is necessary to step to the next voxel in the ray's path. The grid must decide whether to step in the *x*, *y*, or *z* direction. Fortunately, the NextCrossingT variable gives the parametric distance to the next crossing for each direction, and it can choose the smallest one. Traversal can be terminated if this step goes outside of the voxel grid, or if the selected NextCrossingT value is beyond the *t* distance of an already-found intersection. Otherwise, the grid steps to the chosen voxel and increments the chosen direction's NextCrossingT by its DeltaT value, so that future traversal steps will know how far it is necessary to go before stepping in this direction again.

⟨*Advance to next voxel*⟩ ≡   194
    ⟨*Find* stepAxis *for stepping to next voxel* **197**⟩
    if (ray.maxt < NextCrossingT[stepAxis])
        break;
    Pos[stepAxis] += Step[stepAxis];
    if (Pos[stepAxis] == Out[stepAxis])
        break;
    NextCrossingT[stepAxis] += DeltaT[stepAxis];

Choosing the axis along which to step basically requires finding the smallest of three numbers, a straightforward task. However, in this case an optimization is possible because we don't care about the *value* of the smallest number, just its corresponding index in the NextCrossingT array. It is possible to compute this index without any branching, which can lead to performance improvements on modern CPUs, which generally pay a performance penalty for branches.

The following tricky bit of code determines which of the three NextCrossingT values is the smallest and sets stepAxis accordingly. It encodes this logic by setting each of the three low-order bits in an integer to the results of three comparisons between pairs of NextCrossingT values. It then uses a table (cmpToAxis) to map the resulting integer to the direction with the smallest value.

⟨*Find* stepAxis *for stepping to next voxel*⟩ ≡   197
    int bits = ((NextCrossingT[0] < NextCrossingT[1]) << 2) +
            ((NextCrossingT[0] < NextCrossingT[2]) << 1) +
            ((NextCrossingT[1] < NextCrossingT[2]));
    const int cmpToAxis[8] = { 2, 1, 2, 1, 2, 2, 0, 0 };
    int stepAxis = cmpToAxis[bits];

The grid also provides a special GridAccel::IntersectP() method that is optimized for checking for intersection along shadow rays, where we are only interested in the presence of an intersection and not the details of the intersection itself. It is almost identical to the GridAccel::Intersect() routine, except that it calls the Primitive::IntersectP() method of the primitives rather than Primitive::Intersect(), and it immediately stops traversal when any intersection is found. Because of the small number of differences, we won't include the implementation here.

⟨*GridAccel Public Methods*⟩ ≡   **182**
```
bool IntersectP(const Ray &ray) const;
```

4.4 KD-TREE ACCELERATOR

Binary space partitioning (BSP) trees adaptively subdivide space into irregularly sized regions. The most important consequence of this difference with regular grids is that they can be a much more effective data structure for storing irregularly distributed collections of geometry. A BSP tree starts with a bounding box that encompasses the entire scene. If the number of primitives in the box is greater than some threshold, the box is split in half by a plane. Primitives are then associated with whichever half they overlap and primitives that lie in both halves are associated with both of them. This process continues recursively either until each leaf region in the resulting tree contains a sufficiently small number of primitives or until a maximum depth is reached. Because the splitting planes can be placed at arbitrary positions inside the overall bound and because different parts of 3D space can be refined to different degrees, BSP trees can easily handle uneven distributions of geometry.

Two variations of BSP trees are *kd-trees* and *octrees*. A kd-tree simply restricts the splitting plane to be perpendicular to one of the coordinate axes; this makes both traversal and construction of the tree more efficient, at the cost of some flexibility in how space is subdivided. The octree uses three axis-perpendicular planes to simultaneously split the box into eight regions at each step (typically by splitting down the center of the extent in each direction). In this section, we will implement a kd-tree for ray intersection acceleration in the KdTreeAccel class. Source code for this class can be found in the file accelerators/kdtree.cpp.ⓒⓓ

⟨*KdTreeAccel Declarations*⟩ ≡
```
class KdTreeAccel : public Aggregate {
public:
    ⟨KdTreeAccel Public Methods 220⟩
private:
    ⟨KdTreeAccel Private Data 200⟩
};
```

In addition to the primitives to be stored, the KdTreeAccel constructor takes a few parameters that are used to guide the decisions that will be made as the tree is built; these parameters are stored in member variables for later use. For simplicity of implementation, the KdTreeAccel requires that all of the primitives it stores be intersectable. We leave as an exercise the task of improving the implementation to do lazy refinement like the GridAccel does. Therefore, the constructor starts out by refining the given primitives

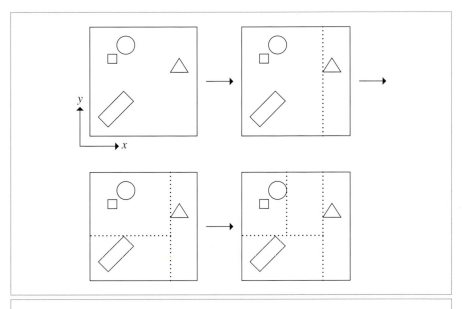

Figure 4.8: The kd-tree is built by recursively splitting the bounding box of the scene geometry along one of the coordinate axes. Here, the first split is along the x axis; it is placed so that the triangle is precisely alone in the right region and the rest of the primitives end up on the left. The left region is then refined a few more times with axis-aligned splitting planes. The details of the refinement criteria—which axis is used to split space at each step, at which position along the axis the plane is placed, and at what point refinement terminates—can all substantially affect the performance of the tree in practice.

until all are intersectable before building the tree. See Figure 4.8 for an overview of how the tree is built.

⟨*KdTreeAccel Method Definitions*⟩ ≡

```
KdTreeAccel::KdTreeAccel(const vector<Reference<Primitive> > &p,
                         int icost, int tcost,
                         float ebonus, int maxp, int maxDepth)
    : isectCost(icost), traversalCost(tcost),
      maxPrims(maxp), emptyBonus(ebonus) {
    vector<Reference<Primitive > > prims;
    for (u_int i = 0; i < p.size(); ++i)
        p[i]->FullyRefine(prims);
    ⟨Initialize mailboxes for KdTreeAccel 200⟩
    ⟨Build kd-tree for accelerator 204⟩
}
```

⟨*KdTreeAccel Private Data*⟩ ≡   **198**

```
int isectCost, traversalCost, maxPrims;
float emptyBonus;
```

As with `GridAccel`, the kd-tree uses mailboxing to avoid repeated intersections with primitives that straddle splitting planes and overlap multiple regions of the tree. In fact, it uses the exact same `MailboxPrim` structure.

⟨*Initialize mailboxes for KdTreeAccel*⟩ ≡   **199**

```
curMailboxId = 0;
nMailboxes = prims.size();
mailboxPrims = (MailboxPrim *)AllocAligned(nMailboxes *
                                  sizeof(MailboxPrim));
for (u_int i = 0; i < nMailboxes; ++i)
    new (&mailboxPrims[i]) MailboxPrim(prims[i]);
```

⟨*KdTreeAccel Private Data*⟩+≡   **198**

```
u_int nMailboxes;
MailboxPrim *mailboxPrims;
mutable int curMailboxId;
```

4.4.1 TREE REPRESENTATION

The kd-tree is a binary tree, where each interior node always has both children and where leaves of the tree store the primitives that overlap them. Each interior node must provide access to three pieces of information:

- Split axis: which of the x, y, or z axes was split at this node
- Split position: the position of the splitting plane along the axis
- Children: information about how to reach the two child nodes beneath it

Each leaf node needs to record only which primitives overlap it.

It is worth going through a bit of trouble to ensure that all interior nodes and many leaf nodes use just 8 bytes of memory (assuming 4-byte `float`s and pointers) because doing so ensures that four nodes will fit into a 32-byte cache line. Because there are many nodes in the tree and because many nodes are accessed for each ray, minimizing the size of the node representation substantially improves cache performance. Our initial implementation used a 16-byte node representation; when we reduced the size to 8 bytes we obtained nearly a 20% speed increase. Both leaves and interior nodes are represented by the following `KdAccelNode` structure. The comments after each `union` member indicate whether a particular field is used for interior nodes, leaf nodes, or both.

⟨*KdAccelNode Declarations*⟩ ≡
```
struct KdAccelNode {
    ⟨KdAccelNode Methods 201⟩
    union {
        u_int flags;    // Both
        float split;    // Interior
        u_int nPrims;   // Leaf
    };
    union {
        u_int aboveChild;         // Interior
        MailboxPrim *onePrimitive; // Leaf
        MailboxPrim **primitives;  // Leaf
    };
};
```

The two low-order bits of the KdAccelNode::flags variable are used to differentiate between interior nodes with *x*, *y*, and *z* splits (where these bits hold the values 0, 1, and 2, respectively) and leaf nodes (where these bits hold the value 3).

It is relatively easy to store leaf nodes in 8 bytes: since the low 2 bits of KdAccelNode::flags are used to indicate that this is a leaf, the upper 30 bits of KdAccelNode::nPrims are available to record how many primitives overlap it. As with GridAccel, if just a single primitive overlaps a KdAccelNode leaf, its MailboxPrim pointer is stored directly in the KdAccelNode::onePrimitive field. If more primitives overlap, memory is dynamically allocated for an array of them pointed to by KdAccelNode::primitives.

Leaf nodes are easy to initialize. The number of primitives must be shifted two bits to the left before being stored so that the low two bits of KdAccelNode::flags can both be set to 1 to indicate that this is a leaf node.

⟨*KdAccelNode Methods*⟩ ≡   201
```
void initLeaf(int *primNums, int np, MailboxPrim *mailboxPrims,
              MemoryArena &arena) {
    nPrims = np << 2;
    flags |= 3;
    ⟨Store MailboxPrim *s for leaf node 202⟩
}
```

For leaf nodes with zero or one overlapping primitives, no dynamic memory allocation is necessary thanks to the KdAccelNode::onePrimitive field. For the case where multiple primitives overlap, the caller passes in a MemoryArena for allocating memory for the arrays of MailboxPrim pointers. (The MemoryArena is introduced in Section A.2.4 of Appendix A.) This utility class helps to reduce wasted space for these allocations and improves cache efficiency by placing all of these arrays together in memory.

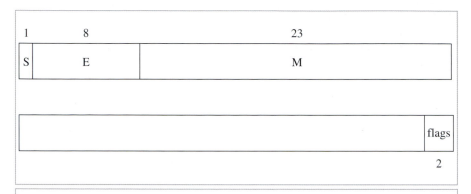

Figure 4.9: Memory layout of IEEE `float`s (top) and the bits of the flags value used to record which splitting plane is used at a kd-tree node. Because the flags overlap the two least-significant bits of the mantissa of the floating-point value, the precision loss from stealing them is minimal.

⟨*Store* `MailboxPrim *s for leaf node`⟩ ≡   **201**
```
if (np == 0)
    onePrimitive = NULL;
else if (np == 1)
    onePrimitive = &mailboxPrims[primNums[0]];
else {
    primitives = (MailboxPrim **)arena.Alloc(np * sizeof(MailboxPrim *));
    for (int i = 0; i < np; ++i)
        primitives[i] = &mailboxPrims[primNums[i]];
}
```

Getting interior nodes down to 8 bytes takes a bit more work. As explained earlier, the lowest 2 bits of `KdAccelNode::flags` are used to record which axis the node was split along. Yet the split position along that axis is stored in `KdAccelNode::split`, a `float` value that occupies the same memory as `KdAccelNode::flags`. This seems impossible—we can't just ask the compiler to use just the top 30 bits of `KdAccelNode::split` as a `float`.

It turns out that as long as the lowest 2 bits of `KdAccelNode::flags` are set after `KdAccelNode::split`, this technique works thanks to the layout of `float`s in memory. For IEEE floating point, the 2 bits used by `KdAccelNode::flags` are the least-significant bits of the mantissa value, so changing their original value only minimally affects the floating-point value that is stored. Figure 4.9 illustrates the layout in memory.

Although this trick is fairly extreme, it is worth it for the performance benefits of having 8-byte tree nodes. In addition, because all of the complexity is hidden behind a small number of `KdAccelNode` methods, the rest of the implementation is insulated from this special representation.

So that we don't need additional memory to store pointers to the two child nodes of an interior node, all of the nodes are allocated in a single contiguous block of memory, and the child of an interior node that is responsible for space below the splitting plane is always stored in the array position immediately after its parent (this also improves cache performance, by keeping at least one child close to its parent in memory). The other child, representing space above the splitting plane, will end up at somewhere else in the array; KdAccelNode::aboveChild stores its position.

Given all those conventions, the code to initialize an interior node is straightforward. The split position is stored before the split axis is written in KdAccelNode::flags. Rather than directly assigning the axis to KdAccelNode::flags, which would clobber the value stored in KdAccelNode::split as well, it is necessary to carefully set just the lower 2 bits of the flags with the axis's value with bit operations.

⟨*KdAccelNode Methods*⟩+≡   **201**
```
void initInterior(int axis, float s) {
    split = s;
    flags &= ~3;
    flags |= axis;
}
```

Finally, we'll provide a few methods to extract various values from the node, so that callers don't have to be aware of the admittedly complex details of its representation.

⟨*KdAccelNode Methods*⟩+≡   **201**
```
float SplitPos() const { return split; }
int nPrimitives() const { return nPrims >> 2; }
int SplitAxis() const { return flags & 3; }
bool IsLeaf() const { return (flags & 3) == 3; }
```

4.4.2 TREE CONSTRUCTION

The kd-tree is built with a recursive top-down algorithm. At each step, we have an axis-aligned region of space and a set of primitives that overlap that region. The region is either split into two subregions and turned into an interior node, or a leaf node is created with the overlapping primitives, terminating the recursion.

As mentioned in the discussion of KdAccelNodes, all tree nodes are stored in a contiguous array. KdTreeAccel::nextFreeNode records the next node in this array that is available, and KdTreeAccel::nAllocedNodes records the total number that have been allocated. By setting both of them to zero and not allocating any nodes at start-up, the implementation here ensures that an allocation will be done immediately when the first node of the tree is initialized.

It is also necessary to determine a maximum tree depth if one wasn't given to the constructor. Although the tree construction process will normally terminate naturally at a reasonable depth, it is important to cap the maximum depth so that the amount of memory used for the tree cannot grow without bound in pathological cases. We have found that the value $8 + 1.3 \log(N)$ gives a reasonable maximum depth for a variety of scenes.

⟨*Build kd-tree for accelerator*⟩ ≡   199
```
nextFreeNode = nAllocedNodes = 0;
if (maxDepth <= 0)
    maxDepth = Round2Int(8 + 1.3f * Log2Int(float(prims.size())));
```
    ⟨*Compute bounds for kd-tree construction* **204**⟩
    ⟨*Allocate working memory for kd-tree construction* **209**⟩
    ⟨*Initialize* primNums *for kd-tree construction* **204**⟩
    ⟨*Start recursive construction of kd-tree* **205**⟩
    ⟨*Free working memory for kd-tree construction*⟩

⟨*KdTreeAccel Private Data*⟩+≡   198
```
KdAccelNode *nodes;
int nAllocedNodes, nextFreeNode;
```

Because the construction routine will be repeatedly using the bounding boxes of the primitives along the way, they are stored in a `vector` before tree construction starts so that the potentially slow `Primitive::WorldBound()` methods don't need to be called repeatedly.

⟨*Compute bounds for kd-tree construction*⟩ ≡   204
```
vector<BBox> primBounds;
primBounds.reserve(prims.size());
for (u_int i = 0; i < prims.size(); ++i) {
    BBox b = prims[i]->WorldBound();
    bounds = Union(bounds, b);
    primBounds.push_back(b);
}
```

⟨*KdTreeAccel Private Data*⟩+≡   198
```
BBox bounds;
```

One of the parameters to the tree construction routine is an array of primitive indices indicating which primitives overlap the current node. Because all primitives overlap the root node, when the recursion begins, we start with an array initialized with values from zero through `prims.size()` − 1.

⟨*Initialize* primNums *for kd-tree construction*⟩ ≡   204
```
int *primNums = new int[prims.size()];
for (u_int i = 0; i < prims.size(); ++i)
    primNums[i] = i;
```

`KdTreeAccel::buildTree()` is called for each tree node. It is responsible for deciding if the node should be an interior node or leaf and updating the data structures appropriately.

The last three parameters, edges, prims0, and prims1, are pointers to data from the ⟨*Allocate working memory for kd-tree construction*⟩ fragment, which will be defined and documented in a few pages.

⟨*Start recursive construction of kd-tree*⟩ ≡   **204**

```
buildTree(0, bounds, primBounds, primNums,
          prims.size(), maxDepth, edges,
          prims0, prims1);
```

The main parameters to KdTreeAccel::buildTree() are the offset into the array of KdAccelNodes to use for the node that it creates, nodeNum; the bounding box that gives the region of space that the node covers, nodeBounds; and the indices of primitives that overlap it, primNums. The remainder of the parameters will be described later, closer to where they are used.

⟨*KdTreeAccel Method Definitions*⟩+≡

```
void KdTreeAccel::buildTree(int nodeNum, const BBox &nodeBounds,
        const vector<BBox> &allPrimBounds, int *primNums,
        int nPrims, int depth, BoundEdge *edges[3],
        int *prims0, int *prims1, int badRefines) {
    ⟨Get next free node from nodes array 205⟩
    ⟨Initialize leaf node if termination criteria met 206⟩
    ⟨Initialize interior node and continue recursion 206⟩
}
```

If all of the allocated nodes have been used up, node memory is reallocated with twice as many entries and the old values are copied. The first time KdTreeAccel::buildTree() is called, KdTreeAccel::nAllocedNodes is zero and an initial block of tree nodes is allocated.

⟨*Get next free node from nodes array*⟩ ≡   **205**

```
if (nextFreeNode == nAllocedNodes) {
    int nAlloc = max(2 * nAllocedNodes, 512);
    KdAccelNode *n = (KdAccelNode *)AllocAligned(nAlloc *
                                                sizeof(KdAccelNode));
    if (nAllocedNodes > 0) {
        memcpy(n, nodes, nAllocedNodes * sizeof(KdAccelNode));
        FreeAligned(nodes);
    }
    nodes = n;
    nAllocedNodes = nAlloc;
}
++nextFreeNode;
```

A leaf node is created (stopping the recursion) either if there are a sufficiently small number of primitives in the region, or if the maximum depth has been reached. The depth parameter starts out as the tree's maximum depth and is decremented at each level.

⟨*Initialize leaf node if termination criteria met*⟩ ≡   205
```
    if (nPrims <= maxPrims || depth == 0) {
        nodes[nodeNum].initLeaf(primNums, nPrims, mailboxPrims, arena);
        return;
    }
```

As described earlier, KdAccelNode::initLeaf() uses a memory arena to allocate space for variable-sized arrays of primitives. Because the arena used here is a member variable, all of the memory it allocates will naturally be freed when the KdTreeAccel object is destroyed.

⟨*KdTreeAccel Private Data*⟩+≡   198
```
    MemoryArena arena;
```

If this is an internal node, it is necessary to choose a splitting plane, classify the primitives with respect to that plane, and recurse.

⟨*Initialize interior node and continue recursion*⟩ ≡   205
    ⟨*Choose split axis position for interior node* 210⟩
    ⟨*Create leaf if no good splits were found* 213⟩
    ⟨*Classify primitives with respect to split* 213⟩
    ⟨*Recursively initialize children nodes* 214⟩

Our implementation chooses a split based on a cost model that estimates the computational expense of performing ray intersection tests, including the time spent traversing nodes of the tree and the time spent on ray-primitive intersection tests. Its goal is to minimize the total cost; we implement a greedy algorithm that minimizes the cost for the node individually. The estimated cost is computed for a series of candidate splitting planes in the node, and the split that gives the lowest cost is chosen.

The idea behind the cost model is straightforward: at any node of the tree we could just create a leaf node for the current region and geometry. In that case, any ray that passes through this region will be tested against all of the overlapping primitives and will incur a cost of

KdAccelNode::initLeaf() 201
KdTreeAccel 198
KdTreeAccel::arena 206
KdTreeAccel::mailboxPrims 200
MemoryArena 845

$$\sum_{i=1}^{N} t_i(i),$$

where N is the number of primitives in the region and $t_i(i)$ is the time to compute a ray-object intersection with the ith primitive.

The other option is to split the region. In that case, rays will incur the cost

$$t_t + p_B \sum_{i=1}^{N_B} t_i(b_i) + p_A \sum_{i=1}^{N_A} t_i(a_i),$$

where t_t is the time it takes to traverse the interior node and determine which of the children the ray passes through, p_B and p_A are the probabilities that the ray passes through each of the two regions below and above the splitting plane, b_i and a_i are the indices of primitives below and above the splitting plane, and N_B and N_A are the number of primitives that overlap the regions below and above the splitting plane, respectively. The choice of splitting plane affects both the values of the two probabilities as well as the set of primitives on each side of the split.

In our implementation, we will make the simplifying assumption that $t_i(i)$ is the same for all of the primitives; this assumption is probably not too far from reality, and any error that it introduces doesn't seem to affect the performance of this accelerator very much. Another possibility would be to add a method to `Primitive` that returns an estimate of the number of CPU cycles its intersection test requires. The intersection cost t_i and the traversal cost t_t can be set by the user; their default values are 80 and 1, respectively. Ultimately, it is the ratio of these two values that determines the behavior of the tree-building algorithm.[5]

Finally, it is worth giving a slight preference to choosing splits where one of the children has no primitives overlapping it, since rays passing through these regions can immediately advance to the next kd-tree node without any ray-primitive intersection tests. Thus, the revised costs for unsplit and split regions are, respectively,

$$t_i N, \text{ and}$$

$$t_t + (1 - b_e)(p_B N_B t_i + p_A N_A t_i),$$

where b_e is a "bonus" value that is zero unless one of the two regions is completely empty, in which case it takes on a value between zero and one.

The probabilities p_B and p_A can be computed using ideas from geometric probability. It can be shown that for a convex volume A contained in another convex volume B, the conditional probability that a random ray passing through B will also pass through A is the ratio of their surface areas, s_A and s_B:

$$p(A|B) = \frac{s_A}{s_B}.$$

Primitive 171

5   Many other implementations of this approach seem to use values for these costs that are much closer together, sometimes even approaching equal values (for example, see Hurley et al. 2002). The values used here gave the best performance for a number of test scenes in pbrt. We suspect that this decrepancy is due to the fact that ray-primitive intersection tests in pbrt require two virtual function calls and a ray world-to-object-space transformation, in addition to the cost of performing the actual intersection test. Highly optimized ray tracers that only support triangle primitives don't pay any of that additional cost. See Section 18.1.2 for further discussion of this design trade-off.

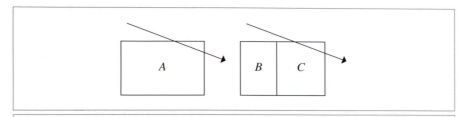

Figure 4.10: If a node of the kd-tree with surface area s_A is split into two children with surface areas s_B and s_C, the probabilities that a ray passing through A also passes through B and C are given by s_B/s_A and s_C/s_A, respectively. Note that $s_B + s_C > s_A$, unless one of them is empty.

Because we are interested in the cost for rays passing through the interior node, we can use this result directly. Thus, given a split of a region A into two subregions B and C (Figure 4.10), the probability that a ray passing through A will also pass through either of the subregions is easily computed.

Given a way to compute the probabilities for the cost model, the last problem to address is how to generate candidate splitting positions and how to efficiently compute the cost for each candidate. It can be shown that the minimum cost with this model will be attained at a split that is coincident with one of the faces of one of the primitive's bounding boxes—there's no need to consider splits at intermediate positions. (To convince yourself of this, consider the behavior of the cost function between the edges of the faces.) Here, we will consider all bounding box faces inside the region for one or more of the three coordinate axes.

The cost for checking all of these candidates thus can be kept relatively low with a carefully structured algorithm. To compute these costs, we will sweep across the projections of the bounding boxes onto each axis and keep track of which gives the lowest cost (Figure 4.11). Each bounding box has two edges on each axis, each of which is represented by an instance of the BoundEdge structure. This structure records the position of the edge along the axis, whether it represents the start or end of a bounding box (going from low to high along the axis), and which primitive it is associated with.

⟨*KdAccelNode Declarations*⟩+≡
```
struct BoundEdge {
    ⟨BoundEdge Public Methods 209⟩
    float t;
    int primNum;
    enum { START, END } type;
};
```

BoundEdge 208

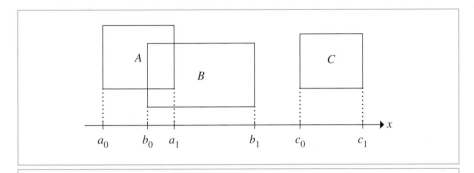

Figure 4.11: Given an axis along which we'd like to consider possible splits, the primitives' bounding boxes are projected onto the axis, which leads to an efficient algorithm to track how many primitives would be on each side of a particular splitting plane. Here, for example, a split at a_1 would leave A completely below the splitting plane, B straddling it, and C completely above it. Each point on the axis, a_0, a_1, b_0, b_1, c_0, and c_1, is represented by an instance of the BoundEdge structure.

⟨*BoundEdge Public Methods*⟩ ≡   **208**

```
BoundEdge(float tt, int pn, bool starting) {
    t = tt;
    primNum = pn;
    type = starting ? START : END;
}
```

At most 2 * prims.size() BoundEdges are needed for computing costs for any tree node, so the memory for the edges for all three axes is allocated once and then reused for each node that is created. The fragment ⟨*Free working memory for kd-tree construction*⟩, not included here, frees this space after the tree has been built.

⟨*Allocate working memory for kd-tree construction*⟩ ≡   **204**

```
BoundEdge *edges[3];
for (int i = 0; i < 3; ++i)
    edges[i] = new BoundEdge[2*prims.size()];
```

After determining the estimated cost for creating a leaf, KdTreeAccel::buildTree() chooses an axis to try to split along and computes the cost function for each candidate split. bestAxis and bestOffset record the axis and bounding box edge index that gave the lowest cost so far, bestCost. invTotalSA is initialized to the reciprocal of the node's surface area; its value will be used when computing the probabilities of rays passing through each of the candidate children nodes.

BoundEdge 208

KdTreeAccel::buildTree() 205

⟨*Choose split axis position for interior node*⟩ ≡　　　　　　　　　　**206**
```
int bestAxis = -1, bestOffset = -1;
float bestCost = INFINITY;
float oldCost = isectCost * float(nPrims);
Vector d = nodeBounds.pMax - nodeBounds.pMin;
float totalSA = (2.f * (d.x*d.y + d.x*d.z + d.y*d.z));
float invTotalSA = 1.f / totalSA;
```
⟨*Choose which axis to split along* **210**⟩
```
int retries = 0;
retrySplit:
```
⟨*Initialize edges for* `axis` **210**⟩
⟨*Compute cost of all splits for* `axis` *to find best* **211**⟩

This method first tries to find a split along the axis with the largest spatial extent; if successful, this choice helps to give regions of space that tend toward being square in shape. This is an intuitively sensible approach. Later, if it was unsuccessful in finding a good split along this axis, it will go back and try the others in turn.

⟨*Choose which axis to split along*⟩ ≡　　　　　　　　　　　　　**210**
```
int axis;
if (d.x > d.y && d.x > d.z) axis = 0;
else axis = (d.y > d.z) ? 1 : 2;
```

First the edges array for the axis is initialized using the bounding boxes of the overlapping primitives. The array is then sorted from low to high along the axis so that it can sweep over the box edges from first to last.

⟨*Initialize edges for* `axis`⟩ ≡　　　　　　　　　　　　　　　　**210**
```
for (int i = 0; i < nPrims; ++i) {
    int pn = primNums[i];
    const BBox &bbox = allPrimBounds[pn];
    edges[axis][2*i]   = BoundEdge(bbox.pMin[axis], pn, true);
    edges[axis][2*i+1] = BoundEdge(bbox.pMax[axis], pn, false);
}
sort(&edges[axis][0], &edges[axis][2*nPrims]);
```

BBox 60
BoundEdge 208
BoundEdge::t 208
INFINITY 856
KdTreeAccel::isectCost 200
Vector 47

The C++ standard library routine `sort()` requires that the structure being sorted define an ordering; this is done using the `BoundEdge::t` values. However, one subtlety is that if the `BoundEdge::t` values match, it is necessary to try to break the tie by comparing the node's types; this is necessary since `sort()` depends on the fact that a < b and b < a is only true if a == b.

⟨*BoundEdge Public Methods*⟩+≡   **208**
```
bool operator<(const BoundEdge &e) const {
    if (t == e.t)
        return (int)type < (int)e.type;
    else return t < e.t;
}
```

Given the sorted array of edges, we'd like to quickly compute the cost function for a split at each one of them. The probabilities for a ray passing through each child node are easily computed using their surface areas, and the number of primitives on each side of the split is tracked by the variables nBelow and nAbove. We would like to keep their values updated such that if we chose to split at edget for a particular pass through the loop, nBelow will give the number of primitives that would end up below the splitting plane and nAbove would give the number above it.[6]

At the first edge, all primitives must be above that edge by definition, so nAbove is initialized to nPrims and nBelow is set to zero. When the loop is considering a split at the end of a bounding box's extent, nAbove needs to be decremented, since that box, which must have previously been above the splitting plane, will no longer be above it if splitting is done at the point. Similarly, after calculating the split cost, if the split candidate was at the start of a bounding box's extent, then the box will be on the below side for all subsequent splits. The tests at the start and end of the loop body update the primitive counts for these two cases.

⟨*Compute cost of all splits for* axis *to find best*⟩≡   **210**
```
int nBelow = 0, nAbove = nPrims;
for (int i = 0; i < 2*nPrims; ++i) {
    if (edges[axis][i].type == BoundEdge::END) --nAbove;
    float edget = edges[axis][i].t;
    if (edget > nodeBounds.pMin[axis] &&
        edget < nodeBounds.pMax[axis]) {
        ⟨Compute cost for split at ith edge 212⟩
    }
    if (edges[axis][i].type == BoundEdge::START) ++nBelow;
}
```

Given all of this information, the cost for a particular split can be computed. belowSA and aboveSA hold the surface areas of the two candidate child bounds; they are easily computed by adding up the areas of the six faces. Given an axis number, the otherAxis array can be used to quickly compute the indices of the other two axes without branching.

BoundEdge 208

---

6   When multiple bounding box faces project to the same point on the axis, this invariant may not be true at those points. However, as implemented here it will only overestimate the counts, and more importantly, will have the correct value for one of the multiple times through the loop at each of those points, so the algorithm functions correctly in the end anyway.

⟨*Compute cost for split at* i*th edge*⟩ ≡   **211**
```
    int otherAxis[3][2] = { {1,2}, {0,2}, {0,1} };
    int otherAxis0 = otherAxis[axis][0];
    int otherAxis1 = otherAxis[axis][1];
    float belowSA = 2 * (d[otherAxis0] * d[otherAxis1] +
                        (edget - nodeBounds.pMin[axis]) *
                        (d[otherAxis0] + d[otherAxis1]));
    float aboveSA = 2 * (d[otherAxis0] * d[otherAxis1] +
                        (nodeBounds.pMax[axis] - edget) *
                        (d[otherAxis0] + d[otherAxis1]));
    float pBelow = belowSA * invTotalSA;
    float pAbove = aboveSA * invTotalSA;
    float eb = (nAbove == 0 || nBelow == 0) ? emptyBonus : 0.f;
    float cost = traversalCost + isectCost * (1.f - eb) *
                (pBelow * nBelow + pAbove * nAbove);
```
⟨*Update best split if this is lowest cost so far* **212**⟩

If the cost computed for this candidate split is the best one so far, the details of the split are recorded.

⟨*Update best split if this is lowest cost so far*⟩ ≡   **212**
```
    if (cost < bestCost)  {
        bestCost = cost;
        bestAxis = axis;
        bestOffset = i;
    }
```

It may happen that there are no possible splits found in the previous tests (Figure 4.12 illustrates a case where this may happen). In this case, there isn't a single candidate position at which to split the node along the current axis. At this point, splitting is tried for the other two axes in turn. If neither of them can find a split (when retries is equal to two), then there is no useful way to refine the node, since both children will still have the same number of overlapping primitives. When this condition occurs, all that can be done is to give up and make a leaf node.

It is also possible that the best split will have a cost that is still higher than the cost for not splitting the node at all. If it is substantially worse and there aren't too many primitives, a leaf node is made immediately. Otherwise, badRefines keeps track of how many bad splits have been made so far above the current node of the tree. It's worth allowing a few slightly poor refinements since later splits may be able to find better ones given a smaller subset of primitives to consider.

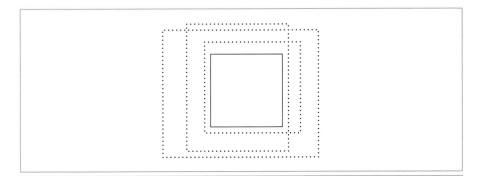

Figure 4.12: If multiple bounding boxes (dotted lines) overlap a kd-tree node (solid lines) as shown here, there is no possible split position that can result in fewer than all of the primitives being on both sides of it.

⟨*Create leaf if no good splits were found*⟩ ≡   206
```
if (bestAxis == -1 && retries < 2) {
    ++retries;
    axis = (axis+1) % 3;
    goto retrySplit;
}
if (bestCost > oldCost) ++badRefines;
if ((bestCost > 4.f * oldCost && nPrims < 16) ||
    bestAxis == -1 || badRefines == 3) {
    nodes[nodeNum].initLeaf(primNums, nPrims, mailboxPrims, arena);
    return;
}
```

Having chosen a split position, the bounding box edges can be used to classify the primitives as being above, below, or on both sides of the split in the same way as was done to keep track of nBelow and nAbove in the earlier code. Note that the bestOffset entry in the arrays is skipped in the loops below; this is necessary so that the primitive whose bounding box edge was used for the split isn't incorrectly categorized as being on both sides of the split.

⟨*Classify primitives with respect to split*⟩ ≡   206
```
int n0 = 0, n1 = 0;
for (int i = 0; i < bestOffset; ++i)
    if (edges[bestAxis][i].type == BoundEdge::START)
        prims0[n0++] = edges[bestAxis][i].primNum;
for (int i = bestOffset+1; i < 2*nPrims; ++i)
    if (edges[bestAxis][i].type == BoundEdge::END)
        prims1[n1++] = edges[bestAxis][i].primNum;
```

Recall that the node number of the "below" child of this node in the kd-tree nodes array is the current node number plus one. After the recursion has returned from that side of the tree, the nextFreeNode offset is used for the "above" child. The only other important detail here is that the prims0 memory is passed directly for reuse by both children, while the prims1 pointer is advanced forward first. This is necessary since the current invocation of KdTreeAccel::buildTree() depends on its prims1 values being preserved over the first recursive call to KdTreeAccel::buildTree() in the following, since it must be passed as a parameter to the second call. However, there is no corresponding need to preserve the edges values or to preserve prims0 beyond its immediate use in the first recursive call.

⟨*Recursively initialize children nodes*⟩ ≡   206
```
float tsplit = edges[bestAxis][bestOffset].t;
nodes[nodeNum].initInterior(bestAxis, tsplit);
BBox bounds0 = nodeBounds, bounds1 = nodeBounds;
bounds0.pMax[bestAxis] = bounds1.pMin[bestAxis] = tsplit;
buildTree(nodeNum+1, bounds0,
          allPrimBounds, prims0, n0, depth-1, edges,
          prims0, prims1 + nPrims, badRefines);
nodes[nodeNum].aboveChild = nextFreeNode;
buildTree(nodes[nodeNum].aboveChild, bounds1, allPrimBounds,
          prims1, n1, depth-1, edges,
          prims0, prims1 + nPrims, badRefines);
```

Thus, much more space is needed for the prims1 array of integers for storing the worst-case possible number of overlapping primitive numbers than for the prims0 array, which only needs to handle the primitives at a single level at a time.

⟨*Allocate working memory for kd-tree construction*⟩+≡   204
```
int *prims0 = new int[prims.size()];
int *prims1 = new int[(maxDepth+1) * prims.size()];
```

4.4.3 TRAVERSAL

Figure 4.13 shows the basic process of ray traversal through the tree. Intersecting the ray with the tree's overall bounds gives initial tmin and tmax values, marked with points in the figure. As with the grid accelerator, if the ray misses the scene bounds, this method can immediately return false. Otherwise, it starts to descend into the tree, starting at the root. At each interior node, it determines which of the two children the ray enters first and processes both children in order. Traversal ends either when the ray exits the tree or when the closest intersection is found.

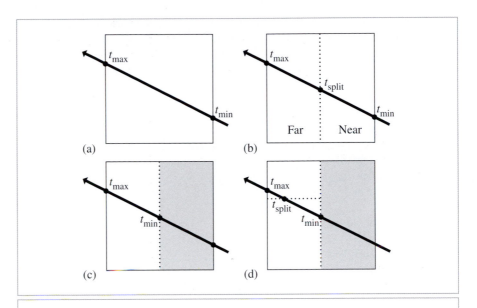

Figure 4.13: Traversal of a Ray through the Kd-Tree. (a) The ray is intersected with the bounds of the tree, giving an initial parametric $[t_{min}, t_{max}]$ range to consider. (b) Because this range is nonempty, it is necessary to consider the two children of the root node here. The ray first enters the child on the right, labeled "near," where it has a parametric range $[t_{min}, t_{split}]$. If the near node is a leaf with primitives in it, ray-primitive intersection tests are performed; otherwise its children nodes are processed. (c) If no hit is found in the node, or if a hit is found beyond $[t_{min}, t_{split}]$, then the far node, on the left, is processed. (d) This sequence continues—processing tree nodes in a depth-first, front-to-back traversal—until the closest intersection is found or the ray exits the tree.

⟨*KdTreeAccel Method Definitions*⟩+≡
```
    bool KdTreeAccel::Intersect(const Ray &ray,
                                Intersection *isect) const {
        ⟨Compute initial parametric range of ray inside kd-tree extent  215⟩
        ⟨Prepare to traverse kd-tree for ray  216⟩
        ⟨Traverse kd-tree nodes in order for ray  216⟩
    }
```

The algorithm starts by finding the overall parametric range $[t_{min}, t_{max}]$ of the ray's overlap with the tree, exiting immediately if there is no overlap.

⟨*Compute initial parametric range of ray inside kd-tree extent*⟩≡   215
```
    float tmin, tmax;
    if (!bounds.IntersectP(ray, &tmin, &tmax))
        return false;
```

Before tree traversal starts, a new mailbox id is found for the ray, and the reciprocals of the components of the direction vector are precomputed so that it is possible to replace divides with multiplies in the main traversal loop. The array of KdToDo structures is used to record the nodes yet to be processed for the ray; it is ordered so that the last active entry in the array is the next node that should be considered. The maximum number of entries needed in this array is the maximum depth of the kd-tree; the array size used in the following should be more than enough in practice.

⟨*Prepare to traverse kd-tree for ray*⟩ ≡   **215**
```
int rayId = curMailboxId++;
Vector invDir(1.f/ray.d.x, 1.f/ray.d.y, 1.f/ray.d.z);
#define MAX_TODO 64
KdToDo todo[MAX_TODO];
int todoPos = 0;
```

⟨*KdTreeAccel Declarations*⟩+≡
```
struct KdToDo {
    const KdAccelNode *node;
    float tmin, tmax;
};
```

The traversal continues through the nodes, processing a single leaf or interior node each time through the loop.

⟨*Traverse kd-tree nodes in order for ray*⟩ ≡   **215**
```
bool hit = false;
const KdAccelNode *node = &nodes[0];
while (node != NULL) {
    ⟨Bail out if we found a hit closer than the current node 216⟩
    if (!node->IsLeaf()) {
        ⟨Process kd-tree interior node 217⟩
    }
    else {
        ⟨Check for intersections inside leaf node 219⟩
        ⟨Grab next node to process from todo list 220⟩
    }
}
return hit;
```

An intersection may have been previously found in a primitive that overlaps multiple nodes. If the intersection was outside the current node when first detected, it is necessary to keep traversing the tree until we come to a node where t_{min} is beyond the intersection. Only then is it certain that there is no closer intersection with some other primitive.

⟨*Bail out if we found a hit closer than the current node*⟩ ≡   **216**
```
if (ray.maxt < tmin) break;
```

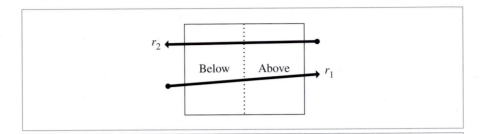

Figure 4.14: The position of the origin of the ray with respect to the splitting plane can be used to determine which of the node's children should be processed first. If the origin of a ray like r_1 is on the "below" side of the splitting plane, we should process the below child before the above child, and vice versa.

For interior tree nodes the first thing to do is to intersect the ray with the node's splitting plane and determine if one or both of the children nodes need to be processed and in what order the ray passes through them.

⟨*Process kd-tree interior node*⟩ ≡   216
    ⟨*Compute parametric distance along ray to split plane* **217**⟩
    ⟨*Get node children pointers for ray* **218**⟩
    ⟨*Advance to next child node, possibly enqueue other child* **219**⟩

The parametric distance to the split plane is computed in the same manner as was done in computing the intersection of a ray and an axis-aligned plane for the ray–bounding box test.

⟨*Compute parametric distance along ray to split plane*⟩ ≡   217
```
    int axis = node->SplitAxis();
    float tplane = (node->SplitPos() - ray.o[axis]) *
        invDir[axis];
```

Now it is necessary to determine the order in which the ray encounters the children nodes, so that the tree is traversed in front-to-back order along the ray. Figure 4.14 shows the geometry of this computation. The position of the ray's origin with respect to the splitting plane is enough to distinguish between the two cases, ignoring for now the case where the ray doesn't actually pass through one of the two nodes.

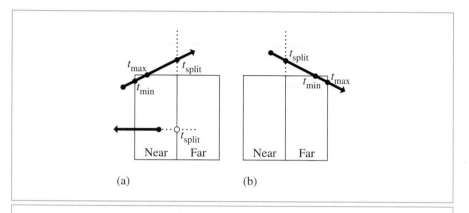

Figure 4.15: Two cases where both children of a node don't need to be processed because the ray doesn't overlap them. (a) The top ray intersects the splitting plane beyond the ray's t_{max} position and thus doesn't enter the far child. The bottom ray is facing away from the splitting plane, indicated by a negative t_{split} value. (b) The ray intersects the plane before the ray's t_{min} value, indicating that the near child doesn't need processing.

⟨*Get node children pointers for ray*⟩ ≡   217

```
const KdAccelNode *firstChild, *secondChild;
int belowFirst = ray.o[axis] <= node->SplitPos();
if (belowFirst) {
    firstChild = node + 1;
    secondChild = &nodes[node->aboveChild];
}
else {
    firstChild = &nodes[node->aboveChild];
    secondChild = node + 1;
}
```

It may not be necessary to process both children of this node. Figure 4.15 shows some configurations where the ray only passes through one of the children. The ray will never miss both children, since otherwise the current interior node should never have been traversed.

The first if test in the following code corresponds to Figure 4.15(a): only the near node needs to be processed if it can be shown that the ray doesn't overlap the far node because it faces away from it or doesn't overlap it because $t_{split} > t_{max}$. Figure 4.15(b) shows the similar case tested in the second if test: the near node may not need processing if the ray doesn't overlap it. Otherwise, the else clause handles the case of both children needing processing; the near node will be processed next, and the far node goes on the todo list.

KdAccelNode **201**
KdAccelNode::SplitPos() **203**
Ray::o **58**

⟨*Advance to next child node, possibly enqueue other child*⟩ ≡   217
```
if (tplane > tmax || tplane < 0)
    node = firstChild;
else if (tplane < tmin)
    node = secondChild;
else {
    ⟨Enqueue secondChild in todo list 219⟩
    node = firstChild;
    tmax = tplane;
}
```

⟨*Enqueue* secondChild *in todo list*⟩ ≡   219
```
todo[todoPos].node = secondChild;
todo[todoPos].tmin = tplane;
todo[todoPos].tmax = tmax;
++todoPos;
```

If the current node is a leaf, intersection tests are performed against the primitives in the leaf, although the mailbox test makes it possible to avoid retesting primitives that have already been considered for this ray.

⟨*Check for intersections inside leaf node*⟩ ≡   216
```
u_int nPrimitives = node->nPrimitives();
if (nPrimitives == 1) {
    MailboxPrim *mp = node->onePrimitive;
    ⟨Check one primitive inside leaf node 219⟩
}
else {
    MailboxPrim **prims = node->primitives;
    for (u_int i = 0; i < nPrimitives; ++i) {
        MailboxPrim *mp = prims[i];
        ⟨Check one primitive inside leaf node 219⟩
    }
}
```

Processing an individual primitive is just a matter of doing the mailbox bookkeeping and passing the intersection request on to the primitive if appropriate.

⟨*Check one primitive inside leaf node*⟩ ≡   219
```
if (mp->lastMailboxId != rayId) {
    mp->lastMailboxId = rayId;
    if (mp->primitive->Intersect(ray, isect))
        hit = true;
}
```

After doing the intersection tests at the leaf node, the next node to process is loaded from the `todo` array. If no more nodes remain, then the ray has passed through the tree without hitting anything.

⟨*Grab next node to process from todo list*⟩ ≡   216
```
if (todoPos > 0) {
    --todoPos;
    node = todo[todoPos].node;
    tmin = todo[todoPos].tmin;
    tmax = todo[todoPos].tmax;
}
else
    break;
```

Like the `GridAccel`, the `KdTreeAccel` has a specialized intersection method for shadow rays that is not shown here. It is largely similar to the `KdTreeAccel::Intersect()` method, just calling `Primitive::IntersectP()` method and returning `true` as soon as it finds any intersection without worrying about finding the closest one.

⟨*KdTreeAccel Public Methods*⟩ ≡   198
```
bool IntersectP(const Ray &ray) const;
```

FURTHER READING

After the introduction of the ray-tracing algorithm, an enormous amount of research was done to try to find effective ways to speed it up, primarily by developing improved ray-tracing acceleration structures. Arvo and Kirk's chapter in *An Introduction to Ray Tracing* (Glassner 1989a) summarizes the state of the art as of 1989 and still provides an excellent taxonomy for categorizing different approaches to ray intersection acceleration. *Ray Tracing News* (*www.acm.org/tog/resources/RTNews/*) is a very good resource for general ray-tracing information and has particularly useful discussions about intersection acceleration approaches, implementation issues, and tricks of the trade.

Clark (1976) first suggested using bounding volumes to cull collections of objects for standard visible-surface determination algorithms. Building on this work, Rubin and Whitted (1980) developed the first hierarchical data structures for scene representation for fast ray tracing, although their method depended on the user to define the hierarchy. Goldsmith and Salmon (1987) described an algorithm for automatically computing bounding volume hierarchies and were also the first to apply techniques for estimating the probability of a ray intersecting a bounding volume based on the volume's surface area.

Fujimoto, Tanaka, and Iwata (1986) were the first to introduce uniform voxel grids for ray tracing, similar to what we describe in this chapter. Snyder and Barr (1987) described a number of key improvements to this approach and showed their use for rendering extremely complex scenes. Some of these improvements are the basis of the exercises at the end of the chapter. Hierarchical grids were first described by Jevans and Wyvill (1989). More complex techniques for hierarchical grids were developed by Cazals, Drettakis, and Puech (1995) and Klimaszewski and Sederberg (1997). The grid traversal method used in this chapter is essentially the one described by Cleary and Wyvill (1988).

Glassner (1984) introduced the use of octrees for ray intersection acceleration; this approach was more robust for scenes with nonuniform distributions of geometry than grids. Use of the kd-tree was first described by Kaplan (1985). Kaplan's tree construction algorithm always split nodes down their middle, although a better approach for building trees and the basis for the method used in the `KdTreeAccel` was introduced by MacDonald and Booth (1990), who estimated ray-node traversal probabilities using relative surface areas. Naylor (1993) has also written on general issues of constructing good kd-trees. Havran and Bittner (2002) have recently revisited many of these issues and introduced useful improvements. Adding a bonus factor for tree nodes that are completely empty, as is done in our implementation, was suggested by Hurley et al. (2002).

Jansen (1986) first developed the efficient ray traversal algorithm for kd-trees. Arvo has also investigated this problem and discusses it in a note in *Ray Tracing News* (Arvo 1988). Sung and Shirley (1992) describe a ray traversal algorithm's implementation for a BSP-tree accelerator; our `KdTreeAccel` traversal code is loosely based on theirs.

Weghorst, Hooper, and Greenberg (1984) discussed the trade-offs of using various shapes for bounding volumes and suggested projecting objects to the screen and using a z-buffer rendering to accelerate finding intersections for camera rays. Other important papers on ray intersection acceleration include Kay and Kajiya (1986), who implemented an object subdivision approach based on bounding objects with collections of slabs, and Arvo and Kirk (1987), who introduced a five-dimensional data structure that subdivided based on both 3D spatial and 2D ray direction.

Arnaldi, Priol, and Bouatouch (1987) Amanatides and Woo (1987) developed the mail-boxing technique.

Kirk and Arvo (1988) introduced the unifying principle of *meta-hierarchies*. They showed that by implementing acceleration data structures to conform to the same interface as is used for primitives in the scene, it's easy to mix and match multiple intersection acceleration schemes. pbrt follows this model since the `Aggregate` inherits from the `Primitive` base class.

Smits (1998) discusses algorithms for fast ray-box intersection on modern architectures and a number of other general issues related to efficient ray tracing.

In the interests of making it easier to compare the performance of different ray intersection algorithms, there have been some efforts to create standard databases of scenes to test various ray intersection algorithms, notably Haines's "standard procedural database" (SPD) (Haines 1987) and Lext et al.'s BART scenes, which include animation (Lext, Assarsson, and Möller 2001). A few of the SPD scenes are available in the pbrt file format on the accompanying CD.

EXERCISES

4.1 What kind of scenes are worst-case scenarios for the two acceleration structures in pbrt? Construct scenes with these characteristics, and measure the performance of pbrt as you add more primitives. How does the worst case for the grid behave when rendered with the kd-tree, and vice versa?

4.2 Render a number of scenes using each of the accelerators in this chapter and record the statistics that the system prints out for each one. What do these statistics tell you about how well the different accelerators handle different types of scenes (uniform distributions of geometry versus nonuniform, etc.)? In particular, assuming the scenes are largely modeled with triangles, what does the fraction of ray-triangle intersection tests that found intersections tell you about the relative effectiveness of the approaches? What about the total number of ray-triangle intersections found?

4.3 Experiment with different techniques for choosing the number of voxels for the uniform grid. Investigate and measure the trade-offs related to time spent building the grid, memory used to represent the grid, and time needed to find ray-object intersections for different grid resolutions.

4.4 Try using bounding box tests to improve the grid's performance: Inside each grid voxel, store the bounding box of the geometry that overlaps the voxel. Use this bounding box to quickly skip intersection tests with geometry if the ray doesn't intersect the bound. Develop criteria based on the number of primitives in a voxel and the size of their bound with respect to the voxel's bound to only do the bounding box tests for voxels where doing so is likely to improve performance. When is this extra work worthwhile?

4.5 Rather than computing a ray–bounding box intersection for the technique described in the previous exercise, it can be more efficient to check to see if the bounding box of a ray's extent as it passes through the voxel overlaps the bounding box of the object (Figure 4.16). (This is a less accurate test than the ray-box intersection, although it is much more efficient.) Snyder and Barr (1987) describe an efficient way to incrementally compute the ray bound. Implement this method and measure its affect on performance. Can you develop good heuristics for choosing between the two approaches?

4.6 Disable the mailbox test in the grid or kd-tree accelerator and measure how much pbrt slows down when rendering various scenes. How effective is mail-

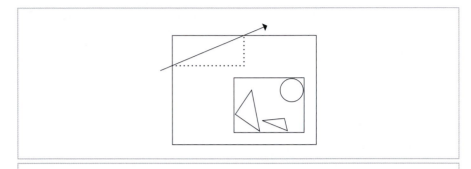

Figure 4.16: If a bounding box of the overlapping geometry is stored in each voxel, it can be used as the basis for fast rejection of unnecessary ray-primitive intersection tests. An alternative to checking for ray–bounding box intersection is to find the bounding box of the ray inside the voxel (shown here with a dotted line) and test to see if that overlaps the geometry bound.

boxing? How many redundant intersection tests are performed without it? One alternative to mailboxing is to set the ray's $[t_{min}, t_{max}]$ range for the accelerator cell that it is currently in so that the primitives will ignore intersections outside that range and may be able to avoid performing a complete intersection test if no intersection is possible in the current range. How does the performance of that approach compare to mailboxing?

❶ 4.7 There is a subtle bug in the mailboxing schemes for both the grid and the kd-tree that may cause intersections to be missed after a few billion rays have been traced. Describe a scenario where this might happen and suggest how this bug could be fixed. How likely is this bug to cause an incorrect result to be returned by the accelerator?

❷ 4.8 Generalize the grid implementation in this chapter to be hierarchical: refine voxels that have an excessive number of primitives overlapping them to instead hold a finer subgrid to store its geometry. (See, for example, Jevans and Wyvill (1989) for one approach to this problem.)

❷ 4.9 Develop a more complex hierarchical grid implementation, following the approach of either Cazals, Drettakis, and Puech (1995) or Klimaszewski and Sederberg (1997). How does its performance compare to hierarchical grids based on Jevans and Wyvill's approach?

❶ 4.10 Implement a primitive list "accelerator" that just stores an array that holds all of the primitives and loops over all of them for every intersection test. How much does using this accelerator make the system slow down? Is this accelerator ever likely to be faster than the `GridAccel` or `KdTreeAccel`? Describe a contrived example where the primitive list would be faster than a grid or kd-tree even for a complex scene.

● 4.11   Implement smarter overlap tests for building accelerators. Using objects' bounding boxes to determine which grid cells and which sides of a kd-tree split they overlap can hurt performance by causing unnecessary intersection tests. (Recall Figure 4.6.) Add a `bool Shape::Overlaps(const BBox &) const` method to the shape interface that takes a world space bounding box and determines if the shape truly overlaps the given bound. A default implementation could get the world bound from the shape and use that for the test, and specialized versions could be written for frequently used shapes. Implement this method for `Spheres` and `Triangles` and modify the accelerators to call it. You may find it helpful to read Akenine-Möller's paper on fast triangle-box overlap testing (Akenine-Möller 2001). Measure the change in `pbrt`'s overall performance due to this change, separately accounting for increased time spent building the acceleration structure and reduction in ray-object intersection time due to fewer intersections. For a variety of scenes, determine how many fewer intersection tests are performed thanks to this improvement.

● 4.12   Fix the `KdTreeAccel` so that it doesn't always immediately refine all primitives before building the tree. One possible approach is to build additional kd-trees as needed, storing these subtrees in the hierarchy where the original unrefined primitive was. Implement this approach, or come up with a better technique to address this problem and measure the change in running time and memory use for a variety of scenes.

● 4.13   Investigate alternative cost functions for building kd-trees for the `KdTreeAccel`. How much can a poor cost function hurt its performance? How much improvement can be had compared to the current one? Are there important factors that the current cost functions don't account for well?

● 4.14   Implement an accelerator based on hierarchical bounding volumes, starting with all of the primitives and progressively partitioning them into smaller spatially nearby subsets, giving a hierarchy of primitives. The top node of the hierarchy should hold a bound that encompasses all of the primitives in the scene and have a small number of children nodes, each of which bounds a subset of the scene. This should continue recursively until the bottom of the tree, at which point the bound around a single primitive is stored. Read Goldsmith and Salmon (1987) about building HBV hierarchies and implement their approach as an `Aggregate` in `pbrt`. Compare its performance against the grid and kd-tree accelerators.

● 4.15   The idea of using spatial data structures for ray intersection acceleration can be generalized to include spatial data structures that themselves hold other spatial data structures, rather than just primitives. Not only could we have a grid that has subgrids inside the grid cells that have many primitives in them (thus partially solving the adaptive refinement problem), but we could also have the scene organized into a hierarchical bounding volume where the leaf

KdTreeAccel 198

nodes are grids that hold smaller collections of spatially nearby primitives. Such hybrid techniques can bring the best of a variety of spatial data structure–based ray intersection acceleration methods. In pbrt, because both geometric primitives and intersection accelerators inherit from the Primitive base class and thus provide the same interface, it's easy to mix and match in this way. Modify pbrt to build hybrid acceleration structures, for example, using a kd-tree to coarsely sort the scene geometry and then uniform grids at the leaves of the tree to manage dense, spatially local collections of geometry. Measure the running time and memory use for rendering schemes with this method compared to the current accelerators.

CHAPTER FIVE

COLOR AND RADIOMETRY

In order to precisely describe how light is represented and sampled to compute images, we must first establish some background in *radiometry*—the study of the propagation of electromagnetic radiation in an environment. Of particular interest in rendering are the wavelengths (λ) of electromagnetic radiation between approximately 370 nm and 730 nm, which account for light visible to humans. The lower wavelengths ($\lambda \approx 400$ nm) are the bluish colors, the middle wavelengths ($\lambda \approx 550$ nm) are the greens, and the upper wavelengths ($\lambda \approx 650$ nm) are the reds.

In this chapter, we will introduce four key quantities that describe electromagnetic radiation: flux, intensity, irradiance, and radiance. These radiometric quantities are each described by their *spectral power distribution* (SPD)—a distribution function of wavelength that describes the amount of light at each wavelength. The Spectrum class, which is defined in Section 5.1, is used in pbrt to represent SPDs.

5.1 SPECTRAL REPRESENTATION

The SPDs of real-world objects can be quite complicated; Figure 5.1 shows graphs of the spectral distribution of emission from a fluorescent light and the spectral distribution of the reflectance of lemon skin. A renderer doing computations with SPDs needs a compact, efficient, and accurate way to represent functions like these. In practice, some trade-off needs to be made between these qualities.

Spectrum 230

227

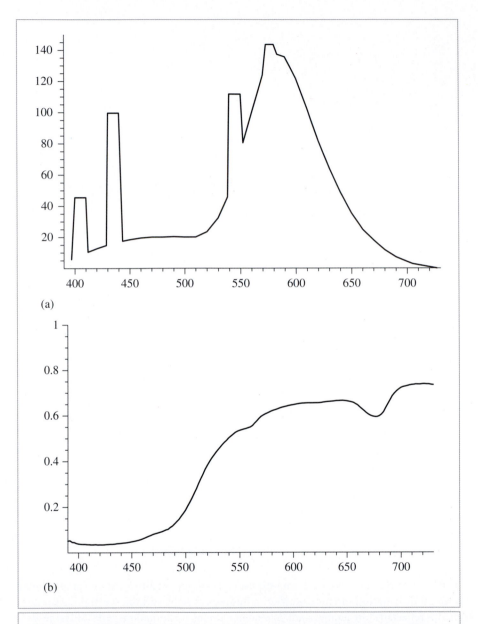

(a)

(b)

Figure 5.1: (a) Spectral power distributions of a fluorescent light and (b) the reflectance of lemon skin. Wavelengths around 400 nm are bluish colors, greens and yellows are in the middle range of wavelengths, and reds have wavelengths around 700 nm. The fluorescent light's SPD is even spikier than shown here, where the SPDs have been binned into 10 nm ranges; it actually emits much of its illumination at single discrete frequencies.

A general framework for investigating these issues can be developed based on the problem of finding good *basis functions* to represent SPDs. The idea behind basis functions is to map the infinite-dimensional space of possible SPD functions to a low-dimensional space of coefficients $c_i \in \mathbb{R}$. For example, a trivial basis function is the constant function $B(\lambda) = 1$. An arbitrary SPD would be represented in this basis by a single coefficient c equal to its average value, so that its approximation would be $cB(\lambda) = c$. This is obviously a poor approximation, since most SPDs are much more complex than this single basis function is capable of representing accurately.

Many different basis functions have been investigated for spectral representation in computer graphics; the "Further Reading" section cites a number of papers and further resources on this topic. Different sets of basis functions can offset substantially different trade-offs in the complexity of the key operations like converting an arbitrary SPD into a set of coefficients (projecting it into the basis), computing the coefficients for the SPD given by the product of two SPDs expressed in the basis, and so on.

5.1.1 SPECTRUM CLASS

Throughout pbrt, we have been careful to implement all computations involving SPDs in terms of the Spectrum class and its built-in operators. The Spectrum class hides the details of the particular spectral representation used, so that changing this detail of the system only requires updating the Spectrum implementation; other code can remain unchanged. The Spectrum class is declared in core/color.h⊙ and defined in core/color.cpp.⊙

However, we have not written the system such that different Spectrum implementations could be provided as plug-ins; if the implementation is changed, the entire system must be recompiled. The advantage to this design is that many of the various Spectrum methods can be implemented as short functions that can be inlined by the compiler, rather than being left as stand-alone functions that have to be invoked through the slow virtual method call mechanism. Inlining frequently used short functions like these can give a substantial improvement in performance.

The standard Spectrum implementation here is based on the most straightforward of the possible representations: it stores a fixed number of samples of the SPD's value at a fixed set of wavelengths. This representation works well for relatively smoothly varying SPDs, and it is useful as a baseline for comparison with other representations. When it is used with a very large number of samples (e.g., with a 1 nm spacing), it can be used to compute reference solutions (at significant computational expense). Basic operations like adding and multiplying SPDs are efficient, with complexity linear in the number of samples.

Spectrum 230

The disadvantage of this representation is that it is particularly ill-suited for SPDs with narrow spikes, such as the fluorescent light SPD. If the samples are placed such that they miss the spike, substantially inaccurate images will be computed. Implementing more complex representations is left for the exercises at the end of the chapter.

The number of samples stored by the Spectrum is set at compile time by COLOR_SAMPLES.

⟨*Global Constants*⟩+≡
```
#define COLOR_SAMPLES 3
```

⟨*Spectrum Declarations*⟩ ≡
```
class COREDLL Spectrum {
public:
    ⟨Spectrum Public Methods  230⟩
    ⟨Spectrum Public Data  235⟩
private:
    ⟨Spectrum Private Data  230⟩
};
```

⟨*Spectrum Private Data*⟩ ≡   **230**
```
float c[COLOR_SAMPLES];
```

Two Spectrum constructors are provided, one initializing a spectrum with the same value for all samples, and one initializing it from an array of sample values:

⟨*Spectrum Public Methods*⟩ ≡   **230**
```
Spectrum(float v = 0.f) {
    for (int i = 0; i < COLOR_SAMPLES; ++i)
        c[i] = v;
}
```

⟨*Spectrum Public Methods*⟩+≡   **230**
```
Spectrum(float cs[COLOR_SAMPLES]) {
    for (int i = 0; i < COLOR_SAMPLES; ++i)
        c[i] = cs[i];
}
```

A variety of arithmetic operations on Spectrum objects are supported; the implementations are all quite straightforward. First are operations to add pairs of spectral distributions. It's easy to show that each sample value for the sum of two SPDs is equal to the sum of the corresponding sample values.

⟨*Spectrum Public Methods*⟩+≡   **230**
```
Spectrum &operator+=(const Spectrum &s2) {
    for (int i = 0; i < COLOR_SAMPLES; ++i)
        c[i] += s2.c[i];
    return *this;
}
```

⟨*Spectrum Public Methods*⟩+≡   230

```
Spectrum operator+(const Spectrum &s2) const {
    Spectrum ret = *this;
    for (int i = 0; i < COLOR_SAMPLES; ++i)
        ret.c[i] += s2.c[i];
    return ret;
}
```

Similarly, subtraction, multiplication, and division of Spectrum objects are defined component-wise. These methods are very similar to the ones already shown, so we won't include them here.

Because pbrt has a performance-critical section of code where a Spectrum is updated with a weighted value of another Spectrum (e.g., s = s+w*s2), the AddWeighted() method is available to do this computation more efficiently than may be possible using the arithmetic operators defined earlier. (Some compilers have trouble eliminating unnecessary temporary variables introduced in expressions like these.)

⟨*Spectrum Public Methods*⟩+≡   230

```
void AddWeighted(float w, const Spectrum &s) {
    for (int i = 0; i < COLOR_SAMPLES; ++i)
        c[i] += w * s.c[i];
}
```

We also provide an equality test:

⟨*Spectrum Public Methods*⟩+≡   230

```
bool operator==(const Spectrum &sp) const {
    for (int i = 0; i < COLOR_SAMPLES; ++i)
        if (c[i] != sp.c[i]) return false;
    return true;
}
```

It is often useful to know if a Spectrum represents an SPD with value zero everywhere. If, for example, a surface has zero reflectance, the light transport routines can avoid the computational cost of casting reflection rays that have contributions that would eventually be multiplied by zeros and thus do not need to be traced.

⟨*Spectrum Public Methods*⟩+≡   230

```
bool Black() const {
    for (int i = 0; i < COLOR_SAMPLES; ++i)
        if (c[i] != 0.) return false;
    return true;
}
```

COLOR_SAMPLES 230
Spectrum 230
Spectrum::c 230

The Spectrum implementation must also provide implementations of a number of slightly more esoteric methods, including ones that take the square root of a spectrum or raise the components of a Spectrum to a given power. These are needed for some of the computations performed by the Fresnel classes and the Lafortune surface reflection model in Chapter 9.

⟨*Spectrum Public Methods*⟩+≡   **230**
```
Spectrum Sqrt() const {
    Spectrum ret;
    for (int i = 0; i < COLOR_SAMPLES; ++i)
        ret.c[i] = sqrtf(c[i]);
    return ret;
}
```

⟨*Spectrum Public Methods*⟩+≡   **230**
```
Spectrum Pow(const Spectrum &e) const {
    Spectrum ret;
    for (int i = 0; i < COLOR_SAMPLES; ++i)
        ret.c[i] = c[i] > 0 ? powf(c[i], e.c[i]) : 0.f;
    return ret;
}
```

For some computations related to participating media in Chapters 12 and 17, being able to perform unary negation and exponentiation of Spectrum values is necessary.

⟨*Spectrum Public Methods*⟩+≡   **230**
```
Spectrum operator-() const;
friend COREDLL Spectrum Exp(const Spectrum &s);
```

Some portions of the image processing pipeline will want to clamp a spectrum to ensure that the function it represents is within some allowable range.

⟨*Spectrum Public Methods*⟩+≡   **230**
```
Spectrum Clamp(float low = 0.f, float high = INFINITY) const {
    Spectrum ret;
    for (int i = 0; i < COLOR_SAMPLES; ++i)
        ret.c[i] = ::Clamp(c[i], low, high);
    return ret;
}
```

Finally, we provide a debugging routine to check if any of the sample values of the SPD is the IEEE not-a-number floating-point value (NaN). This situation can happen due to an accidental division by zero.

⟨*Spectrum Public Methods*⟩+≡   230
```
bool IsNaN() const {
    for (int i = 0; i < COLOR_SAMPLES; ++i)
        if (isnan(c[i])) return true;
    return false;
}
```

5.1.2 XYZ COLOR

A remarkable property of the human visual system makes it possible to represent colors with just three floating-point numbers. The *tristimulus theory* of color perception says that all visible SPDs can be accurately represented for human observers with three values, x_λ, y_λ, and z_λ. Given an SPD $S(\lambda)$, these values are computed by integrating its product with the *spectral matching curves*, $X(\lambda)$, $Y(\lambda)$, and $Z(\lambda)$:

$$x_\lambda = \int_\lambda S(\lambda)\, X(\lambda)\mathrm{d}\lambda$$

$$y_\lambda = \int_\lambda S(\lambda)\, Y(\lambda)\mathrm{d}\lambda$$

$$z_\lambda = \int_\lambda S(\lambda)\, Z(\lambda)\mathrm{d}\lambda.$$

These curves were determined by the Commission Internationale de l'Éclairage (CIE) standards body after a series of experiments with human test subjects and are graphed in Figure 5.2. It is believed that these matching curves are generally similar to the responses of the three types of color-sensitive cones in the human retina. Remarkably, SPDs with substantially different distributions may have very similar x_λ, y_λ, and z_λ values. To the human observer, such SPDs actually appear the same visually. Pairs of such spectra are called *metamers*.

This brings us to a subtle point about representations of spectral power distributions. Most color spaces attempt to model colors that are visible to humans, and therefore use only three coefficients, exploiting the tristimulus theory of color perception. Although XYZ works well to represent a given SPD to be displayed for a human observer, it is *not* a particularly good set of basis functions for spectral computation. For example, although XYZ values would work well to describe the perceived color of lemon skin or a fluorescent light individually (recall Figure 5.1), the product of their respective XYZ values is likely to give a noticeably different XYZ color than the XYZ value computed by multiplying more accurate representations of their SPDs and *then* computing the XYZ value.

With that limitation in mind, we will add a method to the Spectrum class that returns the XYZ values for its SPD. This method is called by the ImageFilm, for example, as it turns the final rendered image (represented by an array of Spectrum values) into display-dependent RGB colors suitable for display. Converting to display-independent XYZ values is the first step in this process.

COLOR_SAMPLES 230
ImageFilm 371
Spectrum 230
Spectrum::c 230

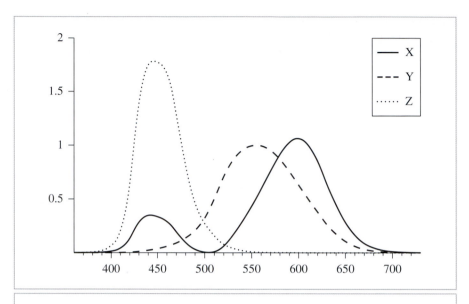

Figure 5.2: Computing the XYZ Values for an Arbitrary SPD. The SPD is convolved with each of the three matching curves.

For a point-sampled spectral representation, the convolution with the XYZ matching functions ends up expressing the x_λ, y_λ, and z_λ values as a weighted sum of the point sample values.

⟨*Spectrum Public Methods*⟩+≡   **230**
```
    void XYZ(float xyz[3]) const {
        xyz[0] = xyz[1] = xyz[2] = 0.;
        for (int i = 0; i < COLOR_SAMPLES; ++i) {
            xyz[0] += XWeight[i] * c[i];
            xyz[1] += YWeight[i] * c[i];
            xyz[2] += ZWeight[i] * c[i];
        }
    }
```

Therefore, we must also decide the wavelengths where the SPD point samples are taken; until now, it has been possible to implement the Spectrum class without facing this issue. Although not sufficient for high-quality spectral computations, an expedient choice is to use the spectra of standard red, green, and blue phosphors for televisions and CRT display tubes. A standard set of these RGB spectra has been defined for high-definition television. The weights to convert from these RGBs to XYZ values are the following:

⟨*Spectrum Method Definitions*⟩ ≡

```
float Spectrum::XWeight[COLOR_SAMPLES] = {
    0.412453f, 0.357580f, 0.180423f
};
float Spectrum::YWeight[COLOR_SAMPLES] = {
    0.212671f, 0.715160f, 0.072169f
};
float Spectrum::ZWeight[COLOR_SAMPLES] = {
    0.019334f, 0.119193f, 0.950227f
};
```

It's also useful to provide a Spectrum creation function that converts from XYZ coefficients to the internal representation. For the point-sampled Spectrum representation, this also works out to be a weighted sum.

⟨*Spectrum Method Definitions*⟩ + ≡

```
Spectrum FromXYZ(float x, float y, float z) {
    float c[3];
    c[0] =  3.240479f * x + -1.537150f * y + -0.498535f * z;
    c[1] = -0.969256f * x +  1.875991f * y +  0.041556f * z;
    c[2] =  0.055648f * x + -0.204043f * y +  1.057311f * z;
    return Spectrum(c);
}
```

For convenience in computing values for XWeight, YWeight, and ZWeight for other spectral basis functions, we will also provide the values of the standard $X(\lambda)$, $Y(\lambda)$, and $Z(\lambda)$ response curves sampled at 1 nm increments from 360 nm to 830 nm.

⟨*Spectrum Public Data*⟩ ≡   **230**

```
static const int CIEstart = 360;
static const int CIEend = 830;
static const int nCIE = CIEend-CIEstart+1;
static const float CIE_X[nCIE];
static const float CIE_Y[nCIE];
static const float CIE_Z[nCIE];
```

COLOR_SAMPLES 230
Spectrum 230

The y coordinate of the XYZ color is closely related to *luminance*, which measures the perceived brightness of a color. (Luminance is discussed in more detail in Section 8.4.1.) For the convenience of methods there, we will provide a method to compute y alone in a separate method.

⟨*Spectrum Public Methods*⟩+≡   **230**
```
float y() const {
    float v = 0.;
    for (int i = 0; i < COLOR_SAMPLES; ++i)
        v += YWeight[i] * c[i];
    return v;
}
```

Luminance also gives a convenient way to order `Spectrum` instances from dark to bright:

⟨*Spectrum Public Methods*⟩+≡   **230**
```
bool operator<(const Spectrum &s2) const {
    return y() < s2.y();
}
```

5.2 BASIC RADIOMETRY

Radiometry provides a set of ideas and mathematical tools to describe light propagation and reflection. It forms the basis of the derivation of the rendering algorithms that will be used throughout the rest of this book. Interestingly enough, radiometry wasn't originally derived from first principles using the physics of light, but was built on an abstraction of light based on particles flowing through space. As such, effects like polarization of light do not naturally fit into this framework, although connections have since been made between radiometry and Maxwell's equations, giving radiometry a solid basis in physics.

Radiative transfer is the phenomenological study of the transfer of radiant energy. It is based on radiometric principles and operates at the *geometric optics* level, where macroscopic properties of light suffice to describe how light interacts with objects much larger than the light's wavelength. It is not uncommon to incorporate phenomena from wave optics models of light, but these results need to be expressed in the language of radiative transfer's basic abstractions.[1] In this manner, it is possible to describe interactions of light with objects of approximately the same size as the wavelength of the light, and thereby model effects like dispersion and interference. At an even finer level of detail, quantum mechanics is needed to describe light's interaction with atoms. Fortunately, direct simulation of quantum mechanical principles is unnecessary for solving rendering problems in computer graphics, so the intractability of such an approach is avoided.

In pbrt, we will assume that geometric optics is an adequate model for the description of light and light scattering. This leads to a few basic assumptions about the behavior of light that will be used implicitly throughout the system:

---

1   Preisendorfer (1965) has connected radiative transfer theory to Maxwell's classical equations describing electromagnetic fields. His framework both demonstrates their equivalence and makes it easier to apply results from one worldview to the other. More recent work was done in this area by Fante (1981).

- *Linearity:* The combined effect of two inputs to an optical system is always equal to the sum of the effects of each of the inputs individually.
- *Energy conservation:* When light scatters from a surface or from participating media, the scattering events can never produce more energy than they started with.
- *No polarization:* We will ignore polarization of the electromagnetic field; therefore the only relevant property of light is its distribution by wavelength (or, equivalently, frequency).
- *No fluorescence or phosphorescence:* The behavior of light at one wavelength is completely independent of light's behavior at other wavelengths or times. As with polarization, it is not too difficult to include these effects, but they would add little practical value to the system.
- *Steady state:* Light in the environment is assumed to have reached equilibrium, so its radiance distribution isn't changing over time. This happens nearly instantaneously with light in realistic scenes, so it is not a limitation in practice. Note that phosphorescence also violates the steady-state assumption.

The most significant loss from adopting a geometric optics model is that diffraction and interference effects cannot easily be accounted for. As noted by Preisendorfer (1965), this is a hard problem to fix because, for example, the total flux over two areas isn't necessarily equal to the sum of flux over each individual area in the presence of those effects (p. 24).

5.2.1 BASIC QUANTITIES

There are four radiometric quantities that are central to rendering: flux, irradiance, intensity, and radiance. All of these quantities are generally wavelength dependent. For the remainder of this chapter, we will not make this dependence explicit, but this property is important to keep in mind.

Flux

Radiant flux, also known as *power*, is the total amount of energy passing through a surface or region of space per unit time. Its units are joules/second (J/s), or more commonly watts (W), and it is normally denoted by the symbol Φ. Total emission from light sources is generally described in terms of flux. Figure 5.3 shows flux from a point light source measured by the total amount of energy passing through an imaginary sphere around the light. Note that the total amount of flux measured on either of the two spheres in Figure 5.3 is the same—although less energy is passing through any local part of the large sphere than the small sphere, the greater area of the large sphere means that the total flux is the same.

Irradiance

Irradiance (E) is the area density of flux (W/m^2). For the point light source example in Figure 5.3, irradiance at a point on the outer sphere is less than the irradiance at a point on the inner sphere, since the surface area of the outer sphere is larger. In particular, for a sphere in this configuration that has radius r,

$$E = \frac{\Phi}{4\pi r^2}.$$

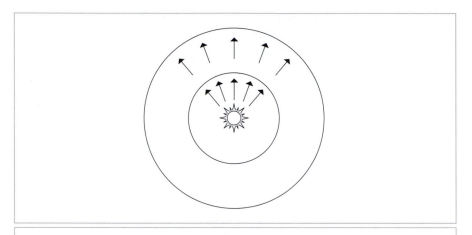

Figure 5.3: Radiant flux, Φ, measures energy passing through a surface or region of space. Here, flux from a point light source is measured at spheres that surround the light.

This fact explains why the amount of energy received from a light falls off with the squared distance from the light.

The irradiance equation can also help us understand the origin of *Lambert's law*, which says that the amount of light arriving at a surface is proportional to the cosine of the angle between the light direction and the surface normal (Figure 5.4). Consider a light source with area A and flux Φ that is illuminating a surface. If the light is shining directly down on the surface (as on the left side of the figure), then the area on the surface receiving light A_1 is equal to A. Irradiance at any point inside A_1 is then

$$E_1 = \frac{\Phi}{A}.$$

However, if the light is at an angle to the surface, the area on the surface receiving light is larger. If A is small, then the area receiving flux, A_2, is roughly $A/\cos\theta$. For points inside A_2, the irradiance is therefore

$$E_2 = \frac{\Phi\cos\theta}{A}.$$

More formally, to cover the general case where the emitted flux distribution is not constant, irradiance at a point is defined as

$$E = \frac{d\Phi}{dA},$$

where the differential flux from the light is computed over the differential area receiving flux.

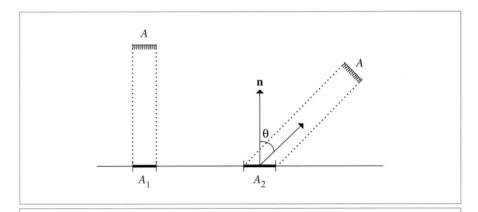

Figure 5.4: Lambert's Law. Irradiance (E) arriving at a surface varies according to the cosine of the angle of incidence of illumination, since illumination is over a larger area at smaller incident angles.

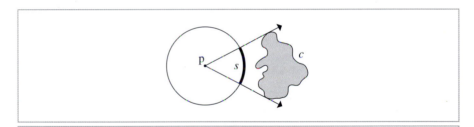

Figure 5.5: Planar Angle. The planar angle of an object c as seen from a point p is equal to the angle it subtends as seen from p, or equivalently as the length of the arc s on the unit sphere.

Solid Angle and Intensity

In order to define *intensity*, we first need to define the notion of a *solid angle*. Solid angles are just the extension of two-dimensional angles in a plane to an angle on a sphere. The *planar angle* is the total angle subtended by some object with respect to some position (Figure 5.5). Consider the unit circle around the point p; if we project the shaded object onto that circle, some length of the circle s will be covered by its projection. The arc length of s (which is the same as the angle θ) is the angle subtended by the object. Planar angles are measured in *radians*.

The solid angle extends the 2D unit circle to a 3D unit sphere (Figure 5.6). The total area s is the solid angle subtended by the object. Solid angles are measured in *steradians*. The entire sphere subtends a solid angle of 4π, and a hemisphere subtends 2π.

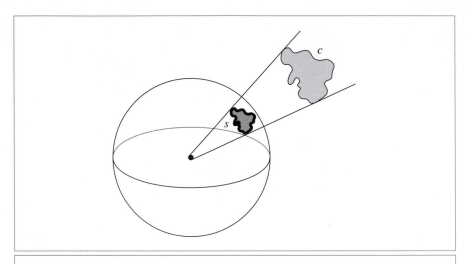

Figure 5.6: Solid Angle. The solid angle s subtended by an object c in three dimensions is computed by projecting c onto the unit sphere and measuring the area of its projection.

The set of points on the unit sphere centered at a point p can be used to describe the vectors anchored at p. We will frequently use the symbol ω to indicate these directions, and we will use the convention that ω is a normalized vector.

Given these definitions, we can now define intensity, which is flux density per solid angle:

$$I = \frac{d\Phi}{d\omega}.$$

Intensity describes the directional distribution of light, but it is only meaningful for point light sources.

Radiance

The final, and most important, radiometric quantity is *radiance*, L. Radiance is the flux density per unit area, per unit solid angle. In terms of flux, it is

$$L = \frac{d\Phi}{d\omega\, dA^{\perp}}, \tag{5.1}$$

where $dA^{\perp}$ is the projected area of dA on a hypothetical surface perpendicular to ω (Figure 5.7). Thus, it is the limit of the measurement of incident light at the surface as a cone of incident directions of interest $d\omega$ becomes very small, and as the local area of interest on the surface dA also becomes very small.

Of all of these radiometric quantities, radiance will be the one used most frequently throughout the rest of the book. An intuitive reason for this is that in some sense it's the

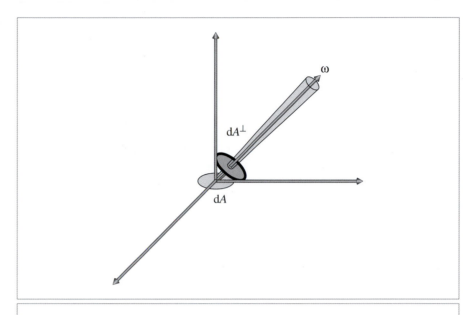

Figure 5.7: Radiance L is defined as flux per unit solid angle $d\omega$ per unit projected area $dA^{\perp}$.

most fundamental of all the radiometric quantities; if radiance is given, then all of the other values can be computed in terms of integrals of radiance over areas and directions. Another nice property of radiance is that it remains constant along rays through empty space. It is thus a natural quantity to compute with ray tracing.

5.2.2 INCIDENT AND EXITANT RADIANCE FUNCTIONS

When discussing radiance at a point in an environment and when writing equations based on radiance, it is useful to make a distinction between radiance arriving at the point (for example, due to illumination from a light source) and radiance leaving that point (for example, due to reflection from a surface). In pbrt we will use the idea of incident and exitant radiance functions to distinguish between these two cases. The approach used here is based on Section 3.5 of Veach (1997).

Consider a point p on the surface of an object. There is some distribution of radiance arriving at the point that can be described mathematically by a function of position and direction. This function is denoted by $L_i(p, \omega)$ (Figure 5.8). The function that describes the outgoing reflected radiance from the surface at that point is denoted by $L_o(p, \omega)$. Note that in both cases the direction vector ω is oriented to point away from p, but be aware that some authors use a notation where ω is reversed for L_i terms so that it points toward p.

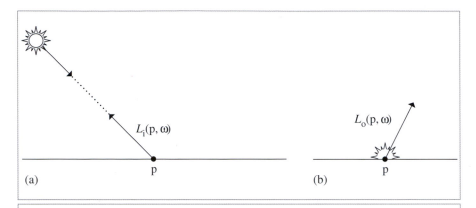

Figure 5.8: (a) The incident radiance function $L_i(p, \omega)$ describes the distribution of radiance as a function of position and direction. (b) The exitant radiance function $L_o(p, \omega)$ gives the distribution of radiance leaving the surface. Note that for both functions, ω is oriented to point away from the surface, and thus, for example, $L_i(p, -\omega)$ gives the radiance arriving on the other side of the surface than the one where ω lies.

It is important to see that, in general,

$$L_i(p, \omega) \neq L_o(p, \omega).$$

Another property to keep in mind is that at a point in space where there is no surface and where there is no participating media causing scattering, these functions are related by

$$L_o(p, \omega) = L_i(p, -\omega).$$

5.3 WORKING WITH RADIOMETRIC INTEGRALS

One of the most frequent tasks in rendering is the evaluation of integrals of radiometric quantities. In this section, we will present some tricks that can make this task easier. To illustrate the use of these techniques, we will often use the computation of irradiance at a point as an example. Irradiance at a point p with surface normal $\mathbf{n}$ due to radiance over a set of directions Ω is

$$E(p, \mathbf{n}) = \int_\Omega L_i(p, \omega) |\cos \theta'| d\omega', \qquad [5.2]$$

where $L_i(p, \omega)$ is the incident radiance function (Figure 5.9) and the $\cos \theta$ term in this integral is due to the $dA^\perp$ term in the definition of radiance. θ is measured as the angle between ω and the surface normal $\mathbf{n}$. Irradiance is usually computed over the hemisphere $\mathcal{H}^2(\mathbf{n})$ of directions about a given surface normal $\mathbf{n}$.

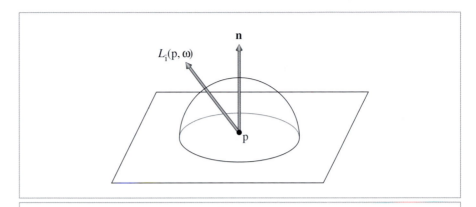

Figure 5.9: Irradiance at a point p is given by the integral of radiance times the cosine of the incident direction over the entire upper hemisphere above the point.

5.3.1 INTEGRALS OVER PROJECTED SOLID ANGLE

The various cosine terms in the integrals for radiometric quantities can often distract from what is being expressed in the integral. This problem can be avoided using *projected solid angle* rather than solid angle to measure areas subtended by objects being integrated over. The projected solid angle subtended by an object is determined by projecting the object onto the unit sphere, as was done for the solid angle, but then projecting the resulting shape down onto the unit disk (Figure 5.10). Integrals over hemispheres of directions with respect to solid angle can equivalently be written as integrals over projected solid angle.

The projected solid angle measure is related to the solid angle measure by

$$d\omega^{\perp} = |\cos\theta| d\omega,$$

so the irradiance-from-radiance integral over the hemisphere can be written more simply as

$$E(\mathrm{p}, \mathbf{n}) = \int_{\mathcal{H}^2(\mathbf{n})} L_i(\mathrm{p}, \omega) \, d\omega^{\perp}.$$

For the rest of this book, we will write integrals over directions in terms of solid angle, rather than projected solid angle. In other sources, however, projected solid angle can be common, and it is always important to be aware of the integrand's actual measure.

5.3.2 INTEGRALS OVER SPHERICAL COORDINATES

It is often convenient to transform integrals over solid angle into integrals over spherical coordinates (θ, ϕ). Recall that an (x, y, z) direction vector can also be written in terms of spherical angles (Figure 5.11):

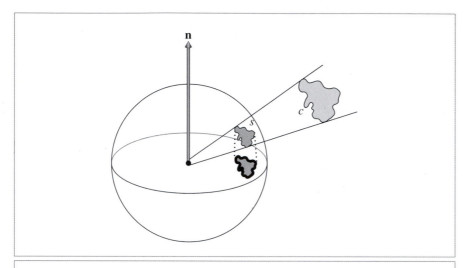

Figure 5.10: The projected solid angle subtended by an object c is the cosine-weighted solid angle that it subtends. It can be computed by finding the object's solid angle s, projecting it down to the plane perpendicular to the surface normal, and measuring its area there. Thus, the projected solid angle depends on the surface normal where it is being measured, since the normal orients the plane of projection.

$$x = \sin \theta \, \cos \phi$$
$$y = \sin \theta \, \sin \phi$$
$$z = \cos \theta.$$

In order to convert an integral over a solid angle to an integral over (θ, ϕ), we need to be able to express the relationship between the differential area of a set of directions $d\omega$ and the differential area of a (θ, ϕ) pair (Figure 5.12). The differential area $d\omega$ is the product of the differential lengths of its sides, $\sin \theta \, d\phi$ and $d\theta$. Therefore,

$$d\omega = \sin \theta \, d\theta \, d\phi.$$

We can thus see that the irradiance integral over the hemisphere, Equation (5.2) with $\Omega = \mathcal{H}^2(\mathbf{n})$, can equivalently be written

$$E(\mathrm{p}, \mathbf{n}) = \int_0^{2\pi} \int_0^{\pi/2} L_i(\mathrm{p}, \theta, \phi) \cos \theta \, \sin \theta \, d\theta \, d\phi$$

If the radiance is the same from all directions, this simplifies to $E = \pi L_i$.

Just as we found irradiance in terms of incident radiance, we can also compute the total flux emitted from some object over the hemisphere surrounding the normal by integrating over the object's surface area A:

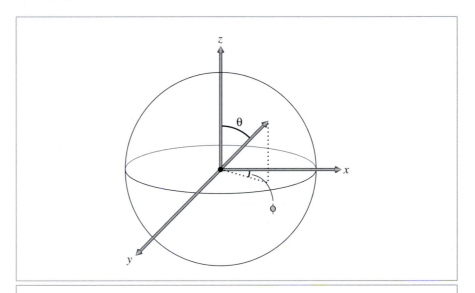

Figure 5.11: A direction vector can be written in terms of spherical coordinates (θ, ϕ) if the x, y, and z basis vectors are given as well. The spherical angle formulae make it easy to convert between the two representations.

$$\Phi = \int_A \int_{\mathcal{H}^2(\mathbf{n})} L_o(\mathrm{p}, \omega) \, \cos\theta \, \mathrm{d}\omega \, \mathrm{d}A.$$

For convenience, we'll define two functions that convert θ and ϕ values into (x, y, z) direction vectors. The first function applies the earlier equations directly. Notice that these functions are passed the sine and cosine of θ, rather than θ itself. This is because the sine and cosine of θ are often already available to the caller. This is not normally the case for ϕ, however, so ϕ is passed in as is.

⟨*Geometry Inline Functions*⟩+≡
```
    inline Vector SphericalDirection(float sintheta,
                                     float costheta, float phi) {
        return Vector(sintheta * cosf(phi),
                      sintheta * sinf(phi),
                      costheta);
    }
```
Vector 47

The second function takes three basis vectors representing the x, y, and z axes and returns the appropriate direction vector with respect to the coordinate frame defined by them:

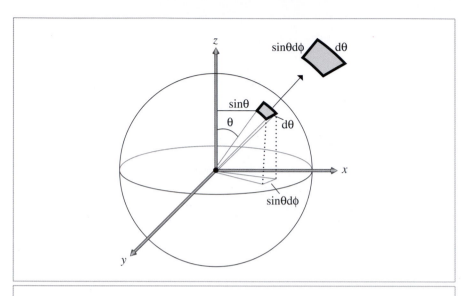

Figure 5.12: The differential area dA subtended by a differential solid angle is the product of the differential lengths of the two edges $\sin\theta d\phi$ and $d\theta$. The resulting relationship, $d\omega = \sin\theta d\theta d\phi$, is the key to converting between integrals over solid angles and integrals over spherical angles.

⟨*Geometry Inline Functions*⟩+≡

```
inline Vector SphericalDirection(float sintheta, float costheta,
                                 float phi, const Vector &x,
                                 const Vector &y, const Vector &z) {
    return sintheta * cosf(phi) * x +
           sintheta * sinf(phi) * y + costheta * z;
}
```

The conversion of spherical angles to a direction can be found by

$$\theta = \arccos z$$
$$\phi = \arctan \frac{y}{x}.$$

The corresponding functions follow. Note that `SphericalTheta()` assumes that the vector v has been normalized before being passed in.

SphericalTheta() 246

Vector 47

⟨*Geometry Inline Functions*⟩+≡

```
inline float SphericalTheta(const Vector &v) {
    return acosf(v.z);
}
```

⟨*Geometry Inline Functions*⟩+≡
```
inline float SphericalPhi(const Vector &v) {
    float p = atan2f(v.y, v.x);
    return (p < 0.f) ? p + 2.f*M_PI : p;
}
```

5.3.3 INTEGRALS OVER AREA

One last transformation of integrals that can simplify computation is to turn integrals over directions into integrals over area. Consider the irradiance integral in Equation (5.2) again, and imagine there is a quadrilateral with constant outgoing radiance and we'd like to compute the resulting irradiance at a point p. Computing this value as an integral over directions is not straightforward, since given a particular direction, it is nontrivial to determine if the quadrilateral is visible in that direction. It's much easier to compute the irradiance as an integral over the area of the quadrilateral.

Differential area is related to differential solid angle (as viewed from a point p) by

$$\mathrm{d}\omega = \frac{\mathrm{d}A \, \cos\theta}{r^2},$$

[5.3]

where θ is the angle between the surface normal of $\mathrm{d}A$ and the vector to p, and r is the distance from p to $\mathrm{d}A$ (Figure 5.13). We will not derive this result here, but it can

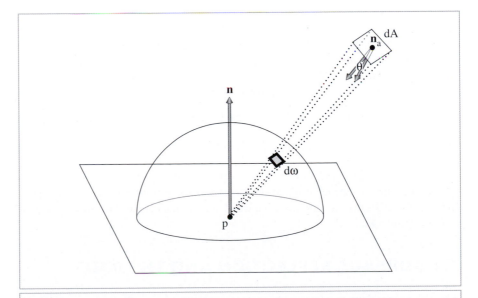

M_PI 855

Vector 47

Figure 5.13: The differential solid angle subtended by a differential area $\mathrm{d}A$ is equal to $\mathrm{d}A \cos\theta/r^2$, where θ is the angle between $\mathrm{d}A$'s surface normal and the vector to the point p and r is the distance from p to $\mathrm{d}A$.

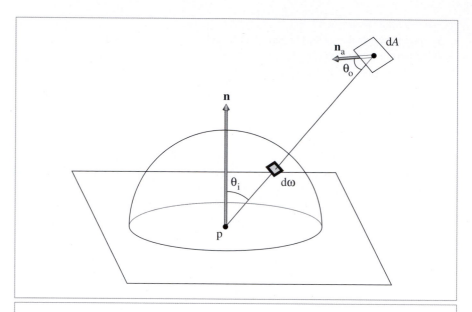

Figure 5.14: To compute irradiance at a point p from a quadrilateral source, it's easier to integrate over the surface area of the source than to integrate over the irregular set of directions that it subtends. The relationship between solid angles and areas given by Equation (5.3) lets us go back and forth between the two approaches.

be understood intuitively: If dA is at distance 1 from p and is aligned exactly so that it is perpendicular to $d\omega$, then $d\omega = dA$, $\theta = 0$, and Equation (5.3) holds. As dA moves farther away from p, or as it rotates so that it's not aligned with the direction of $d\omega$, the r^2 and $\cos\theta$ terms compensate accordingly to reduce $d\omega$.

Therefore, we can write the irradiance integral for the quadrilateral source as

$$E(\mathrm{p}, \mathbf{n}) = \int_A L \, \cos\theta_{\mathrm{i}} \, \frac{\cos\theta_{\mathrm{o}} \, dA}{r^2},$$

where L is the emitted radiance from the surface of the quadrilateral, θ_{i} is the angle between the surface normal at p and the direction from p to the point p' on the light, and θ_{o} is the angle between the surface normal at p' on the light and the direction from p' to p (Figure 5.14).

5.4 SURFACE REFLECTION AND THE BRDF

When light is incident on a surface, the surface scatters the light, reflecting some of it back into the environment. There are two main effects that need to be described to model this

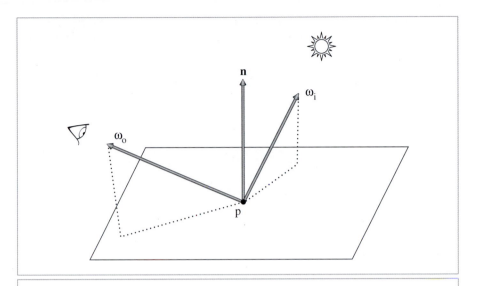

Figure 5.15: The BRDF. The bidirectional reflectance distribution function is a four-dimensional function over pairs of directions ω_i and ω_o that describes how much incident light along ω_i is scattered from the surface in the direction ω_o.

reflection: the spectral distribution of the reflected light and its directional distribution. For example, the skin of a lemon mostly absorbs light in the blue wavelengths, but reflects most of light in the red and green wavelengths (recall the lemon skin reflectance SPD in Figure 5.1). Therefore, when it is illuminated with white light, its color is yellow. The skin has pretty much the same color no matter what direction it's being observed from, although for some directions a highlight—a brighter area that is more white than yellow—is visible. In contrast, the light reflected from a point in a mirror depends almost entirely on the viewing direction. At a fixed point on the mirror, as the viewing angle changes, the object that is reflected in the mirror changes accordingly.

The *bidirectional reflectance distribution function* (BRDF) is a key radiometric concept that gives a formalism for describing these types of reflection. Consider the setting in Figure 5.15: we'd like to know how much radiance is leaving the surface in the direction ω_o toward the viewer, $L_o(p, \omega_o)$, as a result of incident radiance along the direction ω_i, $L_i(p, \omega_i)$.

If the direction ω_i is considered as a differential cone of directions, the differential irradiance at p is

$$dE(p, \omega_i) = L_i(p, \omega_i) \, \cos \theta_i \, d\omega_i. \qquad [5.4]$$

A differential amount of radiance will be reflected in the direction ω_o due to this irradiance. Because of the linearity assumption from geometric optics, the reflected differential radiance is proportional to the irradiance

$$dL_o(p, \omega_o) \propto dE(p, \omega_i).$$

The constant of proportionality defines the surface's BRDF for the particular pair of directions ω_i and ω_o:

$$f_r(p, \omega_o, \omega_i) = \frac{dL_o(p, \omega_o)}{dE(p, \omega_i)} = \frac{dL_o(p, \omega_o)}{L_i(p, \omega_i) \cos \theta_i \, d\omega_i}. \qquad [5.5]$$

Physically based BRDFs have two important qualities:

1. *Reciprocity:* For all pairs of directions ω_i and ω_o, $f_r(p, \omega_i, \omega_o) = f_r(p, \omega_o, \omega_i)$.
2. *Energy conservation:* The total energy of light reflected is less than or equal to the energy of incident light. For all directions ω_o,

$$\int_{\mathcal{H}^2(n)} f_r(p, \omega_o, \omega') \, \cos \theta' \, d\omega' \leq 1.$$

The surface's *bidirectional transmittance distribution function* (BTDF), which describes the distribution of transmitted light, can be defined in a similar manner to the BRDF. The BTDF is generally denoted by $f_t(p, \omega_o, \omega_i)$, where ω_i and ω_o are in opposite hemispheres around p. Interestingly, the BTDF does not obey reciprocity; we will discuss this issue in detail in Section 9.2.

For convenience in equations, we will denote the BRDF and BTDF when considered together as $f(p, \omega_o, \omega_i)$; we will call this the *bidirectional scattering distribution function* (BSDF). Chapter 9 is entirely devoted to describing BSDFs that are used in graphics.

Using the definition of the BSDF, we have

$$dL_o(p, \omega_o) = f(p, \omega_o, \omega_i) L_i(p, \omega_i) |\cos \theta_i| d\omega_i.$$

Here an absolute value has been added to the $\cos \theta_i$ term. This is done because surface normals in pbrt are not reoriented to lie on the same side of the surface as ω_i (many other rendering systems do this, although we find it more useful to leave them in their natural orientation as given by the Shape). Doing so makes it easier to consistently apply conventions like "the surface normal is assumed to point outside the surface" elsewhere in the system. Thus, applying the absolute value to $\cos \theta$ terms like these ensures that the desired quantity is actually calculated.

We can integrate this equation over the sphere of incident directions around p to compute the outgoing radiance in direction ω_o due to the incident illumination at p from all directions:

Shape 90

$$L_o(p, \omega_o) = \int_{\mathcal{S}^2} f(p, \omega_o, \omega_i) L_i(p, \omega_i) |\cos \theta_i| d\omega_i. \qquad [5.6]$$

This is a fundamental equation in rendering; it describes how an incident distribution of light at a point is transformed into an outgoing distribution, based on the scattering properties of the surface. It is often called the *scattering equation* when the sphere $\mathcal{S}^2$ is the domain (as it is here), or the *reflection equation* when just the upper hemisphere $\mathcal{H}^2(\mathbf{n})$ is being integrated over. One of the key tasks of the integration routines in Chapter 16 is to evaluate this integral at points on surfaces in the scene.

FURTHER READING

Meyer was one of the first researchers to closely investigate spectral representations in graphics (Meyer and Greenberg 1980; Meyer et al. 1986). Hall (1989) summarizes the state of the art in spectral representations through 1989, and Glassner's *Principles of Digital Image Synthesis* (1995) covers the topic through the mid-1990s. Hall's more recent survey article (Hall 1999) is another good resource on this topic.

A polynomial representation for spectra was proposed by Raso and Fournier (1991). Peercy (1993) developed a technique based on choosing basis functions in a scene-dependent manner: by looking at the SPDs of the lights and reflecting objects in the scene, a small number of basis functions that could accurately represent the scene's SPDs were found using characteristic vector analysis. Another approach to spectral representation was investigated by Sun et al. (2001), who partitioned SPDs into a smooth base SPD and a set of spikes. Each part was represented differently, using basis functions that worked well for each of these parts of the distribution.

Glassner (1989b) has written an article on the underconstrained problem of converting RGB values (e.g., as selected by the user from a display) to an SPD. Smits (1999) has also investigated this topic.

McCluney's book on radiometry is an excellent introduction to the topic (McCluney 1994). Preisendorfer (1965) also covers radiometry in an accessible manner and delves into the relationship between radiometry and the physics of light. Moon and Spencer (1936, 1948) and Gershun (1939) are classic early introductions to radiometry. Lambert's seminal early writings about photometry from the mid-18th century were recently translated into English by DiLaura (Lambert 1760).

EXERCISES

❷ 5.1   Experiment with different basis functions for spectral representation. How many coefficients are needed for accurate rendering of tricky situations like fluorescent lighting? How much does the particular choice of basis affect the number of coefficients needed?

● 5.2 Implement Peercy's approach of choosing basis functions based on the most important SPDs in the scene (Peercy 1993). In what cases does the improvement in accuracy make up for the additional computational expense of computing the products of spectra versus just using more point samples?

● 5.3 Compute the irradiance at a point due to a unit-radius disk h units directly above its normal with constant outgoing radiance of 10 J/m^2 sr. Do the computation twice, once as an integral over solid angle and once as an integral over area. (Hint: If the results don't match see Section 14.5.2)

● 5.4 Similarly, compute the irradiance at a point due to a square quadrilateral with outgoing radiance of 10 J/m^2 sr that has sides of length 1 and is 1 unit directly above the point in the direction of its surface normal.

CHAPTER SIX

06 CAMERA MODELS

In Chapter 1, we described the pinhole camera model that is commonly used in computer graphics. This model is easy to describe and simulate, but it has serious drawbacks. For example, everything rendered with a pinhole camera is in sharp focus, which can make images look computer generated. In order to make images that appear realistic, it is important to better simulate properties of real-world imaging systems.

Like the Shapes from Chapter 3, cameras in pbrt are represented by an abstract base class. This chapter describes the Camera class and its only method: Camera::GenerateRay(). This method computes the world space ray corresponding to a sample position on the image plane. By generating these rays in different ways based on different models of image formation, the cameras in pbrt can create many types of images of the same 3D scene. Here, we will show a few implementations of the Camera interface, each of which generates rays in a different way.

6.1 CAMERA MODEL

The abstract Camera base class holds generic camera options and defines an interface that all camera implementations must provide.

⟨*Camera Declarations*⟩ ≡
```
class COREDLL Camera {
public:
    ⟨Camera Interface 256⟩
    ⟨Camera Public Data 257⟩
protected:
    ⟨Camera Protected Data 257⟩
};
```

The method that camera subclasses need to implement is Camera::GenerateRay(), which generates a ray for a given image sample. It is important that the camera normalize the direction component of the returned ray—many other parts of the system will depend on this behavior.

This method also returns a floating-point value that gives a weight for the effect that light arriving at the film plane along the generated ray will have on the final image. Most cameras always return a value of one, but cameras that simulate real physical lens systems might need to set this value based on the optics and geometry of the virtual lens system.

⟨*Camera Interface*⟩ ≡   **256**
```
    virtual float GenerateRay(const Sample &sample, Ray *ray) const = 0;
```

The base Camera constructor takes several parameters that are appropriate for all camera types. They include the transformation that places the camera in the scene and the near and far *clipping planes*, which give distances along the camera space *z* axis that delineate the region of the scene that will be visible.[1] Any geometric primitives in front of the near plane or beyond the far plane will not appear in the final image (Figure 6.1).

Real-world cameras have a shutter that opens for a short period of time to expose the film to light. One result of this nonzero exposure time is *motion blur:* objects that move during the film exposure time are blurred. Although pbrt does not currently support motion blur, each Ray does have a time value associated with it to make it easier to add this feature. If a time value between the shutter open time and the shutter close time is associated with each ray such that overall, the complete time range is well covered, it is possible to compute images with motion blur. To make it easier to set these time values, all Cameras store a shutter open and shutter close time.

---

1   Although the names "near" and "far" make clear intuitive sense for these planes, graphics systems frequently refer to them as "hither" and "yon," respectively. A practical reason for this convention is that near and far are reserved keywords in Microsoft's C and C++ compilers.

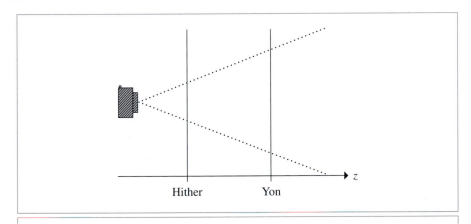

Figure 6.1: Clipping Planes. The camera's clipping planes give the range of space along the *z* axis that will be visible in images. Objects in front of the hither plane or beyond the yon plane will not be visible. Setting the clipping planes to tightly encompass the objects in the scene is important for many scan line algorithms, but is not important for ray tracing.

⟨*Camera Protected Data*⟩ ≡   **256**

```
Transform WorldToCamera, CameraToWorld;
float ClipHither, ClipYon;
float ShutterOpen, ShutterClose;
```

Cameras also contain an instance of the `Film` class to represent the final image to be computed. `Film` will be described in Chapter 8.

⟨*Camera Public Data*⟩ ≡   **256**

```
Film *film;
```

Camera implementations must pass a number of these values to the `Camera` constructor. We will only show its prototype here because its implementation just copies the parameters to the corresponding member variables.

⟨*Camera Interface*⟩+≡   **256**

```
Camera(const Transform &world2cam, float hither, float yon,
       float sopen, float sclose, Film *film);
```

6.1.1 CAMERA COORDINATE SPACES

We have already made use of two important modeling coordinate spaces, object space and world space. We will now introduce four useful coordinate spaces related to the camera and imaging, summarized in Figure 6.2. All together, we now have the following:

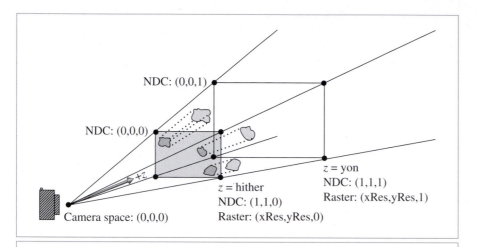

Figure 6.2: A handful of camera-related coordinate spaces help to simplify the implementation of `Cameras`. The camera class holds transformations between them. Scene objects in world space are viewed by the camera, which sits at the origin of camera space and points along the $+z$ axis. Objects between the hither and yon planes are projected onto the image plane at $z =$ hither in camera space. The image plane is at $z = 0$ in raster space, where x and y range from $(0, 0)$ to (xResolution, yResolution). Normalized device coordinate (NDC) space normalizes raster space so that x and y range from $(0, 0)$ to $(1, 1)$.

- *Object space:* This is the coordinate system in which geometric primitives are defined. For example, spheres in pbrt are defined to be centered at the origin of object space.
- *World space:* While each primitive may have its own object space, all objects in the scene are placed in relation to a single world space. Each primitive has an object-to-world transformation that determines where it is located in world space. World space is the standard frame that all spaces are defined in terms of.
- *Camera space:* A virtual camera is placed in the scene at some world space point with a particular viewing direction and orientation. This defines a new coordinate system with its origin at the camera's location. The z axis of this coordinate system is mapped to the viewing direction, and the y axis is mapped to the up direction. This is a handy space for reasoning about which objects are potentially visible to the camera. For example, if an object's camera space bounding box is entirely behind the $z = 0$ plane (and the camera doesn't have a field of view wider than 180 degrees), the object will not be visible to the camera.
- *Screen space:* Screen space is defined on the image plane. The camera projects objects in camera space onto the image plane; the parts inside the *screen window* are visible in the image that is generated. Depth z values in screen space range from zero to one, corresponding to points at the near and far clipping planes, respectively. Note

Camera 256

that although this is called "screen" space, it is still a 3D coordinate system, since z values are meaningful.

- *Normalized device coordinate (NDC) space:* This is the coordinate system for the actual image being rendered. In x and y, this space ranges from $(0, 0)$ to $(1, 1)$, with $(0, 0)$ being the upper-left corner of the image. Depth values are the same as in screen space and a linear transformation converts from screen to NDC space.
- *Raster space:* This is almost the same as NDC space, except the x and y coordinates range from $(0, 0)$ to (xResolution, yResolution).

All cameras store a world-space-to-camera-space transformation; this can be used to transform primitives in the scene into camera space. The origin of camera space is the camera's position, and the camera points along the camera space z axis. The projective cameras in the next section use 4×4 matrices to transform between all of these spaces as needed, but cameras with unusual imaging characteristics can't necessarily represent all of these transformations with matrices.

6.2 PROJECTIVE CAMERA MODELS

One of the fundamental issues in 3D computer graphics is the *3D viewing problem:* how to project a three-dimensional scene onto a two-dimensional image for display. Most of the classic approaches can be expressed by a 4×4 projective transformation matrix. Therefore, we will introduce a projection matrix camera class and then define two camera models based on it. The first implements an orthographic projection, and the other implements a perspective projection—two classic and widely used projections.

⟨*Camera Declarations*⟩+≡
```
class COREDLL ProjectiveCamera : public Camera {
public:
    ⟨ProjectiveCamera Public Methods⟩
protected:
    ⟨ProjectiveCamera Protected Data 260⟩
};
```

In addition to the parameters required by the Camera base class, the ProjectiveCamera takes the projective transformation matrix, screen space extent of the image, and additional parameters for depth of field. Depth of field, which will be described and implemented at the end of this section, simulates the blurriness of out-of-focus objects that occurs in real lens systems.

⟨*Camera Method Definitions*⟩ ≡
```
ProjectiveCamera::ProjectiveCamera(const Transform &w2c,
        const Transform &proj, const float Screen[4],
        float hither, float yon, float sopen,
        float sclose, float lensr, float focald, Film *f)
    : Camera(w2c, hither, yon, sopen, sclose, f) {
    ⟨Initialize depth of field parameters 268⟩
    ⟨Compute projective camera transformations 260⟩
}
```

ProjectiveCamera implementations pass the projective transformation up to the base class constructor shown here. This transformation gives the camera-to-screen projection; from that the constructor can compute most of the others that are needed.

⟨*Compute projective camera transformations*⟩ ≡   260
```
CameraToScreen = proj;
WorldToScreen = CameraToScreen * WorldToCamera;
⟨Compute projective camera screen transformations 260⟩
RasterToCamera = CameraToScreen.GetInverse() * RasterToScreen;
```

⟨*ProjectiveCamera Protected Data*⟩ ≡   259
```
Transform CameraToScreen, WorldToScreen, RasterToCamera;
```

The only nontrivial transformation to compute in the constructor is the screen-to-raster projection. In the following code, note the composition of transformations where (reading from bottom to top), we start with a point in screen space, translate so that the upper-left corner of the screen is at the origin, and then scale by the reciprocal of the screen width and height, giving us a point with x and y coordinates between zero and one (these are NDC coordinates). Finally, we scale by the raster resolution, so that we end up covering the entire raster range from $(0, 0)$ up to the overall raster resolution. An important detail here is that the y coordinate is inverted by this transformation; this is necessary because increasing y values move up the image in screen coordinates, but down in raster coordinates.

⟨*Compute projective camera screen transformations*⟩ ≡   260
```
ScreenToRaster = Scale(float(film->xResolution),
                       float(film->yResolution), 1.f) *
    Scale(1.f / (Screen[1] - Screen[0]),
          1.f / (Screen[2] - Screen[3]), 1.f) *
    Translate(Vector(-Screen[0], -Screen[3], 0.f));
RasterToScreen = ScreenToRaster.GetInverse();
```

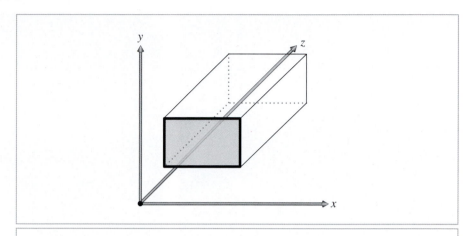

Figure 6.3: The orthographic view volume is an axis-aligned box in camera space, defined such that objects inside the region are projected onto the $z =$ hither face of the box.

⟨*ProjectiveCamera Protected Data*⟩+ ≡   **259**
```
    Transform ScreenToRaster, RasterToScreen;
```

6.2.1 ORTHOGRAPHIC CAMERA

⟨*OrthographicCamera Declarations*⟩ ≡
```
    class OrthoCamera : public ProjectiveCamera {
    public:
        ⟨OrthoCamera Public Methods⟩
    };
```

The orthographic camera, defined in `cameras/orthographic.cpp`, 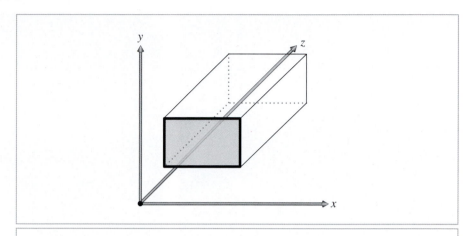 is based on the orthographic projection transformation. The orthographic transformation takes a rectangular region of the scene and projects it onto the front face of the box that defines the region. It doesn't give the effect of *foreshortening*—objects becoming smaller on the image plane as they get farther away—but it does leave parallel lines parallel, and it preserves relative distance between objects. Figure 6.3 shows how this rectangular volume defines the visible region of the scene. Figure 6.4 compares the result of using the orthographic projection for rendering to the perspective projection defined in the next section.

The orthographic camera constructor generates the orthographic transformation matrix with the `Orthographic()` function, which will be defined shortly.

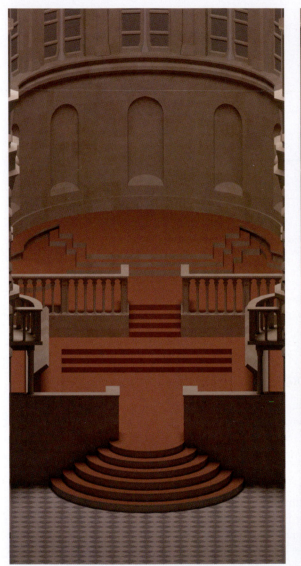

(a)   (b)

Figure 6.4: Images of the Church Model. Rendered with (a) orthographic and (b) perspective cameras. Note that features like the stairs, checks on the floor, and back windows are rendered quite differently with the two models. The lack of foreshortening makes the orthographic view feel like it has less depth, although it does preserve parallel lines, which can be a useful property.

⟨*OrthographicCamera Definitions*⟩ ≡
```
    OrthoCamera::OrthoCamera(const Transform &world2cam,
            const float Screen[4], float hither, float yon,
            float sopen, float sclose, float lensr,
            float focald, Film *f)
      : ProjectiveCamera(world2cam, Orthographic(hither, yon),
                         Screen, hither, yon, sopen, sclose,
                         lensr, focald, f) {
    }
```

The orthographic viewing transformation leaves x and y coordinates unchanged, but maps z values at the hither plane to 0 and z values at the yon plane to 1. To do this, the scene is first translated along the z axis so that the near clipping plane is aligned with $z = 0$. Then, the scene is scaled in z so that the far clipping plane maps to $z = 1$. The composition of these two transformations gives the overall transformation.

⟨*Transform Method Definitions*⟩+≡
```
    Transform COREDLL Orthographic(float znear, float zfar) {
        return Scale(1.f, 1.f, 1.f / (zfar-znear)) *
               Translate(Vector(0.f, 0.f, -znear));
    }
```

We can now go through the code to take a sample point in raster space and turn it into a camera ray. The `Sample::imageX` and `Sample::imageY` components of the camera sample are raster space x and y coordinates on the image plane (the contents of the `Sample` structure are described in detail in Chapter 7). The process is summarized in Figure 6.5.

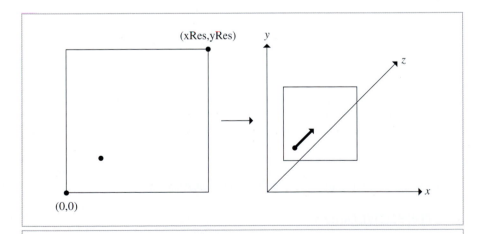

Figure 6.5: To create a ray with the orthographic camera, a raster space position on the image plane is transformed to camera space, giving the ray's origin on the hither plane. The ray's direction in camera space is $(0, 0, 1)$, down the z axis.

First, the raster space sample position is transformed into a point in camera space, giving a point located on the near clipping plane, which is the origin of the camera ray. Because the camera space viewing direction points down the *z* axis, the camera space ray direction is (0, 0, 1). The ray's maxt value is set so that intersections beyond the far clipping plane will be ignored; its value is easily computed from the distance from the near plane to the far plane since the ray's direction is normalized. Finally, the ray is transformed into world space before being returned.

If depth of field has been enabled for this scene, the ray's origin and direction are modified so that depth of field is simulated. Depth of field will be explained later in this section.

⟨*OrthographicCamera Definitions*⟩+≡
```
float OrthoCamera::GenerateRay(const Sample &sample, Ray *ray) const {
    ⟨Generate raster and camera samples 264⟩
    ray->o = Pcamera;
    ray->d = Vector(0,0,1);
    ⟨Set ray time value 264⟩
    ⟨Modify ray for depth of field 269⟩
    ray->mint = 0.;
    ray->maxt = ClipYon - ClipHither;
    ray->d = Normalize(ray->d);
    CameraToWorld(*ray, ray);
    return 1.f;
}
```

Once all of the transformation matrices have been set up, it's easy to set up the raster space sample point and transform it to camera space:

⟨*Generate raster and camera samples*⟩≡　　　　　　　　　　　　　　　　**264, 267**
```
Point Pras(sample.imageX, sample.imageY, 0);
Point Pcamera;
RasterToCamera(Pras, &Pcamera);
```

The Sample structure includes the time at which this ray should be traced, which could be used by a future motion blur extension to pbrt. The Sample's time value ranges between 0 and 1, so here it is used to linearly interpolate between the provided shutter open and close times.

⟨*Set ray time value*⟩≡　　　　　　　　　　　　　　　　　　　　　**264, 267, 275**
```
ray->time = Lerp(sample.time, ShutterOpen, ShutterClose);
```

6.2.2 PERSPECTIVE CAMERA

The perspective projection is similar to the orthographic projection in that it projects a volume of space onto a 2D image plane. However, it includes the effect of foreshortening: objects that are far away are projected to be smaller than objects of the same size that are closer. Furthermore, unlike the orthographic projection, the perspective projection also doesn't preserve distances or angles, and parallel lines no longer remain parallel. The perspective projection is a reasonably close match to how an eye or camera lens generates images of the three-dimensional world. The perspective camera is implemented in the file cameras/perspective.cpp.ⓒⓓ

⟨*PerspectiveCamera Declarations*⟩ ≡
```
class PerspectiveCamera : public ProjectiveCamera {
public:
    ⟨PerspectiveCamera Public Methods⟩
};
```

⟨*PerspectiveCamera Method Definitions*⟩ ≡
```
PerspectiveCamera:: PerspectiveCamera(const Transform &world2cam,
        const float Screen[4], float hither, float yon,
        float sopen, float sclose,
        float lensr, float focald,
        float fov, Film *f)
    : ProjectiveCamera(world2cam, Perspective(fov, hither, yon),
                    Screen, hither, yon, sopen, sclose,
                    lensr, focald, f) {
}
```

The perspective projection describes perspective viewing of the scene. Points in the scene are projected onto a viewing plane at $z = 1$; this is one unit away from the virtual camera at $z = 0$ (Figure 6.6). The Perspective() function computes this transformation; it takes a field-of-view angle in fov, and the distances to the hither and yon planes are passed in n and f, respectively.

⟨*Transform Method Definitions*⟩+ ≡
```
COREDLL Transform Perspective(float fov, float n, float f) {
    ⟨Compute basic perspective matrix  266⟩
    ⟨Scale to canonical viewing volume  267⟩
}
```

The transformation is most easily understood in two steps:

1. Points p in camera space are projected onto the viewing plane. A bit of algebra shows that the projected x' and y' coordinates on the viewing plane can be computed by dividing x and y by the point's z coordinate value. The projected z depth is remapped so that z values at the hither plane are 0 and z values at the yon plane are 1. The computation we'd like to do is

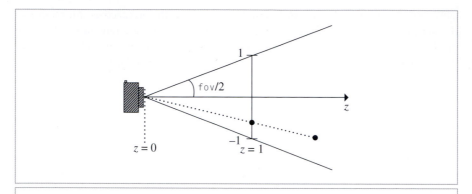

Figure 6.6: The perspective transformation matrix projects points in camera space onto the image plane. The x' and y' coordinates of the projected points are equal to the unprojected x and y coordinates divided by the z coordinate. The projected z' coordinate is computed so that points on the hither plane map to $z' = 0$ and points on the yon plane map to $z' = 1$.

$$x' = x/z$$
$$y' = y/z$$
$$z' = \frac{f(z-n)}{z(f-n)}.$$

All of this computation can be encoded in a 4×4 matrix using homogeneous coordinates:

$$\begin{bmatrix} 1 & 0 & 0 & 0 \\ 0 & 1 & 0 & 0 \\ 0 & 0 & \frac{f}{f-n} & -\frac{fn}{f-n} \\ 0 & 0 & 1 & 0 \end{bmatrix}$$

⟨*Compute basic perspective matrix*⟩ ≡   **265**
```
float inv_denom = 1.f/(f-n);
Matrix4x4 *persp =
    new Matrix4x4(1, 0,              0,                   0,
                  0, 1,              0,                   0,
                  0, 0, f*inv_denom, -f*n*inv_denom,
                  0, 0,              1,                   0);
```

2. The angular field of view (fov) specified by the user is accounted for by scaling the (x, y) values on the projection plane so that points inside the field of view project to coordinates between $[-1, 1]$ on the view plane. For square images, both x and y lie between $[-1, 1]$ in screen space. Otherwise, the direction in which the image is narrower maps to $[-1, 1]$ and the wider direction maps to a proportionally larger range of screen space values.

Matrix4x4 852

Recall that the tangent is equal to the ratio of the opposite side of a right triangle to the adjacent side. Here the adjacent side has length 1, so the opposite side has the length tan(fov/2). Scaling by the reciprocal of this length maps the field of view to range from $[-1, 1]$.

⟨*Scale to canonical viewing volume*⟩ ≡   **265**
```
    float invTanAng = 1.f / tanf(Radians(fov) / 2.f);
    return Scale(invTanAng, invTanAng, 1) * Transform(persp);
```

In a perspective projection, rays originate from the sample position on the hither plane, and their direction is the vector from $(0, 0, 0)$ through the sample position in camera space. In other words, the ray's vector direction is component-wise equal to its point position, so rather than doing a useless subtraction to compute the direction, we just initialize the vector ray->d directly from the point Pcamera.

As with the OrthoCamera, the ray's maxt value is set to lie on the far clipping plane.

⟨*PerspectiveCamera Method Definitions*⟩+≡
```
    float PerspectiveCamera::GenerateRay(const Sample &sample,
                                         Ray *ray) const {
        ⟨Generate raster and camera samples 264⟩
        ray->o = Pcamera;
        ray->d = Vector(Pcamera.x, Pcamera.y, Pcamera.z);
        ⟨Set ray time value 264⟩
        ⟨Modify ray for depth of field 269⟩
        ray->d = Normalize(ray->d);
        ray->mint = 0.;
        ray->maxt = (ClipYon - ClipHither) / ray->d.z;
        CameraToWorld(*ray, ray);
        return 1.f;
    }
```

6.2.3 DEPTH OF FIELD

Real cameras have lens systems that focus light through a finite-sized aperture onto the film plane. Because the aperture has finite area, a single point in the scene may be projected onto an area on the film plane called the *circle of confusion* (Figure 6.7). Correspondingly, a finite area of the scene may be visible from a single point on the image plane, giving a blurred image. Figures 6.8 and 6.9 show this effect, depth of field, in a scene with a series of copies of the dragon model. Figure 6.8(a) is rendered with an infinitesimal aperture and thus without any depth of field effects. Figures 6.8(b) and 6.9 show the increase in blurriness as the size of the lens aperture is increased. Note that the second dragon from the right remains in focus throughout all of the images, as the plane of focus has been placed at its depth. Figure 6.10 shows depth of field used to render the

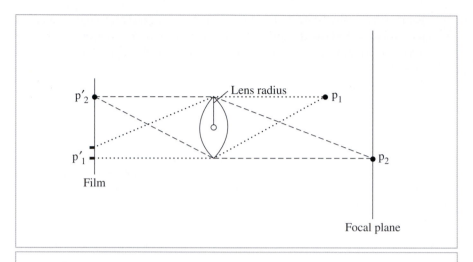

Figure 6.7: Real-world cameras have a lens with finite aperture and lens controls that adjust the lens position with respect to the film plane. Because the aperture is finite, objects in the scene aren't all imaged onto the film in perfect focus. Here, the point p_1 doesn't lie on the plane of points in perfect focus, so it images to an area p_1' on the film and is blurred. The point p_2 does lie on the focal plane, so it images to a point p_2' and is in focus. Either increasing the aperture size or increasing an object's distance from the focal plane will increase an out-of-focus object's blurriness.

ecosystem scene. Note how the effect draws the viewer's eye to the in-focus tree in the center of the image.

The size of the circle of confusion is affected by the radius of the aperture and the distance between the object and the lens. The *focal distance* is the distance from the lens to the plane of objects that project to a zero-radius circle of confusion. These points appear to be perfectly in focus. In practice, objects do not have to be exactly on the focal plane to appear in sharp focus; as long as the circle of confusion is roughly smaller than a pixel, objects appear to be in focus. The range of distances from the lens at which objects appear in focus is called the lens's *depth of field*.

Projective cameras take two extra parameters for depth of field: one sets the size of the lens aperture, and the other sets the focal distance.

⟨*ProjectiveCamera Protected Data*⟩+≡   **259**
    float LensRadius, FocalDistance;

⟨*Initialize depth of field parameters*⟩≡   **260**
    LensRadius = lensr;
    FocalDistance = focald;

ProjectiveCamera::
  FocalDistance 268

ProjectiveCamera::
  LensRadius 268

The math behind computing circles of confusion for simple lenses is not difficult; it mostly involves repeated application of similar triangles and some reasonable approximations about the shape of the lens profile. This process can be easily modeled in a ray

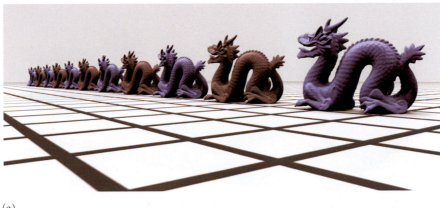

(a)

(b)

Figure 6.8: (a) Scene rendered with no depth of field and (b) depth of field due to a relatively small lens aperture, which gives only a small amount of blurriness in the out-of-focus regions.

tracer with just a few lines of code. All that is necessary is to choose a point on the lens and find the ray from the point on the film that passes through the lens at that point such that objects in the plane of focus are in focus (Figure 6.11). Unfortunately, it is necessary to trace many rays for each image pixel in order to adequately sample the lens for smooth depth of field. Figure 6.12 shows the ecosystem scene from Figure 6.10 with only four samples per pixel (Figure 6.10 had 128 samples per pixel).

⟨*Modify ray for depth of field*⟩ ≡   **264, 267**
    if (LensRadius > 0.) {
        ⟨*Sample point on lens* **270**⟩
        ⟨*Compute point on plane of focus* **272**⟩
        ⟨*Update ray for effect of lens* **272**⟩
    }

ProjectiveCamera::
LensRadius 268

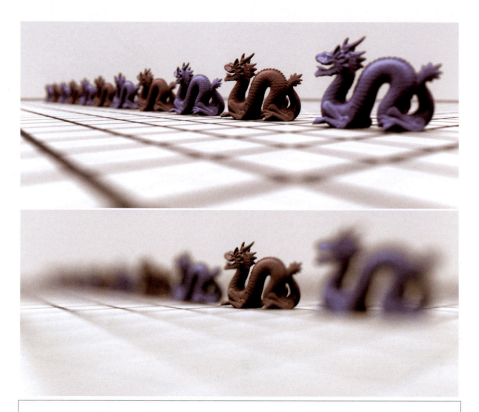

Figure 6.9: As the size of the lens aperture increases, the size of the circle of confusion in the out-of-focus areas increases, giving a greater amount of blur on the image plane.

The ConcentricSampleDisk() function, defined in Chapter 14, takes a (u, v) sample position in $[0, 1]^2$ and maps it to a 2D unit disk. To turn this into a point on the lens, these coordinates are scaled by the lens radius. The Sample class provides the (u, v) lens-sampling parameters in the Sample::lensU and Sample::lensV fields.

⟨*Sample point on lens*⟩ ≡   **269**
```
float lensU, lensV;
ConcentricSampleDisk(sample.lensU, sample.lensV,
                     &lensU, &lensV);
lensU *= LensRadius;
lensV *= LensRadius;
```

The ray's origin is this point on the lens. Now it is necessary to determine the proper direction for the new ray. This direction could be computed using Snell's law, which describes how light refracts when passing from one medium (e.g., air) to another (e.g.,

Figure 6.10: Depth of field gives a greater sense of depth and scale to the ecosystem scene.

glass), but the specifics of this particular problem make this simpler.[2] We know that *all* rays from the given image sample through the lens must converge at the same point on the focal plane. Furthermore, we know that rays through the center of the lens are not refracted, so finding this point of convergence is a matter of intersecting the unperturbed ray from the pinhole model with the focal plane and then setting the ray's direction to be the vector from the point on the lens to the intersection point.

For this simple model, the focal plane is perpendicular to the *z* axis and the ray originates on the near clipping plane, so intersecting the ray through the lens center with the focal plane is straightforward. The *t* value of the intersection is given by

$$t = \frac{\text{focalDistance} - \text{hither}}{\mathbf{d}_z}.$$

---

2   We are also assuming a single thin spherical lens element. Simulating complex lens systems with multiple glass elements is much more involved; see the exercises and the "Further Reading" section.

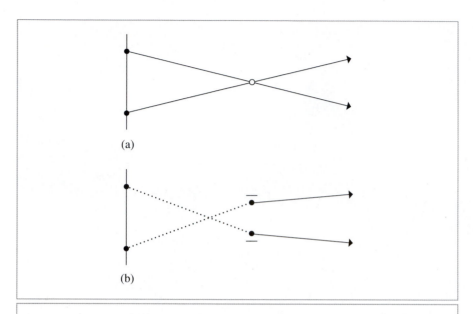

Figure 6.11: (a) For a pinhole camera model, each point on the film plane has a single camera ray associated with it, passing through the single point of the pinhole lens. (b) For a model with a finite aperture, we will sample a point on the disk-shaped lens and find rays' directions by computing the direction from the point on the lens to the point on the plane of focus that the ray through the center of the lens intersects.

⟨*Compute point on plane of focus*⟩ ≡   **269**
```
float ft = (FocalDistance - ClipHither) / ray->d.z;
Point Pfocus = (*ray)(ft);
```

Now the ray is easily initialized. The origin is shifted to the sampled point on the lens and the direction is set so that the ray passes through the point on the plane of focus, `Pfocus`.

⟨*Update ray for effect of lens*⟩ ≡   **269**
```
ray->o.x += lensU;
ray->o.y += lensV;
ray->d = Pfocus - ray->o;
```

6.3 ENVIRONMENT CAMERA

One advantage of ray tracing compared to scan line or rasterization-based rendering methods is that it's easy to employ unusual image projections. We have great freedom in how the image sample positions are mapped into ray directions, since the rendering al-

Figure 6.12: Ecosytem scene with depth of field and only four samples per pixel: the depth of field is undersampled and the image is grainy.

gorithm doesn't depend on properties such as straight lines in the scene always projecting to straight lines in the image.

In this section, we will describe a camera model that traces rays in all directions around a point in the scene, giving a two-dimensional view of everything that is visible from that point. Consider a sphere around the camera position in the scene; choosing points on that sphere gives directions to trace rays in. If we parameterize the sphere with spherical coordinates, each point on the sphere is associated with a (θ, ϕ) pair, where $\theta \in [0, \pi]$ and $\phi \in [0, 2\pi]$. See Section 5.3.2 for more details on spherical coordinates. This type of image is particularly useful because it represents all of the incident light at a point on the scene. It will be useful later when we discuss environment lighting—a rendering technique that uses image-based representations of light in a scene. Figure 6.13 shows this camera in action with the church model. θ values range from 0 at the top of the image

Figure 6.13: The church model rendered with the `EnvironmentCamera`, which traces rays in all directions from the camera position. The resulting image gives a representation of all light arriving at that point in the scene, and can be used for the image-based lighting techniques described in Chapters 13 and 16.

to π at the bottom of the image, and ϕ values range from 0 to 2π, moving from left to right across the image.[3]

⟨*EnvironmentCamera Declarations*⟩ ≡
```
class EnvironmentCamera : public Camera {
public:
    ⟨EnvironmentCamera Public Methods⟩
private:
    ⟨EnvironmentCamera Private Data 274⟩
};
```

Notice that the `EnvironmentCamera` subclass derives directly from the `Camera` class, not the `ProjectiveCamera` class. This is because the environmental projection is nonlinear and cannot be captured by a single 4×4 matrix. It is defined in the file `cameras/environment.cpp`. 🔴

All rays generated by this camera have the same origin. For efficiency, the world space position of the camera is computed and cached in the constructor.

⟨*EnvironmentCamera Private Data*⟩ ≡   **274**
```
    Point rayOrigin;
```

---

3   Readers familiar with cartography will recognize this as an equirectangular projection.

⟨*EnvironmentCamera Method Definitions*⟩ ≡
```
EnvironmentCamera:: EnvironmentCamera(const Transform &world2cam,
                                      float hither, float yon, float sopen,
                                      float sclose, Film *film)
    : Camera(world2cam, hither, yon, sopen, sclose, film) {
    rayOrigin = CameraToWorld(Point(0,0,0));
}
```

Note that the `EnvironmentCamera` still uses the near and far clipping planes to restrict the value of the ray's parameter *t*. In this case, however, these are really *clipping spheres*, since all rays originate at the same point and radiate outward.

⟨*EnvironmentCamera Method Definitions*⟩+ ≡
```
float EnvironmentCamera::GenerateRay(const Sample &sample,
                                     Ray *ray) const {
    ray->o = rayOrigin;
    ⟨Generate environment camera ray direction 275⟩
    ⟨Set ray time value 264⟩
    ray->mint = ClipHither;
    ray->maxt = ClipYon;
    return 1.f;
}
```

To compute the (θ, ϕ) coordinates for this ray, NDC coordinates are computed from the raster image sample position, and then scaled to cover the (θ, ϕ) range. Next, the spherical coordinate formula is used to compute the ray direction, and finally the direction is converted to world space. (Note that because the *y* direction is "up" in camera space, here the *x* and *y* coordinates in the spherical coordinate formula are exchanged in comparison to usage elsewhere in the system.)

⟨*Generate environment camera ray direction*⟩ ≡   275
```
float theta = M_PI * sample.imageY / film->yResolution;
float phi = 2 * M_PI * sample.imageX / film->xResolution;
Vector dir(sinf(theta) * cosf(phi), cosf(theta),
           sinf(theta) * sinf(phi));
CameraToWorld(dir, &ray->d);
```

FURTHER READING

In his seminal Sketchpad system, Sutherland (1963) was the first to use projection matrices for computer graphics. Akenine-Möller and Haines (2002) have a particularly well-written derivation of the orthographic and perspective projection matrices in *Real Time Rendering*. Other good references for projections are Rogers and Adams's *Mathematical*

Elements for Computer Graphics (1990), Watt and Watt (1992), Foley et al. (1990), and Eberly's book on game engine design (Eberly 2001).

Potmesil and Chakravarty (1981, 1982, 1983) did early work on depth of field and motion blur in computer graphics. Cook and collaborators developed a more accurate model for these effects based on *distribution ray tracing*; this is the approach used for the depth of field calculations in this chapter (Cook, Porter, and Carpenter 1984; Cook 1986).

Kolb, Mitchell, and Hanrahan (1995) investigated simulating complex camera lens systems with ray tracing in order to model the imaging effects of real cameras. Another unusual projection method was used by Greene and Heckbert (1986) for generating images for Omnimax theaters. The EnvironmentCamera in this chapter is similar to the camera model described by Musgrave (1992).

EXERCISES

❸ 6.1   Modify one or more of the Cameras implemented in this chapter to support motion blur due to camera motion. For example, the camera might take two transformation matrices, one giving its position at shutter open time and the other giving its position at shutter close. Construct examples that demonstrate why linearly interpolating the components of the two matrices individually will not in general give reasonable transformation matrices for intermediate times.

One accurate approach to interpolating between matrices is to decompose the matrix into translation and rotation components and interpolate each individually (interpolating the rotation with quaternions, for example) (Shoemake and Duff 1992; Shoemake 1994). Alternatively, Alexa (2002) has described a method for interpolating matrices directly without needing a decomposition step. Implement one of these two methods and demonstrate the improvement in results compared to the naive approach of interpolating matrix components directly.

❷ 6.2   Extend your motion blur implementation from the previous exercise to support different shutter models. For example, many cameras expose the film by sliding a rectangular slit across the film. This leads to interesting effects when objects are moving in a different direction than the exposure slit (Glassner 1999). Implement this slit shutter model for both horizontal and vertical slits, and also a leaf shutter. Create scenes that clearly show the effects of each shutter type.

❷ 6.3   The standard model for depth of field in computer graphics models the circle of confusion as imaging a point in the scene to a circle with uniform intensity, although many real lenses produce circles of confusion with nonlinear variation such as a Gaussian distribution. This effect is known as "Bokeh" (Buhler and Wexler 2002). Modify the implementation of depth of field in pbrt to produce images with this effect (for example, by biasing the distribution of lens sam-

Camera 256

ple positions). For example, catadioptric (mirror) lenses produce doughnut-shaped highlights when small points of light are viewed out of focus. Render images showing the difference between this and the standard model.

● 6.4 Write an application that loads images rendered by the `EnvironmentCamera` and uses texture mapping to apply them to a sphere centered at the eyepoint such that they can be viewed interactively. The user should be able to freely change the viewing direction. If the appropriate texture-mapping function is used for generating texture coordinates on the sphere, the image generated by the application will appear as if the viewer was at the camera's location in the scene when it was rendered, thus giving the user the ability to interactively look around the scene.

● 6.5 Kolb, Mitchell, and Hanrahan (1995) have described a camera model for ray tracing based on simulating the lens system of a real camera, which is comprised of a set of glass lenses arranged to form an image on the film plane. Read their paper and implement a camera model in `pbrt` that implements their algorithm for following rays through lens systems. Test your implementation with some of the lens description data from their paper.

CHAPTER SEVEN

07 SAMPLING AND RECONSTRUCTION

Although the final output of a renderer like pbrt is a two-dimensional grid of colored pixels, incident radiance is actually a continuous function defined over the film plane. The manner in which the discrete pixel values are computed from this continuous function can noticeably affect the quality of the final image generated by the renderer; if this process is not performed carefully, artifacts will be present. Fortunately, a relatively small amount of additional computation to this end can substantially improve the quality of the rendered images.

This chapter introduces *sampling theory*—the theory of taking discrete sample values from functions defined over continuous domains and then using those samples to reconstruct new functions that are similar to the original. Building on principles of sampling theory, the Samplers in this chapter select sample points on the image plane at which incident radiance will be computed (recall that in the previous chapter, Cameras used Samples generated by a Sampler to construct their camera rays). Three Sampler implementations are described in this chapter, spanning a variety of approaches to the sampling problem. This chapter concludes with the Filter class. The Filter is used to determine how multiple samples near each pixel are blended together to compute the final pixel value.

279

7.1 SAMPLING THEORY

A digital image is represented as a set of pixel values, typically aligned on a rectangular grid. When a digital image is displayed on a physical device, these values are used to set the intensities and colors of pixels on the display. When thinking about digital images, it is important to differentiate between image pixels, which represent the value of a function at a particular sample location, and display pixels, which are physical objects that emit light with some distribution. For example, in a CRT, each phosphor glows with a distribution that falls off from its center. Pixel intensity has angular distribution as well; it is mostly uniform for CRTs, although it can be quite directional on LCD displays. Displays use the image pixel values to construct a new image function over the display surface. This function is defined at all points on the display, not just the infinitesimal points of the digital image's pixels. This process of taking a collection of sample values and converting them back to a continuous function is called *reconstruction*.

In order to compute the discrete pixel values in the digital image, it is necessary to sample the original continuously defined image function. In pbrt, like most other ray-tracing renderers, the only way to get information about the image function is to sample it by tracing rays. For example, there is no general method that can compute bounds on the variation of the image function between two points on the film plane. While an image could be generated by just sampling the function precisely at the pixel positions, a better result can be obtained by taking more samples at different positions and incorporating this additional information about the image function into the final pixel values. Indeed, for the best-quality result, the pixel values should be computed such that the reconstructed image on the display device is as close as possible to the original image of the scene on the virtual camera's film plane. Note that this is a subtly different goal than expecting the display's pixels to take on the image function's actual value at their positions. Handling this difference is the main goal of the algorithms implemented in this chapter.[1]

Because the sampling and reconstruction process involves approximation, it introduces error known as *aliasing*, which can manifest itself in many ways, including jagged edges or flickering in animations. These errors occur because the sampling process is not able to capture all of the information from the continuously defined image function.

As an example of these ideas, consider a one-dimensional function (which we will interchangeably refer to as a signal), given by $f(x)$, where we can evaluate $f(x')$ at any desired location x' in the function's domain. Each such x' is called a *sample position*, and the value of $f(x')$ is the *sample value*. Figure 7.1 shows a set of samples of a smooth 1D

---

1   In this book, we will ignore the subtle issues related to the characteristics of the physical display pixels and will work under the assumption that the display performs the ideal reconstruction process described later in this section. This assumption is patently at odds with how actual displays work, but it avoids unnecessary complicating of the analysis here. Chapter 3 of Glassner (1995) has a good treatment of nonidealized display devices and their impact on the image sampling and reconstruction process.

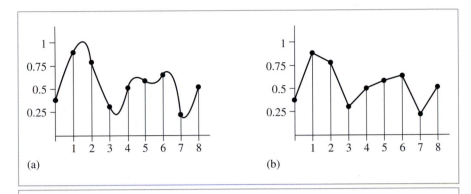

Figure 7.1: (a) By taking a set of *point samples* of $f(x)$ (indicated by black dots), we determine the value of the function at those positions. (b) The sample values can be used to *reconstruct* a function $\tilde{f}(x)$ that is an approximation to $f(x)$. The sampling theorem, introduced in Section 7.1.3, makes a precise statement about the conditions on $f(x)$, the number of samples taken, and the reconstruction technique used under which $\tilde{f}(x)$ is exactly the same as $f(x)$. The fact that the original function can sometimes be reconstructed exactly from point samples alone is remarkable.

function, along with a reconstructed signal $\tilde{f}$ that approximates the original function f. In this example, $\tilde{f}$ is a piecewise-linear function that approximates f by linearly interpolating neighboring sample values (readers already familiar with sampling theory will recognize this as reconstruction with a hat function). Because the only information available about f comes from the sample values at the positions x', $\tilde{f}$ is unlikely to match f perfectly since there is no information about f's behavior between the samples.

Fourier analysis can be used to evaluate the quality of the match between the reconstructed function and the original. This section will introduce the main ideas of Fourier analysis with enough detail to work through some parts of the sampling and reconstruction processes, but will omit proofs of many properties and skip details that aren't directly relevant to the sampling algorithms used in pbrt. The "Further Reading" section of this chapter has pointers to more detailed information about these topics.

7.1.1 THE FREQUENCY DOMAIN AND THE FOURIER TRANSFORM

One of the foundations of Fourier analysis is the Fourier transform, which represents a function in the *frequency domain*. (We will say that functions are normally expressed in the *spatial domain*.) Consider the two functions graphed in Figure 7.2. The function in Figure 7.2(a) varies relatively slowly as a function of x, while the function in Figure 7.2(b) varies much more rapidly. The slower-varying function is said to have lower frequency content. Figure 7.3 shows the frequency space representations of these two functions; the lower-frequency function's representation goes to zero more quickly than the higher-frequency function.

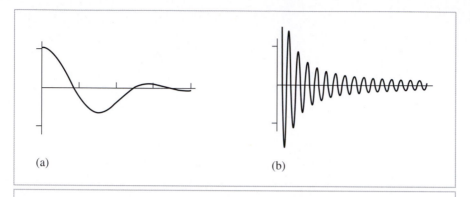

(a)   (b)

Figure 7.2: (a) Low-frequency function, and (b) high-frequency function. Roughly speaking, the higher frequency a function is, the more quickly it varies over a given region.

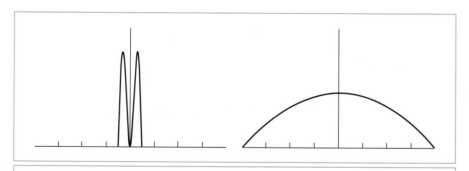

Figure 7.3: Frequency Space Representations of the Functions in Figure 7.2. The graphs show the contribution of each frequency ω to each of the functions in the spatial domain.

Most functions can be decomposed into a weighted sum of shifted sinusoids. This remarkable fact was first described by Joseph Fourier, and the Fourier transform converts a function into this representation. This frequency space representation of a function gives insight into some of its characteristics—the distribution of frequencies in the sine functions corresponds to the distribution of frequencies in the original function. Using this form, it is possible to use Fourier analysis to gain insight into the error that is introduced by the sampling and reconstruction process, and how to reduce the perceptual impact of this error.

> **Table 7.1: Fourier Pairs.** Functions in the spatial domain and their frequency space representations. Because of the symmetry properties of the Fourier transform, if the left column is instead considered to be frequency space, then the right column is the spatial equivalent of those functions as well.

Spatial Domain	Frequency Space Representation
Box: $f(x) = 1$ if $|x| < 1/2$, 0 otherwise	Sinc: $f(\omega) = \text{sinc}(\omega) = \sin(\pi\omega)/(\pi\omega)$
Gaussian: $f(x) = e^{-\pi x^2}$	Gaussian: $f(\omega) = e^{-\pi\omega^2}$
Constant: $f(x) = 1$	Delta: $f(\omega) = \delta(\omega)$
Sinusoid: $f(x) = \cos x$	Translated delta: $f(\omega) = \pi(\delta(1/2 - \omega) + \delta(1/2 + \omega))$
Shah: $f(x) = \text{III}_T(x) = T \sum_i \delta(x - Ti)$	Shah: $f(\omega) = \text{III}_{1/T}(\omega) = (1/T) \sum_i \delta(\omega - i/T)$

The Fourier transform of a one-dimensional function $f(x)$ is[2]

$$F(\omega) = \int_{-\infty}^{\infty} f(x) e^{-i2\pi\omega x} \, \mathrm{d}x. \qquad [7.1]$$

(Recall that $e^{ix} = \cos x + i \sin x$, where $i = \sqrt{-1}$.) For simplicity, here we will consider only *even* functions where $f(-x) = f(x)$, in which case the Fourier transform of f has no imaginary terms. The new function F is a function of *frequency*, ω.[3] We will denote the Fourier transform operator by $\mathcal{F}$, such that $\mathcal{F}\{f(x)\} = F(\omega)$. $\mathcal{F}$ is clearly a linear operator—that is, $\mathcal{F}\{af(x)\} = a\mathcal{F}\{f(x)\}$ for any scalar a, and $\mathcal{F}\{f(x) + g(x)\} = \mathcal{F}\{f(x)\} + \mathcal{F}\{g(x)\}$.

Equation (7.1) is called the *Fourier analysis* equation, or sometimes just the *Fourier transform*. We can also transform from the frequency domain back to the spatial domain using the *Fourier synthesis* equation, or the *inverse Fourier transform*:

$$f(x) = \int_{-\infty}^{\infty} F(\omega) e^{i2\pi\omega x} \, \mathrm{d}\omega. \qquad [7.2]$$

Table 7.1 shows a number of important functions and their frequency space representations. A number of these functions are based on the Dirac delta distribution, a special function that is defined such that $\int \delta(x)\mathrm{d}x = 1$, and for all $x \neq 0$, $\delta(x) = 0$. An important consequence of these properties is that

$$\int f(x)\delta(x)\mathrm{d}x = f(0).$$

---

2   The reader should be warned that the constants in front of these integrals are not always the same in different fields. For example, some authors (including many in the physics community) prefer to multiply both integrals by $1/\sqrt{2\pi}$.

3   In this chapter, we will use the ω symbol to denote frequency. Throughout the rest of the book, ω denotes normalized direction vectors. This overloading of notation should never be confusing, given the contexts where these symbols are used. Similarly, when we refer to a function's "spectrum," we are referring to its distribution of frequencies in its frequency space representation, rather than anything related to color.

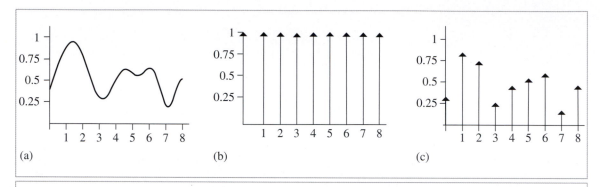

Figure 7.4: Formalizing the Sampling Process. (a) The function $f(x)$ is multiplied by (b) the shah function $III_T(x)$, giving (c) an infinite sequence of scaled delta functions that represent its value at each sample point.

The delta distribution cannot be expressed as a standard mathematical function, but instead is generally thought of as the limit of a unit area box function centered at the origin with width approaching zero.

7.1.2 IDEAL SAMPLING AND RECONSTRUCTION

Using frequency space analysis, we can now formally investigate the properties of sampling. Recall that the sampling process requires us to choose a set of equally spaced sample positions and compute the function's value at those positions. Formally, this corresponds to multiplying the function by a "shah," or "impulse train" function, an infinite sum of equally spaced delta functions. The shah $III_T(x)$ is defined as

$$III_T(x) = T \sum_{i=-\infty}^{\infty} \delta(x - iT),$$

where T defines the period, or *sampling rate*. This formal definition of sampling is illustrated in Figure 7.4. The multiplication yields an infinite sequence of values of the function at equally spaced points:

$$III_T(x) f(x) = T \sum_{i} \delta(x - iT) f(iT).$$

These sample values can be used to define a reconstructed function $\tilde{f}$ by choosing a reconstruction filter function $r(x)$ and computing the *convolution*

$$\big(III_T(x) f(x)\big) \otimes r(x),$$

where the convolution operation $\otimes$ is defined as

$$f(x) \otimes g(x) = \int_{-\infty}^{\infty} f(x')g(x - x') \, dx'.$$

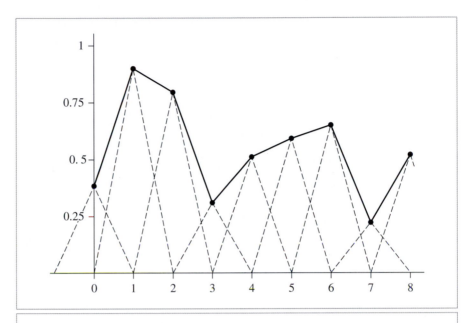

Figure 7.5: The sum of instances of the triangle reconstruction filter, shown with dashed lines, gives the reconstructed approximation to the original function, shown with a solid line.

For reconstruction, convolution gives a weighted sum of scaled instances of the reconstruction filter centered at the sample points:

$$\tilde{f}(x) = T \sum_{i=-\infty}^{\infty} f(iT)r(x - iT).$$

For example, in Figure 7.1, the triangle reconstruction filter, $f(x) = \max(0, 1 - |x|)$, was used. Figure 7.5 shows the scaled triangle functions used for that example.

We have gone through a process that may seem gratuitously complex in order to end up at an intuitive result: the reconstructed function $\tilde{f}(x)$ can be obtained by interpolating among the samples in some manner. By setting up this background carefully, however, Fourier analysis can now be applied to the process more easily.

We can gain a deeper understanding of the sampling process by analyzing the sampled function in the frequency domain. In particular, we will be able to determine the conditions under which the original function can be exactly recovered from its values at the sample locations—a very powerful result. For the discussion here, we will assume for now that the function $f(x)$ is *band-limited*—there exists some frequency ω_0 such that $f(x)$

contains no frequencies greater than ω_0. By definition, band-limited functions have frequency space representations with compact support, such that $F(\omega) = 0$ for all $|\omega| > \omega_0$. Both of the spectra in Figure 7.3 are band-limited.

An important idea used in Fourier analysis is the fact that the Fourier transform of the product of two functions $\mathcal{F}\{f(x)g(x)\}$ can be shown to be the convolution of their individual Fourier transforms $F(\omega)$ and $G(\omega)$:

$$\mathcal{F}\{f(x)g(x)\} = F(\omega) \otimes G(\omega).$$

It is similarly the case that convolution in the spatial domain is equivalent to multiplication in the frequency domain:

$$\mathcal{F}\{f(x) \otimes g(x)\} = F(\omega)G(\omega).$$

These properties are derived in the standard references on Fourier analysis. Using these ideas, the original sampling step in the spatial domain, where the product of the shah function and the original function $f(x)$ is found, can be equivalently described by the convolution of $F(\omega)$ with another shah function in frequency space.

We also know the spectrum of the shah function $III_T(x)$ from Table 7.1; the Fourier transform of a shah function with period T is another shah function with period $1/T$. This reciprocal relationship between periods is important to keep in mind: it means that if the samples are farther apart in the spatial domain, they are closer together in the frequency domain.

Thus, the frequency domain representation of the sampled signal is given by the convolution of $F(\omega)$ and this new shah function. Convolving a function with a delta function just yields a copy of the function, so convolving with a shah function yields an infinite sequence of copies of the original function, with spacing equal to the period of the shah (Figure 7.6). This is the frequency space representation of the series of samples.

Now that we have this infinite set of copies of the function's spectrum, how do we reconstruct the original function? Looking at Figure 7.6, the answer is obvious: just discard all of the spectrum copies except the one centered at the origin, giving the original $F(\omega)$. In order to throw away all but the center copy of the spectrum, we multiply by a box function of the appropriate width (Figure 7.7). The box function $\Pi_T(x)$ of width T is defined as

$$\Pi_T(x) = \begin{cases} 1/(2T) & |x| < T \\ 0 & \text{otherwise.} \end{cases}$$

This multiplication step corresponds to convolution with the reconstruction filter in the spatial domain. This is the ideal sampling and reconstruction process. To summarize:

$$\tilde{F} = \big(F(\omega) \otimes III_{1/T}(\omega)\big)\,\Pi_T(x).$$

This is a remarkable result: we have been able to determine the exact frequency space representation of $f(x)$, purely by sampling it at a set of regularly spaced points. Other

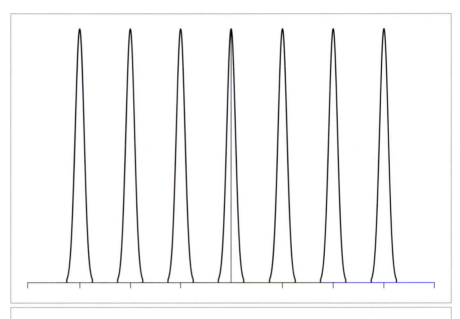

Figure 7.6: The Convolution of $F(\omega)$ and the Shah Function. The result is infinitely many copies of F.

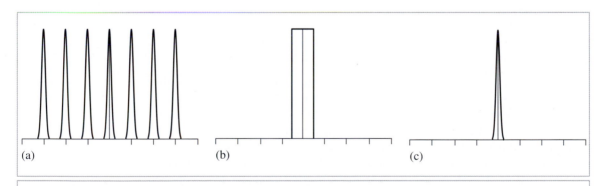

(a)   (b)   (c)

Figure 7.7: Multiplying (a) a series of copies of $F(\omega)$ by (b) the appropriate box function yields (c) the original spectrum.

than knowing that the function was band-limited, no additional information about the composition of the function was used.

Applying the equivalent process in the spatial domain will likewise recover $f(x)$ exactly. Because the inverse Fourier transform of the box function is the sinc function, ideal reconstruction in the spatial domain is found by

$$\tilde{f} = \big(f(x)\mathrm{III}_T(x)\big) \otimes \mathrm{sinc}(x),$$

or

$$\tilde{f}(x) = \sum_{i=-\infty}^{\infty} \mathrm{sinc}(x-i)f(i).$$

Unfortunately, because the sinc function has infinite extent, it is necessary to use all of the sample values $f(i)$ to compute any particular value of $\tilde{f}(x)$ in the spatial domain. Filters with finite spatial extent are preferable for practical implementations even though they don't reconstruct the original function perfectly.

A commonly used alternative in graphics is to use the box function for reconstruction, effectively averaging all of the sample values within some region around x. This is a very poor choice, as can be seen by considering the box filter's behavior in the frequency domain: This technique attempts to isolate the central copy of the function's spectrum by *multiplying by a sinc*, which not only does a bad job of selecting the central copy of the function's spectrum, but includes high-frequency contributions from the infinite series of other copies of it as well.

7.1.3 ALIASING

In addition to the sinc function's infinite extent, one of the most serious practical problems with the ideal sampling and reconstruction approach is the assumption that the signal is band-limited. For signals that are not band-limited, or signals that aren't sampled at a sufficiently high sampling rate for their frequency content, the process described earlier will reconstruct a function that is different than the original signal.

The key to successful reconstruction is the ability to exactly recover the original spectrum $F(\omega)$ by multiplying the sampled spectrum with a box function of the appropriate width. Notice that in Figure 7.6, the copies of the signal's spectrum are separated by empty space, so perfect reconstruction is possible. Consider what happens, however, if the original function was sampled with a lower sampling rate. Recall that the Fourier transform of a shah function III_T with period T is a new shah function with period $1/T$. This means that if the spacing between samples increases in the spatial domain, the sample spacing decreases in the frequency domain, pushing the copies of the spectrum $F(\omega)$ closer together. If the copies get too close together, they start to overlap.

Because the copies are added together, the resulting spectrum no longer looks like many copies of the original (Figure 7.8). When this new spectrum is multiplied by a box function, the result is a spectrum that is similar but not equal to the original $F(\omega)$: High-frequency details in the original signal leak into lower-frequency regions of the spectrum of the reconstructed signal. These new low-frequency artifacts are called *aliases* (because high frequencies are "masquerading" as low frequencies), and the resulting signal is

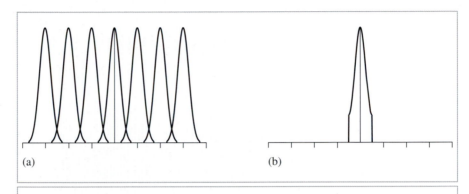

(a)   (b)

Figure 7.8: (a) When the sampling rate is too low, the copies of the function's spectrum overlap, (b) resulting in aliasing when reconstruction is performed.

said to be *aliased*. Figure 7.9 shows the effects of aliasing from undersampling and then reconstructing the one-dimensional function $f(x) = 1 + \cos(4x^2)$.

A possible solution to the problem of overlapping spectra is to simply increase the sampling rate until the copies of the spectrum are sufficiently far apart to not overlap, thereby eliminating aliasing completely. In fact, the *sampling theorem* tells us exactly what rate is required. This theorem says that as long as the frequency of uniform sample points ω_s is greater than twice the maximum frequency present in the signal ω_0, it is possible to reconstruct the original signal perfectly from the samples. This minimum sampling frequency is called the *Nyquist frequency*.

For signals that are not band-limited ($\omega_0 = \infty$), it is impossible to sample at a high enough rate to perform perfect reconstruction. Non-band-limited signals have spectra with infinite support, so no matter how far apart the copies of their spectra are (i.e., how high a sampling rate we use), there will always be overlap. Unfortunately, few of the interesting functions in computer graphics are band-limited. In particular, any function containing a discontinuity cannot be band-limited, and therefore we cannot perfectly sample and reconstruct it. This makes sense because the function's discontinuity will always fall between two samples and the samples provide no information about the location of the discontinuity. Thus, it is necessary to apply different methods besides just increasing the sampling rate in order to minimize the error that aliasing can introduce to the renderer's results.

7.1.4 ANTIALIASING TECHNIQUES

If one is not careful about sampling and reconstruction, myriad artifacts can appear in the final image. It is sometimes useful to distinguish between artifacts due to sampling and those due to reconstruction; when we wish to be precise we will call sampling artifacts *prealiasing*, and reconstruction artifacts *postaliasing*. Any attempt to fix these

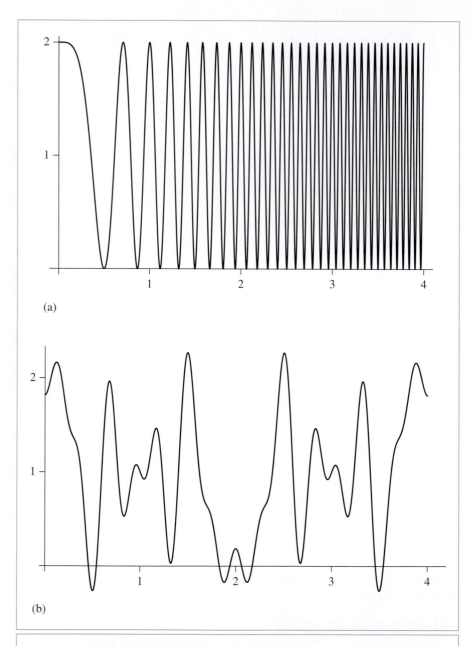

Figure 7.9: Aliasing from Point Sampling the Function $1 + \cos(4x^2)$. (a) The function. (b) The reconstructed function from sampling it with samples spaced 0.125 units apart and performing perfect reconstruction with the sinc filter. Aliasing causes the high-frequency information in the original function to be lost and to reappear as lower-frequency error.

errors is broadly classified as *antialiasing*. This section reviews a number of antialiasing techniques beyond just increasing the sampling rate everywhere.

Nonuniform Sampling

Although the image functions that we will be sampling are known to have infinite-frequency components and thus can't be perfectly reconstructed from point samples, it is possible to reduce the visual impact of aliasing by varying the spacing between samples in a nonuniform way. If ξ denotes a random number between zero and one, a nonuniform set of samples based on the impulse train is

$$\sum_{i=-\infty}^{\infty} \delta \left(x - \left(iT + \frac{1}{2} - \xi \right) \right).$$

For a fixed sampling rate that isn't sufficient to capture the function, both uniform and nonuniform sampling produce incorrect reconstructed signals. However, nonuniform sampling tends to turn the regular aliasing artifacts into noise, which is less distracting to the human visual system. In frequency space, the copies of the sampled signal end up being randomly shifted as well, so that when reconstruction is performed, the result is random error rather than coherent aliasing.

Adaptive Sampling

Another approach that has been suggested to combat aliasing is *adaptive supersampling*: if we can identify the regions of the signal with frequencies higher than the Nyquist limit, we can take additional samples in those regions without needing to incur the computational expense of increasing the sampling frequency everywhere. Unfortunately, it is hard to get this approach to work well in practice, because finding all of the places where supersampling is needed is difficult. Most techniques for doing so are based on examining adjacent sample values and finding places where there is a significant change in value between the two; the assumption is that the signal has high frequencies in that region.

In general, adjacent sample values cannot tell us with certainty what is really happening between them: Even if the values are the same, the function may have huge variation between them. Alternatively, adjacent samples may have substantially different values without any aliasing actually being present. For example, the texture filtering algorithms in Chapter 11 work hard to eliminate aliasing due to image maps and procedural textures on surfaces in the scene; we would not want an adaptive sampling routine to needlessly take extra samples in an area where texture values are changing quickly but no excessively high frequencies are actually present.

Some areas that need supersampling will always be missed by adaptive approaches, leaving an increase in the basic sampling rate as the only recourse. Adaptive antialiasing works well at turning a very aliased image into a less aliased image, but it is usually not able to make a visually flawless image much more efficiently than increasing the sampling rate everywhere, particularly for complex scenes.

Prefiltering

Another approach to eliminating aliasing that sampling theory offers is to filter (i.e., blur) the original function so that no high frequencies remain that can't be captured accurately at the sampling rate being used. This approach is applied in the texture functions of Chapter 11. While this technique changes the character of the function being sampled by removing information from it, it is generally less objectionable than aliasing.

Recall that we would like to multiply the original function's spectrum with a box filter with width chosen so that frequencies above the Nyquist limit are removed. In the spatial domain, this corresponds to convolving the original function with a sinc filter,

$$f(x) \otimes \mathrm{sinc}(2\omega_s x).$$

In practice, we can use a filter with finite extent that works well. The frequency space representation of this filter can help clarify how well it approximates the behavior of the ideal sinc filter.

Figure 7.10 shows the function $1 + \cos(4x^2)$ convolved with a variant of the sinc with finite extent that will be introduced in Section 7.6. Note that the high-frequency details have been eliminated; this function can be sampled and reconstructed at the sampling rate used in Figure 7.9 without aliasing.

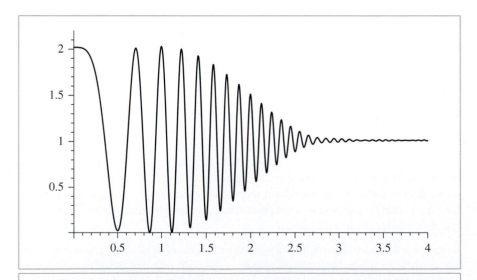

Figure 7.10: Graph of the function $1 + \cos(4x^2)$ convolved with a filter that removes frequencies beyond the Nyquist limit for a sampling rate of $T = .125$. High-frequency detail has been removed from the function, so that the new function can at least be sampled and reconstructed without aliasing.

7.1.5 APPLICATION TO IMAGE SYNTHESIS

The application of these ideas to the two-dimensional case of sampling and reconstructing images of rendered scenes is straightforward: we have an image, which we can think of as a function of two-dimensional (x, y) image locations to radiance values L:

$$f(x, y) \rightarrow L.$$

The good news is that, with our ray tracer, we can evaluate this function at any (x, y) point that we choose. The bad news is that it's not generally possible to prefilter f to remove the high frequencies from it before sampling. Therefore, the samplers in this chapter will use both strategies of increasing the sampling rate beyond the basic pixel spacing in the final image as well as nonuniformly distributing the samples to turn aliasing into noise.

It is useful to generalize the definition of the scene function to a higher-dimensional function that also depends on the time t and (u, v) lens position at which it is sampled. Because the rays from the camera are based on these five quantities, varying any of them gives a different ray and thus a potentially different value of f. For a particular image position, the radiance at that point will generally vary across both time (if there are moving objects in the scene) and position on the lens (if the camera has a finite-aperture lens).

Even more generally, because many of the integrators defined in Chapters 16 and 17 use statistical techniques to estimate the radiance along a given ray, they may return a different radiance value when repeatedly given the same ray. If we further extend the scene radiance function to include sample values used by the integrator (e.g., values used to choose points on area light sources for illumination computations), we have an even higher-dimensional image function

$$f(x, y, t, u, v, i_1, i_2, \ldots) \rightarrow L.$$

Sampling all of these dimensions well is an important part of generating high-quality imagery efficiently. For example, if we ensure that nearby (x, y) positions on the image tend to have dissimilar (u, v) positions on the lens, the resulting rendered images will have less error because each sample is more likely to account for information about the scene that its neighboring samples do not. The Sampler classes in the next few sections will address the issue of sampling all of these dimensions as well as possible.

7.1.6 SOURCES OF ALIASING IN RENDERING

Geometry is one of the most common causes of aliasing in rendered images. When projected onto the image plane, an object's boundary introduces a step function—the image function's value instantaneously jumps from one value to another. Not only do step functions have infinite frequency content as mentioned earlier, but even worse, the perfect reconstruction filter causes artifacts when applied to aliased samples: ringing artifacts appear in the reconstructed function, an effect known as the *Gibbs phenomenon*. Figure 7.11 shows an example of this effect for a 1D function. Choosing an effective

Sampler 296

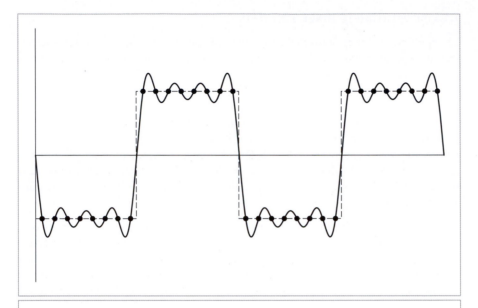

Figure 7.11: Illustration of the Gibbs Phenomenon. When a function hasn't been sampled at the Nyquist rate and the set of aliased samples is reconstructed with the sinc filter, the reconstructed function will have "ringing" artifacts, where it oscillates around the true function. Here a 1D step function (dashed line) has been sampled with a sample spacing of 0.125. When reconstructed with the sinc, the ringing appears (solid line).

reconstruction filter in the face of aliasing requires a mix of science, artistry, and personal taste, as we will see later in this chapter.

Very small objects in the scene can also cause geometric aliasing. If the geometry is small enough that it falls between samples on the image plane, it can unpredictably disappear and reappear over multiple frames of an animation.

Another source of aliasing can come from the texture and materials on an object. *Shading aliasing* can be caused by texture maps that haven't been filtered correctly (addressing this problem is the topic of much of Chapter 11), or from small highlights on shiny surfaces. If the sampling rate is not high enough to sample these features adequately, aliasing will result. Furthermore, a sharp shadow cast by an object introduces another step function in the final image. While it is possible to identify the position of step functions from geometric edges on the image plane, detecting step functions from shadow boundaries is more difficult.

The key insight about aliasing in rendered images is that we can never remove all of its sources, so we must develop techniques to mitigate its impact on the quality of the final image.

7.1.7 UNDERSTANDING PIXELS

There are two ideas about pixels that are important to keep in mind throughout the remainder of this chapter. First, it is crucial to remember that the pixels that constitute an image are point samples of the image function at discrete points on the image plane; there is no "area" associated with a pixel. As Alvy Ray Smith (1995) has emphatically pointed out, thinking of pixels as small squares with finite area is an incorrect mental model that leads to a series of errors. By introducing the topics of this chapter with a signal processing approach, we have tried to lay the groundwork for a more accurate mental model.

The second issue is that the pixels in the final image are naturally defined at discrete integer (x, y) coordinates on a pixel grid, but the Samplers in this chapter generate image samples at continuous floating-point (x, y) positions. The natural way to map between these two domains is to round continuous coordinates to the nearest discrete coordinate; this is appealing since it maps continuous coordinates that happen to have the same value as discrete coordinates to that discrete coordinate. However, the result is that given a set of discrete coordinates spanning a range $[x_0, x_1]$, the set of continuous coordinates that covers that range is $[x_0 - .5, x_1 + .5)$. Thus, any code that generates continuous sample positions for a given discrete pixel range is littered with 0.5 offsets. It is easy to forget some of these, leading to subtle errors.

If we instead truncate continuous coordinates c to discrete coordinates d by

$$d = \lfloor c \rfloor,$$

and convert from discrete to continuous by

$$c = d + .5,$$

then the range of continuous coordinates for the discrete range $[x_0, x_1]$ is naturally $[x_0, x_1 + 1)$ and the resulting code is much simpler (Heckbert 1990a). This convention, which we will adopt in pbrt, is shown graphically in Figure 7.12.

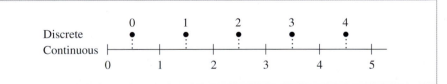

Figure 7.12: Pixels in an image can be addressed with either *discrete* or *continuous* coordinates. A discrete image four pixels wide covers the continuous pixel range [0, 5). A particular discrete pixel d's coordinate in the continuous representation is $d + 0.5$.

7.2 IMAGE SAMPLING INTERFACE

We can now describe the operation of a few classes that generate good image sampling patterns. It may be surprising to see that some of them have a significant amount of complexity behind them. In practice, creating good sample patterns can substantially improve a ray tracer's efficiency, allowing it to create a high-quality image with fewer rays than if a lower-quality pattern was used. Because the run time expense for using the best sampling patterns is approximately the same as for lower-quality patterns, and because evaluating the radiance for each image sample is expensive, doing this work pays dividends (Figure 7.13).

The core sampling declarations and functions are in the files `core/sampling.h` and `core/sampling.cpp` Each of the sample generation plug-ins is in its own source file in the `samplers/` directory.

All of the sampler implementations inherit from an abstract `Sampler` class that defines their interface. The task of `Sampler`s is to generate a sequence of multidimensional sample positions. Two dimensions give the raster space image sample position, and another gives the time at which the sample should be taken; this ranges from zero to one, and is scaled by the camera to cover the time period that the shutter is open. Two more sample values give a (u, v) lens position for depth of field; these also vary from zero to one.

Just as well-placed sample points can help conquer the complexity of the 2D image function, most of the light transport algorithms in Chapter 16 use sample points for tasks like choosing positions on area light sources when estimating illumination. Choosing these points is also the job of the `Sampler`, since it is able to take the sample points chosen for adjacent image samples into account when selecting samples at new points. Doing so can improve the quality of the results of the light transport algorithms.

⟨*Sampling Declarations*⟩ ≡
```
class COREDLL Sampler {
public:
    ⟨Sampler Interface 298⟩
    ⟨Sampler Public Data 298⟩
};
```

All of the `Sampler` implementations take a few common parameters that must be passed to the base class's constructor. These include the overall image resolution in the x and y dimensions and the number of samples the implementation expects to generate for each pixel in the final image. These values are stored in member variables for later use.

COREDLL 904
Sampler 296

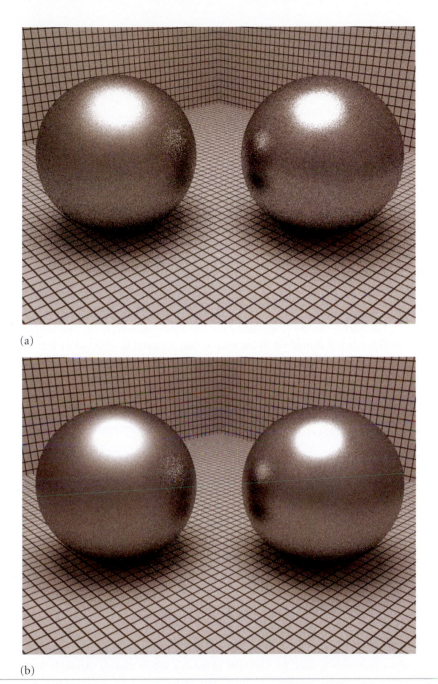

(a)

(b)

Figure 7.13: Scene rendered with (a) a relatively ineffective sampler and (b) a carefully designed sampler, using the same number of samples for each. The improvement in image quality, ranging from the edges of the highlights to the quality of the glossy reflections, is noticeable.

⟨*Sampler Method Definitions*⟩ ≡

```
Sampler::Sampler(int xstart, int xend, int ystart, int yend, int spp) {
    xPixelStart = xstart;
    xPixelEnd = xend;
    yPixelStart = ystart;
    yPixelEnd = yend;
    samplesPerPixel = spp;
}
```

The Sampler implementation should generate samples for pixels with *x* coordinates ranging from xPixelStart to xPixelEnd-1, inclusive, and analogously for *y* coordinates.

⟨*Sampler Public Data*⟩ ≡   296

```
int xPixelStart, xPixelEnd, yPixelStart, yPixelEnd;
int samplesPerPixel;
```

Samplers must implement the Sampler::GetNextSample() method, which is a pure virtual function. The Scene::Render() method calls this function until it returns false; each time it returns true, it should fill in the sample that is passed in with values that specify the next sample to be taken. All of the dimensions of the sample values it generates have values in the range [0, 1], except for imageX and imageY, which are specified with respect to the image size in raster coordinates.

⟨*Sampler Interface*⟩ ≡   296

```
virtual bool GetNextSample(Sample *sample) = 0;
```

In order to make it easy for the main rendering loop to figure out what percentage of the scene has been rendered based on the number of samples processed, the Sampler::TotalSamples() method returns the total number of samples that the Sampler is expected to return.[4]

⟨*Sampler Interface*⟩+≡   296

```
int TotalSamples() const {
    return samplesPerPixel *
           (xPixelEnd - xPixelStart) *
           (yPixelEnd - yPixelStart);
}
```

7.2.1 SAMPLE REPRESENTATION AND ALLOCATION

The Sample structure is used by Samplers to store a single sample. A single Sample is allocated in the Scene::Render() method. For each camera ray to be generated, the

---

4   The low-discrepancy and best-candidate samplers, described later in the chapter, may actually return a few more or less samples than TotalSamples() reports. However, since computing the actual number can't be done quickly, and since an exact number is not really required, the expected number is returned here instead.

Sample's pointer is passed to the Sampler to have its values initialized. It is then passed to the camera and integrators, which read values from it to construct the camera ray and perform lighting calculations.

Depending on the details of the light transport algorithm being used, different integrators may have different sampling needs. For example, the WhittedIntegrator doesn't do any random sampling, so it doesn't need any additional sample values, but the DirectLighting integrator uses values from the Sampler to randomly choose a light source to sample illumination from, as well as to randomly choose positions on area light sources. Therefore, the integrators will be given an opportunity to request additional sample values in various quantities. Information about these requirements is stored in the Sample object. When it is later passed to the particular Sampler implementation, it is the Sampler's responsibility to generate all of the requested types of samples.

⟨*Sampling Declarations*⟩+≡
```
struct Sample {
    ⟨Sample Public Methods  300⟩
    ⟨Camera Sample Data  299⟩
    ⟨Integrator Sample Data  301⟩
};
```

The data in the Sampler for use by the camera is fixed. We've already seen its use by the camera implementations in Chapter 6.

⟨*Camera* Sample *Data*⟩≡   **299**
```
float imageX, imageY;
float lensU, lensV;
float time;
```

The Sample constructor immediately calls the Integrator::RequestSamples() methods of the surface and volume integrators to find out what samples they will need. The integrators can ask for multiple one-dimensional and/or two-dimensional sampling patterns, each with an arbitrary number of entries. For example, in a scene with two area light sources, where the integrator traces four shadow rays to the first source and eight to the second, the integrator would ask for two 2D sample patterns for each image sample, with four and eight samples each. A 2D pattern is required because two dimensions are needed to parameterize the surface of a light. Similarly, if the integrator wanted to randomly select a single light source out of many, it could request a 1D sample with a single value for this purpose and use its float value to randomly choose a light.

By informing the Sampler of as much of its random sampling needs as possible, the Integrator allows the Sampler to carefully construct sample points that cover the entire high-dimensional sample space well. For example, the final image is generally better when neighboring image samples tend to sample different positions on the area lights for their illumination computations, allowing more information to be discovered.

In pbrt, we don't allow integrators to request 3D or higher-dimensional sample patterns because these are generally not needed for the types of rendering algorithms implemented here. If necessary, an integrator can combine points from lower-dimensional patterns to get higher-dimensional sample points (e.g., a 1D and a 2D sample pattern of the same size can form a 3D pattern). Although this is not as good as generating a 3D sample pattern directly, it is usually acceptable in practice. If absolutely necessary, the integrator can always generate a 3D sample pattern itself.

The integrators' implementations of the `Integrator::RequestSamples()` method in turn call the `Sample::Add1D()` and `Sample::Add2D()` methods, which request another sample sequence with a given number of sample values. After they are done calling these methods, the `Sample` constructor can continue, allocating storage for the requested sample values.

⟨*Sample Method Definitions*⟩ ≡
```
    Sample::Sample(SurfaceIntegrator *surf,
                   VolumeIntegrator *vol, const Scene *scene) {
        surf->RequestSamples(this, scene);
        vol->RequestSamples(this, scene);
        ⟨Allocate storage for sample pointers 301⟩
        ⟨Compute total number of sample values needed 302⟩
        ⟨Allocate storage for sample values 302⟩
    }
```

The implementations of the `Sample::Add1D()` and `Sample::Add2D()` methods record the number of samples asked for in an array and return an index that the integrator can later use to access the desired sample values in the `Sample`.

⟨*Sample Public Methods*⟩ ≡   299
```
    u_int Add1D(u_int num) {
        n1D.push_back(num);
        return n1D.size()-1;
    }
```

⟨*Sample Public Methods*⟩+≡   299
```
    u_int Add2D(u_int num) {
        n2D.push_back(num);
        return n2D.size()-1;
    }
```

Most `Sampler`s can do a better job of generating particular quantities of these additional samples than others. For example, the `LDSampler` can generate extremely good patterns, although they must have a size that is a power of two. The `Sampler::RoundSize()` method helps communicate this information. Integrators should call this method with the desired number of samples to be taken, giving the `Sampler` an opportunity to adjust the number of samples to a more convenient one. The integrator should then use the returned value as the number of samples to request from the Sampler.

⟨*Sampler Interface*⟩+≡   296
```
virtual int RoundSize(int size) const = 0;
```

It is the Sampler's responsibility to store the samples it generates for the integrators in the Sample::oneD and Sample::twoD arrays. For 1D sample patterns, it needs to generate n1D.size() independent patterns, where the ith pattern has n1D[i] sample values. These values are stored in oneD[i][0] through oneD[i][n1D[i]-1].

⟨*Integrator* Sample *Data*⟩≡   299
```
vector<u_int> n1D, n2D;
float **oneD, **twoD;
```

To access the samples, the integrator stores the sample tag returned by Add1D() in a member variable (for example, sampleOffset) and can then access the sample values in a loop like

```
for (i = 0; i < sample->n1D[sampleOffset]; ++i) {
    float s = sample->oneD[sampleOffset][i];
        .
        .
        .
}
```

In 2D, the process is equivalent, but the ith sample is given by the two values sample->twoD[offset][2*i] and sample->twoD[offset][2*i+1].

The Sample constructor first allocates memory to store the pointers. Rather than allocating memory twice, it does a single allocation that gives enough memory for both the oneD and twoD sample arrays. twoD is then set to point at an appropriate offset into this memory, after the last pointer for oneD. Splitting up a single allocation like this is useful because it ensures that oneD and twoD point to nearby locations in memory, which is likely to reduce cache misses.

⟨*Allocate storage for sample pointers*⟩≡   300
```
int nPtrs = n1D.size() + n2D.size();
if (!nPtrs) {
    oneD = twoD = NULL;
    return;
}
oneD = (float **)AllocAligned(nPtrs * sizeof(float *));
twoD = oneD + n1D.size();
```

We then use the same trick to allocate memory for the actual sample values so that they are contiguous as well. First, we find the total number of float values needed:

⟨*Compute total number of sample values needed*⟩ ≡   **300**
```
    int totSamples = 0;
    for (u_int i = 0; i < n1D.size(); ++i)
        totSamples += n1D[i];
    for (u_int i = 0; i < n2D.size(); ++i)
        totSamples += 2 * n2D[i];
```

The constructor can now allocate a single chunk of memory and hand it out in pieces for the various collections of samples:

⟨*Allocate storage for sample values*⟩ ≡   **300**
```
    float *mem = (float *)AllocAligned(totSamples * sizeof(float));
    for (u_int i = 0; i < n1D.size(); ++i) {
        oneD[i] = mem;
        mem += n1D[i];
    }
    for (u_int i = 0; i < n2D.size(); ++i) {
        twoD[i] = mem;
        mem += 2 * n2D[i];
    }
```

The Sample destructor, not shown here, just frees the dynamically allocated memory.

7.3 STRATIFIED SAMPLING

The first sample generator that we will introduce divides the image plane into rectangular regions and generates a single sample inside each region. These regions are commonly called *strata*, and this sampler is called the StratifiedSampler. The key idea behind stratification is that by subdividing the sampling domain into nonoverlapping regions and taking a single sample from each one, we are less likely to miss important features of the image entirely, since the samples are guaranteed not to all be close together. Put another way, it does us no good if many samples are taken from nearby points in the sample space, since each new sample doesn't add much new information about the behavior of the image function. From a signal processing viewpoint, we are implicitly defining an overall sampling rate such that the smaller the strata are, the more of them we have, and thus the higher the sampling rate.

The stratified sampler places each sample at a random point inside each stratum by *jittering* the center point of the stratum by a random amount up to half the stratum's width and height. The nonuniformity that results from this jittering helps turn aliasing into noise, as discussed in Section 7.1. The sampler also offers a nonjittered mode, which gives uniform sampling in the strata; this mode is mostly useful for comparisons between different sampling techniques rather than for rendering final images.

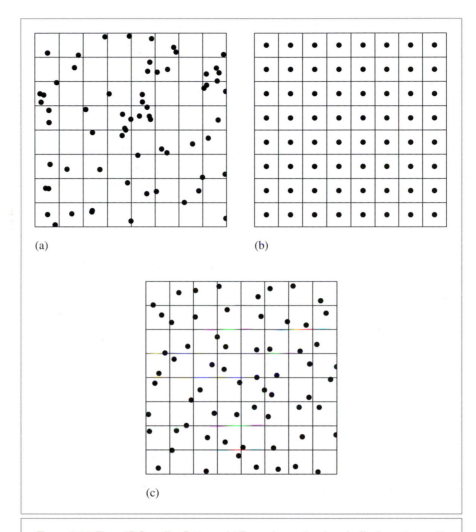

(a)   (b)

(c)

Figure 7.14: Three 2D Sampling Patterns. (a) The random pattern is an ineffective pattern, with many clumps of samples that leave large sections of the image poorly sampled. (b) A uniform stratified pattern is better distributed but can exacerbate aliasing artifacts. (c) A stratified jittered pattern turns aliasing from the uniform pattern into high-frequency noise while still maintaining the benefits of stratification.

Figure 7.14 shows a comparison of a few sampling patterns. The first is a completely random sampling pattern: we have chosen a number of samples and generated that many at random without using the strata at all. The result is a terrible sampling pattern; some regions have few samples and other areas have clumps of many samples. The second is a uniform stratified pattern. In the last, the uniform pattern has been jittered, with a random offset added to each sample's location, keeping it inside its cell. This gives a better overall distribution than the purely random pattern while preserving the benefits of stratification, though there are still some clumps of samples and some regions that are undersampled. We will present more sophisticated image sampling methods in the next two sections that ameliorate some of these remaining shortcomings. Figure 7.15 shows images rendered using the StratifiedSampler and shows how jittered sample positions turn aliasing artifacts into less objectionable noise.

⟨*StratifiedSampler Declarations*⟩ ≡
```
class StratifiedSampler : public Sampler {
public:
    ⟨StratifiedSampler Public Methods  306⟩
private:
    ⟨StratifiedSampler Private Data  304⟩
};
```

The StratifiedSampler generates samples by looping over the pixels from left to right and top to bottom, generating all of the samples for the strata in each pixel before advancing to the next pixel. The constructor takes the range of pixels to generate samples for—[xstart,ystart] to [xend-1,yend-1], inclusive—the number of strata in *x* and *y* (xs and ys) and a boolean (jitter) that indicates whether the samples should be jittered.

⟨*StratifiedSampler Method Definitions*⟩ ≡
```
StratifiedSampler::StratifiedSampler(int xstart, int xend,
        int ystart, int yend, int xs, int ys, bool jitter)
    : Sampler(xstart, xend, ystart, yend, xs * ys) {
    jitterSamples = jitter;
    xPos = xPixelStart;
    yPos = yPixelStart;
    xPixelSamples = xs;
    yPixelSamples = ys;
    ⟨Allocate storage for a pixel's worth of stratified samples  306⟩
    ⟨Generate stratified camera samples for (xPos,yPos)  308⟩
}
```

The sampler holds the coordinate of the current pixel in the xPos and yPos member variables, which are initialized to point to the pixel in the upper left of the image. Note that both the crop window and the sample filtering process can cause this corner to be at a location other than (0, 0).

⟨*StratifiedSampler Private Data*⟩ ≡   **304**
```
int xPixelSamples, yPixelSamples;
bool jitterSamples;
int xPos, yPos;
```

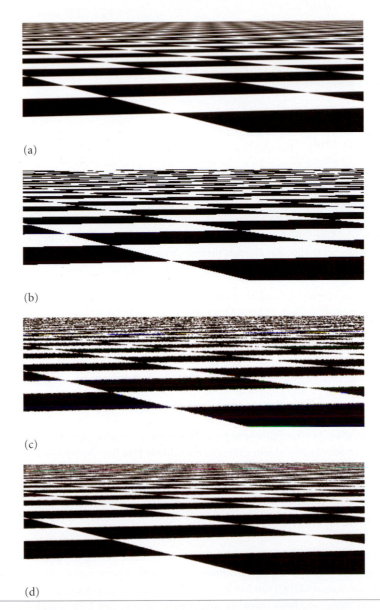

(a)

(b)

(c)

(d)

Figure 7.15: Comparison of Image Sampling Methods with a Checkerboard Texture. This is a difficult image to render well, since the checkerboard's frequency with respect to the pixel spacing tends toward infinity as we approach the horizon. (a) A reference image, rendered with 256 samples per pixel, showing something close to an ideal result. (b) An image rendered with one sample per pixel, with no jittering. Note the jaggy artifacts at the edges of checks in the foreground. Notice also the artifacts in the distance where the checker function goes through many cycles between samples; as expected from the signal processing theory presented earlier, that detail reappears incorrectly as lower-frequency aliasing. (c) The result of jittering the image samples, still with just one sample per pixel. The regular aliasing of the second image has been replaced by less objectionable noise artifacts. (d) The result of four jittered samples per pixel is still inferior to the reference image, but is substantially better than the previous result.

The StratifiedSampler has no preferred sizes for the number of additional samples generated for the Integrators.

⟨*StratifiedSampler Public Methods*⟩ ≡   304
```
int RoundSize(int size) const {
    return size;
}
```

The StratifiedSampler computes image, time, and lens samples for an entire pixel's worth of image samples all at once; doing so allows it to compute better-distributed patterns for the time and lens samples than if it were to compute each sample's values independently. Since the GetNextSample() method only supplies one sample at a time, here the constructor allocates enough memory to store all of the sample values for all of the samples in a single pixel.

⟨*Allocate storage for a pixel's worth of stratified samples*⟩ ≡   304
```
imageSamples = (float *)AllocAligned(5 * xPixelSamples *
                               yPixelSamples * sizeof(float));
lensSamples = imageSamples + 2 * xPixelSamples * yPixelSamples;
timeSamples = lensSamples + 2 * xPixelSamples * yPixelSamples;
```

⟨*StratifiedSampler Private Data*⟩ +≡   304
```
float *imageSamples, *lensSamples, *timeSamples;
```

Naive application of stratification to high-dimensional sampling quickly leads to an intractable number of samples. For example, if we divided the five-dimensional image, lens, and time sample space into four strata in each dimension, the total number of samples per pixel would be $4^5 = 1024$. We could reduce this impact by taking fewer samples in some dimensions (or not stratifying some dimensions, effectively using a single stratum), but we would then lose the benefit of having well-stratified samples in those dimensions. This problem with stratification is known as the *curse of dimensionality*.

We can reap most of the benefits of stratification without paying the price in excessive total sampling by computing lower-dimensional stratified patterns for subsets of the domain's dimensions and then randomly associating samples from each set of dimensions. Figure 7.16 shows the basic idea: we might want to take just four samples per pixel, but still have the samples be stratified over all dimensions. We independently generate four 2D stratified image samples, four 1D stratified time samples, and four 2D stratified lens samples. Then, we randomly associate a time and lens sample value with each image sample. The result is that each pixel has samples that together have good coverage of the sample space. Figure 7.17 shows the improvement in image quality from using stratified lens samples versus using unstratified random samples when rendering depth of field.

Ensuring a good distribution at the pixel level is a reasonable level of granularity: we would like the samples that are close together on the image plane to have dissimilar time and lens samples so that the sample positions are not clumped together in the

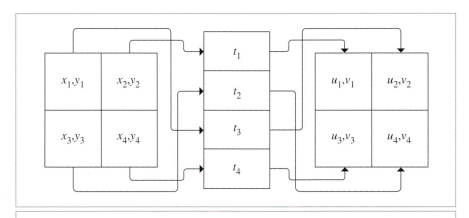

Figure 7.16: We can generate a good sample pattern that reaps the benefits of stratification without requiring that all of the sampling dimensions be stratified simultaneously. Here, we have split (x, y) image position, time t, and (u, v) lens position into independent strata with four regions each. Each is sampled independently, then a time sample and a lens sample are randomly associated with each image sample. We retain the benefits of stratification in each of the individual dimensions without having to exponentially increase the total number of samples.

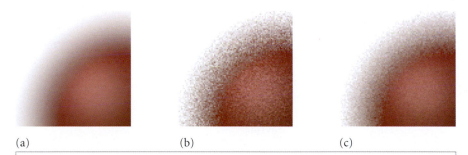

(a)   (b)   (c)

Figure 7.17: Effect of Sampling Patterns in Rendering a Red Sphere Image with Depth of Field.
(a) A high-quality reference image of the blurred edge of a sphere. (b) An image generated with random sampling in each pixel without stratification. (c) An image generated with the same number of samples, but with the `StratifiedSampler`, which stratified both the image and, more importantly for this image, the lens samples. Stratification makes a substantial improvement for this situation.

high-dimensional sampling space. When the samples are widely distributed, the resulting images are generally better, since the samples form a more accurate representation of the image function across the domain. However, it is much less important that samples that are far away on the image plane have uncorrelated time and lens samples.[5].

---

5   Of course, with the approach implemented here, the time and lens sample positions of the image samples for any particular output pixel are well distributed, but the time and lens sample positions of image samples for neighboring pixels are not known, and thus may be similar. The `BestCandidateSampler` can be less susceptible to this problem.

We use this technique to generate the camera samples for the current pixel in the
StratifiedSampler. As GetNextSample() generates new samples, the samplePos variable
tracks the current position in the image, time, and lens sample arrays.

⟨*Generate stratified camera samples for (xPos,yPos)*⟩ ≡   **304, 310**

```
StratifiedSample2D(imageSamples, xPixelSamples, yPixelSamples,
                   jitterSamples);
StratifiedSample2D(lensSamples, xPixelSamples, yPixelSamples,
                   jitterSamples);
StratifiedSample1D(timeSamples, xPixelSamples*yPixelSamples,
                   jitterSamples);
```
⟨*Shift stratified image samples to pixel coordinates* **309**⟩
⟨*Decorrelate sample dimensions* **309**⟩
```
samplePos = 0;
```

⟨*StratifiedSampler Private Data*⟩+≡   **304**
```
int samplePos;
```

We will implement 1D and 2D stratified sampling routines as utility functions, since they
will be useful elsewhere in pbrt. Both of them just loop over the given number of strata
over the [0, 1] domain and place a sample value in each one.

⟨*Sampling Function Definitions*⟩ ≡

```
COREDLL void StratifiedSample1D(float *samp, int nSamples,
                                bool jitter) {
    float invTot = 1.f / nSamples;
    for (int i = 0;  i < nSamples; ++i) {
        float j = jitter ? RandomFloat() : 0.5f;
        *samp++ = (i + j) * invTot;
    }
}
```

⟨*Sampling Function Definitions*⟩+≡

```
COREDLL void StratifiedSample2D(float *samp, int nx, int ny,
                                bool jitter) {
    float dx = 1.f / nx, dy = 1.f / ny;
    for (int y = 0; y < ny; ++y)
        for (int x = 0; x < nx; ++x) {
            float jx = jitter ? RandomFloat() : 0.5f;
            float jy = jitter ? RandomFloat() : 0.5f;
            *samp++ = (x + jx) * dx;
            *samp++ = (y + jy) * dy;
        }
}
```

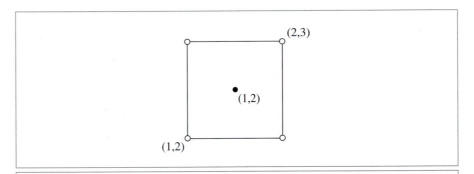

Figure 7.18: To generate stratified samples for a discrete pixel (1, 2), all that needs to be done is to add (1, 2) to the elements of the samples generated over [0, 1]². This gives samples with continuous pixel coordinates from (1, 2) to (2, 3), which end up surrounding the discrete pixel (1, 2).

The StratifiedSample2D() utility function generates samples in the range $[0, 1]^2$, but image samples need to be expressed in terms of continuous pixel coordinates. Therefore, this method loops over all of the new stratified samples and adds the (x, y) pixel number, so that the samples for the discrete pixel (x, y) range over the continuous coordinates $[x, x + 1) \times [y, y + 1)$, following the convention for continuous pixel coordinates described in Section 7.1.7. Figure 7.18 reviews the relationship between discrete and continuous coordinates as it relates to samples for a pixel.

⟨*Shift stratified image samples to pixel coordinates*⟩ ≡   308
```
for (int o = 0; o < 2 * xPixelSamples * yPixelSamples; o += 2) {
    imageSamples[o]   += xPos;
    imageSamples[o+1] += yPos;
}
```

In order to randomly associate a time and lens sample with each image sample, this method shuffles the order of the time and lens sample arrays. Thus, when it later initializes a Sample with the ith precomputed sample value for this pixel, it can just return the ith time and lens sample.

⟨*Decorrelate sample dimensions*⟩ ≡   308
```
Shuffle(lensSamples, xPixelSamples*yPixelSamples, 2);
Shuffle(timeSamples, xPixelSamples*yPixelSamples, 1);
```

The Shuffle() utility function randomly permutes a sample pattern of count samples in dims dimensions.

⟨*Sampling Function Definitions*⟩+≡
```
COREDLL void Shuffle(float *samp, int count, int dims) {
    for (int i = 0; i < count; ++i) {
        u_int other = RandomUInt() % count;
        for (int j = 0; j < dims; ++j)
            swap(samp[dims*i + j], samp[dims*other + j]);
    }
}
```

Given this infrastructure, it's now possible to implement the `GetNextSample()` method of the `StratifiedSampler`. It starts by checking whether it needs to generate a new pixel's worth of samples and whether all the samples have already been generated. It then generates new samples if needed and initializes the `Sample` pointer using the stored samples.

⟨*StratifiedSampler Method Definitions*⟩+≡
```
bool StratifiedSampler::GetNextSample(Sample *sample) {
    ⟨Compute new set of samples if needed for next pixel 310⟩
    ⟨Return next StratifiedSampler sample point 311⟩
    return true;
}
```

The `samplePos` variable keeps track of the current offset into the pixel-sized table of precomputed samples. When it reaches the end of the table, the sampler moves ahead to the next pixel.

⟨*Compute new set of samples if needed for next pixel*⟩ ≡   310
```
if (samplePos == xPixelSamples * yPixelSamples) {
    ⟨Advance to next pixel for stratified sampling 310⟩
    ⟨Generate stratified camera samples for (xPos,yPos) 308⟩
}
```

To advance to the next pixel, the implementation here first tries to move one pixel over in the *x* direction. If doing so takes it beyond the end of the image, it resets the *x* position to the first pixel in the next *x* row of pixels and advances the *y* position. Because the *y* stratum counter `yPos` is advanced only when the end of a row of pixels in the *x* direction is reached, once the *y* position counter has advanced past the bottom of the image, sample generation is complete and then the method returns `false`.

⟨*Advance to next pixel for stratified sampling*⟩ ≡   310
```
if (++xPos == xPixelEnd) {
    xPos = xPixelStart;
    ++yPos;
}
if (yPos == yPixelEnd)
    return false;
```

Since the camera samples have already been computed and stored in the table at this point (either from the current call to GetNextSample() or a previous one), initializing the corresponding Sample fields is easy; the appropriate values are copied from the sample tables.

⟨*Return next* StratifiedSampler *sample point*⟩ ≡   310
    sample->imageX = imageSamples[2*samplePos];
    sample->imageY = imageSamples[2*samplePos+1];
    sample->lensU = lensSamples[2*samplePos];
    sample->lensV = lensSamples[2*samplePos+1];
    sample->time = timeSamples[samplePos];
    ⟨*Generate stratified samples for integrators* 313⟩
    ++samplePos;

Integrators introduce a new complication since they often use multiple samples per image sample in some dimensions rather than a single sample value like the camera does for lens position and time. As we have described the topic of sampling so far, this leaves us with a quandary: if an integrator asks for a set of 64 two-dimensional sample values for each image sample, the sampler has two different goals to try to fulfill:

1. We would like each image sample's 64 integrator samples to themselves be well distributed in 2D (i.e., with an 8×8 stratified grid). Stratification here will improve the quality of the integrator's results for each individual sample.
2. We would like to ensure that the set of integrator samples for one image sample isn't too similar to the samples for its neighboring image samples. As with time and lens samples, we'd like the points to be well distributed with respect to their neighbors, so that over the region around a single pixel, there is good coverage of the entire sample space.

Rather than trying to solve both of these problems simultaneously here, the StratifiedSampler will only address the first one. The other samplers later in this chapter will revisit this issue with more sophisticated techniques and solve both of them simultaneously to various degrees.

A second integrator-related complication comes from the fact that they may ask for an arbitrary number of samples n per image sample, so stratification may not be easily applied. (For example, how do we generate a stratified 2D pattern of seven samples?) We could just generate an $n \times 1$ or $1 \times n$ stratified pattern, but this only gives us the benefit of stratification in one dimension, and no guarantee of a good pattern in the other dimension. The StratifiedSampler::RoundSize() method could round requests up to the next number that's the square of integers, but instead we will use an approach called *Latin hypercube sampling* (LHS), which can generate any number of samples in any number of dimensions with reasonably good distribution.

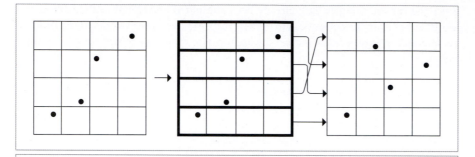

Figure 7.19: Latin hypercube sampling (sometimes called *n*-rooks sampling) chooses samples such that only a single sample is present in each row and each column of a grid. This can be done by generating random samples in the cells along the diagonal and then randomly permuting their coordinates. One advantage of LHS is that it can generate any number of samples with a good distribution, not just *m* × *n* samples, as with stratified patterns.

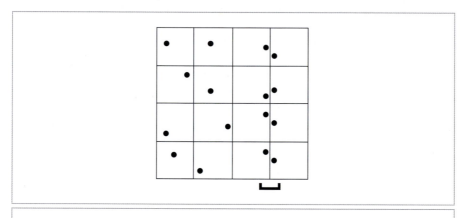

Figure 7.20: A Worst-Case Situation for Stratified Sampling. In an *n* × *n* 2D pattern, up to 2*n* of the points may project to essentially the same point on one of the axes. When "unlucky" patterns like this are generated, the quality of the results computed with them usually suffers.

LHS uniformly divides each dimension's axis into *n* regions and generates a jittered sample in each of the *n* regions along the diagonal, as shown on the left in Figure 7.19. These samples are then randomly shuffled in each dimension, creating a pattern with good distribution. An advantage of LHS is that it minimizes clumping of the samples when they are projected onto any of the axes of the sampling dimensions. This is in contrast to stratified sampling, where 2*n* of the *n* × *n* samples in a 2D pattern may project to essentially the same point on each of the axes. Figure 7.20 shows this worst-case situation for a stratified sampling pattern.

In spite of addressing the clumping problem, LHS isn't necessarily an improvement to stratified sampling; it's easy to construct cases where the sample positions are essentially colinear and large areas of $[0, 1]^2$ have no samples near them (e.g., when the permutation of the original samples is the identity, leaving them all where they started). In particular, as *n* increases, Latin hypercube patterns are less and less effective compared to stratified patterns. We will revisit this issue in the next section, where we will discuss sample patterns that are simultaneously stratified and distributed in a Latin hypercube pattern.

⟨*Generate stratified samples for integrators*⟩ ≡   **311**
```
for (u_int i = 0; i < sample->n1D.size(); ++i)
    LatinHypercube(sample->oneD[i], sample->n1D[i], 1);
for (u_int i = 0; i < sample->n2D.size(); ++i)
    LatinHypercube(sample->twoD[i], sample->n2D[i], 2);
```

The general-purpose `LatinHypercube()` function generates an arbitrary number of LHS samples in an arbitrary dimension. The number of elements in the `samples` array should thus be `nSamples*nDim`.

⟨*Sampling Function Definitions*⟩ + ≡
```
COREDLL void LatinHypercube(float *samples, int nSamples, int nDim) {
    ⟨Generate LHS samples along diagonal 313⟩
    ⟨Permute LHS samples in each dimension 314⟩
}
```

⟨*Generate LHS samples along diagonal*⟩ ≡   **313**
```
float delta = 1.f / nSamples;
for (int i = 0; i < nSamples; ++i)
    for (int j = 0; j < nDim; ++j)
        samples[nDim * i + j] = (i + RandomFloat()) * delta;
```

To do the permutation, this function loops over the samples, randomly permuting the sample points in one dimension at a time. Note that this is a different permutation than the earlier `Shuffle()` routine: that routine does one permutation, keeping all `nDim` sample points in each sample together, while here `nDim` separate permutations of a single dimension at a time are done (Figure 7.21).[6]

---

6   While it's not necessary to permute the first dimension of the LHS pattern, the implementation here does so anyway, since making the elements of the first dimension be randomly ordered means that LHS patterns can be used in conjunction with sampling patterns from other sources without danger of correlation between their sample points.

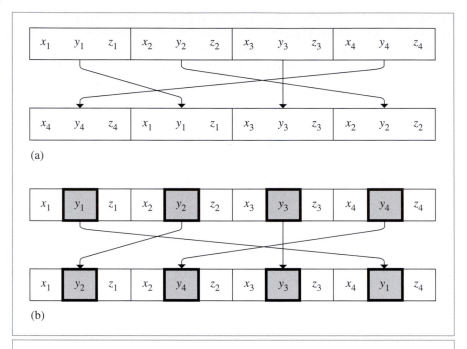

Figure 7.21: (a) The permutation done by the `Shuffle()` routine moves entire blocks of `nDims` elements around. (b) The permutation for Latin hypercube sampling permutes each dimension's samples independently. Here, the shuffling of the second dimension's samples from a four-element pattern of three dimensions is shown.

⟨*Permute LHS samples in each dimension*⟩ ≡   313
```
for (int i = 0; i < nDim; ++i) {
    for (int j = 0; j < nSamples; ++j) {
        u_int other = RandomUInt() % nSamples;
        swap(samples[nDim * j + i],
            samples[nDim * other + i]);
    }
}
```

Starting with the scene in Figure 7.22, Figure 7.23 shows the improvement from good samples for the `DirectLighting` integrator. Image (a) was computed with 1 image sample per pixel, each with 16 shadow samples, and image (b) was computed with 16 image samples per pixel, each with 1 shadow sample. Because the `StratifiedSampler` could generate a good LHS pattern for the first case, the quality of the shadow is much better, even with the same total number of shadow samples taken.

Figure 7.22: Area light sampling example scene.

(a)

(b)

Figure 7.23: Sampling an Area Light with Samples from the Stratified Sampler. (a) shows the result of using 1 image sample per pixel and 16 shadow samples, and (b) shows the result of 16 image samples, each with just 1 shadow sample. The total number of shadow samples is the same in both cases, but because the version with 16 shadow samples per image sample is able to use an LHS pattern, all of the shadow samples in a pixel's area are well distributed, while in the second image, the implementation here has no way to prevent them from being poorly distributed. The difference is striking.

*7.4 LOW-DISCREPANCY SAMPLING

The underlying goal of the StratifiedSampler is to generate a well-distributed but not uniform set of sample points, with no two sample points too close together and no excessively large regions of the sample space that have no samples. As Figure 7.14 showed, a jittered pattern does this much better than a random pattern does, although its quality can suffer when samples in adjacent strata happen to be close to the shared boundary of their two strata.

Mathematicians have developed a concept called *discrepancy* that can be used to evaluate the quality of a pattern of sample positions like these in a way that their quality can be expressed numerically. Patterns that are well-distributed (in a manner to be formalized shortly) have low discrepancy values, and thus the sample pattern generation problem can be considered to be one of finding a suitable *low-discrepancy* pattern of points.[7] A number of deterministic techniques have been developed that generate low-discrepancy point sets, even in high-dimensional spaces. This section will use a few of them as the basis for a low-discrepancy sample generator.

7.4.1 DEFINITION OF DISCREPANCY

Before defining the low-discrepancy sampling class LDSampler, we will first introduce a formal definition of discrepancy. The basic idea is that the "quality" of a set of points in an n-dimensional space $[0, 1]^n$ can be evaluated by looking at regions of the domain $[0, 1]^n$, counting the number of points inside each region, and comparing the volume of each region to the number of sample points inside. In general, a given fraction of the volume should have roughly the same fraction of the sample points inside of it. While it's not possible for this always to be the case, we can still try to use patterns that minimize the difference between the actual volume and the volume estimated by the points (the *discrepancy*). Figure 7.24 shows an example of the idea in two dimensions.

To compute the discrepancy of a set of points, we first pick a family of shapes B that are subsets of $[0, 1]^n$. For example, boxes with one corner at the origin are often used. This corresponds to

$$B = \{[0, v_1] \times [0, v_2] \times \cdots \times [0, v_s]\},$$

where $0 \leq v_i \leq 1$. Given a sequence of sample points $P = x_1, \ldots, x_N$, the discrepancy of P with respect to B is[8]

---

7   Of course, using discrepancy in this way implicitly assumes that the metric used to compute discrepancy is one that has good correlation with the quality of a pattern for image sampling, which may be a slightly different thing, particularly given the involvement of the human visual system in the process.

8   The sup operator is the continuous analog of max. That is, sup $f(x)$ is a constant-valued function of x that passes through the maximum value taken on by $f(x)$.

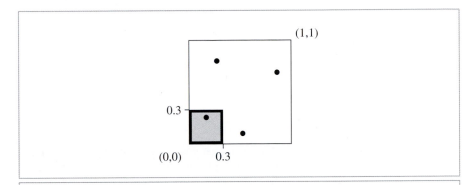

Figure 7.24: The discrepancy of a box (shaded) given a set of 2D sample points in $[0, 1]^2$. One of the four sample points is inside the box, so this set of points would estimate the box's area to be 1/4. The true area of the box is $.3 \times .3 = .09$, so the discrepancy for this particular box is $.25 - .09 = .16$. In general, we're interested in finding the maximum discrepancy of all possible boxes (or some other shape) to compute discrepancy.

$$D_N(B, P) = \sup_{b \in B} \left| \frac{\sharp\{x_i \in b\}}{N} - \lambda(b) \right|,$$

where $\sharp\{x_i \in b\}$ is the number of points in b and $\lambda(b)$ is the volume of b.

The intuition for why this is a reasonable measure of quality is that $\sharp\{x_i \in b\}/N$ is an approximation of the volume of the box b given by the particular points P. Therefore, the discrepancy is the worst error over all possible boxes from this way of approximating volume. When the set of shapes B is the set of boxes with a corner at the origin, this is called the *star discrepancy* $D_N^*(P)$. Another popular option for B is the set of all axis-aligned boxes, where the restriction that one corner be at the origin has been removed.

For a few particular point sets, the discrepancy can be computed analytically. For example, consider the set of points in one dimension

$$x_i = \frac{i}{N}.$$

We can see that the star discrepancy of x_i is

$$D_N^*(x_1, \ldots, x_n) = \frac{1}{N}.$$

For example, take the interval $b = [0, 1/N)$. Then $\lambda(b) = 1/N$, but $\sharp\{x_i \in b\} = 0$. This interval (and the intervals $[0, 2/N)$, etc.) is the interval where the largest differences between volume and fraction of points inside the volume are seen.

The star discrepancy of this sequence can be improved by modifying it slightly:

$$x_i = \frac{i - \frac{1}{2}}{N}.$$

Then

$$D_N^*(x_i) = \frac{1}{2N}.$$

The bounds for the star discrepancy of a sequence of points in one dimension has been shown to be

$$D_N^*(x_i) = \frac{1}{2N} + \max_{1 \leq i \leq N} \left| x_i - \frac{2i-1}{2N} \right|.$$

Thus, the earlier modified sequence has the lowest possible discrepancy for a sequence in 1D. In general, it is much easier to analyze and compute bounds for the discrepancy of sequences in 1D than for those in higher dimensions. For less simply constructed point sequences, and for sequences in higher dimensions and for more irregular shapes than boxes, the discrepancy often must be estimated numerically by constructing a large number of shapes B, computing their discrepancy, and reporting the maximum.

The astute reader will notice that according to the low-discrepancy measure, this uniform sequence in 1D is optimal, but earlier in this chapter we claimed that irregular jittered patterns were perceptually superior to uniform patterns for image sampling in 2D since they replaced aliasing error with noise. In that framework, uniform samples are clearly not optimal. Fortunately, low-discrepancy patterns in higher dimensions are much less uniform than they are in one dimension and thus usually work reasonably well as sample patterns in practice. Nevertheless, their underlying uniformity is probably the reason why low-discrepancy patterns can be more prone to aliasing than patterns with true pseudorandom variation.

7.4.2 CONSTRUCTING LOW-DISCREPANCY SEQUENCES

We will now introduce a number of techniques that have been developed specifically to generate sequences of points that have low discrepancy. Remarkably, few lines of code are necessary to compute many low-discrepancy sampling patterns.

The first set of techniques that we will describe use a construction called the *radical inverse*. It is based on the fact that a positive integer value n can be expressed in a base b with a sequence of digits $d_m \ldots d_2 d_1$ uniquely determined by

$$n = \sum_{i=1}^{\infty} d_i b^{i-1}.$$

The radical inverse function Φ_b in base b converts a nonnegative integer n to a floating-point value in $[0, 1)$ by reflecting these digits about the decimal point:

$$\Phi_b(n) = 0.d_1 d_2 \ldots d_m.$$

Thus, the contribution of the digit d_i to the radical inverse is

$$\frac{d_i}{b^i}.$$

The function `RadicalInverse()` computes the radical inverse for a given number n in the base base. It first computes the value of d_1 by taking the remainder of the number n when divided by the base and adds $d_1 b^{-1}$ to the radical inverse value. It then divides n by the base, effectively chopping off the last digit, so that the next time through the loop, it can compute d_2 by finding the remainder in base base and adding $d_2 b^{-2}$ to the sum, and so on. This process continues until n is zero, at which point it has found the last nonzero d_i value.

⟨*Sampling Declarations*⟩+≡
```
inline double RadicalInverse(int n, int base) {
    double val = 0;
    double invBase = 1. / base, invBi = invBase;
    while (n > 0) {
        ⟨Compute next digit of radical inverse  319⟩
    }
    return val;
}
```

⟨*Compute next digit of radical inverse*⟩≡   319
```
int d_i = (n % base);
val += d_i * invBi;
n /= base;
invBi *= invBase;
```

One of the simplest low-discrepancy sequences is the van der Corput sequence, which is a one-dimensional sequence given by the radical inverse function in base 2:

$$x_i = \Phi_2(i).$$

Table 7.2 shows the first few values of the van der Corput sequence. Notice how it recursively splits the intervals of the 1D line in half, generating a sample point at the center of each interval. The discrepancy of this sequence is

$$D_N^*(P) = O\left(\frac{\log N}{N}\right),$$

which matches the best discrepancy that has been attained for infinite sequences in d dimensions,

$$D_N^*(P) = O\left(\frac{(\log N)^d}{N}\right).$$

RadicalInverse() 319

Two well-known low-discrepancy sequences that are defined in an arbitrary number of dimensions are the *Halton* and *Hammersley* sequences. Both use the radical inverse function as well. To generate an n-dimensional Halton sequence, we use the radical inverse base b, with a different base for each dimension of the pattern. The bases used

Table 7.2: The radical inverse $\Phi_2(n)$ of the first few positive integers, computed in base 2. Notice how successive values of $\Phi_2(n)$ are not close to any of the previous values of $\Phi_2(n)$. As more and more values of the sequence are generated, samples are necessarily closer to previous samples, although with a minimum distance that is guaranteed to be reasonably good.

n	Base 2	$\Phi_2(n)$	
1	1	.1	$= 1/2$
2	10	.01	$= 1/4$
3	11	.11	$= 3/4$
4	100	.001	$= 1/8$
5	101	.101	$= 5/8$
$\vdots$	$\vdots$	$\vdots$	

must all be relatively prime to each other, so a natural choice is to use the first n prime numbers $(p_1, \ldots, p_n)$:

$$x_i = (\Phi_2(i), \Phi_3(i), \Phi_5(i), \ldots, \Phi_{p_n}(i)).$$

One of the most useful characteristics of the Halton sequence is that it can be used even if the total number of samples needed isn't known in advance; all prefixes of the sequence are well distributed, so as additional samples are added to the sequence, low discrepancy will be maintained. This property will be used by the PhotonIntegrator, for example, which doesn't know the total number of photons that will be necessary to emit from lights in the scene ahead of time and thus uses a Halton sequence to get a well-distributed set of photons.

The discrepancy of a d-dimensional Halton sequence is

$$D_N^*(x_i) = O\left(\frac{(\log N)^d}{N}\right),$$

which is asymptotically optimal.

If the number of samples N is fixed, the Hammersley point set can be used, giving slightly lower discrepancy. Hammersley point sets are defined by

$$x_i = \left(\frac{i}{N}, \Phi_{b_1}(i), \Phi_{b_2}(i), \ldots, \Phi_{b_n}(i)\right),$$

where N is the total number of samples to be taken and as before all of the bases b_i are relatively prime. Figure 7.25(a) shows a plot of the first hundred points of the 2D Hammersley sequence. Figure 7.25(b) shows the Halton sequence.

PhotonIntegrator 774

The *folded radical inverse* function can be used in place of the original radical inverse function to further reduce the discrepancy of Hammersley and Halton sequences. The folded radical inverse is defined by adding the offset i to the ith digit d_i and taking the

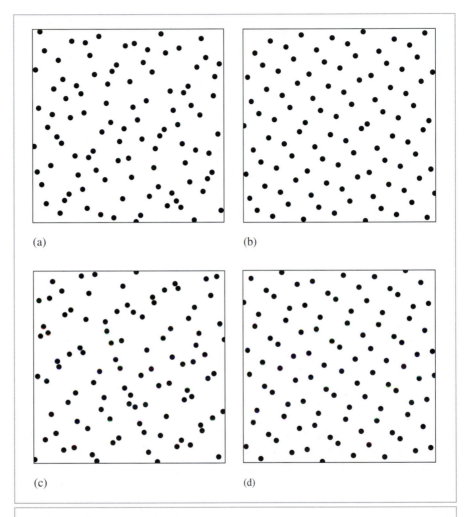

(a)   (b)

(c)   (d)

Figure 7.25: The First 100 Points of Various Low-Discrepancy Sequences in 2D. (a) Halton, (b) Hammersley, (c) Halton with folded radical inverse, (d) Hammersley with folded radical inverse.

result modulus b, then adding that result to the next digit to the right of the decimal point:

$$\Psi_b(n) = \sum_i \frac{(d_i + i - 1) \bmod b}{b^i}.$$

The FoldedRadicalInverse() function computes Ψ_b. It is similar to the original RadicalInverse() function, but with two modifications. First, it needs to track which digit is currently being processed, so that the appropriate offset can be added before the modulus computation; this is done with the modOffset variable. Second, it needs to handle the fact that Ψ_b is actually an *infinite* sum. Even though the digits d_i are zero after a finite number of terms, the offset that is added ensures that most terms beyond this point will be nonzero. Fortunately, the finite precision of computer floating-point numbers has the effect that the implementation can conservatively stop adding digits to the folded radical inverse as soon as it detects that invBi is small enough that adding its contribution to val is certain to leave val unchanged.

⟨*Sampling Declarations*⟩+≡
```
inline double FoldedRadicalInverse(int n, int base) {
    double val = 0;
    double invBase = 1.f/base, invBi = invBase;
    int modOffset = 0;
    while (val + base * invBi != val) {
        ⟨Compute next digit of folded radical inverse 322⟩
    }
    return val;
}
```

⟨*Compute next digit of folded radical inverse*⟩≡   **322**
```
int digit = ((n+modOffset) % base);
val += digit * invBi;
n /= base;
invBi *= invBase;
++modOffset;
```

When the folded radical inverse is used to generate the Hammersley and Halton point sets, they are known as the Hammersley-Zaremba and Halton-Zaramba point sets, after the inventor of the folded radical inverse function. Plots of the first 100 Hammersley-Zaremba and Halton-Zaremba points are shown in Figures 7.25(c) and 7.25(d). It's possible to see visually that the Hammersley sequence has lower discrepancy than the Halton sequence—there are far fewer clumps of nearby sample points. Furthermore, one can see that the folded radical inverse function reduces the discrepancy of the Hammersley sequence; its effect on the Halton sequence is less visually obvious.

7.4.3 (0,2)-SEQUENCES

To generate high-quality samples for the integrators, we can take advantage of a remarkable property of certain low-discrepancy patterns that allows us to satisfy both parts of our original goal for samplers (only one of which was satisfied with the StratifiedSampler): they make it possible to generate a set of sample positions for a pixel's worth of image samples such that each sample is well-stratified with respect not only to the other samples in the set for the pixel but also to the sample positions at the other image samples around the current pixel.

StratifiedSampler 304

A useful low-discrepancy sequence in 2D can be constructed using the van der Corput sequence in one dimension and a sequence based on a radical inverse function due to Sobol' in the other direction. The resulting sequence is a special type of low-discrepancy sequence known as an $(0, 2)$-sequence. $(0, 2)$-sequences are stratified in a very general way. For example, the first 16 samples in an $(0, 2)$-sequence satisfy the previous stratification constraint, meaning there is just one sample in each of the boxes of extent $(\frac{1}{4}, \frac{1}{4})$. However, they also satisfy the Latin hypercube constraint, as only one of them is in each of the boxes of extent $(\frac{1}{16}, 1)$ and $(1, \frac{1}{16})$. Furthermore, there is only one sample in each of the boxes of extent $(\frac{1}{2}, \frac{1}{8})$ and $(\frac{1}{8}, \frac{1}{2})$. Figure 7.26 shows all of the possibilities for dividing the domain into regions where the first 16 samples of an $(0, 2)$-sequence satisfy the stratification properties. Each succeeding sequence of 16 samples from this pattern also satisfies the distribution properties.

In general, any sequence of length $2^{l_1 l_2}$ (where l_i is a nonnegative integer) from an $(0, 2)$-sequence satisfies this general stratification constraint. The set of *elementary intervals* in two dimensions, base 2, is defined as

$$ E = \left\{ \left[\frac{a_1}{2^{l_1}}, \frac{a_1 + 1}{2^{l_1}} \right) \times \left[\frac{a_2}{2^{l_2}}, \frac{a_2 + 1}{2^{l_2}} \right) \right\}, $$

where the integer $a_i = 0, \ldots, 2^{l_i} - 1$. One sample from each of the first $2^{l_1 l_2}$ values in the sequence will be in each of the elementary intervals. Furthermore, the same property is true for each subsequent set of $2^{l_1 l_2}$ values.

To understand now how $(0, 2)$-sequences can be applied to generating 2D samples for the integrators, consider a pixel with 2×2 image samples, each with 4×4 integrator samples. The first $2 \times 2 \times 4 \times 4 = 2^6$ values of an $(0, 2)$-sequence are well-distributed with respect to each other according to the corresponding set of elementary intervals. Furthermore, the first $4 \times 4 = 2^4$ samples are themselves well-distributed according to their corresponding elementary intervals, as are the next 2^4 of them, and the subsequent ones, and so on. Therefore, we can use the first 16 $(0, 2)$-sequence samples for the integrator samples for the first image sample for a pixel, then the next 16 for the next image sample, and so forth. The result is an extremely well-distributed set of sample points.

There are a handful of details that must be addressed before $(0, 2)$-sequences can be used in practice. The first is that we need to generate multiple sets of 2D sample values for each image sample, and we would like to generate different sample values in the areas around different pixels. One approach to this problem would be to use carefully chosen nonoverlapping subsequences of the $(0, 2)$-sequence for each pixel. Another approach, which is used in pbrt, is to randomly *scramble* the $(0, 2)$-sequence, giving a new $(0, 2)$-sequence built by randomly permuting the base b digits of the values in the original sequence.

The scrambling approach we will use is due to Kollig and Keller (2002). It repeatedly partitions and shuffles the unit square $[0, 1]^2$. In each of the two dimensions, it first divides the square in half, then swaps the two halves with 50% probability. Then, it

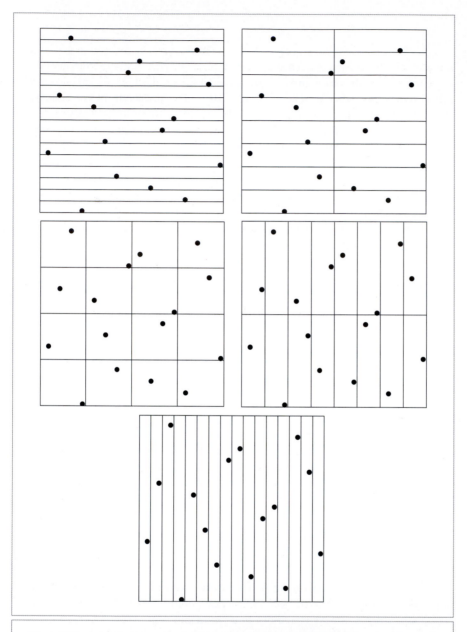

Figure 7.26: A sampling pattern that has a single sample in all of the base 2 elementary intervals. It satisfies both the 4 × 4 stratification and Latin hypercube constraints as well as the other stratification constraints shown.

splits each of the intervals [0, 0.5) and [0.5, 1) in half and randomly exchanges each of those two halves. This process continues recursively until floating-point precision intervenes and continuing the process would no longer change the computed values. This process was carefully designed so that it preserves the low-discrepancy properties of the set of points; otherwise the advantages of the (0, 2)-sequence would be lost from the scrambling. Figure 7.27 shows an unscrambled (0, 2)-sequence and two randomly scrambled variations of it.

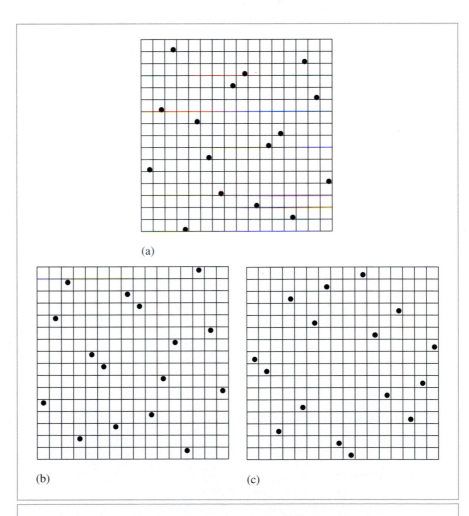

Figure 7.27: (a) A low-discrepancy (0, 2)-sequence-based sampling pattern and (b, c) two randomly scrambled instances of it. Random scrambling of low-discrepancy patterns is an effective way to eliminate the artifacts that would be present in images if we used the same sampling pattern in every pixel, while still preserving the low-discrepancy properties of the point set being used.

Two things make this process efficient: First, because we are scrambling two sequences that are computed in base 2, the digits a_i of the sequences are all 0 or 1, and scrambling a particular digit is equivalent to exclusive-ORing it with 0 or 1. Second, the simplification is made that at each level l of the recursive scrambling, the same decision will be made as to whether to swap each of the 2^{l-1} pairs of subintervals or not. The result of these two design choices is that the scrambling can be encoded as a set of bits stored in a u_int and can be applied to the original digits via exclusive-OR operations.

The Sample02() function generates a sample from a scrambled $(0, 2)$-sequence using the given scramble values. The sequence used here is constructed from two 1D low-discrepancy sequences that together form a $(0, 2)$-sequence. An arbitrary pair of 1D low-discrepancy sequences will not necessarily form a $(0, 2)$-sequence, however.

⟨*Sampling Inline Functions*⟩ ≡
```
inline void Sample02(u_int n, u_int scramble[2], float sample[2]) {
    sample[0] = VanDerCorput(n, scramble[0]);
    sample[1] = Sobol2(n, scramble[1]);
}
```

The implementations of the van der Corput and Sobol' low-discrepancy sequences here are also specialized for the base 2 case. Each of them takes a u_int value scramble that encodes a random permutation to apply and computes the nth value from each of the sequences as it simultaneously applies the permutation. It is worthwhile to convince yourself that the VanDerCorput() function computes the same values as RadicalInverse() in the preceding when they are called with a zero scramble and a base of two, respectively.

⟨*Sampling Inline Functions*⟩+≡
```
inline float VanDerCorput(u_int n, u_int scramble) {
    n = (n << 16) | (n >> 16);
    n = ((n & 0x00ff00ff) << 8) | ((n & 0xff00ff00) >> 8);
    n = ((n & 0x0f0f0f0f) << 4) | ((n & 0xf0f0f0f0) >> 4);
    n = ((n & 0x33333333) << 2) | ((n & 0xcccccccc) >> 2);
    n = ((n & 0x55555555) << 1) | ((n & 0xaaaaaaaa) >> 1);
    n ^= scramble;
    return (float)n / (float)0x100000000LL;
}
```

⟨*Sampling Inline Functions*⟩+≡
```
inline float Sobol2(u_int n, u_int scramble) {
    for (u_int v = 1 << 31; n != 0; n >>= 1, v ^= v >> 1)
        if (n & 0x1) scramble ^= v;
    return (float)scramble / (float)0x100000000LL;
}
```

7.4.4 THE LOW-DISCREPANCY SAMPLER

We need to turn this theory into a practical `Sampler` for the renderer. One potential approach is to consider the problem as a general high-dimensional sampling problem and just use a Hammersley sequence to compute samples for all dimensions—image plane, time, lens, and integration. We have left this approach for an exercise at the end of the chapter and here will instead implement a pattern based on (0, 2)-sequences, since they give the foundation for a particularly effective approach for generating multiple samples per image sample for integration.

Another reason not to use the Hammersley point set is that it can be prone to aliasing in images. Figure 7.28 compares the results of sampling a checkerboard texture using a Hammersley-based sampler to using the stratified sampler from the previous section. Note the unpleasant pattern along edges in the foreground and toward the horizon.

(a)

(b)

Figure 7.28: Comparison of the Stratified Sampler to a Low-Discrepancy Sampler Based on Hammersley Points on the Image Plane. (a) The jittered stratified sampler with a single sample per pixel and (b) the Hammersley sampler with a single sample per pixel. Note that although the Hammersley pattern is able to reproduce the checker pattern farther toward the horizon than the stratified pattern, there is a regular structure to the error in the low-discrepancy pattern that is visually distracting; it doesn't turn aliasing into less objectionable noise as well as the jittered approach. (With one sample per pixel, the `LDSampler` in this section performs similarly to the jittered sampler.)

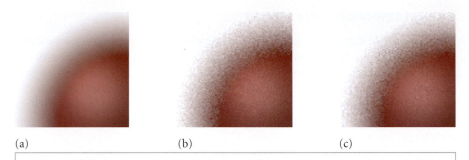

(a)   (b)   (c)

Figure 7.29: Comparisons of the Stratified and Low-Discrepancy Samplers for Rendering Depth of Field. (a) A reference image of the blurred edge of an out-of-focus sphere, (b) an image rendered using the StratifiedSampler, and (c) an image using the LDSampler. The LDSampler's results are better than the stratified image, although the difference is far less than the difference between stratified and random sampling.

The LDSampler uses a (0, 2)-sequence to generate a number of samples for each pixel that must be a power of two. Samples for positions on the lens and for the two-dimensional integrator samples are similarly generated with scrambled (0, 2)-sequences, and one-dimensional samples for time and integrators are generated with a scrambled van der Corput sequence. Similarly to the StratifiedSampler, the LDSampler generates an entire pixel's worth of samples at once and hands them out in turn from GetNextSample(). Figure 7.29 compares the result of using an (0, 2)-sequence for sampling the lens for the depth of field to using a stratified pattern.

⟨*LDSampler Declarations*⟩ ≡
```
    class LDSampler : public Sampler {
    public:
        ⟨LDSampler Public Methods  329⟩
    private:
        ⟨LDSampler Private Data  329⟩
    };
```

The constructor rounds the number of samples per pixel up to a power of two if necessary, since subsets of (0, 2)-sequences that are not a power of two in size are much less well-distributed over [0, 1] than those that are. Note also that the constructor sets up the current pixel (xPos,yPos) and the current pixel sample samplePos in a way that causes the first call to GetNextSample() to immediately generate the samples for the true first pixel, (xPixelStart,yPixelStart).

⟨*LDSampler Method Definitions*⟩ ≡

```
LDSampler::LDSampler(int xstart, int xend,
                     int ystart, int yend, int ps)
    : Sampler(xstart, xend, ystart, yend, RoundUpPow2(ps)) {
    xPos = xPixelStart - 1;
    yPos = yPixelStart;
    if (!IsPowerOf2(ps)) {
        Warning("Pixel samples being rounded up to power of 2");
        pixelSamples = RoundUpPow2(ps);
    }
    else
        pixelSamples = ps;
    samplePos = pixelSamples;
    oneDSamples = twoDSamples = NULL;
    imageSamples = new float[5*pixelSamples];
    lensSamples = imageSamples + 2*pixelSamples;
    timeSamples = imageSamples + 4*pixelSamples;
}
```

⟨*LDSampler Private Data*⟩ ≡   328

```
int xPos, yPos, pixelSamples;
int samplePos;
float *imageSamples, *lensSamples, *timeSamples;
float **oneDSamples, **twoDSamples;
```

As mentioned earlier, the low-discrepancy sequences used here need power-of-two sample sizes.

⟨*LDSampler Public Methods*⟩ ≡   328

```
int RoundSize(int size) const {
    return RoundUpPow2(size);
}
```

The xPos, yPos, and samplePos variables are just like those in the StratifiedSampler. The implementation here, however, precomputes both the image, lens, and time samples for the pixel as well as an entire pixel's worth of all of the samples requested by the integrator. These are stored in the oneDSamples and twoDSamples arrays, respectively.

⟨*LDSampler Method Definitions*⟩+≡
```
bool LDSampler::GetNextSample(Sample *sample) {
    if (!oneDSamples) {
        ⟨Allocate space for pixel's low-discrepancy sample tables 330⟩
    }
    if (samplePos == pixelSamples) {
        ⟨Advance to next pixel for low-discrepancy sampling 330⟩
        ⟨Generate low-discrepancy samples for pixel 331⟩
    }
    ⟨Copy low-discrepancy samples from tables 332⟩
    ++samplePos;
    return true;
}
```

It is not possible to allocate space for the integrator samples in the constructor since the number needed is not yet known when it executes. Therefore, allocation is done the first time this method is called.

⟨*Allocate space for pixel's low-discrepancy sample tables*⟩ ≡   330
```
oneDSamples = new float *[sample->n1D.size()];
for (u_int i = 0; i < sample->n1D.size(); ++i)
    oneDSamples[i] = new float[sample->n1D[i] * pixelSamples];
twoDSamples = new float *[sample->n2D.size()];
for (u_int i = 0; i < sample->n2D.size(); ++i)
    twoDSamples[i] = new float[2 * sample->n2D[i] * pixelSamples];
```

The logic for advancing to the next pixel is just like in the StratifiedSampler.

⟨*Advance to next pixel for low-discrepancy sampling*⟩ ≡   330
```
if (++xPos == xPixelEnd) {
    xPos = xPixelStart;
    ++yPos;
}
if (yPos == yPixelEnd)
    return false;
samplePos = 0;
```

There is a subtle implementation detail that must be accounted for in using these patterns in practice.[9] Often, integrators will use samples from more than one of the sampling patterns that the sampler creates in the process of computing the values of particular integrals. For example, they might use a sample from a one-dimensional pattern to select

---

9   Indeed, the importance of this issue wasn't fully appreciated by the authors until after going through the process of debugging some unexpected noise patterns in rendered images when this sampler was being used.

one of the N light sources in the scene to sample illumination from, and then might use a sample from a two-dimensional pattern to select a sample point on that light source, if it is an area light.

Even if these two patterns are computed with random scrambling with different random scramble values for each one, some correlation can still remain between elements of these patterns, such that the ith element of the one-dimensional pattern and the ith element of the two-dimensional pattern are related. As such, in the earlier area lighting example, the distribution of sample points on each light source would not in general cover the entire light due to this correlation, leading to unusual rendering errors.

This problem can be solved easily enough by randomly shuffling the various patterns individually after they are generated. The LDShuffleScrambled1D() and LDShuffle Scrambled2D() functions take care of this:

⟨*Generate low-discrepancy samples for pixel*⟩ ≡   330
```
    LDShuffleScrambled2D(1, pixelSamples, imageSamples);
    LDShuffleScrambled2D(1, pixelSamples, lensSamples);
    LDShuffleScrambled1D(1, pixelSamples, timeSamples);
    for (u_int i = 0; i < sample->n1D.size(); ++i)
        LDShuffleScrambled1D(sample->n1D[i], pixelSamples,
                             oneDSamples[i]);
    for (u_int i = 0; i < sample->n2D.size(); ++i)
        LDShuffleScrambled2D(sample->n2D[i], pixelSamples,
                             twoDSamples[i]);
```

The LDShuffleScrambled1D() function first generates a scrambled one-dimensional low-discrepancy sampling pattern, giving a well-distributed set of samples across all of the image samples for this pixel. Then, it shuffles these samples into a random order to eliminate correlation between the ith sample from this particular sequence and the ith sample from other sequences in this pixel.

⟨*Sampling Inline Functions*⟩+≡
```
    inline void LDShuffleScrambled1D(int nSamples,
            int nPixel, float *samples) {
        u_int scramble = RandomUInt();
        for (int i = 0; i < nSamples * nPixel; ++i)
            samples[i] = VanDerCorput(i, scramble);
        for (int i = 0; i < nPixel; ++i)
            Shuffle(samples + i * nSamples, nSamples, 1);
        Shuffle(samples, nPixel, nSamples);
    }
```

⟨*Sampling Inline Functions*⟩+≡

```
inline void LDShuffleScrambled2D(int nSamples,
        int nPixel, float *samples) {
    u_int scramble[2] = { RandomUInt(), RandomUInt() };
    for (int i = 0; i < nSamples * nPixel; ++i)
        Sample02(i, scramble, &samples[2*i]);
    for (int i = 0; i < nPixel; ++i)
        Shuffle(samples + 2 * i * nSamples, nSamples, 2);
    Shuffle(samples, nPixel, 2 * nSamples);
}
```

Given the precomputed sample values for the pixel, initializing the Sample structure is a matter of extracting the appropriate values for the current sample in the pixel from the sample tables and copying them to the appropriate places.

⟨*Copy low-discrepancy samples from tables*⟩ ≡   **330**

```
sample->imageX = xPos + imageSamples[2*samplePos];
sample->imageY = yPos + imageSamples[2*samplePos+1];
sample->time = timeSamples[samplePos];
sample->lensU = lensSamples[2*samplePos];
sample->lensV = lensSamples[2*samplePos+1];
for (u_int i = 0; i < sample->n1D.size(); ++i) {
    int startSamp = sample->n1D[i] * samplePos;
    for (u_int j = 0; j < sample->n1D[i]; ++j)
        sample->oneD[i][j] = oneDSamples[i][startSamp+j];
}
for (u_int i = 0; i < sample->n2D.size(); ++i) {
    int startSamp = 2 * sample->n2D[i] * samplePos;
    for (u_int j = 0; j < 2*sample->n2D[i]; ++j)
        sample->twoD[i][j] = twoDSamples[i][startSamp+j];
}
```

Figure 7.30 shows the result of using the (0, 2)-sequence for the area lighting example scene. Note that not only does it give a visibly better image than stratified patterns, but it also does well with one light sample per image sample, unlike the stratified sampler.

★ 7.5 BEST-CANDIDATE SAMPLING PATTERNS

A shortcoming of both the StratifiedSampler and the LDSampler is that they both generate good image sample patterns around a single pixel, but neither has any mechanism for ensuring that the image samples at adjacent pixels are well-distributed with respect to the samples at the current pixel. For example, we would like to avoid having two adjacent pixels choose samples that are very close to their shared edge. The *Poisson disk pattern*

(a)

(b)

Figure 7.30: When the `LDSampler` is used for the area light sampling example, similar results are generated (a) with both 1 image sample and 16 light samples as well as (b) with 16 image samples and 1 light sample, thanks to the (0, 2)-sequence sampling pattern that ensures good distribution of samples over the pixel area in both cases. Compare these images to Figure 7.23, where the stratified pattern generates a much worse set of light samples when only 1 light sample is taken for each of the 16 image samples.

addresses this issue of well-separated sample placement and has been shown to be an excellent image sampling pattern. The Poisson disk pattern is a group of points with no two of them closer to each other than some specified distance. Studies have shown that the rods and cones in the eye are distributed in a similar way, which suggests that this pattern might be effective for imaging. Poisson disk patterns are usually generated by *dart throwing*: a program generates samples randomly, throwing away any that are closer to a previous sample than a fixed threshold distance. This can be a very expensive process, since many darts may need to be thrown before one is accepted.

A related approach due to Don Mitchell is the *best-candidate* algorithm. Each time a new sample is to be computed, a large number of random candidates are generated. All of these candidates are compared to the previous samples, and the one that is farthest away from all of the previous ones is added to the pattern. Although this algorithm doesn't guarantee the Poisson disk property, it usually does quite well at finding well-separated points if enough candidates are generated. It has the additional advantage that any prefix of the final pattern is itself a well-distributed sampling pattern. Furthermore, the best-candidate algorithm makes it easier to generate a good pattern with a predetermined

LDSampler 328

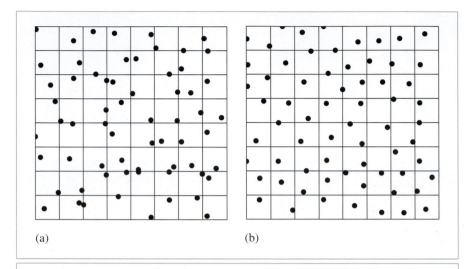

(a)   (b)

Figure 7.31: Comparison of Sampling Patterns. (a) A jittered pattern: note clumping of samples and undersampling in some areas. (b) A pattern generated with the best-candidate algorithm: it is effectively as good as the Poisson disk pattern.

number of samples than the dart-throwing algorithm. A comparison of a stratified pattern to a best-candidate pattern is shown in Figure 7.31.

In this section we will present a `Sampler` implementation that uses the best-candidate algorithm to compute sampling patterns that also have good distributions of samples in the additional sampling dimensions. Because generating the sample positions is computationally intensive, we will compute a good sampling pattern once in a preprocess. The pattern is stored in a table and can be efficiently used at rendering time. Rather than computing a sampling pattern large enough to sample the largest image we'd ever render, we'll compute a pattern that can be reused by tiling it over the image plane. This means that the pattern must have *toroidal topology*—when computing the distance between two samples, we must compute the distance between them as if the square sampling region was rolled into a torus.

7.5.1 GENERATING THE BEST-CANDIDATE PATTERN

We precompute the best-candidate sampling pattern in an offline process. The code described here can be found in the file `tools/samplepat.cpp`. The results are stored in the file `samplers/sampledata.cpp`.

First, we need to define the size of the table used to store the computed sample pattern:

⟨*BestCandidate Sampling Constants*⟩ ≡
```
#define SQRT_SAMPLE_TABLE_SIZE 64
#define SAMPLE_TABLE_SIZE (SQRT_SAMPLE_TABLE_SIZE * \
                           SQRT_SAMPLE_TABLE_SIZE)
```

This program generates sample points in a five-dimensional space: two dimensions for the image sample location, one for the time, and two more to determine a point on the lens. Because we don't know what types of sample patterns the integrators will need a priori, the BestCandidateSampler uses both scrambled (0, 2)-sequences and stratified patterns for their samples.

⟨*Pattern Precomputation Local Data*⟩ ≡
```
static float imageSamples[SAMPLE_TABLE_SIZE][2];
static float timeSamples[SAMPLE_TABLE_SIZE];
static float lensSamples/[SAMPLE_TABLE_SIZE][2];
```

Sample values are computed in a multistage process. First, a well-distributed set of image sample positions is generated. Then, given the image samples, a good set of time samples is found, accounting for the positions of the time samples associated with the nearby image samples. Finally, good samples for the lens are computed, again taking into account the positions of lens samples at nearby image samples, so that close-by image samples tend to have spread-out lens samples.

⟨*Sample Pattern Precomputation*⟩ ≡
```
int main() {
    ⟨Compute image sample positions  336⟩
    ⟨Compute time samples  339⟩
    ⟨Compute lens samples  341⟩
    ⟨Write sample table to disk  342⟩
    return 0;
}
```

In order to speed up the candidate evaluation, the accepted samples are stored in a grid. This makes it possible to check only nearby samples when computing distances between samples. The grid splits up the 2D sample domain $[0, 1]^2$ into BC_GRID_SIZE strata in each direction and stores a list of integer sample numbers identifying the samples that overlap each cell. The GRID() macro maps a position in $[0, 1]$ in one of the two dimensions to the corresponding grid cell.

⟨*Global Forward Declarations*⟩ ≡
```
#define BC_GRID_SIZE 40
typedef vector<int> SampleGrid[BC_GRID_SIZE][BC_GRID_SIZE];
#define GRID(v) (int((v) * BC_GRID_SIZE))
```

To compute the image samples, the program starts by creating a sample grid, and then uses the 2D best-candidate algorithm to fill in the image samples in the grid.

⟨*Compute image sample positions*⟩ ≡   **335**
```
    SampleGrid pixelGrid;
    BestCandidate2D(imageSamples, SAMPLE_TABLE_SIZE, &pixelGrid);
```

⟨*Sample Pattern Precomputation*⟩+≡
```
    void BestCandidate2D(float table[][2], int totalSamples,
                         SampleGrid *grid) {
        SampleGrid localGrid;
        if (!grid) grid = &localGrid;
```
        ⟨*Generate first 2D sample arbitrarily* **336**⟩
```
        for (int currentSample = 1;
             currentSample < totalSamples;
             ++currentSample) {
```
            ⟨*Generate next best 2D image sample* **337**⟩
```
        }
    }
```

The first image sample position is chosen completely at random and recorded in the grid. For all subsequent samples, a set of candidates is generated and compared to the already accepted samples.

⟨*Generate first 2D sample arbitrarily*⟩ ≡   **336**
```
    table[0][0] = RandomFloat();
    table[0][1] = RandomFloat();
    addSampleToGrid(table, 0, grid);
```

A short utility function adds a particular point in the table of samples to a `SampleGrid`:

⟨*Pattern Precomputation Utility Functions*⟩ ≡
```
    static void addSampleToGrid(float sample[][2], int sampleNum,
                                SampleGrid *grid) {
        int u = GRID(sample[sampleNum][0]);
        int v = GRID(sample[sampleNum][1]);
        (*grid)[u][v].push_back(sampleNum);
    }
```

To generate the rest of the samples, a dart-throwing algorithm throws a number of candidate darts for each needed sample. The number of darts thrown is proportional to the number of samples that have been stored already; this ensures that the quality of the samples remains in a sense consistent. After throwing a dart, the program computes how close it is to all of the samples it has accepted so far. If the dart is farther away than the previous best candidate was, it is kept. At the end of the loop, the best remaining candidate is accepted.

⟨*Generate next best 2D image sample*⟩ ≡   **336**
```
float maxDist2 = 0.;
int numCandidates = 500 * currentSample;
for (int currentCandidate = 0;
     currentCandidate < numCandidates;
     ++currentCandidate) {
    ⟨Generate a random candidate sample  337⟩
    ⟨Loop over neighboring grid cells and check distances  337⟩
    ⟨Keep this sample if it is the best one so far  338⟩
}
addSampleToGrid(table, currentSample, grid);
```

Candidate positions are chosen completely at random. Note that image sample locations are being computed in the range [0, 1). It is up to the Sampler that uses the sampling pattern to scale and translate image samples into raster space appropriately.

⟨*Generate a random candidate sample*⟩ ≡   **337**
```
float candidate[2];
candidate[0] = RandomFloat();
candidate[1] = RandomFloat();
```

Given a candidate, it is necessary to compute the distances to all of the nearby samples in the grid, keeping track of the minimum distance to any of them. For efficiency, the implementation actually computes the squared distance, which gives the same result for this test and avoids expensive square root computations.

Distances are computed to only the candidates in the eight neighboring grid cells and the cell that the candidate is in. Although this means that the first few samples are not optimally distributed relative to each other, this won't matter by the time the complete set of samples has been found, as long as BC_GRID_SIZE is less than SQRT_SAMPLE_TABLE_SIZE.

⟨*Loop over neighboring grid cells and check distances*⟩ ≡   **337**
```
float sampleDist2 = INFINITY;
int gu = GRID(candidate[0]), gv = GRID(candidate[1]);
for (int du = -1; du <= 1; ++du) {
    for (int dv = -1; dv <= 1; ++dv) {
        ⟨Compute (u,v) grid cell to check  338⟩
        ⟨Update minimum squared distance from cell's samples  338⟩
    }
}
```

In determining which grid cell to check, it is necessary to handle the toroidal topology of the grid. If the cell that would be considered is out of bounds, the routine wraps around to the other end of the grid.

⟨*Compute (u,v) grid cell to check*⟩ ≡   337, 340, 342

```
int u = gu + du, v = gv + dv;
if (u < 0)              u += BC_GRID_SIZE;
if (u >= BC_GRID_SIZE) u -= BC_GRID_SIZE;
if (v < 0)              v += BC_GRID_SIZE;
if (v >= BC_GRID_SIZE) v -= BC_GRID_SIZE;
```

Given the grid cell, the program then loops over the list of sample numbers. For each sample, it computes the squared distance to the current candidate, tracking the lowest squared distance found so far.

⟨*Update minimum squared distance from cell's samples*⟩ ≡   337

```
for (u_int g = 0; g < (*grid)[u][v].size(); ++g) {
    int s = (*grid)[u][v][g];
    float xdist = Wrapped1DDist(candidate[0], table[s][0]);
    float ydist = Wrapped1DDist(candidate[1], table[s][1]);
    float d2 = xdist*xdist + ydist*ydist;
    sampleDist2 = min(sampleDist2, d2);
}
```

The computation for the 1D distance between two values in [0, 1] also needs to handle the wraparound issue. Consider two samples with x coordinates of .01 and .99. Direct computation will find their distance to be .98, although with wraparound, the actual distance should be .02. Whenever the initial distance is greater than 0.5, the wrapped distance will be lower. In that case, the true distance is just the distance from the higher sample to one, plus the distance from zero to the lower sample.

⟨*Pattern Precomputation Utility Functions*⟩+≡

```
inline float Wrapped1DDist(float a, float b) {
    float d = fabsf(a - b);
    if (d < 0.5f) return d;
    else return 1.f - max(a, b) + min(a, b);
}
```

Once the minimum squared distance has been found, its value is compared to the minimum squared distance for the previous best candidate. If the new one has a higher squared distance to its neighbors, its distance is recorded and it is tentatively put in the output table.

⟨*Keep this sample if it is the best one so far*⟩ ≡   337

```
if (sampleDist2 > maxDist2) {
    maxDist2 = sampleDist2;
    table[currentSample][0] = candidate[0];
    table[currentSample][1] = candidate[1];
}
```

BC_GRID_SIZE 335
currentSample 336
Wrapped1DDist() 338

After generating all of the image samples in this manner, the sample positions for the rest of the dimensions can be found. One approach would be to generalize the Poisson disk concept to a higher-dimensional Poisson sphere. Interestingly enough, it is possible to do better than this, particularly in the five-dimensional case where a very large number of candidate samples would be needed to find good ones.

Consider the problem of choosing time values for two nearby image samples: not only should the time values not be too close together, but in fact they should be as far apart as possible. In any local 2D region of the image, we'd like the best possible coverage of the complete three-dimensional sample space. An intuition for why this is the case comes from how the sampling pattern will be used. Although we're generating a five-dimensional pattern overall, what we're interested in is optimizing its distribution across local areas of the two-dimensional image plane. Optimizing its distribution over the five-dimensional space is at best a secondary concern.

Therefore, a two-stage process is used to generate the sample positions. First, a well-distributed sampling pattern for the time and lens positions is found. Then, these samples are associated with image samples in a way that ensures that nearby image samples have sample values in the other dimensions that are well spread out.[10]

To compute the time samples, a set of one-dimensional stratified sample values over $[0, 1]$ is generated. The timeSamples array is then rearranged so that the ith time sample is a good one for the ith image sample.

⟨*Compute time samples*⟩ ≡   **335**
```
for (int i = 0; i < SAMPLE_TABLE_SIZE; ++i)
    timeSamples[i] = (i + RandomFloat()) / SAMPLE_TABLE_SIZE;
for (int currentSample = 1;
     currentSample < SAMPLE_TABLE_SIZE;
     ++currentSample) {
    ⟨Select best time sample for current image sample 339⟩
}
```

⟨*Select best time sample for current image sample*⟩ ≡   **339**
```
int best = -1;
⟨Find best time relative to neighbors 340⟩
swap(timeSamples[best], timeSamples[currentSample]);
```

As the program looks for a good time sample for the image sample number currentSample, the elements of timeSamples from zero to currentSample-1 have already

---

10 As if that isn't enough to worry about, we should also consider *correlation*. Not only should nearby image samples have distant sample values for the other dimensions, but we should also make sure that, for example, the time and lens values aren't correlated. If samples were chosen such that the time value was always similar to the lens u sample value, the sample pattern is not as good as it would be if the two were uncorrelated. We won't address this issue in our implementation here because the technique used here is not prone to introducing correlation in the first place.

been assigned to previous image samples and are unavailable. The rest of the times, from currentSample to SAMPLE_TABLE_SIZE-1, are the ones to be chosen from.

⟨*Find best time relative to neighbors*⟩ ≡   **339**
```
    float maxMinDelta = 0.;
    for (int t = currentSample; t < SAMPLE_TABLE_SIZE; ++t) {
        ⟨Compute min delta for this time 340⟩
        ⟨Update best if this is best time so far 341⟩
    }
```

Similar to the way image samples were evaluated, only the samples in the adjoining few grid cells are examined here. Of these, the one that is most different from the time samples that have already been assigned to the nearby image samples will be selected.

⟨*Compute min delta for this time*⟩ ≡   **340**
```
    int gu = GRID(imageSamples[currentSample][0]);
    int gv = GRID(imageSamples[currentSample][1]);
    float minDelta = INFINITY;
    for (int du = -1; du <= 1; ++du) {
        for (int dv = -1; dv <= 1; ++dv) {
            ⟨Check offset from times of nearby samples 340⟩
        }
    }
```

The implementation loops through the image samples in each of the grid cells, although it only needs to consider the ones that already have time samples associated with them. Therefore, it skips over the ones with sample numbers greater than the sample it's currently working on. For the remaining ones, it computes the offset from their time sample to the current candidate time sample, keeping track of the minimum difference.

⟨*Check offset from times of nearby samples*⟩ ≡   **340**
```
    ⟨Compute (u,v) grid cell to check 338⟩
    for (u_int g = 0; g < pixelGrid[u][v].size(); ++g) {
        int otherSample = pixelGrid[u][v][g];
        if (otherSample < currentSample) {
            float dt = Wrapped1DDist(timeSamples[otherSample], timeSamples[t]);
            minDelta = min(minDelta, dt);
        }
    }
```

currentSample 336
GRID() 335
imageSamples 335
INFINITY 856
SAMPLE_TABLE_SIZE 335
timeSamples 335
Wrapped1DDist() 338

If the minimum offset from the current time sample is greater than the minimum distance of the previous best time sample, this sample is recorded as the best one so far.

⟨*Update* best *if this is best time so far*⟩ ≡   **340**
```
if (minDelta > maxMinDelta) {
    maxMinDelta = minDelta;
    best = t;
}
```

Finally, the lens positions are computed. Good sampling patterns are again generated with dart throwing and then associated with image samples in the same manner that times were, by selecting lens positions that are far away from the lens positions of nearby image samples.

⟨*Compute lens samples*⟩ ≡   **335**
```
BestCandidate2D(lensSamples, SAMPLE_TABLE_SIZE);
Redistribute2D(lensSamples, pixelGrid);
```

After the `BestCandidate2D()` function generates the set of 2D samples, the `Redistribute2D()` utility function takes the set of lens samples to be assigned to the image samples and reshuffles them so that each sample isn't too close to those in neighboring pixels.

⟨*Sample Pattern Precomputation*⟩+≡
```
static void Redistribute2D(float samples[][2], SampleGrid &pixelGrid) {
    for (int currentSample = 1;
         currentSample < SAMPLE_TABLE_SIZE;
         ++currentSample) {
        ⟨Select best lens sample for current image sample 341⟩
    }
}
```

⟨*Select best lens sample for current image sample*⟩ ≡   **341**
```
int best = -1;
⟨Find best 2D sample relative to neighbors 341⟩
swap(samples[best][0], samples[currentSample][0]);
swap(samples[best][1], samples[currentSample][1]);
```

As with the time samples, we would like to to choose the lens sample that has the minimum distance to the lens sample values that have already been assigned to the neighboring image samples.

⟨*Find best 2D sample relative to neighbors*⟩ ≡   **341**
```
float maxMinDist2 = 0.f;
for (int samp = currentSample; samp < SAMPLE_TABLE_SIZE; ++samp) {
    ⟨Check distance to lens positions at nearby samples 342⟩
    ⟨Update best for 2D lens sample if it is best so far 342⟩
}
```

⟨*Check distance to lens positions at nearby samples*⟩ ≡   341

```
int gu = GRID(imageSamples[currentSample][0]);
int gv = GRID(imageSamples[currentSample][1]);
float minDist2 = INFINITY;
for (int du = -1; du <= 1; ++du) {
    for (int dv = -1; dv <= 1; ++dv) {
        ⟨Check 2D samples in current grid cell 342⟩
    }
}
```

⟨*Check 2D samples in current grid cell*⟩ ≡   342

```
⟨Compute (u,v) grid cell to check 338⟩
for (u_int g = 0; g < pixelGrid[u][v].size(); ++g) {
    int s2 = pixelGrid[u][v][g];
    if (s2 < currentSample) {
        float dx = Wrapped1DDist(samples[s2][0], samples[samp][0]);
        float dy = Wrapped1DDist(samples[s2][1], samples[samp][1]);
        float d2 = dx*dx + dy*dy;
        minDist2 = min(d2, minDist2);
    }
}
```

⟨*Update* best *for 2D lens sample if it is best so far*⟩ ≡   341

```
if (minDist2 > maxMinDist2) {
    maxMinDist2 = minDist2;
    best = samp;
}
```

The last step is to open a file and write out C++ code that initializes the table. When the
BestCandidateSampler is compiled, it will #include this file to initialize its sample table.

⟨*Write sample table to disk*⟩ ≡   335

```
FILE *f = fopen("sampledata.cpp", "w");
if (f == NULL)
    Severe("Couldn't open sampledata.cpp for writing.");
fprintf(f, "\n/* Automatically generated %dx%d sample "
        "table (%s @ %s) */\n\n",
        SQRT_SAMPLE_TABLE_SIZE, SQRT_SAMPLE_TABLE_SIZE,
        __DATE__, __TIME__);
fprintf(f, "const float "
        "BestCandidateSampler::sampleTable[%d][5] = {\n",
        SAMPLE_TABLE_SIZE);
```

```
for (int i = 0; i < SAMPLE_TABLE_SIZE; ++i) {
    fprintf(f, "  { ");
    fprintf(f, "%10.10ff, %10.10ff, ", imageSamples[i][0],
        imageSamples[i][1]);
    fprintf(f, "%10.10ff, ", timeSamples[i]);
    fprintf(f, "%10.10ff, %10.10ff, ", lensSamples[i][0],
        lensSamples[i][1]);
    fprintf(f, "},\n");
}
fprintf(f, "};\n");
```

7.5.2 USING THE BEST-CANDIDATE PATTERN

BestCandidateSampler, the Sampler that uses the sample table, is fairly straightforward. If an average of pixelSamples samples is to be taken in each pixel, a single copy of the sample table covers SQRT_SAMPLE_TABLE_SIZE / sqrt(pixelSamples) pixels in the *x* and *y* directions. Like the StratifiedSampler and LDSampler, this sampler scans across the image from the upper left of the crop window, going left to right and then top to bottom. Here, it generates all samples inside the sample table's extent before advancing to the next region of the image that it covers. Figure 7.32 illustrates this idea.

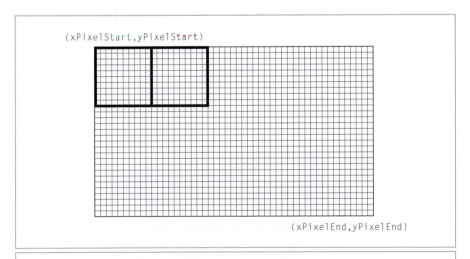

Figure 7.32: Because it is comprised of thousands of samples, the best-candidate sample table will generally cover a large number of pixels. One of the main tasks of the BestCandidateSampler is to tile this pattern over the image plane, mapping its sample positions to image sample positions.

⟨*BestCandidateSampler Declarations*⟩ ≡
```
class BestCandidateSampler : public Sampler {
public:
```
    ⟨*BestCandidateSampler Public Methods* **346**⟩
```
private:
```
    ⟨*BestCandidateSampler Private Data* **344**⟩
```
};
```

The sampler stores the current raster space pixel position in `xTableCorner` and `yTableCorner`, and `tableWidth` is the raster space width in pixels that the precomputed sample table spans. `tableOffset` holds the current offset into the sample table; when it is advanced to the point where it reaches the end of the table, the sampler advances to the next region of the image that the table covers. Figure 7.33 compares the result of using the best-candidate pattern to the stratified pattern for rendering the checkerboard. Figure 7.34 shows the result of using this pattern for depth of field. For the number of samples used in that figure, the low-discrepancy sampler gives a better result, likely because the sample pattern precomputation step searches around a fixed-size region of samples when selecting lens samples. Depending on the actual number of pixel samples used, this region may map to much less or much more than a single pixel area.

⟨*BestCandidateSampler Method Definitions*⟩ ≡
```
    BestCandidateSampler::BestCandidateSampler(int xstart, int xend,
                                               int ystart, int yend,
                                               int pixelSamples)
        : Sampler(xstart, xend, ystart, yend, pixelSamples) {
        tableWidth = (float)SQRT_SAMPLE_TABLE_SIZE / sqrtf(pixelSamples);
        xTableCorner = float(xPixelStart) - tableWidth;
        yTableCorner = float(yPixelStart);
        tableOffset = SAMPLE_TABLE_SIZE;
```
        ⟨*BestCandidateSampler constructor implementation*⟩
```
    }
```

⟨*BestCandidateSampler Private Data*⟩ ≡   **344**
```
    int tableOffset;
    float xTableCorner, yTableCorner, tableWidth;
```

Here we incorporate the precomputed sample data stored in `samplers/sampledata.cpp`.

⟨*BestCandidateSampler Private Data*⟩+≡   **344**
```
    static const float sampleTable[SAMPLE_TABLE_SIZE][5];
```

⟨*BestCandidateSampler Method Definitions*⟩+≡
```
    #include "sampledata.cpp"
```

This sampler usually generates stratified patterns for the samples for integrators (with one exception, explained shortly). In practice, these patterns work best with square-

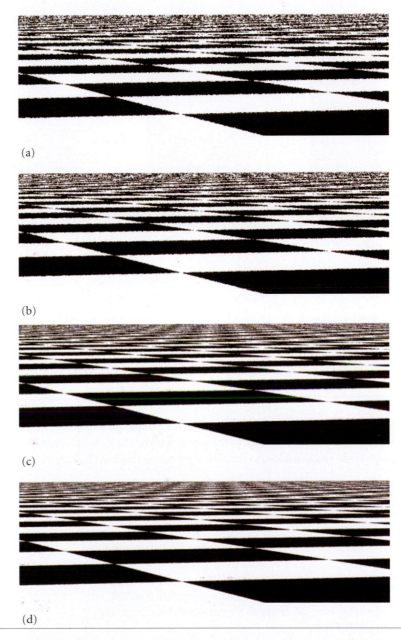

(a)

(b)

(c)

(d)

Figure 7.33: Comparison of the Stratified Sampling Pattern with the Best-Candidate Sampling Pattern. (a) The stratified pattern with a single sample per pixel. (b) The best-candidate pattern with a single sample per pixel. (c) The stratified pattern with four samples per pixel. (d) The four-sample best-candidate pattern. Although the differences are subtle, note that the edges of the checks in the foreground are less aliased when the best-candidate pattern is used, and it also does better at resolving the checks toward the horizon, particularly on the sides of the image. Furthermore, the noise from the best-candidate pattern tends to be higher frequency, and therefore more visually acceptable.

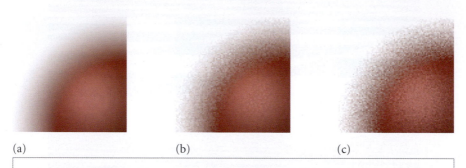

(a)   (b)   (c)

Figure 7.34: (a) Reference depth of field image, and images rendered with (b) the low-discrepancy and (c) best-candidate samplers. Here the low-discrepancy sampler is again the most effective.

shaped strata from an equal number of samples in each direction, so the RoundSize() method rounds up sample size requests so that they are an integer number squared.

⟨*BestCandidateSampler Public Methods*⟩ ≡   **344**
```
    int RoundSize(int size) const {
        int root = Ceil2Int(sqrtf((float)size - .5f));
        return root*root;
    }
```

The BestCandidateSampler::GetNextSample() method has a similar basic approach to the other samplers in this chapter, except that the sample pattern sometimes extends beyond the image's boundaries due to the way it is tiled. These out-of-bounds samples must be ignored, which can lead to multiple tries in order to find an acceptable sample.

⟨*BestCandidateSampler Method Definitions*⟩+≡
```
    bool BestCandidateSampler::GetNextSample(Sample *sample) {
    again:
        if (tableOffset == SAMPLE_TABLE_SIZE) {
            ⟨Advance to next best-candidate sample table position  347⟩
        }
        ⟨Compute raster sample from table  349⟩
        ⟨Check sample against crop window, goto again if outside  349⟩
        ⟨Compute integrator samples for best-candidate sample  350⟩
        ++tableOffset;
        return true;
    }
```

If it has reached the end of the sample table, the sampler tries to move forward by xTableCorner. If this leaves the raster extent of the image, it moves ahead by yTableCorner, and if this takes *y* beyond the bottom of the image, it is finished.

⟨*Advance to next best-candidate sample table position*⟩ ≡   **346**

```
    tableOffset = 0;
    xTableCorner += tableWidth;
    if (xTableCorner >= xPixelEnd) {
        xTableCorner = float(xPixelStart);
        yTableCorner += tableWidth;
        if (yTableCorner >= yPixelEnd)
            return false;
    }
    if (!oneDSamples) {
        ⟨Initialize sample tables and precompute strat2D values 348⟩
    }
    ⟨Update sample shifts 348⟩
    ⟨Generate SAMPLE_TABLE_SIZE-sized tables for single samples 348⟩
```

Samples for integrators are handled here with a hybrid approach: If only a single sample of a particular type is needed per image sample, the sampler uses a value from a shuffled low-discrepancy sequence, extracted from an array of such samples computed for this section of the image. If multiple samples are needed, however, the sampler computes stratified samples for them.

There are three main reasons to use this approach. First, if the integrator needs a large number of samples per image sample, the storage to hold all of the sample values for the thousands of samples in the best-candidate table may be objectionable. Second, as the number of integration samples increases, the effect of not having samples that are well-distributed with respect to the neighbors is reduced, since the integrator samples at the current image sample cover the sample space well themselves. Third, the low-discrepancy sequences can cause some unusual artifacts when used with certain pixel reconstruction filters (as we will see shortly in Figure 7.36). It's still worthwhile to go through the trouble of using low-discrepancy samples for the single-sample case; this is a big help for the PathIntegrator, which uses many single samples like this, for example.

⟨*BestCandidateSampler Private Data*⟩+≡   **344**

```
    float **oneDSamples, **twoDSamples;
    int *strat2D;
```

⟨*BestCandidateSampler constructor implementation*⟩ ≡

```
    oneDSamples = twoDSamples = NULL;
    strat2D = NULL;
```

⟨*Initialize sample tables and precompute* strat2D *values*⟩ ≡   347
```
oneDSamples = new float *[sample->n1D.size()];
for (u_int i = 0; i < sample->n1D.size(); ++i) {
    oneDSamples[i] = (sample->n1D[i] == 1) ?
        new float[SAMPLE_TABLE_SIZE] : NULL;
}
twoDSamples = new float *[sample->n2D.size()];
strat2D = new int[sample->n2D.size()];
for (u_int i = 0; i < sample->n2D.size(); ++i) {
    twoDSamples[i] = (sample->n2D[i] == 1) ?
        new float[2 * SAMPLE_TABLE_SIZE] : NULL;
    strat2D[i] = Ceil2Int(sqrtf((float)sample->n2D[i] - .5f));
}
```

The low-discrepancy samples for the single-sample case are computed with the shuffled random scrambled sampling routines defined earlier.

⟨*Generate* SAMPLE_TABLE_SIZE-*sized tables for single samples*⟩ ≡   347
```
for (u_int i = 0; i < sample->n1D.size(); ++i)
    if (sample->n1D[i] == 1)
        LDShuffleScrambled1D(1, SAMPLE_TABLE_SIZE, oneDSamples[i]);
for (u_int i = 0; i < sample->n2D.size(); ++i)
    if (sample->n2D[i] == 1)
        LDShuffleScrambled2D(1, SAMPLE_TABLE_SIZE, twoDSamples[i]);
```

One problem with using tiled sample patterns is that there may be subtle image artifacts aligned with the edges of the pattern on the image plane due to the same values being used repeatedly for time and lens position in each replicated sample region. Not only are the same samples used and reused (whereas the StratifiedSampler and LDSampler will at least generate different time and lens values for each image sample), but the upper-left sample in each block of samples will always have the same time and lens values, and so on.

A solution to this problem is to transform the set of sample values each time we reuse the pattern. This can be done using *Cranley-Patterson rotations*, which compute

$$X_i' = (X_i + \xi_i) \bmod 1$$

in each dimension, where X_i is the sample value and ξ_i is a random number between zero and one. Because the sampling patterns were computed with toroidal topology, the resulting pattern is still well-distributed and seamless. The table of random offsets for time and lens position ξ_i is updated each time the sample pattern is reused.

⟨*Update sample shifts*⟩ ≡   347
```
for (int i = 0; i < 3; ++i)
    sampleOffsets[i] = RandomFloat();
```

⟨*BestCandidateSampler Private Data*⟩+≡   344
```
float sampleOffsets[3];
```

Computing the raster space sample position from the positions in the table just requires some simple indexing and scaling. We don't use the Cranley-Patterson shifting technique on image samples because this would cause the sampling points at the borders between repeated instances of the table to have a poor distribution. Preserving good image distribution is more important than reducing correlation. The rest of the camera dimensions do use the shifting technique; the WRAP macro ensures that the result stays between zero and one.

⟨*Compute raster sample from table*⟩≡   346
```
#define WRAP(x) ((x) > 1 ? ((x)-1) : (x))
sample->imageX = xTableCorner + tableWidth *
                        sampleTable[tableOffset][0];
sample->imageY = yTableCorner + tableWidth *
                        sampleTable[tableOffset][1];
sample->time  = WRAP(sampleOffsets[0] +
                        sampleTable[tableOffset][2]);
sample->lensU = WRAP(sampleOffsets[1] +
                        sampleTable[tableOffset][3]);
sample->lensV = WRAP(sampleOffsets[2] +
                        sampleTable[tableOffset][4]);
```

The sample table may spill off the edge of the image plane, so some of the generated samples may be outside the appropriate sample region. The sampler detects this case by checking the sample against the region of pixels to be sampled and generating a new sample if it's out of bounds.

⟨*Check sample against crop window, goto* again *if outside*⟩≡   346
```
if (sample->imageX <  xPixelStart ||
    sample->imageX >= xPixelEnd   ||
    sample->imageY <  yPixelStart ||
    sample->imageY >= yPixelEnd) {
    ++tableOffset;
    goto again;
}
```

As explained previously, for integrator samples, the precomputed randomly scrambled low-discrepancy values are used if just one sample of this type is needed; otherwise a stratified pattern is used.

⟨*Compute integrator samples for best-candidate sample*⟩ ≡   346

```
for (u_int i = 0; i < sample->n1D.size(); ++i) {
    if (sample->n1D[i] == 1)
        sample->oneD[i][0] = oneDSamples[i][tableOffset];
    else
        StratifiedSample1D(sample->oneD[i], sample->n1D[i]);
}
for (u_int i = 0; i < sample->n2D.size(); ++i) {
    if (sample->n2D[i] == 1) {
        sample->twoD[i][0] = twoDSamples[i][2*tableOffset];
        sample->twoD[i][1] = twoDSamples[i][2*tableOffset+1];
    }
    else
        StratifiedSample2D(sample->twoD[i], strat2D[i], strat2D[i]);
}
```

7.6 IMAGE RECONSTRUCTION

Given carefully chosen image samples, it is necessary to develop the infrastructure for converting the samples and their computed radiance values into pixel values for display or storage. According to signal processing theory, we need to do three things to compute final values for each of the pixels in the output image:

1. Reconstruct a continuous image function $\tilde{L}$ from the set of image samples.
2. Prefilter the function $\tilde{L}$ to remove any frequencies past the Nyquist limit for the pixel spacing.
3. Sample $\tilde{L}$ at the pixel locations to compute the final pixel values.

Because we know that we will be resampling the function $\tilde{L}$ at only the pixel locations, it's not necessary to construct an explicit representation of the function. Instead, we can combine the first two steps using a single filter function.

Recall that if the original function had been uniformly sampled at a frequency greater than the Nyquist frequency and reconstructed with the sinc filter, then the reconstructed function in the first step would match the original image function perfectly—quite a feat since we only have point samples. But because the image function almost always will have higher frequencies than could be accounted for by the sampling rate (due to edges, etc.), we chose to sample it nonuniformly, trading off noise for aliasing.

The theory behind ideal reconstruction depends on the samples being uniformly spaced. While a number of attempts have been made to extend the theory to nonuniform sampling, there is not yet an accepted approach to this problem. Furthermore, because the sampling rate is known to be insufficient to capture the function, perfect reconstruction isn't possible. Recent research in the field of sampling theory has revisited the issue of reconstruction with the explicit acknowledgment that perfect reconstruction is not generally attainable in practice. With this slight shift in perspective has come powerful new techniques for reconstruction. See, for example, Unser (2000) for a survey of these developments. In particular, the goal of research in reconstruction theory has shifted from perfect reconstruction to developing reconstruction techniques that can be shown to minimize error between the reconstructed function and the original function, *regardless of whether the original was band-limited*.

While the reconstruction techniques used in pbrt are not directly built on these new approaches, they serve to explain the experience of practitioners that applying perfect reconstruction techniques to samples taken for image synthesis generally does not result in the highest-quality images.

To reconstruct pixel values, we will consider the problem of interpolating the samples near a particular pixel. To compute a final value for a pixel $I(x, y)$, interpolation results in computing a weighted average

$$I(x, y) = \frac{\sum_i f(x - x_i, y - y_i) L(x_i, y_i)}{\sum_i f(x - x_i, y - y_i)},$$ [7.3]

where $L(x_i, y_i)$ is the radiance value of the ith sample located at (x_i, y_i), and f is a filter function. Figure 7.35 shows a pixel at location (x, y) that has a pixel filter with extent xWidth in the x direction and yWidth in the y direction. All of the samples inside the

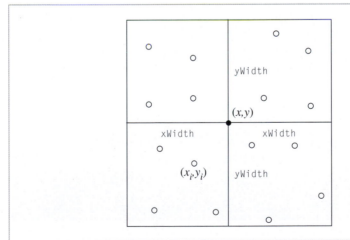

Figure 7.35: 2D Image Filtering. To compute a filtered pixel value for the pixel marked with a filled circle located at (x, y), all of the image samples inside the box around (x, y) with extent xWidth and yWidth need to be considered. Each of the image samples (x_i, y_i), denoted by open circles, is weighted by a 2D filter function, $f(x - x_i, y - y_i)$. The weighted average of all samples is the final pixel value.

box given by the filter extent may contribute to the pixel's value, depending on the filter function's value for $f(x - x_i, y - y_i)$.

The sinc filter is not an appropriate choice here: recall that the ideal sinc filter is prone to ringing when the underlying function has frequencies beyond the Nyquist limit (Gibbs phenomenon), meaning edges in the image have faint replicated copies of the edge in nearby pixels. Furthermore, the sinc filter has *infinite support:* it doesn't fall off to zero at a finite distance from its center, so all of the image samples would need to be filtered for each output pixel. In practice, there is no single best filter function. Choosing the best one for a particular scene takes a mixture of quantitative evaluation and qualitative judgment.

Another issue that influences the choice of image filter is that the reconstruction filter can interact with the sampling pattern in surprising ways. Recall the LDSampler: it generated an extremely well-distributed low-discrepancy pattern over the area of a single pixel, but samples in adjacent pixels were placed without regard for the samples in their neighbors. When used with a box filter, this sampling pattern works extremely well, but when a filter that both spans multiple pixels and isn't a constant value is used, it becomes less effective. Figure 7.36 shows this effect in practice. Using this filter with regular stratified samples

(a)

(b)

Figure 7.36: The choice of pixel reconstruction filter interacts with the results from the sampling pattern in surprising ways. Here, a Mitchell filter has been used to reconstruct pixels in the soft shadows example with the StratifiedSampler (a) and the LDSampler (b). Note the significant difference and artifacts compared to the images in Figures 7.23 and 7.30. Here, we have used 16 image samples and 1 light sample per pixel.

(a)   (b)   (c)

Figure 7.37: The pixel reconstruction filter used to convert the image samples into pixel values can have a noticeable effect on the character of the final image. Here we see blowups of a region of the brick wall in the Sponza atrium scene, filtered with (a) the box filter, (b) Gaussian, and (c) Mitchell-Netravali filter. Note that the Mitchell filter gives the sharpest image, while the Gaussian blurs it. The box is the least desirable, since it allows high-frequency aliasing to leak into the final image. (Note artifacts on the top edges of bricks, for example.)

makes much less of a difference. Given the remarkable effectiveness of patterns generated with the LDSampler, this is something of a quandry: the box filter is the last filter we'd like to use, yet using it instead of another filter substantially improves the results from the LDSampler. Given all of these issues, pbrt provides a variety of different filter functions as plug-ins.

7.6.1 FILTER FUNCTIONS

All filter implementations in pbrt are derived from an abstract Filter class, which provides the interface for the $f(x, y)$ functions used in filtering; see Equation (7.3). The Film (described in the next chapter) stores a pointer to a Filter and uses it to filter the output before writing it to disk. Figure 7.37 shows comparisons of zoomed-in regions of images rendered using a variety of the filters from this section to reconstruct pixel values.

⟨*Sampling Declarations*⟩+≡
```
class Filter {
public:
    ⟨Filter Interface 354⟩
    ⟨Filter Public Data 354⟩
};
```

All filters define a width beyond which they have a value of zero; this width may be different in the x and y directions. The constructor takes these values and stores them along with their reciprocals, for use by the filter implementations. The filter's overall extent in each direction (its *support*) is twice the value of its corresponding width (Figure 7.38).

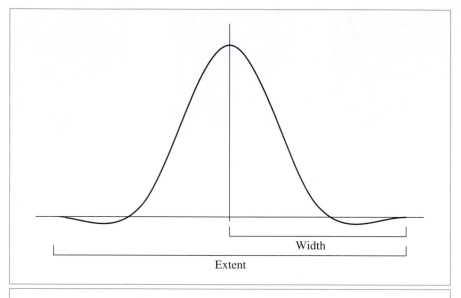

Figure 7.38: The extent of filters in pbrt is specified in terms of their width from the origin to its cutoff point. The support of a filter is its total nonzero extent, here equal to twice its width.

⟨*Filter Interface*⟩ ≡   353
```
Filter(float xw, float yw)
    : xWidth(xw), yWidth(yw), invXWidth(1.f/xw), invYWidth(1.f/yw) {
}
```

⟨*Filter Public Data*⟩ ≡   353
```
const float xWidth, yWidth;
const float invXWidth, invYWidth;
```

The sole function that `Filter` implementations need to provide is `Evaluate()`. It takes *x* and *y* arguments, which give the position of the sample point relative to the center of the filter. The return value specifies the weight of the sample. Code elsewhere in the system will never call the filter function with points outside of the filter's extent, so filter implementations don't need to check for this case.

⟨*Filter Interface*⟩+≡   353
```
virtual float Evaluate(float x, float y) const = 0;
```

Box Filter

One of the most commonly used filters in graphics is the *box filter* (and in fact, when filtering and reconstruction aren't addressed explicitly, the box filter is the de facto result). The box filter equally weights all samples within a square region of the image. Although

Filter 353

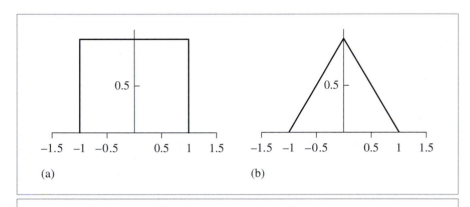

Figure 7.39: Graphs of the (a) box filter and (b) triangle filter. Although neither of these is a particularly good filter, they are both computationally efficient, easy to implement, and good baselines for evaluating other filters.

computationally efficient, it's just about the worst filter possible. Recall from the discussion in Section 7.1 that the box filter allows high-frequency sample data to leak into the reconstructed values. This causes postaliasing—even if the original sample values were at a high enough frequency to avoid aliasing, errors are introduced by poor filtering.

Figure 7.39(a) shows a graph of the box filter, and Figure 7.40 shows the result of using the box filter to reconstruct two 1D functions. For the step function we used previously to illustrate the Gibbs phenomenon, the box does reasonably well. However, the results are much worse for a sinusoidal function that has increasing frequency along the x axis. Not only does the box filter do a poor job of reconstructing the function when the frequency is low, giving a discontinuous result even though the original function was smooth, but it also does an extremely poor job of reconstruction as the function's frequency approaches and passes the Nyquist limit.

⟨*Box Filter Declarations*⟩ ≡

```
class BoxFilter : public Filter {
public:
    BoxFilter(float xw, float yw) : Filter(xw, yw) { }
    float Evaluate(float x, float y) const;
};
```

Because the evaluation function won't be called with (x, y) values outside of the filter's extent, it can always return 1 for the filter function's value.

⟨*Box Filter Method Definitions*⟩ ≡

```
float BoxFilter::Evaluate(float x, float y) const {
    return 1.;
}
```

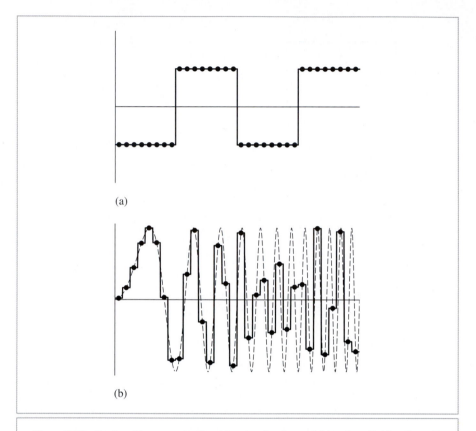

(a)

(b)

Figure 7.40: The box filter reconstructing (a) a step function and (b) a sinusoidal function with increasing frequency as x increases. This filter does well with the step function, as expected, but does an extremely poor job with the sinusoidal function.

Triangle Filter

The triangle filter gives slightly better results than the box: samples at the filter center have a weight of one, and the weight falls off linearly to the square extent of the filter. See Figure 7.39(b) for a graph of the triangle filter.

⟨*Triangle Filter Declarations*⟩ ≡

```
class TriangleFilter : public Filter {
public:
    TriangleFilter(float xw, float yw) : Filter(xw, yw) { }
    float Evaluate(float x, float y) const;
};
```

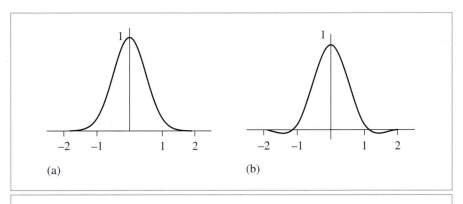

Figure 7.41: Graphs of (a) the Gaussian filter and (b) the Mitchell filter with $B = \frac{1}{3}$ and $C = \frac{1}{3}$, each with a width of two. The Gaussian gives images that tend to be a bit blurry, while the negative lobes of the Mitchell filter help to accentuate and sharpen edges in final images.

Evaluating the triangle filter is simple: the implementation just computes a linear function based on the width of the filter in both the x and y directions.

⟨*Triangle Filter Method Definitions*⟩ ≡
```
float TriangleFilter::Evaluate(float x, float y) const {
    return max(0.f, xWidth - fabsf(x)) *
        max(0.f, yWidth - fabsf(y));
}
```

Gaussian Filter

Unlike the box and triangle filters, the Gaussian filter gives a reasonably good result in practice. This filter applies a Gaussian bump that is centered at the pixel and radially symmetric around it. The Gaussian's value at the end of its extent is subtracted from the filter value, in order to make the filter go to zero at its limit (Figure 7.41). The Gaussian does tend to cause slight blurring of the final image compared to some of the other filters, but this blurring can actually help mask any remaining aliasing in the image.

⟨*Gaussian Filter Declarations*⟩ ≡
```
class GaussianFilter : public Filter {
public:
    ⟨GaussianFilter Public Methods  358⟩
private:
    ⟨GaussianFilter Private Data  358⟩
    ⟨GaussianFilter Utility Functions  358⟩
};
```

The 1D Gaussian filter function of width w is

$$f(x) = e^{-\alpha x^2} - e^{-\alpha w^2},$$

where α controls the rate of falloff of the filter. Smaller values cause a slower falloff, giving a blurrier image. For efficiency, the constructor precomputes the constant term for $e^{-\alpha w^2}$ in each direction.

⟨*GaussianFilter Public Methods*⟩ ≡   357
```
GaussianFilter(float xw, float yw, float a)
    : Filter(xw, yw) {
    alpha = a;
    expX = expf(-alpha * xWidth * xWidth);
    expY = expf(-alpha * yWidth * yWidth);
}
```

⟨*GaussianFilter Private Data*⟩ ≡   357
```
float alpha;
float expX, expY;
```

Since a 2D Gaussian function is separable into the product of two 1D Gaussians, the implementation calls the Gaussian() function twice and multiplies the results.

⟨*Gaussian Filter Method Definitions*⟩ ≡
```
float GaussianFilter::Evaluate(float x, float y) const {
    return Gaussian(x, expX) * Gaussian(y, expY);
}
```

⟨*GaussianFilter Utility Functions*⟩ ≡   357
```
float Gaussian(float d, float expv) const {
    return max(0.f, float(expf(-alpha * d * d) - expv));
}
```

Mitchell Filter

Filter design is notoriously difficult, mixing mathematical analysis and perceptual experiments. Mitchell and Netravali (1988) have developed a family of parameterized filter functions in order to be able to explore this space in a systematic manner. After analyzing test subjects' subjective responses to images filtered with a variety of parameter values, they developed a filter that tends to do a good job of trading off between *ringing* (phantom edges next to actual edges in the image) and *blurring* (excessively blurred results)—two common artifacts from poor reconstruction filters.

Note from the graph in Figure 7.41(b) that this filter function takes on negative values out by its edges; it has *negative lobes*. In practice these negative regions improve the sharpness of edges, giving crisper images (reduced blurring). If they become too large, however, ringing tends to start to enter the image. Also, because the final pixel values

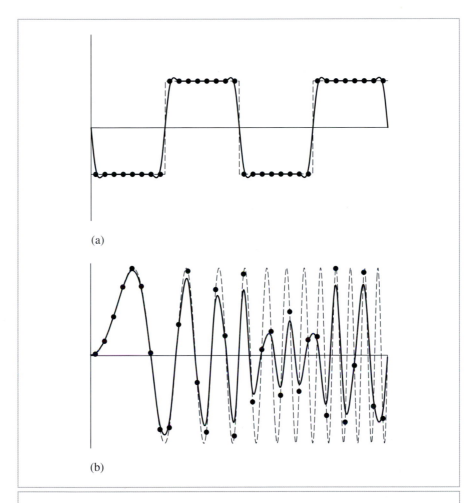

(a)

(b)

Figure 7.42: The Mitchell-Netravali Filter Used to Reconstruct the Example Functions. It does a good job with both of these functions, (a) introducing minimal ringing with the step function and (b) accurately representing the sinusoid until aliasing from undersampling starts to dominate.

can therefore become negative, they will eventually need to be clamped to a legal output range.

Figure 7.42 shows this filter reconstructing the two test functions. It does extremely well with both of them: there is minimal ringing with the step function, and it does a very good job with the sinusoidal function, up until the point where the sampling rate isn't sufficient to capture the function's detail.

⟨*Mitchell Filter Declarations*⟩ ≡
```
class MitchellFilter : public Filter {
public:
    ⟨MitchellFilter Public Methods 360⟩
private:
    float B, C;
};
```

The Mitchell filter has two parameters called B and C. Although any values can be used for these parameters, Mitchell and Netravali recommend that they lie along the line $B + 2C = 1$.

⟨*MitchellFilter Public Methods*⟩ ≡   360
```
MitchellFilter(float b, float c, float xw, float yw)
    : Filter(xw, yw) { B = b; C = c; }
```

Like many 2D image filtering functions, including the earlier Gaussian filter, the Mitchell-Netravali filter is the product of one-dimensional filter functions in the x and y directions. Such filters are called *separable*. In fact, all of the provided filters in pbrt are separable. Nevertheless, the `Filter::Evaluate()` interface does not enforce this requirement, giving more flexibility in implementing new filters in the future.

⟨*Mitchell Filter Method Definitions*⟩ ≡
```
float MitchellFilter::Evaluate(float x, float y) const {
    return Mitchell1D(x * invXWidth) * Mitchell1D(y * invYWidth);
}
```

The 1D function used in the Mitchell filter is an even function defined over the range $[-2, 2]$. This function is made by joining a cubic polynomial defined over $[0, 1]$ with another cubic polynomial defined over $[1, 2]$. This combined polynomial is also reflected around the $x = 0$ plane to give the complete function. These polynomials are controlled by the B and C parameters and are chosen carefully to guarantee C^0 and C^1 continuity at $x = 0$, $x = 1$, and $x = 2$. The polynomials are

$$f(x) = \frac{1}{6}
\begin{cases}
(12 - 9B - 6C)|x|^3 + (-18 + 12B + 6C)|x|^2 + (6 - 2B) & |x| < 1 \\
(-B - 6C)|x|^3 + (6B + 30C)|x|^2 + \\
\quad (-12B - 48C)|x| + (8B + 24C) & 1 \le |x| < 2 \\
0 & \text{otherwise.}
\end{cases}$$

⟨*MitchellFilter Public Methods*⟩+≡ 360

```
float Mitchell1D(float x) const {
    x = fabsf(2.f * x);
    if (x > 1.f)
        return ((-B - 6*C) * x*x*x + (6*B + 30*C) * x*x +
                (-12*B - 48*C) * x + (8*B + 24*C)) * (1.f/6.f);
    else
        return ((12 - 9*B - 6*C) * x*x*x +
                (-18 + 12*B + 6*C) * x*x +
                (6 - 2*B)) * (1.f/6.f);
}
```

Windowed Sinc Filter

Finally, the LanczosSincFilter class implements a filter based on the sinc function. In practice, the sinc filter is often multiplied by another function that goes to zero after some distance. This gives a filter function with finite extent, which is necessary for an implementation with reasonable performance. An additional parameter τ controls how many cycles the sinc function passes through before it is clamped to a value of zero, Figure 7.43 shows a graph of three cycles of the sinc function, along with a graph of the windowing function we use, which was developed by Lanczos. The Lanczos window is just the central lobe of the sinc function, scaled to cover the τ cycles:

$$w(x) = \frac{\sin \pi x/\tau}{\pi x/\tau}.$$

Figure 7.43 also shows the filter that we will implement here, which is the product of the sinc function and the windowing function.

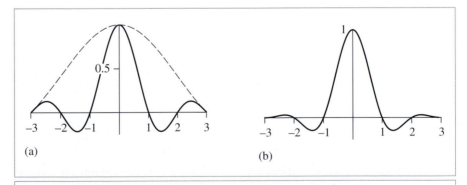

LanczosSincFilter 363

Figure 7.43: Graphs of the Sinc Filter. (a) The sinc function, truncated after three cycles (solid line) and the Lanczos windowing function (dashed line). (b) The product of these two functions, as implemented in the LanczosSincFilter.

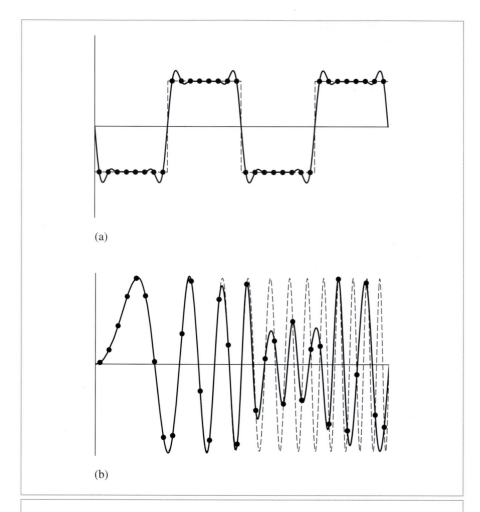

Figure 7.44: Results of Using the Windowed Sinc Filter to Reconstruct the Example Functions.
Here $\tau = 3$. (a) Like the infinite sinc, it suffers from ringing with the step function, although there is much less ringing in the windowed version. (b) The filter does quite well with the sinusoid, however.

Figure 7.44 shows the windowed sinc's reconstruction results for uniform 1D samples. Thanks to the windowing, the reconstructed step function exhibits far less ringing than the reconstruction using the infinite-extent sinc function (compare to Figure 7.11). The windowed sinc filter also does extremely well at reconstructing the sinusoidal function until prealiasing begins.

⟨*Sinc Filter Declarations*⟩ ≡

```
class LanczosSincFilter : public Filter {
public:
    LanczosSincFilter(float xw, float yw, float t)
        : Filter(xw, yw) {
        tau = t;
    }
    float Evaluate(float x, float y) const;
    float Sinc1D(float x) const;
private:
    float tau;
};
```

Like the other filters, the sinc filter is also separable.

⟨*Sinc Filter Method Definitions*⟩ ≡

```
float LanczosSincFilter::Evaluate(float x, float y) const {
    return Sinc1D(x * invXWidth) * Sinc1D(y * invYWidth);
}
```

The implementation computes the value of the sinc function and then multiplies it by the value of the Lanczos windowing function.

⟨*Sinc Filter Method Definitions*⟩+≡

```
float LanczosSincFilter::Sinc1D(float x) const {
    x = fabsf(x);
    if (x < 1e-5) return 1.f;
    if (x > 1.)   return 0.f;
    x *= M_PI;
    float sinc = sinf(x * tau) / (x * tau);
    float lanczos = sinf(x) / x;
    return sinc * lanczos;
}
```

FURTHER READING

One of the best books on signal processing, sampling, reconstruction, and the Fourier transform is Bracewell's *The Fourier Transform and Its Applications* (Bracewell 2000). Glassner's *Principles of Digital Image Synthesis* (Glassner 1995) has a series of chapters on the theory and application of uniform and nonuniform sampling and reconstruction to computer graphics. For an extensive survey of the history of and techniques for interpolation of sampled data, including the sampling theorem, see Meijering (2002). Unser (2000) also surveys recent developments in sampling and reconstruction theory including the recent move away from focusing purely on band-limited functions.

Crow (1977) first identified aliasing as a major source of artifacts in computer-generated images. Using nonuniform sampling to turn aliasing into noise was introduced by Cook (1986) and Dippé and Wold (1985); their work was based on experiments by Yellot (1983), who investigated the distribution of photoreceptors in the eyes of monkeys. Dippé and Wold also first introduced the pixel filtering equation to graphics and developed a Poisson sample pattern with a minimum distance between samples. Lee, Redner, and Uselton (1985) developed a technique for adaptive sampling based on statistical tests that computed images to a given error tolerance.

Heckbert (1990a) has written an article that explains possible pitfalls when using floating-point coordinates for pixels and develops the conventions used here.

Mitchell has investigated sampling patterns for ray tracing extensively. His 1987 and 1991 SIGGRAPH papers on this topic have many key insights, and the best-candidate approach described in this chapter is based on the latter paper (Mitchell 1987, 1991). The general interface for `Samplers` in pbrt is based on an approach he has used in his implementations (Mitchell 1996a). Another efficient technique for generating Poisson disk patterns was developed by McCool and Fiume (1992). Hiller, Deussen, and Keller (2001) applied a technique based on relaxation that takes a random point set and improves its distribution. Cohen et al. (2003) showed how to use Wang tiles to quickly generate large point distributions that are a good approximation to a Poisson disk distribution.

Shirley (1991) first introduced the use of discrepancy to evaluate the quality of sample patterns in computer graphics. This work was built upon by Mitchell (1992), Dobkin and Mitchell (1993), and Dobkin, Eppstein, and Mitchell (1996). One important observation in Dobkin et al.'s paper is that the box discrepancy measure used in this chapter and in other work that applies discrepancy to pixel sampling pattern's isn't particularly appropriate for measuring a sampling pattern's accuracy at randomly oriented edges through a pixel, and that a discrepancy measure based on random edges should be used instead. This observation explains why many of the theoretically good low-discrepancy patterns do not perform as well as expected when used for image sampling.

Mitchell's first paper on discrepancy introduced the idea of using deterministic low-discrepancy sequences for sampling, removing all randomness in the interest of lower discrepancy (Mitchell 1992). Such *quasi-random* sequences are the basis of quasi–Monte Carlo methods, which will be described in Chapter 15. The seminal book on quasi-random sampling and algorithms for generating low-discrepancy patterns was written by Niederreiter (1992).

More recently, Keller and collaborators have investigated quasi-random sampling patterns for a variety of applications in graphics (Keller 1996, 1997, 2001). The (0, 2)-sequence sampling techniques used in the `LDSampler` and `BestCandidateSampler` are based on a paper by Kollig and Keller (2002). They are one instance of a general type of low-discrepancy sequence known as (t, s)-sequences and (t, m, s)-nets. These are discussed further by Niederreiter (1992).

Some of Kollig and Keller's techniques are based on algorithms developed by Friedel and Keller (2000). Wong, Luk, and Heng (1997) compared the numeric error of various low-discrepancy sampling schemes, although one of Mitchell's interesting findings was that low-discrepancy sampling sequences sometimes lead to visually objectionable artifacts in images that aren't present with other sampling patterns. However, Keller (2001) argues that because low-discrepancy patterns tend to converge more quickly than others, they are still preferable if one is generating high-quality imagery at a sampling rate high enough to eliminate artifacts.

Chiu, Shirley, and Wang (1994) suggested a *multijittered* 2D sampling technique that combined the properties of stratified and Latin hypercube approaches, although their technique doesn't ensure good distributions across all elementary intervals as (0, 2)-sequences do.

Mitchell (1996b) has investigated how much better stratified sampling patterns are than random patterns in practice. In general, the smoother the function being sampled is, the more effective they are. For very quickly changing functions (e.g., pixel regions overlapped by complex geometry), sophisticated stratified patterns perform no better than unstratified random patterns. Therefore, for scenes with complex variation in the high-dimensional image function, the advantages of fancy sampling schemes compared to a simple stratified pattern are likely to be minimal.

A unique approach to image sampling was developed by Bolin and Meyer (1995), who implemented a ray tracer that directly synthesized images in the frequency domain. This made it possible to implement interesting adaptive sampling approaches based on perceptual metrics related to the image's frequency content.

Cook (1986) first introduced the Gaussian filter to graphics. Mitchell and Netravali (1988) investigated a family of filters using experiments with human observers to find the most effective ones; the `MitchellFilter` in this chapter is the one they chose as the best. Kajiya and Ullner (1981) have investigated image filtering methods that account for the effect of the reconstruction characteristics of Gaussian falloff from pixels in CRTs, and more recently, Betrisey et al. (2000) described Microsoft's ClearType technology for display of text on LCDs.

There has been quite a bit of research into reconstruction filters for image resampling applications. Although this application is not the same as reconstructing nonuniform samples for image synthesis, much of this experience is applicable. Turkowski (1990b) reports that the Lanczos windowed sinc filter gives the best results of a number of filters for image resampling. Meijering et al. (1999) tested a variety of filters for image resampling by applying a series of transformations to images such that if perfect resampling had been done, the final image would be the same as the original. They also found that the Lanczos window performed well (as did a few others) and that truncating the sinc without a window gave some of the worst results. Other work in this area includes papers by Möller et al. (1997) and Machiraju and Yagel (1996).

EXERCISES

② 7.1 The *multijittered* sampling pattern developed by Chiu, Shirley, and Wang (1994) simultaneously satisfies Latin hypercube and stratified sampling properties. Although it isn't guaranteed to be well-distributed with respect to all elementary intervals, it is easy to implement and can generate good sampling patterns of any number of samples mn, $m \geq 1$, $n \geq 1$; it isn't limited to generating good distributions in quantities of powers of two. Use multijittered sampling patterns to improve the quality of the samples generated for the integrators by the `StratifiedSampler`.

For example, if an integrator requests six two-dimensional samples for each image sample and there are four image samples per pixel, generate a single multijittered pattern of 6×4 samples in each pixel and distribute the samples from the pattern to the image samples in a way that ensures that each image sample's set of samples is well-distributed on its own. Discuss good ways of distributing the multijittered samples to the image samples and discuss bad ways of doing this. Experiment with different approaches, and compare the results to the current implementation of the `StratifiedSampler` when computing direct lighting, for example.

② 7.2 Implement a new low-discrepancy sampler based on an n-dimensional Hammersley pattern, with an appropriate number of sample points such that the requested number of samples are taken per pixel, on average. Render images to compare its results to the samplers implemented in this chapter and discuss the relative merits of them, in theory and in practice. Include both in-focus images with high-frequency detail, in-focus images with smooth variation, out-of-focus images, and images with soft shadows or glossy reflection.

One subtlety in the implementation is handling nonsquare images. Why is scaling the Hammersley pattern in different amounts in the x and y direction to cover the image plane not a good idea? What is an effective way to handle nonsquare images with this sampler instead?

② 7.3 Surprisingly, reordering the series of samples provided by the `Sampler` can noticeably affect the performance of the system, even if doing so doesn't change the total amount of computation being done. This effect is caused by the fact that the coherence of the sampling on the image plane is related to the coherence of the rays traced through the scene, which in turn affects the memory coherence of the accesses to the scene data. Because caches on modern CPUs depend on coherent memory access patterns to give good performance, incoherent rays can reduce overall performance. If two subsequently traced rays are close to each other on the image, they are likely to access a similar subset of the scene data, thus improving performance.

Do a series of experiments to measure this effect. For example, you might want to write a new Sampler that sorts samples generated by another Sampler that it holds a pointer to internally. Try randomly ordering the samples and measure the resulting performance. Then, investigate techniques for sorting the samples to improve their coherence. How do the current samplers benefit differently from this sorting? Discuss reasons for this variation.

7.4   A substantially different software design for sample generation for integration is described in Keller's technical report (Keller 2001). What are the advantages and disadvantages of that approach compared to the one in pbrt? Modify pbrt to support sample generation along the lines of the approach described there and compare flexibility, performance, and image quality to the current implementation.

7.5   Mitchell and Netravali (1988) note that there is a family of reconstruction filters that use both the value of a function and its derivative at the point to do substantially better reconstruction than if just the value of the function is known. Furthermore, they report that they have derived closed-form expressions for the screen space derivatives of Lambertian and Phong reflection models, although they do not include these expressions in their paper. Investigate derivative-based reconstruction and extend pbrt to support this technique. Because it will likely be difficult to derive expressions for the screen space derivatives for general shapes and BSDF models, investigate approximations based on finite differencing. Techniques built on the ideas behind the ray differentials of Section 11.1 may be fruitful for this effort.

Sampler 296

CHAPTER EIGHT

⊘⊠ FILM AND THE IMAGING PIPELINE

The type of film in a camera has a dramatic effect on the way that incident light is eventually transformed into colors in an image. In pbrt, the Film class models the sensing device in the simulated camera. After the radiance is found for each camera ray, a Film implementation determines the sample's contribution to the nearby pixels and updates its representation of the image. When the main rendering loop exits, the Film typically writes the final image to a file on disk.

This chapter has only one Film implementation. It applies the pixel reconstruction equation to compute final pixel values and writes the image to disk with floating-point color values. For a physically based renderer, creating images in a floating-point format provides more flexibility in how the output can be used than if a typical image format with eight-bit unsigned integer values is used; floating-point formats avoid the substantial loss of information that comes from image quantization.

In order to display such images on modern display devices, however, it is necessary to map these floating-point pixel values to discrete values for display. Therefore, this chapter also describes an image processing pipeline that applies a series of transformations to address the limitations of display devices. For example, computer monitors generally expect the color of each pixel to be described by an RGB color triple, not an arbitrary spectral power distribution. Spectra described by general basis function coefficients must therefore be converted to an RGB representation before they can be displayed. A related

Film 370

369

problem, which will be discussed in Section 8.4, is that displays have a substantially smaller range of displayable radiance values than the range present in many real-world scenes. Therefore, the pixel values must be mapped to the displayable range in a way that causes the final displayed image to appear as close as possible to the way it would appear on an ideal display device without this limitation.

8.1 FILM INTERFACE

The `Film` base class, defined in `core/film.h`, defines the abstract interface for `Film` implementations:

⟨*Film Declarations*⟩ ≡
```
class Film {
public:
    ⟨Film Interface 370⟩
    ⟨Film Public Data 370⟩
};
```

The `Film` constructor must be given the overall resolution of the image in the x and y directions; these are stored in the public member variables `Film::xResolution` and `Film::yResolution`. The `Camera`s in Chapter 6 need these values to compute some of the camera-related transformations, such as the raster-to-camera-space transformations.

⟨*Film Interface*⟩ ≡   370
```
Film(int xres, int yres)
    : xResolution(xres), yResolution(yres) {
}
```

⟨*Film Public Data*⟩ ≡   370
```
const int xResolution, yResolution;
```

The first method defined in the `Film` interface is `Film::AddSample()`, which takes a sample and corresponding camera ray, radiance value, and alpha value, and updates the image.

⟨*Film Interface*⟩+≡   370
```
virtual void AddSample(const Sample &sample, const Ray &ray,
                       const Spectrum &L, float alpha) = 0;
```

After the main rendering loop exits, `Scene::Render()` calls the `Film::WriteImage()` method, which allows the film to do any processing necessary to generate the final image and display it or store it in a file.

⟨*Film Interface*⟩+≡   370
```
virtual void WriteImage() = 0;
```

The `Film`'s final responsibility is to determine the range of integer pixel values that the `Sampler` is responsible for generating samples for. While this range would be from (0, 0) to (xResolution − 1, yResolution − 1) for a simple film implementation, in general it is necessary to sample the image plane at locations slightly beyond the edges of the final image due to the finite extent of pixel reconstruction filters.

⟨*Film Interface*⟩+≡   370
```
virtual void GetSampleExtent(int *xstart, int *xend,
                             int *ystart, int *yend) const = 0;
```

8.2 IMAGE FILM

We will provide only one specific Film implementation for pbrt here: ImageFilm. This class simply filters image sample values with a given reconstruction filter and writes the resulting image to disk. It is implemented in the file film/image.cpp.◎

⟨*ImageFilm Declarations*⟩≡
```
class ImageFilm : public Film {
public:
    ⟨ImageFilm Public Methods⟩
private:
    ⟨ImageFilm Private Data 372⟩
};
```

The ImageFilm constructor takes a number of extra parameters beyond the overall image resolution, including a filter function, a crop window that specifies a subrectangle of the pixels to be rendered, the filename for the output image, a boolean parameter that determines whether final pixel colors are multiplied by their alpha values, and a counter that indicates how frequently (if at all) partially complete images are written as rendering progresses.

⟨*ImageFilm Method Definitions*⟩≡
```
ImageFilm::ImageFilm(int xres, int yres,
                     Filter *filt, const float crop[4],
                     const string &fn, bool premult, int wf)
    : Film(xres, yres) {
    filter = filt;
    memcpy(cropWindow, crop, 4 * sizeof(float));
    filename = fn;
    premultiplyAlpha = premult;
    writeFrequency = sampleCount = wf;
    ⟨Compute film image extent 372⟩
    ⟨Allocate film image storage 373⟩
    ⟨Precompute filter weight table 374⟩
}
```

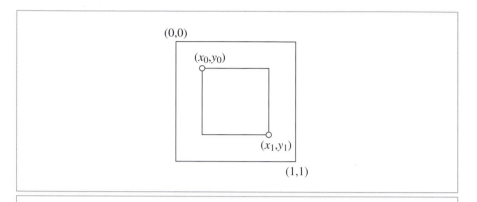

Figure 8.1: The image crop window specifies a subset of the image to be rendered. It is given in NDC space, with coordinates ranging from $(0, 0)$ to $(1, 1)$. The ImageFilm class only allocates space for and stores pixel values in the region inside the crop window.

⟨*ImageFilm Private Data*⟩ ≡   **371**
```
Filter *filter;
int writeFrequency, sampleCount;
string filename;
bool premultiplyAlpha;
float cropWindow[4];
```

In conjunction with the overall image resolution, the crop window gives the extent of pixels that need to be actually stored and written to disk. Crop windows are useful for debugging or for breaking a large image into small pieces that can be rendered on different computers and reassembled later. The crop window is specified in NDC space, with each coordinate ranging from zero to one (Figure 8.1). ImageFilm::xPixelStart and ImageFilm::yPixelStart store the pixel position of the upper-left corner of the crop window, and ImageFilm::xPixelCount and ImageFilm::yPixelCount give the total number of pixels in each direction. Their values are easily computed from the overall image resolution and the crop window, although the calculations must be done carefully such that if an image is rendered in pieces with abutting crop windows, each final pixel will be present in only one of the subimages.

⟨*Compute film image extent*⟩ ≡   **371**
```
xPixelStart = Ceil2Int(xResolution * cropWindow[0]);
xPixelCount = Ceil2Int(xResolution * cropWindow[1]) - xPixelStart;
yPixelStart = Ceil2Int(yResolution * cropWindow[2]);
yPixelCount = Ceil2Int(yResolution * cropWindow[3]) - yPixelStart;
```

⟨*ImageFilm Private Data*⟩+≡   371
```
int xPixelStart, yPixelStart, xPixelCount, yPixelCount;
```

Given the pixel resolution of the (possibly cropped) image, the constructor allocates an array of Pixel structures, one for each pixel. Pixel radiance values are stored in the Pixel::L member variable, their alpha values are stored in Pixel::alpha, and Pixel::weightSum holds the sum of filter weight values for the sample contributions to the pixel. This sum is used to perform pixel filtering as in Equation (7.3). Because small rectangular blocks of pixels are accessed for each image sample, the ImageFilm uses a BlockedArray to store the pixels, which helps reduce the number of cache misses as samples arrive and pixel values are updated.

⟨*Allocate film image storage*⟩≡   371
```
pixels = new BlockedArray<Pixel>(xPixelCount, yPixelCount);
```

⟨*ImageFilm Private Data*⟩+≡   371
```
struct Pixel {
    Pixel() : L(0.f) {
        alpha = 0.f;
        weightSum = 0.f;
    }
    Spectrum L;
    float alpha, weightSum;
};
BlockedArray<Pixel> *pixels;
```

With pbrt's default pixel filter settings, nearly every image sample contributes to 16 pixels in the final image. Particularly for simple scenes, where relatively little time is spent on ray intersection testing and shading computations, the time spent updating the image for each sample can be significant. Therefore, the ImageFilm precomputes a table of filter values so that the Film::AddSample() method can avoid the expense of virtual function calls to the Filter::Evaluate() method as well as the expense of evaluating the filter and can instead use values from the table for filtering. The error introduced by not evaluating the filter at each sample's precise location isn't noticeable in practice.

The implementation here makes the reasonable assumption that the filter is defined such that $f(x, y) = f(|x|, |y|)$, so the table needs to hold values for only the positive quadrant of filter offsets. This assumption is true for all of the Filters currently available in pbrt and is true for most filters used in practice. This makes the table one-fourth the size and improves the coherence of memory accesses, leading to better cache performance.

⟨*Precompute filter weight table*⟩ ≡　　　　　　　　　　　　　　　　　　　　　371

```
#define FILTER_TABLE_SIZE 16
filterTable = new float[FILTER_TABLE_SIZE * FILTER_TABLE_SIZE];
float *ftp = filterTable;
for (int y = 0; y < FILTER_TABLE_SIZE; ++y) {
    float fy = ((float)y + .5f) *
                filter->yWidth / FILTER_TABLE_SIZE;
    for (int x = 0; x < FILTER_TABLE_SIZE; ++x) {
        float fx = ((float)x + .5f) *
                    filter->xWidth / FILTER_TABLE_SIZE;
        *ftp++ = filter->Evaluate(fx, fy);
    }
}
```

⟨*ImageFilm Private Data*⟩+≡　　　　　　　　　　　　　　　　　　　　　371

```
float *filterTable;
```

To understand the operation of ImageFilm::AddSample(), first recall the pixel filtering equation:

$$I(x, y) = \frac{\sum_i f(x - x_i, y - y_i) L(x_i, y_i)}{\sum_i f(x - x_i, y - y_i)}.$$

It computes each pixel's value $I(x, y)$ as the weighted sum of nearby samples' radiance values, using a filter function f to compute the weights. Because all of the Filters in pbrt have finite extent, this method starts by computing which pixels will be affected by the current sample. Then, turning the pixel filtering equation inside out, it updates two running sums for each pixel (x, y) that is affected by the sample. One sum accumulates the numerator of the pixel filtering equation and the other accumulates the denominator. When all of the samples have been processed, the final pixel values are computed by performing the division.

⟨*ImageFilm Method Definitions*⟩+≡

```
void ImageFilm::AddSample(const Sample &sample, const Ray &ray,
                          const Spectrum &L, float alpha) {
    ⟨Compute sample's raster extent 375⟩
    ⟨Loop over filter support and add sample to pixel arrays 375⟩
    ⟨Possibly write out in-progress image 377⟩
}
```

To find which pixels a sample potentially contributes to, Film::AddSample() converts the continuous sample coordinates to discrete coordinates by subtracting 0.5 from x and y. It then offsets this value by the filter width in each direction (Figure 8.2) and takes the ceiling of the minimum coordinates and the floor of the maximum, since pixels outside the bound of the extent are guaranteed to be unaffected by the sample.

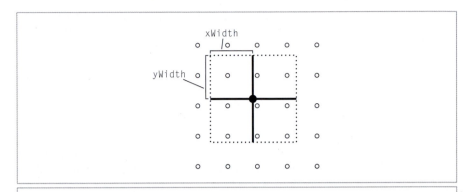

Figure 8.2: Given an image sample at some position on the image plane (solid dot), it is necessary to determine which pixel values (empty dots) are affected by the sample's contribution. This is done by taking the offsets in the x and y directions according to the pixel reconstruction filter's width (solid lines) and finding the pixels inside this region.

⟨*Compute sample's raster extent*⟩ ≡   **374**

```
float dImageX = sample.imageX - 0.5f;
float dImageY = sample.imageY - 0.5f;
int x0 = Ceil2Int (dImageX - filter->xWidth);
int x1 = Floor2Int(dImageX + filter->xWidth);
int y0 = Ceil2Int (dImageY - filter->yWidth);
int y1 = Floor2Int(dImageY + filter->yWidth);
x0 = max(x0, xPixelStart);
x1 = min(x1, xPixelStart + xPixelCount - 1);
y0 = max(y0, yPixelStart);
y1 = min(y1, yPixelStart + yPixelCount - 1);
```

Given the extent of pixels that are affected by this sample—(x0,y0) to (x1,y1), inclusive—the method can now loop over all of those pixels and then filter the sample value appropriately.

⟨*Loop over filter support and add sample to pixel arrays*⟩ ≡   **374**

```
⟨Precompute x and y filter table offsets 376⟩
for (int y = y0; y <= y1; ++y)
    for (int x = x0; x <= x1; ++x) {
        ⟨Evaluate filter value at (x, y) pixel 376⟩
        ⟨Update pixel values with filtered sample contribution 376⟩
    }
```

Each discrete integer pixel (x, y) has an instance of the filter function centered around it. To compute the filter weight for a particular sample, it's necessary to find the offset from the pixel to the sample's position in discrete coordinates and evaluate the filter function. If we were evaluating the filter explicitly, the appropriate computation would be

```
filterWt = filter->Evaluate(x - dImageX, y - dImageY);
```

Instead, the implementation retrieves the appropriate filter weight from the table.

To find the filter weight for a pixel (x', y') given the sample position (x, y), this routine computes the offset $(x' - x, y' - y)$ and converts it into coordinates for the filter weights lookup table. This can be done directly by dividing each component of the sample offset by the filter width in that direction, giving a value between zero and one, and then multiplying by the table size. This process can be further optimized by noting that along each row of pixels in the x direction, the difference in y, and thus the y offset into the filter table, is constant. Analogously, for each column of pixels, the x offset is constant. Therefore, before looping over the pixels here it's possible to precompute these indices, saving repeated work in the loop.

⟨*Precompute x and y filter table offsets*⟩ ≡   375
```
int *ifx = (int *)alloca((x1-x0+1) * sizeof(int));
for (int x = x0; x <= x1; ++x) {
    float fx = fabsf((x - dImageX) *
                    filter->invXWidth * FILTER_TABLE_SIZE);
    ifx[x-x0] = min(Floor2Int(fx), FILTER_TABLE_SIZE-1);
}
int *ify = (int *)alloca((y1-y0+1) * sizeof(int));
for (int y = y0; y <= y1; ++y) {
    float fy = fabsf((y - dImageY) *
                    filter->invYWidth * FILTER_TABLE_SIZE);
    ify[y-y0] = min(Floor2Int(fy), FILTER_TABLE_SIZE-1);
}
```

Now at each pixel, the x and y offsets into the filter table can be found for the pixel, leading to the offset into the array and thus the filter value.

⟨*Evaluate filter value at (x, y) pixel*⟩ ≡   375
```
int offset = ify[y-y0]*FILTER_TABLE_SIZE + ifx[x-x0];
float filterWt = filterTable[offset];
```

⟨*Update pixel values with filtered sample contribution*⟩ ≡   375
```
Pixel &pixel = (*pixels)(x - xPixelStart, y - yPixelStart);
pixel.L.AddWeighted(filterWt, L);
pixel.alpha += alpha * filterWt;
pixel.weightSum += filterWt;
```

Because the pixel reconstruction filter spans a number of pixels, the Sampler must generate image samples a bit outside of the range of pixels that will actually be output. This way, even pixels at the boundary of the image will have an equal density of samples around them in all directions and won't be biased with only values from toward the interior of the image. This is also important when rendering images in pieces with crop windows, since it eliminates artifacts at the edges of the subimages.

⟨*ImageFilm Method Definitions*⟩+≡

```
void ImageFilm::GetSampleExtent(int *xstart, int *xend,
                                int *ystart, int *yend) const {
    *xstart = Floor2Int(xPixelStart - filter->xWidth);
    *xend   = Ceil2Int (xPixelStart + xPixelCount  +
                        filter->xWidth);
    *ystart = Floor2Int(yPixelStart - filter->yWidth);
    *yend   = Ceil2Int (yPixelStart + yPixelCount +
                        filter->yWidth);
}
```

For images that take a long time to render, it can be helpful to the user if the renderer periodically writes out the image that has been computed so far. This is accomplished by repeatedly calling the `ImageFilm::WriteImage()` method if the `ImageFilm::writeFrequency` parameter was set to a positive value, giving the frequency of writing the image in terms of samples processed.

⟨*Possibly write out in-progress image*⟩≡   374

```
if (--sampleCount == 0) {
    WriteImage();
    sampleCount = writeFrequency;
}
```

8.2.1 IMAGE OUTPUT

After the main rendering loop finishes, `Scene::Render()` calls the `Film::WriteImage()` method to store the final image in a file. The `ImageFilm` implementation may also periodically call this method to write partial images to disk, as described earlier.

⟨*ImageFilm Method Definitions*⟩+≡

```
void ImageFilm::WriteImage() {
    ⟨Convert image to RGB and compute final pixel values 378⟩
    ⟨Write RGBA image  379⟩
    ⟨Release temporary image memory  379⟩
}
```

This method starts by making a copy of the pixel values so that the film's pixel values aren't affected by the filter weighting. Thus, this method can be called multiple times during rendering to write partial images.

⟨*Convert image to RGB and compute final pixel values*⟩ ≡   **377**

```
int nPix = xPixelCount * yPixelCount;
float *rgb = new float[3*nPix], *alpha = new float[nPix];
int offset = 0;
for (int y = 0; y < yPixelCount; ++y) {
    for (int x = 0; x < xPixelCount; ++x) {
        ⟨Convert pixel spectral radiance to RGB 378⟩
        alpha[offset] = (*pixels)(x, y).alpha;
        ⟨Normalize pixel with weight sum 379⟩
        ⟨Compute premultiplied alpha color 379⟩
        ++offset;
    }
}
```

Given information about the response characteristics of the display device being used, the pixel values are converted to device-dependent RGB values. First they are converted to device-independent XYZ tristimulus values, which are then converted to RGB. This is another change of spectral basis, where the new basis is determined by the spectral response curves of the red, green, and blue elements of the display device. Here, weights to convert from XYZ to the device RGB based on the HDTV standard are used. This is a good match for most modern display devices.

⟨*Convert pixel spectral radiance to RGB*⟩ ≡   **378**

```
float xyz[3];
(*pixels)(x, y).L.XYZ(xyz);
const float rWeight[3] = { 3.240479f, -1.537150f, -0.498535f };
const float gWeight[3] = {-0.969256f,  1.875991f,  0.041556f };
const float bWeight[3] = { 0.055648f, -0.204043f,  1.057311f };
rgb[3*offset  ] = rWeight[0]*xyz[0] +
                  rWeight[1]*xyz[1] +
                  rWeight[2]*xyz[2];
rgb[3*offset+1] = gWeight[0]*xyz[0] +
                  gWeight[1]*xyz[1] +
                  gWeight[2]*xyz[2];
rgb[3*offset+2] = bWeight[0]*xyz[0] +
                  bWeight[1]*xyz[1] +
                  bWeight[2]*xyz[2];
```

As the pixels are being initialized, their final values from the pixel filtering equation are computed by dividing each pixel sample value by `Pixel::weightSum`. Because reconstructed pixels may end up with negative values due to negative lobes in the reconstruction filter function, they are clamped to zero if necessary.

⟨*Normalize pixel with weight sum*⟩ ≡   378
```
float weightSum = (*pixels)(x, y).weightSum;
if (weightSum != 0.f) {
    float invWt = 1.f / weightSum;
    rgb[3*offset  ] = Clamp(rgb[3*offset  ] * invWt, 0.f, INFINITY);
    rgb[3*offset+1] = Clamp(rgb[3*offset+1] * invWt, 0.f, INFINITY);
    rgb[3*offset+2] = Clamp(rgb[3*offset+2] * invWt, 0.f, INFINITY);
    alpha[offset] = Clamp(alpha[offset] * invWt, 0.f, 1.f);
}
```

Each pixel value is also optionally multiplied by its alpha value; pixel colors scaled by alpha are known as having *premultiplied alpha* (also known as *associated alpha*). This representation has a number of advantages if image compositing operations are being performed by a separate program using images from pbrt (see the "Further Reading" section for additional information).

⟨*Compute premultiplied alpha color*⟩ ≡   378
```
if (premultiplyAlpha) {
    rgb[3*offset  ] *= alpha[offset];
    rgb[3*offset+1] *= alpha[offset];
    rgb[3*offset+2] *= alpha[offset];
}
```

The WriteRGBAImage() function, defined in Section A.6 in Appendix A handles the details of writing the image to a file:

⟨*Write RGBA image*⟩ ≡   377
```
WriteRGBAImage(filename, rgb, alpha, xPixelCount, yPixelCount,
                    xResolution, yResolution, xPixelStart, yPixelStart);
```

After saving the image, the working memory is freed:

⟨*Release temporary image memory*⟩ ≡   377
```
delete[] alpha;
delete[] rgb;
```

8.3 IMAGE PIPELINE

A series of image transformations is necessary to convert general floating-point images to a format suitable for display. These transformations are implemented in the ApplyImagingPipeline() function. A number of tricky issues, ranging from limitations of display devices to the behavior of the human visual system (HVS), need to be carefully addressed during this process. This function isn't used by pbrt or any of its plug-ins, but it is used by external programs that display floating-point images or convert them to non-floating-point image file formats, such as the tools/exrtotiff.cpp program on the CD. This function could also be used by an alternative Film implementation that directly created images stored in integer pixel formats. The parameters to the function guide this conversion process in various ways; their meanings will be explained as they are used through the remainder of this chapter.

There are four main stages in this imaging pipeline. First, tone reproduction algorithms are optionally used to remap the wide range of pixel radiance values to the more limited range that displays are capable of. Next, gamma correction is applied to account for the nonlinear relationship between color values sent to the display and their brightness on the display. Then, the pixel values are scaled to cover the range of input values expected by the display. Finally, a dithering step adds a small amount of random noise to the pixel values to help break up transitions between different colors in different regions of the image.

⟨*Image Pipeline Function Definitions*⟩ ≡
```
    void ApplyImagingPipeline(float *rgb, int xResolution,
            int yResolution, float *yWeight,
            float bloomRadius, float bloomWeight,
            const char *toneMapName, const ParamSet *toneMapParams,
            float gamma, float dither, int maxDisplayValue) {
        int nPix = xResolution * yResolution;
        ⟨Possibly apply bloom effect to image  384⟩
        ⟨Apply tone reproduction to image  388⟩
        ⟨Handle out-of-gamut RGB values  402⟩
        ⟨Apply gamma correction to image  402⟩
        ⟨Map image to display range  403⟩
        ⟨Dither image  403⟩
    }
```

*8.4 PERCEPTUAL ISSUES AND TONE MAPPING

In the early days of computer graphics, shading models always returned color values between zero and one, with no pretense of being associated with actual physical quantities. Thus, pixels had values in this range as well, and images could be directly displayed on a CRT with a frame buffer with RGB components from 0 to 255 just by scaling the pixel values. In the real world, it is not unusual for scenes to have radiance values with magnitudes ranging from roughly 0.01 to 1000, representing five orders of magnitude of variation from the brightest parts to the darkest parts. Remarkably, the HVS handles this extreme range of brightness well, since the human eye is more sensitive to local contrast than to absolute brightness. Not only do computer displays not take general pixel radiance values as input, but they are also unable to display very bright colors or very dim colors. They can generally display only about two orders of magnitude of brightness variation under ideal viewing conditions.

Film 370

ParamSet 877

Because realistic scenes rendered with physically based rendering algorithms also suffer from this mismatch between scene radiance values and the display device's capabilities, it is important to address the issue of displaying the image such that it has as close an appearance to the actual scene as possible. It has recently been an active area of research to find good methods to compress those extra orders of magnitude for image display. This work has been broadly classified as *tone mapping*; it draws on research into the human visual system to guide the development of techniques for image display. By exploiting properties of the HVS, tone mapping algorithms have been developed that do remarkably well at compensating for display device limitations. In this section, we will describe and implement a few such algorithms. Our coverage of this area touches on a representative subset of the possibilities, and the "Further Reading" section gives pointers to many recent papers in this field.

8.4.1 LUMINANCE AND PHOTOMETRY

Because tone mapping algorithms are generally based on human perception of brightness, most tone mapping operators use the unit of *luminance*, which measures how bright a spectral power distribution appears to a human observer. For example, luminance accounts for the fact that an SPD with a particular amount of energy in the green wavelengths will appear brighter to a human than an SPD with the same amount of energy in blue.

Luminance is closely related to radiance: given a spectral radiance value, its luminance value can be computed with a simple conversion formula. In fact, all of the radiometric quantities defined in Chapter 5 have analogs in the field of *photometry*—the study of visible electromagnetic radiation and its perception by the HVS. Each spectral radiometric quantity can be converted to its corresponding photometric quantity by integrating the product of its spectral distribution and the spectral response curve $V(\lambda)$, which describes the relative sensitivity of the human eye to various wavelengths.[1]

Luminance, which we will denote here by Y, is related to spectral radiance $L(\lambda)$ by

$$Y = \int_\lambda L(\lambda)\, V(\lambda) \mathrm{d}\lambda.$$

Luminance and the spectral response curve $V(\lambda)$ are closely related to the XYZ representation of color (Section 5.1.2). The CIE $Y(\lambda)$ tristimulus curve was chosen to be proportional to $V(\lambda)$ so that

$$Y = 683 \int_\lambda L(\lambda)\, Y(\lambda) \mathrm{d}\lambda.$$

---

1   The spectral response curve model is based on experiments done in a normally illuminated indoor environment. Because sensitivity to color decreases in dark environments, it doesn't model HVS response well under all lighting situations. Nonetheless, it forms the basis for the definition of luminance and other related photometric properties.

Table 8.1: Representative luminance values for a number of lighting conditions.

Luminance (cd/m^2, or nits)	
600,000	Sun at horizon
120,000	60-watt light bulb
8000	Clear sky
100–1000	Typical office
1–100	Typical computer display
1–10	Street lighting
0.25	Cloudy moonlight

Thus, given its XYZ representation, we have the luminance of each pixel in the image to within a scale factor. The units of luminance are candelas per meter squared (cd/m^2), where the candela is the photometric equivalent of radiant intensity. The quantity cd/m^2 is often referred to as a *nit*. Some representative luminance values are given in Table 8.1.

The human eye has two types of photoreceptors: rods and cones. Rods help with perception in dark environments (*scotopic* light levels), ranging from approximately 10^{-6} to 10 cd/m^2. Rods give little information about color and are not very good at resolving fine details. Cones handle light ranging from approximately 10^{-2} to 10^8 cd/m^2 (*photopic* light levels). There are three types of cones, with sensitivity to different wavelengths of light. Computer displays generally display luminances from about 1 to 100 cd/m^2.

8.4.2 BLOOM

Before describing tone mapping algorithms for remapping images to the displayable range, we'll describe a technique that can fool the HVS into perceiving that an image on a display is brighter than it actually is. When part of an environment being viewed by the human eye is substantially brighter than the rest of it, an effect called "bloom" often causes a blurred glow in the area around the bright object. The origins of this effect aren't completely understood, but are generally believed to be due to scattering of light inside the human eye. Researchers in computer graphics have found that simulating this effect in rendered images can make images appear substantially more realistic. When this glow is present in part of an image, the HVS naturally perceives that that part of the image is much brighter than the rest of it. Figure 8.3 shows an example of this effect applied to an image with a number of bright specular highlights.

The imaging pipeline can optionally apply a bloom effect to images. The filter used for this effect is empirical and not based on a model of the human visual system, but it works well in practice (the "Further Reading" section has pointers to information about more physically based glare effects). The basic idea is to apply a very wide filter that falls off quickly to all the pixels in the image. Because the filter has a wide support, very bright

(a)

(b)

Figure 8.3: (a) When the bloom effect is applied to an image with bright specular highlights, the human eye perceives glare, which signals that that part of the image is significantly brighter than the rest of it. (b) The same image, but without the bloom effect.

pixels can contribute energy to many pixels around them. Because it falls off quickly, it doesn't change regions of the image that have similar brightness values, but extremely bright pixels are able to overwhelm the low filter weight and spread their contribution to other pixels. This bloom image is then mixed into the original image with a user-supplied weight.

This filter takes two parameters: `bloomRadius`, which gives the fraction of the image that the filter covers, and `bloomWeight`, which gives the weight that the blurred bloom image is given when mixed with the original image. A `bloomRadius` value of zero indicates that the filter is disabled. Values around 0.1 or 0.2 are good starting points when using this filter in practice.

⟨*Possibly apply bloom effect to image*⟩ ≡   **380**
```
    if (bloomRadius > 0.f && bloomWeight > 0.f) {
        ⟨Compute image space extent of bloom effect  384⟩
        ⟨Initialize bloom filter table  385⟩
        ⟨Apply bloom filter to image pixels  385⟩
        ⟨Mix bloom effect into each pixel  386⟩
        ⟨Free memory allocated for bloom effect  386⟩
    }
```

First the width of the filter in pixels must be determined. This value is computed as `bloomRadius` times the larger of the x and y resolutions of the image.

⟨*Compute image space extent of bloom effect*⟩ ≡   **384**
```
    int bloomSupport = Float2Int(bloomRadius *
                              max(xResolution, yResolution));
    int bloomWidth = bloomSupport / 2;
```

Because the bloom filter function is evaluated many times over the image, it is beneficial to precompute a table of its values. The implementation here uses the radially symmetric filter function

$$f(x, y) = \left(1 - \frac{\sqrt{x^2 + y^2}}{d}\right)^4,$$

where d is the width of the filter. This filter is similar to one introduced by Chiu et al. (1993) as an ad hoc model of bloom. This filter is not separable, and thus the number of pixels that must be filtered for each output pixel is quadratic in the filter's width. This property gives extra motivation for precomputing the filter values into a table.

`Float2Int() 856`

⟨*Initialize bloom filter table*⟩ ≡   **384**

```
float *bloomFilter = new float[bloomWidth * bloomWidth];
for (int i = 0; i < bloomWidth * bloomWidth; ++i) {
    float dist = sqrtf(float(i)) / float(bloomWidth);
    bloomFilter[i] = powf(max(0.f, 1.f - dist), 4.f);
}
```

The implementation here first computes a temporary image that holds the bloom contribution. It is important not to update the original image as the bloom values are computed, since doing so would result in errors due to feedback as pixel values with bloom already added would be incorrectly used to determine bloom at nearby pixels.

⟨*Apply bloom filter to image pixels*⟩ ≡   **384**

```
float *bloomImage = new float[3*nPix];
for (int y = 0; y < yResolution; ++y) {
    for (int x = 0; x < xResolution; ++x) {
        ⟨Compute bloom for pixel (x,y) 385⟩
    }
}
```

To compute the value of a pixel in the bloom image, it is first necessary to find the set of pixels that potentially contribute bloom to it. The filter is then applied to all of the pixels in this set.

⟨*Compute bloom for pixel* (x,y)⟩ ≡   **385**

```
⟨Compute extent of pixels contributing bloom 385⟩
int offset = y * xResolution + x;
float sumWt = 0.;
for (int by = y0; by <= y1; ++by)
    for (int bx = x0; bx <= x1; ++bx) {
        ⟨Accumulate bloom from pixel (bx, by) 386⟩
    }
bloomImage[3*offset  ] /= sumWt;
bloomImage[3*offset+1] /= sumWt;
bloomImage[3*offset+2] /= sumWt;
```

The extent of contributing pixels is found by offsetting by the filter width in each direction and clamping to the overall image resolution, similar to how the pixels that an image sample contributes to are found.

⟨*Compute extent of pixels contributing bloom*⟩ ≡   **385**

```
int x0 = max(0, x - bloomWidth);
int x1 = min(x + bloomWidth, xResolution - 1);
int y0 = max(0, y - bloomWidth);
int y1 = min(y + bloomWidth, yResolution - 1);
```

The current pixel isn't included in the bloom computation, since the intent is to add contributions from other pixels to the current one. For other pixels, the bloom filter weights that pixel's contribution to the bloom image.

⟨*Accumulate bloom from pixel* (*bx*, *by*)⟩ ≡   385
```
int dx = x - bx, dy = y - by;
if (dx == 0 && dy == 0) continue;
int dist2 = dx*dx + dy*dy;
if (dist2 < bloomWidth * bloomWidth) {
    int bloomOffset = bx + by * xResolution;
    float wt = bloomFilter[dist2];
    sumWt += wt;
    for (int j = 0; j < 3; ++j)
        bloomImage[3*offset+j] += wt * rgb[3*bloomOffset+j];
}
```

Once the bloom image is complete, it is mixed into the original image according to the bloomWeight value.

⟨*Mix bloom effect into each pixel*⟩ ≡   384
```
for (int i = 0; i < 3 * nPix; ++i)
    rgb[i] = Lerp(bloomWeight, rgb[i], bloomImage[i]);
```

⟨*Free memory allocated for bloom effect*⟩ ≡   384
```
delete[] bloomFilter;
delete[] bloomImage;
```

8.4.3 TONE MAPPING INTERFACE

The basic approach to tone reproduction is to derive a scaling function that maps each pixel's value to the display's dynamic range. For simple tone mapping operators, a single function is often used for all pixels in the image. Such operators are called *spatially uniform* or *global* operators. They give a monotonic mapping from image luminance to display luminance. More sophisticated approaches use a function that varies based on each pixel's brightness and the brightness of nearby pixels; these are *spatially varying* or *local* operators and they do not necessarily guarantee a monotonic mapping.

The fact that spatially varying operators can be more effective than spatially uniform operators is interesting. These approaches work well because the human eye is more sensitive to local contrast than overall luminance. Because of this characteristic, it is often possible to assign different pixel values to different parts of the image that started with the same absolute luminance, without a human observer noticing that anything is amiss.

Therefore, a basic goal of many tone mapping operators is to seek to preserve local contrast in the displayed image rather than to preserve absolute brightness. It's much more important to make sure that enough distinct colors are used in all regions of the image—bright and dim—so that different colors are seen and to not map wide ranges of image intensities to the same pixel values. Thus, an object that is twice as bright as another one in the scene doesn't necessarily need to be twice as bright on the display. Again, local changes in contrast are the most important thing for the human visual system.

The HVS's overall sensitivity to luminance changes varies depending on the *adaptation luminance*, which we will denote by Y^a. The adaptation luminance may vary over different parts of the image. In the following discussion, we will use both the *display adaptation luminance, Y_d^a*, which is the adaptation luminance of the human observer looking at the computer display, and the *world adaptation luminance, Y_w^a*, the adaptation luminance of a human viewing the actual scene.

Since the rods in the human eye take over from the cones in very dim environments, the HVS has substantially different characteristics in the dark. For example, color perception is reduced and everything appears to be varying shades of dark gray. Furthermore, *spatial acuity* is reduced: at an adaptation luminance of 1000 nits, the HVS can resolve about 50 cycles of spatial detail per degree of vision, while at .001 nits, only about 2.2 cycles per degree can be made out. Tone reproduction operators that account for scotopic light levels often introduce some blurring to the image to account for this effect.

All of the tone mapping operators inherit from the `ToneMap` base class, which is defined in `core/tonemap.h` 🔴 and provides the interface method `ToneMap::Map()`.

⟨*ToneMap Declarations*⟩ ≡
```
class ToneMap {
public:
    ⟨ToneMap Interface  387⟩
};
```

The `ToneMap::Map()` method takes a pointer to the array of the image's pixel luminance values, the resolution of the image, and the maximum luminance that the display device being used is capable of generating. It is responsible for computing a scale factor for each pixel and storing it in the `scale` array. The scale should be computed such that the luminances of the scaled pixels will be in the range [0, maxDisplayY].

⟨*ToneMap Interface*⟩ ≡   **387**
```
virtual void Map(const float *y, int xRes, int yRes,
                 float maxDisplayY, float *scale) const = 0;
```

Here is the fragment that applies the tone mapping operator if one was specified in the arguments to `ApplyImagingPipeline()`. First, luminance values are computed for each pixel. Next, the operator computes a scale factor for each pixel, and finally the image is scaled. The maximum luminance that the device is capable of displaying, `maxDisplayY`, is set to a hard-coded (though typical) value.

⟨*Apply tone reproduction to image*⟩ ≡   **380**

```
    ToneMap *toneMap = NULL;
    if (toneMapName)
        toneMap = MakeToneMap(toneMapName,
            toneMapParams ? *toneMapParams : ParamSet());
    if (toneMap) {
        float maxDisplayY = 100.f;
        float *scale = new float[nPix], *lum = new float[nPix];
```
⟨*Compute pixel luminance values* **388**⟩
```
        toneMap->Map(lum, xResolution, yResolution,
                    maxDisplayY, scale);
```
⟨*Apple scale to pixels for tone mapping and map to* [0, 1] **388**⟩
```
        delete[] scale;
        delete[] lum;
    }
```

The `yWeight` argument to `ApplyImagingPipeline()` gives the weights to compute the luminance of an RGB pixel value. If a `NULL` value was passed in, then standard values are used.

⟨*Compute pixel luminance values*⟩ ≡   **388**

```
    float stdYWeight[3] = { 0.212671f, 0.715160f, 0.072169f };
    if (!yWeight) yWeight = stdYWeight;
    for (int i = 0; i < nPix; ++i)
        lum[i] = 683.f * (yWeight[0] * rgb[3*i] +
                          yWeight[1] * rgb[3*i+1] +
                          yWeight[2] * rgb[3*i+2]);
```

Because the scale values returned by the tone mapping operator should leave the pixel luminance values `lum[i]` in the range [0, `maxDisplayY`], the results from the operator now need to be scaled to the range [0, 1] for the rest of the pipeline since current display devices don't take luminance values as input. Furthermore, an additional scale by a factor of 683 is necessary, since the tone mapping operators compute scale values assuming that this scale has already been applied to the pixel values.

⟨*Apple scale to pixels for tone mapping and map to* [0, 1]⟩ ≡   **388**

```
    float displayTo01 = 683.f / maxDisplayY;
    for (int i = 0; i < xResolution * yResolution; ++i) {
        rgb[3*i  ] *= scale[i] * displayTo01;
        rgb[3*i+1] *= scale[i] * displayTo01;
        rgb[3*i+2] *= scale[i] * displayTo01;
    }
```

ApplyImagingPipeline() 380
ParamSet 877
ToneMap 387
ToneMap::Map() 387

8.4.4 MAXIMUM TO WHITE

The most straightforward tone reproduction operator to apply (besides just hoping that the image's pixel values are already in a suitable range for display) is the *maximum to white* operator. It loops over all the pixels to find the one with the greatest luminance and scales all of the pixels uniformly so that the largest luminance maps to the maximum luminance value of the display. Its implementation is in tonemaps/maxwhite.cpp.⊙

⟨*MaxWhiteOp Declarations*⟩ ≡

```
class MaxWhiteOp : public ToneMap {
public:
    ⟨MaxWhiteOp Public Methods 389⟩
};
```

⟨*MaxWhiteOp Public Methods*⟩ ≡   **389**

```
void Map(const float *y, int xRes, int yRes,
        float maxDisplayY, float *scale) const {
    ⟨Compute maximum luminance of all pixels 389⟩
    float s = maxDisplayY / maxY;
    for (int i = 0; i < xRes * yRes; ++i)
        scale[i] = s;
}
```

⟨*Compute maximum luminance of all pixels*⟩ ≡   **389**

```
float maxY = 0.;
for (int i = 0; i < xRes * yRes; ++i)
    maxY = max(maxY, y[i]);
```

There are two main disadvantages to this operator in practice (as its application to the St. Peter's image in Figure 8.4 shows). First, it doesn't account for the human visual system at all: if the lights in the scene are made 100 times brighter and the scene is rerendered, this operator will give the exact same displayed image. Second, a small number of very bright pixels can cause the rest of the image to be too dark to be visible. Nonetheless, it can work well for scenes without too much dynamic range in the image and serves as a baseline that can show off the improvement offered by more sophisticated operators.

8.4.5 CONTRAST-BASED SCALE FACTOR

The next tone reproduction operator focuses on preserving contrast in the displayed image. It was developed by Greg Ward (1994a). Built upon work by researchers who have studied the HVS and developed models that simulate it, this operator is based on a model that describes the smallest change in luminance that is noticeable to a human observer given a particular adaptation luminance—the *just noticeable difference* (JND). The larger the adaptation luminance, the larger a change in luminance is needed to be noticeable. The operator tries to set image luminances such that one JND in the displayed image corresponds to one JND in the actual environment.

ToneMap 387

Figure 8.4: St. Peter's Basilica in Rome. A high dynamic range of St. Peter's accurately encodes the lighting inside the Basilica, including the multiple orders of magnitude of radiance values that are present. The standard approach of choosing a fixed radiance value to map to the brightest displayable color performs poorly on this environment. Here, we have chosen three different maximum radiance values, each greater than the last by a factor of 10. Observe that even in the darkest image, the light from the windows is blown out. In the top and middle images, some areas are too dark to make out details, while in the brightest image, large regions of the image map to the maximum value, so that no detail remains. A human observer inside St. Peter's on the day these photographs were taken would have been able to see detail throughout the environment. The tone reproduction operators in this section will apply more sophisticated algorithms than simple scaling to map the wide range of radiance values to the display device's displayable range.

This uniform scale factor thus attempts to preserve *contrast visibility*—given a region of the original image that would be just noticeably different from its neighbor to a human observer, it tries to scale display pixel values such that the person looking at the display perceives that those two pixel values are just noticeably different. A scale factor that instead increased JNDs would be a waste of precious display dynamic range, while one that reduced JNDs would cause visually detectable features to disappear.

Researchers have found that given an adaptation luminance in the photopic range Y^a, a reasonable model of the minimum change in luminance necessary to be visible is given by

$$\Delta Y(Y^a) = 0.0594(1.219 + (Y^a)^{0.4})^{2.5}.$$

Thus, this operator would like to determine a scale s such that

$$\Delta Y(Y_d^a) = s \Delta Y(Y_w^a),$$

where Y_d^a is the display adaptation luminance and Y_w^a is the world adaptation luminance for someone observing the actual scene.

Substituting the model above and solving for s gives

$$s = \left(\frac{1.219 + (Y_d^a)^{0.4}}{1.219 + (Y_w^a)^{0.4}} \right)^{2.5}. \tag{8.1}$$

⟨*ContrastOp Declarations*⟩ ≡
```
class ContrastOp : public ToneMap {
public:
    ContrastOp(float day) { displayAdaptationY = day; }
    void Map(const float *y, int xRes, int yRes,
            float maxDisplayY, float *scale) const;
    float displayAdaptationY;
};
```

⟨*ContrastOp Method Definitions*⟩ ≡
```
void ContrastOp::Map(const float *y, int xRes, int yRes,
                    float maxDisplayY, float *scale) const {
    ⟨Compute world adaptation luminance, Ywa 392⟩
    ⟨Compute contrast-preserving scale factor, s 392⟩
    for (int i = 0; i < xRes*yRes; ++i)
        scale[i] = s;
}
```

ContrastOp 391
ToneMap 387

One unresolved issue is how to compute the world adaptation luminance Y_w^a. Ideally, this value would be computed based on which part of the scene the viewer was looking at and how long they had been looking at it (it takes some time for the HVS to adapt to luminance changes). Lacking this information, this operator computes a log average of all of the luminances in the original image. Taking the log average rather than a regular

Figure 8.5: Application of the contrast-preserving scale factor to the St. Peters image works well in some parts of the image, although it doesn't do well at preserving detail in the very bright areas. Any operator that uses a single global scale factor is susceptible to this problem.

average of the original luminances helps prevent small bright regions from overwhelming luminance values in the rest of the image.

⟨*Compute world adaptation luminance,* Ywa⟩ ≡   **391, 401**
```
float Ywa = 0.;
for (int i = 0; i < xRes * yRes; ++i)
    if (y[i] > 0) Ywa += logf(y[i]);
Ywa = expf(Ywa / (xRes * yRes));
```

The scale is directly computed from Equation (8.1):

⟨*Compute contrast-preserving scale factor,* s⟩ ≡   **391**
```
float s = powf((1.219f + powf(displayAdaptationY, 0.4f)) /
    (1.219f + powf(Ywa, 0.4f)), 2.5f);
```

Figure 8.5 shows this operator in action. It does a reasonable job on the St. Peter's image, but has trouble maintaining detail in the bright areas. This isn't too surprising; any operator that uses the same scale factor at all pixels will have trouble with images with many orders of magnitude of brightness variation. This operator does work well on typical indoor scenes, however, and is computationally efficient.

8.4.6 VARYING ADAPTATION LUMINANCE

As mentioned earlier, it is often possible to make better use of the display's dynamic range by using a scale factor that varies over the image. Here we will implement a tone reproduction operator tailored for high-contrast scenes with many orders of magnitude of

Figure 8.6: When the adaptation luminance is computed using a fixed search radius at each pixel (here roughly 10 pixels), there are often unsightly halo artifacts at transitions between bright and dim regions of the image. For example, there are black borders around the bright light from the windows, where the adaptation luminance has been computed using the bright window light, such that the tone mapping operator maps adjacent dimmer pixels to very low values.

brightness variation. It computes a local adaptation luminance that smoothly varies over the image. The local adaptation luminance is then used to compute a scale factor using a contrast-preserving tone reproduction operator, in a similar manner to the ContrastOp operator defined earlier.

The main difficulty with methods that compute a spatially varying local adaptation luminance is that they are prone to artifacts at boundaries between very bright and very dim parts of the image. If the tone reproduction operator scales the dim pixels using an adaptation luminance that includes the effects of the bright pixels, the dim pixels will be mapped to black, causing a halo artifact at the boundary of the final image (Figure 8.6).

Instead, it is better if we can make sure that the dim pixels have an adaptation luminance based on just nearby dim pixels. The operator described in this section uses an image processing technique to detect the boundaries between regions with substantially different adaptation luminances. Over local regions of the image where the adaptation luminance is slowly changing, this tone reproduction operator uses a local scale factor tuned to preserve contrast. However, since adaptation is allowed to vary over the image, details are also preserved—bright regions aren't blown out to be white, and dark regions aren't mapped down to black pixels. The approach implemented is based on a tone reproduction operator developed by Ashikhmin (2002). Reinhard et al. (2002) simultaneously developed a different operator that uses the same technique to compute local adaptation. The implementation is in tonemaps/highcontrast.cpp.

ContrastOp 391

The results of applying this operator to the St. Peter's image are shown in Figure 8.7. It does substantially better than the contrast operator, thanks to its spatially varying scale factor.

⟨*HighContrastOp Declarations*⟩ ≡
```
    class HighContrastOp : public ToneMap {
    public:
        void Map(const float *y, int xRes, int yRes,
                 float maxDisplayY, float *scale) const;
    private:
        ⟨HighContrastOp Utility Methods  396⟩
    };
```

The tone mapping function used by HighContrastOp is based on the *threshold versus intensity* (TVI) function, which gives the just noticeable luminance difference for a given adaptation level, $TVI(Y^a)$. It is similar in spirit to the JND function used in ContrastOp, but is based on a more complex model of the human visual system, including a model of response to scotopic light levels.

From the TVI function, we can define the *perceptual capacity*, which tells us, given a particular adaptation level Y_a, how many JNDs a given luminance range (Y_a, Y_b) covers:

$$\frac{Y_a - Y_b}{TVI(Y^a)}.$$

Later, we will use this relationship to remap local regions of the image in a way that preserves their perceptual capacity when displayed.

So that we can quickly compute the perceptual capacity of a given pair of luminance values, the auxiliary capacity function $C(Y)$ is defined as

$$C(Y) = \int_0^Y \frac{\mathrm{d}Y'}{TVI(Y')},$$

where the approximation is made that the adaptation level to compute the differential perceptual capacity at a given luminance is assumed to be equal to that luminance. Then $C(Y_a) - C(Y_b)$ is the perceptual capacity from Y_a to Y_b.

Ashikhmin has made some simplifications to a widely used TVI function in order to be able to integrate it analytically to compute $C(Y)$. The result is the function

$$C(Y) = \begin{cases} Y/0.0014 & Y < 0.0034 \\ 2.4483 + \log(Y/0.0034)/0.4027 & 0.0034 \leq Y < 1 \\ 16.563 + (Y-1)/0.4027 & 1 \leq Y < 7.2444 \\ 32.0693 + \log(Y/7.2444)/0.0556 & \text{otherwise.} \end{cases}$$

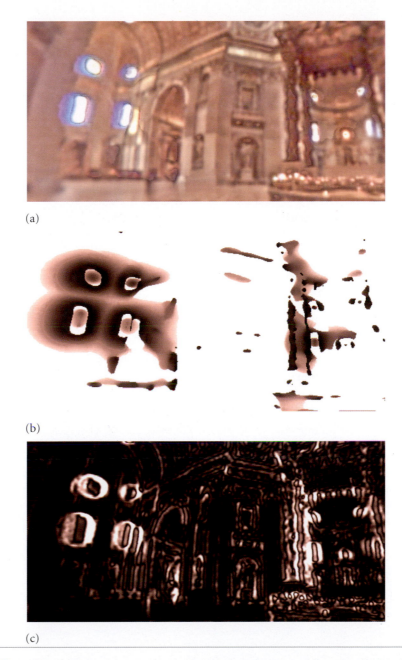

(a)

(b)

(c)

Figure 8.7: The high-contrast tone reproduction operator computes a spatially varying adaptation luminance while paying attention to boundaries between areas with substantially different luminances. (a) The result of its use on the St. Peter's image: it does an excellent job of remapping this image to a small dynamic range. (b) A gray-scale visualization of the blur radius that was used to compute adaptation luminance at each pixel: boundaries with large luminance changes are successfully detected, indicated by small radii, while areas with slower change in luminance compute adaptation luminance over a wider area. (c) The local contrast computed at each pixel with a blur radius of 1.5 and 3 pixels.

⟨*HighContrastOp Utility Methods*⟩ ≡   394
```
static float C(float y) {
    if (y < 0.0034f)
        return y / 0.0014f;
    else if (y < 1)
        return 2.4483f + log10f(y/0.0034f)/0.4027f;
    else if (y < 7.2444f)
        return 16.563f + (y - 1)/0.4027f;
    else
        return 32.0693f + log10f(y / 7.2444f)/0.0556f;
}
```

Given $C(Y)$, we can now take a given luminance value Y and determine how many JND steps it is from the minimum luminance in the image,

$$C(Y) - C(Y_{\min}),$$

and we can also compute, of all of the JND steps that the image goes through, what fraction of the way through all of them it is:

$$\frac{C(Y) - C(Y_{\min})}{C(Y_{\max}) - C(Y_{\min})}.$$

This gives us a sense of how far through the range of display luminances this world luminance should be mapped. Thus, the overall tone mapping operator, giving a scale in terms of display luminance, is

$$T(Y) = Y_{\mathrm{d}}^{\max} \frac{C(Y) - C(Y_{\min})}{C(Y_{\max}) - C(Y_{\min})}.$$

⟨*HighContrastOp Utility Methods*⟩+≡   394
```
static float T(float y, float CYmin, float CYmax, float maxDisplayY) {
    return maxDisplayY * (C(y) - CYmin) / (CYmax - CYmin);
}
```

We can now define the main tone reproduction function. It computes the minimum and maximum luminances of all pixels in the image to give $Y_{\max}$ and $Y_{\min}$. In order to quickly do the searches to compute adaptation luminances, it also builds an image pyramid data structure, where the original image is progressively filtered down into lower-resolution copies of itself. This pyramid is used when the operator loops over all of the pixels and computes each pixel's scale factor.

⟨*HighContrastOp Method Definitions*⟩ ≡
```
void HighContrastOp::Map(const float *y, int xRes, int yRes,
                         float maxDisplayY, float *scale) const {
    ⟨Find minimum and maximum image luminances 397⟩
    ⟨Build luminance image pyramid 398⟩
    ⟨Apply high-contrast tone mapping operator 398⟩
}
```

⟨*Find minimum and maximum image luminances*⟩ ≡   397
```
float minY = y[0], maxY = y[0];
for (int i = 0; i < xRes * yRes; ++i) {
    minY = min(minY, y[i]);
    maxY = max(maxY, y[i]);
}
float CYmin = C(minY), CYmax = C(maxY);
```

Most previous approaches to computing local adaptation luminance used a blurred version of the original image, although this led to the halo artifact described previously. The insight behind the approach implemented here is that adaptation luminance shouldn't be based on a constant-sized region of the image around the pixel (x, y), but should be based on a varying area: as long as the luminance is locally roughly constant, the area can be expanded until a significant change in luminance is reached. This gives the best of both worlds: When luminance is changing slowly, adaptation luminance is computed over a larger area, giving smooth variation of adaptation luminance far from high-contrast features. When contrast is quickly changing, however, this condition is detected and artifacts are avoided by computing a more local adaptation luminance.

A standard technique from image processing is to define the *local contrast* $lc(x, y)$ of a pixel as the magnitude of the difference between that pixel's value in two blurred versions of the image, one blurred with twice as wide a filter than the other:

$$lc(s, x, y) = \frac{B_s(x, y) - B_{2s}(x, y)}{B_s(x, y)}.$$

Here s is the filter width (expressed in pixels) used for blurring the image, and $B_s(x, y)$ is pixel (x, y)'s value in the blurred image. We would like to find the largest local extent around each pixel (x, y) of radius s such that $|lc(s, x, y)|$ is less than some constant value. When it becomes greater than that value, we have passed the amount of acceptable local contrast. Having found such an s, adaptation luminance is computed as

$$Y^a(x, y) = B_s(x, y),$$

HighContrastOp 394
HighContrastOp::C() 396

thus fulfilling the earlier criteria. Figure 8.7(a) shows this operator applied to the St. Peter's Basilica image. Notice how large brightness discontinuities in the original image are detected by the local contrast function, and halo artifacts are avoided.

In order to be able to quickly find the value of pixels in the blurred image $B_s(x, y)$, this operator creates an image pyramid with the MIPMap class, which will be described in Section 11.4.2. For the purposes of this section, we will just make use of the fact that it can accurately and efficiently compute values of $B_s(x, y)$ for arbitrary values of s.

⟨*Build luminance image pyramid*⟩ ≡   397
```
    MIPMap<float> pyramid(xRes, yRes, y, false, 4.f, TEXTURE_CLAMP);
```

Next, the adaptation luminance and scale factor are computed for each pixel. Note that it is necessary to convert from discrete to continuous pixel coordinates in xc and yc to give the correct continuous position for the MIPMap lookup.

⟨*Apply high-contrast tone mapping operator*⟩ ≡   397
```
    for (int y = 0; y < yRes; ++y) {
        float yc = (float(y) + .5f) / float(yRes);
        for (int x = 0; x < xRes; ++x) {
            float xc = (float(x) + .5f) / float(xRes);
            ⟨Compute local adaptation luminance at (x, y) 398⟩
            ⟨Apply tone mapping based on local adaptation luminance 400⟩
        }
    }
```

To compute the adaptation luminance, this method looks up the value of the pixel in images with a given blur amount (specifically those blurred by width and 2 × width) to compute the value of the local contrast function, lc. If it's above the value stored in maxLocalContrast, 0.5 (an arbitrary constant, chosen after some experimentation), the adaptation luminance is set as the average of a slightly smaller region around the pixel and the loop terminates. Otherwise, the blur radius is increased by one pixel's span, dwidth, and a new value of lc is computed. This process eventually stops once it reaches a large blur without finding a sufficient amount of contrast; at that point, just using the wide area to set adaptation luminance works well anyway.

⟨*Compute local adaptation luminance at* (x, y)⟩ ≡   398
```
    float dwidth = 1.f / float(max(xRes, yRes));
    float maxWidth = 32.f / float(max(xRes, yRes));
    float width = dwidth, prevWidth = 0.f;
    float Yadapt;
    float prevlc = 0.f;
    const float maxLocalContrast = .5f;
    while (1) {
        ⟨Compute local contrast at (x, y) 399⟩
        ⟨If maximum contrast is exceeded, compute adaptation luminance 399⟩
        ⟨Increase search region and prepare to compute contrast again 399⟩
    }
```

MIPMap 516
TEXTURE_CLAMP 516

The local contrast computation is made trivial with the MIPMap image pyramid. The MIPMap::Lookup() method applies a filter of a given width to the image at the given pixel position.

⟨*Compute local contrast at* (x, y)⟩ ≡   398

```
float b0 = pyramid.Lookup(xc, yc, width, 0.f, 0.f, width);
float b1 = pyramid.Lookup(xc, yc, 2.f*width, 0.f, 0.f, 2.f*width);
float lc = fabsf((b0 - b1) / b0);
```

If the local contrast exceeds the maximum allowed contrast, an ad hoc approximation determines the width s for which $lc(s, x, y) = \text{maxLocalContrast}$. Given the local contrast that was computed the last time through the loop in prevlc and the fact that

$$\text{prevlc} < \text{maxLocalContrast} < \text{lc},$$

an interpolation amount t is found such that linear interpolation between prevlc and lc gives exactly maxLocalContrast. Under the assumption that contrast varies linearly between the last width at which contrast was computed and the current width, it's easy to compute the width between them where we assume that the contrast constraint was violated.

⟨*If maximum contrast is exceeded, compute adaptation luminance*⟩ ≡   398

```
if (lc > maxLocalContrast) {
    float t = (maxLocalContrast - prevlc) / (lc - prevlc);
    float w = Lerp(t, prevWidth, width);
    Yadapt = pyramid.Lookup(xc, yc, w, 0.f, 0.f, w);
    break;
}
```

⟨*Increase search region and prepare to compute contrast again*⟩ ≡   398

```
prevlc = lc;
prevWidth = width;
width += dwidth;
if (width >= maxWidth) {
    Yadapt = pyramid.Lookup(xc, yc, maxWidth, 0.f, 0.f, maxWidth);
    break;
}
```

Given the tone mapping function $T(Y^a)$, the scale factor at a given pixel (x, y) is defined by

$$s(x, y) = \frac{T(Y^a(x, y))}{Y^a(x, y)}.$$

As long as $Y^a(x, y)$ is slowly varying over the image, this is essentially a locally linear mapping.

Lerp() 853
maxLocalContrast 398
MIPMap 516
MIPMap::Lookup() 528

⟨*Apply tone mapping based on local adaptation luminance*⟩ ≡   398

```
    scale[x + y*xRes] = T(Yadapt, CYmin, CYmax, maxDisplayY) / Yadapt;
```

8.4.7 SPATIALLY VARYING NONLINEAR SCALE

The last tone mapping approach implemented here is not at all grounded in the perception literature, but works remarkably well in practice. It is based on an ad hoc formula that was chosen with perceptual issues in mind and was introduced by Reinhard et al. (2002). Its implementation is in the file tonemaps/nonlinear.cpp.🔴 A spatially varying factor is used to scale each pixel:

$$s(x, y) = \frac{\left(1 + \frac{y(x,y)}{y_{\max}^2}\right)}{1 + y(x, y)}.$$

Note that this operator is not based on luminance Y, but the y component of XYZ color (i.e., the scale factor of 683 is not included).

This scale factor maps black pixels to zero and the brightest pixels to one. In between, darker pixels require relatively less change in brightness to cause a given change in output pixel value than bright pixels do. This is in tune with properties of the HVS, which has a generally logarithmic response curve, rather than a linear one.

⟨*NonLinearOp Declarations*⟩ ≡

```
    class NonLinearOp : public ToneMap {
    public:
        ⟨NonLinearOp Public Methods 400⟩
    private:
        float maxY;
    };
```

The adaptation luminance can optionally be supplied to the constructor. If no value is specified, adaptation luminance will be computed as the log average of pixel luminances, as was done in the ContrastOp.

⟨*NonLinearOp Public Methods*⟩ ≡   400

```
    NonLinearOp(float my) { maxY = my; }
```

The implementation of the operator is straightforward. The only complication is the need to remove the scale of 683 from the luminance values.

Figure 8.8: The ad hoc nonlinear scale factor works remarkably well on the image of St. Peter's Basilica, preserving detail over a wide range of image luminance values.

⟨*NonLinearOp Public Methods*⟩+≡   **400**
```
void Map(const float *y, int xRes, int yRes,
        float maxDisplayY, float *scale) const {
    float invY2;
    if (maxY <= 0.f) {
        ⟨Compute world adaptation luminance, Ywa 392⟩
        Ywa /= 683.f;
        invY2 = 1.f / (Ywa * Ywa);
    }
    else invY2 = 1.f / (maxY * maxY);
    for (int i = 0; i < xRes * yRes; ++i) {
        float ys = y[i] / 683.f;
        scale[i] = maxDisplayY / 683.f *
                    (1.f + ys * invY2) / (1.f + ys);
    }
}
```

Figure 8.8 shows this operator in action. It does an excellent job of mapping the St. Peter's image to a reasonable range, preserving contrast over a wide range of brightnesses.

8.5 FINAL IMAGING PIPELINE STAGES

Unfortunately, there are many colors that modern displays cannot reproduce, such as saturated oranges and purples; such colors are called *out of gamut*. Out-of-gamut colors have values outside the range [0, 1] after they have been converted to the display's RGB space. There aren't any completely satisfactory solutions to the problem of what to do with out-of-gamut pixels. Given that the display device can't reproduce their colors, all that can be done is to trade off different kinds of error in choosing a color that they can display. The imaging pipeline implemented here rescales out-of-gamut colors so that the maximum of the three components has the value one and the others are scaled proportionally.

⟨*Handle out-of-gamut RGB values*⟩ ≡   380
```
for (int i = 0; i < nPix; ++i) {
    float m = max(rgb[3*i], max(rgb[3*i+1], rgb[3*i+2]));
    if (m > 1.f)
        for (int j = 0; j < 3; ++j)
            rgb[3*i+j] /= m;
}
```

Once all of the colors are in the displayable range, it is necessary to adjust the color values for the brightness response exhibited by cathode ray tube (CRT) displays. With these kinds of displays, the displayed brightness doesn't vary linearly with the pixel values: a pixel with value 100 isn't usually twice as bright as a pixel with value 50. Although newer display technologies like LCD screens don't naturally have a nonlinear response like this, they typically mimic this characteristic of CRT display respond (Fairchild and Wyble 1998).

This nonlinear response is generally modeled with a power function:

$$d = v^\gamma,$$

where d is the display brightness, v is the voltage applied to the display's electron gun (which is directly proportional to the image pixel value, unless the hardware or operating system also performs gamma correction), and the *gamma value* γ is generally 2.2. Therefore, given a pixel value v, sending

$$v' = v^{1/\gamma}$$

to the display will cause the displayed color to be linear.

⟨*Apply gamma correction to image*⟩ ≡   380
```
if (gamma != 1.f) {
    float invGamma = 1.f / gamma;
    for (int i = 0; i < 3*nPix; ++i)
        rgb[i] = powf(rgb[i], invGamma);
}
```

The gamma-corrected pixel values are then mapped to the range expected by the display (typically 0 to 255). The maxDisplayValue parameter controls this scaling.

⟨*Map image to display range*⟩ ≡ **380**

```
for (int i = 0; i < 3*nPix; ++i)
    rgb[i] *= maxDisplayValue;
```

Finally, before converting these pixel values to integer values for the display, it is also helpful to *dither* their values, adding a small random value to each pixel's color component. Introducing this very small amount of noise improves the visual quality of displayed images by making slow transitions between areas with one color to another less well-delineated. Failing to dither the image can introduce banding artifacts along slow transitions between similar colors.

⟨*Dither image*⟩ ≡ **380**

```
if (dither > 0.f)
    for (int i = 0; i < 3*nPix; ++i)
        rgb[i] += 2.f * dither * (RandomFloat() - .5f);
```

FURTHER READING

Porter and Duff's paper on compositing digital images is the classic paper on the uses of images with alpha channels and explains why premultiplied alpha is a preferable representation (Porter and Duff 1984). The first use of an extra alpha channel in images in graphics dates to Smith and Catmull (Smith 1979). See also Wallace (1981) for a refinement of Smith and Catmull's approach.

Gamma correction has a long history in computer graphics. Poynton (2002a, 2002b) has written comprehensive FAQs on issues related to color representation and gamma correction. Even though there is no physical reason for LCD displays to have a nonlinear response, Fairchild and Wyble (1998) have measured the response of a widely used LCD and found that gamma correction is also necessary with that display. See also Gibson and Fairchild (2000), where similar results are found for other LCDs.

A number of different approaches have been developed for mapping out-of-gamut colors to the displayable range; see Rougeron and Péroche's survey article for discussion of this issue and references to various approaches (Rougeron and Péroche 1998). This topic is also covered by Hall (1989).

While most image file formats store 8 bits for each red, green, and blue channel (and possibly alpha), many new formats are also able to store floating-point data. Ward (1991b) suggested an efficient technique for compactly storing floating-point image data from realistic image synthesis and has also developed an extension to the TIFF image file format for accurate and compact, high dynamic range color representation (Larson 1998). The OpenEXR format was developed by Kainz and Bogart at Industrial Light and Magic; one of its innovations is a 16-bit floating-point format (Kainz, Bogart, and Hess 2002). Peercy et al. (2000) were the first to use such a format for image representation.

RandomFloat() 857

The images that a renderer generates don't necessarily need to store color values at each pixel. For example, Séquin and Smyrl (1989) described a system that stored the tree of all rays traced at each pixel; this made it possible to modify light and material colors in the scene and generate a new image of the scene without needing to retrace any of the rays. Both Perlin (1985a) and Saito and Takahashi (1990) have shown a number of uses for images that stored 3D position, surface normal, and other geometric and material properties of the first visible object in each pixel, including fast reshading of the scene and illustration-inspired rendering styles.

Tone reproduction for computer graphics became an active area of research around 1993, starting with the work of Tumblin and Rushmeier (1993). Chiu et al. (1993) and Ward (1994a) soon followed with new approaches. The bloom technique in Section 8.4.2 is based on the one described in Chiu et al.'s paper, and the `ContrastOp` is based on Ward's.

Since the initial work in tone reproduction, there has been an explosion of research in this area. The survey article of Devlin et al. (2002) summarizes most of the work in this area through 2002, giving pointers to the original papers. For background information on properties of the human visual system, Wandell's book on vision is an excellent starting point (Wandell 1995). Ferwerda (2001) presents an overview of the human visual system for applications in graphics.

A representative set of papers on tone reproduction includes Ferwerda et al. (1996, 1997), who extended Ward's contrast-based method to handle scotopic lighting levels, including reduced color sensitivity and spatial acuity, and Larson, Rushmeir, and Piatko (1997), who used histogram equalization to distribute pixel values for the final image. See also Pattanaik et al. (1998, 2000); Tumblin, Hodgins, and Guenter (1999); Tumblin and Turk (1999); and Durand and Dorsey (2002).

The ad hoc nonlinear mapping implemented in this chapter was developed by Reinhard et al. (2002), and the local contrast detection approach in the `HighContrastOp` is based on Ashikhmin's technique (Ashikhmin 2002). The same local contrast operator was also introduced for tone mapping by Reinhard et al., who developed an operator based on principles from photography, rather than the human visual system (Reinhard et al. 2002; Reinhard 2002).

Simulating the scattering processes inside the human eye can also improve the perceived realism of the image. Nakamae et al. (1990), Chiu et al. (1993), and Spencer et al. (1995) have modeled glare, where very bright areas in an environment mask dimmer areas next to them. Simulating this effect in displayed images (e.g., by blurring a bit around very bright areas) can substantially increase the perceived brightness of objects, as the ad hoc approach in `pbrt` based on Chiu et al.'s method demonstrates.

ContrastOp 391
HighContrastOp 394

Another interesting application of knowledge of the characteristics of the HVS is perceptually driven rendering, where less work is done in areas of the image that are known to be visually unimportant and more work is done in areas that are known to be important. Both Bolin and Meyer (1998) and Ramasubramanian, Pattanaik, and Greenberg (1999) wrote renderers that performed adaptive sampling based on perceptual models. Walter, Pattanaik, and Greenberg (2002) developed a system that detected and took advantage of masking of noise artifacts due to textures to do faster rendering.

Malacara (2002) gives a concise overview of color theory and basic properties of how the human visual system processes color.

EXERCISES

❷ 8.1 Write a new `Film` implementation that opens a window on the screen and displays pixel values as the scene is rendered. Since the values being stored in the film are floating point and can have a wide range of values, provide controls for interactively controlling the "exposure" of the film.

❷ 8.2 For rendering very large images, the fact that the `ImageFilm` allocates storage for the entire image may have an unacceptable memory cost. Write a new `Film` implementation that allocates space for the image as needed and writes out regions of the image that are finished, freeing the space that was allocated for them. You will need to modify the `Sampler` interface to be able to communicate to the `Film` which parts of the image have been completely sampled, although note that because the image reconstruction filter has nonzero extent, the parts of the image where sampling is complete are not exactly the same as the pixel regions in the output image that are complete.

❶ 8.3 Modify pbrt to create images where each pixel encodes the amount of time spent computing the sample values inside that pixel's filter extent. (A one-pixel-wide box filter is probably the most useful filter for this exercise.) Render images of a variety of scenes with this technique. What insight about the system's performance do the resulting images bring?

❷ 8.4 Replace the random dither computation with a different dithering algorithm such as Bayer matrices or Floyd-Steinberg error diffusion. Construct and render a scene where the differences between these techniques is appreciable.

❷ 8.5 One of the advantages of the linearity assumption in radiometry is that the final image of a scene is the same as the sum of individual images that account for each light source's contribution (assuming a floating-point image file format is used that doesn't clip pixel radiance values). An implication of this property is that if a renderer creates a separate image for each light source, it is possible to write interactive lighting design tools that make it possible to quickly see the effects of scaling the contributions of individual lights in the scene without needing to rerender it from scratch. Instead, a light's individual image can be scaled and the final image regenerated by summing all of the light images again. (This technique was first applied for opera lighting design by Dorsey, Sillion, and Greenberg (1991).) Modify pbrt to output a separate image for each of the lights in the scene and write an interactive lighting design tool that uses them in this manner.

❸ 8.6   Image-based rendering is the general name for a set of techniques that use one or more images of a scene to synthesize new images from viewpoints different than the original ones. One such approach is lightfield rendering, where a set of images from a densely spaced set of positions is used (Levoy and Hanrahan 1996; Gortler et al. 1996). Read these two papers on lightfields and modify pbrt to directly generate lightfields of scenes, without requiring that the renderer be run multiple times, once for each camera position. It will probably be necessary to write a specialized Camera, Sampler, and Film to do this. Also, write an interactive lightfield viewer that loads lightfields generated by your implementation and generates new views of the scene.

❷ 8.7   Implement a tone reproduction operator for low-light environments (e.g., Ferwerda et al. 1996, 1997) and compare its results to the tone reproduction operators described in this chapter.

❷ 8.8   Modify the bloom filter to use a separable kernel, and change the implementation to take advantage of this property to do the filtering with two one-dimensional filtering steps. Because the bloom filter has a wide extent, this approach should be substantially more efficient than the current implementation. Measure the performance improvement with your implementation. Do the halos from the separable filter look as good as the ones from the current filter?

❸ 8.9   The bloom effect implemented in this chapter works reasonably well, but is completely ad hoc. Read the paper by Spencer et al. (1995), which describes glare and bloom algorithms based on a more detailed model of how light scatters in the human eye, and implement their algorithms as a tone reproduction operator.

❸ 8.10   Deep frame buffers: Rather than just storing spectral values and an alpha channel in an image, it's often useful to store additional information about the objects in the scene that were visible at each pixel. See, for example, the SIGGRAPH papers by Perlin (1985a) and Saito and Takahashi (1990). For example, if the 3D position, surface normal, and BRDF of the object at each pixel is stored, then the scene can be efficiently rerendered after moving the light sources (Gershbein and Hanrahan 2000). Alternatively, if each sample stores information about all of the objects visible along its camera ray, rather than just the first one, new images from shifted viewpoints can be rerendered (Shade et al. (1998). Investigate representations for deep frame buffers and algorithms that use them; extend pbrt to support the creation of images like these and develop tools that operate on them.

● 8.11   Rushmeier and Ward (1994) have suggested a nonlinear filter function that
         works well for reducing the visual impact of noise in images generated with
         Monte Carlo light transport algorithms. Their observation was that if a single
         sample is substantially brighter than all of the samples around it, then it is likely
         that the other nearby samples should also have detected the bright feature that
         caused the spike of brightness. If the standard filters described in Chapter 7 are
         used to reconstruct the final image, the spike contributes to a small number of
         pixels, resulting in a visually unappealing bright area in the final image.

         In an effort to reduce noise without changing the overall brightness of the
         image, the Rushmeier-Ward filter widens the extent of the filter function for
         a given sample depending on the brightness of that sample compared to the
         brightness of the nearby samples. For example, if the base filter being used was
         a box filter with extent such that nine samples contributed to each pixel, if any
         of the nine samples contributed more than 25% to the final pixel value, it would
         be detected as a spike and a wider filter extent would be used for it, dispersing
         its energy to a wider set of pixels in the final image.

         However, the filters in `ImageFilm` must be *linear*—the value of the filter func-
         tion is determined solely by the position of the sample with respect to the pixel
         position, and the value of the sample has no impact on the value of the filter
         function. (In a similar manner, it's not currently possible to implement a me-
         dian filter in `pbrt`, where the median of the sample values around each pixel
         is used. The median filter is also effective at eliminating noise.) Because that
         film implementation assumes that filters are linear, and because it doesn't store
         sample values after adding their contribution to the image, implementing the
         Rushmeier-Ward filter in `pbrt` is not straightforward. Investigate approaches
         for modifying that implementation so that this filter can be used. Is it possible
         to support filters like these without storing all of the image samples (which may
         take a large amount of memory for high-resolution images with many sam-
         ples)? Ideas from Exercise 8.2 may be useful to apply here.

CHAPTER NINE

0⑨ REFLECTION MODELS

This chapter defines a set of classes for describing the way that light scatters at surfaces. Recall that in Section 5.4 we introduced the bidirectional reflectance distribution function (BRDF) abstraction to describe light reflection at a surface, the BTDF to describe transmission at a surface, and the BSDF to encompass both of these effects. In this chapter, we will start by defining a generic interface to these surface reflection and transmission functions. Scattering from realistic surfaces is often best described as a mixture of multiple BRDFs and BTDFs; in Chapter 10, we will introduce a BSDF object that combines multiple BRDFs and BTDFs to represent overall scattering from the surface. The current chapter also sidesteps the issue of reflection and transmission properties that vary over the surface; the texture classes of Chapter 11 will address that problem.

Surface reflection models come from a number of sources:

1. *Measured data:* Reflection distribution properties of many real-world surfaces have been measured in laboratories. This data may be used directly in tabular form or to compute coefficients for a set of basis functions.
2. *Phenomenological models:* Equations that attempt to describe the qualitative properties of real-world surfaces can be remarkably effective at mimicking them. These types of BSDFs can be particularly easy to use, since they tend to have intuitive parameters that modify their behavior (e.g., "roughness"). Many of the reflection functions used in computer graphics fall into this category.

3. *Simulation:* Sometimes, low-level information is known about the composition of a surface. For example, we might know that a paint is comprised of colored particles of some average size suspended in a medium, or that a particular fabric is comprised of two types of thread, each with known reflectance properties. In these cases, light scattering from the microgeometry can be simulated to generate reflection data. This simulation can be done either during rendering or as a preprocess, after which it may be fit to a set of basis functions for use during rendering.

4. *Physical (wave) optics:* Some reflection models have been derived using a detailed model of light, treating it as a wave and computing the solution to Maxwell's equations to find how it scatters from a surface with known properties. These models tend to be computationally expensive, however, and usually aren't appreciably more accurate than models based on geometric optics.

5. *Geometric optics:* As with simulation approaches, if the surface's low-level scattering and geometric properties are known, then closed-form reflection models can sometimes be derived directly from these descriptions. Geometric optics makes modeling light's interaction with the surface more tractable, since complex wave effects like polarization are ignored.

In this chapter, we will describe implementations of reflection models based on measured data, phenomenological models, and geometric optics. The "Further Reading" section at the end of this chapter gives pointers to a variety of other models.

Before we define the relevant interfaces, a brief review of how they fit into the overall system is in order. The integrator classes defined in Chapter 16 are responsible for determining which surface is first visible along a ray. Once the hit point is found, the integrator calls the surface shader that is bound to the surface. The surface shader is a short procedure in the Material class that is responsible for deciding what the BSDF is at a particular point on the surface (see Chapter 10); it returns a BSDF object that holds BRDFs and BTDFs that it has allocated and initialized for that point. The integrator then uses the BSDF to compute the scattered light at the point, based on the incoming illumination from the light sources in the scene.

Basic Terminology

In order to be able to compare the visual appearance of different reflection models, we will introduce some basic terminology for describing reflection from surfaces.

Reflection from surfaces can be split into four broad categories: *diffuse*, *glossy specular*, *perfect specular*, and *retro-reflective* (Figure 9.1). Most real surfaces exhibit reflection that is a mixture of these four types. Diffuse surfaces scatter light equally in all directions. Although a perfectly diffuse surface isn't physically realizable, examples of near-diffuse surfaces include dull chalkboards and matte paint. Glossy specular surfaces such as plastic or high-gloss paint scatter light preferentially in a set of reflected directions—they show blurry reflections of other objects. Perfect specular surfaces scatter incident light in a single outgoing direction. Mirrors and glass are examples of perfect specular surfaces. Finally, retro-reflective surfaces like velvet or the Earth's moon scatter light primarily

BSDF 462
Material 468

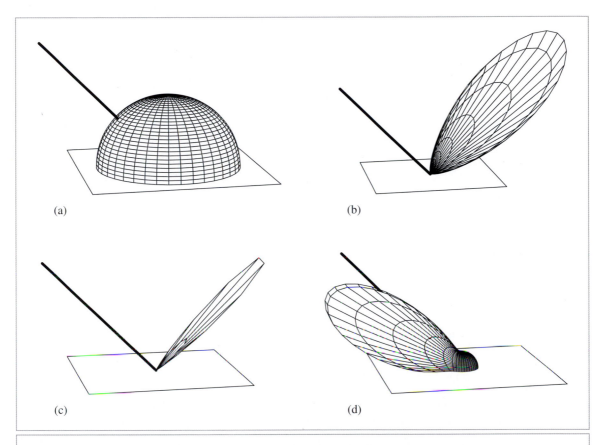

(a)

(b)

(c)

(d)

Figure 9.1: Reflection from a surface can be generally categorized by the distribution of reflected light from an incident direction (heavy lines): (a) diffuse, (b) glossy specular, (c) perfect specular, and (d) retro-reflective distributions.

back along the incident direction. Images throughout this chapter will show the differences between these various types of reflection when used in rendered scenes.

Given a particular category of reflection, the reflectance distribution function may be *isotropic* or *anisotropic*. Most objects are isotropic: if you choose a point on the surface and rotate it around its normal axis around that point, the amount of light reflected doesn't change. In contrast, anisotropic materials reflect different amounts of light as you rotate them in this way. Examples of anisotropic surfaces include brushed metal, phonographic records, and compact disks.

Geometric Setting

Reflection computations in pbrt are evaluated in a reflection coordinate system where the two tangent vectors and the normal vector at the point being shaded are aligned with

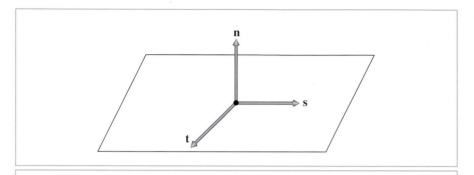

Figure 9.2: The Basic BSDF Interface Setting. The shading coordinate system is defined by the orthonormal basis vectors $(\mathbf{s}, \mathbf{t}, \mathbf{n})$. We will orient these vectors such that they lie along the x, y, and z axes in this coordinate system. Direction vectors ω in world space are transformed into the shading coordinate system before any of the BRDF or BTDF methods are called.

the x, y, and z axes, respectively (Figure 9.2). All direction vectors passed to and returned from the BRDF and BTDF routines will be defined with respect to this coordinate system. It is important to understand this coordinate system in order to understand the BRDF and BTDF implementations in this chapter.

The shading coordinate system also gives a frame for expressing directions in spherical coordinates (θ, ϕ); the angle θ is measured from the given direction to the z axis, and ϕ is the angle formed with the x axis after projection of the direction onto the xy plane. Given a direction vector ω in this coordinate system, it is easy to compute quantities like the cosine of the angle that it forms with the normal direction:

$$\cos \theta = (\mathbf{n} \cdot \omega) = ((0, 0, 1) \cdot \omega) = \omega_z.$$

We will provide a utility function to compute this value; its use serves to make the intent of BRDF and BTDF implementations more clear.

⟨*BSDF Inline Functions*⟩ ≡
```
inline float CosTheta(const Vector &w) { return w.z; }
```

Some additional algebra shows that the value of $\sin \theta$ is

$$\sin \theta = \sqrt{1 - \omega_z^2}.$$

⟨*BSDF Inline Functions*⟩ + ≡
```
inline float SinTheta(const Vector &w) {
    return sqrtf(max(0.f, 1.f - w.z*w.z));
}
```

Vector 47

The value of $\sin^2 \theta$ can be computed using the trigonometric identity $\sin^2 \theta + \cos^2 \theta = 1$.

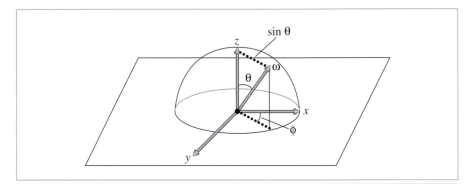

Figure 9.3: The value of $\sin\theta$ can be found by computing the length of the dotted line, which is the magnitude of the xy components of the vector. (Recall that the length of the vector ω is one.) The $\sin\phi$ and $\cos\phi$ values can be computed using the circular coordinate equations $x = r\cos\phi$ and $y = r\sin\phi$, where r, the length of the dashed line, is equal to $\sin\theta$.

⟨*BSDF Inline Functions*⟩+≡

```
inline float SinTheta2(const Vector &w) {
    return 1.f - CosTheta(w)*CosTheta(w);
}
```

We can similarly use the shading coordinate system to simplify the calculations for the sine and cosine of the ϕ angle (Figure 9.3). In the plane of the point being shaded, the vector ω has coordinates (x, y), which are given by $r\cos\phi$ and $r\sin\phi$, respectively. The radius r is $\sin\theta$, so

$$\cos\phi = \frac{x}{r} = \frac{x}{\sin\theta}$$
$$\sin\phi = \frac{y}{r} = \frac{y}{\sin\theta}.$$

⟨*BSDF Inline Functions*⟩+≡

```
inline float CosPhi(const Vector &w) {
    return w.x / SinTheta(w);
}
inline float SinPhi(const Vector &w) {
    return w.y / SinTheta(w);
}
```

Another convention we will follow is that the incident light direction ω_i and the outgoing viewing direction ω_o will both be normalized and outward facing after being transformed into the local coordinate system at the surface. By convention, the surface normal **n** always points to the "outside" of the object, which makes it easy to determine if light is entering or exiting transmissive objects: if the incident light direction ω_i is in the same hemisphere as **n**, then light is entering; otherwise it is exiting.

Therefore, one detail to keep in mind is that the normal may be on the opposite side of the surface than one or both of the ω_i and ω_o direction vectors. Unlike many other renderers, pbrt does not flip the normal to lie on the same side as ω_o. Therefore, it is important that BRDFs and BTDFs be implemented so that they don't expect otherwise.

Furthermore, note that the local coordinate system used for shading may not be exactly the same as the coordinate system returned by the Shape::Intersect() routines from Chapter 3; they can be modified between intersection and shading to achieve effects like bump mapping. See Chapter 10 for examples of this kind of modification.

One final detail to be aware of when reading this chapter is that BRDF and BTDF implementations should not concern themselves with whether ω_i and ω_o lie in the same hemisphere. For example, although a reflective BRDF should in principle detect if the incident direction is above the surface and the outgoing direction is below and always return no reflection in this case, here we will expect the reflection function to instead compute and return the amount of light reflected using the appropriate formulas for their reflection model, ignoring the detail that they are not in the same hemisphere. Higher-level code in pbrt will ensure that only reflective or transmissive scattering routines are evaluated as appropriate. The value of this convention will be explained in Section 10.1.

9.1 BASIC INTERFACE

We will first define the interface for the individual BRDF and BTDF functions. BRDFs and BTDFs share a common base class, BxDF, which defines the basic interface that they implement. Because both have the exact same interface, sharing the same base class reduces repeated code and allows some parts of the system to work with BxDFs generically without distinguishing between BRDFs and BTDFs.

⟨*BxDF Declarations*⟩ ≡
```
class COREDLL BxDF {
public:
    ⟨BxDF Interface 415⟩
    ⟨BxDF Public Data 415⟩
};
```

The BSDF class, which will be introduced in Section 10.1, holds a collection of BxDF objects that together describe the scattering at a point on a surface. Although we are hiding the implementation details of the BxDF behind a common interface for reflective and transmissive materials, some of the light transport algorithms in Chapter 16 will need to distinguish between these two types. Therefore, all BxDFs have a BxDF::type member that holds flags from BxDFType. For each BxDF, the flags should have exactly one of BSDF_REFLECTION or BSDF_TRANSMISSION set, and exactly one of the diffuse, glossy, and specular flags. Note that there is no retro-reflective flag; retro-reflection is treated as glossy reflection in this categorization.

⟨*BSDF Declarations*⟩ ≡
```
enum BxDFType {
    BSDF_REFLECTION    = 1<<0,
    BSDF_TRANSMISSION = 1<<1,
    BSDF_DIFFUSE       = 1<<2,
    BSDF_GLOSSY        = 1<<3,
    BSDF_SPECULAR      = 1<<4,
    BSDF_ALL_TYPES         = BSDF_DIFFUSE |
                             BSDF_GLOSSY |
                             BSDF_SPECULAR,
    BSDF_ALL_REFLECTION    = BSDF_REFLECTION |
                             BSDF_ALL_TYPES,
    BSDF_ALL_TRANSMISSION = BSDF_TRANSMISSION |
                             BSDF_ALL_TYPES,
    BSDF_ALL               = BSDF_ALL_REFLECTION |
                             BSDF_ALL_TRANSMISSION
};
```

⟨*BxDF Public Data*⟩ ≡   **414**
```
const BxDFType type;
```

⟨*BxDF Interface*⟩ ≡   **414**
```
BxDF(BxDFType t) : type(t) { }
```

The `MatchesFlags()` utility method determines if the `BxDF` matches the user-supplied flags:

⟨*BxDF Interface*⟩+≡   **414**
```
bool MatchesFlags(BxDFType flags) const {
    return (type & flags) == type;
}
```

The key method that BxDFs provide is the `BxDF::f()` method. It returns the value of the distribution function for the given pair of directions. This interface implicitly assumes that light in different wavelengths is *decoupled*—energy at one wavelength will not be reflected at a different wavelength. Thus, fluorescent materials are not supported. By making this assumption, the effect of the reflection function can be represented directly with a `Spectrum`.

⟨*BxDF Interface*⟩+≡   **414**
```
virtual Spectrum f(const Vector &wo, const Vector &wi) const = 0;
```

Not all BxDFs can be evaluated with this method. For example, perfectly specular objects like a mirror, glass, or water only scatter light from a single incident direction in a single outgoing direction. Such BxDFs are best described with delta distributions that are zero except for the single direction where light is scattered.

These BxDFs need special handling in pbrt, so we will also provide the method BxDF:: Sample_f(). This method is used both for handling scattering that is described by delta distributions as well as for randomly sampling directions from BxDFs that scatter light along multiple directions; this second application will be explained in Chapter 15. BxDF::Sample_f() computes the direction of incident light ω_i given an outgoing direction ω_o and returns the value of the BxDF for the given pair of directions. For delta distributions, it is necessary for the BxDF to choose the incident light direction in this way, since the caller has no chance of generating the appropriate ω_i direction.[1] The u1, u2, and pdf parameters aren't needed for delta distribution BxDFs, so they will be explained later when we provide implementations of this method for nonspecular reflection functions.

⟨*BxDF Interface*⟩+≡   414
```
virtual Spectrum Sample_f(const Vector &wo, Vector *wi,
    float u1, float u2, float *pdf) const;
```

9.1.1 REFLECTANCE

It can be useful to take the aggregate behavior of the 4D BRDF or BTDF, defined as a function over pairs of directions, and reduce it to a 2D function over a single direction, or even to a constant value that describes its overall scattering behavior.

The *hemispherical-directional reflectance* is a 2D function that gives the total reflection in a given direction due to constant illumination over the hemisphere, or, equivalently, total reflection over the hemisphere due to light from a given direction.[2] It is defined as

$$\rho_{hd}(\omega_o) = \frac{1}{\pi} \int_{\mathcal{H}^2(n)} f_r(p, \omega_o, \omega_i) |\cos \theta_i| \, d\omega_i.$$

The BxDF::rho() method computes the reflectance function ρ_{hd}. Some BxDFs can compute this value in closed form, although most use Monte Carlo integration to compute an approximation to it. For those BxDFs, the nSamples and samples parameters affect the behavior of the Monte Carlo algorithm used; they are explained in Section 15.5.5.

⟨*BxDF Interface*⟩+≡   414
```
virtual Spectrum rho(const Vector &wo, int nSamples = 16,
                    float *samples = NULL) const;
```

---

[1]   Delta distributions in reflection functions have some additional subtle implications for light transport algorithms. Sections 15.5.4 and 16.2.5 describe the issues in detail.

[2]   The fact that these two quantities are equal is due to the reciprocity of real-world reflection functions. If we had a nonphysically based BRDF that did not obey reciprocity, this assumption, along with many others in pbrt, would break down.

The *hemispherical-hemispherical reflectance* of a surface, denoted by ρ_{hh}, is a constant spectral value that gives the fraction of incident light reflected by a surface when the incident light is the same from all directions. It is

$$\rho_{hh} = \frac{1}{\pi} \int_{\mathcal{H}^2(\mathbf{n})} \int_{\mathcal{H}^2(\mathbf{n})} f_r(\mathrm{p}, \omega_o, \omega_i) |\cos \theta_o \cos \theta_i| d\omega_o d\omega_i.$$

We overload the BxDF::rho() method to compute ρ_{hh} if no direction ω_o is provided. The remaining parameters are again used when computing a Monte Carlo estimate, if appropriate.

⟨*BxDF Interface*⟩+≡   **414**
```
    virtual Spectrum rho(int nSamples = 16, float *samples = NULL) const;
```

9.1.2 BRDF→BTDF ADAPTER

It's handy to define an adapter class that makes it easy to reuse an already-defined BRDF class as a BTDF, especially for phenomenological models that may be equally plausible models of transmission. The BRDFToBTDF class takes a BRDF's pointer in the constructor and uses it to implement a BTDF. In particular, doing so involves forwarding method calls on to the BRDF, as well as switching the ω_i direction to lie in the other hemisphere.

⟨*BxDF Declarations*⟩+≡
```
    class COREDLL BRDFToBTDF : public BxDF {
    public:
        ⟨BRDFToBTDF Public Methods 417⟩
    private:
        BxDF *brdf;
    };
```

The constructor for the adapter class is simple. It simply switches the reflection and transmission flags of the BxDF::type member.

⟨*BRDFToBTDF Public Methods*⟩≡   **417**
```
    BRDFToBTDF(BxDF *b)
        : BxDF(BxDFType(b->type ^ (BSDF_REFLECTION | BSDF_TRANSMISSION))) {
        brdf = b;
    }
```

The adapter needs to convert an incoming vector to the corresponding vector in the opposite hemisphere. Fortunately, this is a simple calculation in the shading coordinate system, just requiring negation of the vector's z coordinate.

⟨*BRDFToBTDF Public Methods*⟩+≡   417
```
static Vector otherHemisphere(const Vector &w) {
    return Vector(w.x, w.y, -w.z);
}
```

The `BRDFToBTDF::otherHemisphere()` method is used to reflect a ray into the other hemisphere before calling the BRDF's `BxDF::rho()`, `BxDF::f()`, and `BxDF::Sample_f()` methods.

⟨*BRDFToBTDF Public Methods*⟩+≡   417
```
Spectrum rho(const Vector &w, int nSamples, float *samples) const {
    return brdf->rho(otherHemisphere(w), nSamples, samples);
}
Spectrum rho(int nSamples, float *samples) const {
    return brdf->rho(nSamples, samples);
}
```

⟨*BxDF Method Definitions*⟩≡
```
Spectrum BRDFToBTDF::f(const Vector &wo, const Vector &wi) const {
    return brdf->f(wo, otherHemisphere(wi));
}
```

⟨*BxDF Method Definitions*⟩+≡
```
Spectrum BRDFToBTDF::Sample_f(const Vector &wo, Vector *wi,
                             float u1, float u2, float *pdf) const {
    Spectrum f = brdf->Sample_f(wo, wi, u1, u2, pdf);
    *wi = otherHemisphere(*wi);
    return f;
}
```

9.2 SPECULAR REFLECTION AND TRANSMISSION

The behavior of light at perfectly smooth surfaces is relatively easy to characterize analytically using both the physical and geometric optics models. These surfaces exhibit perfect specular reflection and transmission of incident light; for a given ω_i direction, all light is scattered in a single outgoing direction ω_o. For specular reflection, this direction is the outgoing direction that makes the same angle with the normal as the incoming direction:

$$\theta_i = \theta_o.$$

For transmission, the outgoing direction is given by *Snell's law*, which relates the angle θ_t between the transmitted direction and the surface normal **n** to the angle θ_i between the incident ray and the surface normal **n**. (One of the exercises at the end of this chapter is to derive Snell's law using Fermat's principle from optics.) Snell's law is based on the *index of refraction* for the medium that the incident ray is in and the index of refraction for the medium it is entering. The index of refraction describes how much more slowly light travels in a particular medium than in a vacuum. We will use the Greek letter η, pronounced "eta," to denote the index of refraction. Snell's law is

$$\eta_i \, \sin \theta_i = \eta_t \, \sin \theta_t.$$

In general, the index of refraction varies with the wavelength of light. Thus, incident light generally scatters in multiple directions at the boundary between two different media, an effect known as *dispersion*. This effect can be seen when incident white light is split into spectral components by a prism. Common practice in graphics is to ignore this wavelength dependence, since this effect is generally not crucial for visual accuracy and ignoring it simplifies light transport calculations substantially. Alternatively, the paths of multiple beams of light (e.g., at a series of discrete wavelengths) can be tracked through the environment in which a dispersive object is found. The "Further Reading" section at the end of this chapter has pointers to more information on these issues.

Figure 9.4 shows the effect when the Killeroo model is rendered with a BRDF describing perfect specular reflection and a BTDF describing specular transmission. Note how refraction through the transmissive object distorts the scene behind it.

9.2.1 FRESNEL REFLECTANCE

In addition to the reflected and transmitted directions, it is also necessary to compute the fraction of incoming light that is reflected or transmitted. In simple ray tracers, these fractions are typically just given as "reflectivity" or "transmissiveness" values, which are uniform over the entire surface. For physical reflection or refraction, however, these terms are view dependent and cannot be captured by constant per-surface scaling amounts. The *Fresnel equations* describe the amount of light reflected from a surface; they are the solution to Maxwell's equations at smooth surfaces.

There are two sets of Fresnel equations: one for *dielectric media* (objects that don't conduct electricity, like glass) and one for *conductors* (like metals). For each of these cases, the Fresnel equations have two forms, depending on the polarization of the incident light. Properly accounting for polarization in rendering is a complex task, and so in pbrt we will make the common assumption that light is unpolarized; that is, it is randomly oriented with respect to the light wave. With this simplifying assumption, the Fresnel reflectance is the average of the squares of the parallel and perpendicular polarization terms.

To compute the Fresnel reflectance of a dielectric, we need to know the indices of refraction for the two media. Table 9.1 has the indices of refraction for a number of dielectric materials. A close approximation to the Fresnel reflectance formulae for dielectrics is

$$r_{\parallel} = \frac{\eta_t \cos \theta_i - \eta_i \cos \theta_t}{\eta_t \cos \theta_i + \eta_i \cos \theta_t}$$

$$r_{\perp} = \frac{\eta_i \cos \theta_i - \eta_t \cos \theta_t}{\eta_i \cos \theta_i + \eta_t \cos \theta_t},$$

(a)

(b)

Figure 9.4: Killeroo model rendered with (a) perfect specular reflection and (b) perfect specular refraction. *Model courtesy headus/Rezard.*

Table 9.1: Indices of refraction for a variety of objects, giving the ratio of the speed of light in a vacuum to the speed of light in the medium. These are generally wavelength-dependent quantities; these values are averages over the visible wavelengths.

Medium	Index of refraction η
Vacuum	1.0
Air at sea level	1.00029
Ice	1.31
Water (20° C)	1.333
Fused quartz	1.46
Glass	1.5–1.6
Sapphire	1.77
Diamond	2.42

where $r_{\parallel}$ is the Fresnel reflectance for parallel polarized light and $r_{\perp}$ is the reflectance for perpendicular polarized light. η_i and η_t are the indices of refraction for the incident and transmitted media, and ω_o and ω_t are the incident and transmitted directions, where ω_t was computed with Snell's law.

The cosine terms should all be greater than or equal to zero; for the purposes of computing these values, the geometric normal should be flipped to be on the same side as ω_i and then ω_t.

For unpolarized light, the Fresnel reflectance is

$$F_r = \frac{1}{2}(r_{\parallel}^2 + r_{\perp}^2).$$

The function FrDiel() computes the Fresnel reflection formula for dielectric materials and circularly polarized light. The quantities $\cos\theta_i$ and $\cos\theta_t$ are passed in with the variables cosi and cost.

⟨*BxDF Utility Functions*⟩ ≡
```
COREDLL Spectrum FrDiel(float cosi, float cost,
                        const Spectrum &etai,
                        const Spectrum &etat) {
    Spectrum Rparl = ((etat * cosi) - (etai * cost)) /
                     ((etat * cosi) + (etai * cost));
    Spectrum Rperp = ((etai * cosi) - (etat * cost)) /
                     ((etai * cosi) + (etat * cost));
    return (Rparl*Rparl + Rperp*Rperp) / 2.f;
}
```

COREDLL 904
FrDiel() 421
Spectrum 230

Due to conservation of energy, the energy transmitted by a dielectric is $1 - F_r$.

Table 9.2: Representative Measured Values of η and k for a Few Conductors.

Object	η	k
Gold	0.370	2.820
Silver	0.177	3.638
Copper	0.617	2.63
Steel	2.485	3.433

Unlike dielectrics, conductors don't transmit light, but some of the incident light is absorbed by the material and turned into heat. The Fresnel formula for conductors tells how much is reflected. It depends on the additional quantities η, the index of refraction of the conductor, and k, its *absorption coefficient*. Values of η and k for a few conductors are given in Table 9.2. As with the index of refraction for dielectrics, these quantities are wavelength dependent, but are given as averages here.

A widely used approximation to the Fresnel reflectance for conductors is

$$r_\parallel^2 = \frac{(\eta^2 + k^2)\cos\theta_i^2 - 2\eta\cos\theta_i + 1}{(\eta^2 + k^2)\cos\theta_i^2 + 2\eta\cos\theta_i + 1} \qquad (9.1)$$

$$r_\perp^2 = \frac{(\eta^2 + k^2) - 2\eta\cos\theta_i + \cos\theta_i^2}{(\eta^2 + k^2) + 2\eta\cos\theta_i + \cos\theta_i^2}. \qquad (9.2)$$

⟨*BxDF Utility Functions*⟩+≡
```
COREDLL Spectrum FrCond(float cosi, const Spectrum &eta,
                       const Spectrum &k) {
    Spectrum tmp = (eta*eta + k*k) * cosi*cosi;
    Spectrum Rparl2 = (tmp - (2.f * eta * cosi) + 1) /
                      (tmp + (2.f * eta * cosi) + 1);
    Spectrum tmp_f = eta*eta + k*k;
    Spectrum Rperp2 =
        (tmp_f - (2.f * eta * cosi) + cosi*cosi) /
        (tmp_f + (2.f * eta * cosi) + cosi*cosi);
    return (Rparl2 + Rperp2) / 2.f;
}
```

For many conductors, values for η and/or k aren't known because much less work has gone into measuring these values for conductors than for dielectrics. Two approximation methods have been applied in graphics to find plausible values for these quantities. Both assume that the reflectance of the object has been measured at normal incidence: the viewer and the light are both looking directly down on the surface. By fixing the value of either η or k and substituting into the Fresnel conductor formula, it is possible

COREDLL 904
Spectrum 230

to determine the other value so that the proper reflectance is computed for normal incidence (Cook and Torrance 1982).

The first version of this approach finds an approximate value of η, assuming that the absorption coefficient is equal to zero. If $k = 0$ (assumed) and $\cos \theta_i = 1$ (normal incidence), then Equations (9.1) and (9.2) both simplify to

$$r_{\parallel}^2 = r_{\perp}^2 = \frac{\eta^2 - 2\eta + 1}{\eta^2 + 2\eta + 1} = \left(\frac{\eta - 1}{\eta + 1}\right)^2.$$

Since the Fresnel reflectance F_r is known for normal incidence, we can solve for η, giving

$$\eta = \frac{1 + \sqrt{F_r}}{1 - \sqrt{F_r}}.$$

⟨*BxDF Utility Functions*⟩+≡
```
COREDLL Spectrum FresnelApproxEta(const Spectrum &Fr) {
    Spectrum reflectance = Fr.Clamp(0.f, .999f);
    return (Spectrum(1.) + reflectance.Sqrt()) /
           (Spectrum(1.) - reflectance.Sqrt());
}
```

We can perform the same process to approximate the absorption coefficient k, assuming that $\eta = 1$. In this case, the Fresnel equations simplify to

$$r_{\parallel}^2 = r_{\perp}^2 = \frac{k^2}{k^2 + 4},$$

and we can easily solve for k,

$$k = 2\sqrt{\frac{F_r}{1 - F_r}}.$$

⟨*BxDF Utility Functions*⟩+≡
```
COREDLL Spectrum FresnelApproxK(const Spectrum &Fr) {
    Spectrum reflectance = Fr.Clamp(0.f, .999f);
    return 2.f * (reflectance / (Spectrum(1.) - reflectance)).Sqrt();
}
```

For convenience, we will define an abstract Fresnel class that provides an interface for computing Fresnel reflection coefficients. The FresnelConductor and FresnelDielectric implementations of this interface help simplify the implementation of subsequent BRDFs that may need to support both forms.

⟨*BxDF Declarations*⟩+≡
```
class COREDLL Fresnel {
public:
    ⟨Fresnel Interface 424⟩
};
```

The only method provided by the Fresnel interface is Fresnel::Evaluate(). Given the cosine of the angle made by the incoming direction and the surface normal, it returns the amount of light reflected by the surface.

⟨*Fresnel Interface*⟩≡   424
```
virtual Spectrum Evaluate(float cosi) const = 0;
```

Fresnel Conductors

⟨*BxDF Declarations*⟩+≡
```
class COREDLL FresnelConductor : public Fresnel {
public:
    ⟨FresnelConductor Public Methods 424⟩
private:
    ⟨FresnelConductor Private Data 424⟩
};
```

The FresnelConductor constructor simply stores the given index of refraction η and absorption coefficient k:

⟨*FresnelConductor Private Data*⟩≡   424
```
Spectrum eta, k;
```

⟨*FresnelConductor Public Methods*⟩≡   424
```
FresnelConductor(const Spectrum &e, const Spectrum &kk)
    : eta(e), k(kk) {
}
```

The evaluation routine for FresnelConductor is also simple; it just calls the FrCond() function defined earlier. Note that it takes the absolute value of cosi before calling FrCond(), since FrCond() expects that the cosine will be measured with respect to the normal on the same side of the surface as ω_i, or equivalently that the absolute value of $\cos\theta_i$ should be used.

⟨*BxDF Method Definitions*⟩+≡
```
Spectrum FresnelConductor::Evaluate(float cosi) const {
    return FrCond(fabsf(cosi), eta, k);
}
```

Fresnel Dielectrics

⟨*BxDF Declarations*⟩+≡
```
class COREDLL FresnelDielectric : public Fresnel {
public:
    ⟨FresnelDielectric Public Methods 425⟩
private:
    ⟨FresnelDielectric Private Data 425⟩
};
```

The constructor for FresnelDielectric simply stores the indices of refraction on the two sides of the surface, η_i and η_t:

⟨*FresnelDielectric Private Data*⟩ ≡   **425**
```
float eta_i, eta_t;
```

⟨*FresnelDielectric Public Methods*⟩ ≡   **425**
```
FresnelDielectric(float ei, float et) {
    eta_i = ei;
    eta_t = et;
}
```

⟨*BxDF Method Definitions*⟩+≡
```
Spectrum FresnelDielectric::Evaluate(float cosi) const {
    ⟨Compute Fresnel reflectance for dielectric 425⟩
}
```

Evaluating the Fresnel formula for dielectric media is a bit more complicated than for conductors. First, it is necessary to determine if the incident direction is on the outside of the medium or inside it, so that the two indices of refraction can be interpreted appropriately. Next, Snell's law is applied to compute the sine of the angle between the transmitted direction and the surface normal. Finally, the cosine of this angle is found using the identity $\sin^2 \theta + \cos^2 \theta = 1$.

⟨*Compute Fresnel reflectance for dielectric*⟩ ≡   **425**
```
cosi = Clamp(cosi, -1.f, 1.f);
⟨Compute indices of refraction for dielectric 426⟩
⟨Compute sint using Snell's law 426⟩
if (sint > 1.) {
    ⟨Handle total internal reflection 426⟩
}
else {
    float cost = sqrtf(max(0.f, 1.f - sint*sint));
    return FrDiel(fabsf(cosi), cost, ei, et);
}
```

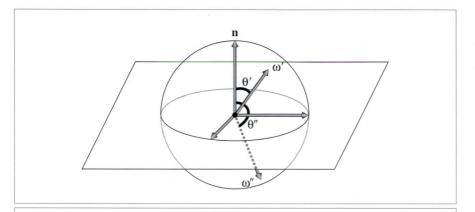

Figure 9.5: The cosine of the angle θ between a direction ω and the geometric surface normal indicates whether the direction is pointing outside the surface (in the same hemisphere as the normal) or inside the surface. In the standard reflection coordinate system, this test just requires checking the z component of the direction vector. Here, ω' is in the upper hemisphere, with a positive-valued cosine, while ω'' is in the lower hemisphere.

The sign of the cosine of the incident angle indicates on which side of the medium the incident ray lies (Figure 9.5). If the cosine is between 0 and 1, the ray is on the outside, and if the cosine is between -1 and 0, the ray is on the inside. The variables ei and et are set such that ei has the index of refraction of the incident medium.

⟨*Compute indices of refraction for dielectric*⟩ ≡   425
```
bool entering = cosi > 0.;
float ei = eta_i, et = eta_t;
if (!entering)
    swap(ei, et);
```

Once the indices of refraction are assigned, it is straightforward to compute $\sin \theta_t$ using Snell's law:

⟨*Compute* sint *using Snell's law*⟩ ≡   425
```
float sint = ei/et * sqrtf(max(0.f, 1.f - cosi*cosi));
```

When light is traveling from one medium to another medium with a lower index of refraction, none of the light at incident angles near grazing passes into the other medium. The largest angle at which this happens is called the *critical angle*; when θ_i is greater than the critical angle, *total internal reflection* occurs, and all of the light is reflected. That case is detected here by a value of $\sin \theta_t$ greater than one; in that case, the Fresnel equations are unnecessary.

⟨*Handle total internal reflection*⟩ ≡   425
```
return 1.;
```

A Special Fresnel Interface

The FresnelNoOp implementation of the Fresnel interface simply returns 100% reflection for all incoming directions. Although this is physically implausible, it is a convenient capability to have available.

⟨*BxDF Declarations*⟩+≡
```
class COREDLL FresnelNoOp : public Fresnel {
public:
    Spectrum Evaluate(float) const { return Spectrum(1.); }
};
```

9.2.2 SPECULAR REFLECTION

We can now implement the SpecularReflection class, which describes physically plausible specular reflection using the Fresnel interface. First, we will derive the BRDF that describes specular reflection. Since the Fresnel equations give the fraction of light reflected, $F_r(\omega_i)$, then we need a BRDF such that

$$L_o(\omega_o) = f_r(\omega_o, \omega_i)L_i(\omega_i) = F_r(\omega_i)\, L_i(\omega_i),$$

where ω_i is the reflection vector for ω_o about the surface normal. (Recall that $\theta_i = \theta_o$ for specular reflection, and therefore $F_r(\omega_o) = F_r(\omega_i)$.)

Such a BRDF can be constructed using the Dirac delta distribution. Recall from Section 7.1 that the delta distribution has the important property that

$$\int f(x)\, \delta(x - x_0)\, dx = f(x_0). \tag{9.3}$$

The delta distribution requires special handling compared to standard functions. In particular, integrals with delta distributions must be evaluated by explicitly accounting for the delta distribution; their values cannot be properly computed without doing so. For example, consider the delta distribution in Equation (9.3): if we tried to evaluate it using the trapezoid rule or some other numerical integration technique, by definition of the delta distribution there would be zero probability that any of the evaluation points x_i would have a nonzero value of $\delta(x_i)$. Rather, we must allow the delta distribution to determine the evaluation point itself. We will see this issue in practice for specular BxDFs as well as for some of the light sources in Chapter 13.

Intuitively, we want the BRDF to be zero everywhere except at the perfect reflection direction, which suggests the use of the delta distribution. A first guess might be to simply use delta functions to restrict the incident direction to the reflection angle ω_r. This would yield a BRDF of

$$f_r(p, \omega_o, \omega_i) = \delta(\omega_i - \omega_r) = \delta(\cos\theta_i - \cos\theta_r)\delta(\phi_o \pm \pi - \phi_r).$$

Although this seems appealing, plugging into the scattering equation, Equation (5.6), reveals a problem:

$$L_o\left(\theta_o, \phi_o\right) = \int_{\mathcal{S}^2} \delta(\cos\theta_i - \cos\theta_r)\delta(\phi_o - \phi_r \pm \pi)L_i\left(\theta_i, \phi_i\right)|\cos\theta_i|\, d\omega_i$$

$$= L_i\left(\theta_r, \phi_r \pm \pi\right)|\cos\theta_i|.$$

This is not correct because it contains an extra factor of $\cos\theta_i$. But we can simply divide out this factor to find the correct BRDF for perfect specular reflection:

$$f_r(p, \omega_o, \omega_i) = F_r(\omega_o)\frac{\delta(\omega_i - R(\omega_o, \mathbf{n}))}{|\cos\theta_i|},$$

where $R(\omega_o, \mathbf{n})$ is the specular reflection vector for ω_o reflected about the surface normal $\mathbf{n}$.

⟨*BxDF Declarations*⟩+≡
```
class COREDLL SpecularReflection : public BxDF {
public:
    ⟨SpecularReflection Public Methods 428⟩
private:
    ⟨SpecularReflection Private Data 428⟩
};
```

The `SpecularReflection` class takes a `Fresnel` object to describe dielectric or conductor Fresnel properties and an additional `Spectrum` object, which is used to scale the reflected color.

⟨*SpecularReflection Public Methods*⟩≡   428
```
SpecularReflection(const Spectrum &r, Fresnel *f)
    : BxDF(BxDFType(BSDF_REFLECTION | BSDF_SPECULAR)),
      R(r), fresnel(f) {
}
```

⟨*SpecularReflection Private Data*⟩≡   428
```
Spectrum R;
Fresnel *fresnel;
```

The rest of the implementation is straightforward. No scattering is returned from `SpecularReflection::f()`, since for an arbitrary pair of directions, the delta function returns no scattering.[3]

⟨*SpecularReflection Public Methods*⟩+≡   428
```
Spectrum f(const Vector &, const Vector &) const {
    return Spectrum(0.);
}
```

---

3   If the caller happened to pass a vector and its perfect mirror direction, this function still returns zero. Although this might be a slightly confusing interface to these reflection functions, we still get the correct answer because reflection functions involving singularities with delta distributions receive special handling by the light transport routines (see Chapter 16).

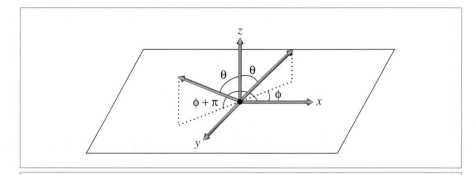

Figure 9.6: Given an incident direction that makes an angle θ with the surface normal and an angle ϕ with the x axis, the reflected ray about the normal makes an angle θ with the normal and $\phi + \pi$ with the x axis. The (x, y, z) coordinates of this direction can be found by scaling the incident direction by $(-1, -1, 1)$.

However, we do implement the `Sample_f()` method, which selects an appropriate direction according to the delta function. It sets the output variable `wi` to be the reflection of the supplied direction `wo` about the surface normal. The `*pdf` value is set to be one, which is the appropriate value for this case, where no Monte Carlo sampling is being done.

⟨*BxDF Method Definitions*⟩+≡
```
Spectrum SpecularReflection::Sample_f(const Vector &wo,
        Vector *wi, float u1, float u2, float *pdf) const {
    ⟨Compute perfect specular reflection direction 429⟩
    *pdf = 1.f;
    return fresnel->Evaluate(CosTheta(wo)) * R / fabsf(CosTheta(*wi));
}
```

The desired direction is the reflection of ω_o around the surface normal. Because all computations take place in a shading coordinate system where the surface normal is $(0, 0, 1)$, we just rotate ω_i by π radians about **n** (Figure 9.6). Recall the transformation matrix from Chapter 2 for a rotation around the z axis; if the angle of rotation is π radians, the matrix is

$$\begin{pmatrix} -1 & 0 & 0 & 0 \\ 0 & -1 & 0 & 0 \\ 0 & 0 & 1 & 0 \\ 0 & 0 & 0 & 1 \end{pmatrix}$$

When a vector is multiplied by this matrix, the effect is just to negate the x and y components.

⟨*Compute perfect specular reflection direction*⟩≡   429
```
*wi = Vector(-wo.x, -wo.y, wo.z);
```

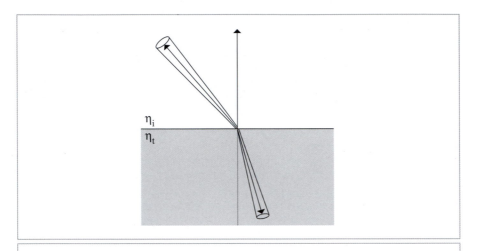

Figure 9.7: The amount of transmitted radiance at the boundary between media with different indices of refraction is scaled by the squared ratio of the two indices of refraction. Intuitively, this can be understood as the result of the radiance's differential solid angle being compressed or expanded as a result of transmission.

9.2.3 SPECULAR TRANSMISSION

We will now derive the BTDF for specular transmission. Snell's law is the basis of the derivation. Not only does it give the direction for the transmitted ray; it can also be used to show that radiance along a ray changes as the ray goes between media with different indices of refraction.

Consider incident radiance arriving at the boundary between two media, with indices of refraction η_i and η_o for the incoming and outgoing media, respectively (Figure 9.7). We use τ to denote the fraction of incident energy that is transmitted to the outgoing direction, as given by the Fresnel equations, so $\tau = 1 - F_r(\omega_i)$. The amount of transmitted differential flux, then, is

$$d\Phi_o = \tau d\Phi_i.$$

If we use the definition of radiance, Equation (5.1), we have

$$(L_o \cos\theta_o dA d\omega_o) = \tau(L_i \cos\theta_i dA d\omega_i).$$

Expanding the solid angles to spherical angles, we have

$$(L_o \cos\theta_o dA \sin\theta_o d\theta_o d\phi_o) = \tau(L_i \cos\theta_i dA \sin\theta_i d\theta_i d\phi_i). \qquad [9.4]$$

We can now differentiate Snell's law with respect to θ, which gives the relation

$$\eta_o \cos\theta_o d\theta_o = \eta_i \cos\theta_i d\theta_i.$$

Rearranging terms, we get

$$\frac{\cos\theta_o d\theta_o}{\cos\theta_i d\theta_i} = \frac{\eta_i}{\eta_o}.$$

Substituting this and Snell's law into Equation (9.4) and simplifying, we have

$$L_o\eta_i^2 d\phi_o = \tau L_i\eta_o^2 d\phi_i.$$

Because $\phi_i = \phi_o + \pi$ and therefore $d\phi_i = d\phi_o$, this gives the final relationship:

$$L_o = \tau L_i \frac{\eta_o^2}{\eta_i^2}. \qquad (9.5)$$

The BTDF for specular transmission is thus

$$f_t(p, \omega_i, \omega_t) = \frac{\eta_o^2}{\eta_i^2}(1 - F_r(\omega_i))\frac{\delta(\omega_i - T(\omega_i, \mathbf{n}))}{|\cos\theta_i|},$$

where $T(\omega_i, \mathbf{n})$ is the specular transmission vector for ω_i about the surface normal $\mathbf{n}$. The $1 - F_r(\omega_i)$ term in this equation corresponds to an easily observed effect: transmission is stronger at near-perpendicular angles. For example, if you look straight down into a clear lake, you can see far into the water, but at grazing angles most of the light is reflected as if from a mirror.

The SpecularTransmission class is almost exactly the same as SpecularReflection except that the sampled direction is the direction for perfect specular transmission. Figure 9.8 shows an image of the Killeroo model using specular reflection and transmission BRDF and BTDF to model glass.

⟨*BxDF Declarations*⟩+≡
```
class COREDLL SpecularTransmission : public BxDF {
public:
    ⟨SpecularTransmission Public Methods  432⟩
private:
    ⟨SpecularTransmission Private Data  432⟩
};
```

The SpecularTransmission constructor stores the two indices of refraction on either side of the surface, as well as a transmission scale factor T.

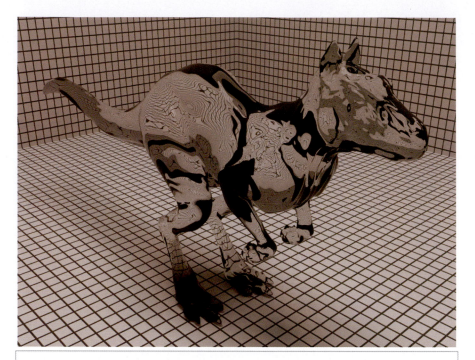

Figure 9.8: When the BRDF for specular reflection and the BTDF for specular transmission are modulated with the Fresnel formula for dielectrics, the realistic angle-dependent variation of the amount of reflection and transmission makes the result more visually convincing. *Model courtesy headus/Rezard.*

⟨*SpecularTransmission Public Methods*⟩ ≡   **431**
```
SpecularTransmission(const Spectrum &t, float ei, float et)
    : BxDF(BxDFType(BSDF_TRANSMISSION | BSDF_SPECULAR)),
      fresnel(ei, et) {
    T = t;
    etai = ei;
    etat = et;
}
```

Because conductors do not transmit light, a FresnelDielectric object is always used to do the Fresnel computations.

⟨*SpecularTransmission Private Data*⟩ ≡   **431**
```
Spectrum T;
float etai, etat;
FresnelDielectric fresnel;
```

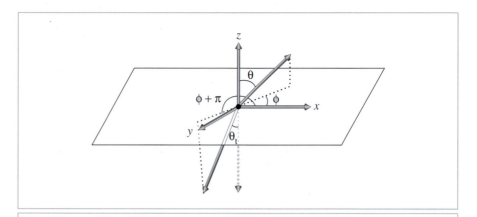

Figure 9.9: The Geometry of Specular Transmission. The specularly transmitted direction makes an angle θ_t with the surface normal. Like specular reflection, the angle it makes with the x axis is π greater than the incident ray's angle.

As in the `SpecularReflection` class, zero is always returned from `SpecularTransmission::f()`, since the BTDF is a scaled delta distribution.

⟨*SpecularTransmission Public Methods*⟩+≡   431
```
Spectrum f(const Vector &, const Vector &) const {
    return Spectrum(0.);
}
```

Figure 9.9 shows the geometry of specular transmission. The incident ray is refracted about the surface normal, with the angle θ_t given by Snell's law.

⟨*BxDF Method Definitions*⟩+≡
```
Spectrum SpecularTransmission::Sample_f(const Vector &wo,
        Vector *wi, float u1, float u2, float *pdf) const {
    ⟨Figure out which η is incident and which is transmitted 434⟩
    ⟨Compute transmitted ray direction 435⟩
    *pdf = 1.f;
    Spectrum F = fresnel.Evaluate(CosTheta(wo));
    return (ei*ei)/(et*et) * (Spectrum(1.)-F) * T /
        fabsf(CosTheta(*wi));
}
```

The method first determines whether the incident ray is entering or exiting the refractive medium. We use the convention that the surface normal, and thus the $(0, 0, 1)$ direction in local reflection space, is oriented such that it points toward the outside of the object. Therefore, if the z component of the ω_i direction is greater than zero, the incident ray is coming from outside of the object.

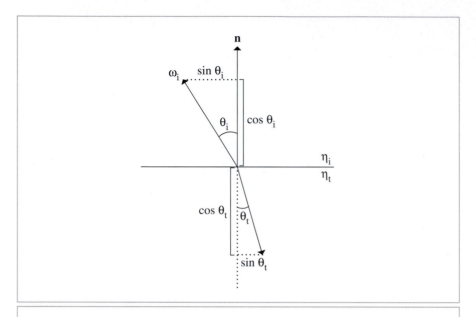

Figure 9.10: Geometry for computing the transmitted direction ω_t from the incident direction ω_i. The $\cos\theta$ terms are equal to the z components of the corresponding direction vectors, and the $\sin\theta$ terms are equal to the xy lengths of the direction vectors.

⟨*Figure out which η is incident and which is transmitted*⟩ ≡   **433**
```
    bool entering = CosTheta(wo) > 0.;
    float ei = etai, et = etat;
    if (!entering)
        swap(ei, et);
```

Figure 9.10 shows the basic setting for computing the transmitted ray direction.

We next compute sini2 and sint2, which are the squares of $\sin\theta_i$ and $\sin\theta_t$, respectively. In the reflection coordinate system, $\sin\theta_i$ is equal to the sum of the squares of the x and y components of ω_o; $\sin^2\theta_t$ can be computed directly from $(\sin\theta_i)^2$ using Snell's law.

We then apply the trigonometric identity $\sin^2\theta + \cos^2\theta = 1$ to compute $\cos\theta_t$ from $\sin\theta_t$; this directly gives us the z component of the transmitted direction. To compute the x and y components, we first mirror ω_i about the normal, as we did for specular reflection, but then scale it by the ratio $\sin\theta_t / \sin\theta_i$ to give it the proper magnitude. From Snell's law, this ratio is just η_i/η_t, which we happen to have computed previously.

⟨*Compute transmitted ray direction*⟩ ≡   **433**
```
float sini2 = SinTheta2(wo);
float eta = ei / et;
float sint2 = eta * eta * sini2;
```
⟨*Handle total internal reflection for transmission* **435**⟩
```
float cost = sqrtf(max(0.f, 1.f - sint2));
if (entering) cost = -cost;
float sintOverSini = eta;
*wi = Vector(sintOverSini * -wo.x, sintOverSini * -wo.y, cost);
```

We need to handle the case of total internal reflection here as well. If the squared value of $\sin\theta_t$ is greater than one, no transmission is possible, so black is returned.

⟨*Handle total internal reflection for transmission*⟩ ≡   **435**
```
if (sint2 > 1.) return 0.;
```

9.3 LAMBERTIAN REFLECTION

One of the simplest BRDFs is the Lambertian model. It models a perfect diffuse surface that scatters incident illumination equally in all directions. Although this reflection model is not physically plausible, it is a good approximation to many real-world surfaces such as matte paint.

⟨*BxDF Declarations*⟩+≡
```
class COREDLL Lambertian : public BxDF {
public:
    ⟨Lambertian Public Methods 435⟩
private:
    ⟨Lambertian Private Data 435⟩
};
```

The Lambertian constructor takes a reflectance SPD R, which gives the fraction of incident light that is scattered. The constructor also precomputes the quantity R/π for convenience in later calculations.

⟨*Lambertian Public Methods*⟩ ≡   **435**
```
Lambertian(const Spectrum &reflectance)
    : BxDF(BxDFType(BSDF_REFLECTION | BSDF_DIFFUSE)),
      R(reflectance), RoverPI(reflectance * INV_PI) {
}
```

⟨*Lambertian Private Data*⟩ ≡   **435**
```
Spectrum R, RoverPI;
```

The reflection distribution function for Lambertian is quite straightforward, since its value is constant. However, the value R/π must be returned, rather than R: the constructor takes the BRDF's reflectance; equating this to the earlier ρ_{hd} integral and solving for the BRDF's value demonstrates why this is the appropriate value to return for the BRDF.

⟨*BxDF Method Definitions*⟩+≡

```
Spectrum Lambertian::f(const Vector &wo, const Vector &wi) const {
    return RoverPI;
}
```

The directional-hemispherical and hemispherical-hemispherical reflectance values for a Lambertian BRDF are trivial to compute analytically, so the derivations are omitted here.

⟨*Lambertian Public Methods*⟩+≡   435

```
Spectrum rho(const Vector &, int, float *) const {
    return R;
}
```

⟨*Lambertian Public Methods*⟩+≡   435

```
Spectrum rho(int, float *) const { return R; }
```

9.4 MICROFACET MODELS

Many geometric-optics-based approaches to modeling surface reflection are based on the idea that rough surfaces can be modeled as a collection of small *microfacets*. A surface comprised of microfacets is essentially a heightfield, where the distribution of faces is described statistically. Figure 9.11 shows cross sections of a relatively rough surface and a much smoother microfacet surface.

Microfacet-based BRDF models work by statistically modeling the scattering of light from a large collection of microfacets. If we assume that the differential area being illuminated, dA, is relatively large compared to the size of individual microfacets, then a large number of microfacets are illuminated, and so their aggregate behavior determines the scattering.

The two main components of microfacet models are an expression for the distribution of facets and a BRDF that describes how light scatters from individual microfacets. Given these, the goal is to derive a closed-form expression giving the BRDF that describes scattering from such a surface. Perfect mirror reflection is typically used for the microfacet BRDF, although the Oren–Nayar model (described in the next section) treats them as Lambertian reflectors.

To compute reflection from such a model, local lighting effects at the microfacet level need to be considered (Figure 9.12). Microfacets may be occluded by another facet, or they may lie in the shadow of a neighboring microfacet, or interreflection may cause

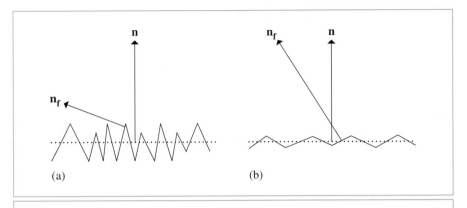

Figure 9.11: Microfacet surface models are often described by a function that gives the distribution of microfacet normals n_f with respect to the surface normal n. (a) The greater the variation of microfacet normals, the rougher the surface is. (b) Smooth surfaces have relatively little variation of microfacet normals.

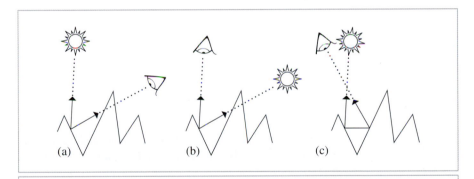

Figure 9.12: Three Important Geometric Effects to Consider with Microfacet Reflection Models. (a) *Masking*: the microfacet of interest isn't visible to the viewer due to occlusion by another microfacet. (b) *Shadowing*: analogously light doesn't reach the microfacet. (c) *Interreflection*: light bounces among the microfacets before reaching the viewer.

a microfacet to reflect more light than predicted by the amount of direct illumination and the low-level microfacet BRDF. A common simplification is to assume that all of the microfacets make up symmetric V-shaped grooves. If this assumption is made, then interreflection with most of the other microfacets can be ignored and only the neighboring microfacet needs to be considered.

Particular microfacet-based BRDF models consider each of these effects with varying degrees of accuracy. The general approach is to make the best approximations possible, while still obtaining an easily evaluated expression.

9.4.1 OREN-NAYAR DIFFUSE REFLECTION

Oren and Nayar (1994) observed that real-world objects tend not to exhibit perfect Lambertian reflection. Specifically, rough surfaces generally appear brighter as the illumination direction approaches the viewing direction. They developed a reflection model that describes rough surfaces as a collection of symmetric V-shaped grooves in an effort to better model effects like these. They further assumed that each individual microfacet (groove face) exhibited perfect Lambertian reflection, and derived a BRDF that models the aggregate reflection of the collection of grooves. The distribution of microfacets was modeled with a Gaussian distribution with a single parameter σ, the standard deviation of the orientation angle.

The resulting model, which accounts for shadowing, masking, and interreflection among the microfacets, does not have a closed-form solution, so they found the following approximation that fit it well:

$$f_r(\omega_i, \omega_o) = \frac{\rho}{\pi} \left(A + B \max(0, \cos(\phi_i - \phi_o)) \sin \alpha \tan \beta \right),$$

where if σ is in radians,

$$A = 1 - \frac{\sigma^2}{2(\sigma^2 + 0.33)}$$

$$B = \frac{0.45\sigma^2}{\sigma^2 + 0.09}$$

$$\alpha = \max(\theta_i, \theta_o)$$

$$\beta = \min(\theta_i, \theta_o).$$

The implementation precomputes and stores the values of the A and B parameters in the constructor to save work in evaluating the BRDF later. Figure 9.13 compares the difference between rendering with ideal diffuse reflection and with the Oren-Nayar model.

⟨*OrenNayar Public Methods*⟩ ≡

```
OrenNayar(const Spectrum &reflectance, float sig)
    : BxDF(BxDFType(BSDF_REFLECTION | BSDF_DIFFUSE)),
      OrenNayarR(reflectance) {
    float sigma = Radians(sig);
    float sigma2 = sigma*sigma;
    A = 1.f - (sigma2 / (2.f * (sigma2 + 0.33f)));
    B = 0.45f * sigma2 / (sigma2 + 0.09f);
}
```

⟨*OrenNayar Private Data*⟩ ≡

```
Spectrum R;
float A, B;
```

Figure 9.19: Spheres rendered with an isotropic microfacet distribution (left) and an anisotropic distribution (right). Note the different specular highlight shapes from the anisotropic model. We have used spheres here instead of the Killeroo, since anisotropic models like these depend on a globally consistent set of tangent vectors over the surface to orient the direction of anisotropy in a reasonable way.

$$\cos^2 \phi = \frac{x^2}{1 - z^2}$$

$$\sin^2 \phi = \frac{y^2}{1 - z^2}.$$

Thus, the implementation is

⟨*Anisotropic Public Methods*⟩+≡   **448**

```
float D(const Vector &wh) const {
    float costhetah = fabsf(CosTheta(wh));
    float e = (ex * wh.x * wh.x + ey * wh.y * wh.y) /
              (1.f - costhetah * costhetah);
    return sqrtf((ex+1)*(ey+1)) * powf(costhetah, e);
}
```

CosTheta() 412
Vector 47

9.5 LAFORTUNE MODEL

A recent trend in computer graphics is to use measured data for rendering realistic images. Although this approach can lead to very realistic renderings, one drawback is the enormous amount of data required to accurately represent a measured BRDF. Lafortune et al. (1997) have developed a BRDF model designed to fit measured BRDF data to a parameterized model with a relatively small number of parameters. Their model is both easy to implement and efficient. The genesis of their model is the *Phong model*— one of the first BRDF models developed for graphics. The original Phong model has a number of shortcomings (in particular it is neither reciprocal nor energy conserving) that the Lafortune model avoids. Figure 9.20 shows this model when used with measured reflectance data from a clay surface.

The *modified Phong BRDF*, which is reciprocal, is

$$f_r(\mathrm{p}, \omega_o, \omega_i) = (\omega_i \cdot R(\omega_o, \mathbf{n}))^e = (\omega_o \cdot R(\omega_i, \mathbf{n}))^e,$$

where $R(\omega, \mathbf{n})$ is the operator that reflects the vector ω about the surface normal $\mathbf{n}$. Like the Blinn microfacet distribution model, the cosine of the angle between the two vectors

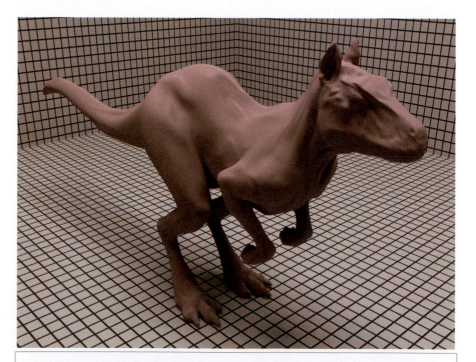

Figure 9.20: Killeroo modeled with a clay material represented with Lafortune et al.'s BRDF model. *Killeroo courtesy headus/Rezard, BRDF data courtesy Cornell Program of Computer Graphics.*

is raised to a given power. In the canonical BRDF coordinate system, the Phong model can be written equivalently as

$$f_r(\mathrm{p}, \omega_o, \omega_i) = (\omega_i \cdot (-\omega_{ox}, -\omega_{oy}, \omega_{oz}))^e = (\omega_o \cdot (-\omega_{ix}, -\omega_{iy}, \omega_{iz}))^e.$$

One of Lafortune et al.'s observations is that the scaling factor $(-1, -1, 1)$ in the modified Phong model that reflects the ω_o direction about the normal can itself be a parameter to the BRDF. We will call this vector the *orientation vector*, since it orients the direction of maximum reflection. For example, if the orientation vector were $(o_x, o_y, o_z) = (-1, -1, 0.5)$, the main reflection vector would be lowered from the perfect specular direction to be closer to the surface. Many glossy surfaces exhibit this type of *off-specular* reflective behavior. If the orientation vector were $(1, 1, 1)$, the surface would be retro-reflective—light would be primarily reflected back along the direction where it arrived.

Using this generalized Phong model as a building block, the Lafortune model expresses the BRDF as the sum of multiple Phong *lobes*, each with a different orientation vector and specular exponent, plus a Lambertian diffuse term. The contribution of each lobe is determined by the magnitude of the orientation vector; the reoriented incident vector is no longer necessarily of unit length, and its length affects the magnitude of the dot product.[4] Thus, we have

$$f_r(\mathrm{p}, \omega_o, \omega_i) = \frac{\rho_d}{\pi} + \sum_{i=1}^{\mathrm{nlobes}} (\omega_o \cdot (\omega_{ix} o_{i,x}, \omega_{iy} o_{i,y}, \omega_{iz} o_{i,z}))^{e_i},$$

where ρ_d is the diffuse reflectance, $(o_{i,x}, o_{i,y}, o_{i,z})$ are the orientation vectors, and e_i are the specular exponents.

As a further generalization, each orientation vector and specular exponent is allowed to vary as a function of wavelength; we represent each of them with Spectrum objects in the following implementation. This gives a natural way to express wavelength-dependent reflection variation in the model. To do this, the orientation vectors are passed as three arrays of Spectrums (one for the x components of o_i, one for the y components, etc.).

In the original paper, the orientation vectors were defined so that the vector $(1, 1, 1)$ would give the classic Phong model. To be consistent with our specular reflection BRDF, we will instead use the convention that $(-1, -1, 1)$ gives the Phong model.

Spectrum 230

---

4   This makes for an unintuitive control for manual adjustment of the BRDF's characteristics, although it is somewhat less troublesome if the BRDF is being automatically fit to measured data.

⟨*BxDF Declarations*⟩+≡
```
class COREDLL Lafortune : public BxDF {
public:
    ⟨Lafortune Public Methods⟩
private:
    ⟨Lafortune Private Data  452⟩
};
```

The Lafortune BxDF here follows a slightly different convention from the rest of the BxDFs for managing the values passed into it: rather than making a local copy of the values in the arrays of coefficients passed to its constructor, it stores pointers to the arrays and assumes that the calling code will be responsible for freeing this memory if necessary. The motivation for this is to save unnecessary copying of data for the common case where the coefficients are statically allocated, as in all of the materials that use Lafortune in Chapter 10. If a material uses textures to compute the coefficients such that they aren't statically allocated, it can use the BSDF_ALLOC() macro from Section 10.1.1 to allocate the coefficient data, which will ensure that it is freed at an appropriate time.

Because the particular values of this BRDF's parameters may affect whether it is diffuse or glossy, the BxDFType is left as an additional parameter to the constructor.

⟨*BxDF Method Definitions*⟩+≡
```
Lafortune::Lafortune(const Spectrum &r, u_int nl,
    const Spectrum *xx, const Spectrum *yy, const Spectrum *zz,
    const Spectrum *e, BxDFType t)
    : BxDF(t), R(r) {
    nLobes = nl;
    x = xx;
    y = yy;
    z = zz;
    exponent = e;
}
```

⟨*Lafortune Private Data*⟩≡   452
```
Spectrum R;
u_int nLobes;
const Spectrum *x, *y, *z, *exponent;
```

BxDF 414
BxDFType 415
COREDLL 904
Lafortune 452
Spectrum 230

To evaluate this reflection model, it is necessary just to sum the contribution of each lobe:

⟨*BxDF Method Definitions*⟩+≡
```
Spectrum Lafortune::f(const Vector &wo, const Vector &wi) const {
    Spectrum ret = R * INV_PI;
    for (u_int i = 0; i < nLobes; ++i) {
        ⟨Add contribution for ith Phong lobe 453⟩
    }
    return ret;
}
```

Evaluating each lobe is done by simultaneously computing the reoriented ω_i vector by multiplying its x, y, and z coefficients with the appropriate spectral orientation coefficients and computing the dot product of the result with ω_o, giving a spectral result that is itself then raised to the spectral exponent provided.

⟨*Add contribution for ith Phong lobe*⟩≡   453
```
Spectrum v = x[i] * wo.x * wi.x +
             y[i] * wo.y * wi.y +
             z[i] * wo.z * wi.z;
ret += v.Pow(exponent[i]);
```

9.6 FRESNEL INCIDENCE EFFECTS

Most BRDF models in graphics do not account for the fact that Fresnel reflection reduces the amount of light that reaches the bottom level of layered objects. Consider a polished wood table or a wall with glossy paint: if you look at their surfaces head-on, you primarily see the wood or the paint pigment color. As you move your viewpoint toward a glancing angle, you see less of the underlying color as it is overwhelmed by increasing glossy reflection due to Fresnel effects.

In this section, we will implement a BRDF model developed by Ashikhmin and Shirley (2000, 2002) that models a diffuse underlying surface with a glossy specular surface above it. The effect of reflection from the diffuse surface is modulated by the amount of energy left after Fresnel effects have been considered. Figure 9.21 shows this idea: When the incident direction is close to the normal, most light is transmitted to the diffuse layer and the diffuse term dominates. When the incident direction is close to glancing, glossy reflection is the primary mode of reflection. The car model in Figures 13.14 and 13.15 uses this BRDF for its paint.

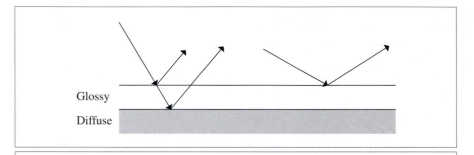

Figure 9.21: The `FresnelBlend` BRDF models the effect of a surface with a glossy layer on top of a diffuse substrate. As the angle of incidence of the vectors ω_i and ω_o heads toward glancing (right), the amount of light that reaches the diffuse substrate is reduced by Fresnel effects and the diffuse layer becomes less visibly apparent.

⟨*BxDF Declarations*⟩+≡
```
class COREDLL FresnelBlend : public BxDF {
public:
    ⟨FresnelBlend Public Methods 455⟩
private:
    ⟨FresnelBlend Private Data 454⟩
};
```

The model takes two spectra, representing diffuse and specular reflectance, and a microfacet distribution for the glossy layer.

⟨*BxDF Method Definitions*⟩+≡
```
FresnelBlend::FresnelBlend(const Spectrum &d, const Spectrum &s,
                          MicrofacetDistribution *dist)
    : BxDF(BxDFType(BSDF_REFLECTION | BSDF_GLOSSY)), Rd(d), Rs(s) {
    distribution = dist;
}
```

⟨*FresnelBlend Private Data*⟩≡   **454**
```
Spectrum Rd, Rs;
MicrofacetDistribution *distribution;
```

This model is based on the weighted sum of a glossy specular term and a diffuse term. Accounting for reciprocity and energy conservation, the glossy specular term is derived as

$$f_r(\mathrm{p}, \omega_o, \omega_i) = \frac{D(\omega_h)F(\omega_o)}{8\pi(\omega_h \cdot \omega_i)(\max((\mathbf{n} \cdot \omega_o), (\mathbf{n} \cdot \omega_i)))},$$

where $D(\omega_h)$ is a microfacet distribution term and $F(\omega_o)$ represents Fresnel reflectance. Note that this is quite similar to the Torrance-Sparrow model.

The key to Ashikhmin and Shirley's model is the derivation of a diffuse term such that the model still obeys reciprocity and conserves energy. The derivation is dependent on an approximation to the Fresnel reflection equations due to Schlick (1993), who approximated Fresnel reflection as

$$F_r(\cos\theta) = R + (1 - R)(1 - \cos\theta)^5,$$

where R is the reflectance of the surface at normal incidence.

Given this Fresnel term, the diffuse term in the following equation successfully models Fresnel-based reduced diffuse reflection in a physically plausible manner:

$$f_r(p, \omega_i, \omega_o) = \frac{28R_d}{23\pi}(1 - R_s)\left(1 - \left(1 - \frac{(\mathbf{n} \cdot \omega_i)}{2}\right)^5\right)\left(1 - \left(1 - \frac{(\mathbf{n} \cdot \omega_o)}{2}\right)^5\right).$$

We will not include the derivation of this result here.

⟨*FresnelBlend Public Methods*⟩ ≡   454

```
Spectrum SchlickFresnel(float costheta) const {
    return Rs + powf(1 - costheta, 5.f) * (Spectrum(1.) - Rs);
}
```

⟨*BxDF Method Definitions*⟩ +≡

```
Spectrum FresnelBlend::f(const Vector &wo, const Vector &wi) const {
    Spectrum diffuse = (28.f/(23.f*M_PI)) * Rd *
        (Spectrum(1.) - Rs) *
        (1 - powf(1 - .5f * fabsf(CosTheta(wi)), 5)) *
        (1 - powf(1 - .5f * fabsf(CosTheta(wo)), 5));
    Vector H = Normalize(wi + wo);
    Spectrum specular = distribution->D(H) /
        (8.f * M_PI * AbsDot(wi, H) *
        max(fabsf(CosTheta(wi)), fabsf(CosTheta(wo)))) *
        SchlickFresnel(Dot(wi, H));
    return diffuse + specular;
}
```

FURTHER READING

Phong (1975) developed an early empirical reflection model for glossy surfaces in computer graphics. Although not reciprocal or energy conserving, it was a cornerstone of the first synthetic images of non-Lambertian objects. The Torrance-Sparrow microfacet model is described in Torrance and Sparrow (1967); it was first introduced to graphics by Blinn (1977) and a variant of it was used by Cook and Torrance (1981, 1982).

Hall's book collected and described the state of the art in physically based surface reflection models for graphics in 1989; it remains a seminal reference (Hall 1989). It discusses the physics of surface reflection in detail, with many pointers to the original literature and with many tables of useful measured data about reflection from real surfaces.

Moravec (1981) was the first to apply a wave optics model to graphics. This area has also been investigated by Bahar and Chakrabarti (1987). Beckmann and Spizzichino (1963) developed an early physical optics model of surface reflection, which was used by Kajiya (1985) to derive an anisotropic reflection model for computer graphics. Beckmann and Spizzichino's work was built upon more recently by He et al. (1991), who developed a sophisticated reflection model that modeled a variety of types of surface reflection, and Stam (1999), who applied wave optics to model diffraction effects.

Nayar, Ikeuchi, and Kanade (1991) have shown that some reflection models based on physical (wave) optics have substantially similar characteristics to those based on geometric optics. The geometric optics approximations don't seem to cause too much error in practice, except on very smooth surfaces. This is a helpful result, giving experimental basis to the general belief that wave optics models aren't usually worth their computational expense for computer graphics applications.

Notable anisotropic BRDF models for computer graphics include those of Poulin and Fournier (1990), Ward (1992), and Schlick (1993). Schlick's model is both computationally efficient and easy to use with importance sampling for Monte Carlo integration. Other good references for anisotropic models are papers by Lu, Koenderink, and Kappers (1999) and Ashikhmin and Shirley (2000, 2002).

Ashikhmin, Premoze, and Shirley (2000) recently developed techniques for computing self-shadowing terms for arbitrary microfacet distributions, without requiring the assumptions that Torrance and Sparrow did. Their solutions cannot be evaluated in closed form, but must be approximated numerically.

The Oren-Nayar Lambertian model is described in their 1994 SIGGRAPH paper (Oren and Nayar 1994). See Lafortune et al. (1997) for a description of the Lafortune BRDF implemented in this chapter. A useful reflection model for simulating skin and other biological tissues is Hanrahan and Krueger's model of subsurface reflection (Hanrahan and Krueger 1993). Stam (2001) describes another approach for subsurface reflection and also derives a generalization of the Cook-Torrance model for transmission; there are a number of important subtleties that are not accounted for in the simple approach taken in the BRDFToBTDF class in this chapter.

The effect of the polarization of light is ignored in pbrt, although for some scenes it can be an important effect; see, for example, the paper by Tannenbaum, Tannenbaum, and Wozny (1994) for information about how to extend a renderer to account for this effect. Similarly, the fact that indices of refraction of real-world objects usually vary as a function of wavelength is also not modeled here; see both Section 11.8 of Glassner's book

(1995) and Devlin et al.'s survey article for information about these issues and references to previous work (Devlin et al. 2002).

Kajiya and Kay (1989) developed a reflection model for hair based on a model of individual hairs as cylinders with diffuse and glossy reflection properties. Their model determines the overall reflection from these cylinders, accounting for the effect of variation in surface normal over the hemisphere along the cylinder. See also the paper by Banks (1994), which discusses shading models for 1D primitives like hair. More recently, Goldman (1997) has developed a probabilistic shading model that models reflection from collections of short hairs, and Marschner et al. (2003) have developed a more accurate model of light scattering from long hair.

A number of researchers have investigated BRDFs based on modeling the small-scale geometric features of a reflective surface. This work includes the computation of BRDFs from bump maps by Cabral, Max, and Springmeyer (1987), Fournier's normal distribution functions (Fournier 1992), and Westin, Arvo, and Torrance (1992), who applied Monte Carlo ray tracing to statistically model reflection from microgeometry and represented the resulting BRDFs with spherical harmonics.

EXERCISES

● 9.1   A consequence of Fermat's principle from optics is that light traveling from a point p_1 in a medium with index of refraction η_1 to a point p_2 in a medium with index of refraction η_2 will follow a path that minimizes the time to get from the first point to the second point. Snell's law can be shown to follow from this fact directly.

Consider light traveling between two points p_1 and p_2 separated by a planar boundary. The light could potentially pass through the boundary while traveling from p_1 to p_2 at any point on the boundary (see Figure 9.22, which shows two such possible points p' and p''.) Recall that the time it takes light to travel between two points in a medium with a constant index of refraction is proportional to the distance between them times the index of refraction in the medium. Using this fact, show that the point p' on the boundary that minimizes the total time to travel from p_1 to p_2 is the point where $\eta_1 \sin \theta_1 = \eta_2 \sin \theta_2$.

● 9.2   Read the papers of Wolff and Kurlander (1990) and Tannenbaum, Tannenbaum, and Wozny (1994) and apply some of the techniques described to modify pbrt to model the effect of light polarization. Set up scenes and render images of them that demonstrate a significant difference when polarization is accurately modeled.

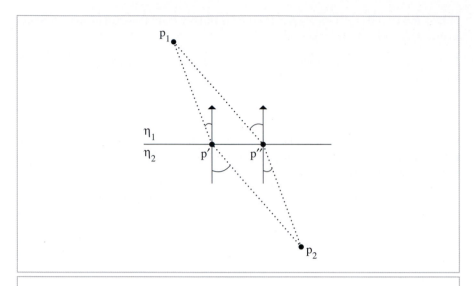

Figure 9.22: Derivation of Snell's Law. Snell's law can be derived using Fermat's principle, which says that light will follow the path that takes the least amount of time to pass between two points. The angle of refraction θ at the boundary between two media can thus be shown to be the one that minimizes the time spent going from p_1 to a point p on the boundary plus the time spent traveling the distance from that point to p_2.

❸ 9.3   Construct a scene with an actual geometric model of a rough plane with a large number of mirrored microfacets and illuminate with an area light source.[5] Place the camera in the scene such that a very large number of microfacets are in each pixel's area, and render images of this scene using hundreds or thousands of pixel samples. Compare the result to using a flat surface with a microfacet-based BRDF model. How well can you get the two approaches to match if you try to tune the microfacet BRDF parameters? Can you construct examples where images rendered with the true microfacets are actually visibly more realistic due to better modeling the effects of masking, self-shadowing, and interreflection between microfacets?

❷ 9.4   Implement the Hanrahan-Krueger subsurface scattering reflection model (Hanrahan and Krueger 1993). Demonstrate and discuss the visual difference between objects rendered with this model compared to objects rendered with microfacet models or the Oren-Nayar model.

---

5   An area light and not a point or directional light is necessary due to subtleties in how lights are seen in specular surfaces. With the light transport algorithms used in pbrt, infinitesimal point sources are never visible in mirrored surfaces. This is a typical limitation of ray-tracing renderers and usually not bothersome in practive.

❸ 9.5 Implement a simulation-based approach to modeling reflection from complex microsurfaces, such as the one described by Westin, Arvo, and Torrance (1992). Modify pbrt so that you can provide a description of the microgeometry of a complex surface (like cloth, velvet, etc.), fire rays at the geometry from a variety of incident directions, and record the distribution and throughput for the rays that leave the surface. (You will likely need to modify the PathIntegrator from Chapter 16 to determine the distribution of outgoing light.) Record the distribution in a three-dimensional table if the surface is isotropic, or a four-dimensional table if it is anisotropic, and use the table to compute BRDF values for rendering images. Demonstrate interesting reflection effects from complex surfaces using this approach. Investigate how the size of the table and the number of samples taken to compute entries in the table affects the accuracy of the final result.

CHAPTER TEN

10 MATERIALS

The low-level BRDFs and BTDFs introduced in the previous chapter address only part of the problem of describing how a surface scatters light. Although they describe how light is scattered at a particular point on a surface, the renderer needs to determine *which* BRDFs and BTDFs to use at that point and how to set their parameters. In this chapter, we describe a procedural shading mechanism that determines the BRDFs and BTDFs to use at points on surfaces.

The basic idea is that a *surface shader* is bound to each primitive in the scene. The surface shader is represented by an instance of the `Material` interface class, which has a method that takes a point to be shaded and returns a `BSDF` object. The `BSDF` class holds a set of `BxDFs` that collectively describe scattering at a point. `Materials`, in turn, use instances of the `Texture` class (to be defined in the next chapter) to determine the material properties at particular points on surfaces. For example, an `ImageTexture` might be used to modulate the color of diffuse reflection across a surface. This is a somewhat different shading paradigm than many rendering systems use; it is common practice to combine the function of the surface shader and the lighting integrator (see Chapter 16) into a single module and have the shader return the color of reflected light at the point. However, by separating these two components and having the `Material` return a `BSDF`, pbrt is able to better handle a variety of light transport algorithms.

10.1 BSDFs

The BSDF class represents a collection of BRDFs and BTDFs. Grouping them in this manner allows the rest of the system to work with composite BSDFs directly, rather than having to consider all of the components they may have been built from. Equally important, the BSDF class hides some of the details of shading normals from the rest of the system. Shading normals, either from per-vertex normals in triangle meshes or from bump mapping, can substantially improve the visual richness of rendered scenes, but because they are an ad hoc construct, they are tricky to incorporate into a physically based renderer. The issues that they introduce are handled in the BSDF implementation.

⟨*BSDF Declarations*⟩+≡
```
class COREDLL BSDF {
public:
    ⟨BSDF Public Methods  464⟩
    ⟨BSDF Public Data  462⟩
private:
    ⟨BSDF Private Methods  468⟩
    ⟨BSDF Private Data  463⟩
};
```

The BSDF constructor takes a DifferentialGeometry object that represents the shading differential geometry, the true surface normal ngeom, and, optionally, the index of refraction of the medium enclosed by the surface. It stores these values in member variables and constructs an orthonormal coordinate system with the shading normal as one of the axes; this will be useful for transforming directions to and from the BxDF coordinate system described in Section 9.1. Throughout this section, we will use the convention that $\mathbf{n}_s$ denotes the shading normal and $\mathbf{n}_g$ the geometric normal (Figure 10.1).

⟨*BSDF Method Definitions*⟩≡
```
BSDF::BSDF(const DifferentialGeometry &dg, const Normal &ngeom, float e)
    : dgShading(dg), eta(e) {
    ng = ngeom;
    nn = dgShading.nn;
    sn = Normalize(dgShading.dpdu);
    tn = Cross(nn, sn);
    nBxDFs = 0;
}
```

BSDF 462
BSDF::nBxDFs 463
BxDF 414
COREDLL 904
Cross() 52
DifferentialGeometry 83
Normal 56
Vector::Normalize() 53

⟨*BSDF Public Data*⟩≡   **462**
```
const DifferentialGeometry dgShading;
const float eta;
```

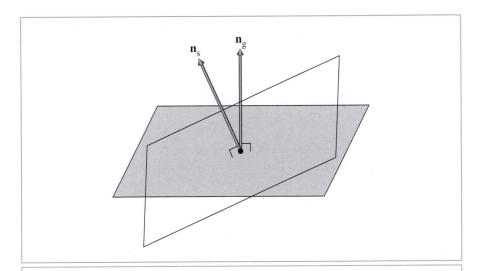

Figure 10.1: The geometric normal, $\mathbf{n_g}$, defined by the surface geometry, and the shading normal, $\mathbf{n_s}$, given by per-vertex normals and/or bump mapping, will generally define different hemispheres for integrating incident illumination to compute surface reflection. This inconsistency is important to handle carefully since it can otherwise lead to artifacts in images.

⟨*BSDF Private Data*⟩ ≡   462
```
Normal nn, ng;
Vector sn, tn;
```

The BSDF implementation stores only a fixed limited number of individual BxDF components. It could easily be extended to allocate more space if more components were given to it, although this isn't necessary for any of the Material implementations in pbrt thus far, and the current limit of eight is plenty for almost all practical applications.

⟨*BSDF Inline Method Definitions*⟩ ≡
```
inline void BSDF::Add(BxDF *b) {
    Assert(nBxDFs < MAX_BxDFS);
    bxdfs[nBxDFs++] = b;
}
```

⟨*BSDF Private Data*⟩+≡   462
```
int nBxDFs;
#define MAX_BxDFS 8
BxDF *bxdfs[MAX_BxDFS];
```

For other parts of the system that need additional information about the particular BRDFs and BTDFs present, two different methods return the number of BxDFs stored by the BSDF; the second only returns the number that match a particular set of BxDFType flags. Note that we could use a single function with a default flag setting of BSDF_ALL, but the no-argument variant of BSDF::NumComponents() is called frequently, so we would like to avoid the overhead of checking the flags of the BxDFs individually in that case.

⟨*BSDF Public Methods*⟩ ≡   462
```
int NumComponents() const { return nBxDFs; }
int NumComponents(BxDFType flags) const;
```

The HasShadingGeometry() method indicates whether the BSDF has a different shading normal than its geometric normal. The PhotonIntegrator, for example, needs to be aware of this.

⟨*BSDF Public Methods*⟩+≡   462
```
bool HasShadingGeometry() const {
    return (nn.x != ng.x || nn.y != ng.y || nn.z != ng.z);
}
```

The BSDF also has methods that perform transformations to and from the local coordinate system expected by BxDFs. Recall that in this coordinate system, the surface normal is along the *z* axis $(0, 0, 1)$, the primary tangent is $(1, 0, 0)$, and the secondary tangent is $(0, 1, 0)$. The transformation of directions into "shading space" simplifies many of the BxDF implementations in Chapter 9. Given three orthonormal vectors **s**, **t**, and **n** in world space, the matrix **M** that transforms vectors in world space to the local reflection space is

$$\mathbf{M} = \begin{pmatrix} \mathbf{s}_x & \mathbf{s}_y & \mathbf{s}_z \\ \mathbf{t}_x & \mathbf{t}_y & \mathbf{t}_z \\ \mathbf{n}_x & \mathbf{n}_y & \mathbf{n}_z \end{pmatrix} = \begin{pmatrix} \mathbf{s} \\ \mathbf{t} \\ \mathbf{n} \end{pmatrix}.$$

To confirm this yourself, consider, for example, the value of **M** times the surface normal **n**, $\mathbf{Mn} = (\mathbf{s} \cdot \mathbf{n}, \mathbf{t} \cdot \mathbf{n}, \mathbf{n} \cdot \mathbf{n})$. Since **s**, **t**, and **n** are all orthonormal, the *x* and *y* components of **Mn** are zero. Since **n** is normalized, $\mathbf{n} \cdot \mathbf{n} = 1$. Thus, $\mathbf{Mn} = (0, 0, 1)$, as expected.

In this case, we don't need to compute the inverse transpose of **M** to transform normals (recall the discussion of transforming normals in Section 2.8.3). Because **M** is an orthogonal matrix (its rows and columns are mutually orthogonal), its inverse is equal to its transpose, so it is its own inverse transpose already.

⟨*BSDF Public Methods*⟩+≡   462
```
Vector WorldToLocal(const Vector &v) const {
    return Vector(Dot(v, sn), Dot(v, tn), Dot(v, nn));
}
```

The method that takes vectors back from local space to world space uses the transpose to invert **M** before doing the appropriate dot products.

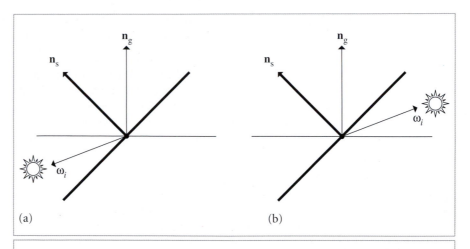

Figure 10.2: The Two Types of Error That Result from Using Shading Normals. (a) A light leak: the geometric normal indicates that the light is on the back side of the surface, but the shading normal indicates the light is visible (assuming a reflective and not transmissive surface). (b) A dark spot: the geometric normal indicates that the surface is illuminated, but the shading normal indicates that the viewer is behind the lit side of the surface.

⟨*BSDF Public Methods*⟩+≡   462
```
Vector LocalToWorld(const Vector &v) const {
    return Vector(sn.x * v.x + tn.x * v.y + nn.x * v.z,
                  sn.y * v.x + tn.y * v.y + nn.y * v.z,
                  sn.z * v.x + tn.z * v.y + nn.z * v.z);
}
```

Shading normals can cause a variety of undesirable artifacts in practice (Figure 10.2). Figure 10.2(a) shows a *light leak:* the geometric normal indicates that ω_i and ω_o lie on opposite sides of the surface, so if the surface is not transmissive, the light should have no contribution. However, if we directly evaluate the scattering equation, Equation (5.6), about the hemisphere centered around the shading normal, we will incorrectly incorporate the light from ω_i. This case demonstrates that $\mathbf{n}_s$ can't just be used as a direct replacement for $\mathbf{n}_g$ in rendering computations.

Figure 10.2(b) shows a similar tricky situation: the shading normal indicates that no light should be reflected to the viewer, since it is not in the same hemisphere as the illumination, while the geometric normal indicates that they are in the same hemisphere. Direct use of $\mathbf{n}_s$ would cause ugly black spots on the surface where this situation happens.

Fortunately, there is an elegant solution to these problems. When evaluating the BSDF, we use the geometric normal to decide if we should be evaluating reflection or transmission: if ω_i and ω_o lie in the same hemisphere with respect to $\mathbf{n}_g$, we evaluate the BRDFs, and otherwise we evaluate the BTDFs. In evaluating the scattering equation, however, the dot product of the normal and the incident direction is still taken with the shading normal, rather than the geometric normal.

Now it should be clear why pbrt requires BxDFs to evaluate their values without regard to whether ω_i and ω_o are in the same or different hemispheres. Thus, light leaks are avoided, since we will only evaluate the BTDFs for the situation in Figure 10.2(a), giving no reflection for a purely reflective surface. Similarly, black spots are avoided since we will evaluate the BRDFs for the situation in Figure 10.2(b), even though the shading normal would suggest that the directions are in different hemispheres.

Given these conventions, the method that evaluates the BSDF for a given pair of directions is straightforward. It starts by transforming the world space direction vectors to local BSDF space and then determines whether it should use the BRDFs or the BTDFs. It then loops over the appropriate set and evaluates the sum of their contributions.

⟨BSDF Method Definitions⟩+≡
```
Spectrum BSDF::f(const Vector &woW, const Vector &wiW,
                 BxDFType flags) const {
    Vector wi = WorldToLocal(wiW), wo = WorldToLocal(woW);
    if (Dot(wiW, ng) * Dot(woW, ng) > 0) // ignore BTDFs
        flags = BxDFType(flags & ~BSDF_TRANSMISSION);
    else // ignore BRDFs
        flags = BxDFType(flags & ~BSDF_REFLECTION);
    Spectrum f = 0.;
    for (int i = 0; i < nBxDFs; ++i)
        if (bxdfs[i]->MatchesFlags(flags))
            f += bxdfs[i]->f(wo, wi);
    return f;
}
```

pbrt also provides BSDF methods that return the summed reflectance values of their individual BxDFs. These methods just loop over the BxDFs and call the appropriate BxDF::rho() methods and therefore won't be shown here.

⟨BSDF Public Methods⟩+≡   462
```
Spectrum rho(BxDFType flags = BSDF_ALL) const;
Spectrum rho(const Vector &wo, BxDFType flags = BSDF_ALL) const;
```

10.1.1 BSDF MEMORY MANAGEMENT

For each camera ray that intersects geometry in the scene, one or more BSDF objects will be created by the SurfaceIntegrator in the process of computing the reflected radiance from the intersection point. (Integrators that account for multiple interreflections of light will generally create a number of BSDFs along the way.) Each of these BSDFs in turn has a number of BxDFs stored inside it, as returned by the Material at the intersection points. A naïve implementation of this process would use `new` and `delete` to dynamically allocate storage for both the BSDF as well as each of the BxDFs that it holds.

Unfortunately, such an approach is inefficient—too much time is spent in the dynamic memory management routines for a series of small memory allocations. Instead, we will use a specialized allocation scheme based on the `MemoryArena` class described in Section A.2.4 in Appendix A. `MemoryArena` allocates a large block of memory and responds to allocation requests via the `MemoryArena::Alloc()` call by returning successive sections of that block. It does not support freeing individual allocations, but instead frees all of them simultaneously when the `MemoryArena::FreeAll()` method is called. The result of this approach is that both allocation and freeing of memory are extremely efficient.

The BSDF class holds a `static` `MemoryArena` instance that is used for BSDF and BxDF allocations. It provides allocation and freeing routines that mirror those in the `MemoryArena`; the requests are just passed on to the `MemoryArena` that it holds. After each camera ray's contribution has been computed, the `Scene::Render()` method frees up all of the memory used for allocating BSDF memory for that ray by calling `BSDF::FreeAll()`. There should be no BSDF pointers held anywhere in the system at this point. If pbrt were modified such that this constraint wasn't the case, it would be necessary to use a different approach for managing BSDF memory.

⟨*BSDF Public Methods*⟩+≡   462
```
static void *Alloc(u_int sz) { return arena.Alloc(sz); }
static void FreeAll() { arena.FreeAll(); }
```

⟨*BSDF Private Data*⟩+≡   462
```
static MemoryArena arena;
```

For the convenience of code that allocates BSDFs and BxDFs (e.g., the Materials in this chapter), there is a macro that hides some of the messiness of using the memory arena approach. Instead of using the `new` operator to allocate those objects like this:

```
BSDF *b = new BSDF;
BxDF *lam = new Lambertian(Spectrum(1.0));
```

code should instead be written with the `BSDF_ALLOC()` macro, like this:

```
BSDF *b = BSDF_ALLOC(BSDF);
BxDF *lam = BSDF_ALLOC(Lambertian)(Spectrum(1.0));
```

The macro calls the `BSDF::Alloc()` routine to allocate the appropriate amount of memory for the object, and then uses the placement operator `new` to run the constructor for the object at the given memory location.

⟨*BSDF Declarations*⟩+≡
```
#define BSDF_ALLOC(T)  new (BSDF::Alloc(sizeof(T))) T
```

We will make the BSDF destructor a private method, in order to ensure that it isn't inadvertently called, for example, due to an attempt to delete a BSDF. Making the destructor private ensures a compile time error if it is called. Trying to delete memory allocated by the MemoryArena could lead to subtle errors, since a pointer to the middle of memory managed by the MemoryArena would be passed to the system's dynamic memory freeing routine. We also declare the BSDF to be a friend of a nonexistent class, in order to silence compiler warnings related to having a private destructor. Thus, a further implication of the allocation scheme here is that BSDF and BxDF destructors are never executed. This isn't a problem for the ones currently in the system.

⟨*BSDF Private Methods*⟩ ≡   **462**
```
~BSDF() { }
friend class NoSuchClass;
```

10.2 MATERIAL INTERFACE AND IMPLEMENTATIONS

The abstract Material class defines a single method that material implementations must provide, Material::GetBSDF(). This method is responsible for determining the reflective properties at the given point on the surface and returning an instance of the BSDF class that describes them. The Material class is defined in the files core/material.h⊙ and core/material.cpp.⊙

⟨*Material Class Declarations*⟩ ≡
```
class COREDLL Material : public ReferenceCounted {
public:
    ⟨Material Interface 468⟩
};
```

The Material::GetBSDF() method is given two differential geometry objects. The first, dgGeom, represents the actual differential geometry at the ray intersection point, and the second, dgShading, represents possibly perturbed shading geometry, such as that from per-vertex normals in a triangle mesh. The material may further perturb the shading geometry with bump mapping in the GetBSDF() method; the returned BSDF holds information about the final shading geometry at the point as well as the BRDF and BTDF components for the point.

⟨*Material Interface*⟩ ≡   **468**
```
virtual BSDF *GetBSDF(const DifferentialGeometry &dgGeom,
                      const DifferentialGeometry &dgShading) const = 0;
```

Since the usual interface to the hit point used by Integrators is through an instance of the Intersection class, we will add a convenience method to Intersection that returns the BSDF at the hit point. It calls the Differentialgeometry::ComputeDifferentials() method to compute information about the projected size of the surface area around the intersection on the image plane for use in texture antialiasing and then forwards the request to the `Primitive`, which in turn will call the `GetBSDF()` method of its `Material`. (See, for example, the `GeometricPrimitive::GetBSDF()` implementation.)

⟨*Intersection Method Definitions*⟩ ≡
```
    BSDF *Intersection::GetBSDF(const RayDifferential &ray) const {
        dg.ComputeDifferentials(ray);
        return primitive->GetBSDF(dg, WorldToObject);
    }
```

10.2.1 MATTE

The `Matte` material is defined in `materials/matte.cpp`.⊙ It is the simplest material in pbrt and describes a purely diffuse surface. It is parameterized by a spectral diffuse reflection value, `Matte::Kd`, and a scalar roughness value, `Matte::sigma`. If `Matte::sigma` has the value zero at the point on a surface, `Matte` returns a `Lambertian` BRDF; otherwise the `OrenNayar` model is used. Like all of the other `Material` implementations in this chapter, it also takes an optional scalar texture that defines an offset function over the surface. If non-`NULL`, this texture is used to compute a shading normal at each point based on the function it defines. Figure 9.13 in the previous chapter shows the `Matte` material with the Killeroo model.

⟨*Matte Class Declarations*⟩ ≡
```
    class Matte : public Material {
    public:
        ⟨Matte Public Methods 469⟩
    private:
        ⟨Matte Private Data 469⟩
    };
```

⟨*Matte Public Methods*⟩ ≡   **469**
```
    Matte(Reference<Texture<Spectrum> > kd,
            Reference<Texture<float> > sig,
            Reference<Texture<float> > bump) {
        Kd = kd;
        sigma = sig;
        bumpMap = bump;
    }
```

⟨*Matte Private Data*⟩ ≡   **469**
```
    Reference<Texture<Spectrum> > Kd;
    Reference<Texture<float> > sigma, bumpMap;
```

The `GetBSDF()` method just puts the pieces together, determining the bump map's effect on the shading geometry, evaluating the textures, and allocating and returning the BSDF.

⟨*Matte Method Definitions*⟩ ≡
```
    BSDF *Matte::GetBSDF(const DifferentialGeometry &dgGeom,
                         const DifferentialGeometry &dgShading) const {
        ⟨Allocate BSDF, possibly doing bump mapping with bumpMap 470⟩
        ⟨Evaluate textures for Matte material and allocate BRDF 470⟩
        return bsdf;
    }
```

If a bump map was provided to the Matte constructor, the Material::Bump() method is called to calculate the shading normal at the point. This method will be defined in the next section.

⟨*Allocate* BSDF, *possibly doing bump mapping with* bumpMap⟩ ≡   **470, 472**
```
    DifferentialGeometry dgs;
    if (bumpMap)
        Bump(bumpMap, dgGeom, dgShading, &dgs);
    else
        dgs = dgShading;
    BSDF *bsdf = BSDF_ALLOC(BSDF)(dgs, dgGeom.nn);
```

Next, the Textures that give the values of the diffuse reflection coefficient and the roughness are evaluated; these may return constant values, look up values from image maps, or do complex procedural shading calculations to compute these values (the texture evaluation process is the subject of Chapter 11). Given these values, all that needs to be done is to allocate a BSDF and the appropriate BRDF component using the BSDF memory allocation macros and return the result. Because Textures may return negative values or values otherwise outside of the expected range, these values are clamped before they are passed to the BRDF constructor.

⟨*Evaluate textures for* Matte *material and allocate BRDF*⟩ ≡   **470**
```
    Spectrum r = Kd->Evaluate(dgs).Clamp();
    float sig = Clamp(sigma->Evaluate(dgs), 0.f, 90.f);
    if (sig == 0.)
        bsdf->Add(BSDF_ALLOC(Lambertian)(r));
    else
        bsdf->Add(BSDF_ALLOC(OrenNayar)(r, sig));
    return bsdf;
```

10.2.2 PLASTIC

Plastic can be modeled as a mixture of a diffuse and glossy scattering function with parameters controlling the particular colors and specular highlight size. The parameters to Plastic are two reflectivities, Kd and Ks, which respectively control the amounts of

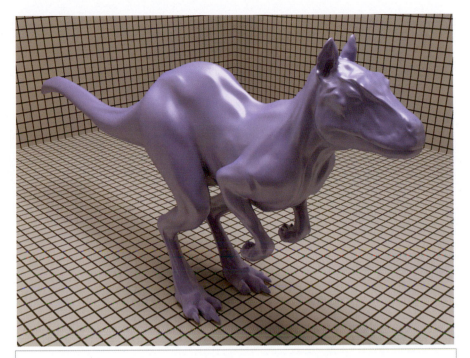

Figure 10.3: Killeroo Rendered with a Plastic Material. Note the combination of diffuse and glossy specular reflection. *Killeroo courtesy headus/Rezard.*

diffuse reflection and glossy specular reflection. Next is a roughness parameter (which ranges from zero to one) that determines the size of the specular highlight; the higher the roughness value, the larger the highlight. Figure 10.3 shows a plastic Killeroo. Plastic is defined in materials/plastic.cpp.

⟨*Plastic Class Declarations*⟩ ≡
```
class Plastic : public Material {
public:
    ⟨Plastic Public Methods 472⟩
private:
    ⟨Plastic Private Data 472⟩
};
```

⟨*Plastic Public Methods*⟩ ≡   **471**
```
Plastic(Reference<Texture<Spectrum> > kd, Reference<Texture<Spectrum> > ks,
        Reference<Texture<float> > rough, Reference<Texture<float> > bump) {
    Kd = kd;
    Ks = ks;
    roughness = rough;
    bumpMap = bump;
}
```

⟨*Plastic Private Data*⟩ ≡   **471**
```
Reference<Texture<Spectrum> > Kd, Ks;
Reference<Texture<float> > roughness, bumpMap;
```

The Plastic::GetBSDF() method follows the same basic structure as Matte::GetBSDF():
it evaluates textures, calls the bump-mapping function, allocates BxDFs, and initializes the
BSDF.

⟨*Plastic Method Definitions*⟩ ≡
```
BSDF *Plastic::GetBSDF(const DifferentialGeometry &dgGeom,
        const DifferentialGeometry &dgShading) const {
    ⟨Allocate BSDF, possibly doing bump mapping with bumpMap 470⟩
    Spectrum kd = Kd->Evaluate(dgs).Clamp();
    BxDF *diff = BSDF_ALLOC(Lambertian)(kd);
    Fresnel *fresnel = BSDF_ALLOC(FresnelDielectric)(1.5f, 1.f);
    Spectrum ks = Ks->Evaluate(dgs).Clamp();
    float rough = roughness->Evaluate(dgs);
    BxDF *spec = BSDF_ALLOC(Microfacet)(ks, fresnel,
                                        BSDF_ALLOC(Blinn)(1.f / rough));
    bsdf->Add(diff);
    bsdf->Add(spec);
    return bsdf;
}
```

10.2.3 ADDITIONAL MATERIALS

Beyond these basic materials, there are 12 more material plug-ins available in pbrt. We
will not show all of their implementations here, since they are all just variations on the
basic themes introduced in Matte and Plastic. All take Textures that define scattering
parameters, these textures are evaluated in their GetBSDF() methods, and appropriate
BxDFs are created and returned in a BSDF. See the documentation on pbrt's file format in
Appendix C for a summary of the parameters that these materials take.

These materials include

- Translucent: Glossy transmission through a surface, as might be seen in frosted
  glass.

- `Mirror`: A simple mirror, modeled with perfect specular reflection.
- `Glass`: Reflection and transmission, weighted by Fresnel terms for accurate angular-dependent variation.
- `ShinyMetal`: A metal surface with perfect specular reflection.
- `Substrate`: A layered model that varies between glossy specular and diffuse reflection depending on the viewing angle (based on the `FresnelBlend` BRDF).
- `Clay`, `Felt`, `Primer`, `Skin`, `BluePaint`, `BrushedMetal`: These materials have no parameters and are all based on measured BRDFs of real surfaces, approximated with the Lafortune et al. model.
- `Uber`: A "kitchen sink" material representing the union of many of the preceding materials. This is a highly parameterized material that is particularly useful when converting scenes from other file formats into pbrt's.

Figure 9.8 in the previous chapter shows the Killeroo model rendered with the glass material, and Figure 9.16 shows it with the `ShinyMetal` material. Figures 10.4 and 10.5 demonstrate the `BluePaint` and `Substrate` materials, respectively.

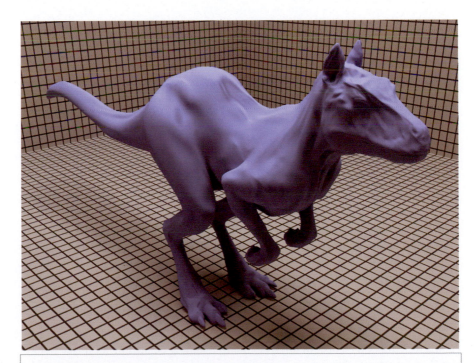

Figure 10.4: Killeroo rendered with a `Lafortune` BRDF that represents measured reflection data from blue paint. *Killeroo courtesy headus/Rezard.*

Figure 10.5: Killeroo rendered with the `Substrate` material, which blends between glossy and diffuse reflection depending on the viewing angle. *Killeroo courtesy headus/Rezard.*

10.3 BUMP MAPPING

All of the `Materials` defined in the previous section take an optional `float` texture map that defines a displacement at each point on the surface: each point p has a displaced point p′ associated with it, defined by $p' = p + d(p)\mathbf{n}(p)$, where $d(p)$ is the offset returned by the displacement texture at p and $\mathbf{n}(p)$ is the surface normal at p (Figure 10.6). We would like to use this texture to compute shading normals so that the surface appears as if it actually had been offset by the displacement function, without modifying its geometry. This process is called *bump mapping*. For relatively small displacement functions, the visual effect of bump mapping can be quite convincing. This idea, and the specific technique to compute these shading normals in a way that gives a plausible appearance of the actual displaced surface, was developed by Jim Blinn (1978).

Figure 10.7 shows the effect of applying bump mapping defined by an image map of a grid of lines to a sphere. A more complex example is shown in Figure 10.8, which shows a scene rendered with and without bump mapping. There, the bump map gives the appearance of a substantial amount of detail in the walls and floors that isn't actually

Material 468

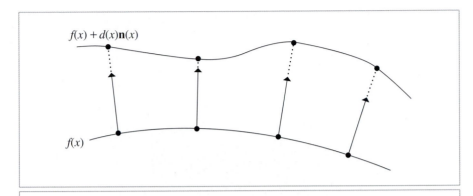

Figure 10.6: A displacement function associated with a material defines a new surface based on the old one, offset by the displacement amount along the normal at each point. pbrt doesn't compute a geometric representation of this displaced surface, but instead uses it to compute shading normals for bump mapping.

present in the geometric model. Figure 10.9 shows one of the image maps used to define the bump function in Figure 10.8.

The Material::Bump() method is a utility routine for use by Material implementations. It is responsible for computing the effect of bump mapping at the point being shaded given a particular displacement Texture. So that future Material implementations aren't required to support bump mapping with this particular mechanism (or at all), we've placed this method outside of the hard-coded material evaluation pipeline and left it as a function that particular material implementations can optionally call.

The implementation of Material::Bump() is based on finding an approximation to the partial derivatives $\partial p/\partial u$ and $\partial p/\partial v$ of the displaced surface and using them in place of the surface's actual partial derivatives to compute the shading normal. (Recall that the surface normal is given by the cross product of these vectors, $\mathbf{n} = \partial p/\partial u \times \partial p/\partial v$.) Assume that the original surface is defined by a parametric function $p(u, v)$, and the bump offset function is a scalar function $d(u, v)$. Then the displaced surface is given by

$$p'(u, v) = p(u, v) + d(u, v)\mathbf{n}(u, v),$$

where $\mathbf{n}(u, v)$ is the surface normal at (u, v).

The partial derivatives of this function can be found using the chain rule. For example, the partial derivative in u is

$$\frac{\partial p'}{\partial u} = \frac{\partial p(u, v)}{\partial u} + \frac{\partial d(u, v)}{\partial u}\mathbf{n}(u, v) + d(u, v)\frac{\partial \mathbf{n}(u, v)}{\partial u}. \tag{10.1}$$

We already have computed the value of $\partial p(u, v)/\partial u$; it's $\partial p/\partial u$ and is available in the DifferentialGeometry, which also stores the surface normal $\mathbf{n}(u, v)$ and the partial

Figure 10.7: Using bump mapping to compute the shading normals for a sphere gives it the appearance of having much more geometric detail than is actually present.

derivative $\partial \mathbf{n}(u, v)/\partial u = \partial \mathbf{n}/\partial u$. The displacement function $d(u, v)$ can be evaluated as needed, which leaves $\partial d(u, v)/\partial u$ as the only unknown term.

There are two possible approaches to finding the values of $\partial d(u, v)/\partial u$ and $\partial d(u, v)/\partial v$. One option would be to augment the Texture interface with a method to compute partial derivatives of the underlying texture function. For example, for image map textures mapped to the surface directly using its (u, v) parameterization, these partial derivatives can be computed by subtracting adjacent texels in the u and v directions. However, this approach is difficult to extend to complex procedural textures like some of the ones defined in Chapter 11. Therefore, pbrt directly computes these values with forward differencing in the Material::Bump() method, without modifying the Texture interface.

Recall the definition of the partial derivative:

$$\frac{\partial d(u, v)}{\partial u} = \lim_{\Delta_u \to 0} \frac{d(u + \Delta_u, v) - d(u, v)}{\Delta_u}.$$

Forward differencing approximates the value using a finite value of Δ_u and evaluating $d(u, v)$ at two positions. Thus, the final expression for $\partial p'/\partial u$ is the following (we have dropped the explicit dependence on (u, v) for some of the terms):

(a)

(b)

Figure 10.8: The Sponza atrium model, rendered (a) without bump mapping and (b) with bump mapping. Bump mapping substantially increases the apparent geometric complexity of the model, without the increased rendering time and memory use that would result from a geometric representation with the equivalent amount of small-scale detail.

$$\frac{\partial p'}{\partial u} \approx \frac{\partial \mathbf{p}}{\partial u} + \frac{d(u + \Delta_u, v) - d(u, v)}{\Delta_u} \mathbf{n} + d(u, v) \frac{\partial \mathbf{n}}{\partial u}.$$

Interestingly enough, most bump-mapping implementations ignore the final term under the assumption that $d(u, v)$ is expected to be relatively small. (Since bump mapping is mostly useful for approximating small perturbations, this is a reasonable assumption.) The fact that many renderers do not compute the values $\partial \mathbf{n}/\partial u$ and $\partial \mathbf{n}/\partial v$ may also

Figure 10.9: One of the image maps used as a bump map for the Sponza atrium rendering in Figure 10.8.

have something to do with this simplification. An implication of ignoring the last term is that the magnitude of the displacement function then does not affect the bump-mapped partial derivatives; adding a constant value to it globally doesn't affect the final result, since only differences of the bump function affect it.

pbrt computes all three terms since it has $\partial\mathbf{n}/\partial u$ and $\partial\mathbf{n}/\partial v$ readily available, although in practice this final term rarely makes a visually noticeable difference.

⟨*Material Method Definitions*⟩ ≡
```
    void Material::Bump(Reference<Texture<float> > d,
                        const DifferentialGeometry &dgGeom,
                        const DifferentialGeometry &dgs,
                        DifferentialGeometry *dgBump) {
        ⟨Compute offset positions and evaluate displacement texture 478⟩
        ⟨Compute bump-mapped differential geometry 479⟩
        ⟨Orient shading normal to match geometric normal 479⟩
    }
```

⟨*Compute offset positions and evaluate displacement texture*⟩ ≡   478
```
    DifferentialGeometry dgEval = dgs;
    ⟨Shift dgEval du in the u direction 479⟩
    float uDisplace = d->Evaluate(dgEval);
    ⟨Shift dgEval dv in the v direction 479⟩
    float vDisplace = d->Evaluate(dgEval);
    float displace = d->Evaluate(dgs);
```

One remaining issue is how to choose the offsets Δ_u and Δ_v for the finite differencing computations. They should be small enough that fine changes in $d(u, v)$ are captured but large enough so that available floating-point precision is sufficient to give a good result. Here we will choose Δ_u and Δ_v values that lead to an offset that is about half the image space pixel spacing and use them to update the appropriate member variables in the DifferentialGeometry to reflect a shift to the offset position. (See Section 11.1.1 for an explanation of how the image space distances are computed.)

⟨*Shift* dgEval du *in the u direction*⟩ ≡   478
```
float du = .5f * (fabsf(dgs.dudx) + fabsf(dgs.dudy));
if (du == 0.f) du = .01f;
dgEval.p = dgs.p + du * dgs.dpdu;
dgEval.u = dgs.u + du;
dgEval.nn = Normal(Normalize(Cross(dgs.dpdu, dgs.dpdv) +
                             du * dgs.dndu));
```

⟨*Shift* dgEval dv *in the v direction*⟩ ≡   478
```
float dv = .5f * (fabsf(dgs.dvdx) + fabsf(dgs.dvdy));
if (dv == 0.f) dv = .01f;
dgEval.p = dgs.p + dv * dgs.dpdv;
dgEval.u = dgs.u;
dgEval.v = dgs.v + dv;
dgEval.nn = Normal(Normalize(Cross(dgs.dpdu, dgs.dpdv) +
                             dv * dgs.dndv));
```

Given the new positions and the displacement texture's values at them, the partial derivatives can be computed directly using Equation (10.1):

⟨*Compute bump-mapped differential geometry*⟩ ≡   478
```
*dgBump = dgs;
dgBump->dpdu = dgs.dpdu + (uDisplace - displace) / du * Vector(dgs.nn) +
               displace * dgs.dndu;
dgBump->dpdv = dgs.dpdv + (vDisplace - displace) / dv * Vector(dgs.nn) +
               displace * dgs.dndv;
dgBump->nn = Normal(Normalize(Cross(dgBump->dpdu, dgBump->dpdv)));
if (dgs.shape->reverseOrientation ^ dgs.shape->transformSwapsHandedness)
    dgBump->nn *= -1.f;
```

Finally, this method flips the shading coordinate frame if needed, so that the shading normal lies in the hemisphere around the geometric normal. Since the shading normal represents a relatively small perturbation of the geometric normal, the two of them should always be in the same hemisphere.

⟨*Orient shading normal to match geometric normal*⟩ ≡   478
```
if (Dot(dgGeom.nn, dgBump->nn) < 0.f)
    dgBump->nn *= -1.f;
```

FURTHER READING

Blinn (1978) invented the bump-mapping technique. Kajiya (1985) generalized the idea of bump mapping the normal to *frame mapping*, which also perturbs the surface's primary tangent vector and is useful for controlling the appearance of anisotropic reflection models.

Snyder and Barr (1987) noted the light leak problem from per-vertex shading normals and proposed a number of work-arounds. The method we have used in this chapter is from Section 5.3 of Veach's thesis (Veach 1997); it is a more robust solution than those of Snyder and Barr.

Shading normals introduce a number of subtle problems for physically based light transport algorithms that we have not addressed here. For example, they can easily lead to surfaces that reflect more energy than was incident upon them, which can wreak havoc with light transport algorithms that are designed under the assumption of energy conservation. Veach (1996) has investigated this issue in depth and developed a number of solutions.

One visual shortcoming of bump mapping is that it doesn't naturally account for self-shadowing, where bumps cast shadows on the surface and prevent light from reaching nearby points. These shadows can have a significant impact on the appearance of rough surfaces. Max (1988) has developed the *horizon mapping* technique, which performs a preprocess on bump maps stored in image maps to compute a term to account for this effect. This approach isn't directly applicable to procedural textures, however. Dana et al. (1999) have measured spatially varying reflection properties from real-world surfaces, including these self-shadowing effects; they convincingly demonstrate this effect's importance for accurate image synthesis.

Another difficult issue related to bump mapping is that antialiasing bump maps that have higher frequency detail than can be represented in the image is quite difficult. In particular, it is not enough to remove high-frequency detail from the bump map function, but in general the BSDF needs to be modified to account for this detail. Fournier (1992) applied *normal distribution functions* to this problem, where the surface normal was generalized to represent a distribution of normal directions. Becker and Max (1993) developed algorithms for blending between bump maps and BRDFs that represented higher-frequency details. More recently, Schilling (1997, 2001) has investigated this issue, particularly for application to graphics hardware.

An alternative to bump mapping is displacement mapping, where the bump function is used to actually modify the surface geometry, rather than just perturbing the normal (Cook 1984; Cook, Carpenter, and Catmull 1987). Advantages of displacement mapping include geometric detail on object silhouettes and the possibility of accounting for self-shadowing. Patterson and collaborators have described an innovative algorithm for displacement mapping with ray tracing where the geometry is unperturbed but the ray's direction is modified such that the intersections that are found are the same as would be found with the displaced geometry (Patterson, Hoggar, and Logie 1991; Logie and Patterson 1994). Heidrich and Seidel (1998) have developed a technique for computing direct intersections with procedurally defined displacement functions.

With the advent of increased memory on computers and caching algorithms, the option of finely tessellating geometry and displacing its vertices for ray tracing has become feasible. Pharr and Hanrahan (1996) describe an approach to this problem based on geometry caching, and Wang et al. (2000) describe an adaptive tessellation algorithm that reduces memory requirements. Smits, Shirley, and Stark (2000) lazily tessellate individual triangles, saving a substantial amount of memory.

The coefficients for the Lafortune BRDF materials in this chapter are from measurements made by Marschner at al. (1999) and are included in the system with the permission of the Program of Computer Graphics, Cornell University.

EXERCISES

❷ 10.1   If the same `Texture` is bound to more than one component of a `Material` (for example, to both `Plastic::Kd` and `Plastic::Ks`), the texture will be evaluated twice. This unnecessarily duplicated work may lead to a noticeable increase in rendering time if the `Texture` is itself computationally expensive. Modify the materials in pbrt to eliminate this problem. Measure the change in the system's performance, both for standard scenes as well as for contrived scenes that show off the redundancy.

❸ 10.2   One form of aliasing that pbrt doesn't try to eliminate is specular highlight aliasing. Glossy specular surfaces with high specular exponents, particularly if they have high curvature, are susceptible to aliasing as small changes in incident direction or surface position (and thus surface normal) may cause the highlight's contribution to change substantially. Read Amanatides's paper on this topic (Amanatides 1992) and extend pbrt to reduce specular aliasing, either using his technique or by developing your own. Most of the quantities needed to do the appropriate computations are already available—$\partial \mathbf{n}/\partial x$ and $\partial \mathbf{n}/\partial y$ in the `DifferentialGeometry`, and so on—although it will probably be necessary to extend the `BxDF` interface to provide more information about the values of specular exponents for glossy specular reflection components.

❷ 10.3   Another approach to specular highlight aliasing is to supersample the BSDF, evaluating it multiple times around the point being shaded. After reading the discussion of supersampling texture functions in Section 11.1, modify the BSDF::f() method to shift around to a set of positions around the intersection point but within the pixel sampling rate around the intersection point and evaluate the BSDF at each one of them when the BSDF evaluation routines are called. (Be sure to account for the change in normal using its partial derivatives.) How well does this approach combat specular highlight aliasing?

❸ 10.4 pbrt doesn't directly represent interfaces between objects that transmit light; instead, it assumes that for transmitted rays entering or leaving an object, the index of refraction outside the object is one. This assumption breaks down for many common cases—for example, a glass of water where rays pass directly from the glass into the water. Furthermore, in pbrt, if such a scene is modeled with the edge of the water coincident with the interior edge of the glass, the transmission from glass to water may be missed completely, since only one of the two ray intersections would be detected. Modify the system to eliminate this problem and render images showing that your approach renders correct images where pbrt currently computes an incorrect result. See, for example, Schmidt and Budge (2002) for one approach to this issue.

❸ 10.5 Read some of the papers on filtering bump maps referenced in the "Further Reading" section of this chapter, choose one of the techniques described there, and implement it in pbrt. Show both the visual artifacts from bump map aliasing without the technique you implement as well as examples of how well your implementation addresses them.

❸ 10.6 Neyret (1996, 1998) has developed algorithms that automatically take descriptions of complex shapes and their reflective properties and turn them into generalized reflection models at different resolutions, each with limited frequency content. The advantage of this representation is that it makes it easy to select an appropriate level of detail for an object based on its size on the screen, thus reducing aliasing. Read these papers and implement the algorithms described in them in pbrt. Show how they can be used to reduce geometric aliasing from detailed geometry and extend them to address bump map aliasing.

❸ 10.7 Use the triangular face refinement infrastructure from the LoopSubdiv shape to implement displacement mapping in pbrt. Rather than just adjusting the surface normal as in bump mapping, the actual surface shape is modified by displacement mapping. The usual approach to displacement mapping is to finely tessellate the geometric shape and then to evaluate the displacement function at its vertices, moving each vertex the given distance along its normal. Because displacement mapping may make the extent of the shape larger, the bounding box of the undisplaced shape will need to be expanded by the maximum displacement distance that a particular displacement function will ever generate.

BSDF::f() 466
LoopSubdiv 136

Refine each face of the mesh until, when projected onto the image, it is roughly the size of the separation between pixels. To do this, you will need to be able to estimate the image pixel-based length of an edge in the scene when it is projected onto the screen. Use the texturing infrastructure in Chapter 11 to evaluate displacement functions. See Pharr and Hanrahan (1996) for discussion of issues related to avoiding cracks in the mesh due to the adaptive refinement.

CHAPTER ELEVEN

11 TEXTURE

We will now describe a set of interfaces and classes that allow us to incorporate *texture* into our material models. Recall that the materials in Chapter 10 are all based on various parameters that describe their characteristics (diffuse reflectance, glossiness, etc.). Because real-world material properties typically vary over surfaces, it is necessary to be able to describe these patterns in some manner. In pbrt, because the texture abstractions are defined in a way that separates the pattern generation methods from the material implementations, it is easy to combine them in arbitrary ways, thereby making it easier to create a wide variety of appearances.

In pbrt, a texture is an extremely general concept: it is a function that maps points in some domain (e.g., a surface's (u, v) parametric space or (x, y, z) object space) to values in some other domain (e.g., spectra or the real numbers). A wide variety of implementations of texture classes are available as plug-ins. For example, pbrt has textures that represent zero-dimensional functions that return a constant in order to accommodate surfaces that have the same parameter value everywhere. Image map textures are two-dimensional functions of (s, t) parameter values that use a 2D array of pixel values to compute values at a particular point (they are described in Section 11.4). There are even texture functions that compute values based on the values computed by other texture functions.

Textures may be a source of high-frequency variation in the final image. Figure 11.1 shows an image with severe aliasing due to a texture. Although the visual impact of this aliasing can be reduced with the nonuniform sampling techniques from Chapter 7, a

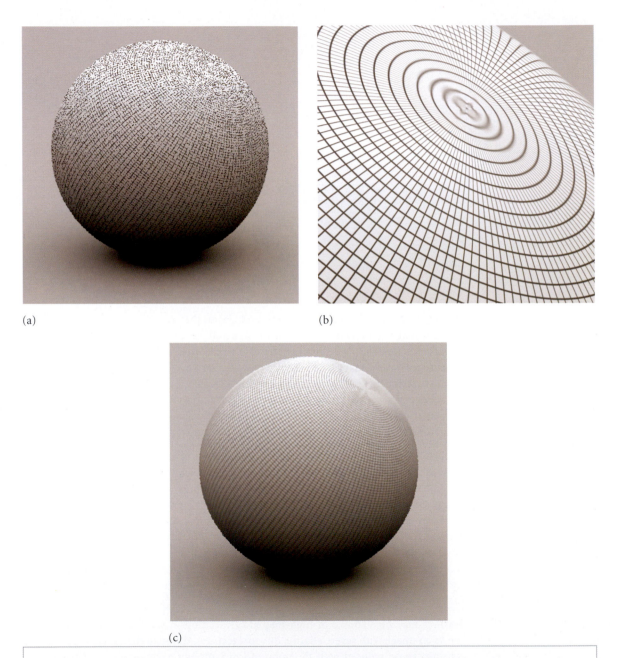

(a)   (b)

(c)

Figure 11.1: Texture Aliasing. (a) An image of a grid texture on a sphere with one sample per pixel has severe aliasing artifacts. (b) A zoomed-in area from near the top of the sphere gives a sense of how much high-frequency detail is present between adjacent pixel sample positions. (c) The texture function has taken into account the image sampling rate to prefilter its function and remove high-frequency detail, resulting in an antialiased image, even with a single sample per pixel.

better solution to this problem is to implement texture functions that eliminate their high-frequency content based on the rate at which they are being sampled. For many texture functions, computing at least a good approximation to the frequency content and antialiasing in this manner isn't too difficult and is substantially more efficient than increasing the image sampling rate.

The first section of this chapter will discuss the problem of texture aliasing and general approaches to solving it. We will then describe the basic texture interface and illustrate its use with a few simple texture functions. Throughout the remainder of the chapter, we will present a variety of more complex texture implementations, demonstrating the use of a number of different texture antialiasing techniques along the way.

11.1 SAMPLING AND ANTIALIASING

The sampling task from Chapter 7 is a frustrating one since the aliasing problem was known to be unsolvable from the start. The infinite frequency content of geometric edges and hard shadows *guarantees* aliasing in the final images, no matter how high the image sampling rate. Fortunately, for textures things are not so hopeless: either there is often a convenient analytic form of the texture function available, which makes it possible to remove excessively high frequencies before sampling it, or it is possible to be careful when evaluating the function so as not to introduce high frequencies in the first place. When this problem is carefully addressed in texture implementations, as is done through the rest of this chapter, there is usually no need for more than one sample per pixel in order to render an image without texture aliasing.

Two problems must be addressed in order to remove aliasing from texture functions:

1. The sampling rate in texture space must be computed. The screen space sampling rate is known from the image resolution and pixel sampling rate, but here we need to determine the resulting sampling rate on a surface in the scene in order to find the rate at which the texture function is being sampled.
2. Given the texture sampling rate, sampling theory must be applied to guide the computation of a texture value that doesn't have higher-frequency variation than can be represented by the sampling rate (e.g., by removing excess frequencies beyond the Nyquist limit from the texture function).

These two issues will be addressed in turn throughout the rest of this section.

11.1.1 FINDING THE TEXTURE SAMPLING RATE

Consider an arbitrary texture function that is a function of position, $T(\mathrm{p})$, defined on a surface in the scene. If we ignore the complications introduced by visibility issues—the possibility that another object may occlude the surface at nearby image samples, or that the surface may have a limited extent on the image plane—this texture function can also be expressed as a function over points (x, y) on the image plane, $T(f(x, y))$,

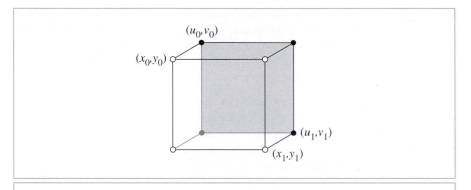

Figure 11.2: If a quadrilateral is viewed with an orthographic perspective such that the quadrilateral precisely fills the image plane, it's easy to compute the relationship between the sampling rate in (x, y) pixel coordinates and the texture sampling rate.

where $f(x, y)$ is the function that maps image points to points on the surface. Thus, $T(f(x, y))$ gives the value of the texture function as seen at pixel (x, y).

As a simple example of this idea, consider a 2D texture function $T(s, t)$ applied to a quadrilateral that is perpendicular to the z axis and has corners at the world space points $(0, 0, 0)$, $(1, 0, 0)$, $(1, 1, 0)$, and $(0, 1, 0)$. If an orthographic camera is placed looking down the z axis such that the quadrilateral precisely fills the image plane and if points p on the quadrilateral are mapped to 2D (s, t) texture coordinates by

$$s = \mathrm{p}_x \qquad t = \mathrm{p}_y,$$

then the relationship between (s, t) and screen (x, y) pixels is straightforward:

$$s = \frac{x}{x_r} \qquad t = \frac{y}{y_r},$$

where the overall image resolution is (x_r, y_r) (Figure 11.2). Thus, given a sample spacing of one pixel in the image plane, the sample spacing in (s, t) texture parameter space is $(1/x_r, 1/y_r)$, and the texture function must remove any detail at a higher frequency than can be represented at that sampling rate.

This relationship between pixel coordinates and texture coordinates, and thus the relationship between their sampling rates, is the key bit of information that determines the maximum frequency content allowable in the texture function. As a slightly more complex example, given a triangle with (s, t) texture coordinates at the vertices and viewed with a perspective projection, it's possible to analytically find the differences in s and t across the sample points on the image plane. This is the basis of basic texture map antialiasing on graphics hardware.

For more complex scene geometry, camera projections, and mappings to texture coordinates, it is much more difficult to precisely determine the relationship between image positions and texture parameter values. Fortunately, for texture antialiasing, we don't need to be able to evaluate $f(x, y)$ for arbitrary (x, y), but just need to find the relationship between changes in pixel sample position and the resulting change in texture sample position at a particular point on the image. This relationship is given by the partial derivatives of this function, $\partial f/\partial x$ and $\partial f/\partial y$. For example, these can be used to find a first-order approximation to the value of f,

$$f(x', y') \approx f(x, y) + (x' - x)\frac{\partial f}{\partial x} + (y' - y)\frac{\partial f}{\partial y}.$$

If these partial derivatives are changing slowly with respect to the distances $x' - x$ and $y' - y$, this is a reasonable approximation. More importantly, the values of these partial derivatives give an approximation to the change in texture sample position for a shift of one pixel in the x and y directions, respectively, and thus directly yield the texture sampling rate. For example, in the previous quadrilateral example, $\partial s/\partial x = 1/x_r$, $\partial s/\partial y = 0$, $\partial t/\partial x = 0$, and $\partial t/\partial y = 1/y_r$.

The key to finding the values of these partial derivatives lies in the `RayDifferential` structure, which was defined in Section 2.5.1. This structure is initialized for each camera ray in the `Scene::Render()` function and contains not only the ray actually being traced through the scene, but also two additional rays, one offset horizontally one pixel from the camera ray and the other offset vertically by one pixel. All of the geometric ray intersection routines use only the main camera ray for their computations; the auxiliary rays are ignored (this is easy to do because `RayDifferential` is a subclass of `Ray`).

Here we will use the offset rays to estimate the partial derivatives of the mapping $p(x, y)$ from image position to world space position and the partial derivatives of the mappings $u(x, y)$ and $v(x, y)$ from (x, y) to (u, v) parametric coordinates, giving the partial derivatives of world space positions $\partial p/\partial x$ and $\partial p/\partial y$ and the partial derivatives of (u, v) parametric coordinates $\partial u/\partial x$, $\partial v/\partial x$, $\partial u/\partial y$, and $\partial v/\partial y$. In Section 11.2, we will see how these can be used to compute the screen space derivatives of arbitrary quantities based on p or (u, v) and consequently the sampling rates of these quantities. The values of these partial derivatives at the intersection point are stored in the `DifferentialGeometry` structure. Note that they are declared as `mutable`, since they are set in a method that takes a const differential geometry object.

⟨*DifferentialGeometry Public Data*⟩+≡   83
```
    mutable Vector dpdx, dpdy;
    mutable float dudx, dvdx, dudy, dvdy;
```

⟨*Initialize* DifferentialGeometry *from parameters*⟩+≡   83
```
    dudx = dvdx = dudy = dvdy = 0;
```

The `DifferentialGeometry::ComputeDifferentials()` method computes these values. It is called by `Intersection::GetBSDF()` before the `Material::GetBSDF()` method is called so that these values will be available for the texture evaluation routines that are called by the material. Because ray differentials aren't available for all rays traced by the system (e.g., rays starting from light sources traced for photon mapping), the `hasDifferentials` field of the `RayDifferential` must be checked before these computations are done. If the differentials are not present, then the derivatives are all assumed to be zero (which will eventually lead to unfiltered point sampling of textures).

⟨*DifferentialGeometry Method Definitions*⟩+≡
```
   void DifferentialGeometry::ComputeDifferentials(
           const RayDifferential &ray) const {
       if (ray.hasDifferentials) {
           ⟨Estimate screen space change in p and (u, v)  491⟩
       }
       else {
           dudx = dvdx = 0.;
           dudy = dvdy = 0.;
           dpdx = dpdy = Vector(0,0,0);
       }
   }
```

The key to computing these estimates is the assumption that the surface is locally flat with respect to the sampling rate at the point being shaded. This is a reasonable approximation in practice, and it is hard to do much better. Because ray tracing is a point-sampling technique, we have no additional information about the scene in between the rays we traced. For highly curved surfaces or at silhouette edges, this approximation can break down, though it is rarely a source of noticeable error in practice. For this approximation, we need the plane through the point intersected by the main ray that is tangent to the surface. This plane is given by the implicit equation

$$ax + by + cz + d = 0,$$

where $a = \mathbf{n}_x$, $b = \mathbf{n}_y$, $c = \mathbf{n}_z$, and $d = -(\mathbf{n} \cdot \mathbf{p})$. We can then compute the intersection points p_x and p_y between the auxiliary rays r_x and r_y with this plane (Figure 11.3). These new points give an approximation to the partial derivatives of position on the surface $\partial \mathrm{p}/\partial x$ and $\partial \mathrm{p}/\partial y$, based on forward differences:

$$\frac{\partial \mathrm{p}}{\partial x} \approx \mathrm{p}_x - \mathrm{p}, \quad \frac{\partial \mathrm{p}}{\partial y} \approx \mathrm{p}_y - \mathrm{p}.$$

Because the differential rays are offset one pixel in each direction, there's no need to divide these differences by a Δ value, since $\Delta = 1$.

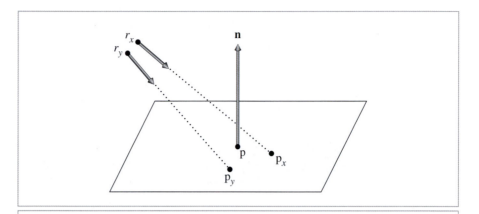

Figure 11.3: By approximating the local surface geometry at the intersection point with the tangent plane through p, approximations to the points at which the auxiliary rays r_x and r_y would intersect the surface can be found by finding their intersection points with the tangent plane p_x and p_y.

⟨*Estimate screen space change in* p *and* (u, v)⟩ ≡   **490**
    ⟨*Compute auxiliary intersection points with plane* **491**⟩
    dpdx = px - p;
    dpdy = py - p;
    ⟨*Compute* (u, v) *offsets at auxiliary points* **493**⟩

The ray-plane intersection algorithm gives the t value where a ray described by origin o and direction **d** intersects a plane described by $ax + by + cz + d = 0$:

$$t = \frac{-((a, b, c) \cdot \mathrm{o}) + d}{(a, b, c) \cdot \mathbf{d}}.$$

To compute this value for the two auxiliary rays, the plane's d coefficient is computed first. It isn't necessary to compute the a, b, and c coefficients, since they're available in dg.nn. We can then apply the formula directly.

⟨*Compute auxiliary intersection points with plane*⟩ ≡   **491**

```
float d = -Dot(nn, Vector(p.x, p.y, p.z));
Vector rxv(ray.rx.o.x, ray.rx.o.y, ray.rx.o.z);
float tx = -(Dot(nn, rxv) + d) / Dot(nn, ray.rx.d);
Point px = ray.rx.o + tx * ray.rx.d;
Vector ryv(ray.ry.o.x, ray.ry.o.y, ray.ry.o.z);
float ty = -(Dot(nn, ryv) + d) / Dot(nn, ray.ry.d);
Point py = ray.ry.o + ty * ray.ry.d;
```

Using the positions p_x and p_y, an approximation to their respective (u, v) coordinates can be found by taking advantage of the fact that the surface's partial derivatives $\partial \mathrm{p}/\partial u$

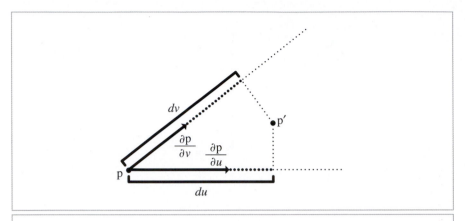

Figure 11.4: An estimate of the difference in (u, v) parametric coordinates from p to p′ can be found by finding the coordinates of p′ with respect to the coordinate system defined by p, $\partial p/\partial u$, and $\partial p/\partial v$.

and $\partial p/\partial v$ form a (not necessarily orthogonal) coordinate system on the plane and that the coordinates of the auxiliary intersection points in terms of this coordinate system are their coordinates with respect to the (u, v) parameterization (Figure 11.4). Given a position p′ on the plane, we can compute its position with respect to the coordinate system by

$$p' = p + \Delta_u \frac{\partial p}{\partial u} + \Delta_v \frac{\partial p}{\partial v}$$

or

$$\begin{pmatrix} p' - p_x \\ p' - p_y \\ p' - p_z \end{pmatrix} = \begin{pmatrix} \partial p_x/\partial u & \partial p_x/\partial v \\ \partial p_y/\partial u & \partial p_y/\partial v \\ \partial p_z/\partial u & \partial p_z/\partial v \end{pmatrix} \begin{pmatrix} \Delta_u \\ \Delta_v \end{pmatrix}.$$

The solutions to this linear system of equations for the two auxiliary intersection points give the screen space partial derivatives $\partial u/\partial x$, $\partial v/\partial x$, $\partial u/\partial y$, and $\partial v/\partial y$. This linear system has three equations with two unknowns—that is, it's overconstrained. However, we need to be careful since one of the equations may be degenerate—for example, if $\partial p/\partial u$ and $\partial p/\partial v$ are in the xy plane such that their z components are both zero, then the third equation will be degenerate. To deal with this case, because we only need two equations to solve the system, we'd like to choose the two that won't lead to a degenerate system. An easy way to do this is to take the cross product of $\partial p/\partial u$ and $\partial p/\partial v$, see which coordinate of the result has the largest magnitude, and use the other two. Since their cross product is already available in nn, this is particularly straightforward. Even after all this, it may happen that the linear system has no solution (usually due to the partial derivatives not forming a coordinate system on the plane). In that case, all that can be done is to return arbitrary values.

⟨*Compute* (*u*, *v*) *offsets at auxiliary points*⟩ ≡ 491
  ⟨*Initialize* A, Bx, *and* By *matrices for offset computation* 493⟩

```
    if (SolveLinearSystem2x2(A, Bx, x)) {
        dudx = x[0]; dvdx = x[1];
    }
    else {
        dudx = 1.; dvdx = 0.;
    }
    if (SolveLinearSystem2x2(A, By, x)) {
        dudy = x[0]; dvdy = x[1];
    }
    else {
        dudy = 0.; dvdy = 1.;
    }
```

⟨*Initialize* A, Bx, *and* By *matrices for offset computation*⟩ ≡ 493

```
    float A[2][2], Bx[2], By[2], x[2];
    int axes[2];
    if (fabsf(nn.x) > fabsf(nn.y) && fabsf(nn.x) > fabsf(nn.z)) {
        axes[0] = 1; axes[1] = 2;
    }
    else if (fabsf(nn.y) > fabsf(nn.z)) {
        axes[0] = 0; axes[1] = 2;
    }
    else {
        axes[0] = 0; axes[1] = 1;
    }
```

  ⟨*Initialize matrices for chosen projection plane* 493⟩

⟨*Initialize matrices for chosen projection plane*⟩ ≡ 493

```
    A[0][0] = dpdu[axes[0]];
    A[0][1] = dpdv[axes[0]];
    A[1][0] = dpdu[axes[1]];
    A[1][1] = dpdv[axes[1]];
    Bx[0] = px[axes[0]] - p[axes[0]];
    Bx[1] = px[axes[1]] - p[axes[1]];
    By[0] = py[axes[0]] - p[axes[0]];
    By[1] = py[axes[1]] - p[axes[1]];
```

11.1.2 FILTERING TEXTURE FUNCTIONS

It is necessary to remove frequencies in texture functions that are past the Nyquist limit for the texture sampling rate. The goal is to compute, with as few approximations as possible, the result of the *ideal texture resampling* process, which says that in order to evaluate $T(f(x, y))$ without aliasing, we must first band-limit it, removing frequencies beyond the Nyquist limit by convolving it with the sinc filter:

$$T_b'(x, y) = \int_{-\infty}^{\infty} \int_{-\infty}^{\infty} \text{sinc}(x')\,\text{sinc}(y')T'\left(f(x + x', y + y')\right)\,\mathrm{d}x'\mathrm{d}y'.$$

The band-limited function in turn should then be convolved with the pixel filter $g(x, y)$ centered at the (x, y) point on the screen at which we want to evaluate the texture function:

$$T_f'(x, y) = \int_{-\text{xWidth}/2}^{\text{xWidth}/2} \int_{-\text{yWidth}/2}^{\text{yWidth}/2} g(x', y')T_b'(x + x', y + y')\mathrm{d}x'\mathrm{d}y'.$$

This gives the theoretically perfect value for the texture as projected onto the screen.[1]

In practice, there are many simplifications that can be made to this process, with little reduction in visual quality. For example, a box filter may be used for the band-limiting step, and the second step is usually ignored completely, effectively acting as if the pixel filter was a box filter, which makes it possible to do the antialiasing work completely in texture space and simplifies the implementation significantly. The EWA filtering algorithm in Section 11.4.4 is a notable exception that doesn't make all of these simplifications.

Even the box filter, with all of its shortcomings, gives acceptable results for texture filtering in many cases. The box can be particularly easy to use, since it can be applied analytically by computing the average of the texture function over the appropriate region. Intuitively, this is a reasonable approach to the texture filtering problem, and it can be computed directly for many texture functions. Indeed, through the rest of this chapter, we will often use a box filter to average texture function values between samples and informally use the term "filter region" to describe the area being averaged over. This is the most common approach when filtering texture functions.

An alternative to using the box filter to filter texture functions is to use the observation that the effect of the ideal sinc filter is to let frequency components below the Nyquist limit pass through unchanged but to remove frequencies past it. Therefore, if we know the frequency content of the texture function (e.g., if it is a sum of terms, each one with known frequency content), then if we replace the high-frequency terms with their average values, we are effectively doing the work of the sinc prefilter. This approach is known as *clamping* and is the basis for antialiasing in the textures based on the noise function in Section 11.6.

---

1 One simplification that is present in this ideal filtering process is the implicit assumption that the texture function makes a linear contribution to frequency content in the image, so that filtering out high frequencies removes high frequencies from the image. This is true for many uses of textures—for example, if an image map is used to modulate the diffuse term of a Matte material. However, if a texture is used to determine the roughness of a glossy specular object, for example, this linearity assumption is incorrect, since the roughness value is both inverted and used as an exponent in a microfacet BRDF. We will ignore this issue here, since it isn't easily solved in general and usually doesn't cause substantial errors.

Matte 469

Finally, for texture functions where none of these techniques is easily applied, the approach of last resort is *supersampling*—the function is evaluated and filtered at multiple locations near the main evaluation point, thus increasing the sampling rate in texture space. If a box filter is used to filter these sample values, this is equivalent to averaging the value of the function. This approach can be expensive if the texture function is complex to evaluate, and as with image sampling, a very large number of samples may be needed to remove aliasing. Although this is a brute-force solution, it is still more efficient than increasing the image sampling rate, since it saves the cost of tracing more rays through the scene.

★ 11.1.3 RAY DIFFERENTIALS FOR SPECULAR REFLECTION AND TRANSMISSION

Given the effectiveness of ray differentials for finding filter regions for texture antialiasing for camera rays, it is useful to extend the method to make it possible to determine texture space sampling rates for objects that are seen indirectly via specular reflection or refraction; objects seen in mirrors, for example, should also no more have texture aliasing than directly visible objects. Igehy (1999) has developed an elegant solution to the problem of how to find the appropriate differential rays for specular reflection and refraction, which is the approach used in pbrt.[2]

Figure 11.5 illustrates the difference that proper texture filtering for specular reflection and transmission can make. Figure 11.5(a) shows a glass ball and a mirrored ball on a plane with a texture map containing high-frequency components. Ray differentials ensure that the images of the texture seen via reflection and refraction from the balls are free of aliasing artifacts. A close-up view of the reflection in the glass ball is shown in Figure 11.5(b) and (c); Figure 11.5(b) was rendered without ray differentials for the reflected and transmitted rays, and Figure 11.5(c) was rendered with ray differentials. The aliasing errors in the left image are eliminated on the right without excessively blurring the texture.

In order to compute the reflected or transmitted ray differentials at a surface intersection point, we need an approximation to the rays that would have been traced at the intersection points for the two offset rays in the ray differential that hit the surface (Figure 11.6). The new ray for the main ray is computed by the BSDF, so here we only need to compute the outgoing rays for the r_x and r_y differentials.

For both reflection and refraction, the origin of each differential ray is easily found. The DifferentialGeometry::ComputeDifferentials() method previously computed approximations for how much the surface position changes with respect to (x, y) position on the image plane $\partial p/\partial x$ and $\partial p/\partial y$. Adding these offsets to the intersection point of the main ray gives approximate origins for the new rays.

DifferentialGeometry::
  ComputeDifferentials() 490

---

2   Igehy's formulation is slightly different than the one here—he effectively tracked the differences between the main ray and the offset rays, while we store the offset rays explicitly. The mathematics all work out to be the same in the end; we chose this alternative since we believe that it makes the algorithm's operation for camera rays easier to understand.

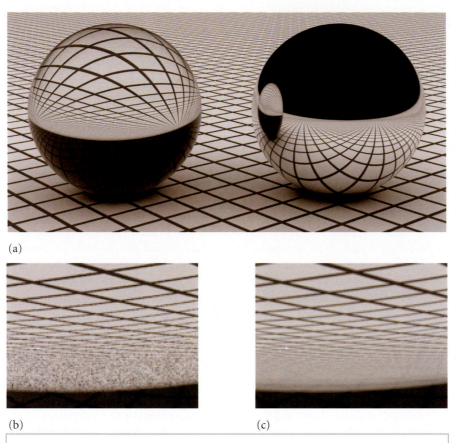

(a)

(b)   (c)

Figure 11.5: (a) Tracking ray differentials for reflected and refracted rays ensures that the image map texture seen in the balls is filtered to avoid aliasing. The left ball is glass, exhibiting reflection and refraction, and the right ball is a mirror, just showing reflection. Note that the texture is well filtered over both of the balls. (b) and (c) show a zoomed-in section of the glass ball; (b) shows the aliasing artifacts that are present if ray differentials aren't used, while (c) shows the result when they are.

⟨*Compute ray differential* rd *for specular reflection*⟩ ≡   **36**
```
    RayDifferential rd(p, wi);
    rd.hasDifferentials = true;
    rd.rx.o = p + isect.dg.dpdx;
    rd.ry.o = p + isect.dg.dpdy;
```
    ⟨*Compute differential reflected directions* **498**⟩

DifferentialGeometry::dpdx 489
DifferentialGeometry::dpdy 489
Intersection::dg 172
RayDifferential 60

Finding the directions of these rays is slightly more tricky. Igehy observed that if we know how much the reflected direction ω_i changes with respect to a shift of a pixel in the x and

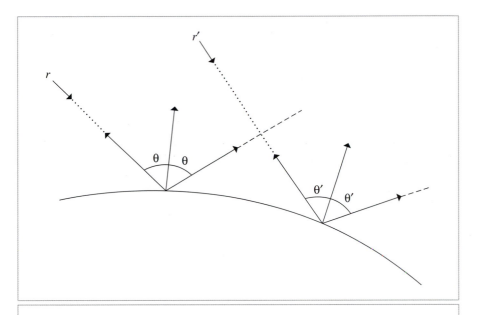

Figure 11.6: The specular reflection formula gives the direction of the reflected ray at a point on a surface. An offset ray for a ray differential (dashed line) will generally intersect the surface at a different point and be reflected in a different direction. The new direction is affected by both the different surface normal at the point as well as the offset ray's different incident direction. The computation to find the reflected direction for the offset ray in pbrt estimates the change in reflected direction as a function of image space position and approximates the ray differential's direction with the main ray's direction added to the estimated change in direction.

y directions on the image plane, we can use this information to approximate the direction of the offset rays:

$$\omega \approx \omega_i + \frac{\partial \omega_i}{\partial x}.$$

For a general world space surface normal and outgoing direction, the direction for perfect specular reflection is

$$\omega_i = -\omega_o + 2(\omega_o \cdot \mathbf{n})\mathbf{n}.$$

Fortunately, the partial derivatives of this expression are easily computed:

$$\frac{\partial \omega_i}{\partial x} = \frac{\partial}{\partial x}\left(-\omega_o + 2(\omega_o \cdot \mathbf{n})\mathbf{n}\right)$$

$$= -\frac{\partial \omega_o}{\partial x} + 2\left((\omega_o \cdot \mathbf{n})\frac{\partial \mathbf{n}}{\partial x} + \frac{\partial(\omega_o \cdot \mathbf{n})}{\partial x}\mathbf{n}\right).$$

Using the properties of the dot product, it can be shown that

$$\frac{\partial(\omega_o \cdot \mathbf{n})}{\partial x} = \frac{\partial \omega_o}{\partial x}\cdot \mathbf{n} + \omega_o \cdot \frac{\partial \mathbf{n}}{\partial x}.$$

The value of $\partial\omega_o/\partial x$ can be found from the difference between the direction of the ray differential's main ray and the direction of the r_x offset ray, and all of the other necessary quantities are readily available from the DifferentialGeometry, so the implementation of this computation for the partial derivatives in x and y is straightforward.

⟨*Compute differential reflected directions*⟩ ≡　　　　　　　　　　　　　　　　**496**
```
Vector dndx = bsdf->dgShading.dndu * bsdf->dgShading.dudx +
              bsdf->dgShading.dndv * bsdf->dgShading.dvdx;
Vector dndy = bsdf->dgShading.dndu * bsdf->dgShading.dudy +
              bsdf->dgShading.dndv * bsdf->dgShading.dvdy;
Vector dwodx = -ray.rx.d - wo, dwody = -ray.ry.d - wo;
float dDNdx = Dot(dwodx, n) + Dot(wo, dndx);
float dDNdy = Dot(dwody, n) + Dot(wo, dndy);
rd.rx.d = wi - dwodx + 2 * (Dot(wo, n) * dndx +
                           Vector(dDNdx * n));
rd.ry.d = wi - dwody + 2 * (Dot(wo, n) * dndy +
                           Vector(dDNdy * n));
```

A similar process of differentiating the equation for the direction of a specularly transmitted ray gives the equation to find the differential change in the transmitted direction. We won't include the derivation or our implementation here, but refer the interested reader to the original paper and to the source code, respectively.

11.2 TEXTURE COORDINATE GENERATION

Almost all of the textures in this chapter are functions that take a two-dimensional or three-dimensional coordinate and return a texture value. Sometimes there are obvious ways to choose these texture coordinates; for parametric surfaces, such as the quadrics in Chapter 3, there is a natural two-dimensional (u, v) parameterization of the surface, and for all surfaces the shading point p is a natural choice for a three-dimensional coordinate.

There is often no natural parameterization of complex surfaces, or the natural parameterization may be undesirable. For instance, the (u, v) values near the poles of spheres are severely distorted. Also, for an arbitrary subdivision surface, there is no simple, general-purpose way to assign texture values so that the entire $[0, 1]^2$ space is covered continuously and without distortion. In fact, creating smooth parameterizations of complex meshes with low distortion is an active area of research in computer graphics.

This section starts by introducing two abstract base classes—TextureMapping2D and TextureMapping3D—that provide an interface for computing these 2D and 3D texture coordinates. We will then implement a number of standard mappings using this interface (Figure 11.7 shows a number of them). Texture implementations store a pointer to a 2D or 3D mapping function as appropriate and use it to compute the texture coordinates at each point. Thus, it's easy to add new mappings to the system without needing

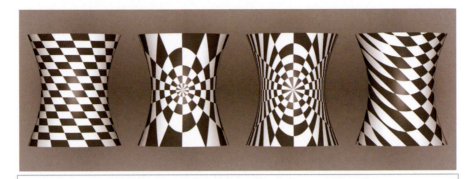

Figure 11.7: A checkerboard texture, applied to a hyperboloid with different texture coordinate generation techniques. From left to right, (u, v) mapping, spherical mapping, cylindrical mapping, and planar mapping.

to modify all of the Texture implementations, and different mappings can be used for different textures associated with the same surface. In pbrt, we will use the convention that 2D texture coordinates are denoted by (s, t); this helps make clear the distinction between the intrinsic (u, v) parameterization of the underlying surface and the (possibly different) coordinate values used for texturing.

The TextureMapping2D base class has a single method, TextureMapping2D::Map(), which is given the DifferentialGeometry at the shading point and returns the (s, t) texture coordinates via float pointers. It also returns estimates for the change in s and t with respect to pixel x and y coordinates in the dsdx, dtdx, dsty, and dtdy parameters so that textures that use the mapping can determine the (s, t) sampling rate and filter accordingly.

⟨*Texture Declarations*⟩ ≡
```
class COREDLL TextureMapping2D {
public:
    ⟨TextureMapping2D Interface 499⟩
};
```

⟨*TextureMapping2D Interface*⟩ ≡   **499**
```
virtual void Map(const DifferentialGeometry &dg,
                 float *s, float *t, float *dsdx, float *dtdx,
                 float *dsdy, float *dtdy) const = 0;
```

11.2.1 2D (u, v) MAPPING

The simplest texture mapping uses the 2D parametric (u, v) coordinates in the DifferentialGeometry to compute the texture coordinates. Their values can be offset and scaled with user-supplied values in each dimension.

⟨*Texture Declarations*⟩+≡
```
class COREDLL UVMapping2D : public TextureMapping2D {
public:
    ⟨UVMapping2D Public Methods⟩
private:
    float su, sv, du, dv;
};
```

⟨*Texture Method Definitions*⟩≡
```
UVMapping2D::UVMapping2D(float _su, float _sv,
                        float _du, float _dv) {
    su = _su; sv = _sv;
    du = _du; dv = _dv;
}
```

The scale-and-shift computation to compute (s, t) coordinates is straightforward:

⟨*Texture Method Definitions*⟩+≡
```
void UVMapping2D::Map(const DifferentialGeometry &dg,
                     float *s, float *t, float *dsdx, float *dtdx,
                     float *dsdy, float *dtdy) const {
    *s = su * dg.u + du;
    *t = sv * dg.v + dv;
    ⟨Compute texture differentials for 2D identity mapping 501⟩
}
```

Computing the differential change in s and t in terms of the original change in u and v and the scale amounts is also easy. Using the chain rule,

$$\frac{\partial s}{\partial x} = \frac{\partial u}{\partial x}\frac{\partial s}{\partial u} + \frac{\partial v}{\partial x}\frac{\partial s}{\partial v}$$

and similarly for the three other partial derivatives. From the mapping method,

$$s = s_u u + d_u,$$

so

$$\frac{\partial s}{\partial u} = s_u, \qquad \frac{\partial s}{\partial v} = 0,$$

and thus

$$\frac{\partial s}{\partial x} = s_u \frac{\partial u}{\partial x},$$

and so forth.

⟨*Compute texture differentials for 2D identity mapping*⟩ ≡   **500**

```
*dsdx = su * dg.dudx;
*dtdx = sv * dg.dvdx;
*dsdy = su * dg.dudy;
*dtdy = sv * dg.dvdy;
```

11.2.2 SPHERICAL MAPPING

Another useful mapping effectively wraps a sphere around the object. Each point is projected along the vector from the sphere's center through the point, up to the sphere's surface. There, the (u, v) mapping for the sphere shape is used. The SphericalMapping2D stores a transformation that is applied to points before this mapping is performed; this effectively allows the mapping sphere to be arbitrarily positioned and oriented with respect to the object.

⟨*Texture Declarations*⟩+≡

```
class COREDLL SphericalMapping2D : public TextureMapping2D {
public:
    ⟨SphericalMapping2D Public Methods⟩
private:
    void sphere(const Point &P, float *s, float *t) const;
    Transform WorldToTexture;
};
```

⟨*Texture Method Definitions*⟩+≡

```
void SphericalMapping2D::Map(const DifferentialGeometry &dg,
        float *s, float *t, float *dsdx, float *dtdx,
        float *dsdy, float *dtdy) const {
    sphere(dg.p, s, t);
    ⟨Compute texture coordinate differentials for sphere (u, v) mapping  502⟩
}
```

A short utility function computes the mapping for a single point. It will be useful to have this logic separated out for computing texture coordinate differentials.

⟨*Texture Method Definitions*⟩+≡

```
void SphericalMapping2D::sphere(const Point &p, float *s, float *t) const {
    Vector vec = Normalize(WorldToTexture(p) - Point(0,0,0));
    float theta = SphericalTheta(vec);
    float phi = SphericalPhi(vec);
    *s = theta * INV_PI;
    *t = phi * INV_TWOPI;
}
```

We could use the chain rule again to compute the texture coordinate differentials, but will instead use a forward differencing approximation to demonstrate another way to compute these values that is useful for more complex mapping functions. Recall that the DifferentialGeometry stores the screen space partial derivatives $\partial p/\partial x$ and $\partial p/\partial y$ that give the change in position as a function of change in image sample position. Therefore, if the s coordinate is computed by some function $f_s(p)$, it's easy to compute approximations like

$$\frac{\partial s}{\partial x} \approx \frac{f_s(p + \Delta \partial p/\partial x) - f_s(p)}{\Delta}.$$

As the distance Δ approaches 0, this gives the actual partial derivative at p.

One other detail is that the sphere mapping has a discontinuity in the mapping formula; there is a seam at $t = 1$, where the t texture coordinate discontinuously jumps back to zero. We can detect this case by checking to see if the value computed with forward differencing is greater than 0.5 and then adjusting it appropriately.

⟨*Compute texture coordinate differentials for sphere* (u, v) *mapping*⟩ ≡   **501**
```
float sx, tx, sy, ty;
const float delta = .1f;
sphere(dg.p + delta * dg.dpdx, &sx, &tx);
*dsdx = (sx - *s) / delta;
*dtdx = (tx - *t) / delta;
if (*dtdx > .5) *dtdx = 1.f - *dtdx;
else if (*dtdx < -.5f) *dtdx = -(*dtdx + 1);
sphere(dg.p + delta * dg.dpdy, &sy, &ty);
*dsdy = (sy - *s) / delta;
*dtdy = (ty - *t) / delta;
if (*dtdy > .5) *dtdy = 1.f - *dtdy;
else if (*dtdy < -.5f) *dtdx = -(*dtdy + 1);
```

11.2.3 CYLINDRICAL MAPPING

The cylindrical mapping effectively wraps a cylinder around the object. It also supports a transformation to orient the mapping cylinder.

⟨*Texture Declarations*⟩+≡
```
class COREDLL CylindricalMapping2D : public TextureMapping2D {
public:
    ⟨CylindricalMapping2D Public Methods⟩
private:
    void cylinder(const Point &P, float *s, float *t) const;
    Transform WorldToTexture;
};
```

The cylindrical mapping has the same basic structure as the sphere mapping; just the mapping function is different. Therefore, we will omit the fragment that computes texture coordinate differentials, since it is essentially the same as the spherical version.

⟨*Texture Method Definitions*⟩+≡

```
void CylindricalMapping2D::Map(const DifferentialGeometry &dg,
        float *s, float *t, float *dsdx, float *dtdx,
        float *dsdy, float *dtdy) const {
    cylinder(dg.p, s, t);
    ⟨Compute texture coordinate differentials for cylinder (u, v) mapping⟩
}
```

⟨*Texture Method Definitions*⟩+≡

```
void CylindricalMapping2D::cylinder(const Point &p,
                                    float *s, float *t) const {
    Vector vec = Normalize(WorldToTexture(p) - Point(0,0,0));
    *s = (M_PI + atan2f(vec.y, vec.x)) / (2.f * M_PI);
    *t = vec.z;
}
```

11.2.4 PLANAR MAPPING

Another classic mapping method is planar mapping. The point is effectively projected onto a plane; a 2D parameterization of the plane then gives texture coordinates for the point. For example, a point p might be projected onto the $z = 0$ plane to yield texture coordinates given by $s = p_x$ and $t = p_y$.

In general, we can define such a parameterized plane with two nonparallel vectors $\mathbf{v}_s$ and $\mathbf{v}_t$ and offsets d_s and d_t. The texture coordinates are given by the coordinates of the point with respect to the plane's coordinate system, which are computed by taking the dot product of the vector from the point to the origin with each vector $\mathbf{v}_s$ and $\mathbf{v}_t$ and then adding the offset. For the example in the previous paragraph, we'd have $\mathbf{v}_s = (1, 0, 0)$, $\mathbf{v}_t = (0, 1, 0)$, and $d_s = d_t = 0$.

⟨*Texture Declarations*⟩+≡

```
class COREDLL PlanarMapping2D : public TextureMapping2D {
public:
    ⟨PlanarMapping2D Public Methods⟩
private:
    Vector vs, vt;
    float ds, dt;
};
```

⟨*Texture Method Definitions*⟩+≡
```
PlanarMapping2D::PlanarMapping2D(const Vector &_v1,
        const Vector &_v2, float _ds, float _dt) {
    vs = _v1;
    vt = _v2;
    ds = _ds;
    dt = _dt;
}
```

The planar mapping differentials can be computed directly by finding the differentials of p in texture coordinate space.

⟨*Texture Method Definitions*⟩+≡
```
void PlanarMapping2D::Map(const DifferentialGeometry &dg,
        float *s, float *t, float *dsdx, float *dtdx,
        float *dsdy, float *dtdy) const {
    Vector vec = dg.p - Point(0,0,0);
    *s = ds + Dot(vec, vs);
    *t = dt + Dot(vec, vt);
    *dsdx = Dot(dg.dpdx, vs);
    *dtdx = Dot(dg.dpdx, vt);
    *dsdy = Dot(dg.dpdy, vs);
    *dtdy = Dot(dg.dpdy, vt);
}
```

11.2.5 3D MAPPING

We will also define a `TextureMapping3D` class that defines the interface for generating three-dimensional texture coordinates.

⟨*Texture Declarations*⟩+≡
```
class COREDLL TextureMapping3D {
public:
    ⟨TextureMapping3D Interface  504⟩
};
```

⟨*TextureMapping3D Interface*⟩≡   **504**
```
virtual Point Map(const DifferentialGeometry &dg,
                Vector *dpdx, Vector *dpdy) const = 0;
```

The natural three-dimensional mapping just takes the world space coordinate of the point and applies a linear transformation to it. This will often be a transformation that takes the point back to the primitive's object space.

⟨Texture Declarations⟩+≡
```
class COREDLL IdentityMapping3D : public TextureMapping3D {
public:
    IdentityMapping3D(const Transform &x)
        : WorldToTexture(x) { }
    Point Map(const DifferentialGeometry &dg, Vector *dpdx,
            Vector *dpdy) const;
private:
    Transform WorldToTexture;
};
```

Because a linear mapping is used, the differential change in texture coordinates can be found by applying the same mapping to the partial derivatives of position.

⟨Texture Method Definitions⟩+≡
```
Point IdentityMapping3D::Map(const DifferentialGeometry &dg,
                            Vector *dpdx, Vector *dpdy) const {
    *dpdx = WorldToTexture(dg.dpdx);
    *dpdy = WorldToTexture(dg.dpdy);
    return WorldToTexture(dg.p);
}
```

11.3 TEXTURE INTERFACE AND BASIC TEXTURES

Texture is a template class parameterized by the return type of its evaluation function. This design makes it possible to reuse almost all of the texturing code between textures that return different types. pbrt currently uses only float and Spectrum textures.

⟨Texture Declarations⟩+≡
```
template <class T> class Texture : public ReferenceCounted {
public:
    ⟨Texture Interface 505⟩
};
```

The key to Texture's interface is its evaluation function; it returns a value of the template type T. The only information it has access to in order to evaluate its value is the DifferentialGeometry at the point being shaded. Different textures in this chapter will use different parts of this structure to drive their evaluation.

⟨Texture Interface⟩≡   505
```
virtual T Evaluate(const DifferentialGeometry &) const = 0;
```

11.3.1 CONSTANT TEXTURE

ConstantTexture returns the same value no matter where it is evaluated. Because it represents a constant function, it can be accurately reconstructed with any sampling rate and therefore needs no antialiasing. Although this texture is trivial, it is actually quite useful. By providing this class, all parameters to all Materials can be represented as Textures, whether they are spatially varying or not. For example, a red diffuse object will have a ConstantTexture that always returns red as the diffuse color of the material. This way, the shading system always evaluates a texture to get the surface properties at a point, avoiding the need for separate textured and nontextured versions of materials. This material's implementation is in textures/constant.cpp.⊙

⟨*ConstantTexture Declarations*⟩ ≡
```
    template <class T> class ConstantTexture : public Texture<T> {
    public:
        ⟨ConstantTexture Public Methods 506⟩
    private:
        T value;
    };
```

⟨*ConstantTexture Public Methods*⟩ ≡   **506**
```
    ConstantTexture(const T &v) { value = v; }
    T Evaluate(const DifferentialGeometry &) const {
        return value;
    }
```

11.3.2 SCALE TEXTURE

We have defined the texture interface in a way that makes it easy to use the output of one texture function when computing another. This is useful since it lets us define generic texture operations using any of the other texture types. The ScaleTexture takes two textures and returns the product of their values when evaluated. It is defined in textures/scale.cpp.⊙

⟨*ScaleTexture Declarations*⟩ ≡
```
    template <class T1, class T2>
    class ScaleTexture : public Texture<T2> {
    public:
        ⟨ScaleTexture Public Methods 507⟩
    private:
        Reference<Texture<T1> > tex1;
        Reference<Texture<T2> > tex2;
    };
```

⟨*ScaleTexture Public Methods*⟩ ≡   **506**
```
ScaleTexture(Reference<Texture<T1> > t1,
             Reference<Texture<T2> > t2) {
    tex1 = t1;
    tex2 = t2;
}
```

ScaleTexture ignores antialiasing, leaving it to its two subtextures to antialias themselves but not making an effort to antialias their product. While it is easy to show that the product of two band-limited functions is also band-limited, the maximum frequency present in the product may be greater than that of either of the two terms individually. Thus, even if the scale and value textures are perfectly antialiased, the result might not be. Fortunately, the most common kind of scale texture is a constant, in which case the other texture's antialiasing is sufficient.

⟨*ScaleTexture Public Methods*⟩+≡   **506**
```
T2 Evaluate(const DifferentialGeometry &dg) const {
    return tex1->Evaluate(dg) * tex2->Evaluate(dg);
}
```

11.3.3 MIX TEXTURES

The MixTexture class is a more general variation of ScaleTexture. It takes three textures as input: two may be of any type, and the third must return a floating-point value. The floating-point texture is then used to linearly interpolate between the two other textures. Note that a ConstantTexture could be used for the floating-point value to achieve a uniform blend, or a more complex Texture to blend in a spatially nonuniform way. This texture is defined in textures/mix.cpp.

⟨*MixTexture Declarations*⟩ ≡
```
template <class T>
class MixTexture : public Texture<T> {
public:
    ⟨MixTexture Public Methods 508⟩
private:
    Reference<Texture<T> > tex1, tex2;
    Reference<Texture<float> > amount;
};
```

⟨*MixTexture Public Methods*⟩ ≡   507

```
MixTexture(Reference<Texture<T> > t1, Reference<Texture<T> > t2,
           Reference<Texture<float> > amt) {
    tex1 = t1;
    tex2 = t2;
    amount = amt;
}
```

To evaluate the mixture, the three textures are evaluated and the floating-point value is used to linearly interpolate between the two. When the blend amount (amt) is zero, the first texture's value is returned, and when it is one, the second one's value is returned. We will generally assume that amt will be between zero and one, but this behavior is not enforced, so extrapolation is possible as well. As with the ScaleTexture, antialiasing is ignored, so the introduction of aliasing here is a possibility.

⟨*MixTexture Public Methods*⟩+≡   507

```
T Evaluate(const DifferentialGeometry &dg) const {
    T t1 = tex1->Evaluate(dg), t2 = tex2->Evaluate(dg);
    float amt = amount->Evaluate(dg);
    return (1.f - amt) * t1 + amt * t2;
}
```

11.3.4 BILINEAR INTERPOLATION

⟨*BilerpTexture Declarations*⟩ ≡

```
template <class T> class BilerpTexture : public Texture<T> {
public:
    ⟨BilerpTexture Public Methods  509⟩
private:
    ⟨BilerpTexture Private Data  509⟩
};
```

The BilerpTexture class provides bilinear interpolation between four constant values. Values are defined at $(0, 0)$, $(1, 0)$, $(0, 1)$, and $(1, 1)$ in (s, t) parameter space. The value at a particular (s, t) position is found by interpolating between them. It is defined in the file textures/bilerp.cpp.

⟨*BilerpTexture Public Methods*⟩ ≡   508
```
BilerpTexture(TextureMapping2D *m,
              const T &t00, const T &t01,
              const T &t10, const T &t11) {
    mapping = m;
    v00 = t00;
    v01 = t01;
    v10 = t10;
    v11 = t11;
}
```

⟨*BilerpTexture Private Data*⟩ ≡   508
```
TextureMapping2D *mapping;
T v00, v01, v10, v11;
```

The interpolated value of the four values at an (s, t) position can be computed by three linear interpolations. For example, we can first use s to interpolate between the values at $(0, 0)$ and $(1, 0)$ and store that in a temporary tmp1. We can then do the same for the $(0, 1)$ and $(1, 1)$ values and store the result in tmp2. Finally, we use t to interpolate between tmp1 and tmp2 and obtain the final result. Mathematically, this is

$$\text{tmp}_1 = (1 - s)v_{00} + sv_{10}$$
$$\text{tmp}_2 = (1 - s)v_{01} + sv_{11}$$
$$\text{result} = (1 - t)\text{tmp}_1 + t\,\text{tmp}_2.$$

Rather than storing the intermediate values explicitly, some algebraic rearrangement gives us the same result from an appropriately weighted average of the four corner values:

$$\text{result} = (1 - s)(1 - t)v_{00} + (1 - s)t\,v_{01} + s(1 - t)v_{10} + st\,v_{11}.$$

⟨*BilerpTexture Public Methods*⟩+≡   508
```
T Evaluate(const DifferentialGeometry &dg) const {
    float s, t, dsdx, dtdx, dsdy, dtdy;
    mapping->Map(dg, &s, &t, &dsdx, &dtdx, &dsdy, &dtdy);
    return (1-s)*(1-t) * v00 +
           (1-s)*(  t) * v01 +
           (  s)*(1-t) * v10 +
           (  s)*(  t) * v11;
}
```

11.4 IMAGE TEXTURE

The ImageTexture class stores a 2D array of point-sampled values of a texture function. It uses these samples to reconstruct a continuous image function that can be evaluated at an arbitrary (s, t) position. These sample values are often called *texels*, since they are similar to pixels in an image but are used in the context of a texture. Image textures are the most widely used type of texture in computer graphics; digital photographs, scanned artwork, images created with image-editing programs, and images generated by renderers are all extremely useful sources of data for this particular texture representation (Figure 11.8). The term *texture map* is often used to refer to this type of texture, although this usage blurs the distinction between the mapping that computes texture coordinates and the texture function itself. The implementation of this texture is in textures/imagemap.cpp.

Figure 11.8: An Example of Image Textures. Here a rendered image is used to modulate the diffuse color of the sphere, making the sphere look painted.

⟨*ImageMapTexture Declarations*⟩ ≡
```
template <class T> class ImageTexture : public Texture<T> {
public:
    ⟨ImageTexture Public Methods⟩
private:
    ⟨ImageTexture Private Methods 513⟩
    ⟨ImageTexture Private Data 511⟩
};
```

The caller provides the ImageTexture with the filename of an image map and parameters that control the filtering of the map for antialiasing. These parameters will be explained in Section 11.4.2. The data in the file are used to create an instance of the MIPMap class that stores the texels in memory and handles the details of reconstruction and filtering to reduce aliasing.

For an ImageTexture that returns Spectrum values from Texture::Evaluate(), the MIPMap stores the image data with type Spectrum. This can be a somewhat wasteful representation, since a single image map may have millions of texels and may not need the full 32 bits of accuracy from the floats used to store Spectrum coefficients for each of them. Exercise 11.1 at the end of this chapter discusses this issue further.

⟨*ImageMapTexture Method Definitions*⟩ ≡
```
template <class T>
ImageTexture<T>::ImageTexture(TextureMapping2D *m,
                             const string &filename,
                             bool doTrilinear,
                             float maxAniso,
                             ImageWrap wrapMode) {
    mapping = m;
    mipmap = GetTexture(filename, doTrilinear,
                        maxAniso, wrapMode);
}
```

⟨*ImageTexture Private Data*⟩ ≡   **511**
```
MIPMap<T> *mipmap;
TextureMapping2D *mapping;
```

11.4.1 TEXTURE CACHING

Because image maps are memory intensive, and because the user may reuse a texture many times within a scene, pbrt maintains a table of image maps that have been loaded so far, so that they are only loaded into memory once even if they are used in more

than one ImageTexture. The ImageTexture constructor calls the static ImageTexture::
GetTexture() method to get a MIPMap representation of the desired texture. If the image
map does need to be loaded from disk, ReadImage() handles the low-level details of this
process and returns an array of texel values.

⟨*ImageMapTexture Method Definitions*⟩+≡
```
template <class T> MIPMap<T> *
ImageTexture<T>::GetTexture(const string &filename,
                           bool doTrilinear, float maxAniso, ImageWrap wrap) {
    ⟨Look for texture in texture cache 512⟩
    int width, height;
    Spectrum *texels = ReadImage(filename, &width, &height);
    MIPMap<T> *ret = NULL;
    if (texels) {
        ⟨Convert texels to type T and create MIPMap 513⟩
    }
    else {
        ⟨Create one-valued MIPMap 513⟩
    }
    textures[texInfo] = ret;
    return ret;
}
```

TexInfo is a simple structure that holds the image map's filename and filtering parameters; all of these must match for a MIPMap to be reused in another ImageTexture. Its
definition is straightforward and won't be included here.

⟨*Look for texture in texture cache*⟩≡   **512**
```
static map<TexInfo, MIPMap<T> *> textures;
TexInfo texInfo(filename, doTrilinear, maxAniso, wrap);
if (textures.find(texInfo) != textures.end())
    return textures[texInfo];
```

Because the image-loading routine returns an array of Spectrum values for the texels, it is
necessary to convert these Spectrum values to the particular type T of texel that this MIPMap
is storing (e.g., float) if the type of T isn't Spectrum. The per-texel conversion is handled
by the utility routine ImageTexture::convert(). This conversion is wasted work in the
common case where the MIPMap is storing Spectrum values, but the flexibility it gives is
worth this relatively small cost in efficiency.[3]

---

3   Additional C++ template trickery could ensure that this step was skipped when T is type Spectrum if the cost of this unnecessary
    work was unacceptable.

⟨*Convert texels to type* T *and create* MIPMap⟩ ≡   512

```
    T *convertedTexels = new T[width*height];
    for (int i = 0; i < width*height; ++i)
        convert(texels[i], &convertedTexels[i]);
    ret = new MIPMap<T>(width, height, convertedTexels, doTrilinear,
                        maxAniso, wrap);
    delete[] texels;
    delete[] convertedTexels;
```

Per-texel conversion is done using C++ function overloading. For every type to which we would like to be able to convert these values, a separate ImageTexture::convert() function must be provided. In the loop over texels earlier, C++'s function overloading mechanism will select the appropriate instance of ImageTexture::convert() based on the destination type. Unfortunately, it is not possible to return the converted value from the function, since C++ doesn't support overloading by return type.

⟨*ImageTexture Private Methods*⟩ ≡   511

```
    static void convert(const Spectrum &from, Spectrum *to) {
        *to = from;
    }
    static void convert(const Spectrum &from, float *to) {
        *to = from.y();
    }
```

If the texture file wasn't found or was unreadable, an image map with a single sample with a value of one is created so that the renderer can continue and generate an image of the scene without needing to abort execution. The ReadImage() function will issue a warning message in this case.

⟨*Create one-valued* MIPMap⟩ ≡   512

```
    T *oneVal = new T[1];
    oneVal[0] = 1.;
    ret = new MIPMap<T>(1, 1, oneVal);
    delete[] oneVal;
```

The ImageTexture::Evaluate() routine is quite simple: it does the usual texture coordinate computation and then hands the image map lookup to the MIPMap, which does the image filtering work for antialiasing.

⟨*ImageMapTexture Method Definitions*⟩+ ≡

```
    template <class T>
    T ImageTexture<T>::Evaluate(const DifferentialGeometry &dg) const {
        float s, t, dsdx, dtdx, dsdy, dtdy;
        mapping->Map(dg, &s, &t, &dsdx, &dtdx, &dsdy, &dtdy);
        return mipmap->Lookup(s, t, dsdx, dtdx, dsdy, dtdy);
    }
```

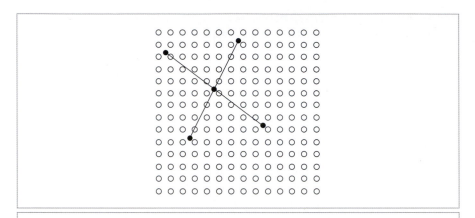

Figure 11.9: Given a point at which to perform an image map (denoted by the solid point in the center) and estimates of the texture space sampling rate (denoted by adjacent solid points), it may be necessary to filter the contributions of a large number of texels in the image map (denoted by open points).

11.4.2 MIP MAPS

As always, if the image function has higher frequency detail than can be represented by the texture sampling rate, aliasing will be present in the final image. Any frequencies higher than the Nyquist limit must be removed by prefiltering before the function is evaluated. Figure 11.9 shows the basic problem we face: an image texture has texels that are samples of some image function at a fixed frequency. The filter region for the lookup is given by its (s, t) center point and offsets to the estimated texture coordinate locations for the adjacent image samples. Because these offsets are estimates of the texture sampling rate, we must remove any frequencies higher than twice the distance to the adjacent samples in order to satisfy the Nyquist criterion.

The texture sampling and reconstruction process has a few key differences from the image sampling process discussed in Chapter 7. These differences make it possible to address the antialiasing problem with more effective and less computationally expensive techniques. For example, here it is inexpensive to get the value of a sample—only an array lookup is necessary (as opposed to having to trace a ray). Further, because the texture image function is fully defined by the set of samples and there is no mystery about what its highest frequency could be, there is no uncertainty related to the function's behavior between samples. These differences make it possible to remove detail from the texture before sampling, thus eliminating aliasing.

However, the texture sampling rate will typically change from pixel to pixel—it is spatially varying. The sampling rate is determined by scene geometry and its orientation, the

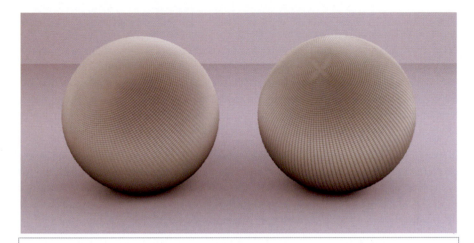

Figure 11.10: Filtering the image map properly substantially improves the image. On the left, trilinear interpolation was used; on the right, the EWA algorithm. Both of these approaches give a much better image than the unfiltered image map in Figure 11.1. Trilinear interpolation is less able to handle strongly anisotropic filter footprints than EWA, which is why the edges of the sphere on the left are a uniform gray color (the overall average value of the texture), while the edges of the sphere on the right are much better able to continue to resolve detail from the image map before fading to gray.

texture coordinate mapping function, and the camera projection and image sampling rate. Because the sampling rate is not fixed, texture filtering algorithms need to be able to filter over arbitrary regions of texture samples efficiently.

The MIPMap class implements two methods for efficient texture filtering with spatially varying filter widths. The first, trilinear interpolation, is fast and easy to implement, and has been widely used for texture filtering in graphics hardware. The second, elliptically weighted averaging, is slower and more complex, but returns extremely high-quality results. Figure 11.1 shows the aliasing errors that result from ignoring texture filtering and just bilinearly interpolating texels from the most detailed level of the image map. Figure 11.10 shows the improvement from using the triangle filter and the EWA algorithm instead.

To limit the potential number of texels that need to be accessed, both of these filtering methods use an *image pyramid* of increasingly lower-resolution prefiltered versions of the original image to accelerate their operation.[4] The original image texels are at the bottom

MIPMap 516

---

4   The name "MIP map" comes from the Latin "multum in parvo," which means "many things in a small place," a nod to the image pyramid.

level of the pyramid, and the image at each level is half the resolution of the previous level, up to the top level, which has a single texel representing the average of all of the texels in the original image. This collection of images needs at most 1/3 more memory than storing the most detailed level alone and can be used to quickly find filtered values over large regions of the original image. The basic idea behind the pyramid is that if a large area of texels needs to be filtered, a reasonable approximation is to use a higher level of the pyramid and do the filtering over the same area there, accessing many fewer texels.

MIPMap is a template class and is parameterized by the data type of the image texels. pbrt creates MIPMaps of both Spectrum and float images; float MIP maps are used for representing directional distributions of intensity from goniometric light sources, for example. The MIPMap implementation requires that the type T support just a few basic operations, including addition and multiplication by a scalar.

The ImageWrap enumerant, passed to the MIPMap constructor, specifies the behavior when the supplied texture coordinates are not in the legal [0, 1] range desired.

⟨*MIPMap Declarations*⟩ ≡
```
typedef enum {
    TEXTURE_REPEAT,
    TEXTURE_BLACK,
    TEXTURE_CLAMP
} ImageWrap;
```

⟨*MIPMap Declarations*⟩+≡
```
template <class T> class MIPMap {
public:
    ⟨MIPMap Public Methods⟩
private:
    ⟨MIPMap Private Methods 519⟩
    ⟨MIPMap Private Data 517⟩
};
```

In the constructor, the MIPMap copies the image data provided by the caller, resizes the image if necessary to ensure that its resolution is a power of two in each direction, and initializes a lookup table used by the elliptically weighted average filtering method in Section 11.4.4. It also records the desired behavior for texture coordinates that fall outside of the legal range in the wrapmode argument.

⟨*MIPMap Method Definitions*⟩ ≡
```
template <class T>
MIPMap<T>::MIPMap(int sres, int tres, const T *img, bool doTri,
                  float maxAniso, ImageWrap wm) {
    doTrilinear = doTri;
    maxAnisotropy = maxAniso;
    wrapMode = wm;
    T *resampledImage = NULL;
    if (!IsPowerOf2(sres) || !IsPowerOf2(tres)) {
        ⟨Resample image to power-of-two resolution 518⟩
    }
    ⟨Initialize levels of MIPMap from image 522⟩
    if (resampledImage) delete[] resampledImage;
    ⟨Initialize EWA filter weights if needed 532⟩
}
```

⟨*MIPMap Private Data*⟩ ≡   **516**
```
bool doTrilinear;
float maxAnisotropy;
ImageWrap wrapMode;
```

Implementation of an image pyramid is substantially easier if the resolution of the original image is an exact power of two in each direction; this ensures that there is a straightforward relationship between the level of the pyramid and the number of texels at that level. If the user has provided an image where the resolution in one or both of the dimensions is not a power of two, then the `MIPMap` constructor starts by resizing the image up to the next power-of-two resolution greater than the original resolution before constructing the pyramid.

Image magnification in this manner involves more application of the sampling and reconstruction theory from Chapter 7: we have an image function that has been sampled at one sampling rate, and we'd like to reconstruct a continuous image function from the original samples to resample at a new set of sample positions. Because this represents an increase in the sampling rate from the original rate, we don't have to worry about introducing aliasing due to undersampling high-frequency components in this step; we only need to reconstruct and directly resample the new function. Figure 11.11 illustrates this task in 1D.

The `MIPMap` uses a separable reconstruction filter for this task; recall from Section 7.6 that separable filters can be written as the product of one-dimensional filters: $f(x, y) = f(x) f(y)$. One advantage of using a separable filter is that if we are using one to resample an image from one resolution (s, t) to another (s', t'), then we can implement the resampling as two one-dimensional resampling steps, first resampling in s to create an

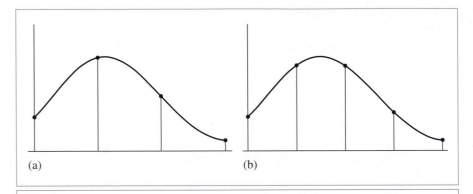

(a)   (b)

Figure 11.11: To increase an image's resolution to be a power of two, the `MIPMap` performs two 1D resampling steps with a separable reconstruction filter. (a) A 1D function reconstructed from four samples, denoted by dots. (b) To represent the same image function with more samples, we just need to reconstruct the continuous function and evaluate it at the new positions.

image of resolution (s', t) and then resampling that image to create the final image of resolution (s', t'). Resampling the image via two 1D steps in this manner simplifies implementation and makes the number of texels accessed for each texel in the final image a linear function of the filter width, rather than a quadratic one.

⟨*Resample image to power-of-two resolution*⟩ ≡   **517**
```
    int sPow2 = RoundUpPow2(sres), tPow2 = RoundUpPow2(tres);
    ⟨Resample image in s direction 519⟩
    ⟨Resample image in t direction⟩
    sres = sPow2;
    tres = tPow2;
```

Reconstructing the original image function and sampling it at a new texel's position is mathematically equivalent to centering the reconstruction filter kernel at the new texel's position and weighting the nearby texels in the original image appropriately. Thus, each new texel is a weighted average of a small number of texels in the original image.

The `MIPMap::resampleWeights()` method determines which original texels contribute to each new texel and what the values are of the contribution weights for each new texel. It returns the values in an array of `ResampleWeight` structures for all of the texels in a 1D row or column of the image. Because this information is the same for all rows of the image when resampling in s and all columns when resampling in t, it's more efficient to compute it once for each of the two passes and then reuse it many times for each one. Given these weights, the image is first magnified in the s direction, turning the original image with resolution (`sres`,`tres`) into an image with resolution (`sPow2`,`tres`), which is stored in `resampledImage`. The implementation here allocates enough space in resampledImage to hold the final zoomed image with resolution (sPow2,tPow2), so two large allocations can be avoided.

⟨*Resample image in s direction*⟩ ≡   518
```
ResampleWeight *sWeights = resampleWeights(sres, sPow2);
resampledImage = new T[sPow2 * tPow2];
```
⟨*Apply* sWeights *to zoom in s direction* **521**⟩
```
delete[] sWeights;
```

For the reconstruction filter used here, no more than four of the original texels will contribute to each new texel after zooming, so ResampleWeight only needs to hold four weights. Because the four texels are contiguous, we only store the offset to the first one.

⟨*MIPMap Private Data*⟩+ ≡   516
```
struct ResampleWeight {
    int firstTexel;
    float weight[4];
};
```

⟨*MIPMap Private Methods*⟩ ≡   516
```
ResampleWeight *resampleWeights(int oldres, int newres) {
    Assert(newres >= oldres);
    ResampleWeight *wt = new ResampleWeight[newres];
    float filterwidth = 2.f;
    for (int i = 0; i < newres; ++i) {
        ⟨Compute image resampling weights for ith texel 520⟩
    }
    return wt;
}
```

Just as it was important to distinguish between discrete and continuous pixel coordinates in Chapter 7, the same issues need to be addressed with texel coordinates here. We will use the same conventions as described in Section 7.1.7. For each new texel, this function starts by computing its continuous coordinates in terms of the old texel coordinates. This value is stored in center, because it is the center of the reconstruction filter for the new texel. Next, it is necessary to find the offset to the first texel that contributes to the new texel. This is a slightly tricky calculation—after subtracting the filter width to find the start of the filter's nonzero range, it is necessary to add an extra 0.5 offset to the continuous coordinate before taking the floor to find the discrete coordinate. Figure 11.12 illustrates why this offset is needed.

Starting from this first contributing texel, this function loops over four texels, computing each one's offset to the center of the filter kernel and the corresponding filter weight. The reconstruction filter function used to compute the weights, Lanczos(), is the same as the one in LanczosSincFilter::Sinc1D().

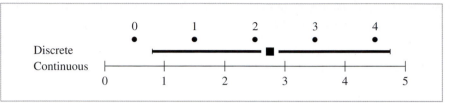

Figure 11.12: The computation to find the first texel inside a reconstruction filter's support is slightly tricky. Consider a filter centered around continuous coordinate 2.75 with width 2, as shown here. The filter's support covers the range [0.75, 4.75], although texel zero is outside the filter's support: adding 0.5 to the lower end before taking the floor to find the discrete texel gives the correct starting texel, number one.

⟨*Compute image resampling weights for* i *th texel*⟩ ≡   519
```
float center = (i + .5f) * oldres / newres;
wt[i].firstTexel = Floor2Int((center - filterwidth) + 0.5f);
for (int j = 0; j < 4; ++j) {
    float pos = wt[i].firstTexel + j + .5f;
    wt[i].weight[j] = Lanczos((pos - center) / filterwidth);
}
```
⟨*Normalize filter weights for texel resampling* **520**⟩

Depending on the filter function used, the four filter weights may not sum to one. Therefore, to ensure that the resampled image won't be any brighter or darker than the original image, the weights are normalized here.

⟨*Normalize filter weights for texel resampling*⟩ ≡   **520**
```
float invSumWts = 1.f / (wt[i].weight[0] + wt[i].weight[1] +
                         wt[i].weight[2] + wt[i].weight[3]);
for (int j = 0; j < 4; ++j)
    wt[i].weight[j] *= invSumWts;
```

⟨*Global Function Declarations*⟩ ≡
```
COREDLL float Lanczos(float, float tau=2);
```

Once the weights have been computed, it's easy to apply them to compute the zoomed texels. For each of the `tres` horizontal scan lines in the original image, a pass is made across the `sPow2` texels in the *s*-zoomed image using the precomputed weights to compute their values.

⟨*Apply* sWeights *to zoom in s direction*⟩ ≡   **519**
```
for (int t = 0; t < tres; ++t) {
    for (int s = 0; s < sPow2; ++s) {
        ⟨Compute texel (s, t) in s-zoomed image 521⟩
    }
}
```

The ImageWrap parameter to the MIPMap constructor determines the convention to be used for out-of-bounds texel coordinates. It either remaps them to valid values with a modulus or clamp calculation, or uses a black texel value as implemented here.

⟨*Compute texel* (*s*, *t*) *in s-zoomed image*⟩ ≡   **521**
```
resampledImage[t*sPow2+s] = 0.;
for (int j = 0; j < 4; ++j) {
    int origS = sWeights[s].firstTexel + j;
    if (wrapMode == TEXTURE_REPEAT)
        origS = Mod(origS, sres);
    else if (wrapMode == TEXTURE_CLAMP)
        origS = Clamp(origS, 0, sres-1);
    if (origS >= 0 && origS < sres)
        resampledImage[t*sPow2+s] += sWeights[s].weight[j] *
                                     img[t*sres + origS];
}
```

The process for resampling in the *t* direction is almost the same as for *s*, so we won't include the implementation here. Once we have an image with resolutions that are powers of two, the levels of the MIP map can be initialized, starting from the bottom (finest) level. Each higher level is found by filtering the texels from the previous level.

Because image maps use a fair amount of memory, and because 8–20 texels are typically used per image texture lookup to compute a filtered value, it's worth carefully considering how the texels are laid out in memory, since reducing cache misses while accessing the texture map can noticeably improve the renderer's performance. Because both of the two texture filtering methods implemented in this section access a set of texels in a rectangular region of the image map each time a lookup is performed, the MIPMap uses the BlockedArray template class to store the 2D arrays of texel values, rather than using a standard C++ array. The BlockedArray reorders the array values in memory in a way that improves cache coherence when the values are accessed with these kinds of rectangular patterns; it is described in Section A.2.5 in Appendix A.

⟨*Initialize levels of MIPMap from image*⟩ ≡   **517**
```
nLevels = 1 + Log2Int(float(max(sres, tres)));
pyramid = new BlockedArray<T> *[nLevels];
```
⟨*Initialize most detailed level of MIPMap* **522**⟩
```
for (int i = 1; i < nLevels; ++i) {
```
⟨*Initialize i th MIPMap level from i − 1st level* **523**⟩
```
}
```

⟨*MIPMap Private Data*⟩+≡   **516**
```
BlockedArray<T> **pyramid;
int nLevels;
```

The base level of the MIP map, which holds the original data (or the resampled data, if it didn't originally have power-of-two resolutions), is initialized by the default BlockedArray constructor.

⟨*Initialize most detailed level of MIPMap*⟩ ≡   **522**
```
pyramid[0] = new BlockedArray<T>(sres, tres, img);
```

Before showing how the rest of the levels are initialized, we will first define a texel access function that will be used during that process. MIPMap::texel() returns a reference to the texel value for the given discrete integer-valued texel position. As described earlier, if an out-of-range texel coordinate is passed in, this method either effectively repeats the texture over the entire 2D texture coordinate domain by taking the modulus of the coordinate with respect to the texture size, clamps the coordinates to the valid range so that the border pixels are used, or returns a black texel for out-of-bounds coordinates.

⟨*MIPMap Method Definitions*⟩+≡
```
template <class T>
const T &MIPMap<T>::texel(int level, int s, int t) const {
    const BlockedArray<T> &l = *pyramid[level];
```
    ⟨*Compute texel* (*s*, *t*) *accounting for boundary conditions* **522**⟩
```
    return l(s, t);
}
```

⟨*Compute texel* (*s*, *t*) *accounting for boundary conditions*⟩ ≡   **522**
```
switch (wrapMode) {
    case TEXTURE_REPEAT:
        s = Mod(s, l.uSize());
        t = Mod(t, l.vSize());
        break;
```

```
              case TEXTURE_CLAMP:
                  s = Clamp(s, 0, l.uSize() - 1);
                  t = Clamp(t, 0, l.vSize() - 1);
                  break;
              case TEXTURE_BLACK: {
                  static const T black = 0.f;
                  if (s < 0 || s >= l.uSize() ||
                      t < 0 || t >= l.vSize())
                      return black;
                  break;
              }
          }
```

For nonsquare images, the resolution in one direction must be clamped to one for the upper levels of the image pyramid, where there is still downsampling to do in the larger of the two resolutions. This is handled by the following max() calls:

⟨*Initialize i th MIPMap level from i − 1st level*⟩ ≡   **522**
```
    int sRes = max(1, pyramid[i-1]->uSize()/2);
    int tRes = max(1, pyramid[i-1]->vSize()/2);
    pyramid[i] = new BlockedArray<T>(sRes, tRes);
    ⟨Filter four texels from finer level of pyramid  523⟩
```

The MIPMap uses a simple box filter to average four texels from the previous level to find the value at the current texel. The Lanczos filter here would give a slightly better result for this computation, although this modification is left as an exercise at the end of the chapter.

⟨*Filter four texels from finer level of pyramid*⟩ ≡   **523**
```
    for (int t = 0; t < tRes; ++t)
        for (int s = 0; s < sRes; ++s)
            (*pyramid[i])(s, t) = .25f * (
                texel(i-1, 2*s,   2*t) +
                texel(i-1, 2*s+1, 2*t) +
                texel(i-1, 2*s,   2*t+1) +
                texel(i-1, 2*s+1, 2*t));
```

11.4.3 ISOTROPIC TRIANGLE FILTER

The first of the two MIPMap::Lookup() methods uses a triangle filter over the texture samples to remove high frequencies. Although this filter function does not give high-quality results, it can be implemented very efficiently. In addition to the (s, t) coordinates of the evaluation point, the caller passes this method a filter width for the lookup, giving the extent of the region of the texture to filter across. This method filters over a square region in texture space, so the width should be conservatively chosen to avoid aliasing

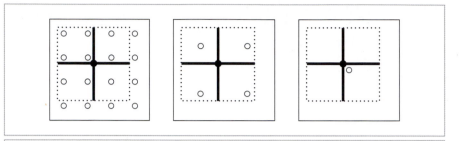

Figure 11.13: Choosing a MIP Map Level for the Triangle Filter. The MIPMap chooses a level such that the filter covers four texels.

in both the *s* and *t* directions. Filtering techniques like this one that do not support a filter extent that is nonsquare or non-axis-aligned are known as *isotropic*. The primary disadvantage of isotropic filtering algorithms is that textures viewed at an oblique angle will appear blurry, since the sampling rate along one axis will be very different from the sampling rate along the other.

Because filtering over many texels for wide filter widths would be inefficient, this method chooses a MIP map level from the pyramid such that the filter region at that level would cover four texels at that level. Figure 11.13 illustrates this idea.

⟨*MIPMap Method Definitions*⟩+≡
```
template <class T>
T MIPMap<T>::Lookup(float s, float t, float width) const {
    ⟨Compute MIPMap level for trilinear filtering 524⟩
    ⟨Perform trilinear interpolation at appropriate MIPMap level 525⟩
}
```

Since the resolutions of the levels of the pyramid are all powers of two, the resolution of level l is $2^{\text{nLevels}-1-l}$. Therefore, to find the level with a texel spacing width w requires solving

$$\frac{1}{w} = 2^{\text{nLevels}-1-l}$$

for l. In general this will be a floating-point value between two MIP map levels.

⟨*Compute MIPMap level for trilinear filtering*⟩ ≡   **524**
```
float level = nLevels - 1 + Log2(max(width, 1e-8f));
```

Log2() 854
MIPMap 516
MIPMap::nLevels 522

As shown by Figure 11.13, applying a triangle filter to the four texels around the sample point will either filter over too small a region or too large a region (except for very carefully selected filter widths). The implementation here applies the triangle filter at both of these levels and blends between them according to how close `level` is to each of them. This helps hide the transitions from one MIP map level to the next at nearby pixels in the final image. While applying a triangle filter to four texels at two levels in this manner doesn't give exactly the same result as applying it to the original highest-resolution texels, the difference isn't too bad in practice and the efficiency of this approach is worth this penalty. In any case, the elliptically weighted average filtering in the next section should be used when texture quality is important.

⟨*Perform trilinear interpolation at appropriate MIPMap level*⟩ ≡   524
```
if (level < 0)
    return triangle(0, s, t);
else if (level >= nLevels - 1)
    return texel(nLevels-1, 0, 0);
else {
    int iLevel = Floor2Int(level);
    float delta = level - iLevel;
    return (1.f-delta) * triangle(iLevel, s, t) +
            delta * triangle(iLevel+1, s, t);
}
```

Given floating-point texture coordinates in $[0, 1]^2$, the `MIPMap::triangle()` routine uses a triangle filter to interpolate between the four texels that surround the sample point, as shown in Figure 11.14. This method first scales the coordinates by the texture resolution at the given MIP map level in each direction, turning them into continuous texel coordinates. Because these are continuous coordinates, but the texels in the image map are defined at discrete texture coordinates, it's important to carefully convert into a common representation. Here, we will do all of our work in discrete coordinates, mapping the continuous texture coordinates to discrete space.

For example, consider the 1D case with a continuous texture coordinate of 2.4: this coordinate is a distance of 0.1 below the discrete texel coordinate 2 (which corresponds to a continuous coordinate of 2.5), and is 0.9 above the discrete coordinate 1 (continuous coordinate 1.5). Thus, if we subtract 0.5 from the continuous coordinate 2.4, giving 1.9, we can correctly compute the correct distances to the discrete coordinates 1 and 2 by subtracting coordinates.

After computing the distances in s and t to the texel at the lower left of the given coordinates, ds and dt, `MIPMap::triangle()` determines weights for the four texels and computes the filtered value. Recall that the triangle filter is

$$f(x, y) = (1 - |x|)(1 - |y|);$$

the appropriate weights follow directly. Notice the similarity between this computation and `BilerpTexture::Evaluate()`.

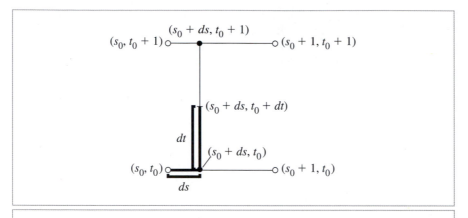

Figure 11.14: To compute the value of the image texture function at an arbitrary (s, t) position, `MIPMap::triangle()` finds the four texels around (s, t) and weights them according to a triangle filter based on their distance to (s, t). One way to implement this is as a series of linear interpolations, as shown here: First, the two texels below (s, t) are linearly interpolated to find a value at $(s, 0)$, and the two texels above it are interpolated to find $(s, 1)$. Then, $(s, 0)$ and $(s, 1)$ are linearly interpolated again to find the value at (s, t).

⟨*MIPMap Method Definitions*⟩+≡

```
template <class T>
T MIPMap<T>::triangle(int level, float s, float t) const {
    level = Clamp(level, 0, nLevels-1);
    s = s * pyramid[level]->uSize() - 0.5f;
    t = t * pyramid[level]->vSize() - 0.5f;
    int s0 = Floor2Int(s), t0 = Floor2Int(t);
    float ds = s - s0, dt = t - t0;
    return (1.f-ds)*(1.f-dt) * texel(level, s0, t0) +
        (1.f-ds)*dt * texel(level, s0, t0+1) +
        ds*(1.f-dt) * texel(level, s0+1, t0) +
        ds*dt * texel(level, s0+1, t0+1);
}
```

★ 11.4.4 ELLIPTICALLY WEIGHTED AVERAGE

The elliptically weighted average (EWA) algorithm fits an ellipse to the two axes in texture space given by the texture coordinate differentials and then filters the texture with a Gaussian filter function (Figure 11.15). It is widely regarded as one of the best texture

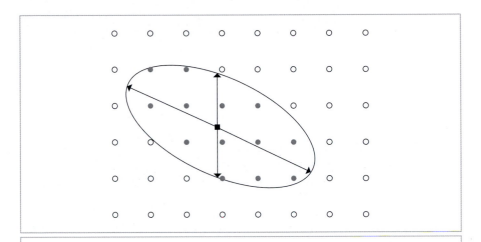

Figure 11.15: The EWA filter applies a Gaussian filter to the texels in an elliptical area around the evaluation point. The extent of the ellipse is such that its edge passes through the positions of the adjacent texture samples as estimated by the texture coordinate partial derivatives.

filtering algorithms in graphics and has been carefully derived from the basic principles of sampling theory. Unlike the triangle filter in the previous section, it can filter over arbitrarily oriented regions of the texture, with some flexibility of having different filter extents in different directions. This type of filter is known as *anisotropic*. This capability greatly improves the quality of its results, since it can properly adapt to different sampling rates along the two image axes.

We won't show the full derivation of this filter here, although we do note that it is distinguished by being a *unified resampling filter*: it simultaneously computes the result of a Gaussian filtered texture function convolved with a Gaussian reconstruction filter in image space. This is in contrast to many other texture filtering methods that ignore the effect of the image space filter, or equivalently assume that it is a box. Even if a Gaussian isn't being used for filtering the samples for the image being rendered, taking some account of the spatial variation of the image filter improves the results, assuming that the filter being used is somewhat similar in shape to the Gaussian, as the Mitchell and windowed sinc filters are.

MIPMap 516

If it was specified in the `MIPMap` constructor that trilinear filtering should always be used, this method computes a conservative isotropic filter width and passes the request on to the trilinear lookup routine.

⟨*MIPMap Method Definitions*⟩+≡
```
    template <class T>
    T MIPMap<T>::Lookup(float s, float t, float ds0, float dt0,
                        float ds1, float dt1) const {
        if (doTrilinear)
            return Lookup(s, t,
                          2.f * max(max(fabsf(ds0), fabsf(dt0)),
                                    max(fabsf(ds1), fabsf(dt1))));
        ⟨Compute ellipse minor and major axes 528⟩
        ⟨Clamp ellipse eccentricity if too large 528⟩
        ⟨Choose level of detail for EWA lookup and perform EWA filtering 529⟩
    }
```

The screen space partial derivatives of the texture coordinates define the axes of the ellipse. The lookup method starts out by determining which of the two axes is the major axis (the longer of the two) and which is the minor, swapping them if needed so that (ds0,dt0) is the major axis. The length of the minor axis will be used shortly to select a MIP map level.

⟨*Compute ellipse minor and major axes*⟩≡   528
```
    if (ds0*ds0 + dt0*dt0 < ds1*ds1 + dt1*dt1) {
        swap(ds0, ds1);
        swap(dt0, dt1);
    }
    float majorLength = sqrtf(ds0*ds0 + dt0*dt0);
    float minorLength = sqrtf(ds1*ds1 + dt1*dt1);
```

Next the *eccentricity* of the ellipse is computed—the ratio of the length of the major axis to the length of the minor axis. A large eccentricity indicates a very long and skinny ellipse. Because this method filters texels from a MIP map level chosen based on the length of the minor axis, highly eccentric ellipses mean that a large number of texels need to be filtered. To avoid this expense (and to ensure that any EWA lookup takes a bounded amount of time), the length of the minor axis may be increased to limit the eccentricity. The result may be an increase in blurring, although this effect usually isn't noticeable in practice.

⟨*Clamp ellipse eccentricity if too large*⟩≡   528
```
    if (minorLength * maxAnisotropy < majorLength) {
        float scale = majorLength / (minorLength * maxAnisotropy);
        ds1 *= scale;
        dt1 *= scale;
        minorLength *= scale;
    }
```

MIPMap 516
MIPMap::doTrilinear 517
MIPMap::maxAnisotropy 517

Like the triangle filter, the EWA filter uses the image pyramid to reduce the number of texels to be filtered for a particular texture lookup, choosing a MIP map level based on the length of the minor axis. Given the limited eccentricity of the ellipse due to the clamping above, the total number of texels used is thus bounded. Given the length of the minor axis, the computation to find the appropriate pyramid level is the same as was used for the triangle filter. Similarly, the implementation here blends between the filtered results at the two levels around the computed level of detail, again to reduce artifacts from transitions from one level to another.

⟨*Choose level of detail for EWA lookup and perform EWA filtering*⟩ ≡   **528**
```
float lod = max(0.f, nLevels - 1.f + Log2(minorLength));
int ilod = Floor2Int(lod);
float d = lod - ilod;
return (1.f - d) * EWA(s, t, ds0, dt0, ds1, dt1, ilod) +
        d * EWA(s, t, ds0, dt0, ds1, dt1, ilod+1);
```

The `MIPMap::EWA()` method actually applies the filter at a particular level.

⟨*MIPMap Method Definitions*⟩+≡
```
template <class T>
T MIPMap<T>::EWA(float s, float t, float ds0, float dt0,
                 float ds1, float dt1, int level) const {
    if (level >= nLevels) return texel(nLevels-1, 0, 0);
    ⟨Convert EWA coordinates to appropriate scale for level  529⟩
    ⟨Compute ellipse coefficients to bound EWA filter region  530⟩
    ⟨Compute the ellipse's (s, t) bounding box in texture space  530⟩
    ⟨Scan over ellipse bound and compute quadratic equation  531⟩
}
```

This method first converts from texture coordinates in [0, 1] to coordinates and differentials in terms of the resolution of the chosen MIP map level. It also subtracts 0.5 from the continuous position coordinate to align the sample point with the discrete texel coordinates, as was done in `MIPMap::triangle()`.

⟨*Convert EWA coordinates to appropriate scale for level*⟩ ≡   **529**
```
s = s * pyramid[level]->uSize() - 0.5f;
t = t * pyramid[level]->vSize() - 0.5f;
ds0 *= pyramid[level]->uSize();
dt0 *= pyramid[level]->vSize();
ds1 *= pyramid[level]->uSize();
dt1 *= pyramid[level]->vSize();
```

It next computes the coefficients of the implicit equation for the ellipse with axes (ds0,dt0) and (ds1,dt1) and centered at the origin. Placing the ellipse at the origin rather than at (s, t) simplifies the implicit equation and the computation of its coefficients, and can be easily corrected for when the equation is evaluated later. The general form of the implicit equation for all points (s, t) inside such an ellipse is

$$e(s, t) = As^2 + Bst + Ct^2 < F,$$

although it is more computationally efficient to divide through by F and express this as

$$e(s, t) = \frac{A}{F}s^2 + \frac{B}{F}st + \frac{C}{F}t^2 = A's^2 + B'st + C't^2 < 1.$$

We will not derive the equations that give the values of the coefficients, although the interested reader can easily verify their correctness.[5]

⟨*Compute ellipse coefficients to bound EWA filter region*⟩ ≡   529
```
float A = dt0*dt0 + dt1*dt1 + 1;
float B = -2.f * (ds0*dt0 + ds1*dt1);
float C = ds0*ds0 + ds1*ds1 + 1;
float invF = 1.f / (A*C - B*B*0.25f);
A *= invF;
B *= invF;
C *= invF;
```

The next step is to find the axis-aligned bounding box in discrete integer texel coordinates of the texels that are potentially inside the ellipse. The EWA algorithm loops over all of these candidate texels, filtering the contributions of those that are in fact inside the ellipse. The bounding box is found by determining the minimum and maximum values that the ellipse takes in the s and t directions. These extrema can be calculated by finding the partial derivatives $\partial e/\partial s$ and $\partial e/\partial t$, finding their solutions for $s = 0$ and $t = 0$, and adding the offset to the ellipse center. For brevity, we will not include the derivation for these expressions here.

⟨*Compute the ellipse's (s, t) bounding box in texture space*⟩ ≡   529
```
float det = -B*B + 4.f*A*C;
float invDet = 1.f / det;
float uSqrt = sqrtf(det * C), vSqrt = sqrtf(A * det);
int s0 = Ceil2Int (s - 2.f * invDet * uSqrt);
int s1 = Floor2Int(s + 2.f * invDet * uSqrt);
int t0 = Ceil2Int (t - 2.f * invDet * vSqrt);
int t1 = Floor2Int(t + 2.f * invDet * vSqrt);
```

Now that the bounding box is known, the EWA algorithm loops over the texels, transforming each one to the coordinate system where the texture lookup point (s, t) is at the origin with a translation. It then evaluates the ellipse equation to see if the texel is inside the ellipse (Figure 11.16) The value of the implicit ellipse equation $e(s, t)$ gives

Ceil2Int() 856

Floor2Int() 856

---

5   Heckbert's thesis has the original derivation (Heckbert 1989, p. 80). A and C have an extra term of 1 added to them so the ellipse
     is a minimum of one texel separation wide. This ensures that the ellipse will not fall between the texels when magnifying at
     the most detailed level.

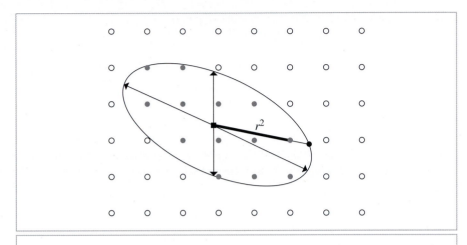

Figure 11.16: Finding the r^2 Ellipse Value for the EWA Filter Table Lookup.

the squared ratio of the distance from the texel to the ellipse center to the distance from the ellipse edge to the center along the line through the texel. If it is inside, the weight of the texel is computed with a Gaussian centered at the middle of the ellipse. The final filtered value returned is a weighted sum over texels (s', t') inside the ellipse, where f is the Gaussian filter function:

$$\frac{\sum f(s' - s, t' - t) t(s', t')}{\sum f(s' - s, t' - t)}.$$

⟨*Scan over ellipse bound and compute quadratic equation*⟩ ≡   **529**
```
T num(0.);
float den = 0;
for (int it = t0; it <= t1; ++it) {
    float tt = it - t;
    for (int is = s0; is <= s1; ++is) {
        float ss = is - s;
        ⟨Compute squared radius and filter texel if inside ellipse 532⟩
    }
}
return num / den;
```

A nice feature of the implicit equation $e(s, t)$ is that its value at a particular texel is the squared ratio of the distance from the center of the ellipse to the texel to the distance from the center of the ellipse to the ellipse boundary along the line through that texel (Figure 11.16). This value is used to index into a precomputed lookup table of Gaussian filter function values.

⟨*Compute squared radius and filter texel if inside ellipse*⟩ ≡   531

```
    float r2 = A*ss*ss + B*ss*tt + C*tt*tt;
    if (r2 < 1.) {
        float weight = weightLut[min(Float2Int(r2 * WEIGHT_LUT_SIZE),
                                     WEIGHT_LUT_SIZE-1)];
        num += texel(level, is, it) * weight;
        den += weight;
    }
```

The lookup table is initialized the first time a MIPMap is constructed. Because it will be indexed with squared distances from the filter center r^2, each entry stores a value $e^{-\alpha r}$, rather than $e^{-\alpha r^2}$.

⟨*MIPMap Private Data*⟩+ ≡   516

```
    #define WEIGHT_LUT_SIZE 128
    static float *weightLut;
```

⟨*Initialize EWA filter weights if needed*⟩ ≡   517

```
    if (!weightLut) {
        weightLut = (float *)AllocAligned(WEIGHT_LUT_SIZE * sizeof(float));
        for (int i = 0; i < WEIGHT_LUT_SIZE; ++i) {
            float alpha = 2;
            float r2 = float(i) / float(WEIGHT_LUT_SIZE - 1);
            weightLut[i] = expf(-alpha * r2);
        }
    }
```

11.5 SOLID AND PROCEDURAL TEXTURING

Once one starts to think of the (s, t) texture coordinates used by 2D texture functions as quantities that can be computed by arbitrary functions and not just from the parametric coordinates of the surface, it is natural to generalize texture functions to be defined over three-dimensional domains (often called *solid textures*) rather than just 2D (s, t). One reason solid textures are particularly convenient is that all objects have a natural three-dimensional texture mapping—object space position. This is a substantial advantage for texturing objects that don't have a natural two-dimensional parameterization (e.g., triangle meshes and implicit surfaces), and for objects that have a distorted parameterization (e.g., near the poles of a sphere). In preparation for this idea, Section 11.2.5 defined a general TextureMapping3D interface to compute 3D texture coordinates as well as an IdentityMapping3D implementation.

Solid textures introduce a new problem, however: texture representation. A three-dimensional image map takes up a fair amount of storage space and is much harder to acquire than a two-dimensional texture map, which can be extracted from photographs or painted by an artist. Therefore, procedural texturing—the idea that short programs could be used to generate texture values at arbitrary positions on surfaces in the scene—came into use at the same time that solid texturing was developed. A simple example of procedural texturing is a procedural sine wave. If we wanted to use a sine wave for bump mapping (for example, to simulate waves in water), it would be inefficient and potentially inaccurate to precompute values of the function at a grid of points and then store them in an image map. Instead, it makes much more sense to evaluate the `sin()` function at points on the surface as needed.

If we can find a three-dimensional function that describes the colors of the grain in a solid block of wood, for instance, then we can generate images of complex objects that appear to be carved from wood. Over the years, procedural texturing has grown in application considerably as techniques have been developed to describe more and more complex surfaces procedurally.

Procedural texturing has a number of interesting implications. First, it can be used to reduce memory requirements for rendering, by reducing the need for the storage of large, high-resolution texture maps. In addition, procedural shading gives the promise of potentially infinite detail; as the viewer approaches an object, the texturing function is evaluated at the points being shaded, which naturally leads to the right amount of detail being visible. In contrast, image texture maps become blurry when the viewer is too close to them. On the other hand, subtle details of the appearance of procedural textures can be much more difficult to control than image maps.

Another difficulty with procedural textures is antialiasing. Procedural textures are often expensive to evaluate, and sets of point samples that fully characterize their behavior aren't available as they are for with image maps. Because we would like to remove high-frequency information in the texture function before we take samples from it, we need to be aware of the frequency content of the various steps we take along the way so we can avoid introducing high frequencies. Although this sounds daunting, there are a handful of techniques that work well to handle this issue.

11.5.1 UV TEXTURE

Our first procedural texture converts the surface's (u, v) coordinates into the first two components of a `Spectrum` (Figure 11.17). It is especially useful when debugging the parameterization of a new `Shape`, for example. It is defined in `textures/uv.cpp`.

⟨*UVTexture Declarations*⟩ ≡
```
class UVTexture : public Texture<Spectrum> {
public:
    ⟨UVTexture Public Methods  534⟩
private:
    TextureMapping2D *mapping;
};
```

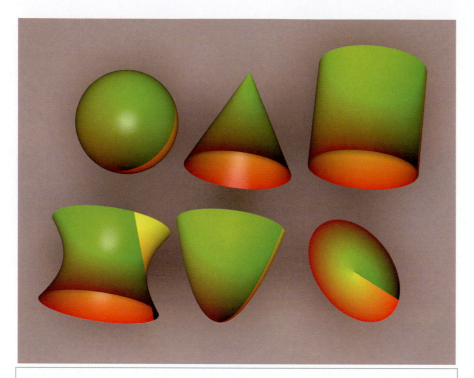

Figure 11.17: The UV Texture Applied to All of pbrt's Quadric Shapes. The u parameter is mapped to the red channel, and the v parameter is mapped to green.

⟨*UVTexture Public Methods*⟩ ≡   533
```
Spectrum Evaluate(const DifferentialGeometry &dg) const {
    float s, t, dsdx, dtdx, dsdy, dtdy;
    mapping->Map(dg, &s, &t, &dsdx, &dtdx, &dsdy, &dtdy);
    float cs[COLOR_SAMPLES];
    memset(cs, 0, COLOR_SAMPLES * sizeof(float));
    cs[0] = s - Floor2Int(s);
    cs[1] = t - Floor2Int(t);
    return Spectrum(cs);
}
```

COLOR_SAMPLES 230
DifferentialGeometry 83
Floor2Int() 856
Spectrum 230
TextureMapping2D::Map() 499
UVTexture::mapping 533

11.5.2 CHECKERBOARD

The checkerboard is the canonical procedural texture (Figure 11.18). The (s, t) texture coordinates are used to break up parameter space into square regions that are shaded with alternating patterns. Rather than just supporting checkerboards that switch between two fixed colors, the implementation here allows the user to pass in two textures to color the

Figure 11.18: The Checkerboard Texture Applied to All of pbrt's Quadric Shapes.

alternating regions. The traditional black-and-white checkerboard is obtained by passing two ConstantTextures. Its implementation is in textures/checkerboard.cpp.

⟨*CheckerboardTexture Declarations*⟩ ≡
```
template <class T> class Checkerboard2D : public Texture<T> {
public:
    ⟨Checkerboard2D Public Methods  536⟩
private:
    ⟨Checkerboard2D Private Data  536⟩
};
```

For simplicity, the frequency of the check function is 1 in (s, t) space: checks are one unit wide in each direction. This can always be changed by the TextureMapping2D class with an appropriate scale of the (s, t) coordinates.

⟨*Checkerboard2D Public Methods*⟩ ≡   **535**
```
    Checkerboard2D(TextureMapping2D *m, Reference<Texture<T> > c1,
                   Reference<Texture<T> > c2, const string &aa) {
        mapping = m;
        tex1 = c1;
        tex2 = c2;
        ⟨Select antialiasing method for Checkerboard2D 536⟩
    }
```

⟨*Checkerboard2D Private Data*⟩ ≡   **535**
```
    Reference<Texture<T> > tex1, tex2;
    TextureMapping2D *mapping;
```

The checkerboard is a good procedural texture for demonstrating trade-offs between various antialiasing approaches for procedural textures. Therefore, we will implement three such approaches, selectable via a string passed to the constructor. The image sequence in Figure 11.23 at the end of this section shows the results of these various antialiasing strategies.

⟨*Select antialiasing method for* Checkerboard2D⟩ ≡   **536**
```
    if (aa == "none") aaMethod = NONE;
    else if (aa == "supersample") aaMethod = SUPERSAMPLE;
    else if (aa == "closedform") aaMethod = CLOSEDFORM;
    else {
        Warning("Anti-aliasing mode \"%s\" not understood "
                "by Checkerboard2D, defaulting"
                "to \"supersample\"", aa.c_str());
        aaMethod = SUPERSAMPLE;
    }
```

⟨*Checkerboard2D Private Types*⟩ ≡
```
    enum { NONE, SUPERSAMPLE, CLOSEDFORM } aaMethod;
```

The evaluation routine does the usual texture coordinate and differential computation and then uses the appropriate fragment to compute an antialiased checkerboard value (or not antialiased, if point sampling has been selected).

⟨*Checkerboard2D Public Methods*⟩+≡   535
```
    T Evaluate(const DifferentialGeometry &dg) const {
        float s, t, dsdx, dtdx, dsdy, dtdy;
        mapping->Map(dg, &s, &t, &dsdx, &dtdx, &dsdy, &dtdy);
        if (aaMethod == CLOSEDFORM) {
            ⟨Compute closed-form box-filtered Checkerboard2D value 538⟩
        }
        else if (aaMethod == SUPERSAMPLE) {
            ⟨Supersample Checkerboard2D 541⟩
        }
        ⟨Point sample Checkerboard2D 537⟩
    }
```

The simplest case is to ignore antialiasing and just point-sample the checkerboard texture at the point. For this case, after getting the (s, t) texture coordinates from the TextureMapping2D, the integer checkerboard coordinates for that (s, t) position are computed, added together, and checked for odd or even parity to determine which of the two textures to evaluate.

⟨*Point sample* Checkerboard2D⟩≡   537, 538
```
    if ((Floor2Int(s) + Floor2Int(t)) % 2 == 0)
        return tex1->Evaluate(dg);
    return tex2->Evaluate(dg);
```

Given how bad aliasing can be in a point-sampled checkerboard texture, we will invest some effort to antialias it properly. The easiest case happens when the entire filter region lies inside a single check (Figure 11.19). In this case, we simply need to determine which

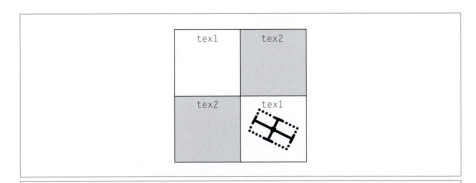

Figure 11.19: The Easy Case for Filtering the Checkerboard. If the filter region around the lookup point is entirely in one check, the checkerboard texture doesn't need to worry about antialiasing and can just evaluate the texture for that check.

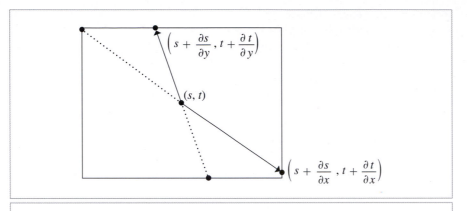

Figure 11.20: It is often convenient to use the axis-aligned bounding box around the texture evaluation point and the offsets from its partial derivatives as the region to filter over. Here, it's easy to see that the lengths of sides of the box are $2\max(|\partial s/\partial x|, |\partial s/\partial y|)$ and $2\max(|\partial t/\partial x|, |\partial t/\partial y|)$.

of the check types we are inside and evaluate that one. As long as the Texture inside that check does appropriate antialiasing itself, the result for this case will be antialiased.

⟨*Compute closed-form box-filtered* Checkerboard2D *value*⟩ ≡   **537**
   ⟨*Evaluate single check if filter is entirely inside one of them* **538**⟩
   ⟨*Apply box filter to checkerboard region* **540**⟩

It's straightforward to check if the entire filter region is inside a single check by computing its bounding box and seeing if its extent lies inside the same check. For the remainder of this section, we will use the axis-aligned bounding box of the filter region given by the partial derivatives $\partial s/\partial x$, $\partial s/\partial y$, and so on, as the area to filter over, rather than trying to filter over the ellipse defined by the partial derivatives as the EWA filter did (Figure 11.20). This simplifies the implementation here, although somewhat increases the blurriness of the filtered values. The variables ds and dt in the following hold half the filter width in each direction, so the total area filtered over ranges from (s-ds, t-dt) to (s+ds, t+dt).

⟨*Evaluate single check if filter is entirely inside one of them*⟩ ≡   **538**
```
    float ds = max(fabsf(dsdx), fabsf(dsdy));
    float dt = max(fabsf(dtdx), fabsf(dtdy));
    float s0 = s - ds, s1 = s + ds;
    float t0 = t - dt, t1 = t + dt;
    if (Floor2Int(s0) == Floor2Int(s1) && Floor2Int(t0) == Floor2Int(t1)) {
        ⟨Point sample Checkerboard2D 537⟩
    }
```

Floor2Int() 856
Texture 505

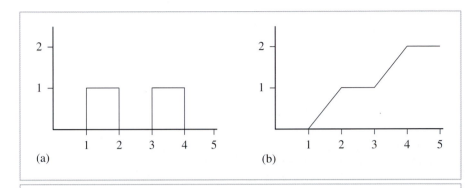

Figure 11.21: Integrating the Checkerboard Step Function. (a) The 1D step function that defines the checkerboard texture function, $c(x)$. (b) A graph of the value of the integral $\int_0^x c(x)\mathrm{d}x$.

Otherwise, the lookup method approximates the filtered value by first computing a floating-point value that indicates what fraction of the filter region covers each of the two check types. This is equivalent to computing the average of the 2D step function that takes on the value 0 when we are in tex1 and 1 when we are in tex2, over the filter region. Figure 11.21(a) shows a graph of the checkerboard function $c(x)$, defined as

$$c(x) = \begin{cases} 0 : & \lfloor x \rfloor \text{ is odd} \\ 1 : & \text{otherwise.} \end{cases}$$

Given the average value, we can blend between the two subtextures, according to what fraction of the filter region each one is visible for.

The integral of the 1D checkerboard function $c(x)$ can be used to compute the average value of the function over some extent. Inspection of the graph reveals that

$$\int_0^x c(x)\mathrm{d}x = \lfloor x/2 \rfloor + 2\max(x/2 - \lfloor x/2 \rfloor - .5, 0).$$

To compute the average value of the step function in one dimension, we separately compute the integral of the checkerboard in each 1D direction in order to compute its average value over the filter region.

⟨*Apply box filter to checkerboard region*⟩ ≡   538

```
#define BUMPINT(x) \
    (Floor2Int((x)/2) + \
     2.f * max((x/2)-Floor2Int(x/2) - .5f, 0.f))
float sint = (BUMPINT(s1) - BUMPINT(s0)) / (2.f * ds);
float tint = (BUMPINT(t1) - BUMPINT(t0)) / (2.f * dt);
float area2 = sint + tint - 2.f * sint * tint;
if (ds > 1.f || dt > 1.f)
    area2 = .5f;
return (1.f - area2) * tex1->Evaluate(dg) +
       area2 * tex2->Evaluate(dg);
```

The final checkerboard antialiasing method implemented here is supersampling. The checkerboard function is evaluated at a set of random stratified positions around the (s, t) point in texture space, jittered so that they roughly cover the filter area. One point in favor of the supersampling approach is that the analytic box filter approach described previously is actually not completely correct. Specifically, it assumes that the correct overall antialiased result can be computed by determining how much of the filter covers each of the two types of check and then evaluating both of them, blending between their values appropriately. The problem with this assumption is that each of the subtextures will evaluate and antialias itself as if it were completely visible throughout all of the filter region.

Figure 11.22 shows a contrived case where this is an incorrect assumption. Here the checkerboard texture has subtextures that are also checkerboards. The textures are all

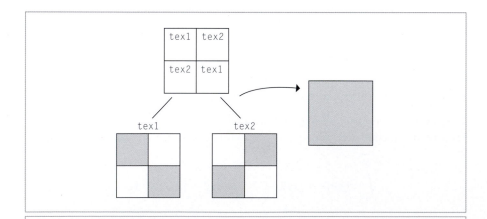

Figure 11.22: If a checkerboard texture is configured with subregions that are themselves checkerboards, it's possible that the overall result will be a solid color. This case illustrates a potential pitfall in how checkerboard texture antialiasing is done because some approaches will return an incorrect result in this case.

configured such that the result of the main checkerboard texture is a solid gray color; all of the white parts of the subtextures are completely hidden. However, if the subtextures filter themselves with the incorrect assumption described earlier, then some of the white will "leak in" to the final computed result. This is a somewhat contrived worst case, and the box filter approach does work correctly for subtextures that are just a constant value, for example. However, the supersampling approach we will implement here does not suffer from this problem.

The supersampling implementation takes a fixed number of samples, N_SAMPLES in the s and t directions. For each sample, the DifferentialGeometry object is updated for the particular sample position, and then the checkerboard texture function is evaluated there.

⟨*Supersample* Checkerboard2D⟩ ≡   **537**

```
#define SQRT_SAMPLES 4
#define N_SAMPLES (SQRT_SAMPLES * SQRT_SAMPLES)
float samples[2*N_SAMPLES];
StratifiedSample2D(samples, SQRT_SAMPLES, SQRT_SAMPLES);
T value = 0.;
float filterSum = 0.;
for (int i = 0; i < N_SAMPLES; ++i) {
    ⟨Compute new differential geometry for supersample location 541⟩
    ⟨Compute (s, t) for supersample and evaluate subtexture 542⟩
}
return value / filterSum;
```

For each sample inside the filter area, the values in the DifferentialGeometry for that sample can be approximated using the partial derivatives of position, and parametric coordinates can be found by shifting the current coordinates according to the sample's offset. The implementation also scales down the screen space differentials for the shifted point, so that any antialiasing done by the subtexture will be over an appropriately reduced area.

⟨*Compute new differential geometry for supersample location*⟩ ≡   **541**

```
float dx = samples[2*i]   - 0.5f;
float dy = samples[2*i+1] - 0.5f;
DifferentialGeometry dgs = dg;
dgs.p += dx * dgs.dpdx + dy * dgs.dpdy;
dgs.u += dx * dgs.dudx + dy * dgs.dudy;
dgs.v += dx * dgs.dvdx + dy * dgs.dvdy;
dgs.dudx /= N_SAMPLES;
dgs.dudy /= N_SAMPLES;
dgs.dvdx /= N_SAMPLES;
dgs.dvdy /= N_SAMPLES;
```

DifferentialGeometry 83
DifferentialGeometry::dudx 489
DifferentialGeometry::dudy 489
DifferentialGeometry::dvdx 489
DifferentialGeometry::dvdy 489

Finally, the sample values are weighted with a Gaussian filter and the result from the appropriate subtexture is accumulated into value.

⟨*Compute (s , t) for supersample and evaluate subtexture*⟩ ≡   **541**

```
float ss, ts, dsdxs, dtdxs, dsdys, dtdys;
mapping->Map(dgs, &ss, &ts, &dsdxs, &dtdxs, &dsdys, &dtdys);
float wt = expf(-2.f * (dx*dx + dy*dy));
filterSum += wt;
if ((Floor2Int(ss) + Floor2Int(ts)) % 2 == 0)
    value += wt * tex1->Evaluate(dgs);
else
    value += wt * tex2->Evaluate(dgs);
```

Figure 11.23 shows these three antialiasing approaches for the checkerboard in practice.

11.5.3 SOLID CHECKERBOARD

The Checkerboard2D class from the previous section wraps a checkerboard pattern *around* the object in parameter space. We can also define a solid checkerboard pattern based on three-dimensional texture coordinates so that the object appears carved out of 3D checker cubes (Figure 11.24). Like the 2D variant, this implementation chooses between texture functions based on the lookup position. Note that these two textures need not be solid textures themselves; the Checkerboard3D merely chooses between them based on the 3D position of the point.

⟨*CheckerboardTexture Declarations*⟩+≡

```
template <class T> class Checkerboard3D : public Texture<T> {
public:
    ⟨Checkerboard3D Public Methods 542⟩
private:
    ⟨Checkerboard3D Private Data 542⟩
};
```

⟨*Checkerboard3D Public Methods*⟩ ≡   **542**

```
Checkerboard3D(TextureMapping3D *m,
              Reference<Texture<T> > c1,
              Reference<Texture<T> > c2) {
    mapping = m;
    tex1 = c1;
    tex2 = c2;
}
```

⟨*Checkerboard3D Private Data*⟩ ≡   **542**

```
Reference<Texture<T> > tex1, tex2;
TextureMapping3D *mapping;
```

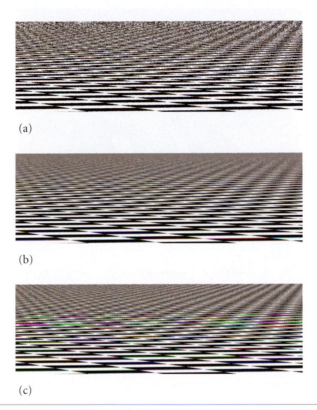

(a)

(b)

(c)

Figure 11.23: Comparisons of the three approaches for antialiasing in procedural textures, applied to the checkerboard texture. All images were rendered with one sample per pixel. (a) No effort has been made to remove high-frequency variation from the texture function, so there are severe artifacts in the image. (b) This image shows the approach based on computing the filter region in texture space and averaging the texture function over that area. (c) Here the checkerboard function was supersampled 16 times in texture space at each shading point. Both the area-averaging and the supersampling approaches give substantially better results than the first approach. In this example, supersampling gives the best results, since the averaging approach has blurred out the checkerboard pattern sooner than was needed because it approximates the filter region with its axis-aligned box. In general, the averaging approach will guarantee that there is no aliasing due to the texture, while supersampling can be susceptible to this error but is less prone to blurring.

Ignoring antialiasing, the basic computation to see if a point is inside a 3D checker region is

```
((Floor2Int(P.x) + Floor2Int(P.y) + Floor2Int(P.z)) % 2 == 0).
```

For antialiasing, the implementation here uses the same general supersampling approach as was used in the 2D checkerboard. The code with the implementation is elided here,

Figure 11.24: The Dragon Model, Textured with the Checkerboard3D Procedural Texture. Notice how the model appears to be carved out of 3D checks, rather than having them pasted on its surface.

however, since it is essentially the same as in the 2D case, just with the inside-check test modified as above.

⟨*Checkerboard3D Public Methods*⟩+≡   **542**
    T Evaluate(const DifferentialGeometry &dg) const {
        ⟨*Supersample* Checkerboard3D⟩
    }

11.6 NOISE

In order to write solid textures that describe complex surface appearances, it is helpful to be able to introduce some controlled variation to the process. Consider a wood floor made of individual planks; each plank's color is likely to be slightly different than the others. Or consider a windswept lake; we might want to have waves of similar amplitude across the entire lake, but we don't want them to be homogeneous over all parts of the lake (as they might be if they were constructed from a sum of sine waves, for example). Modeling this sort of variation in a texture helps make the final result look more realistic.

One difficulty in developing textures like these is that the renderer evaluates the surface's texture functions at an irregularly distributed set of points, where each evaluation is com-

Checkerboard3D 542
DifferentialGeometry 83

pletely independent of the others. As such, procedural textures must *implicitly* define a complex pattern by answering queries about what the pattern's value is at all of these points. In contrast, the *explicit* pattern description approach is embodied by the Post-Script language, for example, which describes graphics on a page with a series of drawing commands. One difficulty that the implicit approach introduces is that the texture can't just call RandomFloat() at each point at which it is evaluated to introduce randomness: because each point would have a completely different random value than its neighbors, no coherence would be possible in the generated pattern.

An elegant way to address this issue of introducing controlled randomness to procedural textures in graphics is the application of what is known as a *noise function*. In general, noise functions used in graphics are smoothly varying functions taking $\mathbb{R}^n \to [-1, 1]$, for at least $n = 1, 2, 3$, without obvious repetition. One of the most crucial properties of a practical noise function is that it be band-limited with a known maximum frequency. This makes it possible to control the frequency content added to a texture due to the noise function so that frequencies higher than allowed by the Nyquist limit aren't introduced.

Many of the noise functions that have been developed are built on the idea of an integer lattice over $\mathbb{R}^3$. First, a value is associated with each integer (x, y, z) position in space. Then, given an arbitrary position in space, the eight adjoining lattice values are found. These lattice values are then interpolated to compute the noise value at the particular point. This idea can be generalized or restricted to more or fewer dimensions d, where the number of lattice points is 2^d. A simple example of this approach is *value noise*, where pseudorandom numbers between -1 and 1 are associated with each lattice point, and actual noise values are computed with trilinear interpolation or with a more complex spline interpolant, which can give a smoother result by avoiding derivative discontinuities when moving from one lattice cell to another.

For such a noise function, given an integer (x, y, z) lattice point, it must be possible to efficiently compute its parameter value in a way that always associates the same value with each lattice point. Because it is infeasible to store values for all possible (x, y, z) points, some compact representation is needed. One option is to use a hash function, where the coordinates are hashed and then used to look up parameters from a fixed-size table of precomputed pseudorandom parameter values.

11.6.1 PERLIN NOISE

In pbrt we will implement a noise function introduced by Ken Perlin (1985a, 2002); as such, it is known as *Perlin noise*. It has a value of zero at all (x, y, z) integer lattice points. Its variation comes from gradient vectors at each lattice point that guide the interpolation of a smooth function in between the points (Figure 11.25). This noise function has many of the desired characteristics of a noise function described above, is computationally efficient, and is easy to implement. Figure 11.26 shows its value rendered on a sphere.

RandomFloat() 857

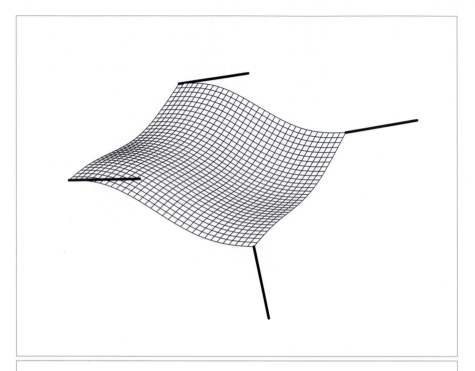

Figure 11.25: The Perlin noise function is computed by generating a smooth function that is zero but with a given derivative at integer lattice points. The derivatives are used to compute a smooth interpolating surface. Here, a 2D slice of the noise function is shown with four gradient vectors.

⟨*Texture Method Definitions*⟩+≡
```
COREDLL float Noise(float x, float y, float z) {
    ⟨Compute noise cell coordinates and offsets  547⟩
    ⟨Compute gradient weights  548⟩
    ⟨Compute trilinear interpolation of weights  550⟩
}
```

For convenience, there is also a variant of Noise() that takes a Point directly:

⟨*Texture Method Definitions*⟩+≡
```
COREDLL float Noise(const Point &P) {
    return Noise(P.x, P.y, P.z);
}
```

Figure 11.26: Perlin's Noise Function Modulating the Diffuse Color of a Sphere.

The implementation first computes the integer coordinates of the cell that contains the given point and the fractional offsets of the point from the lower cell corner:

⟨*Compute noise cell coordinates and offsets*⟩ ≡   **546**
```
int ix = Floor2Int(x);
int iy = Floor2Int(y);
int iz = Floor2Int(z);
float dx = x - ix, dy = y - iy, dz = z - iz;
```

It next computes eight weight values, one for each corner of the cell that the point lies inside. Each integer lattice point has a gradient vector associated with it. The influence of the gradient vector for any point inside the cell is obtained by computing the dot product of the vector from the gradient's corner to the lookup point and the gradient vector (Figure 11.27); this is handled by the Grad() function. Note that the vectors to the corners other than the lower-left one can be easily computed incrementally based on that vector.

Floor2Int() 856
Grad() 549

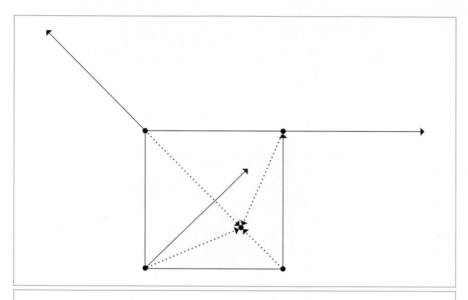

Figure 11.27: The dot product of the vector from the corners of the cell to the lookup point (dotted lines) with each of the gradient vectors (solid lines) gives the influence of each gradient to the noise value at the point.

⟨*Compute gradient weights*⟩ ≡   546

```
ix &= (NOISE_PERM_SIZE-1);
iy &= (NOISE_PERM_SIZE-1);
iz &= (NOISE_PERM_SIZE-1);
float w000 = Grad(ix,   iy,   iz,   dx,   dy,   dz);
float w100 = Grad(ix+1, iy,   iz,   dx-1, dy,   dz);
float w010 = Grad(ix,   iy+1, iz,   dx,   dy-1, dz);
float w110 = Grad(ix+1, iy+1, iz,   dx-1, dy-1, dz);
float w001 = Grad(ix,   iy,   iz+1, dx,   dy,   dz-1);
float w101 = Grad(ix+1, iy,   iz+1, dx-1, dy,   dz-1);
float w011 = Grad(ix,   iy+1, iz+1, dx,   dy-1, dz-1);
float w111 = Grad(ix+1, iy+1, iz+1, dx-1, dy-1, dz-1);
```

The gradient vector for a particular integer lattice point is found by indexing into a precomputed table of integer values, NoisePerm. The four low-order bits of the value for the lattice point determine which of 16 gradient vectors is associated with it. In a preprocessing step, this table of size NOISE_PERM_SIZE was filled with numbers from 0 to NOISE_PERM_SIZE-1 and then randomly permuted. These values were then duplicated, making an array of size 2*NOISE_PERM_SIZE that holds the table twice in succession. The second copy of the table makes lookups in the following code slightly more efficient.

Grad() 549
NOISE_PERM_SIZE 549

Given a particular (ix,iy,iz) lattice point, a series of table lookups gives a value from the random number table:

```
NoisePerm[NoisePerm[NoisePerm[ix]+iy]+iz];
```

By doing three nested permutations in this way, rather than NoisePerm[ix+iy+iz], for example, the final result is more irregular. For example, the first approach usually doesn't generally return the same value if ix and iy are interchanged, as the second always does. Furthermore, since the table was replicated to be twice the original length, the lookups can be done as earlier, eliminating the need for modulus operations in code along the lines of

```
(NoisePerm[ix]+iy) % NOISE_PERM_SIZE
```

Given a final value from the permutation table that determines the gradient number, the dot product with the corresponding gradient vector must be computed. However, the gradient vectors do not need to be represented explicitly. All of the gradients use only -1, 0, or 1 in their coordinates, so that the dot products reduce to addition of some (possibly negated) components of the vector.[6] The final implementation is the following:

⟨*Texture Method Definitions*⟩+≡
```
inline float Grad(int x, int y, int z,
                  float dx, float dy, float dz) {
    int h = NoisePerm[NoisePerm[NoisePerm[x]+y]+z];
    h &= 15;
    float u = h<8 || h==12 || h==13 ? dx : dy;
    float v = h<4 || h==12 || h==13 ? dy : dz;
    return ((h&1) ? -u : u) + ((h&2) ? -v : v);
}
```

⟨*Perlin Noise Data*⟩≡
```
#define NOISE_PERM_SIZE 256
static int NoisePerm[2 * NOISE_PERM_SIZE] = {
    151, 160, 137, 91, 90, 15, 131, 13, 201, 95, 96,
    53, 194, 233, 7, 225, 140, 36, 103, 30, 69, 142,
    ⟨Rest of noise permutation table⟩
};
```

Given these eight contributions from the gradients, the next step is to trilinearly interpolate between them at the point. Rather than interpolating with dx, dy, and dz directly, though, each of these values is passed through a smoothing function. This ensures that

NoisePerm 549
NOISE_PERM_SIZE 549

---

6   The original formulation of Perlin noise also had a precomputed table of pseudorandom gradient directions, although Perlin has more recently suggested that the randomness from the permutation table is enough to remove regularity from the noise function.

the noise function has first- and second-derivative continuity as lookup points move between lattice cells.

⟨*Texture Method Definitions*⟩+≡

```
inline float NoiseWeight(float t) {
    float t3 = t*t*t;
    float t4 = t3*t;
    return 6.f*t4*t - 15.f*t4 + 10.f*t3;
}
```

⟨*Compute trilinear interpolation of weights*⟩≡   546

```
float wx = NoiseWeight(dx);
float wy = NoiseWeight(dy);
float wz = NoiseWeight(dz);
float x00 = Lerp(wx, w000, w100);
float x10 = Lerp(wx, w010, w110);
float x01 = Lerp(wx, w001, w101);
float x11 = Lerp(wx, w011, w111);
float y0 = Lerp(wy, x00, x10);
float y1 = Lerp(wy, x01, x11);
return Lerp(wz, y0, y1);
```

11.6.2 RANDOM POLKA DOTS

A basic use of the noise function is as part of a polka dot texture that divides (s, t) texture space into rectangular cells (Figure 11.28). Each cell has a 50% chance of having a dot inside of it, and the dots are is randomly placed inside their cells. DotsTexture takes the usual 2D mapping function, as well as two Textures, one for the regions of the surface outside of the dots and one for the regions inside. It is defined in textures/dots.cpp. ⓒⓓ

⟨*DotsTexture Declarations*⟩≡

```
template <class T> class DotsTexture : public Texture<T> {
public:
    ⟨DotsTexture Public Methods 550⟩
private:
    ⟨DotsTexture Private Data 551⟩
};
```

⟨*DotsTexture Public Methods*⟩≡   550

```
DotsTexture(TextureMapping2D *m, Reference<Texture<T> > c1,
            Reference<Texture<T> > c2) {
    mapping = m;
    outsideDot = c1;
    insideDot = c2;
}
```

Figure 11.28: The Polka Dot Texture Applied to All of pbrt's Quadric Shapes.

⟨*DotsTexture Private Data*⟩ ≡   550
```
Reference<Texture<T> > outsideDot, insideDot;
TextureMapping2D *mapping;
```

The evaluation function starts by taking the (s, t) texture coordinates and computing integer sCell and tCell values, which give the coordinates of the cell they are inside. We will not consider antialiasing of the polka dots texture here; an exercise at the end of the chapter outlines how this might be done.

⟨*DotsTexture Public Methods*⟩+ ≡   550
```
T Evaluate(const DifferentialGeometry &dg) const {
    ⟨Compute cell indices for dots 552⟩
    ⟨Return insideDot result if point is inside dot 552⟩
    return outsideDot->Evaluate(dg);
}
```

⟨*Compute cell indices for dots*⟩ ≡   **551**
```
float s, t, dsdx, dtdx, dsdy, dtdy;
mapping->Map(dg, &s, &t, &dsdx, &dtdx, &dsdy, &dtdy);
int sCell = Floor2Int(s + .5f), tCell = Floor2Int(t + .5f);
```

Once the cell coordinate is known, it's necessary to decide if there is a polka dot in the cell. Obviously, this computation needs to be consistent so that for each time this routine runs for points in a particular cell, it returns the same result. Yet we'd like the result not to be completely regular (e.g., with a dot in every other cell). Noise solves this problem: by evaluating the noise function at a position that is the same for all points inside this cell—sCell+.5, tCell+.5—we can compute an irregularly varying but consistent value for each cell.[7] If this value is greater than zero, a dot is placed in the cell.

If there is a dot in the cell, the noise function is used again to randomly shift the center of the dot within the cell. The points at which the noise function is evaluated for the center shift are offset by arbitrary constant amounts, however, so that noise values from different noise cells are used from them, eliminating a possible source of correlation with the noise value used to determine the presence of a dot in the first place. (But the dot's radius needs to be small enough so that it doesn't spill over the cell's boundary after being shifted; in that case, points where the texture was being evaluated would also need to consider the dots based in neighboring cells as potentially affecting their value.)

Given the dot center and radius, the texture needs to decide if the (s, t) coordinates are within the radius of the shifted center. It does this by computing their squared distance to the center and comparing it to the squared radius.

⟨*Return* insideDot *result if point is inside dot*⟩ ≡   **551**
```
if (Noise(sCell+.5f, tCell+.5f) > 0) {
    float radius = .35f;
    float maxShift = 0.5f - radius;
    float sCenter = sCell + maxShift *
        Noise(sCell + 1.5f, tCell + 2.8f);
    float tCenter = tCell + maxShift *
        Noise(sCell + 4.5f, tCell + 9.8f);
    float ds = s - sCenter, dt = t - tCenter;
    if (ds*ds + dt*dt < radius*radius)
        return insideDot->Evaluate(dg);
}
```

---

7   Recall that the noise function always returns zero at integer (x, y, z) coordinates, so we don't want to just evaluate it at (sCell, tCell). Although the 3D noise function would actually be evaluating noise at sCell, tCell, .5, slices through noise with integer values for any of the coordinates are not as well-distributed as with all of them offset.

11.6.3 NOISE IDIOMS AND SPECTRAL SYNTHESIS

The fact that noise is a band-limited function means that its frequency content can be adjusted by scaling the domain over which it is evaluated. For example, if Noise(p) has some known frequency content, then the frequency content of Noise(2*p) will be twice as high. This is just like the relationship between the frequency content of $\sin(x)$ and $\sin(2x)$. This technique can be used to create a noise function with a desired rate of variation.

For many applications in procedural texturing, it's useful to have variation over multiple scales—for example, to add finer variations to the base noise function. One effective way to do this with noise is to compute patterns via *spectral synthesis*, where a complex function $f_s(s)$ is defined by a sum of contributions from another function $f(x)$:

$$f_s(x) = \sum_i w_i f(s_i x),$$

for a set of weight values w_i and parameter scale values s_i. If the base function $f(x)$ has a well-defined frequency content (e.g., is a sine or cosine function, or a noise function), then each term $f(s_i x)$ also has a well-defined frequency content as described earlier. Because each term of the sum is weighted by a weight value w_i, the result is a sum of contributions of various frequencies, with different frequency ranges weighted differently.

Typically, the scales s_i are chosen in a geometric progression such that $s_i = 2s_{i-1}$ and the weights are $w_i = w_{i-1}/2$. The result is that as higher-frequency variation is added to the function, it has relatively less influence on the overall shape of $f_s(x)$. Each additional term is called an *octave* of noise, since it has twice the frequency content of the previous one. When this scheme is used with Perlin noise, the result is often referred to as "Fractional Brownian motion" (FBm), after a particular type of random process that varies in a similar manner.

Fractional Brownian motion is a useful building block for procedural textures because it gives a function with more complex variation than plain noise, while still being easy to compute and still having well-defined frequency content. The utility function FBm() implements the Fractional Brownian motion function. Figure 11.29 shows two graphs of it.

FBm() 555

In addition to the point at which to evaluate the function and the function's partial derivatives at that point, the function takes an omega parameter, which ranges from zero to one and affects the smoothness of the pattern by controlling the falloff of contributions at higher frequencies (values around 0.5 work well), and octaves, which gives the maximum number of octaves of noise that should be used in computing the sum.

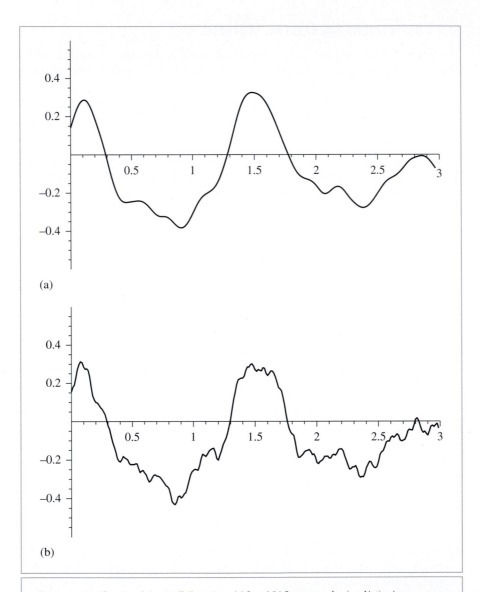

(a)

(b)

Figure 11.29: Graphs of the FBm() Function. (a) 2 and (b) 6 octaves of noise. Notice how as more levels of noise are added, the graph has progressively more detail, although its overall shape remains roughly the same.

⟨*Texture Method Definitions*⟩+≡
```
COREDLL float FBm(const Point &P, const Vector &dpdx,
                  const Vector &dpdy, float omega, int maxOctaves) {
    ⟨Compute number of octaves for antialiased FBm 555⟩
    ⟨Compute sum of octaves of noise for FBm 556⟩
    return sum;
}
```

Antialiasing the FBm function is based on a technique called *clamping* (Norton, Rockwood, and Skolmoski 1982). The idea is that when we are computing a value based on a sum of components, each with known frequency content, we should stop adding in components that would have frequencies beyond the Nyquist limit and instead add their average values to the sum. Because the average value of Noise() is zero, all that needs to be done is to compute the number of octaves such that none of the terms have excessively high frequencies and not evaluate the noise function for any higher octaves.

Noise() (and thus the first term of $f_s(x)$ as well) has a maximum frequency content of roughly $\omega = 1$. Each subsequent term represents a doubling of frequency content. Therefore, we would like to find the appropriate number of terms n such that if the sampling rate in noise space is s, we have

$$2^n s = 2\omega = 2.$$

This condition guarantees that there are no frequencies that can't be represented at the sampling rate. Thus, we have

$$2^{n-1} = \frac{1}{s}$$

$$n - 1 = \log\left(\frac{1}{s}\right)$$

$$n = 1 - \frac{1}{2}\log(s^2).$$

The squared sampling rate s^2 can be computed by finding the maximum of the length of the differentials $\partial p/\partial x$ and $\partial p/\partial y$.

⟨*Compute number of octaves for antialiased FBm*⟩≡   555, 558
```
float s2 = max(dpdx.LengthSquared(), dpdy.LengthSquared());
float foctaves = min((float)maxOctaves, 1.f - .5f * Log2(s2));
int octaves = Floor2Int(foctaves);
```

Finally, the integral number of octaves up to the Nyquist limit are added together and the last octave is faded in, according to the fractional part of foctaves. This ensures that successive octaves of noise fade in gradually, rather than appearing abruptly, which can cause visually noticeable artifacts at the transitions. The implementation here actually increases the frequency between octaves by 1.99, rather than by a factor of 2, in order to

COREDLL 904
Floor2Int() 856
Log2() 854
Noise() 546
Point 54
Vector 47
Vector::LengthSquared() 53

reduce the impact of the fact that the noise function is zero at integer lattice points. This breaks up that regularity across sums of octaves of noise, which can also lead to subtle visual artifacts.

⟨*Compute sum of octaves of noise for FBm*⟩ ≡   **555**

```
float sum = 0., lambda = 1., o = 1.;
for (int i = 0; i < octaves; ++i) {
    sum += o * Noise(lambda * P);
    lambda *= 1.99f;
    o *= omega;
}
float partialOctave = foctaves - octaves;
sum += o * SmoothStep(.3f, .7f, partialOctave) * Noise(lambda * P);
```

The SmoothStep() function takes a minimum and maximum value and a point at which to evaluate a smooth interpolating function. If the point is below the minimum, zero is returned, and if it's above the maximum, one is returned. Otherwise it smoothly interpolates between zero and one using a cubic Hermite spline.

⟨*Global Inline Functions*⟩+≡

```
inline float SmoothStep(float min, float max, float value) {
    float v = Clamp((value - min) / (max - min), 0.f, 1.f);
    return v * v * (-2.f * v  + 3.f);
}
```

Closely related to the FBm() function is the Turbulence() function. It also computes a sum of terms of the noise function, but takes the absolute value of each one:

$$f_s(x) = \sum_i w_i |f(s_i x)|.$$

Taking the absolute value introduces first-derivative discontinuities in the synthesized function and thus the turbulence function has infinite frequency content. Nevertheless, the visual characteristics of this function can be quite useful for procedural textures. Figure 11.30 shows two graphs of the turbulence function.

The Turbulence() implementation here tries to antialias itself in the same way that FBm() did. As described earlier, however, the first-derivative discontinuities in the function introduce infinitely high frequency content, so these efforts can't hope to be perfectly successful. The Turbulence() antialiasing here at least eliminates some of the worst of the artifacts; otherwise, increasing the pixel sampling rate is the best recourse. In practice, this function doesn't alias too terribly when used in procedural textures, particularly compared to the aliasing from infinitely high frequencies from geometric and shadow edges.

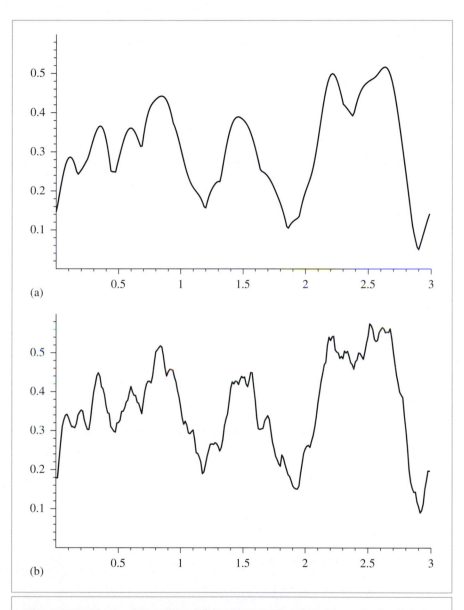

(a)

(b)

Figure 11.30: Graphs of the `Turbulence()` function for (a) 2 and (b) 6 octaves of noise. Note that the first derivative discontinuities introduced by taking the absolute value of the noise function make this function substantially more rough than FBm.

Turbulence() 558

⟨*Texture Method Definitions*⟩+≡
```
COREDLL float Turbulence(const Point &P, const Vector &dpdx,
        const Vector &dpdy, float omega, int maxOctaves) {
    ⟨Compute number of octaves for antialiased FBm 555⟩
    ⟨Compute sum of octaves of noise for turbulence 558⟩
    return sum;
}
```

⟨*Compute sum of octaves of noise for turbulence*⟩ ≡   558
```
float sum = 0., lambda = 1., o = 1.;
for (int i = 0; i < octaves; ++i) {
    sum += o * fabsf(Noise(lambda * P));
    lambda *= 1.99f;
    o *= omega;
}
float partialOctave = foctaves - octaves;
sum += o * SmoothStep(.3f, .7f, partialOctave) *
        fabsf(Noise(lambda * P));
```

11.6.4 BUMPY AND WRINKLED TEXTURES

The FBm and turbulence functions are particularly useful as a source of random variation for bump mapping. The FBmTexture is a float-valued texture that uses FBm() to compute offsets, and WrinkledTexture uses Turbulence() to do so. They are demonstrated in Figures 11.31 and 11.32 and are implemented in textures/fbm.cpp⊙ and textures/wrinkled.cpp.⊙

⟨*FBmTexture Declarations*⟩ ≡
```
template <class T> class FBmTexture : public Texture<T> {
public:
    ⟨FBmTexture Public Methods 558⟩
private:
    ⟨FBmTexture Private Data 559⟩
};
```

⟨*FBmTexture Public Methods*⟩ ≡   558
```
FBmTexture(int oct, float roughness, TextureMapping3D *map) {
    omega = roughness;
    octaves = oct;
    mapping = map;
}
```

Figure 11.31: Sphere with the FBmTexture Used for Bump Mapping.

⟨*FBmTexture Private Data*⟩ ≡   558

```
int octaves;
float omega;
TextureMapping3D *mapping;
```

⟨*FBmTexture Public Methods*⟩+≡   558

```
T Evaluate(const DifferentialGeometry &dg) const {
    Vector dpdx, dpdy;
    Point P = mapping->Map(dg, &dpdx, &dpdy);
    return FBm(P, dpdx, dpdy, omega, octaves);
}
```

The implementation of WrinkledTexture is almost identical to FBmTexture, save for a call to Turbulence() instead of FBm(). As such, it isn't included here.

11.6.5 WINDY WAVES

Application of FBm can give a reasonably convincing representation of waves (Ebert et al. 2003). Both Figures 1.11 and 4.1 use this texture for the water in those scenes. This Texture is based on two observations. First, across the surface of a wind-swept lake (for example), some areas are relatively smooth and some are more choppy; this

Figure 11.32: WrinkledTexture Used as Bump Mapping Function for Sphere.

effect comes from the natural variation of the wind's strength from area to area. Second, the overall form of individual waves on the surface can be described well by the FBm-based wave pattern scaled by the wind strength. This texture is implemented in textures/windy.cpp.⊚

⟨*WindyTexture Declarations*⟩ ≡
```
template <class T> class WindyTexture : public Texture<T> {
public:
    ⟨WindyTexture Public Methods 560⟩
private:
    ⟨WindyTexture Private Data 560⟩
};
```

⟨*WindyTexture Public Methods*⟩ ≡   560
```
WindyTexture(TextureMapping3D *map) {
    mapping = map;
}
```

⟨*WindyTexture Private Data*⟩ ≡   560
```
TextureMapping3D *mapping;
```

The evaluation function uses two calls to the FBm() function. The first scales down the point P by a factor of 10; as a result, the first call to FBm() returns relatively low-frequency variation over the surface of the object being shaded. This value is used to determine the local strength of the wind. The second call determines the amplitude of the wave at the particular point, independent of the amount of wind there. The product of these two values gives the actual wave offset for the particular location.

⟨*WindyTexture Public Methods*⟩+≡   560
```
T Evaluate(const DifferentialGeometry &dg) const {
    Vector dpdx, dpdy;
    Point P = mapping->Map(dg, &dpdx, &dpdy);
    float windStrength = FBm(.1f * P, .1f * dpdx, .1f * dpdy, .5f, 3);
    float waveHeight = FBm(P, dpdx, dpdy, .5f, 6);
    return fabsf(windStrength) * waveHeight;
}
```

11.6.6 MARBLE

Another classic use of the noise function is to perturb texture coordinates before using another texture or lookup table. For example, a facsimile of marble can be made by modeling the marble material as a series of layered strata and then using noise to perturb the coordinate used for finding a value among the strata. The MarbleTexture in this section implements this approach. Figure 11.33 illustrates the idea behind this texture. On the left, the layers of marble are indexed directly using the *y* coordinate of the point on the sphere. On the right, FBm has been used to perturb the *y* value, introducing variation. This texture is implemented in textures/marble.cpp.☺

Figure 11.33: Marble. The MarbleTexture perturbs the coordinate used to index into a one-dimensional table of colors using FBm, giving a plausible marble appearance.

⟨*MarbleTexture Declarations*⟩ ≡
```
class MarbleTexture : public Texture<Spectrum> {
public:
```
    ⟨*MarbleTexture Public Methods* **562**⟩
```
private:
```
    ⟨*MarbleTexture Private Data* **562**⟩
```
};
```

The texture takes the usual set of parameters to control the `FBm()` function that will be used to perturb the lookup coordinate. The `variation` parameter modulates the magnitude of the perturbation.

⟨*MarbleTexture Public Methods*⟩ ≡   **562**
```
MarbleTexture(int oct, float roughness, float sc, float var,
              TextureMapping3D *map) {
    omega = roughness;
    octaves = oct;
    mapping = map;
    scale = sc;
    variation = var;
}
```

⟨*MarbleTexture Private Data*⟩ ≡   **562**
```
int octaves;
float omega, scale, variation;
TextureMapping3D *mapping;
```

An offset into the marble layers is computed by adding the variation to the point's *y* component and using the sine function to remap its value into the range [0, 1]. The ⟨*Evaluate marble spline at* t⟩ fragment uses the *t* value as the evaluation point for a cubic spline through a series of colors that are similar to those of real marble.

⟨*MarbleTexture Public Methods*⟩+ ≡   **562**
```
Spectrum Evaluate(const DifferentialGeometry &dg) const {
    Vector dpdx, dpdy;
    Point P = mapping->Map(dg, &dpdx, &dpdy);
    P *= scale;
    float marble = P.y + variation *
                FBm(P, scale * dpdx, scale * dpdy, omega, octaves);
    float t = .5f + .5f * sinf(marble);
    ⟨Evaluate marble spline at t⟩
}
```

FURTHER READING

Two-dimensional texture mapping with images was first introduced to graphics by Blinn and Newell (1976). Ever since Crow (1977) identified aliasing as the source of many errors in images in graphics, quite a bit of work has been done to find efficient and effective ways of antialiasing image maps. Dungan, Stenger, and Sutty (1978) were the first to suggest creating a pyramid of prefiltered texture images; they used the nearest texture sample at the appropriate level when looking up texture values, using supersampling in screen space to antialias the result. Feibush, Levoy, and Cook (1980) investigated a spatially varying filter function, rather than a simple box filter. (Blinn and Newell were aware of Crow's results and used a box filter for their textures.)

Williams (1983) used a MIP map image pyramid for texture filtering with trilinear interpolation. Shortly thereafter, Crow (1984) introduced summed area tables, which make it possible to efficiently filter over axis-aligned rectangular regions of texture space. Summed area tables handle anisotropy better than Williams's method, although only for primarily axis-aligned filter regions. Heckbert (1986) has written a good general survey of texture mapping algorithms through the mid-1980s.

Greene and Heckbert (1986) originally developed the elliptically weighted average technique, and Heckbert's master's thesis put the method on a solid theoretical footing (Heckbert 1989). Fournier and Fiume (1988) have developed an even higher-quality texture filtering method that focuses on using a bounded amount of computation per lookup. Nonetheless, their method appears to be less efficient than EWA overall. Lansdale's master's thesis has an extensive description of EWA and Fournier and Fiume's method, including implementation details (Lansdale 1991).

More recently, a number of researchers have investigated generalizing Williams's original method using a series of MIP map probes in an effort to increase quality without having to pay the price for the general EWA algorithm. By taking multiple samples from the MIP map, anisotropy is handled well while preserving the computational efficiency. Examples include Barkans's (1997) description of texture filtering in the Talisman architecture, McCormack et al.'s (1999) Feline method, and Cant and Shrubsole's (2000) technique.

Smith's Web site and document on audio resampling gives a good overview of resampling signals in one dimension (Smith 2002). Heckbert's zoom source code is the canonical reference for image resampling (Heckbert 1989). His implementation carefully avoids feedback without using auxiliary storage, unlike ours in this chapter, which allocates additional temporary buffer space to do so.

Three-dimensional solid texturing was originally developed by Gardner (1984, 1985), Perlin (1985a), and Peachey (1985). Norton, Rockwood, and Skolmoski (1982) developed the *clamping* method that is widely used for antialiasing textures based on solid texturing. The general idea of procedural texturing was introduced by Cook (1984), Perlin (1985a), and Peachey (1985).

Peachey's chapter in *Texturing and Modeling* (Ebert et al. 2003) has a thorough summary of approaches to noise functions. After Perlin's original noise function, both Lewis (1989) and van Wijk (1991) developed alternatives that made different time/quality trade-offs. Worley (1996) has developed a quite different noise function for procedural texturing that is well-suited for cellular and organic patterns. Perlin (2002) has revised his noise function to correct a number of subtle shortcomings.

The cone tracing method of Amanatides (1984) was one of the first techniques for automatically estimating filter footprints for ray tracing. The beam tracing algorithm of Heckbert and Hanrahan (1984) was another early extension of ray tracing to incorporate an area associated with each image sample, rather than just an infinitesimal ray. The pencil tracing method of Shinya, Takahashi, and Naito (1987) is another approach to this problem. Other related work on the topic of associating areas or footprints with rays includes Mitchell and Hanrahan's paper on rendering caustics (Mitchell and Hanrahan 1992) and Turkowski's technical report (Turkowski 1993).

Collins (1994) estimated the ray footprint by keeping a tree of all rays traced from a given camera ray, examining corresponding rays at the same level and position. Also, Worley's chapter in *Texturing and Modeling* (Ebert et al. 2003) on computing differentials for filter regions presents an approach similar to ours. The ray differentials used in pbrt are based on Igehy's (1999) formulation, which was extended by Suykens and Willems (2001) to handle glossy reflection in addition to perfect specular reflection.

The first languages and systems that supported the idea of user-supplied procedural shaders were developed by Cook (1984) and Perlin (1985a). (The texture composition model in this chapter is similar to Cook's shade trees.) The RenderMan shading language, described in a paper by Hanrahan and Lawson (1990), remains the classic shading language in graphics. See Ebert et al. (2003) and Apodaca and Gritz (2000) for techniques for writing procedural shaders; both of those have excellent discussions of issues related to antialiasing in procedural shaders.

Many creative methods for computing texture on surfaces have been developed. A sampling of our favorites includes reaction diffusion, which simulates growth processes based on a model of chemical interactions over surfaces and was simultaneously introduced by Turk (1991) and Witkin and Kass (1991); Sims's genetic algorithm-based approach, which finds programs that generate interesting textures through random mutations from which a user selects their favorites (Sims 1991); Fleischer et al.'s cellular texturing algorithms that generate geometrically accurate scales and spike features on surfaces (Fleischer et al. 1995); and Dorsey et al.'s flow simulations that model the effect of weathering on buildings and encode the results in image maps that stored the relative wetness, dirtiness, and so on, at points on the surfaces of structures (Dorsey, Pedersen, and Hanrahan 1996).

EXERCISES

❷ 11.1 Many image file formats don't store floating-point color values but instead use eight bits for each color component, mapping the values to the range [0, 1]. For images originally stored in this format, the MIPMap uses four times more memory than strictly necessary by using floats in Spectrum objects to store these colors. Modify the image reading routines to support an image file format with eight-bit components and return an indication of when an image is read from such a file. Then, modify the MIPMap so that it keeps the data for such textures in an eight-bit representation. How much memory is saved for image texture-heavy scenes? How is pbrt's performance affected? Can you explain the causes of any performance differences?

❷ 11.2 For scenes with many image textures where reading them all into memory simultaneously has a prohibitive memory cost, an effective approach can be to allocate a fixed amount of memory for image maps (a *texture cache*), load textures into that memory on demand, and discard the image maps that haven't been accessed recently when the memory fills up (Peachey 1990). To enable good performance with small texture caches, image maps should be stored in a *tiled* format that makes it possible to load in small square regions of the texture independently of each other. Tiling techniques like these are used in graphics hardware to improve the performance of their texture memory caches (Hakura and Gupta 1997; Igehy, Eldridge, and Proudfoot 1998; Igehy, Eldridge, and Hanrahan 1999). Implement a texture cache in pbrt. Write a conversion program that converts images in other formats to a tiled format. How small can you make the texture cache and still see good performance?

❷ 11.3 The Feline texture filtering technique is a middle ground between trilinear interpolation and EWA filtering. It gives results nearly as good as EWA by doing trilinear filtering at a series of positions along the longer filtering axis in texture space. Read the paper that describes Feline (McCormack et al. 1999) and implement this method in pbrt. How does its performance and quality compare to EWA?

❷ 11.4 Improve the filtering algorithm used for resampling image maps to initialize the MIP map levels using the Lanczos filter instead of the box filter. How does the spheres example image in the file sphere-ewa-vs-trilerp.pbrt⊙ and Figure 11.10 change after your improvements?

❸ 11.5 Modify pbrt to support a shading language to allow user-written programs to compute texture values.

❶ 11.6 Modify the MIPMap so that it never does any texture filtering and always returns a bilinearly interpolated value from the finest level of the pyramid. Using the sphere-ewa-vs-trilerp.pbrt⊙ scene, experiment with how high the number

MIPMap 516
Spectrum 230

of pixel samples needs to be in order to eliminate artifacts due to texture aliasing. (You may find it useful to render a short animated sequence with a slowly moving camera to fully see the effect of texture aliasing.) How much faster is it to do correct texture filtering in the texture lookup routine than to increase the pixel sampling rate to get an equivalently antialiased result?

11.7 Read Worley's paper that describes a new noise function with substantially different visual characteristics than Perlin noise (Worley 1996). Implement this cellular noise function and add `Textures` to `pbrt` that are based on it.

11.8 An additional advantage of properly antialiased image map lookups is that they improve cache performance. Consider, for example, the situation of undersampling a high-resolution image map: nearby samples on the screen will access widely separated parts of the image map, such that there is low probability that texels fetched from main memory for one texture lookup will already be in the cache for texture lookups at adjacent pixel samples. Modify `pbrt` so that it always does image texture lookups from the finest level of the `MIPMap`, being careful to ensure that the same number of texels are still being accessed. How does performance change? What do cache-profiling tools report about the overall change in effectiveness of the CPU cache?

11.9 The implementation of the `DotsTexture` texture in this chapter does not make any effort to avoid aliasing in the results that it computes. Modify this texture to do some form of antialiasing. The `Checkerboard2D` texture offers a guide as to how this might be done, although this case is more complicated, both because the polka dots are not present in every grid cell and because they are irregularly positioned.

At the two extremes of a filter region that is within a single cell and a filter region that spans a large number of cells, the task is easier. If the filter is entirely within a single cell and is entirely inside or outside the polka dot in that cell (if present), then it is only necessary to evaluate one of the two subtextures as appropriate. If the filter is within a single cell but overlaps both the dot and the base texture, then it is possible to compute how much of the filter area is inside the dot and how much is outside and blend between the two. At the other extreme, if the filter area is extremely large, it is possible to blend between the two textures according to the overall average of how much area is covered by dots and how much is not. (Note that this approach potentially makes the same error as was made in the checkerboard, where the subtextures aren't aware that part of their area is occluded by another texture. Ignore this issue for this exercise.)

Implement these approaches and then consider the intermediate cases, where the filter region spans a small number of cells. What approaches work well for antialiasing in this case?

❷ **11.10** Write a general-purpose Texture that stores a reference to another texture and supersamples that texture when the evaluation method is called, thus making it possible to apply supersampling to any Texture. Use your implementation to compare the effectiveness and quality of the built-in antialiasing done by various procedural textures. Also compare the run time efficiency of texture supersampling versus increased pixel sampling.

CHAPTER TWELVE

★ 12 VOLUME SCATTERING

So far, we have assumed that scenes are made up of collections of surfaces in a vacuum, which means that radiance is constant along rays between surfaces. However, there are many real-world situations where this assumption is inaccurate: fog and smoke attenuate and scatter light, and scattering from particles in the atmosphere makes the sky blue and sunsets red. This chapter introduces the mathematics to describe how light is affected as it passes through *participating media*—particles distributed throughout a region of 3D space. Simulating the effect of participating media makes it possible to render images with atmospheric haze, beams of light through clouds, light passing through cloudy water, and subsurface scattering, where light exits an object at a different place from where it entered.

This chapter first describes the basic physical processes that affect the radiance along rays passing through participating media. We then introduce the VolumeRegion base class, an interface for modeling different types of media. Like a BSDF, the volume description characterizes how light is scattered at individual points. In order to determine the global effect on the distribution of light in the scene, VolumeIntegrators are necessary; they are described in Chapter 17.

12.1 VOLUME SCATTERING PROCESSES

There are three main processes that affect the distribution of radiance in an environment with participating media:

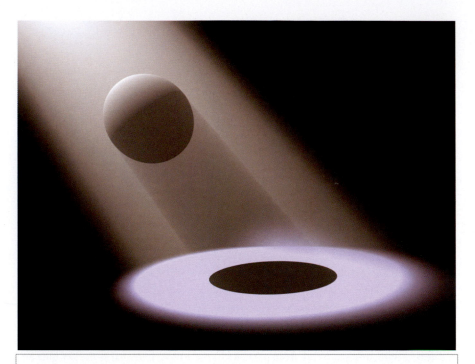

Figure 12.1: Spotlight through Fog. Light scattering from particles in the medium back toward the camera makes the spotlight's illumination visible even in pixels where there are no visible surfaces that reflect it. The sphere blocks light, casting a volumetric shadow in the region beneath it.

- *Absorption*—the reduction in radiance due to the conversion of light to another form of energy, such as heat
- *Emission*—energy that is added to the environment from luminous particles
- *Scattering*—how light heading in one direction is scattered to other directions due to collisions with particles

The characteristics of all of these properties may be *homogeneous* or *inhomogeneous*. Homogeneous properties are constant throughout a given spatial extent, while inhomogeneous properties may vary throughout space. Figure 12.1 shows a simple example of volume scattering, where a spotlight shining through a participating medium illuminates the medium and and casts a volumetric shadow.

12.1.1 ABSORPTION

Consider thick black smoke from a fire: the smoke obscures the objects behind it because its particles absorb light traveling from the object to the viewer. The thicker the smoke, the more light is absorbed. Figure 12.2 shows this effect with a volume density that was

Figure 12.2: If a participating medium primarily absorbs light passing through it, it will have a dark and smoky appearance, as shown here. *Smoke simulation data courtesy Duc Nguyen and Ron Fedkiw.*

created with an accurate physical simulation of smoke formation. Note the shadow on the ground: the participating medium has also absorbed light between the light source to the ground plane, casting a shadow.

Absorption is described by the medium's *absorption cross section* σ_a, which is the probability density that light is absorbed per unit distance traveled in the medium. In general, the absorption cross section may vary with both position p and direction ω, although it is normally just a function of position. It is usually also a spectrally varying quantity. The units of σ_a are a reciprocal distance (m^{-1}). This means that σ_a can take on any positive value; it is not required to be between zero and one, for instance.

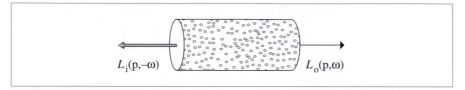

Figure 12.3: Absorption reduces the amount of radiance along a ray through a participating medium. Consider a ray carrying incident radiance at a point p from direction $-\omega$. If the ray passes through a differential cylinder filled with absorbing particles, the change in radiance due to absorption by those particles is $dL_o(p, \omega) = -\sigma_a(p, \omega)L_i(p, -\omega)dt$.

Figure 12.3 shows the effect of absorption along a very short portion of a ray. Some amount of radiance $L_i(p, -\omega)$ is arriving at point p, and we'd like to find the exitant radiance $L_o(p, \omega)$ after absorption in the differential volume. This change in radiance along the differential ray length dt is described by the differential equation

$$L_o(p, \omega) - L_i(p, -\omega) = dL_o(p, \omega) = -\sigma_a(p, \omega)L_i(p, -\omega)dt,$$

which says that the differential reduction in radiance along the beam is a linear function of its initial radiance.[1]

This differential equation can be solved to give the integral equation describing the total fraction of light absorbed for a ray. If we assume that the ray travels a distance d in direction ω through the medium starting at point p, the total absorption is given by

$$e^{-\int_0^d \sigma_a(p+t\omega, \omega)dt}.$$

12.1.2 EMISSION

While absorption reduces the amount of radiance along a ray as it passes through a medium, emission increases it, due to chemical, thermal, or nuclear processes that convert energy into visible light. Figure 12.4 shows emission in a differential volume, where we denote emitted radiance added to a ray per unit distance at a point p in direction ω by $L_{ve}(p, \omega)$. Figure 12.5 shows the effect of emission in the smoke data set. In that figure the absorption coefficient is much lower than in Figure 12.2, giving a very different appearance.

The differential equation that gives the change in radiance due to emission is

$$dL_o(p, \omega) = L_{ve}(p, \omega)dt.$$

---

1   This is another instance of the linearity assumption in radiometry: the fraction of light absorbed doesn't vary based on the ray's radiance, but is always a fixed fraction.

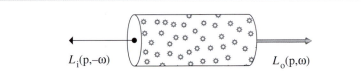

Figure 12.4: The volume emission function $L_{ve}(p, \omega)$ gives the change in radiance along a ray as it passes through a differential volume of emissive particles. The change in radiance per differential distance is $dL = L_{ve}dt$.

Figure 12.5: A Participating Medium Where the Dominant Volumetric Effect Is Emission. Although the medium still absorbs light, still casting a shadow on the ground and obscuring the wall behind it, emission in the volume increases radiance along rays passing through it, making the cloud brighter than the wall behind it.

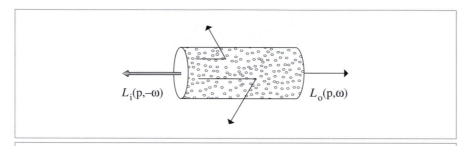

Figure 12.6: Like absorption, out-scattering also reduces the radiance along a ray. Light that hits particles may be scattered in another direction such that the radiance exiting the region in the original direction is reduced.

Note that this equation is based on the assumption that the emitted light L_{ve} is not dependent on the incoming light L_i. This is always true under the linear optics assumptions that pbrt is based on.

12.1.3 OUT-SCATTERING AND EXTINCTION

The third basic light interaction in participating media is scattering. As a beam passes through a medium, it may collide with particles in the medium and be scattered in different directions. This has two effects on the total radiance that the beam carries: It reduces the radiance exiting a differential region of the beam because some of it is deflected to different directions. This effect is called *out-scattering* (Figure 12.6) and is the topic of this section. However, radiance from other rays may be scattered into the path of the current ray; this *in-scattering* process is the subject of the next section.

The probability of an out-scattering event occurring per unit distance is given by the scattering coefficient, σ_s. As with the attenuation coefficient, the reduction in radiance along a differential length $\mathrm{d}t$ due to out-scattering is given by

$$\mathrm{d}L_o(\mathrm{p}, \omega) = -\sigma_s(\mathrm{p}, \omega) L_i(\mathrm{p}, -\omega)\mathrm{d}t.$$

The total reduction in radiance due to absorption and out-scattering is given by the sum $\sigma_a + \sigma_s$. This combined effect of absorption and out-scattering is called *attenuation* or *extinction*. For convenience the sum of these two coefficients is denoted by the attenuation coefficient σ_t:

$$\sigma_t(\mathrm{p}, \omega) = \sigma_a(\mathrm{p}, \omega) + \sigma_s(\mathrm{p}, \omega).$$

Given the attenuation coefficient σ_t, the differential equation describing overall attenuation,

$$\frac{\mathrm{d}L_o(\mathrm{p}, \omega)}{\mathrm{d}t} = -\sigma_t(\mathrm{p}, \omega) L_i(\mathrm{p}, -\omega),$$

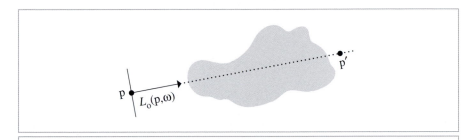

Figure 12.7: The beam transmittance $T_r(\mathrm{p} \to \mathrm{p}')$ gives the fraction of light transmitted from one point to another, accounting for absorption and out-scattering, but ignoring emission and in-scattering. Given exitant radiance at a point p in direction ω (e.g., reflected radiance from a surface), the radiance visible at another point p' along the ray is $T_r(\mathrm{p} \to \mathrm{p}')L_o(\mathrm{p}, \omega)$.

can be solved to find the *beam transmittance*, which gives the fraction of radiance that is transmitted between two points on a ray:

$$T_r(\mathrm{p} \to \mathrm{p}') = e^{-\int_0^d \sigma_t(\mathrm{p}+t\omega,\omega)\mathrm{d}t}$$

where d is the distance between p and p', ω is the normalized direction vector between them, and T_r denotes the beam transmittance between p and p'. Note that the transmittance is always between zero and one. Thus, if exitant radiance from a point p on a surface in a given direction ω is given by $L_o(\mathrm{p}, \omega)$, after accounting for extinction, the incident radiance at another point p' in direction $-\omega$ is

$$T_r(\mathrm{p} \to \mathrm{p}')L_o(\mathrm{p}, \omega).$$

This idea is illustrated in Figure 12.7.

Two useful properties of beam transmittance are that transmittance from a point to itself is one ($T_r(\mathrm{p} \to \mathrm{p}) = 1$), and in a vacuum, $T_r(\mathrm{p} \to \mathrm{p}') = 1$ for all p'. Another important property, true in all media, is that transmittance is multiplicative along points on a ray:

$$T_r(\mathrm{p} \to \mathrm{p}'') = T_r(\mathrm{p} \to \mathrm{p}')T_r(\mathrm{p}' \to \mathrm{p}''),$$

for all points p' between p and p'' (Figure 12.8). This property is important for volume scattering implementations, since it makes it possible to incrementally compute transmittance at many points along a ray by computing the product of each previously computed transmittance with the transmittance for its next segment.

The negated exponent in T_r is called the *optical thickness* between the two points. It is denoted by the symbol τ:

$$\tau(\mathrm{p} \to \mathrm{p}') = \int_0^d \sigma_t(\mathrm{p} + t\omega, -\omega)\mathrm{d}t.$$

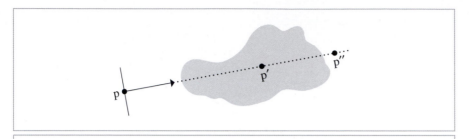

Figure 12.8: A useful property of beam transmittance is that it is multiplicative: the transmittance between points p and p″ on a ray like the one shown here is equal to the transmittance from p to p′ times the transmittance from p′ to p″ for all points p′ between p and p″.

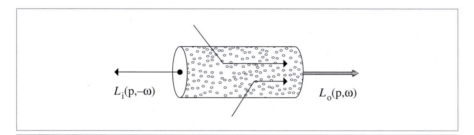

Figure 12.9: In-Scattering accounts for the increase in radiance along a ray due to scattering of light from other directions. Radiance from outside the differential volume is scattered along the direction of the ray and added to the incoming radiance.

In a homogeneous medium, σ_t is a constant, so the τ integral is trivially evaluated and yields *Beer's law:*

$$T_r(\mathrm{p} \to \mathrm{p}') = e^{-\sigma_t d}. \tag{12.1}$$

12.1.4 IN-SCATTERING

While out-scattering reduces radiance along a ray due to scattering in different directions, *in-scattering* accounts for increased radiance due to scattering from other directions (Figure 12.9). Figure 12.10 shows the effect of in-scattering with the smoke data set. Note that the smoke appears much thicker than when absorption or emission was the dominant volumetric effect.

Assuming that the separation between particles is at least a few times the lengths of their radii, it is possible to ignore interparticle interactions when describing scattering at a particular location. Under this assumption, the *phase function* $p(\omega \to \omega')$ describes the

Figure 12.10: In-Scattering with the Smoke Data Set. Note the substantially different appearance compared to the other two smoke images.

angular distribution of scattered radiation at a point; it is the volumetric analog to the BSDF. The BSDF analogy is not exact, however; for example, phase functions have a normalization constraint: for all ω, the condition

$$\frac{1}{4\pi} \int_{\mathbb{S}^2} p(\omega \to \omega')\, \mathrm{d}\omega' = 1 \qquad \text{[12.2]}$$

must hold. This constraint means that phase functions actually define probability distributions for scattering in a particular direction.

The total added radiance per unit distance due to in-scattering is given by the *source term S:*

$$dL_o(p, \omega) = S(p, \omega)dt.$$

It accounts for both volume emission and in-scattering:

$$S(p, \omega) = L_{ve}(p, \omega) + \sigma_s(p, \omega) \int_{S^2} p(p, -\omega' \rightarrow \omega) L_i(p, \omega')d\omega'.$$

The in-scattering portion of the source term is the product of the scattering probability per unit distance, σ_s, and the amount of added radiance at a point, which is given by the spherical integral of the product of incident radiance and the phase function. Note that the source term is very similar to the scattering equation, Equation (5.6); the main difference is that there is no cosine term since the phase function operates on radiance rather than differential irradiance.

12.2 PHASE FUNCTIONS

Just as there are a wide variety of BSDF models to describe scattering from surfaces, many phase functions have been developed. These range from parameterized models that can be used to fit a function with a small number of parameters to measured data, to analytic models that are based on deriving the scattered radiance distribution that results from particles with known shape and material (e.g., spherical water droplets).

In most naturally occurring media, the phase function is a 1D function of only the angle θ between the two directions ω and ω'; such media are called *isotropic*, and these phase functions are often written as $p(\cos\theta)$. In exotic media, such as those with a crystalline structure, the phase function is a 4D function of the two directions. In addition to being normalized, an important property of naturally occurring phase functions is that they are *reciprocal:* the two directions can be interchanged and the phase function's value remains unchanged. Note that isotropic phase functions are trivially reciprocal because $\cos(-\theta) = \cos(\theta)$.

In a slightly confusing overloading of terminology, phase functions themselves can be isotropic or anisotropic as well. An isotropic phase function describes equal scattering in all directions and is thus independent of either of the two directions. Because phase functions are normalized, there is only one such function, and it must be the constant $1/4\pi$:

$$p_{isotropic}(\omega \rightarrow \omega') = \frac{1}{4\pi}.$$

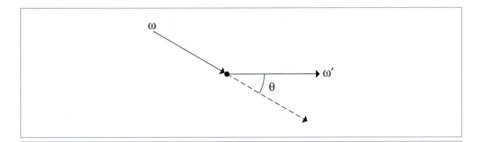

Figure 12.11: Phase functions are written with the convention that the incident direction points toward the point where scattering happens and the outgoing direction ω' points away from it. This is a different convention than was used for BSDFs. The angle between them is denoted by θ.

⟨*Volume Scattering Definitions*⟩ ≡
```
COREDLL float PhaseIsotropic(const Vector &, const Vector &) {
    return 1.f / (4.f * M_PI);
}
```

All of the anisotropic phase functions in the remainder of this section describe isotropic media and are thus defined in terms of the angle between the two directions (Figure 12.11). Phase functions use a different convention for the direction of the vectors at a scattering event than was used for scattering at a surface, where both vectors faced away from the surface. For phase functions, the incident direction points toward the scattering point and the outgoing direction points away from it. This matches the usual convention used for phase functions.

pbrt includes implementations of phase functions that model Rayleigh scattering and Mie scattering. The Rayleigh model describes scattering from very small particles such as the molecules in the Earth's atmosphere. If the particles have radii that are smaller than the wavelength of light λ, $(r/\lambda < 0.05)$, the Rayleigh model accurately describes the distribution of scattered light. Wavelength-dependent Rayleigh scattering is the reason that the sky is blue and sunsets are red. Mie scattering is based on a more general theory; it is derived from Maxwell's equations and can describe scattering from a wider range of particle sizes. For example, it is a good model for scattering in the atmosphere due to water droplets and fog.

We won't include the implementations of these phase functions in the text here. They are straightforward transcriptions of models from the research literature.

COREDLL 904
M_PI 855
Vector 47

⟨*Volume Scattering Declarations*⟩ ≡
```
COREDLL float PhaseRayleigh(const Vector &w, const Vector &wp);
COREDLL float PhaseMieHazy(const Vector &w, const Vector &wp);
COREDLL float PhaseMieMurky(const Vector &w, const Vector &wp);
```

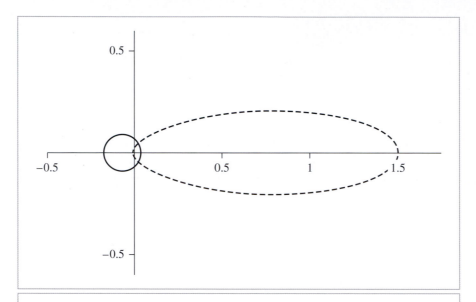

Figure 12.12: Plots of the Henyey-Greenstein Phase Function for Asymmetry g **Parameters** **−.35 and .67.** Negative g values (solid line) describe phase functions that primarily scatter light back in the incident direction, and positive g values (dashed line) describe phase functions that primarily scatter light forward in the direction it was already traveling.

A widely used phase function, particularly in computer graphics, was developed by Henyey and Greenstein (1941). This phase function was specifically designed to be easy to fit to measured scattering data. A single parameter g (called the *asymmetry parameter*) controls the distribution of scattered light:

$$p_{\text{HG}}(\cos\theta) = \frac{1}{4\pi} \frac{1 - g^2}{(1 + g^2 - 2g(\cos\theta))^{3/2}}.$$

Figure 12.12 shows plots of the Henyey-Greenstein phase function with varying asymmetry parameters. The value of g for this model must be in the range $(-1, 1)$. Negative values of g correspond to *back-scattering*, where light is mostly scattered back toward the incident direction, and positive values correspond to forward-scattering. The greater the magnitude of g, the more scattering occurs close to the $-\omega$ or ω directions (for back-scattering and forward-scattering, respectively).

⟨*Volume Scattering Definitions*⟩ $+\equiv$

```
COREDLL float PhaseHG(const Vector &w, const Vector &wp, float g) {
    float costheta = Dot(w, wp);
    return 1.f / (4.f * M_PI) *
        (1.f - g*g) / powf(1.f + g*g - 2.f * g * costheta, 1.5f);
}
```

The asymmetry parameter was carefully chosen to have a precise meaning. It is the average value of the product of the phase function being approximated and the cosine of the angle between ω' and ω. Given an arbitrary phase function, g can be computed as

$$g = \frac{1}{4\pi} \int_{\mathbb{S}^2} p(\omega \to \omega')(\omega \cdot \omega') d\omega' = 2\pi \int_0^\pi p(\cos\theta) \cos\theta \, d\theta.$$

Thus an isotropic phase function gives $g = 0$, as expected.

Any number of phase functions can satisfy this equation; the g value alone is not enough to uniquely describe a scattering distribution. Nevertheless, the convenience of being able to easily convert a complex scattering distribution into a simple parameterized model is often more important than this potential loss in accuracy.

More complex phase functions that aren't described well with a single asymmetry parameter can often be modeled by a weighted sum of phase functions like Henyey-Greenstein, each with different parameter values:

$$p(\omega \to \omega') = \sum_{i=1}^n w_i \, p_i(\omega \to \omega'),$$

where the weights w_i sum to one to maintain normalization.

Blasi, Le Saëc, and Schlick (1993) developed an efficient approximation to the Henyey-Greenstein function that has been widely used in computer graphics due to its computational efficiency. It avoids the expensive `powf()` function:

$$p_{\text{Schlick}}(\cos\theta) = \frac{1}{4\pi} \frac{1 - k^2}{(1 - k\cos\theta)^2}.$$

The k parameter has a similar effect on the distribution to the g term of the Henyey-Greenstein model, where -1 corresponds to total back-scattering, 0 corresponds to isotropic scattering, and 1 corresponds to total forward-scattering. For immediate values, we have found that the polynomial equation

$$k = 1.55g - .55g^3$$

gives an accurate correspondence between k and g values. Figure 12.13 shows a plot of the Schlick model and the Henyey-Greenstein model.

⟨*Volume Scattering Definitions*⟩+≡

```
COREDLL float PhaseSchlick(const Vector &w,
                           const Vector &wp, float g) {
    float k = 1.55f * g - .55f * g * g * g;
    float kcostheta = k * Dot(w, wp);
    return 1.f / (4.f * M_PI) *
        (1.f - k*k) / ((1.f - kcostheta) * (1.f - kcostheta));
}
```

COREDLL 904
M_PI 855
Vector 47

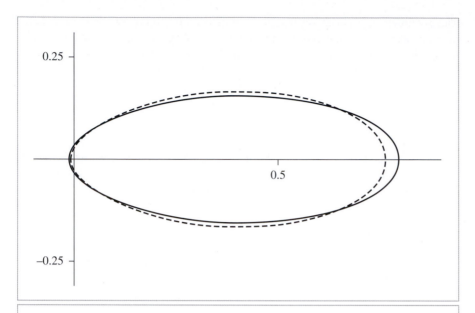

Figure 12.13: Plot of the Schlick phase function with $k = .8112$ (dashed lines) superimposed with plot of the Henyey-Greenstein phase function (solid lines) with $g = .6$. The Schlick model closely matches Henyey-Greenstein and is less computationally expensive to evaluate.

12.3 VOLUME INTERFACE AND HOMOGENEOUS MEDIA

The key abstraction for describing volume scattering in pbrt is the abstract VolumeRegion class—the interface to describe volume scattering in a region of the scene. Multiple VolumeRegions of different types can be used to describe different kinds of scattering in different parts of the scene. In this section, we will describe the basic interface, which is defined in the core/volume.h and core/volume.cpp files, as well as a few useful implementations of that interface, all of which are in the volumes/ directory of the pbrt distribution.

⟨*Volume Scattering Declarations*⟩+≡
```
class COREDLL VolumeRegion {
public:
    ⟨VolumeRegion Interface 583⟩
};
```

All VolumeRegions must be able to compute their axis-aligned world space bounding box, which is returned by the VolumeRegion::WorldBound() method. As with Shapes and Primitives, this bound can be used to place VolumeRegions into acceleration structures.

⟨*VolumeRegion Interface*⟩ ≡   582
```
virtual BBox WorldBound() const = 0;
```

Because `VolumeIntegrators` need to know the parametric range of a world space ray that passes through a volume region, and because a world space bounding box may not tightly bound a particular `VolumeRegion`, a separate method `VolumeRegion::IntersectP()` returns the parametric *t* range of the segment that overlaps the volume, if any.

⟨*VolumeRegion Interface*⟩+ ≡   582
```
virtual bool IntersectP(const Ray &ray, float *t0, float *t1) const = 0;
```

This interface has four methods corresponding to the spatially varying scattering properties introduced earlier in this chapter. Given a world space point and direction, `VolumeRegion::sigma_a()`, `VolumeRegion::sigma_s()`, and `VolumeRegion::Lve()` return the corresponding absorption, scattering, and emission properties. Given a pair of directions, the `VolumeRegion::p()` method returns the value of the phase function at the given point.

⟨*VolumeRegion Interface*⟩+ ≡   582
```
virtual Spectrum sigma_a(const Point &, const Vector &) const = 0;
virtual Spectrum sigma_s(const Point &, const Vector &) const = 0;
virtual Spectrum Lve(const Point &, const Vector &) const = 0;
virtual float p(const Point &, const Vector &,
                const Vector &) const = 0;
```

For convenience, there is also a `VolumeRegion::sigma_t()` method that returns the attenuation coefficient at a point. A default implementation returns the sum of the σ_a and σ_s values, but most of the `VolumeRegion` implementations will override this method and compute σ_t directly. For `VolumeRegions` that need to do some amount of computation to find the values of σ_a and σ_s at a particular point, it's usually possible to avoid some duplicated work when σ_t is actually needed and to compute its value directly.

⟨*Volume Scattering Definitions*⟩+ ≡
```
Spectrum VolumeRegion::sigma_t(const Point &p, const Vector &w) const {
    return sigma_a(p, w) + sigma_s(p, w);
}
```

Finally, the `VolumeRegion::Tau()` method computes the volume's optical thickness from the point ray(ray.mint) to ray(ray.maxt). Some implementations, like the `HomogeneousVolume` in the next section, can compute this value exactly, while others use Monte Carlo integration to compute it. For the benefit of the Monte Carlo approach, this method takes two optional parameters, `step` and `offset`, that are ignored by implementations that compute this value in closed form. These Monte Carlo routines are defined in Section 15.7, and the meanings of these extra parameters are described there.

⟨*VolumeRegion Interface*⟩+≡   **582**
```
virtual Spectrum Tau(const Ray &ray,
                     float step = 1.f, float offset = 0.5) const = 0;
```

12.3.1 HOMOGENEOUS VOLUMES

The simplest volume representation, HomogeneousVolume, describes a box-shaped region
of space with homogeneous scattering properties. Values for σ_a, σ_s, the phase function's
g value, and the amount of emission L_{ve} are passed to the constructor. In conjunction
with a transformation from world space to the volume's object space and an axis-aligned
object space bound, this suffices to describe the region's scattering properties and spatial extent. Its implementation is in volumes/homogeneous.cpp.⓪ Figure 12.14 shows an
image of the dragon model inside a homogeneous volume.

⟨*HomogeneousVolume Declarations*⟩≡
```
class HomogeneousVolume : public VolumeRegion {
public:
    ⟨HomogeneousVolume Public Methods 585⟩
private:
    ⟨HomogeneousVolume Private Data 585⟩
};
```

**Figure 12.14: Dragon Model inside a Homogeneous Volume with Uniform Scattering Proper-
ties throughout Its Spatial Extent.**

The constructor, not shown here, initializes the member variables by copying the corresponding parameters.

⟨*HomogeneousVolume Private Data*⟩ ≡   584
```
Spectrum sig_a, sig_s, le;
float g;
BBox extent;
Transform WorldToVolume;
```

Because the bound is maintained internally in the volume's object space, it must be transformed to world space for the `WorldBound()` method.

⟨*HomogeneousVolume Public Methods*⟩ ≡   584
```
BBox WorldBound() const {
    return WorldToVolume.GetInverse()(extent);
}
```

If the region's world-to-object-space transformation includes a rotation such that the volume isn't axis aligned in world space, it is possible to compute a tighter segment of the ray-volume overlap by transforming the ray to the volume's object space and doing the overlap test there (Figure 12.15).

⟨*HomogeneousVolume Public Methods*⟩+≡   584
```
bool IntersectP(const Ray &r, float *t0, float *t1) const {
    Ray ray = WorldToVolume(r);
    return extent.IntersectP(ray, t0, t1);
}
```

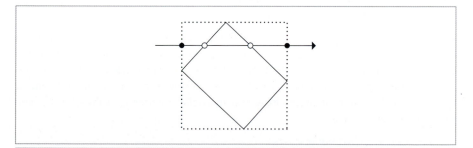

Figure 12.15: Volumes described by axis-aligned bounding boxes in the volume's object space (solid box) can compute a tighter bound on the parametric *t* range of a ray that overlaps the volume by transforming the ray into object space and computing the ray-box intersections there than if they find the intersections with the world space bound (dotted box) and an untransformed ray in world space. Here, the filled circles denote the world space intersections, and the open circles denote the object space intersections.

The rest of the `VolumeRegion` interface methods are straightforward. Each one verifies that the given point is inside the region's extent and returns the appropriate value if so. The `sigma_a()` method illustrates the basic approach; the rest of the methods won't be included here.

⟨*HomogeneousVolume Public Methods*⟩+≡   **584**
```
Spectrum sigma_a(const Point &p, const Vector &) const {
    return extent.Inside(WorldToVolume(p)) ? sig_a : 0.;
}
```

Because σ_a and σ_s are constant throughout the volume, the optical thickness that a ray passes through can be computed in closed form using Beer's law; see Equation (12.1).

⟨*HomogeneousVolume Public Methods*⟩+≡   **584**
```
Spectrum Tau(const Ray &ray, float, float) const {
    float t0, t1;
    if (!IntersectP(ray, &t0, &t1)) return 0.;
    return Distance(ray(t0), ray(t1)) * (sig_a + sig_s);
}
```

12.4 VARYING-DENSITY VOLUMES

The rest of the volume representations in this chapter are based on the assumption that the underlying particles throughout the medium all have the same basic scattering properties, but their density is spatially varying in the medium. One consequence of this assumption is that it is possible to describe the volume scattering properties at a point as the product of the density at that point and some baseline value. For example, we might set the attenuation coefficient σ_t to have a base value of 0.2. In regions where the particle density was 1, a σ_t value of 0.2 would be returned. If the particle density were 3, however, a σ_t value of 0.6 would be the result.

In order to reduce duplicated code and allow the various representations to focus on different methods for defining the density of the particles, we will define a `DensityRegion` class that provides a new pure virtual method to obtain the particle density at a point. Volume representations can then inherit from `DensityRegion` and need not reimplement the substantial amount of shared logic that multiplies the density values by the base values at lookup points.

⟨*Volume Scattering Declarations*⟩+≡
```
class COREDLL DensityRegion : public VolumeRegion {
public:
    ⟨DensityRegion Public Methods 587⟩
protected:
    ⟨DensityRegion Protected Data 587⟩
};
```

The `DensityRegion` constructor takes the basic values of the scattering properties and stores them in corresponding member variables. Note that the interface specifies the volume-to-world transformation, but the class instead stores the world-to-volume transformation.

⟨*DensityRegion Protected Data*⟩ ≡   586
```
Transform WorldToVolume;
Spectrum sig_a, sig_s, le;
float g;
```

⟨*Volume Scattering Definitions*⟩+ ≡
```
DensityRegion::DensityRegion(const Spectrum &sa,
                            const Spectrum &ss, float gg,
                            const Spectrum &emit,
                            const Transform &VolumeToWorld)
    : sig_a(sa), sig_s(ss), le(emit), g(gg)  {
    WorldToVolume = VolumeToWorld.GetInverse();
}
```

All `DensityRegion` implementations must implement the `DensityRegion::Density()` method, which returns the volume's density at the given point in object space. The density is used to scale the basic scattering parameters, so it must be nonnegative everywhere.

⟨*DensityRegion Public Methods*⟩ ≡   586
```
virtual float Density(const Point &Pobj) const = 0;
```

The `DensityRegion::sigma_a()` method is illustrative of how a `DensityRegion` works; it scales `DensityRegion::sig_a` by the local density at the point. The other `VolumeRegion` methods are similar and not shown here.

⟨*DensityRegion Public Methods*⟩+ ≡   586
```
Spectrum sigma_a(const Point &p, const Vector &) const {
    return Density(WorldToVolume(p)) * sig_a;
}
```

One exception is the `DensityRegion::p()` method, which does not scale the phase function's value by the local density. Variations in the amount of scattering from point to point are already accounted for by the scaled σ_s values.

⟨*DensityRegion Public Methods*⟩+ ≡   586
```
float p(const Point &p, const Vector &w, const Vector &wp) const {
    return PhaseHG(w, wp, g);
}
```

The `DensityRegion` cannot implement the `VolumeRegion::Tau()` method, since this method depends on global knowledge of the shape of the `VolumeRegion` as well as the density distribution throughout it. Therefore, this method is left to the implementations.

12.4.1 3D GRIDS

The VolumeGrid class stores densities at a regular 3D grid of positions, similar to the way that the ImageTexture represents images with a 2D grid of samples. These samples are interpolated to compute the density at positions between the sample points. The constructor takes a 3D array of user-supplied density values, thus allowing a variety of sources of data (physical simulation, CT scan, etc.). The smoke data set rendered in Figures 12.2, 12.5, and 12.10 is represented with a VolumeGrid. Because this class is a subclass of DensityRegion, the user also supplies baseline values of σ_a, σ_s, L_{ve}, and g to the constructor. The implementation of the VolumeGrid is in volumes/volumegrid.cpp.

⟨*VolumeGrid Declarations*⟩ ≡
```
class VolumeGrid : public DensityRegion {
public:
    ⟨VolumeGrid Public Methods  590⟩
private:
    ⟨VolumeGrid Private Data  588⟩
};
```

The constructor does the usual initialization of the basic scattering properties, stores an object space bounding box for the region, and makes a local copy of the density values.

⟨*VolumeGrid Method Definitions*⟩ ≡
```
VolumeGrid::VolumeGrid(const Spectrum &sa,
                const Spectrum &ss, float gg,
                const Spectrum &emit, const BBox &e,
                const Transform &v2w,
                int x, int y, int z, const float *d)
    : DensityRegion(sa, ss, gg, emit, v2w),
    nx(x), ny(y), nz(z), extent(e) {
    density = new float[nx*ny*nz];
    memcpy(density, d, nx*ny*nz*sizeof(float));
}
```

⟨*VolumeGrid Private Data*⟩ ≡   **588**
```
float *density;
const int nx, ny, nz;
const BBox extent;
```

The implementations of the WorldBound() and IntersectP() methods are just like the ones for the HomogeneousVolume and so aren't included here.

The task of the Density() method of the VolumeGrid is to use the samples to reconstruct the volume density function at the given point.

⟨*VolumeGrid Method Definitions*⟩+≡

```
float VolumeGrid::Density(const Point &Pobj) const {
    if (!extent.Inside(Pobj)) return 0;
    ⟨Compute voxel coordinates and offsets for Pobj 589⟩
    ⟨Trilinearly interpolate density values to compute local density  589⟩
}
```

Given the eight sample values that surround a point in 3D, this method trilinearly interpolates them to compute the density function's value at the point. It starts by finding the closest volume sample whose integer coordinates are all less than the sample location and then uses the Manhattan distances along each axis, (dx, dy, and dz), as the interpolants. Note that the same conventions for discrete versus continuous texel coordinates are used here as were used in the ImageFilm and MIPMap (Section 7.1.7).

⟨*Compute voxel coordinates and offsets for* Pobj⟩ ≡   589

```
float voxx = (Pobj.x - extent.pMin.x) /
             (extent.pMax.x - extent.pMin.x) * nx - .5f;
float voxy = (Pobj.y - extent.pMin.y) /
             (extent.pMax.y - extent.pMin.y) * ny - .5f;
float voxz = (Pobj.z - extent.pMin.z) /
             (extent.pMax.z - extent.pMin.z) * nz - .5f;
int vx = Floor2Int(voxx);
int vy = Floor2Int(voxy);
int vz = Floor2Int(voxz);
float dx = voxx - vx, dy = voxy - vy, dz = voxz - vz;
```

These distances can be used directly in a series of invocations of Lerp() to estimate the density at the sample point:

⟨*Trilinearly interpolate density values to compute local density*⟩ ≡   589

```
float d00 = Lerp(dx, D(vx, vy, vz),     D(vx+1, vy, vz));
float d10 = Lerp(dx, D(vx, vy+1, vz),   D(vx+1, vy+1, vz));
float d01 = Lerp(dx, D(vx, vy, vz+1),   D(vx+1, vy, vz+1));
float d11 = Lerp(dx, D(vx, vy+1, vz+1), D(vx+1, vy+1, vz+1));
float d0 = Lerp(dy, d00, d10);
float d1 = Lerp(dy, d01, d11);
return Lerp(dz, d0, d1);
```

The D() utility method returns the density at the given sample position. Its only tasks are to handle out-of-bounds sample positions with clamping, and to compute the appropriate array offset for the given sample. Unlike MIPMaps, clamping is almost always the desired solution for out-of-bounds coordinates here. Because all lookup points are inside the VolumeGrid's bounding box, the only time we will have out-of-bounds coordinates is at the edges, either due to the offsets for linear interpolation or the continuous-to-discrete texel coordinate conversion. In both of these cases, clamping is the most sensible solution.

⟨*VolumeGrid Public Methods*⟩ ≡   588
```
float D(int x, int y, int z) const {
    x = Clamp(x, 0, nx-1);
    y = Clamp(y, 0, ny-1);
    z = Clamp(z, 0, nz-1);
    return density[z*nx*ny + y*nx + x];
}
```

12.4.2 EXPONENTIAL DENSITY

Another useful density class is ExponentialDensity, which describes a density that varies as an exponential function of height h within a given 3D extent:

$$d(h) = ae^{-bh}.$$

The a and b values are parameters that control the overall density and how quickly it falls off as a function of height, respectively. This density function is a good model for the Earth's atmosphere as seen from the Earth's surface, where the atmosphere's curvature can generally be neglected (Ebert et al. 2003). It can also be used to model low-lying fog at ground level. It is shown in Figure 12.16 and is defined in volumes/exponential.cpp.

Figure 12.16: ExponentialDensity Used in a Scene with the Dragon Model. Note the reduction in density as a function of height. (Compare to Figure 12.14, for example.)

⟨*ExponentialDensity Declarations*⟩ ≡
```
class ExponentialDensity : public DensityRegion {
public:
    ⟨ExponentialDensity Public Methods 591⟩
private:
    ⟨ExponentialDensity Private Data 591⟩
};
```

The `ExponentialDensity` constructor initializes its member variables directly from its arguments. In addition to the volume scattering properties passed to the `DensityRegion` constructor, the volume's bound, and the *a* and *b* parameter values, this constructor takes a vector giving an "up" direction that orients the volume and is used to compute the height of points for the density computation. While the up direction is not strictly necessary (the world-to-object transformation is sufficient to orient the volume), specifying an explicit up vector can be conceptually easier for the user.

⟨*ExponentialDensity Public Methods*⟩ ≡   591
```
ExponentialDensity(const Spectrum &sa, const Spectrum &ss,
                   float gg, const Spectrum &emit, const BBox &e,
                   const Transform &v2w, float aa, float bb,
                   const Vector &up)
    : DensityRegion(sa, ss, gg, emit, v2w),
      extent(e), a(aa), b(bb) {
    upDir = Normalize(up);
}
```

⟨*ExponentialDensity Private Data*⟩ ≡   591
```
BBox extent;
float a, b;
Vector upDir;
```

The `ExponentialDensity::WorldBound()` and `ExponentialDensity::IntersectP()` methods are the same as their `HomogeneousVolume` counterparts and are not shown here.

The height of a given object space point p along the "up" direction axis can be found by projecting the vector from the lower corner of the bounding box to p onto the "up" direction vector (Figure 12.17). The distance *h* along the up direction to the point of p's perpendicular projection is given by the dot product of these two vectors. The principles behind this are similar to how vectors are transformed to and from the BSDF coordinate system, for example.

⟨*ExponentialDensity Public Methods*⟩+≡   591
```
float Density(const Point &Pobj) const {
    if (!extent.Inside(Pobj)) return 0;
    float height = Dot(Pobj - extent.pMin, upDir);
    return a * expf(-b * height);
}
```

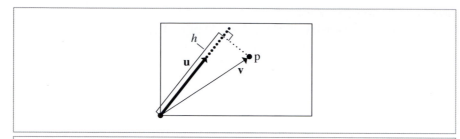

Figure 12.17: For the ExponentialDensity, it's necessary to find the perpendicular projection of the point p onto the "up" direction vector **u** and determine the distance h along **u** of the projection point. This distance is given by the dot product $(\mathbf{u} \cdot \mathbf{v})$, where **v** is the vector from the corner of the box (and the up direction's starting point) to p. This can be verified with basic properties of the dot product.

12.5 VOLUME AGGREGATES

Just as Aggregate implementations can hold sets of Primitives, the AggregateVolume holds one or more VolumeRegions. There are two main reasons to provide volume aggregates in pbrt. First, doing so simplifies the Scene and the implementation of VolumeIntegrators, since they can both be written to make calls to a single aggregate volume region, rather than looping over all of the regions in the scene. Second, AggregateVolume implementations have the potential to use 3D spatial data structures to improve efficiency by culling volumes that are far from a particular ray or lookup point.

Here we will just implement a simple AggregateVolume that stores a list of all the volumes in the scene and loops over them in each of its method implementations. This is inefficient for scenes with many distinct VolumeRegions. Writing a more efficient implementation is left as an exercise at the end of the chapter.

⟨*Volume Scattering Declarations*⟩+≡
```
    class COREDLL AggregateVolume : public VolumeRegion {
public:
        ⟨AggregateVolume Public Methods⟩
private:
        ⟨AggregateVolume Private Data 593⟩
    };
```

The AggregateVolume constructor is simple. It copies the vector of VolumeRegions passed in and computes the bound that encloses them all.

⟨*Volume Scattering Definitions*⟩+≡

```
AggregateVolume::AggregateVolume(const vector<VolumeRegion *> &r) {
    regions = r;
    for (u_int i = 0; i < regions.size(); ++i)
        bound = Union(bound, regions[i]->WorldBound());
}
```

⟨*AggregateVolume Private Data*⟩≡   **592**

```
vector<VolumeRegion *> regions;
BBox bound;
```

As described earlier, the implementations of most of the various VolumeRegion interface methods loop over the individual regions. We will show AggregateVolume::sigma_a() as an example; the rest are similar and not shown here. Note that it simply forwards the call on to each contained VolumeRegion and adds the results. This approach works as desired because the individual VolumeRegion::sigma_a() methods return zero for points outside of their respective extents.

⟨*Volume Scattering Definitions*⟩+≡

```
Spectrum AggregateVolume::sigma_a(const Point &p, const Vector &w) const {
    Spectrum s(0.);
    for (u_int i = 0; i < regions.size(); ++i)
        s += regions[i]->sigma_a(p, w);
    return s;
}
```

The one method of this class that isn't completely trivial is IntersectP(). The parametric t range of the ray over all the volumes is equal to the extent from the minimum of all of the regions' t_{min} values to the maximum of all of the t_{max} values.

⟨*Volume Scattering Definitions*⟩+≡

```
bool AggregateVolume::IntersectP(const Ray &ray,
                                 float *t0, float *t1) const {
    *t0 = INFINITY;
    *t1 = -INFINITY;
    for (u_int i = 0; i < regions.size(); ++i) {
        float tr0, tr1;
        if (regions[i]->IntersectP(ray, &tr0, &tr1)) {
            *t0 = min(*t0, tr0);
            *t1 = max(*t1, tr1);
        }
    }
    return (*t0 < *t1);
}
```

FURTHER READING

The books written by van de Hulst (1980) and Preisendorfer (1965, 1976) are excellent introductions to volume light transport. The seminal book by Chandrasekhar (1960) is another excellent resource, although it is mathematically challenging. See also the "Further Reading" section of Chapter 17 for more references to this topic.

The Henyey-Greenstein phase function was originally described in Henyey and Greenstein (1941). Detailed discussion of scattering and phase functions, along with derivations of phase functions that describe scattering from independent spheres, cylinders, and other simple shapes, can be found in van de Hulst's book (1981). Extensive discussion of the Mie and Rayleigh scattering models is also available there. Hansen and Travis's survey article is also a good introduction to the variety of commonly used phase functions (Hansen and Travis 1974).

Just as procedural modeling of textures is an effective technique for shading surfaces, procedural modeling of volume densities can be used to describe realistic-looking volumetric objects like clouds and smoke. Perlin and Hoffert (1989) describe early work in this area, and the book by Ebert et al. (2003) has a number of sections devoted to this topic, including further references. More recently, accurate physical simulation of the dynamics of smoke and fire has led to extremely realistic volume data sets, including the ones used in this chapter; see, for example, Fedkiw, Stam, and Jensen (2001).

In this chapter, we have ignored all issues related to sampling and antialiasing of volume density functions that are represented by samples in a 3D grid, although these issues should be considered, especially in the case of a volume that occupies just a few pixels on the screen. Furthermore, we have used a simple triangle filter to reconstruct densities at intermediate positions, which is suboptimal for the same reasons as the triangle filter is not a high-quality image reconstruction filter. Marschner and Lobb (1994) present the theory and practice of sampling and reconstruction for three-dimensional data sets, applying ideas similar to those in Chapter 7. See also the paper by Theußl, Hauser, and Gröller (2000) for a comparison of a variety of windowing functions for volume reconstruction with the sinc function and a discussion of how to derive optimal parameters for volume reconstruction filter functions.

EXERCISES

● 12.1   The optical thickness of a ray passing through an `ExponentialDensity` can be computed in closed form, so that the default `Tau()` method based on Monte Carlo integration isn't needed. Derive this expression and add an implementation that computes its value to the `ExponentialDensity` class. Test your implementation to ensure that it computes the same results as the Monte Carlo approach. How much does this speed up `pbrt` for scenes that use an instance of the `ExponentialDensity` volume?

ExponentialDensity 591

❷ **12.2** Given a one-dimensional volume density that is an arbitrary function of height $f(h)$, the optical distance between any two three-dimensional points can be computed very efficiently if the integral $\int_0^{h'} f(h)dh$ is precomputed and stored in a table for a set of h' values (Perlin 1985b; Max 1986; Legakis 1998). Work through the mathematics to show the derivation for this approach and implement it in pbrt, either by modifying ExponentialDensity to use such a lookup table, or by implementing a new VolumeRegion that takes an arbitrary function or a 1D table of density values. How does the efficiency and accuracy of this approach compare to using the default implementation of DensityRegion::Tau()?

❷ **12.3** The VolumeGrid class uses a relatively large amount of memory for complex volume densities. Determine its memory requirements when used for the smoke images in this chapter and modify its implementation to reduce memory use. One approach is to detect regions of space with constant (or relatively constant) density values using an octree data structure and to only refine the octree in regions where the densities are changing. Another possibility is to use less memory to record each density value, for example, by computing the minimum and maximum densities and then using 8 or 16 bits per density value to interpolate between them. What sort of errors appear when either of these approaches is pushed too far?

❷ **12.4** Modify VolumeGrid to use an optimized version of the Tau() method instead of relying on the generic Monte Carlo–based implementation of Density Region::Tau(). Incorporate the available information about the distribution of densities to compute the integral using fewer samples in areas where the density is low. For inspiration, see, for example, Levoy (1988), which describes using a binary volume octree to speed up traversal of empty regions, and Danskin and Hanrahan (1992), which describes various techniques based on 3D pyramid of volume data to use lower-precision computations in regions that have a low contribution to the final result.

❸ **12.5** The AggregateVolume will have poor performance for a scene with more than a handful of VolumeRegions. For example, time will be wasted determining the values of σ_t and σ_s in areas where the point is outside most of the volumes. Write a better volume aggregate based on a 3D data structure like a grid or an octree. Verify that it returns the same results as the AggregateVolume and measure how much faster pbrt is when it is used instead of AggregateVolume. (Don't forget to modify the RenderOptions::MakeScene() method to create an instance of your new aggregate instead of an AggregateVolume.)

❸ **12.6** Implement the atmospheric scattering model described by Preetham, Shirley, and Smits (1999) as a plug-in module to pbrt. Use it to render images of the ecosystem scene and other outdoor scenes.

CHAPTER THIRTEEN

13 LIGHT SOURCES

In order for objects in a scene to be visible, some of them must emit light that is eventually reflected back to the camera. This chapter introduces the abstract `Light` class, which defines the interface used for light sources in pbrt, as well as the implementations of a number of useful light sources. By hiding the implementation of different types of lights behind a carefully designed interface, the light transport routines can operate without knowing which particular types of lights are in the scene, similar to how the acceleration structures can hold collections of primitives without needing to know their actual types. This chapter only defines the basic light functionality because many of the quantities related to complex light sources cannot be computed in closed form. The Monte Carlo routines in Chapter 15 will complete the lighting interface by introducing methods for numerically approximating these quantities.

A range of light source implementations are introduced in this chapter, although the variety is slightly limited by pbrt's physically based design. Many flexible light source models have been developed for computer graphics, incorporating control over properties like the rate at which the light falls off with distance, which objects are illuminated by the light, which objects cast shadows from the light, and so on. While controls such as these are quite useful for artistic effects, many of them are incompatible with physically based light transport algorithms and thus can't be provided in the models here. As an example of this issue, consider a light that doesn't cast shadows: the total energy arriving at surfaces in the scene increases without bound as more surfaces are added. Consider a series of concentric shells of spheres around such a light; if occlusion is ignored, each added shell increases the total received power. This directly violates the principle that the total energy arriving at surfaces illuminated by the light can't be greater than the total energy emitted by the light.

13.1 LIGHT INTERFACE

The core lighting routines and interfaces are in core/light.h ⓒ and core/light.cpp. ⓒ Implementations of particular lights are in individual source files in the lights/ ⓒ directory. All lights share two common parameters: a transformation that defines the light's coordinate system in world space and a parameter that affects Monte Carlo sampling of lights, nSamples. As with shapes, it's often handy to be able to implement a light assuming a particular coordinate system (e.g., that a spotlight is always located at the origin of its light space, shining down the $+z$ axis). The light-to-world transformation makes it possible to place such lights at arbitrary positions and orientations in the scene. The nSamples parameter is used for area light sources where it may be desirable to trace multiple shadow rays to the light to compute soft shadows; it allows the user to have finer-grained control of the number of samples taken on a per-light basis. (This parameter is used, for example, in the DirectLighting integrator in Section 16.1.)

⟨*Light Declarations*⟩ ≡
```
class COREDLL Light {
public:
    ⟨Light Interface 598⟩
    ⟨Light Public Data 598⟩
protected:
    ⟨Light Protected Data 598⟩
};
```

Although storing both the light-to-world and the world-to-light transformations is redundant, having both available simplifies code elsewhere by eliminating the need for calls for Transform::GetInverse(), thus simplifying the code in the implementation. The default number of light source samples taken is one; thus only the light implementations for which taking multiple samples is sensible need to pass in an explicit value here.

⟨*Light Interface*⟩ ≡   598
```
Light(const Transform &l2w, int ns = 1)
    : nSamples(max(1, ns)), LightToWorld(l2w),
      WorldToLight(l2w.GetInverse()) {
}
```

⟨*Light Protected Data*⟩ ≡   598
```
const Transform LightToWorld, WorldToLight;
```

⟨*Light Public Data*⟩ ≡   598
```
const int nSamples;
```

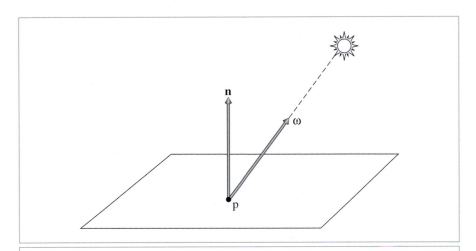

Figure 13.1: The `Light::Sample_L()` method returns incident radiance from the light at a point p and also returns the direction vector ω that gives the direction from which radiance is arriving.

The key method for lights to implement is `Sample_L()`. The caller passes the world space position of a point in the scene, and the light returns the radiance arriving at that point due to that light, assuming there are no occluding objects between them (Figure 13.1). The light is also responsible for initializing the incident direction to the light source ω_i and for initializing the `VisibilityTester` object, which holds information about the shadow ray that must be traced to verify that there are no occluding objects between the light and p. The `VisibilityTester`, which will be described in Section 13.1.1, need not be initialized if the returned radiance value is black—for example, due to the point p being outside of the cone of illumination of a spotlight.

For some types of lights, light may arrive at p from many directions, not just from a single direction as with a point light source, for example. For these types of light sources, the `Sample_L()` method must randomly sample a point on the light source's surface, so that Monte Carlo integration can be used to find the reflected light at p due to illumination from the light. Variants of the `Sample_L()` interface that take additional parameters to guide this sampling will be introduced in Section 15.6.

⟨*Light Interface*⟩+≡   598
```
virtual Spectrum Sample_L(const Point &p, Vector *wi,
                          VisibilityTester *vis) const = 0;
```

All lights must also be able to return their total emitted power; this quantity is useful for light transport algorithms that may want to devote additional computational resources to lights in the scene that make the largest contribution. Because a precise value for emitted power isn't needed elsewhere in the system, a number of the implementations of this method later in this chapter will compute approximations to this value rather than expending computational effort to find a precise value.

⟨*Light Interface*⟩+≡   **598**
```
virtual Spectrum Power(const Scene *) const = 0;
```

Finally, the `IsDeltaLight()` method indicates whether the light is described by a delta distribution. Examples of such lights include point lights, which emit illumination from a single point, and directional lights, where all light arrives from the same direction. The only way to detect illumination from light sources like these is to call their `Sample_L()` methods. It's impossible to randomly choose a direction from a point p that happens to find such a light source. (This is analogous to delta components in BSDFs from specular reflection or transmission.) The Monte Carlo algorithms that sample illumination from light sources need to be aware of which lights are described by delta distributions, since this affects some of their computations.

⟨*Light Interface*⟩+≡   **598**
```
virtual bool IsDeltaLight() const = 0;
```

13.1.1 VISIBILITY TESTING

The `VisibilityTester` is a *closure*—an object that encapsulates a small amount of data and some computation that is yet to be done. It allows lights to return a radiance value under the assumption that the receiving point p and the light source are mutually visible. The integrator can then decide if illumination from the direction ω is relevant before incurring the cost of tracing the shadow ray—for example, light incident on the back side of a surface that isn't translucent contributes nothing to reflection from the other side. If the actual amount of arriving illumination is in fact needed, a call to one of the visibility tester's methods causes the necessary shadow ray to be traced.

⟨*Light Declarations*⟩+≡
```
struct COREDLL VisibilityTester {
    ⟨VisibilityTester Public Methods 600⟩
    Ray r;
};
```

COREDLL 904
Point 54
Ray 59
RAY_EPSILON 59
Scene 23
Spectrum 230
VisibilityTester 600
VisibilityTester::r 600
VisibilityTester::
  SetSegment() 600

There are two methods that initialize `VisibilityTester`s. The first of them, `VisibilityTester::SetSegment()`, indicates that the visibility test is to be done between two points in the scene.

⟨*VisibilityTester Public Methods*⟩≡   **600**
```
void SetSegment(const Point &p1, const Point &p2) {
    r = Ray(p1, p2-p1, RAY_EPSILON, 1.f - RAY_EPSILON);
}
```

The other initialization method, `VisibilityTester::SetRay()`, indicates that the test should indicate whether there is *any* object along a given direction. This is particularly useful for computing shadows from directional lights.

⟨*VisibilityTester Public Methods*⟩+≡   600
```
void SetRay(const Point &p, const Vector &w) {
    r = Ray(p, w, RAY_EPSILON);
}
```

The next pair of methods trace the appropriate ray. First, `VisibilityTester::Unoccluded()` traces the shadow ray and returns a boolean result. Some ray tracers include a facility for casting colored shadows from partially transparent objects and would return a spectrum from a method like this. pbrt does not include this facility explicitly, since those systems typically implement it with a nonphysical hack and thus the `VisibilityTester::Unoccluded()` method here returns a boolean. Scenes where illumination passes through a transparent object should be rendered with an integrator that supports this kind of effect, like the `PhotonIntegrator` described in Section 16.5.

⟨*Light Method Definitions*⟩≡
```
bool VisibilityTester::Unoccluded(const Scene *scene) const {
    return !scene->IntersectP(r);
}
```

`VisibilityTester::Transmittance()` determines the fraction of illumination from the light to the point that is not extinguished by participating media in the scene. If the scene has no participating media, this method returns a constant spectral value of one.

⟨*Light Method Definitions*⟩+≡
```
Spectrum VisibilityTester::Transmittance(const Scene *scene) const {
    return scene->Transmittance(r);
}
```

13.2 POINT LIGHTS

A number of interesting lights can be described in terms of emission from a single point in space with some possibly angularly varying distribution of outgoing light. This section describes the implementation of a number of them, starting with `PointLight`, which represents an isotropic point light source that emits the same amount of light in all directions. It is defined in `lights/point.cpp`.⊙ Figure 13.2 shows a scene rendered with a point light source. Building on this base, a number of more complex lights based on

Figure 13.2: Scene Rendered with a Point Light Source. Notice the hard shadow boundaries from this type of light.

point sources will be introduced, including spotlights and a light that projects an image into the scene.

⟨*PointLight Classes*⟩ ≡
```
    class PointLight : public Light {
    public:
        ⟨PointLight Public Methods  603⟩
    private:
        ⟨PointLight Private Data  603⟩
    };
```

PointLights are positioned at the origin in light space. To place them elsewhere, the light-to-world transformation should be modified as appropriate. Using this transformation, the world space position of the light is precomputed and cached in the constructor by transforming (0, 0, 0) from light space to world space. The constructor also stores the intensity for the light source, which is the amount of power per unit solid angle. Because the light source is isotropic, this is a constant.

Light 598
PointLight 602

⟨*PointLight Method Definitions*⟩ ≡

```
PointLight::PointLight(const Transform &light2world,
                              const Spectrum &intensity)
    : Light(light2world) {
    lightPos = LightToWorld(Point(0,0,0));
    Intensity = intensity;
}
```

⟨*PointLight Private Data*⟩ ≡   602

```
Point lightPos;
Spectrum Intensity;
```

Strictly speaking, it is incorrect to describe the light arriving at a point due to a point light source using units of radiance. Radiant intensity is instead the proper unit for describing emission from a point light source, as explained in Section 5.2. In the light source interfaces here, however, we will abuse terminology and use Sample_L() methods to report the illumination arriving at a point for all types of light sources, dividing radiant intensity by the squared distance to the point p to convert units. Section 15.6 revisits the details of this issue in its discussion of how delta distributions affect evaluation of the integral in the scattering equation. In the end, the correctness of the computation does not suffer from this fudge, and it makes the implementation of light transport algorithms more straightforward by not requiring them to use different interfaces for different types of light.

⟨*PointLight Method Definitions*⟩+≡

```
Spectrum PointLight::Sample_L(const Point &p, Vector *wi,
                                VisibilityTester *visibility) const {
    *wi = Normalize(lightPos - p);
    visibility->SetSegment(p, lightPos);
    return Intensity / DistanceSquared(lightPos, p);
}
```

The total power emitted by the light source can be found by integrating the intensity over the entire sphere of directions:

$$\Phi = \int_{\mathcal{S}^2} I \, d\omega = I \int_{\mathcal{S}^2} d\omega = 4\pi I.$$

⟨*PointLight Public Methods*⟩ ≡   602

```
Spectrum Power(const Scene *) const {
    return Intensity * 4.f * M_PI;
}
```

Finally, since point lights represent singularities that only cast incident light along a single direction, PointLight::IsDeltaLight() returns true.

Figure 13.3: Scene Rendered with a Spotlight. The spotlight cone smoothly cuts off illumination past a user-specified angle from the light's central axis.

⟨*PointLight Public Methods*⟩+≡   **602**
```
bool IsDeltaLight() const { return true; }
```

13.2.1 SPOTLIGHTS

Spotlights are a handy variation on point lights; rather than shining illumination in all directions, they emit light in a cone of directions from their position. For simplicity, we will define the spotlight in the light coordinate system to always be at position $(0, 0, 0)$ and pointing down the $+z$ axis. To place or orient it elsewhere in the scene, the Light::WorldToLight transformation should be set accordingly. Figure 13.3 shows a rendering of the same scene as Figure 13.2, only illuminated with a spotlight instead of a point light. The SpotLight class is defined in lights/spot.cpp.ⓒ

⟨*SpotLight Declarations*⟩≡
```
class SpotLight : public Light {
public:
    ⟨SpotLight Public Methods 607⟩
private:
    ⟨SpotLight Private Data 605⟩
};
```

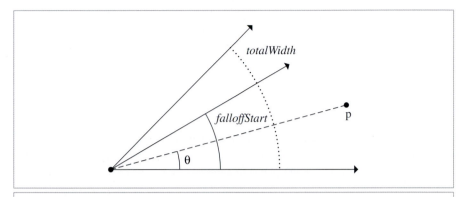

Figure 13.4: Spotlights are defined by two angles, *falloffStart* and *totalWidth*. Objects inside the inner cone of angles, up to *falloffStart*, are fully illuminated by the light. The directions between *falloffStart* and *totalWidth* are a transition zone that ramps down from full illumination to no illumination, such that points outside the *totalWidth* cone aren't illuminated at all. The cosine of the angle between the vector to a point p and the spotlight axis, θ, can easily be computed with a dot product.

Two angles are passed to the constructor to set the extent of the `SpotLight`'s cone: the overall angular width of the cone, and the angle at which falloff starts (Figure 13.4). The constructor precomputes and stores the cosines of these angles for use in the `SpotLight`'s methods.

⟨*SpotLight Method Definitions*⟩ ≡
```
SpotLight::SpotLight(const Transform &light2world,
                     const Spectrum &intensity, float width, float fall)
    : Light(light2world) {
    lightPos = LightToWorld(Point(0,0,0));
    Intensity = intensity;
    cosTotalWidth = cosf(Radians(width));
    cosFalloffStart = cosf(Radians(fall));
}
```

⟨*SpotLight Private Data*⟩ ≡   **604**
```
float cosTotalWidth, cosFalloffStart;
Point lightPos;
Spectrum Intensity;
```

The `SpotLight::Sample_L()` method is almost identical to `PointLight::Sample_L()`, except that it also calls the `Falloff()` method, which computes the distribution of light accounting for the spotlight cone. This computation is encapsulated in a separate method since other `SpotLight` methods will need to perform it as well.

⟨*SpotLight Method Definitions*⟩+≡
```
Spectrum SpotLight::Sample_L(const Point &p, Vector *wi,
                            VisibilityTester *visibility) const {
    *wi = Normalize(lightPos - p);
    visibility->SetSegment(p, lightPos);
    return Intensity * Falloff(-*wi) / DistanceSquared(lightPos, p);
}
```

To compute the spotlight's strength for a receiving point p, this first step is to compute the cosine of the angle between the vector from the spotlight origin to p and the vector along the center of the spotlight's cone. To compute the cosine of the offset angle to a point p, we have (Figure 13.4)

$$\cos \theta = \left(p \widehat{-} (0,0,0)\right) \cdot (0,0,1)$$
$$= p_z / \|p\|.$$

This value is then compared to the cosines of the falloff and overall width angles to see where the point lies with respect to the spotlight cone. We can trivially determine that points with a cosine greater than the cosine of the falloff angle are inside the cone receiving full illumination, and points with cosine less than the width angle's cosine are completely outside the cone. (Note that the computation is slightly tricky since for $\theta \in [0, 2\pi]$, if $\theta > \theta'$, then $\cos \theta < \cos \theta'$.)

⟨*SpotLight Method Definitions*⟩+≡
```
float SpotLight::Falloff(const Vector &w) const {
    Vector wl = Normalize(WorldToLight(w));
    float costheta = wl.z;
    if (costheta < cosTotalWidth)
        return 0.;
     if (costheta > cosFalloffStart)
        return 1.;
    ⟨Compute falloff inside spotlight cone 606⟩
}
```

For points inside the transition range from fully illuminated to outside of the cone, the intensity is scaled to smoothly fall off from full illumination to darkness:

⟨*Compute falloff inside spotlight cone*⟩≡   606
```
float delta = (costheta - cosTotalWidth) /
              (cosFalloffStart - cosTotalWidth);
return delta*delta*delta*delta;
```

The solid angle subtended by a cone with spread angle θ is $2\pi(1 - \cos \theta)$. Therefore, the integral over directions on the sphere that gives power from radiant intensity can be solved to compute the total power of a light that only emits illumination in a cone. For the spotlight, we can reasonably approximate the power of the light by computing the

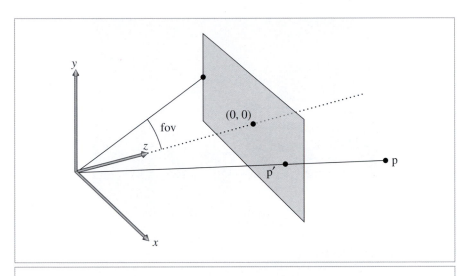

Figure 13.5: The Basic Setting for Projection Light Sources. A point p in the light's coordinate system is projected onto the plane of the image using the light's projection matrix.

solid angle of directions that is covered by the cone with a spread angle cosine halfway between width and fall.

⟨*SpotLight Public Methods*⟩ ≡   **604**

```
Spectrum Power(const Scene *) const {
    return Intensity * 2.f * M_PI *
            (1.f - .5f * (cosFalloffStart + cosTotalWidth));
}
```

13.2.2 TEXTURE PROJECTION LIGHTS

Another useful light source acts like a slide projector; it takes an image map and projects its image out into the scene. The ProjectionLight class uses a projective transformation to project points in the scene onto the light's projection plane based on the field of view angle given to the constructor (Figure 13.5). Its implementation is in lights/projection.cpp.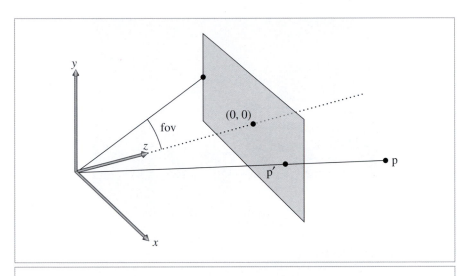 The use of this light in the lighting example scene is shown in Figure 13.6.

⟨*ProjectionLight Declarations*⟩ ≡

```
class ProjectionLight : public Light {
public:
    ⟨ProjectionLight Public Methods 611⟩
private:
    ⟨ProjectionLight Private Data 609⟩
};
```

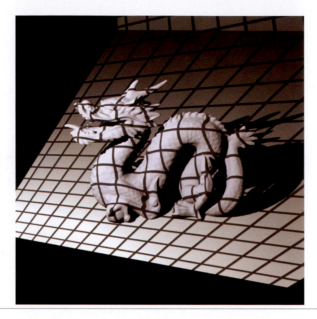

Figure 13.6: Scene Rendered with a Projection Light Using a Grid Texture Map. The projection light acts like a slide projector, projecting an image onto objects in the scene.

⟨*ProjectionLight Method Definitions*⟩ ≡
```
ProjectionLight::ProjectionLight(const Transform &light2world,
        const Spectrum &intensity, const string &texname,
        float fov)
    : Light(light2world) {
    lightPos = LightToWorld(Point(0,0,0));
    Intensity = intensity;
    ⟨Create ProjectionLight MIP-map 609⟩
    ⟨Initialize ProjectionLight projection matrix 609⟩
    ⟨Compute cosine of cone surrounding projection directions 610⟩
}
```

This light could use a Texture to represent the light projection distribution so that procedural projection patterns could be used. However, having a precise representation of the projection function, as is available by using an image in a MIPMap, is useful for being able to sample the projection distribution using Monte Carlo techniques, so we will use that representation in the implementation here.

⟨*Create* ProjectionLight *MIP-map*⟩ ≡   608
```
int width, height;
Spectrum *texels = ReadImage(texname, &width, &height);
if (texels)
    projectionMap = new MIPMap<Spectrum>(width, height, texels);
else
    projectionMap = NULL;
delete[] texels;
```

⟨*ProjectionLight Private Data*⟩ ≡   607
```
MIPMap<Spectrum> *projectionMap;
Point lightPos;
Spectrum Intensity;
```

Similar to the PerspectiveCamera, the ProjectionLight constructor computes a projection matrix and the screen space extent of the projection.

⟨*Initialize* ProjectionLight *projection matrix*⟩ ≡   608
```
float aspect = float(width) / float(height);
if (aspect > 1.f)  {
    screenX0 = -aspect; screenX1 =  aspect;
    screenY0 = -1.f; screenY1 =  1.f;
}
else {
    screenX0 = -1.f;              screenX1 =  1.f;
    screenY0 = -1.f / aspect;   screenY1 =  1.f / aspect;
}
hither = RAY_EPSILON;
yon = 1e30f;
lightProjection = Perspective(fov, hither, yon);
```

⟨*ProjectionLight Private Data*⟩+≡   607
```
Transform lightProjection;
float hither, yon;
float screenX0, screenX1, screenY0, screenY1;
```

Finally, the constructor finds the cosine of the angle between the $+z$ axis and the vector to a corner of the screen window. This value is used elsewhere to define the minimal cone of directions that encompasses the set of directions in which light is projected. This cone is useful for algorithms like photon mapping that need to randomly sample rays leaving the light source. We won't derive this computation here; it is based on straightforward trigonometry.

⟨*Compute cosine of cone surrounding projection directions*⟩ ≡ **608**
```
float opposite = tanf(Radians(fov) / 2.f);
float tanDiag = opposite * sqrtf(1.f + 1.f/(aspect*aspect));
cosTotalWidth = cosf(atanf(tanDiag));
```

⟨*ProjectionLight Private Data*⟩+≡ **607**
```
float cosTotalWidth;
```

Similar to the spotlight's version, ProjectionLight::Sample_L() calls a utility method, ProjectionLight::Projection(), to determine how much light is projected in the given direction. Therefore, we won't include the implementation of Sample_L() here.

⟨*ProjectionLight Method Definitions*⟩+≡
```
Spectrum ProjectionLight::Projection(const Vector &w) const {
    Vector wl = WorldToLight(w);
    ⟨Discard directions behind projection light  610⟩
    ⟨Project point onto projection plane and compute light  610⟩
}
```

Because the projective transformation has the property that it projects points behind the center of projection to points in front of it, it is important to discard points with a negative *z* value. Therefore, the projection code immediately returns no illumination for projection points that are behind the hither plane for the projection. If this check were not done, then it wouldn't be possible to know if a projected point was originally behind the light (and therefore not illuminated) or in front of it.

⟨*Discard directions behind projection light*⟩ ≡ **610**
```
if (wl.z < hither) return 0.;
```

After being projected to the projection plane, points with coordinate values outside the screen window are discarded. Points that pass this test are transformed to get (s, t) texture coordinates inside $[0, 1]^2$ for the lookup in the projection's image map.

⟨*Project point onto projection plane and compute light*⟩ ≡ **610**
```
Point Pl = lightProjection(Point(wl.x, wl.y, wl.z));
if (Pl.x < screenX0 || Pl.x > screenX1 ||
    Pl.y < screenY0 || Pl.y > screenY1) return 0.;
if (!projectionMap) return 1;
float s = (Pl.x - screenX0) / (screenX1 - screenX0);
float t = (Pl.y - screenY0) / (screenY1 - screenY0);
return projectionMap->Lookup(s, t);
```

The total power of this light is approximated as a spotlight that subtends the same angle as the diagonal of the projected image, scaled by the average intensity in the image map. This approximation becomes increasingly inaccurate as the projected image's aspect ratio becomes less square, for example, and it doesn't account for the fact that texels toward the edges of the image map subtend a larger angle than texels in the middle when projected with a perspective projection. Nevertheless, it's a reasonable first-order approximation.

⟨*ProjectionLight Public Methods*⟩ ≡   607

```
Spectrum Power(const Scene *) const {
    return Intensity * 2.f * M_PI * (1.f - cosTotalWidth) *
           projectionMap->Lookup(.5f, .5f, .5f);
}
```

13.2.3 GONIOPHOTOMETRIC DIAGRAM LIGHTS

A *goniophotometric diagram* describes the angular distribution of luminance from a point light source; they are widely used in illumination engineering to characterize lights. Figure 13.7 shows an example of a goniophotometric diagram in two dimensions. In this section, we'll implement a light source that uses goniophotometric diagrams encoded in 2D image maps to describe the emission distribution of the light. The implementation is very similar to the point light sources defined previously in this section; it scales the intensity based on the outgoing direction according to the goniophotometric diagram's values. Figure 13.8 shows a few goniophotometric diagrams encoded as image maps, and Figure 13.9 shows a scene rendered with a light source that uses one of these images to modulate its directional distribution of illumination.

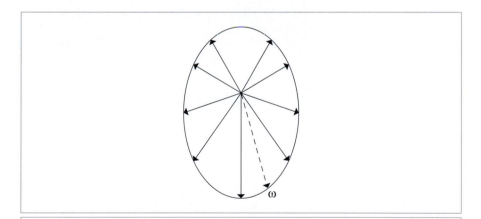

Figure 13.7: An Example of a Goniophotometric Diagram Specifying an Outgoing Light Distribution from a Point Light Source in 2D. The emitted intensity is defined in a fixed set of directions on the unit sphere, and the intensity for a given outgoing direction ω is found by interpolating the intensities of the adjacent samples.

(a)   (b)   (c)

Figure 13.8: Goniophotometric Diagrams for Real-World Light Sources, Encoded as Image Maps with a Parameterization Based on Spherical Coordinates. (a) A light that mostly illuminates in its up direction, with only a small amount of illumination in the down direction. (b) A light that mostly illuminates in the down direction. (c) A light that casts illumination both above and below.

Figure 13.9: Scene Rendered Using a Goniophotometric Diagram from Figure 13.8. Even though a point light source is the basis of this light, including the directional variation of a realistic light improves the visual realism of the rendered image.

⟨*GonioPhotometricLight Declarations*⟩ ≡
```
class GonioPhotometricLight : public Light {
public:
    ⟨GonioPhotometricLight Public Methods 614⟩
private:
    ⟨GonioPhotometricLight Private Data 613⟩

};
```

The `GonioPhotometricLight` constructor takes a base intensity and an image map that scales the intensity based on the angular distribution of light.

⟨*GonioPhotometricLight Method Definitions*⟩ ≡
```
GonioPhotometricLight::GonioPhotometricLight(const Transform &light2world,
        const Spectrum &intensity, const string &texname)
    : Light(light2world) {
    lightPos = LightToWorld(Point(0,0,0));
    Intensity = intensity;
    ⟨Create mipmap for GonioPhotometricLight 613⟩
}
```

Like `ProjectionLight`, `GonioPhotometricLight` constructs a `MIPMap` of the distribution's image map.

⟨*Create* mipmap *for* GonioPhotometricLight⟩ ≡   613
```
int width, height;
Spectrum *texels = ReadImage(texname, &width, &height);
if (texels) {
    mipmap = new MIPMap<Spectrum>(width, height, texels);
    delete[] texels;
}
else mipmap = NULL;
```

⟨*GonioPhotometricLight Private Data*⟩ ≡   613
```
Point lightPos;
Spectrum Intensity;
MIPMap<Spectrum> *mipmap;
```

The `GonioPhotometricLight::Sample_L()` method is not shown here. It is essentially identical to the `SpotLight::Sample_L()` and `ProjectionLight::Sample_L()` methods that use a helper function to scale the amount of irradiance. It assumes that the scale texture is encoded using spherical coordinates, so that the given direction needs to be converted to θ and ϕ values and scaled to $[0, 1]$ before being used to index into the texture. Goniophotometric diagrams are usually defined in a coordinate space where the y axis is up, whereas the spherical coordinate utility routines assume that z is up, so y and z are swapped before doing the conversion.

⟨*GonioPhotometricLight Public Methods*⟩ ≡   **613**
```
    Spectrum Scale(const Vector &w) const {
        Vector wp = Normalize(WorldToLight(w));
        swap(wp.y, wp.z);
        float theta = SphericalTheta(wp);
        float phi   = SphericalPhi(wp);
        float s = phi * INV_TWOPI, t = theta * INV_PI;
        return mipmap ? mipmap->Lookup(s, t) : 1.f;
    }
```

The Power() method's computation is inaccurate because the spherical coordinate parameterization of directions has various distortions, particularly near the $+z$ and $-z$ directions. Again, this error is acceptable for the uses of this method in pbrt.

⟨*GonioPhotometricLight Public Methods*⟩+≡   **613**
```
    Spectrum Power(const Scene *) const {
        return 4.f * M_PI * Intensity * mipmap->Lookup(.5f, .5f, .5f);
    }
```

13.3 DISTANT LIGHTS

Another useful light source type is the *distant light*, also known as a *directional light*. It describes an emitter that deposits illumination from the same direction at every point in space. Such a light is also called a point light "at infinity," since as a point light becomes progressively farther away, it acts more and more like a directional light. For example, the sun (as considered from Earth) can be thought of as a directional light source. Although it is actually an area light source, the illumination effectively arrives at Earth in parallel beams because it is so far away.

⟨*DistantLight Declarations*⟩ ≡
```
    class DistantLight : public Light {
    public:
        ⟨DistantLight Public Methods  616⟩
    private:
        ⟨DistantLight Private Data  615⟩
    };
```

⟨*DistantLight Method Definitions*⟩ ≡
```
    DistantLight::DistantLight(const Transform &light2world,
            const Spectrum &radiance, const Vector &dir)
        : Light(light2world) {
        lightDir = Normalize(LightToWorld(dir));
        L = radiance;
    }
```

(a)

(b)

Figure 13.12: Dragon Model Illuminated by Disk Area Lights. (a) The disk's radius is relatively small; the shadow has soft penumbrae, but otherwise the image looks similar to the one with a point light. (b) The effect of using a much larger disk: not only have the penumbrae become much larger, to the point of nearly eliminating the fully in-shadow areas, but notice how areas like the neck of the dragon and its jaw have noticeably different appearances when illuminated from a wider range of directions.

The AreaLight class implements a basic area light source with a uniform emitted radiance distribution at all points on the shape it is bound to. It emits light with a uniform distribution on the side of the surface with outward-facing surface normal; there is no emission from the other side. (The Shape::reverseOrientation value can be set to true to cause the light to be emitted from the other side of the surface instead.) AreaLight is defined in lights/area.cpp.

⟨*Light Declarations*⟩+≡
```
class AreaLight : public Light {
public:
    ⟨AreaLight Interface 619⟩
protected:
    ⟨AreaLight Protected Data 618⟩
};
```

The constructor caches the surface area of the light source since these area calculations may be computationally expensive:

⟨*AreaLight Method Definitions*⟩≡
```
AreaLight::AreaLight(const Transform &light2world,
                     const Spectrum &le, int ns,
                     const Reference<Shape> &s)
    : Light(light2world, ns) {
    Lemit = le;
    if (s->CanIntersect())
        shape = s;
    else {
        ⟨Create ShapeSet for Shape⟩
    }
    area = shape->Area();
}
```

⟨*AreaLight Protected Data*⟩≡   **618**
```
Spectrum Lemit;
Reference<Shape> shape;
float area;
```

Some shapes can't be used as area lights directly since they don't implement all of the Shape methods that the AreaLight needs to call. One example is subdivision surfaces, which can't compute their surface area. (In general, there aren't closed-form expressions for the surface area of subdivision surfaces.) Later, in the Monte Carlo sampling code in Chapter 15, the AreaLight will need to call Shape methods that sample points on the shape's surface; these methods are also not implemented for some types of shapes.

Shapes like these must be refined into simpler shapes until their `CanIntersect()` methods return true.[1] This refinement is done in the constructor if needed, and if more than one `Shape` is created as a result, a container class called `ShapeSet` is used to store them. This class implements the `Shape` interface, so that the `AreaLight` can be written to only store a single `Shape`, thus simplifying its implementation.

The `ShapeSet` class is just a trivial wrapper for a vector of shapes. Most of its implementation is in Section 15.6, where its methods related to random sampling for Monte Carlo are implemented.

⟨*Shape Declarations*⟩+≡
```
class ShapeSet : public Shape {
public:
    ⟨ShapeSet Public Methods  709⟩
private:
    ⟨ShapeSet Private Data  619⟩
};
```

⟨*ShapeSet Private Data*⟩≡   **619**
```
vector<Reference<Shape> > shapes;
```

The `AreaLight::Sample_L()` method isn't as straightforward as it has been for the light sources described so far. Specifically, at each point in the scene, radiance from area lights can be incident from many directions, not just a single direction as was the case for the other lights (Figure 13.13). This leads to the question, which direction should be chosen for this method? We will defer answering this question and providing an implementation of this method until Section 15.6, after Monte Carlo integration has been introduced.

`AreaLight` adds a new method that is unique to area lights, `AreaLight::L()`. It evaluates the area light's emitted radiance, L, at a point on the surface of the light and in a given outgoing direction, assuming that the given point is on the surface of the light. Because area lights emit light from only one side of the surface, this method just makes sure that the outgoing direction lies in the same hemisphere as the normal.

⟨*AreaLight Interface*⟩≡   **618**
```
virtual Spectrum L(const Point &p, const Normal &n,
                   const Vector &w) const {
    return Dot(n, w) > 0 ? Lemit : 0.;
}
```

---

1   We are thus overloading the semantics of the `Shape::CanIntersect()` method to include both the ability to compute intersections, the ability to compute surface area, and the ability to generate samples.

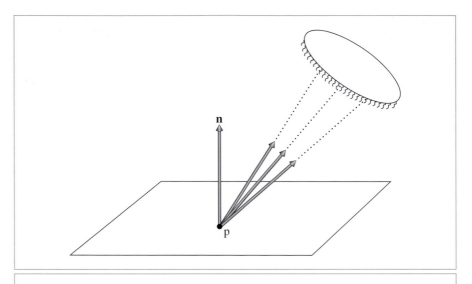

Figure 13.13: An area light casts incident illumination along many directions, rather than from a single direction.

For convenience, there is a method in the Intersection class that makes it easy to compute the emitted radiance at a surface point intersected by a ray. It gets the AreaLight pointer from the primitive and calls its L() method.

⟨*Intersection Method Definitions*⟩+≡
```
Spectrum Intersection::Le(const Vector &w) const {
    const AreaLight *area = primitive->GetAreaLight();
    return area ? area->L(dg.p, dg.nn, w) : Spectrum(0.);
}
```

Emitted power from an area light with uniform emitted radiance over the surface can be directly computed in closed form:

⟨*AreaLight Interface*⟩+≡   **618**
```
Spectrum Power(const Scene *) const {
    return Lemit * area * M_PI;
}
```

Finally, area lights clearly do not represent singularities, so they return false from IsDeltaLight():

⟨*AreaLight Interface*⟩+≡   **618**
```
bool IsDeltaLight() const { return false; }
```

13.5 INFINITE AREA LIGHTS

Another useful kind of light is the infinite area light—an infinitely faraway area light source that surrounds the entire scene. One way to visualize this light is as an enormous sphere that casts light into the scene from every direction. One important use of infinite area lights is for *environment lighting*, where an image that represents illumination in an environment is used to illuminate synthetic objects as if they were in that environment. Figures 13.14 and 13.15 compare illuminating a car model with a standard area light to illuminating it with environment maps that simulate illumination from the sky at a few different times of day (the illumination maps used are shown in Figure 13.16). The increase in realism is striking. The `InfiniteAreaLight` class is implemented in `lights/infinite.cpp`.⑩

A widely used representation for light for this application is the latitude-longitude radiance map. The `EnvironmentCamera` can be used to create image maps for the light, or see the "Further Reading" section for information about techniques for capturing this lighting data from real-world environments. Like the other lights, the `InfiniteAreaLight` takes a transformation matrix; here its use is to orient the image map. It then uses spherical coordinates to map from directions on the sphere to (θ, ϕ) directions, and from there to (u, v) texture coordinates. The provided transformation thus determines which direction is "up."

⟨*InfiniteAreaLight Declarations*⟩ ≡
```
class InfiniteAreaLight : public Light {
public:
    ⟨InfiniteAreaLight Public Methods 625⟩
private:
    ⟨InfiniteAreaLight Private Data 624⟩
};
```

⟨*InfiniteAreaLight Method Definitions*⟩ ≡
```
InfiniteAreaLight::InfiniteAreaLight(const Transform &light2world,
                                     const Spectrum &L, int ns,
                                     const string &texmap)
        : Light(light2world, ns) {
    radianceMap = NULL;
    if (texmap != "") {
        int width, height;
        Spectrum *texels = ReadImage(texmap, &width, &height);
        if (texels)
            radianceMap = new MIPMap<Spectrum>(width, height, texels);
        delete[] texels;
    }
    Lbase = L;
}
```

(a)

(b)

Figure 13.14: Car model (a) illuminated with an area light and a directional light and (b) illuminated with morning skylight from an environment map. Using a realistic distribution of illumination gives an image that is much more visually compelling. In particular, with illumination arriving from all directions, the glossy reflective properties of the paint are much more visually apparent; in (a) there isn't anything to reflect, so the paint inaccurately appears to be dull matte.

(a)

(b)

Figure 13.15: Changing just the environment map used for illumination gives quite different results in the final image: (a) using a midday skylight distribution and (b) using a sunset environment map.

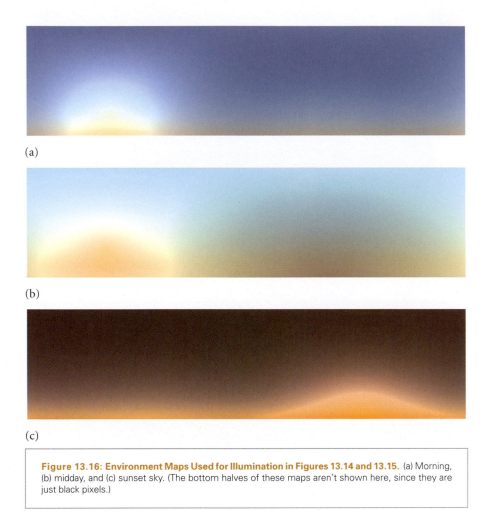

(a)

(b)

(c)

Figure 13.16: Environment Maps Used for Illumination in Figures 13.14 and 13.15. (a) Morning, (b) midday, and (c) sunset sky. (The bottom halves of these maps aren't shown here, since they are just black pixels.)

⟨*InfiniteAreaLight Private Data*⟩ ≡   **621**
```
Spectrum Lbase;
MIPMap<Spectrum> *radianceMap;
```

Because InfiniteAreaLights cast light from all directions, it's also necessary to use Monte Carlo integration to compute reflected light due to illumination from them. Therefore, the InfiniteAreaLight::Sample_L() method will be defined in Section 15.6.

Like directional lights, the total power from the infinite area light is related to the surface area of the scene:

⟨*InfiniteAreaLight Public Methods*⟩ ≡   **621**
```
Spectrum Power(const Scene *scene) const {
    Point worldCenter;
    float worldRadius;
    scene->WorldBound().BoundingSphere(&worldCenter, &worldRadius);
    return Lbase * radianceMap->Lookup(.5f, .5f, .5f) *
            M_PI * worldRadius * worldRadius;
}
```

⟨*InfiniteAreaLight Public Methods*⟩+≡   **621**
```
bool IsDeltaLight() const { return false; }
```

Because infinite area lights need to be able to contribute radiance to rays that don't hit any geometry in the scene, we'll add a method to the base `Light` class that returns emitted radiance due to that light along a ray that didn't hit anything in the scene. (The default implementation for other lights returns no radiance.) It is the responsibility of the integrators to call this method for those rays.

⟨*Light Method Definitions*⟩+≡
```
Spectrum Light::Le(const RayDifferential &) const {
    return Spectrum(0.);
}
```

The `InfiniteAreaLight`'s implementation of this method implements the computation to get radiance for a particular direction in a separate fragment so that it can be reused elsewhere.

⟨*InfiniteAreaLight Method Definitions*⟩+≡
```
Spectrum InfiniteAreaLight::Le(const RayDifferential &r) const {
    Vector w = r.d;
    ⟨Compute infinite light radiance for direction 625⟩
    return L;
}
```

⟨*Compute infinite light radiance for direction*⟩ ≡   **625**
```
Spectrum L = Lbase;
if (radianceMap != NULL) {
    Vector wh = Normalize(WorldToLight(w));
    float s = SphericalPhi(wh) * INV_TWOPI;
    float t = SphericalTheta(wh) * INV_PI;
    L *= radianceMap->Lookup(s, t);
}
```

FURTHER READING

Warn (1983) developed early models of light sources with nonisotropic emission distributions, including the spotlight model used in this chapter. Verbeck and Greenberg (1984) also described a number of techniques for modeling light sources that are now classic parts of the light modeling toolbox. More recently, Barzel (1997) has described a highly parameterized model for light sources, including many controls for controlling rate of falloff, the area of space that is illuminated, and so on. Bjorke (2001) describes a number of additional controls for controlling illumination for artistic effect. (The Barzel and Bjorke approaches are not physically based, which isn't a problem in most applications outside of physically based rendering.)

Blinn and Newell (1976) first introduced the idea of environment maps and their use for simulating illumination, although they only considered illumination of specular objects. Greene (1986) further refined these ideas, considering antialiasing and different representations for environment maps. Nishita and Nakamae (1986) developed algorithms for efficiently rendering objects illuminated by hemispherical skylights and generated some of the first images that showed off that distinctive lighting effect.

Miller and Hoffman (1984) were the first to consider using arbitrary environment maps to illuminate objects with diffuse and glossy BRDFs. Debevec (1998) later extended this work and investigated issues related to capturing images of real environments. The *HDRShop* tool, available from *www.debevec.org/HDRShop*, is invaluable for converting among different environment map formats and parameterizations. Chapter 15 has further references related to Monte Carlo sampling of environment lights.

Algorithms to render soft shadows from area lights were first developed by Amanatides (1984) and Cook, Porter, and Carpenter (1984). See Agrawala et al. (2000) for more recent algorithms for rendering soft shadows and an overview of other related work.

The goniometric light source approximation is widely used to model area light sources in the field of illumination engineering. The rule of thumb there is that once a point is five times an area light source's radius away from it, a point light approximation has sufficient accuracy for most applications. Ashdown (1993) discusses this application in depth and proposes a more sophisticated light source representation for accurate illumination computations. A variety of file format standards have been developed for encoding goniophotometric diagrams for these applications (Illuminating Engineering Society of North America Computer Committee 1986; Stockmar 1986). Many lighting fixture manufacturers provide data in these formats on their Web sites.

Primitive::IntersectP() 172
Shape::IntersectP() 93

As discussed previously, one way to reduce the time spent tracing shadow rays is to have methods like `Shape::IntersectP()` and `Primitive::IntersectP()` that just check for any occlusion along a ray without bothering to compute the geometric information at the intersection point. Other approaches for optimizing ray tracing for shadow rays include the shadow cache, where each light stores a pointer to the last primitive that occluded a shadow ray to the light where that primitive is checked first to see if it occludes subsequent shadow rays before the ray is passed to the acceleration structure (Haines and Greenberg 1986). Pearce (1991) points out that the shadow cache doesn't work well if the scene has finely tessellated geometry; it may be better to cache the voxel that held the last occluder, for instance. (The shadow cache can similarly be defeated when multiple levels of reflection and refraction are present or when Monte Carlo ray-tracing techniques are used.) Hart, Dutré, and Greenberg (1999) have developed a generalization of the shadow cache, which tracks which objects block light from particular light sources and clips their geometry against the light source geometry so that shadow rays don't need to be traced toward the parts of the light that are certain to be occluded.

A related technique, described by Haines and Greenberg (1986), is the light buffer for point light sources, where the light discretizes the directions around it and determines which objects are visible along each set of directions (and are thus potential occluding objects for shadow rays). Another effective optimization is *shaft culling*, which takes advantage of coherence among groups of rays traced in a similar set of directions (e.g., shadow rays from a single point to points on an area light source). With shaft culling, a shaft that bounds a collection of rays is computed and then the objects in the scene that penetrate the shaft are found. For all of the rays in the shaft, it is only necessary to check for intersections with those objects that intersect the shaft, and the expense of ray intersection acceleration structure traversal for each of the rays is avoided (Haines and Wallace 1994).

Woo and Amanatides (1990) classify which lights are visible, not visible, and partially visible in different parts of the scene and store this information in a voxel-based 3D data structure and then use this information to save shadow ray tests. Fernandez, Bala, and Greenberg (2002) developed a similar approach based on spatial decomposition that stores references to important blockers in each voxel, and also builds up this information on demand for applications like walkthroughs.

For complex models, simplified versions of their geometry can be used for shadow ray intersections. For example, the simplification envelopes described by Cohen et al. (1996) can create a simplified mesh that bounds a given mesh from both the inside and the outside. If a ray misses the mesh that bounds a complex model from the outside, or intersects the mesh that bounds it from the inside, then no further shadow processing is necessary. Only the uncertain remaining cases need to be intersected against the full geometry. A related technique is described by Lukaszewski (2001), who uses the Minkowski sum to effectively expand primitives (or bounds of primitives) in the scene so that intersecting one ray against one of these primitives can determine if any of a collection of rays might have intersected the actual primitives.

EXERCISES

❷ 13.1 Shadow mapping is a technique for rendering shadows from point and distant light sources based on rendering an image from the light source's perspective that records depth in each pixel of the image and then projecting points onto the shadow map and comparing their depth to the depth of the first visible object as seen from the light in that direction. This method was first described by Williams (1978), and Reeves, Salesin, and Cook (1987) developed a number of key improvements. Modify pbrt to be able to render depth map images into a file and then use them for shadow testing for lights in place of tracing shadow rays. How much faster can this be? Discuss the advantages and disadvantages of the two approaches.

❶ 13.2 Through algebraic manipulation and precomputation of one more value in the constructor, the SpotLight::Falloff() method can be rewritten to compute the exact same result (modulo floating-point differences) while using no square root computations and no divides (recall that the Vector::Normalize() method performs both a square root and a divide). Derive and implement this optimization. How much is running time improved on a spotlight-heavy scene?

❷ 13.3 Modify the ProjectionLight to also support orthographic projections. This variant is particularly useful even without an image map, since it gives a directional light source with a beam of user-defined extent.

❷ 13.4 Write an improved AreaLight that supports spatially and directionally varying emitted radiance, specified either via image maps or Textures. Use it to render images with effects like a television illuminating a dark room or a stained-glass window lit from behind.

❷ 13.5 Read some of the papers in the "Further Reading" section that discuss the shadow cache and add this optimization to pbrt. Measure how much it speeds up the system for a variety of scenes. What techniques can you come up with that make it work better in the presence of multiple levels of reflection?

❸ 13.6 Modify pbrt to support the shaft culling algorithm (Haines and Wallace 1994). Measure the performance difference for scenes with area light sources. Make sure that your implementation still performs well even with very large light sources (like a hemispherical skylight).

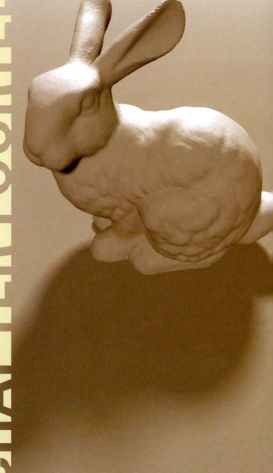

CHAPTER FOURTEEN

14 MONTE CARLO INTEGRATION I: BASIC CONCEPTS

Before we introduce the SurfaceIntegrators and VolumeIntegrators that compute radiance along rays arriving at the camera, we will first lay some groundwork regarding the techniques they will use to compute solutions to the integral equations that describe light scattering. These integral equations generally do not have analytic solutions, so we must turn to numerical methods. Although standard numerical integration techniques like trapezoidal integration or Gaussian quadrature are very effective at solving low-dimensional smooth integrals, their rate of convergence for the higher-dimensional and discontinuous integrals that are common in rendering is poor.

Monte Carlo numerical integration methods provide one solution to this problem. They use randomness to evaluate integrals with a convergence rate that is independent of the dimensionality of the integrand. In this chapter, we review important concepts from probability and lay the foundation for using Monte Carlo techniques to evaluate the key integrals in rendering. The following chapter will then describe techniques for improving the convergence rate of these approaches and will describe the specific algorithms used in pbrt.

Judicious use of randomness has revolutionized the field of algorithm design. Randomized algorithms fall broadly into two classes: *Las Vegas* and *Monte Carlo*. Las Vegas algorithms are those that use randomness but always give the same result in the end (e.g., choosing a random array entry as the pivot element in Quicksort). Monte Carlo algorithms, on the other hand, give different results depending on the particular random numbers used along the way, but give the right answer *on average*. So, by averaging the results of several runs of a Monte Carlo algorithm (on the same input), it is possible to find a result that is statistically very likely to be close to the true answer. Motwani and Raghavan (1995) have written an excellent introduction to the field of randomized algorithms.

Monte Carlo integration[1] is a method for using random sampling to estimate the values of integrals. One very useful property of Monte Carlo is that one needs only to be able to evaluate the integrand at arbitrary points in the domain in order to estimate the value of its integral $\int f(x)\, dx$. This property not only makes Monte Carlo easy to implement, but it also makes the technique applicable to a broad variety of integrands, including those containing discontinuities.

Many of the integrals that arise in rendering are difficult or impossible to evaluate directly. For example, to compute the amount of light reflected by a surface at a point, Equation (5.6), we must integrate the product of the incident radiance and the BSDF over the unit sphere. Because object visibility and thus the incident radiance function at a point in a complex scene varies in difficult-to-predict ways, a closed-form expression for all of the terms in this product is almost never available, and even if it were, performing the integral analytically is generally not possible. Monte Carlo integration makes it possible to estimate the reflected radiance simply by choosing a set of directions over the sphere, computing the incident radiance along them, multiplying by the BSDF's value for those directions, and applying a weighting term. Arbitrary BSDFs, light source descriptions, and scene geometry are easily handled; evaluation of each of these functions at arbitrary points is all that is required.

The main disadvantage of Monte Carlo is that if n samples are used to estimate the integral, the algorithm converges to the correct result at a rate of $O(n^{-1/2})$. In other words, to cut the error in half, it is necessary to evaluate four times as many samples. In rendering, each sample generally requires that one or more rays be traced in the process of computing the value of the integrand, a painful cost to bear when using Monte Carlo for image synthesis. In images, artifacts from Monte Carlo sampling manifest themselves as noise—pixels are randomly too bright or too dark. Most of the current research in Monte Carlo for computer graphics is about reducing this error as much as possible while minimizing the number of additional samples that must be taken.

---

1   For brevity, we will refer to Monte Carlo integration simply as "Monte Carlo."

14.1 BACKGROUND AND PROBABILITY REVIEW

We will start by defining some basic terms and reviewing basic ideas from probability. We assume that the reader is already familiar with basic probability concepts; readers needing a more complete introduction to this topic should consult a textbook such as Sheldon Ross's *Introduction to Probability Models* (2002).

A *random variable* X is a value chosen by some random process. We will generally use capital letters to denote random variables, with exceptions made for a few Greek symbols that represent special random variables. Random variables are always drawn from some domain, which can be either discrete (e.g., a fixed set of possibilities) or continuous (e.g., the real numbers $\mathbb{R}$). Applying a function f to a random variable X results in a new random variable $Y = f(X)$.

For example, the result of a roll of a die is a discrete random variable sampled from the set of events $X_i = \{1, 2, 3, 4, 5, 6\}$. Each event has a probability $p_i = \frac{1}{6}$, and the sum of probabilities $\sum p_i$ is necessarily one. We can take a continuous, uniformly distributed random variable $\xi \in [0, 1]$ and map it to a discrete random variable, choosing X_i if

$$\sum_{j=1}^{i-1} p_j < \xi \le \sum_{j=1}^{i} p_j.$$

For lighting applications, we might want to define the probability of sampling illumination from each light in the scene based on the power Φ_i from each source relative to the total power from all sources:

$$p_i = \frac{\Phi_i}{\sum_j \Phi_j}.$$

Notice that these p_i also sum to one.

The *cumulative distribution function* (CDF) $P(x)$ of a random variable is the probability that a value from the variable's distribution is less than or equal to some value x:

$$P(x) = Pr\{X \le x\}.$$

For the die example, $P(2) = \frac{1}{3}$, since two of the six possibilities are less than or equal to 2.

14.1.1 CONTINUOUS RANDOM VARIABLES

In rendering, discrete random variables are less common than continuous random variables, which take on values over ranges of continuous domains (e.g., the real numbers or directions on the unit sphere).

A particularly important random variable is the *canonical uniform random variable*, which we will write as ξ. This variable takes on all values in its domain $[0, 1)$ with equal probability. This particular variable is important for two reasons. First, it is easy to generate a variable with this distribution in software—most run time libraries have a pseudorandom number generator that does just that.[2] Second, as we will show later, it is possible to generate samples from arbitrary distributions by first starting with canonical uniform random variables and applying an appropriate transformation. The technique described previously for mapping from ξ to the six faces of a die gives a flavor of this technique in the discrete case.

Another example of a continuous random variable is one that ranges over the real numbers between 0 and 2, where the probability of it taking on any particular value x is proportional to the value $2 - x$: it is twice as likely for this random variable to take on a value around zero as it is to take one around one, and so forth. The *probability density function* (PDF) formalizes this idea: it describes the relative probability of a random variable taking on a particular value. The PDF $p(x)$ is the derivative of the random variable's CDF,

$$p(x) = \frac{\mathrm{d}P(x)}{\mathrm{d}x}.$$

For uniform random variables, $p(x)$ is a constant; this is a direct consequence of uniformity. For ξ we have

$$p(x) = \begin{cases} 1 & x \in [0, 1] \\ 0 & \text{otherwise.} \end{cases}$$

PDFs are necessarily nonnegative and always integrate to one over their domains. Given an arbitrary interval $[a, b]$ in the domain, the PDF can give the probability that a random variable lies inside the interval:

$$P(x \in [a, b]) = \int_a^b p(x) \, \mathrm{d}x.$$

This follows directly from the first fundamental theorem of calculus and the definition of the PDF.

14.1.2 EXPECTED VALUES AND VARIANCE

The *expected value* $E_p[f(x)]$ of a function f is defined as the average value of the function over some distribution of values $p(x)$ over its domain. In the next section, we will see how Monte Carlo integration computes the expected values of arbitrary integrals. Expected value over a domain, D, is defined as

$$E_p[f(x)] = \int_D f(x)p(x) \, \mathrm{d}x. \tag{14.1}$$

---

2   Although the theory of Monte Carlo is based on using truly random numbers, in practice a well-written pseudorandom number generator (PRNG) is sufficient. pbrt uses a particularly high-quality PRNG that returns a sequence of pseudorandom values that is effectively as "random" as true random numbers. (Many PRNGs are not as well implemented and have detectable patterns in the sequence of numbers they generate.) True random numbers, found by measuring random phenomena like atomic decay, are available on CD-ROM for those for whom PRNGs are not acceptable.

As an example, consider the problem of finding the expected value of the cosine function between 0 and π, where p is uniform.[3] Because the PDF $p(x)$ must integrate to one over the domain, $p(x) = 1/\pi$, so

$$E[\cos x] = \int_0^\pi \frac{\cos x}{\pi}\,dx = \frac{1}{\pi}(-\sin \pi + \sin 0) = 0,$$

which is precisely the expected result. (Consider the graph of $\cos x$ over $[0, \pi]$ to see why this is so.)

The *variance* of a function is the expected deviation of the function from its expected value. Variance is a fundamental concept for quantifying the error in a value estimated by a Monte Carlo algorithm. It provides a precise way to quantify this error and measure how improvements to Monte Carlo algorithms reduce the error in the final result. Most of Chapter 15 is devoted to techniques for reducing variance and thus improving the results computed by pbrt. The variance of a function f is defined as

$$V[f(x)] = E\left[\left(f(x) - E[f(x)]\right)^2\right].$$

The expected value and variance have three important properties that follow immediately from their respective definitions:

$$E[af(x)] = aE[f(x)]$$

$$E\left[\sum_i f(X_i)\right] = \sum_i E[f(X_i)]$$

$$V[af(x)] = a^2 V[f(x)].$$

These properties, and some simple algebraic manipulation, yield a much simpler expression for the variance:

$$V[f(x)] = E\left[(f(x))^2\right] - E[f(x)]^2. \tag{14.2}$$

Thus, the variance is simply the expected value of the square minus the square of the expected value. Given random variables that are *independent*, variance also has the property that the sum of the variances is equal to the variance of their sum:

$$\sum_i V[f(X_i)] = V\left[\sum_i f(X_i)\right].$$

---

3   When computing expected values with a uniform distribution, we will drop the subscript p from E_p.

14.2 THE MONTE CARLO ESTIMATOR

We can now define the basic Monte Carlo estimator, which approximates the value of an arbitrary integral. It is the foundation of the light transport algorithms defined in Chapters 16 and 17.

Suppose that we want to evaluate a one-dimensional integral $\int_a^b f(x)\mathrm{d}x$. Given a supply of uniform random variables $X_i \in [a, b]$, the Monte Carlo estimator says that the expected value of the estimator

$$F_N = \frac{b-a}{N} \sum_{i=1}^N f(X_i),$$

$E[F_N]$, is in fact equal to the integral.[4] This can be demonstrated with just a few steps. First, note that the PDF $p(x)$ corresponding to the random variable X_i must be equal to $1/(b-a)$, since p must both be a constant and also integrate to one over the domain $[a, b]$. Algebraic manipulation then shows that

$$
\begin{aligned}
E[F_N] &= E\left[\frac{b-a}{N} \sum_{i=1}^N f(X_i)\right] \\
&= \frac{b-a}{N} \sum_{i=1}^N E\left[f(X_i)\right] \\
&= \frac{b-a}{N} \sum_{i=1}^N \int_a^b f(x)p(x)\,\mathrm{d}x \\
&= \frac{1}{N} \sum_{i=1}^N \int_a^b f(x)\,\mathrm{d}x \\
&= \int_a^b f(x)\,\mathrm{d}x.
\end{aligned}
$$

The restriction to uniform random variables can be relaxed with a small generalization. This is an extremely important step, since carefully choosing the PDF from which samples are drawn is an important technique for reducing variance in Monte Carlo (Section 15.4). If the random variables X_i are drawn from some arbitrary PDF $p(x)$, then the estimator

$$F_N = \frac{1}{N} \sum_{i=1}^N \frac{f(X_i)}{p(X_i)} \tag{14.3}$$

---

4   For example, the samples X_i might be computed in an implementation by Lerp(RandomFloat(), a, b).

can be used to estimate the integral instead. The only limitation on $p(x)$ is that it must be nonzero for all x where $|F(x) > 0|$. It is similarly easy to see that the expected value of this estimator is the desired integral of f:

$$E[F_N] = E\left[\frac{1}{N} \sum_{i=1}^{N} \frac{f(X_i)}{p(X_i)}\right]$$

$$= \frac{1}{N} \sum_{i=1}^{N} \int_a^b \frac{f(x)}{p(x)} p(x) \, \mathrm{d}x$$

$$= \frac{1}{N} \sum_{i=1}^{N} \int_a^b f(x) \, \mathrm{d}x$$

$$= \int_a^b f(x) \, \mathrm{d}x.$$

Extending this estimator to multiple dimensions or complex integration domains is straightforward. N samples X_i are taken from a multidimensional (or "joint") PDF, and the estimator is applied as usual. For example, consider the three-dimensional integral

$$\int_{x_0}^{x_1} \int_{y_0}^{y_1} \int_{z_0}^{z_1} f(x, y, z) \, \mathrm{d}x \, \mathrm{d}y \, \mathrm{d}z.$$

If samples $X_i = (x_i, y_i, z_i)$ are chosen uniformly from the box from (x_0, y_0, z_0) to (x_1, y_1, z_1), the PDF $p(X)$ is the constant value

$$\frac{1}{(x_1 - x_0)} \frac{1}{(y_1 - y_0)} \frac{1}{(z_1 - z_0)},$$

and the estimator is

$$\frac{(x_1 - x_0)(y_1 - y_0)(z_1 - z_0)}{N} \sum_i f(X_i).$$

Note that the number of samples N can be chosen arbitrarily, regardless of the dimension of the integrand. This is another important advantage of Monte Carlo over traditional deterministic quadrature techniques. The number of samples taken in Monte Carlo is completely independent of the dimensionality of the integral, while with standard numerical quadrature techniques the number of samples required is exponential in the dimension.

Showing that the Monte Carlo estimator converges to the right answer is not enough to justify its use; a good rate of convergence is important too. Although we will not derive its rate of convergence here, it has been shown that error in the Monte Carlo estimator decreases at a rate of $O(\sqrt{N})$ in the number of samples taken. An accessible treatment of this topic can be found in Veach's thesis (Veach 1997, p. 39). Although standard quadrature techniques converge faster than $O(\sqrt{N})$ in one dimension, their performance becomes exponentially worse as the dimensionality of the integrand increases, while Monte

Carlo's convergence rate is independent of the dimension, making Monte Carlo the only practical numerical integration algorithm for high-dimensional integrals. We have already encountered some high-dimensional integrals in this book, and in Chapter 16 we will see that the path tracing formulation of the light transport equation is an *infinite-dimensional* integral!

14.3 SAMPLING RANDOM VARIABLES

In order to evaluate the Monte Carlo estimator in Equation (14.3), it is necessary to be able to draw random samples from the chosen probability distribution. This section will introduce the basics of this process and demonstrate it with some straightforward examples. The next section will develop the approach for the general multidimensional case, and Sections 15.5 and 15.6 in the next chapter will show how to use these techniques to generate samples from the distributions defined by BSDFs and light sources.

14.3.1 THE INVERSION METHOD

The inversion method uses one or more uniform random variables and maps them to random variables from the desired distribution. To explain how this process works in general, we will start with a simple discrete example. Suppose we have a process with four possible outcomes. The probabilities of each of the four outcomes are given by p_1, p_2, p_3, and p_4, respectively, with the requirement that $\sum_{i=1}^{4} p_i = 1$. The corresponding PDF is shown in Figure 14.1.

In order to draw a sample from this distribution, we first find the CDF $P(x)$. In the continuous case, P is the indefinite integral of p. In the discrete case, we can directly construct the CDF by stacking the bars on top of each other, starting at the left. This idea

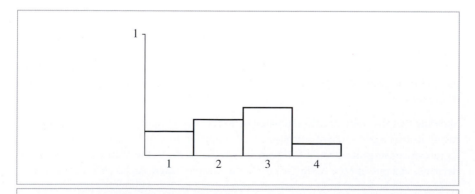

Figure 14.1: A Discrete PDF for Four Events Each with a Probability p_i. The sum of their probabilities $\sum_i p_i$ is necessarily one.

is shown in Figure 14.2. Notice that the height of the rightmost bar must be one because of the requirement that all probabilities sum to one.

To draw a sample from the distribution, we then take a uniform random number ξ and use it to select one of the possible outcomes using the CDF, doing so in a way that chooses a particular outcome with probability equal to its own probability. This idea is illustrated in Figure 14.3, where the events' probabilities are projected onto the vertical axis and a random variable ξ selects among them. It should be clear that this draws from the correct distribution—the probability of the uniform sample hitting any particular bar is exactly equal to the height of that bar. In order to generalize this technique to

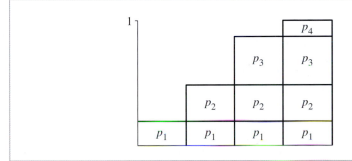

Figure 14.2: A Discrete CDF, Corresponding to the PDF in Figure 14.1. Each column's height is given by the PDF for the event that it represents plus the sum of the PDFs for the previous events, $P_i = \sum_{j=1}^{i} p_i$.

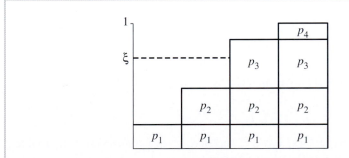

Figure 14.3: To use the inversion method to draw a sample from the distribution described by the PDF in Figure 14.1, a canonical uniform random variable is plotted on the vertical axis. By construction, the horizontal extension of ξ will intersect the box representing the ith outcome with probability p_i. If the corresponding event is chosen for a set of random variables ξ, then the resulting distribution of events will be distributed according to the PDF.

continuous distributions, consider what happens as the number of discrete possibilities approaches infinity. The PDF from Figure 14.1 becomes a smooth curve, and the CDF from Figure 14.2 becomes its integral. The projection process described in the previous paragraph is still the same, although if the function is continuous, the projection has a convenient mathematical interpretation—it represents inverting the CDF and evaluating the inverse at ξ. This technique is thus called the *inversion method*.

More precisely, we can draw a sample X_i from an arbitrary PDF $p(x)$ with the following steps:

1. Compute the CDF[5] $P(x) = \int_0^x p(x')\mathrm{d}x'$.
2. Compute the inverse $P^{-1}(x)$.
3. Obtain a uniformly distributed random number ξ.
4. Compute $X_i = P^{-1}(\xi)$.

14.3.2 EXAMPLE: POWER DISTRIBUTION

As an example of how this procedure works, consider the task of drawing samples from a *power distribution*, $p(x) \propto x^n$. Sampling from this distribution will come up when we are trying to sample the Blinn microfacet model. The PDF of the power distribution is

$$p(x) = cx^n,$$

for some constant c. The first task to tackle is to find the PDF for the function. In most cases, this simply involves computing the value of the proportionality constant c, which can be found using the constraint that $\int p(x)\,\mathrm{d}x = 1$:

$$\int_0^1 cx^n\,\mathrm{d}x = 1$$

$$c\,\frac{x^{n+1}}{n+1}\bigg|_0^1 = 1$$

$$\frac{c}{n+1} = 1$$

$$c = n+1.$$

Therefore, $p(x) = (n+1)x^n$. We can integrate this to get the CDF:

$$P(x) = \int_0^x p(x)\,\mathrm{d}x = x^{n+1},$$

and inversion is simple: $P^{-1}(x) = \sqrt[n+1]{x}$. Therefore, given a uniform random variable ξ, samples can be drawn from the power distribution as

$$X = \sqrt[n+1]{\xi}.$$

---

5   In general, the lower limit of integration should be $-\infty$, although if $p(x) = 0$ for $x \leq 0$, this equation is equivalent.

Another approach is to use a sampling trick that works only for the power distribution, selecting $X = \max(\xi_1, \xi_2, \ldots, \xi_{n+1})$. This random variable is distributed according to the power distribution as well. To see why, note that $Pr\{X < x\}$ is the probability that *all* the $\xi_i < x$. But the ξ_i are independent, so

$$Pr\{X < x\} = \prod_{i=1}^{n+1} Pr\{\xi_i < x\} = x^{n+1},$$

which is exactly the desired CDF. Depending on the speed of your random number generator, this technique can be faster than the inversion method for small values of n.

14.3.3 EXAMPLE: EXPONENTIAL DISTRIBUTION

When rendering images with participating media, it is frequently useful to draw samples from a distribution $p(x) \propto e^{-ax}$. As before, the first step is to normalize this distribution so that it integrates to one. In this case, the range of values x we'd like the generated samples to cover is $[0, \infty)$ rather than $[0, 1]$, so

$$\int_0^\infty ce^{-ax} = -\left.\frac{c}{a}e^{-ax}\right|_0^\infty = \frac{c}{a} = 1.$$

Thus we know that $c = a$, and our PDF is $p(x) = ae^{-ax}$. Now, we integrate to find $P(x)$:

$$P(x) = \int_0^x ae^{-ax'}\,\mathrm{d}x' = 1 - e^{-ax}.$$

This function is easy to invert:

$$P^{-1}(x) = -\frac{\ln(1-x)}{a},$$

and we can draw samples thusly:

$$X = -\frac{\ln(1-\xi)}{a}.$$

This equation can be further simplified by making the observation that if ξ is a uniformly distributed random number, so is $1 - \xi$, so we can safely replace $1 - \xi$ by ξ without changing the distribution. Therefore, our final sampling strategy is

$$X = -\frac{\ln(\xi)}{a}.$$

14.3.4 EXAMPLE: PIECEWISE-CONSTANT 1D FUNCTIONS

An interesting exercise is to work out how to sample from one-dimensional piecewise-constant functions (step functions). Without loss of generality, we will just consider piecewise-constant functions defined over $[0, 1]$.

Assume that the one-dimensional function's domain is split into N equal-sized pieces of size $\Delta = 1/N$. These regions start and end at points $x_i = i\Delta$, where i ranges from

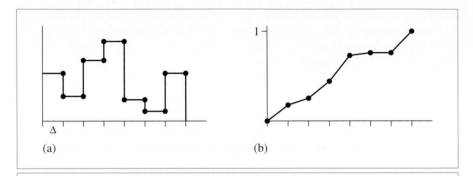

Figure 14.4: (a) Probability density function for a piecewise-constant 1D function and (b) cumulative distribution function defined by this PDF.

0 to N, inclusive. Within each region, the value of the function $f(x)$ is a constant (Figure 14.4(a)). The value of $f(x)$ is

$$f(x) = \begin{cases} v_0 & : & x_0 \leq x < x_1 \\ v_1 & : & x_1 \leq x < x_2 \\ \dots & : & \dots \end{cases}$$

The integral $\int f(x)\mathrm{d}x$ is

$$c = \int_0^1 f(x)\mathrm{d}x = \sum_{i=0}^{N-1} \Delta v_i = \sum_{i=0}^{N-1} \frac{v_i}{N}, \qquad [14.4]$$

and so it is easy to construct the PDF $p(x)$ for $f(x)$ as $f(x)/c$. By direct application of the relevant formulae, the CDF $P(x)$ is a piecewise linear function defined at points x_i by

$$P(x_0) = 0$$

$$P(x_1) = \int_{x_0}^{x_1} p(x)\mathrm{d}x = \frac{v_0}{Nc} = P(x_0) + \frac{v_0}{Nc}$$

$$P(x_2) = \int_{x_0}^{x_2} p(x)\mathrm{d}x = \int_{x_0}^{x_1} p(x)\mathrm{d}x + \int_{x_1}^{x_2} p(x)\mathrm{d}x = P(x_1) + \frac{v_1}{Nc}$$

$$P(x_i) = P(x_{i-1}) + \frac{v_{i-1}}{Nc}.$$

Between two points x_i and x_{i+1}, the CDF is linearly increasing with slope v_i/c.

Recall that in order to sample $f(x)$ we need to invert the CDF to find the value x such that

$$\xi = \int_0^x p(x')\,\mathrm{d}x' = P(x).$$

Because the CDF is monotonically increasing, the value of x must be between the x_i and x_{i+1} such that $P(x_i) \leq \xi$ and $\xi \leq P(x_{i+1})$.

To be able to do this sampling efficiently, we will first provide a function that takes the set of values v_i of $f(x)$ and computes the values of the CDF at x_i. It also returns the integral of $f(x)$ in the user-supplied variable c.

⟨*MC Function Definitions*⟩ ≡
```
void ComputeStep1dCDF(float *f, int nSteps, float *c, float *cdf) {
    ⟨Compute integral of step function at xᵢ 643⟩
    ⟨Transform step function integral into cdf 643⟩
}
```

This function starts by computing the integral of $f(x)$, using Equation (14.4). It stores the result in the cdf array for now so that it doesn't need to allocate additional temporary space for it. The caller must allocate nSteps+1 floats for the cdf array because if $f(x)$ has N step values, then we need to store the value of the CDF at each of the $N + 1$ values of x_i. Storing the CDF value of 1 at the end of the array is redundant, but simplifies code later.

⟨*Compute integral of step function at x_i*⟩ ≡   643
```
int i;
cdf[0] = 0.;
for (i = 1; i < nSteps+1; ++i)
    cdf[i] = cdf[i-1] + f[i-1] / nSteps;
```

Now that the value of the integral over all of $[0, 1]$ is stored in cdf[nSteps], the CDF can be normalized by dividing through by this value:

⟨*Transform step function integral into cdf*⟩ ≡   643
```
*c = cdf[nSteps];
for (i = 1; i < nSteps+1; ++i)
    cdf[i] /= *c;
```

Sampling the function from the CDF is handled by the SampleStep1d() function:

⟨*MC Function Definitions*⟩+≡
```
float SampleStep1d(float *f, float *cdf, float c,
                   int nSteps, float u, float *pdf) {
    ⟨Find surrounding cdf segments 644⟩
    ⟨Return offset along current cdf segment 644⟩
}
```

SampleStep1d() 643

First, it is necessary to find the pair of CDF values that straddle ξ. Because the cdf array is monotonically increasing (and is thus sorted), we can use a binary search function from the C++ standard library: lower_bound() takes a pointer to the start of the array and a pointer one position past the end of the array as well as the value to search for. We can turn the pointer that it returns into an integer offset into the array with a bit of pointer arithmetic.

⟨*Find surrounding cdf segments*⟩ ≡   643
```
    float *ptr = std::lower_bound(cdf, cdf+nSteps+1, u);
    int offset = (int) (ptr-cdf-1);
```

Now that we know the pair of CDF values, we can compute x. First, we determine how far ξ is between cdf[offset] and cdf[offset+1]. Because the CDF is linear, x is that far between x_i and x_{i+1} (Figure 14.4(b)). The PDF for this sample $p(x)$ is easily computed since we have the normalization value c as

$$p(x) = \frac{f(x)}{c}.$$

⟨*Return offset along current cdf segment*⟩ ≡   643
```
    u = (u - cdf[offset]) / (cdf[offset+1] - cdf[offset]);
    *pdf = f[offset] / c;
    return (offset + u) / nSteps;
```

14.3.5 THE REJECTION METHOD

For some functions $f(x)$, it may not be possible to integrate them in order to find their PDFs, or it may not be possible to analytically invert their CDFs. The *rejection method* is a technique for generating samples according to a function's distribution without needing to do either of these steps; it is essentially a dart-throwing approach. Assume that we want to draw samples from some such function $f(x)$ but we do have a PDF $p(x)$ that satisfies $f(x) < cp(x)$ for some scalar constant c, and suppose that we do know how to sample from p. The rejection method is then quite simple:

> loop forever:
>> sample X From p's distribution
>> if $\xi < f(X)/(cp(X))$ then
>>> return X

This procedure repeatedly chooses a pair of random variables (X, ξ). If the point $(X, \xi cp(X))$ lies under $f(X)$, then the sample X is accepted. Otherwise it is rejected and a new sample pair is chosen. This idea is illustrated in Figure 14.5. Without going into too much detail, it should be clear that the efficiency of this scheme depends on how tightly $cp(x)$ bounds $f(x)$. This technique works in any number of dimensions.

In practice, rejection sampling isn't used in any of the Monte Carlo algorithms currently implemented in pbrt. We will normally prefer to find distributions that are similar to

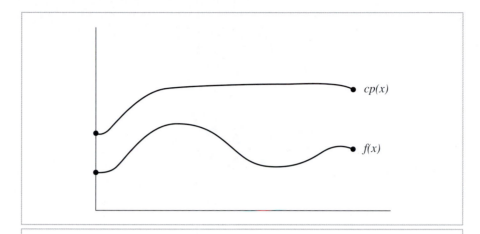

Figure 14.5: Rejection sampling generates samples according to the distribution of an arbitrary function $f(x)$ even if f's PDF is unknown or its CDF can't be inverted. If some distribution $p(x)$ and a scalar constant c are known such that $f(x) < cp(x)$, then samples can be drawn from $p(x)$ and randomly accepted with the rejection method. The closer the fit of $cp(x)$ to $f(x)$, the more efficient this process is.

$f(x)$ that can be sampled directly, for reasons that will be explained in the next chapter. Nevertheless, rejection sampling is an important technique to be aware of, particularly when debugging Monte Carlo implementations. For example, if one suspects the presence of a bug in code that draws samples from some distribution using the inversion method, then one can replace it with a straightforward implementation based on the rejection method and see if the Monte Carlo estimator computes the same result. Of course, it's necessary to take many samples in situations like these, so that variance in the estimates doesn't mask errors.

14.3.6 EXAMPLE: REJECTION SAMPLING A UNIT CIRCLE

Suppose we want to select a uniformly distributed point inside a unit circle. Using the rejection method, we simply select a random (x, y) position inside the circumscribed square and return it if it falls inside the circle. This process is shown in Figure 14.6.

The function RejectionSampleDisk() implements this algorithm. A similar approach will work to generate uniformly distributed samples inside for any complex shape as long as it has an inside-outside test.

RejectionSampleDisk() 646

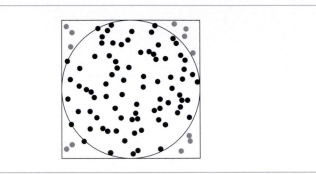

Figure 14.6: Rejection Sampling a Circle. One approach to finding uniform points in the unit circle is to sample uniform random points in the unit square and reject all that lie outside the circle. The remaining points will be uniformly distributed within the circle.

⟨*MC Function Definitions*⟩+≡

```
void RejectionSampleDisk(float *x, float *y) {
    float sx, sy;
    do {
        sx = 1.f - 2.f * RandomFloat();
        sy = 1.f - 2.f * RandomFloat();
    } while (sx*sx + sy*sy > 1.f);
    *x = sx;
    *y = sy;
}
```

In general, the efficiency of rejection sampling depends on the percentage of samples that are expected to be rejected. For the problem of finding uniform points in the 2D case, this is easy to compute. It is the area of the circle divided by the area of the square: $\frac{\pi}{4} \approx 78.5\%$. If the method is applied to generate samples in hyperspheres in the general n-dimensional case, however, the volume of an n-dimensional hypersphere actually goes to *zero* as n increases and this approach becomes increasingly inefficient.

14.4 TRANSFORMING BETWEEN DISTRIBUTIONS

In describing the inversion method, we introduced a technique that generates samples according to some distribution by transforming canonical uniform random variables in a particular manner. Here, we will investigate the more general problem of which distribution results when we transform samples from an arbitrary distribution to some other distribution with a function f.

RandomFloat() 857

Suppose we are given random variables X_i that are already drawn from some PDF $p_x(x)$. Now, if we compute $Y_i = y(X_i)$, we would like to find the distribution of the new random variable Y_i. This may seem like an esoteric problem, but we will see that understanding this kind of transformation is critical for drawing samples from multidimensional distribution functions.

The function $y(x)$ must be a one-to-one transformation; if multiple values of x mapped to the same y value, then it would be impossible to unambiguously describe the probability density of a particular y value. A direct consequence of y being one-to-one is that its derivative must either be strictly greater than zero or strictly less than zero, which implies that

$$Pr\{Y \leq y(x)\} = Pr\{X \leq x\},$$

and therefore

$$P_y(y) = P_y(y(x)) = P_x(x).$$

This relationship between CDFs leads directly to the relationship between their PDFs. If we assume that y's derivative is greater than zero, differentiating gives

$$p_y(y)\frac{dy}{dx} = p_x(x),$$

and so

$$p_y(y) = \left(\frac{dy}{dx}\right)^{-1} p_x(x).$$

In general, y's derivative is either strictly positive or strictly negative, and the relationship between the densities is

$$p_y(y) = \left|\frac{dy}{dx}\right|^{-1} p_x(x)$$

How can we use this formula? Suppose that $p_x(x) = 2x$ over the domain $[0, 1]$, and let $Y = \sin X$. What is the PDF of the random variable Y? Because we know that $dy/dx = \cos x$,

$$p_y(y) = \frac{p_x(x)}{|\cos x|} = \frac{2x}{\cos x} = \frac{2\sin^{-1} y}{\sqrt{1-y^2}}.$$

This procedure may seem backwards—usually we have some PDF that we want to sample from, not a given transformation. For example, we might have X drawn from some $p_x(x)$, and would like to compute Y from some distribution $p_y(y)$. What transformation should we use? All we need is for the CDFs to be equal, or $P_y(y) = P_x(x)$, which immediately gives the transformation

$$y(x) = P_y^{-1}\left(P_x(x)\right).$$

This is a generalization of the inversion method, since if X were uniformly distributed over $[0, 1]$ then $P_x(x) = x$, and we have the same procedure as in the last section.

14.4.1 TRANSFORMATION IN MULTIPLE DIMENSIONS

In the general n-dimensional case, a similar derivation gives the analogous relationship between different densities. We will not show the derivation here; it follows the same form as the one-dimensional case. Suppose we have an n-dimensional random variable X with density function $p_x(x)$. Now let $Y = T(X)$, where T is a bijection. In this case, the densities are related by

$$p_y(y) = p_y(T(x)) = \frac{p_x(x)}{|J_T(x)|},$$

where $|J_T|$ is the absolute value of the determinant of T's Jacobian matrix, which is

$$\begin{pmatrix} \partial T_1/\partial x_1 & \cdots & \partial T_1/\partial x_n \\ \vdots & \ddots & \vdots \\ \partial T_n/\partial x_1 & \cdots & \partial T_n/\partial x_n \end{pmatrix},$$

where T_i are defined by $T(x) = (T_1(x), \ldots, T_n(x))$.

14.4.2 EXAMPLE: POLAR COORDINATES

The polar transformation is given by

$$x = r \cos \theta$$
$$y = r \sin \theta.$$

Suppose we draw samples from some density $p(r, \theta)$. What is the corresponding density $p(x, y)$? The Jacobian of this transformation is

$$J_T = \begin{pmatrix} \frac{\partial x}{\partial r} & \frac{\partial x}{\partial \theta} \\ \frac{\partial y}{\partial r} & \frac{\partial y}{\partial \theta} \end{pmatrix} = \begin{pmatrix} \cos \theta & -r \sin \theta \\ \sin \theta & r \cos \theta \end{pmatrix},$$

and the determinant is $r \left(\cos^2 \theta + \sin^2 \theta \right) = r$. So $p(x, y) = p(r, \theta)/r$. Of course, this is backwards from what we usually want—typically we start with a sampling strategy in Cartesian coordinates and want to transform it to one in polar coordinates. In that case, we would have

$$p(r, \theta) = r p(x, y).$$

14.4.3 EXAMPLE: SPHERICAL COORDINATES

Given the spherical coordinate representation of directions,

$$x = r \sin \theta \cos \phi$$
$$y = r \sin \theta \sin \phi$$
$$z = r \cos \theta,$$

the Jacobian of this transformation has determinant $|J_T| = r^2 \sin \theta$, so the corresponding density function is

$$p(r, \theta, \phi) = r^2 \sin \theta p(x, y, z).$$

This transformation is important since it helps us represent directions as points (x, y, z) on the unit sphere. Remember that solid angle is defined as the area of a set of points on the unit sphere. In spherical coordinates, we previously derived

$$d\omega = \sin \theta \, d\theta \, d\phi.$$

So if we have a density function defined over a solid angle Ω, this means that

$$Pr\{\omega \in \Omega\} = \int_\Omega p(\omega) \, d\omega.$$

The density with respect to θ and ϕ can therefore be derived:

$$p(\theta, \phi) \, d\theta \, d\phi = p(\omega) \, d\omega$$
$$p(\theta, \phi) = \sin \theta p(\omega).$$

14.5 2D SAMPLING WITH MULTIDIMENSIONAL TRANSFORMATIONS

Suppose we have a 2D joint density function $p(x, y)$ that we wish to draw samples (X, Y) from. Sometimes multidimensional densities are separable and can be expressed as the product of one-dimensional densities, for example,

$$p(x, y) = p_x(x)p_y(y),$$

for some p_x and p_y. In this case, random variables (X, Y) can be found by independently sampling X from p_x and Y from p_y. Many useful densities aren't separable, however, so we will introduce the theory of how to sample from multidimensional distributions in the general case.

Given a 2D density function, the *marginal density function* $p(x)$ is obtained by "integrating out" one of the dimensions:

$$p(x) = \int p(x, y) \, dy.$$

This can be thought of as the density function for X alone. More precisely, it is the average density for a particular x over *all* possible y values.

The *conditional density function* $p(y|x)$ is the density function for y given that some particular x has been chosen (it is read "p of y given x"):

$$p(y|x) = \frac{p(x, y)}{p(x)}.$$

The basic idea for 2D sampling from joint distributions is to first compute the marginal density to isolate one particular variable and draw a sample from that density using standard 1D techniques. Once that sample is drawn, compute the conditional density function given that value, and draw a sample from that distribution, again using standard 1D techniques.

14.5.1 EXAMPLE: UNIFORMLY SAMPLING A HEMISPHERE

As an example, consider the task of choosing a direction on the hemisphere uniformly with respect to solid angle. Remember that a uniform distribution means that the density function is a constant, so we know that $p(\omega) = c$. In conjunction with the fact that the density function must integrate to one over its domain, we have

$$\int_{\mathcal{H}^2} p(\omega) \, d\omega = 1 \Rightarrow c \int_{\mathcal{H}^2} d\omega = 1 \Rightarrow c = \frac{1}{2\pi}.$$

This tells us that $p(\omega) = 1/(2\pi)$, or $p(\theta, \phi) = \sin\theta/(2\pi)$ (using a result from the previous example about spherical coordinates). Note that this density function is separable. Nevertheless, we will use the marginal and conditional densities to illustrate the multi-dimensional sampling technique.

Let's sample θ first. To do this, we need θ's marginal density function $p(\theta)$:

$$p(\theta) = \int_0^{2\pi} p(\theta, \phi) \, d\phi = \int_0^{2\pi} \frac{\sin\theta}{2\pi} \, d\phi = \sin\theta.$$

Now, compute the conditional density for ϕ:

$$p(\phi|\theta) = \frac{p(\theta, \phi)}{p(\theta)} = \frac{1}{2\pi}.$$

Notice that the density function for ϕ is itself uniform; this should make intuitive sense given the symmetry of the hemisphere. Now, we use the 1D inversion technique to sample each of these PDFs in turn:

$$P(\theta) = \int_0^\theta \sin\theta' \, d\theta' = 1 - \cos\theta$$

$$P(\phi|\theta) = \int_0^\phi \frac{1}{2\pi} \, d\phi' = \frac{\phi}{2\pi}.$$

Inverting these functions is straightforward, and again noting that we can safely replace $1 - \xi$ with ξ since these are both uniformly distributed random numbers over $[0, 1]$, we get

$$\theta = \cos^{-1} \xi_1$$

$$\phi = 2\pi \xi_2.$$

Converting these back to Cartesian coordinates, we get the final sampling formulae:

$$x = \sin\theta \cos\phi = \cos\left(2\pi\xi_2\right)\sqrt{1 - \xi_1^2}$$

$$y = \sin\theta \sin\phi = \sin\left(2\pi\xi_2\right)\sqrt{1 - \xi_1^2}$$

$$z = \cos\theta = \xi_1.$$

This sampling strategy is implemented in the following code. Two uniform random numbers u1 and u2 are passed in, and a vector on the hemisphere is returned.

⟨*MC Function Definitions*⟩+≡

```
COREDLL Vector UniformSampleHemisphere(float u1, float u2) {
    float z = u1;
    float r = sqrtf(max(0.f, 1.f - z*z));
    float phi = 2 * M_PI * u2;
    float x = r * cosf(phi);
    float y = r * sinf(phi);
    return Vector(x, y, z);
}
```

For each sampling routine like this in pbrt, there is a corresponding function that returns the value of the PDF for a particular sample. For such functions, it is important to be clear which PDF is being evaluated—for example, for a direction on the hemisphere, we have already seen these densities expressed differently in terms of solid angle and in terms of (θ, ϕ). For hemispheres (and all other directional sampling), these functions return values with respect to solid angle. For the hemisphere, the solid angle PDF is a constant $p(\omega) = 1/(2\pi)$.

⟨*MC Function Definitions*⟩+≡

```
COREDLL float UniformHemispherePdf(float theta, float phi) {
    return INV_TWOPI;
}
```

Sampling the full sphere uniformly over its area follows almost exactly the same derivation, which we omit here. The end result is

COREDLL 904
INV_TWOPI 855
M_PI 855
Vector 47

$$x = \cos(2\pi\xi_2)\sqrt{1 - z^2} = \cos(2\pi\xi_2)2\sqrt{\xi_1(1 - \xi_1)}$$

$$y = \sin(2\pi\xi_2)\sqrt{1 - z^2} = \sin(2\pi\xi_2)2\sqrt{\xi_1(1 - \xi_1)}$$

$$z = 1 - 2\xi_1.$$

⟨*MC Function Definitions*⟩+≡
```
    COREDLL Vector UniformSampleSphere(float u1, float u2) {
        float z = 1.f - 2.f * u1;
        float r = sqrtf(max(0.f, 1.f - z*z));
        float phi = 2.f * M_PI * u2;
        float x = r * cosf(phi);
        float y = r * sinf(phi);
        return Vector(x, y, z);
    }
```

⟨*MC Function Definitions*⟩+≡
```
    COREDLL float UniformSpherePdf() {
        return 1.f / (4.f * M_PI);
    }
```

14.5.2 EXAMPLE: SAMPLING A UNIT DISK

Although the disk seems a simpler shape to sample than the hemisphere, it can be more tricky to sample uniformly because it has an (incorrect) intuitive solution. The wrong approach is the seemingly obvious one: $r = \xi_1$, $\theta = 2\pi \xi_2$. Although the resulting point is both random and inside the circle, it is *not* uniformly distributed; it actually clumps samples near the center of the circle. Figure 14.7(a) shows a plot of samples on the unit disk when this mapping was used for a set of uniform random samples (ξ_1, ξ_2). Figure 14.7(b) shows uniformly distributed samples resulting from the following correct approach.

Since we're going to sample uniformly with respect to area, the PDF $p(x, y)$ must be a constant. By the normalization constraint, $p(x, y) = 1/\pi$. If we transform into polar coordinates (see the example in Section 14.4.2), we have $p(r, \theta) = r/\pi$. Now we compute the marginal and conditional densities as before:

$$p(r) = \int_0^{2\pi} p(r, \theta) \, d\theta = 2r$$

$$p(\theta | r) = \frac{p(r, \theta)}{p(r)} = \frac{1}{2\pi}.$$

As with the hemisphere case, the fact that $p(\theta | r)$ is a constant should make sense because of the symmetry of the circle. Integrating and inverting to find $P(r)$, $P^{-1}(r)$, $P(\theta)$, and $P^{-1}(\theta)$, we can find that the correct solution to generate uniformly distributed samples on a disk is

COREDLL 904
M_PI 855
Vector 47

$$r = \sqrt{\xi_1}$$

$$\theta = 2\pi \xi_2.$$

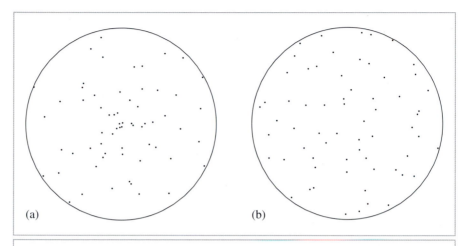

Figure 14.7: (a) When the obvious but incorrect mapping of uniform random variables to points on the disk is used, the resulting distribution is not uniform and the samples are more likely to be near the center of the disk. (b) The correct mapping gives a uniform distribution of points.

Taking the square root of ξ_1 effectively pushes the samples back toward the edge of the disk, counteracting the clumping referred to earlier.

⟨*MC Function Definitions*⟩+≡

```
COREDLL void UniformSampleDisk(float u1, float u2, float *x, float *y) {
    float r = sqrtf(u1);
    float theta = 2.0f * M_PI * u2;
    *x = r * cosf(theta);
    *y = r * sinf(theta);
}
```

Although this mapping solves the problem at hand, it distorts areas on the disk; areas on the unit square are elongated and/or compressed when mapped to the disk (Figure 14.8). Section 15.2.3 will discuss in more detail why this distortion is a disadvantage. Peter Shirley (1997) has developed a "concentric" mapping from the unit square to the unit circle that avoids this problem. The concentric mapping takes points in the square $[-1, 1]^2$ to the unit disk by uniformly mapping concentric squares to concentric circles (Figure 14.9).

The mapping turns wedges of the square into slices of the disk. For example, points in the shaded area of the square in Figure 14.9 are mapped to (r, θ) by

$$r = x$$
$$\theta = \frac{y}{x}.$$

COREDLL 904

M_PI 855

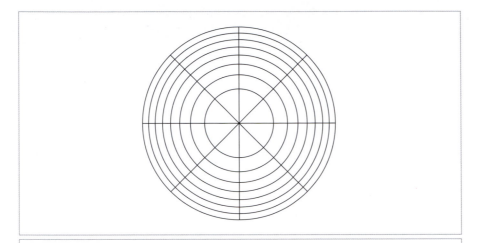

Figure 14.8: The mapping from 2D random samples to points on the disk implemented in `UniformSampleDisk()` distorts areas substantially. Each section of the disk here has equal area and represents $\frac{1}{8}$ of the unit square of uniform random samples in each direction. In general, we'd prefer a mapping that did a better job at mapping nearby (ξ_1, ξ_2) values to nearby points on the disk.

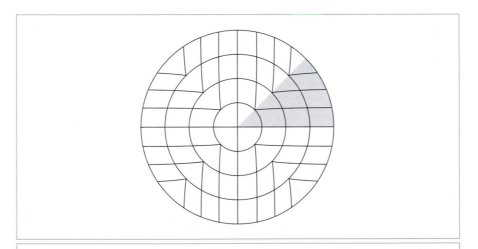

Figure 14.9: The concentric mapping maps squares to circles, giving a less distorted mapping than the first method shown for uniformly sampling points on the unit disk.

See Figure 14.10. The other four quadrants are handled analogously.

⟨*MC Function Definitions*⟩+≡
```
COREDLL void ConcentricSampleDisk(float u1, float u2,
                                  float *dx, float *dy) {
    float r, theta;
    ⟨Map uniform random numbers to [−1, 1]² 655⟩
    ⟨Map square to (r, θ) 655⟩
    *dx = r*cosf(theta);
    *dy = r*sinf(theta);
}
```

⟨*Map uniform random numbers to* $[−1, 1]^2$⟩≡   **655**
```
float sx = 2 * u1 - 1;
float sy = 2 * u2 - 1;
```

⟨*Map square to* $(r, θ)$⟩≡   **655**
```
⟨Handle degeneracy at the origin⟩
if (sx >= -sy) {
    if (sx > sy) {
        ⟨Handle first region of disk  655⟩
    }
    else {
        ⟨Handle second region of disk⟩
    }
}
else {
    if (sx <= sy) {
        ⟨Handle third region of disk⟩
    }
    else {
        ⟨Handle fourth region of disk⟩
    }
}
theta *= M_PI / 4.f;
```

⟨*Handle first region of disk*⟩≡   **655**
```
r = sx;
if (sy > 0.0)
    theta = sy/r;
else
    theta = 8.0f + sy/r;
```

COREDLL 904
M_PI 855

The remaining cases are analogous and are omitted.

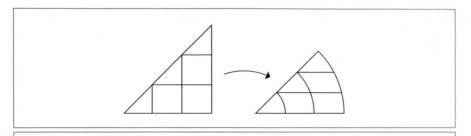

Figure 14.10: Triangular wedges of the square are mapped into (r, θ) pairs in pie-shaped slices of the circle.

14.5.3 EXAMPLE: COSINE-WEIGHTED HEMISPHERE SAMPLING

As we will see later in the next chapter, it is often useful to sample from a distribution that has a similar shape to the integrand being estimated. For example, because the scattering equation weights the product of the BSDF and the incident radiance with a cosine term, it is useful to have a method that generates directions that are more likely to be close to the top of the hemisphere, where the cosine term has a large value, than the bottom, where the cosine term is small.

Mathematically, this means that we would like to sample directions ω from a PDF

$$p(\omega) \propto \cos \theta.$$

Normalizing as usual,

$$\int_{\mathcal{H}^2} cp(\omega)\, \mathrm{d}\omega = 1$$

$$\int_0^{2\pi} \int_0^{\frac{\pi}{2}} c \cos \theta \sin \theta\, \mathrm{d}\theta\, \mathrm{d}\phi = 1$$

$$c2\pi \int_0^{\pi/2} \cos \theta \sin \theta\, \mathrm{d}\theta = 1$$

$$c = \frac{1}{\pi}$$

so

$$p(\theta, \phi) = \frac{1}{\pi} \cos \theta \sin \theta.$$

We could compute the marginal and conditional densities as before, but instead we can use a trick known as *Malley's method* to generate these cosine-weighted points. The idea behind Malley's method is that if we choose points uniformly from the unit disk and then generate directions by projecting the points on the disk up to the hemisphere above it, the resulting distribution of directions will have a cosine distribution (Figure 14.11).

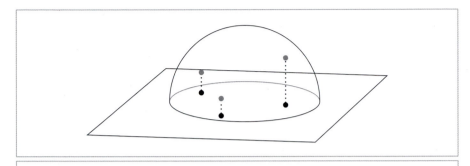

Figure 14.11: Malley's Method. To sample direction vectors from a cosine-weighted distribution, uniformly sample points on the unit disk and project them up to the unit sphere.

Why does this work? Let (r, ϕ) be the polar coordinates of the point chosen on the disk (note that we're using ϕ instead of the usual θ here). From our calculations before, we know that the joint density $p(r, \phi) = r/\pi$ gives the density of a point sampled on the disk.

Now, we map this to the hemisphere. The vertical projection gives $\sin \theta = r$, which is easily seen from Figure 14.11. To complete the $(r, \phi) \rightarrow (\sin \theta, \phi)$ transformation, we need the determinant of the Jacobian

$$|J_T| = \begin{vmatrix} \cos \theta & 0 \\ 0 & 1 \end{vmatrix} = \cos \theta.$$

Therefore, $p(\theta, \phi) = |J_T| p(r, \phi) = \cos \theta r/\pi = (\cos \theta \sin \theta)/\pi$, which is exactly what we wanted! We have used the transformation method to prove that Malley's method generates directions with a cosine-weighted distribution. Note that this technique works regardless of the method used to sample points from the circle, so we can use Shirley's concentric mapping just as well as the simpler $(r, \theta) = (\sqrt{\xi_1}, 2\pi \xi_2)$ method.

⟨*MC Utility Declarations*⟩ ≡

```
inline Vector CosineSampleHemisphere(float u1, float u2) {
    Vector ret;
    ConcentricSampleDisk(u1, u2, &ret.x, &ret.y);
    ret.z = sqrtf(max(0.f, 1.f - ret.x*ret.x - ret.y*ret.y));
    return ret;
}
```

Remember that all of the PDF evaluation routines in pbrt are defined with respect to solid angle, not spherical coordinates, so the PDF function returns a weight of $\cos \theta / \pi$.

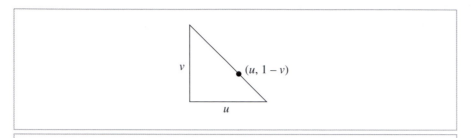

Figure 14.12: Sampling an Isosceles Right Triangle. Note that the equation of the hypotenuse is $v = 1 - u$.

⟨*MC Utility Declarations*⟩+≡

```
inline float CosineHemispherePdf(float costheta, float phi) {
    return costheta * INV_PI;
}
```

14.5.4 EXAMPLE: SAMPLING A TRIANGLE

Our final example will show how to uniformly sample a triangle. Although this might seem like a simple task, it turns out to be more complex than the ones we've seen so far.[6] To simplify the problem, we will assume we are sampling an isosceles right triangle of area $\frac{1}{2}$. The output of the sampling routine that we will derive will be barycentric coordinates, however, so the technique will actually work for any triangle despite this simplification. Figure 14.12 shows the shape to be sampled.

We will denote the two barycentric coordinates here by (u, v). Since we are sampling with respect to area, we know that the PDF $p(u, v)$ must be a constant equal to the reciprocal of the shape's area, $\frac{1}{2}$, so $p(u, v) = 2$.

First, we find the marginal density $p(u)$:

$$p(u) = \int_0^{1-u} p(u, v) \, dv = 2 \int_0^{1-u} dv = 2(1 - u),$$

and the conditional density $p(v|u)$:

$$p(v|u) = \frac{p(u, v)}{p(u)} = \frac{2}{2(1 - u)} = \frac{1}{1 - u}.$$

---

6   It is possible to generate the right distribution by sampling the enclosing parallelogram and reflecting samples on the wrong side of the diagonal back into the triangle. Although this technique is simpler than the one presented here, it is undesirable since it effectively folds the 2D uniform random samples back on top of each other—two samples that are very far away (e.g., (.01, .01) and (.99, .99)) can map to the same point on the triangle. This thwarts variance reduction techniques like stratified sampling that generate sets of well-distributed (ξ_1, ξ_2) samples and expect that they will map to well-distributed points on the object being sampled; see Section 15.2.1 for further discussion.

INV_PI 855

The CDFs are, as always, found by integration:

$$P(u) = \int_0^u p(u')\, du' = 2u - u^2$$

$$P(v) = \int_0^v p(v'|u)\, dv' = \frac{v}{1-u}.$$

Inverting these functions and assigning them to uniform random variables gives the final sampling strategy:

$$u = 1 - \sqrt{\xi_1}$$

$$v = \xi_2 \sqrt{\xi_1}.$$

Notice that the two variables in this case are *not* independent!

⟨*MC Function Definitions*⟩+≡
```
COREDLL void UniformSampleTriangle(float u1, float u2,
                                   float *u, float *v) {
    float su1 = sqrtf(u1);
    *u = 1.f - su1;
    *v = u2 * su1;
}
```

We won't provide a PDF evaluation function for this sampling strategy since the proper value depends on the triangle's area.

FURTHER READING

Many books have been written on Monte Carlo integration. Hammersley and Handscomb (1964), Spanier and Gelbard (1969) and Kalos and Whitlock (1986) are classic references. More recent books on the topic include those by Fishman (1996) and Liu (2001). The Monte Carlo and Quasi Monte Carlo Web site is a useful gateway to recent work in that field *(www.mcqmc.org)*.

COREDLL 904

Good general references about Monte Carlo and its application to computer graphics are the theses by Lafortune (1996) and Veach (1997). This topic is also covered well by Dutré, Bekaert, and Bala (2003). Dutré's *Global Illumination Compendium* (2003) also has much useful information related to this topic. The course notes from the Monte Carlo ray-tracing course at SIGGRAPH also have a wealth of practical information (Jensen et al. 2001, 2003). The square to disk mapping is described by Shirley and Chiu (1997).

EXERCISES

❷ 14.1 Write a program that compares Monte Carlo and one or more alternative numerical integration techniques. Structure this program so that it is easy to replace the particular function being integrated. Verify that the different techniques compute the same result (given a sufficient number of samples for each of them). Modify your program so that it draws samples from distributions other than the uniform distribution for the Monte Carlo estimate and verify that it still computes the correct result when the correct estimator, Equation (14.3), is used. (Make sure that any alternative distributions you use have nonzero probability of choosing any value of x where $f(x) > 0$.)

❶ 14.2 Write a program that computes Monte Carlo estimates of the integral of a given function. Compute an estimate of the variance of the estimates by taking a series of trials and using Equation (14.2) to compute variance. Demonstrate numerically that variance decreases at a rate of $O(\sqrt{n})$.

❷ 14.3 Write a function that takes two uniform random variables (ξ_1, ξ_2) and maps them to a sample from the distribution defined by a piecewise-constant 2D function given as an array of scalar values. (This will be useful for exercises in the next chapter that involve sampling from image maps.) Note that this joint density function is *not* separable. Discuss how you might numerically verify the correctness of your implementation and implement tests that demonstrate that your implementation is in fact correct.

❶ 14.4 The depth-of-field code in Section 6.2.3 uses the `ConcentricSampleDisk()` function to generate samples on the circular lens, since this function gives less distortion than `UniformSampleDisk()`. Try replacing it with `UniformSampleDisk()` and measure the difference in image quality. For example, you might want to compare the error in images from using each approach and a relatively low number of samples to a highly sampled reference image.

Does `ConcentricSampleDisk()` in fact give less error in practice? Does it make a difference if a relatively simple scene is being rendered versus a very complex scene?

CHAPTER FIFTEEN

15 MONTE CARLO INTEGRATION II: IMPROVING EFFICIENCY

Variance in Monte Carlo ray tracing manifests itself as noise in the image—an unpleasant artifact (Figure 15.1). The battle against variance is the basis of most of the work in optimizing Monte Carlo. Recall that Monte Carlo's convergence rate means that it is necessary to quadruple the number of samples in order to reduce the variance by half. Because the run time of the estimation procedure is proportional to the number of samples, the cost of reducing variance can be high. This chapter will develop the theory and practice of techniques for improving the efficiency of Monte Carlo integration without necessarily increasing the number of samples.

The *efficiency* of an estimator F is defined as

$$\epsilon[F] = \frac{1}{V[F]T[F]},$$

where $V[F]$ is its variance and $T[F]$ is the running time to compute its value. According to this metric, an estimator F_1 is more efficient than F_2 if it takes less time to produce the same variance, or if it produces less variance in the same amount of time.

One of the techniques that has been most effective for improving efficiency for rendering problems is a method called *importance sampling*. Recall that there is some freedom in the choice of distribution $p(x)$ to use as the sample distribution for the Monte Carlo

(a)

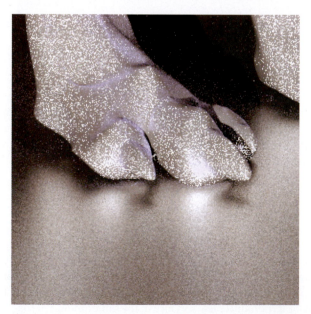

(b)

Figure 15.1: (a) A scene with glossy reflection, where variance from estimating the value of the scattering equation at each pixel is visually disturbing. (b) An image computed with the variance reduction techniques described in this chapter; it has substantially less variance but uses the same amount of computation.

estimator in Equation (14.3). It turns out that choosing a sampling distribution that is similar in shape to the integrand leads to reduced variance. This technique is called importance sampling because samples tend to be taken in "important" parts of the function's domain, where the function's value is relatively large.

The first half of this chapter discusses importance sampling and a number of other techniques for improving the efficiency of Monte Carlo. The second half of the chapter then derives techniques for generating samples according to the distributions of BSDFs, light sources, and functions related to volume scattering so that they can be used as sampling distributions for importance sampling. These sampling methods will be used throughout Chapters 16 and 17.

15.1 RUSSIAN ROULETTE AND SPLITTING

Russian roulette and splitting are two related techniques that can improve the efficiency of Monte Carlo estimates by increasing the likelihood that each sample will have a significant contribution to the result. Russian roulette addresses the problem of samples that are expensive to evaluate but make a small contribution to the final result. We would like to avoid the work of evaluating these samples while still computing a correct estimator.

As an example, consider the problem of estimating the direct lighting integral, which gives reflected radiance at a point due to direct lighting from the light sources in the scene, L_d:

$$L_o(p, \omega_o) = \int_{S^2} f_r(p, \omega_o, \omega_i) L_d(p, \omega_i) |\cos \theta_i| \, d\omega_i.$$

Assume that we have decided to take $N = 2$ samples from some distribution $p(\omega)$ to compute the estimator

$$\frac{1}{2} \sum_{i=1}^{2} \frac{f_r(p, \omega_o, \omega_i) L_d(p, \omega_i) |\cos \theta_i|}{p(\omega_i)}.$$

Most of the computation expense of each of the terms of the sum comes from tracing a shadow ray from the point p to see if the light source is occluded as seen from p.

For all of the directions ω_i where the integrand's value is clearly zero (e.g., because $f_r(p, \omega_o, \omega_i)$ is zero for that direction), we can skip the work of tracing the shadow ray, since tracing it won't change the final value computed. Russian roulette makes it possible to also skip tracing rays when the integrand's value is very low but not necessarily zero, while still computing the correct value on average. For example, we might want to avoid tracing rays where $f_r(p, \omega_o, \omega_i)$ is small, or when ω_i is close to the horizon and thus $|\cos \theta_i|$ is small. Of course, these samples just can't be ignored completely, since the estimator would then consistently underestimate the correct result.

To apply Russian roulette, we select some termination probability q. This value can be chosen in almost any manner; for example, it could be based on an estimate of the value of the integrand for the particular sample chosen, increasing as the integrand's value becomes smaller. With probability q, the integrand is not evaluated for the particular sample and some constant value c is used in its place ($c = 0$ is often used). With probability $1 - q$, the integrand is still evaluated, but is weighted by a term, $1/(1 - q)$, that effectively accounts for all of the samples that were skipped:

$$F' = \begin{cases} \frac{F - qc}{1 - q} & \xi > q \\ c & \text{otherwise.} \end{cases}$$

Remarkably, the expected value of the resulting estimator is the same as the expected value of the original estimator:

$$E[F'] = (1 - q) \left(\frac{E[F] - qc}{1 - q} \right) + qc = E[F].$$

Russian roulette never reduces variance. In fact, unless somehow $c = F$, it will always increase variance. However, it can improve efficiency if probabilities are chosen so that samples that are likely to make a small contribution to the final result are skipped.

One pitfall is that poorly chosen Russian roulette weights can substantially increase variance. Imagine applying Russian roulette to all of the camera rays with a termination probability of .99: we'd only trace 1% of the camera rays, weighting each of them by $1/.01 = 100$. The resulting image would still be "correct" in a strictly mathematical sense, although visually the result would be terrible: mostly black pixels with a few very bright ones. One of the exercises at the end of the next chapter discusses this problem further and describes a technique called *efficiency-optimized Russian roulette* that tries to set Russian roulette weights in a way that minimizes the increase in variance.

15.1.1 SPLITTING

While Russian roulette reduces the effort spent evaluating unimportant samples, splitting increases the number of samples taken in order to improve efficiency. Consider again the problem of computing reflection due only to direct illumination. Ignoring pixel filtering, this problem can be written as a double integral over the area of the pixel A and over the sphere of directions S^2 at the visible points on surfaces at each (x, y) pixel position, where $L_d(x, y, \omega)$ denotes the exitant radiance at the object visible at the position (x, y) on the image due to incident radiance from the direction ω:

$$\int_A \int_{S^2} L_d(x, y, \omega) \, dx \, dy \, d\omega.$$

The natural way to estimate the integral is to generate N samples and apply the Monte Carlo estimator, where each sample consists of an (x, y) image position and a direction ω toward a light source. If there are many light sources in the scene, or if there is an area light casting soft shadows, tens or hundreds of samples may be needed to compute a result with an acceptable variance level. Unfortunately, each sample requires that two rays be traced through the scene: one to compute the first visible surface from position (x, y) on the image plane, and one a shadow ray along ω to a light source.

The problem with this approach is that if $N = 100$ samples are taken to estimate this integral, 200 rays will be traced: 100 camera rays and 100 shadow rays. Yet, 100 camera rays may be many more than are needed for good pixel antialiasing and thus may make relatively little contribution to variance reduction in the final result. Splitting addresses this problem in a straightforward way by formalizing the approach of taking multiple samples in some of the dimensions of integration for each sample taken in other dimensions.

With splitting, the estimator for this integral can be written taking N image samples and M light samples per image sample:

$$\frac{1}{N}\frac{1}{M} \sum_{i=1}^{N} \sum_{j=1}^{M} \frac{L(x_i, y_i, \omega_{i,j})}{p(x_i, y_i) p(\omega_{i,j})}.$$

Thus, we could take just 5 image samples, but take 20 light samples per image sample, for a total of 105 rays traced, rather than 200, while still taking 100 area light samples in order to compute a high-quality soft shadow.

15.2 CAREFUL SAMPLE PLACEMENT

A classic and effective family of techniques for variance reduction is based on the careful placement of samples in order to better capture "important" features of the integrand (or, more accurately, to be less likely to miss important features). These techniques are complementary to techniques like importance sampling and are used extensively in pbrt. Indeed, one of the tasks of Samplers in Chapter 7 was to generate well-distributed samples for use by the integrators for just this reason, although at the time we offered only an intuitive sense of why this was worthwhile. Here we will formally justify that extra work.

15.2.1 STRATIFIED SAMPLING

Stratified sampling was first introduced in Section 7.3, and we now have the tools to motivate its use. Stratified sampling works by subdividing the integration domain Λ into n nonoverlapping regions $\Lambda_1, \Lambda_2, \ldots, \Lambda_n$. Each region is called a *stratum*, and they must completely cover the original domain:

$$\bigcup_{i=1}^{n} \Lambda_i = \Lambda.$$

Sampler 296

To draw samples from Λ, we will draw n_i samples from each Λ_i, according to densities p_i inside each stratum. A simple example is supersampling a pixel. With stratified sampling, the area around a pixel is divided into a $k \times k$ grid, and a sample is drawn from each grid cell. This is better than taking k^2 random samples, since the sample locations are less likely to clump together. Here we will show why this technique reduces variance.

Within a single stratum Λ_i, the Monte Carlo estimate is

$$F_i = \frac{1}{n_i} \sum_{j=1}^{n_i} \frac{f(X_{i,j})}{P_i(X_{i,j})},$$

where $X_{i,j}$ is the jth sample drawn from density p_i. The overall estimate is $F = \sum_{i=1}^{n} v_i F_i$, where v_i is the fractional volume of stratum i ($v_i \in (0, 1]$).

The true value of the integrand in stratum i is

$$\mu_i = E\left[f\left(X_{i,j}\right)\right] = \frac{1}{v_i} \int_{\Lambda_i} f(x)\, dx,$$

and the variance in this stratum is

$$\sigma_i^2 = \frac{1}{v_1} \int_{\Lambda_i} \left(f(x) - \mu_i\right)^2 dx.$$

Thus, with n_i samples in the stratum, the variance of the per-stratum estimator is σ_i^2 / n_i. This shows that the variance of the overall estimator is

$$V[F] = V\left[\sum v_i F_i\right]$$

$$= \sum V\left[v_i F_i\right]$$

$$= \sum v_i^2 V\left[F_i\right]$$

$$= \sum \frac{v_i^2 \sigma_i^2}{n_i}.$$

If we make the reasonable assumption that the number of samples n_i is proportional to the volume v_i, then we have $n_i = v_i N$, and the variance of the overall estimator is

$$V[F_N] = \frac{1}{N} \sum v_i \sigma_i^2.$$

To compare this result to the variance without stratification, we note that choosing an unstratified sample is equivalent to choosing a random stratum I according to the discrete probability distribution defined by the volumes v_i, and then choosing a random sample X in Λ_I. In this sense, X is chosen *conditionally* on I, so it can be shown using conditional probability that

$$V[F] = E_x V_i F + V_x E_i F$$

$$= \frac{1}{N} \left[\sum v_i \sigma_i^2 + \sum v_i \left(\mu_i - Q\right)\right],$$

where Q is the mean of f over the whole domain Λ. See Veach (1997) for a derivation of this result.

There are two things to notice about this expression. First, we know that the right-hand sum must be nonnegative, since variance is always nonnegative. Second, it demonstrates

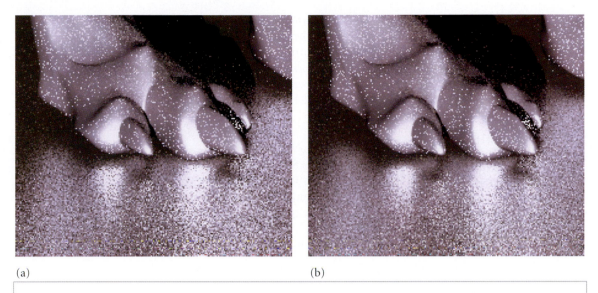

(a)   (b)

Figure 15.2: Variance is higher and the image noisier (a) when random sampling is used to compute the effect of glossy reflection than (b) when a stratified distribution of sample directions is used instead. (Compare the edges of the highlights on the ground, for example.)

that stratified sampling can never increase variance. In fact, stratification always reduces variance unless the right-hand sum is exactly zero. It can only be zero when the function f has the same mean over each stratum Λ_i. In fact, for stratified sampling to work best, we would like to maximize the right-hand sum, so it is best to make the strata have means that are as unequal as possible. This explains why *compact* strata are desirable if one does not know anything about the function f. If the strata are wide, they will contain more variation and will have μ_i closer to the true mean Q.

Figure 15.2 shows the effect of using stratified sampling versus a uniform random distribution for sampling ray directions for glossy reflection. There is a reasonable reduction in variance at essentially no cost in running time.

The main downside of stratified sampling is that it suffers from the same "curse of dimensionality" as standard numeric quadrature. Full stratification in D dimensions with S strata per dimension requires S^D samples, which quickly becomes prohibitive. Fortunately, it is often possible to stratify some of the dimensions independently and then randomly associate samples from different dimensions, as was done in Section 7.3. Choosing which dimensions are stratified should be done in a way that stratifies dimensions that tend to be most highly correlated in their effect on the value of the integrand (Owen 1998). For example, for the direct lighting example in Section 15.1.1, it is far more effective to stratify the (x, y) pixel positions and to stratify (θ, ϕ) ray direction while stratifying (x, θ) and (y, ϕ) would almost certainly be ineffective.

Another solution to the curse of dimensionality that has many of the same advantages of stratification is to use Latin hypercube sampling, which can generate any number of samples independent of the number of dimensions. Unfortunately, Latin hypercube sampling isn't as effective as stratified sampling at reducing variance, especially as the number of samples taken becomes large. Nevertheless, Latin hypercube sampling is provably no worse than uniform random sampling and is often much better.

15.2.2 QUASI MONTE CARLO

The low-discrepancy sampling techniques introduced in Section 7.4 are the foundation of a branch of Monte Carlo called *quasi Monte Carlo*. The key component of quasi–Monte Carlo techniques is that they replace the random numbers used in standard Monte Carlo with low-discrepancy point sets generated by carefully designed deterministic algorithms.

The advantage of this approach is that for many integration problems, quasi–Monte Carlo techniques have asymptotically faster rates of convergence than methods based on standard Monte Carlo. Many of the techniques used in regular Monte Carlo algorithms can be shown to work equally well with quasi-random sample points, including importance sampling. Some others (e.g., Russian roulette and rejection sampling) can not. While the asymptotic convergence rates are not generally applicable to the discontinuous integrands in graphics because the convergence rates depend on smoothness properties in the integrand, quasi Monte Carlo still performs slightly better than regular Monte Carlo for these integrals in practice. See Keller's technical report for discussion of these issues, practical implementation details, as well as many references to related literature (Keller 2001).

In pbrt, we have generally glossed over the differences between these two approaches and have localized them in the Samplers in Chapter 7. This introduces the possibility of subtle errors if a Sampler generates quasi-random sample points that an Integrator then improperly uses as part of an implementation of an algorithm that is not suitable for quasi Monte Carlo. As long as Integrators only use these sample points for importance sampling or other techniques that are applicable in both approaches, this isn't a problem.

15.2.3 WARPING SAMPLES AND DISTORTION

When applying stratified sampling or low-discrepancy sampling to problems like choosing points on light sources for integration for area lighting, pbrt generates a set of samples (ξ_1, ξ_2) over the domain $[0, 1]^2$ and then uses algorithms based on the transformation methods introduced in Sections 14.4 and 14.5 to map these samples to points on the light source. Implicit in this process is the expectation that the transformation to points on the light source will generally preserve the stratification properties of the samples from $[0, 1]^2$—in other words, nearby samples should map to nearby positions on the surface of the light, and faraway samples should map to far-apart positions on the light. If the mapping does not preserve this property, then the benefits of stratification are lost.

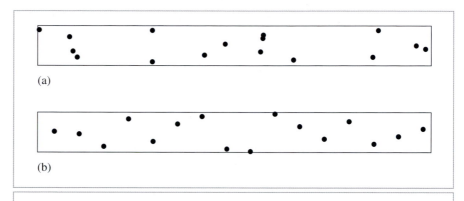

(a)

(b)

Figure 15.3: (a) Transforming a 4 × 4 stratified sampling pattern to points on a long and thin quadrilateral light source effectively gives less than 16 well-distributed samples; stratification in the vertical direction is not helpful. (b) Samples from a (0, 2)-sequence remain well-distributed even after this transformation.

For example, this explains why Shirley's square-to-circle mapping (Figure 14.10) is better than the straightforward mapping (Figure 14.9), since the straightforward mapping has less compact strata away from the center. It also explains why (0, 2)-sequences can be so much better than stratified patterns in practice: they are more robust with respect to preserving their good distribution properties after being transformed to other domains. For example, Figure 15.3 shows what happens when a set of 16 well-distributed sample points are transformed to be points on a skinny quadrilateral by scaling them to cover its surface; the (0, 2)-sequence remains well-distributed, but the stratified pattern fares much less well.

15.3 BIAS

Another approach to variance reduction is to introduce *bias* into the computation: sometimes knowingly computing an estimate that doesn't actually have an expected value equal to the desired quantity can nonetheless lead to lower variance. An estimator is *unbiased* if its expected value is equal to the correct answer. If not, the difference

$$\beta = E[F] - F$$

is the amount of bias.

Kalos and Whitlock (1986, pp. 36–37) give the following example of how bias can sometimes be desirable. Consider the problem of computing an estimate of the mean value of a set of random numbers X_i over the interval from zero to one. One could use the estimator

$$\frac{1}{N} \sum_{i=1}^{N} X_i,$$

or one could use the biased estimator

$$\frac{1}{2} \max(X_1, X_2, \ldots, X_N).$$

The first estimator is in fact unbiased, but has variance with order $O(1/N^{-1})$. The second estimator's expected value is

$$0.5 \frac{N}{N+1} \neq 0.5,$$

so it is biased, although its variance is $O(N^{-2})$, which is much better. For large values of N, the second estimator may be preferred.

The pixel reconstruction method described in Section 7.6 can also be thought of as a biased estimator. Considering it as a Monte Carlo estimation problem, we'd like to compute an estimate of

$$I(x, y) = \iint f(x - x', y - y')L(x', y') \, dx' \, dy',$$

where $I(x, y)$ is a final pixel value, $f(x, y)$ is the pixel filter function (which we assume here to be normalized to integrate to one), and $L(x, y)$ is the image radiance function.

Assuming we have chosen image plane samples uniformly, all samples have the same probability density, which we will denote by p_c. Thus, the unbiased Monte Carlo estimator of this equation is

$$I(x, y) \approx \frac{1}{N p_c} \sum_{i=1}^{N} f(x - x_i, y - y_i)L(x_i, y_i).$$

This gives a different result than the pixel filtering equation we used previously, Equation (7.3), which was

$$I(x, y) = \frac{\sum_i f(x - x_i, y - y_i)L(x_i, y_i)}{\sum_i f(x - x_i, y - y_i)}.$$

Yet the biased estimator is preferable in practice because it gives a result with less variance. For example, if all radiance values $L(x_i, y_i)$ have a value of one, the biased estimator will always reconstruct an image where all pixel values are exactly one—clearly a desirable property. However, the unbiased estimator will reconstruct pixel values that are not all one, since the sum

$$\sum_i f(x - x_i, y - y_i)$$

will generally not be equal to p_c and thus will have a different value due to variation in the filter function depending on the particular (x_i, y_i) sample positions used for the pixel. Thus, the variance due to this effect leads to an undesirable result in the final image. Even for more complex images, the variance that would be introduced by the unbiased estimator is a more objectionable artifact than the bias from Equation (7.3).

15.4 IMPORTANCE SAMPLING

Importance sampling is a variance reduction technique that exploits the fact that the Monte Carlo estimator

$$F_N = \frac{1}{N} \sum_{i=1}^{N} \frac{f(X_i)}{p(X_i)}$$

converges more quickly if the samples are taken from a distribution $p(x)$ that is similar to the function $f(x)$ in the integrand. The basic idea is that by concentrating work where the value of the integrand is relatively high, an accurate estimate is computed more efficiently (Figure 15.4).

For example, suppose we are evaluating the scattering equation, Equation (5.6). Consider what happens when this integral is estimated; if a direction is randomly sampled that is nearly perpendicular to the surface normal, the cosine term will be close to zero. All the expense of evaluating the BSDF and tracing a ray to find the incoming radiance at that sample location will be essentially wasted, as the contribution to the final result will be minuscule. As such, we would be better served if we sampled the sphere in a way that reduced the likelihood of choosing directions near the equator. More generally, if directions are sampled from distributions that match other factors of the integrand (the BSDF, the incoming illumination distribution, etc.), efficiency is similarly improved.

So long as the random variables are sampled from a probability distribution that is similar in shape to the integrand, variance is reduced. We will not provide a rigorous proof of this fact, but will instead present an informal and intuitive argument. Suppose we're trying to use Monte Carlo techniques to evaluate some integral $\int f(x) \, dx$. Since we have freedom in choosing a sampling distribution, consider the effect of using a distribution $p(x) \propto f(x)$, or $p(x) = c f(x)$. It is trivial to show that normalization forces

$$c = \frac{1}{\int f(x) \, dx}.$$

Finding such a PDF requires that we know the value of the integral, which is what we were trying to estimate in the first place. Nonetheless, for the purposes of this example, if we *could* sample from this distribution, each estimate would have the value

$$\frac{f(X_i)}{p(X_i)} = \frac{1}{c} = \int f(x) \, dx.$$

Since c is a constant, each estimate has the same value, and the variance is zero! Of course, this is ludicrous since we wouldn't bother using Monte Carlo if we could integrate f directly. However, if a density $p(x)$ can be found that is similar in shape to $f(x)$, variance decreases.

Importance sampling can actually increase variance if a poorly chosen distribution is used. To understand the effect of sampling from a PDF that is a poor match for the

(a)

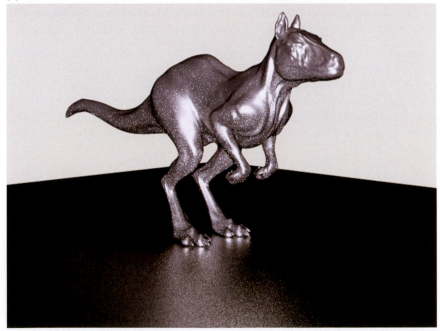

(b)

Figure 15.4: (a) Using a stratified uniform distribution of rays over the hemisphere gives an image with much more variance than (b) applying importance sampling and choosing stratified rays from a distribution based on the BRDF.

integrand, consider using the distribution

$$p(x) = \begin{cases} 99.01 & x \in [0, .01) \\ .01 & x \in [.01, 1) \end{cases}$$

to compute the estimate of $\int f(x)\, dx$ where

$$f(x) = \begin{cases} .01 & x \in [0, .01) \\ 1.01 & x \in [.01, 1). \end{cases}$$

By construction, the value of the integral is one, yet using $p(x)$ to draw samples to compute a Monte Carlo estimate will give a terrible result: almost all of the samples will be in the range $[0, .01)$, where the estimator has the value $f(x)/p(x) \approx 0.0001$. For any estimate where none of the samples ends up being outside of this range, the result will be very inaccurate, almost ten thousand times smaller than it should be. Even worse is the case where some samples do end up being taken in the range $[.01, 1)$. This will happen rarely, but when it does, we have the combination of a relatively high value of the integrand and a relatively low value of the PDF, $f(x)/p(x) = 101$. A large number of samples would be necessary to balance out these extremes to reduce variance enough to get a result close to the actual value, one.

Fortunately, it's not too hard to find good sampling distributions for importance sampling for many integration problems in graphics. For example, in many cases, the integrand is the product of more than one function. While it is frequently very difficult or impossible to construct a PDF that is similar to the product, even finding one that is similar to one of the multiplicands can be helpful. This will be a common strategy in the light transport algorithms in the upcoming two chapters, where we will be trying to estimate integrals that multiply lighting, visibility, scattering, and cosine terms.

In practice, importance sampling is one of the most frequently used variance reduction techniques, since it is easy to apply and is very effective when good sampling distributions are used. It is one of the variance reduction techniques of choice in pbrt, and therefore a variety of techniques for sampling from distributions from BSDFs, light sources, and functions related to participating media will be derived in this chapter.

15.4.1 MULTIPLE IMPORTANCE SAMPLING

Monte Carlo provides tools to estimate integrals of the form $\int f(x)\, dx$. However, we are frequently faced with integrals that are the product of two or more functions: $\int f(x)g(x)\, dx$. If we have an importance sampling strategy for $f(x)$ *and* a strategy for $g(x)$, which should we use? In general it is difficult to directly combine two such sampling strategies to compute a probability density function that is proportional to the product $f(x)g(x)$ that can itself be sampled easily. And as shown in the discussion of importance sampling, a bad choice of sampling distribution can be much worse than just using a uniform distribution.

For example, consider the problem of evaluating direct lighting integrals of the form

$$L_o(p, \omega_o) = \int_{s^2} f(p, \omega_o, \omega_i) L_d(p, \omega_i) |\cos \theta_i| d\omega_i.$$

If we were to perform importance sampling to estimate this integral according to distributions based on either L_d or f_r, one of these two will often perform poorly.

Consider a near-mirror BRDF illuminated by an area light where L_d's distribution is used to draw samples. Because the BRDF is almost a mirror, the value of the integrand will be close to zero at all ω_i directions except those around the mirror direction. This means that almost all of the directions sampled by L_d will have zero contribution, and variance will be quite high. Even worse, as the light source grows large and a larger set of directions is potentially sampled, the value of the PDF decreases, so for the rare directions where the BRDF is nonzero for the sampled direction, we will have a large integrand being divided by a small PDF value. While sampling from the BRDF's distribution would be a much better approach to this particular case, for diffuse or glossy BRDFs and small light sources, sampling from the BRDF's distribution can similarly lead to much higher variance than sampling from the light's distribution.

Unfortunately, the obvious solution of taking some samples from each distribution and averaging the two estimators is hardly any better. Because the variance is additive in this case, this approach doesn't help—once variance has crept into an estimator, we can't eliminate it by adding it to another estimator even if it itself has low variance.

Multiple importance sampling (MIS) addresses exactly these kinds of problems, with a simple and easy-to-implement technique. The basic idea is that when estimating an integral, we should draw samples from multiple sampling distributions, chosen in the hope that at least one of them will match the shape of the integrand reasonably well, even if we don't know which one this will be. MIS provides a method to weight the samples from each technique that can eliminate large variance spikes due to mismatches between the integrand's value and the sampling density. Specialized sampling routines that only account for unusual special cases are even encouraged, as they reduce variance when those cases occur, with relatively little cost in general. Figure 15.5 shows the reduction in variance from using MIS to compute reflection from direct illumination compared to the two approaches described previously.

If two sampling distributions p_f and p_g are used to estimate the value of $\int f(x)g(x) \, dx$, the new Monte Carlo estimator given by MIS is

$$\frac{1}{n_f + n_g} \left(\sum_{i=1}^{n_f} \frac{f(X_i)g(X_i)w_f(X_i)}{p_f(X_i)} + \sum_{j=1}^{n_g} \frac{f(Y_j)g(Y_j)w_g(Y_j)}{p_g(Y_j)} \right),$$

where n_f is the number of samples taken from the p_f distribution method, n_g is the number of samples taken from p_g, and w_f and w_g are special weighting functions chosen such that the expected value of this estimator is the value of the integral of $f(x)g(x)$.

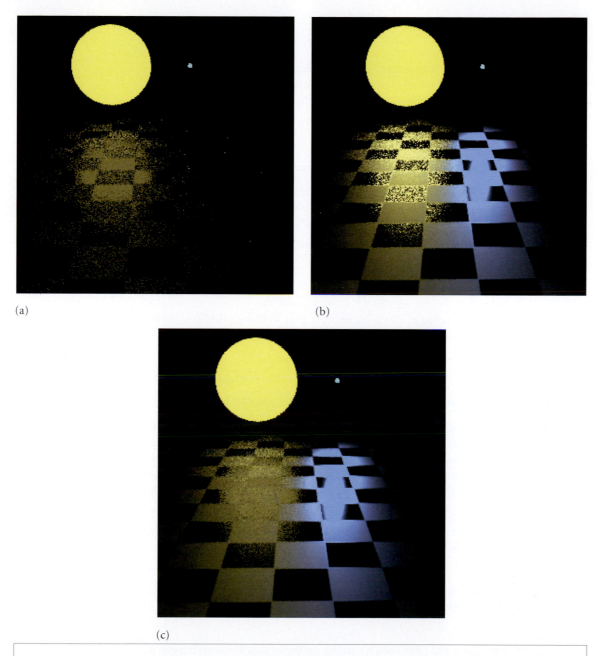

(a)

(b)

(c)

Figure 15.5: Multiple importance sampling is a very effective modification to standard importance sampling methods: (a) A scene with a glossy checkerboard where some checks are nearly perfectly specular and others are nearly diffuse, where direct lighting is computed by sampling the BSDF. This strategy works well for the nearly specular checks but not for the diffuse ones. (b) The result of sampling from the light sources' distributions instead. Again, some reflections look good while others suffer from very high variance. (c) The result of using multiple importance sampling with the power heuristic, giving the best overall result.

The weighting functions take into account *all* of the different ways that a sample X_i or Y_j could have been generated, rather than just the particular one that was actually used. A good choice for this weighting function is the *balance heuristic*:

$$w_s(x) = \frac{n_s p_s(x)}{\sum_i n_i p_i(x)}.$$

The balance heuristic is a provably good way to weight samples to reduce variance.

Consider the effect of this term for the case where a sample X has been drawn from the p_f distribution at a point where the value $p_f(X)$ is relatively low. Assuming that p_f is a good match for the shape of $f(x)$, then the value of $f(X)$ will also be relatively low. But suppose that $g(X)$ has a relatively high value. The standard importance sampling estimate

$$\frac{f(X)g(X)}{p_f(X)}$$

will have a very large value due to $p_f(X)$ being small, and we will have a similar variance problem as in the example in the previous section.

However, with the balance heuristic, the contribution of X will be

$$\frac{f(X)g(X)w_f(X)}{p_f(X)} = \frac{f(X)g(X)n_f p_f(X)}{p_f(X)(n_f p_f(X) + n_g p_g(X))} = \frac{f(X)g(X)n_f}{n_f p_f(X) + n_g p_g(X)}.$$

As long as p_g's distribution is a reasonable match for $g(x)$, then the denominator won't be too small thanks to the $n_g p_g(X)$ term, and the huge variance spike is eliminated, even though X was sampled from a distribution that was in fact a poor match for the integrand. The facts that another distribution will also be used to generate samples and that this new distribution will likely find a large value of the integrand at X are brought together in the weighting term to solve the variance problem.

Here we provide an implementation of the balance heuristic for the specific case of two distributions p_f and p_g. We will not need a more general multidistribution case in pbrt.

⟨*MC Inline Functions*⟩ ≡
```
inline float BalanceHeuristic(int nf, float fPdf, int ng, float gPdf) {
    return (nf * fPdf) / (nf * fPdf + ng * gPdf);
}
```

In practice, the *power heuristic* often reduces variance even further. For an exponent β, the power heuristic is

$$w_s(x) = \frac{(n_s p_s(x))^\beta}{\sum_i (n_i p_i(x))^\beta}.$$

Veach determined empirically that $\beta = 2$ is a good value. We have $\beta = 2$ hard-coded into the implementation here.

⟨*MC Inline Functions*⟩+≡
```
inline float PowerHeuristic(int nf, float fPdf, int ng, float gPdf) {
    float f = nf * fPdf, g = ng * gPdf;
    return (f*f) / (f*f + g*g);
}
```

15.5 SAMPLING REFLECTION FUNCTIONS

Because importance sampling is such an effective variance reduction technique, it's worth going through the effort to find sampling distributions that match functions in the common integrands in graphics. In this section, we will show the derivations and implementations for sampling strategies corresponding to distributions that are similar to many of the BSDF models used in pbrt.

The BxDF::Sample_f() method randomly chooses a direction according to a distribution that is similar to its corresponding scattering function. In Section 9.2, this method was used for finding reflected and transmitted rays from perfectly specular surfaces; later in this section, we will show how that sampling process is a special case of the sampling techniques of the previous chapter. BxDF::Sample_f() takes two sample values in the range $[0, 1]^2$ that are intended to be used by a transformation-based sampling algorithm. Since these are parameters to the method, the routine calling it can easily use stratified or low-discrepancy sampling techniques to generate them, thus ensuring well-distributed directions. If the algorithm used by BxDF::Sample_f() to generate directions doesn't need these sample values (e.g., if it uses rejection sampling), it can just ignore these arguments, although stratified sampling of a distribution that only roughly matches the BSDF is generally a more effective approach than rejection sampling from its distribution exactly.

This method returns the sampled direction in *wi and returns the value of $p(\omega_i)$ in *pdf. The value of the BSDF for the chosen direction is returned in a Spectrum on the stack. The PDF value returned should be measured with respect to solid angle on the hemisphere, and both the outgoing direction ω_o and the sampled incident direction ω_i should be in the standard reflection coordinate system (see "Geometric Setting," page 411).

The default implementation of this method samples the unit hemisphere with a cosine-weighted distribution. Samples from this distribution will give correct results for any BRDF that isn't described by a delta distribution, since there is some probability of sampling all directions where the BRDF's value is nonzero: $p(\omega) > 0$ for all ω. (BTDFs will thus always need to override this method.)

BxDF::Sample_f() 680
Spectrum 230

⟨*BxDF Method Definitions*⟩+≡

```
Spectrum BxDF::Sample_f(const Vector &wo, Vector *wi,
                        float u1, float u2, float *pdf) const {
    ⟨Cosine-sample the hemisphere, flipping the direction if necessary 680⟩
    *pdf = Pdf(wo, *wi);
    return f(wo, *wi);
}
```

There is a subtlety related to the orientation of the normal in the reflection coordinate system that must be accounted for here: the direction returned by Malley's method will always be in the hemisphere around $(0, 0, 1)$. If the ω_o direction is in the opposite hemisphere, then ω_i must be flipped to lie in the same hemisphere as ω_o. This issue is a direct consequence of the fact that pbrt does not flip the normal to be on the same side of the surface as the ω_o direction.

⟨*Cosine-sample the hemisphere, flipping the direction if necessary*⟩≡   **680, 687**

```
    *wi = CosineSampleHemisphere(u1, u2);
    if (wo.z < 0.) wi->z *= -1.f;
```

While `BxDF::Sample_f()` returns the value of the PDF for the direction it chose, the `BxDF::Pdf()` method returns the value of the PDF for an arbitrary given direction. This method is useful for multiple importance sampling, where it is necessary to be able to find the PDF for directions sampled from other distributions. It is crucial that any BxDF subclass that overrides the `BxDF::Sample_f()` method also override the `BxDF::Pdf()` method so that the two return consistent results.

To actually evaluate the PDF for the cosine-weighted sampling method (which we showed earlier was $p(\omega) = \cos\theta/\pi$), it is first necessary to check that ω_o and ω_i lie on the same side of the surface; if not, the sampling probability is zero. Otherwise, the method computes $|\mathbf{n} \cdot \omega_i|$, which simplifies to the absolute value of the z coordinate of ω_i, since $\mathbf{n} = (0, 0, 1)$. One potential pitfall with this method is that the order of the ω_o and ω_i arguments is significant. For the cosine-weighted distribution here, for example, $p(\omega_o) \neq p(\omega_i)$ in general. Code that calls this method must be careful to use the correct argument ordering.

⟨*BSDF Inline Functions*⟩+≡

```
    inline bool SameHemisphere(const Vector &w, const Vector &wp) {
        return w.z * wp.z > 0.f;
    }
```

⟨*BxDF Method Definitions*⟩+≡

```
    float BxDF::Pdf(const Vector &wo, const Vector &wi) const {
        return SameHemisphere(wo, wi) ? fabsf(wi.z) * INV_PI : 0.f;
    }
```

This sampling method is fine for Lambertian BRDFs, and it works well for the Oren-Nayar model as well, so we will not override it for those classes.

15.5.1 SAMPLING THE BLINN MICROFACET DISTRIBUTION

BRDFs based on microfacet distribution functions are more difficult to sample. For these models, the BRDF is a product of three terms, D, G, and F, which is then divided by two cosine terms; recall Equation (9.8). It is impractical to find the probability distribution that matches the complete model, so instead we will derive a method for drawing samples from the distribution described by the microfacet distribution function D alone. This is an effective strategy for importance sampling the complete model, since the D term accounts for most of its variation.

Therefore, all `MicrofacetDistribution` implementations must implement methods for sampling from their distribution and computing the value of their PDF, each with the same signature as the corresponding `BxDF` function, except that their `Sample_f()` methods return void.

⟨*MicrofacetDistribution Interface*⟩+≡   **443**
```
virtual void Sample_f(const Vector &wo, Vector *wi,
                      float u1, float u2, float *pdf) const = 0;
virtual float Pdf(const Vector &wo, const Vector &wi) const = 0;
```

The `Microfacet` `BxDF`, then, forwards the sampling and PDF requests to the distribution function that it holds a pointer to.

⟨*BxDF Method Definitions*⟩+≡
```
Spectrum Microfacet::Sample_f(const Vector &wo, Vector *wi,
                              float u1, float u2, float *pdf) const {
    distribution->Sample_f(wo, wi, u1, u2, pdf);
    if (!SameHemisphere(wo, *wi)) return Spectrum(0.f);
    return f(wo, *wi);
}
```

⟨*BxDF Method Definitions*⟩+≡
```
float Microfacet::Pdf(const Vector &wo, const Vector &wi) const {
    if (!SameHemisphere(wo, wi)) return 0.f;
    return distribution->Pdf(wo, wi);
}
```

Equivalently, Blinn's microfacet distribution function is $D(\cos \theta_h) = (n + 2)(\cos \theta_h)^n$, where $\cos \theta_h = |\mathbf{n} \cdot \omega_h|$. $D(\omega_h) = ((n + 2)/2\pi)(\cos \theta_h)^n$. To use this distribution to sample directions, we will first sample a half-angle direction ω_h according to this distribution, which we will then use to find ω_i by reflecting ω_o about the sampled direction ω_h.

⟨*BxDF Method Definitions*⟩+≡
```
void Blinn::Sample_f(const Vector &wo, Vector *wi,
                     float u1, float u2, float *pdf) const {
    ⟨Compute sampled half-angle vector ωh for Blinn distribution 682⟩
    ⟨Compute incident direction by reflecting about ωh 682⟩
    ⟨Compute PDF for ωi from Blinn distribution 684⟩
    *pdf = blinn_pdf;
}
```

Because the value of ϕ doesn't affect D, the PDF for this distribution, $p_h(\theta, \phi)$, is separable into $p_h(\theta)$ and $p_h(\phi)$. $p_h(\phi)$ is constant with a value of $1/(2\pi)$, and thus ϕ values can be sampled by

$$\phi = 2\pi\xi_2.$$

By construction, microfacet distribution functions are already normalized; they are distribution functions after all. Thus, the PDF is

$$p_h(\cos\theta_h) = (n+2)\cos^n\theta_h.$$

This is a power distribution in $\cos\theta_h$, and thus a uniform random variable can be used to generate a sample by

$$\cos\theta_h = \sqrt[n+1]{\xi_1}.$$

Because pbrt transforms the normal to (0, 0, 1) in the reflection coordinate system, we can almost use the computed direction from spherical coordinates directly. The only additional detail to handle is that if ω_o is in the opposite hemisphere than the normal, then the half-angle vector needs to be in that hemisphere.

⟨*Compute sampled half-angle vector ωh for Blinn distribution*⟩≡　　　　　　　682
```
float costheta = powf(u1, 1.f / (exponent+1));
float sintheta = sqrtf(max(0.f, 1.f - costheta*costheta));
float phi = u2 * 2.f * M_PI;
Vector H = SphericalDirection(sintheta, costheta, phi);
if Dot(wo, H) < 0.f) H = -H;
```

All that's left to do is to apply the formula for reflection of a vector about another vector (Figure 15.6):

⟨*Compute incident direction by reflecting about ωh*⟩≡　　　　682, 685
```
*wi = -wo + 2.f * Dot(wo, H) * H;
```

There's an important detail to take care of to compute the value of the PDF for the sampled direction, however. The microfacet distribution gives the distribution of normals around the *half-angle vector*, but the reflection integral is with respect to the *incoming vector*. These distributions are not the same, and we must convert the half-angle PDF to

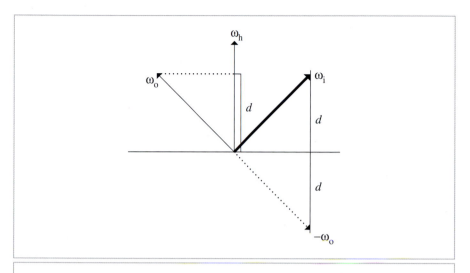

Figure 15.6: The reflection of a direction ω_o about the direction ω_h can be computed by first taking the offset $-\omega_o$ from the origin, giving the vector beneath the surface. We then add two times the distance d, which is given by the projection of ω_o onto ω_h (which is given by their dot product) to give the direction ω_i above the surface.

the incoming angle PDF. In other words, we must change from a density in terms of ω_h to one in terms of ω_i using the techniques developed in Section 14.4. Doing so requires applying the adjustment for a change of variables $d\omega_h/d\omega_i$.

A simple geometric construction gives the relationship between the two distributions. Consider the spherical coordinate system oriented about ω_o (Figure 15.7). The differential solid angles $d\omega_i$ and $d\omega_h$ are $\sin\theta_i\,d\theta_i d\phi_i$ and $\sin\theta_h\,d\theta_h d\phi_h$, respectively, and thus

$$\frac{d\omega_h}{d\omega_i} = \frac{\sin\theta_h\,d\theta_h d\phi_h}{\sin\theta_i\,d\theta_i d\phi_i}.$$

Because ω_i is computed by reflecting ω_o about ω_h, $\theta_i = 2\theta_h$, in conjunction with the fact that $\phi_i = \phi_h$, gives the desired conversion factor:

$$\frac{d\omega_h}{d\omega_i} = \frac{\sin\theta_h\,d\theta_h d\phi_h}{\sin 2\theta_h 2\,d\theta_h d\phi_h}$$

$$= \frac{\sin\theta_h}{4\cos\theta_h\sin\theta_h}$$

$$= \frac{1}{4\cos\theta_h}$$

$$= \frac{1}{4(\omega_i\cdot\omega_h)} = \frac{1}{4(\omega_o\cdot\omega_h)}.$$

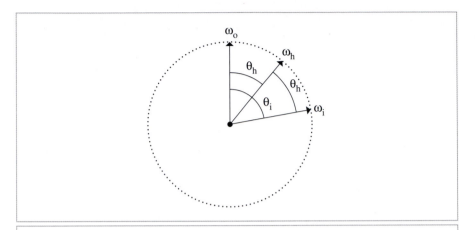

Figure 15.7: The adjustment for change of variable from sampling from the half-angle distribution to sampling from the incident direction distribution can be derived with an observation about the relative angles involved: $\theta_i = 2\theta_h$.

Therefore, the PDF after transformation is

$$p(\theta) = \frac{p_h(\theta)}{4(\omega_o \cdot \omega_h)}.$$

⟨*Compute PDF for ω_i from Blinn distribution*⟩ ≡   **682, 684**
```
float blinn_pdf = ((exponent + 1.f) * powf(costheta, exponent)) /
                  (2.f * M_PI * 4.f * Dot(wo, H));
```

Given all that work, the `Blinn::Pdf()` method's implementation is straightforward. We just reuse the previous code to compute the PDF.

⟨*BxDF Method Definitions*⟩+≡
```
float Blinn::Pdf(const Vector &wo, const Vector &wi) const {
    Vector H = Normalize(wo + wi);
    float costheta = fabsf(H.z);
    ⟨Compute PDF for ωi from Blinn distribution 684⟩
    return blinn_pdf;
}
```

15.5.2 SAMPLING THE ANISOTROPIC MICROFACET MODEL

Ashikhmin and Shirley (2000, 2002) give the equations for sampling from the distribution defined by their anisotropic BRDF model. We will restate their results here without deriving them; interested readers should consult the original publications for details and derivations.

⟨*BxDF Method Definitions*⟩+≡
```
void Anisotropic::Sample_f(const Vector &wo, Vector *wi,
                           float u1, float u2, float *pdf) const {
```
    ⟨*Sample from first quadrant and remap to hemisphere to sample ω_h* **685**⟩
    ⟨*Compute incident direction by reflecting about ω_h* **682**⟩
    ⟨*Compute PDF for ω_i from anisotropic distribution* **686**⟩
```
    *pdf = anisotropic_pdf;
}
```

The sampling method in the `Anisotropic::sampleFirstQuadrant()` function samples a direction in the first quadrant of the unit hemisphere—that is, with spherical angles in the range $(\theta, \phi) \in \left[0, \frac{\pi}{2}\right] \times \left[0, \frac{\pi}{2}\right]$. It's easier to derive a sampling method for this distribution by considering only that part of the problem and using it as a building block for sampling all directions. Here we use ξ_1 to select a quadrant, remap it to $[0, 1]$ to generate a sample from the first quadrant, and then map the sample to the desired quadrant. The remapping of ξ_1 and the sampled ϕ value are all done carefully to preserve stratification: given a small difference in ξ_1 that moves from one quadrant to another, the generated half-angle direction should change only slightly.

⟨*Sample from first quadrant and remap to hemisphere to sample ω_h*⟩≡   685
```
float phi, costheta;
if (u1 < .25f) {
    sampleFirstQuadrant(4.f * u1, u2, &phi, &costheta);
} else if (u1 < .5f) {
    u1 = 4.f * (.5f - u1);
    sampleFirstQuadrant(u1, u2, &phi, &costheta);
    phi = M_PI - phi;
} else if (u1 < .75f) {
    u1 = 4.f * (u1 - .5f);
    sampleFirstQuadrant(u1, u2, &phi, &costheta);
    phi += M_PI;
} else {
    u1 = 4.f * (1.f - u1);
    sampleFirstQuadrant(u1, u2, &phi, &costheta);
    phi = 2.f * M_PI - phi;
}
float sintheta = sqrtf(max(0.f, 1.f - costheta*costheta));
Vector H = SphericalDirection(sintheta, costheta, phi);
if Dot(wo, H) < 0.f) H = -H;
```

The half-angle vector in the first quadrant of the hemisphere can be sampled from this distribution function by

$$\phi = \arctan\left(\sqrt{\frac{e_x + 1}{e_y + 1}} \tan\left(\frac{\pi \xi_1}{2}\right)\right)$$

$$\cos\theta = \xi_2^{(e_x \cos^2 \phi + e_y \sin^2 \phi + 1)^{-1}}.$$

Note that if $e_x = e_y$ and the microfacet distribution is isotropic, this gives the same sampling technique as was used for the earlier Blinn distribution.

⟨*BxDF Method Definitions*⟩ +≡
```
void Anisotropic::sampleFirstQuadrant(float u1, float u2,
        float *phi, float *costheta) const {
    if (ex == ey)
        *phi = M_PI * u1 * 0.5f;
    else
        *phi = atanf(sqrtf((ex+1)*(ey+1)) * tanf(M_PI * u1 * 0.5f));
    float cosphi = cosf(*phi), sinphi = sinf(*phi);
    *costheta = powf(u2, 1.f/(ex * cosphi * cosphi +
                             ey * sinphi * sinphi + 1));
}
```

Finally, the PDF for a direction sampled with this method is straightforward. Again it is the value of the distribution itself, although as before we must be sure to account for the change of variables required to convert from the half-angle distribution to the incident angle distribution just as was done in `Blinn::Pdf()`.

⟨*BxDF Method Definitions*⟩ +≡
```
float Anisotropic::Pdf(const Vector &wo, const Vector &wi) const {
    Vector H = Normalize(wo + wi);
    ⟨Compute PDF for ωᵢ from anisotropic distribution 686⟩
    return anisotropic_pdf;
}
```

⟨*Compute PDF for ωᵢ from anisotropic distribution*⟩ ≡   **685, 686**
```
float anisotropic_pdf = D(H) / (2.f * M_PI * 4.f * Dot(wo, H));
```

15.5.3 SAMPLING FRESNELBLEND

The `FresnelBlend` class is a mixture of a diffuse and glossy term. A straightforward approach to sampling this BRDF is to sample from both a cosine-weighted distribution as well as the microfacet distribution. The implementation here chooses between the two with equal probability based on whether ξ_1 is less than or greater than 0.5. In both cases, it remaps ξ_1 to cover the range $[0, 1]$ after using it to make this decision. (Otherwise, values of ξ_1 used for the cosine-weighted sampling would always be less than 0.5, for example.) Using the sample ξ_1 for two purposes in this manner slightly reduces the quality of the stratification of the (ξ_1, ξ_2) values that are actually used for sampling directions, although this is less of a shortcoming than randomly selecting between the two sampling methods with a new unstratified random number.

⟨*BxDF Method Definitions*⟩+≡
```
Spectrum FresnelBlend::Sample_f(const Vector &wo, Vector *wi,
                                float u1, float u2, float *pdf) const {
    if (u1 < .5) {
        u1 = 2.f * u1;
        ⟨Cosine-sample the hemisphere, flipping the direction if necessary 680⟩
    }
    else {
        u1 = 2.f * (u1 - .5f);
        distribution->Sample_f(wo, wi, u1, u2, pdf);
        if (!SameHemisphere(wo, *wi)) return Spectrum(0.f);
    }
    *pdf = Pdf(wo, *wi);
    return f(wo, *wi);
}
```

The PDF for this sampling strategy is simple; it is just an average of the two PDFs used.

⟨*BxDF Method Definitions*⟩+≡
```
float FresnelBlend::Pdf(const Vector &wo, const Vector &wi) const {
    if (!SameHemisphere(wo, wi)) return 0.f;
    return .5f * (fabsf(wi.z) * INV_PI + distribution->Pdf(wo, wi));
}
```

15.5.4 SPECULAR REFLECTION AND TRANSMISSION

The Dirac delta distributions that were previously used to define the BRDF for specular reflection and the BTDF for specular transmission actually fit into this sampling framework well, as long as a few conventions are kept in mind when using their sampling and PDF functions.

Recall that the Dirac delta distribution is defined such that

$$\delta(x) = 0 \text{ for all } x \neq 0$$

and

$$\int_{-\infty}^{\infty} \delta(x)\, \mathrm{d}x = 1.$$

Thus, it is a probability density function, where the PDF has a value of zero for all $x \neq 0$. Generating a sample from such a distribution is trivial; there is only one possible value for it to take on. When thought of in this way, the implementations of `Sample_f()` for the `SpecularReflection` and `SpecularTransmission` BxDFs can be seen to fit naturally into the Monte Carlo sampling framework.

It is not as simple to determine which value should be returned for the value of the PDF. Strictly speaking, the delta distribution is not a true function, but must be defined as the limit of another function, for example, one describing a box of unit area whose width approaches zero; see Chapter 5 of Bracewell (2000) for further discussion and references. Thought of in this way, the value of $\delta(0)$ tends toward infinity. Certainly, returning an infinite or very large value for the PDF is not going to lead to correct results from the renderer.

Recall that BSDFs defined with delta components also have these delta components in their f_r functions, a detail that was glossed over when we returned values from their `Sample_f()` methods in Chapter 9. Thus, the Monte Carlo estimator for the scattering equation with such a BSDF is written

$$\frac{1}{N} \sum_i^N \frac{f_r(p, \omega_o, \omega_i) L_i(p, \omega_i) |\cos \theta_i|}{p(\omega_i)} = \frac{1}{N} \sum_i^N \frac{\rho_{hd}(\omega_o) \frac{\delta(\omega - \omega_i)}{|\cos \theta_i|} L_i(p, \omega_i) |\cos \theta_i|}{p(\omega_i)},$$

where $\rho_{hd}(\omega_o)$ is the hemispherical-directional reflectance and ω is the direction for perfect specular reflection or transmission.

Because the PDF $p(\omega_i)$ has a delta term as well, $p(\omega_i) = \delta(\omega - \omega_i)$, the two delta distributions cancel out, and the estimator is

$$\rho_{hd}(\omega_o) L_i(p, \omega),$$

exactly the quantity computed by the Whitted integrator, for example.

Therefore, the implementations here return a constant value of one for the PDF for specular reflection and transmission when sampled using `Sample_f()`, with the convention that for specular BxDFs there is an implied delta distribution in the PDF value that is expected to cancel out with the implied delta distribution in the value of the BSDF when the estimator is evaluated. The respective `Pdf()` methods therefore return zero for all directions, since there is zero probability that another sampling method will randomly find the direction from a delta distribution.

⟨*SpecularReflection Public Methods*⟩+≡   428
```
float Pdf(const Vector &wo, const Vector &wi) const {
    return 0.;
}
```

⟨*SpecularTransmission Public Methods*⟩+≡   **431**
```
float Pdf(const Vector &wo, const Vector &wi) const {
    return 0.;
}
```

There is a potential pitfall with this convention: when multiple importance sampling is used to compute weights, PDF values that include these implicit delta distributions can't be freely mixed with regular PDF values. This isn't a problem in practice, since there's no reason to apply MIS when there's a delta distribution in the integrand. The light transport routines in the next chapter have appropriate logic to be sure to avoid this error.

15.5.5 APPLICATION: ESTIMATING REFLECTANCE

As an example of their application, we will show how these BxDF sampling routines can be used in computing estimates of the reflectance integrals defined in Section 9.1.1 for arbitrary BRDFs. For example, recall that the hemispherical-directional reflectance is

$$\rho_{\text{hd}}(\omega) = \frac{1}{\pi} \int_{\mathcal{H}^2(\mathbf{n})} f_{\text{r}}(\omega, \omega') |\cos \theta'| d\omega'.$$

Routines that call this method can optionally specify the number of samples to be taken as well as sample locations to use. If these aren't provided, a Latin hypercube sampling pattern is generated in the method.

The generic BxDF::rho() method computes an estimate of this value for any BxDF, taking advantage of its sampling method to compute the method using importance sampling.

⟨*BxDF Method Definitions*⟩+≡
```
Spectrum BxDF::rho(const Vector &w, int nSamples,
                   float *samples) const {
    if (!samples) {
        samples = (float *)alloca(2 * nSamples * sizeof(float));
        LatinHypercube(samples, nSamples, 2);
    }
    Spectrum r = 0.;
    for (int i = 0; i < nSamples; ++i) {
        ⟨Estimate one term of ρhd 690⟩
    }
    return r / (M_PI * nSamples);
}
```

alloca() 838
BxDF 414
BxDF::rho() 416
LatinHypercube() 313
M_PI 855
Spectrum 230
Vector 47

Actually evaluating the estimator is straightforward; it's a matter of sampling the reflection function's distribution, finding its value, and dividing it by the value of the PDF. Each term of the estimator

$$\frac{1}{N} \sum_{i}^{N} \frac{f_{\text{r}}(\mathbf{p}, \omega, \omega_i) |\cos \theta_i|}{\pi p(\omega_i)}$$

is easily evaluated. The BxDF's Sample_f() method returns all of ω_i, $p(\omega_i)$, and the value of $f_r(p, \omega, \omega_i)$. The only tricky part is the cases where $p(\omega_i) = 0$, which must be detected here, since otherwise a division by zero would place an infinite value in r.

⟨*Estimate one term of* ρ_{hd}⟩ ≡   689
```
Vector wi;
float pdf = 0.f;
Spectrum f = Sample_f(w, &wi, samples[2*i], samples[2*i+1], &pdf);
if (pdf > 0.) r += f * fabsf(wi.z) / pdf;
```

The hemispherical-hemispherical reflectance can be estimated similarly. Given

$$\rho_{hh} = \frac{1}{\pi} \int_{\mathcal{H}^2(\mathbf{n})} \int_{\mathcal{H}^2(\mathbf{n})} f_r(p, \omega', \omega'') |\cos \theta' \cos \theta''| \, d\omega' d\omega'',$$

two vectors, ω' and ω'', must be sampled for each term of the estimate

$$\frac{1}{N} \sum_i^N \frac{f_r(p, \omega_i', \omega_i'') |\cos \theta_i' \cos \theta_i''|}{p(\omega_i') p(\omega_i'')}.$$

⟨*BxDF Method Definitions*⟩+≡
```
Spectrum BxDF::rho(int nSamples, float *samples) const {
    if (!samples) {
        samples = (float *)alloca(4 * nSamples * sizeof(float));
        LatinHypercube(samples, nSamples, 4);
    }
    Spectrum r = 0.;
    for (int i = 0; i < nSamples; ++i) {
        ⟨Estimate one term of ρhh 691⟩
    }
    return r / (M_PI*nSamples);
}
```

The implementation here samples the first direction ω' uniformly over the hemisphere. Given this, the second direction can be sampled with the BxDF::Sample_f() method.[1]

alloca() 838
BxDF 414
BxDF::Sample_f() 680
LatinHypercube() 313
M_PI 855
Spectrum 230
Vector 47

---

1   It could be argued that a shortcoming of the BxDF sampling interface is that there aren't entry points to sample from the four-dimensional distribution of $f_r(p, \omega, \omega')$. This is a reasonably esoteric case for the applications envisioned for pbrt, however.

⟨*Estimate one term of* ρ_{hh}⟩ ≡   **690**
```
Vector wo, wi;
wo = UniformSampleHemisphere(samples[4*i], samples[4*i+1]);
float pdf_o = INV_TWOPI, pdf_i = 0.f;
Spectrum f = Sample_f(wo, &wi, samples[4*i+2], samples[4*i+3], &pdf_i);
if (pdf_i > 0.)
    r += f * fabsf(wi.z * wo.z) / (pdf_o * pdf_i);
```

15.5.6 SAMPLING BSDFs

Given these methods to sample individual BxDFs, we can now define a sampling method for the BSDF class. This method is called by SurfaceIntegrators when they want to sample according to the BSDF's distribution; it calls the individual BxDF::Sample_f() methods to generate samples. The BSDF stores pointers to one or more individual BxDFs that can be sampled individually, but we would like to sample from the density that is the sum of their individual densities,

$$p(\omega) = \frac{1}{N} \sum_{i}^{N} p_i(\omega).$$

The BSDF::Sample_f() method takes three random variables to drive this process; one is used to select among the densities, and the other two are passed along to the particular sampling method chosen.

⟨*BSDF Method Definitions*⟩+≡
```
Spectrum BSDF::Sample_f(const Vector &woW, Vector *wiW,
                        float u1, float u2, float u3, float *pdf,
                        BxDFType flags, BxDFType *sampledType) const {
```
    ⟨*Choose which* BxDF *to sample* **692**⟩
    ⟨*Sample chosen* BxDF **692**⟩
    ⟨*Compute overall PDF with all matching* BxDFs **693**⟩
    ⟨*Compute value of BSDF for sampled direction* **693**⟩
```
}
```

This method first determines which BxDF's sampling method to use for this particular sample. This is complicated by the fact that the caller may pass in flags that the chosen BxDF must match (e.g., specifying that only diffuse components should be considered). Thus, only a subset of the sampling densities may actually be used here.

⟨*Choose which* BxDF *to sample*⟩ ≡   **691**
```
    int matchingComps = NumComponents(flags);
    if (matchingComps == 0) {
        *pdf = 0.f;
        return Spectrum(0.f);
    }
    int which = min(Floor2Int(u3 * matchingComps), matchingComps-1);
    BxDF *bxdf = NULL;
    int count = which;
    for (int i = 0; i < nBxDFs; ++i)
        if (bxdfs[i]->MatchesFlags(flags))
            if (count-- == 0) {
                bxdf = bxdfs[i];
                break;
            }
```

Once the appropriate BxDF is chosen, its BxDF::Sample_f() method is called. Recall that
these methods expect and return vectors in the BxDF's local coordinate system, so the
supplied vector must be transformed to the BxDF's coordinate system and the returned
vector must be transformed back into world coordinates.

⟨*Sample chosen* BxDF⟩ ≡   **691**
```
    Vector wi;
    Vector wo = WorldToLocal(woW);
    *pdf = 0.f;
    Spectrum f = bxdf->Sample_f(wo, &wi, u1, u2, pdf);
    if (*pdf == 0.f) return 0.f;
    if (sampledType) *sampledType = bxdf->type;
    *wiW = LocalToWorld(wi);
```

To compute the actual PDF for sampling the direction ω_i, we need the average of all
of the PDFs of the BxDFs that could have been used, given the BxDFType flags passed
in. Because *pdf already holds the PDF value for the distribution the sample was taken
from, we only need to add in the contributions of the others. It's important that this
step be skipped if the chosen BxDF is perfectly specular, since the PDF has an implicit
delta distribution in it. It would be incorrect to add the other PDF values to this one,
since it is a delta term represented with value one, rather than as an actual delta distribution.

⟨*Compute overall PDF with all matching* BxDF*s*⟩ ≡   **691**
```
if (!(bxdf->type & BSDF_SPECULAR) && matchingComps > 1) {
    for (int i = 0; i < nBxDFs; ++i) {
        if (bxdfs[i] != bxdf &&
            bxdfs[i]->MatchesFlags(flags))
            *pdf += bxdfs[i]->Pdf(wo, wi);
    }
}
if (matchingComps > 1) *pdf /= matchingComps;
```

Given the sampled direction, this method needs to compute the value of the BSDF for the pair of directions (ω_o, ω_i) accounting for all of the relevant components in the BSDF, unless the sampled direction was from a specular component, in which case the value returned from Sample_f() earlier is used. (If a specular component generated this direction, its BxDF::f() method will return black, even if we pass back the direction its sampling routine returned.)

While it could call the BSDF::f() method with the two directions to do this, the value can be more efficiently computed here, taking advantage of the fact that it already has the directions in both world space and the reflection coordinate system available here.

⟨*Compute value of BSDF for sampled direction*⟩ ≡   **691**
```
if (!(bxdf->type & BSDF_SPECULAR)) {
    f = 0.;
    if (Dot(*wiW, ng) * Dot(woW, ng) > 0) // ignore BTDFs
        flags = BxDFType(flags & ~BSDF_TRANSMISSION);
    else // ignore BRDFs
        flags = BxDFType(flags & ~BSDF_REFLECTION);
    for (int i = 0; i < nBxDFs; ++i)
        if (bxdfs[i]->MatchesFlags(flags))
            f += bxdfs[i]->f(wo, wi);
}
return f;
```

The BSDF::Pdf() method does a similar computation, looping over the BxDFs and calling their Pdf() methods to find the PDF for an arbitrary sampled direction:

⟨*BSDF Public Methods*⟩+≡   **462**
```
float Pdf(const Vector &wo, const Vector &wi,
        BxDFType flags = BSDF_ALL) const;
```

15.6 SAMPLING LIGHT SOURCES

Because direct illumination from light sources makes a key contribution to reflected light at a point, it is important to be able to take a point and sample those directions around it where the direct illumination may take on a nonzero value. Consider a diffuse surface illuminated by a small spherical area light source (Figure 15.8): sampling directions using the BSDF's sampling distribution is likely to be very inefficient because the light is only visible along a small cone of directions from the point. A much better approach is to instead use a sampling distribution that is based on the light source. For example, the sampling routine could choose from among only those directions where the sphere is potentially visible. The sphere may actually be occluded for some or all of these directions, though it is not generally feasible to account for this issue in defining the sampling densities.

This section will apply the now familiar Monte Carlo machinery to this problem. Furthermore, it will show the derivations and implementations of techniques for sampling rays leaving light sources. Being able to do this is crucial for bidirectional light transport algorithms like photon mapping and bidirectional path tracing.

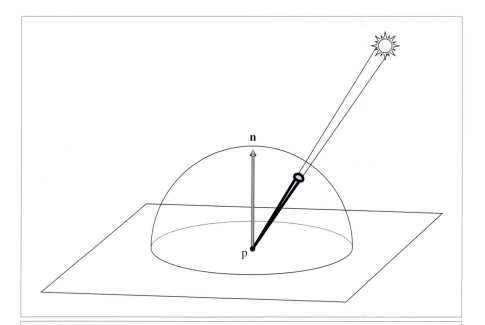

Figure 15.8: Another effective sampling strategy for choosing an incident direction from a point p for direct lighting computations is to use the light source to define a distribution of directions with respect to solid angle at the point. Here, a small spherical light source is illuminating the point. The cone of directions that the sphere subtends is a much better sampling distribution to use than a uniform distribution, for example.

15.6.1 BASIC INTERFACE

There are three main methods related to sampling that all Lights must implement. Two of them, Light::Sample_L() and Light::Pdf(), are comparable to the BxDF::Sample_f() and BxDF::Pdf() methods; they also generate samples from a distribution of directions over the sphere from a point in the scene. Here, the distribution doesn't try to match the BSDF at the point, but instead tries to match the incident radiance distribution from direct illumination from the light source.

The Light::Sample_L() method takes as parameters the point p being illuminated and two-dimensional samples u1 and u2. It returns the sampled incident direction wi from the point p, the value of the PDF for the direction, and a VisibilityTester that can be used to determine if the light source is actually visible from p. Code that calls this method should also check the value returned by the light's IsDeltaLight() method to see if the light source is described by a delta distribution (e.g., a point light). There are similar issues related to how to handle PDF values returned from lights described by delta distributions as there are for perfectly specular BSDFs (recall the discussion in Section 15.5.4).

⟨*Light Interface*⟩+≡   **598**
```
virtual Spectrum Sample_L(const Point &p, float u1,
                          float u2, Vector *wi, float *pdf,
                          VisibilityTester *vis) const = 0;
```

⟨*Light Interface*⟩+≡   **598**
```
virtual float Pdf(const Point &p, const Vector &wi) const = 0;
```

There are also variants of these routines that take the surface normal **n** at the point p; these can be used by lights that can sample with respect to projected solid angle, reducing variance a bit more by accounting for cosine falloff. The version of these routines without the surface normal is necessary for volume scattering where there is no surface normal, so the following versions can't be the only ones for this task. Their default implementations call the versions that don't take a surface normal, so that they only need to be implemented by the lights that do have a specialized sampling algorithm for this case.

⟨*Light Interface*⟩+≡   **598**
```
virtual Spectrum Sample_L(const Point &p, const Normal &n,
                          float u1, float u2, Vector *wi, float *pdf,
                          VisibilityTester *visibility) const {
    return Sample_L(p, u1, u2, wi, pdf, visibility);
}
```

⟨*Light Interface*⟩+≡   **598**
```
virtual float Pdf(const Point &p, const Normal &n,
                  const Vector &wi) const {
    return Pdf(p, wi);
}
```

The third light sampling method is quite different. It samples a ray from a distribution of rays *leaving* the light. This is necessary to support algorithms that consider paths of light from the light source, such as photon mapping (Section 16.5). The returned PDF value should be expressed in terms of the product of the density with respect to surface area on the light and the density with respect to solid angle. The implementations of this method in this section will sample the two distributions separately and compute their product, rather than trying to construct and sample a joint four-dimensional distribution.

⟨*Light Interface*⟩+≡   **598**

```
virtual Spectrum Sample_L(const Scene *scene, float u1,
                          float u2, float u3, float u4,
                          Ray *ray, float *pdf) const = 0;
```

15.6.2 LIGHTS WITH SINGULARITIES

Just as with perfect specular reflection and transmission, light sources that are defined in terms of delta functions fit naturally into this sampling framework, although they require care on the part of the routines that call their sampling methods, since there are implicit delta distributions in the radiance and PDF values that they return. For the most part, these delta distributions naturally cancel out when estimators are evaluated, although multiple importance sampling code must be aware of this case, just as was the case with BSDFs.

Point Lights

Point lights are described by a delta distribution such that they only illuminate a receiving point from a single direction. Thus, the sampling problem is trivial. The implementation of the `Sample_L()` method for incident lighting directions here calls back to the basic `Sample_L()` method implemented in Section 13.2. Indeed, for all of the lights described in terms of delta distributions, we will implement their `Sample_L()` methods in this way (and the rest of their implementations won't be included here).

⟨*PointLight Method Definitions*⟩+≡

```
Spectrum PointLight::Sample_L(const Point &p, float u1,
                             float u2, Vector *wi, float *pdf,
                             VisibilityTester *visibility) const {
    *pdf = 1.f;
    return Sample_L(p, wi, visibility);
}
```

Point 54
PointLight 602
PointLight::Sample_L() 603
Ray 59
Scene 23
Spectrum 230
Vector 47
VisibilityTester 600

Due to the delta distribution, the `PointLight::Pdf()` method returns zero. This reflects the fact that there is no chance for some other sampling process to randomly generate a point on an infinitesimal light source.

⟨*PointLight Method Definitions*⟩+≡
```
float PointLight::Pdf(const Point &, const Vector &) const {
    return 0.;
}
```

The sampling method for generating rays leaving point lights is also straightforward. The origin of the ray must be the light's position; this part of the density is described with a delta distribution. Directions are uniformly sampled over the sphere, and the overall sampling density is the product of these two densities. As usual, we'll ignore the delta distribution that should be included in the PDF because it is canceled out by a (missing) corresponding delta term in the radiance value in the Spectrum returned by the sampling routine.

⟨*PointLight Method Definitions*⟩+≡
```
Spectrum PointLight::Sample_L(const Scene *scene, float u1,
                              float u2, float u3, float u4,
                              Ray *ray, float *pdf) const {
    ray->o = lightPos;
    ray->d = UniformSampleSphere(u1, u2);
    *pdf = UniformSpherePdf();
    return Intensity;
}
```

Spotlights

The SpotLight class also passes requests from the first sampling routine on to the SpotLight::Sample_L() method from Section 13.2.1 and returns zero from its Pdf() method.

The method for sampling an outgoing ray with a reasonable distribution for the spotlight is more interesting. While it could just sample directions uniformly on the sphere as was done for the point light, this distribution is likely to be a bad match for the spotlight's actual distribution. For example, if the light has a very narrow beam angle, many samples will be taken in directions where the light doesn't cast any illumination. Instead, we will sample from a uniform distribution over the cone of directions in which the light casts illumination. Although the sampling distribution does not try to account for the falloff toward the edges of the beam, this isn't a problem in practice.

The PDF $p(\theta, \phi)$ is separable with $p(\phi) = 1/(2\pi)$, as usual. We just need to find the distribution for θ and to sample from this distribution. We would like to sample a direction θ uniformly over the cone of directions around a central direction up to the maximum angle of the beam, θ_{max}:

$$1 = c \int_0^{\theta_{max}} \sin \theta \, d\theta$$

$$= c(-\cos \theta_{max} + 1).$$

So $p(\theta) = 1/(1 - \cos \theta_{max})$.

⟨*MC Function Definitions*⟩+≡
```
COREDLL float UniformConePdf(float cosThetaMax) {
    return 1.f / (2.f * M_PI * (1.f - cosThetaMax));
}
```

The PDF can be integrated to find the CDF, and the sampling technique,

$$\cos\theta = (1 - \xi) + \xi\cos\theta_{\max},$$

follows. There are two `UniformSampleCone()` functions that implement this sampling technique: the first samples about the $(0, 0, 1)$ axis, and the second (not shown here) takes three basis vectors for the coordinate system to be used where samples taken are with respect to the *z* axis of the given coordinate system.

⟨*MC Function Definitions*⟩+≡
```
Vector UniformSampleCone(float u1, float u2, float costhetamax) {
    float costheta = Lerp(u1, costhetamax, 1.f);
    float sintheta = sqrtf(1.f - costheta*costheta);
    float phi = u2 * 2.f * M_PI;
    return Vector(cosf(phi) * sintheta,
                  sinf(phi) * sintheta,
                  costheta);
}
```

The ray sampling method for the light uses these utility routines to choose a random ray inside the spotlight's cone.

⟨*SpotLight Method Definitions*⟩+≡
```
Spectrum SpotLight::Sample_L(const Scene *scene, float u1,
                             float u2, float u3, float u4,
                             Ray *ray, float *pdf) const {
    ray->o = lightPos;
    Vector v = UniformSampleCone(u1, u2, cosTotalWidth);
    ray->d = LightToWorld(v);
    *pdf = UniformConePdf(cosTotalWidth);
    return Intensity * Falloff(ray->d);
}
```

Projection Lights and Goniophotometric Lights

The sampling routines for `ProjectionLights` and `GonioPhotometricLights` are essentially the same as `SpotLights` and `PointLights`, respectively. For sampling outgoing rays, `ProjectionLights` sample uniformly from the cone that encompasses their projected image map (hence the need to compute `ProjectionLight::cosTotalWidth` in the constructor), and those for `GonioPhotometricLights` sample uniformly over the unit sphere. An exercise at the end of this chapter discusses possible improvements to these sampling methods that better account for the directional variation of these lights.

Directional Lights

Sampling a directional light at a given point is trivial. As with `PointLight` and its relatives, the `Sample_L()` method calls back to the one from Chapter 13 and its PDF method returns zero.

Sampling a ray from the light's distribution of outgoing rays is a more interesting problem. The ray's direction is determined in advance by a delta distribution; it must be the same as the light's negated direction. For its origin, there are an infinite number of 3D points where it could start. How should we choose an appropriate one, and how do we compute its density?

The desired property is that rays intersect points in the scene that are illuminated by the distant light with uniform probability. One way to do this is to construct a disk that has the same radius as the scene's bounding sphere and has a normal that is oriented with the light's direction, and then choose a random point on this disk, using the `ConcentricSampleDisk()` function (Figure 15.9). Once this point has been chosen, if the point is displaced along the light's direction by the scene's bounding sphere radius and used as the origin of the light ray, the ray origin will be outside the bounding sphere of the scene, but will intersect it.

This is a valid sampling approach, since by construction it has nonzero probability of sampling all incident rays into the sphere due to the directional light. The area component of the sampling density is uniform and therefore equal to the reciprocal of the area of the disk that was sampled. The directional density is given by a delta distribution based on the light's direction; therefore, it isn't included in the returned PDF value.

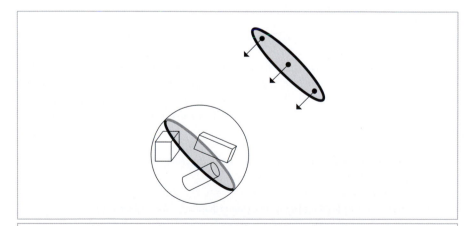

Figure 15.9: To sample an outgoing ray direction for a distant light source, the `DistantLight::Sample_L()` method finds the disk oriented in the light's direction that is large enough so that the entire scene can be intersected by rays leaving the disk in the light's direction. Ray origins are sampled uniformly by area on this disk, and ray directions are given directly by the light's direction.

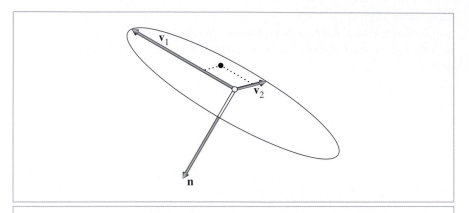

Figure 15.10: Given sample points (d_1, d_2) on the canonical unit disk, points on an arbitrarily oriented and sized disk with normal $\mathbf{n}$ can be found by computing an arbitrary coordinate system $(\mathbf{v}_1, \mathbf{v}_2, \mathbf{n})$, and then computing points on the disk with the offset $d_1\mathbf{v}_1 + d_2\mathbf{v}_2$ from the disk's center.

⟨*DistantLight Method Definitions*⟩+≡

```
Spectrum DistantLight::Sample_L(const Scene *scene,
        float u1, float u2, float u3, float u4,
        Ray *ray, float *pdf) const {
    ⟨Choose point on disk oriented toward infinite light direction 700⟩
    ⟨Set ray origin and direction for infinite light ray 701⟩
    *pdf = 1.f / (M_PI * worldRadius * worldRadius);
    return L;
}
```

Choosing the point on the oriented disk is a simple application of vector algebra. We construct a coordinate system with two vectors perpendicular to the disk's normal (the light's direction); see Figure 15.10. Given a random point on the canonical unit disk, computing the offsets from the disk's center with respect to its coordinate vectors gives the corresponding point.

⟨*Choose point on disk oriented toward infinite light direction*⟩≡   **700**

```
Point worldCenter;
float worldRadius;
scene->WorldBound().BoundingSphere(&worldCenter, &worldRadius);
Vector v1, v2;
CoordinateSystem(lightDir, &v1, &v2);
float d1, d2;
ConcentricSampleDisk(u1, u2, &d1, &d2);
Point Pdisk = worldCenter + worldRadius * (d1 * v1 + d2 * v2);
```

And finally, the point is offset along the light direction and the ray is initialized:

⟨*Set ray origin and direction for infinite light ray*⟩ ≡ **700**
```
ray->o = Pdisk + worldRadius * lightDir;
ray->d = -lightDir;
```

15.6.3 AREA LIGHTS

Recall that area lights are defined by attaching an emission profile to a shape. Therefore, in order to properly sample incident illumination directions from such a light source, it is useful to be able to generate samples over the surface of the shape. To make this possible, we will add sampling methods to the Shape class that sample random points on their surfaces.[2] The AreaLight sampling methods then call these methods.

Sampling Shapes

There are two shape sampling methods, both named Shape::Sample(). The first chooses points on the surface using some sampling distribution with respect to surface area on the shape and returns the position and surface normal of the point chosen. For example, this method is useful for sampling points on the surface of lights for algorithms like photon mapping.

⟨*Shape Interface*⟩+≡ **90**
```
virtual Point Sample(float u1, float u2, Normal *Ns) const {
    Severe("Unimplemented Shape::Sample method called");
    return Point();
}
```

The Shapes that implement this method will almost always sample uniformly by area on their surface. Therefore, we will provide a default implementation of the Shape::Pdf() method corresponding to this sampling method that returns the corresponding PDF: the reciprocal of the surface area.

⟨*Shape Interface*⟩+≡ **90**
```
virtual float Pdf(const Point &Pshape) const {
    return 1.f / Area();
}
```

The second shape sampling method also takes the point from which the surface of the shape is being integrated over. This method is particularly useful for lighting, since the caller can pass in the point to be lit and allow shape implementations to ensure that they only sample the portion of the shape that is potentially visible from that point.

---

2 Notice that the Shape::Sample() method is not a C++ "pure virtual" function. This is deliberate; not all shapes will implement a Sample() method. Some shapes are very difficult to sample (e.g., fractals), and it would be unreasonable to require those shapes to implement a Sample method just to be used as geometry in the system. Shapes like these should return false from their CanIntersect() method and should be able to refine themselves into shapes that do implement this method.

The default implementation ignores the additional point and calls the earlier sampling method.

⟨*Shape Interface*⟩+≡   90
```
virtual Point Sample(const Point &P, float u1, float u2,
                     Normal *Ns) const {
    return Sample(u1, u2, Ns);
}
```

There is an important difference between the two shape sampling methods: the first one generates points on the shape according to a probability density with respect to surface area on the shape, but the second one uses a density with respect to solid angle from the point p. This convention is necessary since the second method is used by the area light sampling routines to generate incident directions from the light at the point being illuminated by sampling a point on the light p′ and computing the direction p′ − p. Because the integrators in pbrt evaluate the direct lighting integral as an integral over directions from p, expressing these sampling densities with respect to solid angle at p is more convenient. The default implementation of the second Pdf() method therefore transforms the density from one defined over area to one defined over solid angle from p.

⟨*Shape Interface*⟩+≡   90
```
virtual float Pdf(const Point &p, const Vector &wi) const {
    ⟨Intersect sample ray with area light geometry 702⟩
    ⟨Convert light sample weight to solid angle measure 703⟩
    return pdf;
}
```

Given a point p and direction ω_i, the Pdf() method determines if the ray (p, ω_i) intersects the shape. If the ray doesn't intersect the shape at all, the probability that the shape would have chosen the direction ω_i is naturally zero, assuming it samples directions by first sampling points on its surface. If there is an intersection, the differential geometry for the corresponding sample point on the light will come in handy in the following. Note that this ray intersection test is only between the ray and the single shape that is the area light source. The rest of the scene geometry is ignored, and thus the intersection test is reasonably efficient.

⟨*Intersect sample ray with area light geometry*⟩≡   702
```
DifferentialGeometry dgLight;
Ray ray(p, wi);
float thit;
if (!Intersect(ray, &thit, &dgLight)) return 0.;
```

To compute the value of the PDF with respect to solid angle from p, this method starts by computing the PDF with respect to surface area. Conversion from a density with respect to area to a density with respect to solid angle requires multiplication by the factor

$$\frac{d\omega_i}{dA} = \frac{r^2}{\cos\theta_o},$$

where θ_o is the angle between the ray from the point on the light to the receiving point p and the light's surface normal, and r^2 is the distance between the point on the light and the point being shaded (recall Section 5.3).

⟨*Convert light sample weight to solid angle measure*⟩ ≡   702
```
float pdf = DistanceSquared(p, ray(thit)) /
                (AbsDot(dgLight.nn, -wi) * Area());
```

Area Light Sampling Methods

Given these sampling methods, the `AreaLight::Sample_L()` methods are quite straight-forward. Most of the hard work is done by the `Shapes`, and the `AreaLight` mostly just needs to compute emitted radiance values.

⟨*AreaLight Method Definitions*⟩+≡
```
Spectrum AreaLight::Sample_L(const Point &p, const Normal &n,
        float u1, float u2, Vector *wi, float *pdf,
        VisibilityTester *visibility) const {
    Normal ns;
    Point ps = shape->Sample(p, n, u1, u2, &ns);
    *wi = Normalize(ps - p);
    *pdf = shape->Pdf(p, *wi);
    visibility->SetSegment(p, ps);
    return L(p, ns, -*wi);
}
```

Because the variant of `Shape::Pdf()` called here returns a density with respect to solid angle, the value can be returned directly.

⟨*AreaLight Method Definitions*⟩+≡
```
float AreaLight::Pdf(const Point &p, const Normal &k,
                        const Vector &wi) const {
    return shape->Pdf(p, n, wi);
}
```

The `Light::Sample_L()` and `Light::Pdf()` interfaces for the case where a point but no normal has been provided, are similar to these and are omitted.

The method for sampling a ray leaving an area light is also easily implemented in terms of the shape sampling methods. The first variant of `Shape::Sample()` is used to find the ray origin, sampled from some density over the surface. Recall that the `AreaLight` emits uniform radiance in all directions, so a uniform distribution of directions is used for ray direction. Because radiance is only emitted from the side of the light the surface normal lies on, if the sampled direction is in the opposite hemisphere than the surface normal, it is flipped to lie in the same hemisphere so that samples aren't wasted in directions where there is no emission.

The PDF for sampling the ray is the product of the PDF for sampling its origin with respect to area on the surface with the PDF for sampling a uniform direction on the hemisphere, $1/(2\pi)$.

⟨*AreaLight Method Definitions*⟩+≡
```
Spectrum AreaLight::Sample_L(const Scene *scene, float u1,
                            float u2, float u3, float u4,
                            Ray *ray, float *pdf) const {
    Normal ns;
    ray->o = shape->Sample(u1, u2, &ns);
    ray->d = UniformSampleSphere(u3, u4);
    if (Dot(ray->d, ns) < 0.) ray->d *= -1;
    *pdf = shape->Pdf(ray->o) * INV_TWOPI;
    return L(ray->o, ns, ray->d);
}
```

Sampling Disks

The `Disk` sampling method uses the concentric disk sampling function to find a point on the unit disk and then scales and offsets this point to lie on the disk of a given radius and height. Note that this method does not account for partial disks due to `Disk::innerRadius` being nonzero or `Disk::phiMax` being less than 2π. Solutions to this bug are discussed in an exercise at the end of the chapter.

⟨*Disk Public Methods*⟩≡   113
```
Point Disk::Sample(float u1, float u2, Normal *Ns) const {
    Point p;
    ConcentricSampleDisk(u1, u2, &p.x, &p.y);
    p.x *= radius;
    p.y *= radius;
    p.z = height;
    *Ns = Normalize(ObjectToWorld(Normal(0,0,1)));
    if (reverseOrientation) *Ns *= -1.f;
    return ObjectToWorld(p);
}
```

Sampling Cylinders

Uniform sampling on cylinders is straightforward. The height and ϕ value are sampled uniformly. Intuitively, it can be understood that this works because a cylinder is just a rolled-up rectangle.

⟨*Cylinder Public Methods*⟩ ≡   **108**

```
Point Cylinder::Sample(float u1, float u2, Normal *Ns) const {
    float z = Lerp(u1, zmin, zmax);
    float t = u2 * phiMax;
    Point p = Point(radius * cosf(t), radius * sinf(t), z);
    *Ns = Normalize(ObjectToWorld(Normal(p.x, p.y, 0.)));
    if (reverseOrientation) *Ns *= -1.f;
    return ObjectToWorld(p);
}
```

Sampling Triangles

The UniformSampleTriangle() function, defined in the previous chapter, returns the barycentric coordinates for a uniformly sampled point on a triangle. The point on a particular triangle for those barycentrics is easily computed.

⟨*TriangleMesh Method Definitions*⟩+≡

```
Point Triangle::Sample(float u1, float u2, Normal *Ns) const {
    float b1, b2;
    UniformSampleTriangle(u1, u2, &b1, &b2);
    ⟨Get triangle vertices in p1, p2, and p3 125⟩
    Point p = b1 * p1 + b2 * p2 + (1.f - b1 - b2) * p3;
    Normal n = Normal(Cross(p2-p1, p3-p1));
    *Ns = Normalize(n);
    if (reverseOrientation) *Ns *= -1.f;
    return p;
}
```

Sampling Spheres

As with Disks, the sampling methods here do not handle partial Spheres; an exercise at the end of the chapter discusses this issue further. If the sampling method is not given an external point that's being lit, sampling a point on a sphere is extremely simple. It just uses the UniformSampleSphere() function to generate a point on the unit sphere and scales the point by the sphere's radius.

⟨*Sphere Public Methods*⟩ ≡   **96**

```
Point Sphere::Sample(float u1, float u2, Normal *ns) const {
    Point p = Point(0,0,0) + radius * UniformSampleSphere(u1, u2);
    *ns = Normalize(ObjectToWorld(Normal(p.x, p.y, p.z)));
    if (reverseOrientation) *ns *= -1.f;
    return ObjectToWorld(p);
}
```

If the sphere is given a point being illuminated, however, it can do better. While uniform sampling over its surface leads to a correct estimate, a better approach is not to sample points on the sphere that are definitely not visible to the point being shaded. The sampling routine will instead uniformly sample directions over the solid angle subtended by the sphere from the point being shaded. It generates directions inside this cone of directions by sampling an offset θ from the center vector ω_c, and then sampling a rotation angle ϕ around the vector.

As seen from the point being shaded p, the sphere subtends an angle of

$$\theta_{\max} = \arcsin\left(\frac{r}{|\mathrm{p} - \mathrm{p_c}|}\right) = \arccos\sqrt{1 - \left(\frac{r}{|\mathrm{p} - \mathrm{p_c}|}\right)^2}, \qquad [15.1]$$

where r is the radius of the sphere and $\mathrm{p_c}$ is its center (Figure 15.11). The implementation uniformly samples directions inside this cone and computes their intersection with the sphere to get the sample position on the light source.

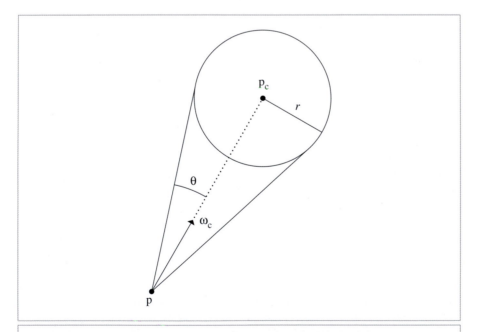

Figure 15.11: To sample points on a spherical light source, we can uniformly sample within the cone of directions around a central vector ω_c with an angular spread of up to θ. Trigonometry can be used to derive the value of $\sin\theta$, $r/|\mathrm{p_c} - \mathrm{p}|$.

⟨*Sphere Public Methods*⟩+≡   **96**
```
Point Sphere::Sample(const Point &p, float u1, float u2,
                     Normal *ns) const {
    ⟨Compute coordinate system for sphere sampling 707⟩
    ⟨Sample uniformly on sphere if p is inside it 707⟩
    ⟨Sample sphere uniformly inside subtended cone 708⟩
}
```

This process is most easily done if we first compute a coordinate system to use for sampling the sphere where the z axis is the vector between the sphere's center and the point being illuminated:

⟨*Compute coordinate system for sphere sampling*⟩≡   **707**
```
Point Pcenter = ObjectToWorld(Point(0,0,0));
Vector wc = Normalize(Pcenter - p);
Vector wcX, wcY;
CoordinateSystem(wc, &wcX, &wcY);
```

It is important to be careful about points that lie inside the sphere. If this happens, the entire sphere should be sampled, since the whole sphere is clearly visible from inside it. Notice that we use a small constant 1e-4 to do this check; this makes the code more robust when points are very close to the sphere.

⟨*Sample uniformly on sphere if* p *is inside it*⟩≡   **707**
```
if (DistanceSquared(p, Pcenter) - radius*radius < 1e-4f)
    return Sample(u1, u2, ns);
```

CoordinateSystem() 54
DistanceSquared() 56
Normal 56
Point 54
Shape::ObjectToWorld 90
Sphere 96
Sphere::Intersect() 99
Sphere::radius 98
Sphere::Sample() 707
UniformSampleCone() 698
Vector 47
Vector::Normalize() 53

If the point being lit is outside the sphere, this method computes the cosine of the subtended angle θ_{max} using Equation (15.1) and then generates a random ray inside the subtended cone using the UniformSampleCone() function and intersects it with the sphere to get the sample point on its surface.

Note that we must be careful about precision errors here. If the generated ray just grazes the edge of the sphere, the Sphere::Intersect() routine might unexpectedly return false. In this case, the implementation arbitrarily chooses to return the point on the line between the shading point and the sphere center. This very slightly biases the sampling routine, although the error introduced by this bias is extremely small.

⟨*Sample sphere uniformly inside subtended cone*⟩ ≡   **707**
```
    float cosThetaMax =
        sqrtf(max(0.f, 1.f - radius*radius / DistanceSquared(p, Pcenter)));
    DifferentialGeometry dgSphere;
    float thit;
    Point ps;
    Ray r(p, UniformSampleCone(u1, u2, cosThetaMax, wcX, wcY, wc));
    if (!Intersect(r, &thit, &dgSphere))
        ps = Pcenter - radius * wc;
    else
        ps = r(thit);
    *ns = Normal(Normalize(ps - Pcenter));
    if (reverseOrientation) *ns *= -1.f;
    return ps;
```

⟨*Sphere Public Methods*⟩+≡   **96**
```
    float Sphere::Pdf(const Point &p, const Vector &wi) const {
        Point Pcenter = ObjectToWorld(Point(0,0,0));
        ⟨Return uniform weight if point inside sphere 708⟩
        ⟨Compute general sphere weight 708⟩
    }
```

To compute the weight for this sampling routine, we must first differentiate between the two sampling strategies for points inside and outside the sphere. If the shading point was inside the sphere, a uniform sampling strategy was used. In this case, the implementation hands off the Pdf() call to the parent class, which takes care of the solid angle conversion.

⟨*Return uniform weight if point inside sphere*⟩ ≡   **708**
```
    if (DistanceSquared(p, Pcenter) - radius*radius < 1e-4f)
        return Shape::Pdf(p, wi);
```

In the general case, we simply recompute the angle subtended by the sphere and call UniformConePdf(). Note that no conversion of sampling measures is required here because UniformConePdf() already returns weights with respect to a solid angle measure.

⟨*Compute general sphere weight*⟩ ≡   **708**
```
    float cosThetaMax =
        sqrtf(max(0.f, 1.f - radius*radius / DistanceSquared(p, Pcenter)));
    return UniformConePdf(cosThetaMax);
```

15.6.4 SHAPESET SAMPLING

A ShapeSet is allocated in the AreaLight constructor if the given shape needs to be refined into multiple shapes in order to be sampled. The ShapeSet conforms to the Shape interface and thus must implement the sampling routine. In order to be able to uniformly sample the overall shape by surface area, we would like to sample individual shapes in the collection with probability based on the ratio of their area to the total area of all of the shapes. Therefore, the ShapeSet constructor computes a discrete CDF for sampling each shape according to individual probabilities given by this ratio. The sampling routine then randomly chooses among the shapes using this distribution. A linear search is used here, which is fine if the ShapeSet has a small number of shapes, although this is obviously not efficient for large collections.

⟨*ShapeSet Private Data*⟩+≡   **619**
```
float area;
vector<float> areaCDF;
```

⟨*ShapeSet Public Methods*⟩≡   **619**
```
Point Sample(float u1, float u2, Normal *Ns) const {
    float ls = RandomFloat();
    u_int sn;
    for (sn = 0; sn < shapes.size()-1; ++sn)
        if (ls < areaCDF[sn]) break;
    return shapes[sn]->Sample(u1, u2, Ns);
}
```

15.6.5 INFINITE AREA LIGHTS

The InfiniteAreaLight can be considered to be an infinitely large sphere that surrounds the entire scene, illuminating it from all directions. We will sample this light with a cosine-weighted distribution around the point being illuminated if a surface normal is available; otherwise a uniform spherical distribution is used. These sampling densities will give correct results, but don't account for the directionally varying radiance distribution that is present from the light's image map. An exercise at the end of this chapter discusses this issue further and explains how to develop improved sampling techniques that do account for this.

⟨*InfiniteAreaLight Method Definitions*⟩+≡
```
Spectrum InfiniteAreaLight::Sample_L(const Point &p,
        const Normal &n, float u1, float u2, Vector *wi,
        float *pdf, VisibilityTester *visibility) const {
    ⟨Sample cosine-weighted direction on unit sphere 710⟩
    ⟨Compute pdf for cosine-weighted infinite light direction 710⟩
    ⟨Transform direction to world space 710⟩
    visibility->SetRay(p, *wi);
    return Le(RayDifferential(p, *wi));
}
```

Choosing a cosine-weighted point on the unit sphere is almost exactly the same as Malley's method from Section 14.5.3, except that we randomly select either the upper or lower hemisphere on which to generate the sample.

⟨*Sample cosine-weighted direction on unit sphere*⟩ ≡   709
```
float x, y, z;
ConcentricSampleDisk(u1, u2, &x, &y);
z = sqrtf(max(0.f, 1.f - x*x - y*y));
if (RandomFloat() < .5) z *= -1;
*wi = Vector(x, y, z);
```

The PDF for the sample is computed similarly to `CosineHemispherePdf()`, except that it is necessary to take into account the solid angle subtended by the entire sphere:

⟨*Compute* pdf *for cosine-weighted infinite light direction*⟩ ≡   709
```
*pdf = fabsf(wi->z) * INV_TWOPI;
```

As with sampling BSDFs, after sampling a direction with respect to a standard coordinate system with the normal in the (0, 0, 1) direction, it is necessary to transform the chosen point to world coordinates. This can be done using an arbitrary coordinate system constructed around the supplied normal.

⟨*Transform direction to world space*⟩ ≡   709
```
Vector v1, v2;
CoordinateSystem(Normalize(Vector(n)), &v1, &v2);
*wi = Vector(v1.x * wi->x + v2.x * wi->y + n.x * wi->z,
             v1.y * wi->x + v2.y * wi->y + n.y * wi->z,
             v1.z * wi->x + v2.z * wi->y + n.z * wi->z);
```

The `Pdf()` method returns the same value as `InfiniteAreaLight::Sample_L()`, (i.e., the cosine-weighted PDF).

⟨*InfiniteAreaLight Method Definitions*⟩+≡
```
float InfiniteAreaLight::Pdf(const Point &, const Normal &n,
                             const Vector &wi) const {
    return AbsDot(n, wi) * INV_TWOPI;
}
```

If no shading normal is supplied (e.g., due to this sampling being done at a point in a participating medium), directions are sampled uniformly on the sphere. The straightforward method that does this and computes its density won't be included here.

Generating a random ray leaving an infinite light source is tricky because we need to ensure that the ray *directions* are themselves uniformly distributed through the scene. Li et al. (2003) show that uniformly distributed lines through the volume enclosed by a sphere can be generated by connecting two uniformly chosen points on the surface of the sphere. The implementation here finds the finite sphere that bounds the scene and samples rays in this manner to get a uniform distribution of random rays passing through it.

⟨*InfiniteAreaLight Method Definitions*⟩+≡
```
Spectrum InfiniteAreaLight::Sample_L(const Scene *scene,
        float u1, float u2, float u3, float u4,
        Ray *ray, float *pdf) const {
    ⟨Choose two points p1 and p2 on scene bounding sphere  711⟩
    ⟨Construct ray between p1 and p2  711⟩
    ⟨Compute InfiniteAreaLight ray weight  711⟩
    return Le(RayDifferential(ray->o, -ray->d));
}
```

Of course, the "sphere" for this light source is only an implicit one surrounding the scene. In order to use the sphere sampling routines, it is necessary to explicitly find the radius and center of the scene's bounding sphere and sample it.

⟨*Choose two points* p1 *and* p2 *on scene bounding sphere*⟩ ≡   711
```
Point worldCenter;
float worldRadius;
scene->WorldBound().BoundingSphere(&worldCenter, &worldRadius);
worldRadius *= 1.01f;
Point p1 = worldCenter + worldRadius * UniformSampleSphere(u1, u2);
Point p2 = worldCenter + worldRadius * UniformSampleSphere(u3, u4);
```

Once the two points p1 and p2 have been chosen on the scene's bounding sphere, it is a simple matter to construct a ray between these two points, using p1 as the origin and p2 − p1 as the direction vector.

⟨*Construct ray between* p1 *and* p2⟩ ≡   711
```
ray->o = p1;
ray->d = Normalize(p2-p1);
```

To compute the PDF for these rays, the area distribution of the first point is multiplied by the directional distribution of the second point. Fortunately, this is simple: p2 is uniformly distributed over the sphere, which means that the directions have a cosine distribution relative to the diameter of the sphere at p1.

⟨*Compute* InfiniteAreaLight *ray weight*⟩ ≡   711
```
Vector to_center = Normalize(worldCenter - p1);
float costheta = AbsDot(to_center, ray->d);
*pdf = costheta / (4.f * M_PI * worldRadius * worldRadius);
```

⋆ 15.7 VOLUME SCATTERING

The equation of transfer is the integral equation that describes the effect of participating media on the distribution of radiance in an environment. It is introduced in Section 17.1, and the VolumeIntegrators in Chapter 17 use Monte Carlo integration to compute estimates of (simplified) instances of this integral. The equation of transfer is an interesting example case for Monte Carlo integration since it can be an integral over an infinite range, of the general form

$$\int_0^{\infty} e^{-g(t)t} f(t) \, dt.$$

Thanks to the exponential term, this integral has a finite value in volume scattering applications.

It's not possible to sample from a uniform distribution to compute estimates of this integral. There's no valid uniform PDF over the range $[0, \infty)$, so some other sampling distribution must be used instead. In some cases, the function $g(t)$ is known to be constant, $g(t) = c$, and a natural sampling distribution is the one based on the exponential term; Section 14.3.3 derived the general sampling process. Thus, if samples T_i are drawn from this distribution, estimates of the integral can be computed by

$$\frac{1}{N} \sum_i^N \frac{e^{-cT_i} f(T_i)}{ce^{-cT_i}} = \frac{1}{N} \sum_i^N \frac{f(T_i)}{c}.$$

More generally, if the function $g(t)$ is not constant, a value of c for the exponential sampling distribution can be chosen arbitrarily (e.g., based on the average value of $g(t)$, if known), and the estimate is

$$\frac{1}{N} \sum_i^N \frac{e^{-g(T_i)T_i} f(T_i)}{ce^{-cT_i}}.$$

Because the extents of `VolumeRegion`s in pbrt must be finite, the system never actually needs to estimate values of these integrals over infinite ranges, and a uniform sampling distribution can still be used. However, as the extents of `VolumeRegion`s increase and as the $g(t)$ term becomes larger, uniform sampling is an increasingly inefficient sampling method as samples are taken in areas where the exponential function is very small, and the variance from not using importance sampling based on the exponential term increases. The implementations of `VolumeIntegrator`s in Chapter 17 use uniform sampling, although an exercise at the end of that chapter discusses how to address this issue.

15.7.1 SAMPLING PHASE FUNCTIONS

It is useful to be able to draw samples from the distribution described by the Henyey-Greenstein phase functions for a number of applications, including applying multiple importance sampling to computing direct lighting in participating media as well as for more general algorithms that compute the effect of multiple scattering in participating media. The PDF for this distribution is separable into θ and ϕ components, with $p(\phi) = 1/(2\pi)$ as usual. The distribution for θ can be shown to be

$$\cos\theta = -\frac{1}{|2g|}\left(1 + g^2 - \left(\frac{1-g^2}{1-g+2g\xi}\right)^2\right)$$

if $g \neq 0$; otherwise $\cos\theta = 1 - 2\xi$.

This sampling technique is implemented here in a routine that takes one vector ω, the asymmetry parameter g and two random numbers, samples from this distribution, and uses the result to construct the corresponding outgoing ray.

⟨*MC Function Definitions*⟩+≡
```
COREDLL Vector SampleHG(const Vector &w, float g,
                        float u1, float u2) {
    float costheta;
    if (fabsf(g) < 1e-3)
        costheta = 1.f - 2.f * u1;
    else
        costheta = -1.f / (2.f * g) *
                   (1.f + g*g - ((1.f-g*g) * (1.f-g+2.f*g*u1)));
    float sintheta = sqrtf(max(0.f, 1.f-costheta*costheta));
    float phi = 2.f * M_PI * u2;
    Vector v1, v2;
    CoordinateSystem(w, &v1, &v2);
    return SphericalDirection(sintheta, costheta, phi, v1, v2, w);
}
```

Because phase functions are already distribution functions, the probability density for sampling any particular direction is the value of the phase function for the given pair of directions.

⟨*MC Function Definitions*⟩+≡
```
COREDLL float HGPdf(const Vector &w, const Vector &wp, float g) {
    return PhaseHG(w, wp, g);
}
```

CoordinateSystem() 54
COREDLL 904
DensityRegion::Tau() 715
M_PI 855
PhaseHG() 580
SphericalDirection() 246
Vector 47

15.7.2 COMPUTING OPTICAL THICKNESS

Section 12.1.3 introduced optical thickness τ, which gives a measure of the total density of participating media that a ray passes through. For media with constant scattering properties, optical thickness can be computed in closed form using Beer's law, Equation (12.1), although that chapter deferred the implementation of a method to compute τ for general media until after Monte Carlo integration had been introduced. Here we will implement the general `DensityRegion::Tau()` method, which computes an estimate of the optical thickness for a ray passing through an arbitrary medium.

Recall the definition of τ:

$$\tau(p \to p') = \int_0^d \sigma_t(p + t\omega, -\omega)dt.$$

Its value can clearly be estimated by

$$\frac{1}{N} \sum_i^N \frac{\sigma_t(p + T_i\omega, -\omega)}{p(T_i)},$$

where random variables T_i are sampled from some distribution p. A natural approach is to apply stratified sampling, dividing the line from 0 to d into N strata and placing one random sample in each one. This could be done by transforming uniform random samples ξ by $d\xi$.

However, recall that Monte Carlo's strength compared to standard numerical integration algorithms comes when we are faced with high-dimensional integrals and discontinuous integrands. Here, we have a one-dimensional integral and an integrand that is often smoothly varying. (Consider the spatially varying density of a cloud or smoke, for example.) Pauly and collaborators have shown that a more efficient integration technique for this problem is to generate a stratified pattern where the sample inside each stratum has the same offset (Pauly 1999; Pauly, Kollig, and Keller 2000):

$$T_i = \frac{\xi + i}{N} d.$$

A single uniform random variable ξ is used for all of the samples. The result is that samples in adjacent strata can't be bunched together, as can happen with regular stratified sampling, thus leading to reduced variance.

The implementation of the `Tau()` method here applies this technique, which is why it only takes a single random variable u. It also indirectly chooses the number of samples N to take for the estimator: the caller passes in `stepSize`, the desired size of the strata, and the method finds the length of the given ray overlapping the medium, d, and then determines N by

$$N = \frac{d}{\text{stepSize}}.$$

N is not computed explicitly in the following implementation. Instead, the `while` loop will execute once for each sample taken until the point t0 exits the region.

Mathematically, the overall estimate should be divided by N and the (constant) PDF value. However, the PDF is just $1/d = 1/(t_1 - t_0)$, so the division by Nd can be simply computed by multiplying by the step size at the end.

⟨*Volume Scattering Definitions*⟩+≡

```
Spectrum DensityRegion::Tau(const Ray &r, float stepSize,
                            float u) const {
    float t0, t1;
    float length = r.d.Length();
    Ray rn(r.o, r.d / length, r.mint * length, r.maxt * length);
    if (!IntersectP(rn, &t0, &t1)) return 0.;
    Spectrum tau(0.);
    t0 += u * stepSize;
    while (t0 < t1) {
        tau += sigma_t(rn(t0), -rn.d);
        t0 += stepSize;
    }
    return tau * stepSize;
}
```

FURTHER READING

Cook and collaborators first introduced random sampling for integration in rendering (Cook, Porter, and Carpenter 1984; Cook 1986), and Kajiya (1986) developed the general-purpose path-tracing algorithm. Other important early work on Monte Carlo in rendering includes Shirley's Ph.D. thesis (Shirley 1990), and articles by Arvo and Kirk on Russian roulette, splitting, and sources of bias in rendering algorithms (Kirk and Arvo 1991). The multiple importance sampling technique was invented by Veach and Guibas (Veach and Guibas 1995; Veach 1997).

Shirley and collaborators have written a number of key papers about Monte Carlo in graphics, including a survey of techniques for light source sampling (Shirley, Wang, and Zimmerman 1996), and recipes for warping uniform random numbers to the surfaces of various shapes (Shirley 1992). Schlick (1994) has developed an efficient BSDF model that is also easy to sample from.

Mitchell (1996b) has written a paper that investigates the effects of stratification for integration problems in graphics (including the two-dimensional problem of pixel antialiasing). In particular, he investigated the connection between the complexity of the function being integrated and the effect of stratification. In general, the smoother or simpler the function, the more stratification helps: for pixels with smooth variation over their areas or with just a few edges passing through them, stratification helps substantially, but as the complexity in a pixel is increased, the gain from stratification is reduced. Nevertheless, because stratification never increases variance, there's no reason not to do it.

A number of papers have been written about techniques for sampling environment lights. See, for example, the papers by Agarwal et al. (2003), and Kollig and Keller (2003).

Keller and collaborators have written extensively on the application of quasi–Monte Carlo integration in graphics (Keller 1996, 2001; Friedel and Keller 2000; Kollig and Keller 2000, 2002).

EXERCISES

❶ 15.1   Fix the buggy `Sphere::Sample()` and `Disk::Sample()` methods, which currently don't properly account for partial spheres and disks when they sample points on the surface. Create a scene that demonstrates the error from the current implementations for which your solution solves the problem.

❷ 15.2   It is possible to derive a sampling method for cylinder area light sources that only chooses points over the visible area as seen from the receiving point, similar to the improved sphere sampling method in this chapter (Gardner et al. 1987; Zimmerman 1995). Learn more about these methods, or rederive them yourself, and write a new implementation of `Cylinder::Sample()` that implements such an algorithm. Verify that pbrt still generates correct images with your method and measure how much the improved version reduces variance for a fixed number of samples taken. How much does it improve efficiency? How do you explain any discrepancy between the amount of reduction in variance and the amount of improvement in efficiency?

❷ 15.3   Discuss situations where the current methods for sampling rays from `ProjectionLights` and `GonioPhotometricLights` may be extremely inefficient, choosing many rays in directions where the light source casts no illumination. Derive improved sampling techniques for each of them based on sampling from a distribution based on the distribution of luminance in their two-dimensional image maps and then properly accounting for the transformation from the 2D image map sampling distribution to the distribution of directions on the sphere. Implement this technique and verify that the system still computes the same images (modulo variance) with your new sampling techniques when using an `Integrator` that calls these methods. Determine how much efficiency is improved by using these sampling methods instead of the default ones.

❷ 15.4   In a similar manner, discribe situations where the current `InfiniteAreaLight` sampling methods may not be very effective. Implement an improved sampling method that chooses directions based on the 2D image map's distribution of luminance values. Determine how to sample from this 2D joint distribution and then work out the appropriate transformation from that distribution to the distribution of directions on the unit sphere. How much does this approach help?

❸ 15.5   Read the papers by Agarwal et al. (2003) or Kollig and Keller (2003) and implement one of these approaches to environment light sampling. Compare performance of the original approach implemented in pbrt, the approach in the previous assignment, and this new approach. Discuss the trade-offs among them.

❸ 15.6 One useful technique not discussed in this chapter is the idea of adaptive density distribution functions that dynamically change the sampling distribution as samples are taken and information is available about the integrand's actual distribution as a result of evaluating the values of these samples. Investigate data structures and algorithms that support such sampling approaches and choose a sampling problem in pbrt to apply them to. (A straightforward approach is to discretize the domain in some manner, record which parts have the highest function values, and then select among the discrete regions according to previous results, sampling uniformly in the chosen domain.) Measure how well this approach works for the problem you selected.

One possible pitfall with methods like this is that different parts of the sampling domain will be the most effective at different times in different parts of the scene. For example, trying to adaptively change the sampling density of points over the surface of an area light source has to contend with the fact that, at different parts of the scene, different parts of the area light may be visible and thus be the important areas. Develop techniques to reduce the impact of this problem in your implementation.

❸ 15.7 The standard Monte Carlo estimator can be written to work with a nonuniform distribution of random numbers used in a transformation method to generate samples X_i,

$$\sum_i^N \frac{f(X_i)}{p(X_i)p_r(\xi_i)},$$

just like the transformation from one sampling density to another. This leads to a useful importance sampling technique, where an algorithm can track which samples ξ_i were effective at finding large values of $f(x)$ and which weren't and then adjusts probabilities toward the effective ones (Booth 1986). A straightforward implementation would be to split $[0, 1]$ into bins of fixed width, track the average value of the integrand in each bin, and use this to change the distribution of ξ_i samples.

Implement this approach and apply it to an integration problem in pbrt. Note that this is somewhat tricky, since it becomes necessary to differentiate all the different places where random numbers are used; the parts of the $[0, 1]^2$ space that are effective for direct lighting will generally be different than the parts that are effective for BSDF sampling, for example. What assumptions about coherence does this approach depend on? This type of method has been applied in graphics by Kelemen et al. (2002) to Metropolis sampling algorithms, although we haven't previously seen it used in the form described in this exercise.

● 15.8   pbrt's routines for using complex shapes like triangle meshes or subdivision meshes as area light sources are written to handle simple shapes and do not scale well to shapes that refine into more than a few tens of triangles in the end. An effective way to sample shapes such as these is to uniformly sample rays from the cone that surrounds the shape as seen from the point being shaded, see if the ray hits the shape, and use the hit location, if any, as the sample point on the area source.

Implement such a sampling method for complex shapes. Test your implementation by using it to render images with simple shapes and then render images using complex shapes as area light sources.

CHAPTER SIXTEEN

16 LIGHT TRANSPORT I: SURFACE REFLECTION

This chapter brings together the ray-tracing algorithms, radiometric concepts, and Monte Carlo sampling algorithms of the previous chapters to implement a set of integrators that compute scattered radiance from surfaces in the scene. Integrators are so named because they are responsible for evaluating the integral equation that describes the equilibrium distribution of radiance in an environment (the light transport equation). As the Camera generates rays, they are passed to the SurfaceIntegrator and the VolumeIntegrator that the user selected; together these two classes are responsible for doing appropriate shading and lighting computations to compute the radiance along the ray, accounting for light reflected from the first surface visible along the ray as well as light attenuated and scattered by participating media along the ray. Surface integrators are covered in this chapter, and volume integrators are the topic of Chapter 17.

Because the light transport equation can be solved in closed form only for trivial scenes, it's necessary to apply a numerical integration technique to approximate its solution. How best to do so has been an active area of research in rendering, and many solution methods have been proposed. In this chapter, we will present implementations of a number of different integrators based on Monte Carlo integration that represent a selection of representative approaches to the problem. Due to basic decisions made in pbrt's design, this chapter does not include methods based on finite-element algorithms (e.g., radiosity), which is the other major approach to solving the light transport equation. See the "Further Reading" section for more information about this method.

Camera 256
SurfaceIntegrator 723
VolumeIntegrator 806

The basic integrator interfaces are defined in core/transport.h, ⓒⒹ and some utility functions used by integrators are in core/transport.cpp. ⓒⒹ The implementations of the various integrators are in the integrators/ⓒⒹ directory.

Both surface and volume integrators inherit from the Integrator abstract base class, which defines the common interface that both of them must implement:

⟨*Integrator Declarations*⟩ ≡
```
class COREDLL Integrator {
public:
    ⟨Integrator Interface 722⟩
};
```

The key method that all integrators must implement is Integrator::Li(), which returns the incident radiance at a point along a given direction, represented by the given ray. The parameters are the following:

- scene: A pointer to the Scene being rendered. The integrator will query the scene for information about the lights and geometry, and so on.
- ray: The ray along which the incident radiance should be evaluated.
- sample: A pointer to a Sample generated by the Sampler for this ray. Some integrators will use this information for Monte Carlo sampling.
- alpha: The opacity of the surface that was hit should be set in this output variable. It should be zero if no surface was hit.

The method returns a Spectrum that holds the radiance along the ray:

⟨*Integrator Interface*⟩ ≡   722
```
    virtual Spectrum Li(const Scene *scene, const RayDifferential &ray,
                        const Sample *sample, float *alpha) const = 0;
```

Optionally, the integrator may implement the Preprocess() method. It is called after the Scene has been fully initialized and gives the integrator a chance to do scene-dependent computation, such as allocating additional data structures that are dependent on the number of lights in the scene, or precomputing a rough representation of the distribution of radiance in the scene. Integrators that don't need to do anything along these lines can leave this method unimplemented.

⟨*Integrator Interface*⟩+≡   722
```
    virtual void Preprocess(const Scene *scene) {
    }
```

If the integrator would like the Sampler to generate sample patterns in the Sample for it to use, it should override the Integrator::RequestSamples() method and call back to the Sample::Add1D() and Sample::Add2D() methods, as described in Section 7.2.1.

⟨*Integrator Interface*⟩+≡   **722**
```
virtual void RequestSamples(Sample *sample, const Scene *scene) {
}
```

The `SurfaceIntegrator` base class doesn't add any new methods beyond those required by the `Integrator`:

⟨*Integrator Declarations*⟩+≡
```
class SurfaceIntegrator : public Integrator {
};
```

16.1 DIRECT LIGHTING

Before we introduce the light transport equation in its full generality, we will implement an integrator that only accounts for direct lighting—light that has traveled directly from a light source to the point being shaded—and ignores indirect illumination from objects that are not themselves emissive. Starting out with this integrator allows us to focus on some of the key details of direct lighting without worrying about the full light transport equation. Furthermore, some of the routines developed here will be used again in subsequent integrators that solve the complete light transport equation.

The implementation here provides two different strategies for computing direct lighting. Each method computes an unbiased estimate of exitant radiance at a point in a given direction. An enumerant records which approach has been selected. The first strategy loops over all of the lights and takes a number of samples based on `Light::nSamples` from each of them, summing the result. The second takes a single sample from just one of the lights, chosen at random.

Depending on the scene being rendered, either of these approaches may be more appropriate. For example, if many image samples are being taken for each pixel (e.g., due to depth of field), a single light sample may be more appropriate, since in the aggregate they will sample the direct lighting enough to give a high-quality image. Alternatively, if few image samples are being taken, sampling all lights may be preferable.

⟨*DirectLighting Declarations*⟩≡
```
enum LightStrategy { SAMPLE_ALL_UNIFORM, SAMPLE_ONE_UNIFORM, };
```

⟨*DirectLighting Declarations*⟩+≡
```
class DirectLighting : public SurfaceIntegrator {
public:
    ⟨DirectLighting Public Methods 724⟩
private:
    ⟨DirectLighting Private Data 724⟩
};
```

The implementation of the constructor isn't included here. It initializes the lighting strategy with a value passed in.

⟨*DirectLighting Private Data*⟩ ≡   **723**
```
   LightStrategy strategy;
```

The number and types of samples needed by this integrator depend on the sampling strategy used:

⟨*DirectLighting Public Methods*⟩ ≡   **723**
```
   void RequestSamples(Sample *sample, const Scene *scene) {
       if (strategy == SAMPLE_ALL_UNIFORM) {
           ⟨Allocate and request samples for sampling all lights 725⟩
       }
       else {
           ⟨Allocate and request samples for sampling one light 725⟩
       }
   }
```

The member variables for direct lighting sampling are declared with a level of indirection in a separate fragment, so that other integrators that use the direct lighting functions defined here can easily incorporate the appropriate member variables.

⟨*DirectLighting Private Data*⟩+≡   **723**
```
   ⟨Declare sample parameters for light source sampling 724⟩
```

⟨*Declare sample parameters for light source sampling*⟩ ≡   **724, 758, 775**
```
   int *lightSampleOffset, lightNumOffset;
   int *bsdfSampleOffset, *bsdfComponentOffset;
```

If all of the lights are being sampled, the integrator needs nLights individual sampling patterns from the Sampler, each one sized according to the number of samples in that light's nSamples member variable. Note that the integrator uses that value as a starting point. The Sampler::RoundSize() method is given an opportunity to change that value to a more appropriate one based on its particular sample generation technique.

One two-dimensional pattern is needed to select points on light sources and another to select BSDF directions; both sampling approaches are combined with multiple importance sampling. Furthermore, a one-dimensional pattern is used to select which BSDF component to sample in the BSDF::Sample_f() method.

BSDF::Sample_f() 691
DirectLighting::
   SAMPLE_ALL_UNIFORM 723
DirectLighting::strategy 724
Sample 299
Sampler 296
Sampler::RoundSize() 301
Scene 23

⟨*Allocate and request samples for sampling all lights*⟩ ≡   724, 758
```
    u_int nLights = scene->lights.size();
    lightSampleOffset = new int[nLights];
    bsdfSampleOffset = new int[nLights];
    bsdfComponentOffset = new int[nLights];
    for (u_int i = 0; i < nLights; ++i) {
        const Light *light = scene->lights[i];
        int lightSamples = scene->sampler->RoundSize(light->nSamples);
        lightSampleOffset[i] = sample->Add2D(lightSamples);
        bsdfSampleOffset[i] = sample->Add2D(lightSamples);
        bsdfComponentOffset[i] = sample->Add1D(lightSamples);
    }
    lightNumOffset = -1;
```

Things are much easier if only a single sample needs to be taken from a single light. Other than the immediate differences from this change, the only other difference is that an additional 1D sample is needed to choose which light to sample.

⟨*Allocate and request samples for sampling one light*⟩ ≡   724
```
    lightSampleOffset = new int[1];
    lightSampleOffset[0] = sample->Add2D(1);
    lightNumOffset = sample->Add1D(1);
    bsdfSampleOffset = new int[1];
    bsdfSampleOffset[0] = sample->Add2D(1);
    bsdfComponentOffset = new int[1];
    bsdfComponentOffset[0] = sample->Add2D(1);
```

The form of the DirectLighting::Li() method is similar to WhittedIntegrator::Li(). The Scene::Intersect() method is called to find the first visible surface along the ray, the BSDF at that point is computed, and so on. We won't include the full implementation of DirectLighting::Li() here in order to focus on its key fragment, ⟨*Compute direct lighting at hit point*⟩, which estimates the value of the integral that gives the reflected radiance.

The scattering equation from Section 5.4 says that exitant radiance $L_o(p, \omega_o)$ from a point p on a surface in direction ω_o is the sum of emitted radiance from the surface at the point plus the integral of incoming radiance over the sphere times the BSDF for each direction and a cosine term. For the DirectLighting integrator, we are only interested in incident radiance directly from light sources, which we denote by $L_d(p, \omega)$:

$$L_o(p, \omega_o) = L_e(p, \omega_o) + \int_{\mathbb{S}^2} f(p, \omega_o, \omega_i) L_d(p, \omega_i) |\cos \theta_i| d\omega_i. \qquad [16.1]$$

The value of $L_e(p, \omega_o)$ is easily found by calling the `Intersection::Le()` method at the intersection point. To estimate the integral over the sphere, we will apply Monte Carlo integration.

⟨*Compute direct lighting for* `DirectLighting` *integrator*⟩ ≡
```
if (scene->lights.size() > 0) {
    ⟨Apply direct lighting strategy⟩
}
```

The fragment ⟨*Apply direct lighting strategy*⟩ is also not included here. It just calls one of the functions that implement the direct lighting approaches—`UniformSampleAllLights()` or `UniformSampleOneLight()`—depending on the value of the `strategy` member variable.

To understand the approaches implemented by the different strategies, first consider the part of the direct lighting equation that we're concerned with here:

$$\int_{\mathcal{S}^2} f(p, \omega_o, \omega_i) L_d(p, \omega_i) |\cos \theta_i| d\omega_i.$$

This can be broken into a sum over the lights in the scene

$$\sum_{j=1}^{\text{lights}} \int_{\mathcal{S}^2} f(p, \omega_o, \omega_i) L_{d(j)}(p, \omega_i) |\cos \theta_i| d\omega_i,$$

where $L_{d(j)}$ denotes incident radiance from the jth light and

$$L_d(p, \omega_i) = \sum_j L_{d(j)}(p, \omega_i).$$

One valid approach is to estimate each term of this sum individually, adding the results together. This is the most basic direct lighting strategy and is implemented in `UniformSampleAllLights()`, which we have implemented as a global function rather than a `DirectLighting` method so that other integrators can use it as well. The `EstimateDirect()` function, which it uses to compute a Monte Carlo estimate of the effect of one sample on one light, will be defined after we have described the other direct lighting strategy.

Note that the number of samples for each light is *not* taken from its `nSamples` member variable but instead from the number of samples available in the `Sample` (the value of which, in turn, was returned by the earlier `Sampler::RoundSize()` call).

⟨*Integrator Utility Functions*⟩ ≡
```
COREDLL Spectrum UniformSampleAllLights(const Scene *scene,
        const Point &p, const Normal &n, const Vector &wo,
        BSDF *bsdf, const Sample *sample,
        int *lightSampleOffset, int *bsdfSampleOffset,
        int *bsdfComponentOffset) {
    Spectrum L(0.);
    for (u_int i = 0; i < scene->lights.size(); ++i) {
        Light *light = scene->lights[i];
        int nSamples = (sample && lightSampleOffset) ?
                            sample->n2D[lightSampleOffset[i]] : 1;
        ⟨Estimate direct lighting from light samples 727⟩
    }
    return L;
}
```

For each light sample the `EstimateDirect()` function computes the value of the Monte Carlo estimator for its contribution. All that has to be done here is to average the values of the estimates.

⟨*Estimate direct lighting from* light *samples*⟩ ≡   **727**
```
    Spectrum Ld(0.);
    for (int j = 0; j < nSamples; ++j)
        Ld += EstimateDirect(scene, light, p, n, wo, bsdf,
            sample, lightSampleOffset[i], bsdfSampleOffset[i],
            bsdfComponentOffset[i], j);
    L += Ld / nSamples;
```

In a scene with a large number of lights, it may not be desirable to always compute direct lighting from all of the lights at every point that is shaded. Monte Carlo gives a way to do this that still computes the correct result on average. Consider as an example computing the expected value of the sum of two functions $E[f(x) + g(x)]$. If we randomly evaluate just one of $f(x)$ or $g(x)$ and multiply the result by two, then the expected value of the result will still be $f(x) + g(x)$. In fact, this generalizes to sums of N terms. This is a straightforward application of conditional probability; see Ross (2002, p. 102) for a proof. Here we estimate direct lighting for only one randomly chosen light and multiply the result by the number of lights to compensate.

⟨*Integrator Utility Functions*⟩+≡
```
    COREDLL Spectrum UniformSampleOneLight(const Scene *scene,
            const Point &p, const Normal &n,
            const Vector &wo, BSDF *bsdf, const Sample *sample,
            int lightSampleOffset, int lightNumOffset,
            int bsdfSampleOffset, int bsdfComponentOffset) {
        ⟨Randomly choose a single light to sample, light 728⟩
        return (float)nLights *
            EstimateDirect(scene, light, p, n, wo, bsdf, sample,
                        lightSampleOffset, bsdfSampleOffset,
                        bsdfComponentOffset, 0);
    }
```

Which of the nLights to sample illumination from is determined using the random sample available in the 1D integrator sample lightNumOffset, if available. Although this is never the case for the DirectLighting integrator, sometimes other integrators will call this function without such a sample available. In that case, they pass −1 for the sample offset and a uniform random number is used here instead.

⟨*Randomly choose a single light to sample,* light⟩ ≡   **728**
```
    int nLights = int(scene->lights.size());
    int lightNum;
    if (lightNumOffset != -1)
        lightNum = Floor2Int(sample->oneD[lightNumOffset][0] * nLights);
    else
        lightNum = Floor2Int(RandomFloat() * nLights);
    lightNum = min(lightNum, nLights-1);
    Light *light = scene->lights[lightNum];
```

It's possible to be even more creative in choosing the individual light sampling probabilities than the uniform method used in UniformSampleOneLight(). In fact, we're free to set the probabilities any way we like, so long as we weight the result appropriately and there is a nonzero probability of sampling any light that contributes to the reflection at the point. The better a job we do at setting the probabilities, the more efficient the Monte Carlo estimator will be, and the fewer rays will be needed to lower variance to an acceptable level. (This is just the discrete instance of importance sampling.) One widely used approach is to base the sample distribution on the total power of the light, for example. In a similar manner, we could take more than one light sample with such an approach; indeed, any number of samples can be taken in the end, so long as they are weighted appropriately. This topic is discussed further in an exercise at the end of the chapter.

16.1.1 ESTIMATING THE DIRECT LIGHTING INTEGRAL

Having chosen a particular light to estimate direct lighting from, we need to estimate the value of the integral

$$\int_{s^2} f(\mathrm{p}, \omega_o, \omega_i) L_d(\mathrm{p}, \omega_i) |\cos \theta_i| d\omega_i$$

for that light. To compute this estimate, we need to choose one or more directions ω_i and apply the Monte Carlo estimator:

$$\frac{1}{N} \sum_{j=1}^{N} \frac{f(\mathrm{p}, \omega_o, \omega_j) L_d(\mathrm{p}, \omega_j) |\cos \theta_j|}{p(\omega_j)}.$$

To reduce variance, we will use importance sampling to choose the directions ω_j. Because both the BSDF and the direct radiance terms are individually complex, it would be difficult to find sampling distributions that match their product well. Instead, we will use the BSDF's sampling distribution for some of the samples and the light's for the rest. Depending on the characteristics of each of them, one of these two sampling methods may be far more effective than the other. Therefore, we will use multiple importance sampling to further improve the results.

Figure 16.1 shows two cases where one of the sampling methods is much better than the other. In Figure 16.1(a), the BSDF is very specular, and the light source is relatively large. Sampling the BSDF will be effective at finding directions where the integrand's value is large, while sampling the light will be less effective: most of the samples will not contribute much since the BSDF is small for most of the directions to the light source. When the light happens to sample a point in the BSDF's glossy region, there will be a spike in the image because the light will return a low PDF, while the value of the integrand will be relatively large. As a result, the variance would be high because the sampling distribution didn't match the actual distribution of the function's values very well.

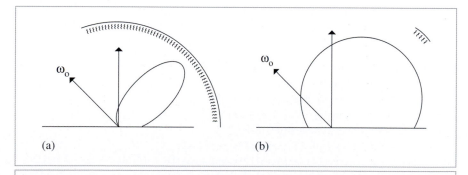

(a)   (b)

Figure 16.1: Depending on the actual distributions of the BSDF and the light source as a function of direction from the point being illuminated, one or the other may be a much more effective distribution to draw samples from for importance sampling.

On the other hand, sometimes sampling the light is the right strategy. Figure 16.1(b), the BSDF is nonzero over many directions, and the light is relatively small. It will be far more effective to choose points on the light to compute ω_i, since the BSDF will have trouble finding directions where there is nonzero incident radiance from the light. Similar to the first case, we would encounter substantial variance since the sampling distribution didn't match the overall function well.

By applying multiple importance sampling, not only can we use both of the two sampling methods, but also we can do so in a way that eliminates the extreme variance from these two situations, since the weighting terms from MIS reduce this variance substantially.

⟨*Integrator Utility Functions*⟩+≡
```
    Spectrum EstimateDirect(const Scene *scene, const Light *light,
            const Point &p, const Normal &n, const Vector &wo,
            BSDF *bsdf, const Sample *sample, int lightSamp,
            int bsdfSamp, int bsdfComponent, u_int sampleNum) {
        Spectrum Ld(0.);
        ⟨Find light and BSDF sample values for direct lighting estimate  730⟩
        ⟨Sample light source with multiple importance sampling  731⟩
        ⟨Sample BSDF with multiple importance sampling  732⟩
        return Ld;
    }
```

First this function finds the values for the various random numbers that it will be using for Monte Carlo integration. A 2D sample (ls1, ls2) is needed for sampling the light source, another 2D sample (bs1, bs2) for sampling the BSDF, and finally a 1D sample bcs is used to select a BxDF component to sample from the complete BSDF. (Recall that the BSDF::Sample_f() takes three random variables, one of them a 1D sample for this purpose.)

If the integrator calling this routine has requested appropriate samples from the Sampler, it can use the corresponding values in the Sample. Otherwise, it gets uniform random values from RandomFloat().

⟨*Find light and BSDF sample values for direct lighting estimate*⟩ ≡   **730**
```
    float ls1, ls2, bs1, bs2, bcs;
    if (lightSamp != -1 && bsdfSamp != -1 &&
        sampleNum < sample->n2D[lightSamp] &&
        sampleNum < sample->n2D[bsdfSamp]) {
        ls1 = sample->twoD[lightSamp][2*sampleNum];
        ls2 = sample->twoD[lightSamp][2*sampleNum+1];
        bs1 = sample->twoD[bsdfSamp][2*sampleNum];
        bs2 = sample->twoD[bsdfSamp][2*sampleNum+1];
        bcs = sample->oneD[bsdfComponent][sampleNum];
    }
```

```
else {
    ls1 = RandomFloat();
    ls2 = RandomFloat();
    bs1 = RandomFloat();
    bs2 = RandomFloat();
    bcs = RandomFloat();
}
```

First, one sample is taken with light's sampling distribution using `Sample_L()`, which also returns the light's emitted radiance and the value of the PDF for the sampled direction. Only if the light successfully samples a direction and returns nonzero emitted radiance does the function here go ahead and evaluate the BSDF for the two directions; otherwise there's no reason to go through the computational expense. For example, a spotlight returns zero radiance for points outside its illumination cone. Then only if the BSDF's value is nonzero is a shadow ray traced to check for occlusion.

⟨*Sample light source with multiple importance sampling*⟩ ≡   **730**
```
    Vector wi;
    float lightPdf, bsdfPdf;
    VisibilityTester visibility;
    Spectrum Li = light->Sample_L(p, n, ls1, ls2,
                                   &wi, &lightPdf, &visibility);
    if (lightPdf > 0. && !Li.Black()) {
        Spectrum f = bsdf->f(wo, wi);
        if (!f.Black() && visibility.Unoccluded(scene)) {
            ⟨Add light's contribution to reflected radiance 732⟩
        }
    }
```

Once it is known that the light is visible and radiance is arriving at the point, the value of the Monte Carlo estimator can be computed. First, radiance from the light to the illuminated point is scaled by the beam transmittance between the two points to account for attenuation due to participating media. Next, recall from Section 15.6.2 that if the light is described by a delta distribution, then there is an implied delta distribution in both the emitted radiance value returned from `Sample_L()` as well as the PDF and that they are expected to cancel out when the estimator is evaluated. In this case, we must not try to apply multiple importance sampling and should compute the standard estimator instead. If this isn't a delta distribution light source, then the `BSDF::Pdf()` method is called to return the BSDF's PDF value for sampling the direction ω_i, and the MIS estimator is used, where the weight is computed here with the power heuristic.

⟨*Add light's contribution to reflected radiance*⟩ ≡   **731**

```
Li *= visibility.Transmittance(scene);
if (light->IsDeltaLight())
    Ld += f * Li * AbsDot(wi, n) / lightPdf;
else {
    bsdfPdf = bsdf->Pdf(wo, wi);
    float weight = PowerHeuristic(1, lightPdf, 1, bsdfPdf);
    Ld += f * Li * AbsDot(wi, n) * weight / lightPdf;
}
```

In a similar manner, a sample is now generated using the BSDF's sampling distribution. This step can be skipped if the light source is a delta distribution because, in that case, there's no chance that sampling the BSDF will give a direction that receives light from the source. If this is not the case, the BSDF can be sampled, although note that the BxDFType flags are set up so that only nonspecular BSDF components are sampled. This is an important detail as well; this function assumes that reflection from perfectly specular BSDF components will be handled separately by the integrator and that it will account for emission from surfaces hit by specular rays elsewhere.

⟨*Sample BSDF with multiple importance sampling*⟩ ≡   **730**

```
if (!light->IsDeltaLight()) {
    BxDFType flags = BxDFType(BSDF_ALL & ~BSDF_SPECULAR);
    Spectrum f = bsdf->Sample_f(wo, &wi, bs1, bs2, bcs,
                                &bsdfPdf, flags);
    if (!f.Black() && bsdfPdf > 0.) {
        lightPdf = light->Pdf(p, n, wi);
        if (lightPdf > 0.) {
            ⟨Add light contribution from BSDF sampling  733⟩
        }
    }
}
```

Given a direction sampled by the BSDF, we need to find out if the ray along that direction intersects this particular light source, and if so, how much radiance from the light reaches the surface. The code must account for both regular area lights, with geometry associated with them, as well as lights like the InfiniteAreaLight that don't have geometry but need to return their radiance for the sample ray via the Light::Le() method.

⟨*Add light contribution from BSDF sampling*⟩ ≡   732
```
float weight = PowerHeuristic(1, bsdfPdf, 1, lightPdf);
Intersection lightIsect;
Spectrum Li(0.f);
RayDifferential ray(p, wi);
if (scene->Intersect(ray, &lightIsect)) {
    if (lightIsect.primitive->GetAreaLight() == light)
        Li = lightIsect.Le(-wi);
}
else
    Li = light->Le(ray);
if (!Li.Black()) {
    Li *= scene->Transmittance(ray);
    Ld += f * Li * AbsDot(wi, n) * weight / bsdfPdf;
}
```

16.2 THE LIGHT TRANSPORT EQUATION

The light transport equation (LTE) is the governing equation that describes the equilibrium distribution of radiance in a scene. It gives the total reflected radiance at a point on a surface in terms of emission from the surface, its BSDF, and the distribution of incident illumination arriving at the point. The key task of the Integrator objects in pbrt is to numerically compute a solution to the LTE to find the incident radiance arriving at the camera. For now we will consider the case where there is no participating media in the scene. Chapter 17 describes the generalizations to this process necessary for scenes that do have participating media.

The detail that makes evaluating the LTE difficult is the fact that incident radiance at a point is affected by the geometry and scattering properties of all of the objects in the scene. For example, a bright light shining on a red object may cause a reddish tint on nearby objects in the scene, or glass may focus light into caustic patterns on a tabletop. Rendering algorithms that account for this complexity are often called *global illumination* algorithms, to differentiate them from *local illumination* algorithms that only use information about the local surface properties in their shading computations.

In this section, we will first derive the LTE and describe some approaches for manipulating the equation to make it easier to solve numerically. We will then describe two generalizations of the LTE that make some of its key properties more clear and serve as the foundation for some of the advanced integrators we will implement later in this chapter.

16.2.1 BASIC DERIVATION

The light transport equation depends on the basic assumptions we have already made in choosing to use radiometry to describe light—that wave optics effects are unimportant and that the distribution of radiance in the scene is in equilibrium. To compute radiance arriving at the film along a camera ray, we would like to express the exitant radiance from the camera ray's intersection point p in the direction ω_o from p to the film sample. We will denote this radiance measurement by $L_o(p, \omega_o)$.

The key principle underlying the LTE is *energy balance*. Any change in energy has to be "charged" to some process, and we must keep track of all the energy. Since we are assuming that lighting is a linear process, the difference between the amount of energy coming in and energy going out of a system must also be equal to the difference between energy emitted and energy absorbed. This idea holds at many levels of scale. On a macro level we have conservation of power:

$$\Phi_o - \Phi_i = \Phi_e - \Phi_a.$$

The difference between the power leaving an object, Φ_o, and the power entering it, Φ_i, is equal to the difference between the power it emits and the power it absorbs, $\Phi_e - \Phi_a$.

In order to enforce energy balance at a surface, exitant radiance must be equal to emitted radiance plus the fraction of incident radiance that is scattered. Emitted radiance is given by L_e, and scattered radiance is given by the scattering equation, which gives

$$L_o(p, \omega_o) = L_e(p, \omega_o) + \int_{\mathcal{S}^2} f(p, \omega_o, \omega_i) L_i(p, \omega_i) |\cos \theta_i| \, d\omega_i.$$

Because we have assumed for now that no participating media is present, radiance is constant along rays through the scene. We can therefore relate the incident radiance at p to the outgoing radiance from another point p', as shown by Figure 16.2. If we define the *ray-casting function* $t(p, \omega)$ as a function that computes the first surface point p' intersected by a ray from p in the direction ω, we can write the incident radiance at p in terms of outgoing radiance at p':

$$L_i(p, \omega) = L_o(t(p, \omega), -\omega).$$

In case the scene is not closed, we will define the ray-casting function to return a special value Λ if the ray (p, ω) doesn't intersect any object in the scene, such that $L_o(\Lambda, \omega)$ is always zero.

Dropping the subscripts from L_o for brevity, this relationship allows us to write the LTE as

$$L(p, \omega_o) = L_e(p, \omega_o) + \int_{\mathcal{S}^2} f(p, \omega_o, \omega_i) L(t(p, \omega_i), -\omega_i) |\cos \theta_i| \, d\omega_i. \quad \text{[16.2]}$$

The key to the above representation is that there is only *one* quantity of interest, exitant radiance from points on surfaces. Of course, it appears on both sides of the equation, so

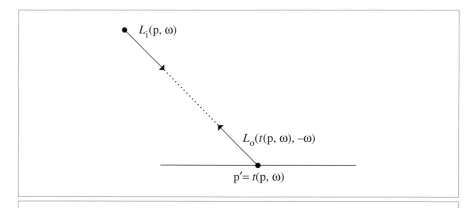

Figure 16.2: Radiance along a Ray through Free Space Is Unchanged. Therefore, to compute the incident radiance along a ray from point p in direction ω, we can find the first surface the ray intersects and compute exitant radiance in the direction $-\omega$ there. The trace operator $t(p, \omega)$ gives the point p' on the first surface that the ray (p, ω) intersects.

our task is still not simple, but it is certainly better. It is important to keep in mind that we were able to arrive at this equation simply by enforcing energy balance in our scene.

16.2.2 ANALYTIC SOLUTIONS TO THE LTE

The brevity of the LTE belies the fact that it is impossible to solve analytically in general. The complexity that comes from physically based BSDF models, arbitrary scene geometry, and the intricate visibility relationships between objects all conspire to mandate a numerical solution technique. Fortunately, the combination of ray-tracing algorithms and Monte Carlo integration gives a powerful pair of tools that can handle this complexity without needing to impose restrictions on various components of the LTE (e.g., requiring that all BSDFs be Lambertian, or substantially limiting the geometric representations that are supported).

It is possible to find analytic solutions to the LTE in extremely simple settings. While this is of little help for general-purpose rendering, it can help with debugging the implementations of integrators. If an integrator that is supposed to solve the complete LTE doesn't compute a solution that matches an analytic solution, then clearly there is a bug in the integrator. As an example, consider the interior of a sphere where all points on the surface of the sphere have a Lambertian BRDF, $f(p, \omega_o, \omega_i) = c$, and also emit a constant amount of radiance in all directions. We have

$$L(p, \omega_o) = L_e + c \int_{\mathcal{H}^2(n)} L(t(p, \omega_i), -\omega_i) |\cos \theta_i| d\omega_i.$$

The outgoing radiance distribution at any point on the sphere interior must be the same as at any other point; nothing in the environment could introduce any variation among different points. Therefore, the incident radiance distribution must be the same at all points, and the cosine-weighted integral of incident radiance must be the same everywhere as well. As such, we can replace the radiance functions with constants and simplify, writing the LTE as

$$L = L_e + c\pi L.$$

While we could immediately solve this equation for L, it's interesting to consider successive substitution of the right-hand side into the L term on the right-hand side. If we also replace πc with ρ_{hh}, the reflectance of a Lambertian surface, we have

$$L = L_e + \rho_{hh}(L_e + \rho_{hh}(L_e + \cdots$$
$$= \sum_{i=0}^{\infty} L_e \rho_{hh}^i.$$

In other words, exitant radiance is equal to the emitted radiance at the point plus light that has been scattered by a BSDF once after emission, plus light that has been scattered twice, and so forth.

Because $\rho_{hh} < 1$ due to conservation of energy, the series converges and the reflected radiance at all points in all directions is

$$L = \frac{L_e}{1 - \rho_{hh}}.$$

This process of repeatedly substituting the LTE's right-hand side into the incident radiance term in the integral can be instructive in more general cases.[1] For example, the DirectLighting integrator effectively computes the result of making a single substitution:

$$L(\mathrm{p}, \omega_o) = L_e(\mathrm{p}, \omega_o) + \int_{\mathcal{S}^2} f(\mathrm{p}, \omega_o, \omega_i) L_d |\cos\theta_i| \, d\omega_i,$$

where

$$L_d = L_e(t(\mathrm{p}, \omega_i), -\omega_i) + \int_{\mathcal{S}^2} f(t(\mathrm{p}, \omega_i), \omega') L(t(t(\mathrm{p}, \omega_i), \omega'), -\omega') |\cos\theta'| \, d\omega'$$

and then ignores the result of multiply scattered light.

Over the next few pages, we will see how performing successive substitutions in this manner and then regrouping the results expresses the LTE in a more natural way for developing rendering algorithms.

---

1   Indeed, this sort of series expansion and inversion can be used in the general case, where quantities like the BSDF are expressed in terms of general operators that map incident radiance functions to exitant radiance functions. This approach forms the foundation for applying sophisticated tools from analysis to the light transport problem. See Arvo's thesis (Arvo 1995) and Veach's thesis (Veach 1997) for further information.

16.2.3 THE SURFACE FORM OF THE LTE

One reason that the LTE as written in Equation (16.2) is complex is that the relationship between geometric objects in the scene is implicit in the ray-tracing operator $t(\mathrm{p}, \omega)$. Making the behavior of the ray-tracing operator explicit in the integrand will shed some light on the structure of this equation. To do this, we will rewrite Equation (16.2) as an integral over *area* instead of an integral over directions on the sphere.

First, we define exitant radiance from a point p' to a point p by

$$L(\mathrm{p}' \to \mathrm{p}) = L(\mathrm{p}', \omega)$$

if p' and p are mutually visible and $\omega = \widehat{\mathrm{p} - \mathrm{p}'}$. We can also write the BSDF at p' as

$$f(\mathrm{p}'' \to \mathrm{p}' \to \mathrm{p}) = f(\mathrm{p}', \omega_{\mathrm{o}}, \omega_{\mathrm{i}})$$

where $\omega_{\mathrm{i}} = \widehat{\mathrm{p}'' - \mathrm{p}'}$ and $\omega_{\mathrm{o}} = \widehat{\mathrm{p} - \mathrm{p}'}$ (Figure 16.3).

Rewriting the terms in the LTE in this manner isn't quite enough, however. We also need to multiply by the Jacobian that relates solid angle to area in order to transform the LTE from an integral over direction to one over surface area. Recall that this is $|\cos \theta'|/r^2$.

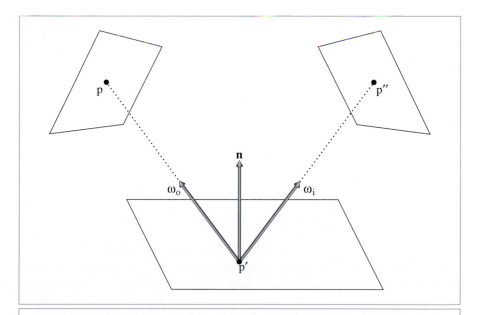

Figure 16.3: The three-point form of the light transport equation converts the integral to be over the domain of points on surfaces in the scene, rather than over directions over the sphere. It is a key transformation for deriving the path integral form of the light transport equation.

We will combine this change-of-variables term, the original $|\cos \theta|$ term from the LTE, and also a binary visibility function V ($V = 1$ if the two points are mutually visible, and $V = 0$ otherwise) into a single geometric coupling term $G(\mathrm{p} \leftrightarrow \mathrm{p}')$:

$$G(\mathrm{p} \leftrightarrow \mathrm{p}') = V(\mathrm{p} \leftrightarrow \mathrm{p}') \frac{|\cos \theta| \, |\cos \theta'|}{\| \, \mathrm{p} - \mathrm{p}' \, \|^2}.$$

Substituting these into the light transport equation and converting to an area integral, we have

$$L(\mathrm{p}' \to \mathrm{p}) = L_{\mathrm{e}}(\mathrm{p}' \to \mathrm{p}) + \int_A f(\mathrm{p}'' \to \mathrm{p}' \to \mathrm{p}) L(\mathrm{p}'' \to \mathrm{p}') G(\mathrm{p}'' \leftrightarrow \mathrm{p}') \, \mathrm{d}A(\mathrm{p}''),$$

[16.3]

where A is all of the surfaces of the scene.

Although Equations (16.2) and (16.3) are equivalent, they represent two different ways of approaching light transport. To evaluate Equation (16.2) with Monte Carlo, we would sample a number of directions from a distribution of directions on the sphere and cast rays to evaluate the integrand. For Equation (16.3), however, we would choose a number of *points* on surfaces according to a distribution over surface area and compute the coupling between those points to evaluate the integrand, tracing rays to evaluate the visibility term $V(\mathrm{p} \leftrightarrow \mathrm{p}')$.

16.2.4 INTEGRAL OVER PATHS

To go from the area integral to a more flexible form of the LTE, a sum over light-carrying paths of different lengths, we can now start to expand the three-point light transport equation, repeatedly substituting the right-hand side of the equation into the $L(\mathrm{p}' \to \mathrm{p}')$ term inside the integral. Here are the first few terms that give incident radiance at a point p_0 from another point p_1, where p_1 is the first point on a surface along the ray from p_0 in direction $\mathrm{p}_1 - \mathrm{p}_0$:

$$L(\mathrm{p}_1 \to \mathrm{p}_0) = L_{\mathrm{e}}(\mathrm{p}_1 \to \mathrm{p}_0) +$$

$$\int_A L_{\mathrm{e}}(\mathrm{p}_2 \to \mathrm{p}_1) f(\mathrm{p}_2 \to \mathrm{p}_1 \to \mathrm{p}_0) G(\mathrm{p}_2 \leftrightarrow \mathrm{p}_1) \mathrm{d}A(\mathrm{p}_2) +$$

$$\int_A \int_A L_{\mathrm{e}}(\mathrm{p}_3 \to \mathrm{p}_2) f(\mathrm{p}_3 \to \mathrm{p}_2 \to \mathrm{p}_1) G(\mathrm{p}_3 \leftrightarrow \mathrm{p}_2)$$

$$f(\mathrm{p}_2 \to \mathrm{p}_1 \to \mathrm{p}_0) G(\mathrm{p}_2 \leftrightarrow \mathrm{p}_1) \, \mathrm{d}A(\mathrm{p}_3) \, \mathrm{d}A(\mathrm{p}_2) + \cdots$$

Each term on the right of this equation represents a path of increasing length. For example, the third term is illustrated in Figure 16.4. This path has four vertices, connected by three segments. The total contribution of all such paths of length four (i.e., a vertex at the eye, two vertices at points on surfaces in the scene, and a vertex on a light source) is given by this term. Here, the first two vertices of the path, p_0 and p_1, are predetermined based on the camera ray and the point that it intersects, but p_2 and p_3 can vary over all points on surfaces in the scene. The integral over all such p_2 and p_3 gives the total contribution of paths of length four to radiance arriving at the eye.

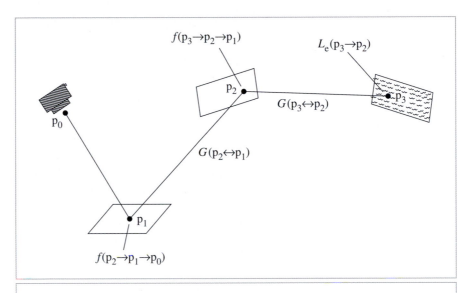

Figure 16.4: The integral over all points p_2 and p_3 on surfaces in the scene given by the light transport equation gives the total contribution of two bounce paths to radiance leaving p_1 in the direction of p_0. The components of the product in the integrand are shown here: the emitted radiance from the light L_e, the geometric terms between vertices G, and scattering from the BSDFs, f.

This infinite sum can be written compactly as

$$L(p_1 \to p_0) = \sum_{i=1}^{\infty} P(\bar{p}_i).$$

[16.4]

$P(\bar{p}_i)$ gives the amount of radiance scattered over a path $\bar{p}_i$ with $i + 1$ vertices,

$$\bar{p}_i = p_0, p_1, \ldots, p_i,$$

where p_0 is on the film plane and p_i is on a light source, and

$$P(\bar{p}_i) = \underbrace{\int_A \int_A \cdots \int_A}_{i-1} L_e(p_i \to p_{i-1})$$

$$\left(\prod_{j=1}^{i-1} f(p_{j+1} \to p_j \to p_{j-1}) G(p_{j+1} \leftrightarrow p_j) \right) \, dA(p_2) \cdots dA(p_i).$$

Before we move on, we will define one additional term that will be helpful in the subsequent discussion. The product of a path's BSDF and geometry terms is called the *throughput* of the path; it describes the fraction of radiance from the light source that arrives at the camera after all of the scattering at vertices between them. We will denote it by

$$T(\bar{p}_i) = \prod_{j=1}^{i-1} f(p_{j+1} \to p_j \to p_{j-1}) G(p_{j+1} \leftrightarrow p_j),$$

so

$$P(\bar{p}_i) = \underbrace{\int_A \int_A \cdots \int_A}_{i-1} L_e(p_i \to p_{i-1}) T(\bar{p}_i) \, dA(p_2) \cdots dA(p_i).$$

Given Equation (16.4) and a particular length i, all that we need to do to compute a Monte Carlo estimate of the radiance arriving at p_0 due to paths of length i is to sample a set of vertices with an appropriate sampling density in the scene to generate a path and then to evaluate an estimate of $P(\bar{p}_i)$ using those vertices. Whether we generate those vertices by starting a path from the camera, starting from the light, starting from both ends, or starting from a point in the middle is a detail that only affects how the weights for the Monte Carlo estimates are computed. We will see how this formulation leads in practice to practical light transport algorithms throughout this chapter.

16.2.5 DELTA DISTRIBUTIONS IN THE INTEGRAND

Delta functions may be present in $P(\bar{p}_i)$ terms due to both BSDF components described by delta distributions as well as certain types of light sources (e.g., point lights and directional lights). These distributions need to be handled explicitly by the light transport algorithm if present. For example, it is impossible to randomly choose an outgoing direction from a point on a surface that would intersect a point light source; instead it is necessary to explicitly choose the single direction from the point to the light source if we want to be able to include its contribution. (The same is true for sampling BSDFs with delta components.) While handling this case introduces some additional complexity to the integrators, it is generally welcome because it reduces the dimensionality of the integral to be evaluated, turning parts of it into a plain sum.

For example, consider the direct illumination term, $P(\bar{p}_2)$, in a scene with a single point light source at point p_{light} described by a delta distribution:

$$P(\bar{p}_2) = \int_A L_e(p_2 \to p_1) f(p_2 \to p_1 \to p_0) G(p_2 \leftrightarrow p_1) \, dA(p_2)$$

$$= \frac{\delta(p_{light} - p_2) L_e(p_{light} \to p_1)}{p(p_{light})} f(p_2 \to p_1 \to p_0) G(p_2 \leftrightarrow p_1).$$

In other words, p_2 must be the same as the light's position in the scene, the delta distribution in the numerator cancels out due to an implicit delta distribution in $p(p_{light})$ (recall the discussion of sampling delta distributions in Section 15.5.4), and we are left with terms that can be evaluated directly, with no need for Monte Carlo. An analogous situation holds for BSDFs with delta distributions in the path throughput $T(\bar{p}_i)$; each one eliminates an integral over area from the estimate to be computed.

16.2.6 PARTITIONING THE INTEGRAND

Many rendering algorithms have been developed that are particularly good at solving the LTE under some conditions, but don't work well (or at all) under others. For example, the Whitted integrator only handles specular reflection from delta BSDFs and ignores multiply scattered light from diffuse and glossy BSDFs, and the irradiance caching technique described later in this chapter handles scattering from diffuse surfaces but would introduce significant error if used for glossy or specular reflection.

Because we would like to be able to derive correct light transport algorithms that account for all possible modes of scattering without ignoring any contributions and without double-counting others, it is important to carefully account for which parts of the LTE a particular solution method accounts for. A nice way of approaching this problem is to partition the LTE in various ways. For example, we might expand the sum over paths to

$$L(\mathrm{p}_1 \to \mathrm{p}_0) = P(\bar{\mathrm{p}}_1) + P(\bar{\mathrm{p}}_2) + \sum_{i=3}^{\infty} P(\bar{\mathrm{p}}_i),$$

where the first term is trivially evaluated by computing the emitted radiance at p_1, the second term is solved with an accurate direct lighting solution technique, but the remaining terms in the sum are handled with a faster but less accurate approach. If the contribution of these additional terms to the total reflected radiance is relatively small for the scene we're rendering, this may be a reasonable approach to take. The only detail is that it is important to be careful to ignore $P(\bar{\mathrm{p}}_1)$ and $P(\bar{\mathrm{p}}_2)$ with the algorithm that handles $P(\bar{\mathrm{p}}_3)$ and beyond (and similarly with the other terms).

It is also useful to partition individual $P(\bar{\mathrm{p}}_i)$ terms. For example, we might want to split the emission term into emission from small light sources, $L_{\mathrm{e,s}}$, and emission from large light sources, $L_{\mathrm{e,l}}$, giving us two separate integrals to estimate:

$$P(\bar{\mathrm{p}}_i) = \int_{A^{i-1}} (L_{\mathrm{e,s}}(\mathrm{p}_i \to \mathrm{p}_{i-1}) + L_{\mathrm{e,l}}(\mathrm{p}_i \to \mathrm{p}_{i-1}))\, T(\bar{\mathrm{p}}_i)\, \mathrm{d}A(\mathrm{p}_2) \cdots \mathrm{d}A(\mathrm{p}_i)$$

$$= \int_{A^i} L_{\mathrm{e,s}}(\mathrm{p}_i \to \mathrm{p}_{i-1})\, T(\bar{\mathrm{p}}_i)\, \mathrm{d}A(\mathrm{p}_2) \cdots \mathrm{d}A(\mathrm{p}_i) +$$

$$\int_{A^i} L_{\mathrm{e,l}}(\mathrm{p}_i \to \mathrm{p}_{i-1})\, T(\bar{\mathrm{p}}_i)\, \mathrm{d}A(\mathrm{p}_2) \cdots \mathrm{d}A(\mathrm{p}_i).$$

The two integrals can be evaluated independently, possibly using completely different algorithms, or different numbers of samples, selected in a way that handles the different conditions well. As long as the estimate of the $L_{\mathrm{e,s}}$ integral ignores any emission from large lights, the estimate of the $L_{\mathrm{e,l}}$ integral ignores emission from small lights, and all lights are categorized as either "large" or "small," the correct result is computed in the end.

Finally, the BSDF terms can be partitioned as well (in fact, this application was the reason that BSDF categorization with `BxDFType` values was introduced in Section 9.1).

For example, if f_Δ denotes components of the BSDF described by delta distributions and $f_{\neg\Delta}$ denotes the remaining components,

$$P(\bar{p}_i) = \int_{A^{i-1}} L_e(p_i \to p_{i-1}) \prod_{j=1}^{i-1} \Big(f_\Delta(p_{j+1} \to p_j \to p_{j-1}) + $$

$$f_{\neg\Delta}(p_{j+1} \to p_j \to p_{j-1}) \Big) G(p_{j+1} \leftrightarrow p_j) dA(p_2) \cdots dA(p_i).$$

Note that because there are $i - 1$ BSDF terms in the product, it is important to be careful not to count only terms with only f_Δ components or only $f_{\neg\Delta}$ components; all of the terms like $f_\Delta f_{\neg\Delta} f_{\neg\Delta}$ must be accounted for as well if a partitioning scheme like this is used.

16.2.7 THE MEASUREMENT EQUATION AND IMPORTANCE

In light of the path integral form of the LTE, it's useful to go back and formally describe the quantity that is being estimated as we compute pixel values for the image. Doing so will help us be able to apply the LTE to a wider set of problems than just computing 2D images (for example, to precomputing scattered radiance distributions at the vertices of a polygonal model, as can be useful for interactive rendering applications). Furthermore, this process leads us to a key theoretical mechanism for understanding particle tracing and the photon mapping algorithm that will be described in Section 16.5.

The *measurement equation* describes the value of an abstract measurement that is found by integrating over some set of rays carrying radiance. For example, when computing the value of a pixel in the image, we want to integrate over rays starting in the neighborhood of the pixel, with contribution weighted by the image reconstruction filter. Ignoring depth of field for now (so that each point on the film plane corresponds to a single outgoing direction from the camera), we can write the pixel's value as an integral over points on the film plane of a weighting function times the incident radiance along the corresponding camera rays:

$$I_j = \int_{A_{film}} \int_{\mathbb{S}^2} W_e(p_{film}, \omega) L_i(p_{film}, \omega) |\cos\theta| \, dA(p_{film}) d\omega$$

$$= \int_{A_{film}} \int_A W_e(p_0 \to p_1) L(p_1 \to p_0) G(p_0 \leftrightarrow p_1) dA(p_0) dA(p_1),$$

where I_j is the measurement for the jth pixel and p_0 is a point on the film. In this setting, the $W_e(p_0 \to p_1)$ term is the product of the filter function around the pixel, f_j, and a delta function that selects the appropriate camera ray direction of the sample from p_0, $\omega_{camera}(p_0)$:

$$W_e(p_0 \to p_1) = f_j(p_0)\delta(t(p_0, \omega_{camera}(p_0)) - p_1).$$

This formulation may initially seem gratuitously complex, but it leads us to an important insight. If we expand the $P(\bar{p}_i)$ terms of the LTE sum, we have

$$I_j = \int_{A_{\text{film}}} \int_A W_e(p_0 \to p_1) L(p_1 \to p_0) G(p_0 \leftrightarrow p_1) dA(p_0) dA(p_1)$$

$$= \sum_i \int_A \int_A W_e(p_0 \to p_1) P(\bar{p}_i) G(p_0 \leftrightarrow p_1) dA(p_0) dA(p_1)$$

$$= \sum_i \int_A \cdots \int_A W_e(p_0 \to p_1) T(\bar{p}_i) L_e(p_{i+1} \to p_i) G(p_0 \leftrightarrow p_1) dA(p_0) \cdots dA(p_i).$$

A nice symmetry between the emitted radiance from light sources (L_e) and the contribution of a sample on the film to the pixel measurement (W_e) has become apparent. The implications of this symmetry are important: it says that we can think of the rendering process in two different ways: Light could be emitted from light sources, bounce around the scene, and arrive at a sensor where W_e describes its contribution to the measurement. Alternatively, we can think of some quantity being emitted from the sensor, bouncing around the scene, and making a contribution when it hits a light source. Either intuition is equally valid.

The value described by the $W_e(p_0 \to p_1)$ term is known as the *importance* for the ray between p_0 and p_1 in the scene. When the measurement equation is used to compute pixel measurements, the importance will often be partially or fully described by delta distributions, as it was in the previous example. Many other types of measurement besides image formation can be described by appropriately constructed importance functions, and thus the formalisms described here can be used to show how the integral over paths described by the measurement equation is the integral that must be estimated to compute them. We will make use of these ideas when describing the photon mapping algorithm later in this chapter.

16.3 PATH TRACING

Now that we have derived the path integral form of the light transport equation, we'll show how it can be used to derive the *path-tracing* light transport algorithm and will present a path-tracing integrator. Figure 16.5 compares images of a scene rendered with only direct lighting and rendered with path tracing. For the scene shown here, indirect illumination is the dominant lighting effect: the image that only includes direct lighting is mostly black, while the one rendered with path tracing accurately represents the complete lighting distribution in the scene.

Path tracing was the first general-purpose unbiased Monte Carlo light transport algorithm used in graphics. Kajiya introduced it in the same paper that first described the light transport equation (1986). Path tracing incrementally generates paths of scattering events starting at the camera and ending at light sources in the scene. One way to think of it is as an extension of Whitted's method to include both delta distribution and nondelta BSDFs and light sources, rather than just accounting for the delta terms.

(a)

(b)

(c)

Figure 16.5: The Sponza Atrium Model. (a) Rendered with direct lighting only. (b) Rendered with path tracing with 1024 samples per pixel, giving a high-quality result. (c) Rendered with just 8 samples per pixel, giving the characteristic grainy noise that is the hallmark of variance. In this scene, indirect illumination is the dominant mode of light transport, so only accounting for direct lighting gives a mostly black image. The disadvantage of path tracing is that a large number of samples may need to be taken in order to reduce variance to an acceptable level. (The light beams are due to the `SingleScattering` volume integrator, to be defined in Section 17.4.)

Although it is slightly easier to derive path tracing directly from the basic light transport equation, we will instead approach it from the path integral form, which helps build understanding of the path integral equation and will make the generalization to bidirectional path tracing easier to understand. Bidirectional path tracing is a technique where paths are generated starting from the lights as well as from the camera; it is discussed (but not implemented) at the end of this section.

16.3.1 OVERVIEW

Given the path integral form of the LTE, we would like to estimate the value of the exitant radiance from the camera ray's intersection point p_1,

$$L(p_1 \rightarrow p_0) = \sum_{i=1}^{\infty} P(\bar{p}_i),$$

for a given camera ray from p_0 that first intersects the scene at p_1. We have two problems that must be solved in order to compute this estimate:

1. How do we estimate the value of the sum of the infinite number of $P(\bar{p}_i)$ terms with a finite amount of computation?
2. Given a particular $P(\bar{p}_i)$ term, how do we generate one or more paths $\bar{p}$ in order to compute a Monte Carlo estimate of its multidimensional integral?

For path tracing, we can take advantage of the fact that for physically valid scenes, paths with more vertices scatter less light than paths with fewer vertices overall (this isn't necessarily true for any particular pair of paths, just in the aggregate). This is a natural consequence of conservation of energy in BSDFs. Therefore, we will always estimate the first few terms $P(\bar{p}_i)$ and will then start to apply Russian roulette to stop sampling after a finite number of terms without introducing bias. Recall from Section 15.1 that Russian roulette allows us to probabilistically stop computing terms in a sum so long as we reweight the terms that are not terminated. For example, if we always computed estimates of $P(\bar{p}_1)$, $P(\bar{p}_2)$, and $P(\bar{p}_3)$ but stopped without computing more terms with probability q, then an unbiased estimate of the sum would be

$$P(\bar{p}_1) + P(\bar{p}_2) + P(\bar{p}_3) + \frac{1}{1-q} \sum_{i=4}^{\infty} P(\bar{p}_i).$$

Using Russian roulette in this way doesn't solve the problem of needing to evaluate an infinite sum, but has pushed it a bit farther out.

If we take this idea a step further and instead randomly consider terminating evaluation of the sum at each term with probability q_i,

$$\frac{1}{1-q_1} \left(P(\bar{p}_1) + \frac{1}{1-q_2} \left(P(\bar{p}_2) + \frac{1}{1-q_3} \left(P(\bar{p}_3) + \cdots, \right. \right. \right.$$

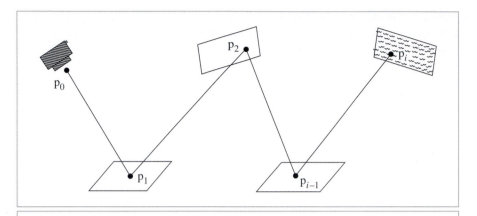

Figure 16.6: A path $\bar{\mathrm{p}}_i$ of $i + 1$ vertices from the camera at p, intersecting a series of positions on surfaces in the scene, to a point on the light p_i. Scattering according to the BSDF occurs at each path vertex from p_1 to p_{i-1} such that the radiance arriving at the camera due to this path is given by the product of the path throughput $T(\bar{\mathrm{p}}_i)$ times the emitted radiance from the light.

we will eventually stop continued evaluation of the sum. Yet because for any particular value of i there is greater than zero probability of evaluating the term $P(\bar{\mathrm{p}}_i)$ and because it will be weighted appropriately if we do evaluate it, the final result is an unbiased estimate of the sum.

16.3.2 PATH SAMPLING

Given this method for evaluating only a finite number of terms of the infinite sum, we also need a way to estimate the contribution of a particular term $P(\bar{\mathrm{p}}_i)$. We need $i + 1$ vertices to specify the path, where the last vertex p_i is on a light source and the first vertex p_0 is determined by the camera ray's first intersection point (Figure 16.6). Looking at the form of $P(\bar{\mathrm{p}}_i)$, a multiple integral over surface area of objects in the scene, the most natural thing to do is to sample vertices p_i according to the surface area of objects in the scene, such that it's equally probable to sample any particular point on an object in the scene for p_i as any other point. (We don't actually use this approach in the PathIntegrator implementation for reasons that will be described later, but this sampling technique could possibly be used to improve the efficiency of our basic implementation and helps to clarify the meaning of the path integral LTE.)

We could define a discrete probability over the n objects in the scene. If each has surface area A_i, then the probability of sampling a path vertex on the surface of the ith object should be

$$p_i = \frac{A_i}{\sum_j A_j}.$$

Then, given a method to sample a point on the ith object with uniform probability, the PDF for sampling any particular point on object i is $1/A_i$. Thus, the overall probability density for sampling the point is

$$\frac{A_i}{\sum_j A_j} \frac{1}{A_i}.$$

And all samples p_i have the same PDF value:

$$p_A(p_i) = \frac{1}{\sum_j A_j}.$$

It's reassuring that they all have the same weight, since our intent was to choose among all points on surfaces in the scene with equal probability.

Given the set of vertices $p_0, p_1, \ldots, p_{i-1}$ sampled in this manner, we can then sample the last vertex p_i on a light source in the scene, defining its PDF in the same way. Although we could use the same technique used for sampling path vertices to sample points on lights, this would lead to high variance, since for all of the paths where p_i wasn't on the surface of an emitter, the path would have zero value. The expected value would still be the correct value of the integral, but convergence would be extremely slow. A better approach is to sample over the areas of only the emitting objects with probabilities updated accordingly. Given a complete path, we have all of the information we need to compute the estimate of $P(\bar{p}_i)$; it's just a matter of evaluating each of the terms.

It's easy to be more creative about how we set the sampling probabilities with this general approach. For example, if we knew that indirect illumination from a few objects contributed to most of the lighting in the scene, we could assign a higher probability to generating path vertices p_i on those objects, updating the sample weights appropriately.

However, there are two interrelated problems with sampling paths in this manner. The first can lead to high variance, while the second can lead to incorrect results. The first problem is that many of the paths will have no contribution if they have pairs of adjacent vertices that are not mutually visible. Consider applying this area sampling method in a complex building model: adjacent vertices in the path will almost always have a wall or two between them, giving no contribution for the path and excessive variance in the estimate.

The second problem is that if the integrand has delta functions in it (e.g., a point light source or a perfectly specular BSDF), this sampling technique will never be able to choose path vertices such that the delta distributions are nonzero. And even if there aren't delta distributions, as the BSDFs become increasingly glossy, almost all of the paths will have low contributions since the points in $f(p_{i+1} \rightarrow p_i \rightarrow p_{i-1})$ will cause the BSDF to have a small or zero value and again we will suffer from high variance. In a similar manner, small area light sources can also be sources of variance if not sampled explicitly.

16.3.3 INCREMENTAL PATH CONSTRUCTION

A solution that solves both of these problems is to construct the path incrementally, starting from the vertex at the camera p_0. At each vertex, the BSDF is sampled to generate a new direction; the next vertex p_{i+1} is found by tracing a ray from p_i in the sampled direction and finding the closest intersection. We are effectively trying to find a path with a large overall contribution by making a series of choices that find directions with important local contributions. While one can imagine situations where this approach could be ineffective, it is a generally a good strategy.

Because this approach constructs the path by sampling BSDFs according to solid angle, and because the path integral LTE is an integral over surface area in the scene, we need to apply the correction to convert from the probability density according to solid angle p_ω to a density according to area p_A (recall Section 5.3):

$$p_A = p_\omega \frac{\|p_i - p_{i+1}\|^2}{|\cos \theta_i|}.$$

This correction causes some of the terms of the geometric term $G(p_i \leftrightarrow p_{i+1})$ to cancel out of $P(\bar{p}_i)$. Furthermore, we already know that p_i and p_{i+1} must be mutually visible since we traced a ray to find p_{i+1}, so the visibility term is trivially one. Therefore, if we use this sampling technique but we still sample the last vertex p_i from some distribution over the surfaces of light sources $p_A(p_i)$, the value of the Monte Carlo estimate for a path is

$$\frac{L_e(p_i \to p_{i-1})}{p_A(p_i)} \left(\prod_{j=1}^{i-1} \frac{f(p_{j+1} \to p_j \to p_{j-1})|\cos \theta_j|}{p_\omega(p_{j+1} - p_j)} \right).$$

16.3.4 IMPLEMENTATION

Our path-tracing implementation computes an estimate of the sum of path contributions $P(\bar{p}_i)$ using the approach described in the previous subsection. Starting at the first intersection of the camera ray with the scene geometry, p_1, it incrementally samples path vertices by importance-sampling from the BSDF's sampling distribution at the current vertex and tracing a ray to the next vertex. To find the last vertex of a particular path, p_i, which must be on a light source in the scene, it uses the multiple importance sampling–based direct lighting code that was developed for the direct lighting integrator. By using the multiple importance sampling weights instead of $p_A(p_i)$ to compute the estimate as described earlier, we have lower variance in the result for cases where sampling the BSDF would have been a better way to find a point on the light.

Another small difference is that as the estimates of the path contribution terms $P(\bar{p}_i)$ are being evaluated, the vertices of the previous path of length $i - 1$ (everything except the vertex on the emitter) are reused as a starting point when constructing the path of length i. This means that it is only necessary to trace one more ray to construct the new path, rather than i rays as we would if we started from scratch. Reusing paths in this manner does introduce correlation among all of the $P(\bar{\mathrm{p}}_i)$ terms in the sum, which slightly reduces the quality of the result, although in practice this is more than made up for by the improved overall efficiency due to tracing fewer rays.

⟨*PathIntegrator Declarations*⟩ ≡
```
class PathIntegrator : public SurfaceIntegrator {
public:
    ⟨PathIntegrator Public Methods 749⟩
private:
    ⟨PathIntegrator Private Data 749⟩
};
```

Although Russian roulette is used here to terminate path sampling in the manner described earlier, the integrator also supports a maximum depth. It can be set to a large number if only Russian roulette should be used:

⟨*PathIntegrator Public Methods*⟩ ≡   **749**
```
PathIntegrator(int md) { maxDepth = md; }
```

⟨*PathIntegrator Private Data*⟩ ≡   **749**
```
int maxDepth;
```

The integrator uses samples from the Sampler for sampling at the first SAMPLE_DEPTH vertices of the path. After the first few bounces, the advantages of well-distributed sample points are greatly reduced, and it switches to using uniform random numbers. The integrator needs light and BSDF samples for multiple importance sampling for the direct lighting calculation at each vertex of the path as well as BSDF samples for sampling directions when generating the outgoing direction for finding the next vertex of the path.

⟨*PathIntegrator Method Definitions*⟩ ≡
```
void PathIntegrator::RequestSamples(Sample *sample,
                                    const Scene *scene) {
    for (int i = 0; i < SAMPLE_DEPTH; ++i) {
        lightPositionOffset[i] = sample->Add2D(1);
        lightNumOffset[i] = sample->Add1D(1);
        bsdfDirectionOffset[i] = sample->Add2D(1);
        bsdfComponentOffset[i] = sample->Add1D(1);
        outgoingDirectionOffset[i] = sample->Add2D(1);
        outgoingComponentOffset[i] = sample->Add1D(1);
    }
}
```

⟨*PathIntegrator Private Data*⟩+≡   **749**

```
#define SAMPLE_DEPTH 3
int lightPositionOffset[SAMPLE_DEPTH];
int lightNumOffset[SAMPLE_DEPTH];
int bsdfDirectionOffset[SAMPLE_DEPTH];
int bsdfComponentOffset[SAMPLE_DEPTH];
int outgoingDirectionOffset[SAMPLE_DEPTH];
int outgoingComponentOffset[SAMPLE_DEPTH];
```

Each time through the for loop of the integrator, the next vertex of the path is found by intersecting the current ray with the scene geometry and computing the contribution of the path to the overall radiance value with the direct lighting code. A new direction is then chosen by sampling from the BSDF's distribution at the last vertex of the path. After a few vertices have been sampled, Russian roulette is used to randomly terminate the path.

⟨*PathIntegrator Method Definitions*⟩+≡

```
Spectrum PathIntegrator::Li(const Scene *scene, const RayDifferential &r,
                            const Sample *sample, float *alpha) const {
    ⟨Declare common path integration variables 751⟩
    for (int pathLength = 0; ; ++pathLength) {
        ⟨Find next vertex of path 751⟩
        ⟨Possibly add emitted light at path vertex 751⟩
        ⟨Evaluate BSDF at hit point 33⟩
        ⟨Sample illumination from lights to find path contribution 752⟩
        ⟨Sample BSDF to get new path direction 752⟩
        ⟨Possibly terminate the path 753⟩
    }
    return L;
}
```

Four variables record the current state of the path. pathThroughput holds the product of the BSDF values and cosine terms for the vertices generated so far, divided by their respective sampling PDFs,

$$\prod_{j=1}^{i-1} \frac{f(\mathrm{p}_{j+1} \to \mathrm{p}_j \to \mathrm{p}_{j-1})|\cos\theta_j|}{p_\omega(\mathrm{p}_{j+1} - \mathrm{p}_j)}.$$

Thus, the product of pathThroughput with scattered light from direct lighting at the final vertex of the path gives the contribution for that overall path. One advantage of this approach is that there is no need to store the positions and BSDFs of all of the vertices of the path, only the last one.

L holds the radiance value from the running total of $\sum P(\bar{\mathrm{p}}_i)$, and ray holds the next ray to be traced to extend the path one more vertex. Finally, specularBounce records if the last outgoing path direction sampled was due to specular reflection; the need to track this will be explained shortly.

⟨*Declare common path integration variables*⟩ ≡   **750**
```
    Spectrum pathThroughput = 1., L = 0.;
    RayDifferential ray(r);
    bool specularBounce = false;
```

Because of the loop invariant that `ray` has been initialized to be the ray to be traced to find the next path vertex, the first task of the loop is quite easy. If no intersection is found along the given ray, processing this path stops. The fragment ⟨*Stop path sampling since no intersection was found*⟩, not included here, does some final cleanup and breaks out of the loop. If an intersection was found, and if this is the first vertex of the path after the point on the film plane, it is also necessary to initialize the `alpha` output variable and the `maxt` member variable of the ray that was originally passed to `PathIntegrator::Li()`. Finally, attenuation along the ray must be accounted for in the path throughput, *unless* this is the camera ray (in which case `Scene::Li()` handles it).

⟨*Find next vertex of path*⟩ ≡   **750**
```
    Intersection isect;
    if (!scene->Intersect(ray, &isect)) {
        ⟨Stop path sampling since no intersection was found⟩
        break;
    }
    if (pathLength == 0) {
        r.maxt = ray.maxt;
        if (alpha) *alpha = 1.;
    }
    else
        pathThroughput *= scene->Transmittance(ray);
```

If the ray hits an object that is emissive, the emission is usually ignored, since the previous path vertex already did a direct lighting computation that was responsible for all direct lighting for paths of this length. There are two exceptions to this: The first is at the initial intersection point of camera rays, since this is the only opportunity to include emission from directly visible objects. The second exception happens when the sampled direction from the last path vertex was from a specular BSDF component. Recall that `EstimateDirect()` deliberately omitted the effect of specular reflection in the direct lighting computation; therefore, if the last bounce was due to specular reflection, any emission at the intersection point must be included here.

EstimateDirect() 730
Intersection 172
Intersection::Le() 620
Ray::d 58
Ray::maxt 58
RayDifferential 60
Scene::Intersect() 29
Scene::Li() 30
Scene::Transmittance() 30
Spectrum 230

⟨*Possibly add emitted light at path vertex*⟩ ≡   **750**
```
    if (pathLength == 0 || specularBounce)
        L += pathThroughput * isect.Le(-ray.d);
```

The direct lighting computation uses the UniformSampleOneLight() function, which gives an estimate of the exitant radiance from direct lighting at the vertex at the end of the current path. Scaling this value by the running product of the path contribution gives its overall contribution to the total radiance estimate.

⟨*Sample illumination from lights to find path contribution*⟩ ≡   **750**

```
const Point &p = bsdf->dgShading.p;
const Normal &n = bsdf->dgShading.nn;
Vector wo = -ray.d;
if (pathLength < SAMPLE_DEPTH)
    L += pathThroughput *
        UniformSampleOneLight(scene, p, n, wo, bsdf, sample,
                              lightPositionOffset[pathLength],
                              lightNumOffset[pathLength],
                              bsdfDirectionOffset[pathLength],
                              bsdfComponentOffset[pathLength]);
else
    L += pathThroughput *
        UniformSampleOneLight(scene, p, n, wo, bsdf, sample);
```

Now it is necessary to sample the BSDF at the vertex at the end of the current path to get an outgoing direction from this vertex for the next ray to trace. The ⟨*Get random numbers for sampling new direction,* bs1, bs2, *and* bcs⟩ fragment, not included here, gets three sample values, either from sample if the current path length is less than the value of SAMPLE_DEPTH, or using RandomFloat() otherwise. BSDF::Sample_f() uses the first two samples, bs1 and bs2, to select a direction from a single BxDF's distribution, and bcs to choose which of potentially multiple BxDFs to sample. The integrator updates the path throughput as described earlier and initializes ray with the ray to be traced to find the next vertex in the next iteration of the for loop.

⟨*Sample BSDF to get new path direction*⟩ ≡   **750**

```
    ⟨Get random numbers for sampling new direction, bs1, bs2, and bcs⟩
    Vector wi;
    float pdf;
    BxDFType flags;
    Spectrum f = bsdf->Sample_f(wo, &wi, bs1, bs2, bcs,
                                &pdf, BSDF_ALL, &flags);
    if (f.Black() || pdf == 0.)
        break;
    specularBounce = (flags & BSDF_SPECULAR) != 0;
    pathThroughput *= f * AbsDot(wi, n) / pdf;
    ray = RayDifferential(p, wi);
```

Path termination kicks in after a few bounces, with a fixed termination probability for all additional bounces. If the path isn't terminated, pathThroughput is updated with the

Russian roulette weight and all subsequent $P(\bar{p}_i)$ terms will be appropriately affected by it.

⟨*Possibly terminate the path*⟩ ≡   750

```
if (pathLength > 3) {
    float continueProbability = .5f;
    if (RandomFloat() > continueProbability)
        break;
    pathThroughput /= continueProbability;
}
if (pathLength == maxDepth)
    break;
```

★ 16.3.5 BIDIRECTIONAL PATH TRACING

The path-tracing algorithm described in this section was the first general light transport algorithm in graphics, handling both a wide variety of geometric objects as well as area lights and general BSDF models. Although it works well for many scenes, it can exhibit high variance in the presence of particular tricky lighting conditions. For example, consider the setting shown in Figure 16.7: a light source is illuminating a small area on the ceiling such that the rest of the room is only illuminated by indirect lighting bouncing from that area. If we only trace paths starting from the camera, we will almost never happen to sample a path vertex in the illuminated region on the ceiling before we trace a shadow ray to the light. Most of the paths will have no contribution, while a few of

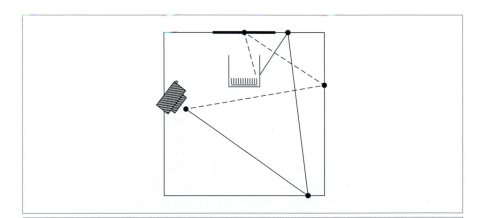

Figure 16.7: A Difficult Case for Path Tracing Starting from the Camera. A light source is illuminating a small area on the ceiling such that only paths with a second-to-last vertex in the area indicated will be able to find illumination from the light. Bidirectional methods, where a path is started from the light and is connected with a path from the camera, can handle situations like these more robustly.

RandomFloat() 857

them—the ones that happen to hit the small region on the ceiling—will have a large contribution. The resulting image will have high variance.

Difficult lighting settings like this can be handled more effectively by constructing paths that start from the camera on one end, from the light on the other end, and are connected in the middle with a visibility ray. This *bidirectional path-tracing* algorithm is a generalization of the standard path-tracing algorithm; for the same amount of computation, it can give substantially lower variance.

The path integral LTE makes it easy to understand how to construct a bidirectional algorithm. As with standard path tracing, the first vertex, p_1, is found by computing the first intersection along the camera ray. The last vertex is found by sampling a point on a light source in the scene. Here we will label the last vertex as q_1, so that we can construct a path of not initially determined length "backward" from the light.

In the basic bidirectional algorithm, we go forward from the camera to create a subpath $p_1, p_2, \ldots, p_i$ and backward from the light to compute a subpath $q_1, q_2, \ldots, q_j$. Each subpath is usually computed incrementally by sampling the BSDF at the previous vertex, although other sampling approaches can be used in the same way as was described for standard path tracing. (Weights for each vertex are computed in the same manner as well.) In either case, in the end, we have a path

$$\bar{p} = p_1, \ldots, p_i, q_j, \ldots, q_1.$$

We need to trace a shadow ray between p_i and q_j to make sure they are mutually visible; if so, the path carries light from the light to the camera, and we can evaluate the path's contribution directly.

There are three refinements to the basic algorithm that improve its performance in practice. The first two are analogous to improvements made to path tracing, and the third is a powerful variance reduction technique on top of the improvement from just starting at the light as well.

- First, subpaths can be reused: given a path $p_1, \ldots, p_i, q_j, \ldots, q_1$, transport over all of the paths can be evaluated by connecting all the various combinations of prefixes of the two paths together. If the two paths have i and j vertices, respectively, then a variety of unique paths can be constructed from them, ranging in length from 2 to $i + j$ vertices long. Each such path built this way only requires that a visibility check be performed by tracing a shadow ray between the last vertices of each of the subpaths. (The BSDFs for each vertex of both paths must be stored to do this.)
- The second optimization is to ignore the paths generated in the path reuse stage that only use one vertex from the light subpath and instead to use the optimized direct lighting code from the direct lighting integrator. This gives a lower-variance result than using the vertex on the light sampled for the light subpath, since it makes it

BSDF 462

possible both to use multiple importance sampling with the BSDF and to use well-distributed sampling patterns for this part of the problem.

- The third optimization is to use multiple importance sampling to reweight paths. Recall the example of a light pointed up at the ceiling, indirectly illuminating a room. As described so far, bidirectional path tracing will improve the result substantially by greatly reducing the number of paths with no contribution, since the paths from the light will be effective at finding those light transport routes. However, the image will still suffer from variance due to paths with unexpectedly large contributions, for example, from paths from the camera that happened to find the bright spot in the ceiling. MIS can be applied to solve this, recognizing that for a path with n vertices, there are actually $n - 1$ ways a path with that length could be generated. For example, a four-vertex path could be built from one camera vertex and three light vertices, two of each kind of vertex, or three camera vertices and one light vertex. Given a particular path sampled in a particular way, we can compute the weights for each of the other ways the path could have been generated and apply the balance heuristic.

pbrt doesn't have a bidirectional path-tracing integrator; implementing one is left as an exercise.

16.4 IRRADIANCE CACHING

With unbiased light transport algorithms like path tracing, some scenes can take a large number of rays (and corresponding compute time) to generate images without objectionable noise. One approach to this problem has been the development of biased approaches to solving the LTE. These approaches generally reuse previously computed results over multiple exitant radiance computations, even when the values used don't estimate the precise quantity that needs to be computed (for example, by reusing an illumination value from a nearby point under the assumption that illumination is slowly changing). Irradiance caching, described in this section, and photon mapping, described in the next, have been two successful biased methods for light transport.

By introducing bias, these methods produce images without the high-frequency noise artifacts that unbiased Monte Carlo techniques are prone to. They can often create good-looking images using relatively little additional computation compared to basic techniques like Whitted ray tracing. This efficiency comes at a price, however: one key characteristic of unbiased Monte Carlo techniques is that variance decreases in a predictable and well-characterized manner as more samples are taken. As such, if an image was computed with an unbiased technique and has no noise, we can be extremely confident that the image correctly represents the lighting in the scene. With a biased solution method, however, error estimates aren't well-defined for the approaches that have been developed so far; if the image doesn't have visual artifacts, it still may have substantial error. Even

Figure 16.8: Indirect Illumination Component of a View of the Sponza Atrium. Note its smoothly varying and slowly changing nature.

worse, given an image with artifacts, increasing the sampling rate with a biased technique doesn't necessarily eliminate artifacts in a predictable way.

The *irradiance caching* algorithm is based on the observation that while direct lighting often changes rapidly from point to point (e.g., consider a hard shadow edge), indirect lighting is often much more slowly changing. Therefore, if we compute an accurate representation of indirect light at a sparse set of sample points in the scene and then interpolate nearby samples to compute an approximate representation of indirect light at any particular point being shaded, we can expect that the error introduced by not recomputing indirect lighting everywhere shouldn't be too bad, and we can achieve a substantial computational savings by not recomputing this information at every point. Figure 16.8, which shows the indirect lighting component of a view of the Sponza atrium scene, illustrates the smoothness of indirect lighting in this environment.

There are two issues that must be addressed in the design of an algorithm such as this one:

1. How is the indirect lighting distribution represented and stored after being computed at a point?
2. When are new representations of indirect light computed, and how often are already existing ones interpolated?

In the irradiance caching algorithm, indirect lighting is computed on demand at a subset of the points that are shaded (as opposed to a fixed set of points chosen in a preprocess) and stored in a spatial data structure. When exitant radiance at a point is being computed, the cache is first searched for one or more acceptable nearby samples, using a set of error metrics to determine if the already existing samples are acceptable. In order to have a compact representation of indirect light, this algorithm only stores the irradiance at each point, rather than a directionally varying radiance distribution, thus reducing the light representation to just a single `Spectrum`.

Recall that irradiance arriving at one side of a surface with normal $\mathbf{n}$ is

$$E(\mathbf{p}, \mathbf{n}) = \int_{\mathcal{H}^2(\mathbf{n})} L_i(\mathbf{p}, \omega_i) |\cos \theta_i| \, d\omega_i.$$

It is in a sense a weighted average of incoming radiance at a point, giving a sense of the aggregate illumination there. Consider the reflection component of the scattering equation for a reflective surface:

$$L_o(\mathbf{p}, \omega_o) = \int_{\mathcal{H}^2(\mathbf{n})} f_r(\mathbf{p}, \omega_o, \omega_i) L_i(\mathbf{p}, \omega_i) |\cos \theta_i| \, d\omega_i;$$

If the surface is Lambertian, the BSDF is constant, and we have

$$L_o(\mathbf{p}, \omega_o) = c \int_{\mathcal{H}^2(\mathbf{n})} L_i(\mathbf{p}, \omega_i) \, |\cos \theta_i| d\omega_i$$

$$= c \, E(\mathbf{p}, \mathbf{n}).$$

In other words, for perfectly diffuse materials, the irradiance alone is enough information to exactly compute the reflection from the surface due to a particular incident lighting distribution. Thus, another key assumption in the irradiance caching algorithm is that many of the surfaces in the scene are diffuse, or that other approaches will be used for the glossy and specular components of the BSDF.

If the surface is nearly Lambertian (e.g., has the Oren-Nayar BRDF or a glossy surface with a very wide specular lobe), we can instead view the irradiance caching algorithm as making the approximation

$$L_o(\mathbf{p}, \omega_o) \approx \left(\int_{\mathcal{H}^2(\mathbf{n})} f_r(\mathbf{p}, \omega_o, \omega_i) \, d\omega_i \right) \left(\int_{\mathcal{H}^2(\mathbf{n})} L_i(\mathbf{p}, \omega_i) \, |\cos \theta_i| d\omega_i \right)$$

$$\approx \left(\frac{1}{2} \, \rho_{hd}(\omega_o) \right) \, E(\mathbf{p}, \mathbf{n}),$$

where ρ_{hd} is the hemispherical-directional reflectance, introduced in Section 9.1.1. This error in this approximation increases as the variation of either of the two integrands increases. As an example of a case with a potential for arbitrarily large error, consider a perfectly specular surface such that only the incident radiance from a single direction contributes to reflected radiance. Using the irradiance and the hemispherical-directional reflectance to compute reflection for such a BSDF incorrectly includes the effect of radiance from all the other incident directions.

⟨*IrradianceCache Declarations*⟩ ≡
```
class IrradianceCache : public SurfaceIntegrator {
public:
    ⟨IrradianceCache Public Methods⟩
private:
    ⟨IrradianceCache Data  758⟩
    ⟨IrradianceCache Private Methods⟩
};
```

Our implementation takes parameters that give the maximum number of bounces of indirect light and the maximum number of levels of specular reflection that the integrator
will account for (it uses basic Whitted ray tracing to account for perfect specular reflection and refraction). The `maxError` value controls how frequently irradiance samples are
reused versus computing a new sample, and `nSamples` controls how many rays are used to
estimate the irradiance integral for each sample computed. Finally, `specularDepth` tracks
the current ray depth as the integrator is recursively called to account for multiply scattered light.

⟨*IrradianceCache Method Definitions*⟩ ≡
```
IrradianceCache::IrradianceCache(int maxspec, int maxind,
                                 float maxerr, int ns) {
    maxError = maxerr;
    nSamples = ns;
    maxSpecularDepth = maxspec;
    maxIndirectDepth = maxind;
    specularDepth = 0;
}
```

⟨*IrradianceCache Data*⟩ ≡   **758**
```
float maxError;
int nSamples;
int maxSpecularDepth, maxIndirectDepth;
mutable int specularDepth;
```

This integrator reuses the direct lighting routines that were defined in the direct lighting
integrator, although here all lights are always sampled. Fragments to request samples for
this are reused from the `DirectLightingIntegrator` as well.

⟨*IrradianceCache Method Definitions*⟩ + ≡
```
void IrradianceCache::RequestSamples(Sample *sample, const Scene *scene) {
    ⟨Allocate and request samples for sampling all lights  725⟩
}
```

⟨*IrradianceCache Data*⟩ + ≡   **758**
```
⟨Declare sample parameters for light source sampling  724⟩
```

(a)   (b)

Figure 16.9: Sponza atrium scene rendered with (a) irradiance caching and (b) path tracing, both with approximately the same amount of computation time. We have intentionally limited the time spent rendering these in order to compare the image artifacts of the two methods when they are not able to take enough samples to sufficiently sample the scene radiance distribution. Path tracing has high-frequency noise, while irradiance caching suffers from circular blotches.

Figure 16.9 shows the irradiance cache in action. Figure 16.9(a) was rendered using the irradiance cache, and Figure 16.9(b) with path tracing, both using approximately the same amount of computation. The artifacts from undersampling with the irradiance cache are quite different than the variance from path tracing. Figure 16.10 shows the locations at which irradiance estimates were computed for this example.

We won't include most of the irradiance cache's Li() method here, but will just focus on its key two fragments, ⟨*Compute direct lighting for irradiance cache*⟩ and ⟨*Compute indirect lighting for irradiance cache*⟩. For direct lighting, the UniformSampleAllLights() function from Section 16.1 is used to apply multiple importance sampling for the direct lighting estimate.

Intersection::Le() 620

UniformSampleAllLights() 727

⟨*Compute direct lighting for irradiance cache*⟩ ≡
```
L += isect.Le(wo);
L += UniformSampleAllLights(scene, p, n, wo, bsdf, sample,
                           lightSampleOffset, bsdfSampleOffset,
                           bsdfComponentOffset);
```

Figure 16.10: The Positions at Which Irradiance Estimates Were Computed for the Image in Figure 16.9. Note that they are mostly near the corners, where indirect illumination is changing most rapidly.

The `IrradianceCache` partitions the BSDF for the indirect lighting computation. Perfect specular reflection is handled by sampling the BSDF and recursively calling the integrator, just as the `WhittedIntegrator` does. The implementation here uses irradiance caching for both the diffuse and glossy components of the BSDF, thus introducing additional error for the glossy components. (An exercise at the end of the chapter describes modifying this integrator to sample from the glossy parts of the BSDF and recursively call the integrator for those rays instead.)

⟨*Compute indirect lighting for irradiance cache*⟩ ≡
```
    if (specularDepth++ < maxSpecularDepth) {
        Vector wi;
        ⟨Trace rays for specular reflection and refraction  36⟩
    }
    --specularDepth;
    ⟨Estimate indirect lighting with irradiance cache  761⟩
```

IrradianceCache 758

IrradianceCache::
  maxSpecularDepth 758

IrradianceCache::
  specularDepth 758

Vector 47

Reflection and transmission must be handled separately, with two independent irradiance values if the surface has both reflective and transmissive nonspecular components, since the irradiance from the hemisphere that is needed for reflective surfaces and the hemisphere on the opposite side of the surface that is needed for transmissive surfaces is completely different. The `IndirectLo()` method handles either case, interpolating a value using the cache or computing a new value and using it to compute exitant radiance using the irradiance values. Before calling these methods, the integrator reorients the normal so that it points in the same hemisphere as the ω_o vector. `IndirectLo()` depends on this convention when it generates sample rays over the hemisphere, since it will ensure that all of these rays are in the same hemisphere as n.

⟨*Estimate indirect lighting with irradiance cache*⟩ ≡   **760**
```
Normal ng = isect.dg.nn;
if (Dot(wo, ng) < 0.f) ng = -ng;
BxDFType flags = BxDFType(BSDF_REFLECTION | BSDF_DIFFUSE | BSDF_GLOSSY);
L += IndirectLo(p, ng, wo, bsdf, flags, sample, scene);
flags = BxDFType(BSDF_TRANSMISSION | BSDF_DIFFUSE | BSDF_GLOSSY);
L += IndirectLo(p, -ng, wo, bsdf, flags, sample, scene);
```

If the `InterpolateIrradiance()` method isn't able to find enough nearby irradiance samples of good enough quality, it computes a new irradiance value and adds it to the cache. Either way, E is initialized with a representation of irradiance for this point, and exitant radiance can be computed with the approximation developed above.

⟨*IrradianceCache Method Definitions*⟩+≡
```
Spectrum IrradianceCache::IndirectLo(const Point &p,
        const Normal &n, const Vector &wo, BSDF *bsdf,
        BxDFType flags, const Sample *sample,
        const Scene *scene) const {
    if (bsdf->NumComponents(flags) == 0)
        return Spectrum(0.);
    Spectrum E;
    if (!InterpolateIrradiance(scene, p, n, &E)) {
        ⟨Compute irradiance at current point 762⟩
        ⟨Add computed irradiance value to cache 763⟩
    }
    return .5f * bsdf->rho(wo, flags) * E;
}
```

Before describing how irradiance values are stored, looked up, and interpolated, first we'll discuss how new estimates are computed; doing so will make more clear how some of the details of reuse work later. We need to estimate the value of the integral

$$E(\mathrm{p}, \mathbf{n}) = \int_{\mathcal{H}^2(\mathbf{n})} L_i(\mathrm{p}, \omega_i) \, |\cos \theta_i| d\omega_i. \qquad [16.5]$$

Because there is no easy available way to importance sample based on the distribution of incident radiance, the implementation uses a cosine-weighted distribution of directions. It is then faced with the problem of computing the amount of incident radiance along each one, $L_i(p, \omega_i)$—precisely the problem that all of the other integrators in this chapter address.

In the implementation here, the IrradianceCache uses standard path tracing to compute these values.[2] Before it starts tracing rays to compute the irradiance estimate, the integrator initializes a pair of random values to use to scramble the two dimensions of a low-discrepancy point sequence that we will map to cosine-weighted directions over the hemisphere. (See Section 7.4.3 for an explanation of how to randomly scramble point sequences so that a different set of sample values is used each time while still preserving the good distribution properties of the point set.) This method also initializes the sumInvDists variable to zero and accumulates the sum of the reciprocal distance each sample ray travels before intersecting an object; this value is used later to help estimate how widely reusable the irradiance estimate is.

To compute the irradiance estimate from the radiance values along the sample rays, the implementation uses the standard Monte Carlo estimator:

$$E(p, \mathbf{n}) = \frac{1}{N} \sum_j \frac{L_i(p, \omega_j)|\cos\theta_j|}{p(\omega_j)}.$$

Because the rays are sampled from a cosine-weighted distribution, $p(\omega) = \cos\theta/\pi$, so

$$\frac{1}{N} \sum_j \frac{L_i(p, \omega_j)|\cos\theta_j|}{|\cos\theta_j|/\pi} = \frac{\pi}{N} \sum_j L_i(p, \omega_j).$$

⟨*Compute irradiance at current point*⟩ ≡   **761**

```
u_int scramble[2] = { RandomUInt(), RandomUInt() };
float sumInvDists = 0.;
for (int i = 0; i < nSamples; ++i) {
    ⟨Trace ray to sample radiance for irradiance estimate 763⟩
}
E *= M_PI / float(nSamples);
```

CosineSampleHemisphere() returns a direction in the canonical reflection coordinate system, with the normal direction mapped to the $+z$ axis. To get a world space ray direction, the convenient BSDF::LocalToWorld() method can be used. This direction may then need to be flipped so that it lies in the same hemisphere as the normal that was passed in. The fragment that estimates the radiance values along the rays, ⟨*Do path tracing to compute radiance along ray for estimate*⟩, is not included here, since it is essentially the same as the code in the PathIntegrator's Li() method. It sets the L variable to hold the incident radiance estimate, which is then added to the E sum.

---

2   Using bidirectional path tracing to compute these values (to capture, for example, indirect lighting due to a spotlight shining at a small area on a ceiling) would be a good improvement to the basic algorithm implemented here.

⟨*Trace ray to sample radiance for irradiance estimate*⟩ ≡ 762
    ⟨*Update irradiance statistics for rays traced*⟩
```
    float u[2];
    Sample02(i, scramble, u);
    Vector w = CosineSampleHemisphere(u[0], u[1]);
    RayDifferential r(p, bsdf->LocalToWorld(w));
    if (Dot(r.d, n) < 0) r.d = -r.d;
    Spectrum L(0.);
```
    ⟨*Do path tracing to compute radiance along ray for estimate*⟩
```
    E += L;
    float dist = r.maxt * r.d.Length();
    sumInvDists += 1.f / dist;
```

So that it can efficiently search for all of the already computed irradiance estimates around a point in the scene, the IrradianceCache uses an octree data structure to store the estimates. The Octree template class, which is described in Section A.4 in Appendix A, recursively splits a given bounding box into subregions, refining the current region into eight subregions at each level of the tree by dividing the box in half at the midpoint of its extent along the *x*, *y*, and *z* axes. Each irradiance estimate has an axis-aligned bounding box associated with it, giving the overall area for which it is potentially a valid sample. The octree uses the extent of this box as a guide for an appropriate level of the tree at which to store the sample. Later, given a point to look up nearby irradiance samples for, the octree just needs to traverse the nodes that the point is inside (there is one such node at each level of the tree) and provide the samples overlapping those nodes to be considered for interpolation (Figure 16.11).

⟨*Add computed irradiance value to cache*⟩ ≡ 761
    ⟨*Update statistics for new irradiance sample*⟩
    ⟨*Compute bounding box of irradiance sample's contribution region* 765⟩
```
    octree->Add(IrradianceSample(E, p, n, maxDist), sampleExtent);
```

Having taken a set of radiance samples, we'd like to estimate over how wide an area we can reuse the irradiance at other points without introducing too much error. For example, indirect irradiance at a point in the middle of the ceiling of a room is likely to be changing more slowly as a function of position than it is at the edge of the ceiling where the wall meets it. In general, the more objects that are close to the sample point, the greater potential there is for rapidly changing irradiance. Therefore, the IrradianceCache computes the harmonic mean of the distance each of the sample rays traveled before intersecting an object,

$$\frac{N}{\sum_i^N 1/d_i},$$

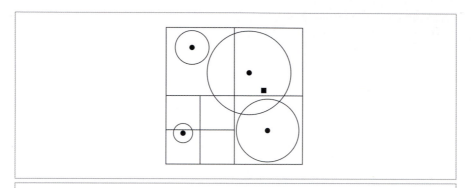

Figure 16.11: Example of Irradiance Sample Storage in 2D (with a Quadtree, Rather than an Octree). Each irradiance sample, denoted by a dot, has a maximum distance over which it potentially can contribute irradiance, denoted here by a circle. Samples are stored in the tree nodes that they overlap, and the tree is refined adaptively so that each sample is stored in a small number of nodes. Given a point at which we want to look up nearby irradiance estimates, here shown with a black square, we just need to traverse the tree nodes that the point overlaps, considering all of the irradiance samples stored in these nodes.

where d_i is the distance that the ith ray traveled. This value serves as an upper bound on the area of influence for the estimate. The harmonic mean is a good way to calculate such a value, as a few rays that go a large distance (or don't intersect anything and have infinite distance, for that matter) can't overwhelm the contributions of close-by distances, which are the most important ones to detect when the irradiance value may be changing rapidly.

Before the maximum potentially valid distance is used to initialize the bounding box for the estimate, it is clamped to a range chosen in an effort to ensure that the bound is neither too small (such that the estimate is never reused) or too large (such that it's reused too much). The values for this range are chosen here in an ad hoc manner; there are certainly scenes where they would be ineffective.

More subtly, the maximum distance is also scaled by the user-supplied error value. Later on, the error metric calculation used for deciding if this estimate can be used at another point incorporates the maximum distance value in a way such that we can equivalently scale maxDist here and compare the computed error estimate to one, or not scale maxDist here and compare the error estimate to maxError. Because maxError should be in the range [0, 1], it's much better to take the former approach, since it makes the bounding box substantially smaller, thereby improving the efficiency of irradiance cache lookups.

⟨*Compute bounding box of irradiance sample's contribution region*⟩ ≡   763
```
static float minMaxDist =
    .001f * powf(scene->WorldBound().Volume(), 1.f/3.f);
static float maxMaxDist =
    .125f * powf(scene->WorldBound().Volume(), 1.f/3.f);
float maxDist = nSamples / sumInvDists;
if (minMaxDist > 0.f)
    maxDist = Clamp(maxDist, minMaxDist, maxMaxDist);
maxDist *= maxError;
BBox sampleExtent(p);
sampleExtent.Expand(maxDist);
```

Each irradiance estimate is represented by an instance of the IrradianceSample structure, which holds the relevant pieces of information. Its constructor, not included here, initializes the member variables with the values passed to it.

⟨*IrradianceCache Declarations*⟩+≡
```
struct IrradianceSample {
    ⟨IrradianceSample Constructor⟩
    Spectrum E;
    Normal n;
    Point p;
    float maxDist;
};
```

The octree is allocated in the integrator's Preprocess() method since the scene is available then and its overall extent, which is needed by the Octree constructor, can be found. It expands the bound by a small amount in each direction so that the octree can gracefully deal with the fact that some of the irradiance samples and some of the lookup points will be marginally outside the scene bounds due to floating-point error from ray intersection computations.

⟨*IrradianceCache Method Definitions*⟩+≡
```
void IrradianceCache::Preprocess(const Scene *scene) {
    BBox wb = scene->WorldBound();
    Vector delta = .01f * (wb.pMax - wb.pMin);
    wb.pMin -= delta;
    wb.pMax += delta;
    octree = new Octree<IrradianceSample, IrradProcess>(wb);
}
```

⟨*IrradianceCache Data*⟩+≡   758
```
mutable Octree<IrradianceSample, IrradProcess> *octree;
```

Now we can define the method that attempts to compute an interpolated irradiance value at a point in the scene using cached values. Much of the work is done by the `Octree::Lookup()` method, which traverses the nodes of the octree that the given point is inside and calls a method of the `IrradProcess` object for each `IrradianceSample` in each of these nodes. This `IrradProcess` method decides if each sample is acceptable and accumulates the value of the interpolated result.

⟨*IrradianceCache Method Definitions*⟩+≡
```
    bool IrradianceCache::InterpolateIrradiance(const Scene *scene,
            const Point &p, const Normal &n, Spectrum *E) const {
        if (!octree) return false;
        IrradProcess proc(n, maxError);
        octree->Lookup(p, proc);
        ⟨Update irradiance cache lookup statistics⟩
        if (!proc.Successful()) return false;
        *E = proc.GetIrradiance();
        return true;
    }
```

`IrradProcess` stores additional information about the point being shaded that it will need for deciding whether irradiance samples can be used at that point as well as information about the interpolated value that is being accumulated. Its constructor initializes the normal `n` and error limit `maxError` with the values passed in and sets the rest of its members to zero.

⟨*IrradianceCache Declarations*⟩+≡
```
    struct IrradProcess {
        ⟨IrradProcess Public Methods 768⟩
        Normal n;
        float maxError;
        mutable int nFound, samplesChecked;
        mutable float sumWt;
        mutable Spectrum E;
    };
```

This `IrradProcess` callback method is invoked for each `IrradianceSample` in an octree node that the lookup point is inside. It is given both the original point p that was passed to `Octree::Lookup()` earlier as well as an irradiance sample from the octree. It first performs a series of tests that may reject the sample as not being acceptable. If the sample passes these tests, the method computes a value that tries to approximate the error from using the sample at the shading point, which is compared to the user-supplied error limit.

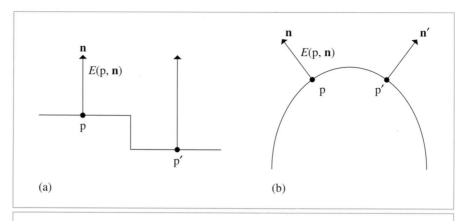

Figure 16.12: Rejection Tests for Samples in the Irradiance Cache. (a) If the irradiance estimate is in front of the lookup point or (b) if the surface normal that orients its hemisphere is substantially different from the normal at the point, reusing irradiance may give substantial errors.

⟨*IrradianceCache Method Definitions*⟩+≡
```
    void IrradProcess::operator()(const Point &p,
            const IrradianceSample &sample) const {
        ++samplesChecked;
        ⟨Skip irradiance sample if surface normals are too different  767⟩
        ⟨Skip irradiance sample if it's too far from the sample point  768⟩
        ⟨Skip irradiance sample if it's in front of point being shaded  768⟩
        ⟨Compute estimate error term and possibly use sample  768⟩
    }
```

If the surface normal of the lookup point and the normal used when computing the irradiance estimate are substantially different, as in Figure 16.12(b), the hemisphere of directions that determines their irradiance values will be different enough that it's unlikely that the sample will accurately represent the actual irradiance, and this estimate is rejected.

⟨*Skip irradiance sample if surface normals are too different*⟩ ≡   767
```
    if (Dot(n, sample.n) < 0.01f)
        return;
```

The next check is to make sure that the point being shaded isn't too far from the sample. This check is redundant given the way the error metric is computed, but it gives an early out before the expensive square root and division operations that will be used in that computation.

⟨*Skip irradiance sample if it's too far from the sample point*⟩ ≡   767
```
    float d2 = DistanceSquared(p, sample.p);
    if (d2 > sample.maxDist * sample.maxDist)
        return;
```

The next check is to see if the irradiance sample is in front of the lookup point, as in Figure 16.12(a). If so, the sample might have a very large maxDist value, reflecting an expected slowly changing indirect irradiance, while the lookup point might be close to a corner or other geometric feature that causes irradiance to actually be changing more quickly there.

⟨*Skip irradiance sample if it's in front of point being shaded*⟩ ≡   767
```
    Normal navg = sample.n + n;
    if (Dot(p - sample.p, navg) < -.01f)
        return;
```

If the sample has passed these four tests, a numerical estimate of the expected error from including the sample in the irradiance value is computed. The expression we use to do this is ad hoc, but it captures the key ideas that error should increase with distance between the sample and the point being shaded and should increase as their normal vectors diverge. If this value is less than the user-supplied error limit, a weight for this irradiance value is found, with higher weight if its error is low, and the weighted irradiance is added to a running sum of interpolated irradiances. (The user-supplied error limit figures into this computation in an indirect way. Recall that the irradiance samples' maxDist values were scaled by the error limit earlier. Thus here the appropriate test works out to be whether err is less than one, not the user-supplied error limit.)

⟨*Compute estimate error term and possibly use sample*⟩ ≡   767
```
    float err = sqrtf(d2) / (sample.maxDist * Dot(n, sample.n));
    if (err < 1.) {
        ++nFound;
        float wt = (1.f - err) * (1.f - err);
        E += wt * sample.E;
        sumWt += wt;
    }
```

When traversing the octree and processing candidate samples is finished, it is necessary to decide if an acceptable interpolated irradiance value has been computed from the irradiance samples. A nonzero sum of weights suffices to indicate that one or more valid estimates have been found.

⟨*IrradProcess Public Methods*⟩ ≡   766
```
    bool Successful() {
        return (sumWt > 0. && nFound > 0);
    }
```

The final interpolated irradiance value is a weighted sum of the irradiance values of the acceptable estimates,

$$E = \frac{\sum_i w_i E_i}{\sum_i w_i}.$$

⟨*IrradProcess Public Methods*⟩+≡   766
```
    Spectrum GetIrradiance() const { return E / sumWt; }
```

16.5 PARTICLE TRACING AND PHOTON MAPPING

Photon mapping is another approach for solving the LTE based on a biased algorithm. Unlike irradiance caching, photon mapping handles both glossy and diffuse reflection well; perfectly specular reflection is handled separately with recursive ray tracing.

Photon mapping is one of a family of *particle-tracing* algorithms, which are based on the idea of constructing paths from the lights where, at each vertex of the path, the amount of incident illumination arriving at the vertex is recorded as an illumination sample. After a certain number of these illumination samples have been computed, a data structure that stores a representation of the distribution of light in the scene is built, and at rendering time, this representation is used to compute values of measurements needed to compute the image. Because the particle-tracing step is decoupled from computing the measurements, many measurements may be able to reuse the work done for a single particle path, thus leading to more efficient rendering algorithms.

In this section, we will start by introducing a theory of particle-tracing algorithms and will discuss the conditions that must be fulfilled by a particle-tracing algorithm so that arbitrary measurements can be computed correctly using the particles created by the algorithm. We will then describe an implementation of a photon mapping integrator that uses particles to estimate illumination by interpolating lighting contributions from particles around the point being shaded.

*16.5.1 THEORETICAL BASIS FOR PARTICLE TRACING

IrradProcess::E 766
IrradProcess::sumWt 766
Spectrum 230

Particle-tracing algorithms in computer graphics are often explained in terms of packets of energy being shot from the light sources in the scene that deposit energy at surfaces they intersect before scattering in new directions. This is an intuitive way of thinking about particle tracing, but the intuition that it provides doesn't make it easy to answer basic questions about how propagation and scattering affect the particles. For example, does their contribution fall off with squared distance like flux density? Or which $\cos\theta$ terms, if any, affect particles after they scatter from a surface?

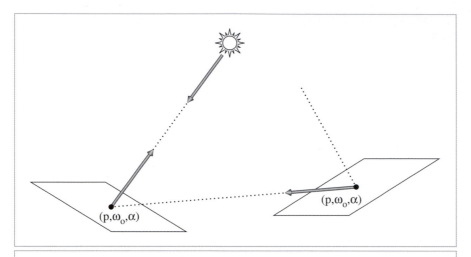

Figure 16.13: When a particle is traced following a path from a light source, an entry in its particle history is recorded at each surface it intersects. Each entry in the history is represented by position p, direction along the ray it arrived along ω_o, and particle weight α.

In order to give a solid theoretical basis for particle tracing, we will describe it with a framework introduced by Veach (1997, Appendix 4.A), which instead interprets the stored particle histories as samples from the scene's equilibrium radiance distribution. Under certain conditions on the distribution and weights of the particles, the particles can be used to compute estimates of nearly any measurement based on the light distribution in the scene. In this framework, it is quite easy to answer questions about the details of particle propagation like the ones earlier. After developing this theory here, the remainder of this section will demonstrate its application to photon mapping.

A particle-tracing algorithm generates a set of N samples of illumination at points p_j, on surfaces in the scene

$$(p_j, \omega_j, \alpha_j),$$

where each sample records incident illumination from direction ω_j and has some weight α_j associated with it (Figure 16.13). We would like to determine the conditions on the weights and distribution of particle positions so that we can use them to compute estimates of arbitrary measurements.

Given an importance function $W_e(p, \omega)$ that describes the measurement to be taken, the natural condition we would like to be fulfilled is that the particles should be distributed and weighted such that using them to compute an estimate has the same expected value as the measurement equation for the same importance function:

$$E\left[\frac{1}{N}\sum_{j=1}^{N}\alpha_j W_e(\mathrm{p}_j, \omega_j)\right] = \int_A \int_{\mathbb{S}^2} W_e(\mathrm{p}, \omega)L_i(\mathrm{p}, \omega)\,\mathrm{d}A\mathrm{d}\omega. \qquad \text{(16.6)}$$

For example, we might want to use the particles to compute the total flux on a wall. Using the definition of flux,

$$\Phi = \int_{A_{\mathrm{wall}}} \int_{\mathcal{H}^2(\mathbf{n})} L_i(\mathrm{p}, \omega)\,|\cos\theta|\,\mathrm{d}A\mathrm{d}\omega,$$

the following importance function selects the particles that lie on the wall and arrived from the hemisphere around the normal:

$$W_e(\mathrm{p}, \omega) = \max((\omega \cdot \mathbf{n}), 0) \times \begin{cases} 1 & : \quad \mathrm{p} \text{ is on wall surface} \\ 0 & : \quad \text{otherwise.} \end{cases}$$

If the conditions on the distribution of particle weights and positions are true for arbitrary importance functions such that Equation (16.6) holds, then the flux estimate can be computed directly as just a sum of the particle weights for the particles on the wall multiplied by the $\cos\theta$ term. If we want to estimate flux over a different wall, a subset of the original wall, and so on, we only need to recompute the weighted sum with an updated importance function. The particles and weights can be reused, and we have an unbiased estimate for all of these measurements. (The estimates will be correlated, however, which is potentially a source of artifacts.)

To see how to generate and weight particles that fulfill these conditions, consider the task of evaluating the measurement equation integral

$$\int_A \int_{\mathbb{S}^2} W_e(\mathrm{p}_0, \omega)L(\mathrm{p}_0, \omega)\mathrm{d}\omega\mathrm{d}A(\mathrm{p}_0) =$$

$$\int_A \int_A W_e(\mathrm{p}_0 \to \mathrm{p}_1)L(\mathrm{p}_1 \to \mathrm{p}_0)G(\mathrm{p}_0 \leftrightarrow \mathrm{p}_1)\,\mathrm{d}A(\mathrm{p}_0)\mathrm{d}A(\mathrm{p}_1),$$

where the importance function W_e that describes the measurement is a black box and thus cannot be used to drive the sampling of the integral at all. We can still compute an estimate of the integral with Monte Carlo integration, but must sample a set of points p_0 and p_1 from all of the surfaces in the scene, using some sampling distribution that doesn't depend on W_e (e.g., by uniformly sampling points by surface area).

By expanding the LTE in the integrand and applying the standard Monte Carlo estimator for N samples, we can find the estimator for this measurement,

$$E\left[\frac{1}{N}\sum_{i=1}^{N} W_e(\mathrm{p}_{i,0} \to \mathrm{p}_{i,1})\left\{\frac{L(\mathrm{p}_{i,1} \to \mathrm{p}_{i,0})G(\mathrm{p}_{i,0} \leftrightarrow \mathrm{p}_{i,1})}{p(\mathrm{p}_{i,0})p(\mathrm{p}_{i,1})}\right\}\right].$$

We can further expand out the L term into the sum over paths and use the fact that $E[ab] = E[aE[b]]$ and the fact that for a particular sample, the expected value

$$E\left[\frac{L(\mathrm{p}_{i,1} \to \mathrm{p}_{i,0})}{P(\mathrm{p}_{i,0})}\right]$$

can be written as a finite sum of n_i terms in just the same way that we generated a finite set of weighted path vertices for path tracing. If the sum is truncated with Russian roulette such that the probability of continuing the sum after j terms is $q_{i,j}$, then the jth term of the ith sample has contribution

$$\frac{L_e(\mathrm{p}_{n_i} \to \mathrm{p}_{n_i-1})}{p(\mathrm{p}_{n_i})} \prod_{j=1}^{n_i-1} \frac{1}{q_{i,j}} \frac{f(\mathrm{p}_{i,j+1} \to \mathrm{p}_{i,j} \to \mathrm{p}_{i,j-1})G(\mathrm{p}_{i,j+1} \leftrightarrow \mathrm{p}_{i,j})}{p(\mathrm{p}_{i,j})}.$$

Looking back at Equation (16.6), we can see that this quantity gives the appropriate value of the particle weights if the particle-generating paths are sampled from a distribution over area:

$$\alpha_{i,j} = \frac{L_e(\mathrm{p}_{n_i} \to \mathrm{p}_{n_i-1})}{p(\mathrm{p}_{n_i})} \prod_{j=1}^{n_i-1} \frac{1}{q_{i,j}} \frac{f(\mathrm{p}_{i,j+1} \to \mathrm{p}_{i,j} \to \mathrm{p}_{i,j-1})G(\mathrm{p}_{i,j+1} \leftrightarrow \mathrm{p}_{i,j})}{p(\mathrm{p}_{i,j})}.$$

Note that we have the freedom to generate a set of particles with these weights in all sorts of different ways. Although the natural approach is to start from points on lights and incrementally sample paths using the BSDFs at the path vertices, similar to how the path-tracing integrator generates paths (starting here from the light, rather than from the camera), we could generate them with any number of different sampling strategies, so long as there is nonzero probability of generating a particle at any point where W_e is nonzero and the particle weights are computed appropriately for the sampling distribution used.

If we only had a single measurement to make, it would be better if we used information about W_e and could compute the estimate more intelligently, since the general particle-tracing approach described here may generate many useless samples if W_e only covers a small subset of the points on scene objects. If we will be computing many measurements, however, the key advantage that particle tracing brings is that we can generate the samples and weights once and can then reuse them over a large number of measurements, potentially computing results much more efficiently than if the measurements were all computed from scratch.

16.5.2 PHOTON INTEGRATOR

The photon mapping integrator traces particles into the scene as described earlier and interpolates among particles to approximate the incident illumination at shading points. For consistency with other descriptions of the algorithm, we will refer to particles generated for photon mapping as photons. The integrator uses a kd-tree data structure to store the photons; this allows it to quickly find the photons around the point being shaded. The kd-tree is referred to as the *photon map*. Because the kd-tree is decoupled from the scene

Figure 16.14: Distribution of photons distributed by the particle tracing algorithm in the Sponza scene.

geometry, this algorithm isn't limited to a particular type of geometric representation (in contrast to using a texture map defined over shapes' (u, v) parameterizations to store illumination, for instance). Figure 16.14 shows the distribution of photons for a view of the Sponza scene.

Photon mapping partitions the LTE in a number of different ways that make it easier to adjust the quality of the results computed. For example, particles from the lights are characterized as being one of three types: direct illumination (light that has arrived directly at a surface, without any scattering), caustic illumination (light that has arrived at a nonspecular surface after interacting with one or more specular surfaces), and indirect illumination (all other types of illumination). Thanks to this partitioning, the integrator has a fair amount of flexibility in how it estimates reflected radiance. For instance, it might use the indirect and caustic photons to estimate reflection due to those modes of light transport, but ignore the direct illumination photons and sample the light sources for direct illumination. As mentioned previously, this integrator also partitions the BSDF: perfect specular components are always handled with recursive ray tracing, while either the photon maps or Monte Carlo ray tracing is used for the rest of it.

⟨*Photonmap Local Declarations*⟩ ≡
```
class PhotonIntegrator : public SurfaceIntegrator {
public:
     ⟨PhotonIntegrator Public Methods⟩
private:
     ⟨PhotonIntegrator Private Methods  776⟩
     ⟨PhotonIntegrator Private Data  775⟩
};
```

Quite a few different parameters control the operation of the integrator. The user must specify a desired number of photons of each type—caustic, direct, and indirect—to store in each of the three types of photon maps. Using more photons increases the quality of results, but takes more time and memory. Because this integrator interpolates nearby photons to estimate illumination at the shading point, the user can also set how many photons are used for the interpolation. The more photons that are used, the smoother the illumination estimate will be, since a larger number of photons will be used to reconstruct it. If too many are used, the result will tend to be too blurry, while too few gives a splotchy appearance. Interpolating 50 to 100 photons is often a good choice.

Finally, the integrator can be configured to do a one-bounce sampling of indirect illumination by sampling the BSDF and tracing rays into the scene, rather than using the indirect photon map. This process, which will be described in more detail later, is known as final gathering.

We won't include the implementation of the `PhotonIntegrator` constructor here, since it just initializes its member variables from the parameters passed to it. Its member variables are the following:

- `nCausticPhotons`, `nDirectPhotons`, and `nIndirectPhotons` give the total number of photons to try to store for each category of illumination stored in the photon map.
- `nLookup` gives the total number of photons to try to use for the interpolation step.
- `maxDistSquared` gives the maximum allowed squared distance from the point where exitant radiance is being computed to a photon that can be used for the interpolation there. If its value is too large, the integrator will waste time searching for nearby photons in dark regions, while if it's too small, it may not be able to find `nLookup` nearby photons, leading to an overly splotchy result.
- `specularDepth` and `maxSpecularDepth` track the current and maximum values of specular reflection, similar to the Whitted integrator.
- `directWithPhotons` determines whether direct illumination is computed with the photon map or by tracing shadow rays to sample the lights.
- `finalGather` controls if final gathering is used for indirect lighting rather than using the indirect photon map directly; if true, `gatherSamples` controls the number of samples taken.

SurfaceIntegrator 723

⟨*PhotonIntegrator Private Data*⟩ ≡   **774**
```
u_int nCausticPhotons, nIndirectPhotons, nDirectPhotons;
u_int nLookup;
mutable int specularDepth;
int maxSpecularDepth;
float maxDistSquared;
bool directWithPhotons, finalGather;
int gatherSamples;
```

The PhotonIntegrator::RequestSamples() method is also quite similar to the others and so is not included in the text. It requests samples for multiple importance sampling for direct lighting and, if final gathering has been enabled, a well-distributed set of samples for sampling the BSDF for the final gather step.

⟨*PhotonIntegrator Private Data*⟩+≡   **774**
```
⟨Declare sample parameters for light source sampling 724⟩
int gatherSampleOffset, gatherComponentOffset;
```

16.5.3 BUILDING THE PHOTON MAPS

When the integrator's Preprocess() method is called, particle paths are followed through the scene until the integrator has accumulated the desired number of particle histories to build the three photon maps. At each intersection of the path with an object, a weighted particle contribution is stored if the map for the corresponding type of illumination is not yet full. Photon objects represent such an illumination sample; the contents of this structure will be defined soon.

⟨*Photonmap Method Definitions*⟩ ≡
```
void PhotonIntegrator::Preprocess(const Scene *scene) {
    if (scene->lights.size() == 0) return;
    vector<Photon> causticPhotons;
    vector<Photon> directPhotons;
    vector<Photon> indirectPhotons;
    ⟨Initialize photon shooting statistics 776⟩
    bool causticDone = (nCausticPhotons == 0);
    bool directDone = (nDirectPhotons == 0);
    bool indirectDone = (nIndirectPhotons == 0);
    while (!causticDone || !directDone || !indirectDone) {
        ++nshot;
        ⟨Give up if we're not storing enough photons 776⟩
        ⟨Trace a photon path and store contribution 776⟩
    }
}
```

The total number of paths started from the lights is maintained in nshot. This value may be larger or smaller than the sizes of the arrays of photons. On the one hand, it may be necessary to shoot many more photons than are stored—for example, due to photons that leave the scene without intersecting any objects. On the other hand, each path may contribute multiple entries to the particle history as it bounces around the scene.

⟨*Initialize photon shooting statistics*⟩ ≡   775
```
static StatsCounter nshot("Photon Map",
    "Number of photons shot from lights");
```

If the integrator finds that it has generated many paths while storing few to no photons of some types, it eventually gives up and exits without creating the corresponding kd-trees. (For example, this might happen if it were trying to populate a caustic map but there weren't any specular objects in the scene to create caustic paths.)

⟨*Give up if we're not storing enough photons*⟩ ≡   775
```
if (nshot > 500000 &&
    (unsuccessful(nCausticPhotons, causticPhotons.size(), nshot) ||
     unsuccessful(nDirectPhotons, directPhotons.size(), nshot) ||
     unsuccessful(nIndirectPhotons, indirectPhotons.size(), nshot))) {
    Error("Unable to store enough photons.  Giving up.\n");
    return;
}
```

⟨*PhotonIntegrator Private Methods*⟩ ≡   774
```
static bool unsuccessful(int needed, int found, int shot) {
    return (found < needed && (found == 0 || found < shot / 1024));
}
```

To create a new path, the integrator samples a ray from one of the lights in the scene and then follows the path, recording particle intersections as it bounces around the scene. The alpha variable is incrementally updated to store the path contribution at each vertex. After path termination, the BSDF memory allocated for the path is freed before going on to start the next one. Freeing the memory after each path is important; if this wasn't done, the system's memory use could grow substantially due to the BSDF memory management scheme.

⟨*Trace a photon path and store contribution*⟩ ≡   775
```
    ⟨Choose 4D sample values for photon  777⟩
    ⟨Choose light to shoot photon from  777⟩
    ⟨Generate photonRay from light source and initialize alpha  777⟩
    if (!alpha.Black()) {
        ⟨Follow photon path through scene and record intersections  778⟩
    }
    BSDF::FreeAll();
```

Since we would like the samples used to generate ray directions to be well-distributed, but we don't know ahead of time how many paths will need to be generated to get the desired number of particle histories, the PhotonIntegrator uses a Halton sequence for these sample values. Recall from Section 7.4 that any set of sequential points starting from the beginning of the Halton sequence has good low-discrepancy properties. Using a Halton sequence here gives a more uniform distribution of photons throughout the scene than uniform random points would, for example. Recall that an n-dimensional Halton sequence is obtained by using the radical inverse function with the first n prime numbers as bases.

⟨*Choose 4D sample values for photon*⟩ ≡   776
```
    float u[4];
    u[0] = RadicalInverse(nshot+1, 2);
    u[1] = RadicalInverse(nshot+1, 3);
    u[2] = RadicalInverse(nshot+1, 5);
    u[3] = RadicalInverse(nshot+1, 7);
```

The implementation here chooses among the lights in the scene with equal probability, using the Halton point from the next dimension to select among them. An exercise at the end of the chapter explains why this is potentially not an optimal light sampling strategy and suggests an improvement.

⟨*Choose light to shoot photon from*⟩ ≡   776
```
    int nLights = int(scene->lights.size());
    int lightNum =
        min(Floor2Int(nLights * RadicalInverse(nshot+1, 11)), nLights-1);
    Light *light = scene->lights[lightNum];
    float lightPdf = 1.f / nLights;
```

Given a light, a ray from the light source is sampled and its α value is initialized with

$$\frac{L_e(p_0, \omega_0)}{p(p_0, \omega_0)},$$

where $p(p_0, \omega_0)$ is the product of the probability for sampling this particular light and the product of the area and directional densities for sampling this particular ray leaving the light.

⟨*Generate* photonRay *from light source and initialize* alpha⟩ ≡   776
```
    RayDifferential photonRay;
    float pdf;
    Spectrum alpha = light->Sample_L(scene, u[0], u[1], u[2], u[3],
                                     &photonRay, &pdf);
    if (pdf == 0.f || alpha.Black()) continue;
    alpha /= pdf * lightPdf;
```

And now the integrator can start following the path through the scene, updating α after each scattering event and recording photons at the path vertices. The specularPath variable records whether the current path has only intersected perfectly specular surfaces after leaving the light source, which indicates that the path is a caustic path.

⟨*Follow photon path through scene and record intersections*⟩ ≡   **776**
```
bool specularPath = false;
Intersection photonIsect;
int nIntersections = 0;
while (scene->Intersect(photonRay, &photonIsect)) {
    ++nIntersections;
    ⟨Handle photon/surface intersection 778⟩
    ⟨Sample new photon ray direction 781⟩
    ⟨Possibly terminate photon path 782⟩
}
```

Given a photon-surface intersection, the particle weight must be updated to account for attenuation due to participating media from the last path vertex to this one. Then, whichever of the three photon maps is the appropriate one for recording this particle's contribution is updated. However, if the current hit is a perfectly specular surface, there's no need to record it in any photon map, since we do not use photons for rendering reflections from specular surfaces.

⟨*Handle photon/surface intersection*⟩ ≡   **778**
```
alpha *= scene->Transmittance(photonRay);
Vector wo = -photonRay.d;
BSDF *photonBSDF = photonIsect.GetBSDF(photonRay);
BxDFType specularType = BxDFType(BSDF_REFLECTION |
    BSDF_TRANSMISSION | BSDF_SPECULAR);
bool hasNonSpecular =
  (photonBSDF->NumComponents() > photonBSDF->NumComponents(specularType));
if (hasNonSpecular) {
    ⟨Deposit photon at surface 779⟩
}
```

BSDF 462
BSDF::NumComponents() 464
BSDF_REFLECTION 415
BSDF_SPECULAR 415
BSDF_TRANSMISSION 415
BxDFType 415
Intersection 172
Intersection::GetBSDF() 469
Ray::d 58
Scene::Intersect() 29
Scene::Transmittance() 30
Vector 47

If this is the first intersection found after the particle has left the light source, then the photon represents direct illumination. Otherwise, if it has only reflected from specular surfaces before arriving at the current intersection point, it must be a caustic photon. Any other case—a path that only hit nonspecular surfaces, or a path that hit a series of specular surfaces before scattering from nonspecular surfaces—represents indirect illumination. The finite-state machine diagram in Figure 16.15 illustrates the possibilities. The nodes of the graph show which of the photon maps should be updated for a photon in that state, and the edges describe whether the photon has scattered from a specular or a nonspecular BSDF component at its previous intersection.

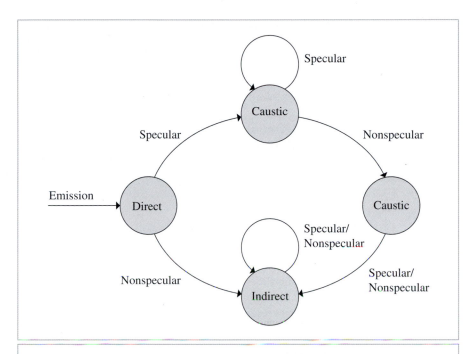

Figure 16.15: Finite-State Machine. An illustration of the transitions photons make from one state to another depending on the type of surface scattering they undergo at path vertices.

⟨*Deposit photon at surface*⟩ ≡   778

```
    Photon photon(photonIsect.dg.p, alpha, wo);
    if (nIntersections == 1) {
        ⟨Process direct lighting photon intersection  780⟩
    }
    else if (specularPath) {
        ⟨Process caustic photon intersection⟩
    }
    else {
        ⟨Process indirect lighting photon intersection⟩
    }
```

DifferentialGeometry::p 83

Intersection::dg 172

Photon 780

The fragments for processing the three types of photon map updates all have equivalent functionality, so we only show the fragment for direct lighting photons here. Until enough photons of a particular type have been found, the photons are stored in the corresponding vector of Photons declared earlier. When the desired number are available, the integrator records how many paths from the lights needed to be constructed before the desired number of photons was found. (This value will be important for the density estimation algorithm used to interpolate among photons around a point being shaded.) It then goes ahead and constructs a kd-tree (the KdTree template class used is described in Section A.5 of Appendix A). After the kd-tree is built, any additional photons of this type that are found while following paths to fill up the other photon maps are ignored.

⟨*Process direct lighting photon intersection*⟩ ≡   **779**
```
if (!directDone) {
    directPhotons.push_back(photon);
    if (directPhotons.size() == nDirectPhotons) {
        directDone = true;
        nDirectPaths = nshot;
        directMap = new KdTree<Photon, PhotonProcess>(directPhotons);
    }
}
```

⟨*PhotonIntegrator Private Data*⟩+≡   **774**
```
int nCausticPaths, nDirectPaths, nIndirectPaths;
mutable KdTree<Photon, PhotonProcess> *causticMap;
mutable KdTree<Photon, PhotonProcess> *directMap;
mutable KdTree<Photon, PhotonProcess> *indirectMap;
```

The Photon structure stores just enough information to record a photon's contribution—the position where it hit the surface, its weight, and the direction it arrived from. Because hundreds of thousands or millions of photons may be stored, using a more compact photon representation than the one used here can be worthwhile. For example, the direction ω_i can be represented in spherical angles (θ, ϕ) and quantized to a small number of directions, using just eight bits for each angle as offsets into a lookup table. To keep the implementation here simple, however, we will just use the straightforward representation below.

⟨*Photonmap Local Declarations*⟩+≡
```
struct Photon {
    ⟨Photon Constructor 780⟩
    Point p;
    Spectrum alpha;
    Vector wi;
};
```

⟨*Photon Constructor*⟩ ≡   **780**
```
Photon(const Point &pp, const Spectrum &wt, const Vector &w)
    : p(pp), alpha(wt), wi(w) {
}
```

Having recorded the particle's contribution in one of the photon maps (or ignoring it if that map type was full), the integrator needs to choose a new outgoing direction from the intersection point and update the α value to account for the effect of scattering of the incident illumination. Equation (16.6) shows how to incrementally update the particle weight after a scattering event: Given some weight $\alpha_{i,j}$ that represents the weight for the jth intersection of the ith particle history, after a scattering event where a new vertex $\mathrm{p}_{i,j+1}$ has been sampled, the weight should be scaled by

$$\frac{1}{q_{i,j+1}} \frac{f(\mathrm{p}_{i,j+1} \to \mathrm{p}_{i,j} \to \mathrm{p}_{i,j-1}) G(\mathrm{p}_{i,j+1} \leftrightarrow \mathrm{p}_{i,j})}{p(\mathrm{p}_{i,j+1})}.$$

As with the path-tracing integrator, there are a number of reasons to choose the next vertex in the path by sampling the BSDF's distribution at the intersection point to get a direction ω' and tracing a ray in that direction, rather than directly sampling by area on the scene surfaces. Therefore, we again apply the Jacobian to account for this change in measure, all of the terms in G except for a single $|\cos \theta|$ cancel out, and the scaling term is

$$\frac{1}{q_{i,j+1}} \frac{f(\mathrm{p}, \omega, \omega') |\cos \theta'|}{p(\omega')}.$$

At the very first intersection, the random numbers used for sampling are the next two dimensions of the point in the Halton sequence that was used to start this path, ensuring a good distribution of directions at the first bounces across all of the paths. For subsequent bounces, the integrator just uses uniform random numbers because the advantages of further low-discrepancy points are mostly lost as more bounces occur.

⟨*Sample new photon ray direction*⟩ ≡   778

```
Vector wi;
float pdf;
BxDFType flags;
⟨Get random numbers for sampling outgoing photon direction⟩
Spectrum fr = photonBSDF->Sample_f(wo, &wi, u1, u2, u3,
                                   &pdf, BSDF_ALL, &flags);
if (fr.Black() || pdf == 0.f)
    break;
specularPath = (nIntersections == 1 || specularPath) &&
               ((flags & BSDF_SPECULAR) != 0);
alpha *= fr * AbsDot(wi, photonBSDF->dgShading.nn) / pdf;
photonRay = RayDifferential(photonIsect.dg.p, wi);
```

As usual, after the first few bounces, Russian roulette either terminates the path or increases its weight to account for the missing contributions of the paths that were terminated.

⟨*Possibly terminate photon path*⟩ ≡   778
```
if (nIntersections > 3) {
    float continueProbability = .5f;
    if (RandomFloat() > continueProbability)
        break;
    alpha /= continueProbability;
}
```

16.5.4 USING THE PHOTON MAP

At rendering time, the photon map is used to compute reflected light at each point being shaded. We would like to estimate the exitant radiance equation at a point p in a direction ω_o, which can equivalently (and cumbersomely) be written as a measurement over all points on surfaces in the scene where a Dirac delta distribution selects only particles precisely at p:

$$\int_{\mathbb{S}^2} L_i(p, \omega_i)\, f(p, \omega_o, \omega_i)\, |\cos\theta_i| d\omega_i =$$

$$\int_A \int_{\mathbb{S}^2} \delta(p - p') L_i(p', \omega_i)\, f(p', \omega_o, \omega_i) |\cos\theta_i|\, d\omega_i dA(p'),$$

and so the function that describes the measurement is

$$W_e(p', \omega) = \delta(p' - p) f(p, \omega_o, \omega) |\cos\theta|.$$

Unfortunately, because there is a delta distribution in W_e, all of the particle histories that were generated during the particle-tracing step have zero probability of having nonzero contribution when Equation (16.6) is used to compute the estimate of the measurement value (just as we will never be able to choose a direction from a surface that intersects a point light source unless the direction is sampled accounting for this).

Here is the point at which bias is introduced into the photon mapping algorithm. Under the assumption that the information about illumination at nearby points can be used to construct an estimate of illumination at the shading point, photon mapping interpolates information about illumination at the point being shaded from nearby photons. The more photons there are around the point and the higher their weights, the more radiance is estimated to be incident at the point. This estimated radiance is used in conjunction with the surface's BSDF to compute the reflected light. Figure 16.16 shows the basic idea.

The error introduced by this interpolation can be difficult to quantify. Storing more photons, so that it isn't necessary to use photons as far away, will almost always improve the results, but in general, error will depend on how quickly the illumination is changing at the point. One can always construct pathological cases where this error is unacceptable, but it usually isn't too bad. Because this interpolation step tends to blur out illumination, high-frequency changes in lighting are sometimes poorly reconstructed with photon mapping. Since indirect illumination tends to be low frequency, this isn't too much of

RandomFloat() 857

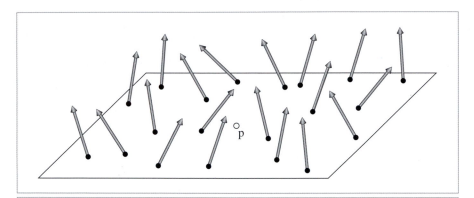

Figure 16.16: The Basic Idea of Using Particle Histories (Photons) to Compute Exitant Radiance. The local density and weights of the photons around the point p, each of which represents (possibly scattered) illumination from a light source, can be used to estimate the illumination at p.

a problem in practice. And although caustics do often have high-frequency variation, photon mapping also works well for them since many photons are focused in caustic regions.

In order to reduce the blurriness in final images from this interpolation, the photon mapping algorithm partitions the integrand and uses photons to evaluate some parts of it, but traces rays to estimate the rest. A number of different partitionings have been proposed. Here we will split the BSDF into delta and nondelta components, and will separate incident radiance from the nondelta component into incident direct ($L_{i,d}$), indirect ($L_{i,i}$), and caustic ($L_{i,c}$) illumination:

$$\int_{\mathbb{S}^2} f(p, \omega_o, \omega_i) L_i(p, \omega_i) |\cos \theta_i| \, d\omega_i =$$

$$\int_{\mathbb{S}^2} f_\Delta(p, \omega_o, \omega_i) L_i(p, \omega_i) |\cos \theta_i| \, d\omega_i +$$

$$\int_{\mathbb{S}^2} f_{\neg\Delta}(p, \omega_o, \omega_i)(L_{i,d}(p, \omega_i) + L_{i,i}(p, \omega_i) + L_{i,c}(p, \omega_i)) |\cos \theta_i| \, d\omega_i.$$

We will elide the complete implementation of `PhotonIntegrator::Li()`, which is similar in form to the `Li()` methods of the other integrators, and will focus on the two key fragments that do the direct and indirect lighting computations. When these fragments run, the specular BSDF components have already been handled in the omitted code, so we only need to consider the nondelta reflection case in the last term of the previous equation.

The delta components of the BSDF can be efficiently and accurately handled with recursive ray tracing. For the nondelta components, it is usually worth sampling direct lighting $L_{i,d}$ by tracing shadow rays to the light sources. Photon maps for direct lighting are normally only useful for large area light sources casting smooth shadows and for quickly rendering preview images. A parameter to the integrator selects between these two options. The LPhoton() function, which will be described shortly, computes reflected radiance in the direction wo for the given BSDF and photon map. Figure 16.17 shows the result of using the photon map for direct lighting.

⟨*Compute direct lighting for photon map integrator*⟩ ≡
```
if (directWithPhotons)
    L += LPhoton(directMap, nDirectPaths, nLookup,
              bsdf, isect, wo, maxDistSquared);
else
    L += UniformSampleAllLights(scene, p, n, wo, bsdf, sample,
        lightSampleOffset, bsdfSampleOffset, bsdfComponentOffset);
```

We will always use the caustic photon map to account for light that has taken one or more specular bounces before hitting a nonspecular surface. These paths are particularly difficult to find when tracing paths starting from the point being shaded; because caustics are focused light, there tend to be enough photons to compute good lighting estimates in areas with caustics. Figure 16.18 shows a caustic cast by the dragon model rendered with the photon map. It does a good job of accounting for this lighting effect.

For some scenes, indirect lighting can be represented well (and computed extremely efficiently) with the photon map. If higher quality is needed, the integrator also provides a method known as *final gathering* (Figure 16.19). At the point where exitant radiance is to be computed, final gathering samples the BSDF and traces rays out into the scene to find incident radiance along those rays. However, at the intersection points of the gather rays, the direct, indirect, and caustic photon maps are used to immediately compute the exitant radiance there. Thus, there is no cost for tracing additional rays to compute exitant radiance at those points (and thus incident radiance for the ray from the original point). Because the error from the interpolation of photons there isn't seen directly at the original point being shaded, the final result can have very high quality.

⟨*Compute indirect lighting for photon map integrator*⟩ ≡
```
L += LPhoton(causticMap, nCausticPaths, nLookup, bsdf,
          isect, wo, maxDistSquared);
if (finalGather) {
    ⟨Do one-bounce final gather for photon map  786⟩
}
else
    L += LPhoton(indirectMap, nIndirectPaths, nLookup,
              bsdf, isect, wo, maxDistSquared);
```

For final gathering, we would like to estimate the reflected radiance due to indirect illumination,

(a)

(b)

(c)

Figure 16.17: (a) When the photon map is used to compute exitant radiance due to direct lighting, the results are much blurrier than (b) if shadow rays are traced as the other integrators always do. (c) Increasing the number of photons for direct lighting (here going from 50,000 to 500,000) improves the result. Note that with this model, the photon map exhibits unsightly "light leaks" where illumination on the back side of some walls is visible on the other side.

Figure 16.18: Caustics Cast by Light Focusing through a Complex Glass Object Have Remarkable Patterns. Photon mapping is particularly effective at capturing this effect.

$$\int_{\mathcal{S}^2} f(\mathrm{p}, \omega_o, \omega_i) L_{i,i}(\mathrm{p}, \omega_i) |\cos \theta_i| d\omega_i.$$

In the implementation here, we will always use the BSDF's importance sampling method to choose sampled directions to estimate the value of this integral. The "Further Reading" section has pointers to a number of techniques that use the incident directions of the photons that are close to p to derive importance sampling techniques that try to match the distribution of $L_{i,i}$. Using both sampling methods along with multiple importance sampling could substantially improve the efficiency of final gathering.

⟨*Do one-bounce final gather for photon map*⟩ ≡   **784**

```
Spectrum Li(0.);
for (int i = 0; i < gatherSamples; ++i) {
    ⟨Sample random direction for final gather ray 787⟩
    RayDifferential bounceRay(p, wi);
    Intersection gatherIsect;
    if (scene->Intersect(bounceRay, &gatherIsect)) {
        ⟨Compute exitant radiance at final gather intersection 788⟩
    }
}
L += Li / float(gatherSamples);
```

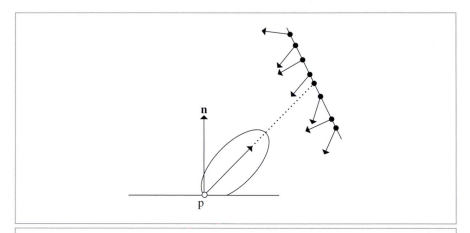

Figure 16.19: The final gathering step with photon mapping traces a set of rays from the BSDF's distribution to sample incident radiance at p in order to compute exitant radiance there. However, rather than continuing recursively and tracing more rays at the gather intersection points, the photon maps are immediately used to do the lighting computation there.

The direction for the final gather ray is sampled by the BSDF's sampling distribution. It is important not to sample specular components of the BSDF here; recall that they are handled separately with the usual recursive ray tracing.

⟨*Sample random direction for final gather ray*⟩ ≡   786

```
Vector wi;
float u1 = sample->twoD[gatherSampleOffset][2*i];
float u2 = sample->twoD[gatherSampleOffset][2*i+1];
float u3 = sample->oneD[gatherComponentOffset][i];
float pdf;
Spectrum fr = bsdf->Sample_f(wo, &wi, u1, u2, u3,
    &pdf, BxDFType(BSDF_ALL & (~BSDF_SPECULAR)));
if (fr.Black() || pdf == 0.f) continue;
```

Having found the first point of intersection of the jth gather ray from p in direction ω_j, we need to compute the outgoing radiance at that point in direction $-\omega_j$, which gives the incident radiance at p, $L_i(p, \omega) = L_o(t(p, \omega), -\omega)$. The three photon maps compute their contribution to this value, attenuate it to account for participating media between the original point and the gather ray intersection point, and apply the estimator

$$\frac{1}{N} \sum_{j=1}^{N} \frac{f(p, \omega_o, \omega_j) L_{i,i}(p, \omega_j) |\cos \theta_j|}{p(\omega_j)}.$$

Note that L_e at the intersection point is ignored, since the direct illumination computation at the original point, however it was done, accounted for its contribution already. Figure 16.20 shows the effect of final gathering.

⟨*Compute exitant radiance at final gather intersection*⟩ ≡   **786**

```
BSDF *gatherBSDF = gatherIsect.GetBSDF(bounceRay);
Vector bounceWo = -bounceRay.d;
Spectrum Lindir =
    LPhoton(directMap, nDirectPaths, nLookup,
            gatherBSDF, gatherIsect, bounceWo, maxDistSquared) +
    LPhoton(indirectMap, nIndirectPaths, nLookup,
            gatherBSDF, gatherIsect, bounceWo, maxDistSquared) +
    LPhoton(causticMap, nCausticPaths, nLookup,
            gatherBSDF, gatherIsect, bounceWo, maxDistSquared);
Lindir *= scene->Transmittance(bounceRay);
Li += fr * Lindir * AbsDot(wi, n) / pdf;
```

16.5.5 PHOTON INTERPOLATION AND DENSITY ESTIMATION

The `LPhoton()` function has two main tasks: First, it needs to find the `nLookup` photons that are closest to the point where the shading is being done. Second, it needs to use those photons to compute the reflected radiance at the point. It uses the kd-tree to do the work of searching for photons around the point, so that it only has to worry about the radiometric part of the computation. It starts by checking that the BSDF has any nonspecular components. If it is purely specular, there's no need to do the lookup, since the BSDF won't return any contribution for any of the photons' incident directions.

⟨*Photonmap Method Definitions*⟩ + ≡

```
Spectrum
PhotonIntegrator::LPhoton(KdTree<Photon, PhotonProcess> *map,
                          int nPaths, int nLookup, BSDF *bsdf,
                          const Intersection &isect, const Vector &wo,
                          float maxDistSquared) {
    Spectrum L(0.);
    if (!map) return L;
    BxDFType nonSpecular = BxDFType(BSDF_REFLECTION |
        BSDF_TRANSMISSION | BSDF_DIFFUSE | BSDF_GLOSSY);
    if (bsdf->NumComponents(nonSpecular) == 0)
        return L;
    ⟨Initialize PhotonProcess object, proc, for photon map lookups 790⟩
    ⟨Do photon map lookup 790⟩
    return L;
}
```

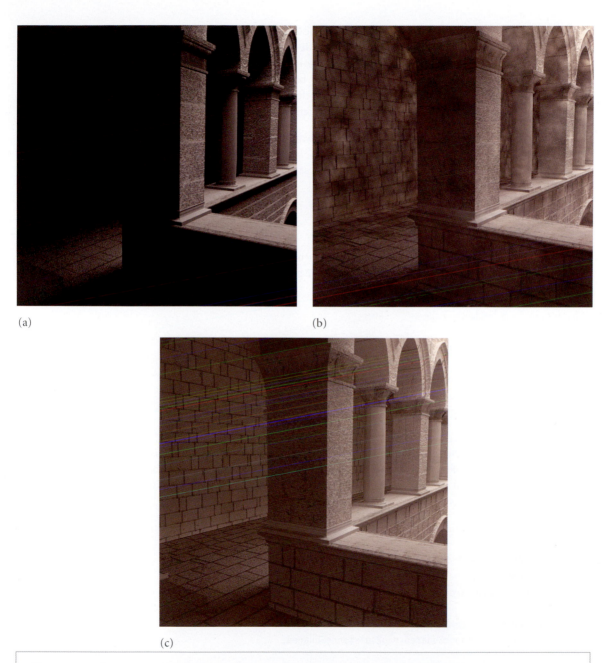

(a)

(b)

(c)

Figure 16.20: Sponza scene (a) with direct illumination only, (b) with photon mapping but without final gathering and (c) with final gathering. Note that the blurriness from using the photon map directly isn't a problem when final gathering is used.

Similar to the octree used for the irradiance cache, the KdTree used to store photons takes a parameter to its Lookup() method that provides an object with a particular method that is called for every item in the search region. PhotonProcess handles that role, storing information about the nearby photons that have been passed to it using the ClosePhoton structure. This method uses alloca() to efficiently allocate space for the array of ClosePhotons rather than incurring the cost of calling new each time it is called.

⟨*Initialize* PhotonProcess *object*, proc, *for photon map lookups*⟩ ≡   **788**
```
    PhotonProcess proc(nLookup, isect.dg.p);
    proc.photons = (ClosePhoton *)alloca(nLookup * sizeof(ClosePhoton));
```

⟨*Do photon map lookup*⟩ ≡   **788**
```
    map->Lookup(isect.dg.p, proc, maxDistSquared);
```
    ⟨*Accumulate light from nearby photons* **794**⟩

In addition to keeping track of the nearby photons, PhotonProcess also needs to record the position of the lookup point, so that it can determine the distance from photons that are passed to it to that point.

⟨*Photonmap Local Declarations*⟩+≡
```
    struct PhotonProcess {
        ⟨PhotonProcess Public Methods⟩
        const Point &p;
        ClosePhoton *photons;
        u_int nLookup;
        mutable u_int foundPhotons;
    };
```

To keep track of a photon close to the lookup point, it is only necessary to store a pointer to it. However, the PhotonProcess structure also caches the squared distance from the photon to the lookup point in order to more quickly be able to discard the farthest-away photon when a closer one is found.

⟨*Photonmap Local Declarations*⟩+≡
```
    struct ClosePhoton {
        ClosePhoton(const Photon *p = NULL, float md2 = INFINITY) {
            photon = p;
            distanceSquared = md2;
        }
        bool operator<(const ClosePhoton &p2) const {
            return distanceSquared < p2.distanceSquared;
        }
        const Photon *photon;
        float distanceSquared;
    };
```

As the KdTree traverses the tree nodes, it calls the following method of PhotonProcess for each photon inside the search radius. This method adds a reference to each such photon in the ClosePhotons array, photons.

⟨*Photonmap Method Definitions*⟩+≡
```
void PhotonProcess::operator()(const Photon &photon,
        float distSquared, float &maxDistSquared) const {
    if (foundPhotons < nLookup) {
        ⟨Add photon to unordered array of photons 791⟩
    }
    else {
        ⟨Remove most distant photon from heap and add new photon 792⟩
    }
}
```

Until nLookup photons have been found around the point, this method stores the nearby photons in an unordered array that is filled in whatever order photons are passed to this callback method. However, once the nLookup+1st photon arrives (if it does), it is necessary to discard the photon that is farthest away and keep only the nLookup closest ones. Therefore, at that point, the photons array is reordered to be a heap, such that the root element is the one with the greatest distance from the lookup point. Recall that a heap data structure can be constructed in linear time and that it can be updated after an item is removed or added in logarithmic time. It is much more efficient to organize photons with a heap than to keep them sorted by distance. The make_heap() function in the C++ standard library reorders a given array into a heap so that the zeroth element is the root of the heap.

Furthermore, once nLookup photons have been found, the search radius that the KdTree uses as it traverses its nodes can be decreased; there's no reason to consider any additional photons that are farther away than the farthest one in the heap. KdTree::Lookup() passes a reference to maxDistSquared into this callback method so that the callback method can reduce its value in situations like this.

⟨*Add photon to unordered array of photons*⟩≡   **791**
```
photons[foundPhotons++] = ClosePhoton(&photon, distSquared);
if (foundPhotons == nLookup) {
    std::make_heap(&photons[0], &photons[nLookup]);
    maxDistSquared = photons[0].distanceSquared;
}
```

As additional photons come in after the heap has been built, we know that the squared distance to new ones must be less than the maxDistSquared, since the KdTree doesn't call the callback method for items that are further away. Thus, any additional photon must be closer than the root node of the heap, which is the farthest-away one that is stored. Therefore, the method immediately calls the standard library routine that removes the root item of the heap and updates the order of the remaining ones in the heap to reestablish a valid heap, pop_heap(). The new photon is added to the end of the array, which will have been left empty after pop_heap() was called and then push_heap() again rebuilds the heap, accounting for a new element added to the end of it. After all of this, maxDistSquared can again be reduced to whatever the distance is to the new farthest-away photon.

⟨*Remove most distant photon from heap and add new photon*⟩ ≡   791
```
    std::pop_heap(&photons[0], &photons[nLookup]);
    photons[nLookup-1] = ClosePhoton(&photon, distSquared);
    std::push_heap(&photons[0], &photons[nLookup]);
    maxDistSquared = photons[0].distanceSquared;
```

Once the search is over and the nearby photons have been found, they need to be inter-polated since none of them will be located precisely at the lookup point. Recall from the original description of the particle-tracing algorithm that both the local density of the particles and their individual weights together affect their contribution (a greater density of particles in the domain where W_e is nonzero will cause more of them to contribute their weights to the sum, and clearly higher weights of individual particles increases their contribution). A statistical technique called *density estimation* builds on this idea and provides the tools to perform this interpolation.

Density estimation constructs a PDF given a set of sample points under the assumption that the samples are distributed according to the overall distribution of some function of interest. Histogramming is a straightforward example of the idea: in 1D, the line is divided into intervals with some width, and one can count how many samples land in each interval and normalize so that the areas of the intervals sum to one.

Kernel methods are a more sophisticated density estimation technique. They generally give better results and smoother PDFs that don't suffer from the discontinuities that histograms do. Given a kernel function $k(x)$ that integrates to one,

$$\int_{-\infty}^{\infty} k(x)\mathrm{d}x = 1,$$

the kernel estimator for N samples at locations x_i is

$$\hat{p}(x) = \frac{1}{Nh} \sum_{i=1}^{N} k\left(\frac{x - x_i}{h}\right),$$

where h is the window width (also known as the smoothing parameter). Kernel methods can be thought of as placing a series of bumps at observation points, where the sum of the bumps forms a PDF since they individually integrate to one and the sum is normalized. Figure 16.21 shows an example of density estimation in 1D, where a smooth PDF is computed from a set of sample points.

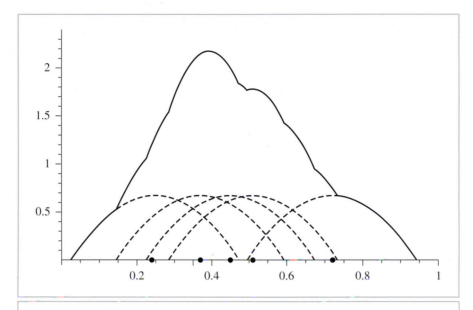

Figure 16.21: 1D example of density estimation, using the Epanechnikov kernel, $k(t) = .75(1 - .2t^2)/\sqrt{5}$, if $t < \sqrt{5}$, 0 otherwise, and a width of 0.1. The points marked with closed circles are the sample points, and an instance of the kernel (dashed lines) is placed over each one. The sum of the kernels gives a properly normalized PDF that attempts to model a distribution that the points could be distributed by.

The key question with kernel methods is how the window width h is chosen. If it is too wide, the PDF will blur out relevant detail in parts of the domain with many samples, while if it is too narrow, the PDF will be too bumpy in the tails of the distribution where there aren't many samples. Nearest-neighbor techniques solve this problem by choosing h adaptively based on local density of samples. Where there are many samples, the width is small; where there are few samples, the width is large. For example, one approach is to pick a number n and find the distance to the nth nearest sample from the point x and use that distance, $d_k(x)$, for the window width. This is the *generalized nth nearest-neighbor estimate:*

$$\hat{p}(x) = \frac{1}{N d_n(x)} \sum_{i=1}^{N} k \left(\frac{x - x_i}{d_n(x)} \right).$$

In d dimensions, this generalizes to

$$\hat{p}(x) = \frac{1}{N (d_n(x))^d} \sum_{i=1}^{N} k \left(\frac{x - x_i}{d_n(x)} \right). \tag{16.7}$$

This is the estimator we will use to construct a PDF from the photons. We will just use a constant kernel function. In 2D, the constant kernel function that fulfills the normalization requirement is

$$k(x) = \begin{cases} \frac{1}{\pi} & |x| < 1 \\ 0 & \text{otherwise.} \end{cases}$$

Substituting into the measurement equation, it can then be shown that the appropriate estimator for the measurement we'd like to compute, the exitant radiance at the point p in direction ω, is given by

$$L_o(\mathrm{p}, \omega_o) \approx \hat{p}(\mathrm{p}) \sum_j^n \alpha_j f(\mathrm{p}, \omega_o, \omega_j),$$

where the sum is over the n nearest photons. Thus, the scale factor for the photons is easily computed based on the density estimation, Equation (16.7).

⟨*Accumulate light from nearby photons*⟩ ≡   **790**

```
float scale = 1.f / (float(nPaths) * maxDistSquared * M_PI);
```
⟨*Estimate reflected light from photons* **794**⟩

For purely diffuse BSDFs, it's wasteful to call the `BSDF::f()` method `nFound` times, since it will always return a constant value. Therefore, that method is only called for each photon if glossy components are present. In either case, reflection or transmission is selected depending on if the photon is on the same or a different side of the surface as the outgoing direction.

⟨*Estimate reflected light from photons*⟩ ≡   **794**

```
ClosePhoton *photons = proc.photons;
int nFound = proc.foundPhotons;
Normal Nf = Dot(wo, bsdf->dgShading.nn) < 0 ? -bsdf->dgShading.nn :
                                              bsdf->dgShading.nn;
if (bsdf->NumComponents(BxDFType(BSDF_REFLECTION |
            BSDF_TRANSMISSION | BSDF_GLOSSY)) > 0) {
    ⟨Compute exitant radiance from photons for glossy surface 794⟩
}
else {
    ⟨Compute exitant radiance from photons for diffuse surface 795⟩
}
```

⟨*Compute exitant radiance from photons for glossy surface*⟩ ≡   **794**

```
for (int i = 0; i < nFound; ++i) {
    BxDFType flag = Dot(Nf, photons[i].photon->wi) > 0.f ?
            BSDF_ALL_REFLECTION : BSDF_ALL_TRANSMISSION;
    L += bsdf->f(wo, photons[i].photon->wi, flag) *
        (scale * photons[i].photon->alpha);
}
```

For diffuse surfaces, the equivalent computation can be done much more efficiently by finding the weighted sum of photon α values and multiplying it by the constant BSDF, found by dividing the surface's reflectance by π.

⟨*Compute exitant radiance from photons for diffuse surface*⟩ ≡ 794

```
Spectrum Lr(0.), Lt(0.);
for (int i = 0; i < nFound; ++i)
    if (Dot(Nf, photons[i].photon->wi) > 0.f)
        Lr += photons[i].photon->alpha;
    else
        Lt += photons[i].photon->alpha;
L += (scale * INV_PI) * (Lr * bsdf->rho(wo, BSDF_ALL_REFLECTION) +
        Lt * bsdf->rho(wo, BSDF_ALL_TRANSMISSION)));
```

FURTHER READING

The first application of Monte Carlo to global illumination for creating synthetic images that we are aware of is described in Tregenza's paper on lighting design (Tregenza 1983). Cook's distribution ray-tracing algorithm computed glossy reflections, soft shadows from area lights, motion blur, and depth of field with Monte Carlo sampling (Cook, Porter, and Carpenter 1984; Cook 1986), although the general form of the light transport equation wasn't stated until papers by Kajiya (1986) and Immel, Cohen, and Greenberg (1986). Kajiya's paper also introduced the path tracing algorithm for solving the light transport equation.

Additional important theoretical work has been done by Arvo (1993, 1995), who has investigated the connection between rendering algorithms in graphics and previous work in *transport theory*, which applies classical physics to particles and their interactions to predict their overall behavior. Our description of the path integral form of the LTE follows the framework in Veach's Ph.D. thesis, which has thorough coverage of different forms of the LTE and its mathematical structure (Veach 1997). Christensen (2003) has written a paper on the application of adjoint functions and importance to solving the LTE; it gives a comprehensive overview of related topics with many pointers to further information.

Russian roulette was introduced to graphics by Arvo and Kirk (1990). Hall and Greenberg (1983) had previously suggested adaptively terminating ray trees by not tracing rays with less than some minimum contribution. Arvo and Kirk's technique is unbiased, although in some situations, bias and less noise may be the less undesirable artifact.

The general idea of tracing light-carrying paths from the light sources was first investigated by Arvo (1986), who stored light in texture maps on surfaces and rendered caustics. Heckbert (1990b) built on this approach to develop a general ray-tracing-based global illumination algorithm, and Pattanaik and Mudur (1995) developed an early particle-tracing technique.

Bidirectional path tracing was independently developed by Lafortune and Willems (1994) and Veach and Guibas (1994). Kollig and Keller (2000) discuss the generalization of bidirectional path tracing to use quasi-random sample patterns.

Ward and collaborators developed the irradiance caching algorithm; it is described in a series of papers (Ward, Rubinstein, and Clear 1988; Ward 1994b). One useful improvement to the basic form of the algorithm implemented here is an improved interpolation scheme described by Ward and Heckbert (1992); they estimate the change in irradiance at sample points as the point moves laterally over the surface and as the surface normal changes, based on the individual radiance samples used to compute the irradiance value. This technique results in a smoother interpolated irradiance function.

Approaches like Arvo's caustic rendering algorithm formed the basis for an improved technique for caustics developed by Collins (1994). Jensen (1995, 1996a) developed the photon mapping algorithm, which had the key innovation of storing the light contributions in a general 3D data structure rather than in textures on surfaces. Density estimation techniques for global illumination were first introduced by Shirley, Walter, and collaborators (Shirley et al. 1995; Walter et al. 1997).

Important improvements to the photon mapping method are described in follow-up papers by Jensen and collaborators and Jensen's book on photon mapping (Jensen 1996b, 1997, 2001; Jensen and Christensen 1998). Other improvements include work by Peter and Pietrek (1998) and Suykens and Willems (2000), who developed techniques to store fewer photons in parts of the scene that are relatively unimportant. Keller and Wald (2000) investigated this issue as well and also developed techniques to use information from photons to optimize direct lighting calculations by using them to determine which light sources were likely to have the largest contribution at a particular point. Christensen (1999) describes an important optimization for the final gathering step; it is the topic of an exercise.

Final gathering for radiosity algorithms was first described in Reichert's thesis (Reichert 1992). One important use of information available in the photon map is optimized final gathering techniques that importance-sample directions for the gathering step using the photons to give information about which directions are likely to have large contributions (Jensen 1995; Hey and Purgathofer 2002).

An innovative approach to solving the LTE was developed by Veach and Guibas (1997), who applied the Metropolis sampling algorithm to the problem. Metropolis is a technique that generates samples from an arbitrary function that are distributed according to the function's PDF; it can do this without requiring that the function be normalized or invertible. Veach and Guibas showed how this method could be applied to image synthesis and that the result was a light transport algorithm that was robust to traditionally difficult lighting configurations (e.g., light shining through a slightly ajar door). Unfortunately, this is a very tricky algorithm to implement in practice.

Approaches for solving the radiosity equations are discussed in books by Cohen and Wallace (1993) and Sillion and Puech (1994). *Principles of Digital Image Synthesis* (Glassner 1995) also covers this topic in depth, and *Advanced Global Illumination* (Dutré, Bekaert, and Bala 2003) has a modern treatment.

EXERCISES

● 16.1 To further improve efficiency, Russian roulette can be applied to skip tracing many of the shadow rays that make a low contribution to the final image. Tentatively compute the potential contribution of each shadow ray to the final overall radiance value before tracing the ray. If the contribution is below some threshold, apply Russian roulette to possibly skip tracing the ray. Recall that Russian roulette always increases variance. When evaluating the effectiveness of your implementation, you should consider its *efficiency*—how long it takes to render an image at a particular level of quality.

● 16.2 Read Veach's description of efficiency-optimized Russian roulette, which adaptively chooses a threshold for applying Russian roulette (Veach 1997, Section 10.4.1). Implement this algorithm in pbrt and evaluate its effectiveness in comparison to manually set thresholds for Russian roulette.

● 16.3 Modify pbrt so that the user can flag certain objects in the scene as being important sources of indirect lighting and modify the PathIntegrator to sample points on those surfaces according to d*A* to generate some of the vertices in the paths it generates. Use multiple importance sampling to compute weights for the path samples, incorporating the probability that they would have been sampled both with BSDF sampling and with this area sampling. How much can this approach reduce variance and improve efficiency for scenes with substantial indirect lighting? How much can it hurt if the user flags surfaces that actually make little or no contribution, or if multiple importance sampling isn't used? Investigate generalizations of this approach that learn which objects are important sources of indirect lighting as rendering progresses so that the user doesn't need to supply this information ahead of time.

PathIntegrator 749

● 16.4 Light transport algorithms that trace paths from the lights like bidirectional path tracing and particle tracing implicitly assume that the BSDFs in the scene are symmetric—that $f(\mathrm{p}, \omega, \omega') = f(\mathrm{p}, \omega', \omega)$. However, both real-world BSDFs like the one describing specular transmission as well as synthetic BSDFs like the ones that are used when shading normals are present are actually not symmetric. Not accounting for this situation can lead to errors in the results computed by these light transport algorithms (Veach 1997, Chapter 5). Fix pbrt to properly handle nonsymmetric BSDFs. Demonstrate that these fixes eliminate errors that are present in the current implementation.

❷ 16.5   Investigate algorithms for rendering scenes with large numbers of light sources: see, for example, the papers by Ward (1991a), Shirley, Wang, and Zimmerman (1996), and Keller and Wald (2000) on this topic, choose one of these approaches, and implement it in pbrt. Run experiments with a number of scenes to evaluate the effectiveness of the approach that you implement.

❸ 16.6   Write an integrator that implements the bidirectional path-tracing algorithm (Lafortune and Willems 1994; Veach and Guibas 1994). Verify its correctness by rendering images using the PathIntegrator with a large number of samples in each pixel. Compare the variance of your implementation to the PathIntegrator for the same total number of rays traced. Then modify your implementation to use multiple importance sampling to weight path contributions. How much is variance further reduced by this improvement?

❷ 16.7   Extend the IrradianceCache to optionally sample the glossy components of the BSDF and recursively trace rays to evaluate indirect radiance along them instead of using irradiance estimates for the glossy term. Set up a scene that illustrates a situation where this gives a substantially better result than using the irradiance estimate for glossy reflection.

❷ 16.8   Read Ward and Heckbert's paper on irradiance gradients (Ward and Heckbert 1992) and implement this technique in the IrradianceCache integrator. How much does it improve the quality of the results that it computes?

❷ 16.9   Improve the IrradianceCache's computation of irradiance values by modifying it to use bidirectional path tracing instead of regular path tracing to compute the individual radiance values. Construct a scene where this approach is much better than path tracing. How much does it improve the results for scenes where the path-tracing approach works well already?

❸ 16.10 By taking a directionally varying distribution of incoming radiance, using it to compute irradiance, and then just storing an irradiance value, the irradiance cache makes a well-chosen engineering trade-off that minimizes the amount of information that must be stored with each entry in the irradiance cache. (Substantially more memory would be needed to store all of the radiance values with each cache entry, for example.) For diffuse BSDFs, irradiance is sufficient to accurately compute reflection, but for glossy BSDFs, the lack of directionally varying illumination information may introduce substantial error. Investigate compact representations for functions on the sphere such as spherical harmonics and spherical wavelets and extend the irradiance cache to represent the incident illumination with coefficients from such a set of basis functions. Modify the IrradianceCache::Li() method to use this representation to compute reflected light from points on surfaces, and compare the accuracy of images rendered with this technique to images rendered by the original irradiance cache, particularly for scenes with glossy surfaces.

❶ **16.11** Experiment with the parameters to the `PhotonIntegrator` until you get a good feel for how they affect results in the final image. At a minimum, experiment with varying the search radius, whether or not photons are used for the direct illumination computation, the number of photons traced, and the number of photons used.

❷ **16.12** If photon mapping is being used only to render caustics in a scene, generation of the caustic map can be accelerated by flagging which objects in the scene potentially have specular components in their BSDFs and then building a directional table around each light source, recording which directions could potentially result in specular paths (Jensen 1996a). Photons are only shot in these directions, saving the work of tracing photons in directions that are certain not to lead to caustics. Extend `pbrt` to support this technique. Note that different solutions will be needed for point light sources, directional light sources, and area light sources. How much does this end up improving efficiency for various scenes?

❷ **16.13** The current implementation of the `PhotonIntegrator` is susceptible to image artifacts if there are a number of light sources in the scene with a wide range of emitted power. Explain the details of a possible situation that this leads to where the fact that the photons stored in the photon map have correspondingly varying weights can lead to increased blotchiness in the radiance computations. Fix the implementation so that it does not have this problem and render images demonstrating the improvement.

❷ **16.14** Modify the photon map integrator so that any photon that was *last* reflected from a specular surface is stored in the caustic map. This would allow `pbrt` to render caustics from very bright indirect illumination (such as a halogen lamp shining on the ceiling). Does this modification ever introduce new artifacts that weren't present in images before?

❷ **16.15** Another approach to improving the efficiency of photon shooting is to start out by shooting photons from lights in all directions with equal probability, but then to dynamically update the probability of sampling directions based on which directions lead to light paths that have high throughput and which directions are less effective. Photons then must be reweighted based on the probability for shooting a photon in a particular direction. So long as there is always nonzero possibility of sending a photon in any direction, this approach doesn't introduce bias into the shooting algorithm. One advantage of this approach compared to the one in Exercise 16.12 is that the user of the renderer doesn't need to flag which objects may cast caustics ahead of time.

`PhotonIntegrator 774`

❷ **16.16** Performance of the photon mapping integrator can be substantially improved by using irradiance caching to compute reflection from diffuse objects—for example, final gathering can be avoided for diffuse surfaces and only needs to be done for glossy surfaces. Extend the photon mapping integrator to compute and interpolate irradiance estimates like the `IrradianceCache`. When an irradiance value needs to be computed at a point, use the photon map to compute the reflected radiance at the intersection points of the rays traced to compute the irradiance estimate. This further improves performance since additional bounces of rays don't need to be traced to compute the estimate.

❸ **16.17** Even if they aren't used directly for computing reflected radiance, the photons around a point carry useful information about the illumination there that can be used for importance sampling. First, see Keller and Wald (2000) and extend the photon mapping integrator to record which light source each direct lighting photon originated from. When computing direct illumination at a point, use the nearby direct lighting photons to choose light source sampling probabilities based on the estimated contribution of each of the light sources.

Next, see Jensen's first paper on photon mapping (Jensen 1995) and Hey and Purgathofer's more recent paper (Hey and Purgathofer 2002). Both of these describe methods for using importance sampling to choose ray directions for path tracing and final gathering based on a PDF built using the photons around a point. Since the distribution of incident directions of these photons gives information about the distribution of indirect illumination there, they can be used to construct a continuous distribution of directions for sampling over the unit sphere. Implement one of these methods and apply it for sampling some of the rays used for the final gathering computation (continue to sample the BSDF for the rest of the rays). Apply multiple importance sampling to compute weights for these samples. How much more efficient is this than pbrt's current basic photon mapping implementation?

❸ **16.18** Christensen (1999) observed that the final gather step in photon mapping can be substantially accelerated by precomputing irradiance at some fraction of the photons in the scene. Then, when a final gather ray hits a surface, it is only necessary to search for the single nearest photon with an irradiance value, which can then be transformed into an outgoing radiance value by multiplying by the BSDF's reflectivity. Implement this technique in the `PhotonIntegrator` and evaluate its effectiveness.

❷ **16.19** When `Textures` are evaluated to compute BSDFs at points along the paths of rays traced from lights or for indirect illumination, it's not necessary to expend as much effort to compute high-quality filtered values as when the BSDF for a directly visible point is being found. Modify pbrt so that the `ImageTexture` always uses a simple trilinear filter for these texture lookups and so that the other textures use more efficient antialiasing techniques than they might otherwise. How much of a difference do these changes make for scenes with relatively large numbers of indirect or light rays?

BSDF 462
ImageTexture 511
PhotonIntegrator 774
Texture 505

❸ 16.20 Modify the IrradianceCache or PhotonIntegrator to use adaptive sampling for computing irradiance estimates or final gather contributions, respectively. Take some number of samples and use them to decide if the function being integrated seems to be relatively smooth or quickly changing. If it is smooth, stop sampling, but otherwise take a larger number of samples in an effort to compute a better estimate. Experiment with different criteria for deciding when to take more samples. How much of an efficiency improvement is your approach able to achieve compared to always taking a large number of samples? Read Kirk and Arvo's paper that discusses how adaptive sampling can introduce bias (Kirk and Arvo 1991). In your implementation, is it worthwhile to use an unbiased adaptive sampling approach, or is the bias unobjectionable in practice?

IrradianceCache 758
PhotonIntegrator 774

CHAPTER SEVENTEEN

17 LIGHT TRANSPORT II: VOLUME RENDERING

Just as SurfaceIntegrators are the meeting point of scene geometry, materials, and lights, applying sophisticated algorithms to solve the light transport equation and determine the distribution of radiance in the scene, VolumeIntegrators are responsible for incorporating the effect of participating media (as described by VolumeRegions) into this process and determining how it affects the distribution of radiance. This chapter briefly introduces the equation of transfer, which describes how participating media change radiance along rays, and then describes the VolumeIntegrator interface as well as a few simple VolumeIntegrator implementations. Many of the general approaches to light transport algorithms for surfaces described in the previous chapter can be extended to handle participating media as well. The "Further Reading" section and this chapter's exercises discuss these connections further.

17.1 THE EQUATION OF TRANSFER

The equation of transfer is the fundamental equation that governs the behavior of light in a medium that absorbs, emits, and scatters radiation (Chandrasekhar 1960). It accounts for all of the volume scattering processes described in Chapter 12—absorption, emission, and in- and out-scattering—to give an equation that describes the distribution of radiance in an environment. The light transport equation is in fact a special case of

803

the equation of transfer, simplified by the lack of participating media and specialized for scattering from surfaces (Arvo 1993).

In its most basic form, the equation of transfer is an integro-differential equation that describes how the radiance along a beam changes at a point in space. It can be transformed into a pure integral equation that describes the effect of participating media from the infinite number of points along a line. It can be derived in a straightforward manner by subtracting the effects of the scattering processes that reduce energy along a beam (absorption and out-scattering) from the processes that increase energy along it (emission and in-scattering). Recall the source term from Section 12.1.4. It gives the change in radiance at a point p in a particular direction ω due to emission and in-scattered light from other points in the medium:

$$S(\mathrm{p}, \omega) = L_{ve}(\mathrm{p}, \omega) + \sigma_s(\mathrm{p}, \omega) \int_{\mathcal{S}^2} p(\mathrm{p}, -\omega' \to \omega) L_i(\mathrm{p}, \omega') \mathrm{d}\omega'.$$

The source term accounts for all of the processes that add radiance to a ray.

The attenuation coefficient, $\sigma_t(\mathrm{p}, \omega)$, accounts for all processes that reduce radiance at a point: absorption and out-scattering. The differential equation that describes its effect is

$$\mathrm{d}L_o(\mathrm{p}, \omega) = -\sigma_t(\mathrm{p}, \omega) L_i(\mathrm{p}, -\omega) \mathrm{d}t.$$

The overall differential change in radiance at a point p' along a ray is found by adding these two effects together to get the integro-differential form of the equation of transfer:[1]

$$\frac{\partial}{\partial t} L_o(\mathrm{p}, \omega) = -\sigma_t(\mathrm{p}, \omega) L_i(\mathrm{p}, -\omega) + S(\mathrm{p}, \omega).$$

With suitable boundary conditions, this equation can be transformed to a purely integral equation. For example, if we assume that there are no surfaces in the scene so that the rays are never blocked and have an infinite length, the integral equation of transfer is

$$L_i(\mathrm{p}, \omega) = \int_0^\infty T_r(\mathrm{p}' \to \mathrm{p}) S(\mathrm{p}', -\omega) \mathrm{d}t,$$

where $\mathrm{p}' = \mathrm{p} + t\omega$ (Figure 17.1). The meaning of this equation is reasonably intuitive: it just says that the radiance arriving at a point from a given direction is contributed to by the added radiance along all points along the ray from the point. The amount of the added radiance at each point along the ray that reaches the ray's origin is reduced by the total beam transmittance from the ray's origin to the point.

More generally, if there are reflecting and/or emitting surfaces in the scene, rays don't necessarily have infinite length and the surface that a ray hits affects its radiance, adding

---

1   It is an integro-differential equation due to the integral over the sphere in the source term.

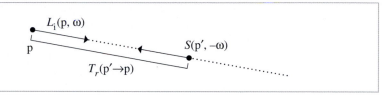

Figure 17.1: The equation of transfer gives the incident radiance at point $L_i(p, \omega)$ accounting for the effect of participating media. At each point along the ray, the source term $S(p', \omega)$ gives the differential radiance added at the point due to scattering and emission. This radiance is then attenuated by the beam transmittance $T_r(p' \to p)$ from the point p' to the ray's origin.

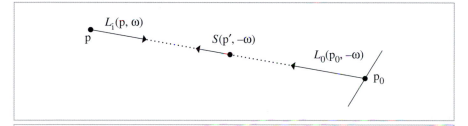

Figure 17.2: For a finite ray that intersects a surface, the incident radiance, $L_i(p, \omega)$, is equal to the outgoing radiance from the surface, $L_o(p_0, -\omega)$, times the beam transmittance to the surface plus the added radiance from all points along the ray from p to p_0.

outgoing radiance from the surface at the point and preventing radiance from points along the ray beyond the intersection point from contributing to radiance at the ray's origin. If a ray (p, ω) intersects a surface at some point p_0 a distance t along the ray, then the integral equation of transfer is

$$L_i(p, \omega) = T_r(p_0 \to p)L_o(p_0, -\omega) + \int_0^t T_r(p' \to p)S(p', -\omega)\mathrm{d}t', \qquad [17.1]$$

where $p_0 = p + t\omega$ is the point on the surface and $p' = p + t'\omega$ are points along the ray (Figure 17.2).

This equation describes the two effects that contribute to radiance along the ray: First, reflected radiance back along the ray from the surface is given by the L_o term, which gives the emitted and reflected radiance from the surface. This radiance may be attenuated by the participating media; the beam transmittance from the ray origin to the point p_0 accounts for this. The second term accounts for the added radiance along the ray due to volume scattering and emission, but only up to the point where the ray intersects the surface; points beyond that one don't affect the radiance along the ray.

In the interest of brevity, we will refrain from further generalization of the equation of transfer here. However, just as the light transport equation could be written in a more general form as a sum over paths of various numbers of vertices and just as an importance function could be introduced to turn it into the measurement equation, the equation of transfer can be generalized in a similar manner. Likewise, we will only present a few simple VolumeIntegrators in the remainder of this chapter, although the general types of algorithms used for the surface integrators in this chapter, such as path tracing, bidirectional path tracing, photon mapping, and so on, can be applied to volume integration as well.

17.2 VOLUME INTEGRATOR INTERFACE

The VolumeIntegrator interface inherits from Integrator, picking up the Preprocess(), RequestSamples(), and Li() methods declared there. The first two of these methods are used by volume integrators in the same way as by surface integrators. The Li() method is similar to the surface integrator versions in that it returns the radiance along the given ray, although volume integrators should assume that the ray has already been intersected with the scene geometry and that if the ray does intersect a surface, its Ray::maxt value will have been set to be at the intersection point. As such, the volume integrator should only compute the effect of volume scattering from the parametric range [mint, maxt] along the ray.

The VolumeIntegrator interface adds an additional method that implementations must provide, Transmittance(), which is responsible for computing the beam transmittance along the given ray from Ray::mint to Ray::maxt.

⟨*Volume Scattering Declarations*⟩+≡
```
class VolumeIntegrator : public Integrator {
public:
    virtual Spectrum Transmittance(const Scene *scene,
        const Ray &ray, const Sample *sample,
        float *alpha) const = 0;
};
```

With this background, the Scene::Li() method can be fully understood. It is a direct implementation of Equation (17.1). The surface integrator computes outgoing radiance L_o at the ray's intersection point, ignoring attenuation back to the ray origin. The volume integrator's Transmittance() method is called to compute the beam transmission T_r to the point on the surface, and its Li() method gives the radiance along the ray due to participating media. The sum of $L_o T_r$ and the additional radiance from participating media gives the total radiance arriving at the ray origin.

17.3 EMISSION-ONLY INTEGRATOR

The simplest possible volume integrator (other than one that ignored participating media completely) simplifies the source term by ignoring in-scattering and only accounting for emission and attenuation. Because in-scattering is ignored, the integral over the sphere in the source term at each point along the ray disappears, and the resulting simplified equation of transfer is

$$L_i(p, \omega) = T_r(p_0 \rightarrow p)L_o(p_0, -\omega) + \int_0^t T_r(p' \rightarrow p)L_{ve}(p', -\omega)dt. \quad [17.2]$$

The EmissionIntegrator, defined in integrators/emission.cpp,⊙ uses Monte Carlo integration to solve this equation. Figure 17.3(a) shows the ecosystem scene without any participating media; Figure 17.3(b), with fog rendered with the EmissionIntegrator.

⟨*EmissionIntegrator Declarations*⟩ ≡
```
class EmissionIntegrator : public VolumeIntegrator {
public:
    ⟨EmissionIntegrator Public Methods 807⟩
private:
    ⟨EmissionIntegrator Private Data 807⟩
};
```

The EmissionIntegrator's Transmittance() and Li() methods both have to evaluate one-dimensional integrals along points t' along a ray. Rather than using a fixed number of samples for each estimate, the implementation here bases the number of samples on the distance the ray travels in the volume—the longer the distance, the more samples are taken. This approach is worthwhile for the naturally intuitive reasons—the longer the ray's extent in the medium, the more accuracy is desirable, and the more samples are likely to be needed to capture greater variation in optical properties along the ray. The number of samples taken is determined indirectly by a user-supplied parameter giving a step size between samples. The ray is divided into segments of the given length, and a single sample is taken in each one.

⟨*EmissionIntegrator Public Methods*⟩ ≡   807
```
    EmissionIntegrator(float ss) { stepSize = ss; }
```

EmissionIntegrator 807
EmissionIntegrator::
  stepSize 807
VolumeIntegrator 806

⟨*EmissionIntegrator Private Data*⟩ ≡   807
```
    float stepSize;
```

The Transmittance() and Li() methods each only need a single 1D sample value to evaluate their respective integrals:

(a)

(b)

Figure 17.3: Ecosystem scene rendered (a) without any participating media and (b) with `ExponentialDensity`-based fog rendered with the `EmissionIntegrator`. Participating media makes the image look substantially more realistic by reducing the contrast of faraway objects.

⟨*EmissionIntegrator Method Definitions*⟩ ≡
```
void EmissionIntegrator::RequestSamples(Sample *sample,
                                        const Scene *scene) {
    tauSampleOffset = sample->Add1D(1);
    scatterSampleOffset = sample->Add1D(1);
}
```

⟨*EmissionIntegrator Private Data*⟩+≡   807
```
int tauSampleOffset, scatterSampleOffset;
```

The `Transmittance()` method is reasonably straightforward. The `VolumeRegion`'s `Tau()` method takes care of computing the optical thickness τ from the ray's starting point to its ending point. The only work for the integrator here is to choose a step size (in case `Tau()` does Monte Carlo integration, as the implementation in Section 15.7 does), pass a single sample value along to that method, and return $e^{-\tau}$. If the `Tau()` method called can compute τ analytically, it will ignore these additional values.

This method takes advantage of the fact that the `Sample` value is only non-`NULL` for camera rays to increase the step size for shadow and indirect rays, thus reducing computational demands (and accuracy). The reduction in accuracy for those rays generally isn't noticeable.

⟨*EmissionIntegrator Method Definitions*⟩+≡
```
Spectrum EmissionIntegrator::Transmittance(const Scene *scene,
        const Ray &ray, const Sample *sample,
        float *alpha) const {
    if (!scene->volumeRegion) return Spectrum(1.f);
    float step = sample ? stepSize : 4.f * stepSize;
    float offset = sample ? sample->oneD[tauSampleOffset][0] :
                            RandomFloat();
    Spectrum tau = scene->volumeRegion->Tau(ray, step, offset);
    return Exp(-tau);
}
```

The `Li()` method is responsible for evaluating the second term of the sum in Equation (17.2). If the ray enters the volume at $t = t_0$ along the ray, then no attenuation or emission happens from the start of the ray up to t_0, and the `Li()` method can instead consider the integral from t_0 to t_1, where t_1 is the minimum of the parametric offset where the ray exits the volume and the offset where it intersects a surface (Figure 17.4). An estimate of the value of this integral,

$$\int_{t_0}^{t_1} T_r(\mathrm{p}' \to \mathrm{p}) L_{\mathrm{ve}}(\mathrm{p}', -\omega)\, dt',$$

can be found by uniformly selecting random points p_i along the ray between t_0 and t_1 and evaluating the estimator

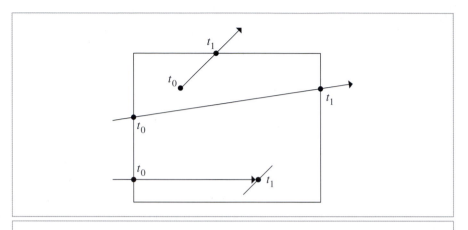

Figure 17.4: The starting point of the ray marching process, t_0, is the maximum of the ray's origin or the point where the ray enters the participating medium. Similarly, the end, t_1, is the minimum of the point where the ray exits the medium and the point where it intersects a surface, if any.

$$\frac{1}{N} \sum_i \frac{T_r(\mathrm{p}_i \to \mathrm{p}) L_{\mathrm{ve}}(\mathrm{p}_i, -\omega)}{p(\mathrm{p}_i)} = \frac{t_1 - t_0}{N} \sum_i T_r(\mathrm{p}_i \to \mathrm{p}) L_{\mathrm{ve}}(\mathrm{p}_i, -\omega)$$

since for uniform points $p(\mathrm{p}_i) = 1/(t_1 - t_0)$. The L_{ve} term in the estimator can be evaluated directly with the corresponding volumeRegion method, and the optical thickness τ to evaluate T_r can either be evaluated directly (for a homogeneous or exponential atmosphere), or via Monte Carlo integration as described in Section 15.7.

In order to do this computation, the implementation of the Li() method thus starts out by finding the t range for the integral and initializing t0 and t1 accordingly:

⟨*EmissionIntegrator Method Definitions*⟩+≡

```
    Spectrum EmissionIntegrator::Li(const Scene *scene,
            const RayDifferential &ray, const Sample *sample,
            float *alpha) const {
        VolumeRegion *vr = scene->volumeRegion;
        float t0, t1;
        if (!vr || !vr->IntersectP(ray, &t0, &t1)) return 0.f;
        ⟨Do emission-only volume integration in vr 811⟩
    }
```

Two additional techniques are used in the implementation here. First, just as the VolumeRegion::Tau() method in Section 15.7 used a uniform step size between sample points, this implementation also steps uniformly for similar reasons. Second, the beam transmittance values T_r can be evaluated efficiently if the points p_i are sorted from the one closest to the ray origin p to the one farthest away. Then, the multiplicative property

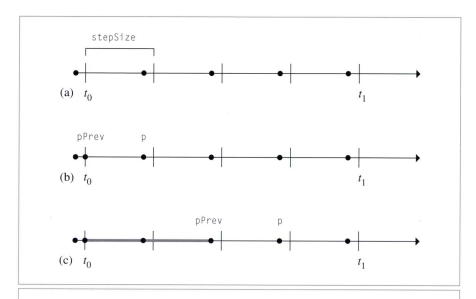

Figure 17.5: Volume Integration Ray Sampling. (a) The ray's extent from t_0 to t_1 is subdivided into a number of segments based on the user-supplied `stepSize` parameter. A single sample is taken in each segment, where the first sample is placed randomly in the first segment and all additional samples are offset by equal-sized steps. (b) Ray marching tracks the previous point to which transmittance was computed, pPrev, as well as the current point, p. Initially, pPrev is the point where the ray enters the volume. (c) At each subsequent step, beam transmittance is computed as the product of transmittance to pPrev and the additional transmittance from pPrev to p.

of T_r can be used to incrementally compute T_r from its value from the previous point:

$$T_r(p_i \to p) = T_r(p_{i-1} \to p)T_r(p_i \to p_{i-1}).$$

Because $T_r(p_i \to p_{i-1})$ covers a shorter distance than $T_r(p_i \to p)$, fewer samples can be used to estimate its value if it is evaluated with Monte Carlo. Both of these ideas are illustrated in Figure 17.5.

⟨*Do emission-only volume integration in* vr⟩ ≡   810
    `Spectrum Lv(0.);`
    ⟨*Prepare for volume integration stepping* **812**⟩
    `for (int i = 0; i < N; ++i, t0 += step) {`
        ⟨*Advance to sample at* t0 *and update* T **812**⟩
        ⟨*Compute emission-only source term at* p **812**⟩
    `}`
    `return Lv * step;`

Spectrum 230

⟨*Prepare for volume integration stepping*⟩ ≡   **811**

```
int N = Ceil2Int((t1-t0) / stepSize);
float step = (t1 - t0) / N;
Spectrum Tr(1.f);
Point p = ray(t0), pPrev;
Vector w = -ray.d;
if (sample)
    t0 += sample->oneD[scatterSampleOffset][0] * step;
else
    t0 += RandomFloat() * step;
```

To find the overall transmittance at the current point, it's only necessary to find the transmittance from the previous point to the current point and multiply it by the transmittance from the ray origin to the previous point, as described earlier.

⟨*Advance to sample at* t0 *and update* T⟩ ≡   **811**

```
pPrev = p;
p = ray(t0);
Spectrum stepTau = vr->Tau(Ray(pPrev, p - pPrev, 0, 1),
                           .5f * stepSize, RandomFloat());
Tr *= Exp(-stepTau);
```
⟨*Possibly terminate ray marching if transmittance is small* **812**⟩

In a thick medium, the transmittance may become very low after the ray has passed a sufficient distance through it. To reduce the time spent computing source term values that are likely to have very little contribution to the radiance at the ray's origin, ray stepping is randomly terminated with Russian roulette when transmittance is sufficiently small.

⟨*Possibly terminate ray marching if transmittance is small*⟩ ≡   **812**

```
if (Tr.y() < 1e-3) {
    const float continueProb = .5f;
    if (RandomFloat() > continueProb) break;
    Tr /= continueProb;
}
```

Having done all this work, computing the source term at the point is trivial:

⟨*Compute emission-only source term at* p⟩ ≡   **811**

```
Lv += Tr * vr->Lve(p, w);
```

17.4 SINGLE SCATTERING INTEGRATOR

In addition to accounting for the emission at each point along the ray, the SingleScattering integrator also considers the incident radiance due to direct illumi-

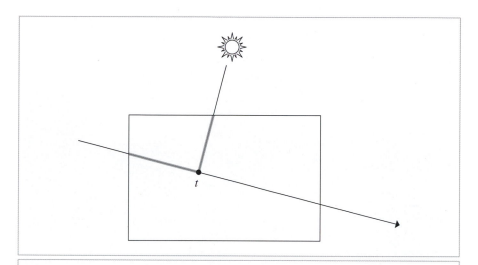

Figure 17.6: When the direct lighting contribution is evaluated at some point t along a ray passing through participating media, it's necessary to compute the attenuation of the radiance from the light passing through the volume to the scattering point as well as the attenuation from that point back to the ray origin.

nation but ignores incident radiance due to multiple scattering. Thus, its `Li()` method estimates the integral

$$\int_0^t T_r(\mathrm{p}' \to \mathrm{p}) \left(L_{\mathrm{ve}}(\mathrm{p}', -\omega) + \sigma_s(\mathrm{p}', \omega) \int_{\mathbb{S}^2} p(\mathrm{p}', -\omega' \to -\omega) L_{\mathrm{d}}(\mathrm{p}', \omega') \mathrm{d}\omega' \right) \mathrm{d}t',$$

where L_{d} only includes radiance from direct lighting. This radiance may be blocked by geometry in the scene and may itself be attenuated by participating media between the light and the point p' along the ray (Figure 17.6). Although accounting for this effect can be much more computationally expensive than just ignoring it as the `EmissionIntegrator` does, it can give striking "beams of light" effects, as seen in Figures 12.1 and 17.7.

Almost all of the implementation of the `SingleScattering` integrator parallels the `EmissionIntegrator`, so only the fragments in the parts that differ are included here. This integrator is defined in the file `integrators/single.cpp`.⊚

EmissionIntegrator 807

Figure 17.7: When the single scattering volume integrator is used with the ecosystem scene, beams of light are visible, giving a striking visual effect.

⟨*SingleScattering Declarations*⟩ ≡
```
class SingleScattering : public VolumeIntegrator {
public:
    ⟨SingleScattering Public Methods⟩
private:
    ⟨SingleScattering Private Data⟩
};
```

This integrator's `Li()` method uses the same general ray-marching approach to evaluate the equation of transfer as the `EmissionIntegrator`. One difference is that this one computes sample values for light source sampling before it enters the `for` loop over sample positions. Because it isn't known how many samples will be necessary until `Li()` is called (since this number depends on the length of the ray segment over which integration is being done), it's not possible to have the `Sampler` generate samples and pass them into `Li()` via the `Sample`. Therefore, a three-dimensional set of Latin hypercube samples is generated here. The first dimension is used to choose which light to sample at each scattering point, and the other two are used by the light to select a point on the light source.

⟨*Compute sample patterns for single scattering samples*⟩ ≡
```
float *samp = (float *)alloca(3 * N * sizeof(float));
LatinHypercube(samp, N, 3);
int sampOffset = 0;
```

The other difference from the `EmissionIntegrator` is how the source term is evaluated. At each sample point along the ray, the following fragment computes the single scattering approximation of the source term at the point p. It serves the same role as the earlier ⟨*Compute emission-only source term at* p⟩ fragment. After including volume emission in the same way that the `EmissionIntegrator` does, it finds the value of σ_s at the point, selects a light to sample using the appropriate Latin hypercube sample, and computes its contribution to scattering at the point. Because the source term is generally evaluated at many points along the ray, only a single light is sampled at each one, and its contribution is scaled by the number of lights, similar to the direct lighting integrator's "sample one light" strategy.

⟨*Compute single scattering source term at* p⟩ ≡
```
Lv += Tr * vr->Lve(p, w);
Spectrum ss = vr->sigma_s(p, w);
if (!ss.Black()) {
    int nLights = scene->lights.size();
    int lightNum = min(Floor2Int(samp[sampOffset] * nLights),
                       nLights-1);
    Light *light = scene->lights[lightNum];
    ⟨Add contribution of light due to scattering at p 815⟩
}
sampOffset += 3;
```

Computing the estimate of the direct lighting contribution at a point p involves estimating the integral

$$\sigma_s(\mathrm{p}, \omega) \int_{\mathcal{S}^2} p(\mathrm{p}, -\omega' \to -\omega) L_d(\mathrm{p}, \omega') \mathrm{d}\omega'.$$

Rather than sampling both the phase function and the light source and applying multiple importance sampling, the implementation here always lets the light choose a sample position on the light source and then computes the estimator directly. For media that aren't extremely anisotropic, this approach works well.

⟨*Add contribution of* light *due to scattering at* p⟩ ≡ 815
```
float pdf;
VisibilityTester vis;
Vector wi;
float u1 = samp[sampOffset+1], u2 = samp[sampOffset+2];
Spectrum L = light->Sample_L(p, u1, u2, &wi, &pdf, &vis);
if (!L.Black() && pdf > 0.f && vis.Unoccluded(scene)) {
    Spectrum Ld = L * vis.Transmittance(scene);
    Lv += Tr * ss * vr->p(p, w, -wi) * Ld * float(nLights) / pdf;
}
```

FURTHER READING

Lommel (1889) was apparently the first to derive the equation of transfer, in a not widely known paper. Not only did he derive the equation of transfer, but he solved it in some simplified cases in order to estimate reflection functions from real-world surfaces (including marble and paper) and compared his solutions to measured reflectance data from these surfaces.

Seemingly unaware of Lommel's work, Schuster (1905) was the next researcher in radiative transfer to consider the effect of multiple scattering. He used the term *self-illumination* to describe the fact that each part of the medium is illuminated by every other part of the medium, and derived differential equations that described reflection from a slab along the normal direction assuming the presence of isotropic scattering. The conceptual framework that he developed remains essentially unchanged in the field of radiative transfer.

Soon thereafter, Schwarzschild (1906) introduced the concept of radiative equilibrium, and Jackson (1910) expressed Schuster's equation in integral form, also noting that "the obvious physical mode of solution is Liouville's method of successive substitutions" (i.e., a Neumann series solution). Finally, King (1913) completed the rediscovery of the equation of transfer by expressing it in the general integral form. Yanovitskij (1997) traces the origin of the integral equation of transfer to Chvolson (1890), but we have been unable to find a copy of this paper.

Blinn (1982b) first used basic volume scattering algorithms for computer graphics. The equation of transfer was first introduced to graphics by Kajiya and Von Herzen (1984). Rushmeier (1988) was the first to compute solutions of it in a general setting. Arvo (1993) first made the essential connections between previous formalizations of light transport in graphics and the equation of transfer and radiative transfer in general.

Other early work in volume scattering for computer graphics includes work by Max (1986) and Nishita, Miyawaki, and Nakamae (1987). Glassner (1995) has a thorough overview of this topic and previous applications of it in graphics, and Max's survey article (Max 1995) also covers the topic well. One key application of volume scattering algorithms in computer graphics has been simulating atmospheric scattering. Work in this area includes papers by Klassen (1987) and Preetham, Shirley, and Smits (1999), who introduced a physically rigorous and computationally efficient atmospheric and sky-lighting model.

Rushmeier and Torrance (1987) used finite-element methods for rendering participating media, and Lafortune and Willems (1996) applied bidirectional path tracing to the problem. Other work includes Bhate and Tokuta's approach based on spherical harmonics (Bhate and Tokuta 1992) and Blasi et al.'s two-pass Monte Carlo algorithm, where the first pass shoots energy from the lights and stores it in a grid and the second pass does final rendering using the grid to estimate illumination at points in the scene (Blasi,

Saëc, and Schlick 1993). Pérez, Pueyo, and Sillion (1997) have written a survey of methods for computing the effect of multiple scattering in participating media. Finally, Jensen and Christensen (1998) have generalized the photon mapping algorithm for participating media, and Pauly, Kollig, and Keller (2000) generalized the Metropolis light transport algorithm to include volume scattering. Pauly's thesis (Pauly 1999) describes the theory and implementation of bidirectional and Metropolis-based algorithms for volume light transport.

There are a number of important applications of visualizing volumetric data sets for medical and engineering applications. This area is called *volume rendering*. In many of these applications, radiometric accuracy is substantially less important than developing techniques that help make structure in the data apparent (e.g., where the bones are in CT scan data). Early papers in this area include those by Levoy (1988, 1990a, 1990b) and Drebin, Carpenter, and Hanrahan (1988).

EXERCISES

● 17.1   With inhomogeneous volume regions, where the optical depth between two points must be computed with ray marching, the SingleScattering volume integrator may spend a lot of time finding the attenuation between lights and points on rays where single scattering is being computed. One approach to reducing this computation is to take advantage of the fact that the amount of attenuation for nearby rays is generally smoothly varying and to use a precomputed approximation to the attenuation. For example, Kajiya and Von Herzen (1984) computed the attenuation to a directional light source at a grid of points in 3D space and then found attenuation at any particular point by interpolating among nearby grid samples. A more memory-efficient approach was developed by Lokovic and Veach (2000) in the form of deep shadow maps, based on a clever compression technique that takes advantage of the smoothness of the attenuation. Implement one of these approaches in pbrt and measure how much it speeds up the SingleScattering integrator. Under what sort of situations do approaches like these result in image errors?

● 17.2   Another effective method to speed up the SingleScattering integrator is to eliminate the need to trace shadow rays from points along the ray passed to the SingleScattering::Li() method by computing shadow maps from each light source (Williams 1978; Reeves, Salesin, and Cook 1987) and use them to determine light source visibility in place of shadow rays. Modify pbrt to optionally use this approach, and measure the performance difference. What resolution do you find to be necessary in the shadow maps for high-quality results?

② **17.3** One shortcoming of the `VolumeIntegrators` in this chapter is that they always take a fixed step size along the ray through the participating medium. If the medium is very dense in some parts but sparse in others, this may be inefficient, as a short step size is needed to accurately resolve detail in the thick parts but is wasteful in the rest of the volume. Modify the implementations in this chapter to vary the step size based on the local scattering properties, and verify that your implementation still computes correct results. How much does adaptive stepping speed up rendering the smoke scene in Figure 12.10? Are there additions to the `VolumeRegion` interface that could make adaptive stepping more robust?

② **17.4** Investigate alternative distributions for sampling t values along rays for estimating the value of the equation of transfer, as discussed in Section 15.7. Construct a scene where the current uniform sampling distribution performs poorly and show the improvement from using an exponential sampling distribution. Also suggest a scenario where the exponential distribution can be a very ineffective distribution to use and where either a uniform distribution or another distribution would perform better.

③ **17.5** Consider a spotlight with a small cone angle shining light through a participating medium. The `SingleScattering` integrator will find it very difficult to efficiently render an image that accurately captures the beam, since a small step size will be needed to find points along rays that lie in the spotlight's cone, yet a small step size will be inefficient for most of the rays that don't pass through the cone at all (Nishita, Miyawaki, and Nakamae 1987). Modify `pbrt`'s light sampling interfaces and modify the `SingleScattering` integrator so that light sources are able to convey information about which parts of particular rays they potentially illuminate. One possibility would be to allow light sources to return a parametric t range to sample for each ray; a default implementation could set the range to $[0, \infty)$. Another possible approach would be to allow the lights the opportunity to sample points along rays directly.

The general problem here is similar to the case of sampling direct illumination at a surface from a small light source: Sampling the BSDF is an inefficient approach, but sampling using the light works quite well. Here, sampling the ray is inefficient, but sampling using the light is effective. Implement one of these techniques in `pbrt` and measure the improvement in running time for difficult-to-render scenes like the one described earlier.

② **17.6** Extend the `SingleScattering` volume integrator to use multiple importance sampling based on sampling points on the light source and sampling the phase function for the direct lighting computation. Under what circumstances will this method give substantially less variance than the current implementation?

③ **17.7** Design and implement a general Monte Carlo path-tracing approach to compute images with multiple scattering in participating media. (To combat the high running times of these algorithms, it may be worthwhile to first implement one of the techniques for reducing the cost of shadow rays described in earlier exercises.) For background information and general approaches, it may be helpful to read Lafortune and Willems's paper about bidirectional path tracing in participating media, even if you don't implement a bidirectional algorithm (Lafortune and Willems 1996). Furthermore, Pauly, Kollig, and Keller (2000) derive the generalization of the path integral form of the LTE for the volume scattering case; their insights may be useful as well.

● 17.8 Photon mapping has also been shown to be an effective way to model the effect of multiple scattering in participating media. Read Jensen and Christensen's paper on this topic (Jensen and Christensen 1998) and implement this method in a new VolumeIntegrator in pbrt. How well does it work to also use photon mapping for direct lighting calculations in participating media?

● 17.9 *Fluence* is the spherical integral of incident radiance at a point, $\int_{S^2} L_i(p, \omega) d\omega$. Implement a volume integrator that performs fluence caching for multiple scattering in participating media, along the basic lines of the IrradianceCache integrator for surfaces; compute fluence at points in the volume as needed and interpolate nearby fluence values when the estimated error from doing so is low. Use the interpolated fluence values to compute reflected light at a point in the volume assuming its phase function is isotropic and thus the angular distribution of incident light is unimportant. Can you get away with also including the direct lighting component in the fluence estimates? How well does fluence caching work for rendering direct lighting alone?

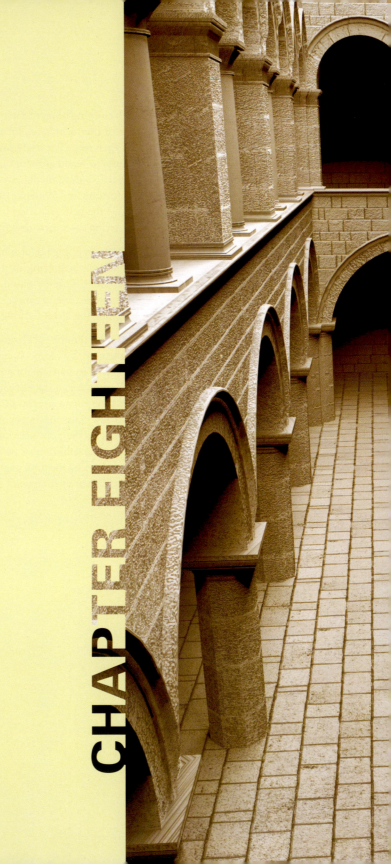

CHAPTER EIGHTEEN

18 SUMMARY AND CONCLUSION

pbrt represents a single point in the space of rendering system designs. The basic decisions we made early on—that ray tracing would be the geometric visibility algorithm used, that physical correctness would be a cornerstone of the system, and that Monte Carlo would be the main approach used for numerical integration—all had pervasive implications for the system's design. An entirely different set of trade-offs would have been made if pbrt were a renderer designed instead for real-time performance or for maximum flexibility for artistic expression. This chapter looks back at some of the details of the complete system, discusses some design alternatives, and also discusses some possible major extensions that are more complex than have been described in the exercises.

18.1 DESIGN RETROSPECTIVE

One of the basic assumptions in pbrt's design was that the most interesting types of images to render are images with complex geometry and lighting. We also assumed that rendering these images well—with good sampling patterns, ray differentials, and antialiased textures—is worth the computational expense. One result of these assumptions is that pbrt is relatively inefficient at rendering simple images.

For example, on a 3.02 GHz Pentium 4 Xeon processor, pbrt takes 2 seconds to render a 512×512 image with no geometry or lights in the scene—a black image! Simple scenes with a few dozen geometric primitives and a small number of lights do not take much longer than this, indicating that the fixed per-ray cost dwarfs the expense of computing intersections and shading for trivial scenes. All of the effort used to compute samples and ray differentials for camera rays and to add the contribution of the rays to the image is clearly a substantial fraction of the time spent rendering simple scenes. For example, with the default parameter settings, each image sample contributes to an average of 16 pixels. If very little time is spent computing the ray's radiance, then the time to update the image using a nontrivial reconstruction filter will generally be much higher than if a one-pixel-wide box filter was used for image reconstruction.

Of course, for a more complex scene, the time spent finding ray intersections, evaluating textures, and applying Monte Carlo integration algorithms dominates running time, and the relative time spent on sample generation and image sample filtering becomes less important. Because we believe that these are the most important types of scenes to render, the fact that some parts of the system hurt performance for simple scenes was never considered a pressing problem to address.

Another performance implication of the basic design is that finding the BSDF at a ray intersection is more computationally intensive than it is in renderers that don't expend as much effort filtering textures and computing ray differentials. We believe that this effort pays off overall by reducing the need to trace more camera rays to address texture aliasing, although again, for simple scenes, texture aliasing is often not a problem. As such, pbrt generally performs better as more samples are taken to compute exitant radiance at a given intersection point. For example, increasing the number of shadow rays traced to an area light source amortizes the antialiasing work done in computing the BSDF's textures, while tracing more camera rays to reduce noise in shadows is less efficient, since a BSDF needs to be computed at each of their intersection points.

The simplicity of some of the interfaces in the system can lead to unnecessary work being done. For example, Samplers always compute lens and time samples, even if they aren't needed by the Camera; there's no way for the Camera to communicate its sampling needs. Similarly, if an Integrator doesn't use all of the samples requested in its GetSamples() method for some ray, the Sampler's work for generating those samples is wasted. This case can occur, for example, if the ray doesn't intersect any geometry.

Another example of potentially wasted computation is that Shapes always compute the partial derivatives of their normal $\partial\mathbf{n}/\partial u$ and $\partial\mathbf{n}/\partial v$, even though these may not be needed. Currently, they are only used if the BSDF has specular components and ray differentials are being computed for the reflected or refracted rays. There's no way for the intersection routine to know if they will be needed at intersection time, however, so their values are always computed. Indeed, there's currently no way to know if the BSDF will have specular components at ray-shape intersection time. The BSDF must be created by the material for this to be known, and the material needs the differential geometry at the intersection point to compute the BSDF!

One way to address this shortcoming would be to allow the material to conservatively describe all of the fields in the DifferentialGeometry that it needs, for example, by setting flags. These flags could be passed to the Shape intersection routines, which could then skip setting the member variables that aren't needed. This approach could further save execution time by allowing shapes to skip computing (u, v) parametric coordinates if they weren't needed, and so on.

18.1.1 ABSTRACTION VERSUS EFFICIENCY

One of the primary tensions when designing interfaces for software systems is making a reasonable trade-off between abstraction and efficiency. For example, many program-mers religiously make all data in all classes private and provide methods to obtain or modify the values of the data items. For simple classes (e.g., Vector), we believe that approach needlessly hides an implementation detail—that the class holds three floating-point coordinates—that we can reasonably expect to never change. Of course, using no information hiding and exposing all details of all classes' internals leads to a code main-tenance nightmare. Yet we believe that there is nothing wrong with judiciously exposing basic design decisions throughout the system. For example, the fact that a Ray is rep-resented with a point, a vector, and two floating-point values that give its extent is a decision that doesn't need to be hidden behind a layer of abstraction. Code elsewhere is shorter and easier to understand when details like these are exposed.

An important thing to keep in mind when writing a software system and making these sorts of trade-offs is expected final size of the system. The core of pbrt (excluding its plug-in modules), where all of the basic interfaces, abstractions, and policy decisions are defined, is just under 9000 lines of code. Adding additional functionality to the system will generally only increase the amount of code in the plug-ins. pbrt is never going to grow to be a million lines of code; this fact can and should be reflected in the amount of information hiding used in the system. It would be a waste of programmer time (and likely a source of run time inefficiency) to design the interfaces to accommodate a system of that level of complexity.

18.1.2 DESIGN ALTERNATIVES: TRIANGLES ONLY

While ray tracing's ability to handle a wide variety of shapes is elegant, this property is not as useful in practice as one might initially expect. Most real-world scenes are either modeled directly with polygons or with smooth surfaces like spline patches and subdivi-sion surfaces that either have difficult-to-implement or inefficient ray-shape intersection algorithms. As such, they are usually tessellated into triangles for ray intersection tests in practice. Unfortunately, not many shapes that are commonly encountered in real-world scenes can be described well with spheres and cones!

There are some advantages to designing a ray tracer around a common low-level shape representation like triangles and only operating on this representation throughout much of the pipeline. Such a renderer could still support a variety of primitives in the scene description but would always tessellate them at some point before performing intersection tests. Advantages of this design include the following:

- The renderer can depend on the fact that the triangle vertices can be transformed into world space in advance, so no transformations of rays into object space are ever necessary.
- The acceleration structures can be specialized so that their nodes directly store the triangles that overlap them. This improves the locality of the geometry in memory and enables ray-primitive intersection tests to be performed directly in the traversal routine, without needing to pass through two levels of virtual function calls, as pbrt does now.
- Displacement mapping, where geometry is subdivided into small triangles, which can then have their vertices perturbed procedurally or with texture maps, can be more easily implemented if all primitives are able to tessellate themselves.

These advantages are substantial, for both increased performance and the complexity that they remove from many parts of the system. For a production renderer, rather than one with pedagogical goals like pbrt, this alternative is probably worth pursuing.

18.1.3 DESIGN ALTERNATIVES: STREAMING COMPUTATION

One of the most exciting recent developments in computer architecture has been the development of *streaming* models of processor design (Kapasi et al. 2003). Streaming architectures differ from conventional CPUs in that they are highly parallel, have many computational units on a single chip, and better expose memory locality, efficiently using bandwidth at all levels of the memory hierarchy. Algorithms that can be expressed in terms of computational kernels that operate on streams of data can enjoy substantial performance advantages on such architectures. In contrast, general-purpose CPUs focus more on making a small number of computational units run quickly than exploiting parallelism over many units.

Modern graphics accelerators are an implementation of the streaming model. This has allowed commodity graphics hardware to achieve performance growth at a substantially faster rate than CPUs—a sustained rate of doubling performance every six months (Hanrahan 2002). Almost all modern computers thus have specialized streaming processors inside them.

Streaming architectures have shown substantial promise in addressing the problem of what to do with the enormous number of transistors now available on a single chip. Streaming processors can allocate additional transistors to additional computational elements, while conventional CPU architectures don't support a programming model that makes it possible to keep more computational units busy. This means that CPUs tend to devote these transistors to control hardware and on-chip cache memory in an effort to keep a single pipeline executing at top speed.

Many graphics and media-related applications fit the streaming programming model well (Owens et al. 2000, 2002; Owens 2002). In particular, Purcell et al. (2002, 2003) and Carr, Hall, and Hart (2002) have demonstrated the implementation of general-purpose ray tracers on streaming graphics hardware. While these systems do not provide many of the features available in pbrt, they demonstrate the feasibility of using GPUs for fast ray tracing.

Writing efficient code for streaming architectures often requires different algorithms than the ones that are most efficient for CPUs. For example, the mechanisms for writing data to memory in streaming architecture are more constrained than on CPUs. However, the performance rewards for writing software for a streaming architecture can be substantial and are likely to increase. Indeed, given the performance potential of these architectures, we believe that should a second edition of this book be written in a few years, the system may well target streaming processor architectures rather than general-purpose CPUs.

18.2 MAJOR PROJECTS

Most of the exercises at the end of the chapters have been reasonably self-contained, involving modifying or extending plug-in modules, rather than making substantial changes to the system's overall architecture. This section outlines a number of more ambitious changes that could be made to the system, involving more wide-reaching changes to its main abstractions and interfaces.

18.2.1 PARALLEL RENDERING

Given the computational cost of ray tracing, there has been interest in parallel algorithms for ray tracing since shortly after the algorithm was first introduced (Cleary et al. 1983; Green and Paddon 1989; Badouel and Priol 1989). With the computational capabilities available in modern CPUs, researchers have started to demonstrate interactive ray tracing using tens of processors. For example, Parker et al. (1999) developed an interactive ray tracer on a shared-memory computer with 64 processors, and Wald and collaborators have ray-traced complex scenes at interactive rates on a cluster of PCs (Wald et al. 2001, 2002; Wald, Slusallek, and Benthin 2001; Wald, Benthin, and Slusallek 2003).[1] Chalmers, Davis, and Reinhard (2002) provide good coverage of the state of the art in parallel ray tracing.

Parallelizing pbrt would require changes to many parts of the system, depending on the particular approach used and the target hardware. One option is to target the system to a cluster of networked machines, with each process running in its own address space and communicating with the others via explicit message passing. The other possibility

---

1   Indeed, even if one isn't writing a parallel ray tracer, there is a wealth of information in papers on this topic about extremely efficient implementation of ray-tracing algorithms, quickly building high-quality acceleration structures, cache-friendly programming for ray tracing, and so forth.

is a shared-memory environment, where a number of threads share the same memory space. This section will focus on issues related to the second approach; see, for example, Wald et al.'s work and Chalmers et al.'s book for information about techniques related to the first.

The key problem to solve when multiple independent threads of execution have access to a shared region of memory is synchronization. It is critical to ensure that one thread isn't modifying a data structure that another is simultaneously reading, thus leading to inconsistent or invalid results. The mechanism that solves this problem is *mutual exclusion:* threads must coordinate among themselves so that this case does not occur. This can sometimes easily be done by convention: if only one thread needs to read or write some data structure and the other threads never access it, this problem can't come up.

More generally, mechanisms like *locks* can be used, where threads can request ownership of a lock object that they later give up, and the operating system ensures that no more than one thread may hold the lock at any time. If shared data structures are protected by locks and all threads follow the convention that they acquire the appropriate lock before accessing or updating the data structures it protects, then the program can execute correctly. This idea is straightforward, but implementing it consistently and correctly in a complex system is quite difficult. Mutual exclusion bugs can be hard to reproduce because some runs show no errors and others may crash due to a chance scheduling of threads by the operating system.

If we were parallelizing pbrt for a shared-memory architecture, we would probably start by parsing the scene description file and building the scene representation, including the acceleration structures, using just a single thread of execution. This phase of the program's execution is difficult to parallelize, since all of the work being done is creation of data structures, and this step generally isn't the main bottleneck in image synthesis. We would then create multiple threads to share the rendering work, but then write out the final image and clean up with just a single thread.

Once the Scene has been created and the rendering threads are ready to start, a mechanism for determining what rendering work each thread should do is needed. An effective and straightforward approach is to partition the image plane into regions and to have different threads work on different regions, taking responsibility for all of the work needed to compute the contributions of a set of image samples.

The image can be partitioned statically or dynamically: A static partition assigns each region to a thread at start-up time (note that there need not be the same number of regions as threads). Each thread can then work on its region without communicating with the other threads. Because some parts of the image may require more computation than others, a better approach is to have threads access a shared data structure to determine what region of the image to work on next. The granularity of the image decomposition must be chosen carefully. If it is too fine, threads will finish work on their image region quickly and spend too much time waiting for access to the shared work queue. On the

Scene 23

other hand, if the regions are too large, a thread working on a complex region may hold up the completion of rendering, as other threads sit idle. In either case, the Samplers would need to be modified to support the partitioning method used (e.g., so that they would generate samples for multiple regions of the image as needed).

In simple ray-tracing systems, the main rendering phase is easily parallelizable, since all of the data structures except for the output image are read only. Many threads can thus easily share the same scene data and only have to coordinate among each other for image output. For this reason ray tracing has often been called "embarrassingly parallel." In more complex ray-tracing systems, there are more issues to address. Fortunately, many of the classes in pbrt are safe for multithreading as they are currently written. For example, the Shapes, Cameras, Filters, VolumeRegions, and Materials all operate on the data passed into their methods and don't modify their member data after they have been created. As such, there is no potential for trouble if multiple threads are calling methods of one of them simultaneously.

Other parts of the system, like Film, would require locking. In pbrt, having threads acquire and release a lock for each image sample would probably lead to poor performance because the time spent acquiring and releasing locks would dwarf the time spent updating the image representation. The easiest way to work around this would be for threads to accumulate sample contributions in local memory and then periodically pass them to the Film in batches. Alternatively, each thread could hold a separate Film object and update it without locking, although the memory cost of this would be higher. When rendering completed, all of the individual Films would be merged into a single Film object for final processing and output.

There are also issues related to the accelerators. If an accelerator refines all of the Primitives at creation time, then the acceleration structure is read only and locking may be avoided. If the accelerator refines primitives for intersection lazily, threads should use a *reader-writer* lock to protect the accelerator. A reader-writer lock allows multiple threads to hold a read lock for read-only access to a data structure, but only allows one to hold a writer lock, and only hands out a writer lock if no threads hold a reader lock. Primitive refinement and updates to the acceleration data structure should only be done by a thread holding a writer lock.

Multithreaded mailboxing introduces a few additional complications to the accelerators. The variable used to assign IDs to rays is a potential source of contention, and having multiple threads try to update the shared mailboxes in the MailboxPrims is a likely source of trouble. The best solution to this is probably for each thread to assign mailbox IDs to rays independently of the other threads, and for each thread to use local private memory to store the ID of the last ray tested against each primitive.

Most of the rest of pbrt is largely already thread safe, although if you were to parallelize the system, you should audit each module with this issue in mind to ensure that you have found all of the places that need mutual exclusion. For example, the statistics system would need to be rewritten to accurately collect statistics in the presence of multiple threads, and the `PhotonIntegrator` and `IrradianceCache` would both need additional locking for their data structures.

18.2.2 INCREASED SCENE COMPLEXITY

Given well-built accelerator structures, one of ray tracing's strengths is that the time spent on ray-primitive intersections grows slowly with added scene complexity. As such, the maximum complexity that a ray tracer can handle may be limited more by memory than by computation. Because rays may pass through many different regions of the scene during a short period of time, virtual memory often performs poorly when ray-tracing complex scenes due to the incoherent memory access patterns.

One way to increase the potential complexity that a renderer is capable of handling is to reduce the memory used to store the scene. For example, pbrt currently uses approximately 300 MB of memory for the one million triangles in the ecosystem scene in Figure 4.1. This works out to 300 bytes per triangle, if all memory use (acceleration structures, geometry, textures and materials, etc.) is amortized over the geometric complexity. We have previously written ray tracers that managed an average of 40 bytes per triangle for scenes like these, including all memory overhead. Clearly, much reduction is possible.

To do this successfully requires careful attention to memory use throughout the system. For example, in the other system, we provided three different `Triangle` implementations, one using 8-bit `u_chars` to store vertex indices, one using 16-bit `u_shorts`, and one using 32-bit `u_ints`. The smallest index size that was sufficient for the range of vertex indices in the mesh was chosen at run time. Deering's paper on geometry compression (Deering 1995) and Ward's packed color format (Ward 1991b) are both good inspirations for thinking along these lines.

A more complex approach is geometry caching (Pharr and Hanrahan 1996), where the renderer holds a fixed amount of geometry in memory and discards geometry that hasn't been accessed recently. This approach is useful for scenes with a lot of tessellated geometry, where a compact higher-level shape representation like a subdivision surface can explode into a large number of triangles. When available memory is low, it can be worthwhile to discard some of this geometry and regenerate it later if needed.

The performance of such a cache can be substantially improved by reordering the rays that are traced in order to improve their spatial and thus memory coherence (Pharr et al. 1997). An easier-to-implement and more effective approach to improving the cache's behavior is described by Christensen et al. (2003), who wrote a ray tracer that uses simplified representations of the scene geometry in a geometry cache. Also, see Rushmeier, Patterson, and Veerasamy (1993) for an example of how to use simplified scene representations to compute indirect illumination.

18.2.3 SUBSURFACE SCATTERING

There is an important assumption implicit in the BSDF and the scattering equation: that the only incident light that has an effect on the exitant radiance at a point p is also

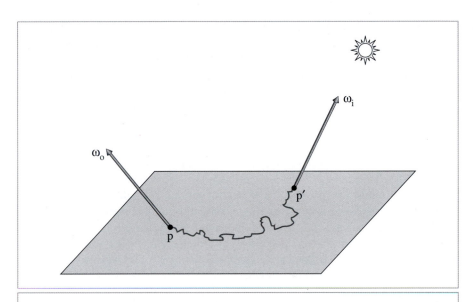

Figure 18.1: The bidirectional scattering-surface reflectance distribution function generalizes the BSDF to account for light that exits the surface at a point other than where it enters. It is more difficult to evaluate than the BSDF, although subsurface light transport can make a substantial contribution to the appearance of many real-world objects.

incident on the surface at p—light that hits the surface at other points p′ is assumed not to affect exitant radiance at p.

For many types of surfaces—human skin, marble, and so on—this assumption is incorrect and there is a significant amount of *subsurface light transport*. The rendering in Figure 1.11 simulates subsurface scattering in the snow, giving it the soft diffused look of real snow. Light that enters such a surface at one location may travel for some distance underneath the surface before exiting at another position (Figure 18.1).

The *bidirectional scattering-surface reflectance distribution function* (BSSRDF) is the formalism that describes this scattering process. It is a distribution function $S(p', \omega_i, p, \omega_o)$ that describes the ratio of exitant differential radiance at point p in direction ω_o to the differential irradiance at p′ from direction ω_i. The generalization of the scattering equation for the BSSRDF requires integration over surface area *and* incoming direction. With two more dimensions to integrate over, it is substantially more complex than the scattering equation, Equation (5.6):

$$L_o(p, \omega_o) = \int_A \int_{\mathcal{S}^2} S(p', \omega_i, p, \omega_o) \, \cos\theta_i \, d\omega_i \, dA.$$

Fortunately, points p′ that are far away from p generally contribute little to $L_o(p, \omega_o)$. This fact can be a substantial help in implementations of subsurface scattering algorithms.

Light transport beneath a surface is described by the same principles as volume light transport in participating media and is described by the equation of transfer; subsurface scattering is based on the same effects as light scattering in clouds, just at a smaller scale. For subsurface scattering, a number of useful simplifications can be made to general volume light transport approaches because, in the end, the quantity of interest is the distribution of light leaving a surface at a point, rather than the actual distribution of light inside the participating medium.

pbrt currently has deep-seated assumptions that the BSDF is the abstraction that will be used to model reflection from surfaces. In order to support subsurface scattering, pbrt would need to be extended to support methods for describing the volume scattering properties of translucent materials. Furthermore, integrators would be needed that applied subsurface light transport algorithms to compute reflection. Because some of these algorithms require the ability to determine more information about local surface geometry than is available in DifferentialGeometry, including the ability to move across points on the surface around the intersection point, the Shape interface will likely require extension to implement these algorithms as well.

Subsurface scattering was first introduced to graphics by Hanrahan and Krueger (1993), although their approach did not attempt to simulate light that entered the object at points other than at the point being shaded. Dorsey et al. (1999) applied photon maps to simulating true subsurface scattering. Other recent work in this area includes papers by Pharr and Hanrahan (2000) and Jensen and collaborators (Jensen et al. 2001; Jensen and Buhler 2002).

The two most easily implemented approaches to this problem are volume photon maps for subsurface scattering, as described by Dorsey et al. (1999) and Jensen et al.'s dipole approach (Jensen et al. 2001; Jensen and Buhler 2002). The latter approach has been the basis of a number of fast implementations for scan line and interactive rendering (Hery 2003; Hao, Baby, and Varshney 2003; Dachsbacher and Stamminger 2003).

18.2.4 PRECOMPUTATION FOR INTERACTIVE RENDERING

Monte Carlo ray-tracing algorithms have applications beyond synthesis of images for display. Recently there has been interest in algorithms for precomputing information about geometric models that encodes a description of how they respond to arbitrary illumination distributions, rather than computing how they reflect a particular distribution of illumination. This information can then be used in scan line or interactive z-buffer rendering to compute realistic shading based on arbitrary illumination conditions. For example, precomputed radiance transfer (PRT) algorithms account for interreflection of light in geometric models, representing it in a way that can be efficiently evaluated in interactive applications (Sloan, Kautz, and Snyder 2002; Sloan, Liu, Shum, and Snyder 2003; Sloan, Hall, Hart, and Snyder 2003).

DifferentialGeometry 83
Shape 90

Because pbrt's overall design is geared toward final image synthesis rather than this type of preprocessing, extending the system to compute this information for a given model isn't just a matter of writing a new `SurfaceIntegrator`. The basic `Integrator::Li()` interface isn't flexible enough to meet the needs of these algorithms. For example, the PRT algorithms in the papers cited earlier need to compute coefficients that encode response to incident illumination at the vertices of a triangle mesh; the task of the integrator is no longer to compute radiance along a set of independent rays. Furthermore, the `Sample` structure isn't rich enough to naturally encode where the samples are to be taken.

Another shortcoming in pbrt's interfaces is that they don't provide access to the scene geometry beyond its bounding boxes and ray-object intersection queries; there's no way to iterate over all of the vertices of a triangle mesh, for example. This was an intentional design decision, since by minimizing the number and variety of methods that `Shapes` must provide, it's easier to add new and unusual shapes to the system. For many types of shapes (e.g., spheres), the very idea of iterating over its vertices has no meaning.

One approach to all of these problems is to write an integrator that overloads the `Integrator::Preprocess()` method and does this precomputation there. The scene description file could then be set up to render an image that was one pixel wide and one pixel tall, which could be ignored. In this case, the integrator would also be responsible for determining the points on the model at which values needed to be computed (e.g., by reading a file from disk or via parameters to the integrator), doing the appropriate computation in `Preprocess()`, and also writing the results to disk.

Alternatively, given an appropriate importance function and leaving the emitted radiance function as an arbitrary function as opposed to a specific function specified by the lights in the scene, it's possible to express some precomputed radiance transfer algorithms in terms of a series of measurements that can be computed with the measurement equation. An alternative thus would be to derive an appropriate importance function for a particular PRT approach, show that the measurement equation gives the value of the appropriate quantity, and design a replacement interface for the `Integrator::Li()` method that takes a representation of an importance function and computes an estimate of the measurement equation for the given importance function.

18.3 CONCLUSION

Over the last five years, pbrt has evolved from a system designed only to support the students taking Stanford's CS348b course to a robust, feature-rich, physically based, extensible rendering package. Since we started working on this project, we have both learned a great deal about what it takes to build a rendering system that doesn't just make pretty pictures, but is one that other people enjoy using and modifying as well. What has been most difficult, however, was designing a large piece of software that others would enjoy *reading*. This has been a far more challenging (and rewarding) task than implementing any of the rendering algorithms themselves. We thank you for reading this book and hope that you have enjoyed reading it as much as we have enjoyed writing it.

▣ UTILITIES

In addition to all of the graphics-related code presented thus far, pbrt makes use of a number of general utility routines and classes. Although these are key to pbrt's operation, it is not necessary to understand their implementation in detail in order to work with the rest of the system. This appendix describes the interfaces to these routines and the implementations of those that are interesting enough to delve into.

This appendix describes routines used for error reporting, memory management, pseudorandom number generation, and other basic details. These sections omit much of the associated source code; their declarations can be found in the file core/pbrt.h, ⓒⓞ and their definitions in core/util.cpp. ⓒⓞ This appendix ends by showing implementations of the generic octree and kd-tree data structures in detail. These are currently used only by the IrradianceCache and PhotonIntegrator, respectively, but were written so that they could be reused for other purposes as well.

A.1 COMMUNICATING WITH THE USER

The functions and classes in this section all communicate information to the user. In addition to consolidating functionality like printing progress bars, hiding user communication behind a small API like the one here also permits easy modification of the communication mechanisms. For example, if pbrt were embedded in an application that had a graphical user interface, errors might be reported via a dialog box or a routine provided by the parent application. If `printf()` calls were strewn throughout the system, it would be more difficult to make the two systems work together well.

A.1.1 ERROR REPORTING

pbrt provides four functions for reporting anomalous conditions. In order of increasing severity, they are `Info()`, `Warning()`, `Error()`, and `Severe()`. All of them take a formatting string as their first argument and a variable number of additional arguments providing values for the format. The syntax is identical to that used by the `printf` family of functions. For example, if the variable `rayNum` has type `int`, then the following call could be made:

```
Info("Now tracing ray number %d\n", rayNum);
```

Some compilers provide a mechanism to indicate that a function processes a formatting string like `printf`. The compiler can then verify that the types of the arguments following the formatting string are correct. Thus, code like

```
int FrameNum;
Info("Finished rendering frame number %f\n", FrameNum);
```

can be properly flagged as incorrect, since the formatting string indicates that `FrameNum` is a `double`, while it is actually an `int`. We define a compiler-specific `PRINTF_FUNC` macro to use this feature. Where it is not possible to do this type of syntax check, `PRINTF_FUNC` has an empty definition.

⟨*Setup printf format*⟩ ≡   **834**
```
#ifdef __GNUG__
#define PRINTF_FUNC __attribute__ \
    ((__format__ (__printf__, 1, 2)))
#else
#define PRINTF_FUNC
#endif // __GNUG__
```

The four error reporting functions can now be declared using this macro:

⟨*Global Function Declarations*⟩+≡
```
    ⟨Setup printf format  834⟩
    extern COREDLL void Info(const char *, ...) PRINTF_FUNC;
    extern COREDLL void Warning(const char *, ...) PRINTF_FUNC;
    extern COREDLL void Error(const char *, ...) PRINTF_FUNC;
    extern COREDLL void Severe(const char *, ...) PRINTF_FUNC;
```

We will not show the implementation of these functions here because they are a straightforward application of the C++ variable argument processing functions.

pbrt also has its own version of the standard `assert()` macro, named `Assert()`. It checks that the given expression's value evaluates to true; if not, `Severe()` is called with information about the location of the assertion failure. `Assert()` is used for basic sanity checks where failure indicates little possibility of recovery. In general, assertions should be used to detect internal bugs in the code, not expected error conditions (such as invalid scene file input), because the message printed will likely be cryptic to anyone other than the developer.

⟨*Global Inline Functions*⟩+≡
```
#ifdef NDEBUG
#define Assert(expr) ((void)0)
#else
#define Assert(expr) \
    ((expr) ? (void)0 : \
        Severe("Assertion " #expr " failed in %s, line %d", \
            __FILE__, __LINE__))
#endif // NDEBUG
```

A.1.2 REPORTING PROGRESS

The `ProgressReporter` class gives the user feedback about how much of a task has been completed and how much longer it is expected to take. For example, the `Scene::Render()` method uses a `ProgressReporter` to show how many of the camera rays have been traced. The current implementation prints a row of plus signs, the elapsed time, and the estimated remaining time.

⟨*Global Classes*⟩≡
```
struct COREDLL ProgressReporter {
    ⟨ProgressReporter Public Methods 835⟩
    ⟨ProgressReporter Data⟩
};
```

The constructor takes the total number of units of work to be done (e.g., the total number of camera rays that will be traced) and a short string describing the task being performed. It also takes an integer indicating the number of characters to use for the progress bar.

⟨*ProgressReporter Public Methods*⟩≡ 835
```
ProgressReporter(int totalWork, const string &title,
                 int barLength=58);
```

Once the `ProgressReporter` has been created, each call to its `Update()` method signifies that one unit of work has been completed. An optional integer value can be passed to indicate that multiple units have been done.

⟨*ProgressReporter Public Methods*⟩+≡ 835
```
void Update(int num = 1) const;
```

Assert() 835
COREDLL 904
ProgressReporter 835
Scene::Render() 24
Severe() 834

The `ProgressReporter::Done()` method lets the user know that the task is complete:

⟨*ProgressReporter Public Methods*⟩+≡   **835**
    `void Done() const;`

A.1.3 STATISTICS

pbrt provides functions for gathering statistics and presenting a single unified format for reporting these statistics. Before pbrt exits, a single function call causes all of the statistics managed by these functions to be printed.

Three types of statistics are supported:

- *Counters:* These provide a way to track the quantity of something, such as the total number of rays that are traced while making an image. They can also track the minimum or maximum of some quantity, such as the number of primitives overlapping a kd-tree leaf node.
- *Percentages:* These record the percentage of times an event happens out of the possible times it could have happened—for example, the percentage of ray-triangle tests that found an intersection.
- *Ratios:* These are similar to percentages, but are reported as a ratio rather than a percentage. For example, a ratio is used to track the average number of grid voxels that the primitives in the scene overlap.

When information is reported to the statistics system, the caller must provide a category and a name for the particular statistic. The category gives a way to gather related types of statistics during output (e.g., all of the statistics gathered by the camera module can be reported together). The name is used as a description for the particular statistic.

A counter is created by creating a `StatsCounter` object, passing it a general category name (e.g., "Camera") and the name of the specific statistic (e.g., "Rays Generated"). The `StatsCounter` should be declared so that it is persistent throughout the program's execution. This can be done by dynamically allocating it, but if the `StatsCounter` is only used in one function, it is usually more convenient to declare it as `static` inside that function.

⟨*Global Classes*⟩+≡
    `class COREDLL StatsCounter {`
    `public:`
        ⟨*StatsCounter Public Methods* **836**⟩
    `private:`
        ⟨*StatsCounter Private Data* **837**⟩
    `};`

COREDLL 904
ProgressReporter::Done() 836
StatsCounter 836

⟨*StatsCounter Public Methods*⟩≡   **836**
    `StatsCounter(const string &category, const string &name);`

StatsCounterType is the type used to count things in the statistics routines. Rather than using an int or long type, double is used in pbrt. This choice was made because doubles are 64 bits on most architectures and provide 52 bits of precision in their mantissa, much more than the 32 bits available in ints on most architectures. This extra precision makes it much less likely that any of the counters will overflow.

⟨*StatsCounter Private Data*⟩ ≡   836
```
    StatsCounterType num;
```

The StatsCounter class overloads the ++ operator, which makes incrementing its value simple:

⟨*StatsCounter Public Methods*⟩+≡   836
```
    void operator++() { ++num; }
    void operator++(int) { ++num; }
```

If the counter is being used to track the minimum or maximum of some range of values, the Min() and Max() methods can be used to report a new value to it:

⟨*StatsCounter Public Methods*⟩+≡   836
```
    void Max(StatsCounterType val) { num = max(val, num); }
    void Min(StatsCounterType val) { num = min(val, num); }
```

Finally, there is a conversion from StatsCounter to double:

⟨*StatsCounter Public Methods*⟩+≡   836
```
    operator double() const { return (double)num; }
```

The interfaces to StatsRatio and StatsPercentage are identical; the only difference is their reporting format. Like StatsCounter, both take the category name and statistic name as the only parameters to their constructors. They both store two values internally, na and nb, such that the final value of the statistic they are tracking is na/nb. The Add() routines provide a way for the user to increment these values.

⟨*StatsRatio Public Methods*⟩ ≡
```
    void Add(int a, int b) { na += a; nb += b; }
```

⟨*StatsPercentage Public Methods*⟩ ≡
```
    void Add(int a, int b) { na += a; nb += b; }
```

The StatsPrint() function prints all of the statistics that have been registered. It sorts them by category and formats the results so that columns of numbers line up and large numbers are reported in units of thousands, millions, or billions, depending on their magnitude.

⟨*Global Function Declarations*⟩+≡
```
    extern void StatsPrint(FILE *dest);
```

When pbrt is about to exit, it calls the StatsCleanup() function, which frees memory allocated by the statistics system:

⟨*Global Function Declarations*⟩+≡
```
    extern void StatsCleanup();
```

A.2 MEMORY MANAGEMENT

Memory management is often a complex issue in a system written in a language without garbage collection. The situation is, for the most part, simple in pbrt, since most dynamic memory allocation is done as the scene description file is parsed, and most of this memory remains in use until rendering is finished. Nevertheless, there are a few issues related to memory management that warrant classes and routines to address them. Many of these issues are performance related, although an automatic reference-counting class is also provided to track the lifetimes of objects that may be referenced by multiple pointers in different parts of the system.

A.2.1 VARIABLE STACK ALLOCATION

Sometimes it is necessary to allocate a variable amount of memory that will be used temporarily in a single function. If only a small amount of memory is needed, the overhead of new and delete (or malloc() and free()) may be high relative to the computation being done. Instead, it is frequently more efficient to use the alloca() call, which allocates memory on the stack with just a few instructions. This memory is automatically deallocated when the routine exits, which also saves bookkeeping work in the routine that uses it.

alloca() is an extremely useful tool, but there are two pitfalls to be aware of when using it. First, because the memory is deallocated when the calling routine completes, the pointer must not be returned from the routine or stored in a data structure with a longer lifetime than the function that allocated it. However, the pointer may be passed to functions called by the allocating function. Second, stack size is limited on some systems, so alloca() shouldn't be used for more than a few kilobytes of storage.

A.2.2 REFERENCE-COUNTED OBJECTS

In programming languages that do not provide automatic memory management, tricky situations can arise when multiple pointers to some object exist. We would like to free an object as soon as it is no longer needed by any other object (but no sooner), so that both memory leaks and errors due to memory corruption are avoided.

As long as there aren't circular references (e.g., object A holds a reference to object B, which holds a reference to object A), a good solution to this problem is to use *reference counting*. Objects that may be pointed to in multiple places store a counter that is incremented when another object stores a reference to it, and decremented when a reference

StatsCleanup() 838

goes away (e.g., due to the holding object being destroyed). When its reference count goes to zero, memory for the object can be safely freed.

We will define two classes to make it easy to use reference-counted objects in pbrt. An object should inherit from the ReferenceCounted class if it is to be managed via reference counting. The ReferenceCounted class just adds an nReferences field; this count will be managed by the Reference class, defined in the following.

⟨*Global Classes*⟩+≡
```
class COREDLL ReferenceCounted {
public:
    ReferenceCounted() { nReferences = 0; }
    int nReferences;
private:
    ReferenceCounted(const ReferenceCounted &);
    ReferenceCounted &operator=(const ReferenceCounted &);
};
```

Rather than holding a pointer to a reference-counted object, an instance of the Reference template is used to hold the reference. The Reference template handles updates to the reference count as appropriate. For example, consider the following function:

```
void func() {
    Reference<Foo> r1 = new Foo;
    Reference<Foo> r2 = r1;
    r1 = new Foo;
    r2 = r1;
}
```

In the first line, a Foo object is allocated; r1 holds a reference to it, and the object's nReferences count is one. A second reference to the object is made in the second line; r1 and r2 refer to the same Foo object, which now has a reference count of two. Next, a new Foo object is allocated. When a reference to it is assigned to r1, the reference count of the original object is decremented to one. Finally, in the last line, r2 is assigned to refer to the newly allocated Foo object. The original Foo object now has zero references and is automatically deleted. At the end of the function, when both r1 and r2 go out of scope, the reference count for the second Foo object goes to zero, causing it to be freed as well. A few C++ language features make this all work transparently.

⟨*Global Classes*⟩+≡
```
template <class T> class Reference {
public:
    ⟨Reference Public Methods  840⟩
private:
    T *ptr;
};
```

The constructors are straightforward. They just need to increment the reference count:

⟨*Reference Public Methods*⟩ ≡   **839**
```
Reference(T *p = NULL) {
    ptr = p;
    if (ptr) ++ptr->nReferences;
}
```

⟨*Reference Public Methods*⟩+≡   **839**
```
Reference(const Reference<T> &r) {
    ptr = r.ptr;
    if (ptr) ++ptr->nReferences;
}
```

When a Reference is assigned to hold a different reference, it is necessary to decrement the old reference count and increment the count of the new object. The increments and decrements are ordered carefully in the following code so that an assignment like r1 = r1 doesn't inadvertently delete the object r1 is referring to if r1 is the only reference.

⟨*Reference Public Methods*⟩+≡   **839**
```
Reference &operator=(const Reference<T> &r) {
    if (r.ptr) r.ptr->nReferences++;
    if (ptr && --ptr->nReferences == 0) delete ptr;
    ptr = r.ptr;
    return *this;
}
```

⟨*Reference Public Methods*⟩+≡   **839**
```
Reference &operator=(T *p) {
    if (p) p->nReferences++;
    if (ptr && --ptr->nReferences == 0) delete ptr;
    ptr = p;
    return *this;
}
```

⟨*Reference Public Methods*⟩+≡   **839**
```
~Reference() {
    if (ptr && --ptr->nReferences == 0)
        delete ptr;
}
```

Reference 839

Reference::ptr 839

ReferenceCounted::
  nReferences 839

We would like to treat References as much like pointers as possible. For example, if the Foo class has a Foo::bar() method and r1 is a Reference<foo> object, we'd like to be able to write expressions like r1->bar(). The following methods take care of these details.

Furthermore, the operator bool method makes it possible to check to see if a reference points to a NULL object with code like if (!r) . . . .

⟨*Reference Public Methods*⟩+≡   839

```
T *operator->() { return ptr; }
const T *operator->() const { return ptr; }
operator bool() const { return ptr != NULL; }
bool operator<(const Reference<T> &t2) const {
    return ptr < t2.ptr;
}
```

A.2.3 CACHE-FRIENDLY MEMORY USAGE

While the speed of modern CPUs has continued to increase at roughly the rate predicted by Moore's law (doubling every 18 months), modern memory technologies haven't been able to keep up with this growth. The speed at which memory can respond to read requests has been getting faster at a rate of roughly 10% per year. Today, a CPU may have to wait 100 or more execution cycles to read from main memory. The CPU is usually idle for much of this time, so a substantial amount of its computational potential may be lost.

One of the most effective techniques to address this problem is the judicious use of small, fast cache memory located either in the CPU itself or closer to it than main memory. The cache holds recently accessed data and is able to service memory requests much faster than main memory.

Because of the high penalty for accessing main memory, designing algorithms and data structures that make good use of the cache can substantially improve overall system performance. This section will discuss general programming techniques for improving cache performance. These techniques are used in many parts of pbrt, particularly the KdTreeAccel, MIPMap, and ImageFilm. We assume that the reader has a basic familiarity with computer architecture and caching technology; readers needing a review are directed to a computer architecture text such as Patterson and Hennessy (1997). In particular, the reader should be generally familiar with topics like cache lines, cache associativity, and the difference between compulsory, capacity, and conflict misses.

One easy way to reduce the number of cache misses incurred by pbrt is to make sure that some key memory allocations are aligned with the blocks of memory that the cache manages. Figure A.1 illustrates the basic technique. pbrt's overall performance was improved by approximately 3% when allocation for the kd-tree accelerator in Section 4.4 was rewritten to use cache-aligned allocation. The AllocAligned() and FreeAligned() functions provide an interface to allocate and release cache-aligned memory blocks. If the preprocessor constant L1_CACHE_LINE_SIZE is not set, a default cache line size of 64 bytes is used, which is representative of many current architectures.

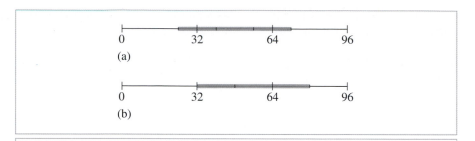

Figure A.1: The Layout of Three 16-Byte Objects in Memory on a System with 32-Byte Cache Lines. Cache-aligned memory allocation ensures that the address returned by the memory allocation routines are aligned with the start of a cache line. (a) The starting address is not cache aligned; the first and last of the three objects span two cache lines, such that two cache misses may be incurred when accessing their elements. (b) The starting address is cache aligned, guaranteeing that a maximum of one cache miss will be incurred per object.

⟨*Memory Allocation Functions*⟩ ≡
```
COREDLL void *AllocAligned(size_t size) {
#ifndef L1_CACHE_LINE_SIZE
#define L1_CACHE_LINE_SIZE 64
#endif
    return memalign(L1_CACHE_LINE_SIZE, size);
}
```

⟨*Memory Allocation Functions*⟩+≡
```
COREDLL void FreeAligned(void *ptr) {
    free(ptr);
}
```

Another family of techniques for improving cache performance is based on reorganizing data structures themselves. For example, using bit fields to reduce the size of a frequently used data structure can be helpful. This approach improves the *spatial locality* of memory access at run time, since code that accesses multiple packed values won't incur more than one cache miss to get them all. Furthermore, by reducing the overall size of the structure, this technique can reduce capacity misses if fewer cache lines are consequently needed to store the structure.

If not all of the elements of a structure are frequently accessed, there are a few possible strategies to improve cache performance. For example, if the structure has a size of 128 bytes and the computer has 64-byte cache lines, two cache misses may be needed to access it. If the commonly used fields are collected into the first 64 bytes rather than being spread

COREDLL 904
L1_CACHE_LINE_SIZE 842

throughout, then no more than one cache miss will be incurred when only those fields are needed (Truong, Bodin, and Seznec 1998).

A related technique is *splitting*, where data structures are split into "hot" and "cold" parts, each stored in separate regions of memory. For example, given an array of some structure type, we can split it into two arrays, one for the more frequently accessed (or "hot") portions, and one for the less frequently accessed (or "cold") portions. This way, cold data doesn't displace useful information in the cache except when it is actually needed.

Cache-friendly programming is a complex engineering task, and we will not cover all the variations here. Readers are directed to the "Further Reading" section of this appendix for more information.

A.2.4 ARENA-BASED ALLOCATION

Conventional wisdom says that the system's memory allocation routines (e.g., `malloc()` and `new()`) are slow, and that custom allocation routines for objects that are frequently allocated or freed can provide a measurable performance gain. However, this conventional wisdom seems to be wrong. Wilson et al. (1995), Johnstone and Wilson (1999), and Berger, Zorn, and McKinley (2001, 2002) have all investigated the performance impact of memory allocation in real-world applications and have found that custom allocators almost always result in *worse* performance than a well-tuned generic system memory allocation, in both execution time and memory use.

One type of custom allocation technique that has proved to be useful in some cases is *arena-based allocation*, which allows the user to quickly allocate objects from a large contiguous region of memory. In this scheme, individual objects are never explicitly freed; the entire region of memory is released when the lifetime of all of the allocated objects ends. This type of memory allocator is a natural fit for many of the objects in pbrt.

There are two main advantages to arena-based allocation. First, allocation is extremely fast, usually just requiring a pointer increment. Second, it can improve locality of reference and lead to fewer cache misses, since the allocated objects are contiguous in memory. A more general dynamic memory allocator will typically prepend a bookkeeping structure to each block it returns, which adversely affects locality of reference.

pbrt provides two classes that implement this type of allocation. The first, `ObjectArena`, is a template parameterized by the type of object to be allocated. The other, `MemoryArena`, supports variable-sized allocation from the arena. Although `MemoryArena` could be used in place of `ObjectArena`, `ObjectArena` allows cleaner syntax for code that only needs an arena for a single object type.

Object Arenas

⟨*Global Classes*⟩+≡
```
    template <class T> class ObjectArena {
    public:
        ⟨ObjectArena Public Methods  844⟩
    private:
        ⟨ObjectArena Private Data  844⟩
    };
```

⟨*ObjectArena Public Methods*⟩≡   844
```
    ObjectArena() {
        nAvailable = 0;
    }
```

⟨*ObjectArena Private Data*⟩≡   844
```
    T *mem;
    int nAvailable;
    vector<T *> toDelete;
```

The ObjectArena::Alloc() method returns a pointer to enough memory to hold a single instance of the type T. If there isn't enough space for another T object in the last allocated block of memory, a new block is allocated. Each block is sized to hold either 16 objects or 64 kB of memory, whichever is larger.

⟨*ObjectArena Public Methods*⟩+≡   844
```
    T *Alloc() {
        if (nAvailable == 0) {
            int nAlloc = max((unsigned long)16,
                             (unsigned long)(65536/sizeof(T)));
            mem = (T *)AllocAligned(nAlloc * sizeof(T));
            nAvailable = nAlloc;
            toDelete.push_back(mem);
        }
        --nAvailable;
        return mem++;
    }
```

A more convenient alternative is provided by its operator T * method, which just calls Alloc() itself. This version makes it possible to use the placement version of C++'s new operator to simultaneously allocate memory and invoke the object's constructor. For example, we could write code like

```
    ObjectArena<Foo> arena;
    Foo *f = new (arena) Foo;
```

⟨*ObjectArena Public Methods*⟩+≡   **844**
```
operator T *() {
    return Alloc();
}
```

The `ObjectArena`'s destructor frees all of the blocks of memory that have been allocated by the arena. To free this memory sooner, the `FreeAll()` method can be called. Note that the `ObjectArena` does not run the objects' destructors when the memory is freed; it is the caller's responsibility to do this manually if appropriate:

```
f->~Foo();
```

Note that the pointers returned from the `ObjectArena` object must *not* be `delete`d, since doing so would likely corrupt the standard library's dynamic memory heap.

⟨*ObjectArena Public Methods*⟩+≡   **844**
```
void FreeAll() {
    for (u_int i = 0; i < toDelete.size(); ++i)
        FreeAligned(toDelete[i]);
    toDelete.erase(toDelete.begin(), toDelete.end());
    nAvailable = 0;
}
```

Memory Arenas

The `MemoryArena` quickly allocates memory for objects of variable size by handing out pointers into a preallocated block. Like `ObjectArena`, it does not support freeing of individual blocks of memory, only freeing of all of the memory in the zone at once. Thus, it is useful when a number of allocations need to be done quickly and all of the allocated objects have similar lifetimes.

⟨*Global Classes*⟩+≡
```
class MemoryArena {
public:
    ⟨MemoryArena Public Methods 846⟩
private:
    ⟨MemoryArena Private Data 846⟩
};
```

The implementation of `MemoryArena` is straightforward. It allocates memory in chunks of size `MemoryArena::blockSize`, the value of which is set by a parameter passed to the constructor. It maintains a pointer to the current block of memory and the offset of the first free location in the block.

⟨*MemoryArena Public Methods*⟩ ≡   **845**
```
MemoryArena(u_int bs = 32768) {
    blockSize = bs;
    curBlockPos = 0;
    currentBlock = (char *)AllocAligned(blockSize);
}
```

MemoryArena also uses two vectors to hold pointers to blocks of memory that have been fully used as well as available blocks that were previously allocated but aren't currently in use.

⟨*MemoryArena Private Data*⟩ ≡   **845**
```
u_int curBlockPos, blockSize;
char *currentBlock;
vector<char *> usedBlocks, availableBlocks;
```

To service an allocation request, the allocation routine first rounds the requested amount of memory up so that it meets the computer's word alignment requirements.[1] It then checks to see if the current block has enough space to handle the request, allocating a new block if necessary. Finally, it returns the pointer and updates the current block offset.

⟨*MemoryArena Public Methods*⟩ + ≡   **845**
```
void *Alloc(u_int sz) {
    ⟨Round up sz to minimum machine alignment 846⟩
    if (curBlockPos + sz > blockSize) {
        ⟨Get new block of memory for MemoryArena 847⟩
        curBlockPos = 0;
    }
    void *ret = currentBlock + curBlockPos;
    curBlockPos += sz;
    return ret;
}
```

Most modern computer architectures impose alignment requirements on the positioning of objects in memory. For example, it is frequently a requirement that float values be stored at memory locations that are word aligned. To be safe, the implementation always hands out double-word-aligned pointers (i.e., their address is a multiple of eight).

⟨*Round up sz to minimum machine alignment*⟩ ≡   **846**
```
sz = ((sz + 7) & (~7));
```

---

1   Some systems (such as those based on Intel processors) can handle non-word-aligned memory accesses, but this is usually 4–12 times slower than word-aligned memory reads or writes. Other architectures do not support this at all and will generate a bus error if a nonaligned access is performed.

If a new block of memory is needed, the MemoryArena stores the pointer to the current block of memory on the usedBlocks list so that it is not lost. Later, when MemoryArena::FreeAll() is called, it will be able to reuse the block for the next series of allocations. The allocation routine then checks to see if there are any already allocated free blocks in the availableBlocks list before calling the system allocation routine to allocate a brand-new block.

⟨*Get new block of memory for* MemoryArena⟩ ≡   846
```
usedBlocks.push_back(currentBlock);
if (availableBlocks.size()&& sz <=blockSize) {
    currentBlock = availableBlocks.back();
    availableBlocks.pop_back();
}
else
    currentBlock = (char *)AllocAligned(max(sz, blockSize));
```

When the user is done with all of the memory, the arena just resets its offset in the current block and moves all of the memory from the usedBlocks list onto the availableBlocks list.

⟨*MemoryArena Public Methods*⟩+ ≡   845
```
void FreeAll() {
    curBlockPos = 0;
    while (usedBlocks.size()) {
        availableBlocks.push_back(usedBlocks.back());
        usedBlocks.pop_back();
    }
}
```

A.2.5 BLOCKED 2D ARRAYS

In C++, 2D arrays are arranged in memory so that entire rows of values are contiguous in memory, as shown in Figure A.2(a). This is not always an optimal layout, however; for such an array indexed by (u, v), nearby (u, v) array positions will often map to distant memory locations. Thus, spatially coherent array indices do not necessarily lead to the spatially coherent memory access patterns that modern memory caches depend on.

For all but the smallest arrays, the adjacent values in the v direction will be on different cache lines, and thus if the cost of a cache miss is incurred to reference a value at a particular location (u, v), there is no chance that handling that miss will also load into memory the data for values $(u, v + 1)$, $(u, v - 1)$, and so on.

To address this problem, the BlockedArray template implements a generic 2D array of values, with the items ordered in memory using a *blocked* memory layout, as shown in Figure A.2(b). The array is subdivided into square blocks of a small fixed size that is a power of two, BLOCK_SIZE. Each block is laid out row by row, as if it were a separate

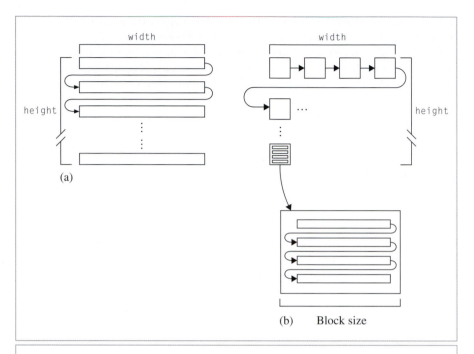

Figure A.2: (a) In C++, the natural layout for a 2D array of size `width*height` is a block of `width*height` entries, where the (u, v) array element is at the `u+v*width` offset. (b) A blocked array has been split into smaller square blocks, each of which is laid out linearly. Although it is slightly more complex to find the memory location associated with a given (u, v) array position in the blocked scheme, the improvement in cache performance due to more coherent memory access patterns often more than makes up for this in overall faster performance.

2D C++ array. This organization substantially improves the memory coherence of 2D array references in practice and requires only a small amount of additional computation to determine the memory address for a particular position (Lam, Rothberg, and Wolf 1991).

To ensure that the block size is a power of two, the caller specifies its logarithm (base 2), which is given by the template parameter `logBlockSize`.

⟨*Global Classes*⟩+≡
```
    template<class T, int logBlockSize> class BlockedArray {
    public:
        ⟨BlockedArray Public Methods 849⟩
    private:
        ⟨BlockedArray Private Data 849⟩
    };
```

The constructor allocates space for the array and optionally initializes its values from a pointer to a standard C++ array. Because the array size may not be an exact multiple of the block size, it may be necessary to round up the size in one or both directions to find the total amount of memory needed for the blocked array. The `BlockedArray::RoundUp()` method rounds both dimensions up to be a multiple of the block size.

⟨*BlockedArray Public Methods*⟩ ≡   848
```
BlockedArray(int nu, int nv, const T *d = NULL) {
    uRes = nu;
    vRes = nv;
    uBlocks = RoundUp(uRes) >> logBlockSize;
    int nAlloc = RoundUp(uRes) * RoundUp(vRes);
    data = (T *)AllocAligned(nAlloc * sizeof(T));
    for (int i = 0; i < nAlloc; ++i)
        new (&data[i]) T();
    if (d)
        for (int v = 0; v < nv; ++v)
            for (int u = 0; u < nu; ++u)
                (*this)(u, v) = d[v * uRes + u];
}
```

⟨*BlockedArray Private Data*⟩ ≡   848
```
T *data;
int uRes, vRes, uBlocks;
```

⟨*BlockedArray Public Methods*⟩+≡   848
```
int BlockSize() const { return 1 << logBlockSize; }
int RoundUp(int x) const {
    return (x + BlockSize() - 1) & ~(BlockSize() - 1);
}
```

For convenience, the `BlockedArray` can also report its size in each dimension:

⟨*BlockedArray Public Methods*⟩+≡   848
```
int uSize() const { return uRes; }
int vSize() const { return vRes; }
```

Looking up a value from a particular (u, v) position in the array requires some indexing work to find the memory location for that value. There are two steps to this process: finding which block the value is in, and finding its offset within that block. Because the block sizes are always powers of two, the `logBlockSize` low-order bits in each of the u and v array positions give the offset within the block, and the high-order bits give the block number (Figure A.3).

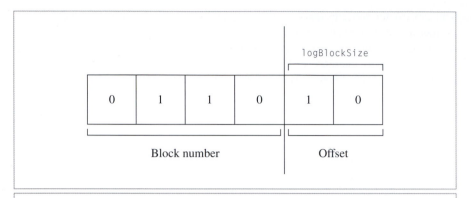

Figure A.3: Given an array coordinate, the (u, v) block number that it is in can be found by shifting off the `logBlockSize` low-order bits for both u and v. For example, with a `logBlockSize` of 2 and thus a block size of 4, we can see that this correctly maps 1D array positions from 0 to 3 to block 0, 4 to 7 to block 1, and so on. To find the offset within the particular block, it is just necessary to mask off the high-order bits, leaving the `logBlockSize` low-order bits. Because the block size is a power of two, these computations can all be done with efficient bit operations.

⟨*BlockedArray Public Methods*⟩+≡   **848**
```
int Block(int a) const { return a >> logBlockSize; }
int Offset(int a) const { return (a & (BlockSize() - 1)); }
```

Then, given the block number (b_u, b_v) and the offset within the block (o_u, o_v), it is necessary to compute what memory location this maps to in the blocked array layout. First consider the task of finding the starting address of the block; since the blocks are laid out row by row, this corresponds to the block number bu + bv * uBlocks, where uBlocks is the number of blocks in the u direction. Because each block has BlockSize()*BlockSize() values in it, the product of the block number and this value gives us the offset to the start of the block. We then just need to account for the additional offset from the start of the block, which is ou + ov * BlockSize().

⟨*BlockedArray Public Methods*⟩+≡   **848**
```
T &operator()(int u, int v) {
    int bu = /Block(u), bv = Block(v);
    int ou = Offset(u), ov = Offset(v);
    int offset = BlockSize() * BlockSize() * (uBlocks * bv + bu);
    offset += BlockSize() * ov + ou;
    return data[offset];
}
```

We will also provide a convenience method to convert a BlockedArray back to a standard C++ array. The caller is responsible for allocating enough memory to hold the uRes * vRes values returned.

⟨*BlockedArray Public Methods*⟩+≡   **848**
```
void GetLinearArray(T *a) const {
    for (int v = 0; v < vRes; ++v)
        for (int u = 0; u < uRes; ++u)
            *a++ = (*this)(u, v);
}
```

A.3 MATHEMATICAL ROUTINES

This section describes a number of useful mathematical functions and classes that support basic operations in pbrt, such as solving small linear systems, manipulating matrices, and linear interpolation.

A.3.1 2 × 2 LINEAR SYSTEMS

There are a number of places throughout pbrt where we need to solve a 2×2 linear system $Ax = B$ of the form

$$\begin{pmatrix} a_{00} & a_{01} \\ a_{10} & a_{11} \end{pmatrix} \begin{pmatrix} x_0 \\ x_1 \end{pmatrix} = \begin{pmatrix} b_0 \\ b_1 \end{pmatrix}$$

for values x_0 and x_1. The SolveLinearSystem2x2() routine finds the closed-form solution to such a system. It returns true if it was successful, and false if the determinant of A is very small, indicating that the system is numerically ill-conditioned and either not solvable or likely to have unacceptable floating-point errors. In this case, no solution is returned.

⟨*Matrix Method Definitions*⟩≡
```
COREDLL bool SolveLinearSystem2x2(const float A[2][2],
        const float B[2], float x[2]) {
    float det = A[0][0]*A[1][1] - A[0][1]*A[1][0];
    if (fabsf(det) < 1e-5)
        return false;
    float invDet = 1.0f/det;
    x[0] = (A[1][1]*B[0] - A[0][1]*B[1]) * invDet;
    x[1] = (A[0][0]*B[1] - A[1][0]*B[0]) * invDet;
    return true;
}
```

A.3.2 4 × 4 MATRICES

The Matrix4x4 structure provides a low-level representation of 4×4 matrices. It is an integral part of the Transform class. Because many Shapes often have identical transformations, Matrix4x4s are reference counted so that the Transform objects can hold shared Matrix4x4 references.

⟨*Global Classes*⟩+≡
```
struct COREDLL Matrix4x4 : public ReferenceCounted {
    ⟨Matrix4x4 Public Methods 852⟩
    float m[4][4];
};
```

The default constructor sets the matrix to the identity matrix:

⟨*Matrix4x4 Public Methods*⟩≡   852
```
Matrix4x4() {
    for (int i = 0; i < 4; ++i)
        for (int j = 0; j < 4; ++j)
            if (i == j) m[i][j] = 1.;
            else m[i][j] = 0.;
}
```

The class also provides constructors that allow the user to pass an array of floats or 16 individual floats to initialize a Matrix4x4:

⟨*Matrix4x4 Public Methods*⟩+≡   852
```
Matrix4x4(float mat[4][4]);
Matrix4x4(float t00, float t01, float t02, float t03,
          float t10, float t11, float t12, float t13,
          float t20, float t21, float t22, float t23,
          float t30, float t31, float t32, float t33);
```

The Matrix4x4 class supports a few low-level matrix operations, each of which returns a reference to a newly allocated matrix that holds the result of the operation. For example, Matrix4x4::Transpose() returns a new matrix that is the transpose of the original matrix.

⟨*Matrix Method Definitions*⟩+≡
```
Reference<Matrix4x4> Matrix4x4::Transpose() const {
    return new Matrix4x4(m[0][0], m[1][0], m[2][0], m[3][0],
                         m[0][1], m[1][1], m[2][1], m[3][1],
                         m[0][2], m[1][2], m[2][2], m[3][2],
                         m[0][3], m[1][3], m[2][3], m[3][3]);
}
```

COREDLL 904
Matrix4x4 852
Matrix4x4::m 852
Matrix4x4::Transpose() 852
Reference 839
ReferenceCounted 839

The product of two matrices $\mathbf{M}_1$ and $\mathbf{M}_2$ is computed by setting the (i, j)th element of the result to the inner product of the ith row of $\mathbf{M}_1$ with the jth column of $\mathbf{M}_2$.

⟨*Matrix4x4 Public Methods*⟩+≡   852
```
static Reference<Matrix4x4>
Mul(const Reference<Matrix4x4> &m1,
    const Reference<Matrix4x4> &m2) {
    float r[4][4];
    for (int i = 0; i < 4; ++i)
        for (int j = 0; j < 4; ++j)
            r[i][j] = m1->m[i][0] * m2->m[0][j] +
                      m1->m[i][1] * m2->m[1][j] +
                      m1->m[i][2] * m2->m[2][j] +
                      m1->m[i][3] * m2->m[3][j];
    return new Matrix4x4(r);
}
```

Finally, `Matrix4x4::Inverse()` returns the inverse of the matrix. The implementation (not shown here) uses a numerically stable Gauss-Jordan elimination routine to compute the inverse.

⟨*Matrix4x4 Public Methods*⟩+≡   852
```
Reference<Matrix4x4> Matrix4x4::Inverse() const;
```

A.3.3 UTILITY FUNCTIONS

A few additional short mathematical functions are useful throughout pbrt.

Linear Interpolation

`Lerp()` performs linear interpolation between two values v1 and v2, with the position given by the t parameter. When t is zero, the result is v1, and when t is one, the result is v2.

⟨*Global Inline Functions*⟩+≡
```
inline float Lerp(float t, float v1, float v2) {
    return (1.f - t) * v1 + t * v2;
}
```

Notice that `Lerp()` is implemented as

$$(1-t)v_1 + tv_2,$$

rather than the more terse and potentially more computationally efficient form of

$$v_1 + t(v_2 - v_1).$$

This is done to reduce floating-point error. If the magnitudes of v1 and v2 are substantially different, it may not be possible to accurately represent the difference $v_2 - v_1$ with a floating-point value in the latter form. When this inaccurate value is scaled by t and added to v_1, the result may be quite inaccurate. With the first formulation, not only is this problem avoided, but `Lerp()` returns *exactly* the values v1 and v2 when pos has values 0 and 1, respectively, and always returns a value in the range $[v_1, v_2]$ if t is in [0, 1]. These properties are not guaranteed by the second formulation.

Clamping

`Clamp()` clamps the given value `val` to be between the values `low` and `high`:

⟨*Global Inline Functions*⟩+≡
```
inline float Clamp(float val, float low, float high) {
    if (val < low) return low;
    else if (val > high) return high;
    else return val;
}
```

Modulus

`Mod()` computes the remainder of a/b. This function is handy since it behaves predictably and reasonably with negative numbers; the C and C++ standards leave the behavior of the % operator undefined in that case.

⟨*Global Inline Functions*⟩+≡
```
inline int Mod(int a, int b) {
    int n = int(a/b);
    a -= n*b;
    if (a < 0) a += b;
    return a;
}
```

Converting between Angle Measures

Two simple functions convert from angles expressed in degrees to radians, and vice versa:

⟨*Global Inline Functions*⟩+≡
```
inline float Radians(float deg) {
    return (M_PI/180.f) * deg;
}
inline float Degrees(float rad) {
    return (180.f/M_PI) * rad;
}
```

Base-2 Logarithms and Exponents

Because the math library doesn't provide a base-2 logarithm function, we provide one here, using the identity $\log_2(x) = \log x / \log 2$.

⟨*Global Inline Functions*⟩+≡
```
inline float Log2(float x) {
    static float invLog2 = 1.f / logf(2.f);
    return logf(x) * invLog2;
}
```

Sometimes we need an integer-valued base-2 logarithm. Rather than computing the logarithm and converting to an integer, it is possible to take advantage of the memory layout of IEEE floating-point values to isolate and return the exponent bits of the input.

⟨*Global Inline Functions*⟩+≡
```
inline int Log2Int(float v) {
    return ((*(int *) &v) >> 23) - 127;
}
```

Finally, some subtle bit manipulation tricks can quickly determine if a given integer is an exact power of two, or round an integer up to the next higher (or equal) power of two.

⟨*Global Inline Functions*⟩+≡
```
inline bool IsPowerOf2(int v) {
    return (v & (v - 1)) == 0;
}
```

⟨*Global Inline Functions*⟩+≡
```
inline u_int RoundUpPow2(u_int v) {
    v--;
    v |= v >> 1;
    v |= v >> 2;
    v |= v >> 4;
    v |= v >> 8;
    v |= v >> 16;
    return v+1;
}
```

Useful Constants

We explicitly redefine M_PI so that it is a 32-bit floating point constant instead of using double precision:

⟨*Global Constants*⟩+≡
```
#ifdef M_PI
#undef M_PI
#endif
#define M_PI        3.14159265358979323846f
```

Other useful constants include $1/\pi$ and $1/2\pi$:

⟨*Global Constants*⟩+≡
```
#define INV_PI    0.31830988618379067154f
#define INV_TWOPI 0.15915494309189533577f
```

Finally, an INFINITY value is defined to be FLT_MAX, the largest representable floating-point number:

⟨*Global Constants*⟩+≡
```
#ifndef INFINITY
#define INFINITY FLT_MAX
#endif
```

A.3.4 FLOATING-POINT TO INTEGER CONVERSION

On the Intel x86 architecture, as many as 80 processor cycles may be necessary to convert a floating-point value to an integer value. The conversion to integer in a simple sequence of code like

```
float a = ..., b = ...;
int i = (int)(a * b);
```

may thus take 80 times longer than the multiplication a*b! The problem is that the floating-point unit's rounding mode needs to be changed from the default before the built-in conversion instruction is used, and this requires an expensive flush of the entire floating-point pipeline.

pbrt needs to convert floats to integers in a number of performance-sensitive areas. These include the sample filtering code, where for every camera sample it is necessary to compute the pixels that are affected by the sample. Similarly, in the Perlin noise evaluation routines it is necessary to find the integer lattice cell that contains a floating-point position.

Herf and Kotay (2000) have developed some techniques to perform these conversions much more quickly without needing to change the rounding mode by taking advantage of the layout of IEEE floating-point values in memory. Using these routines in pbrt yielded a 5% speed increase for some scenes. We will not include the details of their implementation here because they are remarkably arcane, being based on low-level details of the floating-point representation. However, there are four key functions, all of them taking a float value and returning an integer:

- Float2Int(f): This is the same as the basic cast (int)f.
- Round2Int(f): This rounds the floating-point value f to the nearest integer, returning the result as an int.
- Floor2Int(f): The first integer value less than or equal to f is returned.
- Ceil2Int(f): And similarly, the first integer value greater than or equal to f is returned.

A.3.5 PSEUDORANDOM NUMBERS

INFINITY 856

pbrt uses a custom pseudorandom number generator rather than calling the one provided by the system. This is worth the extra effort for two reasons. First, it ensures that pbrt produces the same results regardless of machine architecture and C library implementation. In addition, many systems provide random number generation routines with poor statistical distributions.

The random number generator used in pbrt is the "Mersenne Twister" by Makoto Matsumoto and Takuji Nishimura. The code to the random number generator is both complex and subtle, and we will not attempt to explain it here. Nevertheless, it is one of the best random number generators known, can be implemented very efficiently, and has a period of $2^{19937} - 1$ before it repeats the series again. Pointers to the paper describing its algorithm can be found in the "Further Reading" section.

The RandomFloat() and RandomUInt() routines provide uniformly distributed floating-point values from the range $[0, 1]$ and $[0, 2^{32} - 1]$, respectively.

⟨*Global Inline Functions*⟩+≡
```
inline float RandomFloat();
inline unsigned long RandomUInt();
```

A.4 OCTREES

An octree is a three-dimensional data structure that recursively splits a region of space into eight axis-aligned boxes (Figure A.4). The octree implementation defined in this section is in the file core/octree.h.◉

Octrees have many applications, including acceleration structures for ray tracing. The implementation in this section is specifically designed to determine which of a set of axis-aligned bounding boxes overlaps a given point. Using an octree for these queries can be substantially faster than looping over all of the objects directly. pbrt currently uses these octrees to store the irradiance estimates computed by the IrradianceCache integrator. Each estimate has a bounding box associated with it that gives the spatial region affected by the estimate. The octree implementation is implemented separately from the irradiance cache in order to simplify the description of the IrradianceCache class as well as to make it easier to reuse the octree for other applications.

First, we will define the OctNode structure, which represents a node of the tree. It holds pointers to the eight children of the node (some or all of which may be NULL) and a vector of NodeData objects. NodeData is a template argument that gives the type to be stored in the tree; for the IrradianceCache, it's the IrradProcess structure, which records a single irradiance estimate. The constructor and destructor of the OctNode just initialize the children to NULL and delete them, respectively.

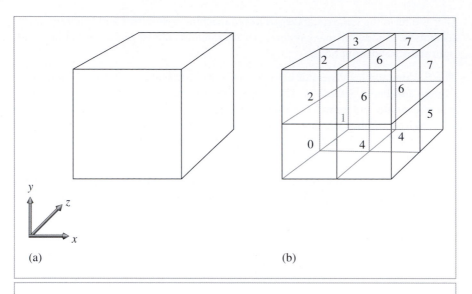

Figure A.4: Basic Octree Refinement. Starting with (a) an axis-aligned bounding box, the octree is defined by (b) progressively splitting each node into eight equal-sized child nodes. The order in which the child nodes are assigned numbers 0 . . . 7 is significant; details will be explained later in this section. Different subtrees may be refined to different depths, giving an adaptive discretization of 3D space.

⟨*Octree Declarations*⟩ ≡
```
template <class NodeData> struct OctNode {
    OctNode() {
        for (int i = 0; i < 8; ++i)
            children[i] = NULL;
    }
    ~OctNode() {
        for (int i = 0; i < 8; ++i)
            delete children[i];
    }
    OctNode *children[8];
    vector<NodeData> data;
};
```

The OctNode template is parameterized by the NodeData type as well as by a "lookup procedure," LookupProc, which is essentially a callback function that lets the Octree communicate back to the caller which elements of NodeData overlap a given lookup position.

⟨*Octree Declarations*⟩+≡
```
template <class NodeData, class LookupProc> class Octree {
public:
    ⟨Octree Public Methods 859⟩
private:
    ⟨Octree Private Methods⟩
    ⟨Octree Private Data 859⟩
};
```

The constructor takes the overall bounds of the tree and a maximum recursion depth beyond which nodes should not be refined:

⟨*Octree Public Methods*⟩≡   859
```
Octree(const BBox &b, int md = 16)
    : bound(b) {
    maxDepth = md;
}
```

⟨*Octree Private Data*⟩≡   859
```
int maxDepth;
BBox bound;
OctNode<NodeData> root;
```

To add an item to the tree, the octree recurses through the tree, creating new nodes as needed, until termination criteria are met, at which point the item is added to the node it overlaps. Similar to the KdTreeAccel of Section 4.4, performance is highly dependent on the specific termination criteria. For example, we could decide never to refine the tree and add all items to the root node. This would be a valid octree, although it would perform poorly for large numbers of objects. However, if the tree is refined too much, items may span many nodes, leading to excessive memory use.

The Octree::Add() method for adding an item forwards the request to a private Octree:: addPrivate() method with a few additional parameters, including the current node being considered, the bounding box of the node, and the squared length of the diagonal of the data item's bounding box. This method calls itself recursively as it works down the octree to the nodes where the item is stored.

⟨*Octree Public Methods*⟩+≡   859
```
void Add(const NodeData &dataItem, const BBox &dataBound) {
    addPrivate(&root, bound, dataItem, dataBound,
            DistanceSquared(dataBound.pMin, dataBound.pMax));
}
```

The internal Octree::addPrivate() method either adds the item to the current node or determines which child nodes the item overlaps, allocates them if necessary, and recursively calls itself to allow the children to decide whether to add the item to their lists.

⟨*Octree Method Definitions*⟩ ≡
```
template <class NodeData, class LookupProc>
void Octree<NodeData, LookupProc>::addPrivate(
        OctNode<NodeData> *node, const BBox &nodeBound,
        const NodeData &dataItem, const BBox &dataBound,
        float diag2, int depth) {
    ⟨Possibly add data item to current octree node 860⟩
    ⟨Otherwise add data item to octree children 860⟩
}
```

The item is added to the current node once the maximum tree depth is reached or when the length of the diagonal of the node is less than the length of the diagonal of the item's bounds. This ensures that the item overlaps a relatively small number of tree nodes while not being too small relative to the extent of the nodes that it's added to. Figure A.5 shows the basic operation of the algorithm in two dimensions (where the corresponding data structure is known as a *quadtree*).

⟨*Possibly add data item to current octree node*⟩ ≡   860
```
if (depth == maxDepth ||
        DistanceSquared(nodeBound.pMin, nodeBound.pMax) < diag2) {
    node->data.push_back(dataItem);
    return;
}
```

If the method continues down the tree, it needs to determine which of the child nodes the item's bounding box overlaps. The fragment ⟨*Determine which children the item overlaps*⟩ initializes an array of boolean values, over[], such that the *i*th element is true only if the bounds of the data item being added overlap the *i*th child of the current node. The method can then loop over the eight children and recursively call addPrivate() for the ones that the object overlaps.

⟨*Otherwise add data item to octree children*⟩ ≡   860
```
Point pMid = .5 * nodeBound.pMin + .5 * nodeBound.pMax;
⟨Determine which children the item overlaps 862⟩
for (int child = 0; child < 8; ++child) {
    if (!over[child]) continue;
    if (!node->children[child])
        node->children[child] = new OctNode<NodeData>;
    ⟨Compute childBound for octree child child 863⟩
    addPrivate(node->children[child], childBound,
            dataItem, dataBound, diag2, depth+1);
}
```

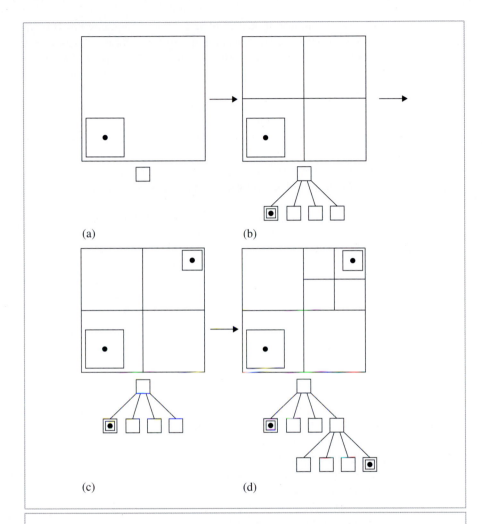

(a)   (b)

(c)   (d)

Figure A.5: Creation of a Quadtree (the 2D Analog of an Octree). (a) The tree contains just the root node, and an object with bounds around a given point is being added. The tree's topology is illustrated with a small box beneath it, corresponding to the root node with no children. (b) The tree is refined one level and the object is added to the single child node that it overlaps (again shown schematically underneath the tree). (c) Another new object with a smaller bounding box than the first is being added. (d) The tree is refined a second time before the item is added. In general, items may be stored in multiple nodes of the tree.

Rather than computing the bounds of each child and doing a bounding box overlap test, it is possible to save work by taking advantage of symmetries of the situation. For example, if the x range of the object's bounding box is entirely on the left side of the plane that splits the tree node in the x direction, it cannot overlap any of the four child nodes on the right side. Careful selection of the child node numbering scheme in Figure A.4 is the key to the success of this approach. The child nodes are numbered such that the low bit of a child's index is zero if its z component is on the low side of the z splitting plane and one if it is on the high side. Similarly, the second bit is set based on which side of the y plane the child is on, and the third bit is set based on its position with respect to the x plane. Given boolean variables that classify a child node with respect to the splitting planes (true if it is above the plane), the child number of a given node is equal to

```
4 * (xHigh ? 1 : 0) + 2 * (yHigh ? 1 : 0) + 1 * (zHigh ? 1 : 0).
```

It is possible to quickly determine which child nodes a given bounding box overlaps by classifying its extent with respect to the center point of the node. For example, if the bounding box's starting x value is less than the midpoint, then the node potentially overlaps children numbers 0, 1, 2, and 3. If its ending x value is greater than the midpoint, it potentially overlaps 4, 5, 6, and 7. The following fragment checks the three dimensions in turn, computing the logical AND of the results; the item only overlaps a child node if it overlaps its extent in all three dimensions.

⟨*Determine which children the item overlaps*⟩ ≡   860
```
bool over[8];
over[0] = over[1] = over[2] = over[3] = (dataBound.pMin.x <= pMid.x);
over[4] = over[5] = over[6] = over[7] = (dataBound.pMax.x  > pMid.x);
over[0] &= (dataBound.pMin.y <= pMid.y);
over[1] &= (dataBound.pMin.y <= pMid.y);
over[4] &= (dataBound.pMin.y <= pMid.y);
over[5] &= (dataBound.pMin.y <= pMid.y);
over[2] &= (dataBound.pMax.y  > pMid.y);
over[3] &= (dataBound.pMax.y  > pMid.y);
over[6] &= (dataBound.pMax.y  > pMid.y);
over[7] &= (dataBound.pMax.y  > pMid.y);
over[0] &= (dataBound.pMin.z <= pMid.z);
over[2] &= (dataBound.pMin.z <= pMid.z);
over[4] &= (dataBound.pMin.z <= pMid.z);
over[6] &= (dataBound.pMin.z <= pMid.z);
over[1] &= (dataBound.pMax.z  > pMid.z);
over[3] &= (dataBound.pMax.z  > pMid.z);
over[5] &= (dataBound.pMax.z  > pMid.z);
over[7] &= (dataBound.pMax.z  > pMid.z);
```

The child node numbering scheme also makes it possible to easily find the bounding box of a particular child based on the child number and the parent node's bound:

⟨*Compute* childBound *for octree child* child⟩ ≡   860, 864
```
    BBox childBound;
    childBound.pMin.x = (child & 4) ? pMid.x : nodeBound.pMin.x;
    childBound.pMax.x = (child & 4) ? nodeBound.pMax.x : pMid.x;
    childBound.pMin.y = (child & 2) ? pMid.y : nodeBound.pMin.y;
    childBound.pMax.y = (child & 2) ? nodeBound.pMax.y : pMid.y;
    childBound.pMin.z = (child & 1) ? pMid.z : nodeBound.pMin.z;
    childBound.pMax.z = (child & 1) ? nodeBound.pMax.z : pMid.z;
```

After items have been added to the tree, the user can use the tree to find the items that have bounds that overlap a given point. The Lookup() method walks down the tree, processing the nodes that the given point overlaps. The user-supplied callback, process, is called for each NodeData item that overlaps the given point. As with the Add() method, the main lookup function directly calls a private version that takes a pointer to the current node and the current node's bounds.

⟨*Octree Public Methods*⟩+≡   859
```
    void Lookup(const Point &p, const LookupProc &process) {
        if (!bound.Inside(p)) return;
        lookupPrivate(&root, bound, p, process);
    }
```

If the private lookup function has been called with a given node, the point p must be inside the node. The user-supplied callback is called for each NodeData item that is stored in the octree node, allowing the user to do whatever processing is appropriate.[2] The callback must either be a pointer to a function that takes a position and a NodeData object, or a class that has an operator() method that takes those arguments.

After the items are processed, this method continues down the tree into the single child node that p is inside until the bottom is reached.

BBox 60
BBox::Inside() 63
LookupProc 859
NodeData 858
Octree::bound 859
Octree::lookupPrivate() 864
Point 54

---

[2]   Note that the Octree actually passes all of the data items in the node to the callback, not just the subset of them that p is inside the bounds of. This isn't too much of a problem in practice, since the node using the Octree can always store a BBox in the NodeData and do the check itself. When it doesn't matter if a few extra NodeData items are passed back, writing the implementation in this way saves the substantial BBox storage space.

⟨*Octree Method Definitions*⟩+≡
```
template <class NodeData, class LookupProc>
void Octree<NodeData, LookupProc>::lookupPrivate(
        OctNode<NodeData> *node, const BBox &nodeBound,
        const Point &p, const LookupProc &process) {
    for (u_int i = 0; i < node->data.size(); ++i)
        process(p, node->data[i]);
    ⟨Determine which octree child node p is inside 864⟩
    if (node->children[child]) {
        ⟨Compute childBound for octree child child 863⟩
        lookupPrivate(node->children[child], childBound, p, process);
    }
}
```

Again taking advantage of the child numbering scheme, it is possible to quickly determine which child a point overlaps by classifying it with respect to the center of the parent node in each direction:

⟨*Determine which octree child node* p *is inside*⟩ ≡   864
```
    Point pMid = .5f * nodeBound.pMin + .5f * nodeBound.pMax;
    int child = (p.x > pMid.x ? 4 : 0) +
                (p.y > pMid.y ? 2 : 0) + (p.z > pMid.z ? 1 : 0);
```

A.5 KD-TREES

Like the octree, the kd-tree is another data structure that accelerates the processing of spatial data. In contrast to the octree, where the data items had a known bounding box and the caller wanted to find all items that overlap a given point, the generic kd-tree presented in this section is useful for handling data items that are just single points in space with no associated bound, but where the caller wants to find all such points within a user-supplied distance of a given point. It is a key component of the implementation of the PhotonIntegrator.

The KdTree class described here is similar to the KdTreeAccel of Section 4.4 in that 3D space is progressively split in half by planes. There are two main differences here:

- Each tree node in the KdTree class stores a single data item. Therefore, there is exactly one kd-tree node for each data item stored in the tree.
- Because each item being stored is just a single point, items never straddle the splitting plane. Therefore, they never need to be stored on both sides of a split.

One result of these differences is that it is possible to build a perfectly balanced tree, which can improve the efficiency of lookups.

Like the KdTreeAccel, the implementation here stores all of the nodes of the tree in a single contiguous array. If a node has a left child, it will immediately follow the node in the array, and the rightChild member of KdNode gives the offset to the right child of the node, if any. rightChild will be set to a very large number if there is no right child.

To further improve the cache efficiency of the kd-tree, we will apply the cache optimization described previously of separating "hot" and "cold" data. Hot data is data that is frequently accessed while the tree is being traversed, while cold data is less frequently accessed. By splitting the kd-tree node data structure into two pieces in this way, it is possible to pack hot data close together in contiguous memory, which improves performance since more tree nodes can be packed into a single cache line. Hot data is stored in KdNode structures, which record information about a node's splitting plane and its children. The additional cold data that the user wants to associate with each node is stored in a separate array, indexed identically to the KdNode array.

⟨KdTree Declarations⟩ ≡
```
    struct KdNode {
        void init(float p, u_int a) {
            splitPos = p;
            splitAxis = a;
            rightChild = ~0;
            hasLeftChild = 0;
        }
        void initLeaf() {
            splitAxis = 3;
            rightChild = ~0;
            hasLeftChild = 0;
        }
        ⟨KdNode Data 865⟩
    };
```

⟨KdNode Data⟩ ≡   865
```
    float splitPos;
    u_int splitAxis:2;
    u_int hasLeftChild:1;
    u_int rightChild:29;
```

The KdTree is a template class that is parameterized by the type of object stored in the nodes (NodeData) and the type of callback function that is used for reporting which nodes are within a given search radius of the lookup position. The KdTree implementation requires that the NodeData class has a Point member variable called NodeData::p that gives its position.

⟨*KdTree Declarations*⟩+≡
```
template <class NodeData, class LookupProc> class KdTree {
public:
    ⟨KdTree Public Methods⟩
private:
    ⟨KdTree Private Methods⟩
    ⟨KdTree Private Data  866⟩
};
```

⟨*KdTree Private Data*⟩≡   866
```
KdNode *nodes;
NodeData *nodeData;
u_int nNodes, nextFreeNode;
```

Because incremental addition or removal of NodeData isn't needed in pbrt, the implementation of the KdTree is made more straightforward by having all of the data to be stored passed to the KdTree constructor. The constructor allocates all of the memory needed for the tree and the data and calls the recursive tree construction function.

⟨*KdTree Method Definitions*⟩≡
```
template <class NodeData, class LookupProc>
KdTree<NodeData, LookupProc>::KdTree(const vector<NodeData> &d) {
    nNodes = d.size();
    nextFreeNode = 1;
    nodes = (KdNode *)AllocAligned(nNodes * sizeof(KdNode));
    nodeData = new NodeData[nNodes];
    vector<const NodeData *> buildNodes;
    for (u_int i = 0; i < nNodes; ++i)
        buildNodes.push_back(&d[i]);
    ⟨Begin the KdTree building process  866⟩
}
```

Tree construction is handled by the recursiveBuild() method. It takes the node number of the current node to be initialized and offsets into the array data, indicating the subset of data items [start, end) from the buildNodes array to be stored beneath this node.

⟨*Begin the KdTree building process*⟩≡   866
```
recursiveBuild(0, 0, nNodes, buildNodes);
```

The tree building process selects the "middle" element of the user-supplied data (this will soon be defined precisely) and partitions the data so that all items below the middle are in the first half of the array and all items above the middle are in the second half. It constructs a node with the middle element as its data item and then recursively initializes the two children of the node by processing the first and second halves of the array (Figure A.6).

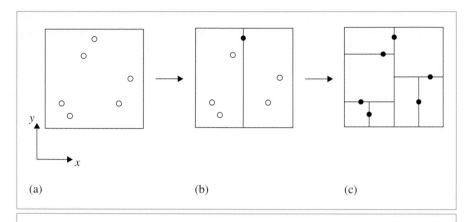

Figure A.6: Creation of a Kd-Tree to Store a Set of Points. (a) A collection of points. (b) A split direction and position are chosen. Here, we have decided to split in the x direction. We choose the point in the middle of the list sorted by x and split along the plane that goes through the point. Roughly half of points are to the left of the splitting plane and half are to the right. (c) We then continue recursively in each half, allocating new tree nodes, splitting and partitioning, until all data points have been processed.

⟨*KdTree Method Definitions*⟩+≡
```
template <class NodeData, class LookupProc> void
KdTree<NodeData, LookupProc>::recursiveBuild(u_int nodeNum,
        int start, int end, vector<const NodeData *> &buildNodes) {
    ⟨Create leaf node of kd-tree if we've reached the bottom  867⟩
    ⟨Choose split direction and partition data  868⟩
    ⟨Allocate kd-tree node and continue recursively  868⟩
}
```

When there is just a single item to be processed, the bottom of the tree has been reached, so the node is flagged as a leaf and the nodeData array item at the appropriate offset is initialized from the appropriate user data.

⟨*Create leaf node of kd-tree if we've reached the bottom*⟩≡   867
```
if (start + 1 == end) {
    nodes[nodeNum].initLeaf();
    nodeData[nodeNum] = *buildNodes[start];
    return;
}
```

Otherwise, the data is partitioned into two halves, and a nonleaf node is initialized. The longest edge of the remaining data's bounding box is used to choose which axis to split along. The standard library nth_element() function then finds the middle node along that axis. It takes three pointers into a sequence, start, mid, and end, and partitions the sequence such that the mid th element is in the position it would be in if the sequence were sorted. It also rearranges the array so that all elements from start to mid-1 are less than mid, and all elements from mid+1 to end are greater than mid. This can all be done more quickly than sorting the entire range—in $O(n)$ time rather than $O(n \log n)$.

⟨*Choose split direction and partition data*⟩ ≡   **867**
```
    ⟨Compute bounds of data from start to end 868⟩
    int splitAxis = bound.MaximumExtent();
    int splitPos = (start+end)/2;
    std::nth_element(&buildNodes[start], &buildNodes[splitPos],
                   &buildNodes[end], CompareNode<NodeData>(splitAxis));
```

It is easy to find the bounds of the entire array range that we're interested in using the Union() method:

⟨*Compute bounds of data from start to end*⟩ ≡   **868**
```
    BBox bound;
    for (int i = start; i < end; ++i)
        bound = Union(bound, buildNodes[i]->p);
```

The nth_element() function needs a "comparison object" that determines the ordering between two data elements. CompareNode compares positions along the chosen axis.

⟨*KdTree Declarations*⟩+≡
```
    template<class NodeData> struct CompareNode {
        CompareNode(int a) { axis = a; }
        int axis;
        bool operator()(const NodeData *d1, const NodeData *d2) const {
            return d1->p[axis] < d2->p[axis];
        }
    };
```

Once the data have been partitioned, the current node is initialized to store the middle item, and its two children are recursively initialized with the two sets of remaining items:

⟨*Allocate kd-tree node and continue recursively*⟩ ≡   **867**
```
    nodes[nodeNum].init(buildNodes[splitPos]->p[splitAxis], splitAxis);
    nodeData[nodeNum] = *buildNodes[splitPos];
    if (start < splitPos) {
        nodes[nodeNum].hasLeftChild = 1;
        u_int childNum = nextFreeNode++;
        recursiveBuild(childNum, start, splitPos, buildNodes);
    }
    if (splitPos+1 < end) {
        nodes[nodeNum].rightChild = nextFreeNode++;
        recursiveBuild(nodes[nodeNum].rightChild, splitPos+1,
                     end, buildNodes);
    }
```

When another part of the system wants to look up items from the tree, it provides a point p, a callback procedure (similar to the one used in the Octree above), and a maximum squared search radius. Using the squared radius rather than the radius directly leads to some optimizations in the following octree traversal code. All data items within that radius will be passed back to the caller.

Rather than being passed by value, the squared search radius is passed into the lookup function by reference. This allows the lookup routine to pass it to the callback procedure by reference, so that the callback can reduce the search radius as the search goes on. This can speed up lookups when the callback routine can determine that a smaller search radius was appropriate after all. As usual, the lookup method immediately calls a private lookup procedure, passing in a pointer to the current node to be processed.

⟨*KdTree Method Definitions*⟩+≡
```
template <class NodeData, class LookupProc> void
KdTree<NodeData, LookupProc>::Lookup(const Point &p,
        const LookupProc &proc, float &maxDistSquared) const {
    privateLookup(0, p, proc, maxDistSquared);
}
```

The lookup function has two responsibilities (Figure A.7): it needs to recursively process each of the children of the current node if they overlap the search region, and it needs to invoke the callback routine, passing it the data item in the current node if it is inside the search radius.

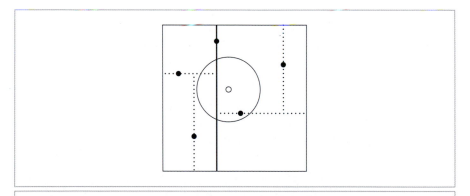

Figure A.7: Basic Process of Kd-Tree Lookups. The point marked with an open circle is the lookup position, and the region of interest is denoted by the circular region around it. At the root node of the tree (indicated by a bold splitting line), the data item is outside the region of interest, so it is not handed to the callback function. However, the region overlaps both children of the node, so we have to recursively consider each of them. The implementation here considers the right child (child number one) first in order to examine the nearby data items before examining the ones farther away.

⟨*KdTree Method Definitions*⟩+≡

```
template <class NodeData, class LookupProc> void
KdTree<NodeData, LookupProc>::privateLookup(u_int nodeNum,
        const Point &p, const LookupProc &process,
        float &maxDistSquared) const {
    KdNode *node = &nodes[nodeNum];
    ⟨Process kd-tree node's children 870⟩
    ⟨Hand kd-tree node to processing function 871⟩
}
```

The tree is traversed depth first, examining the leaf nodes that are close to the lookup point p first. This approach ensures that data points are passed to the callback function in a generally near-to-far order. If the caller is only interested in finding a fixed number of points around the lookup point, after which it will end the search, this is a more efficient order than going far to near.

Therefore, this method first recurses down the side of the tree on which the current point lies. After that lookup has returned, it checks to see if the search radius indicates that the region covers both sides of the tree. Leaf nodes are denoted by a value of 3 in the node's splitAxis field, in which case these steps are skipped.

⟨*Process kd-tree node's children*⟩ ≡   **870**

```
    int axis = node->splitAxis;
    if (axis != 3) {
        float dist2 = (p[axis] - node->splitPos) * (p[axis] - node->splitPos);
        if (p[axis] <= node->splitPos) {
            if (node->hasLeftChild)
                privateLookup(nodeNum+1, p, process, maxDistSquared);
            if (dist2 < maxDistSquared && node->rightChild < nNodes)
                privateLookup(node->rightChild, p, process, maxDistSquared);
        }
        else {
            if (node->rightChild < nNodes)
                privateLookup(node->rightChild, p, process, maxDistSquared);
            if (dist2 < maxDistSquared && node->hasLeftChild)
                privateLookup(nodeNum+1, p, process, maxDistSquared);
        }
    }
```

KdNode 865
KdTree 866
KdTree::nodes 866
LookupProc 859
NodeData 858
Point 54

Finally, at the end of the lookup function, a check is made to see if the point stored in the node is inside the search radius, passing it to the callback function if so. In addition to doing whatever processing it needs to do based on the item, the callback function may decrease maxDistSquared in order to reduce the region of space searched for the remainder of the processing.

⟨*Hand kd-tree node to processing function*⟩ ≡   870

```
float dist2 = DistanceSquared(nodeData[nodeNum].p, p);
if (dist2 < maxDistSquared)
    process(nodeData[nodeNum], dist2, maxDistSquared);
```

A.6 IMAGE FILE HANDLING

Many image file formats have been developed over the years, but for pbrt's purposes we are mainly interested in those that support imagery represented by floating-point pixel values. Because the images generated by pbrt will often have a large dynamic range, such formats are crucial for being able to store the computed radiance values directly, leaving any tone mapping to a postprocess.

pbrt uses the OpenEXR standard as the principal file format for image handling. OpenEXR is a floating-point file format designed by Industrial Light and Magic for use in their movie productions (Kainz, Bogart, and Hess 2002). A library that reads and writes this format is freely available, and support for it is available in a number of other tools. We chose this format because it has a clean design, is easy to use, and has first-class support for floating-point image data.

pbrt uses two functions, ReadImage() and WriteRGBAImage(), to handle image file I/O. ReadImage() is simple. It takes the filename to read from and pointers to two integers that will be initialized with the image resolution, and it returns a freshly allocated array of Spectrum objects, converting RGB data from the file to the native Spectrum format.

⟨*Global Function Declarations*⟩+≡

```
COREDLL Spectrum *ReadImage(const string &name, int *xSize, int *ySize);
```

Writing images is equally simple. The WriteRGBAImage() function takes a filename to be written, a pointer to the beginning of the pixel data, and information about the resolution of the image. The XRes and YRes variables hold the dimensions of the image to be written. If a portion of a larger image is being written, the dimensions of the larger image and the offset of the portion to be written are passed in the remaining variables. Note that these variables are not used to *save* a subimage, but rather to indicate that the pixels being passed are themselves part of a larger image. This information is written into the image header, so that the subimages can later be assembled into a single image by tools like the exrassemble program (located in the tools/⦿ directory on the CD).

⟨*Global Function Declarations*⟩+≡

```
COREDLL void WriteRGBAImage(const string &name,
    float *pixels, float *alpha, int XRes, int YRes,
    int totalXRes, int totalYRes, int xOffset, int yOffset);
```

We will not show the code that interfaces with the OpenEXR libraries. This code can be found in the file core/exrio.cpp.⊚ In addition, the header files and precompiled libraries for OpenEXR can be found on the book's CD or from *www.openexr.com*.

A.7 MAIN INCLUDE FILE

The core/pbrt.h⊚ file is included by all other source files in the system. It contains all global function declarations and inline functions, a few small, widely used classes, and other globally accessible data. All files that include pbrt.h get a number of other include files in the process. This simplifies creation of new source files, almost all of which will want access to these extra headers. However, in the interest of compile time efficiency, we keep the number of these automatically included files to a minimum; the ones here are necessary for almost all modules.

⟨*Global Include Files*⟩ ≡
```
#include <math.h>
#include <stdlib.h>
#include <stdio.h>
#include <string.h>
```

Also, we include files from the C++ standard library to get the C++ classes that we use frequently. The using directive brings these classes into the default namespace.

⟨*Global Include Files*⟩+≡
```
#include <string>
using std::string;
#include <vector>
using std::vector;
#include <iostream>
using std::ostream;
```

We will also define a number of types with typedef here. For convenience, we define shorthand names for unsigned cardinal types: u_char, u_short, u_int, and u_long.

⟨*Global Type Declarations*⟩ ≡
```
typedef unsigned char u_char;
typedef unsigned short u_short;
typedef unsigned int u_int;
typedef unsigned long u_long;
```

We will also define a macro that holds pbrt's current version number. This is a floating-point value that will be increased as future versions of pbrt are developed.

⟨*Global Constants*⟩+≡
```
#define PBRT_VERSION 1.0
```

FURTHER READING

Many papers have been written on cache-friendly programming techniques; only a few are surveyed here. Ericson's chapter on high-performance programming techniques has very good coverage of this topic (Ericson 2004). Lam, Rothberg, and Wolf (1991) investigated blocking (tiling) for improving cache performance and developed techniques for selecting appropriate block sizes, given the size of the arrays and the cache size. Grunwald, Zorn, and Henderson (1993) were one of the first groups of researchers to investigate the interplay between memory allocation algorithms and the cache behavior of applications.

In pbrt, we only worry about cache layout issues for dynamically allocated data. However, Calder et al. (1998) show a profile-driven system that optimizes memory layout of global variables, constant values, data on the stack, and dynamically allocated data from the heap in order to reduce cache conflicts among them all, giving an average 30% reduction in data cache misses for the applications they studied.

Blocking for tree data structures was investigated by Chilimbi, Hill, and Larus (1999); they ensured that nodes of the tree and a few levels of its children were allocated contiguously. Among other applications, they applied their tool to the layout of the acceleration octree in the *Radiance* renderer and reported a 42% speedup in run time. Chilimbi, Davidson, and Larus (1999) also evaluated the effectiveness of reordering fields inside structures to improve locality.

Detailed information about the random number generator used in pbrt, including the original paper that describes its derivation, is available at *www.math.keio.ac.jp/~matumoto/emt.html*.

Sean Anderson has a Web page filled with a collection of bit-twiddling techniques like the ones in the IsPowerOf2() and RoundUpPow2() functions at *graphics.stanford.edu/~seander/bithacks.html*.

Numerical Recipes, by Press et al. (1992), and Atkinson's book (1993) on numerical analysis both discuss algorithms for matrix inversion and solving linear systems.

Samet's book on octrees is the canonical reference on that data structure (Samet 1990), and de Berg et al.'s book on computational geoemtry has extensive information about kd-trees (de Berg et al. 2000).

EXERCISES

❶ A.1 Modify the ObjectArena and MemoryArena so that they just call new for each memory allocation. Render images of a few scenes and measure how much slower pbrt runs (be sure to choose scenes that end up running code that uses these custom allocators.) Can you quantify how much of this is due to different cache behavior and how much is due to overhead in the dynamic memory management routines?

A.2 Change the BlockedArray class so that it doesn't do any blocking and just uses a linear addressing scheme for the array. Measure the change in pbrt's performance as a result. (Scenes with many image map textures are most likely to show differences, since the MIPMap class is a key user of BlockedArray.)

A.3 The KdNode for the KdTree can be brought down to use just four bytes of storage; making this change may further improve its memory performance. Modify the KdNode to just store the split position and split axis in four bytes, using the same technique as was used to overlap the flags and the split position in the KdAccelNode. Then, modify the tree construction routine to build a *left-balanced* kd-tree, where the tree's topology is organized such that for the node at position i in the array of nodes, the left child is at 2*i and the right child is at 2*i+1, and the tree is balanced such that only the first nNodes elements of the array are used. How does this change affect performance for scenes that use photon mapping? Discuss why this change makes the performance difference that it did.

A.4 Software caching is a technique for dynamically gathering recently accessed data in contiguous regions of memory, thus making it less likely that future accesses to them will incur cache misses (Aggarwal 2002). For example, consider the Triangle class. It doesn't store its three vertex positions or even their indices into the shared vertex array. Instead, it needs to get all of this information from the TriangleMesh, possibly incurring multiple cache misses from accessing many different areas in memory. An alternative Triangle implementation would make copies of its vertex position data and store it directly in the Triangle structure. Having this data be contiguous in memory would reduce cache misses by improving locality, but at the cost of substantially increasing the overall storage requirements, possibly then increasing capacity misses.

Software caching charts a middle ground between these extremes: The system would store a relatively small number of these expanded Triangles with all of their data at hand. As regular Triangles are accessed, they copy their data to one of the expanded triangles and record this association in some manner. If the same triangle is accessed again before some other triangle claims its spot from the expanded triangle cache, then the expanded version can be used instead, reaping the benefits of memory coherence at relatively little cost.

Apply this technique in pbrt and measure its performance impact. Both Triangles and KdAccelNodes are possible candidates for this technique. Vary the size of the software cache and measure the performance impact as it gets very large or very small. Evaluate how using different Sampler implementations affects your caching scheme. Why might this make a difference?

℞ SCENE DESCRIPTION INTERFACE

This appendix describes the application programming interface (API) that is used to describe the scene to be rendered to pbrt. Users of the renderer typically don't call the functions in this interface directly, but instead describe their scenes using the text file format described in Appendix C. The statements in these text files have a direct correspondence to the API functions described here.

The need for such an interface to the renderer is clear: there must be a convenient way in which all of the properties of the scene to be rendered can be communicated to the renderer. The interface should be well-defined and general-purpose, so that future extensions to the system fit into its structure cleanly. It shouldn't be too complicated, so that it's easy to describe scenes, but it should be expressive enough that it doesn't leave any of the renderer's capabilities hidden.

A key decision to make when designing a rendering API is whether to expose the system's internal algorithms and structures, or offer a high-level abstraction for describing the scene. These have historically been the two main approaches to scene description in graphics: the interface may specify *how* to render the scene, configuring a rendering pipeline at a low level using deep knowledge of the renderer's internal algorithms, or it may specify *what* the scene's objects, lights, and material properties are, and leave it to the renderer to decide how to transform that description into the best possible image.

The first approach has been successfully used for interactive graphics. In APIs such as OpenGL or Direct3D, it is not possible to just mark an object as a mirror and have reflections appear automatically; rather, the user must choose an algorithm for rendering reflections, render the scene multiple times (e.g., to generate an environment map), store those images in a texture, and then configure the graphics pipeline to use the environment map when rendering the reflective object. The advantage of this approach is that the full flexibility of the rendering hardware is exposed to the user, making it possible to carefully control the actual computation being done and to use the hardware very efficiently. Furthermore, because APIs like these impose a very thin abstraction layer between the user and the renderer, the user can be confident that unexpected inefficiencies won't be introduced by the API.

The second approach to scene description, based on describing the geometry, materials, and lights at a higher level of abstraction, has been most successful for applications like high-end offline rendering. There, users are generally willing to cede control of the low-level rendering details to the renderer in exchange for the ability to specify the scene's properties at a high level. An important advantage of the high-level approach is that the implementations of these renderers have greater freedom to make major changes to the internal algorithms of the system, since the API exposes less of them.

For pbrt, we will use an interface based on the descriptive approach. Because pbrt is fundamentally physically based, the API is necessarily less flexible in some ways than APIs for many nonphysically based rendering packages. For example, it is not possible to have some lights illuminate only some objects in the scene.

Another key decision to make in graphics API design is whether to use an immediate mode or a retained mode style. In an immediate mode API, the user specifies the scene via a stream of commands that the renderer processes as they arrive. In general, the user cannot make changes to the scene description data already specified (e.g., "change the material of that sphere I described previously from plastic to glass"); once it has been given to the renderer, the information is no longer accessible to the user. Retained mode APIs give the user some degree of access to the data structures that the renderer has built to represent the scene. The user can then modify the scene description in a variety of ways before finally instructing the renderer to render the scene.

Immediate mode has been very successful for interactive graphics APIs since it allows graphics hardware to draw the objects in the scene as they are supplied by the user. Since they do not need to build data structures to store the scene and since they can apply techniques like immediately culling objects that are outside of the viewing frustum without worrying that the user will change the camera position before rendering, these APIs have been key to high-performance interactive graphics.

For ray-tracing-based renderers like pbrt, where the entire scene must be described and stored in memory before rendering can begin, some of these advantages of an immediate mode interface aren't applicable. Nonetheless, we will use immediate mode semantics in our API, since it leads to a clean and straightforward scene description language. This choice makes it more difficult to use pbrt for applications like quickly rerendering a scene after making a small change to it (e.g., by moving a light source) and may make rendering animations less straightforward, since the entire scene needs to be redescribed for each frame of an animation. Adding a retained mode interface to pbrt would be a challenging but useful project.

pbrt's rendering API consists of just under 40 carefully chosen functions, all of which are declared in the core/api.h⊙ header file. The implementation of these functions is in core/api.cpp.⊙ This appendix will focus on the general process of turning the API function calls into instances of the classes that represent the scenes.

B.1 PARAMETER SETS

A key problem that a rendering API must address is extensibility: if a developer has created new plug-in modules for pbrt, it shouldn't be necessary to modify the API. In particular, the API should be as unaware as possible of what particular parameters these objects take and what their semantics are. pbrt uses the ParamSet class to address this issue. This class handles collections of named parameters and their values in a generic way. For example, it might record that there is a single floating-point value named "radius" with a value of 2.5, and an array of four color values named "specular" with various color values. The ParamSet provides methods for both setting and retrieving values from these kinds of generic parameter lists. It is defined in core/paramset.h⊙ and core/paramset.cpp.⊙

Most of pbrt's API routines take a ParamSet as one of their parameters; for example, the shape creation routine, pbrtShape(), takes a string giving the name of the shape to make and a ParamSet with parameters for it. The appropriate shape implementation is loaded from disk, and its creation routine is called with the ParamSet passed along as a parameter. This style makes the API's implementation very straightforward.

⟨*ParamSet Declarations*⟩ ≡
    class COREDLL ParamSet {
    public:
        ⟨*ParamSet Public Methods* **878**⟩
    private:
        ⟨*ParamSet Data* **878**⟩
    };

A ParamSet can hold nine types of parameters: booleans, integers, floating-point values, points, vectors, normals, spectra, strings, and the names of Textures that are being used as parameters for Materials and other Textures. Internally, it stores a vector of named values for each of the different types that it stores; each parameter is represented by a ParamSetItem of the appropriate type. This representation means that searching for a given parameter takes $O(n)$ time, where n is the number of parameters of the parameter's type. In practice, there are just a handful of parameters to any function, so a more time-efficient representation isn't necessary.

⟨*ParamSet Data*⟩ ≡   877
```
    vector<ParamSetItem<int> *> ints;
    vector<ParamSetItem<bool> *> bools;
    vector<ParamSetItem<float> *> floats;
    vector<ParamSetItem<Point> *> points;
    vector<ParamSetItem<Vector> *> vectors;
    vector<ParamSetItem<Normal> *> normals;
    vector<ParamSetItem<Spectrum> *> spectra;
    vector<ParamSetItem<string> *> strings;
    vector<ParamSetItem<string> *> textures;
```

The constructor for the ParamSet starts out with unfilled vectors of parameters.

⟨*ParamSet Public Methods*⟩ ≡   877
```
    ParamSet() { }
```

However, because it holds pointers to ParamSetItems in the vectors, it is necessary to do some work when one ParamSet is assigned to another one; we can't just let the default assignment operator or copy constructor copy the contents of all of the vectors, since the ParamSetItem memory would be freed twice in the two ParamSet destructors. The implementations of these methods are straightforward—they just allocate duplicates of all of the ParamSetItems—so we will not include them here. (Another approach would have been to use the automatic reference-counting classes and to store references to ParamSetItems in the vectors instead.)

⟨*ParamSet Public Methods*⟩+≡   877
```
    ParamSet &operator=(const ParamSet &p2);
    ParamSet(const ParamSet &p2);
```

B.1.1 THE ParamSetItem STRUCTURE

The ParamSetItem structure stores all of the relevant information about a single parameter, such as its name, its base type, and its value(s). For example (using the syntax from pbrt's input files), the foo parameter

```
    "float foo" [ 0 1 2 3 4 5 ]
```

has a base type of float, and six values have been supplied for it. It would be represented by a single ParamSetItem<float>.

⟨*ParamSet Declarations*⟩+≡
```
    template <class T> struct ParamSetItem {
        ⟨ParamSetItem Public Methods 879⟩
        ⟨ParamSetItem Data 879⟩
    };
```

The `ParamSetItem` directly initializes its members from the arguments and makes a copy of the values:

⟨*ParamSetItem Methods*⟩ ≡
```
template <class T>
ParamSetItem<T>::ParamSetItem(const string &n, const T *v, int ni) {
    name = n;
    nItems = ni;
    data = new T[nItems];
    for (int i = 0; i < nItems; ++i)
        data[i] = v[i];
    lookedUp = false;
}
```

The boolean value `lookedUp` is set to `true` after the value has been retrieved from the `ParamSet`. This makes it possible to print warning messages if any parameters were added to the parameter set but never used, which typically indicates a misspelling in the scene description file or other user error.

⟨*ParamSetItem Data*⟩ ≡   878
```
string name;
int nItems;
T *data;
bool lookedUp;
```

Naturally, the `ParamSetItem` needs to free allocated memory in its destructor:

⟨*ParamSetItem Public Methods*⟩ ≡   878
```
~ParamSetItem() {
    delete[] data;
}
```

B.1.2 ADDING TO THE PARAMETER SET

To add an entry to the parameter set, the user calls the appropriate `ParamSet` method, passing the name of the parameter, a pointer to its data, and the number of data items. These methods first remove previous values for this parameter, if any.

⟨*ParamSet Methods*⟩ ≡
```
void ParamSet::AddFloat(const string &name,
                        const float *data, int nItems) {
    EraseFloat(name);
    floats.push_back(new ParamSetItem<float>(name, data, nItems));
}
```

We won't include the rest of the methods to add data to the `ParamSet`, but include their prototypes here for reference. The erasure methods are also straightforward and won't be included here.

⟨*ParamSet Public Methods*⟩+≡   877
```
    void AddInt(const string &, const int *, int nItems = 1);
    void AddBool(const string &, const bool *, int nItems = 1);
    void AddPoint(const string &, const Point *, int nItems = 1);
    void AddVector(const string &, const Vector *, int nItems = 1);
    void AddNormal(const string &, const Normal *, int nItems = 1);
    void AddSpectrum(const string &, const Spectrum *, int nItems = 1);
    void AddString(const string &, const string *, int nItems = 1);
    void AddTexture(const string &, const string &);
```

B.1.3 LOOKING UP VALUES IN THE PARAMETER SET

To retrieve a parameter value from a set, it is just necessary to loop through the entries of the requested type and return the appropriate value, if any. There are two versions of the lookup method for each parameter type: a simple one for parameters that have a single data value, and a more general one that returns a pointer to the possibly multiple values of more complex types. The first method mostly serves to reduce the amount of code needed in routines that retrieve parameter values.

The methods that look up a single item (e.g., `FindOneFloat()`) take the name of the parameter and a default value. If the parameter is not found, the default value is returned. This makes it easy to write initialization code like

```
        float radius = params.FindOneFloat("radius", 1.f);
```

In this case, it is not an error if there isn't a "radius" parameter; the default value will be used instead. If the caller wants to detect a missing parameter and issue an error, the second type of lookup methods should be used, since they return a `NULL` pointer if the parameter isn't found.

⟨*ParamSet Methods*⟩+≡
```
    float ParamSet::FindOneFloat(const string &name, float d) const {
        for (u_int i = 0; i < floats.size(); ++i)
            if (floats[i]->name == name && floats[i]->nItems == 1) {
                floats[i]->lookedUp = true;
                return *(floats[i]->data);
            }
        return d;
    }
```

As earlier, here are the declarations of the analogous methods for the remaining types:

⟨*ParamSet Public Methods*⟩+≡   877

```
int FindOneInt(const string &, int d) const;
bool FindOneBool(const string &, bool d) const;
Point FindOnePoint(const string &, const Point &d) const;
Vector FindOneVector(const string &, const Vector &d) const;
Normal FindOneNormal(const string &, const Normal &d) const;
Spectrum FindOneSpectrum(const string &,
    const Spectrum &d) const;
string FindOneString(const string &, const string &d) const;
string FindTexture(const string &) const;
```

The second kind of lookup method returns a pointer to the data if the data is present and returns the number of data items in nItems:

⟨*ParamSet Methods*⟩+≡

```
const float *ParamSet::FindFloat(const string &name, int *nItems) const {
    for (u_int i = 0; i < floats.size(); ++i)
        if (floats[i]->name == name) {
            *nItems = floats[i]->nItems;
            floats[i]->lookedUp = true;
            return floats[i]->data;
        }
    return NULL;
}
```

These are the prototypes for the rest of the lookup functions for the other types:

⟨*ParamSet Public Methods*⟩+≡   877

```
const int *FindInt(const string &, int *nItems) const;
const bool *FindBool(const string &, int *nItems) const;
const Point *FindPoint(const string &, int *nItems) const;
const Vector *FindVector(const string &, int *nItems) const;
const Normal *FindNormal(const string &, int *nItems) const;
const Spectrum *FindSpectrum(const string &, int *nItems) const;
const string *FindString(const string &, int *nItems) const;
```

Because the user may misspell parameter names in the scene description file, the ParamSet also provides a function that goes through the parameter set and reports if any of the parameters present were never looked up. If this happens, it is likely that the user has given an incorrect parameter.

⟨*ParamSet Methods*⟩+≡
```
    void ParamSet::ReportUnused() const {
#define CHECK_UNUSED(v) \
        for (i = 0; i < (v).size(); ++i) \
            if (!(v)[i]->lookedUp) \
                Warning("Parameter \"%s\" not used", \
                    (v)[i]->name.c_str())
        u_int i;
        CHECK_UNUSED(ints);    CHECK_UNUSED(bools);
        CHECK_UNUSED(floats);  CHECK_UNUSED(points);
        CHECK_UNUSED(vectors); CHECK_UNUSED(normals);
        CHECK_UNUSED(spectra); CHECK_UNUSED(strings);
        CHECK_UNUSED(textures);
    }
```

The ParamSet destructor simply calls a separate ParamSet::Clear() method. This makes it possible to clear an existing ParamSet without fully destroying it, as is done in the copy constructor.

⟨*ParamSet Public Methods*⟩+≡   **877**
```
    ParamSet::~ParamSet() {
        Clear();
    }
```

The ParamSet::Clear() method is straightforward: it loops over all of the vectors and deletes their individual ParamSetItems before resetting the vectors to have zero length.

⟨*ParamSet Methods*⟩+≡
```
    void ParamSet::Clear() {
#define DEL_PARAMS(name) \
        for (u_int i = 0; i < (name).size(); ++i) \
            delete (name)[i]; \
        (name).erase((name).begin(), (name).end())
        DEL_PARAMS(ints);    DEL_PARAMS(bools);
        DEL_PARAMS(floats);  DEL_PARAMS(points);
        DEL_PARAMS(vectors); DEL_PARAMS(normals);
        DEL_PARAMS(spectra); DEL_PARAMS(strings);
        DEL_PARAMS(textures);
#undef DEL_PARAMS
    }
```

Finally, the ParamSet::ToString() method returns a string representation of the ParamSet, using the same syntax as would be used to initialize the ParamSet in a pbrt input file. The implementation of this is both straightforward and tedious, and so has been omitted here.

⟨*ParamSet Public Methods*⟩+≡   **877**
    string ToString() const;

B.2 INITIALIZATION AND RENDERING OPTIONS

We now have the machinery to describe the routines that make up the rendering API. Before any other API functions can be called, the rendering system must be initialized by a call to pbrtInit(). Similarly, when rendering is done, pbrtCleanup() should be called; this handles final cleanup of the system. The definitions of these two functions will be filled in throughout the rest of this appendix.

⟨*API Function Definitions*⟩≡
```
COREDLL void pbrtInit() {
    ⟨System-wide initialization⟩
    ⟨API Initialization  884⟩
}
```

⟨*API Function Definitions*⟩+≡
```
COREDLL void pbrtCleanup() {
    StatsCleanup();
    ⟨API Cleanup  884⟩
}
```

After the system has been initialized, a subset of the API routines is available. Legal calls at this point are those that set general rendering options like the camera and sampler properties, the type of film to be used, and so on, but the user is not yet allowed to start to describe the lights, shapes, and materials in the scene.

After the overall rendering options have been set, the pbrtWorldBegin() function locks them in; it is no longer legal to call the routines that set them. At this point, the user can begin to describe the geometric primitives and lights that are in the scene. This separation of global versus scene-specific information can help simplify the implementation of the renderer. For example, consider a spline patch shape that tessellates itself into triangles. This shape might compute the required size of its generated triangles based on the area of the screen that it covers. If the camera's position and image resolution are guaranteed not to change after the shape is created, then the shape can potentially do the tessellation work immediately at creation time.

Once the scene has been fully specified, the pbrtWorldEnd() routine is called. At this point, the renderer knows that the scene description is complete and that rendering can begin. The image will be rendered and written to a file before pbrtWorldEnd() returns. The user may then specify new options for another frame of an animation, and then another pbrtWorldBegin()/pbrtWorldEnd() block to describe the geometry for the next frame, repeating as many times as desired. The remainder of this section will discuss the routines related to setting rendering options. Section B.3 describes the routines for specifying the scene inside the world block.

B.2.1 STATE TRACKING

There are three distinct states that the renderer's API can be in:

- *Uninitialized:* Before pbrtInit() has been called, no other API calls are legal.
- *Option block:* Outside a pbrtWorldBegin() and pbrtWorldEnd() pair, scenewide global options may be set.
- *World block:* Inside a pbrtWorldBegin() and pbrtWorldEnd() pair, the scene may be described.

A module static variable currentApiState starts out with value STATE_UNINITIALIZED, indicating that the API system hasn't yet been initialized. Its value is updated appropriately by pbrtInit(), pbrtWorldBegin(), and pbrtCleanup().

⟨*API Static Data*⟩ ≡
```
#define STATE_UNINITIALIZED  0
#define STATE_OPTIONS_BLOCK   1
#define STATE_WORLD_BLOCK     2
static int currentApiState = STATE_UNINITIALIZED;
```

Now we can start to define the implementation of pbrtInit(). pbrtInit() first makes sure that it hasn't already been called, and then sets the currentApiState variable to STATE_OPTIONS_BLOCK to indicate that the scenewide options can be specified.

⟨*API Initialization*⟩ ≡   **883**
```
if (currentApiState != STATE_UNINITIALIZED)
    Error("pbrtInit() has already been called.");
currentApiState = STATE_OPTIONS_BLOCK;
```

Similarly, pbrtCleanup() makes sure that pbrtInit() has been called and that we're not in the middle of a pbrtWorldBegin()/pbrtWorldEnd() block before resetting the state to the uninitialized state.

⟨*API Cleanup*⟩ ≡   **883**
```
if (currentApiState == STATE_UNINITIALIZED)
    Error("pbrtCleanup() called without pbrtInit().");
else if (currentApiState == STATE_WORLD_BLOCK)
    Error("pbrtCleanup() called while inside world block.");
currentApiState = STATE_UNINITIALIZED;
```

All API procedures that are only valid in particular states invoke one of the state verification macros (VERIFY_UNINITIALIZED(), VERIFY_OPTIONS(), or VERIFY_WORLD()) to make sure that currentApiState holds an appropriate value. If the states don't match, an error message is printed and the function immediately returns.

```
⟨API Macros⟩ ≡
    #define VERIFY_INITIALIZED(func) \
    if (currentApiState == STATE_UNINITIALIZED) { \
        Error("pbrtInit() must be before calling \"%s()\". " \
              "Ignoring.", func); \
        return; \
    } else /* swallow trailing semicolon */
```

```
⟨API Macros⟩+ ≡
    #define VERIFY_OPTIONS(func) \
    VERIFY_INITIALIZED(func); \
    if (currentApiState == STATE_WORLD_BLOCK) { \
        Error("Options cannot be set inside world block; " \
              "\"%s\" not allowed.  Ignoring.", func); \
        return; \
    } else /* swallow trailing semicolon */
```

```
⟨API Macros⟩+ ≡
    #define VERIFY_WORLD(func) \
    VERIFY_INITIALIZED(func); \
    if (currentApiState == STATE_OPTIONS_BLOCK) { \
        Error("Scene description must be inside world block; " \
              "\"%s\" not allowed. Ignoring.", func); \
        return; \
    } else /* swallow trailing semicolon */
```

B.2.2 TRANSFORMATIONS

As the scene is being described, pbrt maintains a *current transformation matrix* (CTM). The CTM is stored in the module-local curTransform variable. When shapes are created, the value of the CTM is used as the object-to-world transformation for that shape. Similarly, the CTM sets the camera-to-world transformation when the camera is created. The scene description API provides a number of routines that update the CTM, most of which just postmultiply the CTM with a given transformation matrix. This is similar to the way OpenGL maintains and updates the current matrix for each of its matrix types.

```
⟨API Static Data⟩+ ≡
    static Transform curTransform;
```

The actual transformation functions are straightforward. Because the CTM is used both for the rendering options and the scene description phases, these routines just verify that pbrtInit() has been called.

⟨*API Function Definitions*⟩+≡
```
COREDLL void pbrtIdentity() {
    VERIFY_INITIALIZED("Identity");
    curTransform = Transform();
}
```

⟨*API Function Definitions*⟩+≡
```
COREDLL void pbrtTranslate(float dx, float dy, float dz) {
    VERIFY_INITIALIZED("Translate");
    curTransform = curTransform * Translate(Vector(dx, dy, dz));
}
```

Most of the rest of the functions are similarly defined, so we will not show their definitions here. pbrt provides the `pbrtConcatTransform()` and `pbrtTransform()` functions to allow the user to specify an arbitrary matrix to postmultiply or replace the CTM, respectively. These correspond to the OpenGL `glMultMatrix()` and `glLoadMatrix()` calls.

⟨*API Function Declarations*⟩≡
```
extern COREDLL void pbrtRotate(float angle,
                               float ax, float ay, float az);
extern COREDLL void pbrtScale(float sx, float sy, float sz);
extern COREDLL void pbrtLookAt(float ex, float ey, float ez,
                               float lx, float ly, float lz,
                               float ux, float uy, float uz);
extern COREDLL void pbrtConcatTransform(float transform[16]);
extern COREDLL void pbrtTransform(float transform[16]);
```

It can be useful to make a named copy the CTM so that it can be referred to later. For example, to place a light at the camera's position, it is useful to first apply the transformation into the camera coordinate system, since then the light can just be placed at the origin (0, 0, 0). This way, if the camera position is changed and the scene is rerendered, the light will move with it. The `pbrtCoordinateSystem()` function copies the CTM into the `namedCoordinateSystems` associative array, and `pbrtCoordSysTransform()` loads a named CTM.

⟨*API Static Data*⟩+≡
```
static map<string, Transform> namedCoordinateSystems;
```

⟨*API Function Definitions*⟩+≡
```
COREDLL void pbrtCoordinateSystem(const string &name) {
    VERIFY_INITIALIZED("CoordinateSystem");
    namedCoordinateSystems[name] = curTransform;
}
```

⟨*API Function Definitions*⟩+≡
```
COREDLL void pbrtCoordSysTransform(const string &name) {
    VERIFY_INITIALIZED("CoordSysTransform");
    if (namedCoordinateSystems.find(name) !=
        namedCoordinateSystems.end())
        curTransform = namedCoordinateSystems[name];
}
```

B.2.3 OPTIONS

All of the rendering options that are set before the pbrtWorldBegin() call are stored in a RenderOptions structure. This structure contains public data members that are set by API calls, and methods that help create objects used by the rest of pbrt for rendering.

⟨*API Local Classes*⟩≡
```
struct RenderOptions {
    ⟨RenderOptions Public Methods⟩
    ⟨RenderOptions Public Data  888⟩
};
```

⟨*API Local Classes*⟩+≡
```
RenderOptions::RenderOptions() {
    ⟨RenderOptions Constructor Implementation  888⟩
}
```

A single static instance of a RenderOptions structure is available to the rest of the API functions:

⟨*API Static Data*⟩+≡
```
static RenderOptions *renderOptions = NULL;
```

When pbrtInit() is called, it allocates a RenderOptions structure that initially holds default values for all of its options:

⟨*API Initialization*⟩+≡   **883**
```
renderOptions = new RenderOptions;
```

The renderOptions variable is freed by pbrtCleanup():

⟨*API Cleanup*⟩+≡   **883**
```
delete renderOptions;
renderOptions = NULL;
```

The API functions for setting rendering options are all quite similar in both their interface and their implementation. For example, pbrtPixelFilter() specifies the kind of Filter to be used for filtering image samples. It takes two parameters: a string giving the name of the filter to use and a ParamSet giving the parameters to the filter. The dynamic loading code in Section B.4 uses the string name to load the appropriate filter implementation from disk. For now, all that needs to be done is to verify that the API is in an appropriate state for `pbrtPixelFilter()` to be called and store the name of the filter and its parameters in `renderOptions`.

⟨*API Function Definitions*⟩+≡

```
COREDLL void pbrtPixelFilter(const string &name,
                            const ParamSet &params) {
    VERIFY_OPTIONS("PixelFilter");
    renderOptions->FilterName = name;
    renderOptions->FilterParams = params;
}
```

⟨*RenderOptions Public Data*⟩≡   887

```
string FilterName;
ParamSet FilterParams;
```

The default filter function is set to the Mitchell filter. Since the default `ParamSet` has no key-value pairs, the filter will be initialized with its default parameter settings by the loader in Section B.4.

⟨*RenderOptions Constructor Implementation*⟩≡   887

```
FilterName = "mitchell";
```

Most of the rest of the rendering option-setting API calls are similar; they simply store their arguments in `renderOptions`. Therefore, we will only include the declarations of these functions here. The options controlled by each function should be apparent from its name; more information about the legal parameters to each of these routines can be found in Appendix C.

⟨*API Function Declarations*⟩+≡

```
extern COREDLL void pbrtFilm(const string &type, const ParamSet &params);
extern COREDLL void pbrtSampler(const string &name,
                                const ParamSet &params);
extern COREDLL void pbrtAccelerator(const string &name,
                                    const ParamSet &params);
extern COREDLL void pbrtSurfaceIntegrator(const string &name,
                                          const ParamSet &params);
extern COREDLL void pbrtVolumeIntegrator(const string &name,
                                         const ParamSet &params);
```

`pbrtCamera()` is slightly different than the other options, since the world-to-camera transformation needs to be set. The CTM is used by `pbrtCamera()` to initialize this value, and the camera coordinate system transformation is also stored for possible future use by `pbrtCoordSysTransform()`.

⟨*RenderOptions Public Data*⟩+≡   **887**
```
    string CameraName;
    ParamSet CameraParams;
    Transform WorldToCamera;
```

⟨*API Function Definitions*⟩+≡
```
    COREDLL void pbrtCamera(const string &name, const ParamSet &params) {
        VERIFY_OPTIONS("Camera");
        renderOptions->CameraName = name;
        renderOptions->CameraParams = params;
        renderOptions->WorldToCamera = curTransform;
        namedCoordinateSystems["camera"] = curTransform.GetInverse();
    }
```

The default camera is set to a perspective projection:

⟨*RenderOptions Constructor Implementation*⟩+≡   **887**
```
    CameraName = "perspective";
```

The only other slightly unusual rendering options API call is pbrtSearchPath(), which provides a list of directories that pbrt uses to search for plug-in implementations. It takes a single string that holds a list of directories, separated by colons in UNIX and semicolons in Windows. Rather than storing the path in the RenderOptions, it passes it to UpdatePluginPath(), which records the path for use by the plug-in loading routines. It also sets a flag indicating that a search path was specified, so that a meaningful warning can be issued if the plug-ins cannot be found.

⟨*API Function Definitions*⟩+≡
```
    COREDLL void pbrtSearchPath(const string &path) {
        VERIFY_OPTIONS("SearchPath");
        UpdatePluginPath(path);
        renderOptions->gotSearchPath = true;
    }
```

⟨*RenderOptions Public Data*⟩+≡   **887**
```
    bool gotSearchPath;
```

By default, this path is set with the PBRT_SEARCHPATH environment variable. If this environment variable is missing, then pbrt will not be able to find its plug-ins unless an explicit search path is set with pbrtSearchPath().

⟨*RenderOptions Constructor Implementation*⟩+≡   **887**
```
   char *searchEnv = getenv("PBRT_SEARCHPATH");
   if (searchEnv == NULL) {
       Warning("PBRT_SEARCHPATH not set in your environment.\n"
               "pbrt won't be able to find plugins if "
               "no SearchPath in input file.\n"
               "PBRT_SEARCHPATH should be a "
               "\"%s\"-separated list of directories.\n",
               PBRT_PATH_SEP);
       gotSearchPath = false;
   }
   else {
       UpdatePluginPath(searchEnv);
       gotSearchPath = true;
   }
```

B.3 SCENE DEFINITION

After the user has set up the overall rendering options, the pbrtWorldBegin() call marks the start of the description of the shapes, materials, and lights in the scene. It sets the current rendering state to STATE_WORLD_BLOCK and resets the CTM to the identity matrix.

⟨*API Function Definitions*⟩+≡
```
   COREDLL void pbrtWorldBegin() {
       VERIFY_OPTIONS("WorldBegin");
       currentApiState = STATE_WORLD_BLOCK;
       curTransform = Transform();
       namedCoordinateSystems["world"] = curTransform;
   }
```

B.3.1 HIERARCHICAL GRAPHICS STATE

As the scene's lights, geometry, and participating media are specified, a variety of attributes can be set as well. In addition to the CTM, these include information about textures and the current material. When a geometric primitive or light source is then added to the scene, the current attributes are used in initializing their specific parameters. These data are all known as *graphics state*.

It is useful for a rendering API to provide some functionality for managing the graphics state. pbrt has API calls that allow the current graphics state to be managed with an *attribute stack;* the user can push the current set of attributes, make changes to their values, and then later pop back to the previously pushed attribute values. For example, a scene description file might contain the following:

```
Material "matte"
AttributeBegin
  Material "plastic"
  Translate 5 0 0
  Shape "sphere" "float radius" [1]
AttributeEnd
Shape "sphere" "float radius" [1]
```

The first sphere is affected by the translation and is bound to the plastic material, while the second sphere is matte and isn't translated. Changes to attributes made inside a pbrtAttributeBegin()/pbrtAttributeEnd() block are forgotten at the end of the block. Being able to save and restore attributes in this manner is a classic idiom for scene description in computer graphics.

The graphics state is stored in the GraphicsState structure. As was done previously with RenderOptions, we'll be adding members to it throughout this section.

⟨*API Local Classes*⟩+≡
```
struct GraphicsState {
    ⟨Graphics State Methods⟩
    ⟨Graphics State 895⟩
};
```

⟨*API Local Classes*⟩+≡
```
GraphicsState::GraphicsState() {
    ⟨GraphicsState Constructor Implementation 896⟩
}
```

When pbrtInit() is called, the current graphics state is initialized to hold default values:

⟨*API Initialization*⟩+≡   **883**
```
graphicsState = GraphicsState();
```

⟨*API Function Definitions*⟩+≡
```
COREDLL void pbrtAttributeBegin() {
    VERIFY_WORLD("AttributeBegin");
    pushedGraphicsStates.push_back(graphicsState);
    pushedTransforms.push_back(curTransform);
}
```

A vector of GraphicsStates is used as a stack to perform hierarchical state management. When pbrtAttributeBegin() is called, the current GraphicsState is copied and pushed onto this stack. pbrtAttributeEnd() then simply pops the state from this stack.

⟨*API Static Data*⟩+≡
```
static GraphicsState graphicsState;
static vector<GraphicsState> pushedGraphicsStates;
static vector<Transform> pushedTransforms;
```

pbrtAttributeEnd() also verifies that we do not have stack underflow by checking to see if there are any entries on the stack:

⟨*API Function Definitions*⟩+≡
```
COREDLL void pbrtAttributeEnd() {
    VERIFY_WORLD("AttributeEnd");
    if (!pushedGraphicsStates.size()) {
        Error("Unmatched pbrtAttributeEnd() encountered. "
            "Ignoring it.");
        return;
    }
    graphicsState = pushedGraphicsStates.back();
    curTransform = pushedTransforms.back();
    pushedGraphicsStates.pop_back();
    pushedTransforms.pop_back();
}
```

We also provide the pbrtTransformBegin() and pbrtTransformEnd() calls. These functions are similar to pbrtAttributeBegin() and pbrtAttributeEnd(), except that they only push and pop the CTM. We frequently want to apply a transformation to a texture, but since the list of named textures is stored in the graphics state, we cannot use pbrtAttributeBegin() to save the transformation matrix. Since the implementations of pbrtTransformBegin() and pbrtTransformEnd() are very similar to pbrtAttributeBegin() and pbrtAttributeEnd(), respectively, they are not shown here.

⟨*API Function Declarations*⟩+≡
```
extern COREDLL void pbrtTransformBegin();
extern COREDLL void pbrtTransformEnd();
```

B.3.2 TEXTURE AND MATERIAL PARAMETERS

Recall that all of the materials in pbrt use textures to describe all of their parameters. For example, the diffuse color of the matte material class is always obtained from a texture, even if the material is intended to have a constant reflectivity (in which case a ConstantTexture would be used).

Before a material can be created, it is necessary to create these textures to pass to the material creation procedures. Textures can be either explicitly created and later referred to by name, or implicitly created on the fly to encapsulate a constant parameter. These two methods of texture creation are hidden by the TextureParams class.

⟨*TextureParams Declarations*⟩ ≡
```
class COREDLL TextureParams {
public:
    ⟨TextureParams Public Methods 893⟩
private:
    ⟨TextureParams Private Data 893⟩
};
```

The TextureParams class contains lists of previously defined float and Spectrum textures, as well as two ParamSets that will be searched for named textures.

⟨*TextureParams Private Data*⟩ ≡   893
```
const ParamSet &geomParams, &materialParams;
map<string, Reference<Texture<float> > > &floatTextures;
map<string, Reference<Texture<Spectrum> > > &spectrumTextures;
```

⟨*TextureParams Public Methods*⟩ ≡   893
```
TextureParams(const ParamSet &geomp, const ParamSet &matp,
              map<string, Reference<Texture<float> > > &ft,
              map<string, Reference<Texture<Spectrum> > > &st)
    : geomParams(geomp),
      materialParams(matp),
      floatTextures(ft),
      spectrumTextures(st) {
}
```

Here we will show the code for finding a texture of Spectrum type; the code for finding a float texture is analogous. The TextureParams::GetSpectrumTexture() method takes a parameter name (e.g., "Kd") , as well as a default Spectrum value. If no texture has been explicitly specified for the parameter, a constant texture will be created that returns the default spectrum value.

Finding the texture is performed in several stages; the order of these stages is crucial. First the parameter list from the Shape for which a Material is being created is searched for a named reference to an explicitly defined texture. If no such texture is found, then the material parameters are searched. Finally, if no explicit texture has been found, the two parameter lists are searched in turn for supplied constant values. If no such constants are found, the default is used.

The order of these steps is crucial, because pbrt allows a shape to override individual elements of the material that is bound to it. For example, the user should be able to create a scene description that contains the lines

```
Material "matte" "color Kd" [ 1 0 0 ]
Shape "sphere" "color Kd" [ 0 1 0 ]
```

These two commands should create a green matte sphere. Because the shape's parameter list is searched first, the Kd parameter from the Shape command will be used when the Matte constructor is called.

⟨*TextureParams Method Definitions*⟩ ≡
```
    Reference<Texture<Spectrum> >
    TextureParams::GetSpectrumTexture(const string &n,
                                      const Spectrum &def) const {
        string name = geomParams.FindTexture(n);
        if (name == "") name = materialParams.FindTexture(n);
        if (name != "") {
            if (spectrumTextures.find(name) != spectrumTextures.end())
                return spectrumTextures[name];
            else
                Error("Couldn't find spectrum"
                      "texture named \"%s\"", n.c_str());
        }
        Spectrum val =
         geomParams.FindOneSpectrum(n, materialParams.FindOneSpectrum(n, def));
        return new ConstantTexture<Spectrum>(val);
    }
```

Because an instance of the TextureParams class is passed to material creation routines that might need to access nontexture parameter values, we also provide ways to access the other parameter list types. These methods return parameters from the geometric parameter list, if found. Otherwise, the material parameter list is searched, and finally the default value is returned.

The TextureParams::FindFloat() method is shown here. The other access methods are similar and omitted.

⟨*TextureParams Public Methods*⟩+≡   **893**
```
    float FindFloat(const string &n, float d) const {
        return geomParams.FindOneFloat(n, materialParams.FindOneFloat(n, d));
    }
```

B.3.3 SURFACE AND MATERIAL DESCRIPTION

The pbrtTexture() method creates a named texture that can be referred to later. In addition to the texture name, its *type* is specified. Currently, pbrt supports only "float" and "color" as texture types. The supplied parameter list is used to create a TextureParams object, which will be passed to the desired texture's creation routine.

⟨*API Function Definitions*⟩+≡
```
COREDLL void pbrtTexture(const string &name, const string &type,
                         const string &texname, const ParamSet &params) {
    VERIFY_WORLD("Texture");
    TextureParams tp(params, params, graphicsState.floatTextures,
                     graphicsState.spectrumTextures);
    if (type == "float")  {
        ⟨Create float texture and store in floatTextures 895⟩
    }
    else if (type == "color")  {
        ⟨Create color texture and store in spectrumTextures⟩
    }
    else
        Error("Texture type \"%s\" unknown.", type.c_str());
}
```

Creating the texture is simple. This function first checks to see if a texture of the same name and type already exists and issues a warning if so. Then, the MakeFloatTexture() routine will find the appropriate plug-in and call its initialization method. The returned texture class is added to the GraphicsState::floatTextures associative array. The code for creating a color texture is similar and not shown.

⟨*Create* float *texture and store in* floatTextures⟩≡   895
```
    if (graphicsState.floatTextures.find(name) !=
        graphicsState.floatTextures.end())
        Warning("Texture \"%s\" being redefined", name.c_str());
    Reference<Texture<float> > ft = MakeFloatTexture(texname,
                                                 curTransform, tp);
    if (ft) graphicsState.floatTextures[name] = ft;
```

⟨*Graphics State*⟩≡   891
```
    map<string, Reference<Texture<float> > > floatTextures;
    map<string, Reference<Texture<Spectrum> > spectrumTextures;
```

The current material is specified by a call to pbrtMaterial(). Its ParamSet is just stored until a Material object needs to be created later when a shape is specified.

⟨*API Function Declarations*⟩+≡
```
    extern COREDLL void pbrtMaterial(const string &name,
                                     const ParamSet &params);
```

⟨*Graphics State*⟩+≡   891
```
    ParamSet materialParams;
    string material;
```

The default material for all objects in the scene is matte:

⟨*GraphicsState Constructor Implementation*⟩ ≡   **891**
```
material = "matte";
```

B.3.4 LIGHT SOURCES

pbrt's API provides two ways for the user to specify light sources for the scene. The first, pbrtLightSource(), defines a light source that doesn't have geometry associated with it (e.g., a point light or a directional light). The second, pbrtAreaLightSource(), specifies an area light source. All shape specifications that appear between the area light source call up to the end of the current attribute block are treated as emissive.

⟨*API Function Definitions*⟩+≡
```
COREDLL void pbrtLightSource(const string &name,
                            const ParamSet &params) {
    VERIFY_WORLD("LightSource");
    Light *lt = MakeLight(name, curTransform, params);
    if (lt == NULL)
        Error("pbrtLightSource: light type "
              "\"%s\" unknown.", name.c_str());
    else
        renderOptions->lights.push_back(lt);
}
```

⟨*RenderOptions Public Data*⟩+≡   **887**
```
mutable vector<Light *> lights;
```

When an area light is specified via pbrtAreaLightSource(), it can't be created immediately since the primitives to follow are needed to define the light source's geometry. Therefore, this function just saves the name of the area light source type and the parameters given to it.

⟨*Graphics State*⟩+≡   **891**
```
ParamSet areaLightParams;
string areaLight;
```

⟨*API Function Definitions*⟩+≡
```
COREDLL void pbrtAreaLightSource(const string &name,
                                const ParamSet &params) {
    VERIFY_WORLD("AreaLightSource");
    graphicsState.areaLight = name;
    graphicsState.areaLightParams = params;
}
```

COREDLL 904
curTransform 885
Error() 834
graphicsState 892
GraphicsState::material 895
Light 598
ParamSet 877
pbrtAreaLightSource() 896
pbrtLightSource() 896
renderOptions 887
RenderOptions::lights 896
VERIFY_WORLD 885

B.3.5 SHAPES AND VOLUME REGIONS

The pbrtShape() function creates a new Shape object and adds it to the scene. It does this by calling MakeShape(), which loads the given shape plug-in, and invoking its creation routine, passing the ParamSet along for its parameters.

⟨*API Function Definitions*⟩+≡

```
COREDLL void pbrtShape(const string &name, const ParamSet &params) {
    VERIFY_WORLD("Shape");
    Reference<Shape> shape = MakeShape(name,
        curTransform, graphicsState.reverseOrientation,
        params);
    if (!shape) return;
    params.ReportUnused();
    ⟨Initialize area light for shape 897⟩
    ⟨Initialize material for shape 897⟩
    ⟨Create primitive and add to scene or current instance 898⟩
}
```

If an area light has been set in the current graphics state by pbrtAreaLightSource(), the new shape is an emitter and an AreaLight needs to be made for it.

⟨*Initialize area light for shape*⟩≡   897

```
AreaLight *area = NULL;
if (graphicsState.areaLight != "")
    area = MakeAreaLight(graphicsState.areaLight, curTransform,
                         graphicsState.areaLightParams, shape);
```

The Material for the shape needs to be created next. Notice that the shape's ParamSet and the current material's ParamSet are passed to the TextureParams constructor, to ensure the proper semantics for material parameter extraction. If the specified material cannot be found (usually due to a typo in the material name), a matte material is created. A warning is issued by the MakeMaterial() call in this case.

⟨*Initialize material for shape*⟩≡   897

```
TextureParams mp(params, graphicsState.materialParams,
                 graphicsState.floatTextures,
                 graphicsState.spectrumTextures);
Reference<Texture<float> > bump = NULL;
Reference<Material> mtl =
    MakeMaterial(graphicsState.material, curTransform, mp);
if (!mtl)
    mtl = MakeMaterial("matte", curTransform, mp);
if (!mtl)
    Severe("Unable to create \"matte\" material?!");
```

If the user is in the middle of defining an object instance, pbrtObjectBegin() (defined in the following section) will have set the currentInstance member of renderOptions to point to a vector that is collecting the shapes that define the instance. In that case, the new shape is added to that array. Otherwise, the shape is stored in the RenderOptions:: primitives array. This array will eventually be passed to the Scene constructor.

⟨*RenderOptions Public Data*⟩+≡   **887**
```
mutable vector<Reference<Primitive> > primitives;
```

⟨*Create primitive and add to scene or current instance*⟩≡   **897**
```
Reference<Primitive> prim = new GeometricPrimitive(shape, mtl, area);
if (renderOptions->currentInstance) {
    if (area)
        Warning("Area lights not supported with object instancing");
    renderOptions->currentInstance->push_back(prim);
}
else {
    renderOptions->primitives.push_back(prim);
    if (area != NULL) {
        ⟨Add area light for primitive to light vector  898⟩
    }
}
```

If this primitive is an area light, it is also added to the RenderOptions::lights array, similar to the pbrtLightSource() call:

⟨*Add area light for primitive to light vector*⟩≡   **898**
```
renderOptions->lights.push_back(area);
```

Volume regions are specified using the pbrtVolume() routine. The VolumeRegion classes returned by the MakeVolumeRegion() call are added to the RenderOptions::volumeRegions array, which is also passed to the Scene constructor.

⟨*RenderOptions Public Data*⟩+≡   **887**
```
mutable vector<VolumeRegion *> volumeRegions;
```

⟨*API Function Definitions*⟩+≡
```
COREDLL void pbrtVolume(const string &name, const ParamSet &params) {
    VERIFY_WORLD("Volume");
    VolumeRegion *vr = MakeVolumeRegion(name, curTransform, params);
    if (vr) renderOptions->volumeRegions.push_back(vr);
}
```

B.3.6 OBJECT INSTANCING

All shapes that are specified between a pbrtObjectBegin() and pbrtObjectEnd() pair are used to create a named object instance (see the discussion of object instancing and

the InstancePrimitive class in Section 4.1.2). pbrtObjectBegin() sets RenderOptions::
currentInstance so that subsequent pbrtShape() calls can add the shape to this instance's
vector of primitive references. This function also pushes the graphics state, so that any
changes made to the CTM while defining the instance don't last beyond the instance
definition.

⟨*API Function Definitions*⟩+≡
```
    COREDLL void pbrtObjectBegin(const string &name) {
        VERIFY_WORLD("ObjectBegin");
        pbrtAttributeBegin();
        if (renderOptions->currentInstance)
            Error("ObjectBegin called inside of instance definition");
        renderOptions->instances[name] = vector<Reference<Primitive> >();
        renderOptions->currentInstance = &renderOptions->instances[name];
    }
```

⟨*RenderOptions Public Data*⟩+≡   **887**
```
    map<string, vector<Reference<Primitive> > > instances;
    vector<Reference<Primitive> > *currentInstance;
```

⟨*RenderOptions Constructor Implementation*⟩+≡   **887**
```
    currentInstance = NULL;
```

⟨*API Function Definitions*⟩+≡
```
    COREDLL void pbrtObjectEnd() {
        VERIFY_WORLD("ObjectEnd");
        if (!renderOptions->currentInstance)
            Error("ObjectEnd called outside of instance definition");
        renderOptions->currentInstance = NULL;
        pbrtAttributeEnd();
    }
```

When an instance is used in the scene, all that needs to be done is to find the instance's
vector of Primitives in the RenderOptions::instances map, create an InstancePrimitive
for it, and add it to the scene. Note that the InstancePrimitive constructor takes the
current transformation matrix from the time when pbrtObjectInstance() is called. The
instance's complete world transformation is the composition of the CTM when it is
instantiated with the CTM when it was originally created.

pbrtObjectInstance() first does some error checking to make sure that the instance is not
being used inside the definition of another instance, and also that the named instance has
been defined. The error checking is simple and not shown here.

⟨*API Function Definitions*⟩+≡
```
COREDLL void pbrtObjectInstance(const string &name) {
    VERIFY_WORLD("ObjectInstance");
    ⟨Object instance error checking⟩
    vector<Reference<Primitive> > &in = renderOptions->instances[name];
    if (in.size() == 0) return;
    if (in.size() > 1 || !in[0]->CanIntersect()) {
        ⟨Refine instance Primitives and create aggregate  900⟩
    }
    Reference<Primitive> prim = new InstancePrimitive(in[0], curTransform);
    renderOptions->primitives.push_back(prim);
}
```

If there is more than one shape in an instance, or if the instance's shape must be refined, an aggregate needs to be built for it. This must be done here rather than in the InstancePrimitive constructor so that the resulting aggregate can be reused if this instance is referred to multiple times.

⟨*Refine instance* Primitives *and create aggregate*⟩≡   **900**
```
    Reference<Primitive> accel =
        MakeAccelerator(renderOptions->AcceleratorName,
                        in, renderOptions->AcceleratorParams);
    if (!accel)
        accel = MakeAccelerator("kdtree", in, ParamSet());
    if (!accel)
        Severe("Unable to find \"kdtree\" accelerator");
    in.erase(in.begin(), in.end());
    in.push_back(accel);
```

B.3.7 WORLD END AND RENDERING

When pbrtWorldEnd() is called, the scene has been fully specified and rendering can begin. This routine makes sure that there aren't excess graphics state structures on the state stack (issuing a warning if so), creates the Scene object, and then calls the Scene::Render() method.

⟨*API Function Definitions*⟩+≡
```
COREDLL void pbrtWorldEnd() {
    VERIFY_WORLD("WorldEnd");
    ⟨Ensure the search path was set  901⟩
    ⟨Ensure there are no pushed graphics states  901⟩
    ⟨Create scene and render  901⟩
    ⟨Clean up after rendering  901⟩
}
```

The user can either set the search path through the environment variable PBRT_SEARCHPATH or through a call to pbrtSearchPath(). If neither of those was done then pbrt cannot continue.

⟨*Ensure the search path was set*⟩ ≡   900
```
if (!renderOptions->gotSearchPath)
  Severe("PBRT_SEARCHPATH environment variable wasn't set and a plug-in\n"
         "search path wasn't given in the input "
         "(with the SearchPath directive).\n");
```

If there are still graphics states remaining on the pushedGraphicsStates stack, a warning is issued for each one:

⟨*Ensure there are no pushed graphics states*⟩ ≡   900
```
while (pushedGraphicsStates.size()) {
    Warning("Missing end to pbrtAttributeBegin()");
    pushedGraphicsStates.pop_back();
    pushedTransforms.pop_back();
}
```

The RenderOptions::MakeScene() method creates the Scene object corresponding to the settings provided by the user. After the Scene has been created, the Scene::Render() method executes the main rendering loop.

⟨*Create scene and render*⟩ ≡   900
```
Scene *scene = renderOptions->MakeScene();
if (scene) scene->Render();
delete scene;
```

Once the rendering is complete, the API transitions back to the "options block" rendering state, prints out all the statistics that were gathered during rendering, and clears the CTM and named coordinate systems so that the next scene, if any, starts with a clean slate.

⟨*Clean up after rendering*⟩ ≡   900
```
currentApiState = STATE_OPTIONS_BLOCK;
StatsPrint(stdout);
curTransform = Transform();
namedCoordinateSystems.erase(namedCoordinateSystems.begin(),
                             namedCoordinateSystems.end());
```

Most of the work in creating the Scene object is handled by the appropriate plug-in creation functions. If any of these routines fail, then pbrt cannot continue and an error message is printed. Otherwise, the Scene constructor is called with the objects created.

⟨*API Function Definitions*⟩+≡

```
Scene *RenderOptions::MakeScene() const {
    〈Create scene objects from API settings 902〉
    〈Initialize volumeRegion from volume region(s) 902〉
    〈Make sure all plug-ins initialized properly 902〉
    Scene *ret = new Scene(camera, surfaceIntegrator, volumeIntegrator,
                           sampler, accelerator, lights, volumeRegion);
    〈Erase primitives, lights, and volume regions from RenderOptions 903〉
    return ret;
}
```

The functions that load and initialize the plug-ins are invoked with the names and parameters that were passed to the rendering API routines. We only show the call that creates the Filter here; the rest are similar and omitted.

⟨*Create scene objects from API settings*⟩ ≡   **902**

```
Filter *filter = MakeFilter(FilterName, FilterParams);
```

If more than one VolumeRegion was specified, an AggregateVolume is created to store them.

⟨*Initialize* volumeRegion *from volume region(s)*⟩ ≡   **902**

```
VolumeRegion *volumeRegion;
if (volumeRegions.size() == 0)
    volumeRegion = NULL;
else if (volumeRegions.size() == 1)
    volumeRegion = volumeRegions[0];
else
    volumeRegion = new AggregateVolume(volumeRegions);
```

If any of the plug-in creation routines fail, they will return NULL. Clearly this is a fatal error; we cannot continue if any of the basic plug-ins are missing, so an error message is printed and no Scene is returned.

⟨*Make sure all plug-ins initialized properly*⟩ ≡   **902**

```
if (!camera || !sampler || !film || !accelerator ||
    !filter || !surfaceIntegrator || !volumeIntegrator) {
    Severe("Unable to create scene due to missing plug-ins");
    return NULL;
}
```

After the scene has been created, RenderOptions clears the vectors of primitives, lights, and volume regions. This ensures that if a subsequent scene is defined, then the scene description from this frame isn't inadvertently included.

⟨*Erase primitives, lights, and volume regions from* RenderOptions⟩ ≡   902
```
    primitives.erase(primitives.begin(), primitives.end());
    lights.erase(lights.begin(), lights.end());
    volumeRegions.erase(volumeRegions.begin(), volumeRegions.end());
```

B.4 DYNAMIC OBJECT CREATION

One of the key elements of pbrt's design is the fact that the pbrt executable holds only the key core logic of the system and that all of the shapes, cameras, lights, integrators, and so on are stored in separate object files on disk and loaded at run time. This makes it easier to extend pbrt with new implementations of various types and helps ensure a clean design by making it harder to sidestep the basic system interfaces.

B.4.1 ADDING NEW PLUG-INS

In this section, we will describe the overall process that pbrt uses to load object implementations at run time, and how plug-ins should be written so that they work with pbrt. We will focus on the details for the Shape class, since the other plug-in types are handled similarly. For platform-specific details about how to compile plug-in implementations so that they can be loaded at run time by pbrt, see either the CD-ROM or the *www.pbrt.org* Web site for examples.

All shape plug-in implementations must provide the CreateShape() function. When pbrt needs to create a shape using the plug-in, it will load the appropriate object file and call this function. For Shapes, the prototype for this function is

⟨*Shape Creation Declaration*⟩ ≡
```
    Shape *CreateShape(const Transform &o2w, bool reverseOrientation,
                       const ParamSet &params);
```

Because all Shapes require an object-to-world transformation and the reverse orientation flag, these are passed directly to this function. Issues like the fact that Spheres require a radius parameter are not exposed at this level of abstraction.

The Sphere's implementation of CreateShape() extracts the necessary parameters from the provided ParamSet and calls the constructor, returning a newly allocated Sphere. This is the only place in the system that calls the sphere's constructor directly. On some operating systems, it is necessary to explicitly indicate that a function should be exported from a shared library. The DLLEXPORT macro takes care of this in a portable way. Also, note that this function is declared with the extern "C" modifier. This is so the C++ compiler will not "mangle" the name, and we can easily refer to this function pointer by name when loading the code manually from the shared library.

⟨*Sphere Method Definitions*⟩+≡

```
extern "C" DLLEXPORT Shape *CreateShape(const Transform &o2w,
        bool reverseOrientation, const ParamSet &params) {
    float radius = params.FindOneFloat("radius", 1.f);
    float zmin = params.FindOneFloat("zmin", -radius);
    float zmax = params.FindOneFloat("zmax", radius);
    float phimax = params.FindOneFloat("phimax", 360.f);
    return new Sphere(o2w, reverseOrientation, radius,
                      zmin, zmax, phimax);
}
```

The prototypes for the remaining creation functions can be found in any of their respective plug-in files on the CD-ROM.

B.4.2 LOADING OBJECT FILES

Loading a plug-in object file and extracting and calling a function from the file can be done relatively easily in modern operating systems. However, the necessary system calls to load shared objects are highly dependent on the operating system. The Plugin base class hides the operating-system-dependent parts of this process.

First, we define a few platform-specific macros. On Windows, classes and methods in the pbrt executable need to be explicitly marked as "exported" in order to make them available from external shared objects. This is done with the __declspec(dllexport) directive. The COREDLL macro marks functions and classes in pbrt's core executable as "exported" when it is being compiled and "imported" when plug-ins are linking against it. On other operating systems, these special compiler directives are not necessary, so these macros are defined to nothing.

⟨*Platform-specific definitions*⟩≡

```
#ifdef WIN32
#ifdef CORE_SOURCE
#define COREDLL __declspec(dllexport)
#else
#define COREDLL __declspec(dllimport)
#endif
#define DLLEXPORT __declspec(dllexport)
#else
#define COREDLL
#define DLLEXPORT
#endif
```

Now, we can define the Plugin class. We will not show the operating-system-specific code here; the interested reader should look at the core/dynload.cpp⊙ and core/dynload.h⊙

files. We provide separate implementations for Apple's Mac OS X, Microsoft Windows, and the UNIX libdl API.

⟨*Runtime Loading Local Classes*⟩ ≡
```
    class Plugin {
    public:
        ⟨Plugin Public Methods 905⟩
    private:
        ⟨Plugin Private Data⟩
    };
```

The Plugin constructor handles the first step of loading the shared object into pbrt's address space. It takes the name of the plug-in file and loads it from disk.

⟨*Plugin Public Methods*⟩ ≡   **905**
```
    Plugin(const string &fname);
```

The Plugin constructor searches a given set of directions to find the plug-in to load. In order to determine where the appropriate plug-in is located, pbrt looks in a list of directories called the *search path*. This list can be updated by calling the UpdatePluginPath() function.

⟨*Runtime Loading Declarations*⟩ ≡
```
    COREDLL void UpdatePluginPath(const string &newpath);
```

The current search path is stored in the PluginSearchPath variable. The code for actually using this search path to find the plug-in will be shown later.

⟨*Runtime Loading Static Data*⟩ ≡
```
    static string PluginSearchPath;
```

Once a plug-in has been loaded into memory, the Plugin::GetSymbol() method searches the shared library for a function with the given name. If that function exists, then a pointer to it is returned. A NULL value is returned if a symbol that does not exist is requested.

⟨*Plugin Public Methods*⟩+≡   **905**
```
    void *GetSymbol(const string &symname);
```

For each pbrt plug-in type, there is a corresponding subclass of Plugin. Here is the implementation of ShapePlugin.

⟨*Runtime Loading Local Classes*⟩+≡
```
    class ShapePlugin : public Plugin {
    public:
        ⟨ShapePlugin Constructor 906⟩
        typedef Shape *(*CreateShapeFunc)(const Transform &o2w,
            bool reverseOrientation, const ParamSet &params);
        CreateShapeFunc CreateShape;
    };
```

The ShapePlugin constructor uses the Plugin::GetSymbol() method to get the pointer to the shape creation function. Notice that the constructor simply casts the returned pointer to a CreateShapeFunc function pointer. This is potentially unsafe; a malicious or poorly written plug-in could crash pbrt by returning the wrong pointer type. In a system with more stringent reliability requirements, we could take extra steps to make sure that the supplied function wasn't able to so easily crash the system.

⟨*ShapePlugin Constructor*⟩≡   906
```
    ShapePlugin(const string &name)
        : Plugin(name) {
        CreateShape = (CreateShapeFunc)(GetSymbol("CreateShape"));
    }
```

When pbrtShape() actually wants to create a Shape, it calls the MakeShape() function, which takes the name of the shape to be created, the current object-to-world transformation, and the ParamSet for the new shape. It calls the template function GetPlugin(), which will be defined shortly. GetPlugin() returns the ShapePlugin for the named shape if it exists. Then, MakeShape() calls the loaded plug-in's CreateShape() function to create the desired object.

⟨*Runtime Loading Method Definitions*⟩≡
```
    COREDLL Reference<Shape> MakeShape(const string &name,
            const Transform &object2world, bool reverseOrientation,
            const ParamSet &paramSet) {
        ShapePlugin *plugin = GetPlugin<ShapePlugin>(name, shapePlugins,
                                                     PluginSearchPath);
        if (plugin)
            return plugin->CreateShape(object2world, reverseOrientation,
                                       paramSet);
        return NULL;
    }
```

The GetPlugin() function maintains a cache of plug-ins in the loadedPlugins map; if the Plugin for name has already been loaded, it can be returned immediately. Otherwise, the searchPath is used to find the plug-in on disk, load it, and add it to the cache.

⟨*Runtime Loading Forward Declarations*⟩ ≡
```
template <class D> D *GetPlugin(const string &name,
        map<string, D *> &loadedPlugins, const string &searchPath) {
    if (loadedPlugins.find(name) != loadedPlugins.end())
        return loadedPlugins[name];
    string filename = name;
```
⟨*Add platform-specific shared library filename suffix*⟩
```
    string path = SearchPath(searchPath, filename);
    D *plugin = NULL;
    if (path != "")
        loadedPlugins[name] = plugin = new D(path.c_str());
    else
        Error("Unable to find Plugin/DLL for \"%s\"",
            name.c_str());
    return plugin;
}
```

⟨*Runtime Loading Static Data*⟩+≡
```
    static map<string, ShapePlugin *> shapePlugins;
```

GetPlugin() uses the SearchPath() utility function, which takes a set of directories and a filename and returns the full path to the first instance of a file found in the given directories.

⟨*Runtime Loading Forward Declarations*⟩+≡
```
    static string SearchPath(const string &searchpath,
                             const string &filename);
```

FURTHER READING

Foley et al. (1990) have discussed hierarchical modeling and retained mode versus immediate mode rendering APIs in depth; their chapter on these issues (Chapter 7) is a good starting point for more information about these topics. The *OpenGL Programming Guide* (Woo et al. 1999) is a good reference for learning the OpenGL interface. The RenderMan API is described in a number of books (Upstill 1989; Apodaca and Gritz 2000) and in its specification document, which is available online (Pixar Animation Studios 2000). A different approach to rendering APIs is taken by the *mental ray* rendering system, which exposes much more internal information about the system's implementation to users, allowing it to be extensible in more ways than is possible in other systems. See Driemeyer and Herken (2002) for further information about it.

EXERCISES

❸ B.1 pbrt's scene file parser is written using the standard lex and yacc tools. While these are an easy way to develop such a parser, carefully implemented hand-written parsers can be substantially more efficient. Replace pbrt's parser with a handwritten parser that parses the same file format. Measure the change in performance with your parser. Profile pbrt when rendering scenes with large scene description files. What fraction of execution time is spent in parsing?

❸ B.2 pbrt's scene description format makes it easy for other programs to export pbrt scenes and makes it easy for users to edit the scene files to make small adjustments to them. However, for complex scenes (such as the ecosystem scene in Figure 4.1), the large text files that are necessary to describe them can take a long time to parse and may occupy a lot of disk space.

Investigate extensions to pbrt to support compact binary file formats for scene files. Two possible ways to approach this problem are the following:

- *Binary encoding for large meshes:* Since most of the complexity in detailed scenes comes from large polygon and subdivision surface meshes, providing specialized encodings for just those shapes may be almost as effective as a binary encoding for the entire scene description format and has the advantage of not requiring that the scene file parser be rewritten. Extend TriangleMesh and/or LoopSubdiv to take an optional string parameter that gives the filename for a binary file that holds some or all of the mesh vertex positions and normals and the array of integers that describes which triangles use which vertices.
- *Binary representation of internal data structures:* For complex scenes, creating the ray acceleration aggregates may take more time than the initial parsing of the scene file. An alternative is to modify the system to have the capability of dumping out a representation of the acceleration structure and all of the primitives inside it after it is first created. The resulting file could then be subsequently read back into memory much more quickly than rebuilding the data structure from scratch. However, because C++ doesn't have native support for saving arbitrary objects to disk and then reading them back during a subsequent execution of the program (a capability known as *serialization* or *pickling* in other languages), adding this feature effectively requires extending many of the objects in pbrt to support this capability on their own.

Both of these approaches have their advantages and disadvantages, although the first is the easiest to implement and will usually solve the basic problem well. The second approach is substantially more involved, but should give the best performance of the two.

❷ B.3   Currently, the material assigned to object instances in pbrt is the current material when the instance was defined inside the pbrtObjectBegin()/ pbrtObjectEnd() block. This can be inconvenient if the user wants to use the same geometry multiple times in a scene, giving it a different material. Fix the API and the InstancePrimitive class so that the material assigned to instances is the current material when the instance is instantiated, or if the user hasn't set a material, the current material when the instance was created.

❸ B.4   Extend pbrt's API to make it possible for the user to supply information about motion over time in the scene, modify pbrt's internal scene representation to store this information, and modify some of the Cameras and Integrators to sample in time to compute images with motion blur.

It may be helpful to investigate how rendering APIs like RenderMan's and *mental ray*'s allow the user to describe motion and use ideas from those APIs for inspiration (Pixar Animation Studios 2000; Driemeyer and Herken 2002). Both of these allow the user to specify *keyframes*—the positions and transformations of objects at individual points in time. For example, the user might be able to supply a set of different transformations for particular times, and the renderer would interpolate among them to find the appropriate transformation for a particular time. (See the discussion of matrix interpolation in the exercises in Chapter 6 for information about approaches for interpolating transformation matrices.)

Motion can be categorized into three types: camera, transformation, and deformation. Supporting a moving camera is the easiest of these; nothing in the core scene representation needs to be modified to support a moving camera, only the Camera implementation. Supporting time-varying transformations for geometry in the scene is more difficult: it is necessary to update the Shape::WorldBound() methods to find the worst-case bounding box that encapsulates the shape over its entire range of motion from the camera's shutter open time to its shutter close time. If a shape is moving quickly, this bounding box may be very large, and many ray intersection tests may be needed as a result.

The most difficult type of motion blur to support in a ray tracer is deformation, or vertex motion. For example, a sphere might be specified as having a radius of .5 at shutter open time but a radius of 1 at shutter close time. Or a subdivision mesh might be specified with a different set of vertex positions at different points in time (with the limitation that the mesh's topology couldn't be changed). This form of motion blur is very important for character animation in many entertainment applications, but the straightforward implementation (linearly interpolating among positions according to the ray's time sample value) is computationally expensive in a ray tracer.

Camera 256
InstancePrimitive 175
Integrator 722
pbrtObjectBegin() 899
pbrtObjectEnd() 899
Shape::WorldBound() 91

❸ B.5   Extend pbrt's API to have some retained mode semantics so that animated
          sequences of images can be rendered without needing to respecify the entire
          scene for each frame. Make sure that it is possible to remove some objects
          from the scene, add others, modify objects' materials and transformations from
          frame to frame, and so on.

⊑ INPUT FILE FORMAT

The scene description files used by pbrt are text files. Each statement in these files corresponds directly to a pbrt API function from Appendix B. For example, when the WorldBegin statement appears in the input, the pbrtWorldBegin() function is called. The file format was designed so that it would be both easy to parse and easy for applications to generate from their own internal representations of scenes. While a binary file format would result in smaller files and faster parsing, a human-readable format is far easier to edit by hand. The input file parser (the implementation of which isn't described here) is very simple. It contains no logic about the validity of any statement beyond its basic syntax; it just calls the corresponding API function. There was no reason for the parsers to duplicate all of the error-checking logic in the API implementation.

Figure C.1 shows a short example of a pbrt input file (this file can be found on the CD-ROM in the file examples/simple.pbrt⦿). Between the start of the file and the WorldBegin statement, overall options for rendering the scene are specified, including the camera type and position, the sampler definition, and information about the image to be generated. After WorldBegin, the lights and geometry in the scene are defined, up until the WorldEnd statement, which causes the image to be rendered. The hash character # denotes that the rest of the line is a comment and should be ignored by the parser.

Some of the statements in the input file, such as WorldBegin, AttributeEnd, and so on, have no additional arguments. Those statements related to specifying transformations,

pbrtWorldBegin() 890

```
LookAt 0 10 100   0 -1 0 0 1 0
Camera "perspective" "float fov" [30]
PixelFilter "mitchell" "float xwidth" [2] "float ywidth" [2]
Sampler "bestcandidate"
Film "image" "string filename" ["simple.exr"]
     "integer xresolution" [200] "integer yresolution" [200]


WorldBegin

AttributeBegin
  CoordSysTransform "camera"
  LightSource "distant"
             "point from" [0 0 0] "point to"   [0 0 1]
             "color L"    [3 3 3]
AttributeEnd

AttributeBegin
  Rotate 135 1 0 0

  Texture "checks" "color" "checkerboard"
          "float uscale" [4] "float vscale" [4]
          "color tex1" [1 0 0] "color tex2" [0 0 1]

  Material "matte"
           "texture Kd" "checks"
  Shape "disk" "float radius" [20] "float height" [-1]
AttributeEnd
WorldEnd
```

Figure C.1: Example of a pbrt scene description file for a red and blue checkered disk.

such as Rotate and LookAt, take a predetermined number of arguments. Most statements, however, take a variable number of arguments and are of the form

identifier "type" parameter-list

For example, Shape describes a shape to be added to the scene, where the type of shape is given by a string and then a list of parameters that define the sphere. Statements of this type all correspond to one of the plug-in types that pbrt supports. The *type* string gives the name of the particular plug-in implementation to use, and the *parameter-list* gives the parameters to pass to the plug-in. With this design, the parser doesn't need to know anything about the semantics of the parameters; it just needs to know how to parse parameter lists and initialize a ParamSet from them. The primary advantage of this approach is that the parser doesn't need to be modified as new plug-in implementations are added to the system.

The only input file directive that does not correspond to a function in the API is the Include statement, which allows other input files to be parsed. Include behaves similarly to the #include directive in C++, except that only the current directory is searched for matching filenames. Of course, a complete pathname or a path relative to the current directory can be specified if appropriate.

```
Include "../geometry/car.pbrt"
```

C.1 PARAMETER LISTS

Variable-length lists of named parameters and their values are the key meeting ground between the parsing system and dynamically loaded plug-ins. Each of these lists holds an arbitrary number of name/value pairs, with the name in quotation marks and the value or values in square brackets:

   "*type name*" *value*

For example,

```
"float fov" [30]
```

specifies a parameter "fov" that is a single floating-point value, with value 30. Or,

```
"float cropwindow" [0 .5 0 .25]
```

specifies that "cropwindow" is a floating-point array with the given four values. Notice that arrays of values are enclosed in square brackets.

The type of each parameter must always be given along with its name; pbrt has no built-in knowledge of any parameter names. This simplifies the parsing system, although it does create a small extra burden for the creator of the input file.

pbrt supports seven basic parameter types: integer, float, point, vector, normal, color, bool, and string. The point, vector, and normal types all take three floating-point values, while color takes COLOR_SAMPLES floating-point values. string parameters must be inside quotation marks:

COLOR_SAMPLES 230

ParamSet 877

```
"string filename" [ "output.exr" ]
```

Finally, bool parameters are set with the strings "true" and "false", quotation marks included.

C.2 STATEMENT TYPES

We will now enumerate the supported statements, what their parameters are, and which API calls they correspond to.

C.2.1 TRANSFORMATIONS

The following set of routines update the current transformation matrix; see Section B.2.2 for further information about the API routines related to transformations. Each of them takes a fixed number of floating-point or string parameters, which is determined by their particular API call.

```
Identity
```
    Arguments: *NONE*
    API Call: `pbrtIdentity()`
```
Translate
```
    Arguments: *x y z*
    API Call: `pbrtTranslate()`
```
Scale
```
    Arguments: *x y z*
    API Call: `pbrtScale()`
```
Rotate
```
    Arguments: *angle x y z*
    API Call: `pbrtRotate()`
```
LookAt
```
    Arguments: *ex ey ez lx ly lz ux uy uz*
    API Call: `pbrtLookAt()`
```
CoordinateSystem
```
    Arguments: *"name"*
    API Call: `pbrtCoordinateSystem()`
```
CoordSysTransform
```
    Arguments: *"name"*
    API Call: `pbrtCoordSysTransform()`
```
Transform
```
    Arguments: $m_{00} \ldots m_{33}$
    API Call: `pbrtTransform()`
```
ConcatTransform
```
    Arguments: $m_{00} \ldots m_{33}$
    API Call: `pbrtConcatTransform()`

C.2.2 SCENEWIDE RENDERING OPTIONS

This section describes rendering options that must be specified before the `WorldBegin` statement.

`SearchPath` can be used to specify the set of directories that `pbrt` looks in to find plug-ins at run time. A search path *must* be specified either in the input file or by setting the `PBRT_SEARCHPATH` environment variable.

SearchPath
> *Arguments:* "path"
> *API Call:* pbrtSearchPath()

The given string *path* can contain multiple directory names separated by colons (semi-colons in Windows). The previous value of the search path can be specified with &. For example,

    SearchPath "/ext/pbrtplugins:&:./plugins"

The rest of the options all specify a particular plug-in to use. These options take the name of the plug-in and its parameter list. Of these, only Camera uses the value of the current transformation matrix when it is encountered in an input file; the CTM is used to initialize the world-to-camera transformation.

Camera
> *Arguments:* "name" parameter-list
> *API Call:* pbrtCamera()

Sampler
> *Arguments:* "name" parameter-list
> *API Call:* pbrtSampler()

PixelFilter
> *Arguments:* "name" parameter-list
> *API Call:* pbrtPixelFilter()

Film
> *Arguments:* "name" parameter-list
> *API Call:* pbrtFilm()

Accelerator
> *Arguments:* "name" parameter-list
> *API Call:* pbrtAccelerator()

SurfaceIntegrator
> *Arguments:* "name" parameter-list
> *API Call:* pbrtSurfaceIntegrator()

VolumeIntegrator
> *Arguments:* "name" parameter-list
> *API Call:* pbrtVolumeIntegrator()

C.2.3 ATTRIBUTES

The WorldBegin statement marks the end of options specification and the start of the description of the lights and geometry in the scene. WorldEnd denotes the end of the scene description; the scene is rendered when it is encountered.

WorldBegin
> *Arguments:* NONE
> *API Call:* pbrtWorldBegin()

WorldEnd
> *Arguments:* NONE
> *API Call:* pbrtWorldEnd()

The current graphics state and transformation matrix are saved and restored using `AttributeBegin` and `AttributeEnd`.

AttributeBegin
    Arguments: *NONE*
    API Call: `pbrtAttributeBegin()`
AttributeEnd
    Arguments: *NONE*
    API Call: `pbrtAttributeEnd()`

The transformation matrix can be saved and restored independently of the graphics state using `TransformBegin` and `TransformEnd`.

TransformBegin
    Arguments: *NONE*
    API Call: `pbrtTransformBegin()`
TransformEnd
    Arguments: *NONE*
    API Call: `pbrtTransformEnd()`

In addition to the current transformation matrix, pbrt stores only the reverse-orientation flag and the current material and active textures in the graphics state. The `Material` statement specifies the plug-in to be used for the current material as well as any parameters needed. The `Texture` statement creates named textures for use as parameters to materials or other textures.

Material
    Arguments: *"name" parameter-list*
    API Call: `pbrtMaterial()`
Texture
    Arguments: *"name" "type" "class" parameter-list*
    API Call: `pbrtTexture()`
ReverseOrientation
    Arguments: *NONE*
    API Call: `pbrtReverseOrientation()`

C.2.4 LIGHTS, SHAPES, AND VOLUMES

Most of the statements inside the `WorldBegin` block will specify shapes and light sources for the scene. All of the following statements make use of the current transformation matrix: For shapes, it is used for the object-to-world transformation; for lights, the light-to-world transformation; and for volumes, volume-to-world. Recall from Section B.3.4 that area lights are defined by specifying an area light source and then specifying one or more shapes. All shapes specified until the area light source goes out of scope (e.g., due to `AttributeEnd`) will be emissive.

Shape
    Arguments: *"name" parameter-list*
    API Call: pbrtShape()

LightSource
    Arguments: *"name" parameter-list*
    API Call: pbrtLightSource()

AreaLightSource
    Arguments: *"name" parameter-list*
    API Call: pbrtAreaLightSource()

Volume
    Arguments: *"name" parameter-list*
    API Call: pbrtVolume()

C.2.5 OBJECT INSTANCING

To create a named object, its definition should be placed within an ObjectBegin/ObjectEnd pair.

ObjectBegin
    Arguments: *"name"*
    API Call: pbrtObjectBegin()

ObjectEnd
    Arguments: *NONE*
    API Call: pbrtObjectEnd()

Then, when the object should be instantiated, it can simply be referred to by name with the ObjectInstance statement.

ObjectInstance
    Arguments: *"name"*
    API Call: pbrtObjectInstance()

C.3 STANDARD PLUG-INS

In this section, we will describe the plug-in classes that are provided with pbrt. Each subsection will describe a different class of plug-ins: cameras, shapes, and so on.

C.3.1 CAMERAS

Each subsection will first repeat the API command that creates the particular plug-in. For cameras, it is

Camera
    Arguments: *"name" parameter-list*
    API Call: pbrtCamera()

Provided Plug-Ins

Next, we will list the kinds of plug-ins that come with pbrt. The "Name" column corresponds to the *"name"* parameter, and the "Class" column indicates which C++ class will be created by the given plug-in name. The default class is indicated in boldface.

Name	Class
"environment"	EnvironmentCamera
"orthographic"	OrthoCamera
"perspective"	PerspectiveCamera

Common Parameters

Some of the plug-in classes have common parameters. For example, all camera plug-ins support the hither and yon parameters.

hither
> *Type:*   float
> *Default:* 10^{-3}
> *Description:*   The distance from the camera origin to the near clipping plane.

yon
> *Type:*   float
> *Default:* 10^{30}
> *Description:*   The distance from the camera origin to the far clipping plane.

shutteropen
> *Type:*   float
> *Default:*   0
> *Description:*   The time at which the virtual camera shutter opens.

shutterclose
> *Type:*   float
> *Default:*   1
> *Description:*   The time at which the virtual camera shutter closes.

lensradius
> *Type:*   float
> *Default:*   0
> *Description:*   The radius of the lens. Used to render scenes with depth of field and focus effects. The default value yields a pinhole camera.

focaldistance
> *Type:*   float
> *Default:* 10^{30}
> *Description:*   The focal distance of the lens. If lensradius is zero, this has no effect. Otherwise, it specifies the distance from the camera origin to the focal plane.

frameaspectratio
> *Type:*   float
> *Default:*   see description
> *Description:*   The aspect ratio of the film. By default, this is computed from the x and y resolutions of the film, but it can be overridden if desired.

EnvironmentCamera 274
OrthoCamera 261
PerspectiveCamera 265

screenwindow

Type:	float[4]
Default:	see description
Description:	The bounds of the film plane in screen space. By default, this is [−1, 1] along the shorter image axis and is set proportionally along the longer axis.

Plug-In Specific Parameters

The remaining parameters are specific to a particular plug-in. Here we will enumerate those parameters and also indicate which, if any, of the common parameters are handled differently in individual plug-ins.

environment::lensradius
environment::focaldistance

Type:	float
Default:	ignored
Description:	The environment camera does not support depth of field.

perspective::fov

Type:	float
Default:	90
Description:	Specifies the field of view for the perspective camera. This is the spread angle of the viewing frustum along the *narrower* of the image's width and height.

C.3.2 SAMPLERS

Sampler

Arguments:	*"name" parameter-list*
API Call:	pbrtSampler()

Provided Plug-Ins

Name	Class
"bestcandidate"	BestCandidateSampler
"lowdiscrepancy"	LDSampler
"stratified"	StratifiedSampler

Common Parameters

None

Plug-In Specific Parameters

bestcandidate::pixelsamples
lowdiscrepancy::pixelsamples

Type:	integer
Default:	4
Description:	The number of samples to take, per pixel. Note that the number of samples is taken per pixel *on average*; individual pixel areas may have slightly more or slightly fewer.

stratified::jitter

Type:	bool
Default:	true
Description:	Whether or not the generated samples should be jittered inside each stratum.

```
stratified::xsamples
```
Type:	integer
Default:	2
Description:	The number of samples per pixel to take in the *x* direction.

```
stratified::ysamples
```
Type:	integer
Default:	2
Description:	The number of samples per pixel to take in the *y* direction.

C.3.3 FILM

```
Film
```
Arguments:	*"name" parameter-list*
API Call:	pbrtFilm()

Provided Plug-Ins

Name	Class
"image"	ImageFilm

Common Parameters

There is only one kind of film provided in pbrt. However, we have separated its parameters into "common" and "specific" ones in anticipation of the needs of future film implementations.

```
xresolution
```
Type:	integer
Default:	640
Description:	The number of pixels in the *x* direction.

```
yresolution
```
Type:	integer
Default:	480
Description:	The number of pixels in the *y* direction.

```
filename
```
Type:	string
Default:	"pbrt.exr"
Description:	The output filename. The ImageFilm always writes files in OpenEXR format, regardless of the file extension.

```
cropwindow
```
Type:	float[4]
Default:	(0, 1, 0, 1)
Description:	The subregion of the image to render. The four values specified should be fractions in the range [0, 1], and they represent x_{min}, x_{max}, y_{min}, and y_{max}, respectively. These values are in normalized device coordinates, with (0, 0) in the upper-left corner of the image.

ImageFilm 371

pbrtFilm() 888

Plug-In Specific Parameters

image::writefrequency

Type:	integer
Default:	−1
Description:	If this is set to a positive value *N*, the film will write the partial image to disk every *N* samples. This is useful for previewing long renders. Negative values cause the film to wait until the rendering is complete before writing an image.

image::premultiplyalpha

Type:	bool
Default:	true
Description:	If true, pixel colors are multiplied by the pixel's alpha value before writing the image to disk.

C.3.4 FILTERS

Filter

Arguments:	*"name" parameter-list*
API Call:	pbrtPixelFilter()

Provided Plug-Ins

Name	Class
"box"	BoxFilter
"gaussian"	GaussianFilter
"mitchell"	MitchellFilter
"sinc"	LanczosSincFilter
"triangle"	TriangleFilter

Common Parameters

xwidth

Type:	float
Default:	2
Description:	The width of the filter in the *x* direction.

ywidth

Type:	float
Default:	2
Description:	The width of the filter in the *y* direction.

Plug-In Specific Parameters

gaussian::alpha

Type:	float
Default:	2
Description:	α controls the falloff rate of the Gaussian filter. Smaller values give a blurrier image.

```
mitchell::B
mitchell::C
```
Type:	float
Default:	$\frac{1}{3}$
Description:	These parameters control the shape of the Mitchell filter. The best results are generally obtained when $B + 2C = 1$.

```
sinc::tau
```
Type:	float
Default:	3
Description:	τ controls how many cycles the sinc function passes through before it is clamped to zero by the windowing function.

```
box::xwidth
box::ywidth
```
Type:	float
Default:	0.5
Description:	The box filter covers one pixel by default.

```
sinc::xwidth
sinc::ywidth
```
Type:	float
Default:	4
Description:	The sinc filter works better with a larger area of support, so it overrides the common default values.

C.3.5 SHAPES

Shape
Arguments:	*"name" parameter-list*
API Call:	pbrtShape()

Provided Plug-Ins

Name	Class
"cone"	Cone
"cylinder"	Cylinder
"disk"	Disk
"hyperboloid"	Hyperboloid
"loopsubdiv"	LoopSubdiv
"nurbs"	NURBS
"paraboloid"	Paraboloid
"sphere"	Sphere
"trianglemesh"	TriangleMesh

Common Parameters
None

Plug-In Specific Parameters

`cone::radius`

Type:	`float`
Default:	1
Description:	The cone's radius.

`cone::height`

Type:	`float`
Default:	1
Description:	The height of the cone along the z axis.

`cone::phimax`

Type:	`float`
Default:	360
Description:	The maximum extent of the cone in ϕ (in spherical coordinates).

`cylinder::radius`

Type:	`float`
Default:	1
Description:	The cylinder's radius.

`cylinder::zmin`

Type:	`float`
Default:	-1
Description:	The height of the cylinder's bottom along the z axis.

`cylinder::zmax`

Type:	`float`
Default:	1
Description:	The height of the cylinder's top along the z axis.

`cylinder::phimax`

Type:	`float`
Default:	360
Description:	The maximum extent of the cylinder in ϕ (in spherical coordinates).

`disk::height`

Type:	`float`
Default:	0
Description:	The location of the disk along the z axis.

`disk::radius`

Type:	`float`
Default:	1
Description:	The outer radius of the disk.

`disk::innerradius`

Type:	`float`
Default:	0
Description:	The inner radius of the disk (if nonzero, the disk is an annulus).

`disk::phimax`

Type:	`float`
Default:	360
Description:	The maximum extent of the disk in ϕ (in spherical coordinates).

`hyperboloid::p1`
>   *Type:*   point
>   *Default:*   0 0 0
>   *Description:*   The first end point of the hyperboloid's line of revolution.

`hyperboloid::p2`
>   *Type:*   point
>   *Default:*   1 1 1
>   *Description:*   The second end point of the hyperboloid's line of revolution.

`hyperboloid::phimax`
>   *Type:*   float
>   *Default:*   360
>   *Description:*   The maximum extent of the hyperboloid in ϕ (in spherical coordinates).

`nurbs::nu`
`nurbs::nv`
>   *Type:*   integer
>   *Default:*   none—must be specified
>   *Description:*   Number of control points for NURBS patch in the u and v parametric directions.

`nurbs::uorder`
`nurbs::vorder`
>   *Type:*   integer
>   *Default:*   see description
>   *Description:*   Order of NURBS surface in u and v directions. (Order is equal to one plus the surface's degree.)

`nurbs::uknots`
>   *Type:*   float[nu+uorder]
>   *Default:*   see description
>   *Description:*   Knot vector for NURBS in the u direction.

`nurbs::vknots`
>   *Type:*   float[nv+vorder]
>   *Default:*   see description
>   *Description:*   Knot vector for NURBS in the v direction.

`nurbs::u0`
`nurbs::v0`
>   *Type:*   float
>   *Default:*   none—must be specified
>   *Description:*   Starting u and v parametric coordinates at which to evaluate NURBS.

`nurbs::u1`
`nurbs::v1`
>   *Type:*   float
>   *Default:*   none—must be specified
>   *Description:*   Ending u and v parametric coordinates at which to evaluate NURBS.

`nurbs::P`

Type:	`point[nu*nv]`
Default:	none
Description:	Either the P or Pw parameter must be specified to give the surface's control points. P gives regular control points.

`nurbs::Pw`

Type:	`float[4*nu*nv]`
Default:	none
Description:	Specifies rational control points, with an additional per-vertex weight value.

`paraboloid::radius`

Type:	`float`
Default:	1
Description:	The paraboloid's radius.

`paraboloid::zmin`

Type:	`float`
Default:	0
Description:	The height of the lower clipping plane along the z axis.

`paraboloid::zmax`

Type:	`float`
Default:	1
Description:	The height of the upper clipping plane along the z axis.

`paraboloid::phimax`

Type:	`float`
Default:	360
Description:	The maximum extent of the paraboloid along ϕ (in spherical coordinates).

`sphere::radius`

Type:	`float`
Default:	1
Description:	The sphere's radius.

`sphere::zmin`

Type:	`float`
Default:	`-radius`
Description:	The height of the lower clipping plane along the z axis.

`sphere::zmax`

Type:	`float`
Default:	`radius`
Description:	The height of the upper clipping plane along the z axis.

`sphere::phimax`

Type:	`float`
Default:	360
Description:	The maximum extent of the sphere in ϕ (in spherical coordinates).

`subdiv::nlevels`

Type:	`integer`
Default:	3
Description:	The number of levels of refinement to compute in the subdivision algorithm.

`subdiv::indices`

Type:	`integer[n]`
Default:	required—no default
Description:	Indices for the base mesh. Indexing is the same as for the triangle mesh primitive.

`subdiv::P`

Type:	`point[n]`
Default:	required—no default
Description:	Vertex positions for the base mesh. This is the same as for the triangle mesh primitive.

`trianglemesh::indices`

Type:	`integer[n]`
Default:	none—must be specified
Description:	An array of integer offsets into the P point array. The triangles are made up of the vertices numbered $3i$, $3(i + 1)$, and $3(i + 2)$. This array's length must be a multiple of 3.

`trianglemesh::P`

Type:	`point[n]`
Default:	none—must be specified
Description:	The vertex positions of the triangle mesh. The order of vertex positions in this array is not important, since the triangles will be constructed using the `indices` array.

`trianglemesh::N`

Type:	`normal[n]`
Default:	none—optional
Description:	Per-vertex normals.

`trianglemesh::S`

Type:	`vector`
Default:	none—optional
Description:	Per-vertex tangents.

`trianglemesh::st`
`trianglemesh::uv`

Type:	`float[2*n]`
Default:	none—optional
Description:	Per-vertex texture coordinates.

C.3.6 ACCELERATORS

`Accelerator`

Arguments:	*"name" parameter-list*
API Call:	`pbrtAccelerator()`

Provided Plug-Ins

Name	Class
`"grid"`	`GridAccel`
`"kdtree"`	`KdTreeAccel`

GridAccel 182
KdTreeAccel 198
pbrtAccelerator() 888

Common Parameters

None

Plug-In Specific Parameters

`grid::refineimmediately`

Type:	bool
Default:	false
Description:	If true, primitives are fully refined as soon as they are added to the grid. Otherwise, they are not refined until a ray enters a voxel that contains the primitive.

`kd-tree::intersectcost`

Type:	integer
Default:	80
Description:	The value of the cost function that estimates the expected cost of performing a ray-object intersection, for use in building the kd-tree (Section 4.4.2).

`kd-tree::traversalcost`

Type:	integer
Default:	1
Description:	Estimated cost for traversing a ray through a kd-tree node.

`kd-tree::emptybonus`

Type:	integer
Default:	0.2
Description:	"Bonus" factor for kd-tree nodes that represent empty space.

`kd-tree::maxprims`

Type:	integer
Default:	1
Description:	Maximum number of primitives to store in kd-tree node. (Not a hard limit; more may be stored if the kd-tree can't find splitting planes that reduce the number of primitives when refining a node.)

`kd-tree::maxdepth`

Type:	integer
Default:	-1
Description:	Maximum depth of the kd-tree. If negative, the kd-tree chooses a maximum depth based on the number of primitives to be stored in it.

C.3.7 MATERIALS

`Material`

Arguments:	*"name" parameter-list*
API Call:	`pbrtMaterial()`

Provided Plug-Ins

Name	Class
`"bluepaint"`	`BluePaint`
`"brushedmetal"`	`BrushedMetal`
`"clay"`	`Clay`
`"felt"`	`Felt`
`"glass"`	`Glass`
`"matte"`	`Matte`
`"mirror"`	`Mirror`
`"plastic"`	`Plastic`

Name	Class
`"primer"`	`Primer`
`"shinymetal"`	`ShinyMetal`
`"skin"`	`Skin`
`"substrate"`	`Substrate`
`"translucent"`	`Translucent`
`"uber"`	`UberMaterial`

Common Parameters

`bumpmap`

Type:	`float texture`
Default:	None
Description:	The floating-point texture to be used as a bump map.

Plug-In Specific Parameters

`matte::Kd`

Type:	`color texture`
Default:	1
Description:	The diffuse reflectivity of the surface.

`matte::sigma`

Type:	`float texture`
Default:	0
Description:	The sigma parameter for the Oren-Nayar model, in degrees. If this is zero, the surface exhibits pure Lambertian reflection.

`plastic::Kd`

Type:	`color texture`
Default:	1
Description:	The diffuse reflectivity of the surface.

`plastic::Ks`

Type:	`color texture`
Default:	1
Description:	The specular reflectivity of the surface.

`plastic::roughness`

Type:	`float texture`
Default:	0.1
Description:	The roughness of the surface, from 0 to 1. Larger values result in larger, more blurry highlights.

`translucent::Kd`

Type:	`color texture`
Default:	1
Description:	The coefficient of diffuse reflection and transmission.

`translucent::Ks`

Type:	`color texture`
Default:	1
Description:	The coefficient of specular reflection and transmission.

`translucent::reflect`

Type: color texture

Default: .5

Description: Fraction of light reflected.

`translucent::roughness`

Type: float texture

Default: 0.1

Description: The roughness of the surface.

`translucent::transmit`

Type: color texture

Default: .5

Description: Fraction of light transmitted.

`mirror::Kr`

Type: color texture

Default: 1

Description: The reflectivity of the mirror. This can be used to make colored or dim reflections.

`glass::Kr`

Type: color texture

Default: 1

Description: The reflectivity of the surface.

`glass::Kt`

Type: color texture

Default: 1

Description: The transmissivity of the surface.

`glass::index`

Type: float texture

Default: 1.5

Description: The index of refraction.

`shinymetal::roughness`

Type: float texture

Default: 0.1

Description: The roughness of the surface.

`shinymetal::Ks`

Type: color texture

Default: 1

Description: The coefficient of glossy reflection.

`shinymetal::Kr`

Type: color texture

Default: 1

Description: The coefficient of specular reflection.

`substrate::Kd`

Type: color texture

Default: .5

Description: The coefficient of diffuse reflection.

substrate::Ks

> *Type:*   color texture
> *Default:*   .5
> *Description:*   The coefficient of specular reflection.

substrate::uroughness

> *Type:*   float texture
> *Default:*   0.1
> *Description:*   The roughness of the surface in the u direction.

substrate::vroughness

> *Type:*   float texture
> *Default:*   0.1
> *Description:*   The roughness of the surface in the v direction.

uber::Kd

> *Type:*   color texture
> *Default:*   1
> *Description:*   The coefficient of diffuse reflection.

uber::Ks

> *Type:*   color texture
> *Default:*   1
> *Description:*   The coefficient of glossy reflection.

uber::Kr

> *Type:*   color texture
> *Default:*   0
> *Description:*   The coefficient of specular reflection.

uber::roughness

> *Type:*   float texture
> *Default:*   0.1
> *Description:*   The roughness of the surface.

uber::opacity

> *Type:*   color texture
> *Default:*   1
> *Description:*   The opacity of the surface. Note that the uber material transmits light without refracting it.

C.3.8 TEXTURES

Texture

> *Arguments:*   "name" "type" "class" parameter-list
> *API Call:*   pbrtTexture()

The Texture statement creates a named texture of a particular type. Currently, the only types that are supported are color and float. See Figure C.1 for an example of how to use the Texture directive to create a texture and then bind it to one of the parameters of a material.

pbrtTexture() 895

Provided Plug-Ins

Name	Class
"bilerp"	BilerpTexture
"checkerboard"	Checkerboard2D
"checkerboard"	Checkerboard3D
"constant"	ConstantTexture
"dots"	DotsTexture
"fbm"	FBmTexture
"imagemap"	ImageTexture
"marble"	MarbleTexture
"mix"	MixTexture
"scale"	ScaleTexture
"uv"	UVTexture
"windy"	WindyTexture
"wrinkled"	WrinkledTexture

Common Parameters

Textures can be separated into three categories: any-D, 2D, and 3D. Any-D textures are ConstantTexture, ScaleTexture, and MixTexture. These kinds of textures do not have a specific dimensionality and have no common arguments.

2D textures use the (u, v) parametric coordinates on a surface for evaluation. They are BilerpTexture, ImageTexture, UVTexture, CheckerboardTexture, and DotsTexture. 2D textures have the following common parameters:

mapping

Type:	string
Default:	"uv"
Description:	A string specifying the kind of texture coordinate mapping to use. Legal values are: "uv", "spherical", "cylindrical", or "planar".

uscale
vscale

Type:	float
Default:	1
Description:	A scaling factor to be applied to the u and v texture coordinates, respectively. These parameters are only meaningful if the texture coordinate mapping type has been set to "uv".

udelta
vdelta

Type:	float
Default:	0
Description:	An offset to be applied to the u and v texture coordinates, respectively. These parameters are only meaningful if the texture coordinate mapping type has been set to "uv" or "planar".

```
v1
v2
```

Type:	vector
Default:	see description
Description:	v_1 and v_2 are two vectors that define a planar mapping. The defaults are $(1, 0, 0)$ and $(0, 1, 0)$, respectively. These parameters are only meaningful if the texture coordinate mapping type has been set to "planar".

3D textures use a texture space point location to evaluate themselves. The current transformation matrix at the time they are created gives the transformation from object space. They are CheckerboardTexture, FBmTexture, WrinkledTexture, MarbleTexture, and WindyTexture. Note that CheckerboardTexture is the only texture that can be either a 2D or 3D texture (see its plug-in specific parameter settings in the following). 3D textures have no common parameters.

Plug-In Specific Parameters

Most of the provided textures can generate either Spectrum or float values, which is why many of the following descriptions have the color/float type.

```
constant::value
```

Type:	color/float texture
Default:	1
Description:	The constant value of this texture.

```
scale::tex1
scale::tex2
```

Type:	color/float texture
Default:	1
Description:	These two textures will be multiplied together by the ScaleTexture.

```
mix::tex1
```

Type:	color/float texture
Default:	0
Description:	One of the two textures to be mixed.

```
mix::tex2
```

Type:	color/float texture
Default:	1
Description:	The other texture to be mixed. These two textures must be of the same type.

```
mix::amount
```

Type:	float texture
Default:	0.5
Description:	The amount to use when linearly interpolating between the two mix textures.

```
bilerp::v00
bilerp::v01
```

`bilerp::v10`
`bilerp::v11`

Type:	float/color
Default:	see description
Description:	The four values to be bilinearly interpolated between. They default to 0, 1, 0, and 1, respectively.

`imagemap::filename`

Type:	string
Default:	required—no default
Description:	The filename of the image to load. Currently pbrt only supports loading OpenEXR files as image textures.

`imagemap::wrap`

Type:	string
Default:	"repeat"
Description:	What to do with texture coordinates that fall outside the legal [0, 1] range. Legal values are "repeat", which simply tiles the texture; "black", which returns black when outside the legal range; and "clamp", which always returns the nearest border texel.

`imagemap::maxanisotropy`

Type:	float
Default:	8
Description:	The maximum elliptical eccentricity for the EWA algorithm.

`imagemap::trilinear`

Type:	bool
Default:	false
Description:	If true, perform trilinear interpolation when looking up pixel values. Otherwise, pbrt uses the EWA algorithm for texture filtering. EWA gives much better results, but is slower.

`checkerboard::dimension`

Type:	integer
Default:	2
Description:	Sets the dimension of the checkerboard texture. Legal values are 2 and 3.

`checkerboard::tex1`

Type:	color/float texture
Default:	1
Description:	The texture to use for even checks.

`checkerboard::tex2`

Type:	color/float texture
Default:	0
Description:	The texture to use for odd checks.

`checkerboard::aamode`

Type:	string
Default:	"closedform"
Description:	Set the antialiasing mode for the checkerboard texture. Legal values are "closedform", "supersample", or "none". This parameter is only legal for 2D checkerboards.

`dots::inside`
`dots::outside`

> *Type:*   color/float texture
> *Default:*   see description
> *Description:*   The textures to use for coloring the dots and the background. The defaults are 1 and 0, respectively.

`fbm::octaves`

> *Type:*   integer
> *Default:*   8
> *Description:*   The number of octaves of noise to use in spectral synthesis.

`fbm::roughness`

> *Type:*   float
> *Default:*   .5
> *Description:*   The "bumpiness" of the resulting texture.

`wrinkled::octaves`

> *Type:*   integer
> *Default:*   8
> *Description:*   The number of octaves of noise to use in spectral synthesis.

`wrinkled::roughness`

> *Type:*   float
> *Default:*   .5
> *Description:*   The "bumpiness" of the resulting texture.

`marble::octaves`

> *Type:*   integer
> *Default:*   8
> *Description:*   The number of octaves of noise to use in spectral synthesis.

`marble::roughness`

> *Type:*   float
> *Default:*   .5
> *Description:*   The "bumpiness" of the resulting texture.

`marble::scale`

> *Type:*   float
> *Default:*   1
> *Description:*   A scaling factor to apply to the noise function inputs.

`marble::variation`

> *Type:*   float
> *Default:*   0.2
> *Description:*   A scaling factor to apply to the noise function output.

C.3.9 VOLUMES

pbrtVolume() 898

`Volume`

> *Arguments:*   "name" parameter-list
> *API Call:*   pbrtVolume()

Provided Plug-Ins

Name	Class
"exponential"	ExponentialDensity
"homogeneous"	HomogeneousVolume

Common Parameters

sigma_a

Type:	color
Default:	0
Description:	The absorption cross section.

sigma_s

Type:	color
Default:	0
Description:	The scattering cross section.

g

Type:	float
Default:	0
Description:	The phase function asymmetry parameter.

Le

Type:	color
Default:	0
Description:	The volume's emission spectrum.

p0

Type:	point
Default:	0 0 0
Description:	One corner of the volume's bounding box.

p1

Type:	point
Default:	1 1 1
Description:	The other corner of the volume's bounding box.

Plug-In Specific Parameters

exponential::a
exponential::b

Type:	float
Default:	1
Description:	The parameters in the exponential volume's ae^{-bh} formula.

exponential::updir

Type:	vector
Default:	(0, 1, 0)
Description:	The "up" direction along which to compute height.

volumegrid::nx
volumegrid::ny
volumegrid::nz

Type:	integer
Default:	1
Description:	The number of voxels in the x, y, and z directions, respectively.

volumegrid::density
  Type: float[nx*ny*nz]
  Default: 0
  Description: The array of density values.

C.3.10 LIGHTS

LightSource
  Arguments: *"name" parameter-list*
  API Call: pbrtLightSource()

AreaLightSource
  Arguments: *"name" parameter-list*
  API Call: pbrtAreaLightSource()

Provided Plug-Ins

Name	Class
"area"	AreaLight
"distant"	DistantLight
"goniometric"	GonioPhotometricLight
"infinite"	InfiniteAreaLight
"point"	PointLight
"projection"	ProjectionLight
"spot"	SpotLight

Common Parameters

None

Plug-In Specific Parameters

area::L
  Type: color
  Default: 1 1 1
  Description: The color of the light.

area::nsamples
  Type: integer
  Default: 1
  Description: Suggested number of shadow samples to take when computing illumination from the light. (Integrators may use a value close to but not necessarily equal to this value or may ignore it completely.)

distant::L
  Type: color
  Default: 1 1 1
  Description: The color of the light.

distant::from
distant::to
  Type: point
  Default: see description
  Description: Two points defining the lighting vector. The defaults are (0, 0, 0) and (0, 0, 1), respectively. This gives a light that is pointing down the *z* axis.

`goniometric::I`

Type:	color
Default:	1 1 1
Description:	The color of the light.

`goniometric::mapname`

Type:	string
Default:	required—no default
Description:	The filename of the goniometric diagram to use for the lighting distribution.

`infinite::L`

Type:	color
Default:	1 1 1
Description:	The color of the light.

`infinite::nsamples`

Type:	integer
Default:	1
Description:	Suggested number of shadow samples to take when computing illumination from the light.

`infinite::mapname`

Type:	string
Default:	none
Description:	The environment map to use for the infinite area light. If this is not provided, the light will be a solid color.

`point::I`

Type:	color
Default:	1 1 1
Description:	The color of the light.

`point::from`

Type:	point
Default:	0 0 0
Description:	The location of the light.

`projection::I`

Type:	color
Default:	1 1 1
Description:	The color of the light.

`projection::fov`

Type:	float
Default:	45
Description:	The spread angle of the projected light, along the shorter image axis.

`projection::mapname`

Type:	string
Default:	required—no default
Description:	The image to project into the scene.

`spot::I`

Type:	color
Default:	1 1 1
Description:	The color of the light.

```
spot::from
```
```
spot::to
```
    Type: point
    Default: see description
    Description: Two points defining the lighting vector. The defaults are $(0, 0, 0)$ and $(0, 0, 1)$, respectively. This gives a light that is pointing down the *z* axis.

```
spot::coneangle
```
    Type: float
    Default: 30
    Description: The angle that the spotlight's cone makes with its primary axis.

```
spot::conedeltaangle
```
    Type: float
    Default: 5
    Description: The angle at which the spotlight intensity begins to fall off at the edges.

C.3.11 SURFACE INTEGRATORS

```
SurfaceIntegrator
```
    Arguments: *"name" parameter-list*
    API Call: pbrtSurfaceIntegrator()

Provided Plug-Ins

Name	Class
"directlighting"	DirectLighting
"irradiancecache"	IrradianceCache
"path"	PathIntegrator
"photonmap"	PhotonIntegrator
"whitted"	WhittedIntegrator

Common Parameters
None

Plug-In Specific Parameters
```
whitted::maxdepth
```
    Type: integer
    Default: 5
    Description: The maximum recursion depth.

```
directlighting::maxdepth
```
    Type: integer
    Default: 5
    Description: The maximum recursion depth.

```
directlighting::strategy
```
    Type: string
    Default: "all"
    Description: The strategy to use for sampling the lighting. Valid options are "all", which samples all the lights uniformly and averages their contribution, and "one", which chooses a single light uniformly at random.

DirectLighting 723
IrradianceCache 758
PathIntegrator 749
pbrtSurfaceIntegrator() 888
PhotonIntegrator 774
WhittedIntegrator 30

`path::maxdepth`
> *Type:*   integer
> *Default:*   5
> *Description:*   The maximum length of a path.

`photonmap::causticphotons`
> *Type:*   integer
> *Default:*   20,000
> *Description:*   The number of photons required to build the caustic photon map.

`photonmap::indirectphotons`
> *Type:*   integer
> *Default:*   100,000
> *Description:*   The number of photons required to build the indirect illumination map.

`photonmap::directphotons`
> *Type:*   integer
> *Default:*   100,000
> *Description:*   The number of photons required to build the direct illumination map.

`photonmap::nused`
> *Type:*   integer
> *Default:*   50
> *Description:*   The number of photons to use in density estimation.

`photonmap::maxdepth`
> *Type:*   integer
> *Default:*   5
> *Description:*   The maximum number of levels of specular reflection and refraction.

`photonmap::maxdist`
> *Type:*   float
> *Default:*   .1
> *Description:*   The maximum distance between a point being shaded and a photon that can contribute to that point.

`photonmap::finalgather`
> *Type:*   bool
> *Default:*   true
> *Description:*   If true, do a final gather when estimating the indirect illumination. Otherwise, just use the photon map at the hit point.

`photonmap::finalgathersamples`
> *Type:*   integer
> *Default:*   32
> *Description:*   Number of samples to use when performing the final gather.

`photonmap::directwithphotons`
> *Type:*   bool
> *Default:*   false
> *Description:*   If true, use the photon map to estimate the direct illumination.

`irradiancecache::maxerror`
> *Type:*   float
> *Default:*   .2
> *Description:*   Controls the maximum allowed estimated error from reusing a previously computed irradiance estimate.

`irradiancecache::maxspeculardepth`
> *Type:*   integer
> *Default:*   5
> *Description:* Maximum recursion depth for tracing specular reflection and refraction rays.

`irradiancecache::maxindirectdepth`
> *Type:*   integer
> *Default:*   3
> *Description:* Maximum recursion depth for tracing paths to compute irradiance estimates.

`irradiancecache::nsamples`
> *Type:*   integer
> *Default:*   4096
> *Description:* How many rays are used to estimate the irradiance value at a point.

C.3.12 VOLUME INTEGRATORS

`VolumeIntegrator`
> *Arguments:*   "name" parameter-list
> *API Call:*   pbrtVolumeIntegrator()

Provided Plug-Ins

Name	Class
"emission"	EmissionIntegrator
"single"	SingleScattering

Common Parameters

`stepsize`
> *Type:*   float
> *Default:*   1
> *Description:* The stepping distance along a ray when doing ray marching.

Plug-In Specific Parameters

None

⧄ INDEX OF FRAGMENTS

Bold numbers indicate the first page of a fragment definition, ***bold italic*** numbers indicate an extension of the definition, and roman numbers indicate a use of the fragment.

Σ INDEX OF CLASSES AND THEIR MEMBERS

Bold numbers indicate the page of a class definition. Class methods and fields are indented.

F INDEX OF MISCELLANEOUS IDENTIFIERS

Finally, this index covers functions, module-local variables, preprocessor definitions, and other miscellaneous identifiers used in the system.

References

Agarwal, S., R. Ramamoorthi, S. Belongie, and H. W. Jensen. 2003. Structured importance sampling of environment maps. *ACM Transactions on Graphics 22*(3), 605–12.

Aggarwal, A. 2002. Software caching vs. prefetching. In *Proceedings of the Third International Symposium on Memory Management*, pp. 157–62. ACM Press.

Agrawala, M., R. Ramamoorthi, A. Heirich, and L. Moll. 2000. Efficient image-based methods for rendering soft shadows. In *Proceedings of ACM SIGGRAPH 2000*, Computer Graphics Proceedings, Annual Conference Series, pp. 375–84.

Akenine-Möller, T. 2001. Fast 3D triangle-box overlap testing. *Journal of Graphics Tools 6*(1), 29–33.

Akenine-Möller, T., and E. Haines. 2002. *Real-Time Rendering*. Natick, Massachussetts: A. K. Peters.

Alexa, M. 2002. Linear combination of transformations. *ACM Transactions on Graphics 21*(3), 380–87.

Amanatides, J. 1984. Ray tracing with cones. In H. Christiansen (Ed.), *Computer Graphics (SIGGRAPH '84 Proceedings),* Volume 18, pp. 129–35.

Amanatides, J. 1992. Algorithms for the detection and elimination of specular aliasing. In *Graphics Interface '92*, pp. 86–93.

Amanatides, J., and D. P. Mitchell. 1990. Some regularization problems in ray tracing. In *Graphics Interface '90*, pp. 221–28.

Amanatides, J., and A. Woo. 1987. A fast voxel traversal algorithm for ray tracing. In *Eurographics '87*, pp. 3–10.

Anderson, S. 2004. *graphics.stanford.edu/~seander/bithacks.html.*

Anton, H. A., I. Bivens, and S. Davis. 2001. *Calculus* (7th ed.). New York: John Wiley & Sons.

Apodaca, A. A., and L. Gritz. 2000. *Advanced RenderMan: Creating CGI for Motion Pictures.* San Francisco: Morgan Kaufmann.

Appel, A. 1968. Some techniques for shading machine renderings of solids. In *AFIPS 1968 Spring Joint Computer Conference.*, Volume 32, pp. 37–45.

Arnaldi, B., T. Priol, and K. Bouatouch. 1987. A new space subdivision method for ray tracing CSG modelled scenes. *The Visual Computer 3*(2), 98–108.

Arvo, J. 1986. Backward ray tracing. *Developments in Ray Tracing, SIGGRAPH '86 Course Notes.*

Arvo, J. 1988. Linear-time voxel walking for octrees. *Ray Tracing News 12*(1).

Arvo, J. 1990. Transforming axis-aligned bounding boxes. In A. S. Glassner (Ed.), *Graphics Gems I*, pp. 548–50. San Diego: Academic Press.

Arvo, J. 1991. Classifying small sparce matrices. In J. Arvo (Ed.), *Graphics Gems II*, pp. 357–61. San Diego: Academic Press.

Arvo, J. 1993. Transfer equations in global illumination. In *Global Illumination, SIGGRAPH '93 Course Notes*, Volume 42.

Arvo, J. 1995. *Analytic Methods for Simulated Light Transport*. Ph.D. thesis, Yale University.

Arvo, J., and D. Kirk. 1987. Fast ray tracing by ray classification. In M. C. Stone (Ed.), *Computer Graphics (SIGGRAPH '87 Proceedings)*, Volume 21, pp. 55–64.

Arvo, J., and D. Kirk. 1990. Particle transport and image synthesis. *Computer Graphics (SIGGRAPH '90 Proceedings) 24*(4), 63–66.

Ashdown, I. 1993. Near-field photometry: a new approach. *Journal of the Illuminating Engineering Society 22*(1), 163–80.

Ashdown, I. 1994. *Radiosity: A Programmer's Perspective*. New York: John Wiley & Sons.

Ashikhmin, M. 2002. A tone mapping algorithm for high contrast images. In *The Proceedings of 13th Eurographics Workshop on Rendering*, Pisa, Italy, pp. 145–55.

Ashikhmin, M., S. Premoze, and P. S. Shirley. 2000. A microfacet-based BRDF generator. In *Proceedings of ACM SIGGRAPH 2000*, Computer Graphics Proceedings, Annual Conference Series, pp. 65–74. ACM Press.

Ashikhmin, M., and P. Shirley 2000. An anisotropic Phong light reflection model. Technical report UUCS-00-014, University of Utah.

Ashikhmin, M., and P. Shirley 2002. An anisotropic Phong BRDF model. *Journal of Graphics Tools 5*(2), 25–32.

Atkinson, K. 1993. *Elementary Numerical Analysis*. New York: John Wiley & Sons.

Badouel, D., and T. Priol. 1989. An efficient parallel ray tracing scheme for highly parallel architectures. In *Fifth Eurographics Workshop on Graphics Hardware*.

Bahar, E., and S. Chakrabarti. 1987. Full-wave theory applied to computer-aided graphics for 3D objects. *IEEE Computer Graphics and Applications 7*(7), 46–60.

Banks, D. C. 1994. Illumination in diverse codimensions. In *Proceedings of SIGGRAPH '94*, Computer Graphics Proceedings, Annual Conference Series, pp. 327–34.

Barkans, A. C. 1997. High-quality rendering using the Talisman architecture. In *1997 SIGGRAPH/Eurographics Workshop on Graphics Hardware*, pp. 79–88.

Barzel, R. 1997. Lighting controls for computer cinematography. *Journal of Graphics Tools 2*(1), 1–20.

Becker, B. G., and N. L. Max. 1993. Smooth transitions between bump rendering algorithms. In *Proceedings of SIGGRAPH '93*, Computer Graphics Proceedings, Annual Conference Series, pp. 183–90.

Beckmann, P., and A. Spizzichino. 1963. *The Scattering of Electromagnetic Waves from Rough Surfaces*. New York: Permagon.

Berger, E. D., B. G. Zorn, and K. S. McKinley. 2001. Composing high-performance memory allocators. In *SIGPLAN Conference on Programming Language Design and Implementation*, pp. 114–24.

Berger, E. D., B. G. Zorn, and K. S. McKinley. 2002. Reconsidering custom memory allocation. In *Proceedings of ACM OOPSLA 2002*.

Betrisey, C., J. F. Blinn, B. Dresevic, B. Hill, G. Hitchcock, B. Keely, D. P. Mitchell, J. C. Platt, and T. Whitted. 2000. Displaced filtering for patterned displays. *Society for Information Display International Symposium. Digest of Technical Papers 31*, 296–99.

Bhate, N., and A. Tokuta. 1992. Photorealistic volume rendering of media with directional scattering. In *Proceedings of the Third Eurographics Rendering Workshop*, pp. 227–45.

Bjorke, K. 2001. Using Maya with RenderMan on Final Fantasy: The Spirits Within. *SIGGRAPH 2001 RenderMan Course Notes*.

Blasi, P., B. L. Saëc, and C. Schlick. 1993. A rendering algorithm for discrete volume density objects. *Computer Graphics Forum (Proceedings of Eurographics '93) 12*(3), 201–10.

Blinn, J. F. 1977. Models of light reflection for computer synthesized pictures. In *Computer Graphics (SIGGRAPH '77 Proceedings)*, Volume 11, pp. 192–98.

Blinn, J. F. 1978. Simulation of wrinkled surfaces. In *Computer Graphics (SIGGRAPH '78 Proceedings)*, Volume 12, pp. 286–92.

Blinn, J. F. 1982a. A generalization of algebraic surface drawing. *ACM Transactions on Graphics 1*(3), 235–56.

Blinn, J. F. 1982b. Light reflection functions for simulation of clouds and dusty surfaces. *Computer Graphics 16*(3), 21–29.

Blinn, J. F., and M. E. Newell. 1976. Texture and reflection in computer generated images. *Communications of the ACM 19*, 542–46.

Bolin, M. R., and G. W. Meyer. 1995. A frequency based ray tracer. In *Proceedings of SIGGRAPH '95*, Computer Graphics Proceedings, Annual Conference Series, pp. 409–18.

Bolin, M. R., and G. W. Meyer. 1998. A perceptually based adaptive sampling algorithm. In *Proceedings of SIGGRAPH '98*, Computer Graphics Proceedings, Annual Conference Series, pp. 299–310.

Bolz, J., and P. Schröder. 2002. Rapid evaluation of Catmull-Clark subdivision surfaces. In *Web3D 2002 Symposium*.

Booth, T. E. 1986. A Monte Carlo learning/biasing experiment with intelligent random numbers. *Nuclear Science and Engineering 92*, 465–81.

Bracewell, R. N. 2000. *The Fourier Transform and Its Applications*. New York: McGraw-Hill.

Bronsvoort, W. F., and F. Klok. 1985. Ray tracing generalized cylinders. *ACM Transactions on Graphics 4*(4), 291–303.

Buck, R. C. 1978. *Advanced Calculus*. New York: McGraw-Hill.

Buhler, J., and D. Wexler. 2002. A phenomenological model for Bokeh rendering. *SIGGRAPH Sketch*. See also *www.flarg.com/bokeh.html*.

Cabral, B., N. Max, and R. Springmeyer. 1987. Bidirectional reflection functions from surface bump maps. In *Computer Graphics (SIGGRAPH '87 Proceedings)*, Volume 21, pp. 273–81.

Calder, B., K. Chandra, S. John, and T. Austin. 1998. Cache-conscious data placement. In *Proceedings of the Eighth International Conference on Architectural Support for Programming Languages and Operating Systems (ASPLOS-VIII)*, San Jose.

Cant, R. J., and P. A. Shrubsole 2000. Texture potential MIP mapping, a new high-quality texture antialiasing algorithm. *ACM Transactions on Graphics 19*(3), 164–84.

Carr, N., J. D. Hall, and J. Hart. 2002. The ray engine. In *Proceedings of Graphics Hardware 2002* (September).

Catmull, E., and J. Clark. 1978. Recursively generated B-spline surfaces on arbitrary topological meshes. *Computer-Aided Design 10*, 350–55.

Cazals, F., G. Drettakis, and C. Puech. 1995. Filtering, clustering and hierarchy construction: a new solution for ray-tracing complex scenes. *Computer Graphics Forum 14*(3), 371–82.

Chalmers, A., T. Davis, and E. Reinhard. 2002. *Practical Parallel Rendering*. Natick, Massachusetts: A. K. Peters.

Chandrasekhar, S. 1960. *Radiative Transfer*. New York: Dover Publications. Originally published by Oxford University Press, 1950.

Chilimbi, T. M., B. Davidson, and J. R. Larus. 1999. Cache-conscious structure definition. In *SIGPLAN Conference on Programming Language Design and Implementation*, pp. 13–24.

Chilimbi, T. M., M. D. Hill, and J. R. Larus. 1999. Cache-conscious structure layout. In *SIGPLAN Conference on Programming Language Design and Implementation*, pp. 1–12.

Chiu, K., M. Herf, P. Shirley, S. Swamy, C. Wang, and K. Zimmerman. 1993. Spatially nonuniform scaling functions for high contrast images. In *Graphics Interface '93*, Toronto, Ontario, Canada, pp. 245–53. Canadian Information Processing Society.

Chiu, K., P. Shirley, and C. Wang. 1994. Multi-jittered sampling. In P. Heckbert (Ed.), *Graphics Gems IV*, pp. 370–74. San Diego: Academic Press.

Christensen, P. H. 1999. Faster photon map global illumination. *Journal of Graphics Tools 4*(3), 1–10.

Christensen, P. H. 2003. Adjoints and importance in rendering: an overview. *IEEE Transactions on Visualization and Computer Graphics 9*(3), 329–40.

Christensen, P. H., D. M. Laur, J. Fong, W. L. Wooten, and D. Batali. 2003. Ray differentials and multiresolution geometry caching for distribution ray tracing in complex scenes. In *Computer Graphics Forum (Eurographics 2003 Conference Proceedings)*, pp. 543–52.

Chvolson, O. D. 1890. Grundzüge einer matematischen Theorie der inneren Diffusion des Lichtes. *Izv. Peterburg. Academii Nauk 33*, 221–65.

Clark, J. H. 1976. Hierarchical geometric models for visible surface algorithms. *Communications of the ACM 19*(10), 547–54.

Cleary, J. G., B. M. Wyvill, R. Vatti, and G. M. Birtwistle. 1983. Design and analysis of a parallel ray tracing computer. In *Graphics Interface '83*, pp. 33–38.

Cleary, J. G., and G. Wyvill. 1988. Analysis of an algorithm for fast ray tracing using uniform space subdivision. *The Visual Computer 4*(2), 65–83.

Cohen, J., A. Varshney, D. Manocha, G. Turk, H. Weber, P. Agarwal, F. P. Brooks Jr., and W. Wright. 1996. Simplification envelopes. In *Proceedings of SIGGRAPH '96*, Computer Graphics Proceedings, Annual Conference Series, pp. 119–28.

Cohen, M., and J. Wallace. 1993. *Radiosity and Realistic Image Synthesis*. San Diego: Academic Press Professional.

Cohen, M. F., J. Shade, S. Hiller, and O. Deussen. 2003. Wang tiles for image and texture generation. *ACM Transactions on Graphics 22*(3), 287–94.

Collins, S. 1994. Adaptive splatting for specular to diffuse light transport. In *Fifth Eurographics Workshop on Rendering*, Darmstadt, Germany, pp. 119–35.

Cook, R. L. 1984. Shade trees. In H. Christiansen (Ed.), *Computer Graphics (SIGGRAPH '84 Proceedings)*, Volume 18, pp. 223–31.

Cook, R. L. 1986. Stochastic sampling in computer graphics. *ACM Transactions on Graphics 5*(1), 51–72.

Cook, R. L., L. Carpenter, and E. Catmull. 1987. The REYES image rendering architecture. In *Computer Graphics (Proceedings of SIGGRAPH '87)*, Anaheim, California, pp. 95–102.

Cook, R. L., T. Porter, and L. Carpenter. 1984. Distributed ray tracing. In *Computer Graphics (SIGGRAPH '84 Proceedings)*, Volume 18, pp. 137–45.

Cook, R. L., and K. E. Torrance. 1981. A reflectance model for computer graphics. In *Computer Graphics (SIGGRAPH '81 Proceedings)*, Volume 15, pp. 307–16.

Cook, R. L., and K. E. Torrance. 1982. A reflectance model for computer graphics. *ACM Transactions on Graphics 1*(1), 7–24.

Crow, F. C. 1977. The aliasing problem in computer-generated shaded images. *Communications of the ACM 20*(11), 799–805.

Crow, F. C. 1984. Summed-area tables for texture mapping. In *Computer Graphics (Proceedings of SIGGRAPH '84)*, Volume 18, pp. 207–12.

Dachsbacher, C., and M. Stamminger. 2003. Translucent shadow maps. In *Proceedings of the 13th Eurographics Workshop on Rendering*, pp. 197–201. Eurographics Association.

Dana, K. J., B. van Ginneken, S. K. Nayar, and J. J. Koenderink. 1999. Reflectance and texture of real-world surfaces. *ACM Transactions on Graphics 18*(1), 1–34.

Danskin, J., and P. Hanrahan. 1992. Fast algorithms for volume ray tracing. In *1992 Workshop on Volume Visualization*, pp. 91–98.

de Berg, M., M. van Kreveld, M. Overmars, and O. Schwarzkopf. 2000. *Computational Geometry: Algorithms and Applications*. New York: Springer-Verlag.

Debevec, P. 1998. Rendering synthetic objects into real scenes: bridging traditional and image-based graphics with global illumination and high dynamic range photography. In *Proceedings of SIGGRAPH '98*, Computer Graphics Proceedings, Annual Conference Series, Orlando, Florida, pp. 189–98. Reading, Massachusetts: Addison-Wesley.

Deering, M. F. 1995. Geometry compression. In *Proceedings of SIGGRAPH '95*, Computer Graphics Proceedings, Annual Conference Series, pp. 13–20.

DeRose, T. D. 1989. A coordinate-free approach to geometric programming. *Math for SIGGRAPH. SIGGRAPH Course Notes # 23*. Also available as Technical Report No. 89-09-16, Department of Computer Science and Engineering, University of Washington, Seattle.

Deussen, O., P. M. Hanrahan, B. Lintermann, R. Mech, M. Pharr, and P. Prusinkiewicz. 1998. Realistic modeling and rendering of plant ecosystems. In *Proceedings of SIGGRAPH '98*, Computer Graphics Proceedings, Annual Conference Series, pp. 275–86.

Devlin, K., A. Chalmers, A. Wilkie, and W. Purgathofer. 2002. Tone reproduction and physically based spectral rendering. In D. Fellner and R. Scopignio (Eds.), *Proceedings of Eurographics 2002*, pp. 101–23. The Eurographics Association.

de Voogt, E., A. van der Helm, and W. F. Bronsvoort. 2000. Ray tracing deformed generalized cylinders. *The Visual Computer 16*(3–4), 197–207.

Dippé, M. A. Z., and E. H. Wold. 1985. Antialiasing through stochastic sampling. In B. A. Barsky (Ed.), *Computer Graphics (SIGGRAPH '85 Proceedings)*, Volume 19, pp. 69–78.

Dobkin, D. P., D. Eppstein, and D. P. Mitchell. 1996. Computing the discrepancy with applications to supersampling patterns. *ACM Transactions on Graphics 15*(4), 354–76.

Dobkin, D. P., and D. P. Mitchell. 1993. Random-edge discrepancy of supersampling patterns. In *Graphics Interface '93*, Toronto, Ontario, pp. 62–69. Canadian Information Processing Society.

Doo, D., and M. Sabin. 1978. Behaviour of recursive division surfaces near extraordinary points. *Computer-Aided Design 10*, 356–60.

Dorsey, J., A. Edelman, J. Legakis, H. W. Jensen, and H. K. Pedersen. 1999. Modeling and rendering of weathered stone. In *Proceedings of SIGGRAPH '99*, Computer Graphics Proceedings, Annual Conference Series, pp. 225–34.

Dorsey, J., H. K. Pedersen, and P. M. Hanrahan. 1996. Flow and changes in appearance. In *Proceedings of SIGGRAPH '96*, Computer Graphics Proceedings, Annual Conference Series, pp. 411–20.

Dorsey, J. O., F. X. Sillion, and D. P. Greenberg. 1991. Design and simulation of opera lighting and projection effects. In *Computer Graphics (Proceedings of SIGGRAPH '91)*, Volume 25, pp. 41–50.

Drebin, R. A., L. Carpenter, and P. Hanrahan. 1988. Volume rendering. In *Computer Graphics (Proceedings of SIGGRAPH '88)*, Volume 22, pp. 65–74.

Driemeyer, T., and R. Herken. 2002. *Programming mental ray*. Wien: Springer-Verlag.

Duff, T. 1985. Compositing 3-d rendered images. In *Computer Graphics (Proceedings of SIGGRAPH '85)*, Volume 19, pp. 41–44.

Dungan, W. Jr., A. Stenger, and G. Sutty. 1978. Texture tile considerations for raster graphics. In *Computer Graphics (Proceedings of SIGGRAPH '78)*, Volume 12, pp. 130–34.

Durand, F., and J. Dorsey. 2002. Fast bilateral filtering for the display of high-dynamic-range images. *ACM Transactions on Graphics 21*(3), 257–66.

Dutré, P. 2003. Global illumination compendium. *www.cs.kuleuven.ac.be/˜phil/GI/*.

Dutré, P., P. Bekaert, and K. Bala. 2003. *Advanced Global Illumination*. Natick, Massachusetts: A. K. Peters.

Eberly, D. H. 2001. *3D Game Engine Design: A Practical Approach to Real-Time Computer Graphics*. San Francisco: Morgan Kaufmann.

Ebert, D., F. K. Musgrave, D. Peachey, K. Perlin, and S. Worley. 2003. *Texturing and Modeling: A Procedural Approach*. San Francisco: Morgan Kaufmann.

Ericson, C. 2004. *Real-Time Collision Detection*. Morgan Kaufmann Series in Interactive 3D Technology. San Francisco: Morgan Kaufmann.

Fairchild, M. D., and D. R. Wyble. 1998. Colorimetric characterization of the Apple studio display (flat panel LCD). Technical report, RIT Munsell Color Science Laboratory, *http://www.cis.rit.edu/research/mcsl/research/reports.shtml*.

Fante, R. L. 1981. Relationship between radiative-transport theory and Maxwell's equations in dielectric media. *Journal of the Optical Society of America 71*(4), 460-468.

Fedkiw, R., J. Stam, and H. W. Jensen. 2001. Visual simulation of smoke. In *Proceedings of ACM SIGGRAPH 2001*, Computer Graphics Proceedings, Annual Conference Series, pp. 15–22.

Feibush, E. A., M. Levoy, and R. L. Cook. 1980. Synthetic texturing using digital filters. In *Computer Graphics (Proceedings of SIGGRAPH '80)*, Volume 14, pp. 294–301.

Fernandez, S., K. Bala, and D. P. Greenberg. 2002. Local illumination environments for direct lighting acceleration. In *Rendering Techniques 2002: 13th Eurographics Workshop on Rendering*, pp. 7–14.

Ferwerda, J. A. 2001. Elements of early vision for computer graphics. *IEEE Computer Graphics and Applications 21*(5), 22–33.

Ferwerda, J. A., S. Pattanaik, P. S. Shirley, and D. P. Greenberg. 1996. A model of visual adaptation for realistic image synthesis. In *Proceedings of SIGGRAPH '96*, Computer Graphics Proceedings, Annual Conference Series, New Orleans, Louisiana, pp. 249–58.

Ferwerda, J. A., S. N. Pattanaik, P. S. Shirley, and D. P. Greenberg. 1997. A model of visual masking for computer graphics. In *Proceedings of SIGGRAPH '97*, Computer Graphics Proceedings, Annual Conference Series, Los Angeles, California, pp. 143–52.

Fishman, G. S. 1996. *Monte Carlo: Concepts, Algorithms, and Applications*. New York: Springer-Verlag.

Fleischer, K., D. Laidlaw, B. Currin, and A. H. Barr. 1995. Cellular texture generation. In *Proceedings of SIGGRAPH '95*, Computer Graphics Proceedings, Annual Conference Series, pp. 239–48.

Foley, J. D., A. van Dam, S. K. Feiner, and J. F. Hughes. 1990. *Computer Graphics: Principles and Practice*. Reading, Massachusetts: Addison-Wesley.

Fournier, A. 1992. Normal distribution functions and multiple surfaces. In *Graphics Interface '92 Workshop on Local Illumination*, pp. 45–52.

Fournier, A., and E. Fiume. 1988. Constant-time filtering with space-variant kernels. In J. Dill (Ed.), *Computer Graphics (SIGGRAPH '88 Proceedings)*, Volume 22, pp. 229–38.

Fournier, A., D. Fussel, and L. Carpenter. 1982. Computer rendering of stochastic models. *Communications of the ACM 25*(6), 371–84.

Fraser, C., and D. Hanson. 1995. *A Retargetable C Compiler: Design and Implementation*. Reading, Massachusetts: Addison-Wesley.

Friedel, I., and A. Keller. 2000. Fast generation of randomized low discrepancy point sets. In *Monte Carlo and Quasi-Monte Carlo Methods 2000*, pp. 257–73. Berlin: Springer-Verlag.

Fujimoto, A., T. Tanaka, and K. Iwata. 1986. Arts: accelerated ray-tracing system. *IEEE Computer Graphics and Applications 6*(4), 16–26.

Gardner, G. Y. 1984. Simulation of natural scenes using textured quadric surfaces. In H. Christiansen (Ed.), *Computer Graphics (SIGGRAPH '84 Proceedings)*, Volume 18, pp. 11–20.

Gardner, G. Y. 1985. Visual simulation of clouds. In *Computer Graphics (Proceedings of SIGGRAPH '85)*, Volume 19, pp. 297–303.

Gardner, R. P., H. K. Choi, M. Mickael, A. M. Yacout, Y. Yin, and K. Verghese. 1987. Algorithms for forcing scattered radiation to spherical, planar circular, and right circular cylindrical detectors for Monte Carlo simulation. *Nuclear Science and Engineering 95*, 245–56.

Gershbein, R., and P. M. Hanrahan. 2000. A fast relighting engine for interactive cinematic lighting design. In *Proceedings of ACM SIGGRAPH 2000*, Computer Graphics Proceedings, Annual Conference Series, pp. 353–58.

Gershun, A. 1939. The light field. *Journal of Mathematics and Physics 18*, 51–151.

Gibson, J. E., and M. D. Fairchild. 2000. Colorimetric characterization of three computer displays (LCD and CRT). Technical report, RIT Munsell Color Science Laboratory, *www.cis.rit.edu/research/mcsl/research/reports.shtml*.

Glassner, A. 1984. Space subdivision for fast ray tracing. *IEEE Computer Graphics and Applications 4*(10), 15–22.

Glassner, A. (Ed.) 1989a. *An Introduction to Ray Tracing*. San Diego: Academic Press.

Glassner, A. 1989b. How to derive a spectrum from an RGB triplet. *IEEE Computer Graphics and Applications 9*(4), 95–99.

Glassner, A. 1993. Spectrum: an architecture for image synthesis, research, education, and practice. In *Developing Large-Scale Graphics Software Toolkits, SIGGRAPH '93 Course Notes*, Volume 3, pp. 1-14–1-43.

Glassner, A. 1995. *Principles of Digital Image Synthesis*. San Francisco: Morgan Kaufmann.

Glassner, A. 1999. An open and shut case. *IEEE Computer Graphics and Applications 19*(3), 82–92.

Goldman, D. B. 1997. Fake fur rendering. In *Proceedings of SIGGRAPH '97*, Computer Graphics Proceedings, Annual Conference Series, pp. 127–34.

Goldman, R. 1985. Illicit expressions in vector algebra. *ACM Transactions on Graphics 4*(3), 223–43.

Goldsmith, J., and J. Salmon. 1987. Automatic creation of object hierarchies for ray tracing. *IEEE Computer Graphics and Applications 7*(5), 14–20.

Goldstein, R. A., and R. Nagel. 1971. 3-D visual simulation. *Simulation 16*(1), 25–31.

Gortler, S. J., R. Grzeszczuk, R. Szeliski, and M. F. Cohen. 1996. The lumigraph. In *Proceedings of SIGGRAPH '96*, Computer Graphics Proceedings, Annual Conference Series, pp. 43–54.

Gray, A. 1993. *Modern Differential Geometry of Curves and Surfaces*. Boca Raton, Florida: CRC Press.

Green, S. A., and D. J. Paddon. 1989. Exploiting coherence for multiprocessor ray tracing. *IEEE Computer Graphics and Applications 9*(6), 12–26.

Greenberg, D. P., K. E. Torrance, P. S. Shirley, J. R. Arvo, J. A. Ferwerda, S. Pattanaik, E. P. F. Lafortune, B. Walter, S.-C. Foo, and B. Trumbore. 1997. A framework for realistic image synthesis. In *Proceedings of SIGGRAPH '97*, Computer Graphics Proceedings, Annual Conference Series, pp. 477–94.

Greene, N. 1986. Environment mapping and other applications of world projections. *IEEE Computer Graphics and Applications 6*(11), 21–29.

Greene, N., and P. S. Heckbert. 1986. Creating raster Omnimax images from multiple perspective views using the elliptical weighted average filter. *IEEE Computer Graphics and Applications 6*(6), 21–27.

Gritz, L., and J. K. Hahn. 1996. BMRT: a global illumination implementation of the RenderMan standard. *Journal of Graphics Tools 1*(3), 29–47.

Grunwald, D., B. G. Zorn, and R. Henderson. 1993. Improving the cache locality of memory allocation. In *SIGPLAN Conference on Programming Language Design and Implementation*, pp. 177–86.

Haines, E. A. 1987. A proposal for standard graphics environments. *IEEE Computer Graphics and Applications 7*(11), 3–5.

Haines, E. A. 1994. Point in polygon strategies. In P. Heckbert (Ed.), *Graphics Gems IV*, pp. 24–46. San Diego: Academic Press.

Haines, E. A., and D. P. Greenberg. 1986. The light buffer: a shadow testing accelerator. *IEEE Computer Graphics and Applications 6*(9), 6–16.

Haines, E. A., and J. R. Wallace. 1994. Shaft culling for efficient ray-traced radiosity. In *Second Eurographics Workshop on Rendering (Photorealistic Rendering in Computer Graphics)*. Also in *SIGGRAPH 1991 Frontiers in Rendering Course Notes*.

Hakura, Z. S., and A. Gupta. 1997. The design and analysis of a cache architecture for texture mapping. In *Proceedings of the 24th International Symposium on Computer Architecture*, Denver, Colorado, pp. 108–20.

Hall, R. 1989. *Illumination and Color in Computer Generated Imagery*. New York: Springer-Verlag.

Hall, R. 1999. Comparing spectral color computation methods. *IEEE Computer Graphics and Applications 19*(4), 36–46.

Hall, R. A., and D. P. Greenberg. 1983. A testbed for realistic image synthesis. *IEEE Computer Graphics and Applications 3*, 10–20.

Hammersley, J., and D. Handscomb. 1964. *Monte Carlo Methods*. New York: John Wiley.

Hanrahan, P. 1983. Ray tracing algebraic surfaces. In *Computer Graphics (Proceedings of SIGGRAPH '83)*, Volume 17, pp. 83–90.

Hanrahan, P. 2002. Why is graphics hardware so fast? *graphics.stanford.edu/~hanrahan/talks/why*.

Hanrahan, P., and W. Krueger. 1993. Reflection from layered surfaces due to subsurface scattering. In *Computer Graphics (SIGGRAPH '93 Proceedings)*, pp. 165–74.

Hanrahan, P., and J. Lawson. 1990. A language for shading and lighting calculations. In F. Baskett (Ed.), *Computer Graphics (SIGGRAPH '90 Proceedings)*, Volume 24, pp. 289–98.

Hansen, J. E., and L. D. Travis. 1974. Light scattering in planetary atmospheres. *Space Science Reviews 16*, 527–610.

Hao, X., T. Baby, and A. Varshney. 2003. Interactive subsurface scattering for translucent meshes. In *ACM Symposium on Interactive 3D Graphics*, pp. 75–82.

Hart, D., P. Dutré, and D. P. Greenberg. 1999. Direct illumination with lazy visibility evaluation. In *Proceedings of SIGGRAPH '99*, Computer Graphics Proceedings, Annual Conference Series, pp. 147–54.

Hart, J. C. 1996. Sphere tracing: a geometric method for the antialiased ray tracing of implicit surfaces. *The Visual Computer 12*(9), 527–45.

Hart, J. C., D. J. Sandin, and L. H. Kauffman. 1989. Ray tracing deterministic 3-d fractals. In *Computer Graphics (Proceedings of SIGGRAPH '89)*, Volume 23, pp. 289–96.

Havran, V., and J. Bittner. 2002. On improving kd-trees for ray shooting. In *Proceedings of WSCG 2002 Conference*, pp. 209–17.

He, X. D., K. E. Torrance, F. X. Sillion, and D. P. Greenberg. 1991. A comprehensive physical model for light reflection. In T. W. Sederberg (Ed.), *Computer Graphics (SIGGRAPH '91 Proceedings)*, Volume 25, pp. 175–86.

Heckbert, P. 1984. The mathematics of quadric surface rendering and SOID. 3-D Technical Memo, New York Institute of Technology Computer Graphics Lab.

Heckbert, P. 1989. Image zooming source code. *www-2.cs.cmu.edu/~ph/src/zoom/*.

Heckbert, P. S. 1986. Survey of texture mapping. *IEEE Computer Graphics and Applications 6*(11), 56–67.

Heckbert, P. S. 1987. Ray tracing JELL-O brand gelatin. In M. C. Stone (Ed.), *Computer Graphics (SIGGRAPH '87 Proceedings)*, Volume 21, pp. 73–74.

Heckbert, P. S. 1989. Fundamentals of texture mapping and image warping. M.S. thesis, Department of Electrical Engineering and Computer Science, University of California, Berkeley.

Heckbert, P. 1990a. What are the coordinates of a pixel? In A. S. Glassner (Ed.), *Graphics Gems I*, pp. 246–48. San Diego: Academic Press.

Heckbert, P. S. 1990b. Adaptive radiosity textures for bidirectional ray tracing. In *Computer Graphics (Proceedings of SIGGRAPH '90)*, Volume 24, pp. 145–54.

Heckbert, P. S., and P. Hanrahan. 1984. Beam tracing polygonal objects. In *Computer Graphics (Proceedings of SIGGRAPH '84)*, Volume 18, pp. 119–27.

Heidrich, W., and H.-P. Seidel. 1998. Ray-tracing procedural displacement shaders. In *Graphics Interface '98*, pp. 8–16.

Henyey, L. G., and J. L. Greenstein. 1941. Diffuse radiation in the galaxy. *Astrophysical Journal 93*, 70–83.

Herf, M., and S. Kotay. 2000. Know your FPU. *www.stereopsis.com/FPU.html*.

Hery, C. 2003. Implementing a skin BSSRDF. *SIGGRAPH 2003 RenderMan Course Notes*.

Hey, H., and W. Purgathofer. 2002. Importance sampling with hemispherical particle footprints. In A. Chalmers (Ed.), *Proceedings of the 18th Spring Conference on Computer Graphics*.

Hiller, S., O. Deussen, and A. Keller. 2001. Tiled blue noise samples. In T. Ertl, B. Girod, G. Greiner, H. Niemann, and H.-P. Seidel (Eds.), *Proceedings of Vision, Modeling and Visualization*.

Hoffmann, C. M. 1989. *Geometric and Solid Modeling: An Introduction*. San Francisco: Morgan Kaufmann.

Hoppe, H., T. DeRose, T. Duchamp, M. Halstead, H. Jin, J. McDonald, J. Schweitzer, and W. Stuetzle. 1994. Piecewise smooth surface reconstruction. In *Proceedings of SIGGRAPH '94*, Computer Graphics Proceedings, Annual Conference Series, Orlando, Florida, pp. 295–302.

Hurley, J., A. Kapustin, A. Reshetov, and A. Soupikov. 2002. Fast ray tracing for modern general purpose CPU. In *Proceedings of GraphiCon 2002*.

Igehy, H. 1999. Tracing ray differentials. In *Proceedings of SIGGRAPH '99*, Computer Graphics Proceedings, Annual Conference Series, pp. 179–86.

Igehy, H., M. Eldridge, and K. Proudfoot. 1998. Prefetching in a texture cache architecture. In *1998 SIGGRAPH/Eurographics Workshop on Graphics Hardware*, pp. 133–42.

Igehy, H., M. Eldridge, and P. Hanrahan. 1999. Parallel texture caching. In *1999 SIG-GRAPH/Eurographics Workshop on Graphics Hardware*, pp. 95–106.

Illuminating Engineering Society of North America. 2002. IESNA standard file format for electronic transfer of photometric data. BSR/IESNA Publication LM-63-2002. *www.iesna.org*.

Illuminating Engineering Society of North America Computer Committee. 1986. IES recommended standard file format for electronic transfer of photometric data. IES LM-63-1986.

Immel, D. S., M. F. Cohen, and D. P. Greenberg. 1986. A radiosity method for non-diffuse environments. In *Computer Graphics (SIGGRAPH '86 Proceedings)*, Volume 20, pp. 133–42.

Institute of Electrical and Electronic Engineers. 1985. IEEE standard 754-1985 for binary floating-point arithmetic. Reprinted in *SIGPLAN 22*(2) 9–25.

Jackson, W. H. 1910. The solution of an integral equation occurring in the theory of radiation. *Bulletin of the American Mathematical Society 16*, 473–75.

Jansen, F. W. 1986. Data structures for ray tracing. In L. R. A. Kessener, F. J. Peters, and M. L. P. Lierop (Eds.), *Data Structures for Raster Graphics, Workshop Proceedings*, pp. 57–73. New York: Springer-Verlag.

Jensen, H. W. 1995. Importance driven path tracing using the photon map. In *Eurographics Rendering Workshop 1995*, pp. 326–35.

Jensen, H. W. 1996a. Global illumination using photon maps. In X. Pueyo and P. Schröder (Eds.), *Eurographics Rendering Workshop 1996*, pp. 21–30.

Jensen, H. W. 1996b. Rendering caustics on non-Lambertian surfaces. In *Graphics Interface '96*, pp. 116–21.

Jensen, H. W. 1997. Rendering caustics on non-Lambertian surfaces. *Computer Graphics Forum 16*(1), 57–64.

Jensen, H. W. 2001. *Realistic Image Synthesis Using Photon Mapping*. Natick, Massachusetts: A. K. Peters.

Jensen, H. W., J. Arvo, P. Dutré, A. Keller, A. Owen, M. Pharr, and P. Shirley. 2003. Monte Carlo ray tracing. *SIGGRAPH 2003 Course,* San Diego.

Jensen, H. W., J. Arvo, M. Fajardo, P. Hanrahan, D. Mitchell, M. Pharr, and P. Shirley. 2001. State of the art in Monte Carlo ray tracing for realistic image synthesis. *SIGGRAPH 2001 Course 29,* Los Angeles.

Jensen, H. W., and J. Buhler. 2002. A rapid hierarchical rendering technique for translucent materials. *ACM Transactions on Graphics 21*(3), 576–81.

Jensen, H. W., and P. H. Christensen. 1998. Efficient simulation of light transport in scenes with participating media using photon maps. In M. Cohen (Ed.), *SIGGRAPH '98 Conference Proceedings*, Annual Conference Series, pp. 311–20. Reading, Massachusetts: Addison-Wesley.

Jensen, H. W., S. R. Marschner, M. Levoy, and P. Hanrahan. 2001. A practical model for subsurface light transport. In *Proceedings of ACM SIGGRAPH 2001*, Computer Graphics Proceedings, Annual Conference Series, pp. 511–18.

Jevans, D., and B. Wyvill. 1989. Adaptive voxel subdivision for ray tracing. In *Graphics Interface '89*, pp. 164–172.

Johnstone, M. S., and P. R. Wilson. 1999. The memory fragmentation problem: solved? *ACM SIGPLAN Notices 34*(3), 26–36.

Kainz, F., R. Bogart, and D. Hess. 2002. OpenEXR image file format. *www.openexr.com.*

Kajiya, J. T. 1982. Ray tracing parametric patches. In *Computer Graphics (SIGGRAPH 1982 Conference Proceedings)*, pp. 245–54.

Kajiya, J. T. 1983. New techniques for ray tracing procedurally defined objects. In *Computer Graphics (Proceedings of SIGGRAPH '83)*, Volume 17, pp. 91–102.

Kajiya, J. T. 1985. Anisotropic reflection models. In *Computer Graphics (Proceedings of SIGGRAPH '85)*, Volume 19, pp. 15–21.

Kajiya, J. T. 1986. The rendering equation. In D. C. Evans and R. J. Athay (Eds.), *Computer Graphics (SIGGRAPH '86 Proceedings)*, Volume 20, pp. 143–50.

Kajiya, J. T., and T. L. Kay. 1989. Rendering fur with three dimensional textures. In *Computer Graphics (Proceedings of SIGGRAPH '89)*, Volume 23, pp. 271–80.

Kajiya, J., and M. Ullner. 1981. Filtering high quality text for display on raster scan devices. In *Computer Graphics (Proceedings of SIGGRAPH '81)*, pp. 7–15.

Kajiya, J. T., and B. P. Von Herzen. 1984. Ray tracing volume densities. In *Computer Graphics (Proceedings of SIGGRAPH '84)*, Volume 18, pp. 165–74.

Kalos, M. H., and P. A. Whitlock. 1986. *Monte Carlo Methods: Volume I: Basics*. New York: Wiley.

Kalra, D., and A. H. Barr. 1989. Guaranteed ray intersections with implicit surfaces. In *Computer Graphics (Proceedings of SIGGRAPH '89)*, Volume 23, pp. 297–306.

Kapasi, U. J., S. Rixner, W. J. Dally, B. Khailany, J. H. Ahn, P. Mattson, and J. D. Owens. 2003. Programmable stream processors. *IEEE Computer 36*(8), 54–62.

Kaplan, M. R. 1985. The uses of spatial coherence in ray tracing. *ACM SIGGRAPH Course Notes 11*.

Kay, D. S., and D. P. Greenberg. 1979. Transparency for computer synthesized images. In *Computer Graphics (SIGGRAPH '79 Proceedings)*, Volume 13, pp. 158–64.

Kay, T., and J. Kajiya. 1986. Ray tracing complex scenes. In *Computer Graphics (SIGGRAPH '86 Proceedings)*, Volume 20, pp. 269–78.

Kelemen, C., L. Szirmay-Kalos, G. Antal, and F. Csonka. 2002. A simple and robust mutation strategy for the Metropolis light transport algorithm. *Computer Graphics Forum 21*(3), 531–40.

Keller, A. 1996. Quasi-Monte Carlo radiosity. In X. Pueyo and P. Schröder (Eds.), *Eurographics Rendering Workshop 1996*, pp. 101–10.

Keller, A. 1997. Instant radiosity. In *Proceedings of SIGGRAPH '97*, Computer Graphics Proceedings, Annual Conference Series, Los Angeles, pp. 49–56.

Keller, A. 2001. Strictly deterministic sampling methods in computer graphics. *mental images Technical Report*. Also in *SIGGRAPH 2003 Monte Carlo Course Notes*.

Keller, A., and I. Wald. 2000. Efficient importance sampling techniques for the photon map. In *Proceedings of Vision, Modeling and Visualization 2000*, pp. 271–79.

King, L. V. 1913. On the scattering and absorption of light in gaseous media, with applications to the intensity of sky radiation. *Philosophical Transactions of the Royal Society of London. Series A. Mathematical and Physical Sciences 212*, 375–433.

Kirk, D., and J. Arvo. 1988. The ray tracing kernel. In *Proceedings of Ausgraph '88*, pp. 75–82.

Kirk, D. B., and J. Arvo. 1991. Unbiased sampling techniques for image synthesis. In T. W. Sederberg (Ed.), *Computer Graphics (SIGGRAPH '91 Proceedings)*, Volume 25, pp. 153–56.

Klassen, R. V. 1987. Modeling the effect of the atmosphere on light. *ACM Transactions on Graphics 6*(3), 215–37.

Klimaszewski, K. S., and T. W. Sederberg. 1997. Faster ray tracing using adaptive grids. *IEEE Computer Graphics and Applications 17*(1), 42–51.

Knuth, D. E. 1984. Literate programming. *The Computer Journal 27*, 97–111. Reprinted in D. E. Knuth, *Literate Programming*, Stanford Center for the Study of Language and Information, 1992.

Knuth, D. E. 1986. *MetaFont: The Program*. Reading, Massachusetts: Addison-Wesley.

Knuth, D. E. 1993a. *TEX: The Program*. Reading, Massachusetts: Addison-Wesley.

Knuth, D. E. 1993b. *The Stanford GraphBase*. New York: ACM Press and Addison-Wesley.

Kolb, C., D. Mitchell, and P. Hanrahan. 1995. A realistic camera model for computer graphics. In R. Cook (Ed.), *SIGGRAPH '95 Conference Proceedings*, Annual Conference Series, pp. 317–24. Reading, Massachusetts: Addison-Wesley.

Kollig, T., and A. Keller. 2000. Efficient bidirectional path tracing by randomized Quasi-Monte Carlo integration. In *Monte Carlo and Quasi-Monte Carlo Methods 2000*, pp. 290–305. Berlin: Springer-Verlag.

Kollig, T., and A. Keller. 2002. Efficient multidimensional sampling. In G. Drettakis and H.-P. Seidel (Eds.), *Computer Graphics Forum (Proceedings of Eurographics 2002)*, Volume 21, pp. 557–63.

Kollig, T., and A. Keller. 2003. Efficient illumination by high dynamic range images. In *Eurographics Symposium on Rendering: 14th Eurographics Workshop on Rendering*, pp. 45–51.

Lafortune, E. 1996. *Mathematical Models and Monte Carlo Algorithms for Physically Based Rendering*. Ph. D. thesis, Katholieke Universiteit Leuven.

Lafortune, E., and Y. Willems. 1994. A theoretical framework for physically based rendering. *Computer Graphics Forum 13*(2), 97–107.

Lafortune, E. P., and Y. D. Willems. 1996. Rendering participating media with bidirectional path tracing. In *Eurographics Rendering Workshop 1996*, pp. 91–100.

Lafortune, E. P. F., S.-C. Foo, K. E. Torrance, and D. P. Greenberg. 1997. Non-linear approximation of reflectance functions. In *Proceedings of SIGGRAPH '97*, Computer Graphics Proceedings, Annual Conference Series, Los Angeles, pp. 117–26.

Lam, M. S., E. E. Rothberg, and M. E. Wolf. 1991. The cache performance and optimizations of blocked algorithms. In *Proceedings of the Fourth International Conference on Architectural Support for Programming Languages and Operating Systems (ASPLOS-IV)*, Palo Alto, California.

Lambert, J. H. 1760. *Photometry, or, On the Measure and Gradations of Light, Colors, and Shade*. The Illuminating Engineering Society of North America. Translated by David L. DiLaura in 2001.

Lang, S. 1986. *An Introduction to Linear Algebra*. New York: Springer-Verlag.

Lansdale, R. C. 1991. Texture mapping and resampling for computer graphics. M.S. thesis, Department of Electrical Engineering, University of Toronto.

Larson, G. W. 1998. LogLUV encoding for full-gamut, high-dynamic range images. *Journal of Graphics Tools 3*(1), 15–31.

Larson, G. W., H. Rushmeier, and C. Piatko. 1997. A visibility matching tone reproduction operator for high dynamic range scenes. *IEEE Transactions on Visualization and Computer Graphics 3*(4), 291–306.

Larson, G. W., and R. A. Shakespeare. 1998. *Rendering with Radiance: The Art and Science of Lighting Visualization*. San Francisco: Morgan Kaufmann.

Lee, M. E., R. A. Redner, and S. P. Uselton. 1985. Statistically optimized sampling for distributed ray tracing. In *Computer Graphics (Proceedings of SIGGRAPH '85)*, Volume 19, pp. 61–67.

Legakis, J. 1998. Fast multi-layer fog. *SIGGRAPH '98 Sketch.*

Levine, J. R., T. Mason, and D. Brown. 1992. *lex & yacc*. O'Reilly & Associates.

Levoy, M. 1988. Display of surfaces from volume data. *IEEE Computer Graphics and Applications 8*(3), 29–37.

Levoy, M. 1990a. Efficient ray tracing of volume data. *ACM Transactions on Graphics 9*(3), 245–61.

Levoy, M. 1990b. A hybrid ray tracer for rendering polygon and volume data. *IEEE Computer Graphics and Applications 10*(2), 33–40.

Levoy, M., and P. M. Hanrahan. 1996. Light field rendering. In *Proceedings of SIGGRAPH '96*, Computer Graphics Proceedings, Annual Conference Series, pp. 31–42.

Levoy, M., and T. Whitted. 1985. The use of points as a display primitive. Technical Report 85-022, Computer Science Department, University of North Carolina at Chapel Hill.

Lewis, J.-P. 1989. Algorithms for solid noise synthesis. In *Computer Graphics (Proceedings of SIGGRAPH '89)*, Volume 23, pp. 263–70.

Lext, J., U. Assarsson, and T. Möller. 2001. A benchmark for animated ray tracing. *IEEE Computer Graphics and Applications 21*(2), 22–30.

Li, X., W. Wang, R. R. Martin, and A. Bowyer. 2003. Using low-discrepancy sequences and the Crofton formula to compute surface areas of geometric models. *Computer Aided Design 35*(9), 771–82.

Liu, J. S. 2001. *Monte Carlo Strategies in Scientific Computing*. New York: Springer-Verlag.

Logie, J. R., and J. W. Patterson. 1994. Inverse displacement mapping in the general case. *Computer Graphics Forum 14*(5), 261–73.

Lokovic, T., and E. Veach. 2000. Deep shadow maps. In *Proceedings of ACM SIGGRAPH 2000*, Computer Graphics Proceedings, Annual Conference Series, pp. 385–92.

Lommel, E. 1889. Die Photometrie der diffusen Zurückwerfung. *Annalen der Physik 36*, 473–502.

Loop, C. 1987. *Smooth Subdivision Surfaces Based on Triangles*. M.S. thesis, University of Utah.

Lu, R., J. J. Koenderink, and A. M. L. Kappers. 1999. Specularities on surfaces with tangential hairs or grooves. *Computer Vision and Image Understanding 78*, 320–35.

Lukaszewski, A. 2001. Exploiting coherence of shadow rays. In *AFRIGRAPH 2001*, pp. 147–150. ACM SIGGRAPH.

MacDonald, J. D., and K. S. Booth. 1990. Heuristics for ray tracing using space subdivision. *The Visual Computer 6*(3), 153–66.

Machiraju, R., and R. Yagel. 1996. Reconstruction error characterization and control: A sampling theory approach. *IEEE Transactions on Visualization and Computer Graphics 2*(4).

Malacara, D. 2002. *Color Vision and Colorimetry: Theory and Applications*. SPIE—The International Society for Optical Engineering.

Mann, S., N. Litke, and T. DeRose. 1997. A coordinate free geometry ADT. Research Report CS-97-15, Computer Science Department, University of Waterloo. Available at *ftp://cs-archive.uwaterloo.ca/cs-archive/CS-97-15/*.

Marschner, S. R., H. W. Jensen, M. Cammarano, S. Worley, and P. Hanrahan. 2003. Light scattering from human hair fibers. *ACM Transactions on Graphics 22*(3), 780–91.

Marschner, S. R., and R. J. Lobb. 1994. An evaluation of reconstruction filters for volume rendering. In *Proceedings of Visualization '94*, Washington, D.C., pp. 100–107.

Marschner, S. R., S. H. Westin, E. P. F. Lafortune, K. E. Torrance, and D. P. Greenberg. 1999. Image-based BRDF measurement including human skin. In *Eurographics Rendering Workshop 1999*, Granada, Spain. Springer Wien/Eurographics.

Martin, W., E. Cohen, R. Fish, and P. S. Shirley. 2000. Practical ray tracing of trimmed NURBS surfaces. *Journal of Graphics Tools 5*(1), 27–52.

Max, N. L. 1986. Atmospheric illumination and shadows. In *Computer Graphics (Proceedings of SIGGRAPH '86)*, Volume 20, pp. 117–24.

Max, N. L. 1988. Horizon mapping: shadows for bump-mapped surfaces. *The Visual Computer 4*(2), 109–17.

Max, N. L. 1995. Optical models for direct volume rendering. *IEEE Transactions on Visualization and Computer Graphics 1*(2), 99–108.

McCluney, W. R. 1994. *Introduction to Radiometry and Photometry*. Boston: Artech House.

McCool, M., and E. Fiume. 1992. Hierarchical Poisson disk sampling distributions. In *Proceedings of Graphics Interface 1992*, pp. 94–105.

McCormack, J., R. Perry, K. I. Farkas, and N. P. Jouppi. 1999. Feline: fast elliptical lines for anisotropic texture mapping. In *Proceedings of SIGGRAPH '99*, Computer Graphics Proceedings, Annual Conference Series, Los Angeles, pp. 243–250.

Meijering, E. 2002. A chronology of interpolation: from ancient astronomy to modern signal and image processing. *Proceedings of the IEEE 90*(3), 319–42.

Meijering, E. H. W., W. J. Niessen, J. P. W. Pluim, and M. A. Viergever. 1999. Quantitative comparison of sinc-approximating kernels for medical image interpolation. In C. Taylor and

A. Colchester (Eds.), *Medical Image Computing and Computer-Assisted Intervention—MICCAI 1999*, pp. 210–17. Berlin: Springer-Verlag. Volume 1679 of *Lecture Notes in Computer Science*.

Meyer, G. W., and D. P. Greenberg. 1980. Perceptual color spaces for computer graphics. In *Computer Graphics (Proceedings of SIGGRAPH '80)*, Volume 14, Seattle, Washington, pp. 254–261.

Meyer, G. W., H. E. Rushmeier, M. F. Cohen, D. P. Greenberg, and K. E. Torrance. 1986. An experimental evaluation of computer graphics imagery. *ACM Transactions on Graphics 5*(1), 30–50.

Miller, G. S., and C. R. Hoffman. 1984. Illumination and reflection maps: simulated objects in simulated and real environments. *Course Notes for Advanced Computer Graphics Animation, SIGGRAPH '84.*

Mitchell, D. P. 1987. Generating antialiased images at low sampling densities. In M. C. Stone (Ed.), *Computer Graphics (SIGGRAPH '87 Proceedings)*, Volume 21, pp. 65–72.

Mitchell, D. P. 1990. Robust ray intersection with interval arithmetic. In *Graphics Interface '90*, pp. 68–74.

Mitchell, D. P. 1991. Spectrally optimal sampling for distributed ray tracing. In T. W. Sederberg (Ed.), *Computer Graphics (SIGGRAPH '91 Proceedings)*, Volume 25, pp. 157–64.

Mitchell, D. P. 1992. Ray tracing and irregularities of distribution. In *Third Eurographics Workshop on Rendering*, Bristol, United Kingdom, pp. 61–69.

Mitchell, D. P. 1996a. Software interface for sampling routines. Personal communication.

Mitchell, D. P. 1996b. Consequences of stratified sampling in graphics. In *Proceedings of SIGGRAPH '96*, Computer Graphics Proceedings, Annual Conference Series, New Orleans, Louisiana, pp. 277–80.

Mitchell, D. P., and P. Hanrahan. 1992. Illumination from curved reflectors. In *Computer Graphics (Proceedings of SIGGRAPH '92)*, Volume 26, pp. 283–91.

Mitchell, D. P., and A. N. Netravali. 1988. Reconstruction filters in computer graphics. In J. Dill (Ed.), *Computer Graphics (SIGGRAPH '88 Proceedings)*, Volume 22, pp. 221–28.

Möller, T., R. Machiraju, K. Mueller, and R. Yagel. 1997. Evaluation and design of filters using a Taylor series expansion. *IEEE Transactions on Visualization and Computer Graphics 3*(2), 184–99.

Möller, T., and B. Trumbore. 1997. Fast, minimum storage ray-triangle intersection. *Journal of Graphics Tools 2*(1), 21–28.

Moon, P., and D. E. Spencer. 1936. *The Scientific Basis of Illuminating Engineering*. New York: McGraw-Hill.

Moon, P., and D. E. Spencer 1948. *Lighting Design*. Reading, Masschusetts: Addison-Wesley.

Moore, R. E. 1966. *Interval Analysis*. Englewood Cliffs, New Jersey: Prentice Hall.

Moravec, H. 1981. 3d graphics and the wave theory. In *Computer Graphics*, Volume 15, pp. 289–96.

Motwani, R., and P. Raghavan. 1995. *Randomized Algorithms*. Cambridge: Cambridge University Press.

Musgrave, K. 1992. A panoramic virtual screen for ray tracing. In D. Kirk (Ed.), *Graphics Gems III*, pp. 288–94. San Diego: Academic Press.

Nakamae, E., K. Kaneda, T. Okamoto, and T. Nishita. 1990. A lighting model aiming at drive simulators. In *Computer Graphics (Proceedings of SIGGRAPH '90)*, Volume 24, pp. 395–404.

Nayar, S. K., K. Ikeuchi, and T. Kanade. 1991. Surface reflection: physical and geometrical perspectives. *IEEE Transactions on Pattern Analysis and Machine Intelligence 17*(7), 611–34.

Naylor, B. 1993. Constructing good partition trees. In *Graphics Interface '93*, pp. 181–91.

Neyret, F. 1996. Synthesizing verdant landscapes using volumetric textures. In *Eurographics Rendering Workshop 1996*, pp. 215–24.

Neyret, F. 1998. Modeling, animating, and rendering complex scenes using volumetric textures. *IEEE Transactions on Visualization and Computer Graphics 4*(1), 55–70.

Niederreiter, H. 1992. *Random Number Generation and Quasi–Monte Carlo Methods*. Philadelphia: Society for Industrial and Applied Mathematics.

Nishita, T., Y. Miyawaki, and E. Nakamae. 1987. A shading model for atmospheric scattering considering luminous intensity distribution of light sources. In *Computer Graphics (Proceedings of SIGGRAPH '87)*, Volume 21, pp. 303–10.

Nishita, T., and E. Nakamae. 1986. Continuous tone representation of three-dimensional objects illuminated by sky light. In *Computer Graphics (Proceedings of SIGGRAPH '86)*, Volume 20, pp. 125–32.

Norton, A., A. P. Rockwood, and P. T. Skolmoski. 1982. Clamping: a method of antialiasing textured surfaces by bandwidth limiting in object space. In *Computer Graphics (Proceedings of SIGGRAPH '82)*, Volume 16, pp. 1–8.

Oren, M., and S. K. Nayar. 1994. Generalization of Lambert's reflectance model. In A. Glassner (Ed.), *Proceedings of SIGGRAPH '94, Computer Graphics Proceedings, Annual Conference Series,* pp. 239–46. New York: ACM Press.

Owen, A. B. 1998. Latin supercube sampling for very high-dimensional simulations. *Modeling and Computer Simulation 8*(1), 71–102.

Owens, J. D. 2002. *Computer Graphics on a Stream Architecture*. Ph.D. thesis, Stanford University.

Owens, J. D., W. J. Dally, U. J. Kapasi, S. Rixner, P. Mattson, and B. Mowery. 2000. Polygon rendering on a stream architecture. In *2000 SIGGRAPH/Eurographics Workshop on Graphics Hardware*, pp. 23–32.

Owens, J. D., B. Khailany, B. Towles, and W. J. Dally. 2002. Comparing REYES and OpenGL on a stream architecture. In *2002 SIGGRAPH / Eurographics Workshop on Graphics Hardware*, pp. 47–56.

Parker, S., W. Martin, P.-P. J. Sloan, P. S. Shirley, B. Smits, and C. Hansen. 1999. Interactive ray tracing. In *1999 ACM Symposium on Interactive 3D Graphics*, pp. 119–26.

Pattanaik, S. N., J. A. Ferwerda, M. D. Fairchild, and D. P. Greenberg. 1998. A multiscale model of adaptation and spatial vision for realistic image display. In *Proceedings of SIGGRAPH '98*, Computer Graphics Proceedings, Annual Conference Series, Orlando, Florida, pp. 287–98.

Pattanaik, S. N., and S. P. Mudur. 1995. Adjoint equations and random walks for illumination computation. *ACM Transactions on Graphics 14*(1), 77–102.

Pattanaik, S. N., J. E. Tumblin, H. Yee, and D. P. Greenberg. 2000. Time-dependent visual adaptation for realistic image display. In *Proceedings of ACM SIGGRAPH 2000*, Computer Graphics Proceedings, Annual Conference Series, pp. 47–54.

Patterson, D., and J. Hennessy. 1997. *Computer Organization and Design*. San Francisco: Morgan Kaufmann.

Patterson, J. W., S. G. Hoggar, and J. R. Logie. 1991. Inverse displacement mapping. *Computer Graphics Forum 10*(2), 129–39.

Pauly, M. 1999. Robust Monte Carlo methods for photorealistic rendering of volumetric effects. Master's thesis, Universität Kaiserslautern.

Pauly, M., T. Kollig, and A. Keller. 2000. Metropolis light transport for participating media. In *Rendering Techniques 2000: 11th Eurographics Workshop on Rendering*, pp. 11–22.

Peachey, D. R. 1985. Solid texturing of complex surfaces. In B. A. Barsky (Ed.), *Computer Graphics (SIGGRAPH '85 Proceedings)*, Volume 19, pp. 279–86.

Peachey, D. R. 1990. Texture on demand. Unpublished manuscript.

Pearce, A. 1991. A recursive shadow voxel cache for ray tracing. In J. Arvo (Ed.), *Graphics Gems II*, pp. 273–74. San Diego: Academic Press.

Peercy, M. S. 1993. Linear color representations for full spectral rendering. In J. T. Kajiya (Ed.), *Computer Graphics (SIGGRAPH '93 Proceedings)*, Volume 27, pp. 191–98.

Peercy, M. S., M. Olano, J. Airey, and P. J. Ungar. 2000. Interactive multi-pass programmable shading. In *Proceedings of ACM SIGGRAPH 2000*, Computer Graphics Proceedings, Annual Conference Series, pp. 425–32.

Pérez, F., X. Pueyo, and F. X. Sillion. 1997. Global illumination techniques for the simulation of participating media. In *Eurographics Rendering Workshop 1997*, pp. 309–20.

Perlin, K. 1985a. An image synthesizer. In *Computer Graphics (SIGGRAPH '85 Proceedings)*, Volume 19, pp. 287–96.

Perlin, K. 1985b. State of the art in image synthesis. *SIGGRAPH Course notes 11*.

Perlin, K. 2002. Improving noise. *ACM Transactions on Graphics 21*(3), 681–82.

Perlin, K., and E. M. Hoffert. 1989. Hypertexture. In *Computer Graphics (Proceedings of SIGGRAPH '89)*, Volume 23, pp. 253–62.

Peter, I., and G. Pietrek. 1998. Importance driven construction of photon maps. In *Eurographics Rendering Workshop 1998*, pp. 269–80.

Pfister, H., M. Zwicker, J. van Baar, and M. Gross. 2000. Surfels: Surface elements as rendering primitives. In *Proceedings of ACM SIGGRAPH 2000*, Computer Graphics Proceedings, Annual Conference Series, pp. 335–42.

Pharr, M., and P. Hanrahan. 1996. Geometry caching for ray-tracing displacement maps. In *Eurographics Rendering Workshop 1996*, pp. 31–40.

Pharr, M., and P. M. Hanrahan. 2000. Monte Carlo evaluation of non-linear scattering equations for subsurface reflection. In *Proceedings of ACM SIGGRAPH 2000*, Computer Graphics Proceedings, Annual Conference Series, pp. 75–84.

Pharr, M., C. Kolb, R. Gershbein, and P. M. Hanrahan. 1997. Rendering complex scenes with memory-coherent ray tracing. In *Proceedings of SIGGRAPH '97*, Computer Graphics Proceedings, Annual Conference Series, pp. 101–08.

Phong, B.-T. 1975. Illumination for computer generated pictures. *Communications of the ACM 18*(6), 311–17.

Phong, B.-T., and F. C. Crow. 1975. Improved rendition of polygonal models of curved surfaces. In *Proceedings of the 2nd USA-Japan Computer Conference*.

Pixar Animation Studios. 2000. The RenderMan interface. Version 3.2.

Porter, T., and T. Duff. 1984. Compositing digital images. In *Computer Graphics (Proceedings of SIGGRAPH '84)*, Volume 18, Minneapolis, Minnesota, pp. 253–59.

Potmesil, M., and I. Chakravarty. 1981. A lens and aperture camera model for synthetic image generation. In *Computer Graphics (Proceedings of SIGGRAPH '81)*, Volume 15, Dallas, Texas, pp. 297–305.

Potmesil, M., and I. Chakravarty. 1982. Synthetic image generation with a lens and aperture camera model. *ACM Transactions on Graphics 1*(2), 85–108.

Potmesil, M., and I. Chakravarty. 1983. Modeling motion blur in computer-generated images. In *Computer Graphics (Proceedings of SIGGRAPH 83)*, Volume 17, Detroit, Michigan, pp. 389–99.

Poulin, P., and A. Fournier. 1990. A model for anisotropic reflection. In *Computer Graphics (Proceedings of SIGGRAPH '90)*, Volume 24, pp. 273–82.

Poynton, C. 2002a. Frequently-asked questions about color. *www.inforamp.net/~poynton/ColorFAQ.html*.

Poynton, C. 2002b. Frequently-asked questions about gamma. *www.inforamp.net/~poynton/GammaFAQ.html*.

Preetham, A. J., P. S. Shirley, and B. E. Smits. 1999. A practical analytic model for daylight. In *Proceedings of SIGGRAPH '99*, Computer Graphics Proceedings, Annual Conference Series, pp. 91–100.

Preisendorfer, R. W. 1965. *Radiative Transfer on Discrete Spaces*. Oxford: Pergamon Press.

Preisendorfer, R. W. 1976. *Hydrologic Optics*. Honolulu, Hawaii: U.S. Department of Commerce, National Oceanic and Atmospheric Administration.

Press, W. H., S. A. Teukolsky, W. T. Vetterling, and B. P. Flannery. 1992. *Numerical Recipes in C: The Art of Scientific Computing* (2nd ed.). Cambridge: Cambridge University Press.

Prusinkiewicz, P. 1986. Graphical applications of L-systems. In *Graphics Interface '86*, pp. 247–53.

Prusinkiewicz, P., M. James, and R. Mech. 1994. Synthetic topiary. In *Proceedings of SIGGRAPH '94*, Computer Graphics Proceedings, Annual Conference Series, pp. 351–58.

Prusinkiewicz, P., L. Mündermann, R. Karwowski, and B. Lane. 2001. The use of positional information in the modeling of plants. In *Proceedings of ACM SIGGRAPH 2001*, Computer Graphics Proceedings, Annual Conference Series, pp. 289–300.

Purcell, T. J., I. Buck, W. R. Mark, and P. Hanrahan. 2002. Ray tracing on programmable graphics hardware. *ACM Transactions on Graphics 21*(3), 703–12.

Purcell, T. J., C. Donner, M. Cammarano, H. W. Jensen, and P. Hanrahan. 2003. Photon mapping on programmable graphics hardware. In *Graphics Hardware 2003*, pp. 41–50.

Ramasubramanian, M., S. N. Pattanaik, and D. P. Greenberg. 1999. A perceptually based physical error metric for realistic image synthesis. In *Proceedings of SIGGRAPH '99*, Computer Graphics Proceedings, Annual Conference Series, Los Angeles, pp. 73–82.

Raso, M., and A. Fournier. 1991. A piecewise polynomial approach to shading using spectral distributions. In *Graphics Interface '91*, pp. 40–46. Canadian Information Processing Society.

Reeves, W. T., D. H. Salesin, and R. L. Cook. 1987. Rendering antialiased shadows with depth maps. In *Computer Graphics (Proceedings of SIGGRAPH '87)*, Volume 21, pp. 283–91.

Reichert, M. C. 1992. A two-pass radiosity method driven by lights and viewer position. Master's thesis, Cornell University.

Reinhard, E. 2002. Parameter estimation for photographic tone reproduction. *Journal of Graphics Tools 7*(1), 45–52.

Reinhard, E., M. Stark, P. Shirley, and J. Ferwerda. 2002. Photographic tone reproduction for digital images. *ACM Transactions on Graphics 21*(3), 267–76. Proceedings of ACM SIGGRAPH 2002.

Rogers, D. F., and J. A. Adams. 1990. *Mathematical Elements for Computer Graphics*. New York: McGraw–Hill.

Ross, S. M. 2002. *Introduction to Probability Models* (8th ed.). San Diego: Academic Press.

Roth, S. D. 1982. Ray casting for modelling solids. *Computer Graphics and Image Processing 18*, 109–44.

Rougeron, G., and B. Péroche. 1998. Color fidelity in computer graphics: a survey. *Computer Graphics Forum 17*(1), 3–16.

Rubin, S. M., and T. Whitted. 1980. A 3-dimensional representation for fast rendering of complex scenes. *Computer Graphics 14*(3), 110–16.

Rushmeier, H. E. 1988. *Realistic Image Synthesis for Scenes with Radiatively Participating Media*. Ph.D. thesis, Cornell University.

Rushmeier, H., C. Patterson, and A. Veerasamy. 1993. Geometric simplification for indirect illumination calculations. In *Graphics Interface '93*, pp. 227–36.

Rushmeier, H. E., and K. E. Torrance. 1987. The zonal method for calculating light intensities in the presence of a participating medium. In *Computer Graphics (Proceedings of SIGGRAPH '87)*, Volume 21, pp. 293–302.

Rushmeier, H. E., and G. J. Ward. 1994. Energy preserving non-linear filters. In *Proceedings of SIGGRAPH '94*, Computer Graphics Proceedings, Annual Conference Series, pp. 131–38.

Rusinkiewicz, S., and M. Levoy. 2000. Qsplat: A multiresolution point rendering system for large meshes. In *Proceedings of ACM SIGGRAPH 2000*, Computer Graphics Proceedings, Annual Conference Series, pp. 343–52.

Saito, T., and T. Takahashi. 1990. Comprehensible rendering of 3-d shapes. In *Computer Graphics (Proceedings of SIGGRAPH '90)*, Volume 24, pp. 197–206.

Samet, H. 1990. *The Design and Analysis of Spatial Data Structures*. Reading, Massachusetts: Addison-Wesley.

Schaufler, G., and H. W. Jensen. 2000. Ray tracing point sampled geometry. In *Rendering Techniques 2000: 11th Eurographics Workshop on Rendering*, pp. 319–28.

Schilling, A. 1997. Toward real-time photorealistic rendering: challenges and solutions. In *1997 SIGGRAPH/Eurographics Workshop on Graphics Hardware*, pp. 7–16.

Schilling, A. 2001. Antialiasing of environment maps. *Computer Graphics Forum 20*(1), 5–11.

Schlick, C. 1993. A customizable reflectance model for everyday rendering. In *Fourth Eurographics Workshop on Rendering*, Paris, France, pp. 73–84.

Schlick, C. 1994. An inexpensive BRDF model for physically-based rendering. *Computer Graphics Forum 13*(3), 233–46.

Schmidt, C. M., and B. Budge. 2002. Simple nested dielectrics in ray traced images. *Journal of Graphics Tools 7*(2), 1–8.

Schneider, P. J., and D. H. Eberly. 2003. *Geometric Tools for Computer Graphics*. San Francisco: Morgan Kaufmann.

Schuster, A. 1905. Radiation through a foggy atmosphere. *Astrophysical Journal 21*(1), 1–22.

Schwarzschild, K. 1906. On the equlibtrium of the sun's atmosphere (Nachrichten von der Koniglichen Gesellschaften der Wissenschaften zu Gottigen). *Göttinger Nachrichten 195*, 41–53.

Séquin, C. H., and E. K. Smyrl. 1989. Parameterized ray tracing. In *Computer Graphics (Proceedings of SIGGRAPH '89)*, Volume 23, pp. 307–14.

Shade, J., S. J. Gortler, L. W. He, and R. Szeliski. 1998. Layered depth images. In *Proceedings of SIGGRAPH 98*, Computer Graphics Proceedings, Annual Conference Series, pp. 231–42.

Shinya, M., T. Takahashi, and S. Naito. 1987. Principles and applications of pencil tracing. In *Computer Graphics (Proceedings of SIGGRAPH '87)*, Volume 21, pp. 45–54.

Shirley, P. 1990. *Physically Based Lighting Calculations for Computer Graphics*. Ph.D. thesis, Department of Computer Science, University of Illinois, Urbana-Champaign.

Shirley, P. 1991. Discrepancy as a quality measure for sample distributions. In W. Purgathofer (Ed.), *Eurographics '91*, pp. 183–194. Amsterdam: North-Holland.

Shirley, P. 1992. Nonuniform random point sets via warping. In D. Kirk (Ed.), *Graphics Gems III*, pp. 80–83. San Diego: Academic Press.

Shirley, P., and K. Chiu. 1997. A low distortion map between disk and square. *Journal of Graphics Tools 2*(3), 45–52.

Shirley, P., and R. K. Morley. 2003. *Realistic Ray Tracing*. Natick, Massachusetts: A. K. Peters.

Shirley, P., B. Wade, P. Hubbard, D. Zareski, B. Walter, and D. P. Greenberg. 1995. Global illumination via density estimation. In *Eurographics Rendering Workshop 1995*, pp. 219–31.

Shirley, P., C. Y. Wang, and K. Zimmerman. 1996. Monte Carlo techniques for direct lighting calculations. *ACM Transactions on Graphics 15*(1), 1–36.

Shoemake, K. 1994. Polar matrix decomposition. In *Graphics Gems IV*, pp. 207–21. San Deigo: Academic Press.

Shoemake, K., and T. Duff. 1992. Matrix animation and polar decomposition. In *Graphics Interface '92*, pp. 258–64.

Sillion, F., and C. Puech. 1994. *Radiosity and Global Illumination*. San Francisco: Morgan Kaufmann.

Sims, K. 1991. Artificial evolution for computer graphics. In *Computer Graphics (Proceedings of SIGGRAPH '91)*, Volume 25, pp. 319–28.

Sloan, P.-P., J. Hall, J. Hart, and J. Snyder. 2003. Clustered principal components for precomputed radiance transfer. *ACM Transactions on Graphics 22*(3), 382–91.

Sloan, P.-P., J. Kautz, and J. Snyder. 2002. Precomputed radiance transfer for real-time rendering in dynamic, low-frequency lighting environments. *ACM Transactions on Graphics 21*(3), 527–36.

Sloan, P.-P., X. Liu, H.-Y. Shum, and J. Snyder. 2003. Bi-scale radiance transfer. *ACM Transactions on Graphics 22*(3), 370–75.

Slusallek, P. 1996. *Vision—An Architecture for Physically-Based Rendering*. Ph.D. thesis, University of Erlangen.

Slusallek, P., and H.-P. Seidel. 1995. Vision—an architecture for global illumination calculations. *IEEE Transactions on Visualization and Computer Graphics 1*(1), 77–96.

Slusallek, P., and H.-P. Seidel. 1996. Towards an open rendering kernel for image synthesis. In *Eurographics Rendering Workshop 1996*, pp. 51–60.

Smith, A. R. 1979. Painting tutorial notes. *SIGGRAPH '79 Course on Computer Animation Techniques*.

Smith, A. R. 1984. Plants, fractals and formal languages. In *Computer Graphics (Proceedings of SIGGRAPH '84)*, Volume 18, pp. 1–10.

Smith, A. R. 1995. A pixel is not a little square, a pixel is not a little square, a pixel is not a little square! (and a voxel is not a little cube). Microsoft Tech Memo 6, *www.alvyray.com*.

Smith, J. O. 2002. Digital audio resampling home page. *www-ccrma.stanford.edu/~jos/resample/*.

Smits, B. 1998. Efficiency issues for ray tracing. *Journal of Graphics Tools 3*(2), 1–14.

Smits, B. 1999. An RGB-to-spectrum conversion for reflectances. *Journal of Graphics Tools 4*(4), 11–22.

Smits, B., P. S. Shirley, and M. M. Stark. 2000. Direct ray tracing of displacement mapped triangles. In *Rendering Techniques 2000: 11th Eurographics Workshop on Rendering*, pp. 307–18.

Snyder, J. M., and A. H. Barr. 1987. Ray tracing complex models containing surface tessellations. In M. C. Stone (Ed.), *Computer Graphics (SIGGRAPH '87 Proceedings)*, Volume 21, pp. 119–28.

Spanier, J., and E. M. Gelbard. 1969. *Monte Carlo Principles and Neutron Transport Problems*. Reading, Massachusetts: Addison-Wesley.

Spencer, G., P. S. Shirley, K. Zimmerman, and D. P. Greenberg. 1995. Physically-based glare effects for digital images. In *Proceedings of SIGGRAPH '95*, Computer Graphics Proceedings, Annual Conference Series, Los Angeles, pp. 325–334.

Stam, J. 1998. Exact evaluation of Catmull-Clark subdivision surfaces at arbitrary parameter values. In *Proceedings of SIGGRAPH '98*, Computer Graphics Proceedings, Annual Conference Series, pp. 395–404.

Stam, J. 1999. Diffraction shaders. In *Proceedings of SIGGRAPH '99*, Computer Graphics Proceedings, Annual Conference Series, pp. 101–10.

Stam, J. 2001. An illumination model for a skin layer bounded by rough surfaces. In *Rendering Techniques 2001: 12th Eurographics Workshop on Rendering*, pp. 39–52.

Stam, J., and C. Loop. 2003. Quad/triangle subdivision. *Computer Graphics Forum 22*(1), 79–85.

Stockmar, A. 1986. Proposal for a data format for exchange of luminaire data (interior, exterior, and/or road lighting luminaires) under the operating systems MS-DOS 2.x/3.xx under condition of unequivocal coordination between luminaire and data set.

Stolfi, J. 1991. *Oriented Projective Geometry*. San Diego: Academic Press.

Stroustrup, B. 1997. *The C++ Programming Language*. Reading, Massachusetts: Addison-Wesley.

Stürzlinger, W. 1998. Ray tracing triangular trimmed free-form surfaces. *IEEE Transactions on Visualization and Computer Graphics 4*(3), 202–14.

Sun, Y., F. D. Fracchia, M. S. Drew, and T. W. Calvert. 2001. A spectrally based framework for realistic image synthesis. *The Visual Computer 17*(7), 429–44.

Sung, K., J. Craighead, C. Wang, S. Bakshi, A. Pearce, and A. Woo. 1998. Design and implementation of the Maya renderer. In *Pacific Graphics '98*.

Sung, K., and P. Shirley. 1992. Ray tracing with the BSP tree. In D. Kirk (Ed.), *Graphics Gems III*, pp. 271–274. San Diego: Academic Press.

Sutherland, I. E. 1963. Sketchpad—a man-machine graphical communication system. In *Proceedings of the Spring Joint Computer Conference (AFIPS)*, pp. 328–46.

Suykens, F., and Y. Willems. 2000. Density control for photon maps. In *Rendering Techniques 2000: 11th Eurographics Workshop on Rendering*, pp. 23–34.

Suykens, F., and Y. Willems. 2001. Path differentials and applications. In *Rendering Techniques 2001: 12th Eurographics Workshop on Rendering*, pp. 257–68.

Szirmay-Kalos, L., and G. Márton. 1998. Worst-case versus average case complexity of ray-shooting. *Computing 61*(2), 103–31.

Tannenbaum, D. C., P. Tannenbaum, and M. J. Wozny. 1994. Polarization and birefringency considerations in rendering. In *Proceedings of SIGGRAPH '94*, Computer Graphics Proceedings, Annual Conference Series, pp. 221–22.

Theußl, T., H. Hauser, and E. Gröller. 2000. Mastering windows: improving reconstruction. In *Proceedings of the 2000 IEEE Symposium on Volume Visualization*, pp. 101–8. New York: ACM Press.

Torrance, K. E., and E. M. Sparrow. 1967. Theory for off-specular reflection from roughened surfaces. *Journal of the Optical Society of America 57*(9), 1105–14.

Tregenza, P. R. 1983. The Monte Carlo method in lighting calculations. *Lighting Research and Technology 15*(4), 163–70.

Trumbore, B., W. Lytle, and D. P. Greenberg. 1993. A testbed for image synthesis. In *Developing Large-Scale Graphics Software Toolkits, SIGGRAPH '93 Course Notes*, Volume 3, pp. 4-7–4-19.

Truong, D. N., F. Bodin, and A. Seznec. 1998. Improving cache behavior of dynamically allocated data structures. In *IEEE PACT*, pp. 322–29.

Tumblin, J., J. K. Hodgins, and B. K. Guenter. 1999. Two methods for display of high contrast images. *ACM Transactions on Graphics 18*(1), 56–94.

Tumblin, J., and H. E. Rushmeier. 1993. Tone reproduction for realistic images. *IEEE Computer Graphics and Applications 13*(6), 42–48.

Tumblin, J., and G. Turk. 1999. LCIS: A boundary hierarchy for detail-preserving contrast reduction. In *Proceedings of SIGGRAPH '99*, Computer Graphics Proceedings, Annual Conference Series, Los Angeles, pp. 83–90.

Turk, G. 1991. Generating textures for arbitrary surfaces using reaction-diffusion. In *Computer Graphics (Proceedings of SIGGRAPH '91)*, Volume 25, pp. 289–98.

Turkowski, K. 1990a. The differential geometry of parametric primitives. Technical Note, Advanced Technology Group, Apple Computer.

Turkowski, K. 1990b. Filters for common resampling tasks. In A. S. Glassner (Ed.), *Graphics Gems I*, pp. 147–65. San Diego: Academic Press.

Turkowski, K. 1990c. Properties of surface-normal transformations. In A. S. Glassner (Ed.), *Graphics Gems I*, pp. 539–47. San Diego: Academic Press.

Turkowski, K. 1993. The differential geometry of texture-mapping and shading. Technical Note, Advanced Technology Group, Apple Computer.

Unser, M. 2000. Sampling—50 years after Shannon. *Proceedings of the IEEE 88*(4), 569–87.

Upstill, S. 1989. *The RenderMan Companion*. Reading, Massachusetts: Addison-Wesley.

van de Hulst, H. C. 1980. *Multiple Light Scattering*. New York: Academic Press.

van de Hulst, H. C. 1981. *Light Scattering by Small Particles*. New York: Dover Publications. Originally published by John Wiley and Sons, 1957.

van Wijk, J. J. 1991. Spot noise-texture synthesis for data visualization. In *Computer Graphics (Proceedings of SIGGRAPH '91)*, Volume 25, pp. 309–18.

Veach, E. 1996. Non-symmetric scattering in light transport algorithms. In X. Pueyo and P. Schröder (Eds.), *Eurographics Rendering Workshop 1996*. Springer Wien.

Veach, E. 1997. *Robust Monte Carlo Methods for Light Transport Simulation*. Ph.D. thesis, Stanford University.

Veach, E., and L. Guibas. 1994. Bidirectional estimators for light transport. In *Fifth Eurographics Workshop on Rendering*, Darmstadt, Germany, pp. 147–62.

Veach, E., and L. J. Guibas. 1995. Optimally combining sampling techniques for Monte Carlo rendering. In *Computer Graphics (SIGGRAPH '95 Proceedings)*, pp. 419–28.

Veach, E., and L. J. Guibas. 1997. Metropolis light transport. In *Computer Graphics (SIGGRAPH '97 Proceedings)*, pp. 65–76.

Verbeck, C. P., and D. P. Greenberg. 1984. A comprehensive light source description for computer graphics. *IEEE Computer Graphics and Applications 4*(7), 66–75.

Wald, I., C. Benthin, and P. Slusallek. 2003. Interactive global illumination in complex and highly occluded environments. In *Eurographics Symposium on Rendering: 14th Eurographics Workshop on Rendering*, pp. 74–81.

Wald, I., T. Kollig, C. Benthin, A. Keller, and P. Slusallek. 2002. Interactive global illumination using fast ray tracing. In *Rendering Techniques 2002: 13th Eurographics Workshop on Rendering*, pp. 15–24.

Wald, I., P. Slusallek, and C. Benthin. 2001. Interactive distributed ray tracing of highly complex models. In *Rendering Techniques 2001: 12th Eurographics Workshop on Rendering*, pp. 277–88.

Wald, I., P. Slusallek, C. Benthin, and M. Wagner. 2001. Interactive rendering with coherent ray tracing. *Computer Graphics Forum 20*(3), 153–64.

Wallace, B. A. 1981. Merging and transformation of raster images for cartoon animation. In *Proceedings of ACM SIGGRAPH '81*, Volume 15, pp. 253–62.

Wallis, B. 1990. Forms, vectors, and transforms. In A. S. Glassner (Ed.), *Graphics Gems I*, pp. 533–538. San Diego: Academic Press.

Walter, B., P. M. Hubbard, P. Shirley, and D. F. Greenberg. 1997. Global illumination using local linear density estimation. *ACM Transactions on Graphics 16*(3), 217–59.

Walter, B., S. N. Pattanaik, and D. P. Greenberg. 2002. Using perceptual texture masking for efficient image synthesis. *Computer Graphics Forum 21*(3), 393–99.

Wandell, B. 1995. *Foundations of Vision*. Sinauer Associates.

Wang, X. C., J. Maillot, E. L. Fiume, V. Ng-Thow-Hing, A. Woo, and S. Bakshi. 2000. Feature-based displacement mapping. In *Rendering Techniques 2000: 11th Eurographics Workshop on Rendering*, pp. 257–68.

Ward, G. 1991a. Adaptive shadow testing for ray tracing. In *Second Eurographics Workshop on Rendering*.

Ward, G. 1991b. Real pixels. In J. Arvo (Ed.), *Graphics Gems II*, pp. 80–83. San Diego: Academic Press.

Ward, G. J. 1992. Measuring and modeling anisotropic reflection. In E. E. Catmull (Ed.), *Computer Graphics (SIGGRAPH '92 Proceedings)*, Volume 26, pp. 265–72.

Ward, G. J. 1994a. A contrast-based scalefactor for luminance display. In P. Heckbert (Ed.), *Graphics Gems IV*, pp. 415–421. Boston: Academic Press.

Ward, G. J. 1994b. The Radiance lighting simulation and rendering system. In A. Glassner (Ed.), *Proceedings of SIGGRAPH '94*, pp. 459–72.

Ward, G. J., and P. Heckbert. 1992. Irradiance gradients. In *Third Eurographics Workshop on Rendering*, Bristol, United Kingdom, pp. 85–98.

Ward, G. J., F. M. Rubinstein, and R. D. Clear. 1988. A ray tracing solution for diffuse interreflection. In J. Dill (Ed.), *Computer Graphics (SIGGRAPH '88 Proceedings)*, Volume 22, pp. 85–92.

Warn, D. R. 1983. Lighting controls for synthetic images. In *Computer Graphics (Proceedings of SIGGRAPH 83)*, Volume 17, Detroit, Michigan, pp. 13–21.

Warren, J. 2002. *Subdivision Methods for Geometric Design: A Constructive Approach*. San Francisco: Morgan Kaufmann.

Watt, A., and M. Watt. 1992. *Advanced Animation and Rendering Techniques*. New York: Addison-Wesley.

Weghorst, H., G. Hooper, and D. P. Greenberg. 1984. Improved computational methods for ray tracing. *ACM Transactions on Graphics 3*(1), 52–69.

Westin, S., J. Arvo, and K. Torrance. 1992. Predicting reflectance functions from complex surfaces. *Computer Graphics 26*(2), 255–64.

Whitted, T. 1980. An improved illumination model for shaded display. *Communications of the ACM 23*(6), 343–49.

Williams, L. 1978. Casting curved shadows on curved surfaces. In *Computer Graphics (Proceedings of SIGGRAPH '78)*, Volume 12, pp. 270–74.

Williams, L. 1983. Pyramidal parametrics. In *Computer Graphics (SIGGRAPH '83 Proceedings)*, Volume 17, pp. 1–11.

Wilson, P. R., M. S. Johnstone, M. Neely, and D. Boles. 1995. Dynamic storage allocation: a survey and critical review. In *Proceedings International Workshop on Memory Management*, Kinross Scotland (UK).

Witkin, A., and M. Kass. 1991. Reaction-diffusion textures. In *Computer Graphics (Proceedings of SIGGRAPH '91)*, Volume 25, pp. 299–308.

Wolff, L. B., and D. J. Kurlander. 1990. Ray tracing with polarization parameters. *IEEE Computer Graphics and Applications 10*(6), 44–55.

Wong, T.-T., W.-S. Luk, and P.-A. Heng. 1997. Sampling with Hammersley and Halton points. *Journal of Graphics Tools 2*(2), 9–24.

Woo, A., and J. Amanatides. 1990. Voxel occlusion testing: a shadow determination accelerator for ray tracing. In *Graphics Interface '90*, pp. 213–20.

Woo, M., J. Neider, T. Davis, D. Shreiner, and the OpenGL Architecture Review Board. 1999. *The OpenGL Programming Guide*. Reading, Massachusetts: Addison-Wesley.

Worley, S. P. 1996. A cellular texture basis function. In *Proceedings of SIGGRAPH '96*, Computer Graphics Proceedings, Annual Conference Series, New Orleans, Louisiana, pp. 291–94.

Wyvill, B., and G. Wyvill. 1989. Field functions for implicit surfaces. *The Visual Computer 5*(1/2), 75–82.

Yanovitskij, E. G. 1997. *Light Scattering in Inhomogeneous Atmospheres*. Berlin: Springer-Verlag.

Yellot, J. I. 1983. Spectral consequences of photoreceptor sampling in the Rhesus retina. *Science 221*, 382–85.

Zimmerman, K. 1995. Direct lighting models for ray tracing with cylindrical lamps. In *Graphics Gems V*, pp. 285–89. San Diego: Academic Press.

Zorin, D., P. Schröder, T. DeRose, L. Kobbelt, A. Levin, and W. Sweldens. 2000. Subdivision for modeling and animation. *SIGGRAPH 2000 Course Notes*.

Index

About the CD-ROM

The accompanying CD-ROM contains the source code to the `pbrt` rendering system, prebuilt binaries for a number of architectures, example scene files and images, and browsable hyperlinked source code to the system. The use of the source code is governed by the following license agreement.

LICENSE AGREEMENT

This Software License Agreement is a legal agreement between you and the Authors and the Publisher of this software. The Software includes computer software, the associated media, any printed materials, and any "online" or electronic documentation. By installing, copying, or otherwise using the Software, you agree to be bound by the terms of this license. If you do not agree to the terms of this license, you may not use the Software, and you should remove the software from your computer. The Software is protected by copyright laws and international copyright treaties, as well as other intellectual property laws and treaties. The Software is licensed, not sold.

1. Grant of License

You may use this Software for any non-commercial purpose, subject to the restrictions in this license. Some purposes which can be non-commercial are teaching, academic research, and personal experimentation.

2. Description of Other Rights and Limitations

You may not use or distribute this Software or any derivative works in any form for commercial purposes. Examples of commercial purposes would be using results or images generated by the software, licensing, leasing, or selling the Software, or distributing the Software for use with commercial products. You may modify this Software and distribute the modified Software for non-commercial purposes; however, you may not grant rights to the Software or derivative works that are broader than those provided by this License. For example, you may not distribute modifications of the Software under terms that would permit commercial use, or under terms that purport to require the Software or derivative works to be sublicensed to others. You must distribute the source code of any modifications you make along with binary executables. Furthermore, you must not remove any copyright or other notices from the Software.

3. DISCLAIMER OF WARRANTY.

THE SOFTWARE IS PROVIDED UNDER THIS LICENSE ON AN "AS IS" BASIS, WITHOUT WARRANTY OF ANY KIND, EITHER EXPRESSED OR IMPLIED, INCLUDING,

WITHOUT LIMITATION, WARRANTIES THAT THE SOFTWARE IS FREE OF DEFECTS, MERCHANTABLE, FIT FOR A PARTICULAR PURPOSE OR NON-INFRINGING. THE ENTIRE RISK AS TO THE QUALITY AND PERFORMANCE OF THE SOFTWARE IS WITH USER. SHOULD SOFTWARE PROVE DEFECTIVE IN ANY RESPECT, YOU (NOT THE AUTHORS OR PUBLISHER) ASSUME THE COST OF ANY NECESSARY SERVICING, REPAIR OR CORRECTION. THIS DISCLAIMER OF WARRANTY CONSTITUTES AN ESSENTIAL PART OF THIS LICENSE. NO USE OF ANY COVERED CODE IS AUTHORIZED HEREUNDER EXCEPT UNDER THIS DISCLAIMER.

4. LIMITATION OF LIABILITY.

UNDER NO CIRCUMSTANCES AND UNDER NO LEGAL THEORY, WHETHER TORT (INCLUDING NEGLIGENCE), CONTRACT, OR OTHERWISE, SHALL THE AUTHORS, THE PUBLISHER, ANY OTHER CONTRIBUTOR, OR ANY DISTRIBUTOR OF COVERED CODE, OR ANY SUPPLIER OF ANY OF SUCH PARTIES, BE LIABLE TO USER OR ANY OTHER PERSON FOR ANY INDIRECT, SPECIAL, INCIDENTAL, OR CONSEQUENTIAL DAMAGES OF ANY CHARACTER INCLUDING, WITHOUT LIMITATION, DAMAGES FOR LOSS OF GOODWILL, WORK STOPPAGE, COMPUTER FAILURE OR MALFUNCTION, OR ANY AND ALL OTHER COMMERCIAL DAMAGES OR LOSSES, EVEN IF SUCH PARTY SHALL HAVE BEEN INFORMED OF THE POSSIBILITY OF SUCH DAMAGES. THIS LIMITATION OF LIABILITY SHALL NOT APPLY TO LIABILITY FOR DEATH OR PERSONAL INJURY RESULTING FROM SUCH PARTY'S NEGLIGENCE TO THE EXTENT APPLICABLE LAW PROHIBITS SUCH LIMITATION. SOME JURISDICTIONS DO NOT ALLOW THE EXCLUSION OR LIMITATION OF INCIDENTAL OR CONSEQUENTIAL DAMAGES, SO THAT EXCLUSION AND LIMITATION MAY NOT APPLY TO USER.

5. Termination of License

All of your rights under this Agreement shall terminate if you fail to comply with any of the material terms or conditions of this Agreement and does not cure such failure in a reasonable period of time after becoming aware of such noncompliance. If all of your rights under this Agreement terminate, you agree to cease use and distribution of the Program as soon as reasonably practicable. However, your obligations under this Agreement and any licenses granted by you relating to the Program shall continue and survive.

6. General

The Authors and the Publisher reserve all rights not expressly granted in this license.

CD-ROM CONTENTS

The contents of this CD-ROM were finalized on April 14, 2004. Please visit the pbrt Web site, *www.pbrt.org*, to check for bug fixes, updates to the system, additional plug-in modules, and scene files:

- Windows Installation Notes
- Building the System under Windows
- Linux, OS X, and UNIX Installation Notes

- Building the System under UNIX
- CD-ROM Acknowledgments

WINDOWS INSTALLATION NOTES

The relevant files are in the `windows/` directory of the CD-ROM. Create a new directory on your hard drive (we'll assume it's `c:\pbrt` for the discussion below) and unzip the files below into it. (You can omit some of these, depending on how you plan to be using the system.)

The `windows/` directory on the CD-ROM contains the following files:

- `source.zip` : source code to the system
- `examples.zip` : example scene files
- `images.zip` : images rendered with the system (PNG and EXR format)
- `binaries.zip` : prebuilt binaries to the system

Next, set your `PBRT_SEARCHPATH` environment variable (Start/Settings/Control Panel/System/Advanced/Environment Variables). If you are running the prebuilt binaries and unzipped them into `c:\pbrt`, this environment variable should be set to `c:\pbrt\bin\win32`. If you are building the system from source, it should be set to `c:\pbrt\src\bin`. You should add this directory to your `PATH` environment variable as well.

After closing the window to set the environment variables, open a new command prompt and change to the example scenes directory:

```
cd c:\pbrt\examples
```

Render a simple scene:

```
pbrt.exe simple.pbrt
```

To view the image, which is stored in EXR format, you can either use the included imageview binary, or you can convert it to a TIFF:

```
imageview.exe pbrt.exr
```

or

```
exrtotiff pbrt.exr pbrt.tif
```

Additional information about the EXR file format is at *www.openexr.com*.

BUILDING THE SYSTEM UNDER WINDOWS

You *must* have Microsoft Visual Studio 2003 installed. You also *must* have bison and flex installed from the Cygwin UNIX tools, available from *www.cygwin.com*. The build process assumes that the Cygwin tools are installed in `c:\cygwin`, the standard location.

After unzipping the sources zip file, open the `pbrt.sln` file from the `src/win32/` directory. Select a debug or release build and build the project. The `pbrt.exe` executable and the plugin DLLs will be stored in src/win32/Projects/Debug or src/win32/Projects/Release, as appropriate.

Make sure that your PBRT_SEARCHPATH and PATH environment variables are set to point to the appropriate binaries that you built and not the supplied prebuilt binaries.

LINUX, OS X, AND UNIX INSTALLATION NOTES

The files you'll need to install the system are stored in gzipped tar files, in the unix/ directory:

- source.tgz : source code to the system
- examples.tgz : example scene files
- images.tgz : images rendered with the system (PNG and EXR format)
- linuxbin.tgz : prebuilt Linux binaries to the system
- macbin.tgz : prebuilt Mac OS X binaries to the system

Create a new directory to store pbrt (we'll assume it is $HOME/pbrt in the discussion below) and untar the appropriate ones into it:

- mkdir $HOME/pbrt
- cd $HOME/pbrt
- tar xvzf /mnt/CDROM/unix/source.tgz
- tar xvzf /mnt/CDROM/unix/examples.tgz
- tar xvfz /mnt/CDROM/unix/images.tgz
- tar xvzf /mnt/CDROM/unix/source.tgz
- tar xvzf /mnt/CDROM/unix/linuxbin.tgz / tar xvzf /mnt/CDROM/unix/macbin.tgz

Note that the path to the CD-ROM's filesystem may be different on your system.

Next, set your PBRT_SEARCHPATH environment variable and add the pbrt binaries directory to your search path. Where to set this depends on the shell you're using. For bash, add the following to your .bashrc file:

- export PBRT_SEARCHPATH=$HOME/pbrt/bin/linux # or bin/osx for Mac OS X
- export PATH=PBRT_SEARCHPATH:$PATH

For tcsh, add the following to your .tcshrc file:

- setenv PBRT_SEARCHPATH $HOME/pbrt/bin/linux # or bin/osx for Mac OS X
- setenv PATH $PBRT_SEARCHPATH:$PATH

For other shells, consult your shell's manual page.

If you are building pbrt from source, instead set the PBRT_SEARCHPATH variable to point to the $HOME/pbrt/src/bin directory.

Now, open a new shell (or otherwise set the above environment variables in an already-existing shell) and render a simple scene:

```
pbrt simple.pbrt
```

After rendering is complete, the file `pbrt.exr` will be created, holding the image. To view it, either use an image-viewing program that supports EXR format or use the included `exrtotiff` program to convert it to TIFF format:

```
exrtotiff pbrt.exr pbrt.tif
```

On Linux, the `imageview` program, found in `bin/linux/imageview`, can be used to view EXR files.

Additional information about the EXR file format is at *www.openexr.com*.

BUILDING THE SYSTEM ON UNIX

In order to easily build the system, you *must* have gcc version 3.3 or later installed. Otherwise, you must download and build the OpenEXR libraries yourself, and modify the Makefile to use the ones you built, as the precompiled ones we supply are not compatible with earlier versions of gcc due to a change in the link format for C++ with gcc version 3.3. (Type `gcc -v` to see its version.)

After untarring the sources, change to the `src/` directory and type `make`. By default, a version with debugging symbols and no optimization is built. (It is much slower than the optimized version.) To build an optimized version, type `make OPT=-O2`, or use your preferred compiler optimization flags as appropriate.

The binaries will be installed in the `src/bin/` directory. Set your `PBRT_SEARCHPATH` and `PATH` environment variables to point to that directory and not the supplied prebuilt binaries.

CD-ROM ACKNOWLEDGMENTS

The bunny, buddha, and dragon models are from the Stanford University Scanning Repository and are included with permission. The TT car model, Sponza atrium, and Sibenik cathedral model are courtesy Marko Dabrovic and Mihovil Odak from RNA Studios. The Killeroo model is included with permission of Phil Dench and Martin Rezard of headus. The ecosystem scene was created by Oliver Deussen and Bernd Lintermann. The smoke datasets are the result of simulations by Duc Nguyen and Ron Fedkiw; Nolan Goodnight created environment maps with a realistic skylight model; and the Cornell Program of Computer Graphics Light Measurement Laboratory allowed us to include measured BRDF data. The imageviewer program was written by Cliff Woolley at UVA.

- `images/figures/01F11.png` is by Guillaume Poncin and Pramod Sharma.
- `images/figures/01F12.png` is by Rui Wang.
- `images/figures/01F13.png` is by Eric Lee.
- `images/figures/01F15.png` is by Jared Jacobs and Michael Turitzin.

Physically Based Rendering
FROM THEORY TO IMPLEMENTATION

This book was typeset with TEX, using the ZzTEX macro package on the Microsoft Windows XP platform. The main body of the text is set in Minion at 9.5/12, and the margin indices are set in Bitstream Letter Gothic 12 Pitch at 5.5/7. Chapter titles are set in East Bloc ICG Open and Univers Black. Cholla Sans Bold is used for other display headings.

The manuscript for this book is written in pyweb, a literate programming markup format of the authors' own design. This input format is based heavily on the noweb system developed by Norman Ramsey. The pyweb scripts simultaneously generate the TEX input for the book as well as the source code that appears on the CD.

In addition, these scripts semi-automatically generate the code identifier cross-references that appears in the margin indices. Wherever possible, these indices are produced automatically by parsing the source code itself. Otherwise, usage and definition locations are marked explicitly in the pyweb input, and these special marks are removed before either the book or the code is generated. These scripts were originally written by the authors, and subsequently partially rewritten by Paul Anagnostopoulos to integrate into the ZzTEX system.

Overall, the book comprises almost 60,000 lines of pyweb input, or nearly 2.5 megabytes of text. The cover image, example renderings, and chapter images were generated by pbrt, the software that is described in this book and appears on the CD. They were produced on two 32-CPU clusters of Intel workstations built by GraphStream.